ADVERTISING AND PROMOTION

AN INTEGRATED MARKETING COMMUNICATIONS PERSPECTIVE 13e

George E. Belch & Michael A. Belch
Both of San Diego State University

ADVERTISING AND PROMOTION: AN INTEGRATED MARKETING COMMUNICATIONS
PERSPECTIVE, THIRTEENTH EDITION

Published by McGraw Hill LLC, 1325 Avenue of the Americas, New York, NY 10019. Copyright ©2024 by
McGraw Hill LLC. All rights reserved. Printed in the United States of America. Previous editions ©2021, 2018,
and 2012. No part of this publication may be reproduced or distributed in any form or by any means, or stored in
a database or retrieval system, without the prior written consent of McGraw Hill LLC, including, but not limited
to, in any network or other electronic storage or transmission, or broadcast for distance learning.

Some ancillaries, including electronic and print components, may not be available to customers outside the
United States.

This book is printed on acid-free paper.

1 2 3 4 5 6 7 8 9 LWI 28 27 26 25 24 23

ISBN 978-1-266-14906-1 (bound edition)
MHID 1-266-14906-6 (bound edition)
ISBN 978-1-266-85466-8 (loose-leaf edition)
MHID 1-266-85466-5 (loose-leaf edition)

Executive Portfolio Manager: *Jessica Dimitrijevic*
Product Developer: *Kelly Delso*
Executive Marketing Manager: *Michelle Sweeden*
Content Project Managers: *Harvey Yep/Bruce Gin*
Buyer: *Laura Fuller*
Content Licensing Specialist: *Beth Cray*
Cover Images: *Market research banner web icon for business and social media marketing, target, survey,
    market gap, customer, trends, analytics and statistics. Flat vector infographic: buffaloboy/Shutterstock;
    Doodle design style concept of creating, marketing and sharing of digital content. Modern line style illustration
    for web banners, hero images, printed materials: rassco/Shutterstock; Vector illustration of a communication
    concept. The word communication with colorful dialog speech bubbles: Artistdesign29/Shutterstock; https safe
    web blue digital binary code background vector illustration EPS10: krissikunterbunt/Shutterstock*
Compositor: *Aptara®, Inc.*

All credits appearing on page or at the end of the book are considered to be an extension of the copyright page.

Library of Congress Cataloging-in-Publication Data

Names: Belch, George E. (George Edward), 1951- author. | Belch, Michael A., author.
Title: Advertising and promotion : an integrated marketing communications perspective /
    George E. Belch & Michael A. Belch, San Diego State University.
Description: Thirteenth edition. | New York, NY : McGraw Hill LLC, [2024] |
    Includes bibliographical references and index.
Identifiers: LCCN 2023013592 (print) | LCCN 2023013593 (ebook) |
    ISBN 9781266149061 (hardcover) | ISBN 9781266854668 (spiral bound) |
    ISBN 9781266856136 (ebook other) | ISBN 9781266857218 (ebook)
Subjects: LCSH: Advertising. | Sales promotion. | Communication in marketing.
Classification: LCC HF5823 .B387 2004 (print) | LCC HF5823 (ebook) |
    DDC 659.1–dc23/eng/20230404
LC record available at https://lccn.loc.gov/2023013592
LC ebook record available at https://lccn.loc.gov/2023013593

mheducation.com/highered

To my family (MAB)

To Ethan and Brooks, welcome to the family (GEB)

About the Authors

Joshua C Mitchell/Your Face is Rad

Dr. George E. Belch

George E. Belch is professor emeritus of marketing in the Fowler College of Business at San Diego State University, where he teaches integrated marketing communications and strategic marketing. He received his PhD in marketing from the University of California, Los Angeles. Before entering academia, Dr. Belch was a marketing representative for the DuPont Company. He also worked as a research analyst for the DDB Worldwide advertising agency.

Dr. Belch's research interests are in the area of consumer processing of advertising information as well as managerial aspects of integrated marketing communications. He has authored or coauthored more than 40 articles in leading academic journals and proceedings, including the *Journal of Marketing Research, Journal of Consumer Research, International Journal of Advertising, Journal of Promotion Management, Journal of Advertising*, and *Journal of Business Research*. He also serves on the editorial review boards of the *Journal of Advertising Research* and the *Journal of Marketing Education*. In 2000, he was selected as Marketing Educator of the Year by the Marketing Educators' Association for his career achievements in teaching and research. He also received the Distinguished Faculty Member Award for the College of Business Administration at San Diego State University in 1994 and 2003.

Dr. Belch has taught in executive education and development programs for various universities around the world. He has also conducted seminars on integrated marketing communications as well as marketing planning and strategy for a number of multinational companies, including Sprint, Microsoft, Qualcomm, Arbitron, Square D Corporation, Armstrong World Industries, and Texas Industries.

Gema Deleon/San Diego State University

Dr. Michael A. Belch

Michael (Mickey) A. Belch is professor emeritus of marketing in the Fowler College of Business at San Diego State University and is also director of the Centre for Integrated Marketing Communications at San Diego State. He received his undergraduate degree from Penn State University, his MBA from Drexel University, and his PhD from the University of Pittsburgh.

Before entering academia he was employed by the General Foods Corporation as a marketing representative and has served as a consultant to numerous companies, including McDonald's, Whirlpool Corporation, Senco Products, GTI Corporation, IVAC, May Companies, Phillips-Ramsey Advertising and Public Relations, and Daily & Associates Advertising. He has conducted seminars on integrated marketing and marketing management for a number of multinational companies and has also taught in executive education programs in France, Amsterdam, Spain, Chile, Peru, Argentina, Colombia, China, Slovenia, and Greece. He is the author or coauthor of more than 50 articles in academic journals and proceedings in the areas of advertising, consumer behavior, and international marketing including the *Journal of Advertising, Journal of Advertising Research, Journal of Business Research, Journal of Promotion Management*, and *International Journal of Advertising*. Dr. Belch is also a member of the editorial review board of the *Journal of Advertising* and the *International Journal of Advertising*. He received outstanding teaching awards from undergraduate and graduate students numerous times. He also received the Distinguished Faculty Member Award for the College of Business Administration at San Diego State University in 2007. He was awarded the Giep Franzen Fellowship from the University of Amsterdam.

Preface

THE CHANGING WORLD OF ADVERTISING AND PROMOTION

Nearly everyone is influenced to some degree by advertising and other forms of promotion. Organizations in both the private and public sectors have learned that the ability to communicate effectively and efficiently with their target audiences is critical to their success. Advertising and other types of promotional messages are used to sell products and services as well as to promote causes, market political candidates, and deal with societal problems such as alcohol and drug abuse. Consumers are finding it increasingly difficult to avoid the efforts of marketers, who are constantly searching for new ways to communicate with them.

Most of the people involved in advertising and promotion will tell you that there is no more dynamic and fascinating field to either practice or study. However, they will also tell you that the field is undergoing dramatic transformations that are changing the ways marketers communicate with consumers forever. We are experiencing perhaps the most dynamic and revolutionary changes of any era in the history of marketing, as well as advertising and promotion. These changes are being driven by advances in technology and developments that have led to the rapid growth of communications through digital and social media, with much of this taking place on mobile devices such as smartphones and tablets. The rapid growth of smartphones has given rise to an entirely new type of marketing, known as *mobile marketing*, which involves promotional activities designed for delivery to these devices. The average consumer spends nearly 7 hours online each day, and marketers are allocating more of their promotional budgets to digital media. Advertising spending on digital media has surpassed traditional media, including television, print, radio, and outdoor in the United States as well as globally.

A major challenge facing marketers is the proliferation of nontraditional media, coupled with the changing media consumption behavior of consumers. Consumers are shifting their media usage patterns and how they utilize different media sources to get the information they want or need to make purchase decisions. Younger generations of consumers in particular are redefining the rules of communication as they determine which forms of media they want to be exposed to, the amount of time they wish to spend consuming various media, and the content they wish to receive. Consumers are no longer mere recipients of advertising messages, as they have been empowered to control the kind of messages or content they want to receive including where, when, and how they want it. The function of integrator has shifted from marketers to the consumers themselves, and in the digital age, the consumer is in control of the integration process.

While digital technology has dramatically changed the world of advertising, changes are occurring in a number of other areas. Consumers are less responsive to advertising, and many are looking for ways to avoid advertising messages from both traditional as well as digital media. Social media platforms such as Facebook, Instagram, TikTok, YouTube, Twitter, and Snapchat have become just as powerful, if not more so, as traditional media, as have the influencers who promote products and brands on them. Marketers are demanding better results from the monies they spend on advertising and promotion and are using a variety of analytics to track performance and measure outcomes, particularly for digital ads. Changes are also occurring among the companies that create and disseminate advertising and other forms of marketing communication as traditional full-service advertising agencies must now compete with digital agencies as well as global accounting and consulting firms that have opened digital divisions and offer a vast array of strategic and data analytic solutions to marketers. The traditional full-service agency model is also being challenged as more marketers bring their advertising, as well as media planning and buying, in-house and use agency services on a limited basis. Many advertising agencies have acquired, started, or become affiliated with direct-marketing, digital, sales promotion, public relations agencies, and analytics companies to better serve clients who have become "media-neutral" and are looking for whatever form of marketing communication works best to reach their target audiences.

In addition to redefining the role and nature of their advertising agencies, marketers are changing the way they communicate with their target audiences. They recognize they are operating in an environment where consumers get much of their news, information, and entertainment online and are cutting the cord from cable in favor of streaming shows on services such as Netflix, Max, Prime Video, Apple TV+, Hulu, and Disney+. New-age advertisers are redefining the notion of what an ad is and where it runs. Companies are using branded entertainment as a way of reaching consumers by creating short films that can be viewed online, arranging product placements, and integrating their brands into movies and television shows to promote their products and services. Marketers are also spending more of their monies in other ways such as event and experiential marketing, sponsorships, cause-related promotions, and viral campaigns.

A number of other factors are affecting the way marketers communicate with consumers in this new environment. Advertising and promotional efforts have become more targeted and are often delivered to target audiences through media that have been purchased programmatically using software that automates the buying, placement, and optimization of media through a bidding system rather than through traditional media analysis and purchasing. The growth of e-commerce is changing the retail industry as traditional brick-and-mortar retailers struggle to compete against Amazon and other online platforms. Many traditional retailers will not survive, while those that remain may become larger and more powerful, forcing marketers to shift money from advertising budgets to sales promotion. Both retailers and marketers often expect their promotional dollars to generate immediate sales and will quickly change the allocation of their budgets if they fail to do so. The digital revolution is in full force, and new ways to communicate with consumers are constantly being developed. Marketers have little choice but to embrace these changes and view them as an opportunity rather than a threat.

This text introduces students to this fast-changing field of marketing communications. While advertising is its primary focus, it is more than just an introductory advertising text because there is more to most organizations' promotional programs than just advertising. The changes discussed here have led marketers and their agencies to approach advertising and promotion from an integrated marketing communications (IMC) perspective, which calls for a "big picture" approach to planning marketing and promotion programs and coordinating the various communication functions. To understand the role of advertising and promotion in today's business world, one must recognize how a firm can use all of the available promotional tools to communicate with its customers. The thirteenth edition of this text addresses the many changes taking place in the world of advertising and promotion and continues to do so by taking this IMC perspective. This new edition also places a heavy emphasis on digital and social media by integrating discussion of these topics throughout the text.

ORGANIZATION OF THIS TEXT

This book is divided into seven major parts. In Part One we examine the role of advertising and promotion in marketing and introduce the concept of integrated marketing communications. Chapter 1 provides an overview of advertising and promotion and its role in modern marketing. The concept of IMC and the factors that have led to its growth are discussed. Each of the promotional-mix elements is defined, and an IMC planning model shows the various steps in the promotional planning process. This model provides a framework for developing the integrated marketing communications program and is followed throughout the text. Chapter 2 examines the role of advertising and promotion in the overall marketing program, with attention to the various elements of the marketing mix and how they interact with advertising and promotional strategy. We have also included

coverage of market segmentation, target marketing, and positioning in this chapter so that students can understand how these concepts fit into the overall marketing programs as well as their role in the development of an advertising and promotional program.

In Part Two we cover the promotional program situation analysis. Chapter 3 describes how firms organize for advertising and promotion and examines the role of ad agencies and other firms that provide marketing and promotional services. We discuss how ad agencies are selected, evaluated, and compensated as well as the changes occurring in the agency business. Attention is also given to other types of marketing communication organizations such as direct marketing, sales promotion, and digital interactive agencies as well as public relations firms. We also consider whether responsibility for integrating the various communication functions lies with the client or the agency. Chapter 4 covers consumer behavior and examines the stages of the consumer decision-making process and both the internal psychological factors and the external factors that influence consumer behavior. The focus of this chapter is on how advertisers can use an understanding of buyer behavior to develop effective advertising and other forms of promotion.

Part Three analyzes the communication process. Chapter 5 examines various communication theories and models of how consumers respond to advertising messages and other forms of marketing communications. This chapter also covers word-of-mouth communication and its role in the viral marketing process. The growth of influencer marketing and the role of social media influencers are also discussed. Chapter 6 provides a detailed discussion of source, message, and channel factors. Various source characteristics are discussed as well as the use of celebrities in advertising. The discussion of message factors includes the use of different types of message structures and appeals.

In Part Four we consider how firms develop goals and objectives for their integrated marketing communications programs and determine how much money to spend and where to spend it in trying to achieve them. Chapter 7 stresses the importance of knowing what to expect from advertising and promotion, the differences between marketing and communication objectives, characteristics of good objectives, and problems in setting objectives. Various methods for determining and allocating the promotional budget are also discussed in this chapter.

The first four parts of the text provide students with a solid background in the areas of marketing, consumer behavior, communications, planning, objective setting, and budgeting. This background lays the foundation for Part Five, where we discuss the development of the integrated marketing communications program.

Part Five examines the various promotional-mix elements that form the basis of the integrated marketing communications program. Chapter 8 discusses advertising creativity and focuses on the creative process and the planning and development of the creative strategy. In Chapter 9 we turn our attention to ways to execute the creative strategy and discuss various options for execution of the message as well as creative tactics for print, television, and digital advertising. We also discuss criteria for evaluating creative work. Chapters 10 through 13 cover media strategy and planning and the various advertising media. Chapter 10 introduces the key principles of media planning and strategy and examines how a media plan is developed. Chapter 11 discusses the advantages and disadvantages of television and radio as media vehicles as well as issues regarding the purchase of radio and TV time and audience measurement. Chapter 12 considers the same issues for the print media (magazines and newspapers). Chapter 13 examines the role of traditional support media such as outdoor and transit advertising, advertising in movie theaters, as well as the tremendous increase in the use of nontraditional branded entertainment strategies such as product placements, product integration, and in-game advertising.

In Chapters 14 through 17 we continue the IMC emphasis by examining other promotional tools that are used in the integrated marketing communications process. Chapter 14 explores the role of direct marketing and examines the ways companies communicate directly with target customers through various media, including direct mail, infomercials, direct-response TV commercials, and digital media. Chapter 15 provides a detailed discussion of marketers' use of the Internet and digital and social media. We examine the increasing use of display ads, blogs, mobile, paid search, and social media. We also give more attention to how the Internet is used to implement various IMC activities as well as mobile marketing. Chapter 16 examines the area of sales promotion, including both consumer-oriented promotions and programs targeted to the trade (retailers, wholesalers, and other intermediaries). Chapter 17 covers the role of publicity and public relations in IMC as well as corporate advertising sponsorships and cause-related marketing.

Part Six consists of Chapter 18, where we discuss ways to measure the effectiveness of various elements of the integrated marketing communications program, including methods for pretesting and post-testing advertising messages and campaigns, in both traditional and new media. In Part Seven we turn our attention to special markets, topics, and perspectives that are becoming increasingly important in contemporary marketing. In Chapter 19 we examine the global marketplace and the role of advertising and other promotional-mix variables such as sales promotion, public relations, and the Internet in international marketing.

The text concludes with a discussion of the regulatory, social, and economic environments in which advertising and promotion operate. Chapter 20 examines industry self-regulation and regulation of advertising by governmental agencies such as the Federal Trade Commission, as well as rules and regulations governing sales promotion, direct marketing, and marketing on the Internet. Because advertising's role in society is constantly changing, our discussion would not be complete without a look at the criticisms frequently levied, so in Chapter 21 we consider the social, ethical, and economic aspects of advertising and promotion. Personal selling and its role in the IMC process is discussed in Chapter 22, which is available online only via the eBook.

CHAPTER FEATURES

The following features in each chapter enhance students' understanding of the material as well as their reading enjoyment.

Chapter-Opening Vignettes

Each chapter begins with a vignette that shows the effective use of integrated marketing communications by a company or ad agency or discusses an interesting issue that is relevant to the chapter. These vignettes engage students by presenting an interesting example, development, or issue that relates to the material covered in the chapter.

IMC Perspectives

These features offer in-depth discussions of interesting issues related to the chapter material and the practical application of integrated marketing communications. Each chapter contains several of these insights into the world of integrated marketing communications.

Global Perspectives

These features provide information similar to that in the IMC Perspectives, with a focus on international aspects of advertising and promotion.

Ethical Perspectives

These features discuss the moral and/or ethical issues regarding practices engaged in by marketers and are also tied to the material presented in the particular chapter.

Digital and Social Media Perspectives

These features provide a detailed discussion of how changes and advances in digital and social media are impacting the practice of integrated marketing communications.

Changes in the Thirteenth Edition

Our goal in writing the thirteenth edition was to continue to provide you with the most comprehensive and current text on the market for teaching advertising and promotion from an IMC perspective. We have made a number of changes in this edition to continue to make it as relevant and current as possible, as well as interesting to students. This new edition focuses on the many changes that are occurring in various areas of marketing communications and how they influence advertising and promotional strategies and tactics. We have updated and made changes to every chapter with a particular focus on digital and social media and how they are being used by marketers. This edition also includes all-new chapter-opening vignettes that have been chosen for their currency and relevancy to IMC. All of the features—including the IMC Perspectives, Digital and Social Media Perspectives, Global Perspectives, and Ethical Perspectives—are also new or have been updated. The chapter-opening vignettes and in-text features provide current examples of how marketers are using various IMC tools as well as insights into many of the current trends and developments taking place in the world of advertising and promotion. The new edition also includes contemporary examples and ads throughout the text as well as updated figures, statistics, and other relevant information.

Chapter-by-Chapter Changes

Chapter 1: A new chapter opener, "Celsius Takes On the Energy Drink Giants," focuses on how the brand has been disrupting the energy drink market with a gender-neutral marketing strategy that targets health-conscious consumers and differs from the extreme sports–focused approach used by other brands such as Red Bull and Monster. Celsius has a unique IMC strategy that uses traditional media but also relies heavily on social media influencers as well as experiential marketing.

- A new Digital and Social Media Perspective, "Advertising Revenue Still Pays the Bill for Media," discusses how consumers are trying to avoid advertising by subscribing to one of the many streaming services now available such as Netflix, Amazon Prime, Apple TV+, Disney+, Hulu, and Max. It also discusses how consumers are using technology to avoid traditional as well as digital ads and the long-run implication of this for the media as well as the advertising industry.
- A new Ethical Perspective, "Brand Activism—Taking a Stand to Build Your Brand," discusses how there have been a number of events and developments recently that have led to greater attention being focused on issues such as economic, social, and racial equality, as well as diversity and inclusion. This has led to an increase in brand equality activism, which involves a company or brand taking a stand on these issues and engaging in efforts to promote social, political, economic, or environmental reform to help drive change and improve society. The pros and cons of brand activism are discussed.
- The chapter provides an updated overview of the promotional mix and the various IMC tools including advertising, direct marketing, and digital/Internet marketing, sales promotion, and publicity/public relations. Attention is given to the growth of digital and social media and how they have surpassed traditional media in terms of media spending and use by marketers.

Chapter 2: A new chapter opener, "Why Are So Many Companies and Brands Changing Their Names?" examines the trend of companies changing their names and why they are doing so. From Facebook and Google to Apple, Dunkin', and KFC, the vignette examines companies who have decided it was time for a name change. Some of these have been significant changes, while others like Dunkin' and KFC are more just keeping with the times. The opener discusses some of the reasons for these changes and how well they have been working.

- A new IMC Perspective, "Segmenting the Online Dating Industry: There's a Site for Everyone," discusses the growth of online dating and how it has led to the development of market segmentation and target marketing in the online dating community. The market segments being targeted and the various positioning strategies employed by the dating sites to reach them are also discussed.
- A new IMC Perspective, "Changing Market Conditions Lead Brands to Reposition—Some Successfully, Some Not," discusses why companies and brands are repositioned and examines some that have undertaken this strategy. The perspective examines a number of examples of companies that have been repositioned including Victoria's Secret, Taco Bell, Gillette, and Spotify and whether they have been successful.

Chapter 3: A new chapter opener, "Accenture's Acquisition of Droga5 Rocks the Advertising Industry," focuses on the disruptions taking place in the advertising industry as a result of the rapid growth of digital media and other emerging technologies marketers are using to communicate with their target audiences. The opener discusses how accounting and management consulting firms such as Accenture, PwC, Deloitte, and IBM have opened divisions that use their digital and analytic capabilities to compete with traditional advertising agencies Accenture Song sent a strong message to the traditional advertising agency industry with its acquisition of Droga5, a leading independent agency widely recognized as a creative powerhouse. The acquisition puts to rest the idea that consultancies pose little threat to advertising agencies as they continue to expand their creative capabilities.

- A new Digital and Social Media Perspective, "Media Buying Moves In-House for Many Companies," discusses how many marketers have begun moving some of their media planning and buying in-house rather than relying on an outside agency. Reasons why marketers are moving media buying in-house are discussed, along with the challenges they face in doing so.

- A new IMC Perspective, "Bud Light Searches for a New Agency," discusses how client–agency relationship breakups are becoming more common as marketers search for a new ad agency that can bring new creative ideas and a fresh perspective to their business. The perspective discusses the process Anheuser-Busch (AB) In-Bev, the world's largest brewer, went through in searching for a new agency for its Bud Light portfolio of brands.
- There is discussion throughout the chapter on changes occurring in the advertising industry and how they are affecting the role of traditional advertising and media agencies.

Chapter 4: A new chapter opener, "Environmental Factors Have Changed Consumer Behavior—Maybe Forever!" examines the impact that recent environmental factors have had on consumers' purchase behavior. COVID-19, inflation, and the war in Ukraine have all affected consumers and forced marketers to adapt to the new normal. A number of articles written by academics as well as industry experts have identified a number of ways people have changed their behavior and discuss whether these changes are likely to be temporary or long lasting.

- A new IMC Perspective, "Are Emotions More Important than Information in Consumer Decision Making?" examines the role of emotions in consumer decision making and compares the importance of them to cognitive information processing factors. The perspective discusses George Boykin's concepts of rational versus emotional persuasion and provide examples of the role of each. Lucas Conley's discussion of Obsessive Branding Disorder (OBD) as related to the luxury fashion industry is introduced.
- A new IMC Perspective, "Storytelling Has Become an Effective Marketing Strategy in Sports," discusses how marketers are constantly exploring new research methods in their efforts to better understand consumers and market to them more effectively. The latest trend involves the use of storytelling to gain deeper insights into consumers' motivations. The perspective describes this research method and how a number of companies, including the New York Yankees baseball team and Nike, have used it to develop marketing campaigns and how athletes themselves might consider it.

Chapter 5: A new chapter opener, "Tesla Uses Word of Mouth to Lead the EV Market," discusses how Tesla has become the most valuable automotive company in the United States and dominates the electric vehicle (EV) market, while spending no money on media advertising. A major reason for Tesla's success is its effective use of word of mouth, as Tesla has a strong referral program that rewards those who share their experiences with the company and its cars with others. Tesla controls all steps of the customer journey and creates a very positive

experience for its customers, which has resulted in very high levels of customer loyalty and satisfaction. The opener also discusses the "Elon Musk" factor in reference to the company's mercurial CEO, who purchased the social media company Twitter in 2022, and the media attention this has created for the company.

- An updated Digital and Social Media Perspective, "Logos Change for the New Era of Business," discusses the importance of logos and how the way marketers think about them has changed, particularly for digital technology companies whose services are accessed primarily through apps and mobile devices. Logo redesigns of other major corporations including General Motors, Kia Motors Corp., and Pfizer are discussed.
- A new Digital and Social Media Perspective, "Influencer Marketing Continues to Grow," discusses how the use of social media influencers by marketers continues to increase. Reasons underlying the use of influencers are discussed along with factors marketers consider when deciding to use both macro and micro influencers.
- A new Digital and Social Media Perspective, "Adapting a Classic Model for the Age of Social Media," discusses how a very popular advertising planning model, the FCB grid, can be adapted for the digital age. The digital planning grid shows how various digital and social media platforms can be integrated into this classic model.
- The discussion of viral marketing and word-of-mouth communication has been updated.

Chapter 6: A new chapter opener, "College Athletes Are the New Endorsers," discusses the 2021 U.S. Supreme Court ruling that the NCAA can no longer limit college athletes from using their name, image, and likeness (NIL) to make money from endorsements and other business ventures. The new NIL rules are discussed, showing how they allow college athletes to earn money in various ways including serving as advertising endorsers, selling ads on their social media pages, and being paid for posts on social media. Concerns over the new NIL rules leading to abuses at many major collegiate athletic programs, such as major donors funding collectives to pay athletes to play for a major college sports program, are discussed.

- A new IMC Perspective, "Tennis Star Roger Federer Joins the Billion-Dollar Club," discusses how the popular Swiss tennis star became the latest athlete to join the $1 billion club in career earnings. Nearly $900 million of Federer's earnings has come from his endorsement portfolio that has included deals with major companies such as Nike, Gillette, Rolex, Mercedes-Benz, Wilson, and Japanese retailer Uniqlo.
- A new Digital and Social Media Perspective, "Are Social Media Influencers Really Celebrities?"

discusses how influencers have become the new celebrities of our age as many of them have amassed large numbers of followers and fans that rival traditional celebrities. Attention is given to whether influencers should be accorded the same status as traditional celebrities who have built their star power based on their talent as singers, actors, entertainers, or athletes. Influencers become popular by posting engaging content on social media platforms and their popularity is often limited to these platforms.

- A new Digital and Social Media Perspective, "The Tweet That Started the #Chicken Wars," discusses a comparative advertising battle involving quick-service restaurants Popeyes and market leader Chick-fil-A that took place primarily on social media platforms. The Twitter battle ensued when Chick-fil-A sent out a Tweet in response to Popeyes launching a test market of its chicken sandwich. Popeyes responded with a simple two-word tweet "y'all good?" that generated nearly 8 billion impressions and an estimated $87 million in earned media.

Chapter 7: A new chapter opener titled "How Much Should a Company Spend on Advertising? It's Complicated!" examines this age-old budgeting issue. Increases in inflation and interest rates are among the numerous environmental factors that have led a number of companies to make significant cuts in their advertising spending. At the same time, a number of other companies and advertising experts in academia and business argue that this is not a smart strategy and suggest the opposite approach. Examples of actions taken by companies such as Coca-Cola and Procter & Gamble are discussed.

- A new Digital and Social Media Perspective, "A Century Later the Consumer Purchase Funnel Continues to Be Debated," discusses the use of consumer purchase funnels for setting objectives. As the use of digital media continues to grow, so too does the belief that traditional consumer funnels are outdated. However, the use of these funnels has continued and adapted to the new digital environment, and shows little sign of going away.
- An updated Digital and Social Media Perspective, "Winners and Losers in the Budget Allocation World: Traditional Media Not Dead Yet?" provides updated numbers showing how companies are moving their monies from traditional media to digital including companies such as Hershey. It also explores some of the long-term implications of the shift to digital for traditional media such as television, magazines, and newspapers.

Chapter 8: A new chapter opener, "TikTok's Impact on Creativity," discusses how the popular social media platform has become the leading destination for short-form videos. Its surge in popularity has been driven by the entertaining user-generated content and creative formats that allow users to participate in and respond to the content they are watching. One of the keys to the success of TikTok is its authenticity—the antithesis of the heavily staged and filtered content often found on social media platforms. Attention is given in the chapter to the political uncertainty TikTok is facing, as it is owned by a Chinese company, which is leading to security concerns over how the data it collects on users of the platform might be used by the Chinese government.

- A new IMC Perspective, "Are Analytics Killing Advertising Creativity?" discusses how many in the advertising industry are concerned that the new focus on analytics and metrics is having a negative impact on advertising creativity, as more emphasis is being placed on data-driven practices rather than creative planning and execution. Most advertising creatives feel that data should be used to inform creative decisions, not to make them. The need for a balance between analytics and creativity, particularly as marketers become more interested in measurable, data-driven results, is discussed.
- A new IMC Perspective, "Auto Insurance Companies Use Different Creative Strategies, But Do They Work?" discusses the different creative strategies used by advertisers of automotive insurance, which is one of the most heavily advertised product/service categories. The creative strategies of various insurance companies including GEICO, State Farm, Progressive, and Allstate are discussed. Attention is also given to the debate over whether all the money spent on advertising by automotive insurance companies is really having an impact on consumers' choice of carriers.

Chapter 9: A new chapter opener, "'Fancy Like' Applebee's," discusses how the neighborly restaurant chain capitalized on being part of the lyrics in the hit song "Fancy Like" by country singer Walker Hayes. Hayes and his daughter created a dance to the song and posted the video on TikTok, which became a viral sensation and spawned a myriad of reenactments on TikTok and other social media platforms. Applebee's capitalized on its viral fame by creating a series of TV commercials featuring Hayes and his hit song and various renditions of the dance.

- A new Digital and Social Media Perspective, "Dove Fights Digital Distortion with 'Reverse Selfie,'" discusses an impactful video created by Unilever's Dove brand as part of it long-running Campaign for Real Beauty that fights against unrealistic beauty standards. The "Reverse Selfie" video features a young woman who drastically edits a picture of herself before posting it online. The film plays backward starting with the posted selfie, then reversing the various editing that went into creating it before revealing that it is not a woman but rather a young girl barely in her teens. The video is part of an integrated campaign that Dove uses as part of its campaign against unrealistic beauty stands and the negative impact they are having on young people.

- A new Digital and Social Media Perspective, "Video Advertising Explodes—But Is More Creativity Needed?" discusses how video is becoming the dominant format for digital marketing as people spend a great deal of their time online, particularly on YouTube and various social media platforms. While the use of online video advertising is increasing, marketers face challenges in getting consumers to pay attention to their advertising messages. The perspective discusses the need for more creativity and the need for marketers to develop online ads that are entertaining and engaging rather than continuing to bombard consumers with more videos that they are likely to ignore.

Chapter 10: A new chapter opener, "The Nielsen Ratings: Will Advertisers Really Say Goodbye?" discusses the controversy currently surrounding the Nielsen Ratings. Since the 1950s these ratings have been the standard by which marketers measure the viewing audience for television programming. The prices charged for TV advertising are based on the ratings, and for years Nielsen has been criticized for numerous problems and weaknesses in its methodology. Despite the criticisms, Nielsen did little to change or improve the ratings system until 2021 when the Media Ratings Council (MRC) revoked their accreditation for having unreliable data. While Nielsen claims they will improve their methodology, a number of competitors are now offering alternatives. The question is, will advertisers abandon a 70-year-old system?

- A new Digital and Social Media Perspective, "Despite Issues, Programmatic Continues to Grow," examines the status of programmatic media buying today and some of the issues leading to potential problems with it. Nevertheless, marketers have increased their use of the media buying technology.
- The chapter opener from the previous edition has been updated and included as an IMC Perspective titled "Do We Really See 10,000 Ads Per Day?" It examines the wearout effect that occurs when viewers see commercials too many times. While advertisers are aware of the problems associated with excessive exposure, they struggle to determine how many times an ad is actually seen and at what point people become tired of it.

Chapter 11: A new chapter opener, "Television Viewers Are Screaming for Streaming," discusses the tremendous growth in the number of streaming services. Nearly 85 percent of U.S. households now subscribe to at least one streaming service and half subscribe to three or more. The chapter opener discusses the impact the growth in streaming is having on the traditional broadcast and cable networks.

- A new IMC Perspective, "Can Live Sports Save Traditional Television?" discusses how the major television and cable networks are relying heavily on live sports programming to compete against the growth of streaming services and the decline in linear television viewing. The networks are willing to pay large amounts of money for the rights to broadcast professional and collegiate football, baseball, and basketball games as well as major sporting events because live sports still attract a very large viewing audience. However, they are also facing competition from major technology companies such as Amazon, Apple, and Google, which have begun acquiring sports rights to provide programming for their streaming services.
- A new Digital and Social Media Perspective, "Podcasts Are Becoming Popular among Listeners and Advertisers," discusses the tremendous growth in podcasts, as there are now more than 2 million active podcasts available for listening. Marketers have recognized that podcasts are a very good medium for delivering advertising messages. Podcast advertising is one of the fastest-growing channels in digital media.
- The chapter covers the changes taking place in the television industry and how they are affecting its use as an advertising media vehicle. Developments such as declining viewership of TV, cord cutting, and changes in audience measurement are discussed.

Chapter 12: A new chapter opener, "Can Newspapers Survive in the Digital World?" discusses the challenges facing the newspaper industry as more people go online to get their news, information, and entertainment. Revenue from advertising has long been the primary source of income for newspapers in the United States but has been in a steady decline for nearly two decades. The newspaper industry reached a major turning point in 2020 when it generated more revenue from circulation than advertising. Factors leading to the decline in newspaper readership are discussed along with how newspapers are responding to the digital disruption.

- An updated Digital and Social Media Perspective, "Magazines Continue to Go Digital," discusses how many magazines are moving to a digital-first or -only strategy and reducing the number of print issues they publish or shuttering their print editions altogether in favor of digital-only editions. The perspective discusses magazines that have moved to digital-only editions and their reasons for doing so.
- A new Ethical Perspective, "The Decline in Newspapers Is Creating More 'News Deserts,'" discusses how the decline in readership and advertising revenue has led to the closing of many newspapers in the United States. As more newspapers go out of business, the number of news deserts, which are communities in which inhabitants have no local newspapers, continues to grow. The importance and value of local newspapers to communities and their citizens and businesses has been recognized by the federal government, which is considering legislation to address the crisis facing local news outlets.
- Factors affecting the magazine and newspaper industries are discussed in the chapter along with how the two major print media are responding to them.

Chapter 13: A new chapter opener, "Now Streaming: Virtual Product Placements," discusses how as more viewers "cut the cord" and opt for streaming versus linear television, advertisers are finding it more difficult to reach their target audiences with TV advertising. As a result, they have increasingly turned to product placements as an option. While not the same as a TV commercial, product placements can be effective and the advertiser still gets their product or brand in front of an audience and with less annoyance to the viewer. The chapter opener discusses new virtual product placement formats being used by marketers, which allow the placement to take place even after the program has been completely developed.

- An updated IMC Perspective, "Now We Are Even Watched in Retail Stores: Is Privacy Dead?" discusses the many new ways marketers are invading consumers' privacy without them being aware of it. While this is nothing new, the ways they are doing so certainly are different. For example, cameras in the cooler aisles of grocery stores read facial expressions and try to determine shoppers' age and gender, as well as their mood, and then use this information to display ads or promotions by posting them on the cooler window.
- The chapter updates various ways marketers are using branded entertainment including product placements, product integrations, advertainment, and advergaming.

Chapter 14: A new chapter opener, "Will Connected TV (CTV) Mean the End for DRTV?" details the sophistication and adaptability of direct marketing on connected TV. While direct-response ads on linear TV continue to be successful, CTV claims to offer a number of advantages over the traditional direct-response model including better targeting, greater appeal to millennials, and more sophisticated ad testing. At the same time, the CTV option has its limitations and has yet to be embraced by many advertisers.

- A new IMC Perspective, "The World of Direct Marketing," discusses how legacy companies are using direct-to-consumer marketing, including Procter & Gamble, Nike, Under Armour, and PetSmart. In addition, the strategies behind successful new brands such as Allbirds and Harry's Shave Club that use direct to consumer marketing are discussed.
- An update on the state of the direct response industry is provided.

Chapter 15: A new chapter opener, "Let's Get Phygital! The Metaverse and the New Web 3.0," discusses what is meant by getting "phygital" and how major companies like Meta, which owns Facebook and Instagram, are preparing themselves for movement into the integration between the digital and "real-life" experiences that will constitute Web 3.0. Augmented and virtual reality are expected to be a major component of the changes that occur as we move into the metaverse.

- A new Digital and Social Media Perspective, "Have the 'Big Three' of the Internet Met Their Match?" discusses the current state of Google, Amazon, and Meta (Facebook), which are the three companies that dominate online advertising. Some of the successful and not so successful moves they have made in recent years are discussed.
- A new Digital and Social Media Perspective, "Changes in Privacy Regulations May Lead to Major Impacts for Consumers and Advertisers," examines how changes allowing consumers to opt out of tracking are affecting digital advertisers as well as consumers.
- The rapidly changing digital environment once again required a major updating and revision of this chapter from the last edition. As we embark on Web 3.0, marketers are increasing their use of digital media at the expense of traditional channels, and social media continues to evolve and offer new alternatives. As difficult as it is to keep up with the changes in digital and social media, some consistent issues are beginning to emerge. Privacy issues remain important and concerns over societal impact are increasing, particularly among young people.
- The chapter provides an update on the status of social media including a discussion of TikTok, which is becoming the most popular platform for most young people. Examples of how companies are using the various social media platforms for a variety of marketing activities are discussed.

Chapter 16: A new chapter opener, "Fast-Food Restaurants Use Loyalty Programs to Engage Customers," discusses how loyalty programs are becoming very popular among the quick-service and fast-food segments of the restaurant industry. While customer loyalty programs have been popular in the travel and hospitality industry as well as among retailers, companies such as McDonald's and Chipotle have just recently begun using them to attract and retain customers. Various features of these loyalty programs are discussed in the chapter-opening vignette.

- A new IMC Perspective, "What's the Deal with Coupons?" discusses how coupon distribution and redemption have been declining over the past decade. A major reason is the decline in newspaper circulation, which has resulted in fewer free-standing inserts (FSIs) being received by households. Other factors affecting the distribution and use of coupons by marketers are discussed.
- A new Digital and Social Media Perspective, "Burger King Gets People to Take a Whopper Detour," discusses an award-winning promotion the fast-food chain developed to challenge McDonald's and encourage consumers to switch to a BK Whopper instead of going to the Golden Arches. The "Whopper Detour" was a very creative and technologically challenging promotion that involved geofencing nearly every

McDonald's restaurant in the country and offering consumers with the BK smartphone app the opportunity to order a Whopper for 1 cent if they placed an order on the app, which would direct them to the nearest Burger King to redeem the offer.

Chapter 17: A new chapter opener, "What Do Kanye West and Cristiano Ronaldo Have in Common? A Lot of Lost Money!" discusses how involvement with the two celebrities has resulted in negative publicity for companies such as Coca-Cola and adidas. A number of other companies that have been on the downside of publicity and their ensuing actions are also discussed.

- A new IMC Perspective, "My Reputation Was Tarnished! Now What Do I Do?" discusses how easy it is for a company to lose a good reputation, and how it often can be very difficult to get it back. Krispy Kreme, Tom's Shoes, BP, and other companies that have suffered damage to their reputations and brand image are discussed along with what they did to try to recapture it.
- An updated Ethical Perspective, "Companies Show Their Good Side for Important Causes," discusses how a number of companies from around the globe support Water Day and Earth Day as philanthropic efforts. The Ethical Perspective discusses how while companies often are on the wrong end of negative publicity, many others are quietly doing good things around the globe, often with little awareness by the public.

Chapter 18: A new chapter opener, "What Are the Best Commercials of All Time?" examines different perspectives on what makes a great TV commercial. Some of the commercials considered the best go as far back as 1968 and 1984 (e.g., Apple's classic "1984" commercial) while others are more recent. The chapter opener discusses some of the factors that lead to effective commercials and notes that not all favorites are necessarily the most effective from a marketing standpoint.

- A new IMC Perspective, "The Winners of the Ogilvy Awards Rely on Research," discusses recent winners of the David Ogilvy Award. This award is given in a number of categories each year to companies and their agencies for the best use of research in the development and/or measurement of advertising campaigns. The perspective describes the award-winning campaigns for Microsoft, the Bank of Montreal, and Michelob and discusses some of the criteria used to measure their effectiveness.
- A new IMC Perspective titled "Advertising Attribution: Is It the Holy Grail for Measuring Effectiveness?" discusses the use of attribution modeling to measure the effectiveness of various IMC elements. While such measures have been available for years, only recently have marketers and academicians put faith in them.

- The various measurement methods discussed in the chapter have been reviewed and updated to ensure they are current and still being used by marketers.

Chapter 19: A new chapter opener, "Australia Invites Tourists to 'Come and Say G'day,'" discusses a new global advertising campaign created by Tourism Australia, which is a government agency responsible for attracting international visitors to the country. Australia was closed to visitors for nearly two years during the COVID-19 pandemic and when it was reopened to tourists in 2022, the country recognized that a global advertising campaign was needed to lure visitors to the land down under. The opener discusses the "Come and Say G'day" integrated campaign that includes TV, print, and out-of-home media, as well as social, digital, and content marketing initiatives.

- An updated Global Perspective, "Qatar Delivers 'Amazing' as Host of the FIFA World Cup," discusses the IMC strategy used by Qatar to help the small Persian Gulf country win the rights to host the 2022 soccer tournament and become the first Middle Eastern and Arab nation to host the prestigious sporting event. Despite considerable controversy over being awarded the rights, Qatar hosted a successful World Cup that was won by Argentina. Two video cases on Qatar's IMC campaign are available and include assignable content for students in Connect.
- A new Global Perspective, "Coca-Cola Wants to Create 'Real Magic' Around the World," discusses the global advertising campaign developed by the Coca-Cola Company as part of its "one brand" strategy that unites various soft drink brands marketed by the company under one personality. "Real Magic" is a global marketing platform that includes a new design identity for the Coke trademark brands, anchored by a fresh expression of the Coca-Cola logo. To launch the "Real Magic" platform, a global IMC campaign was created using the theme "One Coke Away from Each Other" with the tagline serving as a metaphor that celebrates our common humanity.
- A new Digital and Social Media Perspective, "China Leads the Way in Digital Marketing," discusses the opportunities available in the world's largest market as well as the challenges marketers face in trying to compete there. China has moved away from traditional media and has become a "mobile first" market as digital advertising accounts for nearly 80 percent of the total advertising spending in the country. Many feel that the developments occurring in China will soon happen in other countries as the world moves to a digital- and mobile-first mindset.

Chapter 20: A new chapter opener, "High-Profile Celebrities Run into Trouble for Endorsing Failed Cryptocurrencies," discusses how celebrity and social media influencer Kim Kardashian was fined $1.26 million by the Securities and Exchange Commission (SEC) for posting a message on Instagram promoting Ethereum Max (EMAX), a new crypto token. Kardashian violated SEC regulations by not disclosing how much she was paid for the post. The opener also discusses other celebrities named in class-action lawsuits for appearing in ads endorsing the cryptocurrency exchange FTX, which went bankrupt in late 2022.

- A new Ethical Perspective, "False Advertising Lawsuits for Food and Beverage Products Surging," discusses the increase in the number of lawsuits brought against marketers of these products for making claims that cannot be substantiated or may be false and misleading. Many of these are class-action lawsuits brought on behalf of a larger group or class of consumers who may have suffered common injury or damage.
- A new Digital and Social Media Perspective, "Privacy Regulations Are Changing Digital Marketing," discusses how privacy has become a major concern as the growth of digital advertising and marketing overtakes the use of traditional media by marketers. Companies such as Google, Meta (Facebook), and many others have a tremendous amount of data about consumers who use their platforms, and many critics, as well as government regulators, are very concerned over how this information is used. The European Union enacted its General Data Protection Regulation (GDPR) in 2018. The California Consumer Privacy Act went into effect in California in 2020 and a number of other states are implementing similar laws regulating privacy.
- Changes in the self-regulation of advertising are discussed in the chapter along with updates on how the Federal Trade Commission has revised its rules and regulations regarding the use of online endorsements by influencers. Companies that have run into regulatory problems in recent years—such as Tesla, Google, Meta, and Epic Games Inc., which makes the popular video game *Fortnite*—are discussed.

Chapter 21: A new chapter opener, "Why Do Companies Continue to Run Offensive Ads?" discusses a number of companies that have run ads seen as offensive by consumers. A recent example is fashion designer Balenciaga, which ran an ad showing young girls holding Teddy Bears in what appear to be bondage styled harnesses. It was not the first time that Balenciaga was accused of running this style of advertising, and some critics argue it is a purposeful strategy designed to garner attention and publicity.

- An updated Ethical Perspective, "Was the Beginning of #MeToo the End of Sexy Advertising?" discusses how the changing emphasis on women's rights—among other factors—has contributed to less use of sex in advertising. The perspective discusses how women see a difference between sexy ads and sexist ads, having less of a problem with the former. It also discusses how some companies that formerly used sex in ads in the past have now changed their appeals.

- An updated Digital and Social Media Perspective, "As We See More Interracial Ads, How Do Consumers React?" discusses new research by both academics and companies regarding consumers' reactions to the increase in advertising featuring interracial couples.

Chapter 22: A new chapter opener, "B2B Personal Selling in a Virtual Environment," discusses how sales and marketing departments are now breaking down silos that have existed for decades by making effective use of online tools. As communication between departments as well as with customers has continued to increase, both sales and marketing have become more effective.

- Updated IMC Perspective, "Personal Selling and Marketing: Can They Co-exist?" discusses how companies are realizing the importance of marketing and sales working together. The perspective discusses how the two departments often have different objectives and sometimes work against one another to achieve them, but now are improving the relationship.

ACKNOWLEDGMENTS

While this thirteenth edition represents a tremendous amount of work on our part, it would not have become a reality without the assistance and support of many other people. Authors tend to think they have the best ideas, approach, examples, and organization for writing a great book. But we quickly learned that there is always room for our ideas to be improved on by others. A number of colleagues provided detailed, thoughtful reviews that were immensely helpful in making this a better book. We are very grateful to the following individuals who worked with us on earlier editions. They include

Lisa Abendroth, *University of Saint Thomas*
Wendi Achey, *Northampton Community College*
Natalie Adkins, *Creighton University-Omaha*
Bruce Alford, *Louisiana Tech University*
David Allen, *St. Joseph's University*
Neil Alperstein, *Loyola University Maryland*
Craig Andrews, *Marquette University*
Sheila Baiers, *Kalamazoo Valley Community College*
Aysen Bakir, *Illinois State University*
Subir Bandyopadhyay, *University of Ottawa*
Allen Bargfrede, *Berklee College of Music*
Michael Barone, *Iowa State University*
Jerri Beggs, *Illinois State University*
Mike Behan, *Western Technical College and Viterbo University*
John Bennet, *University of Missouri*
Elizabeth Blair, *Ohio University-Athens*
Hulda Black, *Illinois State University*
Janice Blankenburg, *University of Wisconsin-Milwaukee*
Carolyn Bonifield, *University of Vermont*

Karen Bowman, *University of California-Riverside*

Kathy Boyle, *University of Maryland*

Terry Bristol, *Oklahoma State University*

Beverly Brockman, *University of Alabama*

Kendrick Brunson, *Liberty University*

Lauranne Buchanan, *University of Illinois*

Jeffrey Buchman, *Fashion Institute of Technology*

Roy Busby, *University of North Texas*

Victoria Bush, *University of Mississippi*

Christopher Cakebread, *Boston University*

Nathaniel Calloway, *University of Maryland-University College*

Margaret C. Campbell, *University of California, Riverside*

Les Carlson, *Clemson University*

Lindell Chew, *University of Missouri-St. Louis*

Larry Chiagouris, *Lubin School of Business, Pace University*

Oscar Chilabato, *Johnson & Wales University*

Jungsil Choi, *Cleveland State University*

Christina Chung, *Ramapo College of New Jersey*

Theresa Clarke, *James Madison University*

Bob Cline, *University of Iowa-Iowa City*

Catherine Cole, *University of Iowa*

Mary Conran, *Temple University-Philadelphia*

Sherry Cook, *Missouri State University*

Kevin Cumiskey, *Oklahoma State University-Stillwater*

Robert Cutter, *Cleveland State University*

Andrew Czaplewski, *University of Colorado-Colorado Springs*

Robert Daniel Dahlen, *Ohio University*

Richard M. Daily, *University of Texas-Arlington*

Amy Danley, *Wilmington University*

Don Dickinson, *Portland State University*

Sara Dommer, *Georgia Institute of Technology*

Robert H. Ducoffe, *Baruch College*

Mary Edrington, *Drake University*

Roberta Elins, *Fashion Institute of Technology*

Nancy Ellis, *Suffolk Community College*

Mark Elton, *Western Oregon University*

Robert Erffmeyer, *University of Wisconsin-Eau Claire*

John Faier, *Miami University*

Terri Faraone, *Mt. San Antonio College*

Raymond Fisk, *Oklahoma State University*

Theresa Flaherty, *James Madison University*

Alan Fletcher, *Louisiana State University*

Marty Flynn, *Suffolk Community College*

Judy Foxman, *Southern Methodist University*

Amy Frank, *Wingate University*

Bruce Freeman, *Kean University*

Jon B. Freiden, *Florida State University*

Stefanie Garcia, *University of Central Florida*

Geoff Gordon, *University of Kentucky*

Keith Alan Gosselin, *California State University-Northridge*

Kimberly Goudy, *Central Ohio Technical College*

Norman Govoni, *Babson College*

Donald Grambois, *Indiana University*

Nancy Gray, *Arizona State University*

Debora Grossman, *State University of New York-Buffalo*

Stephen Grove, *Clemson University*

Aditi Grover, *Oklahoma State University*

Charles Gulas, *Wright State University-Dayton*

Robert Gulonsen, *Washington University*

Holly Hapke, *University of Kentucky-Lexington*

Bill Hauser, *University of Akron*

Diana Haytko, *East Carolina University*

Yi He, *California State University-East Bay*

Amanda Helm, *University of Wisconsin-Whitewater*

Nikki Hicks, *John Tyler Community College*

Ron Hill, *Villanova University*

JoAnn Hopper, *Western Carolina University*

Paul Jackson, *Ferris State College*

Karen James, *Louisiana State University-Shreveport*

Christopher Joiner, *George Mason University*

Ali Kara, *Penn State University*

Komal Karani, *Lamar University*

Eileen M. Kearney, *Faculty Montgomery County Community College*

Leslie Kendrick, *Johns Hopkins University*

Robert Kent, *University of Delaware*

Don Kirchner, *California State University-Northridge*

Paul Klein, *St. Thomas University*

Susan Kleine, *Arizona State University*

Patricia Knowles, *Clemson University*

David Koehler, *University of Illinois-Chicago*

Gary Kritz, *Seton Hall University*

Ivy Kutlu, *Old Dominion University*

Barbara Lafferty, *University of South Florida-Tampa*

Linda LaMarca, *Tarleton State University*

Dana Lanham, *University of North Carolina-Charlotte*

Clark Leavitt, *Ohio State University*

Rebecca Legleiter, *Tulsa Community College*

Ron Lennon, *Barry University*

Lauren Lev, *Fashion Institute of Technology*

Aron Levin, *Northern Kentucky University*

Tina Lowry, *Rider University*

Rachel Lundbohm, *University of Minnesota-Crookston*

Karen Machleit, *University of Cincinnati*

Scott Mackenzie, *Indiana University*

Stacey Massey, *Texas A&M University*

Jessica Matias, *University of Minnesota-Crookston*

Catherine Mezera, *West Virginia University*

Paula Morris, *Salisbury University*

Elizabeth Moore, *Notre Dame*

Joe Msylivec, *Central Michigan University*

Darrel Muehling, *Washington State University-Pullman*

Barbara Mueller, *San Diego State University*

John H. Murphy II, *University of Texas-Austin*

Richard Murphy, *Jacksonville University*

Mark Neckes, *Johnson & Wales University*

Peter Noble, *Southern Methodist University*

Kathy O'Donnell, *San Francisco State University*

Mandy H. Ortiz, *University of Alabama-Tuscaloosa*

Carol Osborne, *USF Tampa*

Charles Overstreet, *Oklahoma State University*

Jay Page, *University of Cincinnati-Clermont College*

Notis Pagiavlas, *University of Texas-Arlington*

Cara Peters, *Winthrop University*

Paul Prabhaker, *DePaul University, Chicago*

William Pride, *Texas A&M University*

Astrid Proboll, *San Francisco State University*

Sanjay Putrevu, *SUNY University at Albany*

Sekar Raju, *University at Buffalo*

Gregory Rapp, *Portland Community College*

Joel Reedy, *University of South Florida*

Kristen Regine, *Johnson & Wales University*

Glen Reicken, *East Tennessee State University*

Herb Ritchell, *DePaul University*

Scott Roberts, *Old Dominion University*

Michelle Rodriques, *University of Central Florida*

Christopher Ross, *Trident Technical College*

Herbert Jack Rotfield, *Auburn University-Auburn*

Judith Sayre, *University of North Florida*

Allen D. Schaefer, *Missouri State University*

Hope Schau, *University of Arizona*

Carol Schibi, *State Fair Community College*

Denise D. Schoenbachler, *Northern Illinois University*

Lisa Sciulli, *Indiana University of Pennsylvania*

Andrea Scott, *Pepperdine University*

Elaine Scott, *Bluefield State College*

Eugene Secunda, *New York University*

Trina Sego, *Boise State University*

Tanuja Singh, *Northern Illinois University*

Lois Smith, *University of Wisconsin*

Stacy Smulowitz, *University of Scranton*

Harlan Spotts, *Northeastern University*

Melissa St. James, *California State University-Dominguez Hills*

Monique Stampleman, *Fashion Institute of Technology*

LaTonya Steele, *Durham Technical Community College*

Michelle Steven, *St. Francis College*

Mary Ann Stutts, *Southwest Texas State University*

James Swartz, *California State Polytechnic University-Pomona*

Ric Sweeney, *University of Cincinnati*

Janice Taylor, *Miami University*

Robert Taylor, *Radford University*

Brian Tietje, *Cal State Polytechnic*

Frank Tobolski, *DePaul University*

Kevin Toomb, *University North Carolina-Charlotte*

Mindy Treftz, *Columbia College-Christian County*

Lisa Troy, *Texas A&M University*

Ramaprasad Unni, *Tennessee State University*

Deb Utter, *Boston University*

Jim Walker, *Northwest Missouri State University*

Ying Wang, *Youngstown State University*

Rod Warnick, *University of Massachusetts-Amherst*

Judith Washburn, *University of Tampa*

Mike Weigold, *University of Florida-Gainesville*

John Weitzel, *Western Michigan University*

Donna Wertalik, *Virginia Polytechnic Institute*

Kenneth C. Wilbur, *University of Southern California*

Rick Wilson, *Texas State University*

Roy Winegar, *Grand Valley State University*

Richard Wingerson, *Florida Atlantic University*

Terrence Witkowski, *California State University-Long Beach*

Merv H. Yeagle, *University of Maryland-College Park*

Elaine Young, *Champlain College*

Robert Young, *Northeastern University*

We are particularly grateful to the individuals who provided constructive comments on how to make this edition better:

Wendi L. Achey, *Northampton Community College*

Lee Ahern, *Pennsylvania State University*

Carl Bozman, *Gonzaga University*

Michele M. Cauley, *Clemson University*

Traci Freling, *University of Texas-Arlington*

Chung-kue (Jennifer) Hsu, *Virginia Tech*

Sungwoo Jung, *Columbus State University*

Alia Kara, *Pennsylvania State University-York Campus*

Ceyhan Kilic, *Tarleton State University*

Steve Noll, *Madison College*

Lucille Pointer, *University of Houston-Downtown*

Lisa M. Sciulli, *Indiana University of Pennsylvania*

Olga Vilceanu, *Rowan University*

Matthew Watanabe, *California State University-Sacramento*

Susan Westcott Alessandri, *Suffolk University*

Gary B. Wilcox, *University of Texas-Austin*

We would also like to acknowledge the business, advertising, and media communities for their help in providing some of the advertisements throughout the life of this product. A special thanks to all of you.

A manuscript does not become a book without a great deal of work on the part of the publisher. Various individuals at McGraw Hill have been involved with this project over the past several years. Our Product Developer on the thirteenth edition, Kelly Delso, along with Portfolio Manager Jess Dimitrijevic, provided valuable guidance and have been instrumental in making sure we continue to write the best IMC book on the market. A special thanks goes to Claire Hunter, our developmental editor, for all of her efforts and for being so great to work with. Thanks also to Harvey Yep for doing a superb job of managing the production process and Beth Cray for coordinating the permissions and licensing process. We also want to once again acknowledge the outstanding work of David Tietz for most of the ads that appear throughout the book. A special thanks to Lois Olson for her great work on the Connect exercises.

Thanks to the other members of the product team—Terri Schiesl, Robin Lucas, Michele Janicek, Michelle Sweeden, Matt Diamond, and Bruce Gin.

We would like to acknowledge the support we have received from the Fowler College of Business at San Diego State University. As always, a great deal of thanks goes to our families for putting up with us while we were revising this book. Once again we look forward to returning to what we think is normal. Finally, we would like to acknowledge each other for making it through this ordeal for the thirteenth time! We are not sure how many editions we have left in us, but our families and friends will be happy to know that we still get along after all this. Our parents would be proud!

George E. Belch
Michael A. Belch

Instructors
The Power of Connections

A complete course platform

Connect enables you to build deeper connections with your students through cohesive digital content and tools, creating engaging learning experiences. We are committed to providing you with the right resources and tools to support all your students along their personal learning journeys.

65%
Less Time Grading

Laptop: Getty Images; Woman/dog: George Doyle/Getty Images

Every learner is unique

In Connect, instructors can assign an adaptive reading experience with SmartBook® 2.0. Rooted in advanced learning science principles, SmartBook 2.0 delivers each student a personalized experience, focusing students on their learning gaps, ensuring that the time they spend studying is time well-spent.
mheducation.com/highered/connect/smartbook

Affordable solutions, added value

Make technology work for you with LMS integration for single sign-on access, mobile access to the digital textbook, and reports to quickly show you how each of your students is doing. And with our Inclusive Access program, you can provide all these tools at the lowest available market price to your students. Ask your McGraw Hill representative for more information.

Solutions for your challenges

A product isn't a solution. Real solutions are affordable, reliable, and come with training and ongoing support when you need it and how you want it. Visit **supportateverystep.com** for videos and resources both you and your students can use throughout the term.

Students
Get Learning that Fits You

Effective tools for efficient studying

Connect is designed to help you be more productive with simple, flexible, intuitive tools that maximize your study time and meet your individual learning needs. Get learning that works for you with Connect.

Study anytime, anywhere

Download the free ReadAnywhere® app and access your online eBook, SmartBook® 2.0, or Adaptive Learning Assignments when it's convenient, even if you're offline. And since the app automatically syncs with your Connect account, all of your work is available every time you open it. Find out more at
mheducation.com/readanywhere

"I really liked this app—it made it easy to study when you don't have your textbook in front of you."

- Jordan Cunningham,
  Eastern Washington University

iPhone. Getty Images

Everything you need in one place

Your Connect course has everything you need—whether reading your digital eBook or completing assignments for class—Connect makes it easy to get your work done.

Learning for everyone

McGraw Hill works directly with Accessibility Services Departments and faculty to meet the learning needs of all students. Please contact your Accessibility Services Office and ask them to email accessibility@mheducation.com, or visit **mheducation.com/about/accessibility** for more information.

Brief Contents

Detailed Contents

Part Two

Integrated Marketing Communications Program Situation Analysis

NicoElNino/Alamy Stock Photo

Part Three

Analyzing the Communication Process

Slyellow/Shutterstock

Mark Dierker/McGraw Hill

Part Four

Objectives and Budgeting for Integrated Marketing Communications Programs

Part Five

Developing the Integrated Marketing Communications Program

Chris Szagola/AP Images

Mark Dierker/McGraw Hill

Part Six   Monitoring, Evaluation, and Control

Part Seven

Special Topics and Perspectives

DisobeyArt/Shutterstock

19 INTERNATIONAL ADVERTISING AND PROMOTION   640

20 REGULATION OF ADVERTISING AND PROMOTION   680

Carlos Amarillo/Shutterstock

ADVERTISING AND PROMOTION

AN INTEGRATED MARKETING COMMUNICATIONS PERSPECTIVE

An Introduction to Integrated Marketing Communications

Celsius

Learning Objectives

LO1-1 | Describe the role of advertising and other promotional elements in marketing.

LO1-2 | Discuss the evolution of the integrated marketing communications (IMC) concept.

LO1-3 | Explain the increasing value of the IMC perspective in advertising and promotional programs.

LO1-4 | Identify the elements of the promotional mix.

LO1-5 | Identify the contact points between marketers and their target audiences.

LO1-6 | Describe the steps in the IMC planning process.

Celsius Takes On the Energy Drink Giants

In 1987 a new category was born in the beverage market when Austrian entrepreneur Dietrich Mateschitz developed not only a new product but also a unique marketing concept and launched Red Bull Energy Drink. Inspired by functional drinks from East Asia, Mateschtiz launched Red Bull in Austria on April 1, 1987, and within a few years distribution expanded into a number of neighboring European countries. Red Bull continued its international expansion during the 1990s including entry into the U.S. market in 1997. By 2000, Red Bull was sold in more than 50 countries and nearly one billion cans were being sold worldwide.

Red Bull's incredible success was based on marketing it as the drink for periods of increased physical and mental stress as it claimed to improve endurance, alertness, concentration, and reaction time. The company promoted the beverage's ability to vitalize body and mind with the slogan, "Red Bull Gives You Wings," which became one of the most popular and memorable advertising taglines ever. Rather than taking a traditional marketing approach, Red Bull associated itself with the emerging extreme sports movement by sponsoring events such as cliff diving, air races, snowboarding, and freestyle skiing. Its marketing also includes sponsorship of athletes and ownership of multiple sports teams including the New York Red Bulls Major League Soccer (MLS) team, as well as teams in Europe and South America.

While Red Bull enjoyed it first-mover advantage as the founder of the energy drink category, competitors began entering the rapidly growing market. One of the most successful new entrants was Monster Energy, which was introduced in 2002 by the Hansen Natural Company, whose product line focused primarily on natural fruit juices. The company decided to launch an energy drink using a strategy similar to Red Bull that included sponsorships of high adrenaline sports such as auto racing and BMX biking as well as video game players and rappers like Lil Xan. By 2012, Monster Energy had grown to such a large percentage of Hansen's sales that a decision was made to change the name of the company to Monster Beverage Corporation. In 2015, the Coca Cola Company acquired a 17 percent stake in Monster for $2.15 billion and entered into a strategic partnership making it the beverage giant Monster's preferred global distribution partner.

Red Bull and Monster dominate the energy drink market in the United States as well as globally. Red Bull accounts for 38 percent of U.S. energy drink sales at retail while Monster Energy has 23 percent. No other brands have reached a double digit market share, as the next largest are Bang VPX (7 percent), which is owned by Vital Pharmaceuticals, and Rockstar (4 percent), which was purchased by PepsiCo for $3.85 billion in 2020. With the energy drink market being controlled by Red Bull and Monster, many analysts argue there is not much room for another brand to take on the industry heavyweights. However, Celsius is proving them wrong as the brand is rocketing up the sales chart and disrupting the energy drink market with its unique marketing approach. Celsius, which grew its dollar sales by nearly 200 percent in 2022 to nearly $400 million, is carving out a position as a healthier energy drink and has passed Rockstar to become the fourth-largest brand in the category.

Celsius's explosive growth has been driven by a gender-neutral marketing strategy that targets health-conscious consumers and differs from the ego-driven, extreme-sports approach that generally focuses on men. The company positions its drinks as clinically proven to accelerate metabolism and burn calories and fat and as a healthy alternative to other energy drinks, sports drinks, and diet sodas. Advertising for Celsius uses the tagline "Live Fit," and the company's marketing and distribution are designed to reach its key target of health-conscious consumers where they live, work, and play. Its media plan includes digital television, radio, and print advertising. Celsius also relies heavily on influencer marketing to spread its message and has a network of around 1,500 brand ambassadors who range from social media influencers with strong followings to popular fitness instructors. The company also has endorsement deals with a number of professional athletes including Olympic snowboarder Shaun White and NBA star Julius Randle.

Celsius is capitalizing on the strong growth in the functional segment of the beverage market that includes consumers looking for health benefits such as weight control, improved energy, athletic endurance, and hydration. The COVID-19 pandemic accelerated this trend as consumers turned to more health-related foods and drinks to strengthen their

continued

immunity and away from beverages loaded with sugar and other ingredients. As can be seen in the opening ad, Celsius's advertising and packaging highlight the product's natural ingredients, such as green tea, ginger, and guarana seed, and note how it accelerates metabolism and helps burn body fat and calories. This appeals to the brand's target audience of athletes and healthy-minded individuals. Market studies show that Celsius is not only attracting new users to the energy drink category but also converting consumers from Red Bull, Monster, and other competitors to its own brand. Celsius Holdings CEO John Fieldly notes: "What we're seeing is new consumers coming to the category don't want their grandfather's energy drink. They don't want Red Bull. They don't want Monster with all the sugars. These brands that are more traditional energy are just not on trend today and what the consumer wants."

Celsius recognizes that it must continue to push the envelope and out-maneuver and out-execute its much larger competitors with their massive marketing budgets. While the brand has been successful touting its functional attributes to health-conscious 24- to 44-year-olds, it is seeking younger drinkers such as college students by edging into the lifestyle space with its "Vibe" line of flavors. It also expanded its experiential marketing with an "Essential Vibes Tour" that includes sponsorship of a slate of music festivals.

In 2022, *Advertising Age* recognized Celsius as one of America's hottest brands, noting how smart marketing and positioning are making it a major competitor in the highly competitive energy drink market. Competitors are taking note as well. PepsiCo invested $550 million in the company in 2022 as part of a deal that will give the maker of Pepsi, Mountain Dew, and Gatorade a long-term deal to distribute Celsius products. When CEO Fieldly was asked if Celsius might ever be acquired by one of its larger competitors he said, "If it happens it happens," before adding: "We are looking to be the number one energy drink in the world, so maybe we buy them." Stay tuned.

Sources: Connor Hart, "PepsiCo to Take Stake in Celsius," *The Wall Street Journal,* August 2, 2022, p. B3; E. J. Schultz, "America's Hottest Brands—Celsius," *Advertising Age*, July 11, 2022, p. 9; E. J. Schultz, "How Celsius Energy Drink Is Challenging Monster and Red Bull—And Winning," *Advertising Age*, April 12, 2022, https://adage.com/article/marketing-news-strategy/celsius-energy-drink-challenger-brand-monster-and-red-bull/2411081; Christopher Doering, "Celsius Is Luring Consumers That Don't Want 'Grandfather's Energy Drinks,' CEO Says," *Food Dive*, October 28, 2021, https://www.fooddive.com/news/celsius-is-luring-consumers-that-dont-want-grandfathers-energy-drink-c/607026/.

The opening vignette illustrates how Celsius has adapted its marketing strategy and the way it communicates with consumers to become the fastest growing brand of energy drinks. It also provides an excellent example of how the roles of advertising and other forms of marketing communication are changing in the modern world of marketing. In the past, advertising was a relatively simple process as most companies relied primarily on ads run in the mass media to deliver their marketing messages to large numbers of consumers who watched television, listened to radio, and read magazines and newspapers. However, today's marketers recognize that the rapidly changing media environment is making it increasingly difficult to reach their target audiences and communicate effectively with them. The mass media are losing their viewers, listeners, and readers to the highly fragmented but more narrowly targeted digital media that allow consumers to be more actively engaged in the communication process. Consumers are no longer passive message recipients who will sit back and receive unfiltered advertising messages dictated by marketers. They want to have more control of the content they receive from the media, and they are seeking out information, as well as entertainment, from myriad sources.

The marketing strategy used by Celsius Holdings to promote its energy drinks shows how companies are using *integrated marketing communications* (IMC) to reach their target audiences and engage them. Celsius uses traditional mass-media advertising through TV, radio, and magazines as well as out-of-home media such as billboards to build awareness along with its brand identity. The company uses traditional media and various forms of digital advertising to influence online behavior by driving consumers to its website where they can learn more about the brand and where they can purchase it, including retail stores as well as online through Amazon or directly from the company. Celsius also relies heavily on brand ambassadors and other influencers who promote the brand through various social media platforms that have become an important

CELSIUS Energy Drink Retweeted

Trini Tiff @TriniTiffy · May 1
LAST DAY of @SunFestFL

Staying energized with @CelsiusOfficial ✨⚡

#SunFest #SunFestFL #SunFest2020 #SunFestFord #LiveMusic #MusicFestival #ThePalmBeaches #DowntownWPB #WestPalmBeach

SunFest and CELSIUS Energy Drink

♡   ↻ 2   ♡ 9   ↥

EXHIBIT 1–1

Social media is an important part of Celsius's integrated marketing communications program. Brand ambassadors, influencers, and consumers promote the brand on Twitter and other social media platforms.

Celsius/Twitter, Inc.

part of the digital marketing efforts of nearly every company today. Consumers are encouraged to connect with Celsius on Facebook, Instagram, and Twitter while inspirational videos promoting the brand are available on YouTube, Instagram Reels, and TikTok. The social media content follows the same theme as its advertising, which is designed to show how Celsius is part of an active lifestyle and is a healthy alternative to traditional energy drinks (Exhibit 1–1).

Public relations (PR) is also an important part of the marketing communications program for Celsius as the company has to manage its brand and corporate image as well as capitalize on the tremendous amount of publicity and media attention it receives as it emerges as a major competitor in the energy drink market. Sales promotion is another important part of its marketing program. Promotional efforts for Celsius are extended to retail stores, where point-of-purchase displays, special offers, and other tactics are used to encourage retailers such as Target, Walmart, and 7-Eleven, as well as various drug and grocery chains, to stock and promote its products. Celsius also connects with consumers where they like to play by sponsoring running events and using experiential marketing such as its "Live Fit" tour that features pop-up fitness events hosted by popular instructors from fitness chains.

Celsius Holdings, along with thousands of other companies, recognizes that the way it communicates to and connects with consumers to promote its products continues to change, and it must keep pace by integrating a variety of communication tools into its marketing programs. The fragmentation of markets, the decline of traditional media such as magazines and newspapers, the growth of the Internet and new forms of digital and social media, the emergence of global markets, economic uncertainties, and changing lifestyles and media usage patterns of consumers are all changing the ways companies market their products and services and communicate with current and prospective customers.[1] Developing marketing communications programs that are responsive to these changes is critical to the success of nearly every company that competes in the marketplace.

THE GROWTH OF ADVERTISING AND PROMOTION

Advertising and promotion are an integral part of our social and economic systems. In our complex society, advertising has evolved into a vital communications system for both consumers and businesses. The ability of advertising and other promotional methods to deliver carefully prepared messages to target audiences has given them a major role in the marketing programs of most organizations. Companies ranging from large multinational corporations to small retailers increasingly rely on advertising and promotion to help them market products and services. In market-based economies, consumers have learned to rely on advertising and other forms of promotion for information they can use in making purchasing decisions.

In 1980, advertising and sales promotion were the dominant forms of marketing communication used by most companies, and total expenditures in the United States across the two were just over $100 billion. Media advertising accounted for $53 billion, while $49 billion was spent on sales promotion techniques such as product samples, coupons, contests, sweepstakes, premiums, and rebates as well as trade allowances and discounts to retailers. By 1990, $130 billion was being spent on advertising, while sales promotion expenditures increased to $140 billion. By the start of the new millennium, nearly $156 billion was spent on local and national advertising, while spending on sales promotion programs targeted toward consumers and retailers increased to more than $250 billion.[2] This growth has continued over the past two decades as an estimated $330 billion was spent on advertising in 2022, with $129 billion being spent on traditional media advertising (television, radio, magazines, newspaper, out-of-home, and cinema) and $201 billion going to digital/online advertising. In addition to media advertising, nearly $45 billion was spent on direct mail and other forms of direct marketing such as e-mail marketing, $42 billion was spent on sponsorships and event marketing, and more than $300 billion on consumer and trade promotion.[3]

It is particularly interesting to note the shift in advertising spending from traditional media such as television, radio, and print to digital formats, including online search, display and video ads, as well as advertising on social media. In 2019, spending on digital advertising in the United States surpassed that on traditional media advertising (54 percent vs. 46 percent) for the first time, and by 2022, digital ads accounted for nearly two-thirds of all advertising spending. The increase in digital advertising is coming from declines in spending in print versions of magazines and newspapers as well direct mail.[4] The largest category of digital advertising is paid search on search engines such as Google, Yahoo!, and Bing, which account for nearly half of all online ad expenditures. Online display advertising follows close behind and is being driven by the growth in video ads being shown online. Spending on social media platforms such as Facebook, Twitter, Instagram, TikTok, and Snapchat has been the fastest growing digital channel over the past several years. Much of the growth in digital advertising is being driven by mobile marketing whereby ads, text messages, and promotional offers are sent directly to mobile devices such as smartphones and tablets. Digital advertising on mobile devices accounts for nearly two-thirds of all digital ad spending and continues to grow. The shift to mobile marketing is occurring as consumers spend more time on their mobile devices and less time with traditional media such as newspapers, magazines, and television. It is estimated that adults in the United States spend an average of four and a half hours per day on mobile devices, with two-thirds of that time spent on smartphones.[5]

Advertising and promotion have grown globally as well over the past 40 years. Advertising spending outside the United States increased from $55 billion in 1980 to nearly $214 billion by 2002 and by 2022 had grown to $450 billion.[6] The United States accounts for nearly 40 percent of the world's advertising expenditures, while nearly half of global advertising spending is in Western Europe and the Asia/Pacific region. After the United States, the top countries in advertising spending are China, Japan, the United Kingdom, and Germany. Marketers also spend billions more on sales promotion, direct marketing, event sponsorships, and public relations. As is the case in the United States, digital advertising is growing rapidly in countries around the world and is expected to increase its share of total advertising spending to nearly 65 percent by 2023.[7]

Spending on advertising and other forms of promotion will continue to increase as companies around the world strive to market their products and services to their customers, including both consumers and businesses. Integrated marketing communications plays an important role in the marketing programs of consumer product and service companies as well as business-to-business marketers in their efforts to communicate with their current and prospective customers. To understand the role IMC plays in the marketing process, let us first examine the marketing function.

THE ROLE OF MARKETING

Marketing has never been more important or more pervasive than it is today. Organizations ranging from large multinational corporations to small entrepreneurial companies and local businesses recognize that marketing is an important business function and plays a critical role in their ability to compete in the marketplace. For nearly two decades, the American Marketing Association (AMA), the organization that represents marketing professionals in the United States and Canada, defined marketing as *the process of planning and executing the conception, pricing, promotion, and distribution of ideas, goods, and services to create exchanges that satisfy individual and organizational objectives.*[8] This definition of marketing focused on **exchange** as a central concept in marketing and the use of the basic marketing activities to create and sustain

HELP THOSE
AFFECTED BY
THE LOUISIANA
FLOODS

We urgently need your financial support.
We can't do it without you.

PLEASE DONATE TODAY AT REDCROSS.ORG
OR TEXT LAFLOODS TO 90999 TO GIVE $10.*

✚ **American Red Cross**
Louisiana Region

*$10 donation to the American Red Cross. Charges will appear on your wireless bill, or be deducted from your prepaid balance. All purchases must be authorized by account holder. Must be 18 years of age or have parental permission to participate. Message and Data Rates May Apply. Text STOP to 90999 to STOP. Text HELP to 90999 for HELP. Full Terms and Privacy Policy: redcross.org/m

EXHIBIT 1–2

Nonprofit organizations
use advertising to solicit
contributions and support.

American Red Cross

relationships with customers.[9] For exchange to occur there must be two or more parties with something of value to one another, a desire and ability to give up that something to the other party, and a way to communicate with each other. Advertising and promotion play an important role in the exchange process by informing customers of an organization's product or service and convincing them of its ability to satisfy their needs or wants.

Not all marketing transactions involve the exchange of money for a product or service. Nonprofit organizations such as various causes, charities, religious groups, the arts, and colleges and universities (probably including the one you are attending) receive millions of dollars in donations every year. Many nonprofit organizations use ads to solicit contributions from the public such as the one shown in Exhibit 1-2 for the American Red Cross, which responds to approximately 70,000 disasters in the United States every year including floods, fires, tornadoes, hurricanes, and earthquakes that affect tens of thousands. Donors generally do not receive any material benefits for their contributions; they donate in exchange for intangible social and psychological satisfactions such as feelings of goodwill and altruism.

While many still view exchange as the core phenomenon or domain for study in marketing, there is also agreement among most academicians and practitioners that the discipline is rapidly changing. To reflect these changes, the AMA adopted a revised definition of **marketing** in 2007, which is as follows:

> Marketing is the activity, set of institutions, and processes for creating, communicating, delivering and exchanging offerings that have value for customers, clients, partners, and society at large.[10]

This revised definition is viewed as being more reflective of the role of nonmarketers to the marketing process. It also recognizes the important role marketing plays in the process of creating, communicating, and delivering value to customers, as well as society at large. Today, most markets are seeking more than just a one-time exchange or transaction with customers. The focus of market-driven companies is on developing and sustaining *relationships* with their customers. Successful companies recognize that creating, communicating, and delivering *value* to their customers is extremely important. **Value** is the customer's perception of all the benefits of a product or service weighed against all the costs of acquiring and consuming it.[11] Benefits can be functional (the performance of the product), experiential (what it feels like to use the product), and/or psychological (feelings such as self-esteem or status that result from owning a particular brand). Costs include the money paid for the product or service as well as other factors such as time and effort acquiring information about the product/service, making the purchase, learning how to use it, maintaining the product, and disposing of it.

The Marketing Mix

Marketing facilitates the exchange process and the development of relationships by carefully examining the needs and wants of consumers, developing a product or service that satisfies these needs, offering it at a certain price, making it available through a particular place or channel of distribution, and developing a program of promotion or communication to create awareness and interest. These four Ps—product, price, place (distribution), and promotion—are elements of the **marketing mix**. The basic task of marketing is combining these four elements into a marketing program to facilitate the potential for exchange with consumers in the marketplace.

The proper marketing mix does not just happen. Marketers must be knowledgeable about the issues and options involved in each element of the mix. They must also be aware of how these elements can be combined to form an effective marketing program that delivers value to consumers. The market must be analyzed through consumer research, and the resulting information must be used to develop an overall marketing strategy and mix.

The primary focus of this book is on one element of the marketing mix: the promotional variable. However, the promotional program must be part of a viable marketing strategy and be coordinated with other marketing activities. A firm can spend large sums on advertising, sales promotion, or other forms of marketing communication, but it stands little chance of success if the product is of poor quality, is priced improperly, or does not have adequate distribution to consumers. Marketers have long recognized the importance of combining the elements of the marketing mix into a cohesive marketing strategy. Many companies also recognize the need to integrate their various marketing communications efforts, such as traditional media advertising, direct marketing, sales promotion, Internet marketing, social media, event sponsorships, and public relations, to achieve more effective marketing communications.

INTEGRATED MARKETING COMMUNICATIONS

For many years, the promotional function in most companies was dominated by mass-media advertising. Companies relied primarily on their advertising agencies for guidance in nearly all areas of marketing communication. Most marketers did use additional promotional and marketing communication tools, but sales promotion and direct-marketing agencies as well as package design firms were generally viewed as auxiliary services and often used on a per-project basis. Public relations agencies were used to manage the organization's publicity, image, and affairs with relevant publics on an ongoing basis but were not viewed as integral participants in the marketing communications process.

Many marketers built strong barriers around the various marketing and promotional functions and planned and managed them as separate practices, with different budgets, different views of the market, and different goals and objectives. These companies failed to recognize that the wide range of marketing and promotional tools must be coordinated to communicate effectively and present a consistent image to target markets.

The Evolution of IMC

During the 1980s, many companies began taking a broader perspective of marketing communication and recognizing the need for a more strategic integration of their promotional tools. The decade was characterized by the rapid development of areas such as sales promotion, direct marketing, and public relations, which began challenging advertising's role as the dominant form of marketing communication. These firms began moving toward the process of **integrated marketing communications (IMC)**, which involves coordinating the various promotional elements and other marketing activities that communicate with a firm's customers.[12] As marketers embraced the concept of integrated marketing communications, they began asking their ad agencies to coordinate the use of a variety of promotional tools rather than relying primarily on media advertising. A number of companies also began to look beyond traditional advertising agencies and use other types of promotional specialists to develop and implement various components of their promotional plans.

Many large agencies responded to the call for synergy among the promotional tools by acquiring PR, sales promotion, and direct-marketing companies and touting themselves as IMC agencies that offer one-stop shopping for all their clients' promotional needs.[13] Some agencies became involved in these nonadvertising areas to gain control over their clients' promotional programs and budgets and struggled to offer any real value beyond creating advertising. However, the advertising industry soon recognized that IMC was more than just a fad. Terms such as *new advertising*, *orchestration*, and *seamless communication* were used to describe the concept of integration.[14] In 1989, a task force from the American Association of Advertising Agencies (the "4As") developed one of the first definitions of integrated marketing communications:

> a concept of marketing communications planning that recognizes the added value of a comprehensive plan that evaluates the strategic roles of a variety of communication disciplines—for example, general advertising, direct response, sales promotion, and public relations—and combines these disciplines to provide clarity, consistency, and maximum communications impact.[15]

The 4As' definition focused on the process of using all forms of promotion to achieve maximum communication impact. It included the primary marketing communication tools available at that time and, since the Internet revolution had not yet occurred, did not include digital marketing tools such as the Internet and social media. However, critics argued that viewing IMC as simply the coordination of a firm's promotional activities was limited in scope. Advocates of the IMC concept argued for an even broader perspective that considers *all sources of brand or company contact* that a customer or prospect has with a product or service.[16] They noted that the process of integrated marketing communications calls for a "big-picture" approach to planning marketing and promotion programs and coordinating the various communication functions. It requires that firms develop a total marketing communications strategy that recognizes how all of a firm's marketing activities, not just promotion, communicate with its customers.

Consumers' perceptions of a company and/or its various brands are a synthesis of the bundle of messages they receive or contacts they have, such as media advertisements, price, package design, direct-marketing efforts, publicity, sales promotions, websites, point-of-purchase displays, and even the type of store where a product or service is sold. The integrated marketing communications approach seeks to have all of a company's marketing and promotional activities project a consistent, unified image to the marketplace. It recognizes that every customer interaction with a company or brand across a host of contact points represents an opportunity to deliver on the brand promise, strengthen customer relationships, and deepen loyalty. It calls for a centralized messaging function so that everything a company says and does communicates a common theme and positioning.

A company that does this very well is Montblanc, which is a leading international brand of luxury writing instruments as well as watches, jewelry, headphones, leather goods, and other accessories. Montblanc uses its distinctive brand name and image that represent classic design centered on accuracy, craftsmanship, and precision to position its watches, pens, and accessories as high-quality, lifestyle products. This upscale image is enhanced by the company's higher prices as well as its strategy of distributing its products through boutiques, jewelry stores, and other exclusive retail shops, including its own stores.

An example of how Montblanc uses IMC is its global "Mark Makers" campaign that is designed to laud those who live their lives by intuition rather than rules, defying convention for the greater goal of self-actualization.[17] The campaign emphasizes the core belief that everyone can leave a mark, not just by achieving success, but enjoying the journey along the way and pursuing endeavors that inspire. The integrated marketing campaign uses short films, print, digital, and social media and features celebrities who leave their mark on the world through their artistry and creativity and are driven by their passions and a higher purpose. Celebrities featured in the ads, which use the "What Moves You Makes You" tagline, have included writer and director Spike Lee, actors Taron Egerton and Cillian Murphy, and international DJ and entrepreneur Peggy Guo (Exhibit 1–3).

Many companies have adopted this broader perspective of IMC. They see it as a way to coordinate and manage their marketing communication programs to ensure

EXHIBIT 1–3

This ad is part of Montblanc's "Mark Makers" integrated marketing campaign.

Montblanc

that they send customers a consistent message about the company and/or its brands. For these companies, integration represents an improvement over the traditional method of treating the various marketing and promotion elements as virtually separate activities. However, this perspective of IMC has been challenged on the basis that it focuses primarily on the tactical coordination of various communication tools with the goal of making them look and sound alike.[18] It has been criticized as an "inside-out marketing" approach that is a relatively simple matter of bundling promotional-mix elements together so they have one look and speak with one voice.[19] As IMC continued to evolve, academicians as well as practitioners recognized that a broader perspective was needed that would view the discipline from a more strategic perspective.

A Contemporary Perspective of IMC

As marketers become more sophisticated and develop a better understanding of IMC, they are recognizing that it involves more than just coordinating the various elements of their marketing and communications programs into a "one look, one voice" approach. IMC is now recognized as a business process that helps companies identify the most appropriate and effective methods for communicating and building relationships with customers and other stakeholders. Don Schultz of Northwestern University developed what many think is a more appropriate definition of IMC:

> Integrated marketing communication is a strategic business process used to plan, develop, execute and evaluate coordinated, measurable, persuasive brand communications programs over time with consumers, customers, prospects, employees, associates and other targeted relevant external and internal audiences. The goal is to generate both short-term financial returns and build long-term brand and shareholder value.[20]

There are several important aspects of this definition of IMC. First, it views IMC as an ongoing strategic business process rather than just tactical integration of various communication activities. It also recognizes that there are a number of relevant audiences that are an important part of the process. Externally these include customers, prospects, suppliers, investors, interest groups, and the general public. It also views internal audiences such as employees as an important part of the IMC process. This definition also reflects the increasing emphasis that is being placed on the demand for accountability and measurement of the *outcomes* of marketing communication programs as well as marketing in general.

The debate over how to properly define IMC has continued well into the new millennium, and a number of new definitions have been proposed.[21] However, IMC theory and practice has grown and evolved, particularly as a result of the digital revolution that has given rise to the numerous and diverse means of communication options now available to marketers. Today, most companies recognize that communicating effectively with current and prospective customers involves more than just the tactical use of traditional marketing communication tools. These firms, along with most advertising agencies, are embracing IMC and incorporating it into their marketing programs and business practices. Integrated marketing communications has been widely adopted and is proving to be of significant value to companies in the rapidly changing marketing environment they are now facing. IMC has been described as one of the "new generation" marketing approaches used by companies to better focus their efforts in acquiring, retaining, and developing relationships with customers and other stakeholders.[22]

Reasons for the Growing Importance of IMC

The IMC approach to marketing communications planning and strategy is being adopted by companies both large and small and has become popular among firms marketing consumer products and services as well as business-to-business marketers. There are a number of reasons why marketers are adopting IMC. A fundamental reason is that they understand the value of strategically integrating the various communications functions rather than having them operate autonomously. By coordinating their marketing communication efforts, companies can avoid duplication, take advantage of synergy among promotional tools, and develop more efficient and effective marketing communication programs. Advocates of IMC argue that it is an effective way for a company to maximize the return on its investment in marketing and promotion.[23]

The move to integrated marketing also reflects an adaptation by marketers to a changing environment, particularly with respect to consumers, technology, and media consumption behavior. For decades, reaching consumers was relatively easy, as marketers could run their ads in mass media (so named because they reach mass audiences) such as television, radio, magazines, and newspapers. The formula was really very simple, as the mass media had a symbiotic relationship with mass marketers such as automotive firms, consumer packaged-goods companies, and many others. The media companies would develop and deliver expensive but high-quality content that would in turn attract large audiences. The marketers would pay large amounts of money to the television and radio networks and stations and/or magazine and newspaper publishers for access to the mass audiences who would receive the advertising messages that encouraged them to purchase the marketers' products and services. The advertising revenue that the media companies received would be used to produce the high-quality content, which in turn would allow the media to continue to deliver the viewers, listeners, and readers that the marketers coveted. Digital and Social Media Perspective 1–1 discusses the dependence of the media on revenue from advertising and how this business model is being challenged.

There have been major changes in the media landscape that are impacting the traditional mass media and the economic model that has supported them. There continues to be an evolution to *micromarketing* as the mass audiences assembled by the major television networks and augmented by other mass media such as magazines and newspapers are fragmenting and declining.[24] For several decades television viewing audiences moved from the traditional broadcast networks (ABC, CBS, NBC, and Fox) to more narrowly targeted programming on cable networks such as ESPN, HGTV, CNN, and MTV. However, over the past decade, more and more households have been "cutting the cord" from traditional cable services in favor of video streaming alternatives such as Netflix, Max, Apple+, Hulu, Amazon Prime, Sling TV, ESPN+, and YouTube TV. Faster Internet connections and an abundance of video streaming devices such as Apple TV, Roku, Amazon Fire, and Google Chromecast are contributing to the decline of subscribers to cable and satellite services such as DirecTV and Dish. Many younger consumers spend more time watching videos on YouTube, TikTok, and Instagram than watching television. The Internet has become the leading advertising medium, with online versions of nearly every magazine, newspaper, and television and radio station, as well as millions of websites that cater to very specific interests of consumers. The crude banner and pop-up ads that were used in the early days of the Internet have given way to more refined formats such as paid search, which is the most widely used form of online advertising, as well as videos and mobile marketing techniques.

EXHIBIT 1–4

Google Ads is the most popular platform for online search advertising.

Piotr Swat/Alamy Stock Photo

Advertisers can use the Internet in a more targeted way than they can use traditional media. They can run their ads on websites or social media sites that are narrowly targeted to consumer interests or have their ads appear on search engines such as Google, Yahoo!, and Bing, which are seen when people are seeking information about a product or service. For example, Google dominates as the online search advertising marketer with its keyword-targeted advertising program called Google Ads (Exhibit 1-4). Social networking sites such as Facebook, Snapchat, TikTok, Twitter, LinkedIn, Instagram, and YouTube have become pervasive on the Internet and make it possible for people to share content, opinions, insights, and experiences as well as educate one another about companies, brands, and various issues.[25]

Digital and Social Media Perspective 1–1 >>>

Advertising Revenue Still Pays the Bills for Media

If you are like most consumers, you are often annoyed by advertising and would welcome the opportunity to avoid the commercials that disrupt a television show or pop up on the screen of a computer or mobile device when you are surfing the Internet or watching a video online. Consumers have been routinely avoiding television advertising for years by using a remote control to change channels during the commercial break of a television show or fast-forwarding through commercials when watching a recorded show. Studies show that half of the viewers watching a recorded television show routinely skip the commercials, and the number would be higher if it were not for the fact that many of them are multitasking and too busy on their phones, computers, and/or tablets to fast-forward through the ads.

Many consumers have decided to avoid ads altogether by switching to one of the many streaming services now available such as Netflix, Amazon Prime, Apple TV+, Disney+, Hulu, and Max. There has been tremendous growth in streaming over the past 5 years as the number of subscriptions to online streaming services in the United States reached 353 million in 2022 and 1.2 billion globally. Over 80 percent of U.S. households subscribe to at least one streaming service while 50 percent subscribe to three or more of the major services. Netflix dominates the streaming market with 221 million subscribers worldwide including 75 million in the United States and Canada. However, the streaming landscape has changed dramatically over the past 5 years as major companies such as Disney, Amazon, and Apple entered the market while the major networks introduced their own streaming services such as Peacock (NBC) and Paramount+ (CBS).

While streaming services rely primarily on revenue from monthly subscriptions to fund the programming content they provide to viewers, most of the services also offer an advertising-supported tier with lower prices to attract more price-sensitive viewers. Since the inception of its streaming service in 2007, Netflix had resisted offering an ad-supported tier as subscriber growth skyrocketed. However, in 2022 Netflix announced that it would abandon its resistance to advertising and begin testing an ad-supported, lower-priced subscription tier. The announcement came after disclosing that it had lost 200,000 subscribers during the first 3 months of the year as a result of stiffer competition and rising inflation that was pressuring households to tighten their budgets. The new service called "Basic with Ads" was rolled out in November 2022 at a price of $6.99 per month and includes 4 to 5 minutes of advertising content per hour.

Netflix's CEO explained the decision to join the ranks of Hulu, Peacock, Paramount+, Max, and Disney+, which each have ad-supported tiers, by noting, "We've left a big customer segment off the table, which is people who say, 'Hey, Netflix is too expensive for me and I don't mind advertising.' Allowing consumers who like to have a lower price, and

are advertising tolerant, to get what they want makes a lot of sense." The move could also make a lot of sense for Netflix's bottom line as analysts estimate that Netflix could generate $1.2 billion in the United States alone by 2025.

Marketers recognize that it has become more difficult to get consumers to watch traditional television, let alone pay attention to their commercials. They also know that people are spending more time online than with traditional media and are shifting more of their media spending to various forms of digital advertising. However, as marketers shift their ads online, they are dealing with yet another weapon being used by consumers to avoid advertising: ad blockers. While many consumers have installed ad-blocking software on their desktop and laptop computers, more and more are now doing so on their mobile devices and filtering out most ads.

If you are like many people and spend a great amount of time online, ad blocking probably sounds like a good idea because it allows you to avoid being exposed to myriad annoying ads, most of which are of little or no interest to you. However, the advertising industry, as well as online publishers such as newspapers, magazines, blogs, and the multitude of websites available on the Internet, are concerned over the impact ad blockers are having on their digital advertising business. The reason for their concern is that ad blocking has the potential to undermine the central business model for much of the Internet. This model is really quite simple: The companies that offer content online make money by selling advertising space on the search engines, websites, apps, and social media sites that we all visit, and they get paid based on the number of people who see or click on the ads.

Most consumers are glad that they do not have advertising messages cluttering the content on their smartphones and tablets and enjoy being able to fast-forward through television commercials or watch the commercial-free tiers of streaming services. However, those who see ads as something to avoid might want to take a moment to think about what would happen if we lived in an ad-free world. Without advertising, television networks and local stations would have to rely entirely on viewers for revenue, and average households, which are already paying well over $200 a month for subscriptions to cable TV and streaming services, could see their monthly bills increase by 50 percent, and they would get a lot fewer channels. The majority of the social media sites where younger consumers spend their time—such as Facebook, Instagram, YouTube, TikTok, and Snapchat—generate nearly all of their income from advertising. You might ask yourself how much you would be willing to pay per year for an ad-free Facebook or Instagram.

In addition to the television industry and social media sites, web publishers as well as the magazine and newspaper industry would be devastated if they lost all of their advertising revenue. Many people are already reading content from magazines and newspapers for free online because most publications have been unsuccessful in

Pavel Muravev/Alamy Stock Photo

an ad-serving company that generates nearly 90 percent of its revenue from advertising.

So if you are like many consumers and do not like advertising because you find it irritating, annoying, and intrusive, you might want to think twice about what the world would be like without it. Perhaps *Advertising Age* writer Simon Dumenco described it best: "To all the ad haters and ad blockers out there, well, keep this in mind: As famed copywriter Oscar Wilde once wrote, 'When the Gods wish to punish us, they answer our prayers.'"

Sources: Suzanne Vranica, Joe Flint, and Sarah Krouse, "Netflix with Ads Launching as Talks Continue with Studios Over Content," *The Wall Street Journal*, November 2, 2022, https://www.wsj.com/articles/netflix-with-ads-launching-as-talks-continue-with-studios-over-content-11667381403 https://time.com/6175837/netflix-ads-coming/; Bevin Fletcher, "How Many Services Does It Take to Meet Viewer TV Needs? At Least 4, Survey Says," *Fierce Video*, May 11, 2022, https://www.fiercevideo.com/video/how-many-services-does-it-take-meet-viewer-tv-needs-least-4-survey-says; Stephan Shankland, "Ad Blocking Surges as Millions More Seek Privacy, Security and Less Annoyance," *CNET*, May 3, 2021; Simon Dumenco, "Imagine a World without Ads," *Advertising Age*, September 28, 2015, pp. 28–32.

getting people to pay for print and/or digital subscriptions or consumers find a way to get around their firewalls. Thus, digital advertising is critical to their survival. The next time you do a Google search, remember that Google is basically

Challenges Impacting IMC

While IMC has become widely accepted as a strategic business process for brand communications, marketers face a number of challenges in implementing it.[26] A major challenge facing marketers in the practice of IMC is the proliferation of nontraditional media, coupled with the changing media consumption behavior of consumers. Younger generations of consumers in particular are redefining the rules of communication as they determine which forms of media they want to be exposed to, the amount of time they wish to spend consuming various media, and even the content they wish to receive. As Professor Jerry Kliatchko has noted, "Perhaps one of the greatest changes among consumers today in relation to marketing communications is the fact they are no longer mere recipients of messages or media content but can in fact control, create, influence, recreate, alter, and engage in shaping them across platforms and communication channels."[27] He also notes that since audiences have been empowered to control the kind of messages or content they want to receive—including where, when, and how they want them—the function of integrator has shifted from marketers to the consumers themselves, and in the digital age, the consumer is in control of the integration process.

In addition to the proliferation of media options and fragmentation of audiences, marketers are also facing the challenge of consumers being less responsive to and finding ways to avoid their advertising messages. Many consumers are turned off by advertising and other forms of marketing communication because they are tired of being bombarded with sales messages. Younger consumers in the millennial and gen Z age cohorts (which include most college students) are particularly skeptical of advertising. Having grown up in an even more media-saturated and brand-conscious world than their parents did, they respond differently to advertising, and simply pushing messages at them does not work very well.[28] Nearly all of the millennials and gen Zers have smartphones and are spending less time with traditional media. However, like other age cohorts, they are actively seeking ways to avoid advertising messages, not only on television but online as well. They are installing ad blockers on their computers, tablets, and smartphones and skipping out of online ads as quickly as possible (Exhibit 1–5). Recent

EXHIBIT 1–5

The use of AdBlock Plus on computers and mobile devices is increasing.

eyeo GmbH

studies have shown that nearly 43 percent of Internet users worldwide use ad blockers with estimates of their use in the United States ranging from 27 percent to nearly 40 percent.[29] The use of ad blockers is highest for personal computers, but their use on mobile devices has nearly doubled over the past 5 years. The primary reasons consumers use ad blockers is that they feel websites are more manageable without banner ads, they wish to avoid irrelevant or offensive images/messages, and they have privacy concerns such as not wanting their online behavior tracked.[30]

The advertising industry, as well as online publishers such as newspapers, magazines, blogs, and the myriad websites available on the Internet, are very concerned over the impact ad blockers are having on their digital advertising business.[31] Companies that sell advertising space on their websites, apps, and social media sites are paid based on the number of people who see, watch, or click on the ads, so the use of ad blockers has the potential to undermine their basic business model. For example, Spotify, which is one of the most popular music streaming subscription services, changed its terms of service in 2019 to include a ban on ad blockers and notified users that it has the right to suspend any accounts that use them.[32]

The integrated marketing communications movement is also being impacted by fundamental changes in the way companies market their products and services and an ongoing marketing revolution that is changing the rules of marketing.[33] These changes and developments are affecting everyone involved in the marketing and promotional process. Marketers can no longer be tied to a specific communication tool (such as media advertising); rather, they should use whatever contact methods offer the best way of delivering the message to their target audiences. Ad agencies continue to reposition themselves as offering more than just advertising expertise; they strive to convince their clients that they can manage all or any part of clients' integrated marketing communications needs. Most agencies recognize that their future success depends on their ability to understand how to develop and place advertising messages not just for traditional media but also for the rapidly evolving areas of digital marketing, including social media and mobile.

The Role of IMC in Branding

One of the major reasons for the growing importance of integrated marketing communications is that it plays a major role in the process of developing and sustaining brand identity and equity. As branding expert Kevin Keller notes, "Building and properly managing brand equity has become a priority for companies of all sizes, in all types of industries, in all types of markets."[34] With more and more products and services competing for consideration by customers who have less and less time to make choices, well-known brands have a major competitive advantage in today's marketplace. Building and maintaining brand identity and equity require the creation of well-known brands that have favorable, strong, and unique associations in the mind of the consumer.[35] Companies recognize that brand equity is as important an asset as factories, patents, and cash because strong brands have the power to command a premium price from consumers as well as investors. While competitors may be able to duplicate their product designs and manufacturing processes, it is very difficult to duplicate the beliefs, images, and impressions that are ingrained in the minds of consumers as well as the emotions brands evoke. Figure 1-1 shows the world's most valuable brands, as measured by Interbrand, a leading brand consultancy company.

Brand identity is a combination of many factors, including the name, logo, symbols, design, packaging, and performance of a product or service as well as the image or type of associations that come to mind when consumers think about a brand. It encompasses the entire spectrum of consumers' awareness, knowledge, and image of the brand as well as the company behind it. It is the sum of all points of encounter or contact that consumers have with the brand, and it extends beyond the experience or outcome of using it. These contacts can also result from various forms of integrated marketing communications activities used by a company, including mass-media

FIGURE 1-1

Best Global Brands 2022

Rank	Brand	Brand Value (billions)
1	Apple	$482,215
2	Microsoft	278,288
3	Amazon	274,819
4	Google	251,751
5	Samsung	87,689
6	Toyota	59,757
7	Coca-Cola	57,535
8	Mercedes-Benz	56,103
9	Disney	50,325
10	Nike	50,289

Source: "Interbrand's Best Global Brands 2022" is a look at financial performance of the brand, role of brand in the purchase decision process, and the brand strength. For more information go to: https://interbrand.com/best-global-brands/.

advertising, sales promotion offers, sponsorship activities at sporting or entertainment events, websites, social media, and e-mail messages. Consumers can also have contact with or receive information about a brand in stores at the point of sale; through articles or stories they see, hear, or read in the media; or through interactions with a company representative, such as a salesperson. For many companies, mass-media advertising has long been the cornerstone of their brand-building efforts. However, astute marketers recognize that the way consumers relate to brands is changing, and they can no longer build and maintain brand equity merely by spending large sums of money on media advertising and other forms of marketing communication. Brands are becoming less about the actual product or service and more about how people relate to them. Consumers today demand more than just product/service quality or performance, as many view brands as a form of self-expression. It is also widely recognized that marketing is now in the relationship era and companies must connect with consumers based on trust, transparency, engagement, and authenticity. As one chief marketing officer notes: "The future of marketing isn't about getting people to buy your brand, but to buy *into* your brand."[36]

The relationship between brands and their customers has become much more complex. One reason for this is that today's consumer knows much more about brands and the companies that make them than ever before. The value chain of companies has become increasingly visible, and consumers often select brands based on the social, economic, and environmental records and policies of the companies that make them. **Sustainability**, which refers to development that meets the needs of the current generation without compromising the ability of future generations to meet their needs, has become a very important issue for both consumers and corporations.[37] Companies are addressing sustainability by carefully examining the social and environmental impacts of their marketing strategies. This means reevaluating their product and service portfolios, as well as the way these products and services are created, produced, and marketed. A company that is a leader in sustainability is the outdoor apparel company Patagonia, which was founded on the principles of sustainability and transparency and has a 40-year history of environmental conservation and activism. Protecting and preserving the environment is a core business tenet of the company, which is reflected in its mission to "Build the best product, cause no unnecessary harm, use business to inspire and implement solutions to the environmental crisis." Each year the company contributes 1 percent of its annual net revenue to

To Love it is To Respect it.

Patagonia loves nature and we know good gear. To protect our playground, we donate 1% of our revenues to conservation groups throughout the world like the Save the Waves Coalition.

patagonia
patagonia.com

EXHIBIT 1-6

Patagonia is a leader in sustainability and since 1985 has pledged 1 percent of sales to the preservation and restoration of the natural environment.

Patagonia, Inc.

nonprofit charitable organizations that promote environmental conservation and sustainability (Exhibit 1-6).

Marketers are recognizing that many consumers evaluate them based not only on their support of the environment, but on their positions on various social, political, and economic issues as well and often factor this into their purchase decisions. Thus marketing's role is evolving from communicating the value proposition for a company's products and services to an ethical compass that defines its beliefs and values and shapes its behavior. Ethical Perspective 1-1 discusses how this has led to an increase in **brand activism**, which involves a company or brand taking a stand and engaging in efforts to promote social, political, economic, or environmental reform to help drive change in order to improve society.

Cynicism about corporations remains high, and many companies must continue to work hard to gain consumer trust and confidence. Companies are also finding it more difficult to control their brand image because the Internet provides consumers with a wealth of information about their products and services that can be easily accessed and shared. They can use the Internet to make price and quality comparisons or to learn what others think about various brands as well as learn about their experiences or satisfaction with them. The pervasiveness of social media has transformed traditional word-of-mouth into viral "word-of-mouse" messages that fly around Facebook, Twitter, YouTube, or Yelp at the speed of send. Consumers' passion for brands shows no sign of waning and in fact may be getting stronger. However, the ways that companies connect consumers to their companies and brands are changing.

Ethical Perspective 1-1 >>>

Brand Activism—Taking a Stand to Build Your Brand

Traditionally, companies and their brands have not engaged in socially and politically charged conversations for fear of potentially alienating customers. For most companies social responsibility has focused on philanthropic or charitable efforts or on satisfying the environmental, social, and governance (ESG) criteria used by socially conscious investors to screen investments based on corporate polices and to encourage companies to act responsibly. In the past, consumers did not expect companies to take a stand on issues unrelated to their value propositions, and brands could be positioned based on utilitarian or emotional factors such as performance and/ or brand image. However, in recent years there have been a number of events and developments that have led to greater attention being focused on fundamental issues of economic, social, and racial equality as well as diversity and inclusion. This heightened focus is leading consumers to call on companies to take a firm and definitive position on controversial issues and to communicate their stance publicly.

For many companies and brands, neutrality is no longer an option at a time when consumers feel that saying

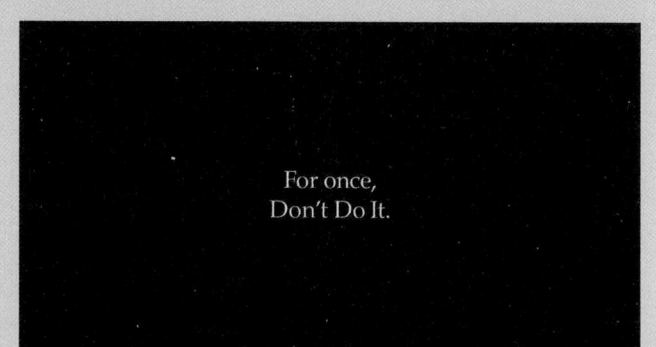

For once,
Don't Do It.

Nike, Inc.

nothing is really saying something after all. Companies no longer have a choice and must determine how to align their values with those of their customers, employees, and society at large. This has led to a new strategy of *brand activism*, which involves a company or brand taking a stand and engaging in efforts to promote social, political, economic, or environmental reform to help drive change in order to improve society. There have been a number of controversial social issues on which companies are being asked to take a stand. Many companies have been forced to confront the issue of racial injustice in America following the tragic deaths of George Floyd, Breonna Taylor, and Ahmaud Arbery. More recent issues include the U.S. Supreme Court's overturning of *Roe v. Wade*, which has led to many states banning or restricting rights to an abortion. Calls for stronger gun control laws have followed numerous mass shootings such as those at a grocery store in Buffalo, New York, a July 4 parade in Highland Park, Illinois, and an elementary school in Uvalde, Texas. The tremendous revulsion over Russia's unprovoked invasion of Ukraine in early 2022 has led a myriad of American and international companies—including McDonald's, Starbucks, Nike, Apple, and Coca-Cola—to stop doing business in that country. Their actions range from limiting access to their products and services to pulling out of Russia altogether as part of economic sanctions against the country.

A number of companies have taken strong positions on these issues and taken steps to address them. For example, Nike was one of the first companies to respond to the protests and unrest following the murder of George Floyd with a series of statements on various social media channels. Putting a spin on its iconic "Just Do It" slogan, the statements read: "For once, don't do it, Don't pretend there's not a problem in America, Don't turn your back on racism." Many other companies followed Nike's lead with campaigns similar in tone and style, and rival adidas retweeted the anti-racism message. Many companies have also taken an activist position with regard to gun violence and mass shootings. In June 2022 the CEOs of more than 250 companies, including Patagonia, Dick's Sporting Goods, Unilever, Lyft, Levi Strauss & Co., and Lululemon, cosigned a letter urging the U.S. Senate to take immediate action to address what they called an epidemic of gun violence following the series of high-profile mass shootings noted previously. The letter from CEOs for Gun Safety urged the Senate to pass bold gun safety legislation to avoid more death and injury.

Companies engaging in brand activism can be rewarded for taking a stance on sociopolitical issues. However, they also are taking a calculated risk as consumers may boycott a brand if it weighs in on the wrong side of an issue or supports in the wrong way. Many branding experts suggest that companies tread carefully when using brand activism as a strategy. They argue that consumers are more divided than ever when it comes to sociopolitical issues, and rhetoric from polarized media outlets and social media can be very damaging to a brand. Before pursuing a brand activism strategy, marketers must consider whether the cause is a good fit for the company and whether it might be polarizing along racial, generational, or political lines. Consideration must also be given to whether a brand's support of a particular cause or issue will be seen as genuine and credible or whether it is viewed as a marketing tool or gimmick instead of authentic brand activism.

While many companies prefer to sit on the sidelines, remaining ambivalent on controversial issues can also be very risky, particularly for brands targeting younger generations of consumers. Studies show that young people around the world are growing up with a deeper sense of purpose than previous generations and prefer companies and brands that directly support causes about which they care. Research shows that millennials and gen Zers, which are very important age cohorts for marketers given their size and spending capacity, are looking for brands that support their values, stand for a cause, and are giving back to the community.

Critics of brand activism argue that it is often little more than a public relations stunt, noting that it is often inauthentic, opportunistic, imitative, or just "woke washing"—which devalue such activism overall. However, many argue that taking a stance or having a point of view on societal issues is no longer a choice but rather is becoming unavoidable. Thus, companies have to determine how their brands can make meaningful contributions and how to communicate this to consumers.

Sources: Ayesha Javed, "CEOs Make the Business Case for Gun Control in Letter Calling for 'Urgent Action,'" *TIME*, June 10, 2022, https://time.com/6186410/ceos-gun-laws-letter/; Detavio Samuels, "Social Responsibility Is a Business Requirement, Not a Make-Good Strategy," *Advertising Age*, March 7, 2022, p. 24; Dick Herbert and Charlie Almond, "Like It or Not, Your Future as an Activist Brand Has Already Begun," *Brand Activism Year in Review 2021—Dentsu*, https://brands.dentsu.com/year-review-2021/brand-activism.

Marketers recognize that in the modern world of marketing, there are many different opportunities and methods for *contacting* current and prospective customers to provide them with information about a company and/or brands. They also recognize that their IMC strategy is an essential part of their strategic brand management process and that strong brand equity requires consistent and effective communication through various brand identify contacts.[38] The challenge is to understand how to use the various IMC tools to make such contacts and deliver the branding message effectively and efficiently. A successful IMC program requires that marketers find the right combination of communication tools and techniques, define their role and the extent to which they can or should be used, and coordinate their use. To accomplish this, the persons responsible for the company's communication efforts must have an understanding of the IMC tools that are available and the ways they can be used.

THE PROMOTIONAL MIX: THE TOOLS FOR IMC

Promotion has been defined as the coordination of all seller-initiated efforts to set up channels of information and persuasion in order to sell goods and services or promote an idea.[39] While implicit communication occurs through the various elements of the marketing mix, most of an organization's communications with the marketplace take place as part of a carefully planned and controlled promotional program. The basic tools used to accomplish an organization's communication objectives are often referred to as the **promotional mix** (Figure 1–2).

Traditionally the promotional mix has included four elements: advertising, sales promotion, publicity/public relations, and personal selling. However, in this text we view direct marketing as well as digital/Internet marketing that takes place online as major promotional-mix elements that marketers use to communicate with their target markets. Each element of the promotional mix is viewed as an integrated marketing communications tool that plays a distinctive role in an IMC program. Each may take on a variety of forms. And each has certain advantages.

Advertising

Advertising is defined as any paid form of nonpersonal communication about an organization, product, service, or idea by an identified sponsor.[40] The *paid* aspect of this definition reflects the fact that the space or time for an advertising message generally must be bought. An occasional exception to this is the public service announcement (PSA), whose advertising space or time is donated by the media, usually to a nonprofit organization or cause.

The *nonpersonal* component means that advertising involves using media (e.g., TV, the Internet, radio, magazines, newspapers) that can transmit a message to groups of individuals, often at the same time. The nonpersonal nature of advertising means that there is generally no opportunity for immediate feedback from the message recipient (except in direct-response advertising). Therefore, before the message is sent, the advertiser must consider how the audience will interpret and respond to it.

Advertising is the best-known and most widely discussed form of promotion, probably because of its pervasiveness. It is also a very important promotional tool, particularly for companies whose products and services are targeted at mass consumer markets, such as automobile manufacturers and packaged-goods and drug companies. Nearly 200 companies spend over $200 million each on advertising in the United States each year, including spending in measured media (television, radio, newspapers, magazines, outdoor, and Internet display advertising) as well as unmeasured media (direct marketing, promotion, online search, social media, and other forms). Figure 1–3 shows the advertising and promotion expenditures of the 25 leading national advertisers.

There are several reasons why advertising is such an important part of many marketers' IMC programs. First, media advertising is still the most cost-effective way to reach large numbers of consumers with an advertising message. Television in particular is an excellent way for marketers to reach mass markets. The four major broadcast networks—CBS, NBC, ABC, and Fox—average around 20 million viewers in total across prime time (7:00 p.m. to 10:00 p.m. or 8:00 p.m. to 11:00 p.m., depending on the time zone)

FIGURE 1–2

Elements of the Promotional Mix

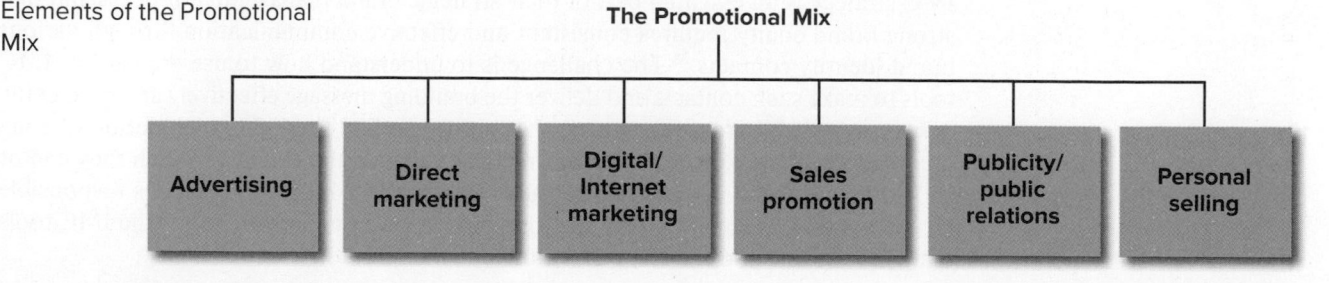

FIGURE 1–3

25 Leading Advertisers in the United States, 2021

Rank	Advertiser	Advertising and Promotion Spending (Millions)
1	Amazon	$10,430
2	Comcast Corp.	6,012
3	Procter & Gamble Co.	5,079
4	American Express Co.	3,376
5	Walt Disney Co.	3,759
6	Alphabet (Google)	3,602
7	Warner Bros. Discovery	3,413
8	Verizon Communications	3,394
9	Walmart	3,105
10	Charter Communications	3,071
11	L'Oreal	2,846
12	Capital One Financial Corp.	2,719
13	General Motors Co.	2,695
14	AT&T	2,541
15	Berkshire Hathaway	2,496
16	Nestle	2,424
17	JP Morgan Chase & Co.	2,313
18	Samsung Electronics Co.	2,256
19	LVMH Moët Hennessy Louis Vuitton	2,229
20	Deutsche Telecom (T-Mobile US)	2,200
21	Progressive Corp.	2,140
22	Expedia Group	2,063
23	Ford Motor Co.	1,978
24	PepsiCo	1,962
25	AbbVie	1,863

Source: "Leading National Advertisers 2022," *Advertising Age*, June 27, 2022, p. 15. Copyright ©Crain Communications 2022.

with the average episode of a program reaching around 6 million viewers either live or within 7 days. Popular shows such as *NCIS*, *The Equalizer*, and *60 Minutes* can reach between 9 to 11 million viewers each week. Live sports programming is particularly good at delivering large audiences as NBC's *Sunday Night Football* has been the highest rated show for the past decade and averages around 18 million viewers.[41] And while the viewing audiences for cable networks such as ESPN, CNN, TNT, HGTV, and MTV are smaller than those for the major networks, their programming appeals to more specific audiences that many marketers are trying to reach. The television viewing landscape has changed dramatically over the past 5 years with the explosive growth in streaming services that has led to significant declines in viewership for broadcast and cable networks. However, these networks can still deliver large numbers of viewers and remain popular among marketers trying to reach mass audiences.

EXHIBIT 1–7

The American Advertising Federation promotes the value of advertising.

Courtesy of American Advertising Federation

Another traditional advertising medium that has declined in audience size, but can still reach large numbers of consumers, is magazines. Magazines such as *Better Homes and Gardens*, *People*, and *Good Housekeeping* have circulation of more than 3 million readers each week or month and can reach more than 10 million people since there are multiple readers of each issue. Thus, for marketers who want to build or maintain brand awareness and reach mass markets with their advertising messages, media advertising remains an excellent way to do so.[42]

Advertising is also a valuable tool for building company or brand equity because it is a powerful way to provide consumers with information as well as to influence their perceptions. Advertising can be used to create favorable and unique images and associations for a brand, which can be very important for companies selling products or services that are difficult to differentiate on the basis of functional attributes. Brand image plays an important role in the purchase of many products and services, and advertising is still recognized as one of the best ways to build a brand. Exhibit 1–7 shows an ad from a campaign run by the American Advertising Federation promoting the value of advertising.

The nature and purpose of advertising differ from one industry to another and/or across situations. Companies selling products and services to the consumer market generally rely heavily on advertising to communicate with their target audiences, as do retailers and other local merchants. However, advertising can also be done by an industry to stimulate demand for a product category such as beef or milk. Advertising is also used extensively by companies who compete in the business and professional markets to reach current and potential customers. For example, business-to-business (B2B) marketers use advertising to perform important functions such as building awareness of the company and its products, generating leads for the sales force, reassuring customers about the purchase they have made, or helping create a favorable image of the company. B2B marketers generally target their advertising to reach key decision makers in other companies and often run their ads in business publications such as magazines and newspapers, although television and the Internet are the largest categories for B2B ad spending. Many products such as personal computers, tablets, smartphones, and printers along with services such as finance and banking, telecommunications, and insurance are marketed to both business customers and consumers. Thus, marketers sometimes develop ad campaigns that serve both markets.[43] Exhibit 1–8 shows an ad from Qualcomm, which designs and markets products and services for the wireless

EXHIBIT 1–8

Qualcomm promotes its leadership role in powering wireless connectivity.

Qualcomm Technologies, Inc.

telecommunications industry. The company is leading the way in fifth-generation (5G) wireless technology that is being used in smartphones, tablets, and many other devices. Qualcomm runs advertising in a variety of media—including print, television, and digital—showing how 5G will help empower the next generation of technological progress and lead the way in wireless connectivity and areas such as on-device artificial intelligence (AI). The company's IMC targets other businesses as well as consumers who are users of wireless devices. Figure 1–4 describes the most common types of advertising.

FIGURE 1–4

Classifications of Advertising

ADVERTISING TO CONSUMER MARKETS

National Advertising
Advertising done by large companies on a nationwide basis or in most regions of the country. Most of the ads for well-known companies and brands that are seen on prime-time TV or in other major national or regional media are examples of national advertising. The goals of national advertisers are to inform or remind consumers of the company or brand and its features, benefits, advantages, or uses and to create or reinforce its image so that consumers will be predisposed to purchase it.

Retail/Local Advertising
Advertising done by retailers or local merchants to encourage consumers to shop at a specific store, use a local service, or patronize a particular establishment. Retail or local advertising tends to emphasize specific patronage motives such as price, hours of operation, service, atmosphere, image, or merchandise assortment. Retailers are concerned with building store traffic, so their promotions often take the form of direct-action advertising designed to produce immediate store traffic and sales.

Primary- versus Selective-Demand Advertising
Primary-demand advertising is designed to stimulate demand for the general product class or entire industry. Selective-demand advertising focuses on creating demand for a specific company's brands. Most advertising for products and services is concerned with stimulating selective demand and emphasizes reasons for purchasing a particular brand.
   An advertiser might concentrate on stimulating primary demand when, for example, its brand dominates a market and will benefit the most from overall market growth. Primary-demand advertising is often used as part of a promotional strategy to help a new product gain market acceptance, since the challenge is to sell customers on the product concept as much as to sell a particular brand. Industry trade associations also try to stimulate primary demand for their members' products, among them cotton, milk, orange juice, pork, and beef.

ADVERTISING TO BUSINESS AND PROFESSIONAL MARKETS

Business-to-Business Advertising
Advertising targeted at individuals who buy or influence the purchase of industrial goods or services for their companies. Industrial goods are products that either become a physical part of another product (raw material or component parts), are used in manufacturing other goods (machinery), or are used to help a company conduct its business (e.g., office supplies, computers). Business services such as insurance, travel services, and health care are also included in this category.

Professional Advertising
Advertising targeted to professionals such as doctors, lawyers, dentists, engineers, or professors to encourage them to use a company's product in their business operations. It might also be used to encourage professionals to recommend or specify the use of a company's product by end-users.

Trade Advertising
Advertising targeted to marketing channel members such as wholesalers, distributors, and retailers. The goal is to encourage channel members to stock, promote, and resell the manufacturer's branded products to their customers.

Direct Marketing

One of the fastest-growing sectors of the U.S. economy is **direct marketing**, in which organizations communicate directly with target customers to generate a response and/or a transaction. Traditionally, direct marketing has not been considered an element of the promotional mix. However, because it has become such an integral part of the IMC program of many organizations and often involves separate objectives, budgets, and strategies, we view direct marketing as a component of the promotional mix.

Direct marketing is much more than direct mail and mail-order catalogs. It involves a variety of activities, including database management, direct selling, telemarketing, and direct-response advertising through direct mail, online, and various broadcast and print media. Some companies, such as Tupperware, Avon, Mary Kay, Herbalife, and Amway, do not use any other distribution channels, relying on independent contractors to sell their products directly to consumers. Companies such as L.L.Bean, Lands' End, J.Crew, and LuLaRoe have been very successful in using direct marketing to sell their clothing products.

One of the major tools of direct marketing is **direct-response advertising**, whereby a product is promoted through an ad that encourages the consumer to purchase directly from the manufacturer. Traditionally, direct mail has been the primary medium for direct-response advertising, although television and the Internet have become increasingly important media. Direct-response advertising and other forms of direct marketing have become very popular over the past two decades, owing primarily to changing lifestyles, particularly the increase in two-income households. This has meant more discretionary income but less time for in-store shopping. The availability of credit cards and toll-free phone numbers has also facilitated the purchase of products from direct-response ads. More recently, the rapid growth of mobile devices to access the Internet is fueling the growth of direct marketing. Many consumers go straight to their smartphones or tablets to search for information about a product or service, and they are very comfortable with making purchases through a mobile device. The convenience of shopping through catalogs or on a company's website and placing orders online has become very appealing to many consumers, and marketers recognize that this can be an effective way to augment their sales through traditional retail channels. For example, athletic shoe and apparel companies such as Nike, adidas, and Under Armour now generate a significant portion of their sales revenue through their e-commerce websites, in addition to selling their products through sports retail stores and their company-owned stores. Nike Direct, which is the direct-to-consumer division of the company, now accounts for nearly 40 percent of the company's revenue. Nike has been investing heavily in digital channels and applications as it pivots away from traditional relationships with retail chains (Exhibit 1–9).

Direct-marketing tools and techniques are also being used by companies that distribute their products through traditional distribution channels or have their own sales force. One of the major trends in marketing that has emerged over the past decade is that of **omnichannel retailing**, whereby companies sell their products through multiple distribution channels including retail stores, online, catalogs, and mobile apps. However, it is about more than just offering a product or service through multiple channels. An omnichannel strategy involves using a combination of physical or offline channels as well as digital or online channels to influence a customer's shopping experience including research before a purchase and service after a sale.[44] Direct marketing plays a big role in the integrated marketing communications programs of consumer-product companies and business-to-business marketers. They use telemarketing to call customers directly and attempt to sell them products and services or qualify them as sales leads. Marketers also send out e-mails, direct-mail pieces ranging from simple letters and flyers to detailed brochures, catalogs, and other promotional materials to give potential customers information about their products or services. Direct-marketing techniques are also used to distribute product samples.

EXHIBIT 1–9

Nike Total Direct-to-Consumer Sales

Sales Year	Sales (in U.S. $billion)
2009	2.18
2010	2.48
2011	2.88
2012	3.57
2013	4.37
2014	5.3
2015	6.63
2016	7.86
2017	9.08
2018	10.43
2019	11.75
2020	12.38
2021	16.37
2022	18.73

Many companies now have extensive databases containing customer names; mail and e-mail addresses; geographic, demographic, and psychographic profiles; purchase patterns, media preferences, credit, and other financial information; and other relevant customer characteristics. Marketers use this information to target their current and prospective customers through a variety of direct-marketing methods such as direct mail, e-mail marketing, telemarketing, and others. These databases are an integral part of companies' customer relationship management (CRM) programs, which involve the systematic tracking of customer preferences and behaviors and modifying a product or service to meet individual needs and wants.[45]

Digital/Internet Marketing

Over the past two decades we have been experiencing perhaps the most dynamic and revolutionary changes in the history of marketing and of integrated marketing communications in particular. These changes are being driven by advances in technology that have led to the dramatic growth of communication through interactive, digital media via the Internet. **Interactive media** allow for a two-way flow of communication whereby users can participate in and modify the form and content of the information they receive in real time. Unlike other forms of marketing communication—such as traditional media advertising—that are one-way in nature, the digital media allow users to perform a variety of activities such as receive, alter, and share information and images; make inquiries; respond to questions; and make purchases online. The rapid growth of the Internet and, more recently, social media has forever changed the nature of how companies do business and the ways they communicate and interact with consumers. Every day more consumers around the world are gaining access to the Internet's World Wide Web of information available to users. There are now more than 5.3 billion Internet users around the world, including 297 million in the United States, where more than 90 percent of the adult population has access to the web.[46] Nearly all marketers are making the Internet an integral part of their marketing communications, as well as overall business strategy.

The Internet is actually a multifaceted marketing communication tool. On one hand, it is an advertising medium as many marketers pay to run display and video ads promoting their products and services on the websites of other companies, organizations, and web publishers. Advertisers also pay Internet search engines such as Google, Bing, and Yahoo! to place ads in or near relevant search results based on keywords. Paid search has become the most widely used form of Internet advertising. The Internet can also be used as a marketing communication tool in its own right because it is a medium that can be used to execute all of the elements of the promotional mix. In addition to advertising on the web, marketers offer sales promotion incentives such as coupons, contests, and sweepstakes online, and they use the Internet to conduct direct marketing, personal selling, and public relations activities more effectively and efficiently.

We are well into the second phase of the Internet revolution, often referred to as "Web 2.0," where the focus is on collaboration and sharing among Internet users. This has given rise to the development and growth of **social media**, which refers to online means of communication and interactions among people that are used to create, share, and exchange content such as information, insights, experiences, perspectives, and even media themselves. It is estimated that nearly three-quarters of Americans have a social network profile and are using one or more social media platforms such as Facebook, Twitter, LinkedIn, Instagram, YouTube, Snapchat, TikTok, and Pinterest. Usage of social media among teens and young adults (18 to 29) is particularly high, with 90 percent of this age group using social networking sites.[47] Social media have revolutionized how companies communicate with, listen to, and learn from their customers and have become a major marketing tool for most companies. Companies and organizations are using social media as well by creating Facebook and Instagram pages, YouTube channels, and Twitter accounts, or by posting advertisements and videos on YouTube, TikTok, and other sites.[48]

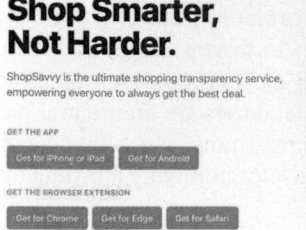

EXHIBIT 1–10

The ShopSavvy app allows shoppers to make price comparisons before making a purchase.

Monolith Technologies, Inc.

For many years consumers accessed the Internet and social media primarily through their personal computers (PCs) including desktops and laptops. However, with the growth of smartphones and tablets there has been a dramatic shift in the way people go online; the majority of those who own these mobile devices prefer to access the Internet on them. The growing popularity of smartphones and tablets has opened up a new way for marketers to connect with consumers. Advertising is already pervasive on the first two screens in most consumers' lives—televisions and personal computers—and more and more ads and promotional messages are appearing on the "third screen" of mobile phones and tablets. This has led to the explosive growth of **mobile marketing**, which is promotional activity designed for delivery to cell phones, smartphones, tablets, and other handheld devices including apps, messaging, commerce, and customer relationship management. Mobile advertising has grown tremendously over the past several years, to an estimated $137 billion in 2022, and now accounts for more than two-thirds of digital advertising spending and just over 40 percent of all ad spending in the United States.[49]

Marketers are extremely interested in mobile marketing since messages can be delivered that are specific to a consumer's location or consumption situation.[50] One of the major factors driving the growth of this medium is the development of mobile shopping services and apps that consumers can use to make shopping more economical, efficient, productive, and fun. Services are now available that provide consumers with mobile coupons sent directly to their phones that can be redeemed at the point of purchase. Other mobile apps that are now available include price comparison apps such as ShopSavvy, BuyVia, Mycartsavings, or RedLaser that allow consumers to scan a barcode and compare prices at a given location against nearby competitors, or online retailers and social sourcing apps such as Bazaarvoice that provide consumers with outside opinions and feedback on their mobile devices while making a purchase (Exhibit 1-10). Marketers are finding a number of creative ways to connect with consumers through their mobile devices by developing their own brand-specific applications as well as games, videos, and ads. For example, Starbucks has developed apps for iPhones and Android mobile devices that allow customers to find Starbucks locations, look up nutritional information, order ahead and pick up drinks to avoid waiting in line, and manage their Starbucks Rewards accounts. Mobile apps have become a widely used marketing tool for most companies today with the vast majority of companies and businesses having a mobile application that consumers can use to access information and interact with them. Mobile apps are particularly important to companies competing in the travel and hospitality industries such as airlines, hotels, rental cars, entertainment venues, and restaurants.

The interactive nature of the Internet and social media is one of their major advantages. This capability enables marketers to gather valuable personal information from customers and prospects and to adjust their offers accordingly, in some cases in real time. For example, a number of companies adjust prices and display different product offers to consumers based on a variety of characteristics such as their web browsing history and location, which includes proximity to rival stores.[51] Another advantage of the Internet is that it provides marketers with the capability to more closely and precisely measure the effects of their advertising and other forms of promotion. There are a number of metrics that can be generated when consumers visit websites or spend time on social media, which allow marketers to determine how consumers are responding to their campaigns, how well they are engaging them, and the return on investment they are receiving from their promotional dollars.

Companies recognize the advantages of the Internet, and many are increasing the role various forms of digital and social media play in their IMC programs. They are developing campaigns that integrate their websites, social media, and mobile marketing with other aspects of their IMC programs such as media advertising.

EXHIBIT 1–11

Coupons, like this one for Bumble Bee Sensations, are a popular consumer-oriented sales promotion tool.

Source: Bumble Bee Foods, LLC

Sales Promotion

The next variable in the promotional mix is **sales promotion**, which is generally defined as those marketing activities that provide extra value or incentives to the sales force, the distributors, or the ultimate consumer and can stimulate immediate sales. Sales promotion is generally broken into two major categories: consumer-oriented and trade-oriented activities.

Consumer-oriented sales promotion is targeted to the ultimate user of a product or service and includes couponing, sampling, premiums, rebates, contests, sweepstakes, and various point-of-purchase materials (Exhibit 1–11). These promotional tools encourage consumers to make an immediate purchase and thus can stimulate short-term sales. *Trade-oriented sales promotion* is targeted toward marketing intermediaries such as wholesalers, distributors, and retailers. Promotional and merchandising allowances, price deals, sales contests, and trade shows are some of the promotional tools used to encourage the trade to stock and promote a company's products.

Among many consumer packaged-goods companies, sales promotion is often 50 to 60 percent of the promotional budget, with much of this money spent on trade promotion.[52] Reasons for the increased emphasis on sales promotion include declining brand loyalty and increased consumer sensitivity to promotional deals. Another major reason is that retailers have become larger and more powerful and are demanding more trade promotion support from their vendors.

Promotion and *sales promotion* are two terms that often create confusion in the advertising and marketing fields. As noted, promotion is an element of marketing by which firms communicate with their customers; it includes all the promotional-mix elements we have just discussed. However, many marketing and advertising practitioners use the term more narrowly to refer to sales promotion activities to either consumers or the trade (retailers, wholesalers). In this book, *promotion* is used in the broader sense to refer to the various marketing communications activities of an organization.

Publicity/Public Relations

Another important component of an organization's promotional mix is publicity/public relations.

Publicity　Publicity refers to nonpersonal communications regarding an organization, product, service, or idea not directly paid for or run under identified sponsorship. It usually comes in the form of a news story, editorial, or announcement about an organization and/or its products and services. Like advertising, publicity involves nonpersonal communication to a mass audience, but unlike advertising, publicity is not directly paid for by the company. The company or organization attempts to get the media to cover or run a favorable story on a product, service, cause, or event to affect awareness, knowledge, opinions, and/or behavior. Techniques used to gain publicity include press releases, press conferences, feature articles, photographs, films, and video news releases.

An advantage of publicity over other forms of promotion is its credibility. Consumers generally tend to be less skeptical toward favorable information about a product or service when it comes from a source they perceive as unbiased. For example, the success (or failure) of a new movie is often determined by the reviews it receives from film critics, who are viewed by many moviegoers as objective evaluators. Another advantage of publicity is its low cost, since the company is not paying for time or space in a mass medium such as TV, radio, or newspapers. While an organization may incur some costs in developing publicity items or maintaining a staff to do so, these expenses will be far less than those for the other promotional programs.

Publicity is not always under the control of an organization and is sometimes unfavorable. Negative stories about a company and/or its products can be very damaging. For example, Facebook and parent company Meta have received a great deal of negative publicity recently over various issues such as their privacy policies and handling of user data, as well as how they have dealt with misinformation and hate speech on their

EXHIBIT 1–12

Honda uses advertising to enhance its corporate image by showing its commitment to building products and creating jobs in America.

American Honda Motor Co., Inc. and Rubin Postaer and Associates

platform. The company faced a major PR crisis in 2021 when a former employee turned whistle blower linked internal documents that exposed some of the internal workings of Facebook and how much the company knew about the harmful effects its platform was having on users and society. The documents showed that the company has studied the negative impact Instagram has on teenage girls yet has done little to mitigate the harms. The company has publicly denied that the social media causes any harm to them. Facebook has also received negative publicity recently over the exposure of Facebook and Instagram user passwords to employees in the company. Concern over these issues has resulted in mounting pressure for the U.S. government to take action to regulate the company and has led many users of Facebook and Instagram to deactivate or even delete their accounts.[53]

Public Relations   It is important to recognize the distinction between publicity and public relations. When an organization systematically plans and distributes information in an attempt to control and manage its image and the nature of the publicity it receives, it is really engaging in a function known as public relations. **Public relations (PR)** is defined as "a strategic communication process that builds mutually beneficial relationships between organizations and their publics."[54] Public relations generally has a broader objective than does publicity, as its purpose is to establish and maintain a positive image of the company among its various publics. Thus, it involves managing relationships with a number of important audiences, including investors, employees, suppliers, communities, and governments (federal, state, and local) as well as consumers.

Public relations uses publicity and a variety of other tools—including special publications, participation in community activities, fund-raising, sponsorship of special events, and various public affairs activities—to enhance an organization's image. Companies also use advertising as a public relations tool. For example, the ad shown in Exhibit 1–12 is part of the American Honda Motor Co.'s corporate social responsibility campaign, which communicates the company's stance on important issues such as social values, business ethics, diversity, environmental stewardship, and community involvement. The ad promotes Honda's commitment to building fuel-efficient products, such as the Honda Jet, and innovating and creating jobs in America.

Traditionally, publicity and public relations have been considered more supportive than primary to the marketing and promotional process. However, many companies now make PR an integral part of their IMC strategy. PR firms are increasingly touting public relations as a communications tool that can take over many of the functions of conventional advertising and marketing.[55]

Personal Selling

The final element of an organization's promotional mix is **personal selling**, a form of person-to-person communication in which a seller attempts to assist and/or persuade prospective buyers to purchase the company's product or service or to act on an idea. Unlike advertising, personal selling involves direct contact between buyer and seller, either face to face or through some form of telecommunications such as telephone sales. This interaction gives the marketer communication flexibility; the seller can see or hear the potential buyer's reactions and modify the message accordingly. The personal, individualized communication in personal selling allows the seller to tailor the message to the customer's specific needs or situation.

Personal selling also involves more immediate and precise feedback because the impact of the sales presentation can generally be assessed from the customer's reactions. If the feedback is unfavorable, the salesperson can modify the message. Personal-selling efforts can also be targeted to specific markets and customer types that are the best prospects for the company's product or service.

While personal selling is an important part of the promotional mix, it will not be covered in this text because it is not a direct part of the IMC program in most companies. Also, personal selling is managed separately in most organizations and is not under the control of the advertising or marketing communications manager. However, throughout the text we will address the many ways and situations in which various IMC tools such as media advertising, digital marketing, and sales promotion must be coordinated with the personal-selling program.

IMC INVOLVES AUDIENCE CONTACTS

The various promotional-mix elements are the major tools that marketers use to communicate with current and/or prospective customers as well as other relevant audiences. However, each of these tools is multifaceted since there are various types of media advertising (print, broadcast, outdoor) and sales promotion as well as ways by which marketers use the Internet (websites, social media, online advertising). Moreover, there are additional ways companies communicate with current and prospective customers that extend beyond the traditional promotional mix. Figure 1–5 provides a more extensive list of the ways by which marketers can communicate with their target audiences.

Many companies are taking an *audience contact* or *touch point* perspective in developing their IMC programs whereby they consider all of the potential ways of reaching their target audience and presenting the company or brand in a favorable manner. A **touch point** refers to each and every opportunity the customer has to see or hear about the company and/or its brands or have an encounter or experience with it. These contacts can range from simply seeing or hearing an ad for a brand to actually having the opportunity to use or experience a brand in a retail store or interacting with the company during a sales transaction or service encounter. Tom Duncan notes that there are four basic categories of contact or touch points.[56] These are as follows:

- *Company-created touch points* are planned marketing communication messages created by the company such as advertisements, websites and social media sites, news/press releases, packaging, brochures and collateral material, sale promotions, and point-of-purchase displays along with other types of in-store décor.

FIGURE 1–5

IMC Audience Contact Tools

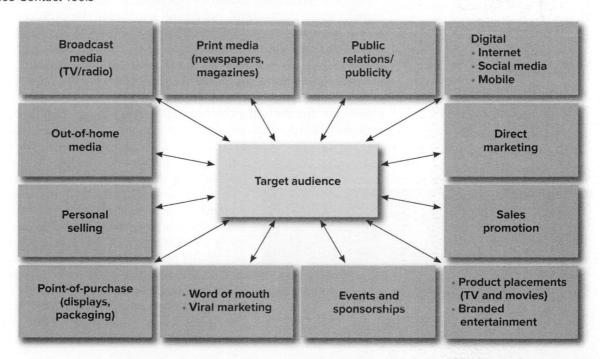

Company-created touch points account for a large part of an IMC program and have the advantage of being under the control of the marketer. However, to be effective these touch points must be relevant to consumers as well as creative and persuasive.

- *Intrinsic touch points* are interactions that occur with a company or brand during the process of buying or using the product or service such as discussions with retail sales personnel or customer service representatives. Intrinsic touch points are often not under the direct control of the marketing department or IMC program. However, Duncan notes that marketers should make suggestions regarding ways to manage and improve these interactions with customers in order to send a positive message about the company or brand. There are also various types of intrinsic touch points that are controlled, or at least may be influenced, by the marketing or IMC manager. These include the design and functioning of the company and/or brand website or social media pages, as well as the packaging, which can contain product information and impact the customers' experience of using a product. Marketers are also finding ways to communicate with consumers during the process of making a purchase by using some of the mobile marketing techniques discussed earlier.

- *Unexpected touch points* are unanticipated references or information about a company or brand that a customer or prospect receives that is beyond the control of the organization. Probably the most influential type of unexpected contact is a word-of-mouth message, which refers to a personal communication that comes from friends, associates, neighbors, co-workers, or family members. Unexpected messages may also come from other sources such as the media, which may print or broadcast stories about a company and/or its brands, as well as experts who write about products and services. Another type of unexpected touch point that has become very influential is websites and apps that provide reviews of products and services. Some of these sites provide expert reviews while others give reviews from other customers. For example, CNET is widely used by consumers looking for reviews of specific brands of consumer electronic products. Tripadvisor has grown to become one of the most popular travel destination and accommodation websites with nearly 500 million unique monthly visitors. Tripadvisor's total number of user reviews and opinions reached one billion in 2022, covering listings for restaurants, hotels, vacation rentals, and attractions. Most of you have probably relied on reviews from Yelp for a variety of local businesses such as restaurants, bars, retail stores, and professional services. Yelp averages 178 million unique visitors each month, and the reviews provided on its website are a very important source of information for many consumers. As shown in Exhibit 1–13, a review of Nick's Del Mar with its 4.5 stars, paired with the photographs, may compel someone to visit or order online, whereas a lower rating may deter consumers. It is important to note that information received from unexpected touch points such as these can be either positive or negative.

- *Customer-initiated touch points* are interactions that occur whenever a customer or prospect contacts a company. Most of these contacts involve inquiries or complaints consumers might have regarding the use of a product or service and occur through calls made directly to the company, via e-mails, or through specific sections of websites to which customers are directed. Many of the customer-initiated contacts are handled through customer service departments, although a number of companies have in-bound telemarketing departments as part of their direct sales efforts. The manner in which marketers handle customer-initiated contacts has a major impact on their ability to attract and retain customers. Moreover, many companies try to differentiate themselves on the basis of customer service and promote their customer orientation in their advertising and other aspects of their IMC programs. They also encourage current or prospective customers to contact them by calling toll-free numbers or by putting their website addresses on packages, in ads, and in various promotional materials.

EXHIBIT 1–13

Reviews on Yelp are a very important touch point and source of information for consumers in selecting restaurants.

Yelp Inc.

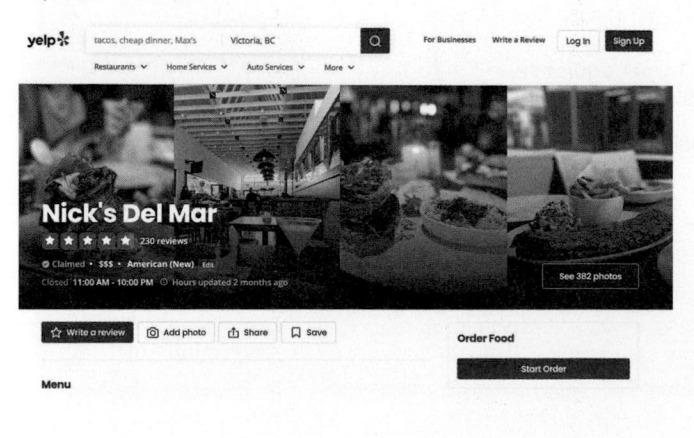

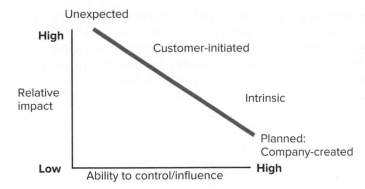

FIGURE 1–6

IMC Touch Points: Control vs. Impact

Marketers who take a contact or touch point perspective recognize that consumers' perceptions and opinions of a brand, as well as their purchase behavior, result from the information they receive and experiences and interactions they have with the company and its products or services. They also recognize that not all touch points are equally effective and they differ in regard to a company's ability to control or influence them. Figure 1–6 plots the four categories of touch points in terms of their relative impact and the marketer's ability to control them.

As can be seen in this figure, company-planned touch points are the easiest to control but are lowest in terms of impact. Marketers can control the nature and type of advertising and other forms of promotion that they send to their target audiences, but consumers often discount these messages since they receive so many of them and they recognize the persuasive intent that underlies them. At the other extreme, unexpected messages are often the most impactful but are the most difficult to control. Duncan notes that an unexpected message can be very powerful because it has the power of third-party credibility since the people who provide the information are often perceived as more believable than company sources because they have no vested interest in the success or failure of the company or brand.[57] Customer-initiated and intrinsic messages fall in between unexpected and company-created messages with respect to impact as well as the ability of the marketer to control them.

Paid, Owned, and Earned Media

Another categorization of the various types of customer touch points that has become very popular is that of paid, owned, and earned media, as shown in Figure 1–7.[58] **Paid media** refers to channels a marketer pays to leverage and includes traditional advertising media such as television, radio, print, outdoor, and direct mail as well as various forms of digital advertising such as paid search and online display and video ads. **Owned media** refers to channels of marketing communication that a company controls, such as its websites, blogs, and mobile apps as well as social media channels such as Facebook, Twitter, Instagram, and YouTube. **Earned media** is exposure for a company or brand that it did not have to pay for and is generated by outside entities such as the media or the general public. Earned media has traditionally been viewed as

FIGURE 1–7

Paid, Owned, and Earned Media

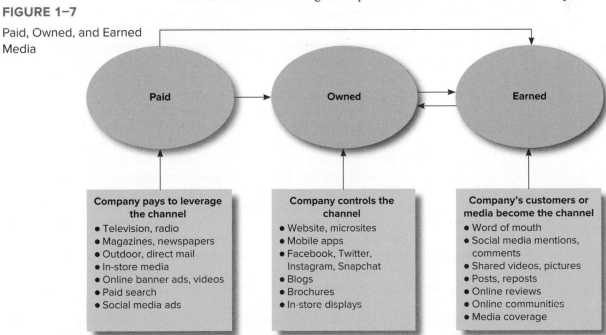

exposure for a company or brand generated by its public relations/publicity efforts or through favorable word of mouth. However, with the growth of digital and social media, earned media exposure is taking place online through social media and as a result of the viral marketing efforts of marketers that focus on getting consumers, as well as the media, to share information about their company and/or brands. This can occur through tweets and re-tweets on Twitter, social media posts on Facebook or Instagram, product reviews, blogs, video sharing, and discussions within online communities.

Marketers making effective use of integrated marketing communications today will use a combination of all three forms of media. For example, advertising through paid media is still an efficient way to generate awareness of and interest in a company or brand, particularly among mass markets. Media advertising can also be used to drive consumers to various forms of owned media such as a Facebook or Instagram page for a company or brand and/or its website where more content can be provided to encourage greater involvement and engagement. Well-executed and coordinated paid and owned media efforts can also serve as a catalyst for generating earned media when the media and/or consumers find information or content about a company or brand to be interesting or valuable enough that they want to write about it or share it with others. An important aspect of earned media is that information about a company or brand that comes from stories in the media or is shared through social media is often perceived as more credible and authentic than paid advertising messages and thus can have a greater influence on consumers.

Marketers must determine how valuable each of the various forms of media and contact tools are for communicating with their current and prospective customers and how they can be combined to form an effective IMC program. This is generally done by starting with the target audience and determining which IMC tools will be most effective in reaching, informing, and persuading them and ultimately influencing their behavior. It is the responsibility of those involved in the marketing communications process to determine how the various contact tools will be used to reach the target audience and help achieve the company's marketing objectives. The IMC program is generally developed with specific goals and objectives in mind and is the end product of a detailed marketing and promotional planning process. We will now look at a model of the process that companies follow in developing and executing their IMC programs.

THE IMC PLANNING PROCESS

In developing an integrated marketing communications strategy, a company combines the various promotional-mix elements, balancing the strengths and weaknesses of each to produce an effective communication program. **Integrated marketing communications management** involves the process of planning, executing, evaluating, and controlling the use of the various promotional-mix elements to effectively communicate with target audiences. The marketer must consider which promotional tools to use and how to integrate them to achieve marketing and communication objectives. Companies also must decide how to distribute the total marketing communications budget across the various promotional-mix elements. What percentage of the budget should be allocated to advertising, sales promotion, the Internet, sponsorships, and personal selling?

As with any business function, planning plays an important role in the development and implementation of an effective integrated marketing communications program. This process is guided by an **integrated marketing communications plan** that provides the framework for developing, implementing, and controlling the organization's IMC program. Those involved with the IMC program must decide on the role and function of the specific elements of the promotional mix, develop strategies for each element, determine how they will be integrated, plan for their implementation, and consider how to evaluate the results achieved and make any necessary adjustments. Marketing communications is but one part of, and must be integrated into, the overall marketing plan and program.

A model of the IMC planning process is shown in Figure 1–8. The remainder of this chapter presents a brief overview of the various steps involved in this process.

Review of the Marketing Plan

The first step in the IMC planning process is to review the marketing plan and objectives. Before developing a promotional plan, marketers must understand where the company (or the brand) has been, its current position in the market, where it intends to go, and how it plans to get there. Most of this information should be contained in the **marketing plan**, a written document that describes the overall marketing strategy and programs developed for an organization, a particular product line, or a brand. Marketing plans can take several forms but generally include five basic elements:

1. A detailed situation analysis that consists of an internal marketing audit and review and an external analysis of the market competition and environmental factors.
2. Specific marketing objectives that provide direction, a time frame for marketing activities, and a mechanism for measuring performance.
3. A marketing strategy and program that include selection of target market(s) and decisions and plans for the four elements of the marketing mix.
4. A program for implementing the marketing strategy, including determining specific tasks to be performed and responsibilities.
5. A process for monitoring and evaluating performance and providing feedback so that proper control can be maintained and any necessary changes can be made in the overall marketing strategy or tactics.

For most firms, the integrated marketing communications plan is an integral part of its marketing strategy and plan. Thus, those involved with the IMC process must know the roles advertising and other promotional-mix elements will play in the overall marketing program. The IMC plan is developed similarly to the marketing plan and often uses its detailed information. Promotional planners focus on information in the marketing plan that is relevant to the promotional strategy.

Promotional Program Situation Analysis

After the overall marketing plan is reviewed, the next step in developing a promotional plan is to conduct the situation analysis. For the IMC program, the situation analysis focuses on the factors that influence or are relevant to the development of a promotional strategy. Like the overall marketing situation analysis, the promotional program situation analysis includes both an internal and an external analysis.

Internal Analysis   The **internal analysis** assesses relevant areas involving the product/service offering and the firm itself. The capabilities of the firm and its ability to develop and implement a successful IMC program, the organization of the marketing communications department, and the successes and failures of past programs should be reviewed. The analysis should study the relative advantages and disadvantages of performing the promotional functions in-house as opposed to hiring an external agency (or agencies). For example, the internal analysis may indicate the firm is not capable of planning, implementing, and managing certain areas of the IMC program. If this is the case, it would be wise to look for assistance from an advertising or digital agency or some other promotional facilitator. If the organization is already using an external agency, the focus will be on the quality of the agency's work and the results achieved by past and/or current campaigns.

In this text we will examine the functions advertising agencies perform for their clients, the agency selection process, compensation, and considerations in evaluating agency performance. We will also discuss the role and function of other promotional facilitators such as digital/interactive agencies, sales promotion firms, direct-marketing companies, public relations agencies, and media specialists as well as marketing and media research firms.

Another aspect of the internal analysis is assessing the strengths and weaknesses of the firm or the brand from an image perspective. Often the brand equity and image a

FIGURE 1–8 An Integrated Marketing Communications Planning Model

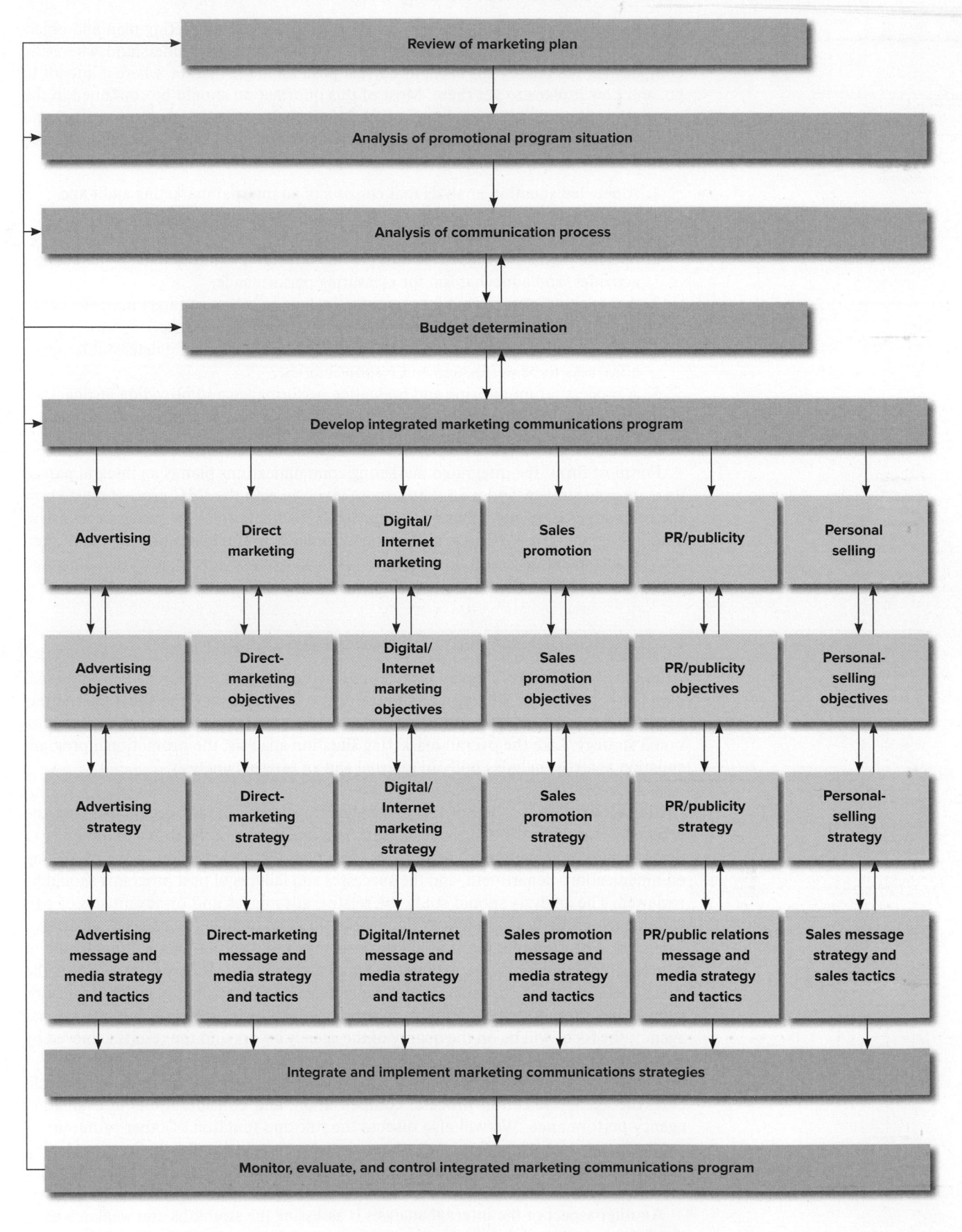

FIGURE 1–8

(Concluded)

Review of Marketing Plan
Examine overall marketing plan and objectives
Role of advertising and promotion
Competitive analysis
Assess environmental influences

Analysis of Promotional Program Situation

Internal analysis
- Promotional department organization
- Firm's ability to implement promotional program
- Agency evaluation and selection
- Review of previous program results

External analysis
- Consumer behavior analysis
- Market segmentation and target marketing
- Market positioning
- Market trends and developments

Analysis of Communication Process
Analyze receiver's response processes
Analyze source, message, channel factors
Establish communication goals and objectives

Budget Determination
Set tentative marketing communications budget
Allocate tentative budget

Develop Integrated Marketing Communications Program

Advertising
- Set advertising objectives
- Determine advertising budget
- Develop advertising message
- Develop advertising media strategy

Direct marketing
- Set direct-marketing objectives
- Determine direct-marketing budget
- Develop direct-marketing message
- Develop direct-marketing media strategy

Digital/Internet marketing
- Set interactive/Internet marketing objectives
- Determine interactive/Internet marketing budget
- Develop interactive/Internet message
- Develop interactive/Internet media strategy

Sales promotion
- Set sales promotion objectives
- Determine sales promotion budget
- Determine sales promotion tools and develop messages
- Develop sales promotion media strategy

Public relations/publicity
- Set PR/publicity objectives
- Determine PR/publicity budget
- Develop PR/publicity messages
- Develop PR/publicity media strategy

Personal selling
- Set personal selling and sales objectives
- Determine personal-selling/sales budget
- Develop sales message
- Develop selling roles and responsibilities

Integrate and Implement Marketing Communications Strategies
Integrate promotional-mix strategies
Create and produce ads
Purchase media time and space
Design and implement direct-marketing programs
Design and distribute sales promotion materials
Design and implement public relations/publicity programs
Design and implement digital/Internet marketing programs

Monitor, Evaluate, and Control Integrated Marketing Communications Program
Evaluate promotional program results/effectiveness
Take measures to control and adjust promotional strategies

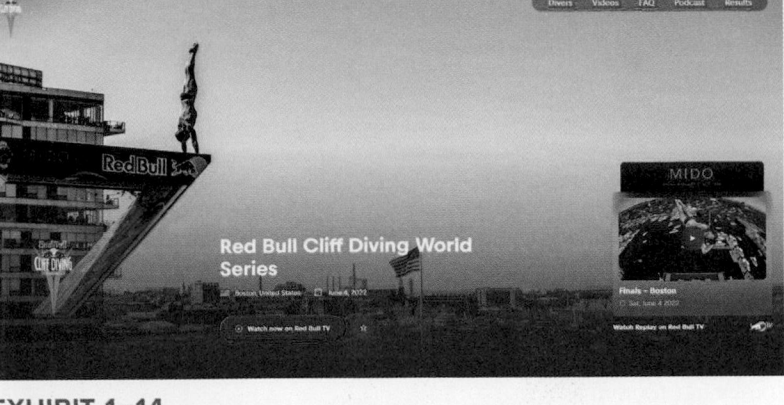

EXHIBIT 1-14

Red Bull's strong brand image is a source of competitive advantage. Red Bull highlights its association with extreme sports by sponsoring events such as the Cliff Diving World Series and featuring the competition on its website.

Red Bull

firm brings to the market will have a significant impact on the way the firm can advertise and promote itself as well as its various products and services. Companies or brands that are new to the market or those for whom perceptions are negative may have to concentrate on their images, not just the benefits or attributes of the specific product or service. On the other hand, a firm with a strong reputation and/or brand image is already a step ahead when it comes to marketing its products or services. For example, brands such as Apple, Samsung, Nike, Tesla, Coca-Cola, Chanel, and Louis Vuitton have very favorable brand images, which can be leveraged in advertising and other elements of their IMC programs. Red Bull is a good example of a brand that has built a very strong brand image through its sponsorship of extreme sports and athletes that give it a source of competitive advantage in the energy drink market (Exhibit 1-14).

The internal analysis also assesses the relative strengths and weaknesses of the product or service; its advantages and disadvantages; any unique selling points or benefits it may have; its packaging, price, and design; and so on. This information is particularly important to the creative personnel who must develop the advertising message for the brand.

Figure 1-9 is a checklist of some of the areas marketers might consider when performing analyses for promotional planning purposes. Addressing internal areas may require information the company does not have available internally and must gather as part of the external analysis.

External Analysis The **external analysis** focuses on factors such as characteristics of the firm's customers, market segments, positioning strategies, and competitors, as shown in Figure 1-9. An important part of the external analysis is a detailed consideration of customers' characteristics and buying patterns, their decision processes, and factors influencing their purchase decisions. Attention must also be given to consumers' perceptions and attitudes, lifestyles, and criteria for making purchase decisions. Often, marketing research studies are needed to answer some of these questions.

A key element of the external analysis is an assessment of the market. The attractiveness and growth potential of various market segments must be evaluated and the segments to target must be identified. Once the target markets are chosen, the emphasis will be on determining how the company or brand should be positioned. What image or place should it have in consumers' minds?

This part of the promotional program situation analysis also includes an in-depth examination of both direct and indirect competitors. While competitors were analyzed in the overall marketing situation analysis, even more attention is devoted to promotional aspects at this phase. Focus is on the firm's primary competitors: their specific strengths and weaknesses; their segmentation, targeting, and positioning strategies; and the promotional strategies they employ. The size and allocation of their promotional budgets, their media strategies, and the messages they are sending to the marketplace should all be considered.

The external phase also includes an analysis of the marketing environment and current trends or developments that might affect the promotional program. Marketers must consider relevant demographic, economic, and sociocultural factors and how they are impacting their markets. For example, consumers have become more focused on health and nutrition, which has had a major impact on the beverage industry. Sales of soft drinks have been declining for more than a decade as a result of consumer concerns over their nutritional value and the high number of calories from added sugar as

Internal Factors	External Factors

Assessment of Firm's Promotional Organization and Capabilities

Organization of promotional department.

Capability of firm to develop and execute promotional programs.

Determination of role and function of ad agency and other promotional facilitators.

Review of Firm's Previous Promotional Programs and Results

Review previous promotional objectives.

Review previous promotional budgets and locations.

Review previous promotional-mix strategies and programs.

Review results of previous promotional programs.

Assessment of Firm or Brand Image and Implications for Promotion

What is the identity and/or reputation of the firm or brand in the market?

Assessment of Relative Strengths and Weaknesses of Product or Service

What are the strengths and weaknesses of product or service?

What are its key benefits?

Does it have any unique selling points?

Assessment of packaging, labeling, and brand image.

How does our product or service compare with competition?

Customer Analysis

Who buys our product or service?

Who makes the decision to buy the product?

Who influences the decision to buy the product?

How is the purchase decision made? Who assumes what role?

What does the customer buy? What needs must be satisfied?

Why do customers buy a particular brand?

Where do they go or look to buy the product or service?

When do they buy? Any seasonality factors?

What are customers' attitudes toward our product or service?

What social factors might influence the purchase decision?

Do the customers' lifestyles influence their decisions?

How is our company or brand perceived by customers?

How do demographic factors influence the purchase decision?

Competitive Analysis

Who are our direct and indirect competitors?

What key benefits and positioning are used by our competitors?

What is our position relative to the competition?

What is the size of our competitors' marketing budgets?

What message, media, and digital strategies are our competitors using?

Environmental Analysis

Are there any current trends or developments that might affect the promotional program?

FIGURE 1–9

Areas Covered in the Situation Analysis

well as the artificial sweetener used in diet sodas. These concerns have led many consumers to turn to alternative beverages such as teas, juices, bottled water, flavored waters, and sports drinks. This has created a market opportunity for marketers who have launched new beverage products that are positioned as being healthier and having more nutritional value.

Another example of a market that has been impacted by changing consumer consumption patterns and industry trends is alcoholic beverages. Sales of beer have been declining as brewers struggle to compete amid the explosion of new products and brands developed for ever narrowing tastes and consumption occasions including hard seltzers and ready-to-drink (RTD) beverages, which include canned cocktails such as mixed drinks and alcoholic iced teas and lemonades. A product category that has experienced tremendous growth over the past several years is hard seltzer as sales reached nearly $5 billion by 2022. More than 150 brands of hard seltzer were launched over the past several years—including line extensions from major brewers such as Corona, Molson Coors, Constellation Brands, and Anheuser Busch InBev—as sales exploded.[59] However, the hard seltzer market is dominated by two brands, White Claw and Truly, which together account for nearly 75 percent of the market, and many have exited the market as growth slows (Exhibit 1–15).

Analysis of the Communication Process

This stage of the promotional planning process examines how the company can effectively communicate with consumers in its target markets. The promotional planner must

EXHIBIT 1–15

Hard seltzer has been a fast growing category of the alcoholic beverage market.

Steve Cukrov/Shutterstock

think about the process consumers will go through in responding to marketing communications. The response process for products or services for which consumer decision making is characterized by a high level of interest is often different from that for low-involvement or routine purchase decisions. These differences will influence the promotional strategy.

Communication decisions regarding the use of various source, message, and channel factors must also be considered. The promotional planner should recognize the different effects various types of advertising messages might have on consumers and whether they are appropriate for the product or brand. Issues such as whether a celebrity spokesperson should be used and at what cost may also be studied. Preliminary discussion of media-mix options (print, TV, radio, digital, direct marketing), including how they can be used to reach the target market and their cost implications, might also occur at this stage.

An important part of this stage of the promotional planning process is establishing communication goals and objectives. In this text, we stress the importance of distinguishing between communication and marketing objectives. **Marketing objectives** refer to what is to be accomplished by the overall marketing program. They are often stated in terms of sales, market share, or profitability.

Communication objectives refer to what the firm seeks to accomplish with its promotional program. They are often stated in terms of the nature of the message to be communicated or what specific communication effects are to be achieved. Communication objectives may include creating awareness or knowledge about a product and its attributes or benefits; creating an image; or developing favorable attitudes, preferences, or purchase intentions. Communication objectives should be the guiding force for development of the overall marketing communications strategy and of objectives for each promotional-mix area.

Budget Determination

After the communication objectives are determined, attention turns to the promotional budget. Two basic questions are asked at this point: How much will the IMC program cost? How will the money be allocated across different media, geographic markets, and time periods? Ideally, the amount a firm needs to spend on advertising and promotion should be determined by what must be done to accomplish its communication objectives. In reality, promotional budgets are often determined using a more simplistic approach, such as how much money is available or a percentage of a company's or brand's sales revenue. At this stage, the budget is often tentative. It may not be finalized until specific promotional-mix strategies are developed.

Developing the Integrated Marketing Communications Program

Developing the IMC program is generally the most involved and detailed step of the promotional planning process. As discussed earlier, each promotional-mix element has certain advantages and limitations. At this stage of the planning process, decisions have to be made regarding the role and importance of each element and their coordination with one another. As Figure 1–8 shows, each promotional-mix element has its own set of objectives and a budget and strategy for meeting them. Decisions must be made and activities performed to implement the promotional programs. Procedures must be developed for evaluating performance and making any necessary changes.

For example, the advertising program will have its own set of objectives, usually involving the communication of some message or appeal to a target audience. A budget will be determined, providing the advertising manager and the agency with some idea of how much money is available for developing the ad campaign and purchasing media to disseminate the ad message.

Two important aspects of the advertising program are development of the message and the media strategy. Message development, often referred to as *creative strategy*, involves determining the basic appeal and message the advertiser wishes to convey to the target audience. To many students this process, along with the ads that result, is the most fascinating aspect of promotion. *Media strategy* involves determining which communication channels will be used to deliver the advertising message to the target audience. Decisions must be made regarding which types of media will be used (e.g., newspapers, magazines, radio, TV, outdoor, digital) as well as specific media selections (e.g., a particular magazine or TV program). This task requires careful evaluation of the media options' advantages and limitations, costs, and ability to deliver the message effectively to the target market.

Once the message and media strategies have been determined, steps must be taken to implement them. Most large companies hire advertising agencies to plan and produce their messages and to evaluate and purchase the media that will carry their ads. However, most agencies work very closely with their clients as they develop the ads and select media, because it is the advertiser that ultimately approves (and pays for) the creative work and media plan.

A similar process takes place for the other elements of the IMC program as objectives are set, an overall strategy is developed, message and media strategies are determined, and steps are taken to implement them. While the marketer's advertising agencies may be used to perform some of the other IMC functions, they may also hire other communication specialists such as direct-marketing and interactive and/or sales promotion agencies, as well as public relations firms.

Monitoring, Evaluation, and Control

The final stage of the IMC planning process is monitoring, evaluating, and controlling the promotional program. It is important to determine how well the IMC program is meeting communication objectives and helping the firm accomplish its overall marketing goals and objectives. The IMC planner wants to know not only how well the promotional program is doing but also why. For example, problems with the advertising program may lie in the nature of the message or in a media plan that does not reach the target market effectively. The manager must know the reasons for the results in order to take the right steps to correct the program.

Most companies are using analytics to measure the effectiveness of their advertising and promotion campaigns, particularly digital advertising. In addition to running ads in traditional media such as television and print, most marketers' IMC programs include digital ads that utilize different formats, such as display and video, and across a number of channels, including search, social media, websites, and mobile. Digital and social media platforms such as Google, Facebook, Instagram, Snapchat, and LinkedIn can provide very detailed analytics that marketers can use to gauge the effectiveness of their digital ads and determine how they move consumers through the purchase funnel.[60] These platforms also provide online courses, training, and certification programs to help marketers understand how to use measurement tools and analytics (Exhibit 1-16).

This final stage of the process is designed to provide managers with continual feedback concerning the effectiveness of the IMC program, which in turn can be used as input into the planning process. As Figure 1-8 shows, information on the results achieved by the IMC program is used in subsequent promotional planning and strategy development.

EXHIBIT 1–16

Google's Analytics Academy provides training in the use of measurement and analytics tools.

Alphabet Inc.

PERSPECTIVE AND ORGANIZATION OF THIS TEXT

Traditional approaches to teaching advertising, promotional strategy, or marketing communications courses have often treated the various elements of the promotional mix as separate functions. As a result, many people who work in advertising, sales promotion, direct marketing, digital/Internet marketing, or public relations tend to approach marketing communications problems from the perspective of their particular specialty. A traditional advertising person may believe marketing communications objectives are best met through the use of media advertising; a digital marketing specialist will advocate for using digital and social media; a promotional specialist argues for a sales promotion program to motivate consumer response; a public relations person advocates for a PR campaign to tackle the problem. These orientations are not surprising, since each person has been trained to view marketing communications problems primarily from one perspective.

In the contemporary business world, however, individuals working in marketing, advertising, and other promotional areas are expected to understand and use a variety of marketing communication tools, not just the one in which they specialize. Ad agencies no longer confine their services to the advertising area. Many are involved in sales promotion, public relations, direct marketing, event sponsorship, digital/interactive, and other marketing communication areas. Individuals working on the client or advertiser side of the business, such as brand, product, or promotional managers, are developing marketing programs that use a variety of marketing communication methods.

This text views advertising and promotion from an integrated marketing communications perspective. We will examine the promotional-mix elements and their roles in an organization's integrated marketing communications efforts. Although media advertising may be the most visible part of the communications program, understanding its role in contemporary marketing requires attention to other promotional areas such as the Internet and digital marketing, direct marketing, sales promotion, and public relations. Not all the promotional-mix areas are under the direct control of the advertising or marketing communications manager. For example, as noted earlier, personal selling is typically a specialized marketing function outside the control of the advertising or promotional department. Likewise, publicity/public relations is often assigned to a separate department. All these departments, however, should communicate with each other to coordinate all the organization's marketing communication tools.

The purpose of this book is to provide you with a thorough understanding of the field of advertising and other elements of a firm's promotional mix and show how they are combined to form an integrated marketing communications program. To plan, develop, and implement an effective IMC program, those involved must understand marketing, consumer behavior, and the communication process. The first part of this book is designed to provide this foundation by examining the roles of advertising and other forms of promotion in the marketing process. We examine the process of market segmentation and positioning and consider their part in developing an IMC strategy. We also discuss how firms organize for IMC and make decisions regarding ad agencies and other firms that provide marketing and promotional services.

We then focus on consumer behavior considerations and analyze the communication process. We discuss various communication models of value to promotional planners in developing strategies and establishing goals and objectives for advertising and other forms of promotion. We also consider how firms determine and allocate their marketing communications budget.

After laying the foundation for the development of a promotional program, this text will follow the integrated marketing communications planning model presented in Figure 1-8. We examine each of the promotional-mix variables, beginning with advertising. Our detailed examination of advertising includes a discussion of creative strategy and the process of developing the advertising message, an overview of media strategy, and an evaluation of the various media (print, broadcast, and support media). The discussion then turns to the other areas of the promotional mix: direct marketing, digital/

Internet marketing, sales promotion, and public relations/publicity. Our examination of the IMC planning process concludes with a discussion of how the program is monitored, evaluated, and controlled. Particular attention is given to measuring the effectiveness of advertising and other forms of promotion.

The final part of the text examines special topic areas and perspectives that have become increasingly important in contemporary marketing. We will examine the area of international advertising and promotion and the challenges companies face in developing IMC programs for global markets as well as various countries around the world. The text concludes with an examination of the environment in which integrated marketing communications operates, including the regulatory, social, and economic factors that influence, and in turn are influenced by, an organization's advertising and promotional program.

Summary

Advertising and other forms of promotion are an integral part of the marketing process in most organizations. Over the past decade, the amount of money spent on advertising, sales promotion, direct marketing, and other forms of marketing communication has increased tremendously, both in the United States and in foreign markets. There has been a very large increase in the amount of monies spent on digital advertising done through the Internet as well as various forms of nontraditional media, some of which did not exist at the beginning of the new millennium, such as social media. To understand the role of advertising and promotion in a marketing program, one must understand the role and function of marketing in an organization. The basic task of marketing is to combine the four controllable elements, known as the marketing mix, into a comprehensive program that facilitates exchange with a target market. The elements of the marketing mix are the product or service, price, place (distribution), and promotion.

For many years, the promotional function in most companies was dominated by mass-media advertising. However, more and more companies are recognizing the importance of integrated marketing communications, coordinating the various marketing and promotional elements to achieve more efficient and effective communication programs. A number of factors underlie the move toward IMC by marketers as well as ad agencies and other promotional facilitators. Reasons for the growing importance of the integrated marketing communications perspective include a rapidly changing environment with respect to consumers, technology, and media. The IMC movement is also being driven by changes in the ways companies market their products and services. A shifting of marketing expenditures from traditional media advertising to digital and social media, a shift in marketplace power from manufacturers to retailers, the growth and development of database marketing, the demand for greater accountability from advertising agencies and other marketing communication firms, and the fragmentation of media markets, as well as changing media consumption patterns, are among the key changes taking place.

Promotion is best viewed as the communication function of marketing. It is accomplished through a promotional mix that includes advertising, personal selling, publicity/public relations, sales promotion, direct marketing, and digital/ Internet marketing. The inherent advantages and disadvantages of each of these promotional-mix elements influence the roles they play in the overall marketing program. In developing the IMC program, the marketer must decide which tools to use and how to combine them to achieve the organization's marketing and communication objectives. Many companies are taking an audience contact or touch point perspective in developing their IMC programs whereby they consider all of the potential ways of reaching their target audience and presenting the company or brand in a favorable manner. The four primary categories of contact points include company planned, intrinsic, unexpected, and customer initiated. These contact points vary with respect to the impact they have on the customer and marketers' ability to control them. Another categorization of the various types of customer contact points that has become very popular is that of paid, owned, and earned media.

Promotional management involves coordinating the promotional-mix elements to develop an integrated program of effective marketing communication. The model of the IMC planning process in Figure 1–8 contains a number of steps: a review of the marketing plan; promotional program situation analysis; analysis of the communication process; budget determination; development of an integrated marketing communications program; integration and implementation of marketing communications strategies; and monitoring, evaluation, and control of the promotional program.

Key Terms

exchange 6
marketing 7
value 7
marketing mix 7
integrated marketing
   communications (IMC) 8

sustainability 15
brand activism 16
promotion 18
promotional mix 18
advertising 18
direct marketing 22

direct-response advertising 22
omnichannel retailing 22
interactive media 23
social media 23
mobile marketing 24
sales promotion 25

Discussion Questions

1. Discuss the role of integrated marketing communications in the marketing program for the energy drink Celsius and how the company uses various IMC tools to compete in the energy drink market. (LO 1-2, 1-5)

2. Evaluate the success of Celsius in competing in the energy drink market against major brands such as Red Bull and Monster. What factors account for the strong growth of the Celsius brand? Do you think the company can continue to increase its market share? Why or why not? (LO 1-1, 1-4, 1-5)

3. Discuss the role that integrated marketing communications plays in the marketing program of companies and organizations. Discuss how the use of the various promotional-mix tools has changed over the past decade and what factors drive these changes. (LO 1-1, 1-4)

4. Spending by marketers on digital advertising has now surpassed spending on traditional media such as television, radio, magazines, and newspapers. Discuss the reasons marketers are spending more on digital than traditional media. Do you expect this trend to continue? (LO 1-2, 1-3, 1-4)

5. Ethical Perspective 1–1 discusses how many companies are becoming involved in brand activism. Discuss the pros and cons of companies becoming involved with and taking a position on controversial social, economic, and political issues. (LO 1-1, 1-2)

6. Discuss some of the ways technology is making it possible for consumers to avoid advertising messages and the impact this is having on the advertising and media industries. (LO 1-2, 1-3)

7. Digital and Social Media Perspective 1–1 discusses how Netflix made a strategic decision to launch an advertising-supported tier to its streaming service. Discuss the reasons Netflix made this strategic decision. Do you think this ad-supported tier of service will be successful? (LO 1-4, 1-5)

8. What is meant by the categorization of touch points into paid, owned, and earned media? Choose a specific company or brand and discuss how it is using these three categories of media. (LO 1-5)

9. Why is it important for those who work in marketing to understand and appreciate all the various IMC tools and how they can be used effectively? (LO 1-5, 1-6)

10. Assume a company is developing an IMC plan for a new product that will compete in a specific category or segment of the beverage market. Discuss some of the factors that should be considered as part of the external analysis when developing the IMC plan. (LO 1-6)

2 The Role of IMC in the Marketing Process

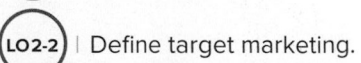

Mitchell Leff/Getty Images

Learning Objectives

LO 2-1 Describe the role of advertising and promotion in an organization's integrated marketing program.

LO 2-2 Define target marketing.

LO 2-3 Discuss the role of market segmentation in an IMC program.

LO 2-4 Describe positioning and repositioning strategies.

LO 2-5 Identify the marketing-mix decisions that influence advertising and promotional strategy.

Why Are So Many Companies and Brands Changing Their Names?

By now you are probably familiar with the company/brand names Meta (formerly Facebook) and Alphabet (formerly Google) but never even knew that USX used to be called United States Steel (USS), Apple, Inc. used to be Apple Computers, or that Tinder was previously Matchbox. Did you know that KFC was Kentucky Fried Chicken, Dunkin' was Dunkin' Donuts, and AirTran was formerly ValuJet? These are just a few of the name changes that have taken place over time in an attempt to not only change the name but also the perceptions of the company or brand itself. But why? Many of these names were quite established and well known, and even doing well as they were. So why change? For a number of reasons. Consider the following examples:

Meta—The social media giant—and perhaps most well-known player in that arena—Facebook changed its name in 2021. The parent company already overseeing other well-known brands such as Instagram, WhatsApp, and Oculus has changed its name as well as its focus, according to founder and CEO Mark Zuckerberg. The new focus would no longer be primarily on social media but on building the metaverse; the new name is designed to reflect that new "metaverse company." (Google's change to Alphabet was to reflect its new diversity into driverless cars and health tech.) But why, you ask? Isn't Facebook already a very successful company? The answer is yes it is, but times are changing. Zuckerberg believes the metaverse is the future and that is where his company wants to be successful. Meanwhile, the social media market is changing as well, and not always in a positive direction. Criticism and concerns with social media are on the increase as the psychological impact, potential for addiction, undesirable and even illegal content continue to raise concerns. Facebook itself has fallen under intense scrutiny for matters ranging from anti-trust issues as well as public trust concerns. While still maintaining a very high market share, the rapid growth of previous years has leveled off. It may be that the change will help.

Alphabet—Like Facebook, Google changed its name as a strategic move when the company decided to move into some higher risk initiatives, like self-driving cars. The company restructured and began to enter new markets, such as life sciences and additional "speculative" experimental areas. The Google name would, of course, be continued for the world's largest search engine, but there were concerns that the Google name was too representative of a "conventional" company. There may also have been concerns about potential anti-trust legislation that might be avoided with the adoption of the new name.

Stoli—When Russia attacked the Ukraine in 2022, the founder of Stolichnaya vodka almost immediately announced the name change as a protest to Russian President Vladimir Putin's actions. Stolichnaya was a Russian name, even though the product was produced in Latvia, and that led to concerns that consumers might boycott the brand. In addition, the company announced plans to only use Slovakian sourced ingredients—ending the use of any imports from Russia—and released a limited edition blue and yellow bottle in support of Ukraine with proceeds going to the World Central Kitchen, a charity feeding millions of refugees from the war.

While these name changes were strategic in nature and initiated by the companies themselves in response to new opportunities and/or to avoid potential threats, this is not necessarily the case for others. Consider just a few companies that changed more in response to adverse social pressures:

Aunt Jemima, Uncle Ben's, and Eskimo Pie—A very popular brand of pancake syrup, Aunt Jemima, had been around since 1889 until its name change in 2021. The product's label featured a Black woman with a kerchief on her head that was often criticized as having emanated from slavery and was changed to feature a different Black woman with a more modern-looking appearance a number of times. Then in 2021, in response to social feedback, the Pearl Milling Company executives acknowledged that the brand's origins were "based on a racial stereotype" and agreed to change the name.

continued

Uncle Ben's rice suffered a similar fate when the name was changed in 2020 to Ben's Original. The Uncle Ben's name had been on the package since the 1940's along with the image of a Black rice farmer (who was actually a maître d' from Chicago) until increased protests over racial injustices in the United States led Mars (the brand's owner) to change both the name and the image in an effort to "evolve." If you grew up eating Eskimo Pie ice cream treats you won't be anymore. You may choose to eat Edy's Pie, the new brand name, but Eskimo Pie and the mascot—a young boy in a hooded robe and boots have been gone since 2020. The parent company Dreyer's believed the term *Eskimo* was derogatory to Inuits.

Washington Commanders and Cleveland Guardians—Known as the Redskins since 1933, the owner of the NFL team finally gave in to fan and sponsor pressures to change the name in 2020. It was not, however, a hasty decision, as the team was simply called the Washington Football Team for 18 months before becoming the Commanders. Eventually, the financial pressure brought upon the owner to drop the Redskins name was too strong to ignore. Some Native Americans and sponsors like FedEx and Nike, among others, protests finally won out. Native Americans had also protested against the Cleveland MLB team bearing the name Indians and having a mascot called Chief Wahoo, calling the names stereotypical for decades before the name was changed.

As you might expect, changing names is not an easy decision. For some companies like Apple and Google, the strategic moves were not changing long-established brand names. For others, the value and reputation of the brand names may have enjoyed many years of recognition, as well as loyalty by consumers. Thus, not only are there significant financial costs, but also the cost of giving up years of brand identity and starting over.

Sources: Saundra Latham, "The Surprising Reasons These Companies and Brands Changed Their Names," *Cheapism*, April 19, 2022, www.cheapism.com; Alex Heath, "Facebook Is Planning to Rebrand the Company with a New Name," *The Verge*, October 19, 2021, www.theverge.com; Chauncey Alcorn, "Aunt Jemima Finally Has a New Name," *CNN*, February 9, 2021, www.cnn.com; Adam Lashinsky, "Why Google Changed Its Name to Alphabet," *Fortune*, August 11, 2015, www.fortune.com.

Marketers know that to be successful they must understand their buyers and potential buyers and develop specific strategies to best reach them. These include the identification of market opportunities, market segmentation, target marketing and positioning, and marketing program development. As you will see in this chapter, this is often a challenging task.

In this chapter, we take a closer look at how marketing strategies influence the role of promotion and how promotional decisions must be coordinated with other areas of the marketing mix. In turn, all elements of the marketing mix must be consistent in a strategic plan that results in an integrated marketing communications program. We use the model in Figure 2–1 as a framework for analyzing how promotion fits into an organization's marketing strategy and programs.

This model consists of four major components: the organization's marketing strategy and analysis, the target marketing process, the marketing planning program development (which includes the promotional mix), and the target market. As the model shows, the marketing process begins with the development of a marketing strategy and analysis in which the company decides the product or service areas and particular markets where it wants to compete. The company must then coordinate the various elements of the marketing mix into a cohesive marketing program that will reach the target market effectively. Note that a firm's promotion program is directed not only to the final buyer but also to the channel or "trade" members that distribute its products to the ultimate consumer. These channel members must be convinced there is a demand for the company's products so they will carry them and will aggressively merchandise and promote them to consumers. Promotions play an important role in the marketing program for building and maintaining demand not only among final consumers but among the trade as well.

As noted in Chapter 1, all elements of the marketing mix—product, price, place (distribution), and promotion—must be integrated to provide consistency and maximum communications impact. Development of a marketing plan is instrumental in achieving this goal.

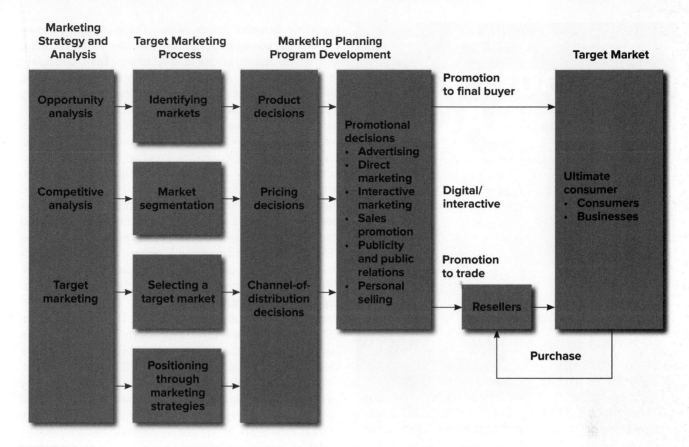

FIGURE 2–1

Marketing and Promotions Process Model

As Figure 2-1 shows, development of a marketing program requires an in-depth analysis of the market. This analysis may make extensive use of marketing research as an input into the planning process. This input, in turn, provides the basis for the development of marketing strategies in regard to product, pricing, distribution, and promotion decisions. Each of these steps requires a detailed analysis, since this plan serves as the road map to follow in achieving marketing goals. Once the detailed market analysis has been completed and marketing objectives have been established, each element in the marketing mix must contribute to a comprehensive integrated marketing program. Of course, the promotional program element (the focus of this text) must be combined with all other program elements in such a way as to achieve maximum impact.

MARKETING STRATEGY AND ANALYSIS

Any organization that wants to exchange its products or services in the marketplace successfully should have a **strategic marketing plan** to guide the allocation of its resources. A strategic marketing plan usually evolves from an organization's overall corporate strategy and serves as a guide for specific marketing programs and policies. As we noted earlier, marketing strategy is based on a situation analysis—a detailed assessment of the current marketing conditions facing the company, its product lines, or its individual brands. From this situation analysis, a firm develops an understanding of the market and the various opportunities it offers, the competition, and the **market segments** or target markets the company wishes to pursue. We examine each step of the marketing strategy and *planning* in this chapter.

Opportunity Analysis

A careful analysis of the marketplace should lead to alternative market opportunities for existing product lines in current or new markets, new products for current markets, or new products for new markets. **Market opportunities** are areas where there are

EXHIBIT 2–1

Chocolate milk has seized a market opportunity.

America's Milk Companies

favorable demand trends, where the company believes customer needs and opportunities are not being satisfied, and where it can compete effectively. Take chocolate milk, for example. Milk is thought to have been around and consumed since 5000 B.C. In recent years, however, white milk has continued a decades-long decline in consumption. But when scientific research showed that chocolate milk was an effective post-workout recovery drink, the Milk Processor Education Program seized on the marketing opportunity, initiating a campaign to create a new drinking occasion for chocolate milk. The board initiated the "Built with Chocolate Milk" campaign, which was designed to deliver a message about chocolate milk and its role in aiding recovery after physical activities (Exhibit 2–1). The campaign leveraged partnerships with on- and offline activities including sampling programs; 360-degree marketing campaigns; social media; advertising; and partnerships with the Rock 'n' Roll Marathon Series, USA Swimming team, and the U.S. Olympic committee. The result was a yearlong steady increase in chocolate milk sales since the campaign started in 2012, and this is forcasted to continue through 2027.[1]

A company usually identifies market opportunities by carefully examining the marketplace and noting demand trends and competition in various market segments. A market can rarely be viewed as one large homogeneous group of customers; rather, it consists of many heterogeneous groups, or segments. In recent years, many companies have recognized the importance of tailoring their marketing to meet the needs and demand trends of different market segments.

For example, different market segments in the personal computer (PC) industry include the home, government, education, science, and business markets. These segments can be even further divided. The coffee industry includes retail for home consumption (e.g., sales through grocery stores) and institutional food services (sales to hotels, hospitals, colleges, and other high-volume users, plus military sales). Each segment requires its own marketing efforts. A company that is marketing its products in the auto industry must decide in which particular market segment or segments it wishes to compete. This decision depends on the amount and nature of competition the brand will face in a particular market. Many auto companies are now competing in the hybrid car market, offering a variety of models (Exhibit 2–2). As can be seen in this exhibit, even luxury cars like Jaguar have now entered the electric car market. Some states have now passed laws that will eventually force all auto makers to offer gas-free selections. Mercedes is now competing in the light-duty truck market and the luxury pickup market. Jaguar and Volvo have both announced that they will make only electric cars in the future, as this market has now become the fastest-growing auto segment.

A competitive analysis is an important part of marketing strategy development and warrants further consideration.

Competitive Analysis

In developing the firm's marketing strategies and plans for its products and services, the manager must carefully analyze the competition to be faced in the marketplace. This may range from direct brand competition (which can also include its own brands) to more indirect forms of competition, such as product substitutes. For example, growth in the bottled water market has led numerous companies to compete in this area and offer different product varieties (Exhibit 2–3). Sales are expected to continue to increase through 2025, reaching over $470 billion.

EXHIBIT 2–2

Many companies are now focusing efforts on the electric car segment, including Jaguar.

Jaguar Land Rover North America, LLC

At a more general level, marketers must recognize they are competing for the consumer's discretionary income, so they must understand the various ways potential customers choose to spend their money. The impact of the worldwide economic downturn has made manufacturers of luxury goods brands rethink their marketing strategies. Sales of luxury products fell during the recession in 2008 and again in 2009. However, by 2013 the top 100 luxury brands rebounded with an 8.2 percent growth rate. Despite the COVID-19 outbreak and the 2022 war in Ukraine, the market has continued to grow better than expected.[2] A market downturn or uncertainty will often have a direct impact on luxury goods sales.

An important aspect of marketing strategy development is the search for a **competitive advantage**, something special a firm does or has that gives it an edge over competitors. Ways to achieve a competitive advantage include having quality products that command a premium price, providing superior customer service, having the lowest production costs and lower prices, and dominating channels of distribution. Competitive advantage can also be achieved through advertising that creates and maintains product differentiation and brand equity, an example of which was the long-running advertising campaign for Michelin tires, which stressed security as well as performance. The strong brand images of Samsung, Nike, BMW, and McDonald's give them a competitive advantage in their respective markets.

The competitive environment in some markets is constantly changing—for example, new market entries and brands reaching the end of their life cycles for a variety of reasons, from failing to adapt to market conditions to negative publicity to superior innovations and so on (think about VCRs and CDs). Sometimes brands that once were popular experience market share losses but are able to stay around and later make a comeback. Consider once-hot brands like Fila, Dr. Martens, Champion, and Polaroid. While all of these brands were popular in the 1980s, each fell on hard times throughout the 1990s and the early 2000s. Now each is enjoying a surge in popularity

EXHIBIT 2–3

SoBe, which is owned by Pepsi, offers a variety of enhanced waters and is an example of direct brand competition.

Steve Cukrov/Alamy Stock Photo

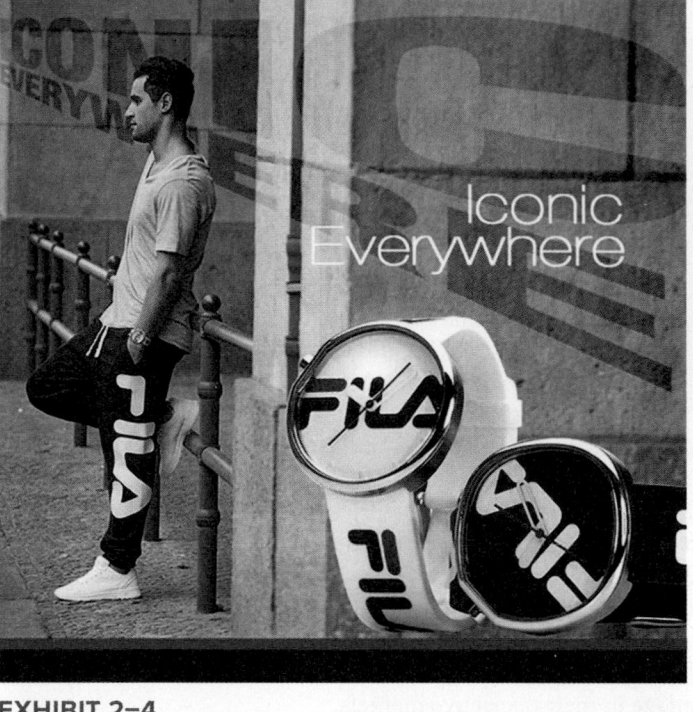

EXHIBIT 2–4

Fila revitalizes its image.

FILA Online, Inc.

with younger market segments, thanks in part to product design changes in some (Fila, Polaroid) and association with social influencers in others (Champion, Dr. Martens).[3] To be successful, or to remain successful, marketers must always be monitoring their competitive environment and adapt, as Fila has done (Exhibit 2–4).

Competitors' marketing programs have a major impact on a firm's marketing strategy, so they must be analyzed and monitored. The reactions of competitors to a company's marketing and promotional strategy are also very important. Competitors may cut prices, increase promotional spending, develop new brands, or attack one another through comparative advertising (Exhibit 2–5). One of the more intense competitive rivalries is the battle between Coca-Cola and Pepsi. A number of other intense competitive rivalries exist in the marketplace, including Hertz and Avis, Verizon and AT&T, and Apple and Samsung.

A final aspect of competition is the growing number of foreign companies penetrating the U.S. market and taking business from domestic firms. In products ranging from beer to cars to electronics, imports are becoming an increasingly strong form of competition with which U.S. firms must contend. As we now compete in a global economy, U.S. companies must not only defend their domestic markets but also learn how to compete effectively in the international marketplace.

Target Market Selection

After evaluating the opportunities presented by various market segments, including a detailed competitive analysis, the company may select one, or more, as a target market. This target market becomes the focus of the firm's marketing effort, and goals and objectives are set according to where the company wants to be and what it hopes to accomplish in this market. As noted in Chapter 1, these goals and objectives are set in terms of specific performance variables such as sales, market share, and profitability. The selection of the target market (or markets) in which the firm will compete is an important part of its marketing strategy and has direct implications for its advertising and promotional efforts. IMC Perspective 2–1 discusses how the growth in online dating has led to a number of sites targeting specific segments.

EXHIBIT 2–5

AT&T and Verizon use comparative ads to compete with each other.

Verizon Communications, Inc.

Recall from our discussion of the integrated marketing communications planning program that the situation analysis is conducted at the beginning of the promotional planning process. Specific objectives—both marketing and communications—are derived from the situation analysis, and the promotional-mix strategies are developed to achieve these objectives. Marketers rarely go after the entire market with one product, brand, or service offering. Rather, they pursue a number of different strategies, breaking the market into segments and targeting one or more of these segments for marketing and promotional efforts. This means different objectives may be established, different budgets may be used, and the promotional-mix strategies may vary, depending on the market approach used.

IMC Perspective 2–1 >>>

Segmenting the Online Dating Industry: There's a Site for Everyone

Cupid Media

While the practice of finding a date online as we know it today is a relatively new phenomenon, trying to find a match through personal ads appeared in British newspapers as early as the late 1600s. The ads were predominantly placed by men looking for a potential spouse before they (the men) got older and the odds of finding someone to marry went down. The ads continued through the 1700s and 1800s in Britain and the United States and saw a marked increase in popularity in the United States in the early 1900s, most commonly by farmers or others living in rural areas and then by lonely veterans returning from duty in World War I.

While personal attempts at finding a partner continued throughout the 20th century in various forms and a variety of media—including newspapers, television, catalogs, and videotapes—a major shift occurred in the 1990s with the establishment and expansion of the World Wide Web. In 1995, Match.com became the first major dating service site to register a domain. JDate.com—a site designed to connect Jewish singles—was established in 1997. Online dating domains began to proliferate in the early 2000s with the establishment of a number of new sites, including eharmony, Ashley Madison, OkCupid, and numerous others. By 2007, online dating became the second highest online industry for paid content. It should be noted, however, that statistics on this industry vary significantly in regard to the number of users of dating sites as well as the number of sites themselves.

Like other industries, when the number of competitors increases, marketers often find that they can no longer compete with everyone or in every market. To market more effectively, they look for segments in the marketplace in which they can compete most effectively. By 2010, segmentation had hit the online dating industry with a bang! There are now thousands of sites and apps frequented by millions of people looking for their match—whether it be a hookup, date, relationship, or marriage. The variety is astounding! Consider just these few:

- *Match.com*—The first and still one of the most popular dating sites now has over 21.5 million users and is ranked among the top by almost every online rating service. It has facilitated the most online dates with the highest success rate.

- *Eharmony and Zoosk*—Also rating high by site evaluators are eharmony and Zoosk. Both are targeted to singles seeking anything from a fun, casual date to a serious relationship. Both have users develop a profile to assist in the match. Both claim to be highly successful for those looking for more serious relationships and/or marriage.

- *Tinder*—Tinder is still considered one of the most popular for casual hookups, though Bumble and Hinge have successfully targeted this market.

Okay, now that you know the biggest players, consider a few sites and apps that target more specific segments:

- *Asian dating sites*—A number of sites are available to those who are interested specifically in dating Asians, including *Asian Honeys*—which claims to have one of the largest membership bases; *The LuckyDate Asia*—"to meet beautiful Asian women that are awesome to You"; *Date Asian Woman*—"the place where lonely Asian singles are looking for life partners"; *Orchidromance*—which has "great matching algorithms with Asian Beauties." A number of other sites including *Asian Melodies*—which claims to have "trending online dating with Asian women"—and *AsianDating*—advertised as the leading Asian dating site with over 4.5 million members—are also available.

- *FarmersOnly.com*—If you live in an urban area or have an urban attitude, this site is not for you. FarmersOnly.com is a site for single farmers who live in rural areas, love animals, or just don't

(continued)

like the urban or suburban lifestyle and are looking for a meaningful relationship. Visiting this site will allow you to "start connecting with other single farmers and down-to-earth folks." The site's tagline is "City Folks Just Don't Get It." The site was founded in 2005 and claims to have grown to over 5 million members and to be responsible for more than 100 marriages. FarmersOnly.com gained notoriety through its quirky television commercials that typically depict a supposed country girl and an urban-type suitor who loses out to the country boy in the end. They also sometimes show animals talking, country scenes like fishing and horseback riding, and the basic country lifestyle.

- *Sites for those over the age of 50*—For those interested in dating others over the age of 50, a number of options are also available. *SilverSingles*—"best for romance and companionship with intelligent matchmaking" for those interested in dating others over the age of 50; *Elite singles*—"for single professionals" with an educated user base and offering personality testing. Again, a number of sites targeting those interested in this specific demographic including *Ourtime, Christianmingle, eharmony,* and *Match* are also available, most for free or a reasonable service charge.

While we could continue to go on (remember there are thousands of sites now out there), it is pretty easy to see how segmented the online dating business has become since the inception of Match.com. Online dating is now estimated to be about a $5.9 billion per year industry that continues to grow and to segment to be attractive to more and more niche markets. Consider these: *beautifulpeople. com*—where people get voted on or off within 48 hours by other members based on their physical attractiveness; *singleparentmeet.com*—for singles with kids looking for a new relationship; and *ghostsingles.com*—ghost singles looking for other ghosts to date.

While beset by somewhat of a negative image in the beginning, online dating has become so mainstream that it no longer appears to be anything other than just another way to meet someone who is similar to you—and an apparently effective way at that. An article in *Wired* magazine in 2002 predicted that, "Twenty years from now, the idea that someone looking for love won't look for it online will be silly, akin to skipping the card catalog to instead wander the stacks because the right books are found only by accident." As long as people have different interests, lifestyles, and needs, it appears marketers will find them and a new online site will be born.

Sources: Amber Brooks, "21 Amazing Online Dating Statistics—The Good, Bad & Weird (2019)," January 14, 2018, www.datingadvice.com; "The Best Online Dating Sites of 2019," January 31, 2019, www.top10bestdatingsites.com; Susie Lee, "The History of Online Dating from 1695 to Now," *Huffington Post,* December 6, 2017, www.huffingtonpost.com; "The History of Online Dating," December 4, 2017, www.onlinedatingadvice.com; Jewel Pi, "7 Unconventional Dating Sites for the Extremely Unique Individual," September 4, 2014, coffeemeetsbagel.com; Anumita Kaur, "South Asians Swipe Right to Find 'the One,'" *LA Times,* May 19, 2022, pp. A1,11; "Leading Asian Women Dating Sites of 2022," July 2022, www.datingchoice.com; "Dating Services in the US—Market Size 2003–2028," February 27, 2022, www.IBISWorld.com; "Best Dating Sites for Singles over 50 in 2022," July 2022, www.top10.com; Jason wise, "How Many People Use Dating Apps in 2022," June 1, 2022, www.earthweb.com.

THE TARGET MARKETING PROCESS

Because few, if any, products can satisfy the needs of all consumers, companies often develop different marketing strategies to satisfy different consumer needs. The process by which marketers do this (presented in Figure 2-2) is referred to as **target marketing** and involves four basic steps: identifying markets with unfulfilled needs, segmenting the market, targeting specific segments, and positioning one's product or service through marketing strategies.

FIGURE 2–2

The Target Marketing Process

FIGURE 2–3

Taprooms

Craft

Large/Non-craft

Regional Craft Breweries

Microbreweries

Brewpubs

Source: Brewers Association.org, May 20, 2022.

LO 2-3

EXHIBIT 2–6

Traditional breweries are now offering craft beers. MillerCoors purchased craft brewery Saint Archer Brewing Co. of San Diego to help it compete more effectively in different market segments, then sold it again 7 years later.

Keith Homan/Alamy Stock Photo

Identifying Markets

When employing a target marketing strategy, the marketer identifies the specific needs of groups of people (or segments), selects one or more of these segments as a target, and develops marketing programs directed to each. This approach has found increased applicability in marketing for a number of reasons, including changes in the market (consumers are becoming much more diverse in their needs, attitudes, and lifestyles); increased use of segmentation by competitors; and the fact that more managers are trained in segmentation and realize the advantages associated with this strategy. Perhaps the best explanation, however, comes back to the basic premise that you must understand as much as possible about consumers to design marketing programs that meet their needs most effectively.

Target market identification isolates consumers with similar lifestyles, needs, and the like and increases our knowledge of their specific requirements. The more marketers can establish this common ground with consumers, the more effective they will be in addressing these requirements in their communications programs and informing and/ or persuading potential consumers that the product or service offering will meet their needs.

Let's use the beer industry as an example. Years ago, beer was just beer, with little differentiation, many local distributors, and few truly national brands. The industry began consolidating; many brands were subsumed by the larger brewers or ceased to exist. As the number of competitors decreased, competition among the major brewers increased. To compete more effectively, brewers began to look at different tastes, lifestyles, and so on of beer drinkers and used this information to design their marketing strategies. This process resulted in the identification of many market segments, each of which corresponds to different customers' needs, lifestyles, and other characteristics.

The beer market has changed dramatically over the past few years, with domestic brands and imports increasing their consolidation efforts. One of the faster-growing segments—craft breweries—itself now consists of a number of segments with numerous offerings available in each (Figure 2–3). Most of the large traditional brewers also have product offerings in each segment, competing with each other as well as smaller craft microbreweries (Exhibit 2-6). Since 2014, the craft market has grown from a $19.6 billion industry to over $26.8 billion by 2021.[4] Each appeals to a different set of needs. Taste is certainly one; others include image, cost, and social appeal. A variety of other reasons for purchasing are also operating, including the consumer's social class, lifestyle, and economic status.

Marketers competing in nearly all product and service categories are constantly searching for ways to segment their markets in an attempt to better satisfy customers' needs. The remainder of this section discusses ways to approach this task.

Market Segmentation

It is not possible to develop marketing strategies for every consumer. Rather, the marketer attempts to identify broad classes of buyers who have the same needs and will respond similarly to marketing actions. **Market segmentation** is dividing a market into distinct groups that (1) have common needs and (2) will respond similarly to a marketing action.

The more marketers segment the market, the more precise is their understanding of it. But the more the market becomes divided, the fewer consumers there are in each segment. Thus, a key decision is: How far should one go in the segmentation

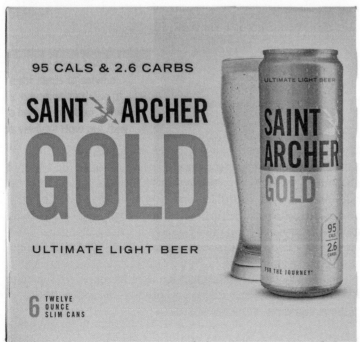

95 CALS & 2.6 CARBS

SAINT ARCHER

GOLD

ULTIMATE LIGHT BEER

6 TWELVE OUNCE SLIM CANS

FIGURE 2–4 Some Bases for Market Segmentation

Basis of Segmentation	Segmentation Variables	Typical Breakdowns
Geographic	Region	Northeast; Midwest; South; West; etc.
	City size	Under 10,000; 10,000–24,999; 25,000–49,999; 50,000–99,999; etc.
	Statistical area	Metropolitan and micropolitan statistical areas; Census tract; etc.
	Media—television	210 designated market areas (DMA) in the United States (Nielsen)
	Density	Urban; suburban; small town; rural
Demographic	Gender	Male; female
	Age	Under 6 yrs; 6–11 yrs; 12–17 yrs; 18–24 yrs; 25–34 yrs; etc.
	Race/ethnicity	African American; Asian; Hispanic; White/Caucasian; etc.
	Life stage	Infant; preschool; child; youth; collegiate; adult; senior
	Birth era	Baby boomer (1946–1964); Gen X (1965–1976); etc.
	Household size	1; 2; 3–4; 5 or more
	Marital status	Never married; married; separated; divorced; widowed; domestic partner
	Income	Under $15,000; $15,000–$24,999; $25,000–$34,999; etc.
	Education	Some high school or less; high school graduate (or GED); etc.
	Occupation	Managerial and professional; technical, sales; farming; etc.
Psychographic	Personality	Gregarious; compulsive; extroverted; aggressive; ambitious; etc.
	Values (VALS2)	Innovators; Thinkers; Achievers; Experiencers; Believers; Strivers; etc.
	Lifestyle (Nielsen PRIZM)	Blue Blood Estates; Single City Blues; etc. (66 total neighborhood clusters)
	Needs	Quality; service; price/value; health; convenience; etc.
Behavioral	Retail store type	Department; specialty; outlet; convenience; mass merchandiser; etc.
	Direct marketing	Mail order/catalog; door-to-door; direct response; Internet
	Product features	Situation-specific; general
	Usage rate	Light user; medium user; heavy user
	User status	Nonuser; ex-user; prospect; first-time user; regular user
	Awareness/intentions	Unaware; aware; interested; intending to buy; purchaser; rejection

process? Where does the process stop? As you can see by the strategy taken in the beer industry, it can go far!

In planning the promotional effort, managers consider whether the target segment is substantial enough to support individualized strategies. More specifically, they consider whether this group is accessible. Can it be reached with a communications program? For example, you will see in Chapter 10 that in some instances there are no media that can efficiently be used to reach some targeted groups. Or the promotions manager may identify a number of segments but be unable to develop the required programs to reach them. The firm may have insufficient funds to develop the required advertising campaign, inadequate sales staff to cover all areas, or other promotional deficiencies. After determining that a segmentation strategy is in order, the marketer must establish the basis on which it will address the market. The following section discusses some of the bases for segmenting markets and demonstrates examples of advertising and promotions applications.

Bases for Segmentation   As shown in Figure 2–4, several methods are available for segmenting markets. Marketers may use one of the segmentation variables

or a combination of approaches. Consider the market segmentation strategy that might be employed to market snow skis. The consumer's lifestyle—active, fun-loving, enjoys outdoor sports—is certainly important. But so are other factors, such as age (participation in downhill skiing drops off significantly at about age 30) and income (have you seen the price of a lift ticket lately?), as well as marital status. Let us review the bases for segmentation and examine some promotional strategies employed in each.

Geographic Segmentation In the **geographic segmentation** approach, markets are divided into different geographic units. These units may include nations, states, counties, or even neighborhoods. Consumers often have different buying habits depending on where they reside. Regional differences may exist in regard to food, drinks, attitudes toward foreign products, and the like. For example, many companies consider California to be a very different market from the rest of the United States and have developed specific marketing programs targeted to the consumers in that state. Other companies have developed programs targeted at specific regions. Exhibit 2-7 shows an ad for Cheerwine, just one of the regional soft-drink "cult brands"—along with Jackson Hole Huckleberry (Wyoming), Vernors (Michigan), and Moxie (New England)—that have found success by marketing in regional areas (in Cheerwine's case, the South). One company—Olde Brooklyn Beverage Company—even went so far as to promote a brand based on a specific section of New York City, differentiating it from bigger brands by promoting the product's "Brooklyn Attitude."

Demographic Segmentation Dividing the market on the basis of demographic variables such as age, sex, family size, education, income, and social class is called **demographic segmentation**. Secret deodorant and the Lady Schick shaver are products that have met with a great deal of success by using the demographic variable of gender as a basis for segmentation. WomensHealth.com, a website and magazine targeting women, may be one of the most successful websites on the Internet addressing issues of particular

importance to women. In Exhibit 2–8, we see how a prominent movie star discusses mental health issues. It is interesting to note that the top 10 websites for women are further segmented by age, lifestyle, fitness, and so forth.

Although market segmentation on the basis of demographics may seem obvious, companies discover that they need to focus more attention on a specific demographic group. For example, IKEA—noting that more than 70 percent of its shoppers are women—has enhanced its store environment to be more "women friendly," as have Home Depot and Walmart. Nike, Reebok, Keds, and Under Armour have all found success through products and ads that empower women. Companies are also finding it difficult to reach the millennial and gen Z age segment. As a result, a number of companies have begun to focus more attention on the baby boomer market—those 76 million Americans born between 1946 and 1964. Given their huge spending power, this age segment has become more attractive to a number of companies including travel agencies and pharmaceutical companies among others. Recognizing their need for

EXHIBIT 2–9

AARP: The Magazine targets the 50 and older segment. The magazine continues to offer print editions and is now available online.

AARP

EXHIBIT 2–10

PRIZM segment profiles like this provide marketers with insights into consumers lifestyles.

Claritas, LLC; wavebreakmedia/ Shutterstock; Ievgen Chepil/Alamy Stock Photo

retirement planning, companies like Fidelity, T. Rowe Price, and Vanguard have very successfully targeted this market. *AARP: The Magazine* is targeted to those who are 50 and older and has 37.5 million readers, making it one of the most read magazines in the United States (Exhibit 2–9).[5]

Other products that have successfully employed demographic segmentation include Dove (gender); Doan's Pills (age); Coca-Cola (race); Mercedes-Benz, Lexus, and BMW cars (income); and Banquet prepackaged dinners (family size).

While demographics may still be the most common method of segmenting markets, it is important to recognize that other factors may be the underlying basis for homogeneity and/or consumer behavior. The astute marketer will identify additional bases for segmenting and will recognize the limitations of demographics. As noted by media strategist Jamie Beckland, many marketers are relying less on demographics and more on psychographic profiling.[6]

Psychographic Segmentation Dividing the market on the basis of personality, lifecycles, and/or lifestyles is referred to as **psychographic segmentation**. While there is some disagreement as to whether personality is a useful basis for segmentation, lifestyle factors have been used effectively. Many consider lifestyle the most effective criterion for segmentation.

The determination of lifestyles is usually based on an analysis of the activities, interests, and opinions (AIOs) of consumers. These lifestyles are then correlated with the consumers' product, brand, and/or media usage. For many products and/or services, lifestyles may be the best discriminator between use and nonuse, accounting for differences in food, clothing, and car selections, among numerous other consumer behaviors.[7]

A leader in the provision of psychographic segmentation is the Claritas PRIZM system. PRIZM provides improved household level segmentation data combined with traditional geodemographics to companies to assist them in their marketing planning and media strategy decisions. The PRIZM program classifies U.S. households into one of 68 consumer segments based on their purchasing preferences allowing companies to better understand consumers lifestyles and their behaviors, including insights into leisure activities, shopping characteristics, media usage, and more. As can be seen in Exhibit 2–10,

PRIZM® Premier Segment Storyboards

▶ claritas

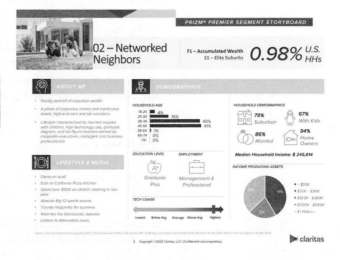

EXHIBIT 2–11

Special K offers a cereal for those who want protein.

Keith Homan/Shutterstock

this information offers insights that go well beyond traditional demographic information. Numerous large companies worldwide have used this system to effectively target potential consumers and reach them more effectively.

Another form of psychographic analysis relies on the use of multiple databases including social profile data (available through almost all social networks), behavioral data (tracking users through their online behaviors), and lifecycle data (stage of the consumer's lifecycle, e.g., buying diapers, graduating high school, etc.). Amazon.com has successfully used this strategy for some time, and others are now starting to see the advantages offered over traditional demographic profiling.[8]

Behavioristic Segmentation Dividing consumers into groups according to their usage, loyalties, or buying responses to a product is **behavioristic segmentation**. For example, product or brand usage, degree of use (heavy vs. light), and/or brand loyalty are combined with demographic and/or psychographic criteria to develop profiles of market segments. In the case of usage, the marketer assumes that nonpurchasers of a brand or product who have the same characteristics as purchasers hold greater potential for adoption than do nonusers with different characteristics. As you will see in Chapter 15, many companies target consumers through social media like Facebook based on behavioristic segmentation.

Degree of use relates to the fact that a few consumers may buy a disproportionate amount of many products or brands. Industrial marketers refer to the **80–20 rule**, meaning 20 percent of their buyers account for 80 percent of their sales volume. Again, when the characteristics of these users are identified, targeting them allows for a much greater concentration of efforts and less wasted time and money. The same heavy-half strategy is possible in the consumer market as well. The majority of purchases of many products (e.g., soaps and detergents, shampoos, cake mixes, beer, dog food, colas, bourbon, and toilet tissue—yes, toilet tissue!) are accounted for by a small proportion of the population. Perhaps you can think of some additional examples.

Benefit Segmentation In purchasing products, consumers are generally trying to satisfy specific needs and/or wants. They are looking for products that provide specific benefits to satisfy these needs. The grouping of consumers on the basis of attributes sought in a product is known as **benefit segmentation** and is widely used. For example, the market for products that contain protein has led to numerous new entries like the Special K Protein in Exhibit 2-11.

Consider the purchase of a wristwatch. While you might buy a watch for particular benefits such as accuracy, water resistance, or stylishness, others may seek a different set of benefits. Watches are commonly given as gifts for birthdays, Christmas, and graduation. Certainly some of the same benefits are considered in the purchase of a gift, but the benefits the purchaser derives are different from those the user will obtain. Ads that portray watches as good gifts stress different criteria to consider in the purchase decision. The next time you see an ad or commercial for a watch, think about the basic appeal and the benefits it offers.

The Process of Segmenting a Market The segmentation process develops over time and is an integral part of the situation analysis. It is in this stage that marketers attempt to determine as much as they can about the market: What needs are not being fulfilled? What benefits are being sought? What characteristics distinguish among the various groups seeking these products and services? A number of alternative segmentation strategies may be used. Each time a specific segment is identified, additional information is gathered to help the marketer understand this group.

For example, once a specific segment is identified on the basis of benefits sought, the marketer will examine psychographic characteristics and demographics to help characterize this group and to further its understanding of this market. Behavioristic segmentation criteria will also be examined. In the purchase of ski boots, for example, specific benefits may be sought—flexibility or stiffness—depending on the type of skiing the buyer does. All this information will be combined to provide a complete profile of the skier.

A number of companies offer research services to help marketing managers define their markets and develop strategies targeting them. The PRIZM system discussed earlier is just one of the services offered; others use demographic, socioeconomic, and geographic data to cluster consumer households into distinct "microgeographic" segments. One of these companies, Claritas, provides demographic and psychographic profiles of geographic areas as small as census track, block group, or zip code +4. Users of the system include Ace Hardware, IBM, Walmart, and numerous others.

Selecting a Target Market

The outcome of the segmentation analysis will reveal the market opportunities available. The next phase in the target marketing process involves two steps: (1) determining how many segments to enter and (2) determining which segments offer the most potential.

Determining How Many Segments to Enter
Three market coverage alternatives are available. **Undifferentiated marketing** involves ignoring segment differences and offering just one product or service to the entire market. For example, when Henry Ford brought out the first assembly-line automobile, all potential consumers were offered the same basic product: a black Ford. For many years, Coca-Cola offered only one product version. While this standardized strategy saves the company money, it does not allow the opportunity to offer different versions of the product to different markets.

Differentiated marketing involves marketing in a number of segments, developing separate marketing strategies for each. For example, the Marriott hotel chain offers a variety of customer services for different travelers, including vacation, business, long or short stay, and so forth.

The third alternative, **concentrated marketing**, is used when the firm selects one segment and attempts to capture a large share of this market. Volkswagen used this strategy in the 1950s when it was the only major automobile company competing in the economy-car segment in the United States. While Volkswagen has now assumed a more differentiated strategy, other companies have found the concentrated strategy effective. For example, Rolls-Royce has focused its automobile business exclusively on the high-income segment; L'Oréal competes in the cosmetics and beauty segment.

Determining Which Segments Offer Potential
The second step in selecting a market involves determining the most attractive segment. The firm must examine the sales potential of the segment, the opportunities for growth, the competition, and its own ability to compete. Then it must decide whether it can market to this group. Stories abound of companies that have entered new markets only to find their lack of resources or expertise would not allow them to compete successfully. After selecting the segments to target and determining that it can compete, the firm proceeds to the final step in Figure 2–2: the market positioning phase.

Market Positioning

Approaches to Positioning
Positioning strategies generally focus on either the consumer or the competition. While both approaches involve the association of product benefits with consumer needs, the former does so by linking the product with the benefits the consumer will derive or creating a favorable brand image, as

EXHIBIT 2-12

Hilton uses positioning that focuses on the consumer.

Hilton

shown in Exhibit 2-12. The Hilton Hotel ad shown in Exhibit 2-12 focuses on creating a favorable brand image in its appeal to consumers. The other approach positions the product by comparing it and the benefit it offers versus the competition. Products like Scope Outlast mouthwash (positioning itself as five times longer lasting than competitors' brands) and Burt's Bees (positioned as a better value than its competitors' brands) have employed this strategy successfully (Exhibit 2-13).

Many advertising practitioners consider market positioning the most important factor in establishing a brand in the marketplace. David Aaker and John Myers note that the term *position* has been used to indicate the brand's or product's image in the marketplace.[9] Jack Trout and Al Ries suggest that this brand image must contrast with those of competitors. They say, "In today's marketplace, the competitors' image is just as important as your own. Sometimes more important."[10] Trout notes that a good branding strategy cannot exist without positioning. He further states that branding is about the process of building a brand, while positioning is about putting that brand in the mind of the consumer.[11] Thus, *positioning*, as used in this text, relates to the image of the product and/or brand relative to competing products or brands. The position of the product or brand is the key factor in communicating the benefits it offers and differentiating it from the competition. Let us now turn to strategies marketers use to position a product.

Positioning has been defined as "the art and science of fitting the product or service to one or more segments of the broad market in such a way as to set it meaningfully apart from competition."[12] As you can see, the position of the product, service, or even store is the image that comes to mind and the attributes consumers perceive as related to it. This communication occurs through the message itself, which explains the benefits, as well as the media strategy employed to reach the target group. Take a few moments to think about how some products are positioned and how their positions are conveyed to you. For example, what comes to mind when you hear the name Mercedes, Dr Pepper, or Apple? What about department stores such as Neiman Marcus, Walmart, and JCPenney? Now think of the ads for each of these products and companies. Are their approaches different from their competitors'? When and where are these ads shown? What is the message they are trying to communicate?

DEVELOPING A POSITIONING STRATEGY

A number of positioning strategies might be employed in developing a promotional program. David Aaker and J. Gary Shansby discuss six such strategies: positioning by product attributes, price/quality, use, product class, users, and competitor.[13] Aaker and Myers add one more approach, positioning by cultural symbols.[14]

Positioning by Product Attributes and Benefits

A common approach to positioning is setting the brand apart from competitors on the basis of the specific characteristics or benefits offered. Sometimes a product may be positioned on more than one product benefit. Marketers attempt to identify **salient attributes** (those that are important to consumers and are the basis for making a purchase decision). For example, when Apple first introduced its computers, the key benefit stressed was ease of use—an effective strategy, given the complexity of computers in the market at that time. While Apple still maintains this position, it is innovative products that come

EXHIBIT 2-13

In this advertisement, Burt's Bees uses a benefit positioning strategy by emphasizing the safe ingredients in baby products.

Burt's Bees

safe.
effective.
natural.

Formulated without parabens, phthalates, petrolatum or SLS

HELPS TO MAINTAIN IMMUNE FUNCTION & OVERALL GOOD HEALTH

EXHIBIT 2–14

Emergen-C positions itself as offering a number of benefits, including a powerful blend of nutrients to support the immune system. The product contains a blend of nutrients to help fortify one's immune system.

GSK Group

EXHIBIT 2–15

Kohl's positions its brand as having good value. Kohl's is a specialty department store that offers "Products You Love for Less."

Kohl's, Inc.

to mind as well, and may be what consumers think about first when thinking of the brand. More recently, there have been a number of new water products that enhance hydration, help the body to exert physical power, increase immunities, and so on. Emergen-C positions itself as a product that fortifies your body, refreshes you, and increases your energy (Exhibit 2-14).

Positioning by Price/Quality

Marketers often use price/quality characteristics to position their brands. One way they do this is with ads that reflect the image of a high-quality brand where cost, while not irrelevant, is considered secondary to the quality benefits derived from using the brand. Premium brands positioned at the high end of the market use this approach to positioning.

Another way to use price/quality characteristics for positioning is to focus on the quality or value offered by the brand at a very competitive price. For example, Kohl's takes the position of a family-oriented specialty store offering good value (Exhibit 2-15). Remember that although price is an important consideration, the product quality must be comparable to, or even better than, competing brands for the positioning strategy to be effective.

Positioning by Use or Application

Another way to communicate a specific image or position for a brand is to associate it with a specific use or application. The Intuit ad shown in Exhibit 2-16 is specifically targeted to small business owners and/or entrepreneurs.

While this strategy is often used to enter a market on the basis of a particular use or application, it is also an effective way to expand the usage of a product. For example, Arm & Hammer baking soda has been promoted for everything from baking to

EXHIBIT 2–16

Intuit offers products specifically useful to small business owners.

Intuit, Inc.

EXHIBIT 2–17

Arm & Hammer baking soda demonstrates numerous product uses.

ZikG/Shutterstock

relieving heartburn to eliminating odors in carpets and refrigerators and has been doing so effectively since 1846 (Exhibit 2–17).

Positioning by Product Class

Often the competition for a product comes from outside the product class. For example, airlines know that while they compete with other airlines, trains and buses are also viable alternatives. Amtrak has positioned itself as an alternative to airplanes, citing cost savings, enjoyment, and other advantages. Dole fruit juices encourage consumers to "drink their fruits," claiming that 8 ounces of juice is the equivalent of two fruits. V8 promotes drinking one's vegetables. Rather than positioning against another brand, an alternative strategy is to position oneself against another product category. The California Avocado Commission launched a major IMC campaign to more strongly position itself as a fruit (as opposed to a vegetable) that is grown on family farms. The print, radio, outdoor, and online campaign took a humorous approach, positioning the avocado as a "fun fruit," while demonstrating the healthy advantages relative to other fruits and vegetables, and providing numerous products for which it might become an alternative, including cream cheese, butter, and dips. Copy points for the ads were provided by the Commission to retailers (Exhibit 2–18). A Mountain High yogurt ad positions the product as a substitute for other baking ingredients such as oils, fats, and so on.

Positioning by Product User

Positioning a product by associating it with a particular user or group of users is yet another approach. An example would be the Globe shoes ad shown in Exhibit 2–19. This ad emphasizes identification or association with a specific group—in this case, skateboarders.

Positioning by Competitor

Competitors may be as important to positioning strategy as a firm's own product or services. Advertisers used to think it was a cardinal sin to mention a competitor in their advertising. However, in today's market, an effective positioning strategy for a product or brand may focus on specific competitors. This approach is similar to positioning by product class, although in this case the competition is within the same product category. Perhaps the best-known example of this strategy was Avis, which positioned itself against the car-rental leader, Hertz, by stating, "We're number two, so we try harder." The Verizon ad shown earlier (Exhibit 2–5) is an example of positioning a brand against the competition. When positioning by competitor, a marketer must often employ another positioning strategy as well to differentiate the brand.

Positioning by Cultural Symbols

Aaker and Myers include an additional positioning strategy in which cultural symbols are used to differentiate brands. When it is associated with a meaningful symbol, the brand is easily identifiable and differentiated from others. Examples are the Jolly Green Giant, the Keebler elves, Speedy Alka-Seltzer, the Pillsbury Doughboy, the Wells Fargo stagecoach, Ronald McDonald, Chiquita Banana, and Mr. Peanut. Tony the Tiger (who has been used by Kellogg's for over 60 years—with a few minor facelifts) clearly qualifies as a cultural symbol (Exhibit 2–20). Each of these symbols has successfully differentiated the product it represents from competitors'.

EXHIBIT 2–18

In this ad, how does the California Avocado Commission use positioning to effectively market California avocados?

California Avocado Commission

EXHIBIT 2–19

Globe positions by product user—in this case, skateboarders.

Globe International Limited

EXHIBIT 2–20

Tony the Tiger has been the mascot of Frosted Flakes since the brand was introduced in 1952, and has become a cultural symbol.

Sheila Fitzgerald/Shutterstock

Repositioning

One final positioning strategy involves altering or changing a product's or brand's position. **Repositioning** a product usually occurs because of declining or stagnant sales or because of anticipated opportunities in other market positions. Repositioning is often difficult to accomplish because of entrenched perceptions about and attitudes toward the product or brand. IMC Perspective 2–2 discusses a number of brands that have been repositioned. As you can see, there are a number of reasons why brands do so. Others who have attempted to change their position include JCPenney, La-Z-Boy, and MTV, with varying degrees of success.

Before leaving this section, you might stop to think for a moment about the positioning (and repositioning) strategies pursued by different companies. Any successful product that comes to mind probably occupies a distinct market position.

DEVELOPING THE MARKETING PLANNING PROGRAM

The development of the marketing strategy and selection of a target market(s) tell the marketing department which customers to focus on and what needs to attempt to satisfy. The next stage of the marketing process involves combining the various elements of the marketing mix into a cohesive, effective marketing program. Each marketing-mix element is multidimensional and includes a number of decision areas. Likewise, each must consider and contribute to the overall IMC program. We now examine product, price, and distribution channels and how each influences and interacts with the promotional program.

Product Decisions

An organization exists because it has some product, service, or idea to offer consumers, generally in exchange for money. This offering may come in the form of a physical product (such as a soft drink, pair of jeans, or car), a service (banking, airlines, or legal assistance), a cause (Special Olympics, American Cancer Society), or even a person (a political candidate). The product is anything that can be marketed and that, when used or supported, gives satisfaction to the individual.

A *product* is more than just a physical object; it is a bundle of benefits or values that satisfy the needs of consumers. The needs may be purely functional, or they may include social and psychological benefits. For example, the campaign for Michelin tires stresses the quality built into Michelin tires (value) as well as their performance and durability (function). The term **product symbolism** refers to what a product or brand means to consumers and what they experience in purchasing and using it.[15] For many products, strong symbolic features and social and psychological meaning may be more important than functional utility.[16] For example, designer clothing such as Versace, Gucci, and Prada is often purchased on the basis of its symbolic meaning and image, particularly by teenagers and young adults. Advertising plays an important role in developing and maintaining the image of these brands.

Product planning involves decisions not only about the item itself, such as design and quality, but also about aspects such as service and warranties as well as brand name and package design. Consumers look beyond the reality of the product and its ingredients. The product's quality, branding, packaging, and even the company standing behind it all contribute to consumers' perceptions.[17] In an effective IMC program, advertising, branding, and packaging are all designed to portray the product as more than just a bundle of attributes. All are coordinated to present an image or positioning of the product that extends well beyond its physical attributes.

Changing Market Conditions Lead Brands to Reposition— Some Successfully, Some Not

Procter & Gamble

There are a number of factors that might lead a brand to reposition—that is, change their positioning strategy. As you might imagine, this is not an easy decision to make as companies may have already invested heavily to establish their current position, and there is no guarantee that the repositioning will be successful. For some brands, however, this may be the last resort in an attempt to save a brand in the decline stage of the product life cycle. While these attempts have failed for some brands, they have also worked for others. Let's explore some of these undertakings and the reasons necessitating the changes.

Victoria's Secret—When one thought of the lingerie retailer Victoria's Secret not that long ago, the vision of sexy "Angels" supermodels was likely the first thing to come to mind. For decades the Angels epitomized a widely accepted stereotype of what is feminine that led to enormous success in the bra and lingerie market. Victoria's Secret was synonymous with sexy, and with success with over 1,400 stores employing over 32,000 employees and over $5 billion in sales. So why change? The brand is still the leader in the women's underwear market and remains the biggest lingerie seller in the United States. Brand shares were near a record high. Why risk it?

Well, for one, times have changed. The #MeToo era led many to look at the company as too male-dominated and out of touch with women. A scandal around the former Chairman and Chief Executive Officer Leslie Wexner and his association with the late financier Jeffery Epstein didn't help either. Interest in the Victoria's Secret fashion show waned. As noted in an article in the *New York Times*, "Rarely has a company so dominant in its sector been exposed as trailing so far behind the culture as Victoria' Secret was in the wake of the #MeToo movement." So while things may have been alright financially, the company's marketing was dated, and a change was imminent.

So in comes the VS Collective and Victoria's Secret becomes a stand-alone company spun off from parent L Brands, Inc. The Collective consists of professional

soccer player Megan Rapinoe, plus-size model Paloma Elsesser, and transgender model Valentina Sampaio. Also included are actress Priyanka Chopra Jonas, world champion skier Eileen Gu, and model Adut Akech. In addition to being featured in its advertising, the group will also help advise the repositioning and hopefully shatter the old brand image. New products, store environment changes, product range increases (for example, larger sizes), and new advertising are in store. The repositioning is considered by many to be "the most extreme and unabashed attempt at a brand turnaround in recent memory." The idea is to redefine what "sexy" means as determined by the masses (and not just sexy models) and to be "What Women Want."

Gillette—For 30 years Gillette's advertising slogan was "The best a man can get." Then in 2019 the shaving company launched a new campaign replacing it with "the best men can be," essentially repositioning the brand from a heavy focus on masculinity to a new, more "positive masculinity" in line with the #MeToo movement. On the Procter & Gamble website (Gillette is owned by P&G), the company noted that "It's time we acknowledge that brands, like ours, play a role in influencing culture. . . . From today on, we pledge to actively challenge the stereotypes and expectations of what it means to be a man everywhere you see Gillette." The first ad featured news clips reporting on the #MeToo movement as well as examples of sexism, sexual harassment, bullying, and toxic masculinity, asking the question "Is this the best a man can get?" In addition, a film, called *We Believe: The Best Men Can Be* was placed on the website and received 4 million views in the first 48 hours. After a year and a half, the video had received 110 million views and over 19.5 billion impressions worldwide.

Not all of the reactions to the new campaign were positive, however. Many of the responses to the new campaign accused Gillette of "an assault on masculinity" or of creating a toxic image of men. A number also said they would never buy Gillette again, and some even called for a boycott. At the same time, many of the responses were positive. A number of critics applauded the brand for taking the risk, and the campaign even received an award by achieving a place on the WARC Creative Effectiveness Ladder, which awards campaigns for "influential ideas that attract attention and controversy."

While Victoria's Secret and Gillette both repositioned their brands to adapt to changing cultural times, this reason may be considered both unique and uncommon. As noted by Bill Viau, blogging on "Marketing Made Human," repositioning often takes place when brands are in trouble due to a number of reasons including decreases in sales, customer disconnect, lack of brand appeal to younger consumers,

(*continued*)

and others. Viau offers examples of a number of brands that have taken the risk and were successful as a result, including:

- *Taco Bell*—The brand successfully changed its positioning from "cheap Mexican food" to a "lifestyle brand" by dropping the "Yo Quiero Taco Bell" (and the chihuahua!) campaign and replacing it with "Live Más" (live more). In addition, changes were made to the menu and the restaurant design, experimenting with new menu items, and a strong social media strategy was put in place focusing more attention on the 20-somethings as its core audience. Eating at Taco Bell now reflects "an experience."
- *Gucci*—The very-high-end luxury brand always did well, but it experienced declines as its prime market aged. As a result, Gucci repositioned itself to maintain its Italian roots and extravagance but also become more contemporary. The new progressive mindset led to a new focus on Instagram-style communications, a new logo, and an empowering stance on gender fluidity. The results were steep gains financially and improvement in the brand's image.
- *Spotify*—When COVID-19 hit, one might have thought that Spotify was in a perfect position given that it was digital, remote, and offered an escape from the reality

going on. But Spotify also relied heavily on advertising revenues. As clients cut their advertising expenditures, Spotify felt the pain and had to make changes. Following on previous success stories like Netflix, Spotify increased their focus on original content like podcasts and Spotify Original and put extra effort into curated playlists from experts, AI, and celebrities. The new Spotify was not just a music provider, but a new content creator and has been successful ever since.

As you can see, a variety of factors can lead to repositioning—not all of which are in the company's control. However, by adapting and changing in response to changing marketing conditions, brands can essentially successfully reinvent themselves. But not always!

Sources: Andrea Felsted, "Victoria's Secret Stakes $5 Billion on a Future with No Angels," *Bloomberg Businessweek*, June 24, 2021, www.Bloomberg.net; Sapna Maheshwari and Vanessa Friedman, "Victoria's Secret Swaps Angels for 'What Women Want.' Will They Buy It?" *New York Times*, June 16, 2021, www.nytimes.com; Lucy Aitken, "How an Influential Idea Repositioned Gillette," WARC, July 2020, www.warc.com; Alexandra Topping, Kate Lyons, and Matthew Weaver, "Gillette#MeToo Razors Ad on 'Toxic Masculinity' Gets Praise—and Abuse," *The Guardian*, January 15, 2019, www.guardian.com; Bill Viau, "6 Examples of Brand Repositioning That Renewed Company Growth," MarketVeep, October 2020, www.marketveep.com.

Branding   Branding is about building and maintaining a favorable identity and image of the company and/or its products or services in the mind of the consumer. The goal of branding is to (1) build and maintain brand awareness and interest; (2) develop and enhance attitudes toward the company, product, or service; and (3) build and foster relationships between the consumer and the brand. The **brand identity** consists of the combination of the name, logo, symbols, design, packaging, image, and associations held by consumers. Think for a minute about the ads for Nike; the product benefits and attributes are usually not even mentioned—yet information about the brand is communicated effectively.

EXHIBIT 2–21

Rolex creates strong brand equity through advertising.

Rolex SA

One important role of advertising in respect to branding strategies is creating and maintaining **brand equity**, which can be thought of as an intangible asset of added value or goodwill that results from the favorable image, impressions of differentiation, and/or the strength of consumer attachment to a company name, brand name, or trademark. Brand equity allows a brand to earn greater sales volume and/or higher margins than it could without the name, providing the company with a competitive advantage. The strong equity position a company and/or its brand enjoys is often reinforced through advertising. For example, Rolex watches command a premium price because of their high quality as well as the strong brand equity they have developed through advertising (Exhibit 2–21).

Packaging   Packaging is another aspect of product strategy that has become increasingly important. Traditionally, the package provided functional benefits such as economy, protection, and storage. However, the role and function of the package have changed because of the self-service emphasis of many stores and the fact that more and more buying decisions are made at the point of purchase. Wrigley's gum, recognizing that as many as two-thirds of all purchases made in the supermarket are unplanned, has increased its efforts to attract attention at the checkout counter. The Chicago company took a close look at how and why

consumers buy impulse items at the checkout as well as how Wrigley's could be more effective in gaining their attention to increase sales.[18] The package is often the consumer's first exposure to the product, so it must make a favorable first impression. A typical supermarket has more than 30,000 items competing for attention. Not only must a package attract and hold the consumer's attention, but it must also communicate information on how to use the product, divulge its composition and content, and satisfy any legal requirements regarding disclosure. Moreover, many firms design the package to carry a sales promotion message such as a contest, sweepstakes, or premium offer.

Many companies view the package as an important way to communicate with consumers and create an impression of the brand in their minds. In other instances packages can extend the brand by offering new uses (Exhibit 2–22). Design factors such as size, shape, color, and lettering all contribute to the appeal of a package and can be as important as a commercial in determining what goes from the store shelf to the consumer's shopping cart. Many companies use packaging to create a distinctive brand image and identity. The next time you walk by a perfume counter, stop to look at the many unique package designs (see Exhibit 2–23).

Price Decisions

The *price variable* refers to what the consumer must give up to purchase a product or service. While price is discussed in terms of the dollar amount exchanged for an item, the cost of a product to the consumer includes time, mental activity, and behavioral effort.[19] The marketing manager is usually concerned with establishing a price level, developing pricing policies, and monitoring competitors' and consumers' reactions to prices in the marketplace. A firm must consider a number of factors in determining the price it charges for its product or service, including costs, demand factors, competition, and perceived value. From an IMC perspective, the price must be consistent with the perceptions of the product, as well as the communications strategy. Higher prices, of course, will communicate a higher product quality, while lower prices reflect bargain or "value" perceptions. A product positioned as highest quality but carrying a lower price than competitors would only confuse consumers. In other words, the price, the advertising, and the distribution channels must present one unified voice speaking to the product's positioning.

Relating Price to Advertising and Promotion Factors such as product quality, competition, and advertising all interact in determining what price a firm can and should charge. Studies have shown that pricing and advertising strategies go together. High relative ad expenditures should accompany premium prices, and low relative ad expenditures should be tailored to low prices. These results obviously support the IMC perspective that one voice must be conveyed. In a comprehensive study, it was shown that exposure to television ads reduces consumers' tendencies to react to price changes. The study further showed that heavy users of the product category were most likely to have their sensitivities reduced.[20]

Distribution Channel Decisions

As consumers, we generally take for granted the role of marketing intermediaries or channel members. If we want a six-pack of soda or a box of detergent, we can buy it at a supermarket, a convenience store, or even a drugstore. Manufacturers understand the value and importance of these intermediaries.

One of a marketer's most important marketing decisions involves the way it makes its products and services available for purchase. A firm can have an excellent product

EXHIBIT 2–22

This ad for WD-40 successfully uses its packaging to show a few of the many uses for the product.

WD-40

EXHIBIT 2–23

This Dior perfume packaging creates a clear product image.

Panther Media GmbH/Alamy Stock Photo

at a great price, but it will be of little value unless it is available where the customer wants it, when the customer wants it, and with the proper support and service. **Marketing channels**, the place element of the marketing mix, are "sets of interdependent organizations involved in the process of making a product or service available for use or consumption."[21]

The distribution strategy should take into consideration the communication objectives and the impact that the channel strategy will have on the IMC program. Stewart and colleagues discuss the need for "integrated channel management," which "reflects the blurring of the boundaries of the communications and distribution functions."[22] Consistent with the product and pricing decisions, where the product is distributed will send a communications message. Does the fact that a product is sold at Neiman Marcus or Saks convey a different message regarding its image than if it were distributed at Kmart or Walmart? If you think about it for a moment, the mere fact that the product is distributed in these channels communicates an image about it in your mind. Stewart gives examples of how channel elements contribute to communication—for example, grocery store displays, point-of-purchase merchandising, and shelf footage. The distribution channel in a well-integrated marketing program serves as a form of reminder advertising. The consumer sees the brand name and recalls the advertising. (Think about the last time you passed a McDonald's. Did it remind you of any of McDonald's ads?)

A company can choose not to use any channel intermediaries but, rather, to sell to its customers through **direct channels**. This type of channel arrangement is sometimes used in the consumer market by firms using direct-selling programs, such as Advocare, Tupperware, and Mary Kay, or firms that use direct-response advertising, telemarketing, or the Internet to sell their products. Direct channels are also frequently used by manufacturers of industrial products and services, which are often selling expensive and complex products that require extensive negotiations and sales efforts, as well as service and follow-up calls after the sale.

Chapter 15 provides a discussion of the role of the Internet and digital media in an IMC program. As will be seen, the Internet is relied on by many companies as a direct channel of distribution, since they offer products and services for sale on their websites. Amazon.com and eBay.com are just two of the many examples of such efforts. The COVID-19 pandemic had a major impact on where consumers shopped. While digital channels were already experiencing increases in sales, the trend was greatly accelerated as consumers were confined to their homes. The impact on on-site shopping was devastating to retail establishments, many of which did not survive. For example, online spending for groceries increased 235 percent year to year in 2020, off-price goods 80 percent, and home improvement 78 percent. Media streaming services increased rapidly with nearly every major U.S. TV studio and network setting up D2C streaming services.[23] As you will see throughout the rest of this text, a major transformation in consumer behaviors has taken place, forcing almost all industries to adapt.

Most consumer-product companies distribute through **indirect channels**, usually using a network of wholesalers (institutions that sell to other resellers) and/or retailers (which sell primarily to the final consumer).

Developing Promotional Strategies: Push or Pull?

Most of you are aware of advertising and other forms of promotion directed toward ultimate consumers or business customers. We see these ads in the media and are often part of the target audience for the promotions. In addition to developing a consumer marketing mix, a company must have a program to motivate the channel members. Programs designed to persuade the trade to stock, merchandise, and promote a manufacturer's products are part of a **promotional push strategy**. The goal of this strategy is to push the product through the channels of distribution by aggressively selling and promoting the item to the resellers, or trade.

Promotion to the trade includes all the elements of the promotional mix. Company sales representatives call on resellers to explain the product, discuss the firm's plans for building demand among ultimate consumers, and describe special programs being offered to the trade, such as introductory discounts, promotional allowances, and cooperative ad programs. The company may use **trade advertising** to interest wholesalers and retailers and motivate them to purchase its products for resale to their customers. Trade advertising usually appears in publications that serve the particular industry.

A push strategy tries to convince resellers they can make a profit on a manufacturer's product and to encourage them to order the merchandise and push it through to their customers. An alternative strategy is a **promotional pull strategy**, spending money on advertising and sales promotion efforts directed toward the ultimate consumer. The goal of a pull strategy is to create demand among consumers and encourage them to request the product from the retailer. Seeing the consumer demand, retailers will order the product from wholesalers (if they are used), which in turn will request it from the manufacturer. Thus, stimulating demand at the end-user level pulls the product through the channels of distribution.

Whether to emphasize a push or a pull strategy depends on a number of factors, including the company's relations with the trade, its promotional budget, and demand for the firm's products. Companies that have favorable channel relationships may prefer to use a push strategy and work closely with channel members to encourage them to stock and promote their products. A firm with a limited promotional budget may not have the funds for advertising and sales promotion that a pull strategy requires and may find it more cost-effective to build distribution and demand by working closely with resellers. When the demand outlook for a product is favorable because it has unique benefits, is superior to competing brands, or is very popular among consumers, a pull strategy may be appropriate. Companies often use a combination of push and pull strategies, with the emphasis changing as the product moves through its life cycle.

THE ROLE OF ADVERTISING AND PROMOTION

As shown in the marketing model in Figure 2-1, the marketing program includes promotion both to the trade (channel members) and to the company's ultimate customers. Marketers use the various promotional-mix elements—advertising, sales promotion, direct marketing, publicity/public relations, digital/Internet marketing, and personal selling—to inform consumers about their products, their prices, and places where the products are available. Each promotional-mix variable helps marketers achieve their promotional objectives, and all variables must work together to achieve an integrated marketing communications program.

To this point, we have discussed the various elements of the marketing plan that serves as the basis for the IMC program. The development and implementation of an IMC program is based on a strong foundation that includes market analysis, target marketing and positioning, and coordination of the various marketing-mix elements. Throughout the following chapters of this text, we will explore the role of various IMC elements in helping achieve marketing objectives.

Summary

Promotion plays an important role in an organization's efforts to market its product, service, or ideas to its customers. Figure 2-1 shows a model for analyzing how promotions fit into a company's marketing program. The model includes a marketing strategy and analysis, target marketing, program development, and the target market. The marketing process begins with a marketing strategy that is based on a detailed situation analysis and guides for target market selection and development of the firm's marketing program.

In the planning process, the situation analysis requires that the marketing strategy be assumed. The promotional program is developed with this strategy as a guide. One of the key decisions to be made pertains to the target marketing process, which includes identifying, segmenting, targeting, and positioning to target markets. There are several bases for segmenting the market and various ways to position a product.

Once the target marketing process has been completed, marketing program decisions regarding product, price, distribution, and promotions must be made. All of these must be coordinated to provide an integrated marketing communications perspective, in which the positioning strategy is supported by one voice. Thus all product strategies, pricing strategies, and distribution choices must be made with the objective of contributing to the overall image of the product or brand. Advertising and promotion decisions, in turn, must be integrated with the other marketing-mix decisions to accomplish this goal.

Key Terms

strategic marketing plan 45
market segments 45
market opportunities 45
competitive advantage 47
target marketing 50
market segmentation 51
geographic segmentation 53
demographic segmentation 53
psychographic segmentation 55

behavioristic segmentation 56
80–20 rule 56
benefit segmentation 56
undifferentiated marketing 57
differentiated marketing 57
concentrated marketing 57
positioning 58
salient attributes 58
repositioning 62

product symbolism 62
brand identity 64
brand equity 64
marketing channels 66
direct channels 66
indirect channels 66
promotional push strategy 66
trade advertising 67
promotional pull strategy 67

Discussion Questions

1. The chapter opening discusses the fact that many companies have been changing their company names. Give a few examples (other than those in the text) of companies that have changed their names. Explain why you think they took this action, and whether you believe it was a positive or negative move on their part. (LO 2-4)

2. Online dating sites have now become a common way for people to meet others that share similar characteristics as themselves. Explain why these sites have become so popular, citing some of the factors leading to their success. (LO 2-2)

3. For many marketers, demographics is the most prevalent form of segmentation employed. Explain why this may not necessarily be the most effective form of segmentation to use. Provide examples to support your position. (LO 2-3)

4. Digital media have become the focus of many companies' media strategies and have experienced strong growth in recent years resulting in traditional media receiving less advertising dollars. Based on what you have learned in this chapter, provide some advantages and disadvantages of focusing so much attention on digital media. (LO 2-5)

5. The chapter identifies five different ways to segment a market. Provide an example of a product or service that employs each and explain how and why they employ this method. (LO 2-3)

6. Discuss the difference between a push and a pull strategy. How do these strategies differ in advertising and promotional strategies? (LO 2-5)

7. What is the difference between product symbolism and functional product attributes? Give examples of brands that reflect each of these in their marketing strategies. (LO 2-5)

8. IMC Perspective 2–1 discusses segmentation in the online dating market. Pick any three online sites and discuss the target market these sites are trying to appeal to. Provide examples to support your position. (LO 2-4)

9. Many companies compete in a number of market segments. Discuss an example of one such company and describe how it communicates with its customers in different market segments. (LO 2-4)

10. The chapter describes various age cohorts including baby boomers, millennials, and gen Z. Describe some of the similarities and differences among these groups and the implications for marketers. (LO 2-3)

3

Organizing for Advertising and Promotion: The Role of Ad Agencies and Other Marketing Communication Organizations

Droga5, LLC

Learning Objectives

LO3-1 Describe how companies organize for advertising and integrated marketing communications functions.

LO3-2 Compare the advantages and disadvantages of different ways to organize for advertising and promotion.

LO3-3 Identify the types of advertising agencies and the roles they play.

LO3-4 Explain how to select, compensate, and evaluate advertising agencies.

LO3-5 Identify the role and functions of specialized marketing communication organizations.

LO3-6 Compare the pros and cons of using an integrated marketing services agency.

Accenture's Acquisition of Droga5 Rocks the Advertising Industry

Throughout the 20th century and into the new millennium, the advertising industry was dominated by traditional advertising agencies. One of the most significant developments was the merger in 1986 of three major agencies (BBDO, Doyle Dane Bernbach, and Needham Harper) into a new holding company called the Omnicom Group. *Advertising Age* termed the merger the "Big Bang" because it served as the catalyst for a flurry of mergers and acquisitions that led to consolidation of the agency business and the formation of the four major agency holding companies that dominated the industry for the next 20 years. However, another major change has been occurring over the past several years that may be just as disruptive as the Big Bang, as old-guard agencies find themselves competing against a different type of agency whose parent companies are known more for their accounting or management consulting expertise than advertising or marketing. In 2017, for the first time ever, the marketing services divisions of four consultancies—Accenture Interactive, PwC, IBM iX, and Deloitte Digital—were among the top 10 largest agency companies in the world, and 5 years later they retained their rankings.

The consultancies do not receive the attention and notoriety of traditional advertising agencies whose focus is often on doing breakthrough creative work for their clients. Most of them have positioned themselves as adjuncts to ad agencies by offering clients consulting services along with expertise and capabilities in technology, data, analytics, content creation, and other areas that have become vital to marketers in the new digital era. They are also leveraging their access to high-level executives, such as chief marketing officers and vice presidents, and wooing them with data-driven approaches to consumer insights and the best ways to communicate with them, particularly through digital media. The major consultancies provide accounting, information technology, and management consulting services to the vast majority of the world's top companies and often can work from the top down—through CEOs and other C-suite executives—rather than working up through marketing departments and corporate hierarchies.

The rapid growth of consultancies is also a reflection of the movement from advertising-dominant marketing to more integrated approaches that consider the entire consumer journey. Brian Whipple, the former managing director of Accenture Interactive (AI), notes that "historically brands have been built by pushed messages with ads that gave suggestions about how you should feel or emote or think about a product or service. We don't believe that is true at all anymore. Instead Accenture's philosophy is that brands are built through hundreds of consumer interactions ranging from e-commerce experiences to how people are treated in physical stores."

Thus far, consultancies have not moved too far into the creative space dominated by the advertising agencies. However, a strong message was sent that they do indeed plan to move deeper into the advertising business when Accenture Interactive (AI) paid nearly $500 million in 2019 to acquire Droga5, a leading independent agency widely recognized as a creative powerhouse. The agency, which began as a small creative boutique in New York City in 2006, has received agency of the year awards more than 10 times over the past decade from various industry organizations such as the Cannes Lions, The One Show, and the Effies as well as by *Adweek* and *Advertising Age*, which are the two major publications that cover the advertising industry. In 2020 Droga5 was named Ad Age Agency of the Decade.

Droga5 was founded by David Droga, who grew up in an Australian ski resort and envisioned himself traveling the world as a ski instructor. However, it was his creative talents that took him abroad as he embarked on an advertising career that took him to Sydney, Singapore, and London before he moved to New York City as the first-ever creative officer of the Publicis Network. After nearly a decade of helping grow agencies owned by major holding companies, he decided to start his own agency and launched Droga5 (which is named for how his mother would label her fifth son's school shirts).

Droga5 experienced tremendous growth after its founding and was widely recognized as one of the leading independent agencies. The agency focuses on creativity connected across the entire brand experience. As shown in the opening image, Droga5 describes itself as creatively led, strategically driven, systems thinkers, and humanity obsessed, all of which have contributed to its tremendous success and growth, and made the

continued

agency an acquisition target for Accenture. Following its acquisition by AI, some questioned whether Droga5 could maintain its unique culture and creative excellence. However, the agency quickly answered by being named Ad Age Agency of the Year in 2021 after a strong performance during the first year of the pandemic, which included increasing its revenue by 26 percent on the back of work for major clients such as Petco, Meta, lululemon, Maserati, Paramount+, and Allstate. Droga5 also acquired a number of new clients including the National Basketball Association and Aspen Skiing.

Thus far, Accenture Interactive's acquisition of Droga5 appears to be working quite well. In 2021 David Droga was named the new CEO and creative chairman of Accenture Interactive. According to Accenture, in his new role Droga will drive creative excellence, customer experience, and business innovation, all of which leverage the unique capabilities of AI. Industry insiders note that Droga's appointment as CEO shows the outside world, their internal staff, and potential acquisitions that Accenture "gets it" when it comes to creative. They also note that Accenture Interactive has rapidly become the leading digital powerhouse at the intersection of data, creativity, and technology. A few months after taking over as CEO, Droga rebranded Accenture Interactive by changing the name of the company to Accenture Song and consolidating more than 40 marketing, communications, and consulting companies under one name. However, Droga5 will continue to operate under its own name, as David Droga noted that it's the only global brand agency that we have and is recognized by clients and talent everywhere.

The acquisition of Droga5 by AI puts to rest the idea that consultancies pose little threat to advertising agencies because their creative capabilities might be limited. Most industry experts argue it is only a matter of time before they move into the creative space dominated by traditional advertising agencies. Digital work now accounts for nearly two-thirds of the revenue for agencies from all disciplines. Moreover, consultancies are already doing digital work for their clients and can use the vast amounts of data and insights they have on consumers to move into the creative turf of advertising agencies.

Many in the advertising industry note that AI's acquisition of Droga5 and the appointment of David Droga to CEO of Accenture Song is just the beginning of a seismic shift that will have a major impact on agencies. Many agencies will have to transform themselves if they hope to survive in the new digital world of advertising.

Sources: Brian Bonilla and Ann-Christian Diaz, "Why Accenture CEO David Droga Rebranded the Company Accenture Song," *Advertising Age*, April 27, 2022, https://adage.com/article/agency-news/why-accenture-interactive-ceo-david-droga-rebranded-company-accenture-song/2414421; Alexandria Jardine, "Droga5 Benefits from Accenture Interactive as Its Founder Moves Up," *Advertising Age*, March 14, 2022, p 18; E. J. Schultz, Brian Bonilla, Bradley Johnson, and Ann-Christine Diaz, "Why David Droga Jumped to Accenture—And How the Industry Is Responding," *Advertising Age*, August 19, 2021, https://adage.com/article/agency-news/why-david-droga-jumped-accenture-and-how-industry-responding/2359566; Judann Pollack, "Behind Accenture's Groundbreaking Droga5 Deal," *Advertising Age*, April 3, 2019, https://adage.com/article/agency-news/accenture-interactive-set-buy-droga5/317215.

Developing and implementing an integrated marketing communications program is usually a complex and detailed process involving the efforts of many persons. As consumers, we generally give little thought to the individuals or organizations that create the clever advertisements that capture our attention, the websites we visit, the videos we watch online, or the contests and sweepstakes we hope to win. But for those involved in the marketing process, it is important to understand the nature of the industry and the structure and functions of the organizations involved. As discussed in the first two chapters, the advertising and promotions business is changing as marketers search for better ways to communicate with their customers. These changes are impacting the way marketers organize for integrated marketing communications, as well as their relationships with advertising agencies and other communication specialists.

This chapter examines the various organizations that participate in the IMC process, their roles and responsibilities, and their relationships to one another. We discuss how companies organize internally for advertising and promotion. For most companies, advertising is planned and executed by an outside ad agency. Many large agencies offer a variety of other IMC capabilities, including public relations, digital/Internet, sales promotion, and direct marketing. Thus, we will devote particular attention to the ad agency's role and the overall relationship between company and agency.

Other participants in the promotional process (such as direct-marketing, sales promotion, and digital/interactive agencies and public relations firms) are becoming increasingly important as more companies take an integrated marketing communications approach to promotion. We examine the role of these specialized marketing communication organizations in the promotional process as well. The chapter concludes with a discussion of whether marketers are best served by using the integrated services of one large agency or the separate services of a variety of communications specialists.

PARTICIPANTS IN THE INTEGRATED MARKETING COMMUNICATIONS PROCESS: AN OVERVIEW

Before discussing the specifics of the industry, we'll provide an overview of the entire system and identify some of the players. As shown in Figure 3–1, participants in the integrated marketing communications process can be divided into five major groups: the advertiser (or client), advertising agencies, media organizations, specialized communication services, and collateral services. Each group has specific roles in the promotional process.

The advertisers, or **clients**, are the key participants in the process. They have the products, services, or causes to be marketed, and they provide the funds that pay for the IMC program. The advertisers also assume major responsibility for developing the marketing plan and making the final decisions regarding the advertising and promotional program that will support it. The organization may perform most of these efforts itself either through its own advertising or marketing communications department or by setting up an in-house agency.

However, many organizations use an **advertising agency**, an outside firm that specializes in the creation, production, and/or placement of the communications message and that may provide other services to facilitate the marketing and promotions process. Many companies have an **agency of record (AOR)**, which is a single agency that has primary responsibility for most of the IMC services that the company or brand might require, such as brand and creative strategy, media planning, development and maintenance of websites, and digital marketing. However, companies that market a large number of products and/or services may have an AOR for each brand or division. For example, Kraft-Heinz has four main agencies that handle its various brands, while General Motors has different AORs for its various automotive divisions, which include Buick, Cadillac, Chevrolet, and GMC. The automotive giant also uses different public relations AORs for its four divisions, as well as a number of digital, promotional, and experiential marketing agencies; an entertainment marketing agency; and several sports marketing agencies. Many large companies often use additional agencies that specialize in developing advertising and digital campaigns for multicultural markets. For example, in addition to its agency of record—Saatchi & Saatchi—Toyota Motor Sales, U.S.A., uses additional agencies in the United

FIGURE 3–1

Participants in the Integrated Marketing Communications Process

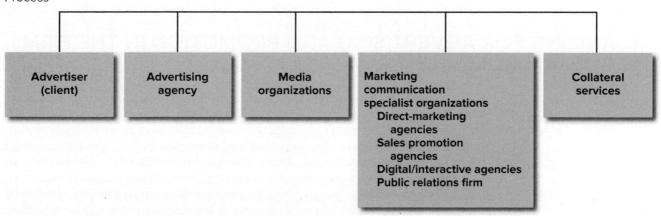

| Advertiser (client) | Advertising agency | Media organizations | Marketing communication specialist organizations
Direct-marketing agencies
Sales promotion agencies
Digital/interactive agencies
Public relations firm | Collateral services |

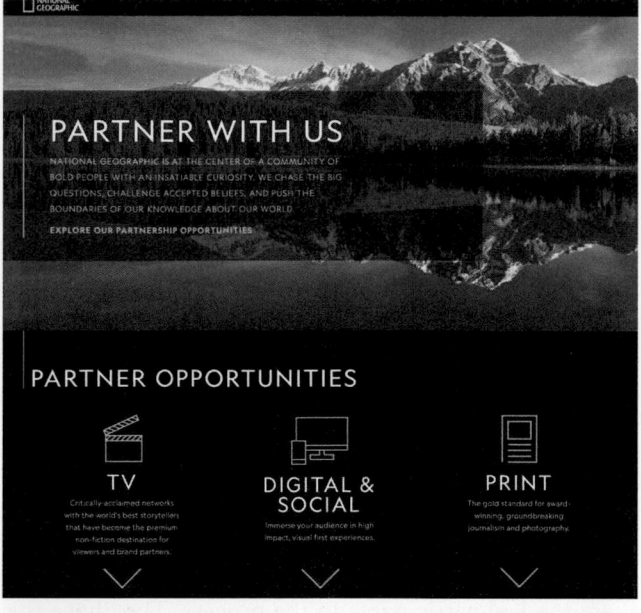

EXHIBIT 3–1

National Geographic promotes the various ways marketers can use its media platforms to connect with consumers.

National Geographic Partners, LLC

States to create ads for the African American, Hispanic, Latino, and Asian American markets. More and more, ad agencies are acting as partners with advertisers and assuming more responsibility for developing the marketing and promotional programs. Distilled spirits giant Pernod Ricard's U.S. division recently hired four multicultural agencies to increase its reach with Black, Latino, Asian, and LGBTQIA+ communities.[1] The agencies will help with the company's DEI and multicultural efforts for brands such as Absolut vodka, Chivas Regal scotch, and Avion tequila.

Media organizations are another major participant in the advertising and promotions process. The primary function of most media is to provide information or entertainment to their subscribers, viewers, or readers. But from the perspective of the promotional planner, the purpose of media is to provide an environment for the firm's marketing communications messages. The media must have editorial or program content that attracts consumers so that advertisers and their agencies will want to buy time or space with them. Exhibit 3-1 shows how *National Geographic* promotes its family of media products such as television, digital and social media, and print as a way to connect with consumers. While the media perform many other functions that help advertisers understand their markets and their customers, a medium's primary objective is to sell itself as a way for companies to reach their target markets with their messages effectively.

The next group of participants are organizations that provide **specialized marketing communication services**. They include direct-marketing agencies, sales promotion agencies, digital/interactive agencies, and public relations firms. These organizations provide services in their areas of expertise. A direct-response agency develops and implements direct-marketing programs, while sales promotion agencies develop promotional programs such as contests and sweepstakes, premium offers, or sampling programs. Digital/interactive agencies are being retained to develop websites for the Internet and help marketers as they move deeper into the realm of interactive media. Public relations firms are used to generate and manage publicity for a company and its products and services as well as to focus on its relationships and communications with its relevant publics.

The final participants shown in the promotions process of Figure 3–1 are those that provide **collateral services**, the wide range of support functions used by advertisers, agencies, media organizations, and specialized marketing communication firms. These individuals and companies perform specialized functions the other participants use in planning and executing advertising and other promotional functions. We will now examine the role of each participant in more detail. (Media organizations will be examined in Chapters 10, 11, 12, 13, and 14.)

ORGANIZING FOR ADVERTISING AND PROMOTION IN THE FIRM: THE CLIENT'S ROLE

Virtually every business organization uses some form of marketing communication. However, the way a company organizes for these efforts depends on several factors, including its size, the number of products it markets, the role of advertising and promotion in its marketing mix, the advertising and promotion budget, and its marketing organization structure. Many individuals throughout the organization may be involved in the advertising and promotion decision-making process. Marketing personnel have the most direct relationship with advertising and are often involved in many aspects of the decision process, such as providing input to the campaign plan, agency selection, media strategy, and evaluation of the effectiveness of the IMC program. Top management is usually interested in how the advertising and other forms of marketing communication represent the firm, and this may also mean being involved in IMC decisions even when the decisions are not part of its day-to-day responsibilities.

While many people both inside and outside the organization have some input into the advertising and promotion process, direct responsibility for administering the program must be assumed by someone within the firm. Many companies have an advertising department headed by an advertising manager operating under a marketing director. In some companies this department may be called marketing communications (marcom). An alternative used by many large multiproduct firms is a decentralized marketing (brand management) system. A third option is to form a separate agency within the firm, an in-house agency. Each of these alternatives is examined in more detail in the following sections.

The Centralized System

In many organizations, marketing activities are divided along functional lines, with advertising placed alongside other marketing functions such as sales, marketing research, and product planning, as shown in Figure 3–2. The **advertising manager** is responsible for all promotions activities except sales (in some companies this individual has the title of marketing communications manager). In the most common example of a **centralized system**, the advertising or marcom manager controls the entire promotions operation, including budgeting, coordinating creation and production of ads, planning media schedules, and monitoring and administering the sales promotions programs for all the company's products or services.

The specific duties of the advertising or marketing communications manager depend on the size of the firm and the importance it places on promotional programs. Basic functions the manager and staff perform include administration and execution, coordination with other departments, and coordination with outside agencies and services.

Administration and Execution   The manager must organize the advertising department and supervise and control its activities. The manager also supervises the execution of the plan by subordinates and/or the advertising agency. This requires working with such departments as production, media, art, copy, digital/interactive, and sales promotion. If an outside agency is used, the advertising department is relieved of much of the executional responsibility; however, it must review and approve the agency's plans.

Coordination with Other Departments   The manager must coordinate the advertising department's activities with those of other departments, particularly those involving other marketing functions. For example, the advertising department must

FIGURE 3–2

The Advertising Department under a Centralized System

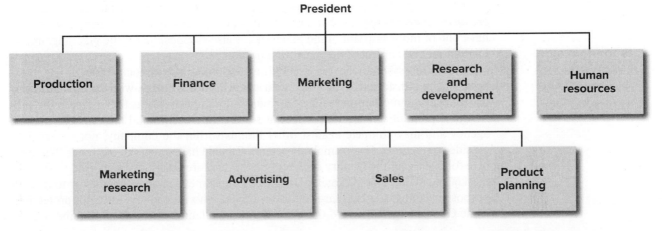

communicate with marketing research and/or sales to determine which product features are important to customers and should be emphasized in the company's communications. Research may also provide information on those who use the product/service or brand, including their demographic and psychographic profiles as well as media usage patterns. The advertising department may also be responsible for preparing material the sales force can use when calling on customers, such as brochures, sales promotion tools, advertising materials, and point-of-purchase displays.

Coordination with Outside Agencies and Services   Many companies have an advertising or marketing communications department but still use an advertising agency as well as other outside services such as digital agencies. For example, companies may develop their advertising programs in-house while employing media buying services to place their ads and/or use collateral services agencies to develop brochures, point-of-purchase materials, and so on. The department serves as a liaison between the company and any outside service providers and also determines which ones to use. Once outside services are retained, the manager will work with other marketing managers to coordinate their efforts and evaluate their performances.

A centralized organizational system is often used when companies do not have many different divisions, product or service lines, or brands to advertise. For example, airlines such as Southwest, American, and JetBlue have centralized advertising or marcom departments, as do major retailers such as Target, Walmart, and Best Buy. Many companies prefer a centralized department because developing and coordinating advertising and marketing programs from one central location facilitates communication regarding the promotions program, making it easier for top management to participate in decision making. A centralized system may also result in a more efficient operation because fewer people are involved in the program decisions, and as their experience in making such decisions increases, the process becomes easier.

At the same time, problems are inherent in a centralized operation. First, it may be difficult for advertising department staff members to understand the overall marketing strategy for the brand, particularly if they are not brought into the planning process. The department may also be slow in responding to specific needs and problems of a product/ service or brand. As companies become larger and develop or acquire new products, services, brands, or even divisions, the centralized system may become impractical.

The Decentralized System

In large corporations with multiple divisions and many different products/services and brands, it is very difficult to manage all the advertising, promotional, and other functions through a centralized department. These types of companies generally have a **decentralized system**, with separate sales and marketing departments for various divisions, product lines, or businesses. Many companies that use a decentralized system, such as Procter & Gamble, Unilever, PepsiCo, Google, and Nestlé, assign each product/ service or brand to a **brand manager** who is responsible for the total management of the brand, including planning, budgeting, sales, and profit performance. (The term *product manager* is also used to describe this position.) The brand manager, who may have one or more assistant brand managers, is also responsible for the planning, implementation, and control of the marketing program.[2]

Under this system, the responsibilities and functions associated with the IMC program are transferred to the brand manager, who works closely with the outside advertising agency and other marketing communications specialists as they develop the promotional program.[3] In a multiproduct or service firm, each brand may have its own ad agency and may compete against other brands within the company, not just against outside competitors. For example, Procter & Gamble has a portfolio of brands that compete for a share of the laundry detergent market and are positioned to appeal to specific market segments. Tide is targeted toward the consumer segment looking for tough, all-purpose cleaning, Cheer is targeted toward those who are looking for color-protection, while Gain is targeted toward those seeking scented laundry detergents (Exhibit 3-2).

EXHIBIT 3-2

Procter & Gamble's laundry detergent brands are positioned for different market segments.

(left) Steve Cukrov/Alamy Stock Photo; (middle, right) Keith Homan/Alamy Stock Photo

As shown in Figure 3-3, the advertising department is part of marketing services and provides support for the brand managers. The role of marketing services is to assist the brand managers in planning and coordinating the integrated marketing communications program. In some companies, the marketing services group may include sales promotion. The brand managers may work with the sales promotion team and/or agency to develop budgets, define strategies, and implement tactical executions for both trade and consumer promotions. Marketing services may also provide other types of support services, such as package design and merchandising.

Some companies may have an additional layer(s) of management above the brand managers to coordinate the efforts of all the brand managers handling a related group of products. This system—generally referred to as a **category management system**—includes category managers as well as brand and advertising managers. The category manager oversees management of the entire product category and focuses on the strategic role of the various brands in order to build profits and market share.[4] Each category manager will have one or more brand managers reporting to him or her for each specific brand as well as an advertising manager.

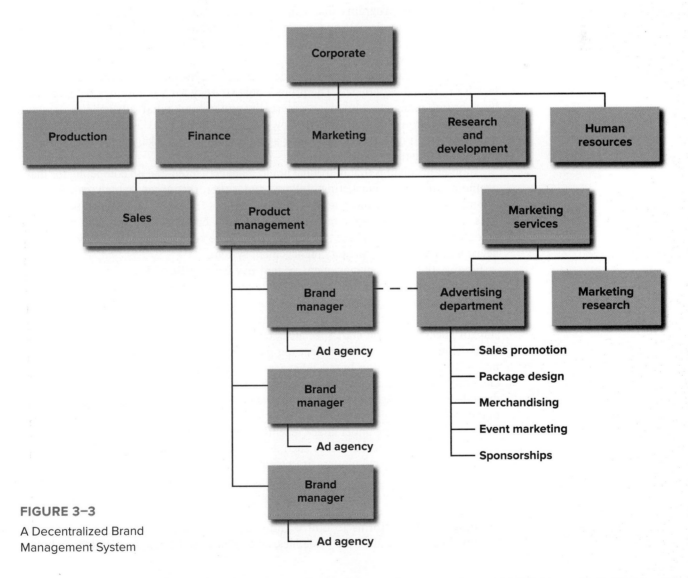

FIGURE 3-3

A Decentralized Brand Management System

EXHIBIT 3–3

P&G's broad portfolio of brands are assigned to various categories for management.

Procter & Gamble

The advertising or marcom manager may review and evaluate the various parts of the IMC program and advise and consult with the brand managers. This person may have the authority to override the brand manager's decisions on advertising and other forms of promotion. In some multiproduct firms that spend a lot on advertising and promotion, the advertising manager may coordinate the work of the various agencies to obtain media discounts for the firm's large volume of media purchases. Category management is often used in large multiproduct or divisional companies such as Procter & Gamble, whose broad portfolio includes 10 product categories with 65 brands—21 of which generate more than a billion dollars in revenue each year (Exhibit 3–3). For example, the hair care category includes brands such as Head & Shoulders, Aussie, Pantene, and Herbal Essences.

An advantage of the decentralized system is that each brand receives concentrated managerial attention, resulting in faster response to problems as well as opportunities. The brand managers have full responsibility for the marketing program, including the identification of target markets as well as the development of integrated marketing communications programs that will differentiate the brand.[5] The brand manager system is also more flexible and makes it easier to adjust various aspects of the advertising and promotional program, such as creative platforms and media and sales promotion schedules.[6]

There are some drawbacks to the decentralized approach. Brand managers often lack training and experience. The promotional strategy for a brand may be developed by a brand manager who does not really understand what advertising or sales promotion can and cannot do and how each should be used. Brand managers may focus too much on short-run planning and administrative tasks, neglecting the development of long-term programs.

Another problem is that individual brand managers often end up competing for management attention, marketing dollars, and other resources, which can lead to unproductive rivalries and potential misallocation of funds. The manager's persuasiveness may become a bigger factor in determining budgets than the long-run profit potential of the brands. These types of problems were key factors in Procter & Gamble's decision to switch to a category management system.

Finally, the brand management system has been criticized for failing to provide brand managers with authority over the functions needed to implement and control the plans they develop.[7] Some companies have dealt with this problem by expanding the roles and responsibilities of the advertising and sales promotion managers and their staff of specialists. The staff specialists counsel the individual brand managers, and advertising or sales promotion decision making involves the advertising and/or sales promotion manager, the brand manager, and the marketing director. For example, General Motors, which is one of the largest advertisers in the United States, decided to drop its brand management system and give division marketing directors more control of the advertising and promotion for its various models.[8] The traditional brand management system has come under attack recently as critics argue that brand managers spend too much time on internal issues such as planning and budgeting and do not devote enough effort to external matters or to creativity and problem solving.[9]

A new challenge facing the brand management system is training managers to keep abreast of the rapidly changing world of digital marketing and managing the identity of a brand across various social media platforms. Brand managers may be involved in deciding which platforms to utilize and how to use them, what to consider when creating internal social media guidelines, and whether to handle social media in-house

Ad Age Insights°

TREND REPORT

MANAGING YOUR BRAND'S SOCIAL LIFE

EXHIBIT 3–4

Brand managers must understand how to use social media to manage brand identity.

Crain Communications Inc.

or outsource it. They also work with various metrics to evaluate the effectiveness of and return on investment for various social media tools. Brand managers are often involved in developing social media strategies that include playbooks for various social media sites such as Facebook, Pinterest, Instagram, YouTube, TikTok, and Snapchat (Exhibit 3–4).[10]

In-House Agencies

Some companies, in an effort to reduce costs and maintain greater control over agency activities, have set up their own advertising agencies internally. An **in-house agency** is an advertising agency that is set up, owned, and operated by the advertiser. Some in-house agencies are little more than advertising departments, but in other companies they are given a separate identity and are responsible for the expenditure of large sums of advertising dollars. Large advertisers that use in-house agencies include Hyundai/Kia, Avon, Revlon, Land Rover, and Spotify. Many companies use in-house agencies exclusively; others combine in-house efforts with those of outside agencies. For example, retail giant Target has an internal creative department that handles the design of its weekly circulars, direct-mail pieces, in-store displays, promotions, and other marketing materials. However, the retailer uses outside agencies to develop most of its branding and image-oriented ads and for specific TV and print assignments. Other retailers such as Benetton and Banana Republic also have in-house advertising departments that work with outside agencies.

A major reason for using an in-house agency is to reduce advertising and promotion costs. Companies with very large advertising budgets pay a substantial amount to outside agencies in the form of media commissions or negotiated fees. With an internal structure, these commissions or fees go to the in-house agency. An in-house agency can also provide related work such as production of collateral materials, digital media, package design, and public relations at a lower cost than outside agencies. In-house agencies are also preferred by some companies because they keep the marketing communications function more closely tied to top management. A study by Forrester Research found that nearly 60 percent of in-house agencies report directly to the company's chief executive officer (CEO) or chief marketing officer (CMO).[11] Another reason is the stability an in-house agency provides because external agencies have much higher turnover levels, which can take a toll on the client–agency relationship. In contrast, in-house agencies are known for retaining their personnel and have a turnover rate of less than 5 percent.[12]

Saving money is not the only reason companies use in-house agencies. Time savings, bad experiences with outside agencies, and the increased knowledge and understanding of the market that come from working on advertising and promotion for the product or service day by day are also reasons. Companies can also maintain tighter control over the process and more easily coordinate promotions with the firm's overall marketing program.

Some companies use an in-house agency simply because they believe it can do a better job than an outside agency could.[13] They may feel they have more knowledge about the market and competitors as well as a better understanding of the intricacies and complexities of their business. Recently, a number of companies have been dropping their outside agencies and developing in-house shops that handle their creative work as well as other areas of the IMC program. An example of a company that has moved its advertising in-house is Chobani, the leader in the Greek yogurt market. The company's chief

EXHIBIT 3–5

World of Whirlpool Studios (WoW) is the in-house agency for Whirlpool Corporation.

Whirlpool Corporation

creative officer noted that it is easier to coordinate its work internally as well as move faster in implementing its advertising telecommunications efforts. He also noted that Chobani could make its marketing budget work harder by putting it toward growth initiatives rather than agency fees.[14]

Another example of a major company that has brought most of its advertising in-house recently is Whirlpool Corp., which launched an internal agency called the World of Whirlpool Studios (WoW). The company has transitioned the IMC for most of its brands—which include Whirlpool, KitchenAid, Maytag, Jennair, and several others—from its agency Digitas to WoW (Exhibit 3–5). Whirlpool stated that it was making the change to streamline its operations and mold them around the customer decision journey. The company also noted that having an in-house agency means that agency employees will have greater access to corporate leaders and data while putting creative talent next to brand partners and supply chain, merchandising, manufacturers, and sales teams.[15]

Opponents of in-house agencies say they can give the advertiser neither the experience and objectivity of an outside agency nor the range of services. They argue that outside agencies have more highly skilled specialists and attract the best creative talent and that using an external firm gives a company a more varied perspective on its advertising problems and greater flexibility. Outside agencies also can provide greater strategic planning capabilities, outside perspectives on customers, and more creative experience with certain media such as digital or television.[16] In-house personnel may become narrow or grow stale while working on the same product line, but outside agencies may have different people with a variety of backgrounds and ideas working on the account. Flexibility is greater because an outside agency can be dismissed if the company is not satisfied, whereas changes in an in-house agency could be slower and more disruptive.

The cost savings of an in-house agency must be evaluated against these considerations. For many companies, high-quality advertising is critical to their marketing success and should be the major criterion in determining whether to use in-house services. Companies often hire outside agencies as they grow and their advertising budgets and IMC needs increase.

For example Under Armour, which has become one of the leading competitors in the athletic shoe and apparel market, handled all of its advertising in-house for nearly two decades. However, as the company grew and expanded into new product categories and international markets, Under Armour management recognized that it would be difficult to handle all of its advertising in-house and in 2015 named its first ever external agency of record.[17]

The use of in-house agencies has grown tremendously in recent years as studies by the Association of National Advertisers as well as the In-House Agency Forum have found that nearly 80 percent of companies now have some type of in-house agency and that they are continuing to bring more IMC assignments in-house.[18] While cost savings was cited in these studies as one of the reasons for the increase in the use of in-house agencies, another major factor was the explosion of new digital advertising tools such as social media, which enable companies to produce more creative content and to do so faster and more nimbly. Many companies feel that they can best handle the volume of content and the quick turnarounds required to keep pace with consumers who are online 24/7 in-house. Marketers also want more insights from analytics and the management of various data sources; they view traditional advertising agencies' capabilities in these areas as limited.

The use of in-house agencies by marketers to handle their advertising is likely to continue and, as is discussed later in the chapter, is expanding to other areas such as media planning and buying. It is important to note that the use of an in-house agency does not mean that marketers have stopped using outside agencies as many continue to use both. The ultimate decision as to which type of agency organization system to use

Organizational System	Advantages	Disadvantages
Centralized	■ Facilitated communications ■ Fewer personnel required ■ Continuity in staff ■ Allows for more top-management involvement	■ Less involvement with and understanding of overall marketing goals ■ Longer response time ■ Inability to handle multiple product lines
Decentralized	■ Concentrated managerial attention ■ Rapid response to problems and opportunities ■ Increased flexibility	■ Ineffective decision making ■ Internal conflicts ■ Misallocation of funds ■ Lack of authority ■ Internal rather than external focus
In-house agencies	■ Cost savings ■ More control ■ Increased coordination ■ Stability ■ Access to top management ■ Faster turnaround times for digital content	■ Less experience ■ Less objectivity ■ Less flexibility ■ Less access to top creative talent

FIGURE 3–4

Comparison of Advertising Organizational Systems

depends on which arrangement works best for the company. The advantages and disadvantages of the three systems are summarized in Figure 3–4. We now turn our attention to the functions of outside agencies and their roles in the promotional process.

ADVERTISING AGENCIES

Many major companies use advertising agencies to assist them in developing, preparing, and executing their promotional programs. An ad agency is a service organization that specializes in planning and executing advertising programs for its clients. More than 14,000 U.S. and international agencies are listed in the REDBOOKs, the leading agency and advertising database; however, most are individually owned small businesses employing fewer than five people. The U.S. ad agency business is highly concentrated. Nearly two-thirds of the domestic **billings** (the amount of client money agencies spend on media purchases and other equivalent activities) are handled by the top 500 agencies. In fact, just 10 U.S. agencies handle nearly 30 percent of the total volume of business done by the top 900 agencies in the United States.[19]

Agency Consolidation

During the late 1980s and into the 90s, the advertising industry underwent major changes as large agencies merged with or acquired other agencies and support organizations to form large advertising organizations, or superagencies. These **superagencies** were formed so that agencies could provide clients with integrated marketing communications services worldwide. Some advertisers became disenchanted with the superagencies and moved to smaller agencies that were flexible and more responsive.[20] However, during the mid-90s the agency business went through another wave of consolidation as a number of medium-size agencies were acquired and became part of large advertising organization holding companies such as Omnicom Group, WPP Group, and the Interpublic Group of Companies. Many of the midsize agencies were acquired by or forged alliances with larger agencies because their clients wanted an agency with international communications capabilities, and their alignment with larger organizations gave them access to a network of agencies around the world. The consolidation of the agency business continued into the new millennium as large agencies such as Fallon Worldwide, Leo Burnett, Saatchi & Saatchi, and Kaplan Thaler were acquired by the giant French holding company Publicis Groupe. Agencies that are owned by the top five holding companies—WPP, Omnicom Group, Interpublic Group, Publicis Groupe, and Accenture Song—account for a little more than half of revenue generated by agencies in the United States. The sixth major holding company is Tokyo-based Dentsu, which controls nearly 30 percent of the media advertising in Japan and is also strong in several other Asian markets.

With the move toward IMC, agencies are now getting much of their revenue from more than just traditional advertising services, which now account for less than 30 percent of the revenue for U.S. agencies. Agencies' revenue comes from other areas such as digital and media buying, public relations, CRM/direct marketing, health care, and promotion.[21] Many of the advertising organizations and major agencies have been acquiring companies specializing in areas such as digital/interactive communications, public relations, customer relationship management (CRM), direct marketing, health care, and sales promotion so that they can offer their clients an ever-broader range of integrated marketing communications services. Particularly noteworthy in these numbers is the percentage of agency revenue that is being generated by digital media. Overall, U.S. agencies now generate nearly two-thirds of their revenue from digital media, versus only 25 percent in 2009. The tremendous increase in digital is not limited to the United States. Major agency holding companies such as Publicis Groupe, Dentsu, and WPP generate much of their worldwide revenue from various forms of digital activities.

While most major advertising agencies have developed digital capabilities, an increasing number of marketers are turning to more specialized agencies to handle their digital marketing work. As discussed in the chapter opener, a major development over the past several years has been the rapid growth of consultancies, which are divisions of major management consulting companies that offer digital marketing, CRM, analytics, and other technology-focused services.[22] Figure 3–5 shows the top 10 agency companies, ranked by their worldwide revenue. As can be seen in this figure, 4 of the top 10 agency companies are owned by consultancies, including Accenture Song, PwC Digital Services, Deloitte Digital, and IBM iX.

FIGURE 3–5

World's Largest Agency Companies

Rank	Agency	Headquarters	Worldwide Revenue (2022) (billions)
1	WPP	London	$17.8B
2	Accenture Song	New York, NY	16.0
3	Publicis Groupe	Paris	15.0
4	Omnicom Group	New York, NY	14.3
5	Interpublic Group of Cos.	New York, NY	10.9
6	Deloitte's Deloitte Digital	New York, NY	10.3
7	Dentsu Group	Tokyo	9.5
8	Hakuhodo DY Holdings	Tokyo	7.4
9	IBM Corp.'s IBM iX	Armonk, NY	6.4
10	Cheil Worldwide	Seoul, South Korea	3.3

Source: *Advertising Age*, Datacenter: Agency Report 2023, April 24, 2023, p. 9.

EXHIBIT 3-6

Gestalt Brand Lab is an agency that specializes in creating strong brands for its clients.

Gestalt Brand Lab

The Ad Agency's Role

The functions performed by advertising agencies might be conducted by the clients themselves through one of the models discussed earlier in this chapter, but most large companies use outside firms. This section discusses some reasons advertisers use external agencies.

Reasons for Using an Agency Probably the main reason outside agencies are used is that they provide the client with the services of highly skilled individuals who are specialists in their chosen fields. An advertising agency staff may include artists, writers, media analysts, researchers, and others with specific skills, knowledge, and experience who can help market the client's products or services. Many agencies specialize in a particular type of business and use their knowledge of the industry to assist their clients with strategic marketing as well as branding. For example, Gestalt Brand Lab is an agency that uses its expertise in IMC to help its clients develop strong brands (Exhibit 3-6).

An outside agency can also provide an objective viewpoint of the market and its business that is not subject to internal company policies, biases, or other limitations. The agency can draw on the broad range of experience it has gained while working on a diverse set of marketing problems for various clients. For example, an ad agency that is handling a travel-related account may have individuals who have worked with airlines, cruise ship companies, travel agencies, hotels, and other travel-related industries. The agency may have experience in this area or may even have previously worked on the advertising account of one of the client's competitors. Thus, the agency can provide the client with insight into the industry (and, in some cases, the competition).

Types of Ad Agencies

Since ad agencies can range in size from a one- or two-person operation to large organizations with over 1,000 employees, the services offered and functions performed will vary. This section examines the different types of agencies, the services they perform for their clients, and how they are organized.

Full-Service Agencies Many companies employ what is known as a **full-service agency**, which offers its clients a full range of marketing, communications, and promotions services, including planning, creating, and producing the advertising; performing research; and selecting media. A full-service agency may also offer nonadvertising services such as strategic market planning; sales promotions, direct marketing, and digital/interactive capabilities; package design; and public relations and publicity.

The full-service agency is made up of departments that provide the activities needed to perform the various advertising functions and serve the client, as shown in Figure 3-6.

Account Services Account services, or account management, is the link between the ad agency and its clients. Depending on the size of the client and its advertising budget, one or more account executives serve as liaison. The **account executive** is responsible for understanding the advertiser's marketing and promotions needs and interpreting them to agency personnel. The person in this role coordinates agency efforts in planning, creating, and producing ads. The account executive also presents agency recommendations and obtains client approval.

As the focal point of agency–client relationships, the account executive must know a great deal about the client's business and be able to communicate this to specialists in the agency working on the account.[23] The ideal account executive has a strong

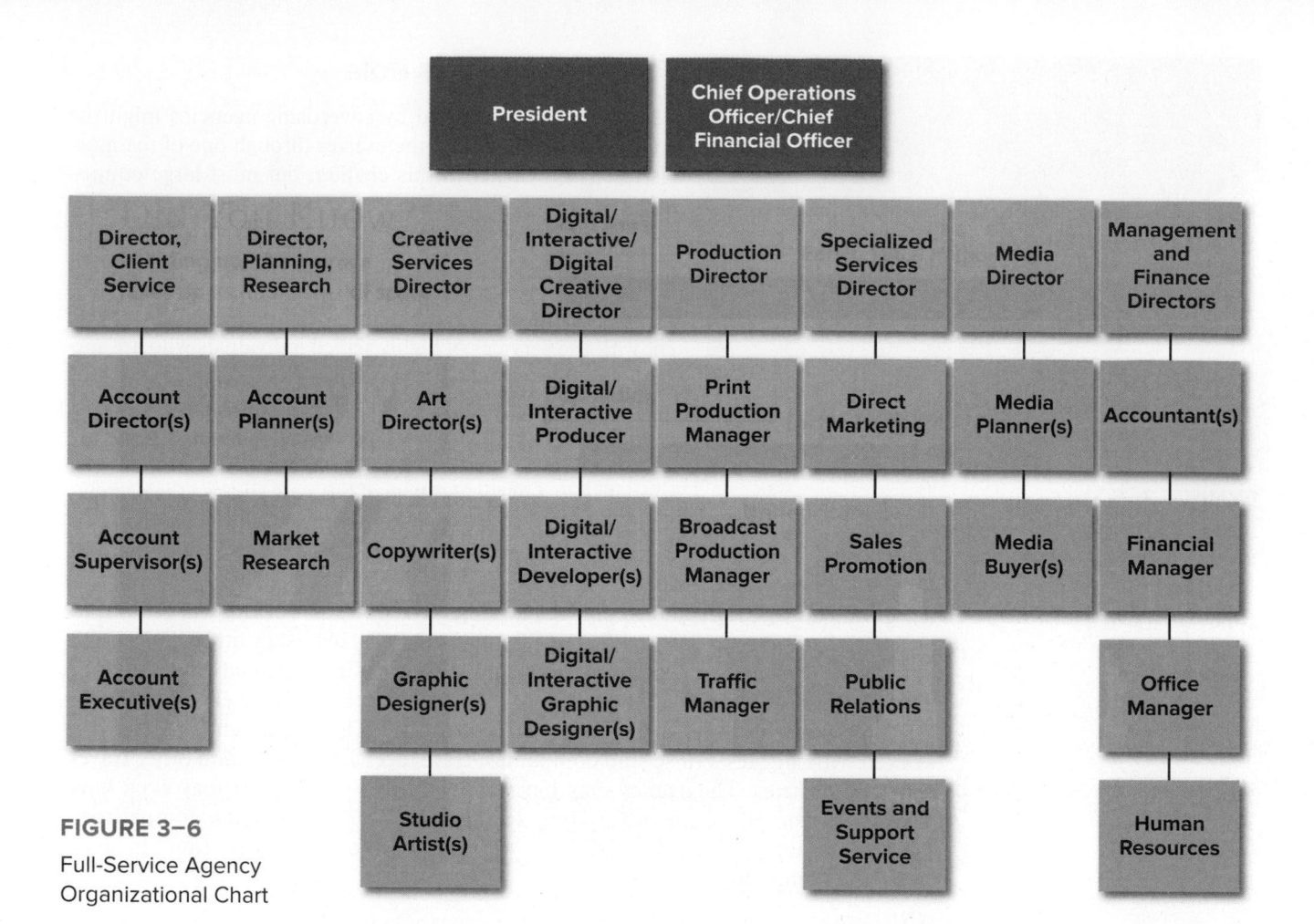

FIGURE 3–6

Full-Service Agency
Organizational Chart

marketing background as well as a thorough understanding of all phases of the advertising process. College graduates with undergraduate and graduate degrees in marketing, advertising, and other disciplines are often hired for account executive positions and go on to have careers in account management. However, with the revolutionary changes sweeping the advertising business, the role of account reps is changing dramatically, and they are struggling to remain relevant.[24] Cost-cutting by marketers has thinned the once-bloated ranks of account management personnel in agencies by as much as 30 percent in recent years. Moreover, for those who remain, the expectations and demands of the position are changing. Agencies want account executives who are good strategic thinkers and have broad-based business acumen, not just expertise in advertising. And as other integrated marketing communications tools such as direct, digital, and social media become more central, they want them to have an understanding of and be able to coordinate activities and relationships in these areas. They also want individuals whose skill set includes solving complex communication problems, communicating in a mature fashion, selling the agency and its capabilities, and knowing when to push back on a client.

Some agencies are developing client-services training programs for their account executives that are designed to educate them in a variety of areas, including basic agency business issues, strategic marketing, the procurement process, and relationship building. Agencies and clients often work together to address this problem by developing communication and indoctrination programs that provide agency personnel with an overview of their clients' business objectives and marketing strategy as well as their financial/budget situation. This allows them to understand the limits within which creative solutions have to be developed.[25] Account representatives will continue to serve an important role in managing the relationships between agencies and their clients.

EXHIBIT 3–7

The role of account executives has changed.

John Kuczala/Getty Images

However, the days of the old-school account executive "in the gray flannel suit" are long gone as agencies look for more from those who work most closely with their clients (Exhibit 3–7).

Marketing Services   Over the past two decades, use of marketing services has increased dramatically. One service gaining increased attention is research, as agencies realize that to communicate effectively with their clients' customers, they must have a good understanding of the target audience. As was discussed in Chapter 1, the advertising planning process begins with a thorough situation analysis, which is based on research and information about the target audience.

Most full-service agencies maintain a *research department* whose function is to gather, analyze, and interpret information that will be useful in developing advertising for their clients. This can be done through primary research—where a study is designed, executed, and interpreted by the research department—or through the use of secondary (previously published) sources of information. Sometimes the research department acquires studies conducted by independent syndicated research firms or consultants. The research staff then interprets these reports and passes on the information to other agency personnel working on that account. The research department may also design and conduct research to pretest the effectiveness of advertising the agency is considering. For example, focus groups as well as other copy testing methods are often used to determine how messages developed by the creative specialists are likely to be interpreted by the target audience.

In many large agencies, the marketing services department may include **account planners** who are individuals that gather information that is relevant to the client's product or service and can be used in the development of the creative strategy as well as other aspects of the IMC campaign. Account planners work with the client as well as other agency personnel including the account executives, creative team members, media specialists, and research department personnel to collect information that can be helpful in gaining a better understanding of the client's target audience and the best ways to communicate with them. They gather and organize information about consumers as well as developments in the marketplace that can be used to prepare the *creative brief*, which is a document that the agency's creative department uses to guide the development of advertising ideas and concepts. Account planners may also be involved in assessing consumers' reactions to the advertising and other elements of the IMC program and providing the creative staff as well as other agency personnel with feedback regarding performance.

Account planning has become a very important function in many agencies because it provides the creative team, as well as other agency personnel, with more insight into consumers and how to use advertising and other IMC tools to communicate with them.[26] However, the account planning function has also become more demanding as the number of marketing communication channels and ways of contacting consumers increases. Account planners increasingly find themselves interacting with individuals from a variety of marketing communication disciplines and have to keep up with developments that are occurring in all of these areas. John Thorpe, the global brand strategy director for Goodby Silverstein & Partners, an agency that is known for its account planning, notes: "No longer can planners just be good at strategy. It's a cross-silo activity. They have to be good at a lot of things that run across advertising. Ambidexterity is required across the house."[27]

The advertising industry recognizes the importance of account planning and the important role it plays in the development of successful IMC campaigns. For example, the 4As, which is the leading trade association representing the advertising agency business in the United States, gives the Jay Chiat Awards for Strategic Excellence each year to agencies in various categories. These awards honor strategic thinking and account planning by planners and other agency professionals who have

EXHIBIT 3–8

The Jay Chiat Awards recognize excellence in account planning.

American Association of Advertising Agencies

developed innovative insights and ideas that are implemented through creative advertising campaigns (Exhibit 3–8). Previously called the 4As Awards for Account Planning, the awards were renamed in 2004 in honor of the late advertising legend Jay Chiat, who is credited with introducing the discipline of planning to agencies in the United States.[28]

The *media department* of an agency analyzes, selects, and contracts for space or time in the media that will be used to deliver the client's advertising message. The media department is expected to develop a media plan that will reach the target market and effectively communicate the message. Since most of the client's ad budget is spent on media time and/or space, this department must develop a plan that both communicates with the right audience and is cost effective.

Media specialists must know what audiences the media reach, their rates, and how well they match the client's target market. The media planning department reviews information on demographics, magazine and newspaper readership, radio listenership, and consumers' Internet/social media usage and TV viewing patterns to develop an effective media plan. The media buyer implements the media plan by purchasing the actual time and space.

Media planning and buying has become a very important part of the agency business. An agency's ability to negotiate prices and effectively use the vast array of media vehicles, as well as other sources of customer contact, is becoming as important as its ability to create ads. Some of the major agencies and/or their holding companies have formed independent media services companies to better serve their clients. These media specialist firms, which are discussed later in the chapter, serve the media needs of the agencies that are part of their parent holding companies but may also offer media services to other clients.

The research and media departments perform most of the functions that full-service agencies need to plan and execute their clients' advertising programs. Some agencies offer additional marketing services to their clients to assist in other promotional areas. An agency may have a sales promotion department, or merchandising department, that specializes in developing contests, premiums, promotions, point-of-sale materials, and other sales materials. It may have direct-marketing specialists and package designers, as well as a PR/publicity department. Many agencies have developed digital/interactive departments to create digital content for their clients. The growing popularity of integrated marketing communications has prompted many full-function agencies to develop capabilities and offer services in these other promotional areas. Advertising agencies are recognizing that they must develop integrated marketing capabilities that extend beyond traditional media advertising.

Creative Services   The creative services department is responsible for the creation and execution of advertisements. The individuals who conceive the ideas for the ads and write the headlines, subheads, and body copy (the words constituting the message) are known as **copywriters**. They may also be involved in determining the basic appeal or theme of the ad campaign and often prepare a rough initial visual layout of the print ad or television commercial.

While copywriters are responsible for what the message says, the *art department* is responsible for how the ad looks. For print ads, the art director and graphic designers prepare *layouts*, which are drawings that show what the ad will look like and from which the final artwork will be produced. For TV commercials, the layout is known as a *storyboard*, a sequence of frames or panels that depict the commercial in still form.

Members of the creative department work together to develop ads that will communicate the key points determined to be the basis of the creative strategy for the client's product or service. Writers and artists generally work under the direction of the agency's creative director, who oversees all the advertising produced by the organization. The director sets the creative philosophy of the department and may even become directly involved in creating ads for the agency's largest clients.

Once the copy, layout, illustrations, and mechanical specifications have been completed and approved, the ad is turned over to the *production department.* Most agencies do not actually produce finished ads; they hire printers, engravers, photographers, typographers, and other suppliers to complete the finished product. For broadcast production, the approved storyboard must be turned into a finished commercial. The production department may supervise the casting of people to appear in the ad and the setting for the scenes as well as choose an independent production studio. The department may hire an outside director to turn the creative concept into a commercial. For example, Nike has used film directors such as David Fincher and Spike Lee to direct some of its commercials; BMW has used film directors such as Guy Ritchie and Ang Lee to direct some of its commercials and webisodes. Academy Award winner Martin Scorsese has directed commercials for Dolce & Gabbana, while Ridley Scott has done ads for Apple and Nissan. Copywriters, art directors, account managers, people from research and planning, and representatives from the client side may all participate in production decisions, particularly when large sums of money are involved.

Creating an advertisement often involves many people and takes several months. In large agencies with many clients, coordinating the creative and production processes can be a major problem. A *traffic department* coordinates all phases of production to see that the ads are completed on time and that all deadlines for submitting the ads to the media are met. The traffic department may be located in the creative services area of the agency, or be part of media or account management, or be separate.

Management and Finance Like any other business, an advertising agency must be managed and perform basic operating and administrative functions such as accounting, finance, and human resources. It must also attempt to generate new business. Large agencies employ administrative, managerial, and clerical people to perform these functions. The bulk of an agency's income (approximately 64 percent) goes to salary and benefits for its employees. Thus, an agency must manage its personnel carefully and get maximum productivity from them.

Agency Organization and Structure Full-function advertising agencies must develop an organizational structure that will meet their clients' needs and serve their own internal requirements. Most medium-size and large agencies are structured under either a departmental or a group system. Under the **departmental system**, each of the agency functions shown in Figure 3–6 is set up as a separate department and is called on as needed to perform its specialty and serve all of the agency's clients. Ad layout, writing, and production are done by the creative department; marketing services is responsible for any research or media selection and purchases; and the account services department handles client contact. Some agencies prefer the departmental system because it gives employees the opportunity to develop expertise in servicing a variety of accounts.

Many large agencies use the **group system**, in which individuals from each department work together in groups to service particular accounts. Each group is headed by an account executive or supervisor and has one or more media people, including media planners and buyers; a creative team, which includes copywriters, art directors, artists, and production personnel; and one or more account executives. The group may also include individuals from other departments such as marketing research, direct marketing, or sales promotion. The size and composition of the group vary depending on the client's billings and the importance of the account to the agency. For very important accounts, the group members may be assigned exclusively to one client. In some agencies, they may serve a number of smaller clients. Many agencies prefer the group system because employees become very knowledgeable about the client's business and there is continuity in servicing the account.

Other Types of Agencies and Services

Not every agency is a large full-service agency. Many smaller agencies expect their employees to handle a variety of jobs. For example, account executives may do their own research, work out their own media schedule, and coordinate the production of ads written and designed by the creative department. Many advertisers, including some large companies, are not interested in paying for the services of a full-service agency but are interested in some of the specific services agencies have to offer. Over the past few decades, several alternatives to full-service agencies have evolved, including creative boutiques and media buying services.

Creative Boutiques   **Creative boutiques** are small ad agencies that provide only creative services and have long been an important part of the advertising industry. These specialized agencies have creative personnel such as writers and artists on staff but do not have media, research, or account planning capabilities. Creative boutiques have developed in response to some companies' desires to use only the creative services of an outside agency while maintaining control of other marketing communication functions internally. While most creative boutiques work directly for companies, full-service agencies often subcontract work to them when they are very busy or want to avoid adding full-time employees to their payrolls. They are usually compensated on a project or hourly fee basis.

Many creative boutiques have been formed by members of the creative departments of full-service agencies who leave the firm and take with them clients who want to retain their creative talents. An advantage of these smaller agencies is their ability to turn out inventive creative work quickly and without the cumbersome bureaucracy and politics of larger agencies. Many companies also prefer working directly with a smaller creative boutique because they can get more attention and better access to creative talent than they would at a larger agency.

Creative boutiques will continue to be an important part of the advertising industry. However, they face challenges as many find themselves competing against larger agencies for business, particularly when there are cutbacks in advertising spending. Moreover, many clients want the range of services that large agencies provide as they are often looking for strategic and business-building ideas rather than just creative work. Many creative boutiques offer additional services as they grow and acquire more clients and become very large and successful independent agencies. For example, Wieden+Kennedy is widely recognized as one of the leading independent agencies for its outstanding creative work for clients such as Nike, Google, McDonald's, ESPN, Old Spice, Sprite, and Evian. The agency has received scores of awards and accolades over the past several decades and has been one of the most honored agencies in the advertising industry. W+K has been the agency of record for Nike since 1982, and its excellent creative work, which includes partnering with talent such as Spike Lee, has helped Nike become one of top 10 brands in the world, (Exhibit 3–9). The agency is very protective of its independence and its creative-driven culture as a former W+K executive notes: "Without real independence, an agency can never truly be creatively led."[29]

There are a number of reasons why some agencies prefer to remain independent rather than being part of a larger agency network. Advocates of independent agencies argue that they can often offer more personalized service for clients, maintain healthier work–life balances, and make nimble choices without have to sit through rounds of approval. Independent agencies can also maintain financial autonomy and be more selective about the clients with whom they choose to work.[30]

EXHIBIT 3–9

Wieden+Kennedy is one of the leading independent agencies and is known for its excellent creative work.

Wieden Kennedy

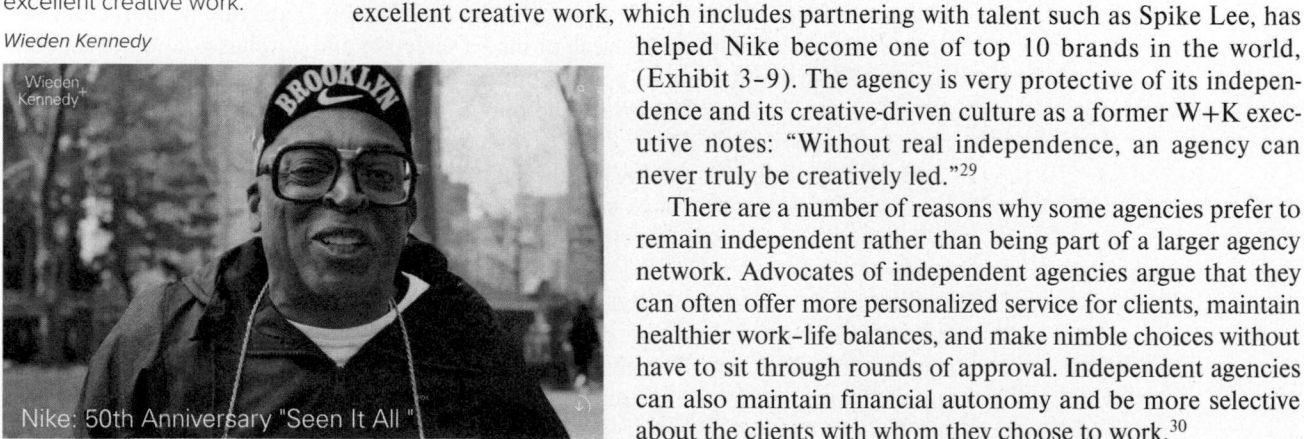

Media Specialist Companies   **Media specialist companies** are organizations that specialize in the buying of media, particularly for television and digital advertising. The task of purchasing advertising media has grown more complex, especially with the fragmentation of media audiences and the growth of digital media. Media buying services have found a niche by specializing in the analysis and purchase of advertising time and space. Agencies and clients often develop their own media strategies and hire a media buying service to execute them. However, some media buying services do help advertisers plan their media strategies. Because media buying services purchase such large amounts of time and space, they receive large discounts and can save the small agency or client money on media purchases. A major development in the purchasing of advertising media in recent years has been the rapid growth of **programmatic buying**, which refers to the wide range of technologies that are automating the buying, placement, and optimization of advertising media.[31] Programmatic buying originated in the purchase of digital advertising space where there are myriad options available to marketers and the purchase process is automated and often based on real-time bidding. However, programmatic buying is expanding beyond digital media, as it is being used to purchase television advertising time as well.[32] Media buying services are generally paid a fee or commission for their work.

Media specialist companies have become a major part of the advertising industry as clients seek alternatives to full-service agency relationships. Many marketers have been unbundling creative work from media services and consolidating their media buying to get more clout for their advertising budgets. Nike, Hyundai/Kia, and Grubhub are among the companies that have moved some or all of their media buying from full-service agencies to media specialist agencies. All of the major agency holding companies own media agencies that can handle media research, planning, and buying for their clients. For example, Starcom is the media agency for Publicis Groupe, while Mindshare and GroupM are owned by WPP.

A number of large advertisers have consolidated their media buying with these large media agencies to save money and improve media efficiencies. Multinational marketers such as PepsiCo, Unilever, Coca-Cola, and many others also use media specialist agencies to handle their global media buying, which helps them achieve economies of scale and more uniform media strategies and implementation across countries. For example, the Coca-Cola Company recently consolidated its nearly $4 billion in worldwide media spending with holding company WPP, which formed a custom-made unit call OpenX to handle the beverage giant's creative, media, data, and marketing solutions. OpenX is responsible for handling all of the media planning and buying for Coca-Cola's entire beverage portfolio, which includes over 200 brands including soft drinks such as Coke, Diet Coke, and Sprite, as well as sports drinks, coffee, tea, and water.[33]

The rise of the media buying services, operating outside the structure of the traditional ad agency media department, and the divestment of these departments from the agency system are two of the most significant developments that have occurred in the advertising industry in recent years. A study conducted for the Association of National Advertisers found a small percentage of companies still use a "general" ad agency to handle their media planning and buying, but the vast majority use a media agency specialist to handle these functions. These media specialists are often part of the same agency holding company as the primary agency that handles their creative work, particularly for large advertisers. However, about a third of the time the media specialist agency is not related to the primary agency.[34] As the media landscape becomes more complex, technological developments such as the use of programmatic buying, big data, and analytics will become even more important in the media planning and buying process. This has led many marketers to carefully review their media planning and buying processes and resulted in greater use of media specialist companies.[35] However, Digital and Social Media Perspective 3–1 discusses how many marketers have been bringing media buying in-house along with other IMC functions.

Media Buying Moves In-House for Many Companies

Maria Vonotna/Shutterstock

Traditionally, most major companies have used outside agencies to plan, develop, and implement their advertising rather than doing so internally, or in-house. They recognize that outside agencies bring a valuable external perspective because they have the benefit of working for a variety of companies across diverse industries. This often gives them a better understanding of market trends and developments, changes in customer behavior and ways they consume media, and other important factors. External agencies also can be more objective because they are not influenced by the internal biases or politics that may exist within the client's organization. Ad agencies are also perceived as having the best creative talent and thus are a good source for the big creative ideas that result in breakthrough advertising campaigns that strike a responsive chord with consumers.

While most marketers continue to use outside agencies to handle their advertising and other parts of their IMC programs, over the past decade many companies have expanded their internal capabilities and are shifting more of these responsibilities in-house. A 2018 study by the Association of National Advertisers (ANA) found that 78 percent of ANA client-side members had some type of in-house agency versus 58 percent in 2012 and 42 percent in 2008. The ANA study concluded that not only has the number of marketers with in-house agencies grown substantially, the workloads for these agencies have increased as well. One area where marketers are expanding their internal capabilities is media strategy and execution as many are moving media planning and buying in-house.

A 2021 study conducted by Forrester Consulting surveyed 300 marketing decision makers in U.S. companies and found that nearly 50 percent indicated that bringing media capabilities in-house is a top marketing objective, and 40 percent expected it will remain a top priority in the coming years. According to the survey, transparency—knowing how much is paid to whom in complex media supply chains—is a major factor driving the goal to bring media capabilities in-house. Other important drivers include

having direct control over consumer data to ensure compliance with increasingly complex privacy regulations and manage the rapid changes brought by the end of third-party cookies and other personal digital identifiers by digital platforms. By bringing media planning and buying in-house, marketers are also able to improve their internal media capabilities and increase customer insights and analytics that will allow them to better reach customers at the right time with the right message.

A number of major marketers have already begun moving some of their media work in-house, including Procter & Gamble, which began in-housing media several years ago. P&G began bringing media planning and buying in-house by having brand management teams handle their own buying on social media platforms such as Meta's Facebook and Instagram. However, the consumer packaged goods giant has expanded its media capabilities and estimates that it now handles nearly 30 percent of its $7 billion in global media spending in-house. Other companies that have brought at least some of their media planning and buying in-house include Netflix, StubHub, Kellogg, and Molson Coors.

While a number of marketers are bringing media in-house, most companies are not yet ready to do so as it requires having the right technologies, processes, and skills-related capabilities. The Forrester Consulting study identified a number of barriers that make the process of taking media planning and buying in-house a challenge for marketers. These include the cultural barrier of the organization's break from its agency-dependent culture and lack of the knowledge and foundation necessary to build a successful in-house practice. Industry experts have also noted that media planning and buying are often too far from most marketers' core competencies and that taking too much media in-house can create tunnel vision, as the external perspective on the market and outside world is lost.

The trend toward taking advertising as well as other areas of the IMC process, such as media planning and buying and digital work, in-house is likely to continue. Traditional advertising as well as media agencies must pay close attention to the increasing use of in-house agencies and consider how they can address the factors leading their clients to handle more of their advertising and other IMC functions in-house. The use of and need for external agencies is not likely to go away, but agencies must find ways to better serve the needs of their clients or risk having them take even more of their business in-house.

Sources: Jack Neff, "Marketers Want to Shift More Media Duties In-House, Forrester Finds," *Advertising Age*, November 16, 2021, https://adage.com/article/media/marketers-want-shift-more-media-duties-house-forrester-finds/2380411; Jennifer Faull, "P&G Now Does 30% of Its Media Planning In-House," *The Drum*, December 4, 2019, https://www.thedrum.com/news/2019/12/04/pg-now-does-30-its-media-planning-house; Adrianne Pasquarelli, "New Report Cites Skyrocketing Growth of Internal Agencies," *Advertising Age*, October 15, 2018, https://adage.com/article/cmo-strategy/report-cites-skyrocketing-growth-internal-agencies/315253/.

AGENCY COMPENSATION

As you have seen, the type and amount of services an agency performs vary from one client to another. As a result, agencies use a variety of methods to get paid for their services. Agencies are typically compensated in three ways: commissions, some type of fee arrangement, or percentage charges.

Commissions from Media

The traditional method of compensating agencies is through a **commission system**, where the agency receives a specified commission (usually 15 percent) from the media on any advertising time or space it purchases for its client. (For outdoor advertising, the commission is 16⅔ percent.) This system provides a simple method of determining payments, as shown in the following example.

Assume an agency prepares a full-page magazine ad and arranges to place the ad on the back cover of a magazine at a cost of $100,000. The agency places the order for the space and delivers the ad to the magazine. Once the ad is run, the magazine will bill the agency for $100,000, less the 15 percent ($15,000) commission. The media will also offer a 2 percent cash discount for early payment, which the agency may pass along to the client. The agency will bill the client $100,000 less the 2 percent cash discount on the net amount, or a total of $98,300, as shown in Figure 3–7. The $15,000 commission represents the agency's compensation for its services.

Appraisal of the Commission System   While the commission system was the primary agency compensation method for many years, it has always been controversial. Critics of the commission system have long argued that it encourages agencies to recommend high-priced media to their clients to increase their commission level. The system has also been criticized on the grounds that it ties agency compensation to media costs, which have been skyrocketing over the past decade. Still others charge that the system encourages agencies to recommend mass-media advertising and avoid noncommissionable IMC tools such as direct mail, sales promotion, public relations, and event sponsorships unless they are requested by the clients.

Defenders of the commission system argue that it is easy to administer and keeps the emphasis in agency compensation on nonprice factors such as the quality of the advertising developed for clients. Proponents of the system argue that agency services are proportional to the size of the commission, since more time and effort are devoted to the large accounts that generate high revenue for the agency. They also note that the system is more flexible than it appears, as agencies often perform other services for large clients at no extra charge as a way of justifying the large commission they receive.

Companies began moving away from the commission system during the 1990s, and most companies no longer use it as the basis for compensating their agencies. The most recent study of agency compensation conducted by the Association of National Advertisers (ANA) in 2022 found that 7 percent of major advertisers in the United States still paid commissions to their agencies, which was a significant decrease from the 12 percent that did so in 2016.[36] Among those companies that do pay commissions, most do not

FIGURE 3–7

Example of Commission System Payment

Media Bills Agency		Agency Bills Advertiser	
Costs for magazine space	$100,000	Costs for magazine space	$100,000
Less 15% commission	−15,000	Less 2% cash discount	−1,700
Cost of media space	85,000	Advertiser pays agency	$ 98,300
Less 2% cash discount	−1,700		
Agency pays media	$ 83,300	Agency income	$ 15,000

pay the traditional 15 percent. Most advertisers use a **negotiated commission** system whereby the commissions are based on a sliding scale that becomes lower as the clients' media expenditures increase. Agencies are also relying less on media commissions for their income as their clients expand their IMC programs to include other forms of promotion and cut back on mass-media advertising. An earlier ANA survey of global ad agency compensation found that reliance on commissions is a more common practice outside the United States, as more than a third of global marketers still use traditional media commissions to compensate their agencies. One reason for the higher use of commissions is that in some countries, such as Brazil and Japan, the use of commissions to compensate agencies is mandated by law or is a common practice.[37]

Fee, Cost, and Incentive-Based Systems

Since many believe the commission system is not equitable to all parties, many agencies and their clients have developed some type of fee arrangement or cost-plus agreement for agency compensation. Some are using incentive-based compensation, which is a combination of a commission and a fee system.

Fee Arrangement   There are two basic types of fee arrangement systems. In the straight or **fixed-fee method**, the agency charges a basic fee for all of its services and credits to the client any media commissions earned. Agency and client agree on the specific work to be done and the amount the agency will be paid for it. This arrangement is similar to the system used by advertisers to pay for other services such as legal, accounting, or consulting. The company and agency agree on a monthly, annual, or overall fee, which can vary according to the salary levels of agency personnel working on the account. In other cases, a flat hourly fee for all work is determined, no matter the salary level of those doing the work. To determine the fee it will charge, the agency assigns costs for salaries, rent, operations, and other expenses and then determines what amount will recover these costs and provide the agency with a profit.

Sometimes agencies are compensated through a **fee–commission combination**, in which the media commissions received by the agency are credited against the fee. If the commissions are less than the agreed-on fee, the client must make up the difference. If the agency does much work for the client in noncommissionable media, the fee may be charged over and above the commissions received.

Both types of fee arrangements require that the agency carefully assess its costs of serving the client for the specified period, or for the project, plus its desired profit margin. To avoid any later disagreement, a fee arrangement should specify exactly what services the agency is expected to perform for the client. The ANA study found that a fee-based structure is the dominant form of compensation, with 82 percent of marketers using this type of plan.

Cost-Plus Agreement   Under a **cost-plus system**, the client agrees to pay the agency a fee based on the costs of its work plus some agreed-on profit margin (often a percentage of total costs). This system requires that the agency keep detailed records of the costs it incurs in working on the client's account. Direct costs (personnel time and out-of-pocket expenses) plus an allocation for overhead and a markup for profits determine the amount the agency bills the client.

Fee agreements and cost-plus systems are commonly used in conjunction with a commission system. The fee-based system can be advantageous to both the client and the agency, depending on the size of the client, advertising budget, media used, and services required. Many clients prefer fee or cost-plus systems because they receive a detailed breakdown of where and how their advertising and promotion dollars are being spent. However, these arrangements can be difficult for the agency, as they require careful cost accounting and may be difficult to estimate when bidding for an advertiser's business. Agencies are also reluctant to let clients see their internal cost figures.

Incentive-Based Compensation   Many clients are demanding more accountability from their agencies and tying agency compensation to performance through some type of **incentive-based system**. Recently a new variation of this system has emerged in the form of *value-based compensation*, whereby agencies are compensated above their basic costs if they achieve or exceed results as measured by agreed-upon metrics.[38] The costs are determined by the tasks that the agency is expected to perform, staffing required, and hourly rates. While there are many variations, the basic idea is that the agency's ultimate compensation level will depend on how well it meets predetermined performance goals. These goals often include objective measures such as sales or market share as well as more subjective measures such as evaluations of the quality of the agency's creative work. Companies using incentive-based systems determine agency compensation through media commissions, fees, bonuses, or some combination of these methods. The use of performance incentives varies by the size of the advertiser, with large advertisers the most likely to use them. Figure 3–8 shows the various performance criteria used, along with the basis for the incentive.

Recognizing the movement toward incentive-based systems, some agencies have agreed to tie their compensation to performance. Agency executives note that pay for performance works best when the agency has complete control over a campaign. Thus, if a campaign fails to help sell a product or service, the agency is willing to assume complete responsibility and take a reduction in compensation. On the other hand, if sales increase, the agency can receive greater compensation for its work.

Percentage Charges

Another way to compensate an agency is by adding a markup of **percentage charges** to various services the agency purchases from outside providers. These may include market research, artwork, printing, photography, and other services or materials. Markups usually range from 17.65 percent to 20 percent and are added to the client's overall bill. Since suppliers of these services do not allow the agency a commission, percentage charges cover administrative costs while allowing a reasonable profit for the agency's efforts. (A markup of 17.65 percent of costs added to the initial cost would yield a 15 percent commission. For example, research costs of $100,000 \times 17.65\% = \$100,000 + \$17,650 = \$117,650$. The \$17,650 markup is about 15 percent of \$117,650.)

FIGURE 3–8

Performance Criteria Used for Incentive Plans

Performance reviews	82%
Sales goals	53
Brand/ad awareness	51
Achieve project objectives	44
Brand perceptions	33
Copy test results	24
Market share goals	24
Profit goals	24
Other criteria	13
Basis for Incentives	
Agency performance	27%
Company performances	13
Both agency and company	53

Source: Association of National Advertisers, *Trends in Agency Compensation,* 14th ed., 2007.

The Future of Agency Compensation

As you can see, there is no one method of agency compensation to which everyone subscribes. Companies have continued to make significant changes in their agency compensation plans over the past decade, including increased use of the commission system and value-based compensation systems.

As more companies adopt IMC approaches, they are reducing their reliance on traditional media advertising, and this is leading to changes in the way they compensate their agencies. The changes in agency compensation are also being driven by economic factors, as most companies cut their advertising and promotion budgets as part of their efforts to save money across all areas of their marketing programs. Most marketers have not increased their marketing budgets and continue to be conservative with their spending for advertising and other forms of marketing communications. While clients recognize that their agencies must be able to make a profit, many are likely to continue to challenge them to reduce internal expenses, identify areas for cost reductions, and tightly manage their controllable spending.[39]

Companies are also making their agencies more accountable for the fees they charge them for services and are asking for more transparency in how agencies structure, determine, and present fee compensation.[40] One of the most significant findings from the ANA agency compensation survey was the increased involvement of senior management, including finance and procurement departments, in the management and negotiation of agency compensation. A previous

ANA compensation survey found that 75 percent of respondents indicated that their procurement departments are involved in the agency compensation negotiations, with nearly half reporting that the process is procurement led with marketing support and only 28 percent saying the process is marketing led.

The involvement of procurement specialists in negotiations continues to affect agency compensation, and a new issue has emerged from the increased emphasis on procurement-driven cost cutting: the practice of media rebates, which are loosely defined as an agency's receipt of a volume discount or compensation from media buys that is not passed on to the client. As discussed earlier, many of the holding companies have spun off their media divisions into freestanding firms that handle only media planning and buying. These large media-buying firms can use their size and power to extract better media prices and cost savings for their clients. However, the issue is whether these savings make their way to the clients or stay with the media buyers. Media rebates are a reviled but tolerated practice outside the United States, and a survey conducted by the ANA revealed that they are becoming more commonplace here as well.[41]

Marketers and agencies agree that rebates are not a problem if they are disclosed and passed on to clients. However, a problem arises in defining exactly what constitutes a media rebate and what should be passed on to clients because rebates seldom take the form of a simple cash payment from the media seller to the agency for reaching a volume target. Industry experts note that they often take more creative forms—such as discounts for early payment of invoices, payment from the media company to the agency for research or other services, or bonus inventory—which the media agency may then be able to sell to clients that do not require an invoice. Rebates can also flow into specialized agency holding-company entities, where they become very difficult to track.

Many working in the advertising industry argue that the two sides must find a way to work together. Marketers must recognize that a relationship in which the agency is barely making any money is not sustainable and respect the right of agencies to make a reasonable profit, while agencies will have to continue to find ways to reduce their costs and accept smaller profit margins. However, they note that clients who continue to tighten the vise on their agencies may find the quality of service they receive may suffer when the agency caves in to their demands.

The ANA publishes an excellent guidebook, *Agency Compensation Methods*, authored by David Beals, which notes that most agency compensation today is still based upon labor-based or deliverables-based fee methods.[42] Beals notes that time will tell whether true performance-based methods will overtake fees, just as fees rapidly overtook traditional media and production commissions. The ANA guidebook also points out that the needs of each client–agency relationship vary in nature and by degree, and includes a list of considerations for developing and analyzing agency compensation methods. These criteria, which are shown Figure 3–9, can be used to evaluate the appropriateness and suitability of existing and alternative agency compensation programs.

FIGURE 3–9

Criteria for Developing and Analyzing Agency Compensation Methods

Equitability/Value	Mutual fairness and the price/value ratio for both parties in the relationship.
Adaptability	The relative ease (or difficulty) with which a compensation agreement can be administered and adapted across the range of services expected of, and provided by, the agency.
Simplicity	Ease/difficulty of structuring and administering a compensation agreement.
Reward	How the compensation method might inherently motivate the agency and/or client in terms of its actions and recommendations.
Predictability	Assurance to both client and agency that their individual and mutual goals are attainable, including the ability to work affordably and profitably within budget parameters.

Source: *Agency Compensation Methods: An ANA Guidebook*, Fourth Edition, p. 14.

EVALUATING AGENCIES

Given the substantial amounts of money being spent on advertising and promotion, demand for accountability of the expenditures has increased. Regular reviews of the agency's performance are necessary. The agency evaluation process usually involves two types of assessments—one financial and operational and the other more qualitative. The **financial audit** focuses on how the agency conducts its business. It is designed to verify costs and expenses, the number of personnel hours charged to an account, and payments to media and outside suppliers. The **qualitative audit** focuses on the agency's efforts in planning, developing, and implementing the client's advertising programs and considers the results achieved.

The agency evaluation is often done on a subjective, informal basis, particularly in smaller companies where ad budgets are low or advertising is not seen as the most critical factor in the firm's marketing performance. However, some companies have developed formal, systematic evaluation systems, particularly when budgets are large and the advertising function receives much emphasis. The top management of these companies wants to be sure money is being spent efficiently and effectively. As the costs of advertising and other forms of promotion rise, more companies are adopting formal procedures for evaluating the performance of their agencies. For example, a survey conducted by the Association of National Advertisers found that 76 percent of marketers have a formal evaluation process for traditional creative agencies while 68 percent have one for traditional media agencies. The survey also found that qualitative performance is weighted more heavily than quantitative factors. Among the leading qualitative performance criteria identified in the survey were innovation, ideas, teamwork, meeting deadlines, strategy, and implementation. An interesting finding of the study was that formal reviews were much less likely to be conducted for digital, public relations, direct, and multicultural agencies.[43]

An important consideration in evaluating agencies is the *value* they provide to their client's business. The 4As, which is the trade association for advertising agencies in the United States, and the Association of National Advertisers conducted a major study to understand how agencies as well as clients define value and the agency activities that provide the most value to the client's business.[44] The top seven dimensions of agency activity that advertisers indicated add the most value to their business are shown in Figure 3-10. The study also considered how clients add value to the client–agency relationship and found that the key value drivers include understanding the brand's problems/opportunities, giving the agency the necessary time and resources to do its best work, articulating expected outcomes, giving clear direction, and providing constructive feedback.[45]

FIGURE 3–10

How Agencies Add Value to a Client's Business

1. Developing and producing creative ideas that are fresh and appropriate.

2. Ensuring that agency disciplines and functions are integrated and that agency teams and divisions collaborate well on behalf of the client.

3. Working in a collaborative way with the client by creating an environment of low egos and high mutual respect.

4. Developing ideas and programs that can be integrated into multiple communication channels.

5. Assigning its best people to the client's business and making its top executives available when needed.

6. Evaluating brand drivers like awareness, consideration, and purchase intent.

7. Providing guidance and solutions in new media and technologies.

Source: "Report on the Agency–Advertiser Value Survey," American Association of Advertising Agencies and Association of National Advertisers, August 2007.

Gaining and Losing Clients

The evaluation process described previously provides valuable feedback to both the agency and the client, such as indicating changes that need to be made by the agency and/or the client to improve performance and make the relationship more productive. Many agencies have had very long-lasting relationships with their clients. For example, General Electric has been with the BBDO Worldwide agency since 1920.[46] Other well-known companies or brands that have had long-lasting relationships include Marlboro/ Leo Burnett (67 years), Unilever/MullenLowe (123 years), and Mars/BBDO (87 years).

While many successful agency–client relationships go on for years, client–agency relationships of 10 years or more are becoming much less common as most agency of record appointments are more likely to last just 3 to 5 years, as marketers seek new ways of connecting with consumers. For example, in 2021 the Richards Group ended its 25-year relationship with retailer Home Depot and named BBDO its new creative agency of record, while United Airlines chose 72andSunny as its global creative agency after 10 years with DentsuMcGarryBowen.[47] A few years earlier, another long-standing relationship ended when Manulife, the parent company for insurance giant John Hancock, ended its 32-year relationship with Hill Holliday and moved its global creative business to Deloitte Digital. The move caught the attention of many in the industry because it was one of the first times a digital consultancy had moved beyond media and was able to win the creative work for a major advertiser.[48]

Some companies switch agencies quite often in search of better creative work or for a variety of other reasons such as reorganizations that lead to changes in top management, changes in marketing or advertising strategy, or conflicts that might arise from mergers and acquisitions among both clients and agencies. A company may also switch agencies in order to consolidate all of its advertising and marketing efforts in one shop. A number of global marketers such as Procter & Gamble, Samsung, IBM, Colgate, Microsoft, and others have reduced the number of agencies they work with in recent years as a way to gain more control over their marketing communications and create a consistent brand image worldwide.[49]

There are a number of reasons clients switch agencies. Understanding these potential problems can help the agency avoid them.[50] In addition, it is important to understand the process agencies go through in trying to win new clients.

Why Agencies Lose Clients   Some of the more common reasons agencies lose clients follow:

- *Poor performance or service.* The client becomes dissatisfied with the quality of the advertising and/or the service provided by the agency.
- *Poor communication.* The client and agency personnel fail to develop or maintain the level of communication necessary to sustain a favorable working relationship.
- *Unrealistic demands by the client.* The client places demands on the agency that exceed the amount of compensation received and reduce the account's profitability.
- *Personality conflicts.* People working on the account on the client and agency sides do not have enough rapport to work well together.
- *Personnel changes.* A change in personnel at either the agency or the advertiser can create problems. New managers may wish to use an agency with which they have established ties. Agency personnel often take accounts with them when they switch agencies or start their own.
- *Changes in size of the client or agency.* The client may outgrow the agency or decide it needs a larger agency to handle its business. If the agency gets too large, the client may represent too small a percentage of its business to command attention.
- *Conflicts of interest.* A conflict may develop when an agency merges with another agency or when a client is part of an acquisition or merger. In the United States, an agency cannot handle two accounts that are in direct competition with each other. In some cases, even indirect competition will not be tolerated.
- *Changes in the client's corporate and/or marketing strategy.* A client may change its marketing strategy and decide that a new agency is needed to carry out the new

program. As more companies adapt an integrated marketing communications approach, they are looking for agencies that have integrated capabilities and can handle more than just their media advertising. A number of companies have changed agencies recently and moved their business to shops that have strong digital marketing capabilities.

- *Declining sales.* When sales of the client's product or service are stagnant or declining, advertising may be seen as contributing to the problem. A new agency may be sought for a new creative approach. IMC Perspective 3–1 discusses the decision by Anheuser-Busch (AB) InBev to part ways with Wieden+Kennedy and search for a new agency for its Bud Light portfolio of brands.

- *Conflicting compensation philosophies.* Disagreement may develop over the level or method of compensation. As more companies move toward incentive-based compensation systems, disagreement over compensation is becoming more common place.

IMC Perspective 3–1 > > >

Bud Light Searches for a New Agency

Anheuser-Busch

Client–agency relationships can last for many years, but breakups are becoming increasingly common, and they can be completely one-sided or mutual. In some cases the reason(s) for the breakup are obvious as the client is not satisfied with the creative work being done by the agency, its sales and/or market share is declining, or the client is looking for a new agency that can bring new creative ideas and a fresh perspective to it business. One might argue that the latter two factors accounted for one of the most notable client–agency splits in recent years that took the advertising world by surprise.

In 2022 Anheuser-Busch (AB) InBev, the world's largest brewer, stunned the industry when it announced that it was putting its creative account for its Bud Light portfolio of brands—which include Bud Light, Bud Light Seltzer, and Bud Light Next—up for review. Since 2015, advertising for Bud Light had been handled by Wieden+Kennedy (W+K), the independent agency widely recognized as a creative powerhouse and noted for its creative-driven culture. W+K has done award-winning creative work for a number of clients through the years, including "The Man Your Man Could Smell Like" commercial for Old Spice body wash, which helped revive a nearly forgotten brand and became the basis of one of the most effective viral marketing campaigns ever done on social media. W+K also helped brand ESPN with its long-running "This is SportsCenter" campaign that focused on behind-the-scenes looks at the network's offices where star athletes, ESPN on-air personalities, and team mascots interacted in mundane but humorous ways. The campaign ran for more than 20 years and became a cultural phenomenon that helped make ESPN the most widely watched cable network and an integral part of the sports world.

W+K also created a number of memorable ads for Bud Light such as the "Dilly Dilly" campaign where the catchphrase used in the commercials quickly became part of popular culture. The campaign centered around a medieval *Game of Thrones*–type universe where a loyal subject is praised by the king for bringing a six-pack of the beer to a banquet as everyone raises a bottle of Bud Light and cheers "dilly dilly." The Bud Light campaign had a major viral lift during the 2018 Super Bowl when Philadelphia Eagles fans began chanting "Philly Philly" as their team upset the New England Patriots with the help of a trick play that the Eagles quarterback referred to using the same phrase.

The decision by AB InBev to put the Bud Light account up for review despite the creative and popular advertising done by W+K over the previous 7 years surprised many in the advertising and beer industries. (Prior to the company's retaining W+K as its lead agency, advertising for Bud Light had been handled by four different agencies in the course of just 2 years.) However, some experts in the beer industry were not surprised, as sales of Bud Light, which is AB InBev's largest brand, had declined for 13 consecutive years, falling from 42.4 million barrels in 2008 to 26 million in 2021. And while a post-COVID-19 rebound helped slow the rate of decline in 2021, the pace of the downfall in Bud Light sales had doubled in the prior 5 years. The decline in Bud Light sales has been attributed to a number of factors including an explosion of new brands and styles, including ready-to-drink beverages, such as hard seltzers and canned

(continued)

cocktails, which are cannibalizing beer sales. Americans are drinking less beer. Although it is still the dominant category in terms of alcohol market share by volume, beer declined from 78 percent in 2017 to 68 percent in 2021.

When AB InBev announced that it was putting the Bud Light account up for review, W+K was invited to participate and make a pitch to retain the business. However, the agency declined the opportunity, although it will continue to work on other AB InBev brands including Budweiser global, Michelob Ultra, Corona, and the AB InBev corporate brand. A number of major agencies jumped at the opportunity. Bud Light is the largest brand of beer in the United States, and to be associated with one of the country's most iconic brands and largest advertisers would be an honor. AB InBev spends nearly $130 million a year on advertising for Bud Light–related brands. However, as they developed their pitches to win the account, the agencies were aware that years of memorable advertising campaigns had failed to move the sales needle for Bud Light, as the light-beer segment of the beer market remains in freefall.

As part of the search for a new agency, AB InBev entertained pitches from five agencies, which were then narrowed to three: the Martin Agency, Anomaly, and Johannes Leonardo (the only shop that had not worked with the brewer in the past). Anomaly had deep ties to AB InBev, having served as the lead agency for Budweiser both in the United States and globally, while the Martin Agency had worked on a Super Bowl spot for Busch Light that was shown regionally during the 2022 big game.

After a review process that lasted several months, AB InBev selected Anomaly as its creative agency of record for the Bud Light beer account, while The Martin Agency was named AOR for the line extensions sold under the brand name including Bud Light Seltzer and zero-calorie Bud Light Next. The vice presidents of marketing for Bud Light and Bud Light Extensions noted that both agencies specialize in transforming brands and throughout the review process demonstrated clear, impactful visions that will help attract new drinkers into the Bud Light family. Both agencies will have to move the sales needle for the Bud Light brands, or InBev may be looking for yet another agency that can meet the challenge to do so.

Sources: Brian Bonilla and E. J. Schultz, "Bud Light Hires Anomaly For Flagship Beer Creative Account, Martin Agency Take Line Extensions," *Advertising Age*, August 23, 2022, https://adage.com/article/agency-news/bud-light-hires-anomaly-flagship-beer-creative-account/2427021; Jon Springer, "Bud Light Is Ailing—Can a New Agency Fix It?" *Advertising Age*, July 11, 2022, pp. 16–18; Brian Bonilla and E. J. Schultz, "Bud Light Narrows U.S. Creative Review to Three Agencies," *Advertising Age*, July 15, 2022, https://adage.com/article/agency-news/bud-light-narrows-us-creative-review-three-agencies/242342; Jameson Fleming and Paul Hiebert, "Bud Light Has Put Its Creative Account Up for Review," *Adweek*, June 8, 2022, https://www.adweek.com/agencies/bud-light-has-put-its-creative-account-up-for-review/

- *Changes in policies.* Policy changes may result when either party reevaluates the importance of the relationship, the agency acquires a new (and larger) client, or either side undergoes a merger or acquisition.
- *Disagreements over marketing and/or creative strategy.* Agencies sometimes disagree with clients over the marketing strategy they want to pursue or the creative approach that might be best for the brand. For example, Wieden + Kennedy terminated relationships with several clients, including the Miller Brewing Co., over disagreements regarding marketing and creative strategy.[51]
- *Lack of integrated marketing capabilities.* Many clients are changing agencies in search of a shop with a broader range of capabilities across various integrated marketing communication areas or greater expertise in a particular area such as digital marketing. In some cases, clients are looking for an agency that can provide more integrated marketing services under one roof. However, many marketers are moving toward an open source model whereby they hire agencies and other marketing communication partners on a project basis, based on their special talents and expertise.[52]

If the agency recognizes various warning signs in its client relationship, it can try to adapt its programs and policies to make sure the client is satisfied. Some of the situations discussed here are unavoidable, and others are beyond the agency's control. But to maintain the account, problems within the agency's control must be addressed.

The time may come when the agency decides it is no longer in its best interest to continue to work with the client. Personnel conflicts, changes in management philosophy, and/or insufficient financial incentives are just a few of the reasons for such a decision. An agency may also decide to leave for a better business opportunity that allows it to grow and make more money. When agencies become known for doing excellent work and developing effective IMC campaigns, they often have the opportunity to pursue larger clients, which may include a company in the same industry. However, conflict of interest policies preclude an agency from working for more than one company in a product or service category.[53]

How Agencies Gain Clients   Competition for accounts in the agency business is intense, since most companies have already organized for the advertising function and only a limited number of new businesses require such services each year. While small agencies may be willing to work with a new company and grow along with it, larger agencies often do not become interested in these firms until they are able to spend at least $1 million per year on advertising. Many of the top agencies won't accept an account that spends less than $5 million per year. Once that expenditure level is reached, competition for the account intensifies.

In large agencies, most new business results from clients that already have an agency but decide to change their relationships. Thus, agencies must constantly search and compete for new clients. Some of the ways they do this follow.

Referrals   Many good agencies obtain new clients as a result of referrals from existing clients, media representatives, and even other agencies. These agencies maintain good working relationships with their clients, the media, and outside parties that might provide business to them.

Solicitations   One of the more common ways to gain new business is through direct solicitation. In smaller agencies, the president may solicit new accounts. In most large agencies, a new business development group seeks out and establishes contact with new clients. The group is responsible for writing solicitation letters, making cold calls, and following up on leads. Cutbacks in ad spending by their clients can lead some agencies to pitch their services on an unsolicited basis to marketers who are satisfied with their agencies. Senior executives recognize that new business is the lifeblood of their agencies and some may encourage their business development teams to pursue advertisers who have not even put their accounts up for review. It is important for agencies to focus on cultivating strong relationships with their clients to ensure they do not consider solications from other agencies.[54]

Presentations   The search process for a new agency usually begins with clients sending out request-for-information documents (RFI) that ask interested agencies to submit basic information. From there, the marketer will narrow its list of contenders and send remaining agencies requests for proposals, or RFPs. For most searches, finalists are asked to prepare a speculative presentation that examines the potential client's marketing situation and develops a tentative campaign that includes creative strategies and ideas. The agency may even be asked to develop rough versions of television ads and other creative work. A goal of any agency pitching an account is to make the finalist list and be invited to make a presentation. This gives the agency the opportunity to sell itself—to describe its experience, personnel, capabilities, and operating procedures—as well as to show its previous creative work.

The search for a new agency can take several months, depending upon the number of finalists and the amount of detail expected in the speculative presentation. Because spec presentations require a great deal of time and preparation and may cost the agency a considerable amount of money without a guarantee of gaining the business, many firms refuse to participate in "creative shootouts." They argue that agencies should be selected on the basis of their experience and the services and programs they have provided for previous clients. Critics also note that in addition to the costs, which can be hundreds of thousands of dollars to pitch a major account, the creative work developed for speculative presentations is often not used and spec presentations do not always give a true indication of how the agency and client will work together.[55] However, many marketers still feel that spec presentations are an important part of the process of selecting a new agency and continue to use them. Thus, most agencies do participate in this form of solicitation, either by choice or because they must do so to gain accounts.

Due in part to the emphasis on speculative presentations, a very important role has developed for *ad agency review consultants*, who specialize in helping clients choose ad agencies. These consultants are often used to bring an objective perspective to the agency review process and to assist advertisers who may lack the resources, experience, or

EXHIBIT 3-10

Many companies use the 4As Agency Search Information Center when conducting an agency search.

American Association of Advertising Agencies

EXHIBIT 3-11

The agency We Believers has won numerous industry awards.

We Believers

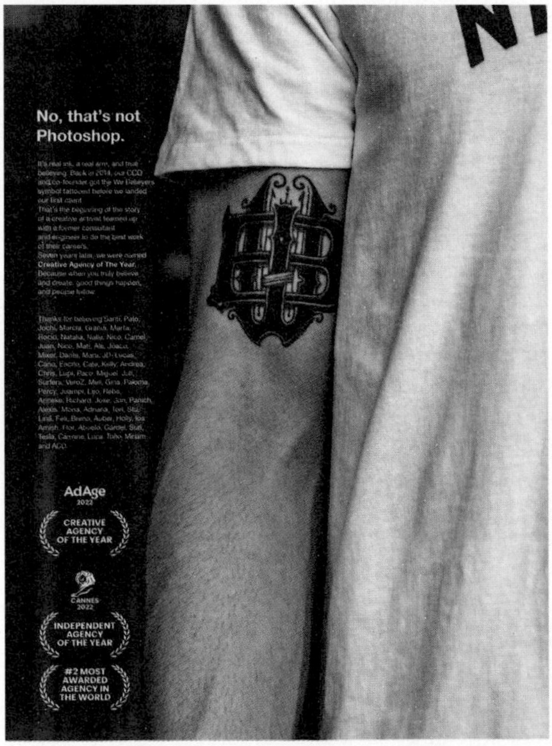

organizational consensus needed to successfully conduct a review. Search consultants are often used in agency reviews where the ad budget for the account is worth $10 million or more.[56] Because their opinions are respected by clients, the entire agency review process may be structured according to their guidelines. However, one study found that while many companies use search consultants to help them with their reviews, they do not always have a direct influence on the final decision regarding which agency they hire.[57]

Many in the advertising industry are calling for changes to the search process, with less emphasis being put on speculative presentations and more on the agency's strategic vision and how it thinks and solves problems. They also suggest that the process needs to be streamlined, with agencies receiving compensation for the time spent preparing their pitch and testing their creative capabilities with specific assignments.[58] However, it is unlikely that many companies will change their agency selection processes, and agencies will have to continue to follow their procedures if they want to compete for the business.

Public Relations Agencies also seek business through publicity/public relations efforts. They often participate in civic and social groups and work with charitable organizations pro bono (at cost, without pay) to earn respect in the community. Participation in professional associations such as the Association of National Advertisers (ANA), the Advertising Research Foundation, and the American Marketing Association can lead to new contacts. Successful agencies often receive free publicity throughout the industry as well as in the mass media. Many agencies are also members of the 4As, which is the leading trade organization for marketing communication agencies ranging from small shops to large holding company agencies. Companies often use the 4As Agency Search Information Center, which includes a searchable database of member agencies including their location and areas of specialization. The information center also provides an agency consultants list along with other resources that can be used to guide the agency search process (Exhibit 3-10).

Image and Reputation Perhaps the most effective way an agency can gain new business is through its reputation for doing excellent work for the clients it serves. Word travels fast through the advertising and marketing industry regarding the agencies that are doing outstanding creative work in advertising as well as in other areas of IMC. There are many award competitions in which advertisers may enter their work and have it recognized, such as the Effie Awards, which are given each year to IMC campaigns based on the results they achieve as well as the strategy that goes into creating them. There are many other awards that recognize outstanding advertising creativity as well as work done in specific areas such as media planning and strategy, digital media, public relations, and sales promotion. For example, the Cannes Lions Awards are presented each year as part of the Cannes International Advertising Festival and have become one of the most prestigious awards in the marketing communications industry. The CLIO Awards are also one of the world's most recognized international advertising, design, and communications competitions and reward creative excellence across a variety of categories and media types.

The major industry publications such as *Advertising Age* and *Adweek* also recognize the top agencies each year based on the quality of their creative work.[59] Being recognized by these publications, as well as other industry groups and associations, enhances the reputation and image of an agency. Exhibit 3-11 shows an ad that appeared in *Advertising Age* for We Believers and notes the various awards the agency received for its outstanding creative work for clients such as Burger King, DoorDash, Corona, and Nestle.

SPECIALIZED SERVICES

Many companies assign the development and implementation of their promotional programs to an advertising agency. But several other types of organizations provide specialized services that complement the efforts of ad agencies. Direct-response agencies, sales promotion agencies, and public relations firms are important to marketers in developing and executing IMC programs in the United States as well as international markets. Let us examine the functions these organizations perform.

Direct-Marketing Agencies

LO 3-5

One of the fastest-growing areas of IMC is direct marketing, where companies communicate with consumers through telemarketing, direct mail, television, the Internet, and other forms of direct-response advertising. As this industry has grown, numerous direct-marketing agencies have evolved that offer companies their specialized skills in both consumer and business markets. Many of the top direct-marketing agencies are subsidiaries of large agency holding companies such as Rapp Worldwide (Omincom), Espsilon (Publicis), and Acxiom (IPG). However, there are also a number of independent direct-marketing agencies including those that serve large companies as well as smaller firms that handle the needs of local companies. Exhibit 3–12 shows how the Anderson agency promotes the various capabilities it offers to clients including strategy, creative, data intelligence, digital, and production.

Direct-marketing agencies provide a variety of services, including database analytics and management, direct mail, research, media services, and creative and production capabilities. While direct mail was traditionally their primary weapon, many direct-marketing agencies are expanding their services to include such areas as infomercial production, digital marketing, analytics, and database management. Database development and management is becoming one of the most important services provided by direct-marketing agencies. Many companies are using database marketing to pinpoint new customers and build relationships and loyalty among existing customers.

A typical direct-marketing agency is divided into three main departments: account management, creative, and media. Some agencies also have a department whose function is to develop and manage databases for their clients. The account managers work with their clients to plan direct-marketing programs and determine their role in the overall integrated marketing communications process. The creative department consists of copywriters, artists, and producers. Creative is responsible for developing the direct-response message, while the media department is concerned with its placement.

Like advertising agencies, direct-marketing agencies must solicit new business and have their performance reviewed by their existing clients, often through formal assessment programs. Most direct-marketing agencies are compensated on a fee basis.

Sales Promotion Agencies

Developing and managing sales promotion programs such as contests, sweepstakes, refunds and rebates,

EXHIBIT 3–12

Agencies such as Anderson provide clients a variety of direct and digital marketing services.

Anderson

EXHIBIT 3–13

Don Jagoda Associates is one
of the leading promotional
agencies.

Don Jagoda Associates, Inc.

premium and incentive offers, and sampling programs are very complex tasks. Most companies use a **sales promotion agency** to develop and administer these programs. Some large ad agencies have created their own sales promotion departments or acquired sales promotion firms. However, most sales promotion agencies are independent companies that specialize in providing the services needed to plan, develop, and execute a variety of sales promotion programs.

Sales promotion agencies often work in conjunction with the client's advertising and/or direct-response agencies to coordinate their efforts with the advertising and direct-marketing programs. Services provided by large sales promotion agencies include promotional planning, creative research, tie-in coordination, fulfillment, premium design and manufacturing, catalog production, and contest/sweepstakes management. Many sales promotion agencies are also developing digital and direct/database marketing to expand their integrated marketing services capabilities. Sales promotion agencies are generally compensated on a fee basis. Exhibit 3–13 shows a page from the website of Don Jagoda Associates, one of the leading sales promotion agencies. The role of sales promotion in the IMC program is covered in Chapter 16.

Public Relations Firms

Many large companies use both an advertising agency and a PR firm. The **public relations firm** develops and implements programs to manage the organization's publicity, image, and affairs with consumers and other relevant publics, including employees, suppliers, stockholders, government, labor groups, citizen action groups, and the general public. The PR firm analyzes the relationships between the client and these various publics, determines how the client's policies and actions relate to and affect these publics, develops PR strategies and programs, implements these programs using various public relations tools, and evaluates their effectiveness.

The activities of a public relations firm include planning the PR strategy and program, generating publicity, conducting lobbying and public affairs efforts, becoming involved in community activities and events, preparing news releases and other communications, conducting research, promoting and managing special events, and managing crises. As companies adopt an IMC approach to promotional planning, they are increasingly coordinating their PR activities with advertising and other promotional areas. Many companies are integrating public relations and publicity into the marketing communications mix to increase message credibility and save media costs.[60] Public relations firms are generally compensated on a fee basis or by retainer. We will examine their role in more detail in Chapter 17.

Digital Agencies

With the rapid growth of the Internet and other forms of digital media, a new type of specialized marketing communications organization has evolved to meet the changing needs of marketers: the digital agency. Many marketers are using **digital agencies** that specialize in the use of various digital marketing tools such as website design and development, apps, search engine optimization (SEO), banner ads, video, mobile marketing, and social media campaigns. They recognize that the development and implementation of digital marketing programs requires an understanding of and expertise in areas such as digital media, content marketing, e-mail marketing and lead generation, database and customer relationship management, measurement, and analytics.

In addition to their advertising agencies, many marketers now choose to work with agencies that specialize in digital marketing and thus have more depth and experience in the field. This has led many large agencies to develop their own digital shops that operate as separate entities within the agency. Also, a number of other large digital agencies such as Publicis Sapient, AKQA, DigitasLBi, and R/GA are owned by major agency holding companies, which provide other agencies in their network with a digital resource. Many traditional advertising agencies have developed digital capabilities ranging from a few specialists within the agency to entire digital departments that work closely with other parts of the agency in developing integrated campaigns for their clients. For example, Wieden+Kennedy began expanding its digital capabilities several years ago as cofounder Dan Wieden noted that the challenge of integrating the digital revolution into the advertising world will either transform the agency or "render us inert."[61] Another agency that has developed strong online capabilities is Deutsch, which handles digital work for clients such as Taco Bell, Patagonia, PetSmart, and Dr Pepper.

While most agencies have developed digital capabilities, a number of marketers are turning to more specialized agencies to handle their digital marketing work. As discussed in the chapter opener, a major development over the past several years has been the rapid growth of consultancies, which are divisions of major management consulting companies that offer digital marketing, CRM, analytics, and other technology-focused services.

As the Internet and digital media become increasingly important marketing tools, more companies will be turning to digital agencies to help them develop successful integrated marketing programs. The growth of social media and mobile marketing is also giving rise to companies that specialize in developing applications and campaigns for Facebook, Twitter, Instagram, Snapchat, and other social platforms. For example, there are a number of companies that help marketers build, monitor, manage, and measure their social media efforts across a variety of social and mobile platforms. These companies work with marketers to develop various ways to engage consumers, including various types of promotions as well as through user-generated photo, essay, and video contests. The number of digital agencies, as well as companies that specialize in the development of campaigns for social and mobile media, will continue to grow, as will their importance, as marketers move more of their IMC efforts away from traditional media into the digital space. In addition, many digital agencies are expanding their capabilities in order to offer clients a variety of services such as strategy and planning, data analysis and modeling, digital creativity, retail activation, and CRM.

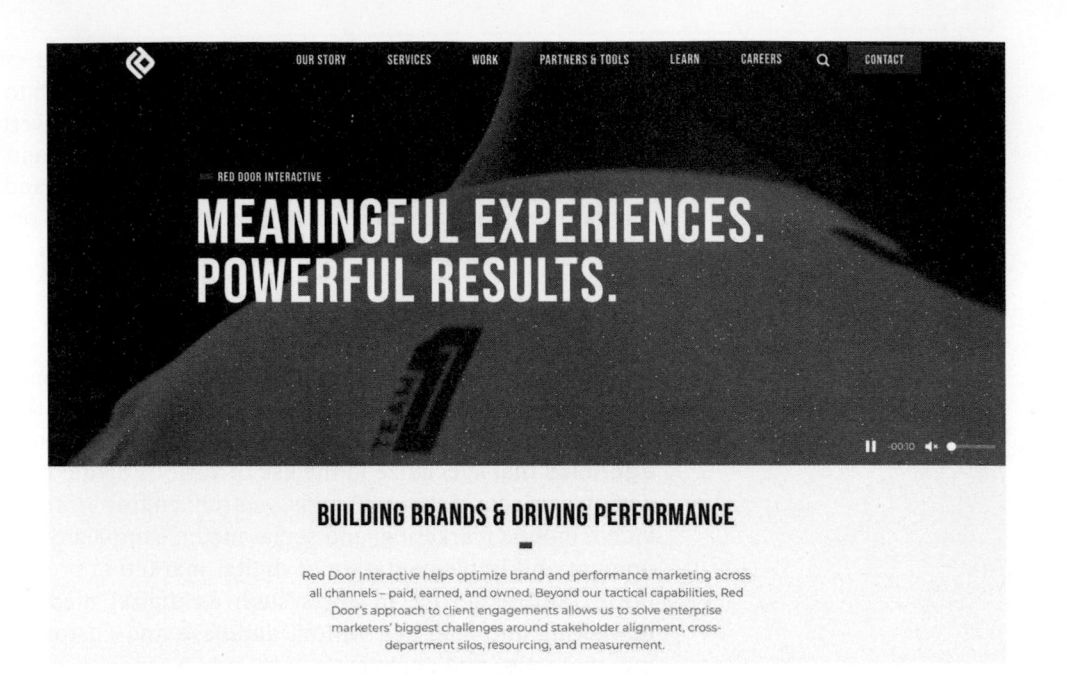

Exhibit 3-14 shows how digital agency Red Door Interactive—whose clients include Asics, Titleist golf, WD-40, and Bosh appliances—promotes its capabilities, which include creative and brand strategy, website development and technology, social media and content marketing services, and search engine optimizatoin (SEO).

COLLATERAL SERVICES

The final participants in the promotional process are those that provide various collateral services. They include marketing research companies, package design firms, consultants, photographers, graphic design companies, talent and influencer agencies, video production houses, and event marketing services companies. One of the more widely used collateral service organizations is the marketing research firm. Companies are increasingly turning to marketing research to help them understand their target audiences and to gather information that will be of value in designing and evaluating their advertising and promotions programs. Even companies with their own marketing research departments often hire outside research agencies to perform some services. Marketing research companies offer specialized services and can gather objective information that is valuable to the advertiser's promotional programs. They conduct *qualitative* research such as in-depth interviews and focus groups, as well as *quantitative* studies such as market surveys.

As more companies make digital marketing an integral part of their IMC programs, new types of marketing technology services have emerged and are being used by marketers as well as agencies. These technologies focus on areas such as mobile, content, and e-mail marketing as well as social media, programmatic media buying, customer experience, analytics, and other specialized areas. Each year, Chief Marketing Technologist blogger Scott Brinker tracks the marketing technology landscape and the number of companies that provide marketing technology solutions and shows them in his popular *Marketing Technology Landscape* super-graphic, which can be found at chiefmartec.com. Exhibit 3-15 shows his 2022 chart, which includes more than 9,000 marketing technology solutions, many of which are used by marketers in developing, implementing, and measuring the effectiveness of their IMC programs.

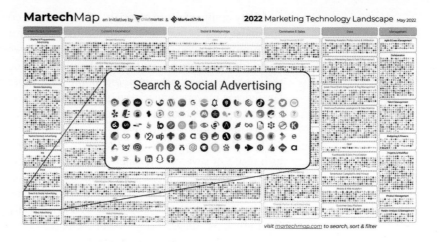

INTEGRATED MARKETING COMMUNICATIONS SERVICES

You have seen that marketers can choose from a variety of specialized organizations to assist them in planning, developing, and implementing an integrated marketing communications program. But companies must decide whether to use a different organization for each marketing communications function or consolidate them with a large advertising agency that offers all of these services under one roof. Many large agencies have broadened their IMC capabilities by developing internal expertise or by acquiring specialists in various fields. We have also seen how many companies are handling more of their IMC programs in-house, not only to save money but also because of the need to have more control over their digital marketing.

Pros and Cons of Integrated Services

There has been an ongoing debate for years as to whether control of the IMC program should be maintained by the client or should be in the hands of the agency. It has been argued that the concept of integrated marketing is nothing new, particularly in smaller companies and communication agencies that have been coordinating a variety of promotional tools for years. And larger advertising agencies have been trying to gain more of their clients' promotional business for several decades. However, in the past, the various services were run as separate profit centers. Each was motivated to push its own expertise and pursue its own goals rather than develop truly integrated marketing programs.

Proponents of integrated marketing services contend that past problems are being solved and the various individuals in the agencies and their subsidiaries are learning to work together to deliver a consistent message to the client's customers. They argue that maintaining control of the entire IMC process achieves greater synergy among each of the communications program elements. They also note that it is more convenient for the client to coordinate all of its marketing efforts—media advertising, direct marketing, digital/social, events, sales promotions, and public relations—through one agency. An agency with integrated marketing capabilities can create a single image for the company or brand and address everyone with one voice.

But not every company wants to turn the entire IMC program over to one agency. Opponents say the providers become involved in political wrangling over budgets, do not communicate with each other as well and as often as they should, and do not achieve synergy. They also claim that agencies' efforts to control all aspects of the promotional program are nothing more than an attempt to hold on to business that might otherwise be lost to independent providers. They note that synergy and economies of scale, while nice in theory, have been difficult to achieve and competition and conflict among agency subsidiaries have been a major problem.[62]

Many companies use a variety of vendors for communication functions, choosing the specialist they believe is best suited for each promotional task, be it advertising, sales promotion, or public relations. While many ad agencies are working to master integration and compete against one another, they still must compete against firms that offer specialized services. As marketing consultant Jack Trout notes, "As long as there are a lot of specialized players, integrating an agency will be tricky. Specialists walk in the door and say 'this is all we do and we're good at it,' which is a hell of an argument. An agency that has all marketing operations in-house will never be perceived as the best in breed."[63]

The already complex client–agency relationship is becoming even more challenging as a result of several other factors, such as reductions in marketing budgets; the accompanying desire of companies to reduce the cost of their IMC programs; and the tremendous increase in the use of social media, mobile marketing, and other nontraditional forms of communication. A study by Forrester Research called "The Future of Agency Relationships" suggests that one of the biggest challenges facing marketers today is knowing who to turn to when they want to change their advertising and/or IMC strategies. The study notes that many of the major agencies are trying to bundle all of the traditional and nontraditional services together and position themselves as being able to offer all of them.[64] However, the more likely scenario is that marketers will have a number of agencies from different areas working on their business, and it is important that they get them to work together. They also must decide who is going to be in charge of managing and coordinating the IMC program. Some companies, particularly those that are heavily involved in e-commerce or that have major technology components to their business, are now opting to have digital agencies, such as consultancies, lead their IMC programs.

Responsibility for IMC: Agency versus Client

Surveys of advertisers and agency executives have shown that both groups believe integrated marketing is important to their organizations' success and that it will be even more important in the future.[65] However, marketers and agency executives have very different opinions regarding who should be in charge of the integrated marketing communications process. Questions regarding leadership, centralization, and control are important organizational design issues.[66] Many advertisers prefer to set strategy for and coordinate their own IMC campaigns, but some agency executives see this as their domain.

While agency executives believe their shops are capable of handling the various elements an integrated campaign requires, many marketers, particularly larger firms, disagree. Marketing executives say the biggest obstacle to implementing IMC is the lack of people with the broad perspective and skills to make it work. Internal turf battles, agency egos, and fear of budget reductions are also cited as major barriers to successful integrated marketing campaigns.[67] A study by the Corporate Executive Board's Advertising and Marketing Roundtable surveyed the heads of advertising and marketing communication departments at global companies as well as agency executives regarding the use of multiple agency partners. The study found that the traditional, static model of a single ad agency or a fixed roster of agencies working on a brand is being supplanted by an open-source model for some marketers. Under this model, marketers hire numerous disparate marketing partners—sometimes on a project basis—to leverage their special talents and expertise as needed.[68] The CEB report notes that clients will increasingly be relegating their lead agencies to be brand stewards and coordinators of a network of specialists in various IMC areas.

Many advertising agencies do not accept the premise that they must accept a new role as stewards and coordinators of specialists. These agencies still view themselves as strategic and executional partners and are adding more resources to offer their clients a full line of services. They are expanding their agencies' capabilities in digital/interactive, multimedia advertising, database management, direct marketing, public relations, and sales promotion. However, many marketers still want to set the strategy for their IMC campaigns and seek specialized expertise, more quality and creativity, and greater control and cost-efficiency by using multiple providers. Steven Center, the former chief marketing officer for Honda of America, takes a position that is probably shared by most top marketing executives. He notes: "Agencies are exposed to much more than us, and they have to bring in raw ideas, market reconnaissance, and intelligence. But they will not tell us how to organize our company to accomplish our marketing mission. That responsibility should always fall entirely with the owner of the brand."[69]

Preparing for the Future

As noted throughout the chapter, much has changed in regard to client–agency relationships, particularly over the past two decades. Traditional advertising agencies are facing competition from a variety of specialist companies, particularly in the areas of digital marketing and information technology, as well as the clients themselves who are bringing more of their IMC functions in-house. Agencies must be able to prove their value to clients and show how they are providing solutions to their marketing communications problems, not just services. Tim Williams, founder of Ignition Consulting Group, a leading advertising agency consulting company, has created a framework that outlines fundamental elements that agencies must work on in order to transform themselves and be prepared for the future. Williams groups them into eight different areas, as shown in Figure 3–11. These elements do not involve simple modifications, such as

FIGURE 3–11

Foundations of the 2020 Agency

Areas	Foundational Elements
Accountability	■ Responsibility for outcomes, not just outputs
	■ Attention to success metrics vs. just cost of service
	■ Measuring what matters: results for clients instead of agency time
Agility	■ Agile philosophy applied to work flow
	■ Prototyping and minimum viable products
	■ Interdisciplinary teams vs. departments
Collaboration	■ Culture that values collaboration over managing hours
	■ Teams of givers, not just takers
	■ Agency partners as peaceful competitors
Digital Fitness	■ Individuals with high digital IQ
	■ Digital as competency across agency, not just a department
	■ Deep understanding of data and personalization
Effectiveness	■ Provider of solutions, not just services
	■ True project management vs. tracking of hours
	■ Focus on effectiveness for clients, not just efficiency for agency
Expertise	■ Knowledge of specific markets or audiences
	■ Best-in-class business model vs. full service
	■ Centers of excellence and best practices
Innovation	■ Revenue streams from intellectual property, not just work for hire
	■ Labs as independent business units
	■ Marketing invention business, not just service business
Pricing	■ Pricing as a core competency versus costing
	■ Aligning the economic incentives of both client and agency
	■ Professional sellers negotiating with professional buyers

adding additional services and capabilities, but rather call for fundamental changes in the way advertising agencies view their business model and serve their clients. Williams argues that agencies need to consider how to refocus and redefine their offerings to clients to make themselves indispensable, which will require them to carefully examine their service models and how they operate their businesses.[70]

Summary

The development, execution, and administration of an advertising and promotions program involve the efforts of many individuals, both within the company and outside it. Participants in the integrated marketing communications process include the advertiser or client, ad agencies, media organizations, specialized marketing communications firms, and providers of collateral services.

Companies use three basic systems to organize internally for advertising and promotion. Centralized systems offer the advantages of facilitated communications, lower personnel requirements, continuity in staff, and more top-management involvement. Disadvantages include a lower involvement with overall marketing goals, longer response times, and difficulties in handling multiple product lines.

Decentralized systems offer the advantages of concentrated managerial attention, more rapid responses to problems, and increased flexibility, though they may be limited by ineffective decision making, internal conflicts, misallocation of funds, and a lack of authority. In-house agencies, while offering the advantages of cost savings, control, and increased coordination, have the disadvantage of less experience, objectivity, and flexibility. However, there has been an increase in the number of companies that are using in-house agencies to handle all, or at least part, of their IMC programs. The move toward greater use of in-house agencies is being driven by the increased use of digital marketing, which requires companies to produce more IMC content and to do so in a timely manner. Many companies are also bringing media planning and buying in-house rather than using an outside media agency.

Many firms use advertising agencies to help develop and execute their programs. These agencies may take on a variety of forms, including full-service agencies, creative boutiques, and media buying services. The first offers the client a full range of services (including creative, account, marketing, and financial and management services); the other two specialize in creative services and media buying, respectively. Agencies are compensated through commission systems, percentage charges, and fee- and cost-based systems. Recently, the emphasis on agency accountability has increased. Agencies are being evaluated on both financial and qualitative aspects, and some clients are using incentive-based compensation systems that tie agency compensation to performance measures such as sales and market share.

In addition to using ad agencies, marketers use the services of other marketing communication specialists, including direct-marketing agencies, sales promotion agencies, public relations firms, and digital agencies. A marketer must decide whether to use a different specialist for each promotional function or have all of its integrated marketing communications done by an advertising agency that offers all of these services under one roof.

Recent studies have found that most marketers believe it is their responsibility, not the ad agency's, to set strategy for and coordinate IMC campaigns. The lack of a broad perspective and specialized skills in nonadvertising areas are seen as major barriers to agencies' increased involvement in integrated marketing communications. Agencies must be able to prove their value to clients and show how they are providing solutions to their marketing communications problems. A framework was presented that outlines fundamental elements that agencies must work on in order to transform themselves and be prepared for the future.

Key Terms

clients 73
advertising agency 73
agency of record (AOR) 73
media organizations 74
specialized marketing communication services 74
collateral services 74
advertising manager 75
centralized system 75
decentralized system 76
brand manager 76
category management system 77
in-house agency 79

billings 81
superagencies 81
full-service agency 83
account executive 83
account planner 85
copywriter 86
departmental system 87
group system 87
creative boutiques 88
media specialist companies 89
programmatic buying 89
commission system 91
negotiated commission 92

fixed-fee method 92
fee–commission combination 92
cost-plus system 92
incentive-based system 93
percentage charges 93
financial audit 95
qualitative audit 95
direct-marketing agencies 101
sales promotion agency 102
public relations firm 102
digital agencies 103

Discussion Questions

1. The chapter opener discusses the acquisition of Droga5 by the consultancy company Accenture Song. Discuss how an independent agency such as Droga5 can benefit from being acquired by a consultancy company. (LO 3-3, 3-5)

2. Who are the various participants in the integrated marketing communications process? Discuss the roles and responsibilities of each and how they are changing, given developments occurring in the advertising industry. (LO 3-1)

3. Discuss the three systems companies generally use to organize for advertising and promotion. What types of companies are most likely to use each system? (LO 3-2)

4. Discuss the pros and cons of using an in-house advertising agency. Why are many companies moving their advertising and other IMC functions such as media planning and buying in-house? (LO 3-2)

5. Discuss the role of account planning in an advertising agency. What are some of the responsibilities of an account planner? (LO 3-3)

6. Why might an advertising agency choose to remain independent rather than being acquired by a larger agency or a holding company? (LO 3-1, 3-3)

7. Discuss the various ways agencies are compensated and how they are changing. Which type of agency compensation model is likely to become dominant, given the changes occurring in the industry? (LO 3-4)

8. Discuss the various criteria a company might use to evaluate the work of its advertising agency. (LO 3-4)

9. Many of the largest advertising agency companies are consultancies such as Accenture Song, Deloitte Digital, and IBM Corp. IBM iX. Discuss the reasons marketers are using consultancies to handle their advertising and other areas of marketing communication versus traditional advertising agencies. How might traditional agencies respond to the threats they are facing from the consultancies? (LO 3-3, 3-6)

10. Discuss the reasons why advertising agencies lose accounts. Find an example of a company that changed advertising agencies and identify the factors that led the company to switch to another agency. (LO 3-4)

11. Discuss the pros and cons of a marketer having one agency handle all of its integrated marketing communications needs versus using specialized marketing communications firms to handle various components of it. (LO 3-6)

4 Perspectives on Consumer Behavior

Joe Raedle/Getty Images

Learning Objectives

 LO4-1 Discuss why an understanding of consumer behavior is valuable in developing advertising and promotional programs.

 LO4-2 Describe the steps in the consumer decision-making process.

 LO4-3 Explain the influence on consumer behavior of psychological processes like perception and motivation.

 LO4-4 Discuss behavioral learning theory and cognitive learning theory.

 LO4-5 Explain the influence of external factors like culture and subculture.

 LO4-6 Identify new ways to study consumer behavior.

Environmental Factors Have Changed Consumer Behaviors—Maybe Forever!

Those who study consumer behavior have known for a long time that changing environmental factors have an impact on shopping and buying behaviors. Sometimes the impact is temporary and consumers later return to their previous behaviors, while at other times it changes consumer behaviors forever. Sometimes the changes are minimal requiring small adjustments, while at others the effects are much more impactful. In the past few years there have been a number of major environmental disruptions that have resulted in significant changes in the way people shop and buy. This raised a number of questions for marketers for the future, and the way they conduct marketing activities may never be the same.

COVID-19—The global pandemic that started in 2019 has resulted in over 500 million infections, the deaths of over 6 million people, and by July 2022 had still not ended. Changes to almost all aspects of peoples' lives occurred and many endure. Of course, consumer behaviors were not immune to the effects of the pandemic. For one thing there was the quarantine, which meant that there were a number of places where consumers could not go, like movie theaters, entertainment events, and so on, because they were not open. Many restaurants and retail stores were also closed, and those that remained open were often avoided by shoppers out of fear of the virus. Even if these stores remained open, they often had limited inventories (remember toilet paper shortages?). So consumers now had to learn to do things from home, shopping, finding entertainment, exercising, and so forth. Companies like Amazon, Peloton, and Netflix saw extremely high growth, while many retail stores and restaurants closed, never to reopen. An article by Consumer behavior expert Jagdish Sheth titled "Impact of COVID-19 on Consumer Behavior: Will the Old Habits Return or Die?" identified some of the immediate effects of the pandemic including (1) hoarding—stockpiling products; (2) improvisation—discarding existing habits and finding new ways to consume; (3) pent-up demand—postponing purchase and consumption of products that results in shifting demand to the future; (4) embracing digital technologies—adopting new technologies (like Zoom) and increasing the use of social media; (5) store comes home—the places we used to go to now come to us, including stores, jobs, education, and health care offerings. He goes on to identify three additional societal changes that have taken place that have more of an indirect impact on consumer behaviors, and he suggests that some of these changes may be temporary while others may become more permanent.

A report by McKinsey & Company titled "How COVID-19 Is Changing Consumer Behavior—Now and Forever" also examined the pandemic's impact leading to changes in shopping and consumption, communications and information use, and the work, learning, travel, and life in home environments. The results showed a surge in the use of e-commerce and reduced shopping frequency. When consumers did go out to shop, they were more likely to go to stores closer to home. There was also a noticeable increase in their preference for trusted brands. Consumers shifted their media consumption usage with a noticeable increase in the use of online and streaming services. Interestingly, the research also indicated that there was a significant acceleration of already existing behaviors including the adoption of online delivery, remote learning, and online entertainment, among others.

Inflation—Due in large part to COVID-19, by July 2022, inflation hit a 40-year high. Increases in the price of food, gasoline, housing, and energy led to a rate of inflation not experienced by consumers since 1981. In an attempt to curb consumer spending, the U.S. government increased federal interest rates, and it seemed like the cost of virtually everything increased. Again, there were a number of changes in the way consumers behaved. Retail giant Walmart noted that inflation-strapped consumers shifted purchases to "need-to-have" goods (like household essentials and groceries) while avoiding "nice-to-have" purchases. Retailer Target noted that shoppers were staying away from larger purchases like televisions, outdoor furniture, and fitness equipment due to their squeezed budgets. On the other hand, McDonald's saw significant sales increases due in part to their value menu, as did LVMH (the world's largest luxury goods company), Louis Vuitton handbags, and Dom Perignon Champagne—obviously not for the same reasons as McDonald's. Coca-Cola proudly announced that their sales increased as well, reflecting the durability of the soft drink. Consumers found themselves driving less, eating at home more, paying more attention to sales, and, if

continued

they could afford it, considering or even purchasing hybrid or electric autos.

War in Ukraine—The Russian attack on Ukraine of course contributed to many environmental factors impacting consumption globally. Food shortages and gasoline price increases affected almost everyone and were a major contributor to inflation, as were disruptions to the supply chain. The war also had an impact on consumer sentiment and consumer confidence. In many ways, the overall impact of the war is yet to be experienced.

These are but some of the environmental factors that have had major impacts on consumers' behaviors, forcing companies to monitor and adapt to them. Clorox, for example, has seen that consumers have taken different strategies when it comes to many of their products. After Clorox initiated a number of price increases, some consumers who continue to purchase the brand will buy smaller-size packages to adapt to the price change, while others will buy in larger sizes to take advantage of the package size savings. While observing other behavioral changes, the company said it will continue to spend 10 percent of their sales on advertising into the near future. Obviously, there are many more challenges ahead including global warming, floods, fires, and more. As noted, there will always be environmental influences directly and/or indirectly altering consumers' decision making and marketers' responses. The question always is, how much of an influence and how long will it last?

Sources: Martha C. White, "How Does Inflation Affect Your Spending Decisions?" *NBC News*, March 28, 2022, www.NBCnews.com; Neal Freyman, "How Inflation Is Shaping Consumer Spending," *Morning Brew*, July 26, 2022, www.morningbrew.com; "Clorox Strategy Continues to Take Inflation and COVID-19 into Account," WARC, August 8, 2022, www.WARC.com; Jagdish Sheth, "Impact of COVID-19 on Consumer Behavior: Will the Old Habits Return or Die?" *Journal of Business Research*, June 4, 2020, www.ncbi.nlm.nih.gov; Sajal Kohli, Bjorn Timelin, Victor Fabius, and Sofia Moulvad Voranen, "How COVID-19 Is Changing Consumer Behavior—Now and Forever," McKinsey & Company, July 30, 2020, www.mckinsey.com.

The lead-in to this chapter describes just one of the many factors influencing consumers' behaviors that marketers need to understand to make their marketing communications more effective. Marketing researchers are constantly conducting research to learn what motivates consumers in their decison making. Consumer research is a major component in helping managers design marketing strategies. Marketers know that many factors may directly or indirectly influence consumers' decision making. What is important for them to know is how and why consumers' needs develop, what they are, and who is likely to use the product or service. Specifically, marketers will study consumer behaviors in an attempt to understand the many factors that lead to and impact purchase decisions. Often, in an attempt to gain insights, marketers will employ techniques borrowed from other disciplines. Research methods used in psychology, anthropology, sociology, and neuroscience are becoming more popular in businesses as managers attempt to explore consumers' purchasing motives. These motives along with consumers' attitudes, lifestyles, and decision-making processes need to be understood before effective marketing strategies can be formulated.

These are just a few of the aspects of consumer behavior that promotional planners must consider in developing integrated marketing communications programs. As you will see, consumer choice is influenced by a variety of factors.

It is beyond the scope of this text to examine consumer behavior in depth. However, promotional planners need a basic understanding of consumer decision making, factors that influence it, and how this knowledge can be used in developing promotional strategies and programs. We begin with an overview of consumer behavior.

AN OVERVIEW OF CONSUMER BEHAVIOR

A challenge faced by all marketers is how to influence the purchase behavior of consumers in favor of the product or service they offer. For companies like Visa, this means getting consumers to charge more purchases on their credit cards. For BMW, it means getting them to purchase or lease a car; for business-to-business marketers like UPS or FedEx, it means getting organizational buyers to purchase more of their products or use their services. While their ultimate goal is to influence consumers' purchase behavior, most marketers understand that the actual purchase is only part of an overall process.

EXHIBIT 4-1

Aspen appeals to those who enjoy the skier lifestyle.

jdross75/Shutterstock

Consumer behavior can be defined as the process and activities people engage in when searching for, selecting, purchasing, using, evaluating, and disposing of products and services to satisfy their needs and desires. For many products and services, purchase decisions are the result of a long, detailed process that may include an extensive information search, brand comparisons and evaluations, and other activities. Other purchase decisions are more incidental and may result from little more than seeing a product prominently displayed at a discount price in a store. Think of how many times you have made impulse purchases while in a store.

Marketers' success in influencing purchase behavior depends in large part on how well they understand consumer behavior. Marketers need to know the specific needs customers are attempting to satisfy and how they translate into purchase criteria. They need to understand how consumers gather information regarding various alternatives and use this information to select among competing brands, and how they make purchase decisions. Where do they prefer to buy a product? How are they influenced by marketing stimuli at the point of purchase? Marketers also need to understand how the consumer decision process and reasons for purchase vary among different types of customers. For example, purchase decisions may be influenced by the personality or lifestyle of the consumer. Notice how the ad shown in Exhibit 4-1 suggests excitement for those who enjoy the skier lifestyle.

The conceptual model in Figure 4-1 will be used as a framework for analyzing the consumer decision process. We will discuss what occurs at the various stages of this model and how advertising and promotion can be used to influence decision making. We will also examine the influence of various psychological concepts, such as motivation, perception, attitudes, and integration processes. Variations in the consumer decision-making process will be explored, as will perspectives regarding consumer learning and external influences on the consumer decision process. The chapter concludes with a consideration of alternative means of studying consumer behavior.

THE CONSUMER DECISION-MAKING PROCESS

As shown in Figure 4-1, the consumer's purchase decision process is generally viewed as consisting of stages through which the buyer passes in purchasing a product or service. This model shows that decision making involves a number of internal psychological processes. Motivation, perception, attitude formation, integration, and learning are important to promotional planners, since they influence the general decision-making process of the consumer. We will examine each stage of the purchase decision model and discuss how the various subprocesses influence what occurs at each phase of the consumer behavior process. We will also discuss how promotional planners can influence this process.

FIGURE 4-1

Basic Model of Consumer Decision Making

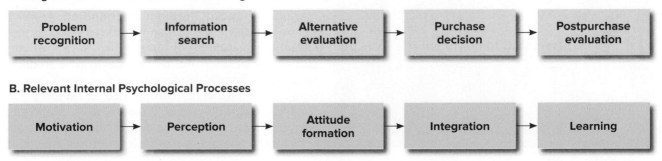

A. Stages in the Consumer Decision-Making Process

Problem recognition → Information search → Alternative evaluation → Purchase decision → Postpurchase evaluation

B. Relevant Internal Psychological Processes

Motivation → Perception → Attitude formation → Integration → Learning

Problem Recognition

Figure 4–1 shows that the first stage in the consumer decision-making process is **problem recognition**, which occurs when the consumer perceives a need and becomes motivated to solve the problem. The problem recognition stage initiates the subsequent decision processes.

Problem recognition is caused by a difference between the consumer's *ideal state* and *actual state*. A discrepancy exists between what the consumer wants the situation to be like and what the situation is really like. (Note that *problem* does not always imply a negative state. A goal exists for the consumer, and this goal may be the attainment of a more positive situation.)

Sources of Problem Recognition

The causes of problem recognition may be very simple or very complex and may result from changes in the consumer's current and/or desired state. These causes may be influenced by both internal and external factors, as discussed in the lead-in to the chapter.

Out of Stock Problem recognition occurs when consumers use their existing supply of a product and must replenish their stock. The purchase decision is usually simple and routine and is often resolved by choosing a familiar brand or one to which the consumer feels loyal, although during and after the COVID-19 pandemic, the out-of-stock issue became more complicated and commonplace due to supply chain disruptions.

Dissatisfaction Problem recognition is created by the consumer's dissatisfaction with the current state of affairs and/or the product or service being used. For example, a consumer may think their snow boots are no longer comfortable or stylish enough. Advertising may be used to help consumers recognize when they have a problem and/or need to make a purchase. The NicoDerm ad shown in Exhibit 4–2 offers assistance for those who may be dissatisfied with smoking and want to quit.

New Needs/Wants Changes in consumers' lives often result in new needs and wants. For example, changes in one's financial situation, employment status, or lifestyle may create new needs and trigger problem recognition. As you will see, when you graduate from college and begin your professional career, your new job may necessitate a change in your wardrobe. (Good-bye blue jeans and T-shirts; hello suits and ties.) Having a baby may necessitate the purchase of a family-style car.

Not all product purchases are based on needs. Some products or services sought by consumers are not essential but are nonetheless desired. A **want** is a desire for something one does not have. Many products sold to consumers satisfy their wants rather than their basic needs.

Related Products/Purchases Problem recognition can also be stimulated by the purchase of a product. For example, the purchase of a new iPhone may lead to the recognition of a need for accessories, such as a charger, ear phones, or a protective cover and apps. The purchase of an iPad may lead to buying a cover and screen cleaner. The purchase of a laptop may prompt the need for software programs, upgrades, a printer, and so on.

Marketer-Induced Problem Recognition Another source of problem recognition is marketers' actions that encourage consumers not to be content with their current state or situation. Ads for personal hygiene products such as mouthwash, deodorant, and foot sprays may be designed to create insecurities that consumers can resolve through the use of these products. Marketers change fashions and clothing designs and create perceptions among consumers that their wardrobes are out of

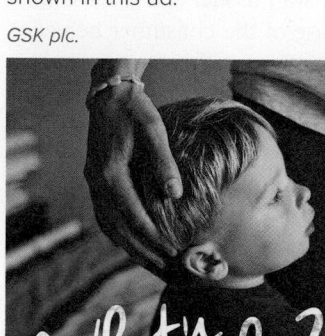

style. Exhibit 4–3 shows how Splat encourages people to change their hair color.

Marketers also take advantage of consumers' tendency toward *novelty-seeking behavior*, which leads them to try different brands. Consumers often try new products or brands even when they are basically satisfied with their regular brand. Marketers encourage brand switching by introducing new brands into markets that are already saturated and by using advertising and sales promotion techniques such as free samples, introductory price offers, and coupons.

New Products Problem recognition can also occur when innovative products are introduced and brought to the attention of consumers. Marketers are constantly introducing new products and services and telling consumers about the types of problems they solve. For example, the smartphone has become much more than a telephone, as more and more apps are now available to do just about anything you can think of. Apple's applications (apps) store has over 2 million free and for-purchase apps for their smartphones and iPads (Exhibit 4–4). As more apps are added, these products will become appealing to more consumers.

Marketers' attempts to create problem recognition among consumers are not always successful. Consumers may not see a problem or need for the product the marketer is selling. Using the smartphone example, for some, all of the potential apps may be considered unnecessary—they just want to be able to send and receive phone calls, texts, and/or e-mails.

Examining Consumer Motivations

LO 4-3

Marketers realize that while problem recognition is often a basic, simple process, the way a consumer perceives a problem and becomes motivated to solve it will influence the remainder of the decision process. For example, one consumer may perceive the need to purchase a new watch from a functional perspective and focus on reliable, low-priced alternatives. Another consumer may see the purchase of a watch as more of a fashion statement and focus on the design and image of various brands. Another may be purchasing the watch as a gift. To better understand the reasons underlying consumer purchases, marketers devote considerable attention to examining **motives**—that is, those factors that compel a consumer to take a particular action.

Hierarchy of Needs One of the most popular approaches to understanding consumer motivations is based on the classic theory of human motivation popularized many years ago by psychologist Abraham Maslow. His **hierarchy of needs** theory postulates five basic levels of human needs, arranged in a hierarchy based on their importance. As shown in Figure 4–2, the five needs are (1) *physiological*—the basic level of primary needs for things required to sustain life, such as food, shelter, clothing, and sex; (2) *safety*—the need for security and safety from physical harm; (3) *social/love and belonging*—the desire to have satisfying relationships with others and feel a sense of love, affection, belonging, and acceptance; (4) *esteem*—the need to feel a sense of accomplishment and gain recognition, status, and respect from others; and (5) *self-actualization*—the need for self-fulfillment and a desire to realize one's own potential.

According to Maslow's theory, the lower-level physiological and safety needs must be satisfied before the higher-order needs become meaningful. Once these basic needs are satisfied, the individual moves on to attempting to satisfy higher-order needs such as self-esteem. In reality, it is unlikely that people move through the needs hierarchy in a stairstep manner. Lower-level needs are an ongoing source of motivation for consumer purchase behavior. However, since basic physiological needs are met in most developed countries, marketers often sell products that fill basic physiological needs by appealing to consumers' higher-level needs.

EXHIBIT 4–3

Splat ads often encourage consumers to try something new.

EXHIBIT 4–4

There are now over 2 million apps available in Apple's store.

Warchi/iStock/Getty Images

FIGURE 4–2

Maslow's Hierarchy of Needs

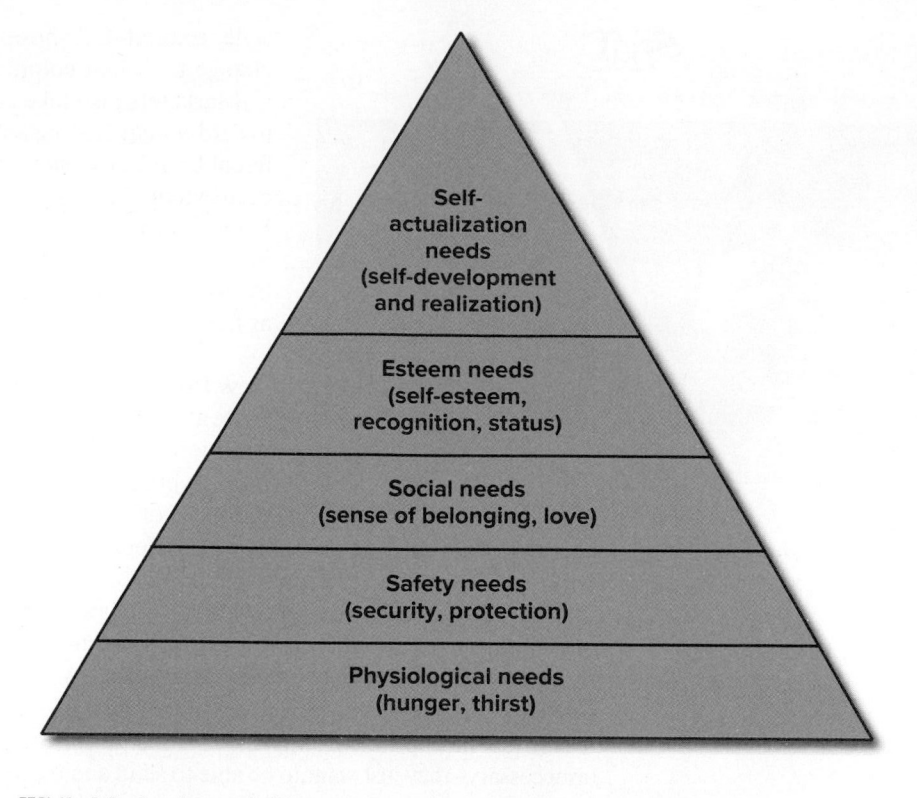

While Maslow's needs hierarchy has flaws, it offers a framework for marketers to use in determining what needs they want their products and services to be shown satisfying. Advertising campaigns can then be designed to show how a brand can fulfill these needs. Marketers also recognize that different market segments emphasize different need levels. For example, a young single person may be attempting to satisfy social or self-esteem needs in purchasing a car, while a family with children will focus more on safety needs. The Volvo ad in Exhibit 4–5 focuses on security needs of consumers, while the Lexus ad addresses self-actualization.

EXHIBIT 4–5

Volvo promotes the fact that their cars are among the safest on the road and provides the ability to meet the consumer's specific need for safety. The Lexus ad is targeted to those who have satisfied the other needs in the hierarchy and now are focusing on self-actualization.

(left) Volvo Car Corporation, (right) Toyota Motor Sales, U.S.A., Inc.

Psychoanalytic Theory   A somewhat more controversial approach to the study of consumer motives is the **psychoanalytic theory** pioneered by Sigmund Freud. Although his work dealt with the structure and development of personality, Freud also studied the underlying motivations for human behavior. Psychoanalytic theory had a strong influence on the development of modern psychology and on explanations of motivation and personality. It has also been applied to the study of consumer behavior by marketers interested in probing deeply rooted motives that may underlie purchase decisions.

Those who attempt to relate psychoanalytic theory to consumer behavior believe consumers' motivations for purchasing are often very complex and unclear to the casual observer—and to the consumers themselves. Many motives for purchase and/or consumption may be driven by deep motives one can determine only by probing the subconscious.

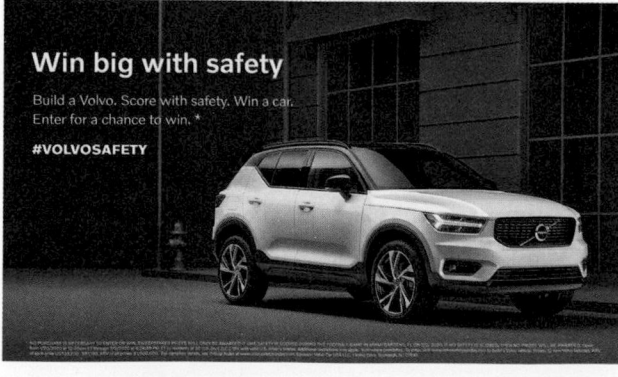

Among the first to conduct this type of research in marketing, Ernest Dichter and James Vicary were employed by a number of major corporations to use psychoanalytic techniques to determine consumers' purchase motivations. The work of these researchers and others who continue to use this approach assumed the title of **motivation research**.

Motivation Research in Marketing   Motivation researchers use a variety of methodologies to gain insight into the underlying causes of consumer behavior. Methods employed include in-depth interviews, projective techniques, association tests, and focus groups in which consumers are encouraged to bring out associations related to products and brands (see Figure 4–3). As one might expect, such associations often lead to interesting insights as to why people purchase. For example:

- A man's purchase of a high-priced fur for his wife proves his potency.[1]
- Consumers prefer large cars because they believe such cars protect them from the "jungle" of everyday driving.[2]
- A man buys a convertible as a substitute mistress.
- Women like to bake cakes because they feel like they are giving birth to a baby.
- Women wear perfume to "attract a man" and "glorify their existence."
- Men like frankfurters better than women do because cooking them (frankfurters, not men!) makes women feel guilty. It's an admission of laziness.
- When people shower, their sins go down the drain with the soap as they rinse.[3]

As you can see from these examples, motivation research has led to some very interesting, albeit controversial, findings and to much skepticism from marketing managers. However, major corporations and advertising agencies continue to use motivation research to help them market their products.

Problems and Contributions of Psychoanalytic Theory and Motivation Research   Psychoanalytic theory has been criticized as being too vague, unresponsive to the external environment, and too reliant on the early development of the individual. It also uses a small sample for drawing conclusions. Because of the emphasis on the unconscious, results are difficult if not impossible to verify, leading motivation research to be criticized for both the conclusions drawn and its lack of experimental validation. Since motivation research studies typically use so few participants, there is

FIGURE 4–3

Some of the Marketing Research Methods Used to Probe the Mind of the Consumer

In-depth interviews
Face-to-face situations in which an interviewer asks a consumer to talk freely in an unstructured interview using specific questions designed to obtain insights into consumers' motives, ideas, or opinions.

Projective techniques
Efforts designed to gain insights into consumers' values, motives, attitudes, or needs that are difficult to express or identify by having them project these internal states upon some external object.

Association tests
A technique in which an individual is asked to respond with the first thing that comes to mind when presented with a stimulus; the stimulus may be a word, picture, ad, and so on.

Focus groups
A small number of people with similar backgrounds and/or interests who are brought together to discuss a particular product, idea, or issue.

also concern that it really discovers the idiosyncrasies of a few individuals and its findings are not generalizable to the whole population.

Still, it is difficult to ignore the psychoanalytic approach in furthering our understanding of consumer behavior. Its insights can often be used as a basis for advertising messages aimed at buyers' deeply rooted feelings, hopes, aspirations, and fears. Such strategies are often more effective than rationally based appeals.

Some corporations and advertising agencies have used motivation research to gain further insights into how consumers think. Examples include the following:

- Chrysler had consumers sit on the floor, like children, and use scissors to cut words out of magazines to describe a car.[4]
- McCann Erickson asked women to draw and describe how they felt about roaches. The agency concluded that many women associated roaches with men who had abandoned them and that this was why women preferred roach killers that let them see the roaches die.
- Saatchi & Saatchi used psychological probes to conclude that Ronald McDonald created a more nurturing mood than did the Burger King (who was perceived as more aggressive and distant).
- Foote Cone & Belding gave consumers stacks of photographs of faces and asked them to associate the faces with the kinds of people who might use particular products.
- The advertising agency Marcus Thomas, LLC, conducted in-depth one-on-one interviews and used projective techniques to determine underlying motivations for choosing one cardiovascular care facility over another.

While often criticized, motivation research has also contributed to the marketing discipline. The qualitative nature of the research is considered important in assessing how and why consumers buy. Focus groups and in-depth interviews are valuable methods for gaining insights into consumers' feelings, and projective techniques are often the only way to get around stereotypical or socially desirable responses. In addition, motivation research is the forerunner of psychographics (discussed in Chapter 2).

Finally, we know that buyers are sometimes motivated by symbolic as well as functional drives in their purchase decisions. Some believe that as competition for advertisers' dollars has increased, the amount and explicitness of sexual content on TV has increased as well, as many programs and commercials now push the limits as to what is acceptable.[5] At the same time, some companies are using sex in advertising in less explicit ways. Some companies have used a range of sexual images in their ads for years primarily to attract attention. The ad shown in Exhibit 4–6 clearly employs sexual content, but not to an excessive degree.

Information Search

The second stage in the consumer decision-making process is *information search*. Once consumers perceive a problem or need that can be satisfied by the purchase of a product or service, they begin to search for information needed to make a purchase decision. The initial search effort often consists of an

EXHIBIT 4–6

Jimmy Choo has successfully used sexy ads to sell their shoes in a tasteful manner. The ads attract attention while creating a favorable image for the brand.

Jimmy Choo S.r.l. P.IVA

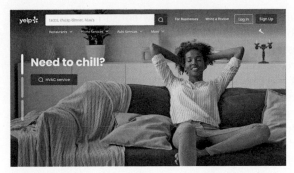

attempt to scan information stored in memory to recall past experiences and/or knowledge regarding various purchase alternatives. This information retrieval is referred to as **internal search**. For many routine, repetitive purchases, previously acquired information that is stored in memory (such as past performance or outcomes from using a brand) is sufficient for comparing alternatives and making a choice.

If the internal search does not yield enough information, the consumer will seek additional information by engaging in **external search**. External sources of information include:

- *Internet sources*, such as organic and sponsored information available through companies' websites, consumer postings, and organizations like Angie's List, Yelp, and so on (Exhibit 4-7). Figure 4-4 shows the results of a study examining where U.S. consumers begin their search process when shopping online.
- *Personal sources*, such as friends, relatives, or co-workers.
- *Marketer-controlled (commercial) sources*, such as information from advertising, salespeople, or point-of-purchase displays and packaging.
- *Public sources*, including articles in magazines or newspapers and reports on TV and so on.
- *Personal experience*, such as actually handling, examining, or testing the product.

Determining how much and which sources of external information to use involves several factors, including the importance of the purchase decision, the effort needed to acquire information, the amount of past experience relevant, the degree of perceived risk associated with the purchase, and the time available. For example, the selection of a movie to see on a Friday night might entail simply talking to a friend or checking the movie guide with an app. A more complex purchase such as a new car might use a number of information sources—perhaps a review in *Kelley Blue Book* or *Consumer Reports* or on Carfax; discussion with family members and friends; an online search; or a test-drive of cars. At this point in the purchase decision, the information-providing aspects of advertising are extremely important.

Perception

Knowledge of how consumers acquire and use information from external sources is important to marketers in formulating communication strategies. Marketers are

FIGURE 4-4

One study revealed where consumers begin their external search.

Jungle Scout, "Consumer Trends Report: Q2 2022," June 23, 2022, eMarketer.

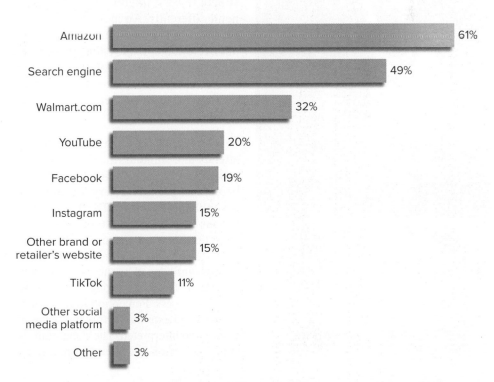

EXHIBIT 4-8

In this ad for Simply Orange, the use of color and context influences the consumer's perception and helps promote the urge to purchase orange juice.

The Coca-Cola Company

EXHIBIT 4-9

This ad reminds consumers of how advertising responds to their needs.

Courtesy of The American Association of Advertising Agencies

particularly interested in (1) how consumers sense external information, (2) how they select and attend to various sources of information, and (3) how this information is interpreted and given meaning. These processes are all part of **perception**, the process by which an individual receives, selects, organizes, and interprets information to create a meaningful picture of the world. Perception is an individual process; it depends on internal factors such as a person's beliefs, experiences, needs, moods, and expectations. The perceptual process is also influenced by the characteristics of a stimulus (such as its size, color, and intensity) and the context in which it is seen or heard (Exhibit 4-8).

Sensation   Perception involves three distinct processes. **Sensation** is the immediate, direct response of the senses (taste, smell, sight, touch, and hearing) to a stimulus such as an ad, package, brand name, or point-of-purchase display. Perception uses these senses to create a representation of the stimulus. Marketers recognize that it is important to understand consumers' reactions to marketing stimuli. For example, the visual elements of an ad or package design must attract consumers' favorable attention and stand out from competitors.

Marketers sometimes try to increase the level of sensory input so that their advertising messages will get noticed. Companies like Bloomingdales, Kraft Foods, and Nike have all used scents to sell their products, while a number of studies conducted in the United States and Europe have shown that using scents can lead to increased sales in retail stores.[6] Scent strips have long been used in magazines, and a study of *Allure* magazine readers showed that 86 percent of readers said they had tried the scent strips, with 72 percent saying they purchased the product as a result.[7]

Selecting Information   Sensory inputs are important but are only one part of the perceptual process. Other determinants of whether marketing stimuli will be attended to and how they will be interpreted include internal psychological factors such as the consumer's personality, needs, motives, expectations, and experiences.

These psychological inputs explain why people focus attention on some things and ignore others. Two people may perceive the same stimuli in very different ways because they select, attend, and comprehend differently. An individual's perceptual processes usually focus on elements of the environment that are relevant to their needs and tune out irrelevant stimuli. Think about how much more attentive you are to advertising for smartphones, automobiles, or electronics when you are in the market for one of these products (a point that is made by the message from the American Association of Advertising Agencies in Exhibit 4-9).

Interpreting the Information   Once a consumer selects and attends to a stimulus, the perceptual process focuses on organizing, categorizing, and interpreting the incoming information. This stage of the perceptual process is very individualized and is influenced by internal psychological factors. The interpretation and meaning an individual assigns to an incoming stimulus also depend in part on the nature of the stimulus. For example, many ads are objective, and their message is clear and straightforward. Other ads are more ambiguous, and their meaning is strongly influenced by the consumer's individual interpretation.

Selectivity occurs throughout the various stages of the consumer's perceptual process. Perception may be viewed as a filtering process in which internal and external factors influence what is received and how it is processed and interpreted. The sheer number and complexity of the marketing stimuli a person is exposed to in any given day require that this filtering

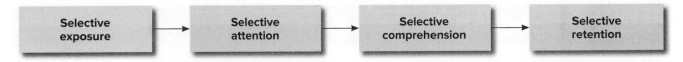

| Selective exposure | → | Selective attention | → | Selective comprehension | → | Selective retention |

FIGURE 4–5

The Selective Perception Process

occur. **Selective perception** may occur at the exposure, attention, comprehension, or retention stage of perception, as shown in Figure 4–5.

Selective Perception   **Selective exposure** occurs as consumers choose whether or not to make themselves available to information. For example, a viewer of a television show may change channels or leave the room during commercial breaks.

Selective attention occurs when the consumer chooses to focus attention on certain stimuli while excluding others. One study of selective attention estimated that the typical consumer is exposed to nearly 5,000 ads per day yet perceives only 150–155 of these messages.[8] Other estimates range as high as 4,000 exposures per day or as low as 362.[9] More recent studies estimate that given our increased time online and with digital this number may be closer to 6,000–10,000[10,11]. Of course the exact number would prove to be extremely difficult to determine. While the numbers may vary, there is agreement that consumers screen out the majority of the ads. This means advertisers must make considerable effort to get their messages noticed. Advertisers often use the creative aspects of their ads to gain consumers' attention. For example, some advertisers set off their ads from others by showing their products in color against a black-and-white background. This creative tactic has been used in advertising for many products, among them Cherry 7UP, Nuprin, Pepto-Bismol, and Coca-Cola. The distinctiveness of the pink color of Pepto Bismol as shown in Exhibit 4–10 not only catches the viewer's attention, but likely immediately leads to brand association as well. IMC Perspective 4–1 discusses other emotional aspects of ads.

Even if the consumer does notice the advertiser's message, there is no guarantee it will be interpreted in the intended manner. Consumers may engage in **selective comprehension**, interpreting information on the basis of their own attitudes, beliefs, motives, and experiences. They often interpret information in a manner that supports their own position. For example, an ad that disparages a consumer's favorite brand may be seen as biased or untruthful, and its claims may not be accepted. This is particularly true in politics.

EXHIBIT 4–10

Color is used to attract attention to this Pepto-Bismol ad.

Procter & Gamble

Eat,
drink,
& be covered.

Pepto-Bismol

The final screening process shown in Figure 4–5 is **selective retention**, which means consumers do not remember all the information they see, hear, or read even after attending to and comprehending it. Advertisers attempt to make sure information will be retained in the consumer's memory so that it will be available when it is time to make a purchase. **Mnemonics** such as symbols, rhymes, associations, and images that assist in the learning and memory process are helpful. Many advertisers use telephone numbers that spell out the company name and are easy to remember (for example, 1-800-GOFEDEX).

Subliminal Perception   Advertisers know consumers use selective perception to filter out irrelevant or unwanted advertising messages, so they employ various creative tactics to get their messages noticed. One controversial tactic advertisers have been accused of using is appealing to consumers' subconscious. **Subliminal perception** refers to the ability to perceive a stimulus that is below the level of conscious awareness. Psychologists generally agree it is possible to perceive things without being consciously aware of them.

As you might imagine, the possibility of using hidden persuaders such as subliminal audio messages or visual cues to influence consumers might be intriguing to advertisers but would not be welcomed by consumers. The idea of marketers influencing

Are Emotions More Important than Information in Consumer Decision Making?

PepsiCo

Those who study how consumers make purchase decisions have focused much of their attention on how consumers use and process information. Physiological research, social psychology, sociology, and cultural anthropology are just a few of the myriad approaches that have been explored in an attempt to gain insights. As noted by George Boykin, there are two ways to persuade people to buy: rational persuasion and emotional persuasion. Rational persuasion employs logical arguments and believable evidence. The conscious mind must be engaged and motivated to process the information. Emotional persuasion relies on the subconscious mind's "auto-pilot" to handle receiving, processing, and evaluating information to make a decision. Emotions and instincts, which reside in the subconscious, kick in as the auto-pilot substitutes for conscious thought. In other words, says Boykin, when decisions are made at the subconscious level, they are based on emotions and instincts, or "gut feeling." So, do consumers' emotions outweigh their use of information in making a purchase decision? Or is it a combination of rational and emotional factors? Following are some studies that indicate that emotions may have more impact than we previously thought.

The Impact of Emotions: A study conducted on befriending brands online by Dr. Tobias Langner, a marketing professor at the University of Wuppertal in Germany, and published in the journal *Psychology and Marketing*, concluded that "Some people feel more warmly to their favorite brands than they do toward their close friends." Langner and his research associates asked study participants to examine a series of photos including those of a close friend, a romantic partner, and a brand they claimed to love (including BMW and adidas) while they responded to a visual rating scale as well as a physiological measure. Respondents demonstrated a greater amount of love for their significant other than they did for the brands. However, when it came to their friends, they reported more positive feelings and a greater physiological response toward the brands, leading the researchers to conclude that "the

emotions we experience when we interact with our loved brands are as intensive as the emotions elicited by close friends."

In his exploration of the branding industry, Lucas Conley discusses Obsessive Branding Disorder (OBD) in relation to the high-end fashion industry. Conley claims that high-end fashions like Louis Vuitton have become so popular among Japanese women that some have admitted to eschewing motherhood in order to make the purchase of their beloved brand more attainable. He concludes that they have developed such an emotional attachment to the brands that the brands are replacing real-life networks of close friends. While sharing the same values, they don't worry about the brands ever disagreeing with them. Emotional bonding with brands?

Color: Research on the impact of color in marketing has been likened to the weather—"everyone has to deal with it, but no one can do anything about it." In other words, while we all believe that color has an impact on the perceptions of brands, personal experiences hinder our ability to translate this impact into specific feelings.

The Importance of Color—A number of studies have explored how color affects both branding and purchasing. These studies have concluded that (1) for some products, 90 percent of snap judgments made about products can be based on color alone; (2) color and brand "fit" (e.g., appropriateness) is important; (3) colors influence the perceived "personality" of the brand; and (4) consumers prefer recognizable brands, which makes color very important in creating a brand identity, among other viable conclusions.

Stanford professor Jennifer Aaker spent years conducting studies on the relationship between color appropriateness and products. Her studies led to the conclusion that brands develop a brand personality to which there are five key dimensions including sincerity, excitement, competence, sophistication, and ruggedness, and that colors align with these specific traits (for example, brown with ruggedness, and red with excitement). While this research does not prescribe how to choose a color for a brand, it does clearly indicate that the feelings, mood, and image created by the color–brand interaction will have an impact on its persuasive capabilities.

Additional studies on the impact of color have concluded that (1) gender affects color preferences, (2) there is no single best color for affecting conversion rates on websites, and (3) the name of the color matters—fancy names are more liked (*mocha* was preferred to *brown*) and unusual and unique names can increase the intent to purchase. All of these studies come to the same conclusion: Color will affect the perceptions of the brand and consumers' decision making.

These studies, among many others, have helped marketers understand that emotional aspects are important in consumers' purchasing decisions, and have an impact on their perceptions of products and brands. As noted by Dan Gartlan, a marketing consultant, "Purely informational advertising can be difficult for people to connect with. One of the issues with that kind of advertising is that the audience might remember the information you've provided but not the brand itself." As a result more companies are increasing their efforts to have their brands connect with consumers' positive emotions (e.g., happiness, pride, altruism) or negative ones (e.g., fear, anger, greed). Anti-smoking and anti-drug use ads frequently employ fear appeals, while political campaigns may try to generate anger. Many companies try to generate a positive emotional attachment to their brands.

Some companies, like Coca-Cola, have done well at implementing this strategy. Coke has been "spreading smiles" for years in its quest to associate happiness with the brand. Coke has offered consumers a 10-step happiness guide, a happiness meter that analyzes mood-related words on Twitter, and more recently a "Choose Happiness" campaign that includes video, outdoor ads, bus wraps, and a #happiestselfie contest on social media. Coke believes that linking the happy emotion to the brand can only help.

Competitor Pepsi has also jumped on the emotion bandwagon. The company's "Say It with Pepsi" campaign employed over 70 uniquely designed emojis to place on its cans and bottles in over 100 global markets. The "Pepsi-Mojis" were designed to deliver marketing messages "graphically, quickly and in a relatable way," according to a Pepsi spokesperson, and will constitute an important role in future campaigns. The campaign was supported by digital and traditional advertising, and the emojis were extended to Pepsi Moji-inspired sunglasses.

It's not just about numbers anymore!

Sources: Dan Gartlan, "Emotional Advertising: How Brands Use Feelings to Get People to Buy," Stevens & Tate, February 18, 2022, www.stevens-tate .com; Tom Welbourne, "Emotional Advertising: How and Why Brands Use It to Drive Sales," *The Drum*, February 14, 2022, www.thedrum.com; E. J. Schultz and Jessica Wohl, "Pepsi Preps Global Emoji Can and Bottle Campaign," *Advertising Age*, February 19, 2016, www.adage.com; Nathan Bomey, "Emojis to Grace Pepsi Products in Summer Campaign," *USA Today*, February 19, 2016, www.usatoday; Tessa Wegert, "Emotion in Ads: Does Sentiment Sell?" ClickZ, July 30, 2015, www.clickz.com; "Does Your Wife Win Out over Your Favorite Brand?" July 30, 2015, www.yahoo.new.com; "The Psychology of Color in Marketing and Branding," www.entrepreneur .com; George Boykin, "How Is Emotional Appeal Used to Persuade?" *Chron*, February 12, 2019, www.smallbusiness.chron.com.

consumers at a subconscious level has strong ethical implications. For years, researchers have had mixed opinions as to whether motivation research and subliminal advertising are likely to be effective in influencing consumer behavior. After 50 years of research and discussion, consumers and researchers no longer feel that they need to be concerned with subliminal advertising. But they certainly haven't lost interest in it.

Alternative Evaluation

After acquiring information during the information search stage of the decision process, the consumer moves to alternative evaluation. In this stage, the consumer compares the various brands or products and services they have identified as being capable of solving the problem and satisfying the needs or motives that initiated the decision process. The various brands identified as purchase options to be considered during the alternative evaluation process are referred to as the consumer's *evoked set*.

The Evoked Set The evoked set is generally only a subset of all the brands of which the consumer is aware. The consumer reduces the number of brands to be reviewed during the alternative evaluation stage to a manageable level. The exact size of the evoked set (sometimes referred to as the consideration set) varies from one consumer to another and depends on such factors as the importance of the purchase and the amount of time and energy the consumer wants to spend comparing alternatives.

The goal of most advertising and promotional strategies is to increase the likelihood that a brand will be included in the consumer's evoked set and considered during alternative evaluation. Marketers use advertising to create *top-of-mind awareness* among consumers so that their brands are part of the evoked set of their target audiences. Popular brands with large advertising budgets use *reminder advertising* to maintain high awareness levels and increase the likelihood they will be considered by

PURE MOBILITY

As the automotive world moves toward fully connected and self-driving cars, it's no surprise who's driving the future of the industry. Michigan. Home to the world's first and only real-world testing facility for autonomous vehicles, Michigan leads the country in research, development, innovation and technology. And it all makes up the epicenter of mobility known as PlanetM. Find out why Michigan is the hands-down choice for your business at michiganbusiness.org/planetm.

MICHIGAN ECONOMIC DEVELOPMENT CORPORATION | PURE MICHIGAN®

EXHIBIT 4–11

Michigan wants to be in the evoked set of business locations.

Source: Michigan Economic Development Corporation

consumers in the market for the product. Marketers of new brands or those with a low market share need to gain awareness among consumers and break into their evoked sets. The ad promoting Michigan as a better place to live and do business (Exhibit 4–11) shows this strategy being used in a different context from products and brands. The ad presents the many benefits of Michigan and encourages prospective businesses to consider it in their evoked set of places to locate or relocate.

Advertising is a valuable promotional tool for creating and maintaining brand awareness and making sure a brand is included in the evoked set. However, marketers also work to promote their brands in the actual environment where purchase decisions are made. Point-of-purchase materials and promotional techniques such as in-store sampling, end-aisle displays, and shelf tags touting special prices encourage consumers to consider brands that may not have initially been in their evoked set.

Evaluative Criteria and Consequences   Once consumers have identified an evoked set and have a list of alternatives, they must evaluate the various brands. This involves comparing the choice alternatives on specific criteria important to the consumer. **Evaluative criteria** are the dimensions or attributes of a product or service that are used to compare different alternatives. Evaluative criteria can be objective or subjective. For example, in buying an automobile, consumers use objective attributes such as price, warranty, and fuel economy as well as subjective factors such as image, styling, and performance.

Evaluative criteria are usually viewed as product or service attributes. Many marketers view their products or services as *bundles of attributes*, but consumers tend to think about products or services in terms of their *consequences* or *outcomes* instead. They distinguish between two broad types of consequences. **Functional consequences** are concrete outcomes of product or service usage that are tangible and directly experienced by consumers. The taste of a soft drink or a potato chip, the acceleration of a car, and the speed of the Internet service provider are examples of functional consequences. **Psychosocial consequences** are abstract outcomes that are more intangible, subjective, and personal, such as how a product makes you feel or how you think others will view you for purchasing or using it.

Product/service attributes and the consequences or outcomes consumers think they will experience from a particular brand are very important, for they are often the basis on which consumers form attitudes and purchase intentions and decide among various choice alternatives. Two subprocesses are very important during the alternative evaluation stage: (1) the process by which consumer attitudes are created, reinforced, and changed; and (2) the decision rules or integration strategies consumers use to compare brands and make purchase decisions. We will examine each of these processes in more detail.

Attitudes

Attitudes are learned predispositions to respond to an object and are some of the most heavily studied concepts in consumer behavior.[12] More recent perspectives view an attitude as a summary construct that represents an individual's overall feelings toward or evaluation of an object.[13] Consumers hold attitudes toward a variety of objects that are important to marketers, including individuals (celebrity endorsers such as Novak Djokovic or Serena Williams), brands (Cheerios, Special K), companies (AT&T and Bank of America), product categories (beef, pork, tuna), retail stores (Walmart, Target), or even advertisements (Nike).

Attitudes are important to marketers because they theoretically summarize a consumer's evaluation of an object (or brand or company) and represent positive or negative feelings and behavioral tendencies. Marketers' keen interest in attitudes is based on the assumption that they are related to consumers' purchase behavior. But attitudes are very important to marketers. Advertising and promotion are used to create favorable attitudes toward new products/services or brands, reinforce existing favorable attitudes, and/or change negative attitudes. An approach to studying and measuring attitudes that are particularly relevant to advertising is multiattribute attitude models.

Multiattribute Attitude Models   Consumer researchers and marketing practitioners have been using multiattribute attitude models to study consumer attitudes for decades. A **multiattribute attitude model** views an attitude object, such as a product or brand, as possessing a number of attributes that provide the basis on which consumers form their attitudes. According to this model, consumers have beliefs about specific brand attributes and attach different levels of importance to these attributes. Using this approach, an attitude toward a particular brand can be represented as

$$A_B = \sum_{i=1}^{n} B_i \times E_i$$

where A_B = attitude toward a brand
 B_i = beliefs about the brand's performance on attribute i
 E_i = importance attached to attribute i
 n = number of attributes considered

For example, a consumer may have beliefs (B_i) about various brands of toothpaste on certain attributes. One brand may be perceived as having fluoride and thus preventing cavities, tasting good, and helping control tartar buildup. Another brand may not be perceived as having these attributes, but consumers may believe it performs well on other attributes such as freshening breath and whitening teeth.

To predict attitudes, one must know how much importance consumers attach to each of these attributes (E_i). For example, parents purchasing toothpaste for their children may prefer a brand that performs well on cavity prevention, a preference that leads to a more favorable attitude toward the first brand. Teenagers and young adults may prefer a brand that freshens their breath and makes their teeth white and thus prefer the second brand.

Consumers may hold a number of different beliefs about brands in any product or service category. However, not all of these beliefs are activated in forming an attitude. Beliefs concerning specific attributes or consequences that are activated and form the basis of an attitude are referred to as **salient beliefs**. Marketers should identify and understand these salient beliefs and recognize that the saliency of beliefs varies among different market segments, over time, and across different consumption situations.

Attitude Change Strategies   Multiattribute models help marketers understand and diagnose the underlying basis of consumers' attitudes. By understanding the beliefs that underlie consumers' evaluations of a brand and the importance of various attributes or consequences, the marketer is better able to develop communication strategies for creating, changing, or reinforcing brand attitudes. The multiattribute model provides insight into several ways marketers can influence consumer attitudes, including:

- Increasing or changing the strength or belief rating of a brand on an important attribute (Colgate Optic White toothpaste has the best whitening power).

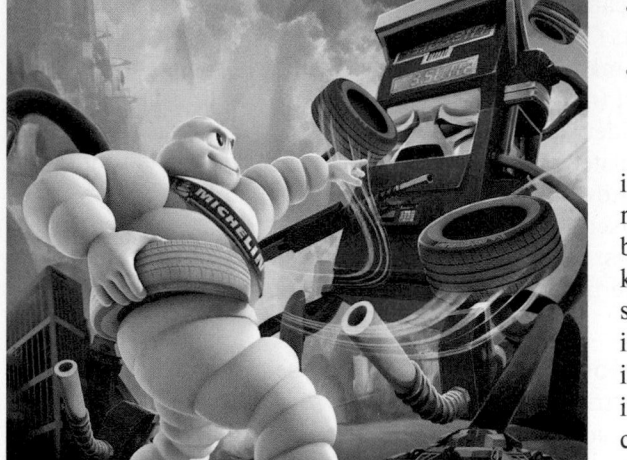

EXHIBIT 4–12

Michelin has stressed the safety aspects of their tires in their ads and has assumed a positioning strategy of being one of the safest tires on the market while also increasing gas mileage.

Michelin North America, Inc.

- Changing consumers' perceptions of the importance or value of an attribute (Michelin tires provide higher gas mileage and safety).
- Adding a new attribute to the attitude formation process (Clorox Green is environmentally friendly).
- Changing perceptions of belief ratings for a competing brand (GM shows its cars can compete with anyone's).

The first strategy is commonly used by advertisers. They identify an attribute or consequence that is important and remind consumers how well their brand performs on this attribute. In situations where consumers do not perceive the marketer's brand as possessing an important attribute or the belief strength is low, advertising strategies may be targeted at changing the belief rating. Even when belief strength is high, advertising may be used to increase the rating of a brand on an important attribute. BMW's "The Ultimate Driving Machine" campaign is a good example of a strategy designed to create a belief and reinforce it through advertising.

Marketers often attempt to influence consumer attitudes by changing the relative importance of a particular attribute. This second strategy involves getting consumers to attach more importance to the attribute in forming their attitude toward the brand. Marketers using this strategy want to increase the importance an attribute has to solve a problem (Exhibit 4–12).

The third strategy for influencing consumer attitudes is to add or emphasize a new attribute that consumers can use in evaluating a brand. Marketers often do this by improving their products or focusing on additional benefits or consequences associated with using the brand. For example, Pottery Barn says they will plant a tree for each wood indoor product sold and for each dollar donated to their tree planting site (Exhibit 4–13).

A final strategy marketers use is to change consumer beliefs about the attributes of competing brands or product categories. This strategy has become much more common with the increase in comparative advertising, where marketers compare their brands to competitors' on specific product attributes.

Integration Processes and Decision Rules

EXHIBIT 4–13

Pottery Barn offers an additional incentive for purchasing.

Williams-Sonoma, Inc.

Another important aspect of the alternative evaluation stage is the way consumers combine information about the characteristics of brands to arrive at a purchase decision. **Integration processes** are the way product knowledge, meanings, and beliefs are combined to evaluate two or more alternatives.[14] Analysis of the integration process focuses on the different types of *decision rules* or strategies consumers use to decide among purchase alternatives.

Consumers often make purchase selections by using formal integration strategies or decision rules that require examination and comparison of alternatives on specific attributes. This process involves a very deliberate evaluation of the alternatives, attribute by attribute. When consumers apply such formal decision rules, marketers need to know which attributes are being considered to provide the information the consumers require.

Sometimes consumers make their purchase decisions using more simplified decision rules known as

heuristics. For familiar products that are purchased frequently, consumers may use price-based heuristics (buy the least expensive brand) or promotion-based heuristics (choose the brand for which I can get a price reduction through a coupon, rebate, or special deal).

One type of heuristic is the **affect referral decision rule**, in which consumers make a selection on the basis of an overall impression or summary evaluation of the various alternatives under consideration. This decision rule suggests that consumers have affective impressions of brands stored in memory that can be accessed at the time of purchase.

Marketers selling familiar and popular brands may appeal to an affect referral rule by stressing overall affective feelings or impressions about their products. Market leaders, whose products enjoy strong overall brand images, often use ads that promote the brand by appealing to affect. Allstate's "You're in Good Hands," Mastercard's "Priceless," and Nationwide's "Nationwide is on your side" are all examples of this strategy.

Purchase Decision

At some point in the buying process, the consumer must stop searching for and evaluating information about alternative brands in the evoked set and make a *purchase decision*. As an outcome of the alternative evaluation stage, the consumer may develop a **purchase intention** or predisposition to buy a certain brand. Purchase intentions are generally based on a matching of purchase motives with attributes or characteristics of brands under consideration. Their formation involves many of the personal subprocesses discussed in this chapter, including motivation, perception, attitude formation, and integration.

A purchase decision is not the same as an actual purchase. Once a consumer chooses which brand to buy, they must still implement the decision and make the actual purchase. Additional decisions may be needed, such as when to buy, where to buy, and how much money to spend. Often, there is a time delay between the formation of a purchase intention or decision and the actual purchase, particularly for highly involved and complex purchases such as automobiles, personal computers, and consumer durables.

For nondurable products, which include many low-involvement items such as consumer packaged goods, the time between the decision and the actual purchase may be short. Before leaving home, the consumer may make a shopping list that includes specific brand names because they have developed **brand loyalty**—a preference for a particular brand that results in its repeated purchase; of course, brand loyalty is not limited to nondurables. Consumers develop loyalties to many types of products and services. Marketers strive to develop and maintain brand loyalty among consumers. They use reminder advertising to keep their brand names in front of consumers, maintain prominent shelf positions and displays in stores, and run periodic promotions to deter consumers from switching brands.

Gaining and maintaining consumers' brand loyalty is not easy. After a scandal in which Wells Fargo bank employees were opening up fraudulent bank accounts for customers without their knowledge, the popular bank was fined by the Consumer Financial Protection Bureau and saw its stock drop to new lows and consumers close their accounts. The situation got so bad, the bank embarked on a rebranding campaign in 2018.[15] Peloton, Facebook, and a number of others had their own mishaps in 2021.[16] Competitors use many techniques to encourage consumers to try their brands, among them new product introductions and free samples. Figure 4–6 shows some of the brands that have achieved this goal. Marketers must continually battle to maintain their loyal consumers while replacing those who switch brands.

FIGURE 4–6

Brands That Have the Most Brand Loyalty

Brand Keys Customer Loyalty Leaders List 2021.

2021 Brand Keys Loyalty Leaders
■ Amazon: online retail (#1)
■ Apple: smartphones (#4)
■ Netflix: video streaming (#2)
■ Domino's pizza (#5)
■ Amazon: video streaming (#3)
■ Disney+: video streaming (#7)
■ Google: search engines (#6)
■ WhatsApp: instant messaging (#9)

Storytelling Has Become an Effective Marketing Strategy in Sports

Elsa/Getty Images

While one of the hottest trends in sports marketing right now is storytelling, the New York Yankees baseball team has been using this technique for over 100 years. The Yankees, established in 1903, are arguably the most successful major league franchise in all of sports. And—love them or hate them—you have to give them credit for their marketing prowess.

To understand why storytelling has been such a successful strategy for the Yankees, and has become so for some others including soccer (football) teams Paris Saint-Germain and Liverpool, one has to understand what storytelling is as it relates to brands and what makes it different from other marketing strategies.

Shaq Abboud, creative director at Scope Productions, explains that from a very early age, our parents read us fairy tales and nursery rhymes and told us stories that were written in interesting, enjoyable, and memorable ways. Good stories can still affect our lives into adulthood. We still love them and we still remember them, Abboud says. He also says that good stories about brands can have the same effect. Other marketers agree, noting that storytelling is a human experience that can drive stronger and deeper connections between consumers and brands if done properly. But, they caution, writing good stories is not easy and is as much of an art as a science.

Marissa Sternberg, senior director of marketing at marketing agency Onespot, examined the science behind what makes storytelling work. Sternberg explains that a story activates parts of the brain that allow the receiver to turn a story into his or her own ideas in a process called neural coupling. This leads to an emotionally charged event causing the brain to release dopamine into the system, thus making it easier to remember and with greater accuracy. Details that help the receiver experience the story from the character's point of view can engage the sensory, motor, visual, auditory, and olfactory sections of the cortex of the brain, resulting in much more effective communication.

As noted by Kimberly A. Whitler, former general manager and CMO and now a professor at the University of Virginia's Darden School of Business, most commercials have only about 30 seconds to communicate with consumers. This means the advertiser has to focus on the single most important idea that he or she needs to convey to the consumer and provide that information. Storytelling, on the other hand, can lead to a story or series of stories that can communicate with consumers, providing them with much more content while keeping them more engaged. It enables marketers to develop a deeper connection with the audience, and rather than focusing on one attribute, stories can communicate what the brand means to the consumer, not just that single attribute.

Take the Yankees, for example. James Warren, CEO of Share More Stories, a storytelling insights company, says that storytelling has been the core of the Yankees brand for over a hundred years, and that George Steinbrenner—the owner of the Yankees for much of this time—was a master storyteller. When things went well, Steinbrenner stoked it. When things did not go well, the stories embraced individual struggles and opportunities for redemption—as in the case of Darryl Strawberry's problems with substance abuse. Now, the YES Network (Yankees Entertainment and Sports Network) shows Yankee stories from the past and present, and others like Stars and PinStripes share stories from celebrity Yankees fans. YES programming also includes the NBA Brooklyn Nets and some minor league and college teams coverage. A shared narrative among New Yorkers, fans, and the Yankees exists, resulting in the Yankees being more than just a brand by making them more human and relatable, according to Warren.

A number of other companies and athletes too have found storytelling to be an effective marketing tool. For example:

Nike—One of the most successful sports-related companies in the world, Nike has "long understood that harnessing emotion in service of storytelling is a far more effective strategy for brand building than rattling off features and benefits," notes author Sam Grawe. Grawe cites Nike founder Phil Knight's comments in 1992 that their advertising "tries to link consumers to the Nike brand through the emotions of sports and fitness." After experiencing an identity crisis in the 1980s, Nike shifted its focus from a production-oriented company talking about design and functional attributes to a marketing one that communicated a change in the way Americans felt about fitness, exercise, and wellness. The commercial for the launch of the Air Max shoe employed the Beatles' song "Revolution" and focused on a new vibe rather than stressing features, and Nike was on its way to being one of the best-known brands in the world. Nike has continued to portray its products through a storytelling technique ever since.

Athletes—The 2021 *NCAA v. Alston* decision by the U.S. Supreme Court ruled that NCAA student athletes could earn compensation via brand deals based on their names, images, and likenesses. The ruling has led to a completely new market for students to market themselves as well as to become brand storytellers and influencers. Sports leaders representing leagues, teams, and brand partners almost immediately got on board to include athletes in their marketing plans, noting that their authenticity and storytelling capabilities would resonate well with the markets they were trying to reach. Fans are often enthralled by the unique stories of the athletes and their passion and loyalty for the specific brands they use. A report by Captiv8, an influencer marketing company, found that by partnering with student athletes, brands could at least double their engagement with prospective consumers. The report also showed that both male and female athletes can be effective, and that athletes' appeal differs by sport as well as social media platform. Many

athletes are already reaping significant financial rewards as a result.

Others—Numerous other brands, both within and outside of sports, have successfully employed storytelling in their marketing plans. Warby Parker, Airbnb, Burt's Bees, Spotify, and Huggies are just a few of the many successful brands employing this strategy. And at least one marketer has claimed that storytelling may be the most effective strategy ever. Or maybe he is just making up a story?

Sources: Paula Minardi, "Athletes as Brand Storytellers: The New Center of Sports Fan Engagement," Greenfly, January 11, 2022, www.greenfly.com; "Student Athletes Get an A+ for Social Media," *Advertising Age*, August 4, 2022, www.adage.com; Audrey Kemp, "Twitter and Opendorse Help Student-Athletes Monetize Game Footage," *The Drum*, August 4, 2022, www.thedrum .com; Sam Grawe, "How Storytelling Is at the Heart of the Nike Brand," *Creative Review*, January 27, 2021, www.creativereview.com; Lizi Hamer, "The Unlimited Potential of Live Storytelling in Sports Marketing," Octagon, March 5, 2021, www.octagon.com; Shaq Abboud, "Unleash Your Secret Weapon: Video Storytelling. Why Is It the Future of Marketing?" *MarTech Advisor*, March 21, 2019, www.martechadvisor.com; Kimberly Whitier, "3 Reasons Why Storytelling Should Be a Priority for Marketers," *Forbes*, July 14, 2018, www.forbes .com; Lorna Keane, "10 Examples of Brand Storytelling (with Data) That Hit the Mark," GWI, April 23, 2018, www.gwi.com; Marissa Sternberg, "Infographic: The Science of Storytelling," OneSpot, July 1, 2017, www.onespot.com.

As seen, purchase decisions for nondurable, convenience items sometimes take place in the store, almost simultaneous with the purchase. Marketers must ensure that consumers have top-of-mind awareness of their brands so that they are quickly recognized and considered. Packaging, shelf displays, point-of-purchase materials, and promotional tools such as on-package coupons or premium offers can influence decisions made through constructive processes at the time of purchase.

Postpurchase Evaluation

The consumer decision process does not end with the purchase. After using the product or service, the consumer compares the level of performance with expectations and is either satisfied or dissatisfied. *Satisfaction* occurs when the consumer's expectations are either met or exceeded; *dissatisfaction* results when performance is below expectations. The postpurchase evaluation process is important because the feedback acquired from actual use of a product will influence the likelihood of future purchases. Positive performance means the brand is likely to be retained in the evoked set and increases the likelihood it will be purchased again. Unfavorable outcomes may lead the consumer to form negative attitudes toward the brand, lessening the likelihood it will be purchased again or even eliminating it from the evoked set.

Another possible outcome of a purchase is **cognitive dissonance**, a feeling of psychological tension or postpurchase doubt that a consumer experiences after making a difficult purchase choice. Dissonance is more likely to occur in important decisions where the consumer must choose among close alternatives (especially if the unchosen alternative has unique or desirable features that the selected alternative does not have).

Consumers experiencing cognitive dissonance may use a number of strategies to attempt to reduce it. They may seek out reassurance and opinions from others to confirm the wisdom of their purchase decision, lower their attitudes or opinions of the unchosen alternative, deny or distort any information that does not support the choice they made, or look for information that does support their choice. An important source of supportive information is advertising, as consumers tend to be more attentive to advertising for the brand they have chosen.[17] Thus, it may be important for companies to advertise to reinforce consumer decisions to purchase their brands.

EXHIBIT 4–14

Ally Bank attempts to capitalize on consumers' dissatisfaction with banks.

Ally Financial

EXHIBIT 4–15

This ad for Lincoln Financial shows how marketers can appeal to consumers engaging in extended problem solving.

Lincoln National Corporation

Marketers have come to realize that postpurchase communication is also important. Some companies send follow-up letters and brochures to reassure buyers and reinforce the wisdom of their decision. Many companies have set up toll-free numbers or e-mail addresses for consumers to call if they need information or have a question or complaint regarding a product. Doesn't it seem like you get a follow-up survey for every service you have performed these days? Some marketers also offer liberalized return and refund policies and extended warranties and guarantees to ensure customer satisfaction. Some have used customers' postpurchase dissatisfaction as an opportunity for gaining new business, as is reflected in Exhibit 4–14.

Variations in Consumer Decision Making

The preceding pages describe a general model of consumer decision making. But consumers do not always engage in all five steps of the purchase decision process or proceed in the sequence presented. They may minimize or even skip one or more stages if they have previous experience in purchasing the product or service or if the decision is of low personal, social, or economic significance. To develop effective promotional strategies and programs, marketers need some understanding of the problem-solving processes their target consumers use to make purchase decisions.

Many of the purchase decisions we make as consumers are based on a habitual or routine choice process. For many low-priced, frequently purchased products, the decision process consists of little more than recognizing the problem, engaging in a quick internal search, and making the purchase. The consumer spends little or no effort engaging in external search or alternative evaluation.

Marketers of products characterized by a routine response purchase process need to get and/or keep their brands in the consumer's evoked set and avoid anything that may result in their removal from consideration. Established brands that have strong market share position are likely to be in the evoked set of most consumers. Marketers of these brands want consumers to follow a routine choice process and continue to purchase their products. This means maintaining high levels of brand awareness through reminder advertising, periodic promotions, and prominent shelf positions in retail stores.

Marketers of new brands or those with a low market share face a different challenge. They must find ways to disrupt consumers' routine choice process and get them to consider different alternatives. High levels of advertising may be used to encourage trial or brand switching, along with sales promotion efforts in the form of free samples, special price offers, high-value coupons, and the like.

A more complicated decision-making process may occur when consumers have limited experience in purchasing a particular product or service and little or no knowledge of the brands available and/or the criteria to use in making a purchase decision. They may have to learn what attributes or criteria should be used in making a purchase decision and how the various alternatives perform on these dimensions. For products or services characterized by problem solving, whether limited or extensive, marketers should make information available that will help consumers decide. Advertising that provides consumers with detailed information about a brand and how it can satisfy their purchase motives and goals is important. Distribution channels should have knowledgeable salespeople available to explain the features and benefits of the company's product or service and why it is superior to competing products.

The Lincoln Financial ad in Exhibit 4–15 is a good example of how advertising can appeal to consumers who may be engaging in extended problem solving when considering financial planning. Notice how the ad communicates with consumers who may be concerned about achieving their dreams. The ad helps the consumer by offering expert advice and planning a variety of options.

THE CONSUMER LEARNING PROCESS

The discussion of the decision process shows that the way consumers make a purchase varies depending on a number of factors, including the nature of the product or service, the amount of experience they have with the product, and the importance of the purchase. One factor in the level of problem solving to be employed is the consumer's *involvement* with the product or brand. Chapter 5 examines the meaning of involvement, the difference between low- and high-involvement decision making, and the implications of involvement for developing advertising and promotional strategies.

Our examination of consumer behavior thus far has looked at the decision-making process from a *cognitive orientation*. The five-stage decision process model views the consumer as a problem solver and information processor who engages in a variety of mental processes to evaluate various alternatives and determine the degree to which they might satisfy needs or purchase motives. There are, however, other perspectives regarding how consumers acquire the knowledge and experience they use in making purchase decisions. To understand these perspectives, we examine various approaches to learning and their implications for advertising and promotion.

Consumer learning has been defined as "the process by which individuals acquire the purchase and consumption knowledge and experience they apply to future related behavior."[18] Two basic approaches to learning are the behavioral approach and cognitive learning theory.

Behavioral Approach

Behavioral learning theories emphasize the role of external, environmental stimuli in causing behavior; they minimize the significance of internal psychological processes. Behavioral learning theories are based on the *stimulus–response orientation (S-R)*, the premise that learning occurs as the result of responses to external stimuli in the environment. Behavioral learning theorists believe learning occurs through the connection between a stimulus and a response. We will examine the basic principles of two behavioral learning theory approaches: classical conditioning and operant conditioning.

Classical Conditioning **Classical conditioning** assumes that learning is an *associative process* with an already existing relationship between a stimulus and a response. Probably the best-known example of this type of learning comes from the studies done with animals by the Russian psychologist Ivan Pavlov. Pavlov noticed that at feeding times, his dogs would salivate at the sight of food. The connection between food and salivation is not taught; it is an innate reflex reaction. Because this relationship exists before the conditioning process, the food is referred to as an *unconditioned stimulus* and salivation is an *unconditioned response.* To see if salivation could be conditioned to occur in response to another neutral stimulus, Pavlov paired the ringing of a bell with the presentation of the food. After a number of trials, the dogs learned to salivate at the sound of the bell alone. Thus, the bell became a **conditioned stimulus** that elicited a **conditioned response** resembling the original unconditioned reaction.

Two factors are important for learning to occur through the associative process. The first is contiguity, which means the unconditioned stimulus and conditioned stimulus must be close in time and space. In Pavlov's experiment, the dog learns to associate the ringing of the bell with food because of the contiguous presentation of the two stimuli. The other important principle is *repetition*, or the frequency of the association. The more often the unconditioned and conditioned stimuli occur together, the stronger the association between them will be.

Applying Classical Conditioning Learning through classical conditioning plays an important role in marketing. Buyers can be conditioned to form favorable impressions and images of various brands through the associative process. Advertisers strive to associate their products and services with perceptions, images, and emotions known to evoke positive reactions from consumers. Many products are promoted through image

FIGURE 4–7

The Classical Conditioning Process

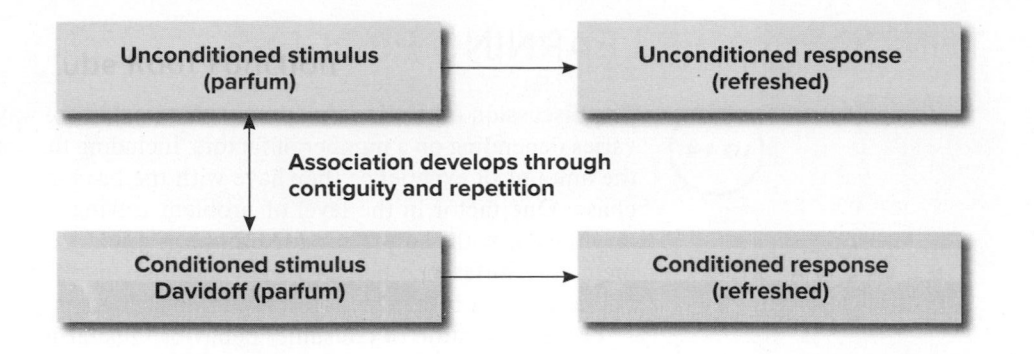

Unconditioned stimulus (parfum)	→	Unconditioned response (refreshed)

Association develops through contiguity and repetition

Conditioned stimulus Davidoff (parfum)	→	Conditioned response (refreshed)

advertising, in which the brand is shown with an unconditioned stimulus that elicits pleasant feelings. When the brand is presented simultaneously with this unconditioned stimulus, the brand itself becomes a conditioned stimulus that elicits the same favorable response.

Figure 4–7 provides a diagram of this process, and the ad for Davidoff Reborn in Exhibit 4–16 shows an application of this strategy. Notice how this ad associates the product with the look and freshness of water. The brand's positioning plays off this association.

Classical conditioning can also associate a product or service with a favorable emotional state. A study by Gerald Gorn used this approach to examine how background music in ads influences product choice.[19] He found that subjects were more likely to choose a product when it was presented against a background of music they liked rather than music they disliked. These results suggest the emotions generated by a commercial are important because they may become associated with the advertised product through classical conditioning. Other studies have shown that music that was congruent with the message enhanced both ad recall and recognition[20] and that music can be used effectively as a mnemonic device to enhance the recall of advertising slogans. Advertisers often attempt to pair a neutral product or service stimulus with an event or situation that arouses positive feelings, such as humor, an exciting sports event, or popular music.

EXHIBIT 4–16

Davidoff employs classical conditioning effectively through this ad showing that the product is refreshing.

Zino Davidoff

Operant Conditioning Classical conditioning views the individual as a passive participant in the learning process who simply receives stimuli. Conditioning occurs as a result of exposure to a stimulus that occurs before the response. In the **operant conditioning** approach, the individual must actively *operate* or act on some aspect of the environment for learning to occur. Operant conditioning is sometimes referred to as *instrumental conditioning* because the individual's response is instrumental in getting a positive reinforcement (reward) or negative reinforcement (a form of reward that occurs when a negative outcome is removed when the desired behavior is performed).

Reinforcement, the reward or favorable consequence associated with a particular response, is an important element of instrumental conditioning. Behavior that is reinforced strengthens the bond between a stimulus and a response. Thus, if a consumer buys a product in response to an ad and experiences a positive outcome, the likelihood that the consumer will use this product again increases. If the outcome is not favorable, the likelihood of buying the product again decreases.

FIGURE 4–8

Instrumental Conditioning
in Marketing

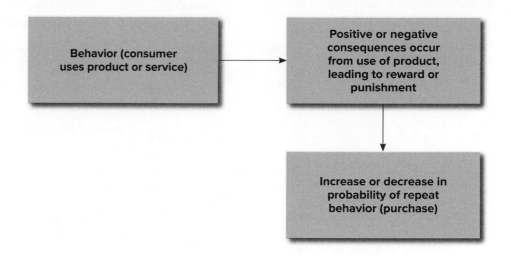

The principles of operant conditioning can be applied to marketing, as shown in Figure 4–8. Companies attempt to provide their customers with products and services that satisfy their needs and reward them to reinforce the probability of repeat purchase. Reinforcement can also be implied in advertising; many ads emphasize the benefits or rewards a consumer will receive from using a product or service. Reinforcement also occurs when an ad encourages consumers to use a particular product or brand to avoid unpleasant consequences. For example, the ad for Carfax in Exhibit 4–17 shows how using this service will help avoid negative consequences—that is, purchasing a used car with problems.

Two concepts that are particularly relevant to marketers in their use of reinforcement through promotional strategies are schedules of reinforcement and shaping. Different **schedules of reinforcement** result in varying patterns of learning and behavior. Learning occurs most rapidly under a *continuous reinforcement schedule*, in which every response is rewarded—but the behavior is likely to cease when the reinforcement stops. Marketers must provide continuous reinforcement to consumers or risk their switching to brands that do.

Learning occurs more slowly but lasts longer when a *partial* or *intermittent reinforcement schedule* is used and only some of the individual's responses are rewarded. Promotional programs have partial reinforcement schedules. A firm may offer consumers an incentive to use the company's product. The firm does not want to offer the incentive every time (continuous reinforcement) because consumers might become dependent on it and stop buying the brand when the incentive is withdrawn. A study that examined the effect of reinforcement on bus ridership found that discount coupons given as rewards for riding the bus were as effective when given on a partial schedule as when given on a continuous schedule.[21] The cost of giving the discount coupons under the partial schedule, however, was considerably less.

Reinforcement schedules can also be used to influence consumer learning and behavior through a process known as **shaping**, the reinforcement of successive acts that lead to a desired behavior pattern or response.

In a promotional context, shaping procedures are used as part of the introductory program for new products. Figure 4–9 provides an example of how samples and discount coupons can be used to introduce a new product and take a consumer from trial to repeat purchase. Marketers must be careful in their use of shaping procedures: If they drop the incentives too soon, the consumer may not establish the desired behavior; but if they overuse them, the consumer's purchase may become contingent on the incentive rather than the product or service.

EXHIBIT 4–17

Carfax shows how to avoid
negative consequences.

CarMax Enterprise Services, LLC

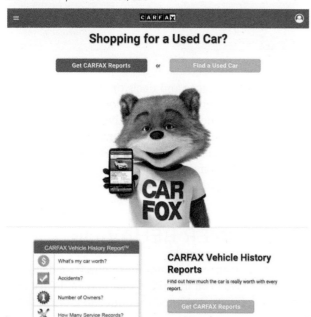

FIGURE 4–9

Application of Shaping
Procedures in Marketing

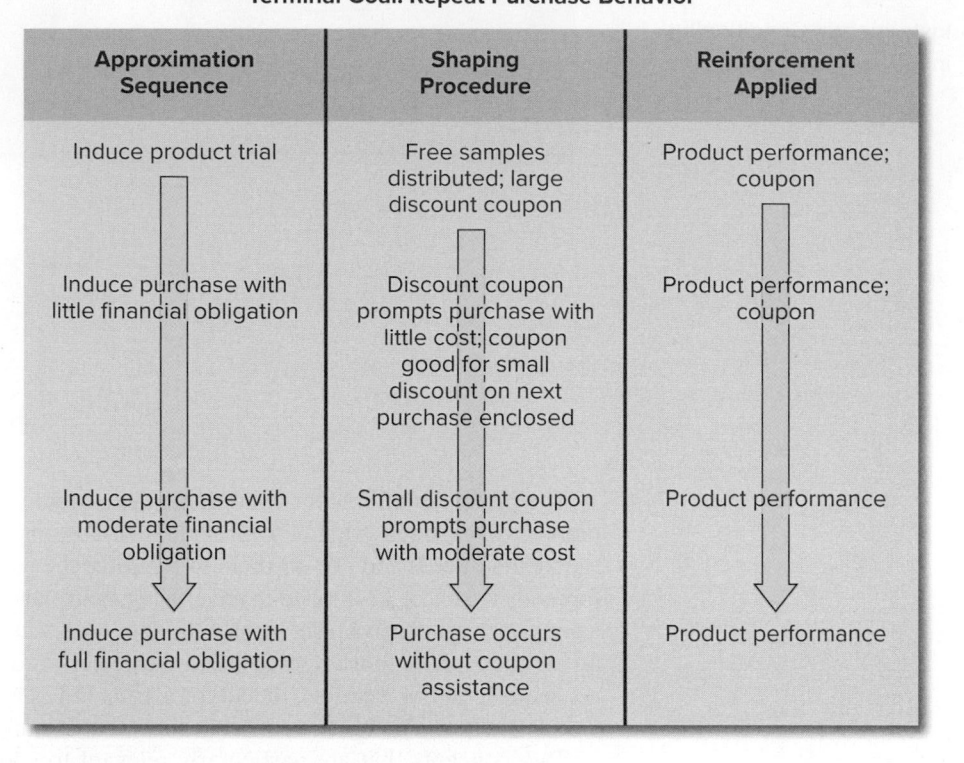

Terminal Goal: Repeat Purchase Behavior

Approximation Sequence	Shaping Procedure	Reinforcement Applied
Induce product trial	Free samples distributed; large discount coupon	Product performance; coupon
Induce purchase with little financial obligation	Discount coupon prompts purchase with little cost; coupon good for small discount on next purchase enclosed	Product performance; coupon
Induce purchase with moderate financial obligation	Small discount coupon prompts purchase with moderate cost	Product performance
Induce purchase with full financial obligation	Purchase occurs without coupon assistance	Product performance

Cognitive Learning Theory

Behavioral learning theories have been criticized for assuming a mechanistic view of the consumer that puts too much emphasis on external stimulus factors. They ignore internal psychological processes such as motivation, thinking, and perception; they assume that the external stimulus environment will elicit fairly predictable responses. Many consumer researchers and marketers disagree with the simplified explanations of behavioral learning theories and are more interested in the complex mental processes that underlie consumer decision making. The cognitive approach to studying learning and decision making has dominated the field of consumer behavior in recent years. Figure 4–10 shows how cognitive theorists view the learning process.

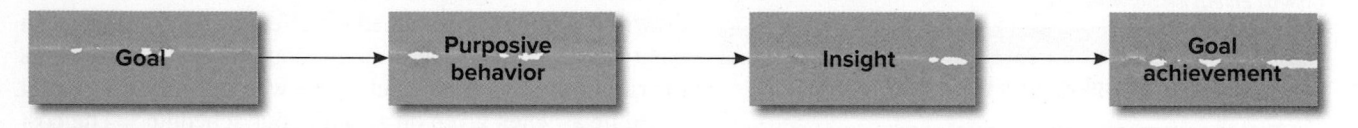

FIGURE 4–10

The Cognitive Learning
Process

Since consumer behavior typically involves choices and decision making, the cognitive perspective has particular appeal to marketers, especially those whose product/service calls for important and involved purchase decisions. Cognitive processes such as perception, formation of beliefs about brands, attitude development and change, and integration are important to understanding the decision-making process for many types of purchases. The subprocesses examined during our discussion of the five-stage decision process model are all relevant to a cognitive learning approach to consumer behavior.

ENVIRONMENTAL INFLUENCES ON CONSUMER BEHAVIOR

As seen in the lead-in to this chapter, the consumer does not make purchase decisions in isolation. A number of external factors have been identified that may influence consumer decision making. They are shown in Figure 4–11 and examined in more detail in the next sections.

FIGURE 4-11

External Influences on
Consumer Behavior

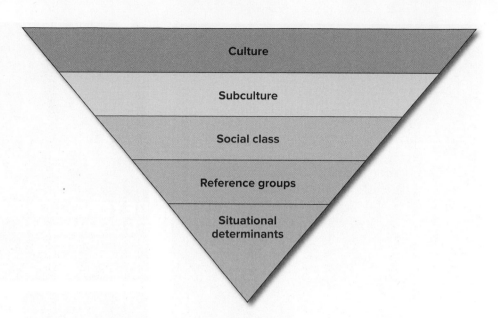

Culture

The broadest and most abstract of the external factors that influence consumer behavior is **culture**, or the complex learned meanings, values, norms, and customs shared by members of a society. Cultural norms and values offer direction and guidance to members of a society in all aspects of their lives, including their consumption behavior. It is becoming increasingly important to study the impact of culture on consumer behavior as marketers expand their international markcting efforts. Each country has certain cultural traditions, customs, and values that marketers must understand as they develop marketing programs.

Marketers must also be aware of changes that may be occurring in a particular culture and the implications of these changes for their advertising and promotional strategies and programs. American culture continually goes through many changes that have direct implications for advertising. Marketing researchers monitor these changes and their impact on the ways companies market their products and services.

While marketers recognize that culture exerts a demonstrable influence on consumers, they often find it difficult to respond to cultural differences in different markets. The subtleties of various cultures are often difficult to understand and appreciate, but marketers must understand the cultural context in which consumer purchase decisions are made and adapt their advertising and promotional programs accordingly.

Subcultures

Within a given culture are generally found smaller groups or segments whose beliefs, values, norms, and patterns of behavior set them apart from the larger cultural mainstream. These **subcultures** may be based on age, geographic, religious, racial, and/or ethnic differences. A number of subcultures exist within the United States. The three largest racial/ethnic subcultures are African Americans, Hispanics, and various Asian groups. These racial/ethnic subcultures are important to marketers because of their size, growth, purchasing power, and distinct purchasing patterns. Marketers develop specific marketing programs for various products and services for these target markets. The ads in Exhibit 4-18 are just two of the many specifically designed to appeal to U.S. subcultures—in these cases, African Americans and Hispanics. Many others can easily be found that target teens, generations X and Y, older adults, and so on.

Social Class

Virtually all societies exhibit some form of stratification whereby individuals can be assigned to a specific social category on the basis of criteria important to members of that society. **Social class** refers to relatively homogeneous divisions in a society into

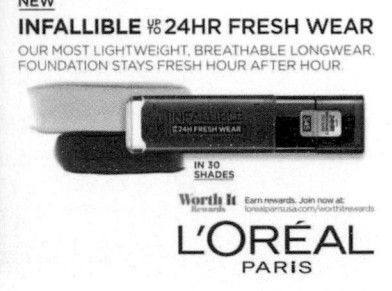

EXHIBIT 4–18

Ads targeted to subcultures.

(left) Giorgio Armani S.p.A., (right) L'Oréal International

which people sharing similar lifestyles, values, norms, interests, and behaviors can be grouped. While a number of methods for determining social class exist, class structures in the United States are usually based on occupational status, educational attainment, and income. Sociologists generally agree there are three broad levels of social classes in the United States: the upper (19 percent), middle (52 percent), and lower (29 percent) classes.[22]

Social class is an important concept to marketers, since consumers within each social stratum often have similar values, lifestyles, and buying behavior. Thus, the various social class groups provide a natural basis for market segmentation. Consumers in the different social classes differ in the degree to which they use various products and services and in their leisure activities, shopping patterns, and media habits. Marketers respond to these differences through the positioning of their products and services, the media strategies they use to reach different social classes, and the types of advertising appeals they develop. The ad in Exhibit 4–19 shows how a product attempts to appeal to the upper classes in both copy and illustration. Clearly the ad is targeted to the upper class individuals that can afford to use this means of travel, and reflects the specific market being targeted.

Reference Groups

Think about the last time you attended a party. As you dressed for the party, you probably asked yourself (or someone else) what others would be wearing. Your selection of attire may have been influenced by those likely to be present. This simple example reflects one form of impact that groups may exert on your behavior.

A group has been defined as "two or more individuals who share a set of norms, values, or beliefs and have certain implicitly or explicitly defined relationships to one another such that their behavior is interdependent."[23] Groups are one of the primary factors influencing learning and socialization, and group situations constitute many of our purchase decisions.

EXHIBIT 4–19

This American Eurocopter ad attempts to appeal to the upper classes.

American Eurocopter Corp

A **reference group** is "a group whose presumed perspectives or values are being used by an individual as the basis for their judgments, opinions, and actions." Consumers use three types of reference groups (associative, aspirational, and disassociative) as a guide to specific behaviors, even when the groups are not present. In the party example, your peers— although not present—provided a standard of dress that you referred to in your clothing selection. Likewise, your college classmates, family, and co-workers, or even a group to which you aspire, may serve as referents, and your consumption patterns will typically conform to the expectations of the groups that are most important to you.

Marketers use reference group influences in developing advertisements and promotional strategies. The ads in Exhibit 4–20 are examples of *aspirational* reference groups (to which we might like to belong) and *disassociative* groups (to which we do not wish to belong), respectively.

Family Decision Making: An Example of Group Influences In some instances, the group may be involved more directly than just as a referent. Family members may serve as referents to each other, or they may actually be involved in the purchase decision process—acting as an individual buying unit. As shown in Figure 4–12, family members may assume a variety of roles in the decision-making process. Each role has implications for marketers.

First, the advertiser must determine who is responsible for the various roles in the decision-making process so messages can be targeted at that person (or those people). These roles will also dictate media strategies, since the appropriate magazines, newspapers, or TV or radio stations must be used. Second, understanding the decision-making process and the use of information by individual family members is critical to the design of messages and choice of promotional program elements. In sum, to create an effective promotional program, a marketer must have an overall understanding of how the decision process works and the role that each family member plays.

EXHIBIT 4–20

The ad on the left from the U.S. Air Force shows an aspirational reference group. Ads like the anti-drinking one shown on the right are designed to bring attention to a problem. Like other ads, such as those in anti-smoking and anti-drug campaigns, part of the goal is to create awareness that the problem exists.

Source: (left) U.S. Air Force, (right) NYC Health

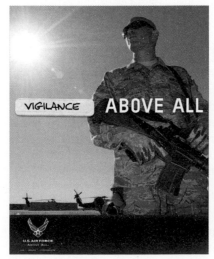

FIGURE 4–12

Roles in the Family Decision-Making Process

The initiator. The person responsible for initiating the purchase decision process—for example, the parent who determines they need a new car.

The information provider. The individual responsible for gathering information to be used in making the decision—for example, the teenage car buff who knows where to find product information in specific magazines or collects it from dealers.

The influencer. The person who exerts influence as to what criteria will be used in the selection process. All members of the family may be involved. The parent may have their criteria, whereas others may each have their own input.

The decision maker(s). The person (or persons) who actually makes (make) the decision. In our example, it may be the one parent alone or in combination with another family member.

The purchasing agent. The individual who performs the physical act of making the purchase. In the case of a car, spouses may decide to choose it together and sign the purchase agreement.

The consumer. The actual user of the product. In the case of a family car, all family members are consumers. For a private car, only one parent might be the consumer.

Situational Determinants

The final external factor is the purchase and usage situation. The specific situation in which consumers plan to use the product or brand directly affects their perceptions, preferences, and purchasing behaviors. Three types of **situational determinants** may have an effect: the specific usage situation, the purchase situation, and the communications situation.

Usage refers to the circumstance in which the product will be used. For example, purchases made for private consumption may be thought of differently from those that will be obvious to the public. The *purchase* situation more directly involves the environment operating at the time of the purchase. Time constraints, store environments, and other factors may all have an impact as was shown by the impact of COVID-19 and inflation discussed earlier. The *communications* situation is the condition in which an advertising exposure occurs (in a car listening to the radio, with friends, etc.). This may be most relevant to the development of promotional strategies because the impact on the consumer will vary according to the particular situation. For example, a consumer may pay more attention to a commercial that is heard alone at home than to one heard in the presence of friends, at work, or anywhere distractions may be present. If advertisers can isolate a particular time when the listener is likely to be attentive, they will probably earn the listener's undivided attention.

In sum, situational determinants may either enhance or detract from the potential success of a message. To the degree that advertisers can assess situational influences that may be operating, they will increase the likelihood of successfully communicating with their target audiences.

ALTERNATIVE APPROACHES TO CONSUMER BEHAVIOR

In addition to the perspectives discussed, consumer researchers complement these psychological approaches with perspectives driven from other scientific disciplines, such as economics, sociology, anthropology, philosophy, semiotics, neuroscience, and history. These cross-disciplinary perspectives have broadened the realm of methodologies used to study consumers and have provided additional insights into consumer decision processes. In addition, new technologies have provided new means for exploring consumers' behaviors.

New Methodologies

Whereas psychologists often study consumer responses to advertising and other forms of communication in controlled settings, where environmental variables can be kept constant, sociologists and anthropologists study behavior in context. For this reason, they often employ qualitative methodologies such as individual interviews, participant observation studies, and/or ethnographies. These methods help capture the social, cultural, and environmental influences that may affect consumer behavior, and may be even more effective in helping us understand than are traditional and/or online survey methods. The humanities have also been a source of new methodologies for consumer research. Historians and semioticians focus their analyses on the advertising messages and other forms of communications themselves. These researchers examine the significance of communications from a linguistic or historical perspective. Research methods such as semiotic and structural analyses examine the symbolic meanings of advertising and different facets of consumption.

New Insights

These alternative perspectives and methodologies provide additional insights and expand our knowledge of consumers. For example, the cultural significance of advertising messages in shaping cultures and triggering communities is now better understood. Likewise, marketers now have a better understanding of how advertising campaigns become popular and help shape our culture. Thanks to the many interpretive analyses of advertisements over recent years, we are also more aware of the influence of advertising images on society.

Some consumer researchers believe that cross-disciplinary research is better suited for the study of consumers because it takes into account their complexity and multidimensionality. When considered along with psychological research, these alternative approaches help us better understand the impact of communications.

Summary

This chapter introduced you to the field of consumer behavior and examined its relevance to promotional strategy. Consumer behavior is best viewed as the process and activities that people engage in when searching for, selecting, purchasing, using, evaluating, and disposing of products and services to satisfy their needs and desires. A five-stage model of the consumer decision-making process consists of problem recognition, information search, alternative evaluation, purchase, and postpurchase evaluation. Internal psychological processes that influence the consumer decision-making process include motivation, perception, attitude formation and change, and integration processes.

The decision process model views consumer behavior primarily from a cognitive orientation. The chapter considered other perspectives by examining various approaches to consumer learning and their implications for advertising and promotion. Behavioral learning theories such as classical conditioning and operant (instrumental) conditioning were discussed. Problems with behavioral learning theories were noted, and the alternative perspective of cognitive learning was discussed.

The chapter also examined relevant external factors that influence consumer decision making. Culture, subculture, social class, reference groups, and situational determinants were discussed, along with their implications for the development of promotional strategies and programs. The chapter concluded with an introduction to alternative perspectives on the study of consumer behavior.

Key Terms

consumer behavior 113
problem recognition 114
want 114
motives 115
hierarchy of needs 115
psychoanalytic theory 116
motivation research 117
internal search 119
external search 119
perception 120
sensation 120
selective perception 121
selective exposure 121
selective attention 121

selective comprehension 121
selective retention 121
mnemonics 121
subliminal perception 121
evaluative criteria 124
functional consequences 124
psychosocial consequences 124
multiattribute attitude model 125
salient beliefs 125
integration processes 126
heuristics 127
affect referral decision rule 127
purchase intention 127
brand loyalty 127

cognitive dissonance 129
classical conditioning 131
conditioned stimulus 131
conditioned response 131
operant conditioning (instrumental conditioning) 132
reinforcement 132
schedules of reinforcement 133
shaping 133
culture 135
subcultures 135
social class 135
reference group 137
situational determinants 138

Discussion Questions

1. In the lead-in to the chapter, Jagdish Sheth noted some factors that have led to major changes in consumer behaviors. Cite examples of how each of the five factors he listed have changed buying behavior. (LO 4-5)

2. Psychoanalytic theory was once considered a good theoretical basis for describing consumer behaviors, then seemingly went out of favor, only to return to prominence in the 1990's. Describe the current state of marketers' use of psychoanalytic theory to explain consumer behaviors. (LO 4-3)

3. The chapter discusses various roles in the family decision-making process. Describe each of these roles. Give examples of purchase decisions that may lead to changes in who assumes responsibilities for these roles. (LO 4-5)

4. Explain what a reference group is. Why is this concept important to marketers? Give examples of ads or other marketing activities that employ this concept. (LO 4-5)

5. What is meant by multiattribute attitude model? Why is this important to marketers? Give examples of how this model has been used in practice. (LO 4-2)

6. The chapter discusses the use of storytelling in advertising to better understand consumer behaviors. Describe what storytelling entails. What are some of the advantages of storytelling? (LO 4-6)

7. What is marketer-induced problem recognition? Give examples of how marketers have created demand for a product or service. (LO 4-2)

8. Explain the difference between a culture and a subculture. Provide examples of how both cultures and subcultures can affect consumer behaviors. (LO 4-5)

9. Marketers have studied family decision-making processes for decades. Why is it important to understand family decision making? How does family decision making impact purchase decisions? (LO 4-5)

10. What are schedules of reinforcement? Why are they important for advertisers to understand? Give an example of the use of schedules of reinforcement in advertising. (LO 4-4)

5 The Communication Process

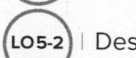

Grzegorz Czapski/Shutterstock

Learning Objectives

LO5-1 | Describe the communication process and its role in IMC.

LO5-2 | Describe the basic model of the communication process.

LO5-3 | Discuss the role of word-of-mouth influence, viral marketing, and influencer marketing.

LO5-4 | Analyze receivers' responses to marketing communications and their implications for promotional planning and strategy.

LO5-5 | Describe the influence of social media on the consumer decision process.

LO5-6 | Discuss consumers' cognitive processing of marketing communications.

Tesla Uses Word of Mouth to Lead the EV Market

When *Advertising Age*, the leading publication for the marketing and advertising industry, named its "marketers of the year" for 2021, number three on the list was Tesla, the company that pioneered the electric vehicle (EV) market in the United States and many other countries. However, there was somewhat of an irony to bestowing Elon Musk's company with this honor, as Tesla spends virtually no money on media advertising and does not even have a marketing department or a chief marketing officer (CMO). According to *Advertising Age*, Tesla spends just 11 cents on measured media per vehicle sold, which is in stark contrast to its competitors in the luxury segment of the automotive market. For example, Ford's Lincoln brand spent $1,812 per vehicle sold in 2021, Jaguar spent $1,235, Lexus spent $956, and Hyundai-owned Genesis spent $682.

Despite doing no advertising, Tesla has become the most valuable car company in the United States and one of the most sought-after brands of automobiles with an extremely loyal fan base. Tesla dominates the EV market in the United States with a 60 percent market share and set records for sales and profit in 2021, with annual revenue of nearly $54 billion, a 71 percent increase over the previous year. The company sold 1.3 million cars around the world in 2022 with much of its soaring sales volume coming from its Model 3 sedan and Model Y crossover. Tesla's market capitalization surged past $1 trillion in 2022, which put the company in an elite club that includes Amazon, Apple, Microsoft, and Google parent Alphabet.

So how does Tesla sell so many cars in an industry where nearly all of its competitors are spending hundreds of millions of dollars on advertising? Automotive experts who have studied the company say that there are a number of factors that account for Tesla's success, such as its first-mover advantage in the EV market and having a revolutionary product. However, *Advertising Age* notes that the forces shaping modern marketing often have nothing to do with big-budget advertising campaigns, and "in the case of Tesla, it means creating a product so differentiated that in many ways it sells itself, fueled by word-of-mouth marketing spread by Tesla zealots."

A major reason for Tesla's success is that it uses one of the most effective methods of marketing: word of mouth. Since its beginning, Tesla has had a strong referral program that rewards those who share their experiences with the company and its cars with others. Consumers trust recommendations from people they know—such as friends, family, and co-workers—more than advertising or other brand-owned channels. Tesla has the highest customer loyalty of all car brands with an overall satisfaction rating of over 90 percent. The company controls all steps of the customer journey and creates a very positive brand experience for its customers. Unlike traditional car companies, Tesla sells directly to consumers so they do not have to deal with a lengthy in-person sales process that often includes a pushy salesperson. The company addresses consumer complaints immediately, often using social media, which makes customers feel like they have a personal relationship with Tesla. The excellent experience Tesla owners have with the company encourages them to share it with others and "spread the good word."

Another reason for Tesla's success is what has been termed the "Elon Musk" factor, in reference to the company's mercurial CEO whose frequent tweeting brings a great deal of attention to the company on social media as well as in the mainstream media. In 2021 *Time* magazine named Musk its Person of the Year noting the positive impact he has had on the automotive market by getting other companies to invest billions in electric vehicles. In 2022 Musk was omnipresent in the news after paying $44 billion to purchase the social media company Twitter. The amount of free publicity Musk creates for Tesla is difficult to replicate and does not require the company to spend money to generate media attention, which led to its dissolving its PR department recently. However, many analysts note that much of the media attention Musk receives has become more negative, particularly given the controversy surrounding his decision to purchase Twitter. There is also concern that the fallout from the Twitter acquisition could have an impact on Tesla.

Marketing professor Kimberly Whitler describes Tesla's success: "While other companies are advertising their virtue or something other than the product they sell, Tesla has focused on, in a way, old-fashioned marketing. They simply built a

continued

spectacular widget, something that is completely different and captures the imagination of consumers. The result? The media talks about it (i.e., earned media) and consumers talk about it (word-of-mouth). . . . How many companies are focusing all of their energy and resources into building noticeably better, superior products that are worthy of earned, positive buzz?"

Some automotive analysts note that Tesla has been able to avoid having to spend money on advertising thus far as demand for it vehicles outstrips supply. They argue competition in the electric market is rapidly increasing, particularly in the luxury segment that Tesla dominates, as larger companies such as BMW, Mercedes, Volvo, Jaguar, and Lexus have added EVs to their product lines. The executive director of insights for the automotive market insights firm Edmunds notes: "Tesla will never be able to hold onto that cool niche forever—no company can. It just seems impossible because somebody will come along that is cooler and hipper. It just so happens they put out a product where there is not a lot of completion right now and that is not going to be the case in five years."

As competition in the EV market intensifies, the true test for Tesla's ability to compete without spending money on media advertising may indeed come over the next several years. It will be interesting to see if the company can continue with its unique business model that relies heavily on word of mouth and other forms of earned media. Elon Musk is confident Tesla can do so, as evidenced by a tweet sent in April 2022: "$1T valuation with $0 advertising spend." However, by the end of 2022 Tesla's market capitalization had declined by 65 percent to $341 billion as vehicle sales fell short of the 50 percent growth target Musk had pledged to meet each year. Also contributing to the decline was his sale of nearly $23 billion worth of Tesla stock to fund his acquisition of Twitter. It will be interesting to see if Musk changes his position on advertising as competition in the EV market intensifies.

Sources: Alan Ohnsman, "How Elon Musk's Twitter Takeover Is Ruining His Own Myth—and Tesla Stock," *Forbes*, November 23, 2022, https://www.forbes.com/sites/alanohnsman/2022/11/23/elon-musk-tesla-stock-twitter/?sh=2d44a3e36f81 "Datacenter: Leading National Advertisers 2022," *Advertising Age*, June 27, 2022, p. 19; E. J. Schultz, "Tesla's Great Year Came without Paid Advertising, but Plenty of Buzz," *Advertising Age*, December 13, 2021, https://adage.com/article/special-report-marketers-year/adage-2021-best-marketers-tesla/2384076; Frank Rojas, "Eight Digital Marketing Lessons We Can Learn from Tesla," *Forbes*, December 10, 2020, https://www.forbes.com/sites/forbesagencycouncil/2020/12/10/eight-digital-marketing-lessons-we-can-learn-from-tesla/?sh=2e5316ac48c8.

The function of all elements of the integrated marketing communications program is to communicate. An organization's IMC strategy is implemented through the various communications it sends to current or prospective customers as well as other relevant publics. Organizations send communications and messages in a variety of ways, such as through advertisements, brand names, logos and graphic systems, websites, social media, press releases, package designs, promotions, and visual images. As discussed in previous chapters, companies are developing more innovative ways to communicate with consumers and deliver their marketing messages, as it is becoming increasingly difficult to do so through traditional media.

The way marketers communicate with their target audiences depends on many factors, including how much current and/or potential customers know and what they think about a company or brand and the image it hopes to create. Those involved in the planning and implementation of an IMC program need to understand the communication process and what it means in terms of how they create, deliver, manage, and evaluate messages about a company or brand. Developing an effective marketing communications program is far more complicated than just choosing a product feature or attribute to emphasize. Marketers must understand how consumers will perceive and interpret their messages and how these reactions will shape consumers' responses to the company and/or its product or service. And as the use of social media and influencers becomes more prevalent, it is important that marketers understand how consumers communicate with one another and how they can participate in and even influence these conversations.

This chapter reviews the fundamentals of communication and examines various perspectives and models regarding how consumers respond to advertising and promotional messages. Our goal is to demonstrate how valuable an understanding of the communication process can be in planning, implementing, and evaluating the marketing communications program.

THE NATURE OF COMMUNICATION

Communication has been variously defined as the passing of information, the exchange of ideas, or the process of establishing a commonness or oneness of thought between a sender and a receiver.[1] These definitions suggest that for communication to occur, there must be some common thinking between two parties and information must be passed from one person to another (or from one group to another). As you will see in this chapter, establishing this commonality in thinking is not always as easy as it might seem; many attempts to communicate are unsuccessful.

The communication process is often very complex. Success depends on such factors as the nature of the message, the audience's interpretation of it, and the environment in which it is received. The receiver's perception of the source and the medium used to transmit the message may also affect the ability to communicate, as do many other factors. Words, pictures, sounds, and colors may have different meanings to different audiences, and people's perceptions and interpretations of them vary. For example, if you ask for a soda on the East Coast or West Coast, you'll receive a soft drink such as Coke or Pepsi. However, in parts of the Midwest and South, a soft drink is referred to as pop. If you ask for a soda, you may get a glass of pop with ice cream in it. Marketers must understand the meanings that words and symbols take on and how they influence consumers' interpretation of products and messages.

Language is one of the major barriers to effective communication; there are different languages in different countries, different languages or dialects within a single country, and subtler problems of linguistic nuance and vernacular. The growth of bilingual, multicultural ethnic markets in the United States is also creating challenges for domestic marketers. For example, while many marketers are recognizing the importance of appealing to the Hispanic market, they find that communicating with this fast-growing segment can be very challenging. They have to decide whether to use ads with a Hispanic-focused creative, dub or remake general market campaigns into Spanish, or run English-language ads and hope that they will appeal to bilingual Hispanics. Many companies are creating ads specifically for the Hispanic market. For example, the California Milk Processor Board recently launched a new version of its "got milk" campaign called "Never Doubt What You Love." The campaign includes Spanish language commercials featuring Afro-Latina actress/writer and Netflix *Gentefied* star Julissa Calderon (Exhibit 5–1). The decision to use Calderon in the Spanish language creative was based on her appeal to California's multicultural, millennial parents who are challenging stereotypes.

Communication can be particularly challenging to companies marketing their products and services abroad because mistranslations and faulty word choices have often created problems for companies in foreign markets. International marketers must also be aware of the connotations of the words, signs, symbols, and expressions they use as brand names or logos in various forms of promotion. Also, advertising copy, slogans, images, and symbols do not always transfer well into other languages. This not only impedes communication but also sometimes results in embarrassing blunders that can damage a company's or a brand's credibility or image. The challenges marketers face in using advertising and other IMC tools for international marketing are discussed in Chapter 19.

EXHIBIT 5–1

The "got milk" campaign uses Spanish language ads featuring Julissa Calderon to appeal to a multicultural market.

Rachel Murray/Getty Images

BASIC MODEL OF COMMUNICATION

Over the years, a basic model of the various elements of the communication process has evolved, as shown in Figure 5-1.[2] Two elements represent the major participants in the communication process: the sender and the receiver. Another two are the major communication tools: message and channel. Four others are the major communication functions and processes: encoding, decoding, response, and feedback. The last element, noise, refers to any extraneous factors in the system that can interfere with the process and work against effective communication.

Source Encoding

The sender, or **source**, of a communication is the person or organization that has information to share with another person or group of people. The source may be an individual (say, a salesperson or hired spokesperson, such as a celebrity, who appears in a company's advertisements) or a nonpersonal entity (such as the corporation or organization itself). For example, the source of many ads is the company, since no specific spokesperson or source is shown. However, many companies use a spokesperson to appear in their ads and to deliver their advertising messages. In some cases, a popular spokesperson can play a very important role in attracting attention to a company's advertising and delivering the message, as well as influencing how well it is received by the target audience. For example, the Citizen Watch Company has featured a variety of athletes and celebrities as brand ambassadors/spokespersons in the "Better Starts Now" global campaign for its Eco-Drive watches. The goal of the campaign is to communicate that Citizen is constantly innovating their watchmaking and that no matter who you are or what you do, it is always possible to make something better and now is the time to start doing it. Exhibit 5-2 shows one of the ads from the campaign featuring Japanese tennis star Naomi Osaka.

Because the receiver's perceptions of the source influence how the communication is received, marketers must be careful to select a communicator the receiver believes is knowledgeable and trustworthy or with whom the receiver can identify or relate in some manner. (How these characteristics influence the receiver's responses is discussed further in Chapter 6.)

The communication process begins when the source selects words, symbols, pictures, and the like to represent the message that will be delivered to the receiver(s). This process, known as **encoding**, involves putting thoughts, ideas, or information into a

FIGURE 5–1

A Model of the Communication Process

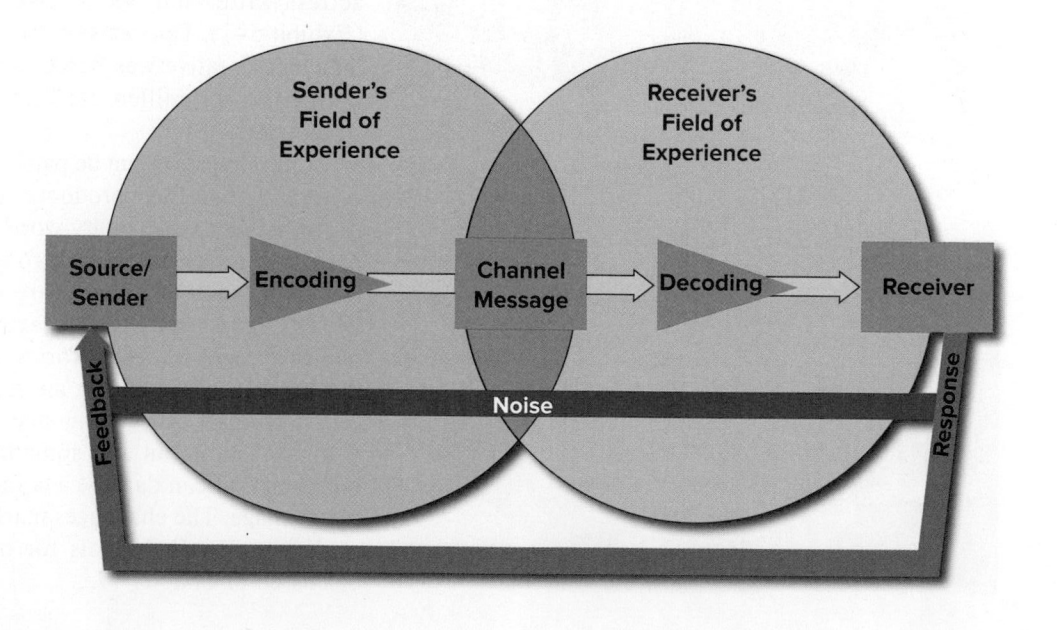

symbolic form. The sender's goal is to encode the message in such a way that it will be understood by the receiver. This means using words, signs, or symbols that are familiar to the target audience. Many symbols have universal meaning, such as the familiar circle with a line through it to denote no parking, no smoking, and so forth. Many companies also have highly recognizable logos—such as McDonald's golden arches, Nike's swoosh, or the Coca-Cola trademark—that are known to consumers around the world. Marketers must pay very close attention to the symbols associated with their company or brand such as logos as they often become a shorthand way for consumers to identify them. In some cases marketers may change their logos as a way of sending a different message to consumers. For example, Starbucks changed its logo and dropped the green ring with the text "Starbucks Coffee" to more prominently display its iconic siren. The change was made to help consumers "think beyond coffee" when they see the Starbucks logo because the company is broadening its strategic focus to include other product categories.[3] The change was also made so the logo would work in countries that do not use Western letters. In some cases, consumers may become very attached to a company's logo and react negatively when they change it. The Gap experienced this a few years ago when the retail chain introduced a redesigned logo that it felt was more contemporary. Responses to the new logo on social media were very negative, and Gap returned to its old design after just 4 days.[4] Digital and Social Media Perspective 5-1 discusses the role of logos and how they have become increasingly important in the new era of business.

Message

The encoding process leads to the development of a **message** that contains the information or meaning the source hopes to convey. The message may be verbal or nonverbal, oral or written, or symbolic. Messages must be put into a transmittable form that is appropriate for the channel of communication being used. In advertising, this may range from simply writing some words or copy that will be read as a radio message to

Megan Thee Stallion
Santa Monica Pier, Los Angeles

producing an expensive television commercial. For many products, it is not the actual words of the message that determine its communication effectiveness but rather the impression or image the ad creates. Notice how the Coach ad shown in Exhibit 5-3 uses only a picture to deliver its message. However, the use of the brand name and picture featuring rapper Megan Thee Stallion is an effective way to communicate Coach's intended message of joy and optimism through the point of view of a new generation. Coach uses a variety of image advertisements in its "That's My Ride" campaign featuring other brand ambassadors such as Jennifer Lopez, TikTok star Parker Kit Hill, and Japanese model and songwriter Koki. The ads used in the campaign debuted Coach's first-ever use of the Horse and Carriage logo, which brings a nostalgia element to the brand.[5]

Marketers must make decisions regarding the *content* of the messages they send to consumers as well as the *structure* and *design* of these messages. Content refers to the information and/or meaning contained in the message, while structure and design refer to the way the message is put together in order to deliver the information or intended meaning. More attention will be given to issues regarding message appeal and structure in the next chapter. Message design is discussed in the chapters on creative strategy (Chapters 8 and 9).

Logos Change for the New Era of Business

Before reading any further, pause for a moment and think about the logos used by well-known companies and brands. Which ones come to mind and are your favorites? Perhaps it is Nike's swoosh, McDonald's golden arches, or Starbucks' siren. In a survey, the brand strategy and design firm Siegel+Gale asked 3,000 people in the United States and United Kingdom to name the most memorable brand marks. Four companies received the majority of the votes: Nike (16 percent), Apple (15.6 percent), McDonald's (11.1 percent), and Coca-Cola (9.7 percent). Logos for some of the other leading global brands such as Google, Microsoft, Amazon, and adidas all received less than 3 percent.

Nike's famous swoosh, considered the most recognizable logo in the world, was created in 1971 by Carolyn Davidson, a graphic design student at Portland State University, for the company then known as Blue Ribbon Sports. Company founder Phil Knight contacted her to design a logo, telling her only that he wanted "something that evokes a sense of motion." Davidson produced a number of design sketches, and eventually Knight settled on the swoosh, which he thought looked like something a runner might leave in his or her wake. In his memoir book, *Shoe Dog*, Knight writes that he was not crazy about it but lacked the time and budget to develop another logo. A short time later, Knight changed the name of the company to Nike, after the Greek goddess of victory, and launched his athletic shoe brand with the swoosh on the side. Davidson was paid $35 for her 17 hours of work and went on her way, although she continued to do some design work for the company.

The use of a logo or visual symbol to distinguish one maker's wares from another has been around for hundreds of years. However, over the years, the practical notion of a logo or trademark as something that identifies the source of a product or service evolved into a more abstract idea of corporate identity. Companies began viewing logos and other visual communication elements as capturing the essence of their brand and adding value to it. They also became very protective of them, developing *standards manuals*, which delineate in very precise detail how company or brand names, logos, and other forms of visual communication can be used. One of the reasons marketers are so protective of their logos is that consumers often develop an emotional attachment to them, which can factor into their perceptions of a company or brand as well as their purchase decisions.

The way marketers think about logos has also changed, particularly for digital technology companies—such as Meta (which owns Facebook and Instagram), Snapchat, Twitter, Uber, and Airbnb—whose services are accessed primarily through apps on smartphones and whose logos are viewed every time a user swipes through a screen. These companies have become *interaction-design-centric* when developing logos and other visual symbols to make them functional as well as aesthetic. A logo or name on a digital device must be more than a branding element; it must be easy to recognize on a small screen where it may be one of many icons.

For example, Uber changed its logo a few years ago to one that shows the Uber name in white letters against a black background with only the letter U capitalized. The creative director at Wolff Olins, the global brand consultancy that led the rebranding efforts, explained the rationale behind the change. "It makes 'Uber' more legible to everyone, as it's easier to read letters of different shapes and sizes—and crucially, it enhances the difference between the first and last letters of the word, which your brain scans first, and keeps words legible even when misspelled."

Logo redesigns are not limited to technology companies as a number of other major corporations have rolled out new logos in the past year as part of their rebranding and changes in business and marketing strategies. For example, pharmaceutical giant Pfizer dispensed with its long-standing blue oval pill-shaped logo in 2021 in favor of a new logo that uses a two-tone double helix and updated font. The new logo was the first significant visual redesign for Pfizer in 70 years and was done as part of a rebranding effort that emphasizes its shift from a drug company to a science company that is in the business of curing and preventing diseases—not just treating them.

Several automotive companies have also made logo changes as part of their rebranding efforts as they move more aggressively into the electric vehicle (EV) market. General Motors recently made the biggest change to its logo in 56 years as part of its marketing push toward the EV market, which includes a $27 billion investment toward electric and autonomous vehicle development. The rebrand swaps out the old logo's dark-blue background with a white lettered uppercase monogram for a light-blue lowercase "gm" with a gradient, which sits in a white box outlined by the same light blue. Instead of having an underline on both letters, there's now a line under just the "m". General Motors' global chief marketing officer said that the new logo is meant "to reflect our modern performance-driven organization and to attract the world's most imaginative thought leaders."

Another automotive company that recently unveiled a new brand logo and slogan is Kia Motors Corp., which moved from its aged emblem showing the word Kia inside an oval to a more modern script-like logo that is composed of a stylized inscription, where all three letters are connected, "K" merged with "I" in the top point, and "I" with "A" at the bottom. As part of the makeover Kia also adopted a new slogan: "Movement that inspires." The company issued a statement noting that the automotive industry is experiencing a period of rapid transformation, and Kia is proactively shaping and adapting to these changes. Kia's CEO noted: "Our new logo represents our desire to inspire customers as their mobility needs evolve, and for our employees to rise to the challenges we face in a fast-changing industry."

Some branding experts argue that while the design of a logo is important, it is really the "logo lockup"—or its use in the context of advertising messages, sponsorships, and

Movement that inspires

Kia Corporation

GK Images/Alamy Stock Photo

GK Images/Alamy Stock Photo

rvlsoft/Shutterstock

strategy in preparation for a post–credit card world where digital payments will dominate. The company's chief marketing and communications officer explained the change by noting: "Reinvention in the digital age calls for modern simplicity. And with more than 80 percent of people spontaneously recognizing the Mastercard symbol without the word 'mastercard,' we felt ready to take this step into our brand evolution."

Redesigning logos and other visual communication elements can be very expensive and often requires a great deal of time and effort. For example, Mastercard conducted nearly 2 years of research to make sure people could identify its wordless logo. So after reading this, you might be feeling bad for Carolyn Davidson, who received only $35 for designing Nike's iconic logo. If so, you will be happy to know that she was eventually honored by Nike and given a generous amount of stock in the company (estimated to be worth nearly $1 million) as well as a diamond and gold ring featuring the swoosh design.

Sources: E. J. Schultz and Hannah Lutz, "GM Changes Logo as Part of Electric Vehicle Push," *Advertising Age*, January 11, 2021, p. 8; E. J. Schultz "Why Logo Redesigns Are on the Rise," *Advertising Age*, January 11, 2021, p. 1; Mike Snider, "Mastercard Ditches Letters for Its New Logo in Iconic Brand Move," *USA Today*, January 8, 2019, p. B1; Mark Wilson, "Uber Has a New Design. Again," *Fast Company*, September 12, 2018, https://www.fastcompany.com/90235065/uber-has-a-new-brand-again; "The $35 Nike Logo and the Woman Who Designed It," *Creative Market*, May 2, 2016, https://creativemarket.com/blog/the-35-nike-logo-and-the-woman-who-designed-it.

other forms of marketing communication—that makes it recognizable and meaningful. Debbie Millman, one of the leading designers and host of the podcast *Design Matters*, notes, "it's not the mark, but rather the marketing" that allows a logo such as the Nike swoosh to stand on its own. However, some companies do achieve the holy grail for their logos, which is the ability to be recognized outside of the logo lockup pairing. For example, Mastercard changed its logo by removing its name from the interlocking red and yellow circles. The change was part of a shift in branding

Channel

LO 5-3

The **channel** is the method by which the communication travels from the source or sender to the receiver. At the broadest level, channels of communication are of two types: nonpersonal and personal. *Nonpersonal channels* of communication are those that carry a message without direct, interpersonal contact between the sender and receiver. Nonpersonal channels are generally referred to as the **mass media** or mass communications, since the message they contain is directed to more than one person and is often sent to many individuals at one time. For example, a TV commercial broadcast on a prime-time show may be seen by 10 million people in a given evening, while a print ad appearing in a popular magazine may be seen by millions of readers over the course of a week or month.

Nonpersonal channels of communication consist of two major types: print and broadcast. Print media include newspapers, magazines, direct mail, and billboards; broadcast media include radio and television. The Internet has characteristics of both nonpersonal and personal forms of communication. It has become a mass-media vehicle as it is now an important source of information for most consumers, and many advertising messages are delivered through various forms of online advertising including banner ads, videos, paid search, and ads on social media sites. In many ways the Internet is nonpersonal in nature because consumers are often just consuming the information or content provided online and there is no personal contact between them and the companies that disseminate this information on their website or through online advertising. However, the Internet is increasingly becoming a form of personal communication since consumers can interact with marketers online as well as communicate and share information with one another through the use of various forms of social media.

Personal channels involve direct communication between two or more persons and can occur through interpersonal contact (face-to-face) or via other methods such as e-mail or through social media. Salespeople serve as personal channels of communication when they deliver a selling message or presentation to a buyer or potential customer. A major advantage of personal channels of communication is that the message or presentation can be tailored to the individual or audience, and the sender receives direct feedback from them. Members of one's social networks, such as friends, neighbors, associates, co-workers, or family members, are also personal channels of communication. They often represent **word-of-mouth (WOM)** influence that involves informal communication among consumers about products and services and is a very powerful source of information.[6]

The way WOM occurs in a marketing context has changed over the years with the emergence of the Internet and social media in particular. Andrew Baker and Naveen Donthu note that there are different forms of word of mouth in marketing including WOM conversation, electronic word of mouth (eWOM), online reviews, and engineered WOM.[7] *WOM conversations* involve an interactive dialogue between two or more consumers about a marketing-relevant topic with no apparent motive for either party. *Electronic word of mouth* is the transmission of information or consumer sentiment about a marketing-relevant topic using a digital device such as a computer or smartphone. This form of WOM generally occurs through social media platforms such as Twitter and Facebook. *Online reviews* are a consumer's evaluation of a marketplace offering submitted through an online platform purposefully designed to aggregate such evaluations. *Engineered WOM* occurs if there is an explicit commercial motive for a consumer to engage in a word-of-mouth conversation such as to earn some type of reward. Social media influencers who receive product samples or other rewards to share information or sway opinions about a brand are an example of engineered WOM often considered to be *artificial* in nature.

Many marketers work hard to generate positive word of mouth for their companies or brands using one or more of these forms of WOM. For example, a marketer may encourage consumers to discuss their product or service with other consumers in person, on social media, or by rating and/or writing a review about it on a site such as Yelp or Amazon. However, with the growth of digital and social media, many marketers are using engineered WOM to bring attention to or generate discussion about their company or brands. **Buzz marketing** is a term used to describe word-of-mouth communication about a company, its products, services, and/or brands, as well as its advertising messages, and is often encouraged by a marketer. Efforts by marketers to generate word-of-mouth discussion about their brands is really nothing new, as tactics such as handing out samples and providing products to influential people and encouraging them to recommend the brand to others have been used for many years. For example, alcoholic beverage marketers have long understood the value of getting bartenders and servers to hype their brands, while pharmaceutical companies often encourage influential physicians to discuss the benefits of their products with peers.

Viral Marketing In the era of digital media, traditional word-of-mouth and buzz marketing techniques have given way to more systematic and organized efforts to encourage people to speak favorably about a company or brand and to recommend it to others in their social network. Many marketers are using **viral marketing**, which refers to the act of propagating marketing-relevant messages through the help and cooperation of individual consumers.[8] Marketers, along with their agencies, work to draw attention to their brands in a variety of ways such as encouraging consumers to create user-generated content (UGC)—pictures, videos, product usage ideas—that can be shared with others on their websites or through social media sites such as Facebook, Twitter, Instagram, and YouTube. For example, GoPro uses viral marketing successfully by encouraging its loyal users to upload their best and most inspirational videos and photos to social media sites such as Twitter, YouTube, and Instagram using the dedicated #GoPro hashtag. User-generated content captured using a GoPro camera can be entered into various challenges and contests where creators are rewarded with cash prizes and merchandise (Exhibit 5-4). GoPro also re-posts its "Photo of the Day" to Instagram to recognize work submitted by its users and has more than 10 million subscribers to its YouTube channel.[9]

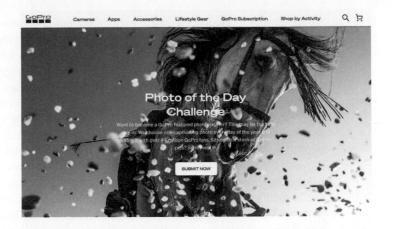

Successful viral marketing can be very difficult to achieve, as the process is affected by many factors that are often beyond a marketer's control. Researchers have identified three major factors that affect the success of a viral marketing program: message characteristics, individual sender or receiver characteristics, and social network characteristics.[10] Message characteristics relate to the content and creative design of a viral message and include factors such as whether the information is entertaining, engaging, novel, humorous, and/or informative. Many videos and commercials have a strong viral component that make them popular and encourage consumers to watch as well as share them. For example, major marketers spend large sums of money to create entertaining and engaging commercials to run during the Super Bowl each year in anticipation that the ads will be previewed and shared leading up to the game as well as watched during and after. The viral component has become an important factor in many companies' decision to advertise during the Super Bowl.[11]

In addition to the message, characteristics of the individual consumer also play an important role in the viral marketing process. Factors such as demographics, personality traits, and motivation for sharing content and messages as well as receiving them impact the effectiveness of viral campaigns.[12] For example, female and younger consumers tend to exert more influence on their target recipients and be more susceptible to viral influences than do male and older consumers, while traits such as extroversion, innovativeness, and altruism are related to tendencies to share messages.[13] Insight into motivations for social sharing comes from a study done by Unruly, an ad marketing technology company that focuses on what is watched and shared online. Its analysis of over 430 billion video views and 100,000 consumer data points revealed that the two most powerful drivers of viral success are psychological response (how the content makes you feel) and social motivation (why you want to share it).[14] Unruly has identified 10 motivations for social sharing, which are shown in Figure 5-2.

With regard to social network characteristics, the structure of networks through which a message spreads as well as the consumers' position in the social network, as defined by relationships with others, can influence the diffusion of a viral message. Many marketers

FIGURE 5-2

Motivations for Social
Sharing of Videos

Adapted from "Why Some Videos Go
Viral" from *Harvard Business Review*,
September 2015. https://hbr.org/
2015/09/ why-some-videos-go-viral.

Opinion Seeking	I want to see what my friends think.
Shared Passion	It lets me connect with my friends about a shared interest.
Conversation Starting	I want to start an online conversation.
Social Utility	This could be useful to my friends.
Self-Expression	It says something about me.
Social in Real Life	It will help me socialize with my friends offline.
Social Good	It's for a good cause and I want to help.
Zeitgeist	It's about a current trend or event.
Kudos: Authority	I want to demonstrate my knowledge.
Kudos: Cool Hunting	I want to be the first to tell my friends.

try to identify individuals who are very influential in various social media domains, such as influencers, bloggers, and persons with a large number of Facebook, Instagram, TikTok, or Twitter fans and followers; then the marketers work hard to get their messages to these individuals in hopes that they pass them on to others in their social network.

Another important aspect of viral marketing is what is often referred to as **seeding**, which involves identifying and choosing the initial group of consumers who will be used to start the diffusion or spreading of a message.[15] Companies that utilize viral marketing must develop a *seeding strategy*, which involves determining how many initial consumers or "seeds" are needed and selecting the right consumers to start and maintain the viral process.

With the growth of social media, most viral marketing is done today through **influencer marketing**, which uses social media to leverage the influence of individuals with a dedicated social media following. These **social media influencers** are often popular social media personalities who constantly create and disseminate useful and organic content within a knowledge domain, project authentic personae, curate intimate relations with a large following, and thus wield influence over followers' purchases and decision making.[16] Joachim Scholz notes that given their origins as "ordinary" consumers, influencers are generally conceptualized as similar to everyday consumers and hence, more authentic than models and celebrities who are traditionally featured in advertising.[17] Since followers often trust influencers and perceive them as experts and/or tastemakers in their areas or domain, marketers can collaborate with them to promote their brands through recommendations or featured content on various social media platforms such as YouTube, Instagram, and TikTok.

Social media influencers have become a major part of the marketing strategy for many companies as global spending on influencer marketing has skyrocketed from around $3 billion in 2017 to an estimated $16.4 billion in 2022.[18] Several factors have changed the shape of influencer marketing recently and led to its increased use by marketers. The COVID-19 pandemic created ideal conditions for influencer marketing to thrive as consumers were spending most of their time at home, and since brands were unable to rely on retail stores to showcase their products, many turned to influencers to do so. Influencers have also become much more sophisticated as many have become content creators who have unique and engaging content to share and collaborate closely with marketers, while others are lifestyle influencers, thought leaders, or brand ambassadors who often become key opinion leaders (KOL) and influential advocates for a company or brand.[19] Figure 5-3 shows

FIGURE 5–3

How Influencers Define Themselves

Source: WARC © Impact.com survey–Influencers.

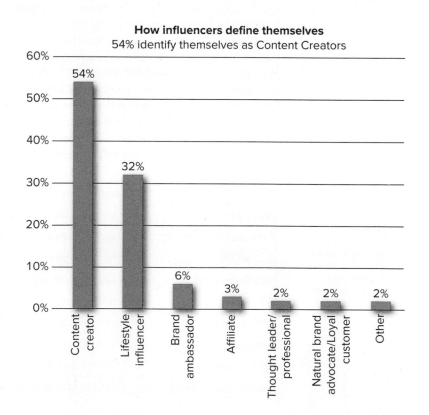

How influencers define themselves
54% identify themselves as Content Creators

EXHIBIT 5–5

Open Influence is an agency that specializes in creating influencer marketing campaigns for companies.

Open Influence Inc.

how influencers define themselves based on a survey conducted by market intelligence firm WARC. Digital and Social Media Perspective 5–2 discusses the explosion in influencer marketing that has occurred in recent years and how marketers are collaborating with social media influencers.

There are advertising agencies and other companies that specialize in working with companies to develop influencer marketing programs. For example, Open Influence is an agency that specializes in influencer marketing and has created campaigns for brands such as Amazon Prime, Bose, Target, and Barilla. The agency collaborates with influencers on content creation as well as brands and social media platforms to assist in the development and execution of influencer marketing campaigns (Exhibit 5–5). Some companies are also building their own online communities so consumers can chat about product experiences and share information online, for example, lululemon, Starbucks, and Gymshark. Procter & Gamble, which is one of the world's largest advertisers, operates a word-of-mouth brand community called Vocalpoint to reach the most influential group of shoppers in America: moms. P&G has broadened the focus of Vocalpoint to include women ages 28 to 45 and now has more than 670,000 members. These women are very involved with their social networks through social media such as Facebook, Twitter, and various blogs and speak or interact with a number of other women during a typical day.

Integrating Word of Mouth with IMC   While viral techniques have become a popular way to generate buzz about a brand, research conducted by the Keller Fay Group—a market research company that focuses on word-of-mouth marketing—has shown that some 90 percent of conversations about products, services, and brands take place offline.[20] Face-to-face interaction accounts for the vast majority of word-of-mouth communications (75 percent) about a brand; phone conversations rank second (15 percent). Only 10 percent of word of mouth takes place through online channels such as e-mail/instant messages, blogs, and chat rooms. Their research also shows that nearly half the word-of-mouth conversations contained references to the various IMC tools used for a brand, including print and television ads, websites, and other marketing tools such as point-of-sale displays and promotions.

Another important finding was that word-of-mouth conversations influenced by advertising are significantly more likely to involve recommendations to buy or try a brand when compared to other WOM-induced discussions about brands. Moreover, these WOM discussions are very powerful, as consumers ascribe a high credibility to the information they hear from others; 50 percent say they are very likely to buy as a result of these conversations.[21]

Subsequent research by Keller Fay has found that the role of advertising in WOM is even stronger, as a quarter of all consumer conversations about brands involve discussions about advertising. And of the brand conversations in which consumers talk about advertising, television advertising is the most prevalent form, which is not

Influencer Marketing Continues to Grow

Marketers have long used influential people to help sell their products and services. When we watch television or read a magazine, many of the ads feature celebrities such as actors, entertainers, or athletes. Companies often pay them large sums of money to attract attention to their advertising messages as well as to have their brands associated with them. However, many marketers are rethinking their use of celebrity endorsers, and rather than using them in TV spots, print ads, or billboards, they are paying them to post messages about their brands on social media. And they are giving them large amounts of money to do so.

Hopper HQ, a company that schedules posts on Instagram, publishes an Instagram Rich list each year to highlight the top influencers on the social media site along with how much they charge per sponsored post. The Kardashian–Jenner family reigns supreme; four of the sisters made the top 10, with Kylie Jenner taking the top spot at a fee of $1.8 million per post to deliver a message to her 329 million followers. Kim Kardashian receives a cool $1.7 million per post and has 312 million followers, while sister Khloe gets $1.3 million for posting to her 237 million followers; Kendall Jenner also pulls down around $1.3 million dollars every time she posts to her 238 million Instagram followers. Two of the top three on the list are international soccer stars who play in the UEFA Champions League. Portugal's Cristian Ronaldo sits at the top of the list with 442 million followers and makes an average of $2.3 million per post, while Lionel Messi from Argentina ranks number 3 and receives nearly $1.8 million per post. Other celebrities in the top 10 on the Instagram Rich list include singer/actor Selena Gomez, actor Dwayne "The Rock" Johnson, and singers Ariana Grande and Beyoncé.

Most of the influencers on the Instagram Rich list do not receive the exorbitant fees that the A-list celebrities command, nor do they have tens of millions of followers. However, many of them are making a very nice living as more marketers rely on influencers to help drive brand mentions, positive sentiment, and favorable associations for their brands. Social media influencers exist on all of the major social media platforms, including Facebook, Instagram, TikTok, Twitter, Snapchat, and YouTube, as well as on smaller platforms such as Twitch and Musical.ly. And many of them have their own blogs where they discuss fashion, sports, food, entertainment, business, and myriad other topics and interests.

The use of influencers has increased dramatically in recent years. Surveys have shown that nearly 90 percent of marketers use at least one viral or influencer marketing campaign each year, and nearly three-quarters plan to maintain or increase their budgets for influencers. There are several reasons marketers are making influencer campaigns an integral part of their IMC programs. Not only is it difficult to reach consumers through traditional media advertising, it is becoming very challenging to reach them online as well. Nearly half of consumers are now using ad blockers, which means that marketers cannot rely on digital advertising through search, display, and social media to target them. However, it is possible to reach them through the Instagram, TikTok, or Facebook sites of influencers because that is where many people now spend time when they go online.

Marketers view influencers as providing targeted exposure to the right kind of consumer: one who is already interested and likely to pay attention. They are also turning to influencers to leverage the authenticity embedded in the connections they have with their friends and followers on social media. These followers don't feel they are being "influenced" or manipulated when they scroll through their Facebook, TikTok, or Instagram feeds and look at pictures or videos from their favorite influencer or blogger. Many of the influencers have become very savvy about how to collaborate with marketers and share their experiences with or opinions about a brand in a subtle but effective way.

While the top celebrities and athletes with mega numbers of followers get much of the attention, many marketers are turning to other categories of influencers, including nano- and micro-influencers. Nano-influencers are generally defined as someone with 500 to 10,000 followers, while micro-influencers have between 10,000 and 100,000 followers. These types of influencers include everyday people, rather than celebrities, who have a real passion or high level of expertise in areas such as fashion, beauty, travel, or fitness, as well as other very specific areas. There are even social media influencers who focus on social media and provide information on how to stay up to date with the latest trends, developments, and content on sites such as LinkedIn, Twitter, Facebook, and Instagram.

There are several reasons many marketers are allocating more of their budgets to nano- and micro-influencers rather than to the macro-influencers with large fan bases. Many experts argue that while these bloggers have a smaller following, they often have higher engagement rates, and their content performs better than the posts of those with large numbers of followers. Research has shown that influencers with 1,000 to 10,000 followers have "like" rates of about 4 percent. This drops to 2.4 percent for those with 10,000 to 100,000 followers, and to just under 2 percent for those with more than a million followers. Many of the macro-influencers with large numbers of followers also have a very diverse fan base, which means marketers may be paying to reach people who are not viable prospects for their brands. Nano- and micro-influencers usually cater to specific, niche audiences that are very interested in the products, services, or topics and are looking for information to help them make purchase decisions. The micro-bloggers often connect better with their followers, which makes them more trustworthy, authentic, and relatable.

Another reason marketers, particularly those with smaller budgets, are collaborating with nano- and micro-influencers is cost, as they charge less per post than do influencers with large followings, which makes them more affordable. Although, brands will need to partner with a number of micro-influencers to reach a large audience, the total costs will often still be lower than the fees required to use a macro-blogger. Pricing of influencer campaigns has become more complex as the cost to use influencers has evolved beyond follower counts. Now, pricing can include considerations such as content type, key performance indicators (KPIs) a marketer is trying to achieve, and whether a brand wants exclusivity for a product or service category. Pricing may also differ depending on whether a marketer goes through an influencer agency, which will take a percentage that can range from 10 to 40 percent, or negotiates a deal directly with influencers.

The use of influencers will continue to grow and become part of the IMC programs for both large and small companies. However, one problem that marketers, as well as social media platforms, are dealing with is measurement of followers, which is an issue for the mega-influencers as well as nano- and micro-bloggers. Some influencers purchase followers or use bots, software that follows and unfollows, comments, and likes other accounts automatically to attract attention to their account. Follower count is meaningless if a substantial number of an influencer's audience is fake. There are warning signs that marketers should pay attention to such as a sudden, erratic spike in followers, which indicates the influencer has purchased followers in order to command a higher price per post.

Social media platforms have been responding to pressure to eradicate the bots, but the problem is far from being solved. Ultimately, the influencers themselves must recognize that consumers' willingness to follow them— as well as marketers' willingness to use them—depends on their ability to build and maintain an active, authentic, and engaged audience of *real* followers.

Sources: Amal Moursi, "The 2022 Instagram Rich List—Who Earns the Most from Sponsored Instagram Posts," *h hopper*, July 13, 2022, https://www.hopperhq.com/blog/2022-instagram-rich-list/; Werner Geyser, "The State of Influencer Marketing 2022," "Benchmark Report, Influencer Marketing Hub, March 2, 2022, https://influencermarketinghub.com/influencer-marketing-benchmark-report/; Erika Wheless, "Why Nano-Influencers Are Important for Brands," *Advertising Age*, September 21, 2021, https://adage.com/article/digital-marketing-ad-tech-news/why-nano-influencers-are-important-brands/2366426; Ilyse Lifrfreing, "Behind the Cost for Brands to Hire Influencers," *Advertising Age*, August 18, 2021, https://adage.com/article/digital-marketing-ad-tech-news/behind-cost-brands-hire-influencers-complex-math-explained/2358736.

surprising given that more money is spent on TV ads than any other medium. However, collectively, other forms of advertising including magazines, newspapers, the Internet, radio, and outdoor are about equal with respect to generating conversations about advertising, which suggests that a variety of IMC tools can be used to drive word of mouth.[22]

These findings are very important from an integrated marketing communications perspective in several respects. First, they show that there can be powerful "pass-along" benefits from consumers talking favorably about a brand and referencing various elements of its IMC program. However, with consumers being bombarded by so many irrelevant marketing messages each day, it is very difficult to get them to talk about them. Thus, marketers must develop creative advertisements and other forms of communication that can trigger conversations and are worthy of sharing. They also reinforce the importance of marketers recognizing that all of the IMC elements work in unison to impact how consumers perceive a brand and the word-of-mouth discussion that is generated by it. The fact that consumers appear to be influenced the most by their conversations with other people shows that marketers need to finds ways to favorably influence these interactions. A recent study by the Publicis agency in conjunction with Twitter studied 9,600 consumers on six social media platforms across the United States, the United Kingdom, India, and Mexico. The survey found that 92 percent of consumers actively seek out comments about brands, products, or services on social media and, more importantly, 68 percent said their impression of a brand was changed as a result of experiencing a brand conversation. The study also found that online conversation is most impactful early in the purchase journey, which suggests people may be more impressionable well before they develop their consideration set of alternatives.[23]

While the use of buzz and viral marketing campaigns is becoming more prevalent, concern has been expressed over its use and whether the person spreading the product message should disclose their affiliation. The Word of Mouth Marketing Association was formed in 2004 to promote and improve the use of word-of-mouth marketing and protect consumers and the industry by providing ethical guidelines for its use. WOMMA has developed a set of rules and guidelines that mandate that marketers must make sure that people recommending products or services disclose whom they are working for. Gary Ruskin, the former executive director of Commercial Alert, a nonprofit organization dedicated to protecting consumers from commercial exploitation, notes that without such disclosures there is "a danger of the basic commercialization of human relations, where friends treat one another as advertising pawns, undercutting social trust."[24]

With the explosion in the use of influencer marketing, there is also concern over endorsements being made on social media by influencers. The Federal Trade Commission now requires anyone endorsing a product or service through social media to disclose whether they have a relationship (material connection) with the company or brand. A *material connection* includes a personal, family, or employment relationship or a financial relationship—such as the brand paying or giving the endorser free or discounted products or services. Regulation of advertising and other areas of IMC is discussed in Chapter 20.

Experts note that viral marketing techniques are very resistant to manipulation, and marketers must be careful about how they use them. Several companies have had viral marketing campaigns backfire when consumers recognized that the companies were artificially trying to promote buzz for their brands. Some argue that the growing popularity of viral marketing could well spell its downfall, because when consumers recognize that everyone is trying to create a buzz for their brand, they are likely to be turned off by the technique.[25] However, with the growth of social media and consumers becoming less attentive to and interested in traditional media advertising, it is likely that marketers will continue to seek ways to develop and deliver branded content and messages that consumers will share with one another. This will extend the reach and impact of their marketing messages and may add an implicit consumer endorsement as well.

The effective use of viral marketing requires that marketers take a strategic approach in the development and implementation of campaigns that are designed to have strong WOM and viral components. For example, Keller and Fay note that marketers should think in terms of social consumers rather than just social media and focus on the stories that consumers share with one another about a brand or a product or service category to ensure that there is a good fit between the consumer story and the brand story. They also suggest that it is the job of brand strategists to identify the people who are most likely to talk about their brand or category and seek to understand when, where, and why people talk.[26]

It is important for marketers to recognize that online and offline conversation channels often work independently of one another, and strategies and tactics may be needed for each. Fay and Larkin analyzed over a decade's worth of research to determine if there are relationships between online and offline conversations and found almost no correlations between the two. They concluded that the online and offline worlds behave like separate ecosystems, with their own features and characteristics. Thus, marketers should not make the mistake of assuming that a social media strategy can substitute for a social influence strategy through offline word-of-mouth conversations.[27]

Receiver/Decoding

The **receiver** is the person(s) with whom the sender shares thoughts or information. Generally, receivers are the consumers in the target market or audience who read, hear, and/or see the marketer's message and decode it. **Decoding** is the process of transforming the sender's message back into thought. This process is heavily influenced by the receiver's frame of reference or **field of experience**, which refers to the experiences, perceptions, attitudes, and values he or she brings to the communication situation.

For effective communication to occur, the message decoding process of the receiver must match the encoding of the sender. Simply put, this means the receiver understands and correctly interprets what the source is trying to communicate. As Figure 5–1 showed, the source and the receiver each have a frame of reference (the circle around each) that they bring to the communication situation. Effective communication is more

EXHIBIT 5–6

This ad uses the concept of common ground.

Ken Stinnett Photography

likely when there is some *common ground* between the two parties. (This is represented by the overlapping of the two circles.) The more knowledge the sender has about the receivers, the better the sender can understand their needs, empathize with them, and communicate effectively. Exhibit 5–6 shows an ad for the Pew Environmental Group's Campaign for America's Wilderness that uses the concept of common ground by noting how both Republicans and Democrats agree on the importance of protecting the American wilderness by passing legislation to give permanent protection to wilderness land in 13 states.

While this notion of common ground between sender and receiver may sound basic, it often causes great difficulty in the advertising communications process. Marketing and advertising people often have very different fields of experience from the consumers who constitute the mass markets with whom they must communicate. Most are college-educated and work and/or reside in large urban areas such as New York, Chicago, or Los Angeles. Many of them are young, fashionable, upwardly mobile people with busy professional and social lives, avid interest in music and movies and the latest clubs and restaurants, and few distractions like children or elderly parents who need looking after. Yet they are often creating ads that must communicate with millions of consumers who have never attended college, work in blue-collar occupations, and/or live in rural areas or small towns. The executive creative director of a large advertising agency described how advertising executives become isolated from the cultural mainstream: "We pull them in and work them to death. And then they begin moving in sushi circles and lose touch with Velveeta and the people who eat it."[28]

Another factor that can lead to problems in establishing common ground between senders and receivers is age. As the population of the United States and many other countries grows older, concern has been expressed over the potential problems that might arise because of age differences between advertising agency personnel and older consumers. It has long been argued that there is a youth bias in advertising and related industries.[29] The claim is that marketers are fixated with reaching younger consumers while paying less attention to those over the age of 50, despite the fact that older consumers control half of the wealth, spend trillions of dollars on products and services each year, and comprise a large percentage of the population in most countries. Studies have shown that professionals working in advertising agencies in the United States, as well as other countries, are much younger than the adult population. According to the Bureau of Labor Statistics, 67 percent of the workers in advertising, public relations, and related services are under the age of 45, with a median age of 39. The youth bias is particularly evident in creative departments because many of those who work in this area are under the age of 40. The age of advertising employees is even younger in other countries such as Australia and the United Kingdom. A recent study found that less than 10 percent of advertising practitioners are over the age of 45.

There are several reasons agencies hire younger personnel. One reason is basic economics: Younger employees cost less, and in an industry notorious for taking every opportunity to cut costs, a 20-year veteran copywriter is more expensive than a recent college graduate. (That younger, less experienced employees are paid less is, of course, true in most industries, not just advertising.) A second reason is creativity; many agencies feel that younger employees are better suited to creative thinking, especially under tight deadlines and high pressure to perform. A third reason is the digital divide, since much of the bias toward younger workers is the result of the advancements in digital

"You use tech language that I don't understand, so I brought an interpreter."

EXHIBIT 5–7

Ageism is an issue in the advertising industry.

Jerry King Cartoons

technology that have transformed the industry over the past two decades. Agencies, as well as marketers, are looking for tech-savvy youth who are digital natives and understand how to reach and engage consumers through mobile marketing, social media, and other digital platforms (Exhibit 5–7).

Critics of the advertising industry argue that ageism is a major problem as it often results in older consumers being shunned and caricatured in ads, perpetuating unrealistic stereotypes and contributing to age discrimination.[30] Martin Eisen notes several reasons why older people are often neglected in advertising in favor of younger people. First, innovators and early adopters of many products are typically younger and thus advertising often targets younger people, even for products used by consumers of all ages. He also notes that the advertising industry has a "hipster" image and, as noted previously, most of the people working in the industry are young. These younger practitioners may consciously or unconsciously choose endorsers or cast people in ads with whom they can identify, which contributes to the high number of young people appearing in ads. Finally, Eisen argues that advertising research has provided evidence that the physical attractiveness of endorsers has positive effects and increases evaluation of ads, brand attitudes, and purchase attentions. Since older people are rated lower in attractiveness than younger people, it is not surprising that advertisers make extensive use of younger people in their ads that resemble the ideal of attractiveness and beauty.[31]

Many argue that most advertising is often about the people who create it, not about the consumers who actually buy the products and services being advertised. It is important that marketers and their agencies understand the frame of reference and perspectives of the consumers in the target markets that are receiving their messages. Many companies spend a considerable amount of time and money pretesting advertising messages to make sure consumers understand them and decode them in the manner intended. Pretesting advertising messages is discussed in more detail in Chapter 18.

Noise

Throughout the communication process, the message is subject to extraneous factors that can distort or interfere with its reception. This unplanned distortion or interference is known as **noise**. Errors or problems that occur in the encoding of the message, distortion in a radio or television signal, and distractions at the point of reception are examples of noise. When you are watching an ad on TV or listening to a radio commercial and a problem occurs in the signal transmission, it will obviously interfere with your reception, lessening the impact of the commercial. Over the past decade a new type of noise has become prevalent in the television viewing environment: the distraction of technology such as laptops, tablets, and mobile phones/smartphones. The majority of people now multitask while watching television, with most of them doing so on a digital device such as a smartphone, tablet, or desktop/laptop computer. Studies by eMarketer have found that nearly three-quarters of the adult population regularly uses another digital device while watching television.[32] Several studies have found that completely undistracted viewers are a minority, as only around 10 percent report doing nothing else while watching television.[33] A survey conducted by digital television technology company TiVo found that more than 80 percent of respondents multitask almost every time or sometimes during a commercial break. A more recent study by Deloitte Media found that 91 percent of Australian viewers multitasked while watching television, up from 79 percent in 2014. Multitasking was even higher among millennials: 96 percent multitasked. Nearly 60 percent of multitasking took place on smartphones while 30 percent was on laptops and tablets. Favorite activities included surfing the Internet, e-mailing, texting, and using social media.[34]

While some types of multitasking involve activities such as reading a magazine or book, the use of digital devices is particularly troublesome for advertisers. A study found that nearly half of the marketing executives surveyed feel that consumers being distracted by a second screen is one of the top factors that limit the effectiveness of their television advertising. The vast majority of the executives noted that it has become difficult to capture consumers' attention solely through TV advertising, which is why many marketers are allocating more of their budgets to digital and social media.[35]

Noise may also occur because the fields of experience of the sender and receiver don't overlap. Lack of common ground may result in improper encoding of the message—using a sign, symbol, or words that are unfamiliar or have different meaning to the receiver. The more common ground there is between the sender and the receiver, the less likely it is this type of noise will occur.

Response/Feedback

The receiver's set of reactions after seeing, hearing, or reading the message is known as a **response**. Receivers' responses can range from nonobservable actions such as storing information in memory to immediate action such as clicking through an online ad to go to a marketer's landing page or website or dialing a toll-free number to order a product advertised on television. Marketers are very interested in **feedback**, that part of the receiver's response that is communicated back to the sender. Feedback, which may take a variety of forms, closes the loop in the communications flow and lets the sender monitor how the intended message is being decoded and received.

For example, in a personal-selling situation, customers may pose questions, comments, or objections or indicate their reactions through nonverbal responses such as gestures and frowns.[36] The salesperson has the advantage of receiving instant feedback through the customer's reactions. But this is generally not the case when mass media are used. Because advertisers are not in direct contact with the customers, they must use other means to determine how their messages have been received. While the ultimate form of feedback occurs through sales, it is often hard to show a direct relationship between advertising and purchase behavior. So marketers use other methods to obtain feedback, among them customer inquiries, store visits, coupon redemptions, and reply cards. Research-based feedback analyzes readership and recall of ads, message comprehension, attitude change, and other forms of response. With this information, the advertiser can determine reasons for success or failure in the communication process and make adjustments.

Successful communication is accomplished when the marketer selects an appropriate source, develops an effective message or appeal that is encoded properly, and then selects the channels or media that will best reach the target audience so that the message can be effectively decoded and delivered. In Chapter 6, we will examine the source, message, and channel decisions and see how promotional planners work with these controllable variables to develop communication strategies. Since these decisions must consider how the target audience will respond to the promotional message, the remainder of this chapter examines the receiver and the process by which consumers respond to advertising and other forms of marketing communications.

ANALYZING THE RECEIVER

To communicate effectively with their customers, marketers must understand who the target audience is, what (if anything) it knows or feels about the company's product or service, and how to communicate with the audience to influence its decision-making process. Marketers must also know how the market is likely to respond to various sources of communication or different types of messages. Before

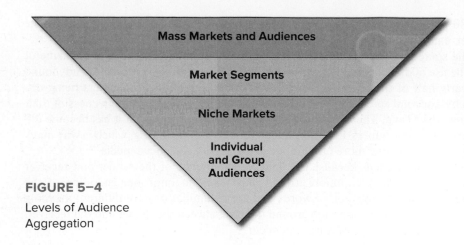

FIGURE 5–4

Levels of Audience
Aggregation

Mass Markets and Audiences

Market Segments

Niche Markets

Individual
and Group
Audiences

they make decisions regarding source, message, and channel variables, promotional planners must understand the potential effects associated with each of these factors. This section focuses on the receiver of the marketing communication. It examines how the audience is identified and the process it may go through in responding to a promotional message. This information serves as a foundation for evaluating the controllable communication variable decisions in the next chapter.

Identifying the Target Audience

The marketing communication process really begins with identifying the audience that will be the focus of the firm's advertising and promotional efforts. The target audience may consist of individuals, groups, niche markets, market segments, or a general public or mass audience (Figure 5-4). Marketers approach each of these audiences differently.

The target market may consist of *individuals* who have specific needs and for whom the communication must be specifically tailored. This often requires person-to-person communication and is generally accomplished through personal selling. Other forms of communication, such as advertising, may be used to attract the audience's attention to the firm, but the detailed message is carried by a salesperson who can respond to the specific needs of the individual customer. Life insurance, financial services, and real estate are examples of products and services promoted this way.

A second level of audience aggregation is represented by the *group*. Marketers often must communicate with a group of people who make or influence the purchase decision. For example, organizational purchasing often involves buying centers or committees that vary in size and composition. Companies marketing their products and services to other businesses or organizations must understand who is on the purchase committee, what aspect of the decision each individual influences, and the criteria each member uses to evaluate a product. Advertising and other forms of marketing communication may be directed at each member of the buying center, and multilevel personal selling may be necessary to reach those individuals who influence or actually make decisions.

Marketers look for customers who have similar needs and wants and thus represent some type of market segment that can be reached with the same basic communication strategy. Very small, well-defined groups of customers are often referred to as *market niches*. They can usually be reached through personal-selling efforts or highly targeted media such as direct mail. The next level of audience aggregation is *market segments*, broader classes of buyers who have similar needs and can be reached with similar messages. As we saw in Chapter 2, there are various ways of segmenting markets and reaching the customers in these segments. As market segments get larger, marketers usually turn to broader-based media such as newspapers, magazines, and TV to reach them.

Marketers of most consumer products attempt to attract the attention of large numbers of present or potential customers (*mass markets*) through mass communication such as advertising or publicity. Mass communication is a one-way flow of information from the marketer to the consumer. Feedback on the audience's reactions to the message is generally indirect and difficult to measure.

TV advertising, for example, lets the marketer send a message to millions of consumers at the same time. But this does not mean effective communication has occurred. This may be only one of several hundred messages the consumer is exposed to that day.

There is no guarantee the information will be attended to, processed, comprehended, or stored in memory for later retrieval. Even if the advertising message is processed, it may not interest consumers or may be misinterpreted by them. Studies by Jacob Jacoby and Wayne D. Hoyer have shown that nearly 20 percent of all print ads and even more TV commercials are miscomprehended by readers.[37]

Unlike personal or face-to-face communications, mass communications do not offer the marketer an opportunity to explain or clarify the message to make it more effective. The marketer must enter the communication situation with knowledge of the target audience and how it is likely to react to the message. This means the receiver's response process must be understood, along with its implications for promotional planning and strategy.

THE RESPONSE PROCESS

Perhaps the most important aspect of developing effective integrated marketing communications programs involves understanding the *response process* the receiver may go through in moving toward a specific behavior (like purchasing a product) and how the promotional efforts of the marketer influence consumer responses. In many instances, the marketer's only objective may be to create awareness of the company or brand name, which may trigger interest in the product. In other situations, the marketer may want to convey detailed information to change consumers' knowledge of and attitudes toward the company/brand and ultimately change their behavior.

Traditional Response Hierarchy Models

A number of models have been developed to show the stages a consumer may pass through in moving from a state of not being aware of a company, product, or brand to actual purchase behavior. These models were developed for different reasons and have different stages. For example, the **AIDA model** was developed to represent the stages a salesperson must take a customer through in the personal selling process.[38] This model depicts the buyer as going through attention, interest, desire, and action stages. The **innovation adoption model** evolved from work on the diffusion of innovations and shows the stages a customer passes through in adopting a new product or service.[39] The steps preceding the final decision to adopt a new product or service include awareness, interest, evaluation, and trial.

FIGURE 5–5

Hierarchy of Effects Model

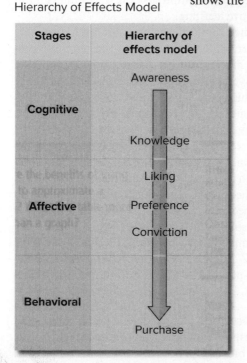

Perhaps the best known of these response hierarchies is the model developed by Robert Lavidge and Gary Steiner as a paradigm for setting and measuring advertising objectives.[40] Their **hierarchy of effects model** shows the stages a consumer goes through in transitioning from being unaware of a brand, to learning about it, forming favorable attitudes or feelings toward it, and ultimately purchasing the brand. The various stages of this model are shown in Figure 5–5. It assumes a consumer passes through these stages in sequential order from initial awareness of a product or service to actual purchase. The model was developed to show how advertising can influence the stages of the response hierarchy. A basic premise of this model is that advertising effects occur over time. Advertising may not lead to immediate behavioral response or purchase; rather, a series of effects must occur, with each step fulfilled before the consumer can move to the next stage in the hierarchy. The hierarchy of effects model is also the basis for the classic *purchase funnel* metaphor that is often used to depict the decision process consumers go through. The consumer starts at the top of funnel with a number of brands in mind, methodically reduces that number as he or she becomes familiar with and evaluates these alternatives, and then emerges with the brand chosen to purchase.[41] As we will see in Chapter 7, the hierarchy of effects model as well as the purchase funnel have become the foundation for setting objectives and measuring the effectiveness of advertising and other forms of marketing communication.

Alternative Response Hierarchies

The hierarchy of effects model, as well as the AIDA and innovation adoption models, view the response process as consisting of movement through a sequence of three basic stages. The *cognitive stage* includes what the consumer knows about the brand. This stage includes awareness that the brand exists and knowledge, information, or comprehension about its attributes, characteristics, or benefits. The *affective stage* refers to the consumer's feelings or affect level (like or dislike) for the particular brand. This stage also includes stronger levels of affect such as preference or conviction. The *conative or behavioral stage* refers to the consumer's action toward the brand such as trial, purchase, and ultimately a decision to repurchase or reject it.

The various response process models assume a similar ordering of these three stages. Cognitive development, such as becoming aware of and knowledgeable about a brand, precedes affective reactions or feelings, which in turn precede behavior such as trial or purchase. While this logical progression is often accurate, the response sequence does not always operate this way. Over the years, considerable research in marketing, social psychology, and communications has led to questioning of the traditional cognitive → affective → behavioral sequence of response. Several other configurations of the response hierarchy have been theorized. For example, Michael Ray developed a model of the response hierarchy based on product/service differentiation and the consumer's level of involvement with the product or service. We will focus on two that are particularly relevant to advertising and promotion—the standard learning model and low-involvement models.

The Standard Learning Hierarchy   In many purchase situations, the consumer will go through the response process in the sequence depicted by the traditional communication models. Ray terms this a **standard learning model**, which consists of a learn → feel → do sequence. Information and knowledge acquired or *learned* about the various brands are the basis for developing affect, or *feelings*, that guide what the consumer will *do* (e.g., actual trial or purchase). In this hierarchy, the consumer is viewed as an active participant in the communication process who gathers information through active learning.

Ray suggests the standard learning hierarchy is likely when the consumer is highly involved in the purchase process and there is much differentiation among competing brands. High-involvement purchase decisions such as those for industrial products and services and consumer durables like personal computers, smartphones, printers, cameras, appliances, and automobiles are areas where a standard learning hierarchy response process is likely. Ads for products and services in these areas are often detailed and provide customers with information that can be used to evaluate brands and help them make a purchase decision. They also may focus on a specific product attribute or feature that is important to consumers in the market segment they are targeting. For example, the ad shown in Exhibit 5-8 for the Samsung Galaxy Z Fold2 smartphone focuses on the foldable feature of the phone that allows it to function as both a phone and a tablet.

The Low-Involvement Hierarchy   Perhaps the most intriguing of the response hierarchies proposed by Ray is the **low-involvement hierarchy**, in which the receiver is viewed

EXHIBIT 5-8

This ad for the Galaxy Z Fold2 phone focuses on the stylish design as well as an important product feature that can be the basis for developing positive feelings toward the product.

Samsung Electronics Co., Ltd.

SAMSUNG

Galaxy Z Fold2 5G

Folded, it's a phone. Unfolded, it's a tablet.

Own now and get Galaxy Wearables worth ₹39980 at just ₹1980*

Galaxy Buds Pro   +   Galaxy Watch Active2

as passing from cognition to behavior to attitude change. Ray suggests this learn → do → feel sequence may occur when involvement in the purchase decision is low, there are minimal differences among brand alternatives, and mass-media (especially television) advertising is important.

The notion of a low-involvement hierarchy is based in large part on Herbert Krugman's theory explaining the effects of television advertising.[42] Krugman wanted to find out why TV advertising produced a strong effect on brand awareness and recall but little change in consumers' attitudes toward the product. He hypothesized that TV is basically a low-involvement medium and the viewer's perceptual defenses are reduced or even absent during commercials. In a low-involvement situation, the consumer does not compare the message with previously acquired beliefs, needs, or past experiences. The commercial results in subtle changes in the consumer's knowledge structure, particularly with repeated exposure. This change in the consumer's knowledge does not result in attitude change but is related to learning something about the advertised brand, such as a brand name, ad theme, or slogan. According to Krugman, when the consumer enters a purchase situation, this information may be sufficient to trigger a purchase. The consumer will then form an attitude toward the purchased brand as a result of experience with it. Thus, in the low-involvement situation the response sequence is as follows:

Message exposure under low involvement →
Shift in cognitive structure → Purchase →
Positive or negative experience → Attitude formation

In the low-involvement hierarchy, the consumer engages in *passive learning* and *random information catching* rather than active information seeking. The advertiser must recognize that a passive, uninterested consumer may focus more on nonmessage elements such as music, characters, symbols, and slogans or jingles than actual message content. The advertiser might capitalize on this situation by developing a catchy jingle that is stored in the consumer's mind without any active cognitive processing and becomes salient when he or she enters the actual purchase situation.

Advertisers of low-involvement products also repeat simple product claims such as a key copy point or distinctive product benefit. A study by Scott Hawkins and Stephen Hoch found that under low-involvement conditions, repetition of simple product claims increased consumers' memory of and belief in those claims.[43] They concluded that advertisers of low-involvement products might find it more profitable to pursue a heavy repetition strategy than to reach larger audiences with lengthy, more detailed messages. For example, Heinz has dominated the ketchup market for over 30 years by repeatedly telling consumers that its brand is the thickest and richest. A variety of advertising campaigns have been used for the brand over the years. However, they all have communicated the same basic message that Heinz is the best and most preferred brand of ketchup (Exhibit 5-9).

Low-involvement advertising appeals prevail in much of the advertising we see for frequently purchased products such as consumer packaged goods: Advertising for Coca-Cola invites consumers to "Taste the feeling" or "Share a Coke." Bounty paper towels claim to be the "quicker picker-upper." Dunkin' uses the slogan "America Runs on Dunkin'" to encourage consumers to purchase coffee and donuts. Each of these slogans is designed to help consumers maintain top-of-mind awareness that can influence their purchase decisions when they are in the market for one of these low-involvement products.

Another popular creative strategy used by advertisers of low-involvement products is what advertising analyst Harry McMahan calls *VIP*, or *visual image personality*.[44] Advertisers often use symbols like the Pillsbury Doughboy, Morris the Cat, and Mr. Clean to develop visual images that will lead consumers to identify and retain ads. Eveready began using the pink bunny in ads for its Energizer batteries in 1989, and he has helped sales of the brand keep going and going for over

EXHIBIT 5–10

The Energizer Bunny is still a
popular personality symbol for
the brand.

Energizer Holdings, Inc.

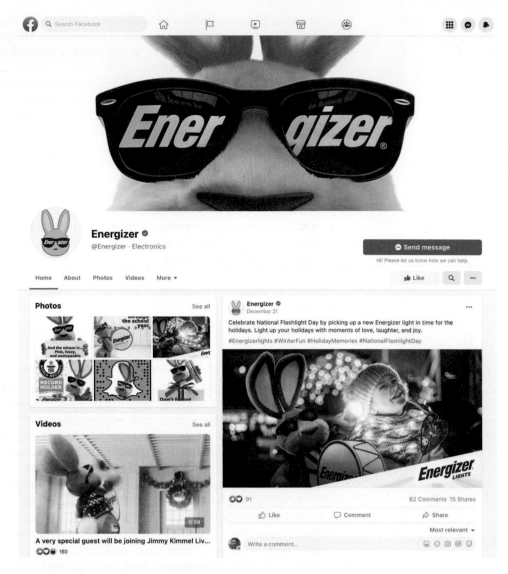

30 years. As can be seen in Exhibit 5-10, the Energizer Bunny even has his own Facebook page, which is used to engage consumers by showing photos and videos as well as
other content related to the use of Energizer batteries.

Implications of the Response Process Models

The hierarchy models of consumers' response processes are useful to promotional planners
from several perspectives. First, they delineate the series of steps potential purchasers must
be taken through to move them from no awareness of a brand to readiness to purchase it.
For example, marketers must not only develop IMC campaigns that make consumers aware
of a brand, they must do so in a manner that compels them to learn more about it and/or
develop an emotional connection with it. Second, potential buyers may be at different stages
in the response hierarchy, so marketers will face different communication challenges. For
example, a company introducing an innovative product such as a smartwatch may use
advertising in traditional media to make people aware of the product along with its features
and benefits. The marketer can provide information about the product in its ads and use
digital and social media to encourage consumers to visit its website or go to a retail store to
learn more about the product. Consumers who visit the website or go to a retail store for a
product demonstration will be more likely to progress through the response hierarchy and
move closer to purchase than will those who see only an ad. Marketers of a mature brand
that enjoys customer loyalty may need only supportive or reminder advertising to reinforce
positive perceptions and maintain top-of-mind awareness for the brand.

The hierarchy models can also be useful as intermediate measures of communication effectiveness. The marketer needs to know where audience members are in the response hierarchy. For example, research may reveal that one target segment has low awareness of the advertiser's brand, whereas another is aware of the brand and its various attributes but has a low level of liking or brand preference. For the first segment of the market, the goal of the IMC program involves increasing the awareness levels for the brand. The number of ads may be increased, or a product sampling program may be used. For the second segment, where awareness is already high but liking and preference are low, the advertiser must determine the reason for the ambivalent or negative feelings and then attempt to address this problem in future advertising.

Advertising and consumer researchers recognize that not all response sequences and behaviors are explained adequately by either the traditional or the alternative response hierarchies. Advertising is just one source of information consumers use in learning about products, forming attitudes, and/or making purchase decisions. Consumers are likely to integrate information from advertising and other forms of marketing communication as well as direct experience in forming judgments about a brand. For example, a study by Robert Smith found that advertising can lessen the negative effects of an unfavorable trial experience on brand evaluations when the ad is processed before the trial. However, when a negative trial experience precedes exposure to an ad, cognitive evaluations of the ad are more negative.[45] More recent research has also shown that advertising can affect consumers' objective sensory interpretation of their experiences with a brand and what they remember about it.[46]

The various response models offer an interesting perspective on the ways consumers respond to advertising and other forms of marketing communication. They also provide insight into promotional strategies marketers might pursue in different situations. A review of these alternative models of the response process shows that the traditional standard learning model does not always apply. The notion of a highly involved consumer who engages in active information processing and learning and acts on the basis of higher-order beliefs and a well-formed attitude may be inappropriate for some types of purchases. Sometimes consumers make a purchase decision on the basis of general awareness resulting from repetitive exposure to advertising, and attitude development occurs after the purchase, if at all. The role of advertising and other forms of promotion may be to induce trial, so consumers can develop brand preferences primarily on the basis of their direct experience with the product.

From a promotional planning perspective, it is important that marketers examine the communication situation for their product or service and determine which type of response process is most likely to occur. They should analyze involvement levels and product/service differentiation as well as consumers' use of various information sources and their levels of experience with the product or service. Once the manager has determined which response sequence is most likely to operate, the integrated marketing communications program can be designed to influence the response process in favor of the company's product or service. Several planning models have been developed that consider involvement levels as well as other factors including response processes and motives that underlie the attitude formation and subsequent brand choice.[47] These models can be of value to marketers as they develop IMC strategies because they recognize that advertising and other promotional tools work differently depending on the type of product involved and the decision process sequence that consumers are likely to follow. Digital and Social Media Perspective 5-3 discusses how a popular advertising planning model developed many years ago was recently modified to show how various digital and social media platforms can be used to influence different types of consumer purchase decisions.

In the past, most marketers of low-involvement products such as consumer packaged goods (CPG) have spent a large portion of their IMC budgets on traditional media such as television and print to build and maintain brand awareness as well as on consumer promotions such as coupons and promotional offers. However, the age of digital marketing has definitely arrived for CPG marketers, as many of them are recognizing that they can connect with consumers through social media as

Adapting a Classic Model for the Age of Social Media

In the 1980s, a very popular advertising planning model was developed by Richard Vaughn and his associates at the Foote Cone & Belding advertising agency. The FCB grid theorized that advertising and other promotional tools work differently depending on the type of product being purchased and the decision-process sequence that consumers are likely to follow. The model built on traditional response theories such as the hierarchy of effects model and its variants and research on high- versus low-involvement decision making. They added the dimension of thinking versus feeling processing at each involvement level based on theorizing regarding brain lateralization and hemispheric specialization. The right/left brain theory suggests that the left side of the brain handles rational, cognitive thinking and processing, while the right side is more visual and emotional and engages more in the affective/feeling functions. The FCB grid delineates four primary advertising planning strategies—informative, affective, habitual, and self-satisfaction—along with the most appropriate variation of the alternative response hierarchies.

Vaughn suggested that the *informative (thinker) strategy* is for high involvement purchase decisions where rational thinking and economic motives prevail and the standard learning hierarchy (learn → feel → do) is the appropriate response model. The *affective (feeler) strategy* recognizes that not all highly involving purchase decisions are motivated predominately by rational components and that emotion or feeling can drive a high-involvement purchase decision. For these types of purchases, the corresponding learning model is one where feelings lead the purchase decision followed by thoughts that lead to action (feel → learn → do). For these products, advertising should focus on psychological and emotional motives such as building self-esteem or enhancing the consumer's ego or self-image.

The *habit formation (doer) strategy* is for low-involvement/thinking products or situations where learning occurs after an exploratory trial purchase. The response process for these products (do → learn → feel) is consistent with a behavioristic learning-by-doing model (remember the discussion of operant conditioning in Chapter 4). The *self-satisfaction (reactor) strategy* is for products or purchase situations where involvement is low but driven primarily by feeling or emotion. Again, the do → feel → learn hierarchy is operating since product experience is the factor triggering the process. Vaughn noted that some minimal level of awareness (passive learning) may precede both types of low-involvement purchase situations but deeper, active learning is not necessary.

The FCB grid provides a useful way for those involved in the advertising planning process, such as the creative team, to analyze consumer/product relationships and develop appropriate promotional strategies. Consumer research can be used to determine how consumers perceive products or brands on the involvement and thinking/feeling dimensions. This information can then be used to develop creative options such as using rational versus emotional advertising appeals, increasing involvement with the product or brand, or even getting consumers to evaluate a think-type product on the basis of feelings and emotions. For low-involvement purchase situations consumers may not need much information prior to purchase, and the goal of advertising or other IMC such as sales promotion might be to stimulate trial.

The FCB grid was popular for many years, and even today it is widely recognized for moving advertising planning away from the assumption that there was only one advertising effects hierarchy. However, it was also developed during the pre-digital era when advertisers relied primarily on traditional media such as print and television and tools such as search engines and social media did not even exist. The contemporary marketing communication environment has changed dramatically over the past two decades, and there are a myriad of digital media platforms available to marketers along with more innovations on the way. However, these media platforms differ in their ability to deliver information to consumers as well as engage them rationally or emotionally. Recognizing these differences, Professors Eric Haley and Matthew Pittman developed an updated grid showing how various digital and social media platforms might work best for the various quadrants of the original FCB grid. Their digital channel grid recognizes that the various social media platforms have different characteristics and consumers' motives and/or needs may vary when using them.

In the informative (thinker) quadrant, paid advertising on websites, search engines such as Google, and social media platforms such as LinkedIn would be ideal as these are places where consumers typically go to find information once a purchase journey has begun. For the affective (feeler) quadrant, they propose that platforms such as Pinterest, YouTube, and Facebook are appropriate as they capitalize on affect or feelings and a preexisting interest in the product or service. In the habit formation (doer) quadrant, which the FCB grid views as being for lower involvement and primarily thinking products, Twitter is proposed as the best platform as it ranks high on topicality or staying up to date with emerging trends. Haley and Pittman argue that Twitter is a platform where users look for new and different ideas and topics and may be willing to try a new low-involvement product, particularly one where they might learn something from its use afterward. For the low-involvement, feeling-based, self-satisfaction reactor quadrant, social media platforms such as Instagram, TikTok, and Snapchat are relevant as all three are based on photo and video sharing. They argue that these platforms are used for entertainment and to share social knowledge, and are also used by influencers, which makes them good options for purchase decisions motivated by feelings. Moreover, their casual nature offering exposure to novelty and entertainment make them good candidates for low-involvement decisions.

	Thinking	Feeling
High Involvement	**1. Informative (thinker)** Car–house–furnishings–new products Model: Learn–feel–do (economic?) **Possible implications** Test: Recall / Diagnostics Media: Long copy format / Reflective vehicles Creative: Specific information / Demonstration	**2. Affective (feeler)** Jewellery–cosmetics–fashion apparel–motorcycles Model: Feel–learn–do (psychological) **Possible implications** Test: Attitude change / Emotional arousal Media: Large space / Image specials Creative: Executional / Impact
Low Involvement	**3. Habit formation (doer)** Food–household items Model: Do–learn–feel (responsive?) **Possible implications** Test: Sales Media: Small space ads / 10-second IDs / Radio; POS Creative: Reminder	**4. Self-satisfaction (reactor)** Cigarettes–alcohol–confectionery Model: Do–feel–learn (social?) **Possible implications** Test: Sales Media: Billboards / Newspapers / POS Creative: Attention

Thinking → Feeling

	Thinking	Feeling
High Involvement	Informative (Thinker) Learn-feel-do Reddit, website, search engine, Linkedin Google, http://www, LinkedIn, reddit	Affective (Feeler) Feel-learn-do Pinterest, Facebook Pinterest, YouTube, facebook
Low Involvement	Habit Formation (doer) Do-learn-feel Twitter twitter	Self-Satisfaction (reactor) Do-feel-learn Instagram, TikTok, Snapchat Instagram, TikTok, snapchat

Source: Google: rvlsoft/Shutterstock; http://www: Guy Erwood/Shutterstock; Linkedin: Artseen/Shutterstock; Reddit: GK Images/Alamy Stock Photo; Twitter: rvlsoft/Shutterstock; Pinterest: tanuha2001/Shutterstock; YouTube: rvlsoft/Shutterstock; Facebook: Artseen/Shutterstock; Instagram: Brilliantist Studio/Shutterstock; TikTok: rvlsoft/Shutterstock; Snapchat: Denys Kalitnyk/Alamy Stock Vector

Haley and Pittman acknowledge that the use of these digital channels may vary across consumers as a platform such as Facebook or YouTube may be a rational endeavor for one person but more emotional for another. They also note that the social media platforms differ in flexibility as platforms such as Facebook are more flexible and allow for the use of text, videos, and photos in a range of size and formats, whereas platforms such as Twitter and TikTok are more rigid due to limitations in text and video formats. Thus their use in multiple FCB quadrants may be limited.

The original FCB grid has been viewed as a valuable planning tool that helped advertising strategists think about how the consumer decision journey might vary depending on two important factors—involvement (high/low) and the mental process or motivation driving the purchase decision (thinking/feeling). The digital channel grid makes an important contribution by showing how various social media platforms and other digital tools can be integrated into this classic model.

Sources: Eric Haley and Matthew Pittman, "Remembering the FCB Grid: Thinking, Feeling, and Involvement in the Age of Social Media," *Journal of Advertising* 51, no. 3 (2022), pp. 323–335; Richard Vaughn, "How Advertising Works: A Planning Model," *Journal of Advertising Research* 20, no. 5 (1980), pp. 27–33; Richard Vaughn, "How Advertising Works: A Planning Model Revisited," *Journal of Advertising Research* 26, no.1 (1986), pp. 57–66.

EXHIBIT 5–11

Charmin uses social media to engage consumers with Enjoy the Go themed ideas such as this.

Procter & Gamble

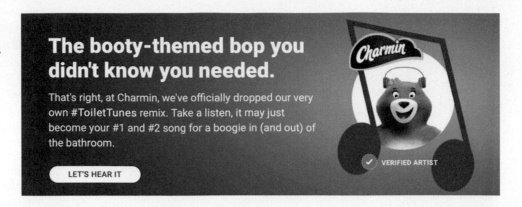

The booty-themed bop you didn't know you needed.

That's right, at Charmin, we've officially dropped our very own #ToiletTunes remix. Take a listen, it may just become your #1 and #2 song for a boogie in (and out) of the bathroom.

LET'S HEAR IT

VERIFIED ARTIST

well. For example, Procter & Gamble has adapted its IMC strategy for Charmin, the leading brand of toilet tissue, and uses social media very effectively to engage consumers. Charmin has become one of the most active brands on social media, with nearly a million fans on Facebook and more than 80,000 Twitter followers; it also has a presence on video platforms such as YouTube and Instagram. The social media strategy for Charmin has created a very engaged brand community by using content that is both relevant and entertaining and relies on humor as its key ingredient. Charmin integrates its social media with its traditional advertising that uses the "Enjoy the Go" theme and focuses not just on toilet paper, but rather on the human experience of everything bathroom related. For example, the brand recently created a #ToiletTunes remix that consumers download on Spotify and listen to in and out of the bathroom (Exhibit 5-11). The toilet tunes remix has gone viral as many consumers have posted videos of themselves dancing to the catchy music on TikTok and Instagram.

The Social Consumer Decision Journey

The response models discussed in the previous section have dominated much of the theorizing, research, and planning regarding how consumers respond to advertising and other IMC tools. However, over the past decade the environment in which consumers evaluate brands and make purchase decisions has changed dramatically as digital content—including social media—has become pervasive in our daily lives and is influencing consumer behavior. With the advent of social networking tools and the availability of digital devices such as smartphones and tablets, consumers are more empowered than ever before as they can access and retrieve information, connect with one another to share it, discuss products/services and brands, and interact with marketers quickly and easily.

A major study commissioned by the Advertising Research Foundation (ARF) examined how digital and social media are used in the purchase decision process along with how and when consumers turn to them to help manage this process. One of the major findings of this study is that "consumers, in effect, are always on as they are constantly considering potential purchases and evaluating the various providers of products and service" and that they can be in both an active and passive shopping mode.[48] When they are in a "passive" shopping mode, the information and advice consumers need to make a purchase comes to them unsolicited, such as a comment on a social media site; an ad seen on a TV show, in a magazine, or on a website; or by observing someone using a product or service. At other times, consumers are in an "active" shopping mode whereby they are purposefully seeking information and/or assistance so they can make informed purchase decisions with confidence. Consumers in an active shopping mode may visit the website or Facebook page of a company or brand; go to a search engine such as Google, Yahoo!, or Bing; go to a retail store; or have a conversation with a friend or associate (either online or in person).

Another important conclusion from this study, as well as research conducted by the McKinsey & Company's Global Digital Marketing Strategy practice group, is that consumers do not make purchase decisions in the linear manner depicted by the traditional hierarchy of effects and purchase funnel models whereby they start at the wide part of the funnel with many brands in mind and narrow them down to a final choice.[49] The research conducted by McKinsey as well as the ARF study show that consumers go through a much more iterative and less reductive process and that they can enter a purchase path at various points, depending on whether they first engage with a brand, research a product or service, or hear about a product through their social networks. Based on these findings, David Edelman and his associates at McKinsey proposed a "consumer decision journey" framework for understanding how consumers interact with companies and brands during the purchase decision process. The decision journey has four basic stages: *consider*, *evaluate*, *buy*, and *enjoy-advocate-bond*.[50] This framework views the consumer decision-making process as a winding journey with multiple feedback loops rather than a linear, single uniform path to purchase based on active shopping and influenced by marketer-dominated and controlled touch points such as media advertising.

Recognizing the increasing importance and influence of social media on consumer behavior, Edelman and his colleagues expanded the consumer decision journey framework to include social media, as shown in Figure 5-6. The social consumer decision journey framework recognizes that consumers connect with large numbers of brands through digital and social media channels that are often beyond the marketers' or retailers' control, evaluate a shifting array of them, and often expand the pool before narrowing it. After a purchase, consumers may remain very engaged and publicly promote or disparage the products or services they have purchased, often through digital and social media.[51] The McKinsey group notes that "social media is a unique component of the consumer decision journey: it's the only form of marketing that can touch consumers at each and every stage, from when they're pondering brands and products right through the period after a purchase, as their experience influences the brands they prefer and their potential advocacy influences others."[52] As can be seen in Figure 5-6, there are a number of ways various digital and social media tools such as YouTube, Twitter, Facebook, and Foursquare can influence consumers at various stages of the decision journey.

FIGURE 5–6

The Social Consumer
Decision Journey

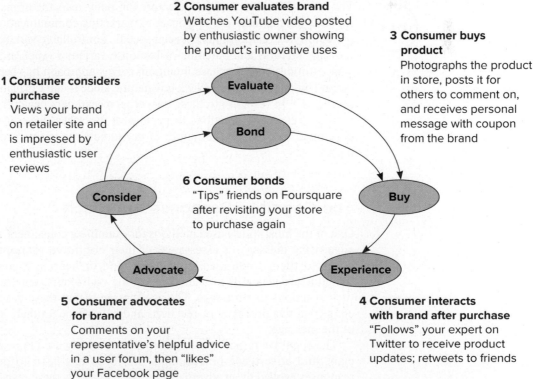

1 Consumer considers purchase
Views your brand on retailer site and is impressed by enthusiastic user reviews

2 Consumer evaluates brand
Watches YouTube video posted by enthusiastic owner showing the product's innovative uses

3 Consumer buys product
Photographs the product in store, posts it for others to comment on, and receives personal message with coupon from the brand

6 Consumer bonds
"Tips" friends on Foursquare after revisiting your store to purchase again

5 Consumer advocates for brand
Comments on your representative's helpful advice in a user forum, then "likes" your Facebook page

4 Consumer interacts with brand after purchase
"Follows" your expert on Twitter to receive product updates; retweets to friends

The consumer decision journey framework has a number of implications for marketers as they develop their IMC programs. Edelman notes that instead of determining how to allocate spending across the various IMC tools such as various forms of media advertising, marketers should target stages in the decision journey. Marketers often spend a large percentage of their IMC budgets on advertising and sales promotion that are designed to influence consumers at the consider and buy stages. However, consumers may often be influenced more during the evaluate and enjoy-advocate-bond stages. For many consumers the most important incentive to buy may be another person's advocacy or recommendation. He notes that it is also important for marketers to focus not only on the portion of their budget allocated to paid media—or what is sometimes referred to as "working media spend"—but also consider the role of *owned* media that a brand controls (such as websites and social media platforms) as well as *earned media* (customer-created content on blogs, forums, and social media).

Some of the findings from the ARF-commissioned study also are relevant to the role of social and digital media on the consumer decision journey. This study found that consumers like to tout their effectiveness and prowess as shoppers to others, which means that marketers can leverage this desire by providing forums for consumers to share their stories and experiences with others. The study also found that much online activity occurs after products are purchased, which points to an opportunity for marketers to develop a dialogue with consumers, engage them in discussions, and deepen their loyalty and affinity for their brands. The ARF study noted that the purchase journey of consumers varies by product or service category because high-risk/involvement products have longer cycles than do lower-risk/involvement products. It is also important to note that the ARF research indicates that brand perceptions and offline advertising are still important in driving consideration throughout the cycle. Thus it is important for marketers to build and maintain strong brands and be visible and pervasive throughout the decision journey.

COGNITIVE PROCESSING OF COMMUNICATIONS

The hierarchical response models were for many years the primary focus of approaches for studying the receivers' responses to marketing communications. Attention centered on identifying relationships between specific controllable variables (such as source and message factors) and outcome or response variables (such as attention, comprehension, attitudes, and purchase intentions). This approach has been criticized on a number of fronts, including its black-box nature, since it can't explain what is causing these reactions.[53] In response to these concerns, researchers began trying to understand the nature of cognitive reactions to persuasive messages. Several approaches have been developed to examine the nature of consumers' cognitive processing of advertising messages.

The Cognitive Response Approach

One of the most widely used methods for examining consumers' cognitive processing of advertising messages is assessment of their **cognitive responses**, the thoughts that occur to them while reading, viewing, and/or hearing a communication.[54] These thoughts are generally measured by having consumers write down or verbally report their reactions to a message. The assumption is that these thoughts reflect the recipient's cognitive processes or reactions and help shape ultimate acceptance or rejection of the message.

The cognitive response approach has been widely used in research by both academicians and advertising practitioners. Its focus has been to determine the types of responses evoked by an advertising message and how these responses relate to attitudes

FIGURE 5–7

A Model of Cognitive
Response

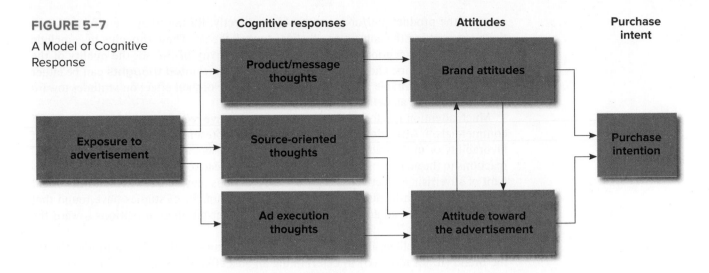

toward the ad, brand attitudes, and purchase intentions. Figure 5–7 depicts the three basic categories of cognitive responses researchers have identified—product/message, source-oriented, and ad execution thoughts—and how they may relate to attitudes and intentions.

Product/Message Thoughts The first category of thoughts comprises those directed at the product or service and/or the claims being made in the communication. Much attention has focused on two particular types of responses: counterarguments and support arguments.

Counterarguments are thoughts the recipient has that are opposed to the position taken in the message. For example, consider the ad for Ultra Tide shown in Exhibit 5-12. A consumer may express disbelief or disapproval of a claim made in an ad. ("I don't believe that any detergent could get that stain out!") Other consumers who see this ad may generate **support arguments**, or thoughts that affirm the claims made in the message. ("Ultra Tide looks like a really good product—I think I'll try it.")

The likelihood of counterarguing is greater when the message makes claims that oppose the receiver's beliefs. For example, a consumer viewing a commercial that attacks a favorite brand is likely to engage in counterarguing. Counterarguments relate negatively to message acceptance; the more the receiver counterargues, the less likely he or she is to accept the position advocated in the message.[55] Support arguments, on the other hand, relate positively to message acceptance. Thus, the marketer should develop ads or other promotional messages that minimize counterarguing and encourage support arguments.

EXHIBIT 5–12

Consumers often generate support arguments in response to ads for quality products.

The Procter & Gamble Company

Source-Oriented Thoughts A second category of cognitive responses is directed at the source of the communication. One of the most important types of responses in this category is **source derogations**, or negative thoughts about the spokesperson or organization making the claims. Such thoughts generally lead to a reduction in message acceptance. If consumers find a particular spokesperson annoying or untrustworthy, they are less likely to accept what this source has to say.

Of course, source-related thoughts are not always negative. Receivers who react favorably to the source generate favorable thoughts, or **source bolsters**. As you would expect, most advertisers attempt to hire spokespeople their target audience likes to carry this effect over to the message. Considerations involved in choosing an appropriate source or spokesperson will be discussed in Chapter 6.

Ad Execution Thoughts The third category of cognitive responses shown in Figure 5–7 consists of the individual's thoughts about the ad itself. Many of the thoughts receivers have when reading or viewing an ad do not concern the product and/or message claims directly. Rather, they are affective reactions representing the consumer's feelings toward the ad. These thoughts may include reactions to ad execution factors such as the creativity of the ad, the quality of the visual effects, colors, and voice tones. **Ad execution–related thoughts** can be either favorable or unfavorable. They are important because of their effect on attitudes toward the advertisement as well as the brand.

Much attention has focused on consumers' affective reactions to ads, especially TV commercials.[56] **Attitude toward the ad** (Aad) represents the receivers' feelings of favorability or unfavorability toward the ad. Advertisers are interested in consumers' reactions to the ad because they know that affective reactions are an important determinant of advertising effectiveness, since these reactions may be transferred to the brand itself or directly influence purchase intentions. A number of studies have found that people who like an ad are more likely to have higher purchase intentions toward the product or service.[57]

Consumers' feelings about the ad may be just as important as their attitudes toward the brand (if not more so) in determining an ad's effectiveness.[58] The importance of affective reactions and feelings generated by the ad depends on several factors, among them the nature of the ad and the type of processing engaged in by the receiver.[59] Many advertisers use emotional appeals designed to evoke positive feelings and affective reactions as the basis of their creative strategy. The success of this strategy depends in part on the consumers' involvement with the brand and their likelihood of attending to and processing the message. Another way marketers try to create favorable attitudes toward their ads is by using humor, which can put consumers in a positive mood and increase their liking of not only the ad itself, but also the brand. For example, many of the ads shown during the Super Bowl each year use humorous appeals since marketers know consumers will be watching them closely and discussing them with others both during and after the game.

We end our analysis of the receiver by examining a popular model that considers how involvement and other factors may influence the route to persuasion consumers follow and their cognitive processing of a message.

The Elaboration Likelihood Model

Differences in the ways consumers process and respond to persuasive messages are addressed in the **elaboration likelihood model (ELM)** of persuasion, shown in Figure 5-8.[60] The ELM was devised by Richard Petty and John Cacioppo to explain the process by which persuasive communications (such as ads) lead to persuasion by influencing attitudes. According to the ELM, the attitude formation or change process depends on the amount and nature of *elaboration*, or processing, of relevant information that occurs in response to a persuasive message. High elaboration means the receiver engages in careful consideration, thinking, and evaluation of the information or arguments contained in the message. Low elaboration occurs when the receiver does not engage in active information processing or thinking but rather makes inferences about the position being advocated in the message on the basis of simple positive or negative cues.

The ELM shows that elaboration likelihood is a function of two elements: motivation and ability to process the message. *Motivation* to process the message depends on such factors as involvement, personal relevance, and individuals' needs and arousal levels. *Ability* depends on the individual's knowledge, intellectual capacity, and opportunity to process the message. For example, an individual viewing a humorous commercial or one containing an attractive model may be distracted from processing the information about the product.

According to the ELM, there are two basic routes to persuasion or attitude change. Under the **central route to persuasion**, the receiver is viewed as a very active, involved participant in the communication process, whose ability and motivation to attend, comprehend, and evaluate messages are high. When central processing of an advertising message occurs, the consumer pays close attention to message content and scrutinizes the message arguments. A high level of cognitive response activity or processing occurs,

FIGURE 5–8

The Elaboration Likelihood
Model of Persuasion

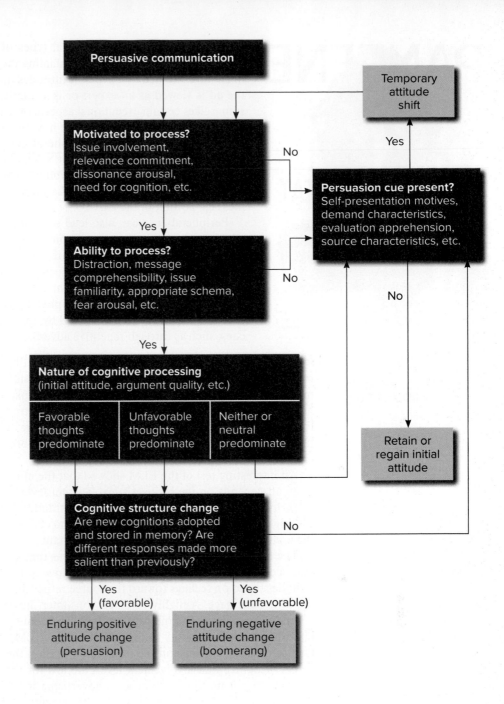

and the ad's ability to persuade the receiver depends primarily on the receiver's evaluation of the quality of the arguments presented. Predominantly favorable cognitive responses (support arguments and source bolsters) lead to favorable changes in cognitive structure, which lead to positive attitude change, or persuasion.

Conversely, if the cognitive processing is predominantly unfavorable and results in counterarguments and/or source derogations, the changes in cognitive structure are unfavorable and *boomerang*, or result in negative attitude change. Attitude change that occurs through central processing is relatively enduring and should resist subsequent efforts to change it.

Under the **peripheral route to persuasion**, shown on the right side of Figure 5–8, the receiver is viewed as lacking the motivation or ability to process information and is not likely to engage in detailed cognitive processing. Rather than evaluating the information presented in the message, the receiver relies on peripheral cues that may be incidental to the main arguments. The receiver's reaction to the message depends on how he or she evaluates these peripheral cues.

STRONG IS
TAKING THE HEAT

Pantene's rich, creamy Daily Moisture
Renewal Shampoo and Conditioner sends powerful
Pro-V moisture deep into your hair. So even the dry
damage from 100 blowdries transforms into silky amazing.

STRONG IS BEAUTIFUL

EXHIBIT 5–13

This ad contains peripheral cues, most notably a celebrity endorser.

Procter & Gamble

The consumer may use several types of peripheral cues or cognitive shortcuts rather than carefully evaluating the message arguments presented in an advertisement.[61] Favorable attitudes may be formed if the endorser in the ad is viewed as an expert or is attractive and/or likable or if the consumer likes certain executional aspects of the ad such as the way it is made, the music, or the imagery. Notice how the ad in Exhibit 5–13 for Pantene shampoo contains several peripheral cues, including an attractive and relevant celebrity endorser (singer Selena Gomez) and visual imagery that is consistent with the brand positioning. These cues might help consumers form a positive attitude toward the brand even if they do not process the message portion of the ad.

Peripheral cues can also lead to rejection of a message. For example, ads that advocate extreme positions, use endorsers who are not well liked or have credibility problems, or are not executed well (such as low-budget ads for local retailers) may be rejected without any consideration of their information or message arguments. As shown in Figure 5–8, the ELM views attitudes resulting from peripheral processing as temporary. So favorable attitudes must be maintained by continual exposure to the peripheral cues, such as through repetitive advertising.

Implications of the ELM The elaboration likelihood model has important implications for marketing communications, particularly with respect to involvement. For example, if the involvement level of consumers in the target audience is high, an ad or sales presentation should contain strong arguments that are difficult for the message recipient to refute or counterargue. If the involvement level of the target audience is low, peripheral cues may be more important than detailed message arguments.

An interesting test of the ELM showed that the effectiveness of a celebrity endorser in an ad depends on the receiver's involvement level.[62] When involvement was low, a celebrity endorser had a significant effect on attitudes. When the receiver's involvement was high, however, the use of a celebrity had no effect on brand attitudes; the quality of the arguments used in the ad was more important.

The explanation given for these findings was that a celebrity may serve as a peripheral cue in the low-involvement situation, allowing the receiver to develop favorable attitudes based on feelings toward the source rather than engaging in extensive processing of the message. A highly involved consumer, however, engages in more detailed central processing of the message content. The quality of the message becomes more important than the identity of the endorser. The ELM suggests that the most effective type of message depends on the route to persuasion the consumer follows. Many marketers recognize that involvement levels are low for their product categories and consumers are not motivated to process advertising messages in any detail. That's why marketers of low-involvement products often rely on creative tactics that emphasize peripheral cues and use repetitive advertising to create and maintain favorable attitudes toward their brand.

The ELM is one of the most frequently cited theories of how advertising impacts consumers and is considered one of the most influential theoretical contributions to the academic literature in advertising and other forms of persuasion.[63] However, the model has been the subject of debate and criticism by a number of academic researchers as attempts to replicate the findings from the study discussed previously have not been successful.[64] A recent effort to replicate this study with subjects from three countries (United States, United Kingdom, and Australia) was only partially successful and did not support the key finding that attitudes formed via the central route to persuasion are more predictive of behavior than those formed via the peripheral route. The authors suggest that changes in the media environment, particularly the shift to the dominance of digital and social media, call into question the relevancy of advertising theories developed during the era when traditional mass media was dominant.[65]

SUMMARIZING THE RESPONSE PROCESS AND THE EFFECTS OF ADVERTISING

As you have seen from our analysis of the receiver, the process consumers go through in responding to marketing communications can be viewed from a number of perspectives. Vakratsas and Ambler reviewed more than 250 journal articles and books in an effort to better understand how advertising works and affects the consumer.[66] On the basis of their review of these studies, they concluded that although effects hierarchies have been actively employed for nearly 100 years, there is little support for the concept of a hierarchy of effects in the sense of temporal sequence. They note that in trying to understand the response process and the manner in which advertising works, there are three critical intermediate effects between advertising and purchase (Figure 5-9). These include *cognition*, the "thinking" dimension of a person's response; *affect*, the "feeling" dimension; and *experience*, which is a feedback dimension based on the outcomes of product purchasing and usage. They conclude that individual responses to advertising are mediated or filtered by factors such as motivation and ability to process information, which can radically alter or change the individual's response to advertising. They suggest that the effects of advertising should be evaluated using these three dimensions, with some intermediate variables being more important than others, depending on factors such as the product category, stage of the product life cycle, target audience, competition, and impact of other marketing-mix components.

Other researchers have been critical of the hierarchy models as well. For example, Hall argues that advertisers need to move away from explicit and implicit reliance on hierarchical models of advertising effects and develop models that place affect and experience at the center of the advertising process.[67] The implication of these criticisms is that marketers should focus on cognition, affect, and experience as critical variables that advertising may affect. However, they should not assume a particular sequence of responses but, rather, engage in research and analysis to better understand how advertising and other forms of promotion may affect these intermediate variables in various product/market situations.

While a number of issues and concerns regarding hierarchy of effects models have been noted, many believe that they are of value to advertising practice and research. For example, Thomas Barry contends that despite their limitations, hierarchical models do help predict behavior. He notes that these models also provide insight into whether advertising strategies need to focus on impacting cognition, affect, and/or behavior based on audience or segmentation experiences. They also provide valuable planning, training, and conceptual frameworks.[68]

Those responsible for planning the IMC program need to learn as much as possible about their target audience and how it may respond to advertising, along with other forms of marketing communication. For example, William Weilbacher has noted that marketing communications programs include more than just advertising.[69] Consumers are continually immersed in brand-sponsored communications that also include public relations, a broad range of sales promotion activities, social media, direct marketing, event sponsorships, movie and TV show product placements, and other forms of marketing communication. He argues that hierarchy models must move beyond just explaining the effects of advertising and consider how, and with what effects, consumers synthesize information from all the various integrated marketing communications activities for a brand. As we have seen from the discussion of the social consumer decision journey, information from the numerous forms of social media and other digital sources is adding to the number of factors that influence the consumer response process and decision making.

FIGURE 5-9

A Framework for Studying How Advertising Works

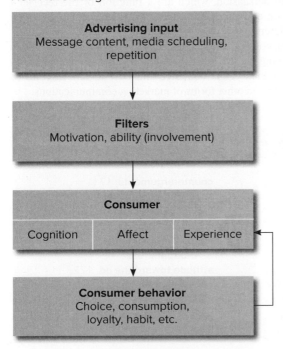

The various models discussed in this chapter are important as they present the basic elements of communication and provide insight into how consumers process and respond to advertising and other IMC tools. It is vital to understand the communication process as it provides a foundation for studying and evaluating integrated marketing communications. Those involved in various aspects of IMC find that understanding the communication process helps them make better decisions in planning, implementing, and evaluating their marketing communication programs.

Summary

The function of all elements of the IMC program is to communicate, so promotional planners must understand the communication process. This process can be very complex; successful marketing communications depend on a number of factors, including the nature of the message, the audience's interpretation of it, and the environment in which it is received. For effective communication to occur, the sender must encode a message in such a way that it will be decoded by the receiver in the intended manner. Feedback from the receiver helps the sender determine whether proper decoding has occurred or whether noise has interfered with the communication process.

Nonpersonal channels of communication are those that carry a message without direct, interpersonal contact between the sender and receiver and are generally referred to as the mass media. Personal channels involve direct communication between two or more persons and can occur through interpersonal contact (face to face) or via other methods such as e-mail or through social media. Members of one's social networks such as friends, neighbors, associates, co-workers, or family members are also personal channels of communication and represent word-of-mouth (WOM) influence, which can be a very powerful source of information. Marketers often try to generate WOM through viral marketing, which refers to the act of propagating marketing-relevant messages through the help and cooperation of individual consumers. With the growth of social media, most viral marketing is done today through influencer marketing, which uses social media to leverage the influence of individuals with a dedicated social media following. These social media influencers create and disseminate content to a large following and often wield influence over followers' purchases and decision making.

Promotional planning begins with the receiver or target audience, as marketers must understand how the audience is likely to respond to various sources of communication or types of messages. For promotional planning, the receiver can be analyzed with respect to both its composition (i.e., individual, group, or mass audiences) and the response process it goes through. Several models of the response process have been developed, including the AIDA, innovation adoption, and hierarchy of effects model. Alternative orderings of the traditional response hierarchy are possible, including the standard learning and low-involvement models.

The environment in which consumers evaluate brands and make purchase decisions has changed dramatically as digital content—including social media—has become pervasive in our daily lives and is influencing consumer behavior. The social consumer decision journey framework recognized that consumers can enter the purchase path at various points, depending on whether they first engage with a brand, research a product or service, or hear about it through their social networks.

The cognitive response approach examines the thoughts evoked by a message and how they shape the receiver's ultimate acceptance or rejection of the communication. The elaboration likelihood model of attitude formation and change recognizes two forms of message processing: the central and peripheral routes to persuasion, which are a function of the receiver's motivation and ability to process a message. There are three critical intermediate effects between advertising and purchase: including cognition, affect, and experience. Those responsible for planning the IMC program should learn as much as possible about their target audience and how it may respond to advertising and other forms of marketing communications.

Key Terms

communication 145
source 146
encoding 146
message 147
channel 149
mass media 149
word-of-mouth (WOM) 150
buzz marketing 150
viral marketing 150
seeding 152
influencer marketing 152
social media influencers 152

receiver 156
decoding 156
field of experience 156
noise 158
response 159
feedback 159
AIDA model 161
innovation adoption model 161
hierarchy of effects model 161
standard learning model 162
low-involvement hierarchy 162
cognitive responses 170

counterarguments 171
support arguments 171
source derogations 171
source bolsters 171
ad execution–related
   thoughts 172
attitude toward the ad 172
elaboration likelihood
   model (ELM) 172
central route to persuasion 172
peripheral route to persuasion 173

1. Discuss why Tesla has been able to dominate the electric vehicle segment of the automotive market despite spending almost no money on media advertising. Do you think Tesla will be able to compete without advertising as more competitors enter the EV market? (LO 5-1, 5-3)

2. Discuss the importance of logos and why a company might make a decision to change its logo. Evaluate the logo changes made by General Motors, Pfizer, or Kia Motors Corp. Do you think these new logos are good or bad? (LO 5-1, 5-2)

3. Discuss the role of logos for digital technology companies such as Uber, Amazon, Airbnb, and others. Why is the design of a logo for these companies so important? (LO 5-1, 5-2)

4. Discuss the four types of word-of-mouth communication and how they are used by marketers. (LO 5-3)

5. Discuss the reasons why companies are using social media influencers as part of their integrated marketing communication programs. Why might a marketer choose to use a nano- or micro-influencer rather than a popular macro-influencer such as a celebrity? (LO 5-3)

6. It is well recognized that an age bias exists in the advertising industry. Do you think it is acceptable for advertising and digital agencies to favor younger people in the hiring process? (LO 5-1, 5-3)

7. Discuss how marketers of a low-involvement product such as soft drinks or paper towels would use various IMC tools differently than a marketer of a high-involvement product such as a laptop computer or an automobile. (LO 5-4)

8. Choose one of the four quadrants of the FCB planning grid and the FCB digital channel grid shown in Digital and Social Media Perspective 5–3. Discuss the type of advertising strategy a marketer of a product in this quadrant might use. How might digital and social media platforms be used for products in this quadrant? (LO 5-4)

9. Discuss how marketers can use the cognitive response approach to analyze consumers' reactions to and processing of their advertising messages. Choose a print ad or TV commercial and discuss the types of cognitive responses that it might generate using the model shown in Figure 5–7. (LO 5-6)

10. Explain the differences between the central versus peripheral route to persuasion and the factors that determine when each might be used by consumers in response to an advertisement or other form of marketing communication. (LO 5-6)

6

Source, Message, and Channel Factors

Kyle Okita/Cal Sport Media/Newscom

Learning Objectives

LO 6-1 Discuss the variables in the communication system and how they influence consumers' processing of promotional messages.

LO 6-2 Identify decision factors involved in selecting a source for a promotional message.

LO 6-3 Compare the different types of message structures and appeals that can be used in advertising.

LO 6-4 Explain how different types of channels influence the marketing communications process.

College Athletes Are the New Endorsers

Sports have long been an important part of the college experience; many students love football weekends at their schools, going to a basketball game, or watching a game on television and cheering for their team. The United States has a unique culture of college athletics, with all the different school traditions, alumni engagement, and scholarship opportunities for athletes. Amateurism has been a keynote of collegiate sports. The National Collegiate Athletic Association was formed in 1906 to regulate college athletics and protect young athletes. Under the NCAA rules, college athletes could not be paid to play a sport and could only receive scholarships and stipends for some living expenses. They also could not engage in certain activities such as working at summer instructional camps or making money from contracts not related to the sport in which they participated.

The NCAA enforced its amateurism rules with a vengeance, and athletes could lose their eligibility and scholarships for violating them. However, after going largely unchanged for more than a century, in June 2021, the U.S. Supreme Court unanimously ruled in the case of *NCAA v. Alston* that the NCAA is not legally allowed to limit any education-related payments to student athletes. From there the NCAA deferred to individual states to create their own rules allowing college athletes to make money in business ventures without losing their eligibility. Two NCAA regulations did remain in place: Schools are not allowed to pay a player or provide compensation for performance, and recruited athletes cannot sign any "name, image, and likeness" (NIL) deal contingent upon going to a particular school.

The new NIL rules essentially allow college athletes to profit off themselves because they can earn money in a number of ways, including appearing in advertisements and promotions for a business, making personal appearances, selling ads on their social media accounts, being paid for posts on social media, selling signed memorabilia, selling merchandise, running a sports camp, and starting their own businesses. Some schools and athletes responded quickly to the new rules, and a wave of endorsements followed: deals for athletic shoes and apparel, deals with local businesses such as automotive dealers, and payment for posts on social media. For example, Paige Bueckers, a star guard on the University of Connecticut Huskies basketball team and the first freshman in women's college basketball history to win the Wooden Award as the most outstanding player of the year, who has nearly 1 million followers on Instagram, charges an estimated $3,600 per post and has partnered with brands such as Gatorade and StockX. The female athlete who made the most money on NIL deals in 2022 was Louisiana State University (LSU) gymnast Olivia Dunne whose 2.2 million followers on Instagram and 6 million on TikTok helped her make more than $2 million in endorsements. Many schools have begun helping their athletes secure NIL deals by hiring dedicated staff in athletic departments and creating websites and social media pages to promote their athletes. Under the new NIL rules, athletes are also allowed to hire agents to help them secure endorsement deals.

While many argue that the new NIL rules were long overdue, critics are concerned that the program is quickly getting out of control as boosters at many large schools become involved. State laws and NCAA regulations contain limitations on NIL such as that money cannot come from the schools or be used for recruiting athletes. The idea was that NIL money would come from businesses that actually wanted the athletes' endorsements and would pay a fair price for endorsements. However, at many schools that play big-time college sports, big-money donors are funding "collectives," which are formed by wealthy alumni and supporters and collect financial resources that are directed to athletes for the right to use their name, image, and likeness. The collectives are supposed to help facilitate NIL deals for athletes, but critics argue they are just a way to pay athletes to play for a college sports team. One expert has estimated that every men's basketball and football player on a major Division I team could be making six figures or more within a few years. Booster involvement in recruiting has always been against the rules, and the NCAA announced that it is stepping up its enforcement to include any NIL violations that may involve boosters using collectives to lure recruits to their schools with the promise of a big NIL deal.

The majority of college athletes are not football or basketball players at major universities but rather participate in niche sports that have limited NIL potential. However, NIL advocates argue that all college athletes should have the right to earn additional money and profit off their name, image, and likeness.

continued

Moreover they note that the NCAA and college sports have long had an exploitive business model that has resulted in billions of dollars being made by universities and media companies from college athletes. They argue that it is long overdue for some of the money generated by the billion-dollar world of college sports to hit the wallets of the players, and NIL is a legitimate way to do so.

Critics of NIL argue that it is not working as planned and has become the "Wild, Wild West," is out of control, and getting dramatically worse. The NCAA is working on creating new NIL guidelines, but legal experts question whether it will be successful in doing so. For anyone who thinks the NIL genie can be put back in the bottle, they might consider that the state athletic association in Pennsylvania recently paved the way for high school athletes to be paid under an NIL plan. One can only wonder if youth sports will be next.

Sources: The Athletic College Football Staff, "What Is NIL? Everything You Need to Know about the NCAA and Name, Image and Likeness," *The Athletic*, May 10, 2022, https://theathletic.com/3301694/2022/05/10/nil-ncaa-definition/; Erika Wheless, "5 NIL Deals Marketers Should Know About," *Advertising Age*, April 1, 2022, https://adage.com/article/digital-marketing-ad-tech-news/5-nil-deals-marketers-should-know-about/2409976; Eddie Pells, "It's 1st Final Four in NIL Era," *San Diego Union Tribune*, March 21, 2022, pp. C1, 3.

In this chapter, we analyze the major variables in the communication system: the source, the message, and the channel. We examine the characteristics of sources, how they influence reactions to promotional messages, and why one type of communicator is more effective than another. We then focus on the message itself and how structure and type of appeal influence its effectiveness. Finally, we consider how factors related to the channel or medium affect the communication process.

PROMOTIONAL PLANNING THROUGH THE PERSUASION MATRIX

LO 6-1

To develop an effective advertising and promotional campaign, a firm must select the right spokesperson to deliver a compelling message through appropriate channels or media. Source, message, and channel factors are controllable elements in the communication model. The **persuasion matrix** (Figure 6-1) helps marketers see how each controllable element interacts with the consumer's response process.[1]

FIGURE 6-1

The Persuasion Matrix

Dependent variables: Steps in being persuaded	Independent variables: The communication components				
	Source	Message	Channel	Receiver	Destination
Message presentation/exposure			(2)		
Attention/awareness	(4)				
Knowledge/comprehension				(1)	
Yielding/liking		(3)			
Retention					
Behavior					

The matrix has two sets of variables. *Independent variables* are the controllable components of the communication process, outlined in Chapter 5; *dependent variables* are the steps a receiver goes through in being persuaded. Marketers can choose the person or source who delivers the message, the type of message appeal used, and the channel or medium. And although they can't control the receiver, they can select their target audience. The destination variable is included because the initial message recipient may pass on information to others, such as friends or associates, through word of mouth.

Promotional planners need to know how decisions about each independent variable influence the stages of the response hierarchy so that they don't enhance one stage at the expense of another. A humorous message may gain attention but result in decreased comprehension if consumers fail to process its content. Many ads that use humor, sexual appeals, or celebrities capture consumers' attention but result in poor recall of the brand name or message. The following examples, which correspond to the numbers in various cells of Figure 6–1, illustrate decisions that can be evaluated with the persuasion matrix.

1. *Receiver/comprehension: Can the receiver comprehend the ad?* Marketers must know the receivers in their target market so they can determine the best way to develop advertising messages for them. Consideration has to be given to factors such as demographic and psychographic characteristics of the receiver as well as their purchase patterns. A less educated person may have difficulty interpreting a complicated message, while certain terms or jargon may be unfamiliar to some receivers. The more insight a marketer has into the target audience, the easier it is to use words, symbols, and expressions that will make an advertising message clear and easy to understand.

2. *Channel/presentation: Which media vehicles should be used to present the advertising message?* When advertisers purchase media, they do so based on exposure potential, or the opportunity for consumers to see their message. Media decisions are based in large part on the size and composition of the audience reached as well as cost. A popular prime-time TV show such as *NCIS* is seen by as many as 10 million people each week, while magazines such as *Time* and *People* reach over 3 million readers with each weekly publication and millions more through their digital editions. But the important point is how well a media vehicle reaches the marketer's target audience. Most popular shows on network television reach an older viewing audience as the median age of the prime-time viewing audience for the major networks during the 2021–22 television season ranged from 56 to 63.[2] Thus, marketers trying to reach a younger target audience may find it difficult to do so by advertising on network television. A recent survey that examined the television viewing tastes of gen Z and millennial viewers in the United States and Canada found that two-thirds of 13- to 39-year-olds watch TV shows on streaming services weekly while about half watch cable and network shows. The most popular network shows were *Grey's Anatomy* and *Family Guy.*[3]

3. *Message/yielding: What type of message will create favorable attitudes or feelings?* Marketers generally try to create advertising messages that lead to positive feelings toward the product or service. Humorous messages often put consumers in a good mood and evoke positive feelings that may become associated with the brand being advertised. Music adds emotion that makes consumers more receptive to the message. Many advertisers use explicit sexual appeals designed to arouse consumers or suggest they can enhance their attractiveness. Some marketers compare their brands to competitors and show how they are better than them.

4. *Source/attention: Who will be effective in getting consumers' attention?* The large number of ads we are bombarded with every day makes it difficult for advertisers to break through the clutter. Marketers deal with this problem by using sources who will attract the target audience's attention—actors, athletes, entertainers, or attractive models.

SOURCE FACTORS

The source component is a multifaceted concept. When an athlete such as LeBron James appears in a Nike ad, is the source James himself, the company, or some combination of the two? And, of course, consumers get information from friends, relatives, and neighbors; in fact, personal sources may be the most influential factor in a purchase decision. Word-of-mouth information transmitted from one individual to another is often perceived as more reliable and trustworthy than that received through more formal marketing channels such as advertising. As was discussed in Chapter 5, marketers are using influencers and viral marketing methods to generate favorable word-of-mouth discussion and recommendations for their products and services.

We use the term **source** to mean the person involved in communicating a marketing message, either directly or indirectly. A *direct source* is a spokesperson who delivers a message and/or endorses a product or service, like professional tennis star Sloane Stephens who appears in an ad that is part of the "Built With Chocolate Milk" campaign sponsored by the Milk Processor Education Program. The campaign promotes the benefits of recovering from a tough workout or competition with the high quality protein and nutrients found in chocolate milk (Exhibit 6-1). An *indirect source*, say, a model, doesn't actually deliver a message but draws attention to and/or enhances the appearance of the ad. Some ads use neither a direct nor an indirect source; the source is the organization with the message to communicate. Since most research focuses on individuals as a message source, our examination of source factors follows this approach.

EXHIBIT 6–1

Tennis star Sloane Stephens endorses milk as part of the "Built With Chocolate Milk" campaign.

America's Milk Companies

Companies are very careful when selecting individuals to deliver their selling messages. Many firms spend huge sums of money for a specific person to endorse their product or company. They also spend millions recruiting, selecting, and training salespeople to represent the company and deliver sales presentations. They recognize that the characteristics of the source affect the sales and advertising message.

Marketers try to select individuals whose traits will maximize message influence. The source may be knowledgeable, popular, and/or physically attractive; may typify the target audience; or have the power to reward or punish the receiver in some manner. Herbert Kelman developed three basic categories of source attributes: credibility, attractiveness, and power.[4] Each influences the recipient's attitude or behavior through a different process (see Figure 6-2).

Source Credibility

Credibility is the extent to which the recipient sees the source as having relevant knowledge, skill, or experience and trusts the source to give unbiased, objective information. There are two important dimensions to credibility: expertise and trustworthiness.

A communicator seen as knowledgeable—someone with expertise—is more persuasive than one with less expertise. But the source also has to be trustworthy—honest, ethical, and believable. The influence of a knowledgeable source will be lessened if audience members think he or she is biased or has underlying personal motives for advocating a position (such as being paid to endorse a product).

FIGURE 6–2

Source Attributes and Receiver Processing Modes

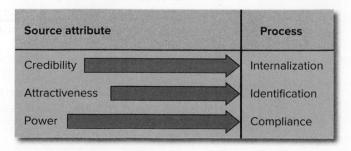

Source attribute	Process
Credibility	Internalization
Attractiveness	Identification
Power	Compliance

One of the most reliable effects found in communications research is that expert and/or trustworthy sources are more persuasive than sources who are less expert or trustworthy.[5] Information from a credible source influences beliefs, opinions, attitudes, and/or behavior through a process known as **internalization**, which occurs when the receiver adopts the opinion of the credible communicator since he or she believes information from this source is accurate. Once the receiver internalizes an opinion or attitude, it becomes integrated into the receiver's belief system and may be maintained even after the source of the message is forgotten.

A highly credible communicator is particularly important when message recipients have a negative position toward the product, service, company, or issue being promoted, because the credible source is likely to inhibit counterarguments. As discussed in Chapter 5, reduced counterarguing should result in greater message acceptance and persuasion.

Applying Expertise   Because attitudes and opinions developed through an internalization process become part of the individual's belief system, marketers want to use communicators with high credibility. Companies use a variety of techniques to convey source expertise. Sales personnel are trained in the product line, which increases customers' perceptions of their expertise. Marketers of highly technical products recruit sales reps with specialized technical backgrounds in engineering, computer science, and other areas to ensure their expertise.

Spokespeople are often chosen because of their knowledge, experience, and expertise in a particular product or service area. Endorsements from individuals or groups recognized as experts, such as doctors or dentists, are also common in advertising. For example, Dove has promoted the fact that its skin cleansing products are the most recommended by dermatologists in ads for more than 60 years (Exhibit 6–2). The importance of using expert sources was shown in a study by Roobina Ohanian, who found that the perceived expertise of celebrity endorsers was more important in explaining purchase intentions than their attractiveness or trustworthiness. She suggests that celebrity spokespeople are most effective when they are knowledgeable, experienced, and qualified to talk about the product they are endorsing.[6] A number of other studies have shown that celebrities perceived as having expertise with a product or service can lend persuasive power to an advertising message.[7]

Applying Trustworthiness   While expertise is important, the target audience must also find the source believable. Finding celebrities or other figures with trustworthy images is often difficult. Many trustworthy public figures hesitate to endorse products because of the potential impact on their reputation and image. E-Poll Market Research conducts ongoing consumer surveys to gauge the popularity and marketability of celebrities by surveying consumers and having them rate celebrities on 46 different personality attributes such as trustworthiness, sincerity, trendsetting, and influence. The company's annual E-Score Celebrity Report includes a spokesperson index score that reflects a celebrity's perceived credibility and authority and suggests the celebrity's potential as a spokesperson.[8] The company conducts ongoing research to determine the popularity of celebrities among different consumer demographic groups. For example, in its most recent poll the most popular female celebrities among women under 40 included actors Zendaya, Kristen Bell, and Jennifer Aniston, Olympic gymnast Simone Biles, and music artists Rihanna and Doja Cat. The celebrities appealing most to men under 40 included actors Dwayne "The Rock" Johnson, Keanu Reeves, and Kevin Hart. The athletes rated as the most powerful endorsers included NBA stars Stephen Curry and LeBron James, retired NBA superstar Michael Jordan, and tennis great Roger Federer.[9]

Marketers can also deal with the source-trustworthiness issue by using other IMC tools such as publicity. Information received from sources such as newscasters is often very influential because these individuals are perceived as unbiased and thus more credible, even though they are often presenting stories that stem from press releases. In some situations, celebrities may appear on news programs or talk shows and promote an upcoming cause or

event such as the release of a new movie or music. With the increase in stealth marketing techniques, many consumers are becoming wary of endorsements made by celebrities on news programs and talk shows. For example, a *New York Times* article revealed that drug companies were making payments to celebrities or their favorite charities in return for the celebrities' touting the companies' pharmaceutical products on news and talk shows. As a result of the controversy from the article, CNN and the major broadcast networks announced that they would disclose any such financial deals during interviews.[10]

With the growth of social media, another area of concern has arisen regarding the trustworthiness of sources that endorse companies and brands and make recommendations on sites such as Facebook, Instagram, TikTok, and Twitter as well as through online reviews or on blogs. In 2009 the Federal Trade Commission passed a set of guidelines requiring online endorsers and bloggers to disclose any material connection they might have to a company. The FTC developed the guidelines in response to studies that showed as many as 30 percent of online reviews were fake and were coming from someone who had been paid to write them or failed to reveal their association with a company or brand. In 2015, the FTC issued an update to its endorsement guidelines clarifying how much disclosure is required.[11]

Using Corporate Leaders as Spokespeople Another way of enhancing source credibility is to use the company president or chief executive officer as a spokesperson in the firm's advertising. Many companies believe the use of their president or CEO is the ultimate expression of the company's commitment to quality and customer service. Research has also shown that CEOs often are effective advertising spokespeople because they are seen as embodying the expertise and trust consumers require from advertising.[12] For some firms, the use of a president or CEO in their ads can help create an identity and personality for the company and/or brand. For example, Richard Branson's irreverence and zeal for life have helped personify the image of Virgin's empire of megastores, airlines, mobile phones, and soft drinks. Branson has been used occasionally in ads for various Virgin brands. Another popular CEO spokesperson is Sir James Dyson, who has appeared in ads for the company's vacuum cleaners, hair dryers, and other innovative products. Dyson is perceived to be authentic and genuine, which are two important traits for corporate leaders who appear in ads for their companies (Exhibit 6-3). The practice of using company founders, owners, and presidents as advertising spokespersons is particularly prevalent among small and midsize companies such as retailers and auto dealers serving local markets.

Many marketing and advertising experts question the strategy of using company presidents or owners in ads and note that it is often ego rather than logic that is the reason for their use.[13] The experts suggest that businesspeople should get in front of the camera only if they exude credibility and possess the intangible quality of provoking a warm, fuzzy feeling in viewers. For example, Microsoft chair Bill Gates appeared in several TV commercials that were designed to help build a stronger image for the company. Gates was paired with comedian Jerry Seinfeld in the spots, which attempted to use quirky humor to get consumers to think about Microsoft in a different way. However, the ads aired for only a short time, and many ad critics noted that Gates did not come across well in them.[14]

Another concern is that a CEO spokesperson who becomes very popular may get more attention than the company's product/service or advertising message. And if a firm's image becomes too closely tied to a popular leader, there can be problems if that person leaves the company or is involved in any type of controversy such as

EXHIBIT 6–3

James Dyson is one of the most effective CEO spokespersons.

Dyson, Inc.

James Dyson
Inventor of cyclonic vacuum technology

a labor dispute, political issue, or personal problem. For example, John Schnatter appeared in more than 60 commercials for the Papa John's pizza chain over the past two decades, and he was considered one of the most effective CEO spokespersons because he was perceived as authentic and genuine.[15] However, during an earnings report conference call in 2017, Schnatter blamed the National Football League's handling of its players' kneeling protests during the national anthem for the chain's declining pizza sales. Papa John's had been the official pizza sponsor of the NFL since 2010. Several white supremacist groups praised Schnatter for his comments and called Papa John's "the official pizza of the alt-right." The controversy resulted in an extensive amount of negative publicity for the company, which pulled all advertising featuring Schnatter, who resigned as CEO less than 2 months later.[16] It has also been argued that scandals involving top executives in some companies have eroded confidence in executives, which affects their ability to come across as trustworthy as they would have a few years ago. Moreover, in the new era of social media it is very easy to criticize corporate leaders who do not come across as trustworthy and believable.[17]

Major corporations are likely to continue to use their top executives in their advertising, particularly when they have celebrity value that helps enhance the firm's image. Some research suggests the use of a company president or CEO can improve attitudes and increase the likelihood that consumers will inquire about a company's product or service.[18] Defenders of the practice argue that the use of top executives or business owners in ads is an effective way of projecting an image of trust and honesty and, more important, the idea that the company isn't run by some faceless corporate monolith. As one expert notes: "These guys come into people's living rooms every night and, over the course of weeks and years, become like members of the family. It gets to the point that when you think of a certain product category, you think of the guy you see all the time on TV."[19]

Limitations of Credible Sources   Several studies have shown that a high-credibility source is not always an asset, nor is a low-credibility source always a liability. High- and low-credibility sources are equally effective when they are arguing for a position opposing their own best interest.[20] A very credible source is more effective when message recipients are not in favor of the position advocated in the message.[21] However, a very credible source is less important when the audience has a neutral position, and such a source may even be less effective than a moderately credible source when the receiver's initial attitude is favorable.[22]

Another reason a low-credibility source may be as effective as a high-credibility source is the **sleeper effect**, whereby the persuasiveness of a message increases with the passage of time. The immediate impact of a persuasive message may be inhibited because of its association with a low-credibility source. But with time, the association of the message with the source diminishes and the receiver's attention focuses more on favorable information in the message, resulting in more support. However, many studies have failed to demonstrate the presence of a sleeper effect.[23] Many advertisers hesitate to count on the sleeper effect, since exposure to a credible source is a more reliable strategy.[24]

Source Attractiveness

A source characteristic frequently used by advertisers is **attractiveness**, which encompasses similarity, familiarity, and likability.[25] *Similarity* is a supposed resemblance between the source and the receiver of the message, while *familiarity* refers to knowledge of the source through exposure. *Likability* is an affection for the source as a result of physical appearance, behavior, or other personal traits. Even when the sources are not athletes or movie stars, consumers often admire their physical appearance, talent, and/or personality.

Source attractiveness leads to persuasion through a process of **identification**, whereby the receiver is motivated to seek some type of relationship with the source and thus adopts similar beliefs, attitudes, preferences, or behavior. Maintaining this position depends on the source's continued support for the position as well as the receiver's continued identification with the source. If the source changes position, the receiver may also change. Unlike internalization, identification does not usually integrate information from an attractive source into the receiver's belief system. The receiver may maintain the attitudinal position or behavior only as long as it is supported by the source or the source remains attractive.

Marketers recognize that receivers of persuasive communications are more likely to attend to and identify with people they find likable or similar to themselves. Similarity and likability are the two source characteristics marketers seek when choosing a communicator.

Applying Similarity   Marketers recognize that people are more likely to be influenced by a message coming from someone with whom they feel a sense of similarity.[26] If the communicator and receiver have similar needs, goals, interests, and lifestyles, the position advocated by the source is better understood and received. Similarity is used in various ways in marketing communications. Companies select salespeople whose characteristics match well with their customers'. A sales position for a particular region may be staffed by someone local who has background and interests in common with the customers. Global marketers often hire foreign nationals as salespeople so customers can relate more easily to them. Companies may also try to recruit former athletes to sell sporting goods or beer, since their customers usually have a strong interest in sports. Several studies have shown that customers who perceive a salesperson as similar to themselves are more likely to be influenced by the salesperson's message.[27]

Similarity is also used by creating a situation where the consumer feels empathy for the person shown in the commercial. In a slice-of-life commercial, the advertiser usually starts by showing an event or predicament that consumers often face, with the hope of getting the consumer to think, "I can see myself in that situation." This can help establish a bond of similarity between the communicator and the receiver, increasing the source's level of persuasiveness. Marketers like to cast actors in their commercials that consumers will notice, recognize, identify with, and remember, as well as help differentiate their products and services. In some cases they try to create a personality figure for the company or brand that consumers will find likable. For example, one of the most popular advertising personalities for more than a decade has been Flo, the fictional salesperson character who has appeared in more than 100 commercials for Progressive Insurance. Her popularity prompted other companies to develop likeable characters such as Jan, the charming and sassy receptionist at the Toyota dealership, and Lily, the retail store employee who has appeared in ads for AT&T's mobile service for a number of years (Exhibit 6–4). Her perky enthusiasm and somewhat quirky wit and charm, along with the way she presents the mobile plans to customers, has made the ad campaign very popular with consumers.[28] Casting directors consider factors such as similarity and how the audience will identify with people when looking for talent to use in commercials.

Many companies feel that the best way to connect with consumers is by using regular-looking, everyday people with whom the average person can easily identify. For example, some of the most popular commercials for many years were those from the "Whassup?" campaign for Budweiser beer. In these ads the DDB agency cast a group of real-life friends from Philadelphia, rather than actors, who greet each other with the slang word "Whassup?" when they speak on the phone or get together to watch a game and enjoy a Bud. *Advertising Age* named "Whassup?" one of the top ad campaigns of the 21st century, noting how it was very effective at tapping into popular culture and what young people are actually like and how they speak to each other.[29]

EXHIBIT 6–4

AT&T commercials featuring Lily, the store employee, have been very popular.

AT&T Inc.

Applying Likability: Using Celebrities Marketers recognize the value of using popular celebrities to endorse their companies and brands, such as TV and movie stars, athletes, entertainers, musicians, and other well-known public figures. And they are willing to pay them large amounts of money to do so. Many of the top endorsers are professional athletes. According to *Forbes'* annual report, athletes making the most from global endorsement deals in 2022 included Swiss tennis star Roger Federer, who made an estimated $90 million per year, followed by NBA basketball star LeBron James at $80 million, and golfer Tiger Woods at $68 million.[30] IMC Perspective 6-1 discusses how Federer achieved great success and wealth as an endorser. Several other athletes make more than $50 million a year in endorsements, including soccer stars Cristiano Ronaldo and Lionel Messi, and NBA star Kevin Durant. For women, the top athlete endorser was tennis star Naomi Osaka, who makes $58 million from endorsement deals with Nike, Louis Vuitton, Gatorade, Workday, and a number of other companies, followed by Serena Williams at $45 million. Other top female endorsers include former tennis star Maria Sharapova and gymnast Simone Biles. A number of top female endorsers are entertainers, including actor-singer Jennifer Lopez and singers Beyoncé and Taylor Swift. Actors making the most from endorsement deals include Charlize Theron and Sofia Vergara, whose endorsements include Pepsi, Head & Shoulders shampoo, and Cover Girl cosmetics.[31]

There are a number of reasons marketers spend huge sums of money to have celebrities appear in TV commercials or print ads to endorse their company or brand or promote them on social media. Many marketers recognize that celebrities have *stopping power*. That is, they draw attention to advertising messages in very cluttered media environments, as the human brain recognizes celebrities in a manner similar to how it recognizes people we actually know. This in turn leads to greater recall and/or recognition of the company or brand. Celebrities can also favorably influence consumers' feelings, attitudes, and purchase behavior, as they may give more attention to and place higher value on products and services celebrities are endorsing.

Another reason for using celebrity endorsers is that they can enhance the target audience's perceptions of the product or service in terms of image and/or performance. Most marketers of sporting goods equipment use athletes to endorse their products because a well-known athlete may convince potential buyers that the product will enhance their own performance. For example, most of the companies that make golf equipment have endorsement deals with professional golfers who appear in ads and can be seen using their clubs and balls in televised tournaments. Exhibit 6-5 shows an ad for Srixon's Z Star Series golf ball featuring professional golfer Hideki Matsuyama.

A number of factors must be considered when a company decides to use a celebrity spokesperson, including the dangers of overshadowing the product and being overexposed, the target audience's receptivity, and risks to the advertiser.

Overshadowing the Product How will the celebrity affect the target audience's processing of the advertising message? Consumers may focus their attention on the celebrity and fail to notice or recall the brand or advertising message. Carsten Erfgen and his colleagues refer to this as the "vampire effect" and note that it occurs when the personality of the celebrity endorser overshadows the brand he or she is advertising and thus has a negative impact rather than helping to sell it.[32] Advertisers should select a celebrity spokesperson who will attract attention and enhance the sales message yet not overshadow the brand. For example, high-end clothing brand St. John decided that it was best to drop actor Angelina Jolie from its advertising after a few years. The company felt that she was overshadowing the brand. Jolie was viewed as a very good fit for St. John, including her role as the voice of its children's charity—a cause she is well known for supporting. However, the company felt that she was simply too famous and decided to use a top British fashion model in its ads.[33] A recent study found that celebrity overshadowing can be particularly problematic when the consumers have low attachment to or interest in the celebrity.[34]

EXHIBIT 6-5

Golf equipment companies such as Srixon use professional golfers to endorse their products.

SRI Sports Limited

Tennis Star Roger Federer Joins the Billion-Dollar Club

Mohamed Farag/Getty Images

Companies have been using popular athletes to endorse their products and services and serve as advertising spokespersons for decades. Marketers realize the value of using athletes who are recognized and often admired by their target audience as a way to draw attention to their advertising messages. Sports stars usually promote products such as athletic shoes, apparel, and sports equipment. However, the popularity of high-profile athletes often transcends sports, and they endorse a variety of other products including automobiles, fast food, soft drinks, clothing, airlines, and watches, as well as consulting and financial services.

Star athletes often make large amounts of money from the contracts they sign with professional teams or the prize money they earn from tournaments or competitions in sports such as tennis, golf, and boxing. However, for many athletes most of the money they make comes from endorsement deals with major companies around the world. The latest athlete to join the $1 billion club in career earnings while still active was 41-year-old Swiss tennis star Roger Federer, who joined golfer Tiger Woods, boxer Floyd Mayweather, NBA star LeBron James, and soccer stars Cristiano Ronaldo and Lionel Messi in the prestigious 10-figure club. As of 2022, $130 million of Federer's bankroll had come from prize money as a professional tennis player while nearly $900 million had come from his unmatched endorsement portfolio of blue-chip companies.

There are a number of reasons for Federer's tremendous popularity as an endorser. First of all, Federer is considered one of the greatest tennis players of all time as he has won an astounding 103 ATP tournaments and holds 20 Grand Slam singles titles, third behind Novak Djokovic with 21 and Rafael Nadal at 22. His eight singles titles at Wimbledon, which is the oldest tennis tournament in the world and widely regarded as the most prestigious, is also a record. He has been viewed as perhaps the most marketable athlete in the world for more than a decade. He has incredible

demeanor both on and off the court and has handled both wins and losses with grace and style, which has made him endearing to fans as well as sponsors.

Another major reason for Federer's success as an endorser is the way he has managed his career off the court. Like many tennis stars, Federer originally signed an endorsement deal with Nike in 1994 when he was just a teenager. By 2002, he was making an average of $100,000 a year. In 2002 he renewed the deal for an estimated $2 million annually, which most experts considered as being way too low given his on-court potential and the endorsements of other tennis stars such Maria Sharapova, Andy Roddick, and Andre Agassi, which were much higher. In 2005 Federer re-signed with the sports management company IMG, which he had left in 2002 to go on his own, and by 2008 Federer renewed his Nike deal for 10 years, reportedly at more than $10 million per year, which was believed to be a record for a tennis endorsement. IMG also helped Federer secure lucrative global endorsement deals with Gillette, Rolex, Mercedes-Benz, Wilson, Credit Suisse, and Moët & Chandon.

By 2012 Federer was making an estimated $70 million in endorsements, which put him second on the list of the world's highest-paid athletes, trailing only golfer Tiger Woods. However, that same year he made a major decision to take greater control of his career off the court when he left the sports agency giant IMG and launched his own sports agency company called TEAM 8 with his longtime agent Tony Godsick. In 2018, Federer made perhaps the biggest sponsorship gamble of his career when he walked away from Nike and signed a 10-year apparel deal with Japanese fast fashion brand Uniqlo, which guaranteed him $30 million per year, even after he retired from competition. The deal with Uniqlo covered only apparel and not shoes, and Federer also signed a deal with Swiss sneaker brand On as a global ambassador that gave him equity in the company. It is estimated the deal could be worth several hundred million dollars to Federer when the company goes public.

Experts noted that Uniqlo's offer was clearly far more than Nike was prepared to pay an aging superstar, no matter how popular. Moreover, tennis is not a major money-making division as it accounts for only about $350 million of the company's $45 billion in annual revenue. The rule of thumb in the world of sponsorships is that you don't spend over 10 percent of overall revenue on athlete sponsorship deals, and Nike already had a loaded roster of tennis stars including Serena Williams, Rafael Nadal, Maria Sharapova, and rising star Nick Kyrgios under contract. The company had also signed a $1 billion lifetime endorsement deal with basketball star LeBron James.

Federer retired from tennis in September 2022, saying his body would no longer allow him to compete at a high level. However, he shows no signs of slowing down as a corporate pitchman. He has 12.7 million followers on Twitter, placing him just behind Rafael Nadal in popularity, and he boasts 18 million Facebook followers, which is far ahead of every other tennis professional. Tennis players, like professional golfers and soccer players, are very popular from a marketing perspective as they are part of a global sport that appeals to both men and women. Federer is very likely to join the list of athletes who have been popular endorsers even in retirement including David Beckham, Michael Jordan, Peyton Manning, and Maria Sharapova. Most of Federer's sponsors have extended their endorsement deals with Federer and will go with him into his retirement and beyond. University of Oregon sports sponsorship expert T. Bettina Cornwell sums it up best when asked if these companies are taking a risk: "Federer is timeless."

Sources: Christopher Clarey, "The Chief Tennis Officer," *The New York Times Magazine*, August 29, 2021, pp. 26–31, 57; James Booth, "Roger Federer's Sponsor Gamble Pays Off Big Time," *Dmarge*, October 12, 2021, https://www.dmarge.com/roger-federer-sponsor; Kurt Badenhausen, "How Roger Federer Became Tennis' First $1 Billion Star," *Sportico.com*, June 29, 2021, https://www.yahoo.com/video/roger-federer-became-tennis-first-140023231.html.

Overexposure Consumers are often skeptical of endorsements because they know the celebrities are being paid.[35] This problem is particularly pronounced when a celebrity endorses too many products or companies and becomes overexposed. For example, former NFL quarterback Peyton Manning has had endorsement deals and appeared in commercials for a number of companies/brands including Nike, ESPN, Frito Lay, Pepsi, Michelob Ultra, Workday, and Caesar's Sports Book. Advertisers can protect themselves against overexposure with an exclusivity clause limiting the number of products a celebrity can endorse. However, such clauses are usually expensive, and most celebrities agree not to endorse similar products anyway. Many celebrities, knowing their fame is fleeting, try to earn as much endorsement money as possible, yet they must be careful not to damage their credibility by endorsing too many products. For example, singer-actor Cher damaged her credibility as an advertising spokesperson by appearing in too many infomercials. When she realized that appearing in so many infomercials was hurting her acting career as well, she ceased doing them.[36]

Target Audiences' Receptivity One of the most important considerations in choosing a celebrity endorser is how well the individual matches with and is received by the advertiser's target audience. Marketers have to consider the reputation and image of the celebrity endorsers they are considering as spokespersons and how well they align with the image of their company or brand, as well as the advertising message. Consideration must also be given to whether celebrities resonate with the audience they are targeting because many consumers are not influenced by celebrity endorsements. For example, consumers who are particularly knowledgeable about a product or service or have strongly established attitudes may be less influenced by a celebrity than would those with little knowledge or neutral attitudes. Several studies have found celebrity endorsements are more effective with younger consumers such as gen Z and millennials because these age cohorts have a higher level of trust of celebrities and are more likely to have a positive attitude toward companies or brands endorsed by them.[37]

The teen and young adult markets are generally very receptive to celebrity endorsers, as evidenced by the frequent use of entertainers and athletes in ads targeted to this group for products such as apparel, cosmetics, and beverages. Many marketers are taking advantage of this by utilizing the social media communities of celebrities to engage and build connections with celebrities they follow. As was discussed in Chapter 5, many celebrities promote brands on their personal Instagram or Facebook pages. For example, pop star Selena Gomez has endorsement deals with a number of companies/brands, including Coach, Coca-Cola, and Pantene shampoo. Luxury brand marketer Louis Vuitton signed Gomez to an endorsement deal a few years ago by rolling out ads on Instagram, where she has a huge global following. The post scored more than 1 million likes in the first 2 hours it was posted.[38]

While young celebrities with large followings on social media are often used as endorsers, recent research has shown that their older counterparts are just as effective, if not more so. A study by Spotted, a research company that focuses on celebrity endorsements, analyzed the effectiveness of endorsement deals, taking into

EXHIBIT 6–6

Dwayne "The Rock" Johnson is a very effective spokesperson for a number of companies and brands. Under Armour has created a signature product line that is built around his image and authenticiy.

Under Armour, Inc.

consideration factors such as the likability; relatability; attractiveness; trustworthiness; authenticity; and facial, name, and voice recognition of 400 celebrities. Their study found that the most effective campaigns were those using older celebrities such as Dwayne "The Rock" Johnson for Under Armour, Mark Wahlberg for AT&T, Kristen Bell for Old Navy, and Reese Witherspoon for Crate & Barrel. The least effective campaigns used younger celebrities such as Bella Thorne for BUXOM cosmetics, Shay Mitchell for Toyota, and Ansel Elgort for Polo Ralph Lauren. Spotted's CEO noted that older celebrities may be more effective because the sheer volume of their work gives them more exposure to different subsets of consumers, and they enjoy a higher level of familiarity and trustworthiness.[39]

Under Armour recently collaborated with Dwayne Johnson to create a new product line called "Outlaw Mana," which features a full line of clothing and shoes for both men and women (Exhibit 6–6). Johnson also has endorsement deals with a number of other brands including Apple, Ford, and Voss water.

A number of marketers do not use celebrities because they have determined that they do not influence the markets they are targeting, and/or they do not want to pay the large sums of money often required to do so. Many are also concerned that consumers have become more skeptical and cynical toward the use of celebrity endorsers and respond better to ads using humor, irony, and unvarnished truth. There is also concern over tying a company or brand's image to a celebrity endorser, which we discuss next.

Risk to the Advertiser A celebrity's behavior may pose a risk to a company.[40] A number of entertainers and athletes have been involved in activities that could embarrass the companies whose products they endorsed. For example, golfer Tiger Woods was making more than $100 million per year from various endorsement deals when he was dominating professional golf. However, a number of companies, including Accenture, Gillette, Gatorade, and Tag Heur, terminated their deals with him when his infidelity and other character issues became public in 2009. Woods retained his endorsement deal with Nike and has signed endorsement deals with other companies such as Monster Energy, TaylorMade Golf, and Bridgestone Golf after rebuilding his image.[41] Several high-profile athletes have lost lucrative endorsement deals after testing positive for performance-enhancing drugs including former tennis star Maria Sharapova and seven-time Tour De France cycling champion Lance Armstrong. More recently, adidas ended its endorsement deal with San Diego Padres baseball star Fernando Tatis Jr. after 2 years when he tested positive for a banned substance.[42]

Problems regarding endorsers are not limited to athletes; they can occur with other types of celebrities as well, including social media influencers. In 2019 several celebrities were among a group of individuals indicted for allegedly paying large sums of money to help their children gain admission into prestigious universities. Actor Lori Loughlin and her fashion designer husband Mossimo Giannulli were charged with paying $500,000 to help their two daughters get into the University of Southern California by designating them as recruits to the university's crew team. One of the daughters, Olivia Jade Giannulli, was a popular social media influencer with nearly 2 million subscribers on YouTube and 1.3 million followers on Instagram. However, within a few weeks most of the companies whose brands she was representing cut ties with her, including cosmetics giant Sephora, hair care brand TRESemmé, fashion brand Lulus, and consumer electronics company HP Inc.[43] Jade is still an active influencer but most of her deals are with smaller brands such as denim line Garage and sneakers from Banana Bread.

Marketers recognize that the use of celebrity endorsers can be a very expensive and high-risk strategy because what the celebrities do in their personal lives can impact their image and the way they are viewed by the public. Some companies may face a dilemma in selecting celebrity endorsers: While they prefer them to be upright, they still want them to have an edge or be somewhat irreverent to be able to connect with consumers. This may be particularly true for companies marketing their products to teens and young adults. To avoid problems, companies often research a celebrity's personal life and background. Many endorsement contracts include a morals clause allowing the company to terminate the contract if a controversy arises. Several companies, including luxury brands Burberry and Chanel as well as fashion retailer H&M, canceled their contracts with supermodel Kate Moss in the wake of a British tabloid photo that showed her using cocaine.[44] However, marketers should remember that adding morals clauses to their endorsement contracts only gets them out of a problem; it does not prevent it from happening. Thus, it is important that they carefully consider the character of a celebrity as well as the potential risk associated with using him or her as a spokesperson or endorser for the company or one of its brands.[45]

Return on Investment Perhaps the most important factor a company must consider regarding the use of celebrity endorsers is the return on investment from using them. Marketers use celebrities to increase awareness of and attention to their company and/or brands, as well as their advertisements, and to develop strong associations between the celebrity and the brand that will result in higher purchase intentions. Many companies do not reveal the increases in sales and/or market share that result from the use of celebrity endorsers. However, an interesting study was conducted by Anita Elberse and Jeroen Verleun that examined the economic impact of a sample of 347 endorsement deals for 180 athletes across six packaged-goods product categories. The results of their study found that sales did increase significantly over the first 6 months that the athlete endorsers were used—about 4 percent. However, subsequent major achievements by the athletes did not improve the sales of the brands studied relative to their competitors, which calls into question the long-term value of endorsement deals.[46]

It should be noted that there are many examples of companies that have seen sales increase, and there can be other factors that marketers consider in determining the value gained from using a celebrity endorser. Thus it is likely that many marketers will continue to use them despite some of the drawbacks associated with their use that have been discussed. Some companies are changing their relationships with celebrity endorsers and having them become more involved with their companies and brands rather than just appearing in advertisements (Exhibit 6–7). A number of high-profile celebrities have become involved in areas such as product design and development as well as the advertising creative process. For example, Selena Gomez's endorsement deal with Coach included her collaborating with the luxury brand's creative director to develop her own line of accessories, leather goods, and clothing.[47] Actor Jennifer Aniston entered into a partnership with collagen powder company Vital Proteins that included making her the company's chief creative officer.[48] Some marketing experts argue that these celebrity deals are little more than window dressing, while others argue that they can be valuable.

Marketers are also becoming more creative in the way they pay celebrities, sometimes even by giving them a stake in the company. For example, rapper 50 Cent (Curtis Jackson) received a minority stake in Glacéau Vitaminwater, which increased his involvement with the company. He developed a flavor, appeared in ads, and even mentioned the brand in some of this songs. When the company was acquired by Coca-Cola, Jackson made an estimated $100 million.[49] When Under Armour signed New England Patriots quarterback Tom Brady to an endorsement deal, he received an equity stake in the company. According to Under Armour CEO Kevin Plank, it was an ideal arrangement for the firm, as it makes Brady fully invested in the company's success.[50]

More recently, a number of high-profile athletes received large payouts after forgoing cash payment in exchange for equity in endorsement deals with the sports drink BodyArmor, which was purchased by the Coca-Cola Company for $5.6 billion in 2021. The estate of late NBA star Kobe Bryant received more than $400 million from his stake in

EXHIBIT 6–7

Marketers are using celebrities for more than just appearing in ads.

Mark Dierker/McGraw Hill

the company while some of the earliest endorsers such as NBA star James Harden, former NFL quarterback Andrew Luck, and Major League Baseball player Mike Trout also received eight-figure payouts.[51]

Understanding the Meaning of Celebrity Endorsers   Advertisers must try to match the product or company's image, the characteristics of the target market, and the personality of the celebrity.[52] The image celebrities project to consumers can be just as important as their ability to attract attention. An interesting perspective on celebrity endorsement was developed by Grant McCracken.[53] He argues that credibility and attractiveness don't sufficiently explain how and why celebrity endorsements work and offers a model based on meaning transfer (Figure 6–3).

According to this model, a celebrity's effectiveness as an endorser depends on the culturally acquired meanings he or she brings to the endorsement process. Each celebrity contains many meanings, including status, class, gender, and age as well as personality and lifestyle. In explaining stage 1 of the meaning transfer process, McCracken notes:

> Celebrities draw these powerful meanings from the roles they assume in their television, movie, military, athletic, and other careers. Each new dramatic role brings the celebrity into contact with a range of objects, persons, and contexts. Out of these objects, persons, and contexts are transferred meanings that then reside in the celebrity.[54]

The advertising industry sometimes refers to the cultural meaning a celebrity spokesperson can bring to an endorsement as "borrowed equity." An excellent example of a celebrity who has acquired cultural meaning that she brings to her many endorsements is actor Jennifer Aniston. In addition to being very attractive, she is funny, charismatic, authentic, and wholesome—a persona developed from the Rachel character she played on the hit sitcom *Friends* for many years. She is also perceived as very likeable, relatable, and aspirational, which are traits stemming from the roles she has played in movies such as *The Breakup*, *Marly & Me*, *Horrible Bosses*, and *Office Space* and more recently the Apple TV+ series *The Morning Show*. Aniston's cultural meaning works very well in endorsements she has done for brands such as Heineken, Shire Eyelove, and Emirates Airlines.[55]

McCracken suggests celebrity endorsers bring their meanings and image into the ad and transfer them to the product they are endorsing (stage 2 of the model in Figure 6–3). For example, Jennifer Aniston is also known for living a healthy lifestyle and promoting wellness, which is reflected in her ageless beauty. This aspect of her cultural meaning helped make her a very effective endorser in advertising for brands such as Aveeno Skin Care and Glaceau Smartwater. More recently she has been appearing in ads for the

FIGURE 6–3

Meaning Movement and the Endorsement Process

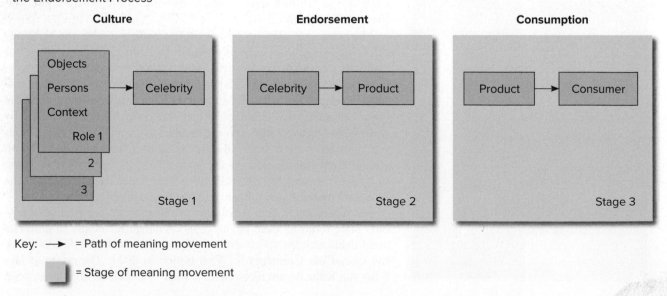

Key: → = Path of meaning movement

▢ = Stage of meaning movement

EXHIBIT 6–8

Jennifer Aniston's image works well in advertising for wellness products such as Vital Proteins.

Vital Proteins LLC

collagen powder brand Vital Proteins, which is positioned as a supplement that can help support healthy skin, hair, nails, bones, and joints (Exhibit 6–8).

In the final stage of McCracken's model, the meanings the celebrity has given to the product are transferred to the consumer. The use of Aniston in its advertising helps Vital Proteins communicate its branding and positioning message of how use of the product along with a proper diet and exercise can lead to health and vitality. McCracken notes that this final stage is complicated and difficult to achieve. The way consumers take possession of the meaning the celebrity has transferred to a product is probably the least understood part of the process.

The meaning transfer model has some important implications for companies using celebrity endorsers. Marketers must first decide on the image or symbolic meanings important to the target audience for the particular product, service, or company. They must then determine which celebrity best represents the meaning or image to be projected. An advertising campaign must be designed that captures that meaning in the product and moves it to the consumer. Marketing and advertising personnel often rely on intuition in choosing celebrity endorsers for their companies or products, but some companies conduct research studies to determine consumers' perceptions of celebrities' meaning.

Marketers may also pretest ads to determine whether they transfer the proper meaning to the product. When celebrity endorsers are used, the marketer should track the campaign's effectiveness. Does the celebrity continue to be effective in communicating the proper meaning to the target audience? Celebrities who are no longer in the limelight may lose their ability to transfer any significant meanings to the product.

CHOOSING A CELEBRITY ENDORSER

As we have seen, marketers must consider many factors when choosing a celebrity to serve as an advertising spokesperson for the company or a particular brand. Studies have shown that advertising and marketing managers take these various factors into account when choosing a celebrity endorser.[56] Among the most important factors are the celebrity's match with the target audience and the product/service or brand, the overall image of the celebrity, the cost of acquiring the celebrity, trustworthiness, the risk of controversy, and the celebrity's familiarity and likability among the target audience. Another consideration for marketers is whether to use mainstream celebrities such as athletes, actors, and entertainers or spend their promotional budget on social media influencers and YouTube personalities who have become quasi-celebrities and are often more influential with younger audiences. Over the past two decades, the growth of social media platforms such as Facebook, YouTube, Instagram, Snapchat, and TikTok has dramatically changed the way many people consume media and entertainment. YouTube has nearly 2 billion monthly users who spend an average of an hour a day on the YouTube mobile app alone. Digital and Social Media Perspective 6–1 discusses how social media influencers and YouTube personalities are becoming celebrities who are very influential among the gen Z cohort and younger millennials who have grown up with YouTube and social media as their primary source of entertainment.

While some advertising and marketing executives rely on their own intuition and gut feeling, many turn to research that measures a celebrity's familiarity and appeal among their target audience as well as other factors. Many companies and their advertising agencies rely on Q-scores that are commercially available from the New York–based firm Marketing Evaluations, Inc. To determine its Q-scores for various types of

Are Social Media Influencers Really Celebrities?

If you took a survey of baby boomers or gen Xers and asked them to name the most influential celebrities, it is likely the list would include television and movie stars, entertainers, musicians, and athletes. Depending on their age, they would probably mention popular celebrities such as Jennifer Anniston, Tom Cruise, Adele, Jennifer Lopez, Beyoncé, George Clooney, Brad Pitt, LeBron James, and perhaps even one of the Kardashians. However, if you were to ask many millennials and gen Zers the same question, the list would be quite different and include names that many people have never heard of—such as Khaby Lame, Huda Kattan, Charli D'Amelio, Rickey Thompson, or MrBeast—unless they spend a lot of time on Instagram, TikTok, YouTube, and other popular social media sites.

The 21st century has become the age of social media, and a myriad of influencers have emerged since the launch of various platforms such as YouTube, Facebook, Instagram, Snapchat, and more recently TikTok. Gone are the days when marketers relied primarily on celebrity endorsements in ads to promote their brands. Now many are allocating a significant part of their marketing budget to influencers who have a large following on social media and are viewed as experts in their niche. Influencer marketing works because of the high level of trust influencers have built with their audience, which makes their endorsement a form of social proof that can influence the behavior of their followers.

It has been argued that social media influencers have become the new celebrities of our age as many of them have amassed large numbers of follower and fans that rival traditional celebrities. For example, Charli D'Amelio, who has become famous for posting dancing and choreography videos on TikTok, has 125 million followers on the platform and another 50 million on Instagram. She has clearly achieved celebrity status among her many followers on these social media platforms. However, an interesting debate has emerged regarding whether social media influencers should be viewed the same as traditional celebrities as there are differences in the ways they have acquired their fandom.

Gillian Brooks and her colleagues note that traditional celebrities acquire celebrity capital through institutional intermediaries such as sport, television, music, and movies. Their capital is also built through the attention they receive in the media, that is, magazines and television talk and entertainment shows. The traditional celebrification process is controlled by gatekeepers of media visibility such as publicists, red carpet events, paparazzi, and the endorsement deals for which they often exchange their celebrity capital. Social media influencers, on the other hand, gain popularity without such institutional intermediaries as they are famous online for becoming famous online, often on specific platforms such as TikTok, YouTube, or Instagram. Their celebrity capital is built through direct interaction with their followers. Their fans share their content, which helps influencers gain new audiences every day.

Taylor Hill/FilmMagic/Getty Images

The question is whether influencers should be accorded the same status as traditional celebrities who have built their "star power" based on their talent as singers, actors, entertainers, or athletes. Social media influencers become popular by posting engaging content on social media platforms, and their popularity is often limited to these platforms. While it is possible for most celebrities to become social media influencers, most influencers cannot be celebrities.

However, there are several reasons YouTubers influence teens and millennials more than mainstream celebrities do. According to a study conducted by Google, and many other studies, YouTube subscribers say that their favorite YouTubers understand them better and can relate to them more than do traditional celebrities. YouTube content creators develop relationships with their fan base, which leads to higher engagement, as evidenced by more views, comments, and other actions such as liking and sharing. Teens and young adults feel that YouTube personalities are more influential in setting trends and shaping popular culture than traditional celebrities. A new generation of social media influencers who create their own content and deliver it on TikTok, YouTube, Instagram, Facebook, and other platforms are becoming household names and legitimate influencers among young consumers.

Chris Foster, the former chief operating officer of the Saatchi & Saatchi advertising agency, notes that the Internet and social media are clearly changing the nature of celebrity in ways that have major implications for advertising and other forms of marketing. He argues that the traditional image of a celebrity as remote, unknowable, and highly controlled by publicists is no longer persuasive or effective because members of today's plugged-in generation want to feel connected to their idols and have a sense of how they spend their lives.

Foster argues that a democratization of celebrity is taking place that includes three key factors—expertise, access, and identification—and popular social media personalities often stack up as well, if not better, on all three than do traditional celebrities who are paid to promote brands. He notes that the use of endorsements in advertising will never go away but is changing dramatically in ways that give advertisements more meaning. Technology is enabling ordinary consumers themselves to do the marketing for brands and do it in ways that are more authentic and may remove the need for celebrity endorsers. As Foster notes: "We've seen the future of celebrity endorsers and it's us."

Sources: Gillian Brooks, Jenna Drenten, and Mikolaj Jan Piskorski, "Influencer Celebrification: How Social Media Influencers Acquire Celebrity Capital," *Journal of Advertising* 50, no. 5 (October–December 2021), pp. 528–547; Loveleen Kaur, "Are Social Media Influencers Turning into New Age Celebrities?" *Thinkbizarre*, March 1, 2022, https://thinkbizarre.com/social-media-influencers-turning-into-celebrities/; Chris Foster, "Why J-Law & George Clooney Don't Matter: Saatchi & Saatchi COO," *USA Today*, June 15, 2015, www.usatoday.com/story/opinion/2015/06/12/internet-celebrity-endorsement-advertising-column/71084290/.

celebrities—including athletes, news and sports personalities, performers such as actors and entertainers, and influencers—the company surveys a representative national panel of consumers several times a year. Respondents are asked to indicate whether they have ever seen or heard of the performer or sports personality and, if they have, to rate him or her on a scale that includes "one of my favorites," very good, good, fair, and poor. The *familiarity score* indicates what percentage of people have heard of the person; the *one of my favorites score* is an absolute measure of the appeal or popularity of the celebrity. The well-known *Q-score* is calculated by taking the percentage of respondents who indicate that a person is "one of my favorites" and then dividing that number by the percentage of respondents who indicate they have heard of that person. Q-scores are important because they answer the question: How appealing is the person among those who do know him or her? The average Q-score for performers is generally around 18 and about 17 for sports personalities. Marketing Evaluation's Q-scores are also broken down on the basis of various demographic criteria such as a respondent's age, income, location, occupation, education, and race as well as social media usage so that marketers have some idea of how a celebrity's popularity varies among different groups of consumers. Marketing Evaluations also now reports a negative Q-score, which is the percentage of respondents who rate the personality as fair or poor divided by only those who are familiar with the person. Exhibit 6–9 shows a sample page from the Performer Q study.

In addition to Q-scores, marketers use information provided by a number of other research firms that provide them with data on the popularity of various celebrities and insight into how well their image might fit with their company or brand. For example, consumer research firm GfK MRI and market research firm E-Poll launched a new service, MRI/E-Poll Celebrity Fusion, that provides detailed insight into consumer/celebrity compatibility. The service combines MRI's consumer research data, which covers purchase patterns for over 6,500 products and services, with E-Polls research on awareness, appeal, and attribute measures for more than 10,000 celebrities. The service allows marketers insight into how the interest and appeal of celebrities align with consumers' purchase behavior for various brands.[57]

Applying Likability Decorative Models

Advertisers often draw attention to their ads by featuring a physically attractive person who serves as a passive or decorative model rather than as an active communicator. Research suggests that physically attractive communicators generally have a positive impact and generate more favorable evaluations of both ads and products than do less attractive models.[58] The gender appropriateness of the model for the product being advertised and the model's relevance to the product are also important considerations.[59] Products such as cosmetics or fashionable clothing are likely to benefit from the use of attractive models, since physical appearance is very relevant in marketing these items.

	PERSONALITY NAME						
	ONE OF MY FAVORITES	VERY GOOD	GOOD	FAIR/ POOR	TOTAL FAMILIAR	POSITIVE Q SCORE	NEGATIVE Q SCORE
TOTAL SAMPLE	9	18	30	25	83	11	31
6 - 11 YEARS	16	12	18	9	56	29	17
12 - 17 YEARS	11	21	30	23	86	13	27
18 - 34 YEARS	11	22	33	29	95	11	31
35 - 49 YEARS	11	20	34	26	90	12	29
50 AND OVER	4	13	28	27	72	6	37
18 - 49 YEARS	11	21	34	28	93	11	30
18 YEARS AND OVER	8	18	32	27	85	10	32
25 - 54 YEARS	11	20	32	28	91	12	31
TOTAL MALES							
6 AND OVER	9	16	31	25	81	11	31
18 - 34 YEARS	10	21	33	29	94	10	31
35 - 49 YEARS	13	18	33	25	89	15	28
50 AND OVER	4	11	28	25	67	5	36
18 - 49 YEARS	11	20	33	27	91	13	30
18 YEARS AND OVER	9	17	31	26	83	11	32
25 - 54 YEARS	12	21	30	27	90	13	30
TOTAL FEMALES							
6 AND OVER	10	19	30	26	84	12	31
18 - 34 YEARS	12	22	33	30	97	12	31
35 - 49 YEARS	8	21	35	27	91	9	30
50 AND OVER	5	15	28	29	76	7	38
18 - 49 YEARS	10	22	34	28	94	10	30
18 YEARS AND OVER	8	19	32	29	87	9	33
25 - 54 YEARS	10	20	34	29	92	11	31
HOUSEHOLD INCOME							
UNDER $20,000	8	13	30	20	71	11	28
$20,000 - $39,999	9	18	31	26	85	11	31
$40,000 - $59,999	11	14	34	27	86	13	31
$60,000 AND OVER	9	21	28	27	85	11	31
$75,000 AND OVER	9	19	29	28	85	11	32
EDUCATION (ADULT)							
HIGH SCHOOL GRADUATE/LESS	10	19	30	23	80	12	28
SOME COLLEGE/DEGREE	7	17	34	32	90	8	36
OCCUPATION (ADULT)							
WHITE COLLAR	7	21	35	29	91	7	32
BLUE COLLAR	10	16	32	28	85	12	32
RACE							
NON BLACK	7	17	31	27	81	9	33
BLACK	26	25	23	16	90	29	17
ETHNICITY							
HISPANIC	12	17	37	23	89	13	26
NIELSEN COUNTY SIZE							
A	11	18	32	26	87	12	30
B	9	19	30	25	83	11	30
C & D	8	16	28	24	75	10	32
REGION							
NORTHEAST	10	21	25	30	85	12	35
NORTH CENTRAL	9	19	32	24	83	11	28
SOUTH	11	18	32	21	82	13	26
WEST	7	13	30	30	80	9	38

EXHIBIT 6–9

Sample page from Marketing Evaluations, Inc., Performer Q Study.

Marketing Evaluations, Inc.

Some models draw attention to the ad but not to the product or message. Studies show that an attractive model facilitates recognition of the ad but does not enhance copy readership or message recall. Thus, advertisers must ensure that the consumer's attention will go beyond the model to the product and advertising message.[60] Marketers must also consider whether the use of highly attractive models might negatively impact advertising effectiveness. Several studies have shown that some women experience negative feelings when comparing themselves with beautiful models used in ads and the images of physical perfection they represent.[61] A recent study by Rachelle Jantzon and Michael Basil suggests that it is possible for models or endorsers to be too attractive, particularly when an ad is targeted at an audience that is the same sex as the endorser.[62] Their study found that endorser attractiveness generally makes an ad more effective with viewers not of the same sex. However, when an ad is evaluated by viewers of the same sex, the use of a highly attractive model may result in less interest in the advertisement, suggesting that marketers should be cautious about unrealistically attractive models in their ads.

The only models we'll ever use are role models.

We feature women who reflect the real beauty diversity in society
#RealBeauty #DovePromise

Mario Testiono & *Dove*

EXHIBIT 6-10

Dove takes a social advocacy approach in promoting its beauty products.

Unilever

Some companies have developed marketing campaigns that undermine the traditional approach to beauty care advertising by telling women, as well as young girls, that they're beautiful just the way they are. For example, Unilever's Dove brand has long eschewed the use of supermodels in its ads and uses everyday women and girls who resemble its typical consumers. Since 2004, Dove has been running various versions of the "Campaign for Real Beauty," which is designed to appeal to everyday women and offer a broader, healthier, and more democratic view of beauty.[63] The campaign has included magazine ads, online videos, extensive public relations, cause marketing, social media, and a website where women can discuss beauty-related issues. Recently, the company took the campaign in a related but slightly different direction with the "Dove Real Beauty Pledge," which is based on the principle that beauty is for everyone and should be a source of confidence and not anxiety (Exhibit 6-10). As part of the Real Beauty Pledge, Dove is committed to three vows: always featuring real women, never models; portraying women as they are in real life; and helping young girls build confidence and self-esteem.

Source Power

The final characteristic in Kelman's classification scheme is **source power**. A source has power when he or she can actually administer rewards and punishments to the receiver. As a result of this power, the source may be able to induce another person(s) to respond to the request or position he or she is advocating. The power of the source depends on several factors. The source must be perceived as being able to administer positive or negative sanctions to the receiver (*perceived control*), and the receiver must think the source cares about whether or not the receiver conforms (*perceived concern*). The receiver's estimate of the source's ability to observe conformity is also important (*perceived scrutiny*).

EXHIBIT 6-11

Actor Clint Eastwood's authoritative image makes him an effective source.

Take Pride in America

YOURS.

Public lands make up over one-third of this great country, and they belong to each of us. From sidewalks outside our doors to beaches to distant mountain streams, we share it all. And together, we can protect it. Whether you'd like to organize a cleanup, be a campground host or do something else, there's a way you can help. To find out more about the volunteer opportunities available, visit www.TakePride.gov.

TAKE PRIDE IN AMERICA
It's your land, lend a hand.

When a receiver perceives a source as having power, the influence process occurs through a process known as **compliance**. The receiver accepts the persuasive influence of the source and acquiesces to the advocate's position in hopes of obtaining a favorable reaction or avoiding punishment. The receiver may show public agreement with the source's position but not have an internal or private commitment to this position. Persuasion induced through compliance may be superficial and last only as long as the receiver perceives that the source can administer some reward or punishment.

Power as a source characteristic is very difficult to apply in a nonpersonal influence situation such as advertising. A communicator in an ad generally cannot apply any sanctions to the receiver or determine whether compliance actually occurs. An indirect way of using power is by using an individual with an authoritative personality as a spokesperson. For example, Take Pride in America is a U.S. Department of the Interior program that encourages individuals, civic groups, corporations, and others to volunteer in caring for the public lands that it controls. The program has used actor-director Clint Eastwood, whose movie roles earned him an image as a rugged tough guy, in public service campaigns commanding people not to pollute or damage public lands (Exhibit 6-11). Eastwood has used his imposing image in TV commercials calling for people who abuse public lands "to clean up their act or get out of town."

The use of source power applies more in situations involving personal communication and influence. For example, in a personal-selling situation, the sales rep may have some power over a buyer if the latter anticipates receiving special rewards or favors for complying with the salesperson. Some companies provide their sales reps with large expense accounts to spend on customers for this very purpose. Representatives of companies whose product demand exceeds supply are often in a position of power; buyers may comply with their requests to ensure an adequate supply of the product. Sales reps must be very careful in their use of a power position, since abusing a power base to maximize short-term gains can damage long-term relationships with customers.

MESSAGE FACTORS

The way marketing communications are presented is very important in determining their effectiveness. Marketers must consider not only the content of their persuasive messages but also how this information will be structured for presentation and what type of message appeal will be used. Advertising, in all media except radio, relies heavily on visual as well as verbal information. Many options are available with respect to the design and presentation of a message. This section examines the structure of messages and considers the effects of different types of appeals used in advertising.

Message Structure

Marketing communications usually consist of a number of message points that the communicator wants to get across. An important aspect of message strategy is knowing the best way to communicate these points and overcome any opposing viewpoints audience members may hold. Extensive research has been conducted on how the structure of a persuasive message can influence its effectiveness, including order of presentation, conclusion drawing, message sidedness, refutation, and verbal versus visual message characteristics.

Order of Presentation   A basic consideration in the design of a persuasive message is the arguments' order of presentation. Should the most important message points be placed at the beginning of the message, in the middle, or at the end? Research on learning and memory generally indicates that items presented first and last are remembered better than those presented in the middle (see Figure 6–4).[64] This suggests that a communicator's strongest arguments should be presented early or late in the message but never in the middle.

Presenting the strongest arguments at the beginning of the message assumes a **primacy effect** is operating, whereby information presented first is most effective. Putting the strong points at the end assumes a **recency effect**, whereby the last arguments presented are most persuasive.

FIGURE 6–4

Ad Message Recall as a Function of Order of Presentation

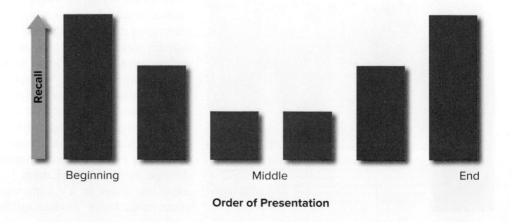

Order of Presentation

Whether to place the strongest selling points at the beginning or the end of the message depends on several factors. If the target audience is opposed to the communicator's position, presenting strong points first can reduce the level of counterarguing. Putting weak arguments first might lead to such a high level of counterarguing that strong arguments that followed would not be believed. Strong arguments work best at the beginning of the message if the audience is not interested in the topic, so they can arouse interest in the message. When the target audience is predisposed toward the communicator's position or is highly interested in the issue or product, strong arguments can be saved for the end of the message. This may result in a more favorable opinion as well as better retention of the information.

The order of presentation can be critical when a long, detailed message with many arguments is being presented. Most effective sales presentations open and close with strong selling points and bury weaker arguments in the middle. For short communications, such as a 15- or 30-second TV or radio commercial, the order may be less critical. However, many product and service messages are received by consumers with low involvement and minimal interest. Thus, an advertiser may want to present the brand name and key selling points early in the message and repeat them at the end to enhance recall and retention. Order of presentation is also an important consideration in other forms of marketing communication. For example, many press releases use the "pyramid style" of writing, whereby most of the important information is presented up front to ensure that it is read, since editors often cut from the end of articles.

Conclusion Drawing Marketing communicators must decide whether their messages should explicitly draw a firm conclusion or allow receivers to draw their own conclusions. Research suggests that, in general, messages with explicit conclusions are more easily understood and effective in influencing attitudes. However, other studies have shown that the effectiveness of conclusion drawing may depend on the target audience, the type of issue or topic, and the nature of the situation.[65]

More highly educated people prefer to draw their own conclusions and may be annoyed at an attempt to explain the obvious or to draw an inference for them. But stating the conclusion may be necessary for a less educated audience, who may not draw any conclusion or may make an incorrect inference from the message. Marketers must also consider the audience's level of involvement in the topic. For highly personal or ego-involving issues, message recipients may want to make up their own minds and resent any attempts by the communicator to draw a conclusion. One study found that open-ended ads (without explicit conclusions) were more effective than closed-ended arguments that did include a specific conclusion—but only for involved audiences.[66]

Whether to draw a conclusion for the audience also depends on the complexity of the topic. Even a highly educated audience may need assistance if its knowledge level in a particular area is low. Does the marketer want the message to trigger immediate action or a more long-term effect? If immediate action is an objective, the message should draw a definite conclusion. This is a common strategy in political advertising, particularly for ads run close to election day. When immediate impact is not the objective and repeated exposure will give the audience members opportunities to draw their own conclusions, an open-ended message may be used.

Drawing a conclusion in a message may make sure the target audience gets the point the marketer intended. But many advertisers believe that letting customers draw their own conclusions reinforces the points being made in the message. For example, a health services agency in Kentucky found that open-ended ads were more memorable and more effective in getting consumers to use health services than were ads stating a conclusion. Ads that posed questions about alcohol and drug abuse and left them unanswered resulted in more calls by teenagers to a help line for information than did a message offering a resolution to the problem.[67] The ad shown in Exhibit 6-12, which is from the Montana Meth Project (MMP) drug prevention messaging

EXHIBIT 6-12

This ad is a good example of the use of open-ended messaging.

Montana Meth Project

campaign, is a good example of this strategy. The ad challenges teens to consider what they know about methamphetamine and prompts them to learn more by visiting the MMP website.

Message Sidedness   Another message structure decision facing the marketer involves message sidedness. A **one-sided message** mentions only positive attributes or benefits. A **two-sided message** presents good as well as bad points. The logic of a two-sided message is that acknowledging a limitation or shortcoming can be a way to enhance credibility and make the message more effective. One-sided messages are most effective when the target audience already holds a favorable opinion about the topic. They also work better with a less educated audience.[68]

Two-sided messages are more effective when the target audience holds an opposing opinion or is highly educated. Two-sided messages may enhance the credibility of the source.[69] A better-educated audience usually knows there are opposing arguments, so a communicator who presents both sides of an issue is likely to be seen as less biased and more objective. Martin Eisend conducted a meta-analysis of the research conducted on the effects of one- versus two-sided advertising messages. The results of his analysis showed that the persuasive impact of message sidedness depends on a number of factors, including the amount and importance of negative information in the ad, attribute quality, placement of the negative information, the correlation between negative and positive attributes, and whether the advertiser discloses negative information voluntarily or because it is required to do so.[70]

Most advertisers use one-sided messages. They are concerned about the negative effects of acknowledging a weakness in their brand or don't want to say anything positive about their competitors. There are exceptions, however. Sometimes advertisers compare brands on several attributes and do not show their product as being the best on every one. There also may be situations in which a company feels that it is best to acknowledge its shortcomings and let its customers know that it has addressed them.

An example of a company that used a two-sided message very effectively is the Domino's Pizza chain, which took the strategy to a whole new level in an integrated marketing campaign used to introduce its new, reformulated pizza. Domino's recognized that changes were needed after conducting research that revealed many consumers had issues with the taste of its pizza. As part of its "Oh Yes We Did" campaign, Domino's used commercials showing the chain's new CEO in front of the camera admitting that he had heard what the focus groups had to say and that he took it to heart. The spots then pointed viewers to a special website (www.pizzaturnaround.com) that featured a 4-minute documentary chronicling Domino's employees' reactions to the negative comments coming from the focus groups and telling about the company's quest to make a better pizza. The website also showed positive as well as negative viewer comments that were linked in from Twitter. While Domino's and its agency knew the campaign might be risky, they moved forward with it and the results were very favorable. They received a great deal of publicity regarding the ads, much of which praised the company for conceding the shortcomings of its product and explaining what it was doing about it. The two-sided message strategy also had a very positive impact on sales as the chain generated a record increase in same-store sales during the campaign.[71] Domino's has become the largest pizza company in the world over the past decade, and the company traces its tremendous growth back to the decision to reamp its recipe and launch the bold "Oh Yes We Did" campaign that called itself out for having an inferior product.[72]

A more recent example of the high profile use of a two-sided message is advertising done by German automaker Volkswagen in 2019, which addressed the global diesel emissions scandal that began in 2015 and had a negative impact on the company's image for several years. Governmental regulatory agencies in the United States and Europe discovered that special software installed in Volkswagen diesel-powered vehicles was designed to defeat emissions testing making them appear far cleaner and safer for the environment than they actually were. The vehicles were actually emitting more toxic fumes than permitted. The scandal drew major media attention and tarnished Volkswagen's

After the bad buzz, here's a better one.

It's funny how a negative can give you a positive. Just like two sides of a battery. On one side, you have the not-so-good buzz.

But on the other, you have plans for an almost $800 million assembly plant expansion in Chattanooga, Tennessee to build electric vehicles. And 1,000 newly employed Chattanoogans who'll work there. You also have a brand-new platform for how

to build electric cars, that will make them accessible to more people, with the ultimate goal of being carbon neutral globally by 2050. See, sometimes the bad can make you better. Sometimes it pushes you to learn from the past. To make the future something that belongs to everyone.

You might call it a lesson. We call it our all-electric ID. Buzz.

Volkswagen

EXHIBIT 6–13

Volkswagen used a two-sided advertising message acknowledging the diesel scandal as part of an ad campaign for its electric vehicles.

Volkswagen of America, Inc.

long-held pro-environment positioning, in addition to costing the company billions of dollars in legal settlement costs.

In 2019 Volkswagen launched a new branding campaign called "Drive Something Bigger Than Yourself," which was designed to showcase its plan to put 22 million electric vehicles on the road by 2028 and be carbon neutral by 2050. In the initial phase of the campaign, Volkswagen aired a 1 minute 45 second TV commercial that begins with a lone figure in an open doorway surrounded by darkness. Flashbacks of news reports about VW's 2015 diesel scandal can be heard in the darkness as the scene shifts to a lone designer, working late and sketching electric vehicle renderings in a dimly lit room. A few seconds later we hear the opening of the classic Simon & Garfunkel hit "The Sound of Silence." While the song plays, the designer grows frustrated but is inspired by looking at old drawings of VW's classic Microbus. Scenes of modern-day vehicle manufacturing are followed by the big reveal: The ID. Buzz, an electric version of the Microbus VW that is set to arrive in the United States in 2023, emerges from the darkness. The ad ends with white lettering against a black background stating: "In the darkness, we found the light. Introducing a new era of electric driving." The campaign also included print ads that utilized a two-sided message as shown in Exhibit 6–13.

The two-sided advertisements marked the first time Volkswagen had addressed the diesel scandal head-on in its advertising in the United States. Some ad critics questioned the strategy of using the two-sided message. For example, in a review of the ad, *Advertising Age* wrote: "But by mentioning the scandal now in a new ad, the brand risks reminding buyers about an issue that many probably had forgotten about. The ad also does not explicitly apologize for VW's actions, which could risk angering some consumers."[73] However, many praised Volkswagen and argued that the company needed to address the scandal again in a very public way to gain the credibility needed to be successful in the electric vehicle market. The chief creative officer of the Johannes Leonardo agency that created the ad noted that Volkswagen needed a clearing-of-the-air moment and a big idea that would help the company turn the page and move forward.[74]

Refutation   In a special type of two-sided message known as a **refutational appeal**, the communicator presents both sides of an issue and then refutes the opposing viewpoint. Since refutational appeals tend to "inoculate" the target audience against a competitor's counterclaims, they can be more effective than one-sided messages in making consumers resistant to an opposing message.[75]

Refutational messages may be useful when marketers wish to build attitudes that resist change and/or must defend against attacks or criticism of their products or the company. For example, SeaWorld Parks & Entertainment has used refutational messaging as part of an integrated campaign to defend itself against criticism by PETA and other animal activist groups. In addition to the refutational ads, SeaWorld has created a website (seaworldcares.com) that provides information refuting many of the attacks made against the company regarding its treatment of marine mammals such as dolphins, orcas, and sea lions. It also serves to educate the public about the many programs and initiatives it has to protect and help marine life (Exhibit 6–14). Market leaders, who are often the target of comparative messages, may find that acknowledging competitors' claims and then refuting them can help build resistant attitudes and customer loyalty.

EXHIBIT 6-14

SeaWorld uses refutational messaging to defend itself against criticism by PETA and other animal activist groups.

SeaWorld

Year In Review: SeaWorld's Work With Animals in Need of Rescue, Rehabilitation, and Return

December 31, 2021

During 2021, SeaWorld Rescue teams across all three parks mobilized to help rescue and rehabilitate animals in need with the end goal of being able to return them to their natural habitat.

Animal care Conservation Rescue

Celebrating Walrus Awareness Week

December 10, 2021

The first full week of December serves as Walrus Awareness Week, and we couldn't be happier to be talking about these massive marine mammals.

Animal care

With Threats On The Rise, Ocean Animals Need SeaWorld Now More Than Ever

May 10, 2019

Jody Westberg, a member of SeaWorld San Diego's rescue team, explains how humans impact ocean environments and why rescue teams serve as a crucial line of defense for some of marine life's most insurmountable threats.

Animal care Conservation Rescue

Verbal versus Visual Messages   Thus far our discussion has focused on the information, or verbal, portion of the message. However, the nonverbal, visual elements of an ad are also very important. Many ads provide minimal amounts of information and rely on visual elements to communicate. Pictures are commonly used in advertising to convey information or reinforce copy or message claims.

Both the verbal and visual portions of an ad influence the way the advertising message is processed.[76] Consumers may develop images or impressions based on visual elements such as an illustration in an ad or the scenes in a TV commercial. In some cases, the visual portion of an ad may reduce its persuasiveness, since the processing stimulated by the picture may be less controlled and consequently less favorable than that stimulated by words.[77]

Pictures affect the way consumers process accompanying copy. A study showed that when verbal information was low in imagery value, the use of pictures providing examples increased both immediate and delayed recall of product attributes.[78] However, when the verbal information was already high in imagery value, the addition of pictures did not increase recall. Advertisers often design ads where the visual image supports the verbal appeal to create a compelling impression in the consumer's mind. Notice how the ad for Arrowhead Mountain Spring Water shown in Exhibit 6-15 uses a beautiful visual image of the mountains to communicate the key product attribute of purity.

EXHIBIT 6-15

Visual images are an effective way to communicate an important product attribute.

Arrowhead by Nestle Waters North America

Born Better.

Message Appeals

One of the advertiser's most important creative strategy decisions involves the choice of an appropriate appeal. Some ads are designed to appeal to the rational, logical aspect of the consumer's decision-making process; others appeal to feelings in an attempt to evoke some emotional reaction. Many believe that effective advertising combines the practical reasons for purchasing a product with emotional values. In this section we will examine several common types of message appeals, including comparative advertising, fear, and humor.

Comparative Advertising   **Comparative advertising** is the practice of either directly or indirectly naming competitors in an ad and comparing one or more specific attributes.[79] This form of advertising became popular after the Federal Trade Commission (FTC) began advocating its use in 1972. The FTC reasoned that direct comparison of brands would provide better product information, giving consumers a more rational basis for making purchase decisions. Television networks cooperated with the FTC by lifting their ban on comparative ads, and the result was a flurry of comparative commercials.

Initially, the novelty of comparative ads resulted in greater attention. But since they have become so common, their attention-getting value has declined. Some studies show that recall is higher for comparative than noncomparative messages, but comparative ads are generally not more effective for other response variables, such as brand attitudes or purchase intentions.[80] Advertisers must also consider how comparative messages affect credibility. Users of the brand being attacked in a comparative message may be especially skeptical about the advertiser's claims.

Comparative advertising may be particularly useful for new brands, since it allows a new market entrant to position itself directly against the more established brands and to promote its distinctive advantages. Direct comparisons can help position a new brand in the evoked, or choice, set of brands the customer may be considering. Comparative advertising is often used for brands with a small market share. They compare themselves to an established market leader in hopes of creating an association and tapping into the leader's market.

An example of a brand that has used comparative advertising effectively is the sports drink BodyArmor, which has become the fastest-growing brand in the category by challenging market leader Gatorade. The ads feature a number of high-profile athletes—such as NBA stars James Harden, Klay Thompson, and Donovan Mitchell, NFL quarterback Kyler Murray and running back Christian McCaffrey, and baseball star Mike Trout—and communicate the need for athletes to evolve all aspects of their game in order to compete, including their choice of sports drinks. The ads take aim at Gatorade by noting how the star athletes would not choose an outdated sports drink and that BodyArmor is the more natural and better choice. The comparative ads end with the tagline: "Thanks Gatorade. We'll take it from here" (Exhibit 6-16). The use of comparative advertising helped BodyArmor, which was founded in 2011, become the second largest sports drink with sales of nearly $1.4 billion in 2021. As noted earlier, the Coca-Cola Co. bought full control of the company for $5.6 billion, making it the largest acquisition in Coke's history.[81]

The use of comparative advertising is not limited to new brands or those with a small market share; a number of high-profile marketers have been using comparative appeals to differentiate their brands in a competitive marketplace.[82] For example, comparative advertising has become common in the mobile phone industry as the three major providers (Verizon, AT&T, and T-Mobile) often run ads comparing themselves against one another on key attributes such as network coverage, signal quality, and price. Samsung has used comparative ads to gain market share in the smartphone market by comparing its Samsung Galaxy smartphone to Apple's iPhone.

EXHIBIT 6–16

BodyArmor uses comparative advertising to challenge Gatorade in the sports drink market.

BA Sports Nutrition, LLC.

EXHIBIT 6–17

Molson Coors ran this ad in *The New York Times* in response to a comparative ad for Bud Light that aired on the Super Bowl.

Source: Miller Brewing Company

Market leaders often hesitate to use comparison ads, as most believe they have little to gain by featuring competitors' products in their ads. There are exceptions, of course; Coca-Cola resorted to comparative advertising in response to challenges made by Pepsi that were reducing Coke's market share. One of the longest-running and intense comparative advertising battles has been waged for decades between Anheuser-Busch InBev's Bud Light and Molson Coors Miller Lite brands. The two brands have traded superiority claims centered on how fewer calories and carbohydrates doesn't mean sacrificing taste. However, the battle took a new turn a few years ago when Anheuser-Bush aired an ad for Bud Light on the 2019 Super Bowl accusing Miller Lite and Coors Light of using corn syrup in the brewing process for their beers. The attack continued after the game as AB InBev continued to run the commercial—as well as using print and digital ads, billboards, and its website—to point out that Bud Light has "100 percent less corn syrup than Miller Lite or Coors Lite." The corn syrup accusations drew a quick rebuttal from Molson Coors, which began its counterattack against Bud Light by running a full-page ad in major newspapers defending its use of corn syrup. The ad was addressed to "beer drinkers of America" and made the distinction between corn syrup and high fructose corn syrup, which Miller Lite does not use (Exhibit 6–17).

Molson Coors filed a lawsuit in federal court 6 weeks after the Super Bowl, accusing AB InBev of false advertising as well as trademark dilution. In the lawsuit, Molson Coors claimed the Bud Light ads are misleading, arguing that while the brewer uses corn syrup in the fermentation process, the yeast consumes and breaks it down, leaving no corn syrup in the final product when the brewing process is completed. Molson Coors also claimed AB InBev purposely intermingled corn syrup and high fructose corn syrup in its messaging to encourage consumers to switch to Bud Light because high fructose corn syrup has been linked to obesity. AB InBev responded by stating that the lawsuit is baseless because its ads are intended to point out a key difference in Bud Light versus its two competitors. The lawsuit was initially successful and Anheuser-Busch was required to stop mentioning corn syrup in its advertising and promotional materials. However, the decision was overturned on appeal and the court even suggested that if Molson Coors did not like the sneering tone of Anheuser-Busch's ads, it could mock Bud Light in return.[83] A study by Fred Beard suggests that marketers must be careful when using comparative advertising because the potential for negative reactions by consumers is high when prominent brands compare themselves against one another. He also found that comparative ads work better with a younger audience than they do for older consumers.[84] Digital and Social Media Perspective 6–2 discusses the #Chicken Wars, a recent comparative advertising battle involving quick-serve restaurants Popeyes and market leader Chick-fil-A that took place primarily on social media.

Another area where comparative messages are quite commonly used is political advertising. Political advertising is viewed as an important component of political speech and thus enjoys more First Amendment protection than does commercial speech and less regulation by either government or self-policing agencies. Thus, it has become quite common for political ads to contain negative, one-sided attacks on an opposing candidate's weaknesses such as character flaws, voting record, public misstatements, broken promises, and the like.[85] The goal of these ads is to discredit the character, record, or position of an opponent and create doubt in voters' minds about their ability to govern effectively. A major reason why negative political ads are used successfully is that voters often tend to weight negative information more heavily than positive information when forming impressions of political candidates.[86] However, studies have shown that the use of "attack advertising" by politicians can result in negative perceptions of both candidates.[87]

The Tweet That Started the #Chicken Wars

Quick-service restaurants (QSR) are a major part of the restaurant industry in the United States, accounting for more than $300 billion in sales each year. The QSR segment has long been dominated by hamburger-focused restaurants such as McDonald's and Burger King, pizza restaurants such as Domino's and Pizza Hut, and sandwich shops such as Subway. However, over the past decade the chicken segment of the QSR industry has experienced the greatest growth as chicken consumption in the United States has risen nearly 17 percent per capita compared to a 2.5 percent decline for beef. It seems like chicken is everywhere as consumer perceptions of chicken as a healthier alternative have taken hold and many are choosing a chicken sandwich over a Big Mac or Whopper.

Many of these healthy chicken eaters are getting their fill at hamburger-focused restaurants such as McDonald's, Burger King, and Wendy's, which have been trying to raise their game by developing more and better chicken sandwiches and other items. And people in search of a chicken sandwich are going to regional chicken QSRs such as Zaxby's, Raising Cane, and Bojangles. However, the company that is dominating the chicken sandwich market and has been an absolute juggernaut is Chick-fil-A, which has quietly become the third-most-popular fast-food restaurant in the United States. The Atlanta-based company's revenue increased by 33 percent in 2021 to $5.8 billion while profits were $1.2 billion, an increase of 67 percent from the previous year. Chick-fil-A manages to have impressive sales numbers despite having fewer locations as each store makes significantly more money than rivals' restaurants. Chick-fil-A has set itself apart from rivals with its long-term focus on customer service, investments in technology, and a unique franchise system in which each owner runs only a single location.

When you are the market leader in an industry, it is not uncommon for competitors to compare themselves to you in their ads. What is less common is for a rival to upend an industry with a simple two-word tweet rather than a high-profile comparative advertising campaign in major media such as television or online. However, this was the case in the now famous Chicken Sandwich War of 2019, which lasted for over 2 years.

The war began in 2019 when Popeyes, which is owned by Restaurant Brands International, launched its first chicken sandwich after spending 2 years in development and testing. The Miami-based chain was late to the chicken sandwich market, long dominated by Chick-fil-A, which owned over 50 percent of the market despite being closed on Sundays. The new sandwich was Popeyes' biggest product launch in 30 years, and the company recognized that it needed to steal market share and attention from Chick-fil-A. A traditional media advertising campaign was used to launch the new sandwich and build awareness as well as generate media attention. However, Popeyes and

Popeyes Chicken ✔
@PopeyesChicken

... y'all good?

Chick-fil-A, Inc. ✔ @ChickfilA
Bun + Chicken + Pickles = all the ❤ for the original.

Bun Chicken + Pickles Love

♡ 326K   12:58 PM - Aug 19, 2019

Popeyes Louisiana Kitchen, Inc.

its agency GSD&M was also developing a strategy that would use social media to take advantage of the hype that was building among its core customers in test markets. A decision was made to use Twitter as its main social media tool, as that was where its customers spent much of their time and a real-time response strategy could be used.

Popeyes took a listen-first approach as the chicken sandwich launched in test markets. Popeyes saw that the momentum was building and also noted that Chick-fil-A was viewed as a guilty pleasure for many people who disagreed with the company's conservative stance on various social issues. By the time the sandwich was launched nationally on August 12, the agency knew the right tweet could generate a deluge of earned media. The right moment came a week later when Chick-fil-A sent out a Tweet stating: "Bun+Chicken+Pickles = all the (heart emoji) for the original." Based on the plan it had in place, Popeyes' Twitter response was simply two words, "y'all good?"

Popeyes' tweet received more than 320,000 likes and earned nearly 8 billion impressions worth an estimated $87 million in earned media. The "tweet heard around the

(continued)

world," as one media outlet described it, put Popeyes' chicken sandwich at the center of popular culture as Black Twitter made memes, celebrities posted on social media without getting paid, and talk show hosts made jokes about it. Popeyes also added more Twitter followers during the week of the tweet than it did in the first half of 2019 plus all of the previous 2 years combined and became the leading search on Google. The media attention generated by the tweet resulted in several days of long lines in Popeyes stores and at drive-through windows, and many locations ran out of product as the new sandwich became more popular.

The week after the tweet, Popeyes increased its market share by 30 percent, the largest QSR share increase ever tracked by analytics firm Sense360. Sales of the chicken sandwich were 16 times more than forecasted, which led to Popeyes selling out of their 10-week sandwich supply in just 8 days. Sandwich-crazed fans went to extraordinary lengths to get a chance to try the new chicken sandwich, in some stores fights broke out, and an angry customer pulled a gun at a Popeyes in Houston after learning that the sandwich was sold out.

Sales continued to surge at Popeyes after it debuted its new chicken sandwich. Average sales per store in 2021 increased to about $1.8 million a year, compared with $1.4 million in 2019. Popeyes stopped short of proclaiming outright victory in the war as Chick-fil-A sales increased as well. Popeyes found a clever way to end the war in July of 2021, not through surrender but rather though a peace offering that doubled as a creative product launch and an impactful charitable move. Popeyes' entry into the chicken nugget market was accompanied by an ad stating "We Come in Piece. 8 Piece" and a single tweet stating "It's over, y'all." The olive branch also included news that Popeyes nugget launch would be celebrated by the chain donating the equivalent of $1 million of nuggets, both its own and product purchased from competitors, to the Second Harvest Food Bank of New Orleans. The gesture generated another 3.3 billion media impressions worth an estimated $33.7 million in ad value for Popeyes.

Sources: Jon Springer, "Popeyes' Call for Peace Signals Victory in the Chicken War," *Advertising Age*, April 25, 2022, p. 20; Clara Malley, "Everything You Need to Know about the 'Chicken Wars,'" *Hypebeast*, March 1, 2021, https://hypebeast.com/2021/3/everything-you-need-to-know-about-the-chicken-wars; "Popeyes–Chicken Wars, Winner in Restaurants," 12th Annual Shorty Awards, https://shortyawards.com/12th/gsdm-and-popeyes-chicken-wars.

EXHIBIT 6–18

The Ad Council uses a fear appeal to discourage buzzed driving.

National Highway Traffic Safety Administration and Ad Council

YOU JUST BLEW $10,000.

Buzzed. Busted. Broke.
Get caught, and you could be paying around $10,000 in fines, legal fees and increased insurance rates.

Buzzed driving is drunk driving.
buzzeddriving.adcouncil.org

Ad Council NHTSA

Fear Appeals Fear is an emotional response to a threat that expresses, or at least implies, some sort of danger. Ads sometimes use **fear appeals** to evoke this emotional response and arouse individuals to take steps to remove the threat. Some, like the antidrug ads used by the Partnership for a Drug-Free America, stress physical danger that can occur if behaviors are not altered. Others—like those for deodorant, mouthwash, or dandruff shampoos—threaten disapproval or social rejection. Fear appeals are often used to discourage unsafe behaviors such as drinking and driving and, more recently, texting and driving. For example, the Ad Council, which is the leading producer of public service advertising in the United States, has created a number of campaigns that use fear appeal messages to deal with these behaviors. Exhibit 6–18 shows an ad created by the Ad Council to discourage buzzed driving by showing how getting arrested for a DUI can cost nearly $10,000 in legal fees. The ad was part of a campaign created by the council after its research found that too many drivers thought drunk driving messages didn't apply to them: that driving "buzzed" after only a few drinks was different than driving drunk.

How Fear Operates Before deciding to use a fear appeal-based message strategy, the advertiser should consider how fear operates, what level to use, and how different target audiences may respond. One theory suggests that the relationship between the level of fear in a message and acceptance or persuasion is curvilinear, as shown in Figure 6–5.[88] This means that message acceptance increases as the amount of fear used rises—to a point. Beyond that point, acceptance decreases as the level of fear rises.

This relationship between fear and persuasion can be explained by the fact that fear appeals have both facilitating and inhibiting effects.[89] A low level of fear can have facilitating effects; it attracts attention and interest in the message and may motivate the receiver

FIGURE 6–5

Relationship between
Fear Levels and Message
Acceptance

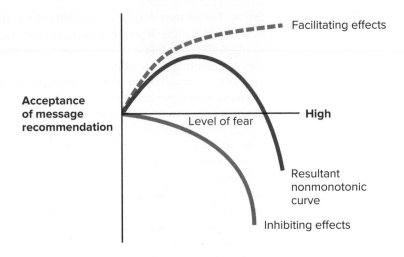

to act to resolve the threat. Thus, increasing the level of fear in a message from low to moderate can result in increased persuasion. High levels of fear, however, can produce inhibiting effects; the receiver may emotionally block the message by tuning it out, perceiving it selectively, or denying its arguments outright. Figure 6–5 illustrates how these two countereffects operate to produce the curvilinear relationship between fear and persuasion.

A study by Punam Anand Keller and Lauren Goldberg Block provides support for this perspective on how fear operates.[90] They examined the conditions under which low- and high-fear appeals urging people to stop smoking are likely to be effective. Their study indicated that a communication using a low level of fear may be ineffective because it results in insufficient motivation to elaborate on the harmful consequences of engaging in the destructive behavior (smoking). However, an appeal arousing high levels of fear was ineffective because it resulted in too much elaboration on the harmful consequences. This led to defensive tendencies such as message avoidance and interfered with processing of recommended solutions to the problem.

Another approach to the curvilinear explanation of fear is the protection motivation model.[91] According to this theory, four cognitive appraisal processes mediate the individual's response to the threat: appraising (1) the information available regarding the severity of the perceived threat, (2) the perceived probability that the threat will occur, (3) the perceived ability of a coping behavior to remove the threat, and (4) the individual's perceived ability to carry out the coping behavior.

This model suggests that both the cognitive appraisal of the information in a fear appeal message and the emotional response mediate persuasion. An audience is more likely to continue processing threat-related information, thereby increasing the likelihood that a coping behavior will occur.

The protection motivation model suggests that ads using fear appeals should give the target audience information about the severity of the threat, the probability of its occurrence, the effectiveness of a coping response, and the ease with which the response can be implemented.[92] For example, the ad shown in Exhibit 6–19 uses a mild fear appeal for Seagate Technology's Replica product, which is used to back up computer hard

EXHIBIT 6–19

Seagate uses a mild fear appeal that alerts consumers to a problem and offers a solution.

Seagate Technology LLC

State 1

State 2

State 3

State 4

State 5

State 6

drives. The ad uses playful illustrations in a graphic style to communicate the message of what can happen if your computer crashes and all of the files are lost. Notice how the ad also offers a solution to the threat by showing the ease of using the Replica product and the resulting peace of mind.

It is also important to consider how the target audience may respond. Fear appeals are more effective when the message recipient is self-confident and prefers to cope with dangers rather than avoid them.[93] They are also more effective among nonusers of a product than among users. Thus, a fear appeal may be better at keeping nonsmokers from starting than persuading smokers to stop.

In reviewing research on fear appeals, Herbert Rotfeld has argued that some of the studies may be confusing different types of threats and the level of potential harm portrayed in the message with fear, which is an emotional response.[94] He concludes that the relationship between the emotional responses of fear or arousal and persuasion is not curvilinear but rather is monotonic and positive, meaning that higher levels of fear do result in greater persuasion. However, Rotfeld notes that not all fear messages are equally effective because different people fear different things. Thus they will respond differently to the same threat, so the strongest threats are not always the most persuasive. This suggests that marketers using fear appeals must consider the emotional responses generated by the message and how they will affect reactions to the message.

While research suggests that message recipients might tune out a message that uses too much fear, there are examples of advertising campaigns where high levels of fear have been effective at changing behavior. For example, the Montana Meth Project (MMP) is a large-scale prevention program aimed at reducing methamphetamine use, particularly among teenagers, through public service messaging, policy, and community outreach. The integrated campaign uses hard-hitting TV, radio, print, digital, and social media messaging to communicate the risks of meth use.[95] Many of the ads used in the campaign use a high level of fear to communicate the risks of meth use and addiction such as the one shown in Exhibit 6-20. The MMP has been very successful: Meth use in Montana has declined significantly, and the campaign has been expanded to a number of other states. A study of fear appeals by Andrea Morales, Eugenia Wu, and Gavan Fitzsimons suggests that ads such as those used in the MMP campaign may be effective because they activate disgust as well as fear through some of the disturbing images they contain.[96]

Humor Appeals   Humorous ads are often the best known and best remembered of all advertising messages. Many advertisers, including GEICO, Old Spice, Snickers, Frito Lay, Amazon, Budweiser, and Bud Light, use humor appeals effectively. Humor is usually presented primarily through TV commercials and online video and to a lesser extent through radio, as these media lend themselves to the execution of humorous messages. However, humor is occasionally used in print ads as well, as images can be used in combination with clever headlines and ad copy to develop humorous messages.

EXHIBIT 6–20

The Montana Meth Project uses ads with a high level of fear to communicate the risks of methamphetamne use.

Montana Meth Project

EXHIBIT 6–21

This Volkswagen ad shows
how humor can be used
effectively in a print message.

Volkswagen of America, Inc.

The ad for Volkswagen's new park assist feature shown in Exhibit 6–21 is a very good example of how humor can be used in a print ad. The image puts a focus on VW's park assist feature by using a humorous image to highlight the challenge drivers often face when trying to park between two other tightly parked vehicles. The ad uses humor to effectively communicate a message of being able to safely park using Volkswagen's new feature.

Advertisers use humor for many reasons.[97] Humorous messages attract and hold consumers' attention. They enhance effectiveness by putting consumers in a positive mood, increasing their liking of the ad itself and their feeling toward the product or service. And humor can distract the receiver from counterarguing against the message. A meta-analytic test of various models of how humor works in advertising showed that its effects are primarily based on affective processes and that it can distract from the processing of cognitive information such as brand beliefs and benefits. This suggests that the peripheral processing of humorous messages is dominant and that effort devoted to processing of ad-related affective elements comes at the expense of attention to brand-related cognitions.[98]

Critics argue that funny ads draw people to the humorous situation but distract them from the brand and its attributes. Also, effective humor can be difficult to produce and some attempts are too subtle for mass audiences. And, there is concern that humorous ads may wear out faster than serious appeals. **Wearout** refers to the tendency of a television or radio commercial to lose its effectiveness when it is seen and/or heard repeatedly.[99] Wearout may occur if consumers no longer pay attention to a commercial after several exposures or become annoyed at seeing or hearing an ad multiple times. Some experts argue that humorous ads wear out faster than other formats because once the consumer gets the joke, the ad becomes boring. However, advocates of humor argue that funny ads are effective longer, as consumers will respond more favorably to a well-executed humorous ad than to a serious message.[100] One way marketers deal with the wearout problem is by creating "pool-outs" or multiple executions around a campaign theme that can be rotated so no one ad airs repeatedly during a short time period. For example, large advertisers such as GEICO, Snickers, Old Spice, and Anheuser-Busch InBev generally have a number of commercials available to rotate. However, this can be a problem for smaller companies that do not have a large enough budget to produce multiple commercials.

Clearly, there are valid reasons both for and against the use of humor in advertising. Not every product or service lends itself to a humorous approach. A number of studies have found that the effectiveness of humor depends on several factors, including the type of product or service and audience characteristics.[101] For example, humor has been more prevalent and more effective with low-involvement, feeling products than with high-involvement, thinking products.[102] A recent study examined how audience involvement moderates the effects of humorous ads. The researchers found that for products that are not intrinsically humorous, the use of humor in an advertising message is more effective when involvement is relatively low rather than high. These findings support the idea that high-involvement products may not be as well suited for advertising humor as low-involvement products.[103]

CHANNEL FACTORS

The final controllable variable of the communication process is the channel, or medium, used to deliver the message to the target audience. While a variety of methods are available to transmit marketing communications, as noted in Chapter 5, they can be classified into two broad categories: personal and nonpersonal media.

Personal versus Nonpersonal Channels

There are a number of basic differences between personal and nonpersonal communications channels. Information received from personal influence channels is generally more persuasive than information received via the mass media. Reasons for the differences are summarized in the following comparison of advertising and personal selling:

> From the standpoint of persuasion, a sales message is far more flexible, personal, and powerful than an advertisement. An advertisement is normally prepared by persons having minimal personal contact with customers. The message is designed to appeal to a large number of persons. By contrast, the message in a good sales presentation is not determined in advance. The salesman has a tremendous store of knowledge about his product or service and selects appropriate items as the interview progresses. Thus, the salesman can adapt this to the thinking and needs of the customer or prospect at the time of the sales call. Furthermore, as objections arise and are voiced by the buyer, the salesman can treat the objections in an appropriate manner. This is not possible in advertising.[104]

Personal channels are used in several ways in an IMC program. As was discussed in Chapter 5, many marketers are recognizing the importance of word-of-mouth communications, which are becoming more prevalent with the growth of social media. The more traditional use of personal communications is through sales programs that are implemented through a company's sales force as well as at the point of purchase through retail sales personnel. However, the advertising and promotion programs for most marketers rely heavily on traditional media advertising as well as digital and social media. Thus, we will discuss some of the important factors that marketers must consider with respect to these media.

Effects of Alternative Mass Media

The various mass media that advertisers use to transmit their messages differ in many ways, including the number and type of people they reach, costs, information processing requirements, and qualitative factors. The mass media's costs and efficiency in exposing a target audience to a communication will be evaluated in Chapters 10 through 12. However, we should recognize differences in how information is processed and how communications are influenced by context or environment.

Differences in Information Processing   There are basic differences in the manner and rate at which information from various forms of media is transmitted and can be processed. Information from ads in print media, such as newspapers, magazines, or direct mail, as well as online through websites, social media, and other forms of owned media is *self-paced*; readers process the ad or information at their own rate and can study it as long as they desire. In contrast, information from advertising messages that run on radio and television is *externally paced*; the transmission rate is controlled by the medium.

The difference in the processing rate for print and broadcast media has some obvious implications for advertisers. Self-paced print media make it easier for the message recipient to process a long, complex message. Advertisers often use print ads when they want to present a detailed message with a lot of information. Broadcast media are more effective for transmitting shorter messages or, in the case of TV, presenting images along with words.

While there are limits to the length and complexity of broadcast messages, advertisers can deal with this problem. One strategy is to use a radio or TV ad to get consumers' attention and direct them to a website for a more detailed message. Some advertisers develop broadcast and digital/print versions of the same message. The copy portion is similar in both media, but the print ad can be processed at a rate comfortable to the receiver.

Effects of Context and Environment

Interpretation of an advertising message can be influenced by the context or environment in which the ad appears. Communication theorist Marshall McLuhan's thesis,

EXHIBIT 6–22

Travel + Leisure magazine creates an excellent reception environment for travel-related ads as the editorial content focuses on popular destinations.

Dotdash Meredith

"The medium is the message," implies that the medium communicates an image that is independent of any message it contains.[105] A **qualitative media effect** is the influence the medium has on a message. The image of the media vehicle can affect reactions to the message. For example, an ad for a high-quality men's clothing line might have more of an impact in a fashion magazine like *GQ* than in *Sports Afield*. Airlines, destination resorts, and travel-related services advertise in publications such as *Travel + Leisure* partly because the articles, pictures, and other ads help excite readers about travel (Exhibit 6–22).

A media environment can also be created by the nature of the program in which a commercial appears. One study found that consumers reacted more positively to commercials seen during a happy TV program than a sad one.[106] Advertisers pay premium dollars to advertise on popular programs that create positive moods, like sitcoms, sporting events, award shows such as the Oscars and Grammys, and holiday specials. Conversely, advertisers tend to avoid programs that create a negative mood among viewers or may be detrimental to the company or its products. Many companies won't advertise on programs with excessive violence or sexual content. Coca-Cola never advertises on TV news programs because it thinks bad news is inconsistent with Coke's image as an upbeat, fun product. A study by Andrew Aylesworth and Scott MacKenzie found that commercials placed in programs that induce negative moods are processed less systematically than ads placed in programs that put viewers in positive moods.[107] They suggest that media buyers might be well advised to follow the conventional wisdom of placing their ads during "feel-good" programming, especially if the message is intended to work through a central route to persuasion. However, messages intended to operate through a peripheral route to persuasion might be more effective if they are shown during more negative programs, where presumably viewers will not analyze the ad in detail because of their negative mood state.

Clutter

Another aspect of the media environment that is important to advertisers is the problem of **clutter**, which has been defined as the amount of advertising in a medium.[108] However, for television, clutter is often viewed as including all the nonprogram material that appears in the broadcast environment—commercials, promotional messages for shows, public service announcements (PSAs), and the like. Clutter is of increasing concern to advertisers since there are so many messages in various media competing for the consumer's attention. Traditionally, nearly half of the average magazine's pages would contain ads, and in some publications such as fashion magazines, the ratio of ads to editorial content was even higher. However, in recent years, many marketers have shifted their ad spending to digital media, which has resulted in a significant decline in the number of ad pages in many magazines. However, clutter remains a problem for television and radio advertising, as well as online, where consumers are often bombarded with ad messages. On average, around a quarter of a broadcast hour on TV is devoted to commercials, while most radio stations carry an average of 10 to 12 minutes of commercial time per hour. The average length of a commercial break during prime time on the major networks is just over 3 minutes, which means viewers are exposed to a large number of ads in a short time period, making it difficult for commercials to attract and hold the attention of viewers as well as communicate effectively.

Louisa Ha and Kim McCann note that clutter is a concern among marketers for several reasons.[109] First, advertisers believe that their advertising messages will receive less attention from consumers in a cluttered media environment, who may be irritated by the number of ads, which may lead them to avoid them altogether. Television viewers can easily switch channels during commercial breaks or, as noted in the previous chapter, engage in multitasking and turn their attention to digital devices. A second major concern with clutter is that consumers simply will not be able to remember ads if too many are presented at the same time because of limited processing and memory capacity. A number of studies have examined clutter from an information processing perspective and used *overload theory* to explain why clutter reduces advertising effectiveness. This theory suggests that when an individual is overloaded with too many ads at one time, the absorption of one ad will be at the expense of another.[110]

Clutter is also a concern among advertisers as it is viewed as contributing to **advertising disengagement**, which the Advertising Research Foundation refers to as a lack of excitement, interest, attention, or involvement intended to be aroused by an advertisement or advertising campaign.[111] Even if consumers do not take steps to avoid advertising messages in a cluttered media environment, being exposed to a large number of ads may result in an overall feeling of being disengaged or detached from advertising in general. Research on disengagement has shown that it may have a negative impact on a variety of factors including consumer–brand relationships, commitment, brand loyalty, message recall and effectiveness, and consumer attitudes toward an advertisement.[112]

Clutter has become a major concern among television advertisers as a result of increases in nonprogram time and the trend toward shorter commercials. While the 30-second commercial replaced 60-second spots as the industry standard in the 1970s, many advertisers are now using 15-second spots. The advertising industry continues to express concern over the highly cluttered viewing environment on TV; the amount of clutter increased as much as 30 percent during the 1990s and has continued to increase over the past two decades.[113] Several factors are causing the increased clutter, including lower ratings for TV shows as consumers spend more time online and the fact that many marketers are reducing their spending on television advertising and shifting these monies into digital ads, thus causing the TV networks to begin inserting more commercials into programs to offset these factors and avoid revenue declines whenever possible.

The four major broadcast networks average around 13 minutes of commercial time per hour during prime time; cable networks average nearly 15 minutes, with some being even higher.[114] Thus, a viewer watching 3 hours of television during prime time on the broadcast and/or cable networks would be exposed to more than 100 commercials—in addition to programming promotions and public service announcements. The clutter rate is often higher during popular shows, as the networks may add more commercials because they can charge more for them. And, of course, advertisers and their agencies often perpetuate the problem by pressuring the networks to squeeze their ads into top-rated shows with the largest audiences.

Advertisers and agencies have been pressuring the networks to reduce the amount of advertising time on their programs. In 2018, several of the major networks, including Fox and NBC, announced that they were reducing the number of commercials they would show during prime-time programming to address the clutter problem. In 2019, NBC Universal reduced commercial time another 10 percent in an effort to bring audiences a better viewing experience and provide marketers with more engaging advertising opportunities.[115] The problem is not likely to go away, however, and advertisers will continue to search for ways to break through the clutter, such as using humor, celebrity spokespeople, or novel creative approaches.[116]

Clutter in Online Advertising   While television has received most of the criticism regarding advertising clutter, the problem is prevalent in online advertising as well. Ha and McCann provide an excellent discussion of the differences in clutter between online and offline media.[117] They note that there are differences between online and offline media environments that can impact consumer response to advertising clutter. A major difference that distinguishes online from offline media environments is that in the online environment the concept of "audience" is replaced by that of "users," because consumers actively use online media with specific goals, and online media have interactive capability with user input and advertisers' programming control.[118] They also note that even when someone is surfing the Internet, they have to pay attention to the computer or mobile device screen whereas offline media users can treat television and radio as background noise without having any specific media consumption goals.

Ha and McCann note that the Internet has the dual characteristics of being both a captive medium and a self-paced medium. A major factor regarding clutter in online media is that advertising formats vary greatly for Internet advertising and the captivity of the advertising to the user is determined not by the ad medium, but rather by the specific ad format. For example, pop-up ads or pre-roll video advertising are captive formats that sometimes force users to pay attention to the ad by not allowing them to proceed with their online content consumption without viewing the message or taking action to dismiss it. As is the case with offline media, the clutter problem in online media can have negative effects including ad avoidance and disengagement, ad memory reduction, and more negative attitudes toward the Internet site as well as advertising in general. As noted in earlier chapters, a lack of control over online advertising as well as the large number of ads appearing on many websites have led many consumers to install ad blockers on their computers and mobile devices and to opt out of being tracked online to avoid receiving ads targeted to them.

Summary

This chapter focuses on the controllable variables that are part of the communication process—source, message, and channel factors. Decisions regarding each of these variables should consider their impact on the various steps of the response hierarchy the message receiver passes through. The persuasion matrix helps assess the effect of controllable communication decisions on the consumer's response process.

Selection of the appropriate source or communicator to deliver a message is an important aspect of communications strategy. Three important attributes are source credibility, attractiveness, and power. Marketers enhance message effectiveness by hiring communicators who are experts in a particular area and/or have a trustworthy image. The use of celebrities to deliver advertising messages has become very popular; advertisers hope they will catch the receivers' attention and influence their attitudes or behavior through an identification process. The chapter discusses the meaning a celebrity brings to the endorsement process and the importance of matching the image of the celebrity with that of the company or brand.

The design of the advertising message is a critical part of the communication process. There are various options regarding message structure, including order of presentation of message arguments, conclusion drawing, message sidedness, refutation, and verbal versus visual traits. The advantages and disadvantages of different message appeal strategies were considered, including comparative messages and emotional appeals such as fear and humor.

Finally, the channel or medium used to deliver the message was considered. Differences between personal and nonpersonal channels of communication were discussed. Alternative mass media can have an effect on the communication process as a result of information processing and qualitative factors. The context in which an ad appears and the reception environment are important factors to consider in the selection of mass media. Clutter continues to be a serious problem for advertisers, particularly on TV, where commercials have become shorter and more numerous. Clutter is also a problem for online advertising as the number of ads on websites and social media increases.

Key Terms

persuasion matrix 180
source 182
credibility 182
internalization 183
sleeper effect 185
attractiveness 185
identification 185

source power 197
compliance 197
primacy effect 198
recency effect 198
one-sided message 200
two-sided message 200
refutational appeal 201

comparative advertising 203
fear appeals 206
wearout 209
qualitative media effect 211
clutter 211
advertising disengagement 212

1. The chapter opener discusses how the NCAA's new name, image, and likeness (NIL) program allows college athletes to accept money from businesses for using them in advertisements and other promotions. Discuss the pros and cons of NIL. Find an example of a company using college athletes as endorsers and evaluate the use of them. (LO 6-2)

2. Discuss how marketers can use the persuasion matrix shown in Figure 6–1 to plan their integrated marketing communication programs. Choose a TV commercial, online video, or print ad and use the persuasion matrix to evaluate how it might influence consumers' response processes. (LO 6-1)

3. Discuss the three primary source attributes shown in Figure 6–2 and the processes by which they can influence attitude and/or behavior change. Find an example of an advertisement or other type of promotional message that uses each source attribute. (LO 6-2)

4. IMC Perspective 6–1 discusses the tremendous success of tennis star Roger Federer as an endorser. Discuss the reasons Federer has been successful as an endorser. Find an example of a company using Federer as an endorser and evaluate its use of him. (LO 6-2)

5. Find a celebrity who is currently being used in an advertising campaign for a specific company or brand and use McCracken's meaning transfer model (shown in Figure 6–3) to analyze the use of this individual as a spokesperson. (LO 6-2)

6. Should popular social media influencers be viewed as having the same celebrity status as more traditional celebrities such as athletes, actors, and entertainers? Why or why not? (LO 6-2)

7. Discuss Volkswagen's decision to use a two-sided advertising message acknowledging the diesel emissions scandal that occurred in 2015. Do you think this was an effective way for the company to address this issue? (LO 6-3)

8. Go to the website for the Montana Meth Project (https://www.montanameth.org/) and choose three ads that use various levels of fear in the message. Discuss why each ad may or may not be effective. (LO 6-3)

9. Discuss the pros and cons of using humor as the basis for an advertising appeal. Find an example of an advertising message that uses humor and evaluate its effectiveness. (LO 6-3)

10. What is meant by a qualitative media effect? Choose a television program or magazine and discuss the reception environment created by the show or publication. Which type of companies or brands might be interested in advertising on this program or in this magazine? (LO 6-4)

11. Discuss what is meant by advertising clutter and how it is a problem in various media such as television, radio, and online. What are some of the ways the media and advertisers can address the clutter problem? (LO 6-4)

7 Establishing Objectives and Budgeting for the Promotional Program

Charles LaGreca/Shutterstock

Learning Objectives

LO7-1 | Discuss the value of setting objectives for advertising and promotion.

LO7-2 | Describe the relationship between promotional objectives and marketing objectives.

LO7-3 | Discuss sales versus communications objectives.

LO7-4 | Compare the value of sales objectives and communications objectives as goals for promotional programs.

LO7-5 | Describe the process of budgeting for IMC.

LO7-6 | Compare the economic and sales response perspectives on budgeting.

LO7-7 | Compare different methods of setting budgets.

How Much Should a Company Spend on Advertising? It's Complicated!

One of the most difficult decisions that a company has to make is determining the amount of the marketing communications budget. Unfortunately, there is no formula or algorithm that provides a simple and straightforward answer to this problem. Add to this that the amount of the budget may not always be determined exclusively by the marketing department, it is tied to sales and/or stage in the product life cycle, and it may be impacted significantly by external factors such as economic and competitive conditions, and you can understand why companies take different approaches to this decision with varying degrees of success.

According to the U.S. Ad Market Tracker, July 2022 ad spending was down 12.7 percent—the worst monthly decline since July 2020, which was itself down 17.8 percent from the previous July. As noted by Daniel Konstantinovic of *eMarketer.com*, a variety of factors combined to lead to this decline: (1) the pandemic lockdown was over and people were getting out of the home and back to a more normal life, (2) rising inflation led to cutbacks in consumer spending, (3) consumers were wary of a recession, and (4) advertisers were still uncertain about new privacy regulations. Konstantinovic noted that "one in five marketers have cut their ad spending" leading to layoffs in nearly every sector of advertising. Big spenders in the automotive and tech industries led the budget cutbacks, with automakers spending down 23 percent, and Microsoft halting TV ad spending in June citing increases in inflation and interest rates. Ford considered cutting the entire ad budget for its electric vehicles. As noted by Michaela Jefferson of the Ehrenberg-Bass Institute, "Ford CEO Jim Farley said he sees little reason for the automaker to bother using traditional ad campaigns for electric vehicles." It seems like it has always been like that.

But a number of companies argue that this is exactly what *not* to do. They argue that if you believe that advertising works, then you should increase—not decrease—spending in these times. P&G, for example, believes that when factors like inflation, the pandemic, and so on occur, companies should continue to spend, citing the need to retain "mental availability" of the brand. During the peak of the pandemic, P&G increased its budget by 1.9 percent over the previous year. CFO Jon Moeller cited a number of factors for the increase, including the need to retain existing buyers by reminding them of the benefits of P&G brands, promote trial from non-buyers, and the opportunity to gain brand visibility. He also noted that media consumption was much higher during this period. The strategy was borne out by sales increases of 5 percent.

Marketing strategist Mark Ritson contrasted Moeller's approach to that taken by Coca-Cola. Like a number of other companies, Coca-Cola "went dark," pausing its global advertising efforts during the worst of the pandemic months, cutting advertising investment in the UK by 35 percent. Ritson notes that unlike P&G, Coca-Cola made a mistake, which allowed rival PepsiCo a 5 percent increase in net revenue growth, as CEO James Quincey did not want to spend money on advertising when he felt he couldn't get a return given the lockdown.

A number of studies also support the belief that a hiatus in ad spending is detrimental to the brand. The Ehrenberg-Bass Institute conducted a study of 70 Australian consumer goods companies' media spend and volume sales for more than two decades. The researchers concluded "When financial pressures hit or a brand's net profit needs boosting, advertising spend is often one of the first budgets to be cut," noting that the COVID-19 pandemic was one such period that led to numerous marketers making cuts when they shouldn't have, as "on the average brands' sales fall 16 percent after one year without advertising and by 25 percent after two years." After 4 years, none of the brands reported sales higher than in the last year in which they advertised. A Nielsen report concluded that as many as 50 percent of companies globally underspend in their media plans. One of the conclusions in the report was that too many "brands spend based on their previous spending patterns, rather than what will make an impact." According to the study, "Spending doesn't have to be risky when you use research."

Can it be that simple?

Sources: Daniel Konstantinovic, "July Was the Worst Month for Ad Spending in 2 Years," *eMarketer*, August 18, 2022, www.eMarketer.com; Daniel Konstantinovic, "Economic Uncertainty Comes for the Advertising Industry," *eMarketer*, July 18, 2022, www.eMarketer.com; Landon Oakum, "Nielsen Report Finds Underspending in 50% of Media Plans Jeopardizing Maximum ROI," Nielsen, July 6, 2022, www.nielsen.com; Shauna Lewis,

continued

"Nielsen Report: Advertisers Aren't Spending Enough Money," Nielsen, July 18, 2022, www.nielsen.com; Katie Deighton, "P&G Ramps Up Marketing amid Coronavirus Demand: 'This Is Not a Time to Go Off-Air,'" *TheDrum*, April 17, 2020, www.thedrum.com; Mark Ritson, "P&G and Coke's Pandemic Performances Prove It: You Don't Cut Ad Spend in a Crisis," *Marketing Week*, August 11, 2021, www.marketingweek.com; Michaela Jefferson, "Ehrenberg-Bass Reveals the Negative Effect an Advertising Hiatus Has on Brand Growth" *Marketing Week*, August 10, 2021, www.marketingweek.com; Matt Posky "Ford Decides Paying for Ads Is Stupid", www.theTruthAboutCars.com, June 2, 2022.

The lead-in to this chapter demonstrates the importance of continuing to budget for advertising during difficult times. Too often, companies become complacent and assume that their brand name will allow them to cut back, essentially resting on their laurels. At other times, such as during a downturn in the economy or when companies find that sales are starting to decrease, they cut their marketing budgets to save money and/or maintain profits. History has shown that this is not always a good idea. As will be seen in this chapter, marketers must establish sound communications objectives and allocate the monies required to achieve them. Both objective setting and budgeting must be seen as an ongoing process. These objectives should be based on purchase decision models that guide the budget allocation to various media and not just the fact that a particular media category is trending. As you will see, many large companies have been using these purchase decision models for a number of years, and continue to do so. At the same time not everyone agrees with their use or their validity, arguing that the models are either outdated or should never have been used in the first place. As the media environment continues to change, marketers continue to examine these models and their value in guiding the IMC program. As this chapter will demonstrate, the success of a program can and should be measured by both marketing and communications objectives. The chapter will examine how the goals for the integrated marketing communications program follow the company's overall marketing strategy and how these goals determine and are determined by the promotional budget.

Unfortunately, many companies have difficulty with the most critical step in the promotional planning process—setting realistic objectives that will guide the development of the IMC program. Complex marketing situations, conflicting perspectives regarding what advertising and other promotional-mix elements are expected to accomplish, and uncertainty over resources make the setting of marketing communications objectives an attempt to create order out of chaos. While the task of setting objectives can be complex and difficult, it must be done properly because specific goals and objectives are the foundation on which all other promotional decisions are made. Budgeting for advertising and other promotional areas, as well as creative and media strategies and tactics, evolves from these objectives. They also provide a standard against which performance can be measured.

Setting specific objectives should be an integral part of the planning process. However, many companies either fail to use specific marketing communications objectives or set ones that are inadequate for guiding the development of the promotional plan or measuring its effectiveness. Many marketers are uncertain as to what integrated marketing communications should be expected to contribute to the marketing program. The goal of their company's advertising and promotional program is simple: to generate sales. They fail to recognize the specific tasks that advertising and other promotional-mix variables must perform in preparing customers to buy a particular product or service.

As we know, advertising and promotion are not the only marketing activities involved in generating sales. Moreover, it is not always possible or necessary to measure the effects of advertising in terms of sales. For example, the Allianz ad shown in Exhibit 7-1 has

EXHIBIT 7–1

The objective of this ad is to demonstrate Allianz's support for the future.

Allianz SE

EXHIBIT 7–2

Gillette's objectives for this campaign are more than just generating sales.

Procter & Gamble

a goal beyond just supporting its company and attracting new customers. It is also designed to build trust and credibility on the brand.

Consider the Gillette ad shown in Exhibit 7–2. The goal of this campaign was to establish Gillette as the "go-to choice" for women's hair removal. What objectives might the company have for this ad? How might its effectiveness be measured?

This chapter examines the nature and purpose of objectives and the role they play in guiding the development, implementation, and evaluation of an IMC program. Attention is given to the various types of objectives appropriate for different situations. We will also examine the budget-setting process and the interdependence of objective setting and budgeting.

THE VALUE OF OBJECTIVES

Perhaps one reason many companies fail to set specific objectives for their integrated marketing communications programs is that they don't recognize the value of doing so. Another may be disagreement as to what the specific objectives should be. Advertising and promotional objectives are needed for several reasons, including the functions they serve in communications, planning and decision making, and measurement and evaluation.

Communications

Specific objectives for the IMC program facilitate coordination of the various groups working on the campaign. Many people are involved in the planning and development of an integrated marketing communications program on the client side as well as in the various promotional agencies. The advertising and promotional program must be coordinated within the company, inside the ad agency, and between the two. Any other parties involved in the promotional campaign, such as public relations and/or sales promotion firms, research specialists, and media buying services, must also know what the company hopes to accomplish through its marketing communications program. Many problems can be avoided if all parties have written, approved objectives to guide their actions and serve as a common base for discussing issues related to the promotional program.

Planning and Decision Making

Specific promotional objectives also guide development of the integrated marketing communications plan. All phases of a firm's promotional strategy should be based on the established objectives, including budgeting, creative, and media decisions as well as direct-marketing, public relations/publicity, sales promotion, and/or reseller support programs.

Meaningful objectives can also be a useful guide for decision making. Promotional planners are often faced with a number of strategic and tactical options in terms of choosing creative options, selecting media, and allocating the budget among various elements of the promotional mix. Choices should be made based on how well a particular strategy matches the firm's promotional objectives.

Measurement and Evaluation of Results

An important reason for setting specific objectives is that they provide a benchmark against which the success or failure of the promotional campaign can be measured. Without specific objectives, it is extremely difficult to determine what the firm's advertising and promotion efforts accomplished. One characteristic of good objectives is that they are *measurable*; they specify a method and criteria for determining how well the promotional program is working. By setting specific and meaningful objectives, the promotional planner provides a measure(s) that can be used to evaluate the effectiveness of the marketing communications program. Most organizations are concerned about the return on their promotional investment, and comparing actual performance against measurable objectives is the best way to determine if the return justifies the expense.

DETERMINING INTEGRATED MARKETING COMMUNICATIONS OBJECTIVES

Integrated marketing communications objectives should be based on a thorough situation analysis that identifies the marketing and promotional issues facing the company or a brand. The situation analysis is the foundation on which marketing objectives are determined and the marketing plan is developed. IMC objectives evolve from the company's overall marketing plan and are rooted in its marketing objectives. Advertising and promotional objectives are not the same as marketing objectives (although many firms tend to treat them as synonymous).

Marketing versus Communications Objectives

Marketing objectives are generally stated in the firm's marketing plan and are statements of what is to be accomplished by the overall marketing program within a given time period. Marketing objectives are usually defined in terms of specific, measurable outcomes such as sales volume, market share, profits, or return on investment. Good marketing objectives are *quantifiable*; they delineate the target market and note the time frame for accomplishing the goal (often one year). For example, a copy machine company may have as its marketing objective "to increase sales by 10 percent in the small-business segment of the market during the next 12 months." To be effective, objectives must also be *realistic* and *attainable*.

A company with a very high market share may seek to increase its sales volume by stimulating growth in the product category. It might accomplish this by increasing consumption by current users or encouraging nonusers to use the product. Some firms have as their marketing objectives expanding distribution and sales of their product in certain market areas. Companies often have secondary marketing objectives that are related to actions they must take to solve specific problems and thus achieve their primary objectives.

Once the marketing communications manager has reviewed the marketing plan, he or she should understand where the company hopes to go with its marketing program, how it intends to get there, and the role advertising and promotion will play. Marketing goals defined in terms of sales, profit, or market share increases are usually not appropriate promotional objectives. They are objectives for the entire marketing program, and achieving them depends on the proper coordination and execution of all the marketing-mix elements, including not just promotion but product planning and production, pricing, and distribution. For example, a company may be very successful in its promotional program, creating interest and/or trial for a product. But what if the product is unavailable when the consumer goes to buy it, or what if, once in the store, the consumer feels the product is overpriced and decides not to buy? Should the promotional program be blamed when the product's poor performance is due to other marketing strategies or tactics?

Integrated marketing communications objectives are statements of what various aspects of the IMC program will accomplish. They should be based on the particular communications tasks required to deliver the appropriate messages to the target audience. Managers must be able to translate general marketing goals into communications goals and specific promotional objectives.

Sometimes companies do not have a formal marketing plan, and the information needed may not be readily available. In this case, the promotional planner must attempt to gather as much information as possible about the product and its markets from sources both inside and outside the company.

After reviewing all the information, the promotional planner should see how integrated marketing communications fits into the marketing program and what the firm hopes to achieve through advertising and other promotional elements. The next step is to set objectives in terms of specific communications goals or tasks.

Many planners approach promotion from a communications perspective and believe the objective of advertising and other promotional-mix elements is usually to communicate information or a selling message about a product or service. Other managers argue that sales or some related measure, such as market share, is the only meaningful goal for advertising and promotion and should be the basis for setting objectives. These two perspectives have been the topic of considerable debate and are worth examining further.

SALES VERSUS COMMUNICATIONS OBJECTIVES

Sales-Oriented Objectives

To many managers, the only meaningful objective for their promotional program is sales. They take the position that the basic reason a firm spends money on advertising and promotion is to sell its product or service. Promotional spending represents an investment of a firm's resources that requires an economic justification. Managers generally compare investment options on a common financial basis, such as return on investment (ROI). However, determining the specific return on advertising and promotional dollars is often quite a difficult task. A study by Webmarketing123 of both business-to-business (B2B) and business-to-consumer (B2C) marketers indicated that a majority admit they don't know which channels make the biggest impact on revenues. For example, while 87 percent of B2B marketers used social media, only 17 percent claimed they were able to measure ROI. Likewise, with B2C marketers, 87 percent said they used social media with only 27 percent able to measure ROI.[1] Colgate Palmolive attempted to employ artificial intelligence in an attempt to determine the ROI of its retail promotions. Unfortunately—as is often the case in attempting to determine ROI—the company had limited success. Due to a number of obstacles, including the lack of data availability, competitive activities, and other factors, the system was unable to provide trustworthy and verifiable results.[2] At the same time, many managers believe that monies spent on advertising and other forms of promotion should produce measurable results, such as increasing sales volume by a certain percentage or dollar amount or increasing the brand's market share. They believe objectives (as well as the success or failure of the campaign) should be based on the achievement of sales results.

As a result, many managers have increased their efforts to make agencies more accountable for their performances. In turn, some agencies have developed their own tools to attempt to provide more ROI information in regard to how their integrated communications programs are performing. These agencies often attempt to differentiate themselves from others on this premise.

Some managers prefer sales-oriented objectives to make the individuals involved in advertising and promotion think in terms of how the promotional program will influence sales. For example, GEICO, once ranked fourth behind State Farm, Allstate, and Progressive insurance companies, increased its advertising budget by 75 percent—nearly double that of its competitors—and broadened its media placements. As a result, GEICO took over as the number one insurance company in new customer acquisitions and is now the second-largest insurance company in the United States.[3] Likewise, as noted in the lead-in to

EXHIBIT 7–3

A number of companies like P&G decided to increase their advertising budgets in an attempt to bolster sales.

Procter & Gamble

this chapter, a number of companies like P&G benefited from budget increases (Exhibit 7–3).

Problems with Sales Objectives It appears that increases in advertising expenditures seemed to work for GEICO as it experienced sales increases. Does this mean that these results can be attributed directly to the increased advertising budgets? Not necessarily. It might help to compare this situation to a football game and think of advertising as a quarterback. The quarterback is one of the most important players on the team but can be effective only with support from the other players. If the team loses, is it fair to blame the loss entirely on the quarterback? Of course not. Just as the quarterback is but one of the players on the football team, promotion is but one element of the marketing program, and there are many other reasons why the targeted sales level was not reached. The quarterback can lead his team to victory only if the linemen block, the receivers catch his passes, and the running backs help the offense establish a balanced attack of running and passing. Even if the quarterback plays an outstanding game, the team can still lose if the defense gives up too many points.

In the business world, sales results can be due to any of the other marketing-mix variables, including product design or quality, packaging, distribution, or pricing. Advertising can make consumers aware of and interested in the brand, but it can't make them buy it, particularly if it is not readily available or is priced higher than a competing brand. As shown in Figure 7–1, sales are a function of many factors, not just advertising and promotion. There is an adage in marketing that states, "Nothing will kill a poor product faster than good advertising." Taken with the other factors shown in Figure 7–1, this adage demonstrates that all the marketing elements must work together if a successful plan is to be implemented.

Another problem with sales objectives is that the effects of advertising often occur over an extended period. Many experts recognize that advertising has a lagged or **carryover effect**; monies spent on advertising do not necessarily have an immediate

FIGURE 7–1

Factors Influencing Sales

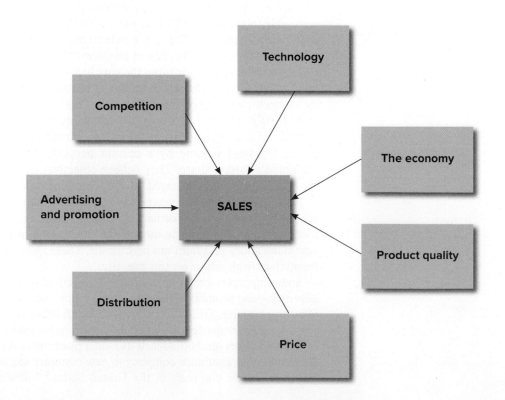

EXHIBIT 7–4

Kayem Foods' marketing
strategy led to sales increases.

James Borchuck/ZUMApress/
Newscom

impact on sales.[4] Advertising may create awareness, interest, and/or favorable attitudes toward a brand, but these feelings will not result in an actual purchase until the consumer enters the market for the product, which may occur later. A review of econometric studies that examined the duration of cumulative advertising effects found that for mature, frequently purchased, low-priced products, advertising's effect on sales lasts up to 9 months.[5] Models have been developed to account for the carryover effect of advertising and to help determine the long-term effect of advertising on sales.[6] The carryover effect adds to the difficulty of determining the precise relationship between advertising and sales.

Another problem with sales objectives is that they offer little guidance to those responsible for planning and developing the promotional program. The creative and media people working on the account need some direction as to the nature of the advertising message the company hopes to communicate, the intended audience, and the particular effect or response sought. As you will see shortly, communications objectives are recommended because they provide operational guidelines for those involved in planning, developing, and executing the advertising and promotional program.

Where Sales Objectives Are Appropriate   While there can be many problems in attempting to use sales as objectives for a promotional campaign, there are situations where sales objectives are appropriate. Certain types of promotion efforts seek direct action in nature; they attempt to induce an immediate behavioral response from the prospective customer. A major objective of most sales promotional programs is to generate short-term increases in sales. At the same time, short-term strategies hopefully will lead to longer-term gains as well. A good example is Kayem Foods of Chelsea, Massachusetts. To celebrate its 100th anniversary, Kayem changed the design of its frankfurter package. After consumer research suggested changing the copy and label on the package, the product was reintroduced. In the first 12 weeks Kayem saw sales rise by 15.7 percent[7] (Exhibit 7–4). Thirteen years later the company maintains the same label and has become the official hot dog of the Boston Red Sox, Florida Marlins, and Washington Nationals, among other sports teams, and now employs over 500 people.

Direct-response advertising is one type of advertising that evaluates its effectiveness on the basis of sales. Merchandise is advertised in material mailed to customers, in newspapers and magazines, through the Internet, or on television. The consumer purchases the merchandise by mail, on the Internet, or by calling a toll-free number. The direct-response advertiser generally sets objectives and measures success in terms of the sales response generated by the ad. For example, objectives for and the evaluation of a direct-response ad on TV are based on the number of orders received each time a station broadcasts the commercial. Because advertising is really the only form of communication and promotion used in this situation and response is generally immediate, setting objectives in terms of sales is appropriate. The credit card ad shown in Exhibit 7–5 is an example of a product sold through direct-response advertising.

EXHIBIT 7–5

Many credit card companies
use direct-response
advertising to sell products.

American Airlines

EXHIBIT 7–6

JCPenney seeks sales from this ad.

Penney IP LLC

Retail advertising, which accounts for a significant percentage of all advertising expenditures, is another area where the advertiser often seeks an immediate response, particularly when sales or special events are being promoted. The ad for JCPenney's sale shown in Exhibit 7–6 is designed to attract consumers to stores during the sales period (and to generate sales volume). JCPenney's management can determine the effectiveness of its promotional effort by analyzing store traffic and sales volume during the sale and comparing them to figures for nonsale days. But retailers may also allocate advertising and promotional dollars to image-building campaigns designed to create and enhance favorable perceptions of their stores. For example, after Subway spokesperson Jarod Fogle pleaded guilty to having sex with minors and possessing child pornography, Subway immediately disassociated itself with Fogle, who had been in its ads for 15 years. Fogle had lost 245 pounds and had become the center of the Subway campaign stressing a healthy diet and weight-loss benefits of eating at the sandwich chain rather than at hamburger outlets. Subway's new campaign focused on the 50-year history of the brand and reminded people that it had been selling "fresh" long before Chipotle and Panera—who the company felt got all the credit for "fresh." The campaign was successful, Subway experienced little or no negative impact from the Fogle association, and the campaign enhanced the "fresh" image for the brand. Fogle began his prison sentence in 2015.

Sales-oriented objectives are also used when advertising plays a dominant role in a firm's marketing program and other factors are relatively stable. For example, many packaged-goods companies compete in mature markets with established channels of distribution, stable competitive prices and promotional budgets, and products of similar quality. They view advertising and sales promotion as the key determinants of a brand's sales or market share, so it may be possible to isolate the effects of these promotional-mix variables. Many companies have accumulated enough market knowledge with their advertising, sales promotion, and direct-marketing programs to have considerable insight into the sales levels that should result from their promotional efforts. Mark Baynes, vice president of Kellogg's Morning Foods Division, attributed a turnabout in sales to effective advertising, brand repositioning, and more emotional appeals that generate interest.[8] Thus, many companies believe it is reasonable to set objectives and evaluate the success of their promotional efforts in terms of sales results.

Advertising and promotional programs tend to be evaluated in terms of sales, particularly when expectations are not being met. Marketing and brand managers under pressure to show sales results often take a short-term perspective in evaluating advertising and sales promotion programs. They are often looking for a quick fix for declining sales or loss of market share. They ignore the pitfalls of making direct links between advertising and sales, and campaigns—as well as ad agencies—may be changed if sales expectations are not being met. As discussed in Chapter 3, many companies want their agencies to accept incentive-based compensation systems tied to sales performance. Thus, while sales may not be an appropriate objective in many advertising and promotional situations, managers are inclined to keep a close eye on sales and market share figures and make changes in the promotional program when these numbers become stagnant or decline.

Communications Objectives

Some marketers do recognize the problems associated with sales-oriented objectives. They recognize that the primary role of an IMC program is to communicate and that planning should be based on communications objectives. Advertising and other promotional efforts

EXHIBIT 7–7

This ad satisfies its communication objective by creating a favorable image of Minnesota Power.

Minnesota Power

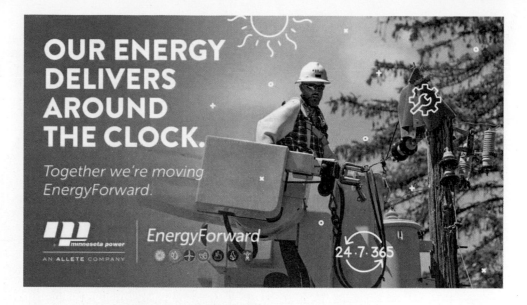

are designed to achieve communications such as brand knowledge and interest, favorable attitudes and image, and purchase intentions. Consumers are not expected to respond immediately; rather, advertisers realize they must provide relevant information and create favorable predispositions toward the brand before purchase behavior will occur.

For example, the ad in Exhibit 7–7 is designed to inform consumers of the company's importance. While there is no call for immediate action, the ad creates favorable impressions about the company by demonstrating the importance of electricity. The Minnesota Power ad portrays the company as more than just a utility company, but rather a partner in enhancing the user's life.

Advocates of communications-based objectives generally use some form of the hierarchical models discussed in Chapter 5 when setting advertising and promotional objectives. In all these models, consumers pass through three successive stages: cognitive (thinking), affective (feeling), and conative (behavioral). As consumers proceed through the three stages, they move closer to making a purchase.

Communications Effects Pyramid   Advertising and promotion perform communications tasks in the same way that a pyramid is built, by first accomplishing lower-level objectives such as awareness and knowledge or comprehension. Subsequent tasks involve moving consumers who are aware of or knowledgeable about the product or service to higher levels in the pyramid (Figure 7–2). The initial stages, at the base of the pyramid, are easier to accomplish than are those toward the top, such as trial and repurchase or regular use. Thus, the percentage of prospective customers will decline as they move up the pyramid (or down the funnel).

The communications pyramid can also be used to determine promotional objectives for an established brand. The promotional planner must determine where the target audience lies with respect to the various blocks in the pyramid. If awareness levels for a brand and knowledge of its features and benefits are low, the communications objective should be to increase them. If these blocks of the pyramid are already in place, but liking or preference is low, the advertising goal may be to change the target markets' image of the brand and move consumers through to purchase. Think about the iconic shoe brand Vans, for example. As shown in the ad in Exhibit 7–8, the company's creative and cutting-edge advertising embraces the off-the-wall athleticism of Van's classic shoe wearers. Vans started in 1966 in a small storefront in Anaheim, California, with shoe boxes on the shelves that didn't even have shoes in them. Once an order was placed, the shoes would be manufactured on the spot and ready to be picked up the next day. Targeted to surfers and skateboarders, you could buy a pair for $8 or just one shoe for $4 (skateboarders tend to wear out one shoe that they use to drag or as a

FIGURE 7–2

Communications Effects
Pyramid

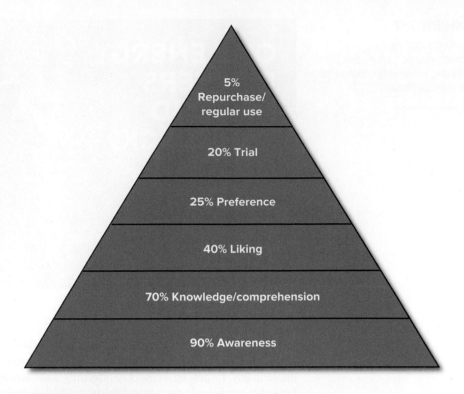

EXHIBIT 7–8

Vans has successfully targeted
skateboarders with iconic
brand advertising like this one.

Vans, A VF Company

brake). With successful advertising, a spot in the movie *Fast Times at Ridgemont High*, and the attractiveness of the Southern California image, sales took off. Vans now has over 18 million fans and continues to grow.[9] Think about the company's movement through the communications pyramid and how the objectives and strategies had to change to achieve such success.

Problems with Communications Objectives

Not all marketing and advertising managers accept communications objectives; some say it is too difficult to translate a sales goal into a specific communications objective. But at some point a sales goal must be transformed into a communications objective. If the marketing plan for an established brand has an objective of increasing sales by 10 percent, the promotional planner will eventually have to think in terms of the message that will be communicated to the target audience to achieve this. Possible objectives include the following:

- Increasing the percentage of consumers in the target market who associate specific features, benefits, or advantages with our brand.
- Increasing the number of consumers in the target audience who prefer our product over the competition's.
- Encouraging current users of the product to use it more frequently or in more situations.
- Encouraging consumers who have never used our brand to try it.

In some situations, promotional planners may gain insight into communications objectives' relationship to sales from industry research. Figure 7–3 provides an example of the GfK International purchase funnel used by many in the automobile industry as a diagnostic model of consumer decision making. While there are some marketers who contend the consumer funnels no longer are applicable, Digital and Social Media Perspective 7–1 provides another perspective.

FIGURE 7–3

GfK Purchase Funnel

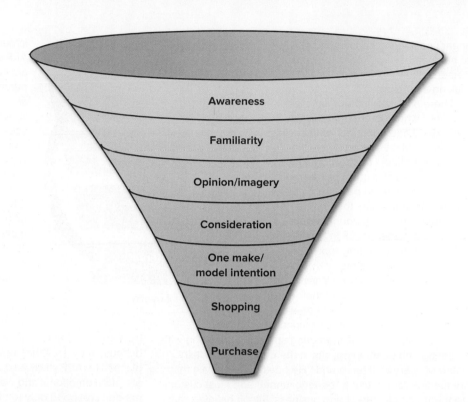

Digital and Social Media Perspective 7–1 > > >

A Century Later the Consumer Purchase Funnel Continues to Be Debated

Consumer response hierarchies were first introduced over a century ago and have been used by marketers in sales and advertising ever since. Likewise, discussions of the hierarchies have appeared in the marketing literature for over a half century. Just a few years ago a number of marketers were writing about the demise of the consumer funnel. Its death, they said, was caused by the growth of digital and social media. They went on to say that it had lived a long and prosperous life and had served marketers well but—like other concepts—had outlived its time. But, to paraphrase Mark Twain (or Elvis), the death of the consumer funnel has been extremely exaggerated.

Discussions of consumer response hierarchies have appeared in the marketing literature for over a half century and have had probably as many opponents as proponents regarding their usefulness in developing marketing and communications strategies. Nevertheless, a number of large companies including BMW, Sprint, Honda, and General Motors have employed their own hierarchies, typically referring to them as *purchase funnels*. These purchase funnels have been used as planning guides to move consumers from awareness to final purchase. While consumer purchase funnels have their advocates, there are still some nonbelievers out there who contend that the funnels are too linear, and the impact of digital, social, and mobile have changed the way consumers make decisions.

For example, Joe Ayyoub calls the funnel paradigm aged and says it's time for a reboot, arguing that we can no longer capture customers by taking them through the linear awareness to purchase sequence. He attributes this change to the increase in digital information, including product reviews, pricing information, and social media recommendations, as well as the use of mobile by the customer while in the store. According to Ayyoub, it is time to split the funnel, with the top focusing on awareness, but once customers become aware, they are moved to the bottom half, where monies should be allocated to conversion strategies. At that point marketers can focus on delivering the right offers at the right time on the right platform and to the right audience. Essentially, one-to-one marketing replaces mass marketing.

Cynthia Clark agrees with Ayyoub, noting that the funnel has "morphed considerably from a decade ago." Clark contends that the buying journey has changed, with control shifting from the organization to the consumers, who are taking it upon themselves to learn as much as they can about a brand before making a purchase.

Tom Roach refers to the funnels as "the cockroach of marketing concepts," arguing that it does not seem right that most of the marketing industry uses a template that is "mostly wrong and not strongly supported by marketing science." Like others, he also argues that the concept needs to be adapted to today's media environment and is too

(continued)

linear considering consumers tend to have entirely unpredictable and personal journeys on their way to making a purchase.

There are many other marketers out there who contend that the funnel is dead and no longer of value to marketers. Most contend that with the advent of new media, consumers have changed and can't be treated like they were in the past. And, given the new technologies that provide a seemingly endless amount of data to marketers, they shouldn't be. Mass marketing is being replaced by one-to-one marketing.

However, not everyone is convinced that we need to bury the funnel. Mark Ritson notes, "I do not know of a way to build strategy without a funnel. It is the backbone of all marketing strategy and, along with targeting and positioning, sits at the centre of the dashboard of every well run brand." He goes on to explain that companies cannot use a "generic funnel" and must customize them to their market and business. Ritson believes that "funnel juggling" is the answer to marketing effectiveness.

One of the more in-depth examinations of how the consumer decision process works comes from an extensive three-phase study commissioned by the Advertising Research Foundation (ARF), which examined many of the issues addressed in the previously mentioned studies while adding valuable new insights.

The ARF study does not consider the traditional decision-making models to be dead or even of limited value. Rather, the study was based on the assumption that the models have value but need to be examined in a new light given the

The Buying Funnel Is Dead

impact of social and digital media. The ARF study contends that consumers are constantly considering potential purchases and evaluating brands, but at some times are in a more active shopping mode and purposefully seeking assistance so they can make a purchase decision with confidence. While various media may have an impact in the more passive state, it is in the active state where consumers rely more heavily on social media to gain information from websites, friends, product experts, and so on. Thus, no single source is driving the purchase decision, but all can make a contribution in different ways.

If all this is true, then one has to wonder if all these new technologies actually increase the consumers' trust and confidence. Are they likely to purchase just because they are being reached at the right time and place? The ARF study also showed that purchase decisions are often emotional and well thought out. Maybe consumers don't respond only to the last best offer?

Sources: Tom Roach, "Why the Sales Funnel Is the Cockroach of Marketing Concepts," *Marketing Week*, September 2021, www.marketingweek.com; Mark Ritson, "Wondering Why Netflix Wants to Stop Password Sharing? It's All about Funnels," *Marketing Week*, March 25, 2021, www.marketingweek.com; Ellen Hammett, "How BMW Is Using Content to 'Enlarge the Upper Sales Funnel,'" *Marketing Week*, February 25, 2019, www.marketingweek.com; Mark Meyerson, "Rethinking the Marketing Funnel with Consumer Decision Journeys," *MarTech*, February 25, 2019, www.martech.com; Aaron Brooks, "Marketing Funnel Strategies: 5 Steps to Increase Sales in 2019," Venture Harbour, January 3, 2019, www.ventureharbour.com; Joe Ayyoub, "How to Break Out of the Funnel," *ClickZ*, July 2, 2015, www.clickz.com; Cynthia Clark, "Winning in the New and Improved Sales and Marketing Funnel," 1to1 Media, May 12, 2014, www.1to1media.com.

In attempting to translate sales goals into specific communications objectives, promotional planners often are not sure what constitutes adequate levels of awareness, knowledge, liking, preference, or conviction. There are no formulas to provide this information. The promotional manager will have to use his or her personal experience and that of the brand or product managers, as well as the marketing history of this and similar brands. Average scores on various communications measures for this and similar products should be considered, along with the levels achieved by competitors' products. This information can be related to the amount of money and time spent building these levels as well as the resulting sales or market share figures. However, at some point, sales-oriented objectives must be translated into what the company hopes to communicate and to whom it hopes to communicate.

Many marketing and promotional managers recognize the value of setting specific communications objectives and their important role as operational guidelines to the planning, execution, and evaluation of the promotional program. Communications objectives are the criteria used in the DAGMAR approach to setting advertising goals and objectives, which has become one of the most influential approaches to the advertising planning process.

DAGMAR: AN APPROACH TO SETTING OBJECTIVES

In 1961, Russell Colley prepared a report for the Association of National Advertisers titled *Defining Advertising Goals for Measured Advertising Results* (DAGMAR).[10] In it, Colley developed a model for setting advertising objectives and measuring the results of an ad campaign. The major thesis of the **DAGMAR** model is that communications effects are the logical basis for advertising goals and objectives against which success or failure should be measured.

Under the DAGMAR approach, an advertising goal involves a **communications task** that is specific and measurable. A communications task, as opposed to a marketing task, can be performed by, and attributed to, advertising rather than to a combination of several marketing factors. Colley proposed that the communications task be based on a hierarchical model of the communication process with four stages:

- *Awareness*—making the consumer aware of the existence of the brand or company.
- *Comprehension*—developing an understanding of what the product is and what it will do for the consumer.
- *Conviction*—developing a mental disposition in the consumer to buy the product.
- *Action*—getting the consumer to purchase the product.

As discussed earlier, other hierarchical models of advertising effects can be used as a basis for analyzing the communications response process. Some advertising theorists prefer the Lavidge and Steiner hierarchy of effects model, since it is more specific and provides a better way to establish and measure results.[11]

While the hierarchical model of advertising effects was the basic model of the communications response process used in DAGMAR, Colley also studied other specific tasks that advertising might be expected to perform in leading to the ultimate objective of a sale. He developed a checklist of 52 advertising tasks to characterize the contribution of advertising and serve as a starting point for establishing objectives.

Characteristics of Objectives

A second major contribution of DAGMAR to the advertising planning process was its definition of what constitutes a good objective. Colley argued that advertising objectives should be stated in terms of concrete and measurable communications tasks, specify a target audience, indicate a benchmark starting point and the degree of change sought, and specify a time period for accomplishing the objective(s).

Concrete, Measurable Tasks   The communications task specified in the objective should be a precise statement of what appeal or message the advertiser wants to communicate to the target audience. Advertisers generally use a copy platform to describe their basic message. The objective or copy platform statement should be specific and clear enough to guide the creative specialists who develop the advertising message. For example, Hyundai, after years of being at or near the bottom of the list of automobiles in customer satisfaction ratings, focused its attention on increasing the quality, as well as improving consumers' perceptions, of its cars. The result is that Hyundai is among the top of the list of a number of websites' ratings for mid-size cars (Exhibit 7-9). According to DAGMAR, the objective must also be measurable.

Target Audience   Another important characteristic of good objectives is a well-defined target audience. The primary target audience for a company's product or service is described in the situation analysis. It may be based on descriptive variables such as geography, demographics, and psychographics (on which advertising media selection decisions are based) as well as on behavioral variables such as usage rate or benefits sought.

EXHIBIT 7–9

Hyundai's sedans, like this one, have won a number of awards.

Hyundai Motor Company

Benchmark and Degree of Change Sought

To set objectives, one must know the target audience's present status concerning response hierarchy variables such as awareness, knowledge, image, attitudes, and intentions and then determine the degree to which consumers must be changed by the campaign. Determining the target market's present position regarding the various response stages requires **benchmark measures**. Often a marketing research study must be conducted to determine prevailing levels of the response hierarchy. In the case of a new product or service, the starting conditions are generally at or near zero for all the variables, so no initial research is needed.

Establishing benchmark measures gives the promotional planner a basis for determining what communications tasks need to be accomplished and for specifying particular objectives. For example, a preliminary study for a brand may reveal that awareness is high but consumer perceptions and attitudes are negative. The objective for the campaign must then be to change the target audience's perceptions of and attitudes toward the brand.

Quantitative benchmarks are not only valuable in establishing communications goals and objectives but also essential for determining whether the campaign was successful. Objectives provide the standard against which the success or failure of a campaign is measured. An ad campaign that results in a 90 percent awareness level for a brand among its target audience cannot really be judged effective unless one knows what percentage of the consumers were aware of the brand before the campaign began. A 70 percent precampaign awareness level would lead to a different interpretation of the campaign's success than would a 30 percent level.

Specified Time Period

A final consideration in setting advertising objectives is specifying the time period in which they must be accomplished. Appropriate time periods can range from a few days to a year or more. Most ad campaigns specify time periods from a few months to a year, depending on the situation facing the advertiser and the type of response being sought. For example, awareness levels for a brand can be created or increased fairly quickly through an intensive media schedule of widespread, repetitive advertising to the target audience. Repositioning of a product requires a change in consumers' perceptions and takes much more time.

Assessment of DAGMAR

The DAGMAR approach to setting objectives has had considerable influence on the advertising planning process. Many promotional planners use this model as a basis for setting objectives and assessing the effectiveness of their promotional campaigns. DAGMAR also focused advertisers' attention on the value of using communications-based rather than sales-based objectives to measure advertising effectiveness and encouraged the measurement of stages in the response hierarchy to assess a campaign's impact. Colley's work has led to improvements in the advertising and promotional planning process by providing a better understanding of the goals and objectives toward which planners' efforts should be directed. This usually results in less subjectivity and leads to better communication and relationships between client and agency.

Criticism of DAGMAR   While DAGMAR has contributed to the advertising planning process, it has not been totally accepted by everyone in the advertising field. A number of problems have led to questions regarding its value as a planning tool:[12]

- *Problems with the response hierarchy.* A major criticism of the DAGMAR approach is its reliance on the hierarchy of effects model. The fact that consumers do not always go through this sequence of communications effects before making a purchase has been recognized, and alternative response models have been developed. As indicated in Digital and Social Media Perspective 7–1, much of the criticism stems from the argument that digital and social media have significantly changed the consumer's decision-making process from a linear one-to-one in which consumers can enter or leave at any stage, resulting in a more circular process (Exhibit 7–10). DAGMAR MOD II recognizes that the appropriate response model depends on the situation and emphasizes identifying the sequence of decision-making steps that apply in a buying situation.[13]

- *Sales objectives.* Another objection to DAGMAR comes from those who argue that the only relevant measure of advertising objectives is sales. They have little tolerance for ad campaigns that achieve communications objectives but fail to increase sales. Advertising is seen as effective only if it induces consumers to make a purchase. The problems with this logic were addressed in our discussion of communications objectives.

- *Practicality and costs.* Another criticism of DAGMAR concerns the difficulties involved in implementing it. Money must be spent on research to establish quantitative benchmarks and measure changes in the response hierarchy. This is costly and time-consuming and can lead to considerable disagreement over method, criteria, measures, and so forth. Many critics argue that DAGMAR is practical only for large companies with big advertising and research budgets. Many firms do not want to spend the money needed to use DAGMAR effectively.

- *Inhibition of creativity.* A final criticism of DAGMAR is that it inhibits advertising creativity by imposing too much structure on the people responsible for developing the advertising. Many creative personnel think the DAGMAR approach is too concerned with quantitative assessment of a campaign's impact on awareness, brand-name recall, or specific persuasion measures. The emphasis is on passing the numbers test rather than developing a message that is truly creative and contributes to brand equity.

EXHIBIT 7–10

Performics suggests that consumers go through a marketing spiral.

Performics

ARE YOU ACTIVATING YOUR PARTICIPANTS?

Performics, the global digital performance marketing agency, inspires participation by applying the principles of search marketing to drive performance across paid, owned and earned media.

Argentina • Australia • Canada • China • Colombia • Czech Republic • Denmark • Egypt • France • Germany
Kuwait • Lebanon • India • Italy • Mexico • Netherlands • Norway • Philippines • Poland • Russia • Saudi Arabia
Singapore • Spain • Sweden • Taiwan • United Arab Emirates • United Kingdom • United States • Vietnam
www.performics.com

PROBLEMS IN SETTING OBJECTIVES

Although the DAGMAR model suggests a logical process for advertising and promotion planning, most advertisers and their agencies fail to follow these basic principles. They fail to set specific objectives for their campaigns and/or do not have the proper evidence to determine the success of their promotional programs. Many advertising agencies do not state appropriate objectives for determining success and thus can't demonstrate whether a supposedly successful campaign was really a success. Even though these campaigns may be doing something right, they generally do not know what it is.

One study examined the advertising practices of business-to-business marketers to determine whether their ads used advertising objectives that met Colley's four DAGMAR criteria.[14] Entries from the annual Business/Professional Advertising Association Gold Key Awards competition, which solicits the best marketing communications efforts from business-to-business advertisers, were evaluated with respect to their campaigns' objectives and summaries of results. Most of these advertisers did not set concrete advertising objectives, specify objective tasks, measure results in terms of stages of a hierarchy of effects, or match objectives to evaluation measures.

Improving Promotional Planners' Use of Objectives

As we have seen, it is important that advertisers and their agencies pay close attention to the objectives they set for their campaigns. They should strive to set specific and measurable objectives that not only guide promotional planning and decision making but also can be used as a standard for evaluating performance. Unfortunately, many companies do not set appropriate objectives for their integrated marketing communications programs.

Many companies fail to set appropriate objectives because top management has only an abstract idea of what the firm's IMC program is supposed to be doing. In an extensive review of thousands of case studies, Jerry Thomas concluded that most advertisers don't know if their advertising works and some ads may have a negative impact on sales. Thomas notes that the advertising industry has a very poor quality assurance system and turns out a very inconsistent product (the ads). He cites a number of reasons why this happens, one of which is the fact that clients don't define the role of advertising in the marketing program and do not precisely specify communications objectives.[15]

Few firms will set objectives that meet all the criteria set forth in DAGMAR. However, promotional planners should set objectives that are specific and measurable and go beyond basic sales goals. Even if specific communications response elements are not always measured, meeting the other criteria will sharpen the focus and improve the quality of the IMC planning process.

Setting Objectives for the IMC Program

One reason so much attention is given to advertising objectives is that for many companies advertising has traditionally been the major way of communicating with target audiences. Other promotional-mix elements such as sales promotion, direct marketing, and public relations are used intermittently to support and complement the advertising program.

Another reason is that traditional advertising-based views of marketing communications planning, such as DAGMAR, have dominated the field for so long. These approaches are based on a hierarchical response model and consider how marketers can develop and disseminate advertising messages to move consumers along an effects path. This approach, shown in Figure 7-4, is what professor Don Schultz calls *inside-out planning*. He says, "It focuses on what the marketer wants to say, when the marketer wants to say it, about things the marketer believes are important about his or her brand, and in the media forms the marketer wants to use."[16]

Schultz advocates an *outside-in planning* process for IMC that starts with the customer and builds backward to the brand. This means that promotional planners study the

FIGURE 7–4

Traditional Advertising-Based View of Marketing Communications

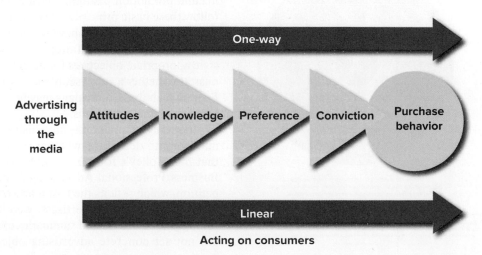

FIGURE 7–5

Objectives and Strategies
in the Social Consumer
Decision Journey

Sources: Expert interviews; McKinsey
analysis.

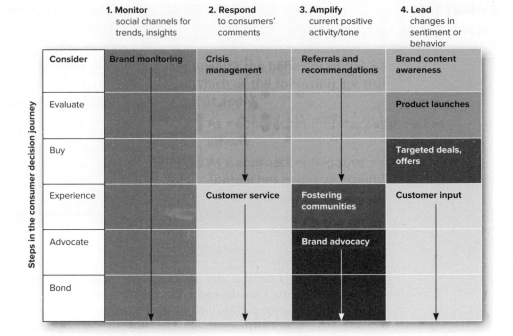

Steps in the consumer decision journey	1. Monitor social channels for trends, insights	2. Respond to consumers' comments	3. Amplify current positive activity/tone	4. Lead changes in sentiment or behavior
Consider	Brand monitoring	Crisis management	Referrals and recommendations	Brand content awareness
Evaluate				Product launches
Buy				Targeted deals, offers
Experience		Customer service	Fostering communities	Customer input
Advocate			Brand advocacy	
Bond				

various media customers and prospects use, when the marketer's messages might be most relevant to customers, and when they are likely to be most receptive to the message.

A similar approach is suggested by Professor Tom Duncan, who argues that IMC should use **zero-based communications planning**, which involves determining what tasks need to be done and which marketing communications functions should be used and to what extent.[17] This approach focuses on the task to be done and searches for the best ideas and media to accomplish it. Duncan suggests that an effective IMC program should lead with the marketing communications function that most effectively addresses the company's main problem or opportunity and should use a promotional mix that draws on the strengths of whichever communications functions relate best to the particular situation.

While Schultz and Duncan discuss strategies for setting objectives based on traditional response hierarchies, attention should also be given to competing models. As seen in Chapter 5, considering decision making as a "social consumer decision journey" necessitates the establishment of communications objectives as viewed from a different perspective. The rows in Figure 7–5 show the steps in the consumer decision journey ranging from consideration to bonding. The columns depict the objectives that marketers need to accomplish at each stage, while the 10 marketing responses necessary to achieve these objectives are listed within the matrix. In this perspective, the marketer must *monitor*—that is, know what is being said online about the product or brand to gain insights as to how it is being perceived in the marketplace and then respond accordingly. This process—according to the model—must take place continuously. Second, marketers must *respond* to specific issues at a personal level. Responses may be positive in nature (customer service or sales leads) or (more likely) be part of crisis management, dealing with negative issues regarding the product or brand. *Amplification* deals with designing the communications program—particularly as it relates to social media—to foster engagement and sharing, as well as loyalty. The objective of amplifying is to get consumers more involved in the brand, extending the experience the brand has to offer, and have them communicate their positive experiences to others in the social network. The final objective, *lead*, is designed to take the consumer to long-term behavioral changes. At the early stages of the process it may simply include creating more brand awareness. Later in the process, lead may be designed to create buzz or promote time-sensitive issues like sales or promotions. The model also advocates the solicitation of consumer input upon completion of the purchase for the purpose of creating continuous inputs.

EXHIBIT 7–11

The San Diego Zoo ran this ad to support its Wildlife Alliance program.

San Diego Zoo Wildlife Alliance

While the social consumer decision journey may differ from traditional response hierarchies, it is also similar in that it envisions going through stages in the purchase decision. Like the traditional model, marketers need to take specific marketing actions to help consumers through the process.

Many of the considerations for determining advertising objectives are relevant to setting goals for other elements of the integrated marketing communications program. The promotional planner should determine what role various sales promotion techniques, publicity and public relations, direct marketing, digital media, and personal selling will play in the overall marketing program and how they will interact with advertising as well as with one another.

For example, the marketing communications program for the San Diego Zoo has a number of objectives. First, it must provide funding for the zoo's programs and maintain a large and powerful base of supporters for financial strength. The communications must educate the public about the zoo's various programs and maintain a favorable image on a local, regional, and even international level. A major objective of the IMC program is drawing visitors to the zoo and its many experiences while supporting the San Diego Zoo Wildlife Alliance, its international, nonprofit conservation organization that integrates wildlife health and care, science, and education to develop sustainable conservation solutions (Exhibit 7–11).

Like the San Diego Zoo, other zoos may establish similar objectives. As can be seen in Figure 7–6, these programs may employ a variety of integrated marketing communications tools. When setting objectives for these promotional elements, planners must consider what the firm hopes to communicate through the use of this element, among what target audience, and during what time period. As with advertising, results should be measured and evaluated against the original objectives, and attempts should be made to isolate the effects of each promotional element. Objectives for marketing communications elements other than advertising are discussed more thoroughly in Part Five of the text.

ESTABLISHING AND ALLOCATING THE PROMOTIONAL BUDGET

If you take a minute to look back at the IMC planning model in Chapter 1, you will see that while the arrows from the review of the marketing plan and the promotional situation analysis to analysis of the communication process are *unidirectional*, the flow between the communications analysis and budget determination is a *two-way interaction*. What this means is that whereas establishing objectives is an important part of the planning process, recognizing the limitations of the budget is important too. No organization has an unlimited budget, so objectives must be set with the budget in mind.

Often when we think of promotional expenditures of firms, we think only about the huge amounts being spent. We don't usually take the time to think about how these monies are being allocated and about the recipients of these dollars. The budgeting

Advertising

Objectives: Drive attendance to Zoo. Uphold image and educate target audience and inform them of new attractions and special events and promotions.

Audience: Members and nonmembers of Zoological Society. Households in local and national markets. Tourist and group sales markets.

Timing: As allowed and determined by budget. Mostly timed to coincide with promotional efforts.

Tools/media: Television, radio, newspaper, magazines, direct mail, outdoor, tourist media (television and magazine).

Sales Promotions

Objectives: Use price, product, and other variables to drive attendance when it might not otherwise come.

Audience: Targeted, depending on co-op partner, mostly to local market.

Timing: To fit needs of Zoo and co-sponsoring partner.

Tools/media: Coupons, sweepstakes, tours, broadcast tradeouts, direct mail: statement stuffers, fliers, postcards, online ticket discounts.

Public Relations

Objectives: Inform, educate, create, and maintain image for Zoological Society and major attractions; reinforce advertising message.

Audience: From local to international, depending on subject, scope, and timing.

Timing: Ongoing, although often timed to coincide with promotions and other special events. Spur-of-the-moment animal news and information such as acquisitions, births, and so on.

Tools/media: Coverage by major news media, articles in local, regional, national, and international newspapers, magazines and other publications such as visitors' guides, tour books, and guides, appearances by Zoo spokepersons on news and talk shows, zoo newsletter, adopt an animal program, support conservation program.

Cause Marketing/Corporate Sponsorships/Events Underwriting

Objectives: To provide funding for Zoological Society programs and promote special programs and events done in cooperation with corporate sponsor. Must be win-win business partnership for Society and partner.

Audience: Supporters of both the Zoological Society and the corporate or product/service partner.

Timing: Coincides with needs of both partners, and seasonal attendance generation needs of Zoo.

Tools: May involve advertising, publicity, discount co-op promotions, ticket trades, hospitality centers. Exposure is directly proportional to amount of underwriting by corporate sponsor, both in scope and duration, education programs.

Direct Marketing

Objectives: Maintain large powerful base of supporters for financial and political strength.

Audience: Local, regional, national, and international. Includes children's program, seniors (60+), couples, single memberships, and incremental donor levels.

Timing: Ongoing, year-round promotion of memberships.

Tools: Direct mail and on-grounds visibility.

Group Sales

Objectives: Maximize group traffic and revenue by selling group tours to Zoo.

Audience: Conventions, incentive groups, bus tours, associations, youth, scouts, schools, camps, seniors, clubs, military, organizations, domestic and foreign travel groups.

Timing: Targeted to drive attendance in peak seasons or at most probable times such as convention season.

Tools: Travel and tourism trade shows, telemarketing, direct mail, trade publication advertising.

Internet

Objectives: Provide information regarding the Zoo, programs, memberships, and public relations activities.

Audience: All audiences interested in acquiring more information about the Zoo.

Timing: Ongoing, updated frequently over time

Tools: Website, blog, including videos, Facebook, Twitter, and other social media.

FIGURE 7–6 An Example of a Zoo's Objectives for Various Promotional Elements

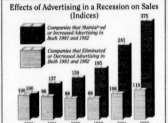

IN A RECESSION, THE BEST DEFENSE IS A GOOD OFFENSE.

It's a recession. Your instincts demand that you cut the ad budget. But, as the McGraw-Hill Research[1] analysis of business-to-business advertising expenditures during the 1981-82 recession shows, it's those with the courage to maintain or increase advertising in a recession who reap a major sales advantage over their competitors who panic and fall back into a defensive posture.

Effects of Advertising in a Recession on Sales (Indices)

And this advantage continues to expand long after the recession is over.

Recessions last an average of 11 months, but any advertising decision made during one can have permanent repercussions. The McGraw-Hill study demonstrates that nervous advertisers lose ground to the brave and can't gain it back. In 1980, according to the chart seen here, sales indices were identical, but by 1985 the brave had racked up a 3.2 to 1 sales advantage. A similar study done by McGraw-Hill during the 1974-75 recession corroborates the 1980's research.

A recession is the single greatest period in which to make short- and long-term gains. And, surprisingly, increasing advertising modestly during one has much the same effect on your profits as cutting advertising does. According to The Center for Research & Development's October 1990 study of consumer advertising during a recession, advertisers who yield "to the natural inclination to cut spending in an effort to increase profits in a recession find that it doesn't work."[1] This study, relying on the PIMS[2] database, also uncovered that aggressive recessionary advertisers picked up 4.5 *times* as much market share gain as their overcautious competitors, leaving them in a far better position to exploit the inevitable recovery and expansion.

Chevrolet countered its competitors during the 1974-75 recession by aggressively beefing up its ad spending and attained a two percent market share increase. Today, two share points in the automotive industry are worth over $4 billion. Delta Airlines and Revlon also boosted ad spending in the 1974-75 recession and achieved similar results.

Continuous advertising sustains market leadership. And it's far easier to sustain momentum than it is to start it up again. Consider this list of market category leaders: Campbell's, Coca-Cola, Ivory, Kellogg, Kodak, Lipton and Wrigley. This is the leadership list for 1925. And 1990. These marketers have maintained a relentless commitment to their brands in both good times and bad. Kellogg had the guts to pump up its ad spending during the Great Depression and cemented a market leadership it has yet to relinquish.

These are the success stories. Space and diplomacy don't allow the mention of the names of those who lacked gusto and chose to cut their ad spending in recessionary times.

But if you would like to learn more about how advertising can help make the worst of times the best of times, please write to Department C, American Association of Advertising Agencies, 666 Third Avenue, New York, New York 10017, enclosing a check for five dollars. You will receive a booklet covering the pertinent research done on all the U.S. recessions since 1923. Please allow 4 to 6 weeks for delivery.

McGraw-Hill Research, 1986. The Center for Research and Development ©1990.
Profit Impact of Market Strategies, The Strategic Planning Institute, Cambridge, MA.

AAAA

EXHIBIT 7–12

The American Association of Advertising Agencies (4As) promotes the continued use of advertising in a recession.

American Association of Advertising Agencies

decisions have a significant impact not only on the firm itself but also on numerous others involved either directly or indirectly. The remainder of this chapter provides insight into some underlying theory with respect to budget setting, discusses how companies budget for promotional efforts, and demonstrates the inherent strengths and weaknesses associated with these approaches. Essentially, we focus on two primary budgeting decisions: establishing a budget amount and allocating the budget.

Establishing the Budget

The size of a firm's advertising and promotions budget can vary from a few thousand dollars to more than a billion. When companies like AT&T and Verizon spend more than $3 billion per year to promote their products, they expect such expenditures to accomplish their stated objectives. The budget decision is no less critical to a firm spending only a few thousand dollars; its ultimate success or failure may depend on the monies spent. One of the most critical decisions facing the marketing manager is how much to spend on the promotional effort.

Unfortunately, many managers fail to realize the value of advertising and promotion. They treat the communications budget as an expense rather than an investment. Instead of viewing the dollars spent as contributing to additional sales and market share, they see budget expenses as cutting into profits. As a result, when times get tough, the advertising and promotional budget is the first to be cut—even though there is strong evidence that exactly the opposite should occur, as Exhibit 7–12 argues. Figure 7–7 shows the results of an extensive review of research involving advertising during a recession. The review covers 40 studies in the United States over an 83-year period. As can be seen, the argument for continuing to advertise during an economic downturn outweighs that of decreasing ad expenditures.[18] Moreover, the decision is not a one-time responsibility. A new budget is formulated every year, each time a new product is introduced, or when either internal or external factors necessitate a change to maintain competitiveness.

While it is one of the most critical decisions, budgeting has perhaps been the most resistant to change. A comparison of advertising and promotional texts over the past 20 years would reveal the same methods for establishing budgets. The theoretical basis for this process remains rooted in economic theory and marginal analysis. (Advertisers also use an approach based on **contribution margin**—the difference between the total revenue generated by a brand and its total variable costs. But, as

FIGURE 7–7

Conclusions on Research of Advertising in a Recession

Source: G. Tellis and K. Tellis, "Research on Advertising in a Recession," *Journal of Advertising Research* 49, no. 3 (2009), pp. 304–27.

- Advertising is strongly related to economic cycles across major world economies.

- The single most compelling reason for cutting back advertising during a recession is that sales during a recession are likely to be lower than they would be during an expansion.

- There is strong, consistent evidence that cutting back on advertising can hurt sales during and after a recession.

- Not cutting back on advertising during a recession could increase sales during and after the recession.

- Firms that increased advertising during a recession experienced higher sales, market share, or earnings during or after the recession.

- Most firms tend to cut back on advertising during a recession, reducing noise and increasing the effectiveness of advertising of the firm that advertises.

FIGURE 7–8

Marginal Analysis

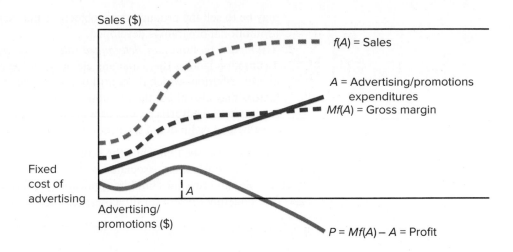

Robert Steiner says, *marginal analysis* and *contribution margin* are essentially synonymous terms.)[19] We begin our discussion of budgeting with an examination of these theoretical approaches.

Theoretical Issues in Budget Setting   Most of the models used to establish advertising budgets can be categorized as taking an economic or a sales response perspective.

Marginal Analysis   Figure 7–8 graphically represents the concept of **marginal analysis**. As advertising/promotional expenditures increase, sales and gross margins also increase to a point, but then they level off. Profits are shown to be a result of the gross margin minus advertising expenditures. Using this theory to establish its budget, a firm would continue to spend advertising/promotional dollars as long as the marginal revenues created by these expenditures exceeded the incremental advertising/promotional costs. As shown on the graph, the optimal expenditure level is the point where marginal costs equal the marginal revenues they generate (point *A*). If the sum of the advertising/promotional expenditures exceeded the revenues they generated, one would conclude the appropriations were too high and scale down the budget. If revenues were higher, a higher budget might be in order. (We will see later in this chapter that this approach can also be applied to the allocation decision.)

Whereas marginal analysis seems logical intuitively, certain weaknesses limit its usefulness. These weaknesses include the assumptions that (1) sales are a direct result of advertising and promotional expenditures and this effect can be measured, and (2) advertising and promotion are solely responsible for sales. Let us examine each of these assumptions in more detail.

1. *Assumption that sales are a direct measure of advertising and promotion efforts.* Earlier in this chapter we discussed the fact that the advertiser needs to set communications objectives that contribute to accomplishing overall marketing objectives but at the same time are separate. One reason for this strategy is that it is often difficult, if not impossible, to demonstrate the effects of advertising and promotions on sales. In studies using sales as a direct measure, it has been almost impossible to establish the contribution of advertising and promotion. In the words of David Aaker and James Carman, "Looking for the relationship between advertising and sales is somewhat worse than looking for a needle in a haystack."[20] Thus, to try to show that the size of the budget will directly affect sales of the product is misleading. A more logical approach would be to examine the impact of various budgets on the attainment of communications objectives.

As we saw in the discussion of communications objectives, sales are not the only goal of the promotional effort. Awareness, interest, attitude change, and other communications objectives are often sought, and while the bottom line may be to sell the product, these objectives may serve as the basis on which the promotional program is developed.

2. *Assumption that sales are determined solely by advertising and promotion.* This assumption ignores the remaining elements of the marketing mix—price, product, and distribution—which do contribute to a company's success. Environmental factors may also affect the promotional program, leading the marketing manager to assume the advertising was or was not effective when some other factor may have helped or hindered the accomplishment of the desired objectives.

Overall, you can see that while the economic approach to the budgeting process is a logical one, the difficulties associated with determining the effects of the promotional effort on sales and revenues limit its applicability. Marginal analysis is seldom used as a basis for budgeting (except for direct-response advertising).

Sales Response Models You may have wondered why the sales curve in Figure 7–8 shows sales leveling off even though advertising and promotions efforts continue to increase. The relationship between advertising and sales has been the topic of much research and discussion designed to determine the shape of the response curve.

Almost all advertisers subscribe to one of two models of the advertising/sales response function: the concave-downward function or the S-shaped response curve.

- *The concave-downward function.* After reviewing more than 100 studies of the effects of advertising on sales, Julian Simon and Johan Arndt concluded that the effects of advertising budgets follow the microeconomic law of diminishing returns.[21] That is, as the amount of advertising increases, its incremental value decreases. The logic is that those with the greatest potential to buy will likely act on the first (or earliest) exposures, while those less likely to buy are not likely to change as a result of the advertising. For those who may be potential buyers, each additional ad will supply little or no new information that will affect their decision. Thus, according to the **concave-downward function model**, the effects of advertising quickly begin to diminish, as shown in Figure 7–9A. Budgeting under this model suggests that fewer advertising dollars may be needed to create the optimal influence on sales.

- *The S-shaped response function.* Many advertising managers assume the **S-shaped response curve** (Figure 7–9B), which projects an S-shaped response function to the budget outlay (again measured in sales). Initial outlays of the advertising budget have little impact (as indicated by the essentially flat sales curve in range *A*). After a certain budget level has been reached (the beginning of range *B*), advertising and promotional efforts begin to have an effect, as additional increments of expenditures result in increased sales. This incremental gain continues only to a point, however, because at the beginning of range *C*, additional expenditures begin to return little or nothing in the way of sales. This model suggests a small advertising budget is likely to have no impact beyond the sales that may have been

FIGURE 7–9

Advertising Sales/Response Functions

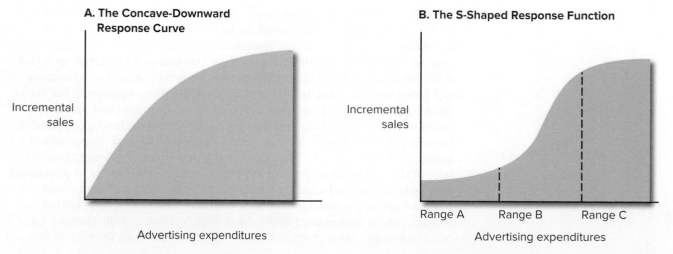

A. The Concave-Downward Response Curve

B. The S-Shaped Response Function

generated through other means (for example, word of mouth). At the other extreme, more does not necessarily mean better: Additional dollars spent beyond range *B* have no additional impact on sales and for the most part can be considered wasted. As with marginal analysis, one would attempt to operate at that point on the curve in area *B* where the maximum return for the money is attained.

Weaknesses in these sales response models render them of limited use to practitioners for direct applications. Many of the problems seen earlier—the use of sales as a dependent variable, measurement problems, and so on—limit the usefulness of these models. At the same time, keep in mind the purpose of discussing such models. Even though marginal analysis and the sales response curves may not apply directly, they give managers some insight into a theoretical basis of how the budgeting process should work. There's some empirical evidence indicating the models may have validity.

The studies discussed in earlier chapters on learning and the hierarchy of effects also demonstrate the importance of repetition for gaining awareness and for subsequent higher-order objectives such as adoption. Thus, while these models may not provide a tool for setting the advertising and promotional budget directly, we can use them to guide our appropriations strategy from a theoretical basis. As you will see later in this chapter, such a theoretical basis has advantages over many of the methods currently being used for budget setting and allocation.

Additional Factors in Budget Setting While the theoretical bases just discussed should be considered in establishing the budget appropriation, a number of other issues must also be considered. A weakness in attempting to use sales as a *direct* measure of response to advertising is that various situational factors may have an effect. Some of the factors that have been shown to affect the advertising/sales ratio are shown in Figure 7-10. For a product characterized by emotional buying motives, hidden

FIGURE 7–10

Factors Influencing Advertising Budgets

Factor	Relationship of Advertising/Sales	Factor	Relationship of Advertising/Sales
Product Factors		Competition:	
Basis for differentiation	+	Active	+
Hidden product qualities	+	Concentrated	+
Emotional buying motives	+	*Customer Factors*	
		Concentration of users	+
		Strategy Factors	
Purchase frequency	Curvilinear	Early stage of brand life cycle	+
Market Factors		Long channels of distribution	+
Stage of product life cycle:		High prices	+
Introductory	+	High quality	+
Growth	+	Media strategy	+
Maturity	–	Creative strategy	+
Decline	–	Promotional strategy	+
Inelastic demand	+	*Cost Factors*	
Market share	–	High profit margins	+

Note: + relationship means the factor leads to a positive effect of advertising on sales; – relationship indicates little or no effect of advertising on sales.

FIGURE 7–11

Factors Considered in
Budget Setting

Changes in advertising strategy and/or creative approach	51%
Competitive activity and/or spending levels	47%
Profit contribution goal or other financial target	43%
Level of previous year's spending, with adjustment	17%
Senior management dollar allocation or set limit	11%
Volume share projections	8%
Projections/assumptions on media cost increases	25%
Modifications in media strategy and/or buying techniques	17%

product qualities, and/or a strong basis for differentiation, advertising would have a noticeable impact on sales. Products characterized as large-dollar purchases and those in the maturity or decline stages of the product would be less likely to benefit.

As we will see later in this chapter, the percentage-of-sales method of budgeting has inherent weaknesses in that the advertising and sales effects may be reversed. So we cannot be sure whether the situation actually led to the advertising/sales relationship or vice versa. Thus, while these factors should be considered in the budget appropriation decision, they should not be the sole determinants of where and when to increase or decrease expenditures.

A survey of executives from some of the largest advertising companies, advertising agencies, and consultants yielded the factors shown in Figure 7–11 that are important in budget setting.

Overall, the responses reflect in part their perceptions as to factors of importance in how budgets are set. To understand the differences in the relative importance of these factors, it is important to understand the approaches currently employed in budget setting. The next section examines these approaches.

Budgeting Approaches

The theoretical approaches to establishing the promotional budget are seldom employed. In smaller firms, they may never be used. Instead, a number of methods developed through practice and experience are implemented. This section reviews some of the more traditional methods of setting budgets and the relative advantages and disadvantages of each. First, you must understand two things: (1) Many firms employ more than one method, and (2) budgeting approaches vary according to the size and sophistication of the firm.

Top-Down Approaches   The approaches discussed in this section may be referred to as **top-down approaches** because a budgetary amount is established (usually at an executive level) and then the monies are passed down to the various departments (as shown in Figure 7–12). These budgets are essentially predetermined and have no true theoretical basis. Top-down methods include the affordable method, arbitrary allocation, percentage of sales, competitive parity, and return on investment (ROI).

The Affordable Method   In the **affordable method** (often referred to as the "all-you-can-afford method"), the firm determines the amount to be spent in various areas such as production and operations. Then it allocates what's left to advertising and promotion, considering this to be the amount it can afford. The task to be performed by the advertising/promotions function is not considered, and the likelihood of under- or overspending is high, as no guidelines for measuring the effects of various budgets are established.

Strange as it may seem, this approach is common among small firms. Unfortunately, it is also used in large firms, particularly those that are not marketing-driven and do not

FIGURE 7–12

Top-Down versus Bottom-Up
Approaches to Budget
Setting

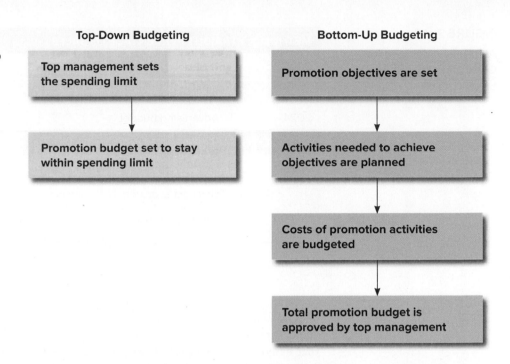

Top-Down Budgeting

Top management sets
the spending limit

↓

Promotion budget set to stay
within spending limit

Bottom-Up Budgeting

Promotion objectives are set

↓

Activities needed to achieve
objectives are planned

↓

Costs of promotion activities
are budgeted

↓

Total promotion budget is
approved by top management

understand the role of advertising and promotion. For example, many high-tech firms focus on new product development and engineering and assume that the product, if good enough, will sell itself. In these companies, little money may be left for performing the advertising and promotions tasks.

The logic for this approach stems from "We can't be hurt with this method" thinking. That is, if we know what we can afford and we do not exceed it, we will not get into financial problems. While this may be true in a strictly accounting sense, it does not reflect sound managerial decision making from a marketing perspective. Often this method does not allocate enough money to get the product off the ground and into the market. In terms of the S-shaped sales response model, the firm is operating in range *A*. Or the firm may be spending more than necessary, operating in range *C*. When the market gets tough and sales and/or profits begin to fall, this method is likely to lead to budget cuts at a time when the budget should be increased.

Arbitrary Allocation Perhaps an even weaker method than the affordable method for establishing a budget is **arbitrary allocation**, in which virtually no theoretical basis is considered and the budgetary amount is often set by fiat. That is, the budget is determined by management solely on the basis of what is felt to be necessary. In a discussion of how managers set advertising budgets, Melvin Salveson reported that these decisions may reflect "as much upon the managers' psychological profile as they do economic criteria."[22] While Salveson was referring to larger corporations, the approach is no less common in small firms and nonprofit organizations.

The arbitrary allocation approach has no obvious advantages. No systematic thinking has occurred, no objectives have been budgeted for, and the concept and purpose of advertising and promotion have been largely ignored. Other than the fact that the manager believes some monies must be spent on advertising and promotion and then picks a number, there is no good explanation why this approach continues to be used. Yet budgets continue to be set this way, and our purpose in discussing this method is to point out only that it is used—not recommended.

Percentage of Sales Perhaps the most commonly used method for budget setting (particularly in large firms) is the **percentage-of-sales method**, in which the advertising and promotions budget is based on sales of the product. Management determines the amount by either (1) taking a percentage of the sales dollars or (2) assigning a fixed amount of the unit product cost to promotion and multiplying this amount by the number of units sold. These two methods are shown in Figure 7–13.

FIGURE 7–13

Alternative Methods for
Computing Percentage of
Sales

METHOD 1: STRAIGHT PERCENTAGE OF SALES		
2023	Total dollar sales	$1,000,000
	Straight % of sales at 10%	$100,000
2024	Advertising budget	$100,000
METHOD 2: PERCENTAGE OF UNIT COST		
2023	Cost per product to manufacturer	$4.00
	Unit cost allocated to advertising	$1.00
2023	Forecasted sales, 100,000 units	
2024	Advertising budget (100,000 × $1)	$100,000

A variation on the percentage-of-sales method uses a percentage of projected future sales as a base. This method also uses either a straight percentage of projected sales or a unit cost projection. In the straight-percentage method, sales are projected for the coming year based on the marketing manager's estimates. The budget is a percentage of these sales, often an industry standard percentage like those presented in Figure 7–14.

One advantage of using future sales as a base is that the budget is not based on last year's sales. As the market changes, management must factor the effect of these changes on sales into next year's forecast rather than relying on past data. The resulting budget is more likely to reflect current conditions and be more appropriate.

Figure 7–14 reveals that the percentage allocated varies from one industry to the next. Some firms budget a very small percentage (for example, 0.07 percent in mining and extraction industries), and others spend a much higher proportional amount

FIGURE 7–14

Advertising-to-Sales Ratios
by Industry Sector

SAI Books/Schonfeld & Associates, Inc.

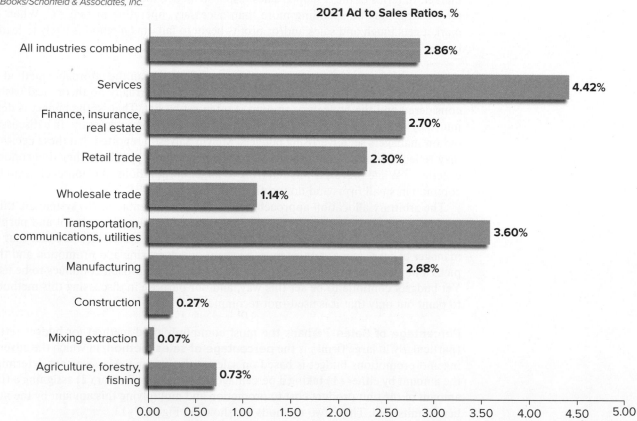

2021 Ad to Sales Ratios, %

- All industries combined: 2.86%
- Services: 4.42%
- Finance, insurance, real estate: 2.70%
- Retail trade: 2.30%
- Wholesale trade: 1.14%
- Transportation, communications, utilities: 3.60%
- Manufacturing: 2.68%
- Construction: 0.27%
- Mixing extraction: 0.07%
- Agriculture, forestry, fishing: 0.73%

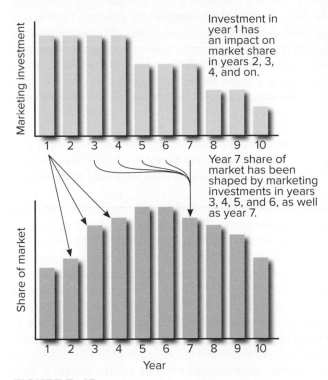

Investment in year 1 has an impact on market share in years 2, 3, 4, and on.

Year 7 share of market has been shaped by marketing investments in years 3, 4, 5, and 6, as well as year 7.

FIGURE 7–15

Investments Pay Off in Later Years

(4.42 percent in the service industry). Actual dollar amounts spent vary markedly according to the company's total sales figure. Thus, a smaller percentage of sales in computer and office equipment industry may actually result in significantly more advertising dollars being spent.

Proponents of the percentage-of-sales method cite a number of advantages. It is financially safe and keeps ad spending within reasonable limits, as it bases spending on the past year's sales or what the firm expects to sell in the upcoming year. Thus, there will be sufficient monies to cover this budget, with increases in sales leading to budget increases and sales decreases resulting in advertising decreases. The percentage-of-sales method is simple, straightforward, and easy to implement. Regardless of which basis—past or future sales—is employed, the calculations used to arrive at a budget are not difficult. Finally, this budgeting approach is generally stable. While the budget may vary with increases and decreases in sales, as long as these changes are not drastic the manager will have a reasonable idea of the parameters of the budget.

At the same time, the percentage-of-sales method has some serious disadvantages, including the basic premise on which the budget is established: sales. Letting the level of sales determine the amount of advertising and promotions dollars to be spent reverses the cause-and-effect relationship between advertising and sales. It treats advertising as an expense associated with making a sale rather than an investment. As shown in Figure 7–15, and discussed in the chapter lead-in, companies that consider promotional expenditures an investment reap the rewards.

A second problem with this approach was actually cited as an advantage earlier: stability. Proponents say that if all firms use a similar percentage, that will bring stability to the marketplace. But what happens if someone varies from this standard percentage? The problem is that this method does not allow for changes in strategy either internally or from competitors. An aggressive firm may wish to allocate more monies to the advertising and promotions budget, a strategy that is not possible with a percentage-of-sales method unless the manager is willing to deviate from industry standards.

The percentage-of-sales method of budgeting may result in severe misappropriation of funds. If advertising and promotion have a role to perform in marketing a product, then allocating more monies to advertising will, as shown in the S-shaped curve, generate incremental sales (to a point). If products with low sales have smaller promotion budgets, this will hinder sales progress. At the other extreme, very successful products may have excess budgets, some of which may be better appropriated elsewhere.

The percentage-of-sales method is also difficult to employ for new product introductions. If no sales histories are available, there is no basis for establishing the budget. Projections of future sales may be difficult, particularly if the product is highly innovative and/or has fluctuating sales patterns.

Finally, if the budget is contingent on sales, decreases in sales will lead to decreases in budgets when they most need to be increased. Continuing to cut the advertising and promotion budgets may just add impetus to the downward sales trend. On the other hand, some of the more successful companies have allocated additional funds during hard times or downturns in the cycle of sales as shown earlier. Companies that maintain or increase their ad expenditures during recessions achieve increased visibility and higher growth in both sales and market share (compared to those that reduce advertising outlays).

While the percentage-of-future-sales method has been proposed as a remedy for some of the problems discussed here, the reality is that problems with forecasting, cyclical growth, and uncontrollable factors limit its effectiveness.

Competitive Parity If you asked marketing managers if they ever set their advertising and promotions budgets on the basis of what their competitors allocate, they would probably deny it. Yet if you examined the advertising expenditures of these companies, both as a percentage of sales and in respect to the media where they are allocated, you would see little variation in the percentage-of-sales figures for firms within a given industry. Such results do not happen by chance alone. Companies that provide competitive advertising information, trade associations, and other advertising industry periodicals are insights into competitors' expenditures. Larger corporations often subscribe to services such as Competitive Media Reporting, also known as Kantar Competitive Media Spending, which provides estimates of companies' spending in traditional and digital media. Smaller companies often use a **clipping service**, which clips competitors' ads from local print media, allowing the company to work backward to determine the cumulative costs of the ads placed.

In the **competitive parity method**, managers establish budget amounts by matching the competition's percentage-of-sales expenditures. The argument is that setting budgets in this fashion takes advantage of the collective wisdom of the industry. It also takes the competition into consideration, which leads to stability in the marketplace by minimizing marketing warfare. If companies know that competitors are unlikely to match their increases in promotional spending, they are less likely to take an aggressive posture to attempt to gain market share. This minimizes unusual or unrealistic ad expenditures.

The competitive parity method has a number of disadvantages, however. For one, it ignores the fact that advertising and promotions are designed to accomplish specific objectives by addressing certain problems and opportunities. Second, it assumes that because firms have similar expenditures, their programs will be equally effective. This assumption ignores the contributions of creative executions and/or media allocations, as well as the success or failure of various promotions. Further, it ignores possible advantages of the firm itself; some companies simply make better products than others. A study by Yoo and Mandhachitara indicates that a competitive parity strategy must consider the fact that a competitor's advertising can actually benefit one's own firm, and that one competitor's gain is not always the other's loss. As shown in Figure 7–16 there are four different situations to determine how the competitive budgets may impact sales—only one of which involves the zero-sum scenario.[23]

Also, there is no guarantee that competitors will continue to pursue their existing strategies. Since competitive parity figures are determined by examination of competitors' previous years' promotional expenditures (short of corporate espionage), changes in

FIGURE 7–16

Competitors' Advertising Outlays Do Not Always Hurt

market emphasis and/or spending may not be recognized until the competition has already established an advantage. Further, there is no guarantee that a competitor will not increase or decrease its own expenditures, regardless of what other companies do. Finally, competitive parity may not avoid promotional wars. Coke versus Pepsi and AT&T versus Verizon have been notorious for their spending wars, each responding to the other's increased outlays.

In summary, few firms employ the competitive parity method as a sole means of establishing the promotional budget. This method is typically used in conjunction with the percentage-of-sales or other methods. It is never wise to ignore the competition; managers must always be aware of what competitors are doing. But they should not just emulate them in setting goals and developing strategies.

Return on Investment (ROI) In the percentage-of-sales method, sales dictate the level of advertising appropriations. But advertising causes sales, not the other way around. In the marginal analysis and S-shaped curve approaches, incremental investments in advertising and promotions lead to increases in sales. The keyword here is *investment*. In the **ROI budgeting method**, advertising and promotions are considered investments, like plant and equipment. Thus, the budgetary appropriation (investment) leads to certain returns. Like other aspects of the firm's efforts, advertising and promotion are expected to earn a certain return. ROI has received a great deal of attention by practitioners over the past few years, with many still disagreeing as to how it should be measured. Figure 7–17 shows the results of *Advertising Age*'s report of the Aegis Group rating of how various media perform under this criterion (5 equals best).

While the ROI method looks good on paper, the reality is that it is rarely possible to assess the returns provided by the promotional effort—at least as long as sales continue to be the basis for evaluation. Thus, while managers are certain to ask how much return they are getting for such expenditures, the question remains unanswered and depends on the criteria used to determine effectiveness. ROI remains a difficult method to employ.

Summary of Top-Down Budgeting Methods You are probably asking yourself why we even discussed these budgeting methods if they are not recommended for use or have severe disadvantages that limit their effectiveness. But you must understand the various methods used in order to recognize their limitations, especially since these flawed methods are commonly employed by marketers. Research conducted over a number of years by various researchers indicates that the affordable, competitive parity, percentage-of-sales, and objective and task methods are the most commonly employed budgeting methods. As noted, the emphasis on ROI has dramatically increased over the past few years.[24, 25, 26, 27, 28] Tradition and top management's desire for control are probably the major reasons why top-down methods continue to be popular.

Build Up Approaches The major flaw associated with the top-down methods is that these judgmental approaches lead to predetermined budget appropriations often not linked to objectives and the strategies designed to accomplish them. A more effective budgeting strategy would be to consider the firm's communications objectives and budget what is deemed necessary to attain these goals. As noted earlier, the promotional planning model shows the budget decision as an interactive process, with the communications objectives on one hand and the promotional-mix alternatives on the other. The idea is to budget so these promotional-mix strategies can be implemented to achieve the stated objectives.

Objective and Task Method It is important that objective setting and budgeting go hand in hand rather than sequentially. It is difficult to establish a budget without specific objectives in mind, and setting objectives without regard to how much money is available makes no sense. For example, a company may wish to create awareness among X percent of its target market. A minimal budget amount will be required to accomplish this goal, and the firm must be willing to spend this amount.

FIGURE 7–17   Aegis-Rated ROI of Various Media

Medium	The Measurement Challenge	ROI Measurability
Direct Response	Direct mail, telemarketing, and other forms are the most measurable of media listed here. Direct can have a synergistic effect, especially for pharma, telecom, and financial services.	5
Sales Promotion	Offers such as coupons and discounts generate a lot of consumer response and therefore a bounty of data. The data lend themselves to measurement, especially for package goods via syndicated scanner data. Freestanding inserts generate much valuable data.	5
Internet	The Internet can be influential for big-ticket purchases like cars. Very measurable, with the cautionary note that "Internet is a very broad net," ranging from search engines to ads in content to websites such as in the auto market, where such marques as Saab get lots of hits, and all should be looked at separately. The goal is to understand how the consumer is interacting online with the brand.	5
TV	While promotions have very pronounced, short-term effects that allow precise measurement, TV has a subtler and more gradual effect that may show greater variability. But ROI can be measured with a high degree of accuracy, and there's no excuse for TV not to show a measurable effect. MMA clients have been using a lot more analysis to create a better mix between :15s and :30s, and better allocation across dayparts.	4.5
Print	The experts can slice and dice print by weekly vs. monthly publications, by targeted vs. general market, by promotional ads vs. equity-building. Print promotional materials, like freestanding inserts, are a separate—and much more measurable—matter. As with all other media, accuracy and timing of the data are crucial in determining how measurable the medium is. Print can play a strong role in expanding the reach of the media mix.	4.5
Public Relations	There are companies that specialize in the measurement of PR campaigns' quality; they can measure the number of impressions delivered—via positive or negative PR—for a brand name or category. PR can have a measurable impact on sales (think trans fats in food). The problem: Many marketers aren't buying these PR data.	4
Video Games	Whether the game is played online or offline is crucial. An ad embedded in a game cartridge is very hard to measure because there's no way to know how often it's played, though there's no denying "True Crime's" Nick Kang is a big hit. With online games, there are great data available through the Internet.	Online Offline
	Scale: 5 = Best	
Radio	The available data typically aren't as strong as those for its traditional-media colleagues of TV and print, and this hampers radio.	3
Cinema	Movie advertising can be measured by the number of impressions delivered, much like outdoor or kiosk advertising would be measured.	3
Sponsored Events	Measurability depends on whether sponsorship is likely to spark short-term effect. A major recurring event like the Olympics is very measurable. Others can be difficult to measure short term. Measurement can be complex because events have so many pieces, including how the event is advertised, the PR buzz, signage, and the recollection of the event itself.	3
Product Placement	There are companies that measure quality of placement as well as the quantity of exposures. Treated much like TV advertising, with the caveat that not every product placement is the same. Fox's *American Idol* is a great example: AT&T Wireless's tie-in, which involves voting by text message, is interactive—even part of the entertainment—while the judges drinking from a Coke cup is not. (P.S. AT&T Wireless, now owned by Cingular, isn't an MMA client.) So the question becomes: How do you score the quality of placement?	3
Outdoor	Available data are limited due to the nature of outdoor advertising; there's no syndicated vendor that sells the needed data on outdoor. And outdoor lacks "variance"—the billboard is up X number of months and seen by an unchanging X number of people each day.	2
Guerrilla Marketing	Hard to measure if the variable you're using is sales. If 10,000 people at an event get free T-shirts, it's difficult to measure the effect on the 400,000 people living in that market. Because guerrilla can encompass so many different kinds of tactics, getting useful data can be a problem—it depends on how measurable the response is. Marketers' ROI expectations for guerrilla are lower than for other media, so the urgency to measure is less. Not to mention they spend a lot less on guerrilla than on traditional media like TV.	1

The **objective and task method** of budget setting uses a **build up approach** consisting of three steps: (1) defining the communications objectives to be accomplished, (2) determining the specific strategies and tasks needed to attain them, and (3) estimating the costs associated with performance of these strategies and tasks. The total budget is based on the accumulation of these costs.

Implementing the objective and task approach is somewhat more involved. The manager must monitor this process throughout and change strategies depending on how well objectives are attained. As shown in Figure 7–18, this process involves several steps:

1. *Isolate objectives.* When the promotional planning model is presented, a company will have two sets of objectives to accomplish—the marketing objectives for the product and the communications objectives. After the former are established, the task involves determining what specific communications objectives will be designed to accomplish these goals. Communications objectives must be specific, attainable, and measurable, as well as time limited.

2. *Determine tasks required.* A number of elements are involved in the strategic plan designed to attain the objectives established. (These strategies constitute the remaining chapters in this text.) These tasks may include advertising in various media, sales promotions, and/or other elements of the promotional mix, each with its own role to perform.

3. *Estimate required expenditures.* Build up analysis requires determining the estimated costs associated with the tasks developed in the previous step. For example, it involves costs for developing awareness through advertising, trial through sampling, and so forth.

4. *Monitor.* As you will see in Chapter 18 on measuring effectiveness, there are ways to determine how well one is attaining established objectives. Performance should be monitored and evaluated in light of the budget appropriated.

5. *Reevaluate objectives.* Once specific objectives have been attained, monies may be better spent on new goals. Thus, if one has achieved the level of consumer awareness sought, the budget should be altered to stress a higher-order objective such as evaluation or trial.

The major advantage of the objective and task method is that the budget is driven by the objectives to be attained. The managers closest to the marketing effort will have specific strategies and input into the budget-setting process.

The major disadvantage of this method is the difficulty of determining which tasks will be required and the costs associated with each. For example, specifically what tasks are needed to attain awareness among 50 percent of the target market? How much will it cost to perform these tasks? While these decisions are easier to determine for certain

FIGURE 7–18

The Objective and Task Method

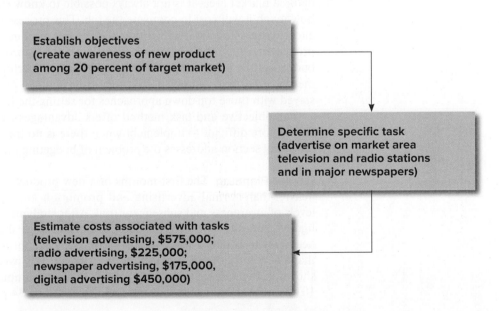

Establish objectives
(create awareness of new product among 20 percent of target market)

Determine specific task
(advertise on market area television and radio stations and in major newspapers)

Estimate costs associated with tasks
(television advertising, $575,000;
radio advertising, $225,000;
newspaper advertising, $175,000,
digital advertising $450,000)

FIGURE 7–19

Share of Advertising Sales
Relationship (Two-Year
Summary)

A. New Brands of Food Products

Brand	Average share of advertising	Attained share of sales	Ratio of share of advertising to share of sales
101	34%	12.6%	2.7
102	16	10.0	1.6
103	8	7.6	1.1
104	4	2.6	1.5
105	3	2.1	1.4

B. New Brands of Toiletry Products

Brand	Average share of advertising	Attained share of sales	Ratio of share of advertising to share of sales
401	30%	19.5%	1.5
402	25	16.5	1.5
403	20	16.2	1.2
404	12	9.4	1.3
405	16	8.7	1.8
406	19	7.3	2.6
407	14	7.2	1.9
408	10	6.0	1.7
409	7	6.0	1.2
410	6	5.9	1.0
411	10	5.9	1.7
412	6	5.2	1.2

objectives—for instance, estimating the costs of sampling required to stimulate trial in a defined market area—it is not always possible to know exactly what is required and/or how much it will cost to complete the job. This process is easier if there is past experience to use as a guide, with either the existing product or a similar one in the same product category. But it is especially difficult for new product introductions. As a result, budget setting using this method is not as easy to perform or as stable as some of the methods discussed earlier. Given this disadvantage, many marketing managers have stayed with those top-down approaches for setting the total expenditure amount.

The objective and task method offers advantages over methods discussed earlier but is more difficult to implement when there is no track record for the product. The following section addresses the problem of budgeting for new product introductions.

Payout Planning The first months of a new product's introduction typically require heavier-than-normal advertising and promotion appropriations to stimulate higher levels of awareness and subsequent trial. After studying more than 40 years of Nielsen figures, James O. Peckham estimated that the average share of advertising-to-sales ratio necessary to launch a new product successfully is approximately 1.5:2.0.[29] This means that a new entry should be spending at approximately twice the desired market share, as shown in the two examples in Figure 7–19. For example, in the food industry, brand 101 gained a 12.6 percent market share by spending 34 percent of the total advertising

FIGURE 7–20

Example of Three-Year
Payout Plan ($ millions)

	Year 1	Year 2	Year 3
Product sales	15.0	35.50	60.75
Profit contribution (@ $0.50/case)	7.5	17.75	30.38
Advertising/promotions	15.0	10.50	8.50
Profit (loss)	(7.5)	7.25	21.88
Cumulative profit (loss)	(7.5)	(0.25)	21.63

dollars in this category. Likewise, brand 401 in the toiletry industry had a 30 percent share of advertising dollars to gain 19.5 percent of sales.

To determine how much to spend, marketers often develop a **payout plan** that determines the investment value of the advertising and promotion appropriation. The basic idea is to project the revenues the product will generate, as well as the costs it will incur, over 2 to 3 years. Based on an expected rate of return, the payout plan will assist in determining how much advertising and promotions expenditure will be necessary and when the return might be expected. A 3-year payout plan is shown in Figure 7–20. The product would lose money in year 1, almost break even in year 2, and finally begin to show substantial profits by the end of year 3.

The advertising and promotion figures are highest in year 1 and decline in years 2 and 3. This appropriation is consistent with Peckham's findings and reflects the additional outlays needed to make as rapid an impact as possible. (Keep in mind that shelf space is limited, and store owners are not likely to wait around for a product to become successful.) The budget also reflects the firm's guidelines for new product expenditures, since companies generally have established deadlines by which the product must begin to show a profit. Finally, keep in mind that building market share may be more difficult than maintaining it—thus the substantial dropoff in expenditures in later years.

While the payout plan is not always perfect, it does guide the manager in establishing the budget. When used in conjunction with the objective and task method, it provides a much more logical approach to budget setting than do the top-down approaches previously discussed. Yet on the basis of the studies reported on earlier, payout planning does not seem to be a widely employed method.

Quantitative Models Attempts to apply *quantitative models* to budgeting have met with limited success. For the most part, these methods employ **computer simulation models** involving statistical techniques such as multiple regression analysis to determine the relative contribution of the advertising budget to sales. Because of problems associated with these methods, their acceptance has been limited, and quantitative models have yet to reach their potential. As requirements for accountability continue to increase, more sophisticated models may be forthcoming. Specific discussion of these models is beyond the scope of this text, however. Such methods do have merit but may need more refinement before achieving widespread success.

Summary of Budgeting Methods There is no universally accepted method of setting a budget figure. Weaknesses in each method may make it unfeasible or inappropriate. As earlier studies have shown, the use of the objective and task method continues to stay high, whereas less sophisticated methods vary in their rates of adoption. More advertisers are also employing the payout planning approach.

In a study of how managers make decisions regarding advertising and promotion budgeting decisions, George Low and Jakki Mohr interviewed 21 managers in eight consumer-product firms. Their research focused on the decision processes and procedures used to set spending levels on the factors that influence the allocation of advertising and promotion dollars.

On the basis of their results (shown in Figure 7–21), the authors concluded that the budget-setting process is still a perplexing issue to many managers and that institutional

FIGURE 7–21

How Advertising and
Promotions Budgets Are Set

The Nature of the Decision Process
■ Managers develop overall marketing objectives for the brand.
■ Financial projections are made on the basis of the objectives and forecasts.
■ Advertising and promotions budgets are set on the basis of quantitative models and managerial judgment.
■ The budget is presented to senior management, which approves and adjusts the budgets.
■ The plan is implemented (changes are often made during implementation).
■ The plan is evaluated by comparing the achieved results with objectives.

Factors Affecting Budget Allocations
■ The extent to which risk taking is encouraged and/or tolerated.
■ Sophistication regarding the use of marketing information.
■ Managerial judgment.
■ Use of quantitative tools.
■ Brand differentiation strategies.
■ Brand equity.
■ The strength of the creative message.
■ Retailer power.
■ Short- versus long-term focus.
■ Top-down influences.
■ Political sales force influences.
■ Historical inertia.
■ Ad hoc changes.

pressures lead to a greater proportion of dollars being spent on sales promotions than managers would prefer. In addition, the authors concluded that to successfully develop and implement the budget, managers must (1) employ a comprehensive strategy to guide the process, avoiding the piecemeal approach often employed, (2) develop a strategic planning framework that employs an integrated marketing communications philosophy, (3) build in contingency plans, (4) focus on long-term objectives, and (5) consistently evaluate the effectiveness of programs.[30]

By using these approaches in combination with the percentage-of-sales methods, these advertisers are likely to arrive at a more useful, accurate budget. For example, many firms now start the budgeting process by establishing the objectives they need to accomplish and then limit the budget by applying a percentage-of-sales or another method to decide whether or not it is affordable. Competitors' budgets may also influence this decision.

Allocating the Budget

Once the budget has been appropriated, the next step is to allocate it. The allocation decision involves determining which markets, products, and/or promotional elements will receive which amounts of the funds appropriated.

Allocating to IMC Elements As shown in Digital and Social Media Perspective 7-2, many advertisers are shifting much of their budget dollars away

Winners and Losers in the Budget Allocation World: Traditional Media Not Dead Yet?

If you believe some of the media pundits (and think of your own lifestyle), you no doubt believe that traditional media like television, magazines, newspapers, and maybe even radio may not even exist in the not too distant future. You probably do not subscribe to a print magazine or newspaper, and if you do read a magazine or get the news at all, it is probably online. There is little argument that we now live in a digital world. Those who purchase advertising time know this too. Digital is the new media darling.

In 2022 in the United States, digital ad spending was expected to hit $239.89 billion at the time of this writing. From 2017 to 2022 ad expenditures increased by 67.7 percent at a 12.1 percent annual growth rate! If forecasters are correct, from 2020 to 2025 the digital ad market will grow at an average rate of 16 percent annually. Companies in the retail and packaged-goods industry have shown the largest increases in digital media expenditures, followed by entertainment, computer products, consumer electronics, and travel. Given that media budgets have not increased at nearly these rates, it is obvious that the monies are being reallocated from traditional to digital media. In the United States, projections are that newspaper advertising will decline from $30.25 million in 2021 to $24.98 million in 2025, and magazine ads will decline from $13.9 million to $10.64 million. Television now accounts for 57 percent of video ad spending and connected TV (CTV) has gone down by 16 percent, with both expected to continue to decline. Overall, upper funnel media have experienced the greatest losses in the new allocations. Things have looked pretty bleak for about a decade.

So are traditional media really dead? Not so fast! An article in the *Harvard Business Review* by Christine Moorman, Megan Ryan, and Nader Tavassoli suggests that traditional advertising is alive and well and actually headed for growth for the first time in a decade. The expected shift back to traditional advertising is expected to be led by service companies followed by product companies. Interestingly, companies that make 100 percent of their sales through the Internet are leading the way back!

The authors note seven drivers behind the shift, including (1) consumers believe there is too much clutter in digital advertising, (2) consumers trust traditional ads more than digital ones, (3) they fear the coming change in third-party cookies that allow for tracking of consumers' activities, (4) they support the growth of podcasts (consumers trust their hosts and are influenced by their endorsements), (5) advertisers like the synergy of traditional media and digital working together, (6) companies think traditional media are sometimes a better fit for some brands than digital is, and (7) businesses are concerned that digital advertising may be less effective than claimed. While there is no guarantee that this movement will continue into the future, it may be a new beginning for traditional media—or a rebirth for digital, particularly if and when companies recognize the potential for digital and traditional to work together rather than compete for media dollars!

Sources: Christine Moorman, Megan Ryan, and Nader Tavassoli, "Why Marketers Are Returning to Traditional Advertising," *Harvard Business Review*, April 29, 2022, www.hbr.com; "US Digital Ad Spending (2020–2025)," Oberlo, August 31, 2022, www.oberlo.com; "Linear TV's Shrinking Ad Share Gets Even Smaller," *eMarketer*, June 8, 2022, www.emarketer.com; Louie Andre, "26 Relevant Print Marketing Statistics: 2022 Ad Spending and Impact," *Finances Online*, February 28, 2022, www.financesonline.com; Jeremy Goldman, "CTV Ads Look to Be One of the Advertising Channels Hit Hardest by Marketers' Economic Concerns," *eMarketer*, July 15, 2022, www.emarketer.com.

from traditional advertising media and into digital and social media. Numerous industry studies have shown that most traditional media advertisers expect to decrease their expenditures in these media into the future as well.

Some marketers have also used the allocation decision to stretch their advertising dollar and get more impact from the same amount of money. Companies have taken a number of steps, including consolidating and cutting division expenditures, reducing agency fees, producing fewer campaigns, and relying more on targeted media.

Client–Agency Policies Another factor that may influence budget allocation is the individual policy of the company or the advertising agency. The agency may discourage the allocation of monies to sales promotion, preferring to spend them on the advertising area. The agency may take the position that these monies are harder to track in terms of effectiveness and may be used improperly if not under its control. (In many cases commissions are not made on this area, and this fact may contribute to the agency's reluctance.)

The orientation of the agency or the firm may also directly influence where monies are spent. Many ad agencies are managed by officers who have ascended through the creative ranks and are inclined to emphasize the creative budget. Others may have preferences for specific media. For example, some agencies position themselves as experts in nontraditional media and often spend more client money in this medium. Both the agency and the client may favor certain aspects of the promotional program, perhaps on the basis of past successes, that will substantially influence where dollars are spent.

Market Size   While the budget should be allocated according to the specific promotional tools needed to accomplish the stated objectives, the *size* of the market will affect the decision. In smaller markets, it is often easier and less expensive to reach the target market. Too much of an expenditure in these markets will lead to saturation and a lack of effective spending. In larger markets, the target group may be more dispersed and thus more expensive to reach. Think about the cost of purchasing media in Chicago or New York City versus a smaller market like Columbus, Ohio, or Birmingham, Alabama. The former would be much more costly and would require a higher budget appropriation.

Market Potential   For a variety of reasons, some markets hold more potential than others. Marketers of snow skis would find greater returns on their expenditures in Denver, Colorado, than in Fort Lauderdale, Florida. Imported Mexican beers sell better in the border states (Texas, Arizona, California) than in the Midwest. A disproportionate number of imported cars are sold in California and New England. When particular markets hold higher potential, the marketing manager may decide to allocate additional monies to them. (Keep in mind that just because a market does not have high sales does not mean it should be ignored. The key is *potential*—and a market with low sales but high potential may be a candidate for additional appropriations.)

Market Share Goals   Two studies in the *Harvard Business Review* discussed advertising spending with the goal of maintaining and increasing market share.[31] John Jones compared the brand's share of market with its share of advertising voice (the total value of the main media exposure in the product category). Jones classified the brands as "profit taking brands, or underspenders" and "investment brands, those whose share of voice is clearly above their share of market." His study indicated that for those brands with small market shares, profit takers are in the minority; however, as the brands increase their market share, nearly three out of five have a proportionately smaller share of voice.

Jones noted that three factors can be cited to explain this change. First, new brands generally receive higher-than-average advertising support. Second, older, more mature brands are often "milked"—that is, when they reach the maturity stage, advertising support is reduced. Third, there's an advertising economy of scale whereby advertising works harder for well-established brands, so a lower expenditure is required. Jones concluded that for larger brands, it may be possible to reduce advertising expenditures and still maintain market share. Smaller brands, on the other hand, have to continue to maintain a large share of voice (SOV).

James Schroer addressed the advertising budget in a situation where the marketer wishes to increase market share. His analysis suggests that marketers should:

- Segment markets, focusing on those markets where competition is weak and/or underspending instead on a national advertising effort.
- Determine their competitors' cost positions (how long the competition can continue to spend at the current or increased rate).
- Resist the lure of short-term profits that result from ad budget cuts.
- Consider niching strategies as opposed to long-term wars.

Figure 7-22 shows Schroer's suggestions for spending priorities in various markets.

Economies of Scale in Advertising   Some studies have presented evidence that firms and/or brands maintaining a large share of the market have an advantage

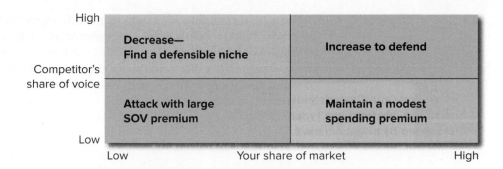

over smaller competitors and thus can spend less money on advertising and realize a better return.[32] Larger advertisers can maintain advertising shares that are smaller than their market shares because they get better advertising rates, have declining average costs of production, and accrue the advantages of advertising several products jointly. In addition, they are likely to enjoy more favorable time and space positions, cooperation of middle people, and favorable publicity. These advantages are known as **economies of scale**.

Reviewing the studies in support of this position and then conducting research over a variety of small package products, Kent Lancaster found that this situation did not hold true and that in fact larger brand share products might actually be at a disadvantage.[33] His results indicated that leading brands spend an average of 2.5 percentage points more than their brand share on advertising. More specifically, his study concluded:

1. There is no evidence that larger firms can support their brands with lower relative advertising costs than can smaller firms.
2. There is no evidence that the leading brand in a product group enjoys lower advertising costs per sales dollar than do other brands.
3. There is no evidence of a static relationship between advertising costs per dollar of sales and the size of the advertiser.

The results of this and other studies suggest there really are no economies of scale to be accrued from the size of the firm or the market share of the brand.[34]

Organizational Characteristics   In a review of the literature on how allocation decisions are made between advertising and sales promotion, George Low and Jakki Mohr concluded that organizational factors play an important role in determining how communications dollars are spent.[35] The authors note that the following factors influence the allocation decision. These factors vary from one organization to another, and each influences the relative amounts assigned to advertising and promotion:

- The organization's structure—centralized versus decentralized, formalization, and complexity.
- Power and politics in the organizational hierarchy.
- The use of expert opinions (for example, consultants).
- Characteristics of the decision maker (preferences and experience).
- Approval and negotiation channels.
- Pressure on senior managers to arrive at the optimal budget.

One example of how these factors might influence allocations relates to the level of interaction between marketing and other functional departments, such as accounting and operations. The authors note that the relative importance of advertising versus sales promotion might vary from department to department. Accountants, being dollars-and-cents minded, would argue for the sales impact of promotions, while operations would argue against sales promotions because the sudden surges in demand that might result would throw off production schedules. The marketing department might be influenced by the thinking of either of these groups in making its decision.

The use of outside consultants to provide expert opinions might also affect the allocation decision. Trade journals, academic journals, and even books might also be valuable inputs into the decision maker's thinking. In sum, it seems obvious that many factors must be taken into account in the budget allocation decision. Market size and potential, specific objectives sought, and previous company and/or agency policies and preferences all influence this decision.

Summary

This chapter has examined the role of objectives in the planning and evaluation of the IMC program and how firms budget in an attempt to achieve these objectives. Specific objectives are needed to guide the development of the promotional program, as well as to provide a benchmark against which performance can be measured and evaluated. Objectives serve important functions as communications devices, as a guide to planning the IMC program and deciding on various alternatives, and for measurement and evaluation.

Objectives for IMC evolve from the organization's overall marketing plan and are based on the roles various promotional-mix elements play in the marketing program. Many managers use sales or a related measure such as market share as the basis for setting objectives. However, many promotional planners believe the role of advertising and other promotional-mix elements is to communicate and communications objectives should be measured because of the various problems associated with sales-based objectives. They use communications-based objectives like those in the response hierarchy as the basis for setting goals.

Much of the emphasis in setting objectives has been on traditional advertising-based views of marketing communications. However, many companies are moving toward zero-based communications planning, which focuses on what tasks need to be done, which marketing communications functions should be used, and to what extent. Many of the principles used in setting advertising objectives can be applied to other elements in the promotional mix.

As you have probably concluded, the budget decision is not typically based on supporting experiences or strong theoretical foundations. Nor is it one of the more soundly established elements of the promotional program. The budgeting methods used now have some major problems. Economic models are limited, often try to demonstrate the effects on sales directly, and ignore other elements of the marketing mix. Some of the methods discussed have no theoretical basis and ignore the roles advertising and promotion are meant to perform.

One possible way to improve the budget appropriation is to tie the measures of effectiveness to communications objectives rather than to the broader-based marketing objectives. Using the objective and task approach with communications objectives may not be the ultimate solution to the budgeting problem, but it is an improvement over the top-down methods. Marketers often find it advantageous to employ a combination of methods.

As with determining the budget, managers must consider a number of factors when allocating advertising and promotions dollars. Market size and potential, agency policies, and the preferences of management itself may influence the allocation decision.

Key Terms

marketing objectives 220
integrated marketing communications
objectives 220
carryover effect 222
DAGMAR 229
communications task 229
benchmark measures 230
zero-based communications
planning 233

contribution margin 236
marginal analysis 237
concave-downward function
model 238
S-shaped response curve 238
top-down approaches 240
affordable method 240
arbitrary allocation 241
percentage-of-sales method 241

clipping service 244
competitive parity method 244
ROI budgeting method 245
objective and task method 247
build up approach 247
payout plan 249
computer simulation models 249
economies of scale 253

Discussion Questions

1. During difficult times, many companies cut their advertising budgets to save money, despite the fact that evidence does not support this strategy. Explain why so many companies take this approach and why they should not. (LO 7-7)

2. Why are sales and/or marketing objectives problematic for determining the effectiveness of advertising campaigns? What are some of the values offered by communication objectives? (LO 7-1)

3. Explain the S-shaped response curve and the concave-downward curve as they relate to budget setting. What are the differences in these two curves? Give examples of how each might be more appropriate for different products. (LO 7-6)

4. Consumer purchase funnels have been criticized recently as being of little use for setting communications objectives. Some argue that their linear focus and the fact that consumers may now enter the funnel at any point make them outdated. Discuss whether this position is well founded and why or why not. (LO 7-3)

5. Sometimes it seems as though marketers have abandoned traditional media and have focused their attention on digital media only as allocations to digital media have increased so significantly while traditional media have lost allocations. Explain if this is a true fact, and discuss why, if so, it is either a smart or not-so-smart allocation of resources. (LO 7-6)

6. Some very successful companies have gained sales and market share by increasing their advertising budgets during a recession. Explain why this could be a successful strategy. (LO 7-7)

7. As more and more advertising dollars move to digital media, traditional media are losing revenue. Will traditional media no longer exist in the future? (LO 7-5)

8. Discuss an example of how a company's media strategy might change as they progress through a hierarchy of effects model (funnel). Choose any model you wish to use. (LO 7-4)

9. Explain why it is so difficult to use sales as an indicator of advertising effectiveness and why communications objectives may work better. (LO 7-3).

10. Explain some of the factors that might lead to success in increasing sales and achieving communications when competitors decrease their budgets. (LO 7-7)

8

Creative Strategy: Planning and Development

Rafael Henrique/SOPA Images/LightRocket/Getty Images

Learning Objectives

LO8-1 Describe the role of creative strategy in advertising.

LO8-2 Discuss the creative process for advertising and inputs to this process.

LO8-3 Describe the development of creative strategy.

LO8-4 Examine approaches to developing the major selling ideas that are used as the basis for an advertising campaign.

TikTok's Impact on Creativity

Digital technology is changing the world and advertising is changing with it. The explosive growth of the Internet, mobile devices, and various social media platforms has transformed the way people consume media, and the way they respond to advertising has changed as well. Yet while entertainment and connectivity keep evolving, digital advertising formats have not kept up but remained largely the same for years. As a result consumers usually mute them, skip over them, or simply tune them out. Creative breakthroughs in digital advertising have remained elusive, and as a result web surfers click on less than 2 percent of the online banner ads that appear on the screens of their computers and/or mobile devices and choose the skip option for 95 percent of pre-roll video ads.

While advertisers struggle to find ways to connect with consumers, many of those working in creative are finding inspiration from the social media platform TikTok, which has grown from what many considered a copycat short-video app for lip-syncing and dance videos to global dominance with over 1 billion active monthly users worldwide. Mona Hasan, creative director at Fortnite Collective, notes that Tiktok is the new ad school and is teaching a more modern approach to communicating to current and future generations. She argues that TikTok doesn't just allow users to share videos, it inspires them to create them; as a result, they are creating new ways of thinking, living, and buying—in addition to dancing. Advertisers should pay attention.

TikTok has become the leading destination for short-form mobile videos and has been heralded as the future of entertainment. TikTok's mission is "to inspire creativity and bring joy," and its surge in popularity has been driven in part by the joyful and entertaining user-generated content on the platform. Users of the app can enjoy an endless stream of fun, compelling, and engaging content tailored to their interests on the personalized "For You Feed" while participating in the creation themselves. One of the things that sets TikTok apart is its engagement factor as many of the platform's creative formats are made for interaction and allow users to actively participate in and respond to the content they are watching. Features like "react" allow users to film themselves reacting to another video; "duet"

calls on people to join in and remix, which lets users film reactionary videos that appear next to the original video.

One of the keys to the success of TikTok is its authenticity as it is the antithesis of the heavily staged and filtered content found across other social media platforms. TikTok's tagline is "Real People, Real Videos," and the videos are from real people tapping into different lifestyles, trends, insights, and perspectives from around the country and the world. This all suggests that advertisers should find ways to integrate such realness into their messages rather than the usual hyper-polished, aspirational content. Experts note that there are a number of other things advertisers can learn from TikTok, such as marketers do not need to spend large sums of money or have an elaborate team of decision makers to create impactful content. Advertisers should pay attention to TikTok to gain insights into what is trending or about to happen in popular culture.

TikTok itself is encouraging marketers to embrace the creativity, positivity, and authenticity of TikTok and create content that truly speaks to people. They introduced TikTok for Business globally with a campaign called "Don't Make Ads. Make Tiktoks" that challenges marketers to transform the way they connect with their audiences. A TikTok executive notes, "TikTok is a diverse and entertaining window into people's joyful moments. But it's not just about consuming content—it's an engine of culture creation where anybody can easily create, participate, and be discovered. The same holds true for brands: because our users are highly engaged in a sound-on, discovery-based environment, good branded content becomes part of the experience and has the power to create cultural movements."

Many marketers are finding creative ways to connect with their target audience on TikTok. For example, fast-food chain Chipotle used irreverent and engaging content in its #GuacDance challenge, encouraging fans to show off their avocado-themed dance moves inspired by Dr. Jean's "Guacamole Song." The challenge generated 250,000 video submissions and 430 million video starts in 6 days and became TikTok's highest-performing branded challenge in the United States to date. The promotion resulted

continued

in Chipotle's biggest guacamole day ever. With more than 800,000 sides served, the chain's avocado usage increased by 68 percent for National Avocado Day.

Microsoft found a clever way to use TikTok when it launched its newest operating system, Windows 11, in 2022 by engaging TikTok comedian Emily Zugay, who is known for making fun of brand logos and offering her own goofy redesigns. Microsoft used its Windows account, which is one of several brand accounts the company has on TikTok, to comment relentlessly on her videos and get her to give the Windows' four-paned blue window-shaped logo the Zugay treatment, replacing the blue squares with a photo of her face. The Zugay stunt became the most watched video on the Windows account and helped it surpass 1 million TikTok followers less than a year after starting. Its videos have received over 11 million likes and more than 10 million views.

TikTok is likely to shape the future of entertainment as well as the way marketers communicate with their customers, through the platform features or in their advertising messages. However, Tiktok is facing some political uncertainty as it is owned by the Chinese company ByteDance Ltd. Former president Donald Trump issued an executive order to try to ban the app and force the parent company to sell TikTok's U.S. business over what he claimed were security risks. The action was challenged in court, and President Biden revoked Trump's ban in June 2021. However, in 2022 a member of the Federal Communications Commission called on Apple and Google to remove TikTok from their app stores over concerns that user data from the wildly popular social media platform is being accessed in China.

While the future of TikTok in the United States is uncertain, one thing that is for certain is that the social media giant is inspiring marketers to find new ways to connect with consumers and take more chances. As Mona Hasan notes: "The platform is shaping the future of ads by helping us remember what being creative is all about."

Sources: Catherine Perloff, "How Microsoft Windows Reached 1 Million TikTok Followers in Nine Months," *Adweek*, September 2, 2022, https://www.adweek.com/media/how-microsoft-windows-reached-1-million-tiktok-followers-in-nine-months/; Aron Gregg, "FCC Commissioner Calls on Google and Apple to Ban Tiktok App," *The Washington Post*, June 29, 2022, https://www.washingtonpost.com/business/2022/06/29/fcc-tiktok-ban-apple-google/; Mona Hasan, "TikTok Is the New Ad School," *Advertising Age*, November 12, 2021, https://adage.com/article/opinion/tiktok-new-ad-school/2379736; TikTok Editorial Team, "What We Mean When We Say 'Don't Make Ads'" *TikTok for Business*, June 29, 2021, https://www.tiktok.com/business/en-US/blog/what-we-mean-when-we-say-dont-make-ads; Alisio Kelso, "Why Chipotle's Bet on TikTok Is Paying Off, *Forbes*, August 7, 2019, https://www.forbes.com/sites/aliciakelso/2019/08/07/why-chipotles-bet-on-tiktok-is-paying-off/?sh=735be2874080.

One of the most important components of an integrated marketing communications program is the advertising message. While the fundamental role of an advertising message is to communicate information, it does much more. The commercials we watch on TV or hear on radio, the print ads we see in magazines and newspapers, and the videos, banner ads, and other forms of advertising on the Internet and social media sites are a source of entertainment, motivation, fascination, fantasy, and sometimes irritation as well as information. Ads and commercials appeal to, and often create or shape, consumers' problems, desires, and goals. From the marketer's perspective, the advertising message is a way to tell consumers how the product or service can solve a problem or help satisfy desires or achieve goals. Advertising can also be used to create images or associations and position a brand in the consumer's mind as well as transform the experience of buying and/or using a product or service. Many consumers who have never driven or even ridden in a BMW perceive it as "the ultimate driving machine." Ads such as the one shown in Exhibit 8–1 focus on the pleasure and excitement of driving a BMW and play an important role in creating the ultimate driving machine brand image. Many people purchase Nike athletic shoes and apparel because they have internalized the company's "Just Do It" advertising slogan and ethos.

One need only watch an evening of commercials, peruse a few magazines, or spend some time surfing the Internet to realize there are myriad ways to convey an advertising message. Underlying all of these messages are a **creative strategy** that determines what the advertising message will say or communicate and **creative tactics** for how the

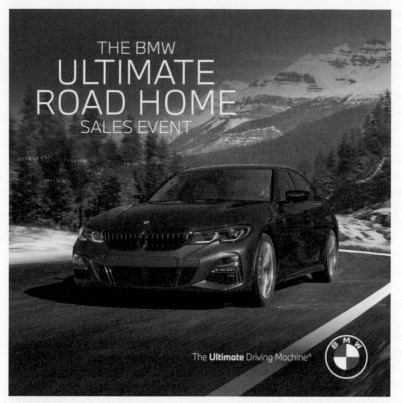

EXHIBIT 8–1

Excellent advertising helps create an image for BMW automobiles as "the ultimate driving machine."

BMW of North America, LLC

message strategy will be executed. In this chapter, we focus on advertising creative strategy. We consider what is meant by creativity, particularly as it relates to advertising, and examine a well-known approach to creativity in advertising.

We will examine the creative strategy development process and various approaches to determining the *big idea* that will be used as the central theme of the advertising campaign and be translated into attention-getting, distinctive, and memorable messages. Creative specialists are finding it more and more difficult to come up with big ideas that will break through the clutter and still satisfy the concerns of their risk-averse clients. Their clients are continually challenging them to find the creative message that will strike a responsive chord with their target audience.

Some of you may not be directly involved in the design and creation of ads; you may choose to work in another agency department such as digital or media, or work on the client side of the business. However, because creative strategy is often so crucial to the success of the firm's IMC effort, everyone involved in the promotional process should understand the creative strategy and tactics that underlie the development of advertising campaigns and messages, as well as the creative options available to the advertiser. Also, individuals on the client side as well as agency people outside the creative department must work with the creative specialists in developing the advertising campaign, implementing it, and evaluating its effectiveness. Thus, marketing and product managers, account representatives, researchers, and media personnel must appreciate the creative process and develop a productive relationship with creative personnel.

THE IMPORTANCE OF CREATIVITY IN ADVERTISING

For many students, as well as many advertising and marketing practitioners, the most interesting aspect of advertising is the creative side. We have all at one time or another been intrigued by an ad and admired the creative insight that went into it. A great ad is a joy to behold and often an epic to create, as the cost of producing a TV commercial can exceed $1 million. Many companies see this as money well spent. They realize that the manner in which the advertising message is developed and executed is often critical to the success of the promotional program, which in turn can influence the effectiveness of the entire marketing program. Major advertisers such as Procter & Gamble, Verizon, AT&T, Unilever, GEICO, FedEx, Apple, McDonald's, Coca-Cola, and many other companies spend millions of dollars each year to develop advertising messages that hopefully will win the hearts and minds of consumers. They also spend hundreds of millions of dollars more to purchase media time and space to run these messages. While these companies sell excellent products and services, they realize creative advertising is also an important part of their marketing success. The importance of creativity is summarized very well by Stephan Vogel, the chief creative officer of Ogilvy EMEA and creative chairman of Ogilvy

Germany: "Nothing is more efficient than creative advertising. Creative advertising is more memorable, longer lasting, works with less media spending, and builds a fan community . . . faster."[1]

Good creative strategy and execution can often be central to determining the success of a product or service or reversing the fortunes of a struggling brand. For example, creative advertising was able to revive Procter & Gamble's Old Spice brand and make it the market leader in the body wash category as well as one of the leading brands of other personal care products for men. Conversely, an advertising campaign that is poorly conceived or executed can be a liability. Many companies have solid marketing and promotional plans and spend substantial amounts of money on advertising, yet have difficulty coming up with a creative campaign that will differentiate them from their competitors.

It is important to understand that just because an ad or commercial is creative or popular does not mean it will increase sales or revive a declining brand. Many ads have won awards for creativity but failed to increase sales.[2] For example, Anheuser-Busch InBev terminated its 30-year relationship with the DDB agency, which had created a number of award-winning campaigns for Budweiser such as the "Whassup?" ads as well as many critically acclaimed commercials featuring the iconic Clydesdales.[3] Sales of both Budweiser and Bud Light had declined over the past several years and AB InBev felt that a change was needed in creative strategy for the brands. As discussed in Chapter 3, the two major competitors in the U.S. beer industry, Anheuser-Busch InBev and Molson Coors, have both experienced major sales declines in the light beer category as craft beers, and more recently hard seltzers, have become more popular. Both companies switched agencies several times as they struggled to find ad campaigns that would help move the sales needle for brands such as Bud Light, Miller Lite, and Coors Light.[4] Sales of Coors Light declined for a number of years as the brand struggled to find an ad campaign that resonated with consumers. For several years, the brand used the "Climb On" campaign that encouraged men and women to celebrate the mountains they climb with a refreshing Coors Light. However, the campaign did not improve sales for the brand, and in early 2019, Molson Coors announced they were switching agencies and taking the advertising for Coors Light in a new direction. Leo Burnett was retained as the lead agency for the brand, and in 2019 a new campaign was unveiled called "Made To Chill" that focuses on millennials and gen Z consumers who live in an always on, hyper-connected world where there is always pressure for their time and attention. The chief marketing officer for Molson Coors noted that the advertising positions Coors Light as the perfect antidote to a world that is always "on" as it shifted Coors Light from being a brand that's just another light beer to something that gives you a moment of refreshment.[5] The advertising also combines the attributes consumers have come to associate with Coors Light, refreshment and cold, but with a sense of purpose (Exhibit 8-2). The "Made To Chill" campaign has been successful in reviving the brand as sales of Coors Light have increased over the past 3 years.[6]

Many advertising and marketing people have become ambivalent toward, and in some cases even critical of, advertising awards.[7] They argue that agency creative people are often more concerned with creating ads that win awards than ones that sell their clients' products. Other advertising people believe awards are a good way to recognize creativity that often does result in effective advertising. They note that there are a number of studies that have shown that award-winning advertising is almost always more effective advertising.[8] As we saw in Chapter 7, the success of an ad campaign cannot always be judged in terms of sales. However, many advertising and marketing personnel, particularly those on the client side, believe advertising must ultimately lead the consumer to purchase the product or service. Finding a balance between creative advertising and effective advertising is difficult. To better understand this dilemma, we turn to the issue of creativity and its role in advertising.

EXHIBIT 8–2

Coors Light targets beer drinkers in New York City with this ad, which is part of the brand's "Made to Chill" campaign.

Coors Brewing Company

ADVERTISING CREATIVITY

What Is Creativity?

Creativity is probably one of the most commonly used terms in advertising. Ads are often called creative. The people who develop ads and commercials are known as creative types. And advertising agencies develop reputations for their creativity. Perhaps so much attention is focused on the concept of creativity because many people view the specific challenge given to those who develop an advertising message as being creative. It is their job to turn all of the information regarding product features and benefits, marketing plans, consumer research, and communication objectives into a creative concept that will bring the advertising message to life. This raises the question: What is meant by *creativity* in advertising?

Different Perspectives on Advertising Creativity

Perspectives on what constitutes creativity in advertising differ. At one extreme are people who argue that advertising is creative only if it sells the product. An advertising message's or campaign's impact on sales counts more than whether it is innovative or wins awards. At the other end of the continuum are those who judge the creativity of an ad in terms of its artistic or aesthetic value and originality. They contend creative ads can break through the competitive clutter, grab the consumer's attention, and have some impact.

As you might expect, perspectives on advertising creativity often depend on one's role. A study by Elizabeth Hirschman examined the perceptions of various individuals involved in the creation and production of TV commercials, including management types (brand managers and account executives) and creatives (art director, copywriter, commercial director, and producer).[9] She found that product managers and account executives view ads as promotional tools whose primary purpose is to communicate favorable impressions to the marketplace. They believe a commercial should be evaluated in terms of whether it fulfills the client's marketing and communications objectives. The perspective of those on the creative side was much more self-serving, as Hirschman noted:

> In direct contrast to this client orientation, the art director, copywriter, and commercial director viewed the advertisement as a communication vehicle for promoting their own aesthetic viewpoints and personal career objectives. Both the copywriter and art director made this point explicitly, noting that a desirable commercial from their standpoint was one which communicated their unique creative talents and thereby permitted them to obtain "better" jobs at an increased salary.[10]

In her interviews, Hirschman also found that brand managers were much more risk-averse and wanted a more conservative commercial than did the creative people, who wanted to maximize the impact of the message.

What constitutes creativity in advertising is probably somewhere between the two extremes. To break through the clutter and make an impression on the target audience, an ad often must be unique and entertaining. As noted in Chapter 5, research has shown that a major determinant of whether a commercial will be successful in changing brand preferences is its "likability," or the viewer's overall reaction.[11] TV commercials, videos, and print ads that are well designed and executed and generate emotional responses can create positive feelings that are transferred to the product or service being advertised. Many creative people believe this type of advertising can come about only if they are given considerable latitude in developing advertising messages. But ads that are creative only for the sake of being creative often fail to communicate a relevant or meaningful message that will lead consumers to purchase the product or service.

Everyone involved in planning and developing an advertising campaign must understand the importance of balancing the "it's not creative unless it sells" perspective with the novelty/uniqueness and impact position. Marketing and brand managers or account executives must recognize that imposing too many sales- and marketing-oriented communications objectives on the creative team can result in mediocre advertising, which is often ineffective in today's competitive, cluttered media environment. At the same time, the creative specialists must recognize that the goal of advertising is to assist in selling the product or service, and good advertising must communicate in a manner that helps the client achieve this goal. Despite having different perspectives on creativity, both sides are likely to agree that creative advertising is important because it often garners more attention and can lead to deeper processing by consumers.[12] Marketing professor Scott Koslow also notes that "creativity gives permission to consumers to be open to what appears to be new information about a brand and brings a fresh perspective—the ultimate 'new-news'."[13]

Determinants of Creativity

Advertising creativity is the ability to generate fresh, unique, and appropriate or relevant ideas that can be used as solutions to communication problems. Those who study as well as work in advertising generally agree on these two central determinants of creativity, which are often viewed in terms of divergence and relevance.[14] **Divergence** refers to the extent to which an ad contains elements that are novel, different, or unusual. Robert Smith and his colleagues have identified five major factors that could account for the ways divergence can be achieved in advertising, which they describe as follows:[15]

OVERFED BIRDS ARE MAYHEM
And if you have a sketchy F&I provider, you could be paying for your customers' claims yourself.
VISIT US AT NADA BOOTH #319.

Allstate
DEALER SERVICES

1. *Originality.* Ads that contain elements that are rare, surprising, or move away from the obvious and commonplace.
2. *Flexibility.* Ads that contain different ideas or switch from one perspective to another.
3. *Elaboration.* Ads that contain unexpected details or finish and extend basic ideas so they become more intricate, complicated, or sophisticated.
4. *Synthesis.* Ads that combine, connect, or blend normally unrelated objects or ideas.
5. *Artistic value.* Ads that contain artistic verbal impressions or attractive shapes and colors.

There are other ways divergence can be achieved in developing creative advertising such as through the use of humor, fantasy, emotion, and imagery, which are discussed in Chapter 9 as the basis for advertising execution techniques. In some cases the focus of the creative strategy may be to achieve *fluency*, which refers to the ability to generate a variety of messages around a creative idea. For example, Allstate Insurance has developed a very effective integrated marketing campaign around the "mayhem" theme that includes TV commercials, as well as print and online ads. The campaign has run since 2010 and features scores of ads showing a villainous character who wreaks havoc on vehicles and property (Exhibit 8–3). GEICO has developed myriad humorous TV commercials as well as print and online ads around the "Fifteen seconds can save you 15 percent or more on car insurance" theme.

The second major determinant of creativity is **relevance**, which reflects the degree to which the various elements of the ad are meaningful, useful, or valuable to the consumer.[16] Smith and colleagues suggest that relevance can be achieved in two ways. *Ad-to-consumer relevance* refers to situations where the ad contains execution

EXHIBIT 8–4

This ad for KFC Hot and Spicy chicken uses divergence based on originality and artistic value.

KFC Corporation

elements that are meaningful to consumers. For example, advertisers may use celebrities with whom consumers identify, music that they like, or visual images and other execution techniques that capture their interest and attention. *Brand-to-consumer relevance* refers to situations where the advertised brand of a product or service is of personal interest to consumers. Relevance or appropriateness can also be viewed in terms of the degree to which an advertisement provides information or an image that is pertinent to the brand. Ads for many products such as fashionable clothing, jewelry, cosmetics, and liquor often rely on visual images to deliver their message rather than providing specific product information. However, these images are important to consumers in forming impressions and attitudes toward these brands and deciding whether to select one brand over another.

An example of creative advertising that uses originality and artistic value aspects of divergence is a campaign developed by the Ogilvy Hong Kong agency for KFC's Hot and Spicy fried chicken. The print and outdoor ads replaced fire with different images of spicy fried chicken, such as pictures of the Space Shuttle leaving the launching pad or a rocket-fired race car (Exhibit 8–4). The images were a simple and effective metaphoric way to communicate a message regarding the intense flavor of the KFC product.

A number of studies have been conducted showing that advertising creativity impacts consumers' responses to advertising messages across various stages of the response hierarchy, including cognitive, affective, and behavioral responses.[17] For example, advertising that is more novel has been shown to require consumer processing time, resulting in longer exposure and greater attention. Studies have also shown that creative ads draw more attention to the advertised brand and have higher levels of recall, greater motivation to process the information, and deeper levels of processing.[18] In addition to these cognitive outcomes, studies have also shown that creative advertising positively impacts emotional reactions including attitudes and purchase intentions.[19]

Sara Rosengren and her colleagues conducted a very detailed meta-analysis that examined the results of 67 different studies to synthesize the literature on advertising creativity and test different theoretical explanations for its effects.[20] Their analysis focused on the originality and appropriateness/relevance aspects of creativity and how they impact consumer response. Their study showed that advertising creativity has an impact on consumer responses such as attitudes toward the ad, brand attitudes, and memory. However, the effects of creativity are weaker when only originality is assessed compared with using both originality and appropriateness. They also found that advertising creativity has stronger effects for high-involvement versus low-involvement products and for unfamiliar versus familiar brands. The finding that creativity involves more than originality and that incorporating appropriateness leads to more positive consumer response is important. They noted that ads that won creative awards, which tended to be higher in originality, had a weaker impact on consumer response and that effects were stronger when consumers judged creativity compared with when advertising experts did the judging. These findings point to the importance of involving consumers and getting their input during the development of advertising.

While most of the research on advertising creativity has been focused on measures such as attention, attitudes, and purchase intentions, German professors Reinartz and Saffert conducted an interesting study that related the five creativity factors to purchase behavior.[21] They analyzed more than 400 German television ad campaigns across nine different consumer packaged-goods categories, examining the impact of creativity on actual sales figures for the products. Their findings showed that highly creative campaigns had a greater impact on sales than did campaigns that were low in creativity, although the impact of creativity differed by product category. They also found big variations in the impact that different creative elements had on advertising

FIGURE 8–1

Impact of Combinations of
Creative Elements on Sales

What Creativity Combinations Work Best?		% Relative Effectiveness (Sales Uplift of Pairing Relative to Average Effectiveness)
Originality + Elaboration	**More effective**	+96
Originality + Artistic value		+89
Elaboration + Artistic value		+28
Originality + Synthesis		+ 1
Originality + Flexibility		– 1
Synthesis + Elaboration		– 5
Flexibility + Synthesis		–20
Synthesis + Artistic value		–29
Flexibility + Elaboration		–59
Flexibility + Artistic value	**Less effective**	–99

effectiveness. Although all of the creativity factors had a positive impact, elaboration was the most powerful, followed by artistic value; synthesis was least important. However, an important finding from their study is that it was the combination of different creative elements that accounted for the most variation in sales. As can be seen in Figure 8-1, campaigns that combined originality with elaboration had the greatest impact, followed by those combining originality with artistic value.

Several studies have shown that divergence achieved through novelty/originality and/or elaboration is a particularly important component of advertising creativity. However, clients often favor relevance over divergence, as they want their agencies to create ads that communicate pertinent information such as specific product features and benefits. Smith and his colleagues suggest that clients should be less resistant to divergent approaches and note that there is a fundamental need for divergent thinkers in the ad development process.[22] Considering that most advertising messages are seen and/or heard in a very cluttered media environment where marketers must compete for the attention of consumers, it is important that attention be given to creating ads that are novel and divergent as well as relevant and meaningful. Creativity is often a key success factor in advertising, although questions remain regarding why it works better in some situations than others. The results of the meta-analysis done by Rosengren and her colleagues showed that consumers' response to advertising is impacted by the originality and appropriateness/relevance of an advertising message, while the findings from Reinartz and Saffert's research found that originality combined with elaboration and artistic value drives sales. It is no surprise that originality has a significant impact on the effectiveness of an ad. However, other creative elements such as flexibility, artistic value, and elaboration are only likely to be worthwhile if they can connect to the overall purpose of the campaign and the larger brand identity. Thus marketers need to pay close attention to all of the creative elements of their ads.

PLANNING CREATIVE STRATEGY

The Creative Challenge

Those who work on the creative side of advertising often face a challenge. They must take all the research, creative briefs, strategy statements, communications objectives, and other inputs and transform them into an advertising message. Their job is to write copy, design layouts and illustrations, or produce commercials that effectively communicate the central theme on which the campaign is based. Rather than simply stating the features or benefits of a product or service, they must put the advertising message into a form that will engage the audience's interest and make the ads memorable.[23]

The job of the creative team is challenging because every marketing situation is different and each campaign or advertisement may require a different creative approach. Numerous guidelines have been developed for creating effective advertising,[24] but there is no magic formula. As copywriter Hank Sneiden notes in his book *Advertising Pure and Simple*:

> Rules lead to dull stereotyped advertising, and they stifle creativity, inspiration, initiative, and progress. The only hard and fast rule that I know of in advertising is that there are no rules. No formulas. No right way. Given the same problem, a dozen creative talents would solve it a dozen different ways. If there were a sure-fire formula for successful advertising, everyone would use it. Then there'd be no need for creative people. We would simply program robots to create our ads and commercials and they'd sell loads of product—to other robots.[25]

Sneiden's book was written nearly 50 years ago, and his tongue-in-cheek comment regarding robots creating ads is actually becoming a reality as the role of artificial intelligence in advertising creativity is increasing.

Taking Creative Risks

Many creative people follow proven formulas when creating ads because the formulas are safe. Clients often feel uncomfortable with advertising that is too different. Bill Tragos, former chair of TBWA, the advertising agency noted for its excellent creative work for Absolut vodka, Evian, and many other clients, says, "Very few clients realize that the reason that their work is so bad is that they are the ones who commandeered it and directed it to be that way. I think that at least 50 percent of an agency's successful work resides in the client."[26] Koslow and his colleagues have examined the influence of clients on the creativity of their agencies and found that the main reason some marketers receive better creative work than others is that they are open to exploring new ideas. They also found that access to consumer research is important as it provides agencies with insights needed to produce highly creative works. They noted that highly creative campaigns do not just appear; planning and insightful research are important for agencies to develop new ideas.[27]

Many who work on the creative side in agencies argue that it is important for clients to take some risks if they want breakthrough advertising that gets noticed. One agency that has been successful in getting its clients to take risks is Wieden+Kennedy, best known for its excellent creative work for companies such as Nike and ESPN over the years and more recently for clients such as Budweiser and Intuit/TurboTax. The agency's founders believe a key element in its success has been a steadfast belief in taking risks when most agencies and their clients have been retrenching and becoming more conservative.[28] The agency can develop great advertising partly because clients like Nike are willing to take risks and go along with the agency's priority system, which places the creative work first and the client–agency relationship second. The agency has even terminated relationships with large clients like Gallo when they interfered too much with the creative process. Exhibit 8–5 shows an example of a creative ad developed by W+K for Nike to honor tennis great Serena Williams on her retirement and acknowledge her impact on the sport.

Not all companies or agencies agree that advertising has to be risky to be effective, however. Many marketing managers are more comfortable with advertising that simply communicates product or service features and benefits and gives the consumer a reason to buy. They see their ad campaigns as multimillion-dollar investments whose goal is to sell the product rather than finance the whims of their agency's creative staff. They argue that some

EXHIBIT 8–5

Wieden+Kennedy's belief in taking risks has led to creative advertising for clients such as Nike.

Nike, Inc.

creative people have lost sight of advertising's bottom line: Does it sell? There has been an ongoing debate over the artsy, image-oriented approach to advertising taken by many creative types versus the more hard-sell approach that many clients prefer.

The Perpetual Debate: Creative versus Hard-Sell Advertising

For decades there has been a perpetual battle over the role of advertising in the marketing process. The war for the soul of advertising has been endlessly fought between those who believe ads should move people and those who just want to move product. On one side are the "suits" or "rationalists" who argue that advertising must sell the product or service, and that the more selling points or information in an ad, the better its chance of moving the consumer to purchase. On the other side are the "poets" or proponents of creativity who argue that advertising has to build an emotional bond between consumers and brands or companies that goes beyond product advertising. The debate over the effectiveness of creative or artsy advertising is not new. The rationalists have taken great delight in pointing to long lists of creative and award-winning campaigns over the years that have failed in the marketplace. Some note that even legendary advertising executive David Ogilvy, whom many consider the greatest copywriter of all time, once said: "If it doesn't sell, it's not creative."[29]

The "poets" argue that the most important thing good advertising does is make an emotional connection with consumers. They note that consumers do not want to be bombarded by ads; they want to be entertained and inspired. Indeed numerous studies have found that consumers look for ways to avoid TV commercials as well as online video and banners ads rather than watch or click through on them.[30] Thus, advertising has to be creative and enjoyable enough that consumers will not avoid it yet still be able to help sell a product or service. It is the second part of this mandate that causes concern among the "suits." They note that there are many examples of creative campaigns that moved consumers' emotions but were terminated because they did not increase sales and/or market share and put accounts and reputations on the line. As noted earlier, a number of major advertisers have dismissed agencies that earned critical acclaim and awards for their creative work but failed to move the sales needle.[31]

Most of the "poets" who support advertising that connects on an emotional level insist that selling product is as much a priority for them as it is for those on the rational side of the debate. One top agency executive notes that "we've proven that this kind of advertising works, otherwise we wouldn't be in business, us or the agencies that practice the craft at this level." However, Brent Bouchez, former executive creative director at the Bozell agency, argues the poets are losing sight of the fact that advertising is about selling things, and being really creative in advertising means solving problems and building interesting brands that people want to buy. He notes, "It's time we stopped teaching young creative people to consider it a victory if the logo in an ad is hard to find, or if the product doesn't appear in the commercial at all. It's time we stopped using 'break through the clutter' as an excuse to say nothing about what it is we're selling or why you should buy it."[32]

The issue of how much latitude creative people should be given and how much risk the client should be willing to take is open to considerable debate. However, clients and agency personnel generally agree that the ability to develop novel yet appropriate approaches to communicating with the customer makes the creative specialist valuable—and often hard to find.

Creative Personnel

The image of the creative advertising person perpetuated in novels, movies, and TV shows is often one of a freewheeling, freethinking, eccentric personality. The educational background of creative personnel is often in nonbusiness areas such as art, literature, music, humanities, or journalism, so their interests and perspectives tend to differ

EXHIBIT 8–6

Awards for creativity are given for media planning as well as other components of an IMC program.

MediaCom

from those of managers with a business education or background. Creative people tend to be more abstract and less structured, organized, or conventional in their approach to a problem, relying on intuition more often than logic. For example, Arthur Kover conducted a study of advertising copywriters and found that they work without guidance from any formal theories of communication. However, those interviewed in his study did have similar informal, implicit theories that guide them in creating ads. These theories are based on finding ways to break through the ad clutter, open the consciousness of consumers, and connect with them to deliver the message.[33]

It is important to note that creativity is not the exclusive domain of those who work in the creative department of ad agencies. Integrated marketing communications requires creative thinking from everyone involved in the planning and execution of IMC programs. Personnel from other parts of the agency such as account services and planning, media planners, digital media specialists and researchers, as well as those on the client side, such as marketing and brand managers, must all seek creative solutions to challenges faced in planning, developing, and executing an IMC campaign. For example, awards are given each year for creativity in areas such as media planning, sales promotion, and digital and interactive media. MediaCom, a division of the WPP group, was named *Adweek*'s Global Media Agency of the Year in both 2020 and 2021. The agency was honored for its creativity in media planning and strategy for clients such as Coca-Cola, Google, Bayer, and JP Morgan Chase and helping them redefine their media and investment strategy in response to the dramatic changes brought on by the COVID-19 pandemic.[34] The agency was also recognized for nurturing and growing relationships with clients while taking care of its employees and cultivating new capabilities. MediaCom's credo is "People First. Better Results" (Exhibit 8–6).

It is also important that those working on the client side do not create a relationship with their agencies that inhibits the creative processes required to produce good advertising. Shelia Sasser and Scott Koslow point out that the most highly skilled creatives aspire to work with open-minded clients who are receptive to new ideas. They also note some of the best creative work developed by agencies does not get used because clients are resistant to taking creative risks, unless they are under pressure to perform.[35] Advertising agencies as well as other IMC specialist organizations thrive on creativity because it is at the heart of what they do. Thus, agencies, as well as clients, must create an environment that fosters the development of creative thinking and creative advertising. Clients must also understand the differences between the perspectives of the creative personnel and marketing and product managers. Differences between creative and managerial personalities and perspectives must be recognized and tolerated so that creative people can do their best work and all those involved in the advertising process can cooperate. While the client has ultimate approval of the advertising, the opinions of creative specialists must be respected when advertising ideas and content are evaluated. (Evaluation of the creatives' ideas and work is discussed in more detail in Chapter 9.)

THE CREATIVE PROCESS

Some advertising people say creativity in advertising is best viewed as a process, and creative success is most likely when some organized approach is followed. This does not mean there is an infallible blueprint to follow to create effective advertising; as we saw earlier, many advertising people reject attempts to standardize creativity or develop rules. However, most do follow a process when developing an ad.

One of the most popular approaches to creativity in advertising was developed by James Webb Young, a former creative vice president at the J. Walter Thompson agency. Young said, "The production of ideas is just as definite a process as the production of Fords; the production of ideas, too, runs an assembly line; in this production the mind follows an operative technique which can be learned and controlled; and its effective use is just as much a matter of practice in the technique as in the effective use of any tool."[36] Young's model of the creative process contains five steps:

1. *Immersion.* Gathering raw material and information through background research and immersing yourself in the problem.
2. *Digestion.* Taking the information, working it over, and wrestling with it in the mind.
3. *Incubation.* Putting the problems out of your conscious mind and turning the information over to the subconscious to do the work.
4. *Illumination.* The birth of an idea—the "Eureka! I have it!" phenomenon.
5. *Reality or verification.* Studying the idea to see if it still looks good or solves the problem; then shaping the idea to practical usefulness.

Young's process of creativity is similar to a four-step approach outlined much earlier by English sociologist Graham Wallas in his classic book *The Art of Thought.*[37]

1. *Preparation.* Gathering background information needed to solve the problem through research and study.
2. *Incubation.* Getting away and letting ideas develop.
3. *Illumination.* Seeing the light or solution.
4. *Verification.* Refining and polishing the idea and seeing if it is an appropriate solution.

Models of the creative process are valuable to those working in the creative area of advertising, since they offer an organized way to approach an advertising problem. Preparation or gathering of background information is the first step in the creative process. As we saw in earlier chapters, the advertiser and agency start by developing a thorough understanding of the product or service, the target market, and the competition. They also focus on the role of advertising and other IMC tools in the marketing and promotional program.

These models do not say much about how this information will be synthesized and used by the creative specialist because this part of the process is unique to the individual. In many ways, it's what sets apart the great creative minds and strategists in advertising. However, many agencies are now using a process called *account planning* to gather information and help creative specialists as they go through the creative process of developing advertising.

Account Planning

To facilitate the creative process, many agencies now use **account planning**, which is a process that involves conducting research and gathering all relevant information about a client's product or service, brand, and consumers in the target audience. Account planning began in Great Britain during the 1960s and 70s and is now used by many agencies throughout the world.

Jon Steel, a former vice president and director of account planning at Goodby, Silverstein & Partners's San Francisco office, has written an excellent book on the process titled *Truth, Lies & Advertising: The Art of Account Planning.*[38] He notes that the account planner's job is to provide the key decision makers with all the information they require to make an intelligent decision. According to Steel, "Planners may have to work very hard to influence the way that the advertising turns out, carefully laying out a strategic foundation with the client, handing over tidbits of information to creative people when, in their judgment, that information will have the greatest impact, giving feedback on ideas, and hopefully adding some ideas of their own."

A recent study of account planners found that they often play a very complex role in the creative development process. They search for insights using various mechanisms, such as conducting consumer research; tapping into their personal domain knowledge, including experiences and observations; and challenging conventions, such as the nature of consumer decision making and consumers' relationships with a brand. They also borrow from other sources by studying best practices and advertising problem approaches used by other brands and extend the brand narrative by having a clear understanding of the brand essence or DNA and the role it plays in future advertising executions.[39]

Account planning plays an important role during creative strategy development by driving the process from the customers' point of view. Planners will work with the client as well as other agency personnel, such as the creative team and media specialists. They discuss how the knowledge and information they have gathered can be used in the development of the creative strategy as well as other aspects of the advertising campaign. Account planners are usually responsible for all the research (both qualitative and quantitative) conducted during the creative strategy development process. In the following section we examine how various types of research and information can provide input to the creative process of advertising. This information can be gathered by account planners or others whose job it is to provide input to the process.

Inputs to the Creative Process: Preparation, Incubation, Illumination

Background Research   Only the most foolish creative person or team would approach an assignment without first learning as much as possible about the client's product or service, the target market, the competition, and any other relevant background information. The creative specialist should also be knowledgeable about general trends, conditions, and developments in the marketplace, as well as research on specific advertising approaches or techniques that might be effective. The creative specialist can acquire background information in numerous ways. Some informal fact-finding techniques have been noted by Sandra Moriarty:

- Reading anything related to the product or market—books, trade publications, general interest articles, research reports, and the like.
- Asking everyone involved with the product for information—designers, engineers, salespeople, and consumers.
- Listening to what people are talking about. Visits to stores, malls, restaurants, and even the agency cafeteria can be informative. Listening to the client can be particularly valuable, since the client often knows the product and market best.
- Using the product or service and becoming familiar with it. The more you use a product, the more you know and can say about it.
- Working in and learning about the client's business to understand better the people you're trying to reach.[40]

To assist in the preparation, incubation, and illumination stages, many agencies provide creative people with both general and product-specific preplanning input. **General preplanning input** can include books, periodicals, trade publications, websites, scholarly journals, pictures, and clipping services, which gather and organize magazine, newspaper, and online articles on the product or service, the market, and the competition, including competitors' ads. This input can also come from research studies conducted by the client, the agency, the media, or other sources.

Another useful general preplanning input concerns trends, developments, and happenings in the marketplace. Information is available from a variety of sources, including local, state, and federal governments, secondary research suppliers, and various industry trade associations, as well as advertising and media organizations. For example, advertising industry groups like the American Advertising Federation (AAF), the 4As (formerly called the American Association of Advertising Agencies), and media organizations like the Video Advertising Bureau, Radio Advertising Bureau, and News/Media Alliance publish research reports and newsletters that provide information on market trends and developments and how they might affect consumers. An industry trade group that has become very important with the growth of digital advertising is the Interactive Advertising Bureau (IAB). Its membership comprises more than 650 leading media and technology companies that are responsible for selling, delivering, and optimizing digital

← HOME

Standards, Guidelines & Best Practices

Featured Content

IAB CCPA Compliance Framework for Publishers & Technology Companies

Standard Terms and Conditions for Internet Advertising for Media Buys One Year...

Digital Video Ad Serving Template (VAST)

EXHIBIT 8–7

The Interactive Advertising Bureau is an excellent source of information for marketers using online advertising.

The Interactive Advertising Bureau

advertising or marketing campaigns. The trade group also develops industry standards and guidelines for online advertising, conducts research, and promotes best practices for digital advertising (Exhibit 8–7). Those involved in developing creative strategy can also gather relevant and timely information by reading publications like *Adweek, Advertising Age,* and *Marketing News.* Many individuals who work in creative departments read *Communication Arts* magazine, which covers topics such as design, advertising, illustration, photography, interactive media, and typography.

Product- or Service-Specific Research   In addition to getting general background research and preplanning input, creative people receive **product- or service-specific preplanning input.** This information generally comes in the form of specific studies conducted on the product or service, the target audience, or a combination of the two. Types of product-specific preplanning input include quantitative and qualitative consumer research such as demographic and psychographic profiles of users of a product, service, or brand; focus groups and/or in-depth interviews; and perceptual mapping and positioning studies.

Many product- or service-specific studies helpful to the creative team are conducted by the client or the agency. Many of these studies use a variation of an approach called **problem detection** for finding ideas around which creative strategies could be based.[41] This research technique involves asking consumers familiar with a product (or service) to generate an exhaustive list of things that bother them or problems they encounter when using it and how often they arise. The consumers rate these problems in order of importance and evaluate various brands in terms of their association with each problem. A problem detection study can provide valuable input for product improvements, reformulations, or new products. It can also give the creative people ideas regarding attributes or features to emphasize and guidelines for positioning new or existing brands.

A number of advertising agencies conduct branding research to help better identify clients' customers and how they connect to their brands. For example, the Y&R Group developed a proprietary tool called the BrandAsset Valuator (BAV) for building and managing a brand. The model uses four pillars: energized differentiation, relevance, esteem, and knowledge. These pillars identify cores issues for the brand and evaluate current and future financial performance and potential (Exhibit 8–8). The agency formed a separate corporate research group to handle the BAV, which is now the world's largest database of brand perceptions; it contains ratings for nearly 60,000 brands in 52 countries on more than 70 dimensions.

Nearly all of the major agencies are conducting branding research and/or developing models or systems that they can use to gain better insight into consumers and develop more effective campaigns for their clients. The importance of building and maintaining strong brands is likely to become even greater in the future. This will put even more pressure on agencies to develop new and better tools and techniques that can be used to guide their clients' advertising campaigns.

EXHIBIT 8–8

BrandAsset Valuator is used to manage brands.

BAV Group, Inc.

+BAVGROUP   ABOUT BAV | SOLUTIONS | BRANDS & CULTURE | WHO WE ARE | CAREERS | CONTACT US   SEARCH

HOME

HOW IT WORKS

BAV® MEASURES EXTENSIVE BRAND QUALITIES AND METRICS THAT DRIVE FINANCIAL AND MARKETPLACE SUCCESS

BRAND STRENGTH
Future growth potential

BRAND STATURE
Current operating value

DIFFERENTIATION   RELEVANCE   ESTEEM   KNOWLEDGE

Qualitative Research Input   Many agencies, particularly larger ones with strong research departments, have their own research programs and specific techniques they use to assist in the development of creative strategy and provide input to the creative process. In addition to the various quantitative research studies, qualitative research techniques such as in-depth interviews or focus groups can provide the creative team with valuable insight at the early stages of the creative process. **Focus groups** are a research method whereby consumers (usually 10 to 12 people) from the target market are led through a discussion regarding a particular topic. Focus groups give insight as to why and how consumers use a product or service, what is important to

EXHIBIT 8-9

Marketers often use online
focus group services to
pretest ads.

Invoke

CLIENT STORY: ORBITZ
Invoke helps Orbitz win the David Ogilvy award

"The team – Orbitz, BBDO and Invoke — all sat in the room together monitoring the live feedback, which was translated into improvement ideas on-the-spot. This close collaboration made it possible for the creative team to cycle more ideas through and develop more relevant creative than previously."

– Stacey Symonds, Sr. Director of Consumer Insights at Orbitz

them in choosing a particular brand, what they like and don't like about various products or services, and any special needs they might have that aren't being satisfied. A focus group session might also include a discussion of types of ad appeals to use or evaluation of the advertising of various companies.

Focus group interviews bring the creative people and others involved in creative strategy development into contact with the customers. Listening to a focus group gives copywriters, art directors, and other creative specialists a better sense of who the target audience is, what the audience is like, and whom the creatives need to write, design, or direct to in creating an advertising message. Focus groups can also be used to evaluate the viability of different creative approaches under consideration and suggest the best direction to pursue.[42] Many marketers are now conducting focus groups online using groups of consumers who are part of an online community, as well as Internet research panels of 80 to 100 consumers organized by research firms such as Greenfield Online and Invoke Solutions. Concepts can be presented to these panels using instant-message and chat room styles, and detailed feedback can be gathered and processed in a few hours versus the several weeks that are needed to get comparable results from traditional focus groups.[43] Exhibit 8-9 shows how Invoke Solutions promotes the value of its online focus groups by showing how they were used by Orbitz and its agency, BBDO, in developing the "Take Vacation Back" ad campaign, which won a David Ogilvy Award from the Advertising Research Foundation.

Agency creative personnel have long expressed concern over the idea of having their ideas and work critiqued by consumers. Many creatives insist that good ideas don't need to be tested and that testing can often weaken a creative execution. Moreover, they argue that it interferes with the creative process and limits their ability to develop innovative and breakthrough advertising messages.[44] Those critical of focus groups note that highly successful campaigns such as the one featuring the Aflac duck

EXHIBIT 8-10

The Aflac duck is a very
popular and recognizable
personality symbol for the
supplemental insurance
company and is often featured
in its advertising.

Aflac Inc.

get the
Aflacts
#5

Aflac belongs to you, not your company.
So make sure you take it with you.

would never have made it on the air if the company had heeded the responses of focus group participants. While many participants found the duck funny, others found it insulting. The duck survived only after executives from the Kaplan Thaler Group convinced the company to allow the Ipsos-ASI research firm to test the ad along with four others it created and four spots from other agencies competing for the account.[45] The recall score of the spot featuring the duck was the highest score Ipsos-ASI had seen in the insurance category at the time. Kaplan Thaler won the account, and the award-winning campaign featuring the duck has been running for more than 20 years and led to significant increases in sales for the supplemental insurance provider (Exhibit 8-10).

While some creative personnel may be opposed to having their ideas scrutinized in a focus group, there are, of course, numerous examples of situations where input from focus groups has proved to be very valuable and insightful. Creative personnel must recognize that companies want to ensure that the ads that are being developed for their brands have the best possible chance of evoking favorable reactions from consumers and encouraging them to purchase their product and/or services. Joe Plummer, the former chief research officer of the Advertising Research Foundation, explains their position pretty well by noting, "Any creative director worth his salt who really thinks a client is going to lay down $100 million without a high level of confidence of success is naïve."[46] IMC Perspective 8-1 discusses how the growth of analytics and the practice of using data to make marketing decisions has created a challenge for advertising creatives.

Another form of qualitative input that has become popular among advertising agencies is **ethnographic research**, which involves observing consumers in their natural environment.[47] This form of research has its roots in the social science discipline of anthropology, where it has long been used to gather information on human societies and cultures. It has been adapted for use in marketing by sending anthropologists or trained researchers into the field to study and observe consumers in their homes, at work, or at play. For example, the Ogilvy & Mather agency has a research unit that moves into consumers' homes, follows consumers in their leisure pursuits, or trails them as they move through their daily lives. For Ogilvy client Molson Coors, Discovery staffers traveled around the country filming Miller drinkers, as well as those drinking competitive brands. They used the tapes to study group dynamics and how the dynamics changed while people were drinking. The agency used the insights gained from the study to help develop a new advertising campaign for Miller Lite beer.

Many marketing and agency researchers prefer ethnographic research over the use of focus groups, as the latter technique has a number of limitations. Strong personalities can often wield undue influence in focus groups, and participants often will not admit, or may not even recognize, their behavior patterns and motivations. However, ethnographic studies can cost more to conduct and are more difficult to administer.

Generally, creative people are open to any research or information that will help them understand the client's target market better and assist in generating creative ideas. The advertising industry is recognizing the importance of using research to guide the creative process. The Advertising Research Foundation initiated the David Ogilvy Awards, named after the advertising legend who founded Ogilvy & Mather. These awards are presented to teams of advertising agencies, client companies, and research companies in recognition of research that has been used successfully to determine the strategy and effectiveness of ad campaigns.

One of the 2021 David Ogilvy Award winners was a campaign developed by FCB New York for Michelob ULTRA Organic Seltzer. When Anheuser-Busch InBev launched Michelob ULTRA in 2021, there were more than 65 brands of hard seltzer saturating the market with competing claims of refreshment, flavor, and taste. Moreover, two early entrants in the market, White Claw and Truly, held 75 percent market share. FCB used primary and secondary market research to identify consumers' biggest complaint about the product, which was that most hard seltzers taste fake. The agency also used research to identify a market segment that none of the seltzer brands were speaking to—affluent drinkers looking for a real-tasting, healthier low-carb/low-sugar option. Qualitative research was used to identify the motivating product claims that the advertising campaign could be centered around, and real taste, natural ingredients, and zero grams of sugar rose to the top. Quantitative research was then used to validate the claims and ensure they were both unique and would drive purchase intent.

Based on the research, the motivating product truth was identified: Michelob ULTRA Organic Seltzer has no artificial flavoring and is USDA Certified Organic, so it tastes real, unlike the artificial-tasting competition. The creative strategy for Michelob

IMC Perspective 8–1 >>>

Are Analytics Killing Advertising Creativity?

Advertising used to be reserved for the artistic, creative types who could develop imaginative ideas and connect with consumers who often make emotionally driven decisions, rather than purely logical ones. Today, however, advertising is becoming more science and less art, like most other areas of marketing. Data-savvy marketers have access to a seemingly never-ending stream of information and insights into their customers and are relying heavily upon data and analytics, which is forcing creativity to take a back seat to more data-driven approaches. Just about every element of an IMC campaign can be tracked, tested, and reported, particularly for digital advertising where impressions, click-throughs, bounce rates, time on site, and many other metrics are now readily available.

While marketing is still geared toward connecting with the audience, it now relies heavily upon data that can be measured and reproduced, and many in the advertising industry argue that this focus on analytics and metrics is killing creativity, as it is leaving important concepts such as brand building, emotional connections, and customer loyalty low on the list of priorities for many companies. Studies have shown that a high percentage of those working in marketing and advertising feel that a culture of measurement is stifling creativity as more emphasis is placed on data-driven practices, rather than creative methods of campaign planning and execution.

This controversy, although heated now, is nothing new. The use of research and metrics has long been an important part of the advertising creative process. Major marketers often spend hundreds of thousands of dollars to develop and test creative ideas and concepts that are turned into advertisements for their companies and/or brands, and for good reason. Many of the commercials and videos you see on television or online for big brands cost an average of $500,000 just to produce, while some can cost more than $1 million when all of the preproduction, production, and postproduction costs are added up. And once a commercial, video, or print ad is produced, marketers may spend millions more in traditional and online media to deliver the ads to consumers. But marketers also have to consider opportunity costs, which, from an advertising perspective, means wondering whether another creative approach might have worked better than the data-driven one chosen.

Traditionally, many marketers have used some form of copy or A/B testing to compare the effectiveness of different creative concepts or advertising messages prior to making a decision on which one to use. Various forms of copy testing are often used, and there are many examples of how marketers have relied on the test results to avoid costly mistakes and choose the best alternative. Today, most copy testing methods involve showing ads online to a panel of consumers and measuring their reactions using measures such as recall, likability, persuasiveness, and purchase intentions. Ads can be tested at various stages of production, starting with layouts of print messages and ad copy to early versions of TV commercials and videos shown in rough form such as animatics, all the way through to a finished ad, commercial, or video. Pretesting results often are analyzed by comparing them to norms of previous ads used by the marketer, industry and category averages, or other ads currently being used by advertisers.

While most advertising creatives are not opposed to pretesting of their ideas, most feel that the data should be used to inform creative decisions, not to make them. They argue that too heavy a reliance on ad testing and meeting norms and other metrics hinders the creative process and often stops innovative ideas from coming to life. Moreover, they note that ad-testing methods elicit only conscious responses and cannot truly capture how consumers might respond emotionally and subconsciously to a creative message. Some cite the famous quote by the late Apple co-founder Steve Jobs who once said, "It's really hard to design products by focus groups. A lot of times people don't know what they want until you show it to them."

The challenge facing advertising is finding the right balance between analytics and creativity, particularly as marketers become more and more interested in measurable, datadriven results. Much of advertising is about creative and effective storytelling that makes a connection with the target audience and can be used to build brand and/or position it in the market. Michelle Beh notes that the core of creativity is the idea, and ideas come from insights, which in turn are often informed by data. She suggests that creative teams need to understand how and where they can get data and what the data really says, while researchers should understand how creative teams use their data to create solutions and outcomes for clients. Beh also argues that marketers are often testing unfinished creative executions, hoping that consumers can understand the intended outcome of the idea, which is a reason many creative concepts do not test well. Thus, data and analytics should be used to guide and inform creative thinking and provide guard rails rather than to prematurely find fault with or derail possibly good ideas.

Ultimately, creativity and analytics need to be balanced and marketers must find ways to achieve a symbiotic relationship between art and science. Those working on both the agency side and client side of the business must recognize that it is a combination of creativity and analytics that is likely to yield the best outcomes, not just one of them alone.

Sources: Terence D'Souza, "Combining Analytics with Creativity: How Advertisers Can Leverage Both," *Financial Express*, June 11, 2022, https://www.financialexpress.com/brandwagon/combininganalytics-with-creativity-how-advertisers-can-leverage-both/2556976/; Michele Beh, "Does Data Kill or Amplify Creativity?" *The Media Online*, September 27, 2021, https://themediaonline.co.za/2021/09/does-data-kill-or-amplify-creativity/; Diogo Felippelli, "How Much Should Data Influence Your Creative Marketing Decisions?" *Tagger*, March 2022, https://www.taggermedia.com/blog/marketing-strategy-balance-data-creativity/.

EXHIBIT 8–11

The "As Real as It Tastes" campaign for Michelob ULTRA Organic Seltzer won a David Ogilvy Award for an IMC campaign based on consumer research.

Anheuser-Busch Companies, LLC

ULTRA that evolved from the research was centered around the theme "As Real as It Tastes," and the advertising campaign was launched during the 2021 Super Bowl by taking on the biggest fakery at the world's biggest advertising event—the relationship between celebrities and brands in Super Bowl ads. The Super Bowl featured what appeared to be various A-list celebrities talking about the real reasons to crave Michelob ULTRA Organic Seltzer. Singer Usher wanted no carbs, actor Lucy Liu wanted no sugar, Megan Fox wanted no artificial aftertaste, and tennis star Serena Williams just wanted a hard seltzer. However, the real truth came at the end when viewers learned that the cast of celebrities were really lookalikes, and the commercial had only one real celebrity, award-winning actor Don Cheadle, who revealed the punchline: Sometimes things aren't as real as they seem, just like hard seltzer.

To keep the real over fake conversation going, a Twitter promotion was launched that showed people how to identify which of their followers were bots, and the fake followers could be exchanged for real Michelob ULTRA Organic seltzer. The campaign also included an Ultra Summer Getaway Sweepstakes, giving consumers a chance to win a real rather than a virtual vacation. Hard seltzer drinkers could snap a photo of the QR code featured in the ads, which would route them to a website where they could enter to win an exclusive, curated vacation with three of their friends or family inspired by the real fruit flavors of Michelob ULTRA Organic Seltzer's Classic Collection (Exhibit 8–11). The "As Real as It Tastes" campaign achieved strong results and helped establish the brand in the highly competitive market. In just 2 months the brand joined White Claw and Truly as one of the three most talked about brands of hard seltzer, became the brand most recognized as 'better for you,' and was the second biggest gainer in market share.[48]

Inputs to the Creative Process: Verification, Revision

The verification and revision stage of the creative process evaluates ideas generated during the illumination stage, rejects inappropriate ones, refines and polishes those that remain, and gives them final expression. Techniques used at this stage include directed focus groups to evaluate creative concepts, ideas, or themes; message communication studies; portfolio tests; and evaluation measures such as viewer reaction profiles.

At this stage of the creative process, members of the target audience may be asked to evaluate rough creative layouts and to indicate what meaning they get from the ad, what they think of its execution, or how they react to a slogan or theme. The creative team can gain insight into how a TV commercial might communicate its message by having members of the target market evaluate the ad in storyboard form. A **storyboard** is a series of drawings used to present the visual plan or layout of a proposed commercial. It contains a series of sketches of key frames or scenes along with the copy or audio portion for each scene (see Exhibit 8–12).

Testing a commercial in storyboard form can be difficult because storyboards are too abstract for many consumers to understand. To make the creative layout more realistic and easier to evaluate, the agency may produce an **animatic**, a videotape of the storyboard along with an audio soundtrack. Storyboards and animatics are useful for research purposes as well as for presenting the creative idea to other agency personnel or to the client for discussion and approval.

At this stage of the process, the creative team is attempting to find the best creative approach or execution style before moving ahead with the campaign themes and going into actual production of the ad. The verification/revision process may include more formal, extensive pretesting of the ad before a final decision is made. Pretesting and related procedures are examined in detail in Chapter 18.

EXHIBIT 8–12

Marketers can gain insight into consumers' reactions to a commercial by showing them a storyboard or an animatic.

Courtesy of The Lambesis Agency

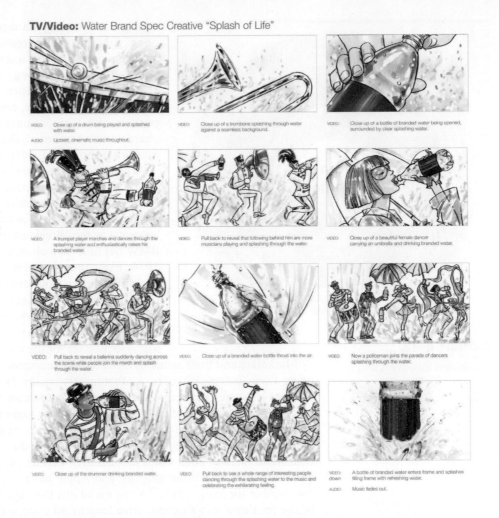

TV/Video: Water Brand Spec Creative "Splash of Life"

CREATIVE STRATEGY DEVELOPMENT

Advertising Campaigns

Most ads are part of a series of messages that make up an IMC or **advertising campaign**, which is a set of interrelated and coordinated marketing communications activities that center on a single theme or idea that appears in different media across a specified time period. Determining the unifying theme around which the campaign will be built is a critical part of the creative process, as it sets the tone for the individual ads and other forms of marketing communications that will be used. A **campaign theme** should be a strong idea, as it is the central message that will be communicated in all the advertising and other promotional activities. The theme for the advertising campaign is usually expressed through a **slogan (tagline)** that reduces the key idea into a few words or a brief statement. The advertising slogan should serve as a summation line that succinctly expresses the company or brand's positioning, as well as the message it is trying to deliver to the target audience.[49] The slogan usually appears in every advertisement and is often used in other forms of marketing communications to serve as a reminder of, and to reinforce, the marketer's branding message. Kohli, Leuthesser, and Suri note that slogans are a key element of a brand's identity as they can enhance a brand's image, aid in its recognition and recall, and help differentiate it in the minds of consumers, thus contributing to brand equity.[50] They note that while a brand name and/or logo cannot say much in a literal sense, slogans can bridge this gap and say something about the image of the product or service. They can also serve as a "hook" or "handle" that helps capture the meaning of a brand and relay what makes it special.[51]

EXHIBIT 8–13

Guidelines for advertising slogans.

Kumail Hemani

FIGURE 8–2

Examples of Effective Advertising Slogans

Company or Brand	Slogan
1. Toyota	Let's Go Places
2. Home Depot	How Doers Get More Done
3. Amazon	Spend Less. Smile More
4. McDonald's	I'm Lovin' It!
5. Sony PlayStation	Play Has No Limits
6. Walmart	Save Money. Live Better.
7. Bounty	The Quicker Picker Upper
8. Airbnb	Belong Anywhere
9. Capital One	What's In Your Wallet?
10. Dunkin'	America Runs on Dunkin'

Digital marketing manager Kumail Hemani has developed guidelines for creating effective slogans, which include recognizing that a slogan is a shadow for a brand as it is used everywhere along with it and thus has a key role in communicating the essence of a brand. He also notes that slogans should be simple, catchy, and predictable as well as connect with the consumer on an emotional level. Other characteristics of good slogans/taglines that he recommends are shown in Exhibit 8–13.

While some marketers change their campaign themes often, a successful campaign theme may last for decades. Philip Morris has been using the "Marlboro country" campaign for over 50 years, General Mills has positioned Wheaties cereal as the "Breakfast of Champions" since 1933, and BMW has used "the ultimate driving machine" theme since 1974. Even though BMW has changed agencies several times over the past four decades, the classic tagline has been retained. Figure 8–2 lists some of the advertising slogans currently being used by marketers that are recognized as being very effective because they are memorable and communicate a unique message for the company or brand.

Marketers and their agencies often develop campaign themes with the intention of using them for many years. Unfortunately, many last only a short time, usually because they are ineffective and do not communicate a distinct identity for a company or brands. While many marketers and their agencies spend a great deal of time and effort developing slogans, some experts argue that taglines are becoming less important because many companies and brands do not use them. Brand-building consultant Denise Yohn notes that admired brands such as Starbucks, Whole Foods, and lululemon do not use slogans, and Apple has not used its famous "Think different" tagline for many years.[52] Yohn maintains that advertisers relied on slogans more in the past as a way to summarize lengthy ad copy with a memorable catchphrase. However, many marketers are relying more on targeted digital advertising and word of mouth and running fewer big campaigns that require taglines. She also points out that taglines work best when a brand's differentiation is derived from a product or service attribute. However, today many brands try to distinguish themselves by connecting with consumers' values and personalities, which can be difficult to convey through a tagline.

Like any other area of the marketing and promotional process, the creative aspect of advertising and the development of the campaign theme is guided by specific goals and objectives. A creative strategy that focuses on what must be communicated will guide the selection of the campaign theme and the development of all messages used in the ad campaign. The creative strategy is based on several factors, including identification of the target audience; the basic problem, issue, or opportunity the advertising must address; the major selling idea or key benefit the message needs to communicate; and any supportive information that needs to be included in the ad. Once these factors are determined, a creative strategy statement should describe the message appeal and execution style that will be used. Many ad agencies outline these elements in a document known as the copy or creative platform.

1. Basic problem or issue the communication must address or solve

2. Communication objectives

3. Target audience

4. Insights to drive creative work

5. Key benefits or major selling idea to communicate

6. Reason to believe/supporting information

7. Tone and manner/brand personality

8. Deliverables (what is needed and when)

9. Measures of success (should be tied back to objectives)

FIGURE 8-3

Key Elements of a
Creative Brief

Creative Brief

The **creative brief** is a document that specifies the key elements of the creative strategy for an advertising campaign and serves as the basis for communication between the client and the advertising agency. Some agencies and/or companies have a different name for this document, such as *creative platform* or *work plan, creative blueprint,* or *creative contract.* Just as there are different names for the creative brief, there are variations in the outline and format used and in the level of detail included. Recently, the Association of National Advertisers (ANA), the trade association that represents more than 600 of the leading advertisers in the United States, published a report titled "Better Creative Briefs" that provides guidelines for developing effective briefs.[53] The "must have elements" of a creative brief are shown in Figure 8-3.

The ANA report notes that the traditional way of developing the creative brief has been a two-step process. The client first creates the *assignment brief* (sometimes called a *business* or *marketing brief*) that includes what the client wants the agency to do, as well as what the agency needs to know to succeed. The second step is the development of the *creative brief* by the agency, which is usually done by the account planner and/or representative assigned to the account. Those from the agency team or group assigned to the account—including creative personnel as well as representatives from digital, media, and research departments—may have input. The advertising and/or marketing and brand managers from the client side ultimately approve the creative brief, and it then becomes the roadmap to guide the creative process.

The ANA notes that some clients and agencies are moving to one collaborative brief rather than a two-step process, where the client takes the lead and develops the brief collaboratively with a representative from the agency, such as the account planner or representative. The agency can then rework and refine the brief and work with the client to ensure alignment on the changes.[54]

Several components of the creative brief were discussed in previous chapters. For example, Chapter 7 examined the DAGMAR model and showed how the setting of advertising objectives requires specifying a well-defined target audience and developing a communication task statement that spells out what message must be communicated to this audience. Determining what problem the product or service will solve or what issue must be addressed in the ad helps in establishing communication objectives for the campaign to accomplish. Two critical components of the brief are the development of the major selling idea and creative strategy development. These two steps are often the responsibility of the creative team or specialist and form the basis of the advertising campaign theme.

Many creative briefs also include supporting information and requirements (brand identifications, disclaimers, and the like) that should appear in any advertising message. This information may be important in ensuring uniformity across various executions of the ads used in a campaign or in meeting any legal requirements. Exhibits 8-14A and B show an example of a creative brief used by the Lambesis agency to create a print campaign for Tacori and an ad that was created based on the brief. As noted in the brief, the primary objective of the advertising for Tacori is to establish the Tacori collection as a more accessible fashion jewelry line.

Obtaining information regarding customers, the product or service, and the market that can be used in developing the creative brief is an important part of the creative planning process. While it is important that this basic information is provided to agency creatives, this may not always occur due to breakdowns in communication on the client as well as the agency side or between the two.

John Sutherland and colleagues conducted an extensive survey of agency creative directors, copywriters, and art directors on the specific types of marketing information

Lambesis

2800 Roosevelt Street, Carlsbad California, 92008 Main 760.547.2333 Fax 760.547.2331 lambesis.com

Creative Brief

Client: Tacori

Assignment
Develop new print concepts for the launch of the 18K925 line by Tacori

Objectives
- Support the long-term goal of growing 18K925 to become 50% of Tacori's business by clearly establishing the new Tacori collection as a more accessible, fashion jewelry line

Target
- Women, Age 25-49, HHI $75K+, Urban dwellers, Brand driven consumers, in market for fashion jewelry for self or as a gift for someone special.

- *What do they currently think?*
  I know and love Tacori as a high-end jewelry brand that's gifted for special occasions (=expressions of love)

- *What do we want them to think?*
  Tacori is also a brand with bold, statement-making, accessible designs that still have that distinctly artisanal Tacori touch (=expressions of style)

Product positioning
Tacori's 18K925 designer jewelry line is the ultimate expression of passion, with modern, accessible style and lasting quality.

Reasons to believe
- Accessible price points between $400 - $3000
- Bold, fun, wearable designs fuse colorful gemstones and gold+silver metals, with classic Tacori design cues
- Distinct Tacori brand name and image

Tonality
Modern meets heirloom, bold, aspirational, unique

Creative considerations
- Develop concepts within the Iconic Passion campaign
- Creative requirements:
  - Demonstrate aspirational, yet attainable luxury
  - Accommodate a variety of product imagery including necklaces, bracelets and/or rings to showcase the range of jewelry
  - Use the Tacori logo
- Other considerations that need be addressed:
  - Concepts must be able to work for print and horizontal OOH and B&W newspaper
  - Concepts need to ensure that retailer tags added to the bottom of the ad are legible

EXHIBIT 8–14A

Creative brief for Tacori jewelry.

Lambesis Agency

EXHIBIT 8–14B

Print ad created based on creative brief to establish Tacori as an accessible fashion jewelry line.

Tacori

that is made available to them for use in developing and executing a creative strategy.[55] They identified six specific types of marketing information: the demographic profile of the target audience, customer product usage information, client's product performance information, competitors' product performance information, marketing strategy information, and the main selling point supplied by the client. Their study showed that agency creative personnel often lack the information needed to effectively design and execute creative strategies. They found that information in these specific categories was provided to creatives only around one-half to two-thirds of the time. Even the most basic target demographic profile was not provided 30 percent of the time. This study indicates that there is a gap in the information that creative personnel need to develop effective advertising and what they are being provided, which points to the need for better communication between clients and agencies.

An ANA survey conducted among member clients and agencies also found a gap between how each side rated the quality of creative briefs provided by clients to their agencies. While the majority of clients felt they provide clear assignment briefings to the agency, only about a quarter of agencies agreed.[56] Another recent survey conducted by the World Advertising Federation on creative briefs found that most agencies feel that clients are briefing their work with specific media channels and outputs in mind rather than taking an integrated communications perspective. The survey also found significant misalignment between clients on key elements of creative briefs. While nearly three-quarters of clients believe they have a single-minded proposition or single view of the customer in their briefs, the vast majority of agency representatives did not agree with their assessment.[57] Clearly, there is room for improvement in the development of creative briefs as well as communication between clients and their agencies.

The information contained in the creative brief provides the agency with important background information and the basic elements of the overall advertising strategy. The next step in the creative process is the development of the message strategy and begins with the search for the *big idea* that will build on the creative brief and bring it to life. One of the major challenges for the creative team is determining the major selling idea that will be used as the basis of the campaign. We will examine some approaches often used for determining the major selling idea and campaign theme.

The Search for the Major Selling Idea

An important part of creative strategy is determining the central theme that will become the **major selling idea** of the ad campaign. As A. Jerome Jeweler states in his book *Creative Strategy in Advertising*:

> The major selling idea should emerge as the strongest singular thing you can say about your product or service. This should be the claim with the broadest and most meaningful appeal to your target audience. Once you determine this message, be certain you can live with it; be sure it stands strong enough to remain the central issue in every ad and commercial in the campaign.[58]

Some advertising experts argue that for an ad campaign to be effective it must contain a big idea that attracts the consumer's attention, gets a reaction, and sets the advertiser's product or service apart from the competition's. Well-known ad executive John O'Toole describes the *big idea* as "that flash of insight that synthesizes the purpose of the strategy, joins the product benefit with consumer desire in a fresh, involving way, brings the subject to life, and makes the reader or audience stop, look, and listen."[59]

Of course, the real challenge to the creative team is coming up with the big idea to use in the ad. Many products and services offer virtually nothing unique, and it can be difficult to find something interesting to say about them. The late David Ogilvy, discussed the difficulty of generating big ideas for an advertising campaign by noting:

> I doubt if more than one campaign in a hundred contains a big idea. I am supposed to be one of the more fertile inventors of big ideas, but in my long career as a copywriter I have not had more than 20, if that.[60]

While really great ideas in advertising are difficult to come by, there are many big ideas that became the basis of very creative, successful advertising campaigns. Classic examples include Nike's "Just Do It" campaign, the "Intel Inside" campaign that positioned the company's microprocessors as the key component in personal computers, the "Got Milk?" theme used to promote milk consumption, and the "Priceless" campaign for MasterCard that focused on special moments and experiences that money cannot buy.

A number of more recent campaigns are examples of successful big ideas as well. In 2015, *Advertising Age* had a panel of influential and acclaimed advertising creatives and executives pick the best campaigns of the new millennium.[61] The campaign selected as the best of the 21st century up to that point was Dove's "Campaign for Real Beauty," which was discussed in Chapter 6.

An integrated campaign that combined paid, owned, and earned media was "The Man Your Man Could Smell Like" effort for Old Spice Body Wash. The humorous ads developed for the campaign included a well-built, handsome, and bare-chested character telling women that Old Spice body wash will make their male partners smell like him if they stopped using lady-scented body wash and switched to Old Spice (Exhibit 8-15). The Wieden+Kennedy agency built on the popularity of the ads with the "Responses" campaign, which involved soliciting questions for the Old Spice guy via Twitter and Facebook and having him answer them with short video clips. The videos made Old Spice the most popular brand online and helped it become the market leader in the body-wash category.

IMC Perspective 8-2 discusses the different creative approaches used by advertisers for automotive insurance, which is one of the most heavily promoted product/service categories.

EXHIBIT 8-15

The Man Your Man Could Smell Like campaign for Old Spice is one of the best campaigns of the new millennium.

Old Spice by Procter & Gamble

Auto Insurance Companies Use Different Creative Strategies, But Do They Work?

If you have watched television lately, surfed the Internet, listened to radio, or read a magazine, chances are you have seen a commercial for automotive insurance. Automotive insurance is one of the most advertised product/service categories, accounting for $6.7 billion in measured media spending in 2021. Four of the top 10 most advertised brands in the United States in 2021 were insurance companies led by GEICO, which spent $1.4 billion, followed by Progressive, Allstate, and Liberty Mutual. Automobile insurance companies face a unique marketing challenge because regardless of age, gender, or socio-economic status, all drivers need insurance. In fact, some form of liability coverage is required by law in all 50 states. This opportunity presents a challenge as auto insurers must market their service to a wide range of consumers who represent a broad spectrum of characteristics including age, education, and income, as well as purchase motives.

As a result, in recent years we have seen auto insurance companies create a diverse range of advertisements designed to appeal to many different types of consumers. The goal of these campaigns, of course, is to attract and retain as many customers as possible by encouraging consumers to switch from one insurance company to another. The ease of purchasing auto insurance online has intensified the competition and made automotive insurance a fluid market. Studies have shown that nearly one in six consumers switch their auto insurance providers in a given year, based primarily on price and convenience. Because it is difficult to differentiate their insurance programs, the major companies emphasize entertainment, humor, lifestyle, and characters rather than hard-sell informational techniques in their ads. Their goal is to attraction attention, build awareness and brand recall, or make consumers feel uncomfortable with their current auto insurance provider, often without ever mentioning costs or features.

The advertising strategy of some auto insurers is to use a big-budget, multi-pronged advertising approach with several creative campaigns running simultaneously. GEICO, for example, which has an advertising budget nearly twice as large as most of its competitors, has at any given time as many as five different ad campaigns running at once, which breaks a basic commandment of marketing: Thou shalt not confuse the consumer. However, while the look, style, and creative approaches vary, the core message is the same from one campaign to another, which is that consumers should take time to compare rates because "Fifteen minutes could save you 15 percent or more on car insurance." The idea behind using multiple campaigns simultaneously is to break through advertising clutter and attract attention, as well as avoid the problem of wear-out that often results when consumers tire of seeing and/or hearing the same advertising message repeatedly.

Over the past two decades, the Martin Agency has developed what seems like an endless parade of amusing commercials for GEICO that often use very different creative strategies. The company first began using its popular gecko character in 1999, and the lizard with the Cockney English accent still appears in many of the company's print and TV ads. GEICO has also used a variety of other characters, including the metrosexual caveman who is insulted by the tagline, "So easy a caveman can do it." There have also been myriad commercials using popular clichés, fairy tales, animals, reality shows, and soap operas for creative inspiration.

In an effort to keep pace with GEICO's aggressive spending and humor-based, multi-pronged ad campaigns, other insurers have increased their advertising spending and created ad campaigns based on humor (or at least *attempted* humor) as well as casting individuals who become personality symbols for their brands. For example, State Farm has used the Green Bay Packers star quarterback Aaron Rodgers in its ads for more than a decade, initially running a series of "discount double check" ads. State Farm added the Jake character, who appears in the ads as a real State Farm salesman, in 2011, but who was recast in 2020 and is now played by actor Kevin Mimms. The most recent State Farm ads have featured other athletes and celebrities such as singer Drake, NBA star Chris Paul, and Kansas City Chiefs quarterback Patrick Mahomes. The most recent ads feature Rodgers and Mahomes discussing State Farm's Personal Price Plan and Jake letting them know they don't need to reveal personal secrets to get a price tailored to their needs.

Progressive still uses its popular Flo character, who has been featured in its ads since 2008, and originally debuted as a cashier character working in the insurer's fictional superstore. With her trademark red lipstick and retro eyeliner, Flo has appeared in over 200 commercials for Progressive over the past 14 years and become an iconic figure in the world of advertising. The latest series of Progressive ads feature Flo navigating an unexpected encounter with an old love interest played by Hollywood star Jon Hamm. While he seems eager to rekindle their relationship, Flo only has room for one love in her life: insurance.

In some cases, *not* following the industry trend toward using humorous campaigns has been a recipe for success. Allstate's "Mayhem" campaign, which was first launched in 2010, features actor Dean Winters playing a villainous character who wreaks havoc on other cars and property as a way of showing that many accidents involve more than your average fender bender. The Mayhem ads utilize both dry humor and a mild fear appeal to show the serious consequences, as well as personal liability, that can result from an auto accident. The campaign is intended to be disruptive in an industry whose primary focus is on price. The Mayhem ads have been well received among young people. The Mayhem character has a large social media following, including nearly 120,000 followers on Twitter. The campaign has been an effective counter to GEICO and Progressive's discount-focused advertising as it is encourages consumers to recognize that you get what you pay for when purchasing insurance.

Given their varying levels of success across the industry, there is significant debate by industry analysts as to whether the approaches used by car insurance companies are effective. The goal of many of these ads is to encourage consumers to call a toll-free number, visit the advertiser's website, or call one of their agents to compare rates and coverage and consider switching carriers. A study by professors Yi-Lin Tsai and Elisabeth Honka found that auto insurance advertising did pay off by increasing general brand awareness but had no impact on which companies consumers chose to get quotes from, nor in the final step of choosing which insurer to go with. Thus, one could argue that all those insurance ads may be doing little more than providing consumers with a good laugh during a commercial break.

Sources: Sara Routhier, "The Best Car Insurance Commercials (Big Laughs & True Stats)," *Car Insurance Comparison*, May 24, 2022, https://www.carinsurancecomparison.com/top-car-insurance-commercials/; E. J. Schultz and Adrianne Pasquarelli, "The 9 Most Popular Insurance Ad Characters, Ranked," *Advertising Age*, January 13, 2022, https://adage.com/article/marketing-news-strategy/most-popular-insurance-ad-characters-ranked/2392531; Yi-Lin Tsai and Elisabeth Honka, "Non-Informational Advertising Informing Consumers: How Advertising Affects Consumers' Decision-Making in the U.S. Auto Insurance Industry," *SSRN Electronic Journal*, 10.2139/ssrn.3094448.

Developing the Major Selling Idea

It is difficult to pinpoint the inspiration for a big idea or teach advertising creatives an easy way to find one. As noted earlier, Arthur Kover conducted a study of advertising copywriters to understand how they approach the creative process and search for big ideas. He found that they view the purpose of a big idea as breaking through the advertising clutter and delivering a message.[62] Advertising professor John Rossiter argues that most copywriters focus on communicating the *key benefit claim*, which refers to the benefit thought by the copywriter to be the key to selling the advertised product. He notes that most creative ideas are based on finding ways to dramatically and effectively convey the key benefit claim.[63] As noted earlier, the key benefit claim is often explicit in the tagline that is used as the basis for the advertising campaign, such as the "quicker picker upper" theme for Bounty paper towels or "the ultimate driving machine" for BMW. However, the creative team must still work to develop effective ways to communicate this message in the executions of the advertising and other components of the IMC program.

There are myriad ways that creative personnel can approach the search for big ideas and how to execute them. However, over the years several classic approaches have emerged that can guide the creative team's search for a major selling idea and the development of effective advertising. Among the four best-known approaches are:

- Using a unique selling proposition.
- Creating a brand image.
- Finding the inherent drama.
- Positioning.

Unique Selling Proposition   The concept of the **unique selling proposition (USP)** was developed by Rosser Reeves, former chair of the Ted Bates agency, and is described in his influential book *Reality in Advertising*. Reeves noted three characteristics of unique selling propositions:

1. Each advertisement must make a proposition to the consumer. Not just words, not just product puffery, not just show-window advertising. Each advertisement must say to each reader: "Buy this product and you will get this benefit."
2. The proposition must be one that the competition either cannot or does not offer. It must be unique either in the brand or in the claim.
3. The proposition must be strong enough to move the mass millions—that is, pull over new customers to your brand.[64]

EXHIBIT 8–16

This ThermaCare ad uses a unique selling proposition.

ThermaCare

Reeves said the attribute claim or benefit that forms the basis of the USP should dominate the ad and be emphasized through repetitive advertising. An example of a brand that uses a USP approach for its advertising is ThermaCare heatwraps (Exhibit 8–16). The brand has patented heat cells that penetrate to increase circulation and accelerate healing as well as provide relief from back pain, which is a problem for many people.

For Reeves's approach to work, there must be a truly unique product or service attribute, benefit, or inherent advantage that can be used in the claim. The approach may require considerable research on the product and consumers, not only to determine the USP but also to document the claim. As we will see in Chapter 20, the Federal Trade Commission objects to advertisers' making claims of superiority or uniqueness without providing supporting data. Also, some companies have sued their competitors for making unsubstantiated uniqueness claims.

Advertisers must also consider whether the unique selling proposition affords them a *sustainable competitive advantage* that competitors cannot easily copy. In the packaged-goods field in particular, companies quickly match a brand feature for feature, so advertising based on USPs becomes ineffective. For example, a few years ago Molson Coors introduced MGD 64, a 64-calorie version of its Miller Genuine Draft brand and the lowest-calorie domestic beer on the market. However, within a year its major rival Anheuser-Busch launched Bud Select 55, which contained only 55 calories, after noting the success Miller had with its ultra-low-calorie beer.[65]

Some advertising experts question the USP approach, noting that few products have meaningful differences and today's speed of innovation makes it very difficult to maintain a performance edge. They also note that research from behavioral economics shows that consumer motivations are often more emotional than rational and argue that the brand is the only USP that really matters. Thus, marketers must be careful not to have such a singular focus on a USP that it interferes with creative advertising that contributes to the emotional aspect of a brand.[66]

Creating a Brand Image In many product and service categories, competing brands are so similar that it is very difficult to find or create a unique attribute or benefit to use as the major selling idea. Many of the packaged-goods products that account for most of the advertising dollars spent in the United States are difficult to differentiate on a functional or performance basis. The creative strategy used to sell these products is based on the development of a strong, memorable identity for the brand through **image advertising**.

David Ogilvy popularized the idea of brand image in his famous book *Confessions of an Advertising Man*. Ogilvy said that with image advertising, "every advertisement should be thought of as a contribution to the complex symbol which is the brand image." He argued that the image or personality of the brand is particularly important when brands are similar:

> The greater the similarity between brands, the less part reason plays in brand selection. There isn't any significant difference between the various brands of whiskey, or cigarettes, or beer. They are all about the same. And so are the cake mixes and the detergents and the margarines. The manufacturer who dedicates his advertising to building the most sharply defined personality for his brand will get the largest share of the market at the highest profit. By the same token, the manufacturers who will find themselves up the creek are those shortsighted opportunists who siphon off their advertising funds for promotions.[67]

EXHIBIT 8–17

Tory Burch uses advertising to build an image of style and sophistication.

Tory Burch LLC

Image advertising has become increasingly popular and is used as the main selling idea for a variety of products and services, including soft drinks, liquor, cigarettes, cars, airlines, financial services, perfume/colognes, and clothing. Many consumers wear various brands of jeans, such as Levi's, Madewell, or AG, and drink certain brands of beer or soft drinks because of the image of these brands. The key to successful image advertising is developing an image that will appeal to product users. This is often done by associating a brand with certain symbols or artifacts that have cultural meaning. For example, Marlboro became the leading brand of cigarettes by using advertising that associates the brand with the cowboy, who is perceived as rugged, individualistic, and a symbol of freedom and independence. Many fashion brands build an image for their clothing and accessories by using ads that feature attractive models and visual appeals that convey psychosocial associations and feelings such as sexy, stylish, glamorous, and sophisticated. Advertising for brands such as Gucci, Michael Kors, and Tory Burch embody many of these image characteristics as a way of building an emotional connection with young women who are interested in style and fashion. The Tory Burch ad shown in Exhibit 8–17 is a good example of this as it creates an image of style and sophistication for the brand.

Finding the Inherent Drama Another approach to determining the major selling idea is finding the **inherent drama** or characteristic of the product that makes the consumer purchase it. The inherent drama approach expresses the advertising philosophy of Leo Burnett, founder of the Leo Burnett agency in Chicago. Burnett believed that there is almost always something about a brand that separates it from all other brands and keeps it in the marketplace. He argued that this inherent drama "is often hard to find but it is always there, and once found it is the most interesting and believable of all advertising appeals."[68] Burnett believed that good creative minds know how to bring inherent drama to life through advertising that is based on a foundation of consumer benefits with an emphasis on the dramatic element in expressing those benefits.

Burnett advocated a down-home type of advertising that presents the message in a warm and realistic way. Some of the more famous ads developed by his agency using the inherent drama approach are for McDonald's, Maytag appliances, Kellogg's cereals, and Hallmark cards. Leo Burnett has created a number of poignant and dramatic advertising campaigns for Hallmark cards over the past 25 years based on the approach. An excellent example of advertising based on the approach is an awarding-winning campaign created by Leo Burnett Madrid for Pernod Ricard liqueur brand Ruavieja called "The Time We Have Left," which centered on an online calculator that helped people determine how much longer in their lifetime they had to spend with family and friends. In Spain it is common to take time to enjoy a digestive liqueur like Ruavieja after lunch or dinner to make the moment last longer with the people around you. However, the challenge facing the brand was that it was caught up in a world where people were no longer participating in slow-paced traditions because they are in a constant state of rush, and time was becoming a scarce commodity.

The "Time We Have Left" campaign encouraged people to change their behavior and find more time to see each other by telling them exactly how much time they had left together. Leo Burnett and client Pernod Ricard gathered data from the National Institute of Statistics on life expectancy as well as studies related to the likelihood of maintaining the frequency of encounters over time. Based on this information they built a fairly accurate tool that predicted how much time you had left with someone in terms

EXHIBIT 8–18

The "Time We Have Left" campaign for Ruavieja liqueur used an inherent drama approach for the big idea.

Licores Ruavieja

of days and hours. A very poignant video was created to promote the tool that captured real people's reactions when confronted with the algorithm's results and compelled people to reassess their perception of time and spend more time with loved ones (Exhibit 8–18). The spot went viral and Pernod Ricard followed it up by sponsoring people's trips within Spain to reconnect with loved ones.[69]

Positioning   The concept of *positioning* as a basis for advertising strategy was introduced by Jack Trout and Al Ries in the early 1970s and has become a popular basis of creative development.[70] The basic idea is that advertising is used to establish or "position" the product or service in a particular place in the consumer's mind. Positioning is done for companies as well as for brands. Many of the top brands in various product and service categories have retained their market leadership because they have established and maintained a strong position or identity in the minds of consumers.[71] For example, Crest has built and maintained the success of its toothpaste based on the position of cavity prevention, while BMW's positioning as "the ultimate driving machine" transcends and helps differentiate its entire product line.

Trout and Ries originally described positioning as the image consumers had of the brand in relation to competing brands in the product or service category, but the concept has been expanded beyond direct competitive positioning. As discussed in Chapter 2, companies and brands can be positioned on the basis of product or service attributes, price/quality, usage or application, type of user, cultural symbols, or product class. Any of these can spark a major selling idea that becomes the basis of the creative strategy and results in the brand's occupying a particular place in the minds of the target audience. Since positioning can be done on the basis of a distinctive attribute, the positioning and unique selling proposition approaches can overlap. Positioning approaches have been used as the foundation for a number of successful creative strategies. In some situations marketers recognize that they must adapt their positioning strategy for different market segments or modify it to connect better with their target market. And in some cases, a repositioning of the whole company or brand may be needed.

For example, Subway, which is the largest restaurant chain based on the number of locations, introduced its "Eat Fresh Refresh" repositioning strategy in 2021 after seven consecutive years of sales decline in the United States. The effort included the largest menu overhaul in Subway's history, including adding 12 new sandwiches with updated ingredients, and changes in its stores and on its app to better facilitate its growing delivery and pickup business. In 2022 Subway launched its largest advertising campaign ever to explain how each sandwich earned a coveted spot in the all-star Subway series roster. The star athlete–studded campaign features former NBA star and television analyst Charles Barkley and former Dallas Cowboys quarterback and NFL television analyst Tony Romo as the voices of Subway's Eat Fresh Refresh special series draft telecast. They provide color commentary on the 12 sandwiches that earned the coveted spots on the roster (Exhibit 8–19). A number of other star athletes are featured in the campaign including Olympic gymnast Simone Biles, NBA star Stephen Curry, and former NFL stars Rob Gronkowski and Marshawn Lynch.[72]

Contemporary Approaches to the Big Idea

The USP, brand image, inherent-drama, and positioning approaches are often used as the basis of the creative strategy for ad campaigns. These creative styles have become associated with some of the most successful creative minds in advertising and their agencies.[73] Agencies are by no means limited to any one creative approach. The famous "Marlboro Country" campaign, a classic example of image advertising, was

EXHIBIT 8-19
Subway used the "Eat Fresh Refresh" campaign to reposition the sandwich chain around freshness.

Subway IP LLC

developed by Leo Burnett Co. Many different agencies have followed the unique selling proposition approach advocated by Rosser Reeves. The challenge to the creative specialist or team is to find a major selling idea—whether it is based on a unique selling proposition, brand image, inherent drama, position in the market, or some other approach—and use it as a guide in developing an effective creative strategy. While these classic approaches are used by many creative specialists, many other styles are available and are indeed necessary given the changes that have occurred in media and technology over the past two decades.

Advertisers are facing major challenges in their search for the big idea in today's world. They must develop creative ideas that can differentiate their brands and extend beyond traditional mass media. Most marketers and their agencies recognize that they must come up with big ideas that can be used across a variety of media, engage consumers, and enter into a dialogue with them. Many of the approaches that have worked well in the traditional media-centric world of print and television advertising may not be effective in the complex, multiscreen world in which consumers live today. Jean Lin, CEO of the digital network Isobar, argues that technology and accessibility to information has forever changed people's relationship with brands along with how they form perceptions and opinions. She argues that the role of a contemporary creative agency must change, and notes: "In this new world, how we come up with creative solutions has to change. We must embrace interactive and nonlinear messaging. Hand-held devices and mobility means everywhere; stories need to be told seamlessly across screens. And business ideas need to be nurtured through creativity, innovation, and imagination."[74]

The challenge of developing creative advertising that captures the attention of consumers and impacts them has clearly become even greater with the proliferation of new media. Lee Clow, chairman emeritus of TBWA/Media Arts Lab, which is Apple's lead creative agency and a recipient of the prestigious Lion of St. Mark Award given to an individual for a contribution to creativity in advertising, was asked to comment on how advertising has changed over the past several decades and the creative challenge facing agencies. Clow responded:

> "Brands have the ability to connect with people in all kinds of ways and have an ongoing dialogue and relationship with them as opposed to the monologue, how it used to be. We haven't come close to figuring out how to use all these new-media opportunities and most clients are very conflicted about what media they should use and why. They keep thinking there's some new silver bullet in the new media world that will allow them to save money or find a new way to twist consumers' arms."[75]

Clow summarizes the challenge facing those who work on the creative side in the new world of advertising quite well. Marketers will continue to challenge their agencies, as well as themselves, to find innovative ideas and creative solutions for advertising and other forms of marketing communications.

Summary

The creative development and execution of the advertising message are crucial parts of a firm's integrated marketing communications program and are often the key to the success of a marketing campaign. Marketers generally turn to ad agencies to develop, prepare, and implement their creative strategy since these agencies are specialists in the creative function of advertising. The creative specialist or team is responsible for developing an effective way to communicate the marketer's message to the customer. Other individuals on both the client and the agency sides work with the creative specialists to develop the creative strategy, implement it, and evaluate its effectiveness.

The challenge facing the writers, artists, and others who develop ads is to be creative and come up with fresh, unique, and appropriate ideas that can be used as solutions to communications problems. Creativity in advertising is a process of several stages, including preparation, incubation, illumination, verification, and revision. Various sources of information are available to help the creative specialists determine the best campaign theme, appeal, or execution style. Many companies use research for input to the creative process including qualitative techniques such as focus groups and ethnographic studies. Research is also used to pretest advertising messages to determine how consumers evaluate and will respond to them, although some companies are foregoing copy testing, as the changing media consumption environment of consumers requires them to develop more content and move more quickly.

Most advertising is part of a series of messages that make up an IMC or advertising campaign that is based on a central theme or idea. The campaign theme is usually expressed through a slogan or tagline. Creative strategy development is guided by specific goals and objectives and is based on a number of factors, including the target audience, the basic problem the advertising must address, the objectives the message seeks to accomplish, and the major selling idea or key benefit the advertiser wants to communicate. These factors are generally stated in a copy platform, which is a work plan used to guide development of the ad campaign. An important part of creative strategy is determining the major selling idea that will become the central theme of the campaign. There are several approaches to doing this, including using a unique selling proposition, creating a brand image, looking for inherent drama in the brand, and positioning.

Advertisers are facing major challenges in their search for big ideas that extend beyond traditional mass media. They must develop big ideas that can be used across a variety of media, engage consumers, and enter into a dialogue with them. Many of the approaches that have worked well in the traditional media-centric world of print and television advertising may not be effective in the complex, multiscreen world in which consumers live today.

Key Terms

creative strategy 258
creative tactics 258
advertising creativity 262
divergence 262
relevance 262
account planning 268
general preplanning
   input 269

product- or service-specific
   preplanning input 270
problem detection 270
focus groups 270
ethnographic research 272
storyboard 274
animatic 274
advertising campaign 275

campaign theme 275
slogan (tagline) 275
creative brief 277
major selling idea 279
unique selling proposition
   (USP) 281
image advertising 282
inherent drama 283

Discussion Questions

1. Discuss how the social media platform TikTok is impacting advertising creativity. Do you think TikTok's impact will continue into the future? Why or why not? (LO 8-1, 8-2, 8-3)

2. Discuss the role and importance of creativity in advertising. Do you think advertising agencies often emphasize creativity at the expense of developing ads that can help generate sales for a product or service? What can clients do to avoid this problem? (LO 8-1)

3. Advertising creativity is viewed as the ability to generate unique and appropriate ideas that can be used as solutions to communication problems. This definition suggests that a creative ad is one that is novel but also relevant or appropriate. Find an example of an advertisement (either a print ad, TV commercial, or online ad/video) that is novel but not necessarily relevant to the product or service. Discuss why the client would have approved this ad. (LO 8-1)

4. Discuss the various factors that account for the way divergence can be achieved in advertising creativity. Find an example of an advertisement that reflects these various factors and explain how it does so. (LO 8-1)

5. The meta-analysis study of advertising creativity found that ads that have won creative awards tend to be higher in originality but had a weaker impact on consumer response. Discuss the implications of these findings for the significance of advertising creative awards. Why do you think so many agencies spend time and effort entering creative award competitions? (LO 8-1, 8-2)

6. Assume that you have been hired as an account planner by an advertising agency and assigned to work on the advertising campaign for a new brand of bottled water. Describe the various types of general and product-specific preplanning input you might provide to the creative team. (LO 8-2)

7. Many advertising creative personnel are opposed to research and analytics as they argue that they stifle the creative process. Discuss the problems, as well as the value, of using research and analytics as input to the process of creating advertisements. (LO 8-2, 8-3)

8. IMC Perspective 8–2 discusses the various creative approaches used by companies to advertise automotive insurance. Research has shown that advertising by insurance companies has little impact on consumers' final decision of what insurer to go with. Given this, why do you think auto insurance companies such as GEICO, State Farm, Progressive, or Allstate spend so much money on advertising? (LO 8-3, 8-4)

9. Discuss the role of an advertising slogan in an advertising campaign and some of the factors that should be considered in developing an effective slogan. Find an example of a good slogan or tagline as well as one that does not communicate effectively. Discuss the reasons why you view these as either good or bad examples of advertising slogans. (LO 8-3)

10. What is a creative brief? Discuss the various elements that should be included in a creative brief and why they are important. (LO 8-3)

11. Find an example of an ad or campaign that you think reflects one of the approaches used to develop a major selling idea such as unique selling proposition, brand image, inherent drama, or positioning. Discuss how the major selling idea is reflected in this ad or campaign. (LO 8-4)

Creative Strategy:
Implementation and Evaluation

Applebee's Restaurants LLC

Learning Objectives

LO 9-1 | Compare the different types of appeals used in advertising.

LO 9-2 | Identify creative execution styles and their most appropriate applications.

LO 9-3 | Discuss tactics for the creation of print ads and TV commercials as well as online advertising.

LO 9-4 | Discuss guidelines for clients to evaluate creative work.

"Fancy Like" Applebee's

In May 2021 Applebee's President John Cywinski received a text message from a friend about a song he had just heard on the radio with lyrics about eating at Applebee's. The song was "Fancy Like," by country singer Walker Hayes, which was about to become a viral sensation. The irresistible song was about how, when an average couple with simple tastes is looking to live it up for a night of fine dining, Applebee's is a big step up from a drive-through restaurant. When Cywinski heard the song, he was blown away. "Holy smokes, these lyrics are so much about our brand!" In the song, Hayes sings about going to Applebee's on a date night and getting a Bourbon Street Steak with an Oreo Shake.

Cywinski recognized that the lyrics captured Applebee's image as an unpretentious, inviting, welcoming, and neighborly restaurant. The chain has regulars that are there on a daily or weekly basis for lunch or dinner and have great relationships with Applebee's team members. He quickly reached out to Walker Hayes, who he learned is a loyal Applebee's customer in real life, as a typical date night for the Nashville-based country star and his wife really is Applebee's.

Applebee's struck a deal with Hayes and began working with him to create a commercial around the song, which was not yet the chart-topping crossover hit it was about to become in mid-June. That's when Hayes's 15-year-old daughter Lila (one of the family's six kids), who often teamed up to do dance videos for his songs, told him: "Dad, it needs a dance." Father and daughter (shown in the opening photo) spent 30 minutes making up the dance and then posted it on TikTok, and the video was like lightning in a bottle. Overnight, the TikTok video hit 2.3 million views and within a few days it reached 14 million. The video spawned a myriad of reenactments across TikTok and beyond—including people filming themselves doing the dance at Applebee's. "Fancy Like" became the number one country song and quickly rose to the top of the Billboard Hot 100 chart. By November nearly 900,000 different TikTok videos had been created using the song along with 100 million Spotify streams and more than 50 million YouTube views of the original music video.

Applebee's capitalized on its newfound viral fame and the free exposure by creating a series of TV commercials featuring the song and various renditions of the dance from TikTok. It also brought back the Oreo Shake, which got a shout out in the song but had been cut from the menu during the pandemic because it was too hard to make. They photographed Walker and his wife eating Bourbon Street Steak and having shakes and used the photos for in-store merchandising. A "Fancy Like" meal was added to the menu as well. The advertising campaign also added to the popularity of "Fancy Like" as many people were waiting for Applebee's to do something to capitalize on the hit song and TikTok video to take advantage of the momentum that had built up.

In addition to being part of a pop culture phenomenon, the Applebee's ad campaign and viral attention had a big impact on Applebee's sales. Same-store sales increased each month from July to September by 12 percent, and Applebee's outpaced sales of its casual-dining competitors by 9.3 percent. Applebee's and its agency, Grey New York, received the Grand Effie Award for 2022 for the "Fancy Like" campaign with one of the judges noting, "It was clear that the team was following the lead of culture versus trying to create it, which made it feel organic and authentic. 'Fancy Like' Applebee's also shows that a great idea can come from anywhere—if you're ready."

Applebee's chief marketing officer, Joel Yashinsky, noted the importance of capitalizing on cultural moments but also doing so in a way that was natural, not forced, and authentic to Hayes. Yashinsky says: "Brands can pay a lot of money for something to happen or to work with an athlete, movie star or musician. But, when its authentic, lean into that. Those are really special and unique. It's been so fun to work on this idea, song, this moment because it's so real and authentic."

Walker Hayes and Applebee's now have a partnership and future collaborations are planned. When asked about the success of "Fancy Like" and the ad campaign, Walker noted that one of his favorite things was the return of the Oreo Shake to the menu and being part of a song that changed a massive food chain's menu. He is still a patron of Applebee's although crowd control can be a problem when he and his wife are there for date night. True to his down-home country style, he says: "There's a picture of my wife and me laminated on every table at Applebee's around the country. We

continued

steal 'em every time we go there—maybe we'll get in trouble one day."

Probably not, Walker.

Sources: Tony Hao, "Applebee's Tiktok-Viral Walker Hayes Collab Wins 2022 U.S. Grand Effie," *Advertising Age*, June 14, 2022, https://adage.com/article/agency-news/applebees-tiktok-viral-walker-hayes-collab-wins-2022-us-grand-effie/242025; Alexandra Bower, "Applebee's Didn't Commission 'Fancy Like,' but It Was Happy to Have an Organic Brand Partner," *Adweek*, March 2, 2022, https://www.adweek.com/brand-marketing/applebees-fancy-like-walker-hayes-brand-partner/; Joe Guskowski, "How the Viral Song 'Fancy Like' Rocked Applebee's Summer," *Restaurant Business*, November 5, 2021, https://www.restaurantbusinessonline.com/marketing/how-viral-song-fancy-rocked-applebees-summer.

In Chapter 8 we discussed the importance of advertising creativity and examined the various stages of the creative process. We also focused on determining what the advertising message should communicate. This chapter focuses on *how* the message will be executed. A successful advertising campaign requires creative strategy that uses the right type of appeal and is executed properly. We examine various advertising appeals and execution styles as well as tactics for implementing print, television, and online advertising. The chapter concludes by presenting criteria marketers can use to evaluate the creative work of their agencies.

APPEALS AND EXECUTION STYLES

The **advertising appeal** refers to the approach used to attract the attention of consumers and/or to influence their feelings toward the product, service, or cause. An advertising appeal can also be viewed as "something that moves people, speaks to their wants or needs, and excites their interest."[1] The **creative execution style** is the way a particular appeal is turned into an advertising message presented to the consumer. According to William Weilbacher:

> The appeal can be said to form the underlying content of the advertisement, and the execution the way in which that content is presented. Advertising appeals and executions are usually independent of each other; that is, a particular appeal can be executed in a variety of ways and a particular means of execution can be applied to a variety of advertising appeals. Advertising appeals tend to adapt themselves to all media, whereas some kinds of executional devices are more adaptable to some media than others.[2]

Advertising Appeals

Many different appeals can be used as the basis for advertising messages. At the broadest level, these approaches are generally broken into two categories: informational/rational appeals and emotional appeals. In this section, we focus on ways to use rational and emotional appeals as part of a creative strategy. We also consider how rational and emotional appeals can be combined in developing the advertising message.

Informational/Rational Appeals **Informational/rational appeals** focus on the consumer's practical, functional, or utilitarian need for the product or service and emphasize features of a product or service and/or the benefits or reasons for owning or using a particular brand. The content of these messages emphasizes facts, learning, and the logic of persuasion.[3] Rational-based appeals tend to be informative, and advertisers using them generally attempt to convince consumers that their product or service has a particular attribute(s) or provides a specific benefit that satisfies their needs. Their objective is to persuade the target audience to buy the brand because it is the best available or does a better job of meeting consumers' needs. For example, Exhibit 9–1 shows a rational appeal ad for the Honda Pilot SUV that focuses on its advanced technological features and dependability.

Many rational motives can be used as the basis for advertising appeals, including comfort, convenience, economy, health, and sensory benefits such as touch, taste, and smell. Other rational motives or purchase criteria commonly used in advertising include quality, dependability, durability, efficiency, efficacy, and performance. The particular features, benefits, or evaluative criteria that are important to consumers and can serve as the basis of an informational/rational appeal vary from one product or service category to another as well as among various market segments.

Weilbacher identified several types of advertising appeals that fall under the category of rational approaches, among them feature, competitive advantage, price, news, and product/service popularity appeals.

Ads that use a *feature appeal* focus on the dominant traits of the product or service. These ads tend to be highly informative and present the customer with a number of important product attributes or features that will lead to favorable attitudes and can be used as the basis for a rational purchase decision. Technical and high-involvement products such as consumer electronics and automobiles often use this type of advertising appeal. However, a feature appeal can be used for a variety of products and services. These types of appeals often show how product attributes can result in specific benefits for consumers. For example, advertisements using this type of appeal will list and/or discuss the specific features or benefits of the product or service in the ad copy. The ad shown in Exhibit 9-2 for the Blue Cash Everyday Card from American Express is a good example of advertising that uses a feature appeal. The copy lists the various places where card users receive cash back on their purchases as well other security-related

EXHIBIT 9–3

Southwest Airlines uses a variation of a price appeal to promote its Wanna Get Away Plus fare option.

Southwest Airlines Co.

EXHIBIT 9–4

Titleist uses a popularity appeal by promoting that it is the #1 ball in golf and is committed to being the best.

Titleist

BEING #1 IS A MINDSET

Being #1 is more than a number, it's a mindset.
It's a commitment to being the best you can be, no matter what you're striving for.
Titleist. The #1 ball in golf.

#1 ball in golf.

features of the Blue Cash Everyday Card, such as purchase protection, extended warranty, and mobile fraud alerts.

When a *competitive advantage appeal* is used, the advertiser makes either a direct or an indirect comparison to another brand (or brands) and usually claims superiority on one or more attributes. This type of appeal was discussed in Chapter 6 under Comparative Advertising.

A *favorable price appeal* makes the price offer the dominant point of the message. Price appeal advertising is used most often by retailers to announce sales, special offers, or low everyday prices. Price appeal ads are often used by national advertisers, particularly during economic down times or to reach price sensitive market segments. Most fast-food chains have made price an important part of their marketing strategy through promotional deals and "value menus" or lower overall prices, and their advertising strategy is designed to communicate this. Price-based appeals are also often used by business-to-business marketers to advertise products and/or services and promote their value or affordability. Many other types of advertisers use price appeals as well, such as airlines and car-rental companies. For example, Southwest Airlines uses a variation of price appeal with ads such as the one shown in Exhibit 9–3 promoting "Wanna Get Away Plus," a new fare product that adds more flexibility, options, and rewards to the carrier's fare lineup. The new fare class offers a fourth option in Southwest's fare system that is just above the more discounted and restrictive "Wanna Get Away" fare.

News appeals are those in which some type of news or announcement about the product, service, or company dominates the ad. This type of appeal can be used for a new product or service or to inform consumers of significant modifications or improvements. This appeal works best when a company has important news it wants to communicate to its target market. For example, airlines sometimes use news appeals when they begin offering service to new cities or opening new routes as a way of informing consumers as well as generating media interest that can result in publicity for them.

Product/service popularity appeals stress the popularity of a product or service by pointing out the number of consumers who use the brand, the number who have switched to it, the number of experts who recommend it, or its leadership position in the market. The main point of this type of advertising appeal is that the wide use of the brand proves its quality or value and other customers should consider using it. The ad for Titleist golf balls shown in Exhibit 9–4 uses a popularity appeal. The ad notes that Titleist is the #1 ball in golf and, like many top players, is committed to being the best. Titleist is the leading brand of golf balls, and its popularity among tour professionals has a strong influence on the purchase decisions of amateur golfers.

Emotional Appeals Emotional appeals relate to the customers' social and/or psychological needs for purchasing a product or service. Many consumers' motives for their purchase decisions are emotional, and their feelings about a brand can be more important than knowledge of its features or

FIGURE 9–1

Bases for Emotional Appeals

Personal States or Feelings		Social-Based Feelings
Safety	Arousal/stimulation	Recognition
Security	Sorrow/grief	Status
Fear	Pride	Respect
Love	Achievement/accomplishment	Involvement
Affection	Self-esteem	Embarrassment
Happiness	Actualization	Affiliation/belonging
Joy	Pleasure	Rejection
Nostalgia	Ambition	Acceptance
Sentiment	Comfort	Approval
Excitement		

attributes. Advertisers for many products and services view rational, information-based appeals as dull. Many advertisers believe appeals to consumers' emotions work better at selling brands that do not differ markedly from competing brands, since rational differentiation of them is difficult.[4] Many feelings or needs can serve as the basis for advertising appeals designed to influence consumers on an emotional level, as shown in Figure 9–1. These appeals are based on the psychological states or feelings directed to the self (such as pleasure or excitement), as well as those with a more social orientation (such as status or recognition).

Advertisers can use emotional appeals in many ways in their creative strategy. Kamp and Macinnis note that commercials often rely on the concept of *emotional integration*, whereby they portray the characters in the ad as experiencing an emotional benefit or outcome from using a product or service.[5] Ads using humor, sex, and other appeals that are very entertaining, arousing, upbeat, and/or exciting can affect the emotions of consumers and put them in a favorable frame of mind. Many TV advertisers use poignant ads that bring a lump to viewers' throats. Hallmark, Campbell's Soup, Procter & Gamble, and McDonald's often create commercials that evoke feelings of warmth, nostalgia, and/or sentiment. Marketers use emotional appeals in hopes that the positive feelings they evoke will transfer to the brand and/or company. Research shows that positive mood states and feelings created by advertising can have a favorable effect on consumers' evaluations of a brand.[6] Studies also show that emotional advertising is better remembered than nonemotional messages.[7]

The effectiveness of emotion-based appeals has also been documented in research conducted by Hamish Pringle and Peter Field and is discussed in their book *Brand Immortality*.[8] Pringle and Field analyzed 880 case studies of successful advertising campaigns submitted for the United Kingdom–based Institute of Practitioners in Advertising Effectiveness Award competition over the past three decades and included campaigns from the UK as well as international competitions. Their analysis compared advertising campaigns that relied primarily on emotional appeals versus those that used rational persuasion and information. A key finding from their study is that advertising campaigns with purely emotional content are nearly twice as likely to generate large profit gains than are campaigns using only rational content. The emotional-only campaigns were also more effective than those that used a combination of emotional and rational content. Their research also showed that one of the reasons why emotional campaigns work so well is that they reduce price sensitivity and strengthen the ability of brands to charge a price premium, which contributes to profitability. They also found that emotional campaigns continue to work well during economic downturns.[9]

While emotional appeals are often executed through television commercials, many marketers are now implementing them online through videos that provide an opportunity for popular messages to go viral. Digital and Social Media Perspective 9–1 discusses a campaign created by Unilever's Dove brand that highlights the insecurity created among young girls and women by heavily edited selfies on social media. The campaign features a

Dove Fights Digital Distortion with "Reverse Selfie"

Ogilvy UK

The media and the advertising industry have long been criticized for setting an unrealistic standard of beauty that most women believe they cannot achieve. A few years into the new millennium, Unilever's Dove brand conducted research showing that only 2 percent of the women around the world considered themselves conventionally beautiful and 75 percent said they wanted to see a more accurate portrayal of beauty in the media. Based on these findings, Unilever embarked on an integrated marketing campaign designed to challenge the stereotypical view of beauty, celebrate diversity, and make all women feel beautiful. In 2004 Unilever launched the Campaign for Real Beauty globally featuring everyday women whose physical appearance was outside the stereotypical norms of beauty presented by supermodels.

Two years into the campaign, Dove released Evolution, an impactful video that uncovered the truth behind the images of beautiful women seen in magazines, on television, and online. The video used time-lapse photography to show a woman going from make-up free and ordinary to a glamorous supermodel after spending hours on makeup artistry, hair stylists, and Photoshop enhancements. The video ended with the message: "It's no wonder our perception of beauty is distorted." The video became a viral phenomenon as it received millions of viewings after being posted on YouTube and social media. In 2015 *Advertising Age* had a panel of influential and acclaimed advertising creatives and executives pick the best campaigns of the new millennium. Dove's Campaign for Real Beauty was selected as the best of the 21st century so far. The panel used terms such as *ground-breaking*, *bold*, *transparent*, and *authentic* to describe it.

Dove and its long-time global agency Ogilvy have remained on the frontlines of the fight against unrealistic beauty standards for the past two decades and are now facing a new challenge with the ubiquity of social media—the selfie. Research conducted by the Dove Self-Esteem Project has shown that by the age of 13, 80 percent of girls have downloaded a filter or used an app to change how they look in photos; two-thirds try to hide or change at least one body part or feature before posting a picture, and more than one-third say they don't look good enough without some form of photo editing. Some survey respondents admitted spending up to 30 minutes editing a picture before posting.

In 2021 Dove renewed its fight against unrealistic beauty standards with a new campaign that highlights the damage caused by heavily edited selfies on social media. At the heart of the campaign is a 60-second film called "Reverse Selfie," which is a sequel to Evolution and other videos Dove has created to expose the impossible beauty ideals of the advertising industry and media. The video features a young woman who drastically edits a picture of herself before posting it online. The film plays backward, starting with the posted selfie, then reversing the various tweaks and staging that went into creating the image before finally revealing that it's not a woman at all behind the picture but actually a young girl, barely in her teens. The spot ends with the statement, "The pressure of social media is hurting our girl's self-esteem. More screen time during the pandemic has made things worse."

Ogilvy executives noted that the agency's creative team spent a long time finding the right girl for the video, talking to girls about their experiences of how they used these apps and how they felt about themselves. The young girl shown in the video was cast specifically because she'd had very real experiences about losing confidence and self-esteem. Ogilvy noted: "It was a very emotional performance from her which was close to the experience she went through."

The focus of the campaign is on reversing the damage social media continues to have on young women and girls as the practice of making digital edits to one's facial features in photos has soared as a consequence of unrealistic beauty ideals in social media. The executive vice president of Dove notes: "Digital distortion is happening more than ever as tools once only available to professionals can now be accessed by young girls at the touch of a button without regulation. There has been intensifying pressure on young people to edit and distort their appearance to reflect an unachievable ideal."

The reverse selfie video has been delivered on television globally as well as on social media using the hashtag #TheSelfieTalk. It has a high presence on Instagram given the platform's focus on the sharing of photos. The social media posts often repurpose the campaign's video and images into shorter snippets and some simple graphics posted with statistics about the prevalence of selfie editing. The integrated campaign also includes a set of posters, each split in half and depicting natural faces of girls against heavily edited versions, in order to emphasize the impact of retouching apps.

While "Reverse Selfie" is designed to shock girls and young women by showing them how manipulated photos can leave them feeling inadequate, Dove also wanted to offer a solution to the problem, so the video ends with a message of support that urges parents to have 'The Selfie Talk' with their children. The video directs them to a dedicated section of the Dove website that has a confidence kit that empowers teachers, parents, and young people to go online to understand how to fight back against social pressures. Dove has also joined forces with several celebrities to tackle the problem and promote 'The Selfie Talk' including Grammy award–winning singer and body confidence advocate Lizzo. Social media platform TikTok also entered into a partnership with Dove in a campaign to promote body inclusivity and acceptance.

The metrics shown in the accompanying image clearly demonstrate the tremendous impact the "Reverse Selfie" IMC campaign has had thus far, as it has generated billions of impressions globally and is helping reverse the negative effects of retouching apps. However, in the age of social media the battle against unrealistic beauty standards will continue, and Dove is likely to be there to fight it.

Sources: Rebecca Fulleylove, "Dove Tackles Self-Esteem and Heavily Edited Selfies in Latest Campaign," *Creative Review*, April 23, 2021, https://www.creativereview.co.uk/dove-reverseselfie-ad-campaign/; Sara Spray, "Dove and Lizzo Unite in Powerful Campaign Against Unrealistic Selfies," *Adweek*, April 21, 2021, https://www.adweek.com/brand-marketing/doveand-lizzo-unite-in-powerful-campaign-against-unrealistic-selfies/; Imogen Watson, "Reverse Selfie: Dove's Mission to Combat Social Media's Negative Effects," *The Drum*, April 28, 2021, https://www.thedrum.com/news/2021/04/28/reverse-selfie-dove-s-mission-combat-social-media-snegative-effects; Ad Age Staff, "Top Campaigns of the 21st Century," *Advertising Age*, January 12, 2015, pp. 14–22.

video called "Reverse Selfie" that shows a young girl who drastically edits a picture of herself before posting it online. The video has amassed millions of views online.

Another reason for using emotional appeals is to influence consumers' interpretations of their product usage experience. One way of doing this is through what is known as transformational advertising. A **transformational ad** is defined as "one which associates the experience of using (consuming) the advertised brand with a unique set of psychological characteristics which would not typically be associated with the brand experience to the same degree without exposure to the advertisement."[10]

Transformational ads create feelings, images, meanings, and beliefs about the product or service that may be activated when consumers use it, transforming their interpretation of the usage experience. Christopher Puto and William Wells note that a transformational ad has two characteristics:

1. It must make the experience of using the product richer, warmer, more exciting, and/or more enjoyable than that obtained solely from an objective description of the advertised brand.
2. It must connect the experience of the advertisement so tightly with the experience of using the brand that consumers cannot remember the brand without recalling the experience generated by the advertisement.[11]

Transformational advertising can help differentiate a product or service by making the consumption experience more enjoyable by suggesting the type of experiences consumers might have when they consume the product or service. This type of advertising is often used by companies in the travel industry to help consumers envision the experience or feeling they might have when they take a trip such as a cruise, visit a particular destination, or go on vacation with friends and/or family.

An example of the effective use of transformational advertising is the recent "Only Your People" campaign for Vrbo. The vacation home rental company's strategy is to focus on friends and families that want to book an entire large home. With millions of vacation homes to choose from, its app makes it easy to find the perfect place to be together with whoever you call family, which it views as broad and

EXHIBIT 9–5

Vrbo uses transformational advertising as part of the "Only Your People" campaign, which focuses on enjoying a vacation home with friends and family.

Vrbo

inclusive (Exhibit 9–5). The campaign launched with a pre-game ad on the 2022 Super Bowl called "A Place for Together" that followed families, and friends who are like family, as they experience the powerful moments of togetherness that take place at Vrbo vacation homes.[12] The spot was set to the nostalgic tune "Right Where I Belong" by the Muppets that was featured in the movie *The Muppets Take Manhattan*. The campaign included a series of transformational ads featuring different destinations and types of vacation homes to show that no matter what type of vacation you're going on or who you're traveling with, staying in Vrbo's whole homes is the best way to enjoy time together with your loved ones. The campaign also included a TikTok challenge that invited users to post a video of themselves surrounded by their favorite people with three $5,000 Vrbo vacations awarded to the winners.[13]

Combining Rational and Emotional Appeals   In many advertising situations, the decision facing the creative specialist is not whether to choose an emotional or a rational appeal but, rather, to determine how to combine the two approaches. As noted copywriters David Ogilvy and Joel Raphaelson have stated:

> Few purchases of any kind are made for entirely rational reasons. Even a purely functional product such as laundry detergent may offer what is now called an emotional benefit—say, the satisfaction of seeing one's children in bright, clean clothes. In some product categories the rational element is small. These include soft drinks, beer, cosmetics, certain personal care products, and most old-fashioned products. And who hasn't experienced the surge of joy that accompanies the purchase of a new car?[14]

Consumer purchase decisions are often made on the basis of both emotional and rational motives, and attention must be given to both elements in developing effective advertising. Purchase decisions regarding services can also be based on both rational and emotional motives. For example, many consumers choose an airline based on factors such as price, availability, arrival and/or departure time, and the ability to earn miles or points for their travel. However, airlines recognize that it is also important to appeal to emotional factors in competing for passengers.

Automotive marketers also recognize that it is important to connect with prospective customers on an emotional as well as rational level. For example, Subaru changed its creative strategy from rational to more emotional-based advertising a number of years ago when it began using the "Love" campaign. For several decades Subaru cycled through advertising agencies and campaigns using rational-based appeals with taglines such as "What to Drive," "The Beauty of All-Wheel Drive," "Driven by What's Inside," and "Think, Feel, Drive." The rational-based advertising appeals failed to move the sales needle, so Subaru of America management knew it was time for a change and hired a new agency, Carmichael Lynch, which began by doing research to understand why automotive customers were not considering or buying Subarus. While awareness was a problem, they also learned that those who were aware did not know enough about the brand to form the favorable attitudes that would lead to consideration and ultimately, purchase. A major insight came when research was conducted among existing owners that asked why they *did* purchase a Subaru. Typically, the answers revolved around rational motives such as safety, quality, all-wheel drive, and other factors that were mentioned in ads for the brand. However, the majority of the owners would also answer by expressing their strong affection and devotion to the brand and how much they loved it. The insight gained from the research was the impetus for a new campaign that was launched in 2007 using the tagline: "Love. It's what makes a Subaru a Subaru."

Rather than focusing on logical reasons for buying a vehicle, such as product attributes and benefits, the "Love" campaign tugs at the heartstrings of car buyers. The commercials used in the campaign show friends going on camping trips in their Subaru and memories and experiences families have had with a Subaru, such as handing down the car to their children, sending them off to college, and surviving an accident

EXHIBIT 9-6

The "Share the Love" event is part of the emotion-based "Love" campaign for Subaru that helped the company achieve record sales for 13 consecutive years.

Subaru of America, Inc.

EXHIBIT 9-7

This clever reminder ad reminds people to keep Tic Tac breath mints handy.

tic tac

because of the safety features of a Subaru. The "Love" campaign has tied together the attributes Subaru had been highlighting for decades in its advertising but were not really resonating with consumers.

In addition to advertising, the "Love" campaign has also become the umbrella for other integrated marketing efforts for Subaru, including promotions, sponsorships, corporate- and dealer-owned media, and cause-related marketing. The theme is used in a charitable campaign called "Share the Love," which Subaru has run at the end of every year since 2008 (Exhibit 9-6). Rather than using year-end discounts and rebates, Subaru donates $250 to charities for every car sold during December and has contributed more than $200 million over the past 15 years.

Additional Types of Appeals   Not every ad fits neatly into the categories of rational or emotional appeals. For example, ads for some brands can be classified as **reminder advertising**, which has the objective of building brand awareness and/or keeping the brand name in front of consumers. Well-known brands and market leaders often use reminder advertising to maintain top-of-mind awareness among consumers in their target markets. For example, Exhibit 9-7 shows a reminder ad for Tic Tac breath mints that uses a clever play on the iconic romantic line from the hit movie *Jerry Maguire* that became part of popular culture. In one of the film's most memorable scenes at the end of the movie, Tom Cruise's title character gives out a heartfelt speech to Renee Zellweger's character, Dorothy Boyd; Zellweger stops Cruise and tearfully says, "You had me at 'hello.'"

Products and services that have a seasonal pattern to their consumption also use reminder advertising, particularly around the appropriate period. For example, marketers of candy products often increase their media budgets and run reminder advertising around Halloween, Valentine's Day, Christmas, and Easter.

Online ads often serve as a form of reminder advertising. Many of the banner ads that are pervasive on Internet websites have very low click-through rates but still can be effective and serve a valuable function by fostering familiarity, even though most consumers may never click through to the source of the ads. Research into the psychology of online advertising has shown that repeated exposure to banner advertising can enhance familiarity with and generate positive feelings toward a brand.[15] These favorable feelings often occur through what psychologists have identified as the *mere exposure effect*, whereby repeated exposure to a stimulus (such as a brand name) can result in favorable feelings toward it.[16] While digital advertising may have positive effects through the incidental exposure that takes place when consumers visit a website, many advertising experts argue that consumers tune out most of the banner ads, as well as other forms of Internet advertising. They note that it is becoming increasingly difficult to get people visiting a website to attend to, let alone engage with, digital ads.[17]

Advertisers introducing a new product often use **teaser advertising**, which is designed to build curiosity, interest, and/ or excitement about a product or brand by talking about it but not actually showing it. Teasers, or *mystery ads* as they are sometimes called, are also used by marketers to draw attention to upcoming product launches and/or advertising campaigns and generate interest and publicity for them. For example, Under Armour has used teaser ads to create interest and excitement around new product introductions such as running and basketball shoes. It is very likely you have received a teaser ad from a marketer in your e-mail inbox as they are often used to capture

HAVENLY

Keep your eyes open,

AND YOUR INBOX REFRESHED.

Next week, we're launching something new,
that we *know* you'll love.

That's all we can say for now...

EXHIBIT 9–8

Teaser ads are often used as
part of e-mail marketing
campaigns.

Havenly Inc.

EXHIBIT 9–9

Airbnb's "Made Possible
By Hosts" campaign is an
example of the effective use
of user-generated content.

Airbnb, Inc.

Made possible by Hosts

airbnb

attention interest so you will open the message and hopefully respond to it. While teaser e-mail messages are used in a variety of e-mail marketing contexts, they are most popular for product launches, sale or promotion announcements, and event invitations. Exhibit 9–8 shows a teaser ad that was part of an e-mail campaign used by Havenly, an online interior design and decorating service. Notice how the ad encourages consumers to pay attention to their e-mail inbox for upcoming news from the company.

Teaser ads also are often used to generate interest and excitement for new movies or TV shows. They are also used by automotive advertisers for introducing a new model or announcing significant changes in a vehicle. A study by Thorbjorsen and his colleagues found that online teaser advertising pre-announcing a new product is more effective in generating product interest and positive word of mouth than merely advertising a new product at the time of launch.[18] While teaser campaigns can generate interest in a new product, advertisers must be careful not to extend them too long or they will lose their effectiveness. As one advertising executive says, "Contrary to what we think, consumers don't hold seminars about advertising. You have to give consumers enough information about the product in teaser ads to make them feel they're in on the joke."[19]

Another form of advertising that is becoming increasingly popular is **user-generated content (UGC)**, whereby ads or other types of messages are created by consumers rather than by the company and/or its agency.[20] A number of marketers have developed contests that involve having consumers create ads and submit them for consideration. Frito-Lay was one of the first marketers to use UGC on a major level when it sponsored a "Crash the Super Bowl" creative competition and ran a user-generated ad during the big game that was entirely conceived and produced by amateurs rather than advertising professionals. A number of other marketers have made UGC part of their IMC campaigns by using various types of messages that have been crowdsourced.

The growth of social media platforms such as Facebook, YouTube, Snapchat, TikTok, and Instagram has led many marketers to use user-generated content material such as pictures, videos, and stories as part of their integrated marketing campaigns.[21] For example, Ben & Jerry's uses UGC as a source of inexpensive, authentic marketing content by incorporating images of its products that were tagged on social media by its customers into its website, blog, newsletter, and various social media sites such as Facebook and Instagram. Airbnb ran a very effective UGC campaign in 2021 to connect with both travelers and renters still facing lockdowns and restrictions from the COVID-19 pandemic. The company felt that, given the state of the world, a traditional advertising campaign would be perceived as too commercial and opted for an approach using user-generated content. The "Made Possible By Hosts" campaign consisted of a series of short films using real photo shots by photographers on real trips staying in the homes of Airbnb hosts around the world.[22] The goal was to have the user-generated content trigger feelings of nostalgia and hope for a brighter future. The campaign's videos attracted over 17 million views globally. Exhibit 9–9 shows one of the photos from the campaign to educate people on the magical experiences that Airbnb hosts make possible for their guests.

Many ads are not designed to sell a product or service but rather to enhance the image of the company or meet other corporate goals such as soliciting investment or recruiting employees. These are generally referred to as corporate image advertising and are discussed in detail in Chapter 17.

Advertising Execution

Once the specific advertising appeal that will be used as the basis for the advertising message has been determined, the creative specialist or team begins its execution. *Creative execution* is the way an advertising appeal is presented. While it is obviously important for an ad to have a meaningful appeal or message to communicate to the consumer, the manner in which the ad is executed is also important.

One of the best-known advocates of the importance of creative execution in advertising was William Bernbach, founder of the Doyle Dane Bernbach agency. In his famous book on the advertising industry, *Madison Avenue*, Martin Mayer notes Bernbach's reply to David Ogilvy's rule for copywriters that "what you say in advertising is more important than how you say it." Bernbach replied, "Execution can become content, it can be just as important as what you say. A sick guy can utter some words and nothing happens; a healthy vital guy says them and they rock the world."[23] Bernbach was one of the revolutionaries of his time who changed advertising creativity on a fundamental level by redefining how headlines and visuals were used, how art directors and copywriters worked together, and how advertising could be used to arouse feelings and emotions.

An advertising message can be presented or executed in numerous ways. We will examine the following most frequently used execution approaches:

- Straight-sell or factual message
- Scientific/technical evidence
- Demonstration
- Comparison
- Testimonial
- Slice of life
- Animation
- Personality symbol
- Imagery
- Dramatization
- Humor
- Combinations

EXHIBIT 9–10

This ad for ELVIVE Total Repair 5 uses a straight sell execution.

L'Oreal International

Straight-Sell or Factual Message   One of the most basic types of creative executions is the straight-sell or factual message. This type of ad relies on a straightforward presentation of information concerning the product or service. The execution is often used with informational/rational appeals, where the focus of the message is the product or service and its specific attributes and/or benefits.

Straight-sell executions are commonly used in print ads. A picture of the product or service occupies part of the ad, and the factual copy takes up the rest of the space. They are also used in TV advertising, with an announcer generally delivering the sales message while the product/service is shown on the screen. Ads for high-involvement consumer products as well as industrial and other business-to-business products generally use this format. Straight-sell advertising executions are often used for various types of consumer products and services as well and can be very effective when done creatively. For example, personal care products such as shampoos, deodorants, and cosmetics often use straight-sell executions that focus on the problem a product can solve for a consumer by using it. The ad shown in Exhibit 9–10 for L'Oréal's ELVIVE Total Repair 5 balm is a good example of a straight-sell execution because the copy discusses how use of the product can help repair damaged hair.

EXHIBIT 9–11

Neutrogena uses a scientific evidence appeal by promoting how the product has been tested in the lab and is the brand most recommended by dermatologists.

Johnson & Johnson Inc.

EXHIBIT 9–12

This Varilux ad is an effective way to demonstrate the superiority of its progressive lenses.

Varilux by Essilor of America

Scientific/Technical Evidence   In a variation of the straight sell, scientific or technical evidence is presented in the ad to support performance or efficacy claims. Advertisers often cite technical information, results of scientific or laboratory studies, or endorsements by scientific bodies, doctors, or agencies to support their advertising claims. For example, an endorsement from the American Council on Dental Therapeutics on how fluoride helps prevent cavities was the basis of the campaign that made Crest the leading brand of toothpaste. The ad for Neutrogena's Rapid Wrinkle Repair product shown in Exhibit 9–11 uses this execution style by noting how the product has been tested in the lab and is the retinol brand most recommended by dermatologists.

Demonstration   Demonstration advertising is designed to illustrate the key advantages of the product/service by showing it in actual use or in some staged situation. Demonstration executions can be very effective in convincing consumers of a product's utility or quality and of the benefits of owning or using the brand. TV and online videos are particularly well suited for demonstration executions, since the benefits or advantages of the product can be shown on the screen using sight, sound, and motion. Although perhaps a little less dramatic than TV, demonstration ads can also work in print. The ad for Varilux Progressive Lenses shown in Exhibit 9–12 is an excellent example of the use of this technique. The ad shows the superiority of its progressive lenses with W.A.V.E. technology over ordinary progressive lenses by contrasting the clarity of the two images. The company also uses demonstrations in TV and online ads.

Comparison   Brand comparisons can also be the basis for the advertising execution. The comparison execution approach is increasingly popular among advertisers, since it offers a direct way of communicating a brand's particular advantage over its competitors or positioning a new or lesser-known brand with industry leaders. Comparison executions are often used to execute competitive advantage appeals, as discussed earlier.

Testimonial   Many advertisers prefer to have their messages presented by way of a testimonial, where a consumer praises the product or service on the basis of his or her personal experience with it. Testimonial executions can have ordinary satisfied customers discuss their own experiences with the brand and the benefits of using it. This approach can be very effective when the person delivering the testimonial is someone with whom the target audience can identify or who has an interesting story to tell. The testimonial must be based on actual use of the product or service to avoid legal problems, and the spokesperson must be credible.

A number of marketers, such as weight-loss companies, use testimonials to advertise their products, services, and programs. For example, Jenny Craig uses television commercials, online videos, and print ads featuring ordinary consumers discussing how they have been able to lose weight by following the company's programs.

A related execution technique is the *endorsement*, where a well-known or respected individual such as a celebrity or expert in the product or service area speaks on behalf of the company or the brand. For example, Jenny Craig recently retained reality television star and social media influencer Brittany Cartwright as the brand ambassador for its new Max Up weight-loss program. Cartwright showcased her weight-loss journey using the new program in a series of television commercials, digital media, and

EXHIBIT 9–13

Jenny Craig uses testimonials featuring social influencer Brittany Cartwright to promote its new Max Up weight-loss program.

Jenny Craig, Inc.

social media promotions (Exhibit 9–13). When endorsers promote a company or its products or services, the message is not necessarily based on their personal experiences.

Slice-of-Life   A widely used advertising format, particularly for consumer products and services, is the slice-of-life execution, which is generally based on a problem–solution approach. This type of execution portrays a problem or conflict that consumers might face in their daily lives. The ad then shows how the advertiser's product or service can resolve the problem.

Slice-of-life or problem–solution execution approaches are not limited to consumer-product advertising. Many business-to-business marketers use this type of advertising to demonstrate how their products and services can be used to solve business problems.[24] Some business-to-business marketers use a variation of the problem–solution execution that is sometimes referred to as *slice-of-death advertising*.[25] This execution style is used in conjunction with a fear appeal, as the focus is on the negative consequences that result when businesspeople make the wrong decision in choosing a supplier or service provider. For example, FedEx used this type of advertising for nearly three decades through humorous but to-the-point commercials that show what might happen when important packages and documents aren't received on time.

Many marketers like to use the slice-of-life genre because they believe it can genuinely be an effective way of addressing a problem or issue and offering a solution. Execution is critical in using the technique effectively, as these ads are designed to be dramatizations of a supposedly real-life situation that consumers might encounter. Getting viewers to identify with the situation and/or characters depicted in the ad can be very challenging. Since the success of slice-of-life ads often depends on how well the actors come across and execute their roles, professional actors are often used to achieve credibility and to ensure that the commercial is of high quality. Smaller companies and local advertisers often do not have ad budgets large enough to hire the talent or to pay for the production quality needed to effectively create slice-of-life spots. Thus, this execution technique is more likely to be used by companies with ad budgets that are large enough to fund the use of professional talent and high-quality production.

Slice-of-life commercials can also be used as an effective way to execute humor appeals. For example, one of the most popular commercials in 2022 was a spot for Amazon's Alexa voice-assistant featuring actor Scarlett Johansson and her husband, *Saturday Night Live* "Weekend Update" host Colin Jost, in which the couple imagine that Alexa can read their minds, injecting some paranoia into their relationship. The "Mind Reader" spot opens with Jost saying, "Alexa, it's game day." That prompts the home assistant to set the mood, switching to the game on the TV, closing the blinds, dimming the lights, and chilling rosé. "It's like she can read your mind," the actors say in unison. They then experience a series of strange use cases for a psychic Alexa such as the assistant ordering mouthwash just by judging Jost's reaction to Johansson's morning breath; or the scene shown in Exhibit 9–14 where Alexa powers up a blender to spare Johansson

EXHIBIT 9–14

Amazon used a humorous slice-of-life execution for its popular "Mind Reader" commercial for its Alexa voice-assistant.

Amazon.com, Inc.

when Jost drones on in the kitchen. Humorously, the spot uses various everyday situations to play on a common fear about ever-present devices—that they hear everything. In the commercial, Alexa even acts on silent cues. The commercial ends by reassuring consumers as Jost says: "It's probably better Alexa can't read your mind." "Bad idea," Johansson agrees.[26]

Animation   An advertising execution approach that has become popular in recent years is animation. With this technique, animated scenes are drawn by artists or created on the computer, and cartoons, puppets, or other types of fictional characters may be used. Cartoon animation is especially popular for commercials targeted at children. Animated cartoon characters have also been used in many campaigns, including Green Giant vegetables (the Jolly Green Giant) and Keebler cookies (the Keebler elves). Kraft Foods revitalized its Mr. Peanut character a few years ago to make him more appealing to young consumers. They ran animated commercials with actor Robert Downey Jr. and, later, Bill Hader of *Saturday Night Live* doing the voice of Mr. Peanut.[27]

A number of major marketers use animation for TV commercials, online videos, or short films. For example, as discussed in Chapter 5, Procter & Gamble has been using the animated bears in commercials for Charmin toilet tissue for nearly two decades. Chipotle has also used computer-generated animation to create short films as part of its "Food with Integrity" campaign, including the award-winning "Back to the Start" spot. The two-minute short film depicts the life of a farmer as he slowly turns his family farm into an industrial animal factory. He soon sees the errors of his ways and realizes the benefits of sustainable farming and turns it back. The animated spot was named one of the top 15 commercials of the 21st century by *Advertising Age.* Chipotle built on the success of "Back to the Start" by developing several other animated short films that generated a large amount of earned media attention and were widely shared on social media.[28] In 2021 Chipotle released another popular animated film called "A Future Begins" that supports the next generation of farmers by shining a light on the enormous challenges facing the U.S. farming industry, which has lost over 40 times more farmers than it has gained over the past 5 years (Exhibit 9–15).[29] The soundtrack for the video features Kacey Musgraves singing a reimagined version of Coldplay's "Fix You." The use of animation as an execution style may increase as creative specialists find more ways to use computer-generated graphics and other technological innovations.[30]

Personality Symbol   Another type of advertising execution involves developing a central character or personality symbol that can deliver the advertising message and with which the company or brand can be identified. This character can be a person, like

EXHIBIT 9–15

Chipotle has used computer-generated animation for a series of short films, such as "A Future Begins," to support sustainable farming practices.

Chipotle Mexican Grill, Inc.

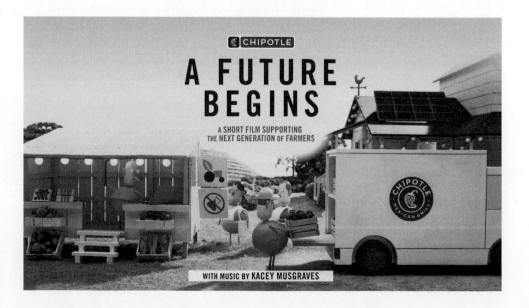

the iconic Mr. Whipple, who asked shoppers, "Please don't squeeze the Charmin," or the Maytag repairman, who sits anxiously by the phone but is never needed because the company's appliances are so reliable. Over the past decade, several companies have developed successful advertising campaigns that use personality symbols for the company or brand, including Dos Equis beer and KFC.

Personality figures can also be built around animated characters and animals. As discussed in Chapter 5, personality symbols such as the Pillsbury Doughboy, Tony the Tiger, and Charlie the Tuna have been used for decades to promote Pillsbury's refrigerated dough products, Kellogg's Frosted Flakes, and Star-Kist tuna, respectively. Other popular personality symbols that have been used more recently include the Energizer Bunny, Mr. Clean, and the Burger King character. One of the most popular and effective advertising personality symbols has been the Aflac duck, which has been very successful in raising awareness, as well as sales, for the supplemental insurance company over the past two decades.[31] Aflac has even integrated the duck into the company's redesigned corporate logo to take advantage of the tremendous equity that has resulted from the ads featuring the character.

As discussed in Chapter 8, a number of other insurance companies use characters and mascots as personality symbols for their brands. Exhibit 9–16 shows the various

Farmers Insurance Group   Liberty Mutual Group   The Allstate Corporation   The Progressive Corporation

GEICO   Aflec Incorporated   State Farm Insurance

EXHIBIT 9–16

Various characters and mascots are used as personality symbols in advertising by insurance companies.

FIGURE 9–2

Ratings of Insurance
Company Ad Characters

Company/Character	Awareness Level	Favorability Rating
GEICO/Gecko	98%	75%
Progressive/Flo	95	66
Aflac/Duck	92	66
Progressive/Jamie	87	52
Liberty Mutual/Limu Emu and Doug	84	54
State Farm/Jake	83	69
Allstate/Mayhem	79	67
Farmers/Professor Burke	76	67
Progressive/Dr. Rick	59	54

Source: "The 9 Most Popular Insurance Ad Characters, Ranked," *Advertising Age*, January 13, 2022.

personality symbols used in advertising by insurance companies. Figure 9–2 shows the results of a recent *Advertising Age*-The Harris Poll survey regarding consumers' opinions of nine fictional insurance characters. The survey found that all of the characters had awareness levels of 75 percent or higher except for Progressive's Dr. Rick character, a life coach who dishes out tough love advice. The GEICO gecko still reigns supreme with a 98 percent awareness level and favorability rating of 75 percent while Progressive's Jamie was the least liked character.

Imagery   You have probably noticed that some ads contain little or no information about the brand or company and are almost totally visual. These advertisements use imagery executions whereby the ad consists primarily of visual elements such as pictures, illustrations, and/or symbols rather than information. An imagery execution is used when the goal is to encourage consumers to associate the brand with the symbols, characters, and/or situation shown in the ad. Imagery ads are often the basis for emotional appeals that are used to advertise products or services where differentiation based on physical characteristics is difficult, such as soft drinks, liquor, designer clothing, and cosmetics. However, image is important for all types of products and services, as marketers want the target audience to hold a favorable set of psychosocial associations for their company or brand.

An imagery execution may be based on *usage imagery* by showing how a brand is used or performs and the situation in which it is used. For example, advertising for trucks and SUVs often shows the vehicles navigating tough terrain or in challenging situations such as towing a heavy load. An excellent example of usage imagery is the award-winning outdoor ad for Michelin tires shown in Exhibit 9–17. This clever ad shows the arm of the iconic "Michelin Man" helping an SUV make it up a hill in the snow. Usage imagery executions are also often used in the marketing of services as well as experiences such

EXHIBIT 9–17

This outdoor ad for Michelin utilizes usage imagery to promote the superior traction of its tires in the snow.

Michelin North America Inc.

EXHIBIT 9–18

Advertising for Yes To creates a fun and irreverent image for the brand.

YESTO, Inc.

as hotels and destination resorts to show favorable images related to the use of a company's service offering. This type of execution can also be based on *user imagery* where the focus is on the type of person who uses the brand. Advertising for products such as cosmetics, jewelry, and designer clothing often rely on user imagery by associating the brand with the characteristics of the person shown in the ad. The image can be based on factors such as the lifestyle, values, personality, or other characteristics of the user of the brand. Image executions rely heavily on visual elements such as photography, color, tonality, and design to communicate the desired image to the consumer. The ad for Yes To natural skin care products shown in Exhibit 9–18 is a good example of advertising based on user imagery. The "Yes To" campaign was designed to create a fun, playful, and irreverent image for the brand that breaks through standard conventions of natural skin care. This campaign includes a series of banner ads and videos used online and in social media to engage viewers by asking the question, "What do you say yes to?" and showing users of the brand in playful behaviors. Marketers who rely on image executions have to be sure that the usage or user imagery with which they associate their brand evokes the right feelings and reactions from the target audience.

Dramatization   Another execution technique particularly well suited to television is dramatization, where the focus is on telling a short story with the product or service as the star. Dramatization is somewhat akin to slice-of-life execution in that it often relies on the problem–solution approach, but it uses more excitement and suspense in telling the story. The purpose of using drama is to draw the viewer into the action it portrays. Advocates of drama note that when it is successful, the audience becomes lost in the story and experiences the concerns and feelings of the characters.[32] According to Sandra Moriarty, there are five basic steps in a dramatic commercial:

> First is exposition, where the stage is set for the upcoming action. Next comes conflict, which is a technique for identifying the problem. The middle of the dramatic form is a period of rising action where the story builds, the conflict intensifies, the suspense thickens. The fourth step is the climax, where the problem is solved. The last part of a drama is the resolution, where the wrap-up is presented. In advertising that includes product identification and call to action.[33]

In his excellent book *Creative Advertising*, Mario Pricken lists several relevant questions that should be considered when telling a story through a dramatic execution: What everyday situations could you develop around the product to show its advantages in the best light? What sort of story could involve the product as best friend or partner? In what everyday situation could it attract attention in a provocative way? In what situation could it become a star, a lifesaver, or a helper? In what everyday story could it make people laugh? He also notes that there are a number of dramatic styles that might be best suited for telling the story. These include, but are not limited to, genres such as thriller, adventure, comedy, slapstick, love story, and documentary.[34]

The challenge facing the creative team when using a dramatic execution is how to encompass the various elements and tell the story effectively in 30 seconds, which is the length of the typical commercial.

Many marketers are using dramatization as part of short films that can be viewed on their websites, as well as on various social media platforms such as YouTube, Facebook, and Instagram. An example of the effective use of dramatization is the "Truth About Opioids" campaign created by the Truth Initiative, which is a nonprofit public health organization dedicated to preventing tobacco and drug use among young people. The campaign uses dramatic TV commercials, such as a spot showing a young girl intentionally crashing her car into a wall and a construction worker slamming his arm in a door to break his arm so they can get more prescription opioids. Each spot ends with a clear

EXHIBIT 9–19

The "Truth About Opioids" uses dramatization in commercials and videos to educate young people about the opioid crisis.

Rhode Island Department of Health

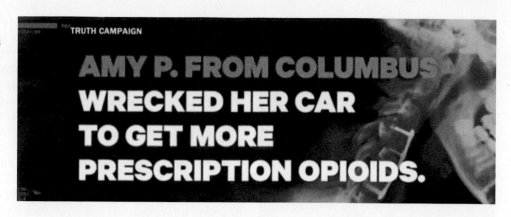

call to action, "Know the truth, spread the truth" (Exhibit 9–19). A second phase of the campaign uses a short film called Rebekkah's story that focuses on a young woman's withdrawal, treatment, and recovery from opioid addiction.[35] The campaign is a collaboration among the Truth Initiative, the Office of National Drug Control Policy, and the Ad Council to prevent and reduce the misuse of opioids among youth and young adults, destigmatize addiction, and highlight the importance of treatment.

Humor   Like comparisons, humor was discussed in Chapter 6 as a type of advertising appeal, but this technique can also be used as a way of presenting other advertising appeals. Humorous executions are particularly well suited to television or radio, although some print ads attempt to use this style. The pros and cons of using humor as an executional technique are similar to those associated with its use as an advertising appeal. However, it is important to recognize that the success of humorous appeals often depends on how well they are executed. Advertising professor Charles Taylor notes that there are two fundamental factors that determine whether humorous appeals are effective—the concept and the execution—and it is the latter that is usually most important. For example, Taylor argues that the success of the Progressive insurance ads using Flo as a personality symbol is due, in large part, to how well the ads have been executed by the Arnold Worldwide agency.[36]

Combinations   Many of the execution techniques can be combined to present the advertising message. For example, animation is often used to create personality symbols or present a fantasy. Slice-of-life ads are often used to demonstrate a product or service or as the basis for various types of emotional appeals. Comparisons are sometimes made using a humorous approach. FedEx has used humorous executions of the slice-of-death genre depicting business people experiencing dire consequences when they use another delivery service and an important document doesn't arrive on time. It is the responsibility of the creative specialist(s) to determine whether more than one execution style should be used in creating the ad.

CREATIVE TACTICS

Our discussion thus far has focused on the development of creative strategy and various appeals and execution styles that can be used for the advertising message. Once the creative approach, type of appeal, and execution style have been determined, attention turns to creating the actual advertisement. The design and production of advertising messages involve a number of activities, among them writing copy, developing illustrations and other visual elements of the ad, and bringing all of the pieces together to create an effective message. In this section, we examine the verbal and visual elements of an ad and discuss tactical considerations in creating print ads and TV commercials.

Creative Tactics for Print Advertising

The basic components of a print ad are the headline, the body copy, the visual or illustrations, and the layout (the way they all fit together). The headline and body copy portions of the ad are the responsibility of the copywriters; artists, often working under the direction of an art director, are responsible for the visual presentation. Art directors also work with the copywriters to develop a layout, or arrangement of the various components of the ad: headlines, subheads, body copy, illustrations, captions, logos, and the like. We briefly examine the three components of a print ad and how they are coordinated.

Headlines The **headline** is the words in the leading position of the ad—the words that will be read first or are positioned to draw the most attention. Headlines are usually set in larger type and are often set apart from the body copy or text portion of the ad to give them prominence. Most advertising people consider the headline the most important part of a print ad.

The most important function of a headline is attracting readers' attention and interesting them in the rest of the message. While the visual portion of an ad is obviously important, the headline often shoulders most of the responsibility of attracting readers' attention. Research has shown the headline is generally the first thing people look at in a print ad, followed by the illustration. Only 20 percent of readers go beyond the headline and read the body copy.[37] So in addition to attracting attention, the headline must give the reader good reason to read the copy portion of the ad, which contains more detailed and persuasive information about the product or service. To do this, the headline must put forth the main theme, appeal, or proposition of the ad in a few words. Some print ads contain little if any body copy, so the headline must work with the illustration to communicate the entire advertising message.

Headlines also perform a segmentation function by engaging the attention and interest of consumers who are most likely to buy a particular product or service. Advertisers begin the segmentation process by choosing to advertise in certain types of publications (e.g., a business, travel, or fashion magazine). An effective headline goes even further in selecting good prospects by addressing their specific needs, wants, or interests. For example, the headline of the Pedialyte Sport drink ad shown in Exhibit 9–20 ran in sports and exercise magazines such as *Sports Illustrated* and *Bicycling* and is designed to appeal to cyclists who often go on long rides when the weather is hot. The headline attracts attention by challenging competitive cyclists not to get beat by the heat when riding. It draws readers to the picture of the product as well as to the ad copy that explains how Pedialyte Sport has more electrolytes and less sugar than the leading sports drink and can help them stay hydrated.

EXHIBIT 9–20

The headline of this Pedialyte Sport ad is designed to attract the attention of cyclists.

Abbott Laboratories Co.

Types of Headlines There are numerous headline possibilities. The type used depends on several factors, including the creative strategy, the particular advertising situation (e.g., product type, media vehicle[s] being used, timeliness), and its relationship to other components of the ad, such as the illustration or body copy. Headlines can be categorized as direct and indirect. **Direct headlines** are straightforward and informative in terms of the message they are presenting and the target audience they are directed toward. Common types of direct headlines include those offering a specific benefit, making a promise, or announcing a reason the reader should be interested in the product or service.

Indirect headlines are not straightforward about identifying the product or service or getting to the point. But they are often more effective at attracting readers' attention and interest because they provoke curiosity and lure readers into the body copy to learn an answer or get an explanation. Techniques for writing indirect headlines include using questions, provocations, how-to statements, and challenges.

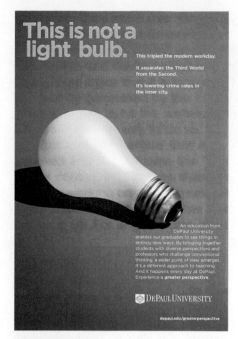

This is not a light bulb.

This tripled the modern workday.

It separates the Third World from the Second.

It's lowering crime rates in the inner city.

An education from DePaul University enables our graduates to see things in entirely new ways. By bringing together students with diverse perspectives and professors who challenge conventional thinking, a wider point of view emerges. It's a different approach to teaching. And it happens every day at DePaul. Experience a **greater perspective**.

DEPAUL UNIVERSITY

depaul.edu/greaterperspective

EXHIBIT 9–21

This ad for DePaul University uses an indirect headline that creates curiosity and encourages people to read the body copy.

DePaul University

EXHIBIT 9–22

This GEICO ad uses subheads to make the copy easier to read as well as to highlight features and benefits.

GEICO

"You could save hundreds by switching to GEICO."

WITH GEICO, IT'S EASY TO SAVE.
I'm here to save you money. Well…not really here in your kitchen, but you know what I mean.

People say to me, I don't have time to shop for car insurance. And I say to them, have you ever made $500 in 15 minutes? Go to **geico.com**. Answer some quick questions and you get an accurate rate quote. You buy right then, or if you want, call **1-800-947-AUTO** to buy over the phone. Either way, you could save $500.

VALUE. IT'S SAVINGS AND SERVICE.
People know they could save hundreds. But what about GEICO's service? I tell people, GEICO isn't just about saving hundreds. There's also the 24/7 service with real live people. They're on the phones at all hours answering your questions. And you can also get the help you need at **geico.com**.

CLAIMS MADE EASY.
A friend gets into a small accident. Everyone is OK. When he gets home he goes to **geico.com**, reports the claim and schedules an appointment. Later he goes back to the website, prints out his estimate and views photos of the damage. He then goes to a GEICO-approved shop and his claim repairs are guaranteed for as long as he owns his car. Now that's what I call service.

DEPENDABILITY. IT'S THE GEICO WAY.
I get asked, how dependable is GEICO? They've been consistently protecting drivers and delivering great value for more than 70 years. That sounds dependable to me.

PROTECT LOTS OF THINGS WITH GEICO.
Sure, GEICO does cars. Everyone knows that. But, you could also save big when GEICO insures your motorcycle or ATV. Homeowner's and renter's insurance? GEICO can help you with those, and boats and PWCs, too.

LOOK, IT ALL MAKES A LOT OF SENSE.
It's easy to switch, so contact GEICO. You'll get the value and claim service all my mates love.

15 minutes could save you 15%.

GEICO.
geico.com
1-800-947-AUTO
or call your local office.

Average savings based on GEICO New Policyholder Survey Data through February 2007. Some discounts, coverages, payment plans, and features are not available in all states or in all GEICO companies. Government Employees Insurance Co. • GEICO General Insurance Co. • GEICO Indemnity Co. • GEICO Casualty Co. These companies are subsidiaries of Berkshire Hathaway Inc. GEICO auto insurance is not available in MA. Homeowner's, motorcycle and ATV insurance are currently not available in some states. Homeowner's, renter's, boat, and PWC coverages are written through non-affiliated insurance companies and are secured through Insurance Counselors Inc., the GEICO Property Agency. The GEICO gecko image © GEICO 1999 - 2007 GEICO. Washington, DC 20076. © 2006-2007 GEICO.

GEN

Indirect headlines rely on their ability to generate curiosity or intrigue so as to motivate readers to become involved with the ad and read the body copy to find out the point of the message. This can be risky if the headline is not provocative enough to get the readers' interest. Advertisers deal with this problem by using indirect headlines that are interesting enough to generate interest or curiosity as well as employing a strong visual appeal that will attract attention and offer a reason for reading more of the message. An excellent example of this is the ad for DePaul University shown in Exhibit 9-21. The headline contradicts the picture of the light bulb and is designed to grab the reader's attention and generate curiosity that will encourage people to read the body copy. Those doing so learn how DePaul graduates learn to see things in entirely new ways by bringing together students with diverse perspectives and professors who challenge conventional thinking.

Subheads While many ads have only one headline, it is also common to see print ads containing the main head and one or more secondary heads, or **subheads**. Subheads are usually smaller than the main headline but larger than the body copy. Subheads are often used to enhance the readability of the message by breaking up large amounts of body copy and highlighting key sales points. Their content reinforces the headline and advertising slogan or theme. The ad for GEICO auto insurance shown in Exhibit 9-22 is a good example of the effective use of subheads to present a large amount of advertising copy and highlight the major points of the message.

Body Copy The main text portion of a print ad is referred to as the **body copy** (or sometimes just *copy*). While the body copy is usually the heart of the advertising message, getting the target audience to read it is often difficult. The copywriter faces a dilemma: The body copy must be long enough to communicate the advertiser's message yet short enough to hold readers' interest.

Body copy content often flows from the points made in the headline or various subheads, but the specific content depends on the type of advertising appeal and/or execution style being used. For example, straight-sell copy that presents relevant information, product features and benefits, or competitive advantages is often used with the various types of rational appeals discussed earlier in the chapter. Emotional appeals often use narrative copy that tells a story or provides an interesting account of a problem or situation involving the product.

Advertising body copy can be written to go along with various types of creative appeals and executions—comparisons, price appeals, demonstrations, humor, dramatizations, and the like. Copywriters choose a copy style that is appropriate for the type of appeal being used and effective for executing the creative strategy and communicating the advertiser's message to the target audience.

Visual Elements The third major component of a print ad is the visual element. The illustration is often a dominant part of a print ad and plays an important role in determining its effectiveness. The visual portion of an ad must attract attention, communicate an idea or image, and work in a synergistic fashion with the headline and body copy to produce an effective message. In some print ads, the visual portion of the ad is essentially the message and thus must convey a strong and meaningful image. For example, the ad for McDonald's shown in Exhibit 9-23 uses a simple, clever image of French fries in the shape of a strong signal to promote the availability of free Wi-Fi at its restaurants.

EXHIBIT 9–23

This ad uses a clever visual image to remind people that McDonald's offers free Wi-Fi.

McDonald's Corporation

Many decisions have to be made regarding the visual portion of the ad: what identification marks should be included (brand name, company or trade name, trademarks, logos); whether to use photos or hand-drawn or painted illustrations; what colors to use (or even perhaps black and white or just a splash of color); and what the focus of the visual should be.

Layout   While each individual component of a print ad is important, the key factor is how these elements are blended into a finished advertisement. A **layout** is the physical arrangement of the various parts of the ad, including the headline, subheads, body copy, illustrations, and any identifying marks. The layout shows where each part of the ad will be placed and gives guidelines to the people working on the ad. The layout helps the copywriter determine how much space he or she has to work with and how much copy should be written. It can also guide the art director in determining the size and type of photos. Layouts are often done in rough form and presented to the client so that the advertiser can visualize what the ad will look like before giving preliminary approval. The agency should get client approval of the layout before moving on to the more costly stages of print production. While the layout of a print ad is often straightforward, creative layouts can be a very effective way to deliver a branding message.

Creative Tactics for Television

As consumers, we see so many TV commercials that it's easy to take for granted the time, effort, and money that go into making them. Creating and producing commercials that break through the clutter on TV and communicate effectively is a detailed, expensive process. On a cost-per-minute basis, commercials are the most expensive productions seen on television.

TV is a unique and powerful advertising medium because it contains the elements of sight, sound, and motion, which can be combined to create a variety of advertising appeals and executions. Unlike print, the viewer does not control the rate at which the message is presented, so there is no opportunity to review points of interest or reread things that are not communicated clearly. As with any form of advertising, one of the first goals in creating TV commercials is to get the viewers' attention and then maintain it. This can be particularly challenging because of the clutter and because people often view TV commercials while doing other things (reading a book or magazine, talking).

Like print ads, TV commercials have several components. The video and audio must work together to create the right impact and communicate the advertiser's message.

Video   The video elements of a commercial are what is seen on the screen. The visual portion generally dominates the commercial, so it must attract viewers' attention and communicate an idea, message, and/or image. A number of visual elements may have to be coordinated to produce a successful ad. Decisions have to be made regarding the product, the presenter, action sequences, demonstrations, and the like, as well as the setting(s), the talent or characters who will appear in the commercial, and such other factors as lighting, graphics, color, and identifying symbols.

Audio   The audio portion of a commercial includes voices, music, and sound effects. Voices are used in different ways in commercials. They may be heard through the direct presentation of a spokesperson or as a conversation among various people appearing in the commercial. A common method for presenting the audio portion of a commercial

EXHIBIT 9–24

Voice123 provides advertisers with access to voice professionals who can be used to do voiceover for their commercials.

Voice123

is through a **voiceover**, where the message is delivered or action on the screen is narrated or described by an announcer who is not visible. A number of major advertisers have celebrities with distinctive voices do the voiceovers for their commercials.[38] Actor Morgan Freeman does the voiceover commercials for Visa and Under Armour; Allison Janney is the voice behind Kaiser Permanente commercials, and Hyundai has used actors Paul Rudd and Judd Apatow in some of its TV spots. Other celebrities who have been paid large sums of money to do voiceovers for commercials include Jon Hamm for Mercedes-Benz, George Clooney for Budweiser, Julia Roberts for Nationwide Insurance, Viola Davis for Delta Air Lines, and Bill Hader of *SNL* fame for Planters peanuts.

While some companies use celebrities or professionals to do the voiceover for their commercials, digital disruption is rapidly changing the voiceover industry as an online marketplace has emerged that connects voice actors to companies who need them. For decades, voiceovers were done primarily by professionals who were members of the Screen Actors Guild (SAG) and often had agents represent them. However, today voice actors are setting up home studios by hooking up a microphone and mixer and marketing their services through companies such as Voices.com, Voice123, and others that connect companies with voiceover talent (Exhibit 9–24). Voice actors often still need agents and SAG membership for most of the high-paying jobs such as advertising campaigns done by major marketers. However, many smaller companies are using online voice services for their commercials and videos.[39]

Music is also an important part of many TV commercials and can play a variety of roles.[40] In many commercials, the music provides a pleasant background or helps create the appropriate mood. Advertisers often use **needledrop**, which Linda Scott describes as follows:

> Needledrop is an occupational term common to advertising agencies and the music industry. It refers to music that is prefabricated, multipurpose, and highly conventional. It is, in that sense, the musical equivalent of stock photos, clip art, or canned copy. Needledrop is an inexpensive substitute for original music; paid for on a one-time basis, it is dropped into a commercial or film when a particular normative effect is desired.[41]

In some commercials, music is much more central to the advertising message. It can be used to get attention, break through the advertising clutter, communicate a key selling point, help establish an image or position, or add feeling.[42] For example, Google used The Beatles song "Help!" as part of its "Here to Help" ad campaign, which included a 60-second commercial set to the classic song. The ad featured user-generated content to show relatable, real-life moments where Google products and technology can help

EXHIBIT 9–25

Google licensed the master recording of The Beatles song "Help!" for its "Here to Help" campaign.

Denys Prykhodov/Shutterstock

people in their everyday lives, such as getting directions to a destination or instructions on how to do something or finding a way around traffic (Exhibit 9–25).

Steve Oakes conducted a review and analysis of research on consumers' cognitive and affective responses to music in advertising.[43] He found that increased congruity between the music and advertising with respect to variables such as mood, genre, score, image, and tempo contributes to the communication effectiveness of an advertisement by enhancing recall, brand attitude, affective response, and purchase intention. Research has also shown that music can work through a classical conditioning process to create a positive mood that makes consumers more receptive to an advertising message.[44] These studies underscore the importance of considering the mood induced by music and how it might influence responses to ads.

Because music can play such an important role in the creative strategy, many companies have paid large sums for the rights to use popular songs in their commercials. There are two kinds of works to which companies negotiate rights when licensing music for use in commercials. The *musical composition* includes the music notes and the words, while the *master recording* includes the voice(s) of the original artist.[45] The latter is usually much more expensive to buy, so advertisers will often negotiate for the rights to use the music and have it performed by someone with a similar voice. Rights to music can be held by various parties, such as the original artist, the artist's estate, or a music publishing company. For example, the rights to songs done by the late reggae star Bob Marley are held by his estate, while the rights to songs by Michael Jackson are controlled by music publishing company Sony/ATV. Google purchased the rights to the master recording of The Beatles song "Help!" for the campaign discussed previously. Google feels that the large amount of money paid to license the soundtrack was worth it because it works so well with the theme of the commercial and campaign.

Some advertising experts argue that music can account for as much as 50 percent of the effectiveness of a commercial and are encouraging their clients to invest in popular songs and soundtracks that can help them connect with their customers on an emotional level. They note that marketers who align themselves with popular songs and artists are often perceived as more cutting-edge and trendy, particularly if they are seen as exposing consumers to new artists and/or songs. There was a time when artists felt having their music used in commercials or creating songs for ads was "selling out." However, most artists now recognize that it is more beneficial and lucrative to "sell in" and have become open to having their music used in commercials. Artists can clearly benefit from having their songs used in commercials. For example, Apple often used music in its ad campaigns and is known for featuring songs by relatively obscure artists that benefit from the "Apple Bump," as they become very popular once they appear in the company's commercials. Apple used the Space Rangers song "The Move" as the soundtrack for the commercial used to launch the iPhone 14. So many songs have been used in Apple campaigns over the years that the editors at Apple Music recently curated a playlist titled "Heard in Apple Ads" that is available on Apple Music.[46]

Some advertisers are willing to pay large amounts of money to use the voices of the original artists in their commercials. A recent study by Nielsen, "I Second That Emotion: The Emotive Power of Music in Advertising," found that commercials with some form of music performed better across four important metrics—creativity, empathy, emotive power, and information power—than those that did not have music. The study notes that music not only can create a positive emotional response but can also help motivate consumers to buy a brand.[47]

Another important musical element in both TV and radio commercials is **jingles**, catchy, short songs about a product or service that usually carry the advertising theme and a simple message. Jingles are a specific type of **audio logo**, which is a sound, an effect, a short music clip, a musical riff, or a voiceover. Jingles typically last between 3 and 5 seconds and generally are heard at the end of a commercial. They are important as they tap into the inherent power of sound to create a memorable and distinct identity for a brand that often can connect with consumers at an emotional level, such as the jingles for Kay Jewelers ("Every kiss begins with Kay") or Folgers coffee ("The best part of waking up is Folgers in your cup"). Veritonic, an audio research and analytics company, does a survey each year on the most effective audio logos based on how successfully consumers could recall the company/brand associated with them and how well they resonated with the advertising content. In their 2022 annual report, the companies/brands with the most effective logos included fast-food chain Arby's ("We have the meats"), windshield repair and replacement company Safelite ("Safelite repair. Safelite replace"), Ace Hardware ("Ace is the place with the helpful hardware folks"), and several insurance companies including Farmers ("We are Farmers") and State Farm ("Like a good neighbor, State Farm is there"). The audio logo rated the highest was the iconic jingle for Folgers coffee.[48]

Jingles are often composed by companies that specialize in writing commercial music for advertising. These "jingle houses" work with the creative team to determine the role music will play in the commercial and the message that needs to be communicated. While the use of jingles in advertising dates back to the 1950s, the catchy music and songs, along with other types of audio logos, have become increasingly important as marketers strive to enhance their sound profile as part of their branding strategy. Companies and their marketers recognize that audio logos are an effective way to keep their company name and/or slogan in the minds of their customers and prospects. The position of many advertisers regarding the use of jingles is summed up by a Procter & Gamble brand manager who believes jingles work, noting that "if they are humming it, they are buying it."[49]

Planning and Production of TV Commercials   One of the first decisions that has to be made in planning a TV commercial is the type of appeal and execution style that will be used. Television is well suited to both rational and emotional advertising appeals or combinations of the two. Various execution styles used with rational appeals, such as a straight sell or announcement, demonstration, testimonial, or comparison, work well on TV. Television is particularly well suited to emotional appeals such as humor, fear, romance, and fantasies, which are often executed using dramatizations and slice-of-life commercials.

Advertisers recognize that they need to do more than talk about, demonstrate, or compare their products or services. Their commercials have to break through the clutter and grab viewers' attention, which is becoming increasingly difficult in today's multitasking viewing environment. Television is essentially an entertainment medium, and many advertisers recognize that their commercials are most successful when they entertain as well as inform. Many of the most popular advertising campaigns are characterized by commercials with strong entertainment value, like the engaging ads for Nike, McDonald's, Apple, and AT&T as well as humorous spots for companies/brands such as GEICO, State Farm, Hyundai, and Budweiser/Bud Light.

Television commercials are an integral part of the IMC program for most marketers, particularly larger companies that are advertising their products and services to mass markets. However, the costs of planning and producing a TV commercial can be very high and must be considered as part of the budget for an advertising campaign. While it is possible to produce a commercial for a few thousand dollars (such as many spots that air for local retailers and businesses), marketers recognize that a poorly produced TV ad will not be effective and may have a negative impact on the company and/or brand's image. Thus, large amounts of money are often required to produce high-quality TV commercials. For 25 years a Television Production Cost Survey was done by the American Association of Advertising Agencies (4As) that provided an

FIGURE 9–3

Production Costs for a
30-Second Television
Commercial

Big Time Productions
1234 Production Place
Santa Monica, CA 90404

Bid Date 3/25				Firm Bid (x) Cost Plus Fixed Fee ( )	
Production Co:	Big Time Productions			Agency:	Awesome Ads
Address:	1234 Production Place			Address:	1234 Advertising Way
	Santa Monica, CA 90404				Santa Monica, CA 90404
Telephone:	(310)555-5555			Telephone:	(310)555-5555
Fax:	(310)444-4444			Fax:	(310)444-4444
Job #:	M10-340			Agency Prod:	Ashley Producer
Director:				Agency Art Dir:	Brian Artist
Executive Producer:				Agency Writer:	Deborah Writer
Production Contact:				Agency Bus Mgr:	Alan Business
DP:				Client:	FAST FOOD CHAIN
Art Director:				Product:	Sandwich, Burger,
Editor:	Fine Edits			Bid Name:	
Pre-Production					
Days:					
Build & Strike Days:				Commercial Title:	Length:
Pre-Light Days:	One			1) "Delicious Sandwich"	:30
Studio Shoot Days:				2) "Yummy Burger"	:30
Location Days:	Two	Hours: 10 & 14			
Locations(s)	Los Angeles				

SUMMARY OF PRODUCTION COSTS	TOTAL
PRE-PRODUCTION & WRAP	$76,676
SHOOTING LABOR	$93,901
LOCATIONS & TRAVEL	$65,690
PROPS, WARDROBE & ANIMALS	$18,670
STUDIO & SET CONSTRUCTION	$88,056
EQUIPMENT	$42,750
FILMSTOCK DEVELOP & PRINT	$22,920
DIRECTOR/CREATIVE FEES	$32,400
INSURANCE	$12,288
PRODUCTION MARK UP	$92,153
NEEDLEDROP MUSIC	$2,000
EDITING	$66,504
TALENT	$33,905
GRAND TOTAL	$647,913

estimate of the average cost for producing a 30-second commercial for a national brand. The last survey done was more than 10 years ago, and the cost data supplied by 10 agencies for 506 national commercials of varying length estimated the average cost to be $354,000.[50] It is likely that the production costs for quality commercials have increased since the last 4As survey, particularly for major marketers who rely heavily on TV ads. Figure 9–3 shows an example of the production costs for a commercial that was produced for a major fast-food chain.

There are many factors that contribute to the costs of producing a TV commercial, including production personnel, equipment, location fees, video editing, sound recording and mixing, music fees, and talent. Increases in television commercial production costs are a major concern among marketers, and many companies are looking for ways to reduce them. For example, a large expense item is talent costs, as actors who appear in commercials receive *residuals* that are based primarily on how many times a commercial airs. The Joint Policy Committee on Broadcast Relations, an advertising industry group that represents advertisers and agencies in bargaining with talent unions, negotiated a new compensation system that will base pay for commercial actors on the size of the audience the spot reaches as well as the number of times it is run. In 2019, the Screen Actors Guild-American Federation of Television and Radio Artists (SAG-AFTRA) union and the Joint Policy Committee reached a new agreement on terms for successor television and audio commercial contracts that addresses changes occurring in the advertising industry, such as provisions for digital and social media.[51]

The cost of producing the high-quality TV commercials and videos used by many marketers remains high. However, today marketers are producing a variety of video content in addition to TV commercials for use across a variety of platforms and are learning to do so more efficiently to control production costs. And marketers and their agency partners have gotten smarter over the years and have learned to produce video content more efficiently.

Planning the Commercial The various elements of a TV commercial are brought together in a **script**, a written version of a commercial that provides a detailed description of its video and audio content. The script shows the various audio components of the commercial—the copy to be spoken by voices, the music, and sound effects. The video portion of the script provides the visual plan of the commercial—camera actions and angles, scenes, transitions, and other important descriptions. The script also shows how the video corresponds to the audio portion of the commercial.

Once the basic script has been conceived, the writer and art director get together to produce a storyboard, a series of drawings used to present the visual plan or layout of a proposed commercial. The storyboard contains still drawings of the video scenes and descriptions of the audio that accompanies each scene. Like layouts for print ads, storyboards provide those involved in the production and approval of the commercial with a good approximation of what the final commercial will look like. In some cases an animatic (a videotape of the storyboard along with the soundtrack) may be produced if a more finished form of the commercial is needed for client presentations or pretesting.

Production Once the storyboard or animatic of the commercial is approved, it is ready to move to the production phase, which involves three stages:

1. *Preproduction*—all the work and activities that occur before the actual shooting/recording of the commercial.
2. *Production*—the period during which the commercial is filmed or videotaped and recorded.
3. *Postproduction*—activities and work that occur after the commercial has been filmed and recorded.

The various activities of each phase are shown in Figure 9-4. Before the final production process begins, the client must usually review and approve the creative strategy and the various tactics that will be used in creating the advertising message.

Creative Tactics for Online Advertising

While a great deal of attention has been given to advertising creativity over the years, much of the focus has been on its application to traditional forms of advertising such as print, television, radio, or outdoor. However, marketers are allocating more of their media budgets to digital ads that appear on websites, social media, and mobile devices, which are creating a new set of challenges from a creative perspective. Compared to traditional media such as television or magazines, the Internet is a more goal-oriented medium.

FIGURE 9–4

The Three Phases of Production for Commercials

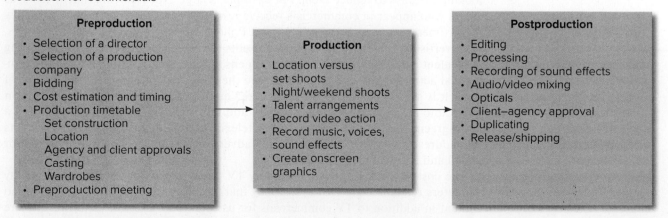

EXHIBIT 9–26

This online ad for Pepsi was designed to send a message that Pepsi is better with burgers from fast-food chains that don't serve Pepsi at all.

PepsiCo

Getting consumers to pay attention to, let alone engage or interact with, a digital ad is very difficult since doing so takes them away from the content on the web page or social media site they are visiting on their computers, tablets, or phones. Online ads often interrupt our viewing sessions, and unless they are providing relevant information and/or are very creative or entertaining, it is likely they will be ignored. Doubleclick, which is the display advertising division of Google, reports that the click-through rates (CTRs) for online display advertising across all format and placements is just 0.05 percent.[52] Rich media such as video ads have the highest average click-through rate (0.1 percent) of all digital ad formats, but the CTR is still very low. Moreover, many of the pre-roll ads shown prior to a video being viewed do not give the viewer the option to skip the advertisement and thus are often perceived as intrusive and annoying.

Role of Digital Ads   A variety of digital advertising formats are available to marketers, including banner ads, search ads, interstitials, native ads, and videos. The type of online ad used by marketers will vary depending on the goal(s) they are trying to achieve. Peter Minnium of the Interactive Advertising Bureau notes that digital advertising is trifurcating into three types of advertising—concept, content, and commerce ads—and their use varies based on the goals and/or objectives the marketer is trying to achieve all along the purchase funnel.

The goal of digital concept ads is to drive top-of-the-funnel goals such as awareness and interest, which can be achieved through banner ads or videos such as commercials. For example, the digital agency for Pepsi created a clever online ad as part of the #BetterWithPepsi campaign featuring the Pepsi logo in the crumpled folds of easily identifiable hamburger wrappers from the top three fast-food restaurants—Burger King, McDonald's, and Wendy's—all of which serve Coke instead of Pepsi (Exhibit 9–26). The goal of the ad was to make the point that burgers simply taste better with Pepsi and send a message that the top three burger chains deny their customers the opportunity to enjoy their hamburgers with an ice-cold Pepsi.[53]

Content ads typically have a mid-funnel goal of enhancing consumers' knowledge or understanding of a product or service, which can be done by providing high-quality content with which the viewer can engage. Different types of online ads can be used to provide content such as videos, webisodes, in-feed ads to Facebook or Twitter with sponsored content, and native ads. **Native advertising** is a type of paid placement designed to fit seamlessly into the content that surrounds it. The design, content, and writing style of a native ad mirrors the nonpaid content around it, giving the user the impression that it really belongs. Native advertising is becoming a dominant form of content advertising, particularly in digital editions of magazines and newspapers.

EXHIBIT 9–27

Mercedes-Benz developed a native advertising campaign in cooperation with *The Washington Post* to promote the Intelligent Drive system in the E-class automobile.

Mercedes-Benz USA, LLC

For example, Exhibit 9–27 shows an ad from a native campaign run by Mercedes-Benz called "The rise of the superhuman" that appeared in the online edition of *The Washington Post*. To pique interest and engage readers, the native content used an interactive quiz with questions and hot spots the reader could click to get more information about various technologies that turn ordinary people into superhumans, such as virtual reality, robotic suits, and facial recognition. The content tied into information about the Intelligent Drive system in the Mercedes-Benz E-class automobile.

The third form of digital advertising is commerce ads, which primarily have a bottom-of-the-funnel goal of getting consumers to take action and make a purchase. Commerce ads are the dominant form of display advertising, particularly retargeting types that follow consumers across the Web, and typically are not visually rich, as their success is based on serving the right offer to consumers and can be easily measured in terms of clicks and conversions. While digital advertising is discussed in more detail in Chapter 15, we will consider the creative issues associated with display ads and online videos, which are the dominant forms used by marketers.

Display Ads There are many different formats available for online display advertising. Many online display ads use large-size ad formats such as rectangular ads, horizontally oriented leaderboards, or skyscrapers that are vertically oriented and give advertisers the ability to place an ad adjacent to the website content. A study conducted by Dynamic Logic analyzed results from 4,800 online campaigns and found that the best-performing ad unit in terms of metrics such as brand awareness, recall, and purchase intent was the traditional pixel rectangular banner ad. The study also noted that ads surrounding content, such as well-worn skyscraper and leaderboard units, are the least effective, as people have developed "banner blindness."[54] Rectangular banner ads can be more effective because they are often closer to and interrupt the content, which means that as you read the information on the site, your eye naturally has to roll over the ad. However, ads that cover content are also among the most annoying online advertising formats.

In another study the company analyzed the highest and lowest performers from its database of more than 170,000 digital ads and found that creative factors such as persistent branding, strong calls to action, and the use of human faces result in better ad recall, brand awareness, and purchase intentions than do highly targeted or high-profile online ad placements. The results of the study support past research conducted by the company, which has shown that creative quality accounts for more than 50 percent of the success or failure of online advertising; factors such as ad size, technology, context, and targeting make up the remainder.

Critics argue that one of the major problems with online advertising is that it has been too focused on ubiquitous banner ads as marketers often try to build awareness and/or brand identity by simply buying large amounts of banner ads across myriad online platforms. A great deal of time and effort is devoted to optimizing media placement, retargeting, and measuring the effects of digital advertising campaigns, but less attention is given to creative considerations and the fundamentals of great advertising.[55] However, the domination of banner ads at the top or side of a page is weakening as new online display formats are being developed that are larger, richer, and take up more of a page, either initially or upon expansion. The Interactive Advertising Bureau refers to these new formats as "Rising Stars," which include ad unit formats such as billboard sidekicks and sliders as well as various video formats. One format that has become very popular is expanding pushdown ad units that push page content down

AD PLACEMENTS ON COX.COM

Medium Rectangle
300x250

Leaderboard
728x90*

Billboard
970x250

Pushdown Ad Unit
970x90 expands to 970x415

Half-Page
300x600

Mobile Ad Unit
320x50

EXHIBIT 9–28

Online display ad formats.

Cox Media, LLC

EXHIBIT 9–29

The Interactive Advertising Bureau developed the "New Ad Portfolio" guidelines for various forms of online advertising.

IAB

rather than expanding over it, which helps address the annoyance issue. Exhibit 9–28 shows examples of various online display advertising formats.

Although the design of most display ads is straightforward, there are certain rules and restrictions that must be adhered to in order to avoid having them rejected. For example, display ads should be distinguishable from normal webpage content, and there are rules that restrict ads from having a white background without an outline border. Various social media sites have restrictions regarding banner ads. Facebook has a rule that ad images can contain only 20 percent text, including logos. The Interactive Adverting Bureau (IAB), marketers, and online advertising networks have developed a range of display ad best practices. In 2017, the IAB released the "New Ad Portfolio" guidelines, which provide comprehensive recommendations for display advertising on websites, mobile apps, and social media as well as new digital experiences such as virtual reality and augmented reality (Exhibit 9–29). Before developing online display ads, marketers and/or their agencies must check with the ad networks and publisher to determine their specific requirements. These requirements also apply to the use of rich media such as online video, to which we now turn our attention.

Online Video The use of online video advertising is growing rapidly and is part of the tremendous growth in the viewing of videos across all online platforms, including websites, YouTube, Facebook, Instagram, Twitter, Snapchat, TikTok, and other popular social media sites. The use of video for online advertising can include multiple formats ranging from the airing of a digital video or commercial in a program streaming online to more customized formats for viewing on mobile devices. Online advertisers using video can choose from a number of options regarding the placement of the ad such as pre-roll, which runs before the piece of video content that is being viewed; mid-roll, which runs somewhere in the middle of the content; or post-roll, where the video plays at the completion of the content. They can also choose to use interactive ads that take over the full screen and preempt or pause the video content and allow a variety of interactions, like clicking for more information, signing up for a newsletter, or locating a store. These types of ads allow for further viewer engagement with the brand as well as interactivity that either expands in play or clicks out to an advertiser website. Different online advertising formats have also been developed as part of the IAB's "Rising Stars" program, such as control bars that allow viewers to share ads, watch extended versions, overlay videos with ad content, and more.

IAB New Ad Portfolio

Transition Now to the IAB New Standard Ad Unit Portfolio: Lightweight, Cross-Screen, and Flexible size ads that implement LEAN principles

The New Ad Portfolio guidelines developed by the IAB Tech Lab Ad Portfolio Working Group are comprehensive recommendations of advertising experiences across diverse digital landscape including websites, mobile apps, social media, communication, and messaging experiences as well as new digital experiences like virtual reality and augmented reality.

The IAB New Standard Ad Unit Portfolio ("IAB New Ad Portfolio") is comprised of:

1. Display ads
2. Native ads
3. New media experiences like Emoji ads, 360-degree image and video ads, Virtual reality ads and Augmented reality ads

It emphasizes on better user experience, faster load performance and non disruptive ad content based on the following principles:

1. Respect: A consumer's primary objective is consuming publisher content
2. Control: A consumer has control over his/her advertising experience
3. Choice: A consumer decides what content he/she wants to experience and for how long

Creative decisions regarding online videos and ads are often similar to those for television as far as the type of appeal, execution style, and use of video and audio elements. However, online video advertising must consider other factors such as intrusiveness, length, and content. For example, most online video ads are inserted pre-roll and shown prior to the video being viewed and provide little or no options to skip the advertisement, which means they can interfere with intended viewer activity. A study by Goodrich, Schiller, and Galletta found that online ads that are perceived as intrusive had a negative impact on attitudes and intentions toward both the advertised brand and the host website and also resulted in higher abandonment of ad viewing.[56] Length of the online video or ad is also an important factor because consumers are likely to be annoyed by longer ad formats or abandon them if they have the option to do so, unless they find them useful or entertaining. However, short-form commercials such as five-second spots may have trouble delivering a meaningful message.

Content is also an important consideration when creating online videos and advertisements. However, many creative directors note that the content of video ads that work well online is not that different from their TV counterparts. Videos and ads that provide relevant and/or valuable information are less likely to be perceived as intrusive and thus avoided. Emotional appeals often work better for longer videos, while humor can be very effective for online ads and perhaps have a greater likelihood of being shared. Marketers are recognizing that more attention has to be given to developing commercials and videos specifically for online use rather than simply uploading the same ads they use for television. Digital and Social Media Perspective 9–2 discusses how advances in smartphones, tablets, and streaming services is impacting video advertising.

Marketers will continue to spend more of their advertising budgets online since this is where their target audiences are spending their time. Moreover, many feel that the targeting and measurement capabilities of digital more than make up for the creative limitations of online advertising. However, it is also important for marketers to challenge their agencies to adopt and experiment with new types of formats and develop digital ads that are informative, entertaining, and/or engaging rather than continuing to bombard consumers with banner and/or video ads that they can easily avoid by clicking a mouse or button.

CLIENT EVALUATION AND APPROVAL OF CREATIVE WORK

While the creative specialists have much responsibility for determining the advertising appeal and execution style to be used in a campaign, the client must evaluate and approve the creative approach before any ads are produced. A number of people on the client side may be involved in evaluating the creative work of the agency, including the advertising or communications manager, product or brand managers, marketing director or vice president, representatives from the legal department, and sometimes even the president or chief executive officer (CEO) of the company or the board of directors. The amount of input each of these individuals has in the creative evaluation and approval process varies depending on the company's policies, the importance of the product to the company, the role of advertising in the marketing program, and the advertising approach being recommended.

In many cases, top management is involved in selecting an ad agency and must approve the theme and creative strategy for the campaign. Evaluation and approval of the individual ads proposed by the agency often rest with the advertising and product managers who are primarily responsible for the brand. The account executive and a member of the creative team present the creative concept to the client's advertising and product and/or marketing managers for their approval before beginning production. A careful evaluation should be made before the ad actually enters production, since this

Video Advertising Explodes—But Is More Creativity Needed?

Traditionally, marketers who wanted to advertise their company or brands using video would create commercials that would be shown on broadcast or cable television networks. However, a new era of advertising has arrived as marketers are spending more of their budgets online and video is rapidly becoming the dominant format for digital marketing. Several factors are driving the explosion in video advertising. A major factor is the way people consume media, as most are spending a great deal of their time online, particularly on YouTube and various social media platforms, watching videos. The increased usage of social media has been identified as the prime factor driving the growth in video advertising. A second factor is advances in technology as mobile phones in particular have gotten bigger, faster, and more conducive to video advertising. Research has shown the click-through rate (CTR) for online video advertising in mobile apps is much higher than for display ads. Facebook video ads also have a higher CTR than image ads.

While the use of online video advertising is expected to continue to surge in the coming years, marketers still face challenges in getting consumers to pay attention to their advertising messages. Take a moment to think about the last time you went to YouTube to watch a video and a pre-roll ad appeared before the video started. Did you watch the commercial or quickly hit the skip button so you could get on with watching the video? Advertisers usually have less than five seconds on YouTube to convince someone that their ad is worth watching before they have the option to skip it; more than 90 percent of people skip pre-roll ads after that five-second mark.

As marketers shift more of their advertising to using videos online on websites and social media, more attention needs to be given to creativity for such digital advertising. Getting consumers to pay attention to, not to mention engage with, an online ad is very difficult because doing so takes them away from the content on websites or their social media page. Television and radio ads air during commercial breaks and do not compete for viewers' or listeners' attention during a program, while print ads often appear on separate pages of a magazine or newspaper and can easily be ignored by simply turning the page. However, online ads often interrupt our viewing sessions, and unless they provide information that is relevant and/or of interest to a consumer, it is likely they will be ignored.

Many question the progress made in creativity in online advertising. They argue that the growth of digital and social media has lowered the bar and allows anyone to advertise, and that the increase in online advertising has been accompanied by a decrease in the quality of the ads. Many marketers use a digital, PR, or social media agency to create a number of ads very quickly using nothing more than free online tools such as Canva rather than engage the creative team at more comprehensive advertising agencies. Moreover, companies with smaller marketing budgets are afraid of overspending on video production. Thus, rather than developing impactful creative concepts, they focus on simple ideas that are easy to execute and can hopefully drive sales.

Another practice that is impacting online advertising is the growing use of short-form videos. Marketers have taken notice of the popularity of short-form video on social media platforms, such as TikTok, Instagram Reels, YouTube Shorts, Google, and Pinterest. Short-form videos first gained popularity through viral content based on dances, songs, and challenges. Seeing the success of this content, many marketers are using tactics such as songs, challenges, and teasers, as well as interactive elements such as polls to attract the attention and interest of consumers. They are developing partnerships with social media sites as well as collaborating with influencers to create short-form videos online. Research has shown that short-form video has the highest return on investment (ROI) of any social media marketing tactic. Shorter videos have been shown to be effective at influencing consumers throughout the purchase funnel. In addition to increasing awareness, they can boost brand preference and purchase intentions. Short-form videos are shared twice as frequently as any other type of information, according to reports.

Marketers will continue to move their advertising to digital media because they know that is where consumers now spend much of their time. They believe that the targeting and measurement capabilities of digital media more than make up for the creative limitations of online advertising. But to be successful they will have to challenge their agencies to develop online ads that are entertaining and engaging rather than continue to bombard consumers with yet more videos that they are likely to ignore.

Sources: Martina Bretous, "6 Short-Form Video Trends Marketers Should Watch in 2022," *HubSpot*, July 18, 2022, https://blog.hubspot.com/marketing/short-form-video-trends; Lisa Montenegro, "In 2022, Video Is Where We All Need to Be," *Forbes*, January 28, 2022, https://www.forbes.com/sites/forbesagencycouncil/2022/01/28/in-2022-video-is-where-we-all-need-to-be/?sh=9ca4eec7e5ad; Robert Williams, "Short Video Ads Impact All Stages of Purchase Funnel, Study Says," *Marketing Dive*, December 14, 2020, https://www.marketingdive.com/news/short-video-ads-impact-all-stages-of-purchase-funnelstudy-says/592095/; Karen X. Cheng, "Common Video Marketing Mistakes," *Adweek*, April 8, 2019, p. 11.

stage requires considerable time and money as suppliers are hired to perform the various functions required to produce the actual ad.

The client's evaluation of the print layout or commercial storyboard can be difficult, since the advertising or brand manager is generally not a creative expert and must be careful not to reject viable creative approaches or accept ideas that will result in inferior advertising. However, personnel on the client side can use the guidelines discussed next to judge the efficacy of creative approaches suggested by the agency.

Guidelines for Evaluating Creative Output

Advertisers use numerous criteria to evaluate the creative approach suggested by the ad agency. In some instances, the client may want to have the rough layout storyboard or animatic pretested to get quantitative information to assist in the evaluation. (Various methods for pretesting print ads and TV commercials will be discussed in Chapter 18.) However, the evaluation process is usually more subjective; the advertising or brand manager relies on qualitative considerations. The following are the basic criteria for evaluating creative approaches:

- *Is the creative approach consistent with the brand's marketing and advertising objectives?* One of the most important factors the client must consider is whether the creative appeal and execution style recommended by the agency are consistent with the marketing strategy for the brand and the role advertising and promotion have been assigned in the overall marketing program. This means the creative approach must be compatible with the image of the brand and the way it is positioned in the market. The approach should also be consistent with marketing and advertising objectives and contribute to building or maintaining brand equity.

- *Is the creative approach consistent with the creative strategy and objectives? Does it communicate what it is supposed to?* The advertising appeal and execution must meet the communications objectives laid out in the copy platform, and the ad must say what the advertising strategy calls for it to say. Creative specialists can lose sight of what the advertising message is supposed to be and come up with an approach that fails to execute the advertising strategy. Individuals responsible for approving the ad should ask the creative specialists to explain how the appeal or execution style adheres to the creative strategy and helps meet communications objectives.

- *Is the creative approach appropriate for the target audience?* Generally, much time has been spent defining, locating, and attempting to understand the target audience for the advertiser's product or service. Careful consideration should be given to whether the ad appeal or execution recommended will appeal to, be understood by, and communicate effectively with the target audience. This involves studying all elements of the ad and how the audience will respond to them. Advertisers do not want to approve advertising that they believe will receive a negative reaction from the target audience. For example, it has been suggested that advertising targeted to older consumers should use models who are 10 years younger than the average age of the target audience, since most people feel younger than their chronological age.[57] Advertisers also face a considerable challenge developing ads for the teen market because teenagers' styles, fashions, language, and values change so rapidly. They may find they are using an advertising approach, a spokesperson, or even an expression that is no longer popular among teens.

- *Does the creative approach communicate a clear and convincing message to the customer?* Most ads are supposed to communicate a message that will help sell the brand. Many ads fail to communicate a clear and convincing message that motivates consumers to use a brand. While creativity is important in advertising, it is also important that the advertising communicate information attributes, features and benefits, and/or images that give consumers a reason to buy the brand.

- *Does the creative execution keep from overwhelming the message?* A common criticism of advertising, and TV commercials in particular, is that so much emphasis is placed on creative execution that the advertiser's message gets overshadowed. Many creative, entertaining commercials have failed to register the brand name and/or selling points effectively. For example, Aflac had to modify the commercials using its iconic duck character after several research studies showed that many consumers were not exactly sure what Aflac insurance was. Consumers indicated that the advertising didn't explain what supplemental insurance is and what Aflac does, so recent ads focus more attention on explaining the product and the company.[58]

  With the increasing amount of clutter in most advertising media, it may be necessary to use a novel creative approach to gain the viewer's or reader's attention. However, the creative execution cannot overwhelm the message. Clients must walk a fine line: Make sure the sales message is not lost, but be careful not to stifle the efforts of the creative specialists and force them into producing dull, boring advertising.

- *Is the creative approach appropriate for the media environment in which it is likely to be seen?* Each media vehicle has its own specific climate that results from the nature of its editorial content, the type of reader or viewer it attracts, and the nature of the ads it contains. Consideration should be given to how well the ad fits into the media environment in which it will be shown. For example, the Super Bowl has become a showcase for commercials. People who care very little about advertising know how much a 30-second commercial costs and pay as much attention to the ads as to the game itself, so many advertisers feel compelled to develop new ads for the Super Bowl or to save new commercials for the game. In some cases, marketers may develop ads specifically for certain media vehicles such as magazines. For example, many of the ads run in the popular *Sports Illustrated Swimsuit Issue* that is published each year are adapted to fit with the theme of the magazine. Exhibit 9–30 shows an example of a clever ad for Snickers that appeared on the back cover of the annual SI swimsuit issue.

IF YOU BOUGHT THIS MAGAZINE FOR THE SNICKERS BIKINI, YOU'RE PROBABLY HUNGRY.

- *Is the ad truthful and tasteful?* Marketers also have to consider whether an ad is truthful, as well as whether it might offend consumers. Marketers sometimes use various tactics on social media and other digital platforms to draw attention to their messages that may backfire. For example, Burger King UK made unintended headlines after posting a controversial "joke" tweet on International Women's Day 2021 stating that "Women belong in the kitchen." The fast-food chain in fact made the tweet to announce their culinary scholarship program for female employees. Although it was clear from the rest of the thread that the tweet was intended as a joke, few people bothered to read it through and thousands of users bombarded the thread calling out Burger King for misogyny and insensitivity. Burger King initially tried to explain that its intention had been to promote the culinary scholarship program, but they eventually apologized and deleted the entire Twitter thread.

  An interesting example of clever but somewhat controversial advertising that might offend some people is a print ad that KFC used in the United Kingdom in response to a crisis marketing situation a few years ago.[59] An operational issue with a delivery provider resulted in the chain running

EXHIBIT 9–31

KFC ran this clever apology ad in the United Kingdom, but it may be seen as inappropriate in some countries.

Yum! Brands, Inc.

WE'RE SORRY

A chicken restaurant without any chicken. It's not ideal. Huge apologies to our customers, especially those who travelled out of their way to find we were closed. And endless thanks to our KFC team members and our franchise partners for working tirelessly to improve the situation. It's been a hell of a week, but we're making progress, and every day more and more fresh chicken is being delivered to our restaurants. Thank you for bearing with us.

Visit kfc.co.uk/crossed-the-road for details about your local restaurant.

out of chicken and being forced to close hundreds of stores temporarily. Disappointed customers were very vocal on social media and even tried to get the police involved in some cities when the chain ran out of chicken. The marketing team and its agency, Mother London, knew they had to respond and decided to do so with a creative stunt by rearranging the letters in its name in the apology ad, which is shown in Exhibit 9–31. The ad won numerous creative awards because many felt that it was appropriate for a company that does not take itself too seriously with its marketing. While the ad worked well in the United Kingdom, there are some countries where the ad might be seen as inappropriate or distasteful.

The ultimate responsibility for determining whether an ad deceives or offends the target audience lies with the client. It is the job of the advertising or brand manager to evaluate the approach suggested by the creative specialists against company standards. The firm's legal department may be asked to review the ad to determine whether the creative appeal, message content, or execution could cause any problems for the company. It is much better to catch any potential legal problems before the ad is shown to the public.

The chief marketing officer, brand manager, advertising manager, and/or other personnel on the client side can use these basic guidelines in reviewing, evaluating, and approving the ideas offered by the creative specialists. There may be other factors specific to the firm's advertising and marketing situation. Also, there may be situations where it is acceptable to deviate from the standards the firm usually uses in judging creative output. As we will see in Chapter 18, the client may want to move beyond these subjective criteria and use more sophisticated pretesting methods to determine the effectiveness of a particular approach suggested by the creative specialist or team.

Summary

In this chapter, we examined how the advertising message is implemented and executed. Once the creative strategy that will guide the ad campaign has been determined, attention turns to the specific type of advertising appeal and execution format to carry out the creative plan. The appeal is the central message used in the ad to elicit some response from consumers or influence their feelings. Appeals can be broken into two broad categories: rational and emotional. Rational appeals focus on consumers' practical, functional, or utilitarian need for the product or service; emotional appeals relate to social and/or psychological reasons for purchasing a product or service. Numerous types of appeals are available to advertisers within each category.

The creative execution style is the way the advertising appeal is presented in the message. A number of common execution techniques were examined in the chapter, along with considerations for their use. Attention was also given to

tactical issues involved in creating print, television, and digital advertising. The components of a print ad include headlines, body copy, illustrations, and layout. We also examined the video and audio components of TV commercials and various considerations involved in the planning and production of commercials. The role of creativity in digital advertising was discussed along with tactical considerations for display and online video ads.

Creative specialists are responsible for determining the advertising appeal and execution style as well as the tactical aspects of creating ads. However, the client must review, evaluate, and approve the creative approach before any ads are produced or run. A number of criteria were discussed that can be used by advertising, product, or brand managers and others involved in the promotional process to evaluate the advertising messages before approving final production.

Key Terms

advertising appeal 290
creative execution style 290
informational/rational appeals 290
emotional appeals 292
transformational ad 295
reminder advertising 297
teaser advertising 297

user-generated content (UGC) 298
headline 307
direct headlines 307
indirect headlines 307
subheads 308
body copy 308
layout 309

voiceover 310
needledrop 310
jingles 312
audio logos 312
script 314
native advertising 315

Discussion Questions

1. The chapter opener discusses how Applebee's collaborated with country singer Walker Hayes to develop an advertising campaign around his hit song "Fancy Like." Discuss how Applebee's was able to capitalize on the popularity of the song. Do you think Applebee's will be able to partner with Hayes on future ad campaigns or will this turn out to be a short-lived advertising opportunity? (LO 9-1, 9-2, 9-3)

2. What types of products or services are most likely to use an informational/rational appeal as the basis for an advertising message? Find an example of a specific type of informational/rational ad and analyze its use by the advertiser. (LO 9-1)

3. Discuss some of the reasons emotion-based advertising appeals are effective. Find an example of a company or brand that is using an advertising campaign based on an emotional appeal and analyze its effectiveness. (LO 9-1)

4. Digital and Social Media Perspective 9–1 discusses the "Reverse Selfie" video used by Dove to address the issue of heavily edited selfies that young girls post on social media. Watch the video on YouTube and discuss whether you think it will be effective in addressing the problem of unrealistic beauty standards. (LO 9-1, 9-4)

5. Explain the concept of transformational advertising. Find an example of a company that is using

transformational ads and discuss how the ads might enhance the experience of using the product or service. (LO 9-1)

6. Choose three of the advertising execution techniques discussed in the chapter and find examples of advertisements that are using them. Discuss why these companies or brands might be using these particular ad execution techniques. (LO 9-2)

7. Discuss the role of headlines in a print advertisement. What is the difference between a direct headline and an indirect headline, and when might each type be used? (LO 9-3)

8. Discuss the role of music in advertising. Find an example of a television commercial that is using a specific song and discuss the role the music plays in delivering the message. (LO 9-3)

9. Discuss the challenges marketers face in developing online video advertising messages given the advances in technology around mobile devices and streaming services. (LO 9-3)

10. Choose a current advertising campaign and analyze it with respect to the creative guidelines discussed in the last section of the chapter. Identify any areas where you feel the campaign does or does not meet the guidelines and discuss why this is so. (LO 9-4)

10 Media Planning and Strategy

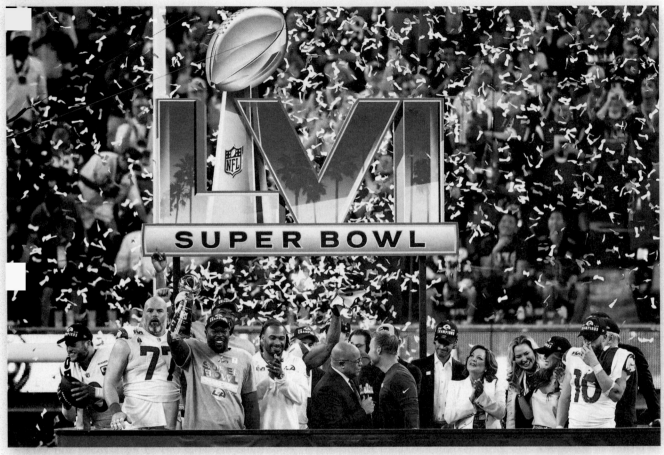

Ronald Martinez/Getty Images

Learning Objectives

LO10-1 | Define the key terminology in media planning.

LO10-2 | Explain how to develop a media plan.

LO10-3 | Describe the purpose of media objectives.

LO10-4 | Describe how to develop and implement media strategies.

LO10-5 | Compare the characteristics of various media.

The Nielsen Ratings: Will Advertisers Really Say Goodbye?

Even if you have never studied or read an article about advertising, worked in the television industry, or had any interest in business at all, you probably have at least heard of the Nielsen Ratings. Maybe it was something you heard on television or read in the newspaper or a magazine after the Super Bowl or the Academy Awards, or just because your favorite TV program was no longer on and you found out it was because its ratings were down. The Nielsen Ratings are a measure of the size and composition of television audiences in the United States and have been the standard upon which the costs of television commercials is based. Since the Nielsen Ratings started in 1950, the higher your show was rated, the more you could charge for your advertising time. Even today the ratings are a critical metric that guides decisions regarding where ads will be placed, programming, scheduling, and even employment decisions (news anchors' jobs are particularly vulnerable). And for over 70 years the Nielsen Ratings have been criticized and demonized in scores of negative articles in magazines, academic journals, and advertising books as well as other media sources.

So what is it that makes the ratings so controversial? Over the years numerous articles have attacked the Nielsen research methodology from a variety of perspectives. Concerns include sampling issues (nonrepresentative of the overall viewer audience, respondents being aware of being tested leading to response bias, samples too small to be representative, etc.), how and where data collection took place, and even how the results were used. As recently as 2021 critics claimed the Nielsen methodology was no more current than it was in the 1950s, and when the ratings indicated that television viewership was down during the pandemic they were skeptical to say the least. The Media Rating Council (MRC), an independent monitoring service that establishes standards, audits, and accredits organizations in the media measurement industry, revoked Nielsen's accreditation in 2021 for "potentially unreliable data," while confirming that Nielsen had incorrectly counted viewership.

Nielsen (finally, some would say) announced that they were going to overhaul their system by 2024, leading Scott Brown, the general manager for audience measurement at Nielsen, to say that it "would change the whole concept of what TV ratings are." The new system would incorporate digital viewing on a smartphone or computer while including streaming TV as well as traditional metrics. The new system called Nielsen One would allow advertisers to see directly where the viewer sees the ad and compare the metrics. The company is working with executives throughout the television industry as well as the Association of National Advertisers and MRC throughout the development process, which will require a massive undertaking.

Meanwhile some advertisers may not be just waiting around for Nielsen's new system. A number of competitors, recognizing that the decades old standard is no longer invincible, have developed their own systems. Through the years a number of competitors have tried to offer an alternative to the Nielsen ratings with little or no success. Whereas in the past it was very difficult to use someone else's measurement system when everyone relied on Nielsen, some advertisers are now more open to new options. After all, the Nielson upgrade is not the Nielsen ratings that have been relied upon for the past 70 years, it is a new and different system. Some companies and agencies have already decided to use other measurement providers along with Nielsen to offer parallel metrics. Others are taking a wait and see approach. After all, these new entries haven't proven their systems will be any better. And as noted by Tim Peterson of digiday.com, "And then there's the fact that advertisers are moving from an era in which they had a single source of truth for decades to a current landscape in which they will have to verify a new world order." Almost everyone agrees that it will take more than a year to test out the new Nielsen system, which is currently in its alpha stage of testing. Many are waiting to see what happens after that!

Sources: Tim Peterson, "Advertisers, TV Networks Plan to Set Nielsen Alternatives as 'Shadow Currencies' in This Year's Upfront Negotiations," *Digiday*, January 21, 2022, www.digiday.com; Sahil Patel, "Nielsen Sets Timeline for Big Change in TV Ratings," *Wall Street Journal*, December 8, 2020, www.wsj.com; Brian Steinberg, "Nielsen Plans TV-Ratings Overhaul by 2024 with Focus on Multi-Screen Audience," *Variety*, December 8, 2020, www.variety.com.

As discussed in the lead-in to this chapter, the Nielsen Ratings have been a critical component of media planning for almost as long as there has been television in spite of the well-known fact that there have always been methodological issues with the system. In defense of Nielsen, the enormous task of accurately determining what households were watching on television was at least in part one of the reasons why no one else came up with a more acceptable methodology. But times have changed. Media research has advanced and become more sophisticated, and the media environment has changed and become more complex. Digital has created new opportunities for advertisers to the point where spending on digital now exceeds that allocated to television advertising. As they should, marketers are now demanding more, and more reliable, metrics.

The ability to gain even more data on the target audience, the proliferation of new media, and pressure to place the ad in pretty much real time, as well as the use of different metrics has resulted in a whole new media buying landscape. As a result, media planning has become more complex than ever before—despite the contention that some technological advances simplify it. As you will see in the following chapters, these changes offer marketers opportunities not previously available, but they also require in-depth knowledge of all the media alternatives. Integrated marketing communications programs are no longer a luxury; they are a necessity. Media planners must now consider multiple new options as well as recognize the changes that are occurring in traditional sources. New and evolving media contribute to the already difficult task of media planning. Planning when, where, and how the message will be delivered is a complex and involved process that is constantly evolving. The primary objective of the media plan is to develop a framework that will deliver the message that communicates what the product, brand, and/or service can do for the target audience in the most efficient, cost-effective manner possible.

This chapter examines some key considerations in making media decisions and discusses the development of media strategies and plans. Later chapters will explore the relative advantages and disadvantages of the various media and examine each in more detail.

It should be noted that while new media often use their own terms and concepts, many also use the more traditional metrics as well. Much of the focus in this chapter will be on traditional concepts, with subsequent chapters dealing with media-specific terminology. For example, in social media a medium would be user-generated video, YouTube is a platform, and a channel would be 60secondmarketer.com.[1] Nevertheless, the value and necessity of a planning framework still exists across all media.

AN OVERVIEW OF MEDIA PLANNING

The media planning process is not an easy one. Options include traditional mass media such as television, newspapers, radio, and magazines (and the choices available within each of these categories) as well as out-of-home media such as outdoor advertising, transit advertising, and electronic billboards. A variety of other media such as direct marketing, promotional products, sales promotions, and in-store point-of-purchase options must also be considered. A proliferation of new media, including branded entertainment, social media, the Internet, and mobile, have also provided marketers with many options to consider.

While at first glance the choices among these alternatives might seem relatively straightforward, this is rarely the case. Part of the reason media selection becomes so involved is the nature of the media themselves. TV combines both sight and sound, an advantage not offered by most other media. Magazines can convey more information and may keep the message available to the potential buyer for a much longer time. Newspapers also offer their own advantages, as do outdoor, direct media, and each of the others. The new digital media offer many of the advantages of other media but also have limitations in their capabilities. The characteristics of each alternative must be considered, along with many other factors. This process becomes even more complicated when the manager has to choose between alternatives within the same medium—for example, between *Vanity Fair* and *Vogue* in print, between *FBI* and *NCIS* on TV, between two streaming channels' programming, or TikTok and Instagram on the Internet.

Many companies, large and small, have come to realize the importance of a sound media strategy. They are focusing additional attention on the integration of creative work and media as well as the use of multiple media vehicles to achieve the optimal impact. For example, ads that have been shown on TV now appear for viewing on the company's Internet site or YouTube. In the past the commercials to be shown during the Super Bowl were surrounded by secrecy in an attempt to heighten expectations. Now, many of the commercials that appear during the Super Bowl are first released on YouTube or other media outlets to gain more exposure. Advertisers still disagree as to which strategy is more effective.

The product and/or service being advertised affects the media planning process. As demonstrated in Figure 10-1, firms have found some media more useful than others in conveying their messages to specific target audiences. For example, Procter & Gamble and Walt Disney spend a larger percentage of their overall budget in measured media (traditional media like TV, magazines) than do others in the top ten, while Amazon spends the lowest percentage. Note that many of these companies have recently decreased their spending in traditional media while increasing unmeasured expenditures. The result is placement of advertising dollars in these preferred media—and significantly different media strategies.

Some Basic Terms and Concepts

Before beginning our discussion of media planning, we review some basic terms and concepts used in the media planning and strategy process.

Media planning is the series of decisions involved in delivering the promotional message to the prospective purchasers and/or users of the product or brand. Media planning is a process, which means a number of decisions are made, each of which may be altered or abandoned as the plan develops.

The media plan is the guide for media selection. It requires development of specific **media objectives** and specific **media strategies** (plans of action) designed to attain these objectives. Once the decisions have been made and the objectives and strategies formulated, this information is organized into the media plan.

The **medium** is the general category of available delivery systems, which includes broadcast media (like TV and radio), digital media, print media (like newspapers and magazines), direct marketing, outdoor advertising, and other support media. The **media vehicle** is the specific carrier within a medium category. For example, *Vanity Fair* and *In Style* are print vehicles; *The Voice* and *60 Minutes* are broadcast vehicles; Facebook and Instagram are social media vehicles. As you will see in later chapters, each vehicle has its own characteristics as well as its own relative advantages and disadvantages. Specific decisions must be made as to the value of each in delivering the message.

Reach is a measure of the number of different audience members exposed at least once to a media vehicle in a given period of time. **Coverage** refers to the potential audience that might receive the message through a vehicle. Coverage relates to potential audience; reach refers to the actual audience delivered. (The importance of this distinction will become clearer later in this chapter.) Finally, **frequency** refers to the number of times the receiver is exposed to the media vehicle in a specified period. While there are numerous more media planning terms that are important and commonly used, we will begin our discussion with these as they are critical to your understanding of the planning process.

FIGURE 10–1 *Ad Age*'s Leading National Advertisers

Rank	Marketer	Headquarters	Total U.S. Advertising Spending 2021		U.S. Measured-Media Ad Spending 2021
1	**Amazon**	Seattle	**$10,430**	Estimated advertising and promotion spending	**$1,455**
2	**Comcast Corp.**	Philadelphia	**6,012**	Estimated advertising, marketing and promotion spending	**1,091**
3	**Procter & Gamble Co.**	Cincinnati	**5,079**	Estimated marketing spending. Year ended June 2021	**2,363**
4	**American Express Co.**	New York	**3,976**	Estimated marketing and promotion expenses	**152**
5	**Walt Disney Co.**	Burbank, California	**3,759**	Estimated ad spending. Year ended October 2021	**1,090**
6	**Alphabet (Google)**	Mountain View, California	**3,602**	Estimated advertising and promotion spending	**767**
7	**Warner Bros. Discovery**	New York	**$3,413**	Estimated pro forma ad spending	**$994**
8	**Verizon Communications**	New York	**3,394**	Ad spending. Verizon in November 2021 bought TracFone Wireless. Verizon in September 2021 sold Verizon Media (now Yahoo)	**728**
9	**Walmart**	Bentonville, Arkansas	**3,105**	Estimated ad spending	**477**
10	**Charter Communications**	Stamford, Connecticut	**3,071**	Marketing expenses	**258**

*Ranked by total U.S. advertising spending in 2021. Dollars in millions. Ranking of top 200 advertisers: AdAge.com/lna2022. Database with ad spending, brands, profiles, executives and agency rosters for 100 biggest advertisers: AdAge.com/marketertrees2022.

Source: https://adage.com/article/datacenter/25-biggest-us-advertisers-include-amazon-and-pg-leading-national-advertisers-2022/2419581.

The Media Plan

The media plan determines the best way to get the advertiser's message to the market. In a basic sense, the goal of the media plan is to find that combination of media that enables the marketer to communicate the message in the most effective manner to the largest number of potential customers at the lowest cost.

The activities involved in developing the media plan and the purposes of each are presented in Figure 10-2. As you can see, a number of decisions must be made throughout this process. As the plan evolves, events may occur that necessitate changes. Many advertisers find it necessary to alter and update their objectives and strategies frequently.

FIGURE 10-2 Activities Involved in Developing the Media Plan

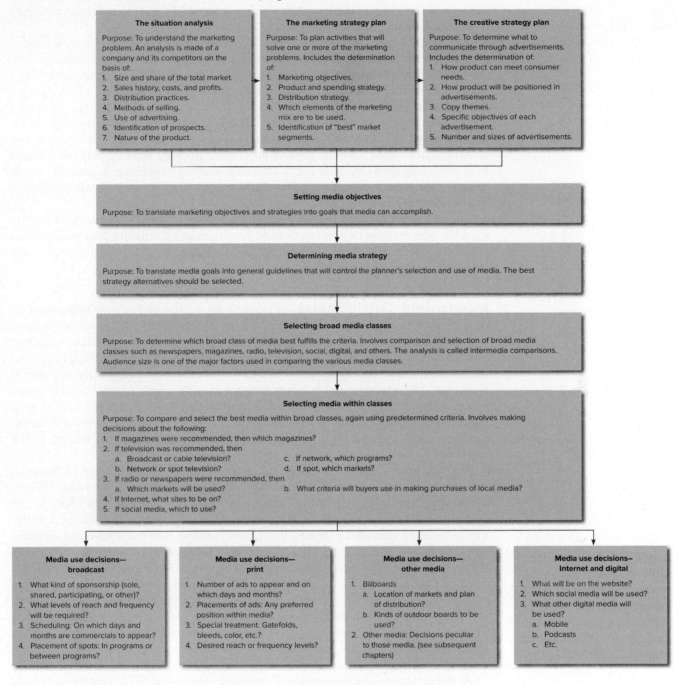

Problems in Media Planning

Unfortunately, the media strategy decision has not become a simple task. A number of problems contribute to the difficulty of establishing the plan and reduce its effectiveness. These problems include insufficient information, inconsistent terminologies, time pressures, and difficulty measuring effectiveness.

Insufficient Information While a great deal of information about markets and the media exists, media planners often require more than is available. Some data are just not measured, either because they cannot be or because measuring them would be too expensive. For example, continuous measures of radio listenership exist, but only periodic listenership studies are reported due to sample size and cost constraints. There are problems with some measures of audience size in other media as well. As you will see later in this chapter, there is often a lack of information and transparency asociated with some media.

The timing of measurements is also a problem; some audience measures are taken only at specific times of the year. (For example, **sweeps periods** in February, May, July, and November are used for measuring TV audiences and setting advertising rates.) This information is then generalized to succeeding months, so future planning decisions must be made on past data that may not reflect current behaviors. (In the largest TV markets, meters are used to provide information.) Think about planning for TV advertising for the fall season. There are no data on the audiences of new shows, and audience information taken on existing programs during the summer may not indicate how these programs will do in the fall because summer viewership is generally much lower. While the advertisers can review these programs before they air, all markets do not have actual audience figures.

The lack of information is even more of a problem for small advertisers, or smaller markets, who may not be able to afford to purchase the information they require. As a result, their decisions are based on limited or out-of-date data that were provided by the media themselves, or no data at all.

Inconsistent Terminologies   Problems arise because the cost bases used by different media often vary and the standards of measurement used to establish these costs are not always consistent. For example, print media may present cost data in terms of the cost to reach a thousand people (cost per thousand, or CPM), broadcast media use the cost per ratings point (CPRP), and outdoor media use the number of showings. The advent of the Internet brought about a whole new lexicon of terminologies. Audience information that is used as a basis for these costs has also been collected by different methods. Finally, terms that actually mean something different (such as *reach* and *coverage*) may be used synonomously by some, adding to the confusion.

In 2006, a joint task force composed of members of the Association of National Advertisers (ANA), American Association of Advertising Agencies (4As), Direct Marketing Association (DMA), Advertising Research Foundation (ARF), and Interactive Advertising Bureau (IAB) launched an initiative to determine a better way to measure consumer exposure to an advertisement. The group unveiled an initiative that would significantly change the way exposure was measured, essentially replacing the use of frequency (the number of exposures to an ad) with engagement, a measure they said would better reflect the growing number of media choices available to consumers. Although the committee agreed on backing the new term, others were not so willing, asking for a more precise definition of *engagement*. The committee agreed to further examine and validate the concept.[2] However, even today there is no consensus as to the meaning of the term, and some in the ad industry have called for a return to a focus on awareness.[3]

At the same time, the importance of engagement has been recognized by marketers. The Nielsen Company, which was discussed in the lead-in, is just one of many firms now providing engagement data. A quick Google search will show numerous companies offering a variety of metrics particularly in the digital domain. Figure 10–3 shows the results of a study that demonstrates that there is a strong correlation between program involvement and ad recall, which may be part of the reason advertisers are interested in learning more than just awareness figures.

Time Pressures   It seems that advertisers are always in a hurry—sometimes because they need to be, other times because they think they need to be. Actions by a competitor—for example, the cutting of airfares by one carrier—require immediate response. But sometimes a false sense of urgency dictates time pressures. In either situation, media selection decisions may be made without proper planning and analysis of the markets and/or media.

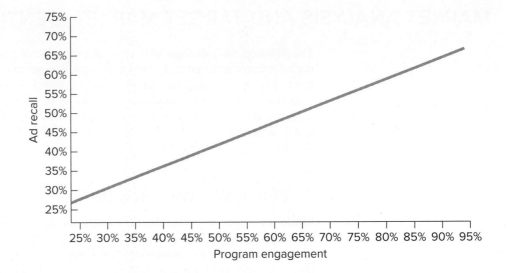

Difficulty Measuring Effectiveness Because it is so hard to measure the effectiveness of advertising and promotions in general, it is also difficult to determine the relative effectiveness of various media or media vehicles. (Recall the discussion of ROI from Chapter 7.) While progress is being made in this regard, the media planner may have little more than an estimate of or a good guess at the impact of these alternatives. In fact, in a study reported in *eMarketer*, only 25 percent of brand marketers reported that they were confident that their media mix was optimal, due to the inability to make this determination.[4]

Because of these problems, not all media decisions are quantitatively determined. Sometimes managers have to assume the image of a medium in a market with which they are not familiar, anticipate the impact of recent events, or make judgments without full knowledge of all the available alternatives.

While these problems complicate the media decision process, they do not render it an entirely subjective exercise. The remainder of this chapter explores in more detail how media strategies are developed and ways to increase their effectiveness.

DEVELOPING THE MEDIA PLAN

The promotional planning model in Chapter 1 discussed the process of identifying target markets, establishing objectives, and formulating strategies for attaining them. The development of the media plan and strategies follows a similar path, except that the focus is more specifically keyed to determining the best way to deliver the message. The process, shown in Figure 10-4, involves a series of stages: (1) market analysis, (2) establishment of media objectives, (3) media strategy development and implementation, and (4) evaluation and follow-up. Each of these is discussed in turn, with specific examples.

FIGURE 10–4 Developing the Media Plan

MARKET ANALYSIS AND TARGET MARKET IDENTIFICATION

The situation analysis stage of the overall promotional planning process involves a complete review of internal and external factors, competitive strategies, and the like. In the development of a media strategy, a market analysis is again performed, although this time the focus is on the media and delivering the message. The key questions at this stage are these: To whom will we advertise (who is the target market)? What internal and external factors may influence the media plan? Where (geographically) and when should we focus our efforts?

To Whom Will We Advertise?

While a number of target markets might be derived from the situation analysis, to decide which specific groups to go after, the media planner may work with the client, account representative, marketing department, and creative directors. A variety of factors can assist media planners in this decision. Some will require primary research, whereas others will be available from published (secondary) sources.

Experian Simmons, formerly the Simmons Market Research Bureau (SMRB), provides information through its annual *Experian National Consumer Study.* The study provides information regarding traditional media usage (English and Spanish languages), product, brands and services used, and demographic and psychographic characteristics. Similarly, Gfk-owned MRI-Simmons also provides information that is more specific to the media usage of consumers. Once competitors, the two companies (Gfk and Experian-Simmons) have combined efforts in 2021 (and is now called MRI-Simmons) to provide insights into consumers' media usage of eleven traditional and digital media platforms.

Media planners are often more concerned with the percentage figures and index numbers than with the raw numbers. This is largely due to the fact that they may have their own data from other sources, both primary and secondary; the numbers provided may not be specific enough for their needs; or they question the numbers provided because of the methods by which they were collected. The total (raw) numbers provided by MRI-Simmons are used in combination with the media planner's own figures.

On the other hand, the **index number** is considered a good indicator of the potential of the market. This number is derived from the formula

$$\text{Index} = \frac{\text{Percentage of users in a demographic segment}}{\text{Percentage of population in the same segment}} \times 100$$

An index number over 100 means use of the product is proportionately greater in that segment than in one that is average (100) or less than 100. For example, the data in Figure 10-5 show that people in the age groups 18-54 are more likely to engage in jogging/running, while participation in this activity drops off significantly after age 54. Men are slightly more likely than women to participate. Depending on their overall strategy, marketers may wish to use this information to determine which groups are now using the product and target them or to identify a group that is currently using the product less and attempt to develop that segment. Figure 10-6 provides more instruction on how to read an MRI-Simmons report.

While the index is helpful, it should not be used alone. Percentages and product usage figures are also needed to get an accurate picture of the market. Just because the index for a particular segment of the population is very high, that doesn't always mean it is an attractive segment to target. The high index may be a result of a low denominator (a very small proportion of the population in this segment). In Figure 10-7, the 18- to 24-year-old age segment has the highest index, but it also has both the lowest product usage and the lowest population percentage. A marketer who relied solely on the index would be ignoring a full 82 percent of product users.

Keep in mind that while MRI-Simmons provides demographic, geographic, and some psychographic information, other factors may also be useful in defining specific markets and media usage.

Study Universe	Study Universe					Sports: How Often Engaged in/Jogging/Running_ Participated in Last 12 Months				
	Unweighted	Weighted (000)	Vertical (%)	Horizontal (%)	Index	Unweighted	Weighted (000)	Vertical (%)	Horizontal (%)	Index
	51,697	254,237	100.00%	100.00%	→ 100	6,191	26,936	100.00%	10.59%	→ 100
Adults	51,697	254,237	100.00%	100.00%	→ 100	6,191	26,936	100.00%	10.59%	→ 100
Men	25,535	122,919	48.35%	100.00%	→ 100	3,286	13,631	50.61%	11.09%	→ 105
Women	26,162	131,318	51.65%	100.00%	→ 100	2,905	13,305	49.39%	10.13%	→ 96
Respondent is parent of child under 18 currently living in the household	13,777	63,637	25.03%	100.00%	→ 100	2,128	9,401	34.90%	14.77%	↑ 139
Respondent is mom of child under 18 currently living in the household	7,475	34,252	13.47%	100.00%	→ 100	1,088	5,041	18.71%	14.72%	↑ 139
Respondent is dad of child under 18 currently living in the household	6,302	29,386	11.56%	100.00%	→ 100	1,040	4,360	16.19%	14.84%	↑ 140
Respondent is parent of a child under 18 not currently living in the household	4,247	19,988	7.86%	100.00%	→ 100	542	2,267	8.42%	11.34%	→ 107
Respondent is parent of an adult aged 18 or over not currently living in the household	16,475	93,814	36.90%	100.00%	→ 100	1,050	5,394	20.03%	5.75%	↓ 54
Any parent (Any parent of an adult or child, living in home or out of the household)	30,606	162,819	64.04%	100.00%	→ 100	3,182	15,027	55.79%	9.23%	↓ 87
Age 18–24	5,697	29,213	11.49%	100.00%	→ 100	902	4,332	16.08%	14.83%	↑ 140
Age 25–34	10,833	45,588	17.93%	100.00%	→ 100	1,887	7,305	27.12%	16.02%	↑ 151
Age 35–44	9,510	41,849	16.46%	100.00%	→ 100	1,546	6,538	24.27%	15.62%	↑ 147
Age 45–54	7,747	39,899	15.69%	100.00%	→ 100	922	4,367	16.21%	10.95%	→ 103
Age 55–64	8,150	42,381	16.67%	100.00%	→ 100	630	2,957	10.98%	6.98%	↓ 66
Age 65+	9,760	55,308	21.75%	100.00%	→ 100	304	1,437	5.33%	2.60%	↓ 25
Mean respondent age	N/A	47.4	N/A	N/A	→ 100	N/A	39.2	N/A	N/A	↓ 83
Median respondent age	N/A	47.7	N/A	N/A	→ 100	N/A	37.6	N/A	N/A	↓ 79
Adults 18–34	16,530	74,801	29.42%	100.00%	→ 100	2,789	11,637	43.20%	15.56%	↑ 147
Adults 18–49	29,768	136,360	53.63%	100.00%	→ 100	4,810	20,495	76.09%	15.03%	↑ 142
Adults 25–54	28,090	127,336	50.09%	100.00%	→ 100	4,355	18,211	67.61%	14.30%	↑ 135
Adults 35–54	17,257	81,748	32.15%	100.00%	→ 100	2,468	10,905	40.48%	13.34%	↑ 126
Men 18–24	2,982	14,686	5.78%	100.00%	→ 100	467	2,045	7.59%	13.92%	↑ 131
Men 18–34	8,514	37,586	14.78%	100.00%	→ 100	1,499	5,817	21.60%	15.48%	↑ 146
Men 18–49	14,676	67,777	26.66%	100.00%	→ 100	2,497	10,101	37.50%	14.90%	↑ 141
Men 25–34	5,532	22,900	9.01%	100.00%	→ 100	1,032	3,772	14.00%	16.47%	↑ 155

(continued)

Study Universe	Study Universe					Sports: How Often Engaged in/Jogging/Running_ Participated in Last 12 Months				
Study Universe	Unweighted	Weighted (000)	Vertical (%)	Horizontal (%)	Index	Unweighted	Weighted (000)	Vertical (%)	Horizontal (%)	Index
Men 25–54	13,627	62,854	24.72%	100.00%	→ 100	2,273	9,153	33.98%	14.56%	↑ 137
Men 35–44	4,405	20,657	8.13%	100.00%	→ 100	741	3,124	11.60%	15.12%	↑ 143
Men 35–54	8,095	39,954	15.72%	100.00%	→ 100	1,241	5,381	19.98%	13.47%	↑ 127
Men 45–54	3,690	19,297	7.59%	100.00%	→ 100	500	2,257	8.38%	11.70%	→ 110
Men 55–64	3,855	20,315	7.99%	100.00%	→ 100	345	1,625	6.03%	8.00%	↓ 75
Men 65+	5,071	25,064	9.86%	100.00%	→ 100	201	808	3.00%	3.22%	↓ 30
Women 18–24	2,715	14,526	5.71%	100.00%	→ 100	435	2,286	8.49%	15.74%	↑ 149
Women 18–34	8,016	37,215	14.64%	100.00%	→ 100	1,290	5,820	21.61%	15.64%	↑ 148
Women 18–49	15,092	68,583	26.98%	100.00%	→ 100	2,313	10,394	38.59%	15.16%	↑ 143
Women 25–34	5,301	22,689	8.92%	100.00%	→ 100	855	3,534	13.12%	15.58%	↑ 147
Women 25–54	14,463	64,482	25.36%	100.00%	→ 100	2,082	9,058	33.63%	14.05%	↑ 133
Women 35–44	5,105	21,192	8.34%	100.00%	→ 100	805	3,414	12.67%	16.11%	↑ 152
Women 35–54	9,162	41,794	16.44%	100.00%	→ 100	1,227	5,524	20.51%	13.22%	↑ 125
Women 45–54	4,057	20,602	8.10%	100.00%	→ 100	422	2,110	7.83%	10.24%	→ 97
Women 55–64	4,295	22,066	8.68%	100.00%	→ 100	285	1,332	4.95%	6.04%	↓ 57
Women 65+	4,689	30,244	11.90%	100.00%	→ 100	103	629	2.34%	2.08%	↓ 20
Highest Degree Received by Respondent: 12th grade or less	2,458	24,788	9.75%	100.00%	→ 100	226	2,257	8.38%	9.11%	↓ 86
Highest Degree Received by Respondent: Graduated high school	8,543	71,031	27.94%	100.00%	→ 100	706	5,152	19.13%	7.25%	↓ 68
Highest Degree Received by Respondent: Some college, no degree	10,157	43,658	17.17%	100.00%	→ 100	1,064	4,492	16.68%	10.29%	→ 97
Highest Degree Received by Respondent: Associate degree	5,830	26,134	10.28%	100.00%	→ 100	589	2,552	9.47%	9.77%	→ 92
Highest Degree Received by Respondent: Bachelor's degree	14,731	51,870	20.40%	100.00%	→ 100	2,169	7,295	27.08%	14.06%	↓ 133
Highest Degree Received by Respondent: Post-graduate degree	9,978	36,755	14.46%	100.00%	→ 100	1,437	5,189	19.26%	14.12%	↑ 133
Highest Degree Received by Respondent: Some college (no degree) OR Associate Degree	15,987	69,792	27.45%	100.00%	→ 100	1,653	7,044	26.15%	10.09%	→ 95
Highest Degree Received by Respondent: Bachelor's degree OR Post-Graduate Degree	24,709	88,625	34.86%	100.00%	→ 100	3,606	12,483	46.34%	14.09%	↑ 133

Mediamark Research & Intelligence, LLC (GfK MRI).

Study Universe Weighted (000): In the Spring 2022 MRI-Simmons USA Study, the Weighted Study Universe (projected population) is 254,257, when calculated in thousands, represents 254,257,000 Adults 18+.

Target Weighted (000): Projected to population is 38,466,000 women 18+ who drank Sparkling Water/Seltzer in the last 6 months

Target Vertical %: Of Adults 18+ who drank Sparking Water/Seltzer in the last 6 months, 55.83% were women.

Target Horizontal %: Of Women 18+, 29.29% drank Sparking Water/Seltzer in the last 6 months.

Target Index: Women 18+ are 8% more likely than Adults 18+ to have drunk Sparking Water/Seltzer in the last 6 months.

	Study Universe					Sparkling Water/Seltzer: Drank in Last 6 Months				
Study Universe	Unweighted	Weighted (000)	Vertical(%)	Horizontal(%)	Index	Unweighted	Weighted (000)	Vertical(%)	Horizontal(%)	Index
	51,697	254,237	100.00%	100.00%	100	14,905	68,903	100.00%	27.10%	100
Adults	51,697	254,237	100.00%	100.00%	100	14,905	68,903	100.00%	27.10%	100
Men	25,535	122,919	48.35%	100.00%	100	6,880	30,437	44.17%	24.76%	91
Women	26,162	131,318	51.65%	100.00%	100	8,025	38,466	55.83%	29.29%	108
Respondent is parent of child under 18 currently living in the household	13,777	63,637	25.03%	100.00%	100	4,369	19,739	28.65%	31.02%	114
Respondent is mom of child under 18 currently living in the household	7,475	34,252	13.47%	100.00%	100	2,456	11,492	16.68%	33.55%	124
Respondent is dad of child under 18 currently living in the household	6,302	29,386	11.56%	100.00%	100	1,913	8,247	11.97%	28.06%	104
Respondent is parent of a child under 18 not currently living in the	4,247	19,988	7.86%	100.00%	100	1,202	5,204	7.55%	26.04%	96
Respondent is parent of an adult aged 18 or over not currently living in the	16,475	93,814	36.90%	100.00%	100	4,112	21,666	31.44%	23.09%	85
Any parent (Any parent of an adult or child, living in home or out of home)	30,606	162,819	64.04%	100.00%	100	8,572	42,375	61.50%	26.03%	96
Age 18-24	5,697	29,213	11.49%	100.00%	100	1,400	7,356	10.68%	25.18%	93
Age 25-34	10,833	45,588	17.93%	100.00%	100	3,581	14,608	21.20%	32.04%	118
Age 35-44	9,510	41,849	16.46%	100.00%	100	3,158	13,662	19.83%	32.65%	120
Age 45-54	7,747	39,899	15.69%	100.00%	100	2,361	11,454	16.62%	28.71%	106
Age 55-64	8,150	42,381	16.67%	100.00%	100	2,190	10,554	15.32%	24.90%	92

FIGURE 10–6

How to Read an MRI-Simmons Report

Mediamark Research & Intelligence, LLC (GfK MRI).

What Internal and External Factors Are Operating?

Media strategies are influenced by both internal and external factors operating at any given time. *Internal factors* may involve the size of the media budget, managerial and administrative capabilities, or the organization of the agency. *External factors* may include the economy (the rising costs of media), changes in technology (the availability of new media and new buying methods), competitive factors, and the like. While some of this information may require primary research, much information is available through secondary sources, including magazines, syndicated services, news sources, and online.

One service's competitive information was shown in Figure 10–1. Another is Kantar, although there are numerous other sources.

Where to Promote?

The question of where to promote relates to geographic considerations. As noted in Chapter 7, companies often find that sales are stronger in one area of the country or the world than another and may allocate advertising expenditures according to the market potential of an area. For example, the Mexican beer Pacifico has a much greater brand share of the beer market in the Pacific census region than in the Midwest census region. The question is, where will the ad dollars be more wisely spent? Should Pacifico allocate additional promotional monies to those markets where the brand is already among

FIGURE 10–7

How High Indexes Can Be Misleading

Age Segment	Population in Segment (%)	Product Use in Segment (%)	Index
18–24	15.1	18.0	119
25–34	25.1	25.0	100
35–44	20.6	21.0	102
45 +	39.3	36.0	91

the leaders to maintain and expand market share, or does more potential exist in those markets where the firm is not doing as well and there is more room to grow? Perhaps the best answer is that the firm should spend advertising and promotion dollars where they will be the most effective—that is, in those markets where they will achieve the desired objectives. Unfortunately, as we have seen so often, it is not always possible to directly measure the impact of promotional efforts. At the same time, certain tactics can assist the planner in making this determination.

Using Indexes to Determine Where to Promote In addition to the indexes from MRI-Simmons, three other indexes may also be useful:

1. The **survey of buying power index** is conducted for every major metropolitan market in the United States and is based on a number of factors, including population, effective buying income, and total retail sales in the area. Each of these factors is individually weighted to drive a buying power index that charts the potential of a particular metro area, county, or city relative to the United States as a whole. The resulting index gives media planners insight into the relative value of that market. When used in combination with other market information, the survey of buying power index helps the marketer determine which geographic areas to target.

2. The **brand development index (BDI)** helps marketers factor the rate of product usage by geographic area into the decision process.

$$BDI = \frac{\text{Percentage of brand to total U.S. sales in the market}}{\text{Percentage of total U.S. population in the market}} \times 100$$

The BDI compares the percentage of the brand's total U.S. sales in a given market area with the percentage of the total population in the market to determine the sales potential for that brand in that market area. An example of this calculation is shown in Figure 10–8. The higher the index number, the more market potential exists. In this case, the index number indicates this market has high potential for brand development.

3. The **category development index (CDI)** is computed in the same manner as is the BDI, except it uses information regarding the product category (as opposed to the brand) in the numerator:

$$CDI = \frac{\text{Percentage of product category total sales in market}}{\text{Percentage of total U.S. population in market}} \times 100$$

The CDI provides information on the potential for development of the total product category rather than specific brands. When this information is combined with the BDI, a much more insightful promotional strategy may be developed. For example, consider the market potential for coffee in the United States. One might first look at how well the product category does in a specific market area. In Utah and Idaho, for example, the category potential is low (see Figure 10–9). The marketer analyzes the BDI to find how the brand is doing relative to other brands in this area. This information can then be used in determining how well a particular product category and a particular brand are performing and figuring

FIGURE 10–8

Calculating BDI

$$BDI = \frac{\text{Percentage of brand sales in South Atlantic region}}{\text{Percentage of U.S. population in South Atlantic region}} \times 100$$

$$= \frac{50\%}{16\%} \times 100$$

$$= 312$$

FIGURE 10–9

Using CDI and BDI to
Determine Market Potential

$$\text{CDI} = \frac{\text{Percentage of product category sales in Utah/Idaho}}{\text{Percentage of total U.S. population in Utah/Idaho}} \times 100$$

$$= \frac{1\%}{1\%} \times 100$$

$$= 100$$

$$\text{BDI} = \frac{\text{Percentage of total brand sales in Utah/Idaho}}{\text{Percentage of total U.S. population in Utah/Idaho}} \times 100$$

$$= \frac{2\%}{1\%} \times 100$$

$$= 200$$

what media weight (or quantity of advertising) would be required to gain additional market share, as shown in Figure 10-10.

While these indexes provide important insights into the market potential for the firm's products and/or brands, this information is supplemental to the overall strategy determined earlier in the promotional decision-making process. In fact, much of this information may have already been provided to the media planner. Since it may be used more specifically to determine the media weights to assign to each area, this decision ultimately affects the budget allocated to each area as well as other factors such as reach, frequency, and scheduling.

ESTABLISHING MEDIA OBJECTIVES

Just as the situation analysis leads to establishment of marketing and communications objectives, the media situation analysis should lead to determination of specific media objectives. The media objectives are not ends in themselves. Rather, they are designed to lead to the attainment of communications and marketing objectives. Media objectives

FIGURE 10–10

Using BDI and CDI Indexes

	High BDI	Low BDI
High CDI	High market share Good market potential	Low market share Good market potential
Low CDI	High market share Monitor for sales decline	Low market share Poor market potential

High BDI and high CDI	This market usually represents good sales potential for both the product category and the brand.
High BDI and low CDI	The category is not selling well, but the brand is; probably a good market to advertise in but should be monitored for declining sales.
Low BDI and high CDI	The product category shows high potential but the brand is not doing well; the reasons should be determined.
Low BDI and low CDI	Both the product category and the brand are doing poorly; not likely to be a good place for advertising.

are the goals for the media program and should be limited to those that can be accomplished through media strategies. An example of media objectives: Create awareness in the target market through the following:

- Use broadcast media to provide coverage of 80 percent of the target market over a six-month period.
- Reach 60 percent of the target audience at least three times over the same six-month period.
- Create a positive brand image through mood and creativity.

DEVELOPING AND IMPLEMENTING MEDIA STRATEGIES

LO 10-4

Having determined what is to be accomplished, media planners consider how to achieve these objectives. That is, they develop and implement media strategies, which evolve directly from the actions required to meet objectives and involve the criteria in Figure 10-11.

The Media Mix

A wide variety of media and media vehicles are available to advertisers. While it is possible that only one medium and/or vehicle might be employed, it is much more likely that a number of alternatives will be used. The objectives sought, the characteristics of the product or service, the size of the budget, and individual preferences are just some of the factors that determine what combination of media will be taken into consideration.

As an example, consider a promotional situation in which a product requires a visual demonstration to be communicated effectively. In this case, TV or digital media may be the most effective medium. If the promotional strategy calls for coupons to stimulate trial, print media may be necessary. (Many companies also provide the capability to print coupons from their websites.) For in-depth information, digital media may be best; social media may be best for spreading the word among friends.

By employing a media mix, advertisers can add more versatility to their media strategies, since each medium contributes its own distinct advantages (as demonstrated in later chapters). By combining media, marketers can increase coverage, reach, and frequency levels while improving the likelihood of achieving overall communications and marketing goals.

FIGURE 10–11

Criteria Considered in the Development of Media Plans

- The media mix
- Target market coverage
- Geographic coverage
- Scheduling
- Reach and frequency
- Recency
- Creative aspects and mood
- Flexibility
- Budget considerations

Target Market Coverage

The media planner determines which target markets should receive the most media emphasis. Developing media strategies involves matching the most appropriate media to this market by asking, "Through which media and media vehicles can I best get my message to prospective buyers?" The issue here is to get coverage of the market, as shown in Figure 10-12. The optimal goal is full market coverage, shown in the second pie chart. But this is a very optimistic scenario. More realistically, conditions shown in the third and fourth charts are most likely to occur. In the third chart, the coverage of the media does not allow for coverage of the entire market, leaving some potential customers without exposure to the message. In the fourth chart, the marketer is faced with a problem of overexposure (also called **waste coverage**), in which the media coverage exceeds the targeted audience. If media coverage reaches people who are not sought as buyers and are not potential users, then it is wasted. (This term is used for coverage that reaches people who are not potential buyers and/or users. Consumers may not be part of the intended target market but may still be considered as potential—for example, those who buy the product as a gift for someone else.)

FIGURE 10-12

Marketing Coverage
Possibilities

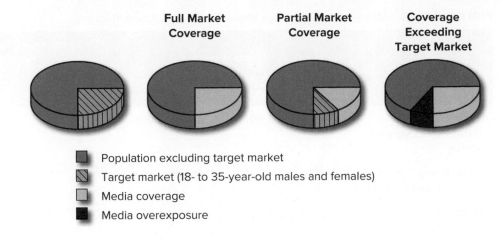

Full Market
Coverage

Partial Market
Coverage

Coverage
Exceeding
Target Market

■ Population excluding target market

▨ Target market (18- to 35-year-old males and females)

▢ Media coverage

■ Media overexposure

The goal of the media planner is to extend media coverage to as many of the members of the target audience as possible while minimizing the amount of waste coverage. The situation usually involves trade-offs. Sometimes one has to live with less coverage than desired; other times, the most effective media expose people not sought. In this instance, waste coverage is justified because the media employed are likely to be the most effective means of delivery available and the cost of the waste coverage is exceeded by the value gained.

When watching football games on TV, you may have noticed commercials for stock brokerage firms such as Charles Schwab, Ameritrade, and E*Trade. Not all viewers are candidates for stock market services, but a very high percentage of potential customers can be reached with this strategy. So football programs are considered a good media buy because the ability to generate market coverage outweighs the disadvantages of high waste coverage.

Figure 10-13 shows how information provided by MRI-Simmons can be used to match media to target markets. This excerpt is from the report that profiles magazines read, cable TV show types watched, websites visited, and so forth by the joggers/runners identified in Figure 10-5. (You can practice using index numbers here.) From Figure 10-13, you can see that the NFL Network, NHL Network, and ESPN would likely be wise selections, whereas the Outdoor Channel and the Oprah Winfrey Network would be less likely to lead to the desired exposures.

Geographic Coverage

Snow skiing is much more popular in some areas of the country than in others. It would not be the wisest of strategies to promote skis in those areas where interest is not high, unless you could generate an increase in interest. It may be possible to promote an interest in skiing in the Southeast, but a notable increase in sales of ski equipment is not very likely, given the market's distance from snow. The objective of weighting certain geographic areas more than others makes sense, and the strategy of exerting more promotional efforts and dollars in those areas follows naturally.

Scheduling

Obviously, companies would like to keep their advertising in front of consumers at all times as a constant reminder of the product and/or brand name. In reality, this is not possible for a variety of reasons (not the least of which is the budget). Nor is it necessary. The primary objective of *scheduling* is to time promotional efforts so that they will coincide with the highest potential buying times. For some products these times are not easy to identify; for others they are very obvious. Three scheduling methods available to

FIGURE 10–13 MRI-Simmons Provides Media Usage of Joggers/Runners

Study Universe	Study Universe					Sports: How Often Engaged in/Jogging/Running_ Participated in Last 12 Months				
	Unweighted	Weighted (000)	Vertical (%)	Horizontal (%)	Index	Unweighted	Weighted (000)	Vertical (%)	Horizontal (%)	Index
Any Watching Past 30 Days_Discovery en Español	791	5,590	2.20%	100.00%	➜100	82	384	1.43%	6.87%	↓ 65
Any Watching Past 30 Days_Discovery Family	1,283	6,997	2.75%	100.00%	➜100	121	539	2.00%	7.70%	↓ 73
Any Watching Past 30 Days_Discovery Life Channel	1,383	6,917	2.72%	100.00%	➜100	133	572	2.12%	8.27%	↓ 78
Any Watching Past 30 Days_Disney Channel	7,497	37,863	14.89%	100.00%	➜100	790	3,721	13.81%	9.83%	➜ 93
Any Watching Past 30 Days_Disney Junior	3,831	19,375	7.62%	100.00%	➜100	468	2,181	8.10%	11.26%	➜106
Any Watching Past 30 Days_Disney XD	2,533	12,730	5.01%	100.00%	➜100	317	1,481	5.50%	11.63%	➜110
Any Watching Past 30 Days_E! (Entertainment Television)	6,285	30,267	11.91%	100.00%	➜100	683	2,931	10.88%	9.68%	➜ 91
Any Watching Past 30 Days_ESPN	13,835	67,050	26.37%	100.00%	➜100	1,735	7,460	27.70%	11.13%	➜105
Any Watching Past 30 Days_ESPN2	8,520	42,509	16.72%	100.00%	➜100	1,020	4,286	15.91%	10.08%	➜ 95
Any Watching Past 30 Days_ESPNU	3,456	17,273	6.79%	100.00%	➜100	446	1,871	6.95%	10.83%	➜102
Any Watching Past 30 Days_ESPNews	4,355	21,543	8.47%	100.00%	➜100	476	1,983	7.36%	9.20%	↓ 87
Any Watching Past 30 Days_ESPN SEC	3,114	15,936	6.27%	100.00%	➜100	339	1,433	5.32%	8.99%	↓ 85
Any Watching Past 30 Days_Estrella TV	490	3,608	1.42%	100.00%	➜100	*47	*328	*1.22%	*9.09%	↓ *86
Any Watching Past 30 Days_FETV (Family Entertainment TV)	541	3,024	1.19%	100.00%	➜100	*37	*128	*0.48%	*4.23%	↓ *40
Any Watching Past 30 Days_Flix	1,048	4,906	1.93%	100.00%	➜100	87	374	1.39%	7.62%	↓ 72
Any Watching Past 30 Days_FM	239	1,004	0.39%	100.00%	➜100	*30	*86	*0.32%	*8.57%	↓ *81
Any Watching Past 30 Days_Food Network	12,709	62,694	24.66%	100.00%	➜100	1,426	6,437	23.90%	10.27%	➜ 97
Any Watching Past 30 Days_FOX	19,778	99,360	39.08%	100.00%	➜100	2,107	9,236	34.29%	9.30%	↓ 88
Any Watching Past 30 Days_Fox Business Network	3,270	16,511	6.49%	100.00%	➜100	284	1,169	4.34%	7.08%	↓ 67

Study Universe	Study Universe					Sports: How Often Engaged in/Jogging/Running_ Participated in Last 12 Months				
	Unweighted	Weighted (000)	Vertical (%)	Horizontal (%)	Index	Unweighted	Weighted (000)	Vertical (%)	Horizontal (%)	Index
Any Watching Past 30 Days_National Geographic Channel	9,985	51,121	20.11%	100.00%	→ 100	1,018	4,343	16.12%	8.50%	↓ 80
Any Watching Past 30 Days_National Geographic Wild	4,614	23,888	9.40%	100.00%	→ 100	420	1,846	6.85%	7.73%	↓ 73
Any Watching Past 30 Days_NBA TV	3,312	15,562	6.12%	100.00%	→ 100	413	1,757	6.52%	11.29%	→107
Any Watching Past 30 Days_NBC	23,693	116,474	45.81%	100.00%	→ 100	2,476	10,416	38.67%	8.94%	↓ 84
Any Watching Past 30 Days_NEWSMAX TV	2,361	12,517	4.92%	100.00%	→ 100	188	851	3.16%	6.80%	↓ 64
Any Watching Past 30 Days_NewsNation	951	4,676	1.84%	100.00%	→ 100	69	241	0.89%	5.15%	↓ 49
Any Watching Past 30 Days_NFL Network	5,689	27,244	10.72%	100.00%	→ 100	687	2,878	10.68%	10.56%	→100
Any Watching Past 30 Days_NHL Network	1,687	7,856	3.09%	100.00%	→ 100	220	1,061	3.94%	13.51%	↑127
Any Watching Past 30 Days_Nick at Nite	2,003	9,453	3.72%	100.00%	→ 100	231	983	3.65%	10.40%	→ 98
Any Watching Past 30 Days_Nick Jr.	3,339	16,864	6.63%	100.00%	→ 100	362	1,527	5.67%	9.05%	↓ 85
Any Watching Past 30 Days_Nickelodeon	5,263	26,124	10.28%	100.00%	→ 100	622	2,785	10.34%	10.66%	→101
Any Watching Past 30 Days_Outdoor Channel	1,422	8,174	3.22%	100.00%	→ 100	131	598	2.22%	7.32%	↓ 69
Any Watching Past 30 Days_Ovation TV	677	3,190	1.25%	100.00%	→ 100	*46	*213	*0.79%	*6.68%	↓ *63
Any Watching Past 30 Days_OWN (Oprah Winfrey Network)	4,280	20,403	8.03%	100.00%	→ 100	328	1,364	5.06%	6.69%	↓ 63
Any Watching Past 30 Days_Oxygen	3,850	19,466	7.66%	100.00%	→ 100	322	1,410	5.23%	7.24%	↓ 68
Any Watching Past 30 Days_Paramount Network	8,109	39,950	15.71%	100.00%	→ 100	850	3,609	13.40%	9.03%	↓ 85
Any Watching Past 30 Days_PBS	11,832	57,202	22.50%	100.00%	→ 100	1,016	4,357	16.18%	7.62%	↓ 72
Any Watching Past 30 Days_PBS KIDS	3,612	17,878	7.03%	100.00%	→ 100	457	2,135	7.93%	11.94%	↑113
Any Watching Past 30 Days_POP	1,374	6,534	2.57%	100.00%	→ 100	169	718	2.67%	10.99%	→104

*Indicates small sample
Mediamark Research & Intelligence, LLC (GfK MRI).

FIGURE 10–14

Three Methods of
Promotional Scheduling

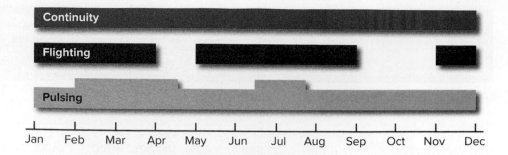

the media planner—continuity, flighting, and pulsing—are shown in Figure 10-14. Appendix A at the end of this chapter shows how running shoe brand ASICS uses scheduling in its media plan.

Continuity refers to a continuous pattern of advertising, which may mean every day, every week, or every month. The key is that a regular (continuous) pattern is developed without gaps or nonadvertising periods. Such strategies might be used for advertising for food products, laundry detergents, toiletries, or other products consumed on an ongoing basis without regard for seasonality.

A second method, **flighting**, employs a less regular schedule, with intermittent periods of advertising and nonadvertising. At some time periods there are heavier promotional expenditures, and at others there may be no advertising. Many banks, for example, spend no money on advertising in the summer but maintain advertising throughout the rest of the year. Snow skis are advertised heavily between October and April; less in May, August, and September; and not at all in June and July.

Pulsing is actually a combination of the first two methods. In a pulsing strategy, continuity is maintained, but at certain times promotional efforts are stepped up. In the beer industry, advertising continues throughout the year but may increase at holiday periods such as Memorial Day, Labor Day, or the Fourth of July. The scheduling strategy depends on the objectives, buying cycles, and budget, among other factors. There are certain advantages and disadvantages to each scheduling method, as shown in Figure 10-15. One comprehensive study (acclaimed by many in the TV research community as "the most comprehensive study ever to shed light on scheduling") indicated that continuity is more effective than flighting. On the basis of the idea that it is important to get exposure to the message as close as possible to when the consumer is going to make the purchase, the study concludes that advertisers should continue weekly schedules as long as possible.[5] The key here may be the "as long as possible" qualification. Given a significant budget, continuity may be more of an option than it is for those with more limited budgets.

Reach versus Frequency

Since advertisers have a variety of objectives and face budget constraints, they usually must trade off reach and frequency. They must decide whether to have the message be seen or heard by more people (reach) or by fewer people more often (frequency).

How Much Reach Is Necessary?   Thinking back to the hierarchies discussed in Chapter 5, you will recall that the first stage of each model requires awareness of the product and/or brand. The more that people are aware during each stage, the more they are likely to move to each subsequent stage. Achieving awareness requires reach—that is, exposing potential buyers to the message. New brands or products need a very high level of reach, since the objective is to make all potential buyers aware of the new entry. High reach is also desired at later stages of the hierarchy. For example, at the trial stage of the adoption hierarchy, a promotional strategy might use cents-off coupons or free samples. An objective of the marketer is to reach a larger number of people with these samples in an attempt to make them learn of the product, try it, and develop favorable attitudes toward it. (In turn, these attitudes may lead to purchase.)

FIGURE 10–15

Characteristics of
Scheduling Methods

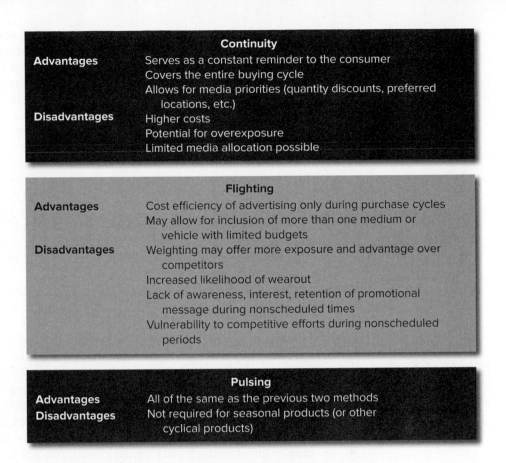

Continuity

Advantages · Serves as a constant reminder to the consumer
· Covers the entire buying cycle
· Allows for media priorities (quantity discounts, preferred
locations, etc.)

Disadvantages · Higher costs
· Potential for overexposure
· Limited media allocation possible

Flighting

Advantages · Cost efficiency of advertising only during purchase cycles
· May allow for inclusion of more than one medium or
vehicle with limited budgets

Disadvantages · Weighting may offer more exposure and advantage over
competitors
· Increased likelihood of wearout
· Lack of awareness, interest, retention of promotional
message during nonscheduled times
· Vulnerability to competitive efforts during nonscheduled
periods

Pulsing

Advantages · All of the same as the previous two methods

Disadvantages · Not required for seasonal products (or other
cyclical products)

The problem arises because there is no known way of determining how much reach is required to achieve levels of awareness, attitude change, or buying intentions; nor can we be sure an ad placed in a vehicle will actually reach the intended audience. Digital and Social Media Perspective 10-1 which appears later in this chapter demonstrates how this problem may be compounded with the use of programmatic buying. (There has been some research on the first problem, which will be discussed in the following section on effective reach.)

If you buy advertising time on *60 Minutes*, will everyone who is tuned to the program see the ad? No. Many viewers will leave the room, be distracted during the commercial, and so on, as shown in Figure 10-16 (which also provides a good example of the

FIGURE 10–16

Who's Still There to Watch
the Ads?

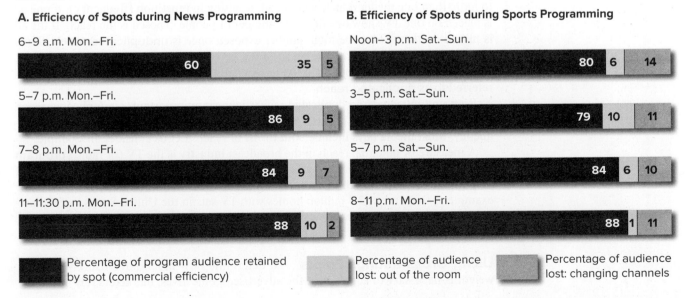

A. Efficiency of Spots during News Programming

6–9 a.m. Mon.–Fri.

60 | 35 | 5

5–7 p.m. Mon.–Fri.

86 | 9 | 5

7–8 p.m. Mon.–Fri.

84 | 9 | 7

11–11:30 p.m. Mon.–Fri.

88 | 10 | 2

B. Efficiency of Spots during Sports Programming

Noon–3 p.m. Sat.–Sun.

80 | 6 | 14

3–5 p.m. Sat.–Sun.

79 | 10 | 11

5–7 p.m. Sat.–Sun.

84 | 6 | 10

8–11 p.m. Mon.–Fri.

88 | 1 | 11

■ Percentage of program audience retained
by spot (commercial efficiency)

■ Percentage of audience
lost: out of the room

■ Percentage of audience
lost: changing channels

difference between reach and coverage). This figure demonstrates that depending on the program, this number may range from 12 to 40 percent. If I expose everyone in my target group to the message once, will this be sufficient to create a 100 percent level of awareness? The answer again is no. This leads to the next question: What frequency of exposure is necessary for the ad to be seen and to have an impact?

What Frequency Level Is Needed?   With respect to media planning, *frequency* carries a slightly different meaning. (Remember when we said one of the problems in media planning is that terms often take on different meanings?) Here frequency is the number of times one is exposed to the media vehicle in a specified time period (usually 13 weeks), not necessarily to the ad itself. Marketers have always known that everyone who is watching a program is not going to stay in the room to watch the commercials. Given the rise in the number of people able to skip ads, one can be sure the number of those not exposed to the ad is on the increase. As noted, marketers continue to seek ways to increase engagement, hoping to reduce the number leaving the room during commercial breaks.

Most advertisers do agree that a 1:1 exposure ratio does not exist. So while your ad may be placed in a certain vehicle, the fact that a consumer has been exposed to that vehicle does not ensure that your ad has been seen. As a result, the frequency level expressed in the media plan overstates the actual level of exposure to the ad. This overstatement has led some media buyers to refer to the reach of the media vehicle as "opportunities to see" an ad rather than actual exposure to it.

Because the advertiser has no sure way of knowing whether exposure to a vehicle results in exposure to the ad, the media and advertisers have adopted a compromise: One exposure to the vehicle constitutes reach, given that this exposure must occur for the viewer even to have an opportunity to see the ad. Thus, the exposure figure is used to calculate reach and frequency levels. But this compromise does not help determine the frequency required to make an impact. The creativity of the ad, the involvement of the receiver, noise, and many other intervening factors confound any attempts to make a precise determination.

At this point, you may be thinking, "If nobody knows this stuff, how do they make these decisions?" That's a good question, and the truth is that the decisions are not always made on hard data. Says Joseph Ostrow, executive vice president/director of communications services with Young and Rubicam, "Establishing frequency goals for an advertising campaign is a mix of art and science but with a definite bias toward art."[6] Let us first examine the process involved in setting reach and frequency objectives and then discuss the logic of each.

Establishing Reach and Frequency Objectives   It is possible to be exposed to more than one media vehicle with an ad, resulting in repetition (frequency). If one ad is placed on one TV show one time, the number of people exposed is the reach. If the ad is placed on two shows, the total number exposed once is **unduplicated reach**. Some people will see the ad twice. The reach of the two shows, as depicted in Figure 10–17, includes a number of people who were reached by both shows (C). This overlap is referred to as **duplicated reach**.

Both unduplicated and duplicated reach figures are important. Unduplicated reach indicates potential new exposures, while duplicated reach provides an estimate of frequency. Most media buys include both forms of reach. Let us consider an example.

A measure of potential reach in the broadcast industry is the TV (or radio) **program rating**. This number is expressed as a percentage. For an estimate of the total number of homes reached, multiply this percentage times the number of homes with TV sets. For example, if there are 122.4 million homes with TV sets in the United States and the program has a rating of 30, then the calculation is 0.30 times 122.4, or 36.72 million homes. (We go into much more detail on ratings and other broadcast terms in Chapter 11.)

Using Gross Ratings Points   To determine how much advertising volume or weight is necessary to accomplish the advertiser's objectives, marketers rely on ratings

FIGURE 10–17

Representation of Reach and Frequency

A. Reach of One TV Program

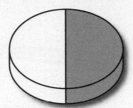

Total market audience reached

B. Reach of Two Programs

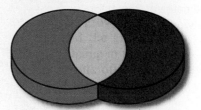

Total market audience reached

C. Duplicated Reach

Total market reached
with both shows

D. Unduplicated Reach

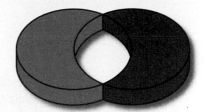

Total reach less
duplicated reach

(the number of people reached) and frequency (the average number of times exposed) figures. A summary measure that combines the program rating and the average number of times the home is reached during this period (frequency of exposure) is a commonly used reference point known as **gross ratings points (GRPs)**:

$$GRP = Reach \times Frequency$$

GRPs are based on the total audience the media schedule may reach using a duplicated reach estimate. **Target ratings points (TRPs)** refer to the number of people in the primary target audience the media buy will reach—and the number of times. Unlike GRP, TRP does not include waste coverage.

Given that GRPs do not measure actual reach, the advertiser must ask: How many GRPs are needed to attain a certain reach? How do these GRPs translate into effective reach? For example, how many GRPs must one purchase to attain an unduplicated reach of 50 percent, and what frequency of exposure will this schedule deliver? The following example may help you to understand how this process works.

First you must know what these ratings points represent. A purchase of 100 GRPs could mean 100 percent of the market is exposed once or 50 percent of the market is exposed twice or 25 percent of the market is exposed four times, and so on. As you can see, this information must be more specific for the marketer to use it effectively. To know how many GRPs are necessary, the manager needs to know how many members of the intended audience the schedule actually reaches. The graph in Figure 10–18 helps make this determination.

In Figure 10–18, a purchase of 100 TRPs on one network would yield an estimated reach of 32 percent of the total households in the target market. This figure would climb to 37.2 percent if two networks were used and 44.5 percent with three. Working backward through the formula for GRPs, the estimate of frequency of exposure—3.125, 2.688, and 2.247, respectively—demonstrates the trade-off between reach and frequency.

An interesting example of the use of GRPs is provided by a race to be the Republican candidate for California governor. With the election to be held in June, the advertising schedule for March for the leading candidate consisted of 1,000 GRPs per week in 11 California media markets. This buy was expected to yield a frequency of approximately 10 exposures per week to the average TV watcher in the largest markets, and approximately 6 per week in the smaller ones. The opposing candidate spent an

FIGURE 10–18

Estimates of Reach for
Network TRPs

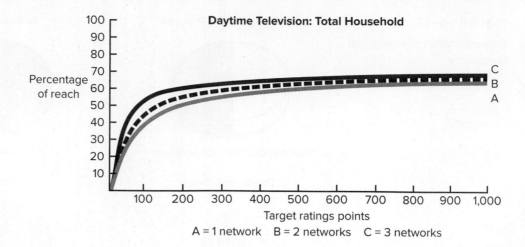

Daytime Television: Total Household

A = 1 network   B = 2 networks   C = 3 networks

estimated 15 to 50 percent of this amount, depending on the specific market.[7] The candidate that spent the most won the race.

The overriding question is: How many GRPs are necessary to achieve our objectives? According to Scott Walker, most advertisers prefer to get 500 to 700 GRPs to be sure their message is seen and seen often.[8] A number of researchers have explored this issue. David Berger, vice president and director of research at Foote, Cone & Belding, has determined that 2,500 GRPs are likely to lead to roughly a 70 percent probability of high awareness, 1,000 to 2,500 would yield about a 33 percent probability, and less than 1,000 would probably result in almost no awareness.[9] David Olson obtained similar results and further showed that as awareness increased, trial of the product would also increase, although at a significantly slower rate.[10] In both cases, it was evident that high numbers of GRPs were required to make an impact.

Figure 10–19 summarizes the effects that can be expected at different levels of exposure, on the basis of research in this area. A number of factors may be operating, and direct relationships may be difficult to establish. In addition to the results shown in Figure 10–19, Joseph Ostrow has shown that while the number of repetitions increases awareness rapidly, it has much less impact on attitudinal and behavioral responses.[11]

You can imagine how expensive it was for the candidate mentioned earlier to purchase 1,000 GRPs per week in 11 markets well before the election. To spend at that

FIGURE 10–19

The Effects of Reach and
Frequency

1. One exposure of an ad to a target group within a purchase cycle has little or no effect in most circumstances.

2. Since one exposure is usually ineffective, the central goal of productive media planning should be to enhance frequency rather than reach.

3. The evidence suggests strongly that an exposure frequency of two within a purchase cycle is an effective level.

4. Beyond three exposures within a brand purchase cycle or over a period of 4 or even 8 weeks, increasing frequency continues to build advertising effectiveness at a decreasing rate but with no evidence of decline.

5. Although there are general principles with respect to frequency of exposure and its relationship to advertising effectiveness, differential effects by brand are equally important.

6. Nothing we have seen suggests that frequency response principles or generalizations vary by medium.

7. The data strongly suggest that wearout is not a function of too much frequency; it is more of a creative or copy problem.

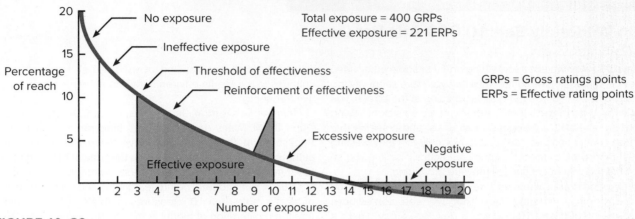

**Total Exposure versus Effective Exposure
of a Prime-Time Television Schedule**

Total exposure = 400 GRPs
Effective exposure = 221 ERPs

No exposure
Ineffective exposure
Threshold of effectiveness
Reinforcement of effectiveness
Excessive exposure
Negative exposure
Effective exposure

GRPs = Gross ratings points
ERPs = Effective rating points

Percentage of reach

Number of exposures

FIGURE 10–20

Graph of Effective Reach

level for an extended period of time could result in overexposure (not to mention a major hit on the pocketbook), as viewers might get tired of the ads.

Determining Effective Reach   Since marketers have budget constraints, they must decide whether to increase reach at the expense of frequency or increase the frequency of exposure but to a smaller audience. A number of factors influence this decision. For example, a new product or brand introduction will attempt to maximize reach, particularly unduplicated reach, to create awareness in as many people as possible as quickly as possible. At the same time, for a high-involvement product or one whose benefits are not obvious, a certain level of frequency is needed to achieve effective reach.

Effective reach represents the percentage of a vehicle's audience reached at each effective frequency increment. This concept is based on the assumption that one exposure to an ad may not be enough to convey the desired message. As we saw earlier, no one knows the exact number of exposures necessary for an ad to make an impact, although for years advertisers have settled on three as the minimum. (The following discussion relates to and has been considered the standard over the past decades. While a number of studies have demonstrated this may no longer be exactly correct, no defining research has led to its being replaced. We offer the information more for exemplary purposes than fact.) Effective reach (exposure) is shown in the shaded area in Figure 10-20 in the range of 3 to 10 exposures. Fewer than 3 exposures is considered insufficient reach, while more than 10 is considered overexposure and thus ineffective reach. This exposure level is no guarantee of effective communication; different messages may require more or fewer exposures. More recently, a number of scholars have argued that the three-exposure theory was applicable in the 1970s when consumers were exposed to only about 1,000 ads per day. Now that they are exposed to as many as 3,000 to 5,000 per day, this number may no longer be valid.[12] (Some have estimated that the number today may be as much as 10,000 exposures per day.) In addition, the fact that there are so many more media available to viewers today would increase the number of exposures required.[13] The complexity of the message, message length, and recency of exposure also impact this figure as evidenced in IMC Perspective 10-1.

Since they do not know how many times the viewer will actually be exposed, advertisers typically purchase GRPs that lead to more than three exposures to increase the likelihood of effective reach and frequency. Surmanek also argues that effective reach can be as low as one exposure, if the exposure is very recent or close to the purchase occasion (thus, recency is more important than frequency). He contends that more exposures arc necessary when the message is complex and requires several exposures to be understood.[14]

Do We Really See 10,000 Ads Per Day?

Have you ever watched something on TV or some other video device and up pops a commercial that you have seen way too many times? After you get done screaming at the screen, you ask, "Why do they do that?" and say, "I am so sick of seeing that commercial!" It happens to all of us, and it seems that some companies just don't get it. Not only are they wasting their money on all these ads, they are actually turning you off toward the product or service they are promoting.

Depending on whom you believe and the methodology they employ, estimates are that we see somewhere between 6,000 and 10,000 ads a day. Yes, a day! That's a wide range, you say, and you are right because no one really knows for sure. But whatever number is more accurate, it is still a heck of a lot of ads. As might be expected, the introduction of online advertising is a major factor underlying this increase. And that is the problem—nobody really knows for sure how many times someone sees an ad. But as you might expect, this is important for the advertiser to know. If I don't buy enough advertising time or space, my ad may not get seen at all. On the other hand, if I buy too much, the viewer sees it too often, it becomes less and less effective each time it is seen, and it may become irritating and do more harm than good.

While marketers have wrestled with this question for a long time, in both academic and practitioner domains, there is no absolute answer. Perhaps the most relied-upon research was conducted by Herbert Krugman way back in the 1970s. Krugman postulated that the optimal number of exposures to a television commercial was between 3 and 10 times. Fewer than 3 would be an ineffective number of exposures, while more than 10 would be excessive, and subsequent exposures would start to lead to negative exposures. Even though Krugman's work is now a half century old, the magic number three still seems to be the conventional wisdom. Numerous articles have appeared in the literature over the past decades critiquing Krugman's work, but it seems no one has come up with a better number proven and accepted by advertisers.

But think how different times are now compared to the 1970s. Television was the dominant advertising medium. Newspapers and magazines were going strong. The Internet wouldn't exist for more than two decades. There were no cell phones. The estimated number of daily exposures to ads was thought to be around 1,500! Is it this reliance on the rule of three that is causing overexposure? Have all the changes in the media environment had no impact on effective frequency?

Jennifer Lee Burton, Jan Gollins, Linda E. McNeely, and Daniellle M. Walls decided it was time for a fresh look. Publishing in the *Journal of Advertising Research*, the authors felt it was time to reexamine the "rule of three," given consumers' viewing experiences today, to determine if it was still true or out of date. Their research focused on the impact of having more than 10 exposures to an ad, hypothesizing that the proliferation of media in the life of consumers today would lead to a higher threshold for advertising repetition. Their research supported this idea, with those seeing the ad 10 or more times reporting higher purchase intentions than those seeing it less often. The research is consistent with that conducted by Susanne Schmidt and Martin Eisend, who also argued for a repetitionist approach rather than a minimalist approach as their study indicated that ad recall continues to increase after 10 exposures, and attitudes toward the ad do not level off after 8 exposures.

In an article in *Ad Age*, Jack Neff, reporting on a number of studies conducted by Facebook, the Mobile Marketing Association, and Procter & Gamble across a variety of media—including TV, Facebook, and mobile—found that the level of optimal exposure varied across media, viewing habits, and time and programs watched, among other factors. The conclusion was that "universal rules of thumb are hard to come by."

So, given that these were all well-conducted studies and that we still have no concrete evidence to support what the optimal frequency should be, it appears that the answer may very well be "it depends." Unfortunately for the viewer, it may be that we are going to continue to see some ads "ad nauseam" because the one thing advertisers do agree on is that they would rather have their ad seen too often than not enough.

Sources: Sam Carr, "How Many Ads Do We See A Day In 2021?" *PPC Protect*, February 15, 2021. www.insightly.com; Jennifer Lee Burton, Jan Gollins, Linda E. McNeely, and Danielle M. Walls, "Revisiting the Relationship between Ad Frequency and Purchase Intentions," *Journal of Advertising Research*, March 2019, pp. 27–39; Jack Neff, "What's the Frequency, Pritchard?" *Ad Age*, November 7, 2018, www.adage.com; "A New 'Wearout' Standard for a New Era of Advertising," WARC, March 15, 2019. www.warc.com; Susanne Schmidt, and Martin Eisend, "Advertising Repetition: A Meta-analysis on Effective Frequency in Advertising," *Journal of Advertising*, 44, no. 4 (2015), p. 415.

Erwin Ephron, an expert in media planning, disagrees. Ephron notes that while increasing reach at minimum frequency was popular in the 1990s, it is no longer a viable strategy because changes in the marketplace (commercial avoidance, multitasking, and technological innovations) have made it more difficult to get exposure to an ad. As a result, it is important to create plans that value both reach and frequency to ensure that the ad gets seen and has an impact. In other words, higher frequency results in higher reach.[15] Determining effective reach is further complicated by the fact that when calculating GRPs, advertisers use a figure that they call **average frequency**, or the average number of times the target audience reached by a media schedule is exposed to the vehicle over a specified period.

The problem with this figure is revealed in the following scenario:

> Consider a media buy in which:
> 50 percent of audience is reached 1 time.
> 30 percent of audience is reached 5 times.
> 20 percent of audience is reached 10 times.
> Average frequency = 4

In this media buy, the average frequency is 4, which is slightly more than the number established as effective. Yet a full 50 percent of the audience receives only one exposure. Thus, the average frequency number can be misleading, and using it to calculate GRPs might result in underexposing the audience.

Complicating this even further, Sheree Johnson reports on research conducted by Media Dynamics Inc. in 2014 that examined how many daily ads consumers are exposed to in a day. Johnson distinguishes between ad and/or brand exposures and "ad only" exposures. While she agrees that the number of brand and ad exposures may be 5,000+ per day, the average number of "ads only" exposures is closer to 362, with 86 creating some level of awareness and only 12 making an impression.[16] Johnson notes that despite the fact that commercial clutter has risen steadily, consumers have more options by which they can avoid ads, which impacts exposures. The bottom line is that no one really knows how many exposures occur in one day, so we have to use our best estimates.

Although GRPs have their problems, they can provide useful information to the marketer. A certain level of GRPs is necessary to achieve awareness, and increases in GRPs are likely to lead to more exposures and/or more repetitions—both of which are necessary to have an effect on higher-order objectives. Perhaps the best advice for purchasing GRPs is offered by Ostrow, who recommends the following strategies:[17]

1. Instead of using average frequency, the marketer should decide what minimum frequency goal is needed to reach the advertising objectives effectively and then maximize reach at that frequency level.
2. To determine effective frequency, one must consider marketing factors, message factors, and media factors. (See Figure 10–21.)

Effective Frequency   While the previous discussion focused on the number of exposures that are necessary to achieve effective reach, it is also necessary to know how much frequency is necessary to impact other communications objectives. As IMC Perspective 10–1 indicates, there has been disagreement on this number for years. In research presented in the *Journal of Advertising*, Susanne Schmidt and Martin Eisend report on a meta-analysis that examined 37 studies that impact consumers' response to an ad. Specifically, the focus was on the number of exposures necessary to impact recall and attitude toward the brand. The results indicated that 10 exposures are necessary to maximize attitudes while recall increases linearly. The authors also note that other factors, including the consumer's involvement and time between exposures, will also have an effect.[18]

In summary, the reach-versus-frequency decision, while critical, is very difficult to make. A number of factors must be considered, and concrete rules do not always apply. The decision is often more of an art than a science.

Recency   As noted by Ephron, the idea that one exposure to an ad had a greater impact than additional exposures did if it was shown in the week preceding a purchase led many advertisers to focus more attention on reach, less on frequency, and an emphasis on **recency**. Campaigns employed **recency planning**—focusing on short interval reach at minimum frequency levels as close to the purchase decision as possible. Rather than focusing on a four-week planning period for reach, recency planning

FIGURE 10–21

Factors Important in
Determining Frequency
Levels

Marketing Factors

- *Brand history.* Is the brand new or established? New brands generally require higher frequency levels.
- *Brand share.* An inverse relationship exists between brand share and frequency. The higher the brand share, the lower the frequency level required.
- *Brand loyalty.* An inverse relationship exists between loyalty and frequency. The higher the loyalty, the lower the frequency level required.
- *Purchase cycles.* Shorter purchasing cycles require higher frequency levels to maintain top-of-mind awareness.
- *Usage cycle.* Products used daily or more often need to be replaced quickly, so a higher level of frequency is desired.
- *Competitive share of voice.* Higher frequency levels are required when a lot of competitive noise exists and when the goal is to meet or beat competitors.
- *Target group.* The ability of the target group to learn and to retain messages has a direct effect on frequency.

Message or Creative Factors

- *Message complexity.* The simpler the message, the less frequency required.
- *Message uniqueness.* The more unique the message, the lower the frequency level required.
- *New versus continuing campaigns.* New campaigns require higher levels of frequency to register the message.
- *Image versus product sell.* Creating an image requires higher levels of frequency than does a specific product sell.
- *Message variation.* A single message requires less frequency; a variety of messages requires more.
- *Wearout.* Higher frequency may lead to wearout. This effect must be tracked and used to evaluate frequency levels.
- *Advertising units.* Larger units of advertising require less frequency than smaller ones to get the message across.

Media Factors

- *Clutter.* The more advertising that appears in the media used, the more frequency is needed to break through the clutter.
- *Editorial environment.* The more consistent the ad is with the editorial environment, the less frequency is needed.
- *Attentiveness.* The higher the level of attention achieved by the media vehicle, the less frequency is required. Low-attention-getting media require more repetitions.
- *Scheduling.* Continuous scheduling requires less frequency than does flighting or pulsing.
- *Number of media used.* The fewer media used, the lower the level of frequency required.
- *Repeat exposures.* Media that allow for more repeat exposures (for example, monthly magazines) require less frequency.

calls for a continuous schedule over a one-week period, and less targeting to gain exposure to reach as many potential consumers as possible.[19] While one might argue that many of the exposures are then wasted, Ephron would disagree, noting that people are in the market at different times and that awareness and image building also can benefit by the exposures. Both Ephron and Herbert Krugman suggest that advertising needs to act like a brand, and "Advertising needs to be like a product sitting on the shelf, because you never know when the consumer is going to be looking for you, so advertising has to rent the shelf-space all the time."[20] Political advertising seems to adhere to this rule, as the number of ads aired increases significantly as election day gets closer. For some television stations, the availability of spots decreases for other products and services and the political ads buy most of the available times.

Creative Aspects and Mood

The context of the medium in which the ad is placed may also affect viewers' perceptions. A specific creative strategy may require certain media. Because TV provides both sight and sound, it may be more effective in generating emotions than are other media; magazines may create different perceptions from newspapers. In developing a media strategy, marketers must consider both creativity and mood factors. Let us examine each in more detail.

Creative Aspects   It is possible to increase the success of a product significantly through a strong creative campaign. But to implement this creativity, you must employ a medium that will support such a strategy. McDonald's, IKEA, and Fanta among others have run very creative and successful print ad campaigns over the years. Hallmark, among many others, has effectively used TV to create emotional appeals. In some situations, the media strategy to be pursued may be the driving force behind the creative strategy, as the media and creative departments work closely together to achieve the greatest impact with the audience of the specific media.

Mood   Certain media enhance the creativity of a message because they create a mood that carries over to the communication. For example, think about the moods created by the following magazines: *Gourmet*, *Skiing*, *Travel and Leisure*, and *House Beautiful*. Each of these special-interest vehicles puts the reader in a particular mood. The promotion of fine wines, ski boots, luggage, and home products is enhanced by this mood. On the other hand, advertisers are always concerned about their ads being adjacent to negative news stories that may place the viewer in a negative mood and the impact that mood might have on the ad and product. What different images might be created for your product if you advertised it in the following media?

> *The New York Times* versus the *National Enquirer*
> *Architectural Digest* versus *Reader's Digest*
> A highly rated prime-time TV show versus an old rerun
> Television versus the Internet

The message may require a specific medium and a certain media vehicle to achieve its objectives. Likewise, certain media and vehicles have images that may carry over to the perceptions of messages placed within them.

A study reported in the *Journal of Marketing* showed that TV viewers skip commercials based on the feeling created by a television program and a "mood mismatch," and the mismatch also makes it more difficult to recall when it is watched. For example, viewers watching a show that creates a sad, quiet mood are annoyed when it is interrupted by a loud and active commercial, resulting in a lower likelihood of remembering the brand message and an increased likelihood of ignoring or skipping through it.[21] While advertisers typically create exciting ads to get attention and interest, the study suggests that the advertiser may want to tone down the ad to fit the mood of the context within which it is shown.

Flexibility

An effective media strategy requires a degree of flexibility. Because of the rapidly changing marketing environment, strategies may need to be modified. If the plan has not built in some flexibility, opportunities may be lost and/or the company may not be able to address new threats. Flexibility may be needed to address the following:

1. *Market opportunities.* Sometimes a market opportunity arises that the advertiser wishes to take advantage of. For example, wine companies have attempted to

capitalize on the increasing interest in this drink created by changing trends in the U.S. marketplace. The development of a new advertising medium may offer an opportunity that was not previously available. Think of how the Internet has created opportunities for smaller companies.

2. *Market threats.* Internal or external factors may pose a threat to the firm, and a change in media strategy is dictated. For example, a competitor may alter its media strategy to gain an edge. Failure to respond to this challenge could create problems for the firm.

3. *Availability of media.* Sometimes a desired medium (or vehicle) is not available to the marketer. Perhaps the medium does not reach a particular target segment or has no time or space available. There are still some geographic areas that certain media do not reach. Even when the media are available, limited advertising time or space may have already been sold or cutoff dates for entry may have passed. Alternative vehicles or media must then be considered.

4. *Changes in media or media vehicles.* A change in the medium or in a particular vehicle may require a change in the media strategy. For example, the advent of cable TV opened up new opportunities for message delivery, as did the introduction of interactive media. The Internet has led many consumer companies to adopt this medium and use it in different ways such as a primary source of information or for e-commerce; a number of new technologies such as tablets and smartphones have provided additional options. New special-interest magazines, podcasts, social networks, and video game ads are just a few new options available to advertisers. Likewise, a drop in ratings or a change in editorial format may lead the advertiser to use different alternatives. The shifting of advertising dollars to digital has led to a number of print media either ceasing to exist or offering online versions only. Some online streaming services' premium subscriptions have made it possible for viewers to be free of ads completely while eliminating the availability of the media option for advertisers.

Fluctuations in these factors mean the media strategy must be developed with enough flexibility to allow the manager to adapt to specific market situations.

Budget Considerations

One of the more important decisions in the development of media strategy is cost estimating. The value of any strategy can be determined by how well it delivers the message to the audience with the lowest cost and the least waste. We have already explored a number of factors, such as reach, frequency, and availability, that affect this decision. The marketer tries to arrive at the optimal delivery by balancing cost with each of these. As the following discussion shows, understanding cost figures may not be as easy as it seems.

Advertising and promotional costs can be categorized in two ways. The **absolute cost** of the medium or vehicle is the actual total cost required to place the message. For example, a full-page ad in *Sports Illustrated* costs about $78,000, which also includes an online ad version. **Relative cost** refers to the relationship between the price paid for advertising time or space and the size of the audience delivered; it is used to compare the cost of an ad in different media vehicles. Relative costs are important because the manager must try to optimize audience delivery within budget constraints. Since a number of alternatives are available for delivering the message, the advertiser must evaluate the relative costs associated with these choices. The way media costs are provided and problems in comparing these costs across media often make such evaluations difficult.

Determining Relative Costs of Media   To evaluate alternatives, advertisers must compare the relative costs of media as well as vehicles within these media. Unfortunately, the broadcast, print, digital, and out-of-home media do not always

FIGURE 10-22

Cost per Thousand
Computations: *Time* versus
The Week

	Time	The Week
Cost per page	$278,400	$72,800
Circulation	3.5 million	500,000
Calculation of CPM	$$CPM = \frac{Page\ cost \times 1,000}{Circulation}$$	
	$$\frac{\$278,400 \times 1,000}{3,500,000}$$	$$\frac{\$72,800 \times 1,000}{500,000}$$
CPM	$79.54	$145.60

provide the same cost breakdowns, nor necessarily do vehicles within the print media. Following are the cost bases used:

1. **Cost per thousand (CPM).** For years the magazine industry has provided cost breakdowns on the basis of cost per thousand people reached. The formula for this computation is

$$CPM = \frac{Cost\ of\ ad\ space\ (absolute\ cost)}{Circulation} \times 1,000$$

Figure 10-22 provides an example of this computation for two vehicles in the same medium—*Time* and *The Week*—and shows that (all other things being equal) *Time* is a more cost-effective buy, even though its absolute cost is higher. (We will come back to "all other things being equal" in a moment.)

2. **Cost per ratings point (CPRP).** The broadcast media provide a different comparative cost figure, referred to as cost per ratings point or *cost per point (CPP)*, based on the following formula:

$$CPRP = \frac{Cost\ of\ commercial\ time}{Program\ rating}$$

An example of this calculation for a spot ad is shown in Figure 10-23. It indicates that *Thursday Night Football* would be more cost-effective than *Sunday Night Football*.

3. **Daily inch rate.** For newspapers, cost-effectiveness is based on the daily inch rate, which is the cost per column inch of the paper. Like magazines, newspapers now use the cost-per-thousand formula discussed earlier to determine relative costs. As shown in Figure 10-24, the *Pittsburgh Post Gazette* costs significantly less to advertise in than does the *Cleveland Plain Dealer* (again, all other things being equal). A number of newspapers also include **modular pricing**. In this form of pricing, costs are based on the size of a set module such as full page, half page, quarter page, or eighth page. The modules can also be described in terms of column inches, but because the size of the ad is simpler to understand and determines the price many buyers prefer modular pricing.

FIGURE 10-23

Comparison of Cost per
Ratings Point

	Sunday Night Football	Thursday Night Football
Cost per ad	$811,679	$635,439
Rating	12.3	10.8
Reach (millions HH)	18	15.4
Calculation	$811,679/12.3	$635,439/10.8
CPRP (CPP)	$65,990	$58,837

FIGURE 10-24

Comparative Costs in
Newspaper Advertising

	Pittsburgh Post Gazette	Cleveland Plain Dealer
Cost per page	$20,969	$59,598
Cost per inch	303.90	473
Circulation	184,234	271,180
Calculation	$CPM = \dfrac{\text{Page cost} \times 1{,}000}{\text{Circulation}}$	
	$\dfrac{\$20{,}969 \times 1{,}000}{184{,}234}$	$\dfrac{\$59{,}598 \times 1{,}000}{271{,}180}$
CPM	$113.81	$219.77

Digital Pricing Models   Purchasing an ad in digital media again entails a different basis for pricing and a different means for determining relative cost comparisons. While a number of options are available for buying ad space on digital media and each has its own potential advantages and disadvantages, our discussion here is to provide a basic understanding of the need to make relative cost comparisons when developing the media plan.

For example, one **digital pricing** structure involves **bidding** in which the buyer participates in an auction to purchase placement for the ad format. The bidding process may be done manually by a manager who is involved in the campaign, or through an automatic process referred to as programmatic that takes place in milliseconds through designed software. While **programmatic** makes the purchasing process much easier, and is increasing in use, there are some who are not as enamored with this process as seen in Digital and Social Media Perspective 10-1.

Digital and Social Media Perspective 10–1 >>>

Despite Issues, Programmatic Continues to Grow

Not long ago, if marketers wanted to purchase an online display ad they had to contact the website, negotiate the terms for each ad placement, and sign an insertion order. If they wanted to do the same in traditional media, the process would be essentially the same—that is, determine which medium they wanted the ad in, negotiate the deal, and place an order. Now, thanks to big data, algorithms, and something called real-time bidding (RTB), all this can be done through technology almost instantly and, depending on whom you believe, more effectively. The latest trend in media buying, known as programmatic buying, is upon us, and online and social ad buyers seemingly can't adopt it fast enough.

Consider these numbers: In 2012, advertisers spent just shy of $2 billion on real-time bidding. By 2021, expectations were that this amount would reach $418 billion worldwide. Predictions are by 2023 that 86 percent of all placements would be programmatic. While mobile video ads accounted for about two-thirds of programmatic ad expenditures in the United States in 2021, connected TV (CTV) is quickly on the increase.

But what is programmatic? It's hard to pin down exactly what the term means. While it started off as an acceptable synonym to *real-time bidding*, as it has grown in usage it has also become more confusing. According to *Adweek*, real-time bidding essentially means the use of big data to figure out the right ad, targeted to the right person, at the right time. A more formal definition is offered by MarTech (martech.org). "Programmatic advertising helps automate the decision-making process of media buying by targeting specific audiences and demographics. Programmatic ads are placed using artificial intelligence (AI) and real-time bidding (RTB) for online display, social media advertising, mobile and video campaigns, and is expanding to traditional TV advertising marketplaces." So basically programmatic is computer-based advertising buying using a real-time bidding process. When an opening is available, the software advises advertisers which page it is and supplies demographic and behavioral data about the user. Each advertiser's software puts in its bid and in real time the transaction is completed along with the ad of the winning bidder. While originally used to buy and sell online display advertising, and used primarily by direct marketers, programmatic is now commonly used to buy mobile and video display advertising, and many expect that it will become the way to purchase ads on television as well. It is considered highly targeted, resulting in improved results and efficiencies, and because it is automated it makes the buyer's life easier. Proponents believe that it will replace all other types of ad buying in the not-too-distant future.

A variety of companies are committed to programmatic already. While Kellogg's moved more monies into digital advertising, the company continues to use TV and print. However, for its digital ad placements, programmatic is the method most commonly used. The company believes that it has increased return on investment (ROI) primarily through the improved frequency, control, and targeting using programmatic. Movies Unlimited, an online store for movie collectors specializing in hard-to-find titles while also carrying nearly every title currently available, had a tremendous amount of site traffic but also a 75 percent cart abandonment problem. By using programmatic to assist in e-mail retargeting efforts, the online company experienced a 500 percent increase in ROI. Meliá Hotels International, McDonald's, and Telstra also claim success using programmatic, and P&G continues to increase its use to the point where the majority of the company's online buying will employ the automated method.

But, as is to be expected, not everyone is so enthralled with the concept. There are those who believe they have found the holy grail of media buying, but there are others who are not convinced. Fraud, brand safety, along with a lack of uniform standards and viewability are of major concern to many programmatic buyers. So too is transparency—or concrete evidence the ad is even being placed. These concerns are reflected in the brand managers' not knowing where the ads are being placed: What if the ad appears somewhere that is surrounded by offensive content? How would this impact their brand image? Another issue is what many consider to be "remnant inventory'"—that is, leftover availabilities that no one else wanted, and not providing information that allows buyers to know why this inventory was not sold. Reports have also indicated that more than 50 percent of

the placements can't even be viewed. In 2020, the ISBA (originally known as The Advertisers Protection Society) of the United Kingdom in association with the Association of Online Publishers conducted an extensive study of online publishing. The study concluded that approximately 50 percent of the monies spent by online advertisers is lost in the programmatic advertising supply chain, and 15 percent cannot be attributed at all, leading to a call for reform of the system. The ISBA study noted a need for standardization across a range of contractual and technology areas—essentially stating a need to clean up the system. Integral Ad Science (IAS)—a U.S. company that places value on digital ad placements and monitors issues regarding viewability, fraud, and so on—issued a report indicating that improvements were being made. The report also indicated that ad fraud remained steady. In addition, many ads may be placed on illegal, inappropriate, and low-quality sites. Many, if not all, of these concerns are eliminated in direct buying, providing the manager with a greater sense of comfort.

Despite these concerns, however, it appears that programmatic is here to stay (at least for the near future) and is likely to find its way into television and maybe even radio ad buying. When companies like P&G, Time, Inc., News Corp., and ESPN continue to embrace it, it will seemingly take a lot to stop the train!

Sources: "What Is Programmatic Advertising," *MarTech*, April 26, 2019, www.martech.org; Joe Mandese, "Report Reveals 86% of European Brands Have Shifted Programmatic In-House" *MediaDailyNews*, April 24, 2019, www.mediapost.com; Ross Benes, "How Digitization Affects TV Ad Sellers," *eMarketer*, November 20, 2018, www.emarketer.com; "65% of Digital Media Will Be Programmatic in 2019," WARC, November 19, 2018, www.warc.com; Robin Kurzer, "IAS Media Quality Report Paints a Slightly More Optimistic Picture for Programmatic Ad Buyers," *MarTech*, September 26, 2018, www.martech.org; "Programmatic TV Ushers in 'Golden Era,'" WARC, March 14, 2016, www.warc.com; "US Advertisers Are Investing Heavily in Programmatic, but Obstacles Remain," *eMarketer*, March 29, 2016, www.emarketer.com; Tim Nichols, "Why Programmatic Ad Buying Is More Important Than You Think," *ClickZ*, November 13, 2015, www.clickz.com; "Programmatic Buyers Demand Placement Transparency," *eMarketer*, April 8, 2015, www.emarketer.com; "Fraud, Brand Safety Take Center Stage among Ad Buyers," *eMarketer*, January 12, 2015, www.emarketer.com; "Global Programmatic Advertising Spending from 2017 to 2026," *Statista*, September 12, 2022, www.statista.com; "US Programmatic Video 2022," *eMarketer*, January 26, 2022, www.emarketer.com; "There Is a Big Hole in the Value Chain: Brands Lose 50% of the Money They Invest in Programmatic Ads," *Marketing Week*, May 11, 2020, www.marketingweek.com.

As you can see, it is difficult to make comparisons across various media. What is the broadcast equivalent of cost per thousand or the column inch rate? In an attempt to standardize relative costing procedures, the broadcast and newspaper media have begun to provide costs per thousand, using the following formulas:

$$\text{Television: } \frac{\text{Cost of 1 unit of time} \times 1{,}000}{\text{Program rating}} \qquad \text{Newspapers: } \frac{\text{Cost of ad space} \times 1{,}000}{\text{Circulation}}$$

The adoption of the various media to use CPM as a standard basis helps to at least provide some ability to compare relative costs, however, problems remain given the differences in the media characteristics themselves. In addition, there are some problems inherent with the use of CPM's themselves.

FIGURE 10–25

Cost-per-Thousand
Estimates

Scenario A: Overestimation of Efficiency	
Target market	18–49
Magazine circulation	3,250,000
Circulation to target market	65% (2,112,500)
Cost per page	$287,440

$$\text{CPM} = \frac{\$287,440}{3,250.00}$$

$$\text{CPM (actual target audience)} = \frac{\$287,440 \times 1,000}{2,112,500} = \$136.07$$

Scenario B: Underestimation of Efficiency	
Target market	All age groups, male and female
Magazine circulation	3,250,000
Cost per page	$287,440
Pass-along rate	3* (33% of households)

$$\text{CPM (based on readers per copy)} = \frac{\text{Page cost} \times 1,000}{\text{Circulation} + 3(1,072,500)} = \frac{(287,440 \times 1,000)}{4,322,500} = \$66.50$$

*Assuming pass-along was valid.

While the comparison of media on a cost-per-thousand basis is important, intermedia comparisons can be misleading. The ability of TV to provide both sight and sound, the longevity of magazines, and other characteristics of each medium make direct comparisons difficult. The media planner should use the cost-per-thousand numbers but must also consider the specific characteristics of each medium and each media vehicle in the decision.

The cost per thousand may overestimate or underestimate the actual cost-effectiveness. Consider a situation where some waste coverage is inevitable. The circulation (using hypothetical magazine figures to demonstrate our point) exceeds the target market. If the people reached by this message are not potential buyers of the product, then having to pay to reach them results in too low a cost per thousand, as shown in scenario A of Figure 10-25. We must use the potential reach to the target market—the destination sought—rather than the overall circulation figure. A medium with a much higher cost per thousand may be a wiser buy if it is reaching more potential receivers. (Most media buyers rely on **target CPM [TCPM]** which calculates CPMs based on the target audience, not the overall audience.)

CPM may also underestimate cost-efficiency. Magazine advertising space sellers have argued for years that because more than one person may read print copy, the actual reach is underestimated. They want to use the number of **readers per copy** as the true circulation. This would include a **pass-along rate**, estimating the number of people who read the magazine without buying it. Scenario B in Figure 10-25 shows how this underestimates cost-efficiency. Consider a family in which a father, mother, and two teenagers read each issue of a magazine. Assume such families constitute 33 percent of the magazine's circulation base, based on 3,250,000. While the circulation figure includes only one magazine, in reality there are four potential exposures in these households, increasing the total reach to 4.32 million.

While the number of readers per copy makes intuitive sense, it has the potential to be extremely inaccurate. The actual number of times the magazine changes hands is difficult to determine. How many people in a fraternity read each print issue of *Sports Illustrated* or *GQ* that is delivered? How many people in a sorority or on a dorm floor read each issue of *Cosmopolitan* or *Vanity Fair*? How many of either group read each issue of *Bloomberg Businessweek*? While research is conducted to make these determinations, pass-along estimates are very subjective and using them to estimate reach is speculative. These figures are regularly provided by the media, but managers are selective about using them. At the same time, the art of media buying enters, for many magazines' managers have a good idea how much greater the reach is than their circulation figures provided. (Of course this may be less of an issue with digital editions.)

In addition to the potential for over- or underestimation of cost-efficiencies, CPMs are limited in that they make only *quantitative* estimates of the value of media. Although they may be good for comparing very similar vehicles (such as news magazines like *Time* and *The Week*), they are less valuable in making intermedia comparisons—for example, CPM for magazines versus Internet banner ads. We have already noted some differences among media that preclude direct comparisons.

You can see that the development of a media strategy involves many factors. Ostrow may be right when he calls this process an art rather than a science, as so much of it requires going beyond the numbers.

EVALUATION AND FOLLOW-UP

All plans require some evaluation to assess their performances. The media plan is no exception.

In outlining the planning process, we stated that objectives are established and strategies developed for them. Having implemented these strategies, marketers need to know whether or not they were successful. Measures of effectiveness must consider two factors: (1) How well did these strategies achieve the media objectives? (2) How well did this media plan contribute to attaining the overall marketing and communications objectives? If the strategies were successful, they should be used in future plans. If not, their flaws should be analyzed.

The problem with measuring the effectiveness of media strategies is probably obvious to you at this point. At the outset of this chapter, we suggested the planning process was limited by problems with measurements and lack of consistent terminology (among others). While these problems limit the degree to which we can assess the relative effectiveness of various strategies, it is not impossible to make such determinations.

Even if the evaluation procedure is not foolproof, it is better than no attempt. We will discuss more about measuring effectiveness in Chapter 18.

CHARACTERISTICS OF MEDIA

To this point, we have discussed the elements involved in the development of media strategy. One of the most basic elements in this process is the matching of media to markets. In the following chapters, you will see that each medium has its own characteristics that make it better or worse for attaining specific objectives. First, Figure 10–26 provides an overall comparison of media and some of the characteristics by which they are evaluated. This is a very general comparison, and the various media options must be analyzed for each situation. Nevertheless, it is a good starting point and serves as a lead-in to subsequent chapters.

FIGURE 10–26

Media Characteristics

Media	Advantages	Disadvantages
Television	Mass coverage High reach Impact of sight, sound, and motion High prestige Low cost per exposure Attention getting Favorable image	Low selectivity Short message life High absolute cost High production costs Clutter
Radio	Local coverage Low cost High frequency Flexible Low production costs Well-segmented audiences	Audio only Clutter Low attention getting Fleeting message
Magazines	Segmentation potential Quality reproduction High information content Longevity Multiple readers	Long lead time for ad placement Visual only Lack of flexibility
Newspapers	High coverage Low cost Short lead time for placing ads Ads can be placed in interest sections Timely (current ads) Reader controls exposure Can be used for coupons	Short life Clutter Low attention-getting capabilities Poor reproduction quality Selective reader exposure
Outdoor	Location specific High repetition Easily noticed	Short exposure time requires short ad Poor image Local restrictions
Direct mail	High selectivity Reader controls exposure High information content Opportunities for repeat exposures	High cost/contact Poor image (junk mail) Clutter
Digital/ interactive	User selects product information User attention and involvement Interactive relationship Direct selling potential Flexible message platform	Privacy concerns Potential for deception Clutter Few valid measurement techniques

Summary

This chapter has presented an overview of the determination of media objectives, development of the media strategy, and formalization of objectives and strategy in the form of a media plan. Sources of media information, characteristics of media, and key media decisions were also discussed.

The media strategy must be designed to supplement and support the overall marketing and communications objectives. The objectives of this plan are designed to deliver the message the program has developed.

The basic task involved in the development of media strategy is to determine the best matching of media to the target market, given the constraints of the budget. The media planner attempts to balance reach and frequency and to deliver the message to the intended audience with a minimum of waste coverage. At the same time, a number of additional factors affect the media decision. Media strategy development has been called more of an art than a science because while many quantitative data are available, the planner also relies on creativity and nonquantifiable factors.

This chapter discussed many factors, including developing a proper media mix, determining target market and geographic coverage, scheduling, and balancing reach and frequency. Creative aspects, budget considerations, the need for flexibility in the schedule, and the use of programmatic buying programs in the media planning process were also considered.

The chapter also introduced a number of resources available to the media planner. A summary chart of advantages and disadvantages of various media was provided.

Key Terms

media planning 327
media objectives 327
media strategies 327
medium 327
media vehicle 327
reach 327
coverage 327
frequency 327
sweeps periods 330
index number 332
survey of buying power index 336
brand development index (BDI) 336
category development index (CDI) 336

waste coverage 338
continuity 342
flighting 342
pulsing 342
unduplicated reach 344
duplicated reach 344
program rating 344
gross ratings points (GRPs) 345
target ratings points (TRPs) 345
effective reach 347
average frequency 349
recency 349
recency planning 349

absolute cost 352
relative cost 352
cost per thousand (CPM) 353
cost per ratings point (CPRP) 353
daily inch rate 353
modular pricing 353
digital pricing models 354
bidding 354
programmatic 354
target CPM (TCPM) 356
readers per copy 356
pass-along rate 356

Discussion Questions

1. If you watch linear television for any length of time, you are certain to see a number of commercials repeated to the point of overkill. Why do advertisers show the same ads so many times over and over again? What impact does this have on the viewers? (LO 10-4)

2. Explain the differences between the three methods of scheduling. Give examples of products and/or services that might use each form. (LO 10-1)

3. Describe some of the factors important in determining frequency levels. Pick at least one from each of the categories and give an example of how it might impact frequency levels. (LO 10-4)

4. Marketers often rely on demographics as the basis for target marketing and as a result look to differences in product usage based on these criteria as well as their media habits. Explain why relying strictly on demographics could cause a less than optimal media strategy. (LO 10-2)

5. What is "pass-along rate"? Does this figure have any relevance to media buyers these days? Explain why or why not. (LO 10-1)

6. Media use different cost bases to provide measures of relative costs (for example CPM, CPRP, etc). In an attempt to provide a standard basis for comparison across media, many have adopted CPM as the standard to make these costs easier to understand. Marketers have argued that CPMs cannot be used as a comparison across media. Explain why they feel this way and why you agree or disagree with this position. (LO 10-5)

7. Explain what an MRI-Simmons report is. How do advertisers use this report? Pick any product and discuss what the report would tell you about that product's users. (LO 10-2)

8. Given we know that sometimes print media may be passed on to more than one viewer (for example more than one member of a household may read the newspaper), why don't advertisers rely more on the readers-per-dollar figure than CPM? (LO 10-1)

9. Figure 10–10 in the text discusses how to use BDI and CDI indexes. Give an example of products that may be at each of the four positions described in the figure. Explain your reasoning. (LO 10-2)

10. Explain the meaning of reach and frequency as it may relate to digital media. Are these traditional measures of any value to digital advertisers? Explain your answer. (LO 10-1).

A

ASICS America Summary Flowchart

	January				February				March				April				May				June	
	29	5	12	19	26	2	9	16	23	2	9	16	23	30	6	13	20	27	4	11	18	25	1	8
Global/Branding																								
TV											▬▬▬▬													
Hulu-online TV															▬▬▬									
Performance Running																								
Print									▬▬▬▬▬▬▬▬▬▬▬▬▬▬▬▬▬▬▬▬▬▬														
Online														▬▬▬▬▬▬▬▬▬▬▬▬▬▬▬▬▬▬▬										
Onitsuka Tiger																								
Print									▬▬▬▬▬▬▬▬▬▬▬▬▬▬▬▬▬▬▬▬▬▬▬▬														
Online																								
NYC Marathon																								
Outdoor/Online/TV																								
Trade																								
Print		▬▬▬▬▬																						

	June			July				August					September				October				November				December			
	8	15	22	29	6	13	20	27	3	10	17	24	31	7	14	21	28	5	12	19	26	2	9	16	23	30	7	14	21

11 Evaluation of Media: Television and Radio

Tada Images/Shutterstock

Learning Objectives

 LO11-1 Describe the role of television as an advertising medium and its advantages and limitations.

 LO11-2 Discuss how television advertising time is purchased for network and local television as well as cable television.

 LO11-3 Discuss how television viewing audiences are measured and developments in audience measurement.

 LO11-4 Discuss the role of radio as an advertising medium and its advantages and limitations.

 LO11-5 Discuss how radio advertising time is purchased.

 LO11-6 Discuss how radio audiences are measured and developments in audience measurement.

Television Viewers Are Screaming for Streaming

Television has long been considered the primary form of entertainment for most people as well as the quintessential advertising medium for many marketers who want to reach large audiences and use its combination of sight, sound, and motion to deliver an impactful message. However, it would be hard to overstate the changes that have impacted the television industry over the past few years. The world has never been more connected nor had as many options to access content and listen, watch, read, or interact with media. People have myriad media consumption options today and many would prefer to spend time on social media, watch YouTube videos, or read articles online while listening to podcasts. And among those who still watch TV, many—including those in the 18–49 demographic target that advertisers covet—are not watching television in the traditional *linear* fashion, whereby they view a TV program on a network or cable channel at the specific time it is scheduled.

For a number of years, the traditional broadcast and cable networks were primarily concerned with time shifting, where TV viewers record a show on a digital video recorder (DVR) and watch it whenever they want, usually fast-forwarding through the commercials. In an effort to deal with time-shifted viewing, most cable and satellite TV providers began offering video-on-demand (VOD) services so viewers could watch their favorite shows on their own schedule. Although most VOD services do not allow viewers to fast-forward through commercials and the programs have fewer ads, advertisers are willing to pay less for them. Despite these challenges, advertising-supported VOD has maintained a steady level of growth across all demographics.

Contributing to the problems facing the traditional broadcast and cable networks is the increase in cord cutting, which refers to households dropping traditional pay-TV services such as cable or satellite. The percentage of U.S. households with cable or an alternative delivery system has steadily declined over the past decade going from 88 percent in 2013 to 66 percent in 2022. In 2013, there were over 100 million households paying for cable, but it is forecasted that by 2026 there will be less than 60 million. While a major reason for cord cutting is the cost of pay-TV services, an increasingly important factor is the rapid growth of streaming services. More than 80 percent of television households in the United States have a TV set that can access the Internet through a smart TV or connected device such as Apple TV, Roku, Amazon Fire TV, or Google Chromecast. In 2022, nearly 85 percent of U.S. households subscribed to at least one streaming service such as Netflix, Amazon Prime, Max, Hulu, Disney+, Peacock, ESPN+ and Paramount+.

Over the past 6 years, the streaming landscape has seen many new players enter the market, all of whom have been creating their own content as well as licensing existing movies and television shows to attract viewers. The streaming market is still dominated by Netflix, which has 221 million subscribers globally and 75 million in the United States and Canada. However, Netflix has been losing market share as new services enter the market. In 2016 Netflix had 71 percent of the streaming market while Amazon Prime had 8 percent and Hulu 7 percent. By 2022 Netflix's market share in the United States had dropped to 42 percent as it lost share to new services such as Max, Apple TV+, Disney+, Paramount+, and Peacock.

While the cost of pay TV is a major reason TV viewers are switching to streaming, the second most important driver is that consumers feel that streaming services meet their viewing needs. With new and existing content spread across a broad and diverse set of streaming options, many TV viewers are opting to subscribe to more than one service. A 2022 survey from Hub Entertainment Research showed that 50 percent of households subscribe to three or more of the five biggest streaming services (Netflix, Amazon Prime, Hulu, Max, and Disney+).

While many households are willing to pay for streaming services, many are opting for ad-supported streaming that they can watch for free. These streaming services are available from Hulu, Disney+, Max, Peacock, Paramount+, and others. And as discussed in Chapter 1, Netflix began offering an ad-supported option in late 2022. The ad load varies across the different platforms, but many of the services have about 4 to 5 minutes of commercials per hour. A major problem viewers have noted with ad-supported streaming services is seeing the same ad multiple times per viewing session.

The growth in streaming services and their ability to attract viewers has become a major problem for the traditional broadcast and cable networks. In

continued

2022 streaming viewership reached new highs as streaming accounted for 3 percent of total TV viewing time in the United States—an increase of 23 percent compared to the previous year. Cable TV viewership was a little behind at 34 percent, while broadcast's share of TV viewing was at 21 percent, down 25 percent from a year earlier. The new viewership numbers show that streaming has become a top choice for TV viewers, mainly driven by exclusive and original content that can't be found on cable or broadcast television. The major networks have recognized the shift to streaming by TV viewers and are developing their own streaming services. NBC programs can be viewed on Peacock while CBS has the Paramount+ streaming service. The ABC Network is owned by The Walt Disney Company which has the Disney+ streaming service. Disney also owns ESPN and launched the ESPN+ streaming service in 2018, which is targeted to avid sports fans.

Predictions of traditional television's imminent demise have come and gone through the years like fast-forwarded commercial breaks. Media experts have argued that all of the technological developments would lead to the demise of TV's traditional advertising-based business model because consumers want to watch what they want when they want, and this does not include commercials. It is very possible that the experts' predictions are slowly but surely coming true.

Sources: Sarah Krouse, "Streaming Tops Cable-TV Viewing for the First Time," *The Wall Street Journal*, August 18, 2022, https://www.wsj.com/articles/americans-spent-more-time-streaming-than-watching-cable-tv-in-julya-first-11660827184; Bevin Fletcher, "How Many Services Does It Take to Meet Viewer TV Needs?" *FIERCE Video*, May 11, 2022, https://www.fiercevideo.com/video/how-many-services-does-it-take-meet-viewer-tv-needs-least-4-survey-says #:~; Ethan Jakob Kraft, "What Viewers Dislike about Streaming TV Ads," *Advertising Age*, October 21, 2021, https://adage.com/article/marketing-news-strategy/what-viewers-dislike-about-streaming-tv-ads/2374826.

Television has been the dominant form of entertainment in most households for more than three-quarters of a century. Advertising has been the lifeblood of the industry for nearly as long. Ever since Bulova ran the first TV ad in 1941, at a cost of $10, the commercial has been considered the quintessential form of advertising for many marketers. Television advertising has gone through many changes over the past 80 years. For decades it was dominated by three major broadcast networks (ABC, CBS, and NBC), which could deliver more than 90 percent of the prime-time viewing audience on any given evening. However, with the growth of cable and direct broadcast satellite services, most television households can receive more than 100 channels that offer various types of shows, news, sports, music, information, and other entertainment genres. The device that delivers all of this has evolved, as most homes have large flat-panel, high-definition televisions (HDTVs) that offer high-resolution digital images along with high-quality sound. Moreover, these HDTVs are often connected to digital video recorders (DVRs), gaming consoles, streaming devices, and computers, while the cable and satellite companies that deliver the signals also offer access to movies, sports, and other forms of entertainment through their on-demand services. However, as discussed in the chapter opener, many households are spending much of their viewing time watching TV through streaming services. Media experts note that it is only a matter of time before all of this content is delivered to TV sets online via the Internet.

The changes that are occurring in the television industry are important because they are having a profound impact on the largest advertising medium. TV has virtually saturated households throughout the United States and most other countries and is still a very important part of the lives of most people. The average American household watches nearly 6 hours of TV a day, including just over 3 hours with traditional linear TV and 2:41 with digital viewing. "The tube" has become the predominant source of news and entertainment for many people. Nearly two-thirds of TV households in the United States have digital video recorders (DVRs), and over 80 percent have HDTVs on which they can watch their favorite television programs and movies. On any given evening during the prime-time hours of 8 to 11 P.M., more than 100 million people are watching TV. Popular shows like *NCIS*, *FBI*, and *The Voice* can draw between 8 to 10 million viewers each week. The large numbers of people who watch television are important to the TV networks and stations because they can sell time on these programs to marketers who want to reach that audience with their advertising messages. Moreover, the qualities that make TV a great medium for news and entertainment also make it an excellent medium for creative ads that can have a strong impact on consumers.

Radio is also an integral part of our lives. Many of us wake up to clock radios and rely on radio programs to inform and/or entertain us while we drive to work or school. For many people, radio is a constant companion in their cars, at home, even at work. The average American listens to the radio nearly 2 hours each day.[1] Like TV viewers, radio listeners are an important audience for marketers.

In this chapter, we examine the media of TV and radio, including the general characteristics of each as well as their specific advantages and disadvantages. We examine how advertisers use TV and radio as part of their advertising and media strategies, how they buy TV and radio time, and how audiences are measured and evaluated for each medium. We also examine the factors that are changing the role of TV and radio as advertising media.

TELEVISION

It has often been said that television is the ideal advertising medium. Its ability to combine visual images, sound, motion, and color presents the advertiser with the opportunity to develop the most creative and imaginative appeals of any medium. However, TV does have certain problems that limit or even prevent its use by many advertisers.

Advantages of Television

TV has numerous advantages over other media, including creativity and impact, coverage and cost-effectiveness, captivity and attention, and selectivity and flexibility.

Creativity and Impact   Perhaps the greatest advantage of TV is the opportunity it provides for presenting the advertising message. The interaction of sight and sound offers tremendous creative flexibility and makes possible dramatic, lifelike representations of products and services. TV commercials can be used to convey a mood or image for a brand as well as to develop emotional or entertaining appeals that help make a dull product appear interesting.

Television is also an excellent medium for demonstrating a product or service as well as telling a story about a brand to highlight its features and benefits or create an emotional attachment. For example, as part of the "Love" campaign for Subaru (which was discussed in Chapter 9), the Carmichael Lynch agency created a poignant commercial called "Cut the Cord," which shows a father putting his daughter on the school bus for the first time and then driving alongside it to make sure she's okay (Exhibit 11-1). As he drives, the dad says, "I'm overprotective. That's why I got a Subaru," while the voiceover at the end of the spot says, "Love. It's what makes a Subaru a Subaru." The various emotional appeals that Subaru uses for the "Love" campaign lend themselves to television and have played an important role in helping Subaru of America achieve record sales increases for 13 consecutive years.[2]

EXHIBIT 11-1

Subaru uses television commercials to create an emotional attachment to its cars.

Subaru of America, Inc.

Coverage and Cost-Effectiveness   Television advertising makes it possible to reach large audiences. Nearly everyone, regardless of age, sex, income, or educational level, watches at least some TV. Most people do so on a regular basis. According to Nielsen's National Television Household Universe Estimates, 307.9 million people aged 2 or older live in the 122.4 million TV households in the United States.

Marketers selling products and services that appeal to broad target audiences find that TV lets them reach mass markets, often very cost-efficiently. The average prime-time TV show reaches several million homes; a top-rated show like *NCIS* may reach nearly 6 million homes and almost twice that many viewers. The average cost per thousand (CPM) viewers reached averages around $45 for prime-time network shows and $42 for national cable shows.[3]

Because of its ability to reach large audiences in a cost-efficient manner, TV is a popular medium among companies selling mass-consumption products. Companies with widespread distribution and availability of their products and services use TV to reach the mass market and deliver their advertising messages at a very low cost per thousand. Television advertising accounts for a large portion of the media budget for large consumer packaged-goods marketers such as Procter & Gamble, automotive marketers, insurance companies, telecommunication firms, and major retailers. Telecommunication companies like Verizon, T-Mobile, and AT&T spend more than $3 billion per year on advertising, with much of their budgets being allocated to various forms of television—including network, spot, cable, and syndicated programs. Major retailers such as Walmart, Target, Macy's, and Kohl's also spend heavily on television. Figure 11–1 shows the top 10 network and cable TV advertisers and their expenditures.

FIGURE 11–1

Top 10 Broadcast Network and Cable TV Advertisers, 2021.

"100 Leading National Advertisers," *Advertising Age*, June 27, 2022, p. 18.

	Network TV Ad Spending	
Rank	**Company**	**Measured Broadcast (millions)**
1.	Procter & Gamble Co.	$844
2.	Amazon	496
3.	Berkshire Hathaway	490
4.	Deutsche Telecom (T-Mobile)	428
5.	AbbVie	402
6.	Progressive Corp.	400
7.	Verizon Communications	390
8.	General Motors Co.	379
9.	Apple	368
10.	Walt Disney Co.	347
	Cable TV Ad Spending	
1.	Procter & Gamble Co.	$877
2.	Berkshire Hathaway	642
3.	Warner Bros. Discovery	629
4.	Amazon	495
5.	Walt Disney Co.	490
6.	Abbvie	370
7.	PepsiCo	341
8.	Progressive Corp.	336
9.	Deutsche Telecom (T-Mobile)	332
10.	Yum! Brands	327

BET is the leading provider of media and entertainment for African Americans and consumers of Black culture globally. Our brands reflect a full range of the Black experience and connect with fans of hip hop, gospel, jazz, comedy, drama, news, and more. BET Networks inspires its audiences to make a difference in their lives and communities with their pro-social agenda.

EXHIBIT 11-2

The BET network is the leading provider of media and entertainment for African Americans.

Black Entertainment Television LLC

Captivity and Attention   Television is basically intrusive in that commercials impose themselves on viewers as they watch their favorite programs. Unless we make a special effort to avoid commercials, most of us are exposed to thousands of them each year. The increase in viewing options and the penetration of DVDs, DVRs, remote controls, and other automatic devices have made it easier for TV viewers to avoid commercial messages.[4] However, the remaining viewers are likely to devote some attention to many advertising messages. As discussed in Chapter 5, the low-involvement nature of consumer learning and response processes may mean TV ads have an effect on consumers simply through heavy repetition and exposure to catchy slogans and jingles.

Selectivity and Flexibility   Television has often been criticized for being a non-selective medium, since it is difficult to reach a precisely defined market segment through the use of TV advertising. But some selectivity is possible due to variations in the composition of audiences as a result of program content, broadcast time, and geographic coverage. For example, Saturday morning TV caters to children; Saturday and Sunday afternoon programs are geared to the sports-oriented male; and weekday daytime shows appeal heavily to homemakers.

With the availability of cable TV, advertisers refine their coverage further by appealing to groups with specific interests such as sports, news, history, the arts, or music, as well as specific demographic groups. Exhibit 11-2 shows an ad promoting the BET network, which is the leading provider of entertainment including music, news, style and public affairs for African Americans and those interested in Black culture.

Advertisers can also adjust their media strategies to take advantage of different geographic markets through local or spot ads in specific market areas. Television ads can be scheduled to run repeatedly to achieve continuity in media scheduling, or flighting or pulsing can be used to take advantage of special events or occasions as well as time periods. For example, marketers targeting males often advertise during sporting events such as golf and tennis tournaments as well as MLB, NBA, or NFL games. Sports programming has become particularly popular among advertisers since sporting events are usually watched live. This increases the likelihood of viewers seeing an advertiser's commercials rather than fast-forwarding through them, as is often the case when playing back a program on a DVR.

Many marketers advertise on sporting events such as college football and basketball games because they are a good way to reach young men, who are a valuable and elusive target audience. A number of companies and brands also use sponsorship deals with the networks that broadcast the games as a way to reach college students, as well as football and basketball fans. For example, Home Depot has sponsored ESPN's popular *College GameDay*, which airs from the campus where one of the biggest games of the week is being played and televised, since 2003 (Exhibit 11-3). Dr Pepper renewed its deal with ESPN to continue as the presenting sponsor for the College Football National Championship Trophy through 2026, paying an estimated $35 million per year to do so.[5]

The popularity of college football and basketball has led to tremendous increases in revenue for many universities' athletic programs. The television networks have agreed to pay about $30 billion in rights fees to college conferences and their member schools over the next 15 years. ESPN currently pays the National Collegiate Athletic Association $470 million a year for the rights to televise the four-team College Football Playoff (CFP) through 2025. However, the CFP is expanding to 12 teams in 2026 and the rights fees are expected to reach close to $2 billion annually.[6] CBS and Turner Broadcasting extended their deal with the NCAA for the rights to televise the popular men's basketball tournament,

EXHIBIT 11-3

Home Depot sponsors ESPN's popular *College GameDay* show during football season.

Chris Szagola/AP Images

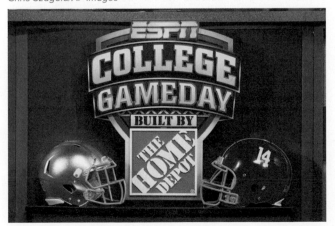

known as "March Madness," through 2032. The NCAA will receive $1.1 billion annually for the broadcast rights to the tournament.[7]

As mentioned, sports programming has become particularly popular among advertisers since sporting events are usually watched live, which increases the likelihood of viewers seeing an advertiser's commercial. Live sports have long been an integral part of the programming for the major broadcast and cable networks. However, competition for the rights to live sports has intensified in recent years as tech companies such as Apple, Google, and Amazon have entered the market as part of their strategy for using sports programming to build their streaming services. IMC Perspective 11–1 discusses the importance of live sports to the broadcast and cable networks and the challenges they are facing from streaming services.

IMC Perspective 11–1 >>>

Can Live Sports Save Traditional Television?

As discussed in the chapter opener, traditional broadcast and cable television is facing major challenges from streaming services, which have had a major impact on the way many people watch TV today. Linear television viewing, where viewers watch programs as scheduled, has been in decline as the streaming era has defined itself in opposition to live viewing. However, there is still one form of content TV viewers insist on watching live: sports. People love watching National Football League (NFL), National Basketball Association (NBA), Major League Baseball (MLB), and college football and basketball games live, which reduces the number of people who record the games and fast-forward through the commercials. Major League Soccer (MLS) is also growing in popularity, particularly among younger audiences.

The major television and cable networks have been willing to pay large amounts of money for the rights to broadcast football, baseball, and basketball games as well as events such as the Olympics and FIFA World Cup because live sports still attract a very large viewing audience. During the 2021–22 television season, sports games and events accounted for 95 of the top 100 most-watched broadcasts with NFL games making up 75 of the top 100. The major networks know that they can recoup their investment from advertisers who are willing to pay more for commercial time on sporting events because they are a good way to reach younger consumers, who are a valuable and elusive target audience for marketers. As one media analyst notes: "Sports are kind of the last bastion of the linear television model."

With its large audiences and attractive demographics, live sports programming has long been the foundation of broadcast and cable network programming. The Fox broadcast network relied heavily on sports in its early days by paying large rights fees for NFL games, which served as the lead-in programming for shows such as The Simpsons and Married With Children. Fox used sports programming to become the fourth major network and is still highly dependent on live sports today. During the 2021–22 season Fox pulled nearly 37 percent of its prime-time viewing audience from sports programs such as Thursday Night Football, MLB games, and WWE Smackdown, which is considered a sports program. NBC also owes a sizeable portion of its viewership to sports as 28 percent of its prime-time viewership in 2021–22 came from programming such as the Winter Olympics and Sunday Night Football, which has been the number-one-rated prime-time show for 11 consecutive years and averaged 19.9 million viewers in 2022. ESPN has used college football and basketball games to become the most popular cable network and has paid large rights fees for Monday Night Football games as well as NBA and MLB games.

Historically the major television networks and sports rights owners have had a very symbiotic relationship. The professional leagues, NCAA, collegiate conferences, and sporting events provided broadcast rights to their games that drive the mass audiences while the broadcast and cable networks provided distribution and monetization in the form of rights fees. As the number of cable channels grew, competition for sports rights intensified and rights fees increased dramatically. In 2021 the NFL signed media rights agreements with CBS, NBC, Fox, and ESPN collectively worth $100 billion over 11 years, nearly doubling the value of its previous contract. The NBA's current deal is up after the 2024–25 season, and the league is expected to triple its current annual take of $2.6 billion. Rights fees for collegiate football and basketball games are likely to skyrocket as well, particularly as conference realignment takes place as the Big Ten and SEC expand.

The surge in sports rights fees in recent years is largely attributable to increased competition, changing consumer TV viewing habits, and the continued ratings erosion for non-sports programming. However, a new variable has been entered into the equation for determining sports rights as the behemoth tech companies, bolstered by their deep pockets and strong desire to boost viewership of their streaming-subscription services, have entered the bidding arena for media rights held by the NFL, NBA, and MLB. The new rights deal for NFL games sent a shock wave through the media industry as streaming service Amazon Prime acquired the exclusive rights to the NFL's *Thursday Night Football*, reportedly paying $1 billion a year for 11 years. Amazon shelled out a multiple of what the networks were willing to pay after they lost hundreds of millions of dollars on the package over the past several years.

Amazon.com, Inc

Apple made a major statement in 2022 with a deal to become the primary carrier of Major League Soccer, guaranteeing the league around $200 million annually in the 10-year pact, which was far more than any traditional TV network was willing to pay. Many industry experts believe Apple will use the MLS rights to demonstrate its ability to grow and nurture the league as well as its viability as a media partner for other sports entities. Apple also competed with Amazon and Google, which owns YouTube TV, to replace DirecTV for the rights to the NFL's "Sunday Ticket" package that shows out-of-market Sunday NFL games that are not being aired on local television. In late 2022, the NFL awarded its "Sunday Ticket" subscription package to Google's YouTube TV starting with the 2023 season. It is estimated that YouTube will pay the NFL $2 billion a year for the 7 year deal.

Apple, Amazon, and Google have set their sights on live sports as they see it as a market that is ripe for change and an arena in which they are all well positioned to compete with their streaming services. The tech giants are eager to position themselves for a future without cable as traditional television viewers continue to cut the cord and trade cable packages for streaming services. They recognize that most new television entertainment platforms have been built around sports rights such as ESPN and its multiple networks and Fox's aforementioned using NFL rights to fast-track its ascendance as the fourth major broadcast network. Expansion into sports will also provide the tech companies with the opportunity to expand deeper into media by selling more subscriptions to their streaming services. Amazon is using *Thursday Night Football* to drive more Prime memberships, while Apple plans to use live sports to get more users for its iPhones, iPads, MacBooks, and other products and services.

The traditional broadcast and cable networks recognize that their hold on live sports is tenuous. However, with TV viewing habits being so closely tied to sports programming, they risk major disruption to their businesses if they are unwilling to pay the exorbitant fees to retain marquee live sports rights. Several of the major networks such as ABC and CBS are already less dependent on live sports and have focused on attracting viewers with non-sports programming. However, live sports is really the last category of exclusively must-see programming on television. It will be interesting to see if the traditional business model of the networks can survive or will succumb to the competition from the big tech companies who are likely to use sports to build their streaming services.

Sources: Tripp Mickle, Kevin Draper, and Benjamin Mullin, "Why Big Tech Is Making a Big Play for Live Sports," *The New York Times*, July 24, 2022, https://www.nytimes.com/2022/07/24/technology/sports-streaming-rights.html; Stephen Battaglio, "Will Live Sports Disappear From Traditional TV?" *Los Angeles Times*, June 25, 2022, https://www.latimes.com/entertainment-arts/business/story/2022-06-25/are-sports-going-to-disappear-from-traditional-tv; Rick Porter, "How Much Sports Matter (or Don't) to Network Viewership," *The Hollywood Reporter*, May 9, 2022, https://www.hollywoodreporter.com/tv/tv-news/how-much-broadcast-networks-depend-sports-1235143456/.

Limitations of Television

Although television is unsurpassed from a creative perspective, the medium has several disadvantages that limit or preclude its use by many advertisers. These problems include high costs, the lack of selectivity, the fleeting nature of a television message, commercial clutter, limited viewer attention, and distrust of TV ads.

Costs Despite the efficiency of TV in reaching large audiences, it is an expensive medium in which to advertise. The high cost of TV stems not only from the expense of buying airtime but also from the costs of producing a quality commercial. Production costs for a national brand 30-second spot average more than $350,000 and can reach over $1 million for more elaborate commercials.[8] Many advertisers also develop commercials specifically for certain ethnic markets such as African Americans and

Hispanics.[9] More advertisers are using media-driven creative strategies that require production of a variety of commercials, which drive up their costs. Even local ads can be expensive to produce and often are not of high quality. The high costs of producing and airing commercials often price small and medium-size advertisers out of the market.

Lack of Selectivity   Some selectivity is available in television through variations in programs and cable TV. But advertisers who are seeking a very specific, often small, target audience find the coverage of TV often extends beyond their market, reducing its cost effectiveness (as discussed in Chapter 10). Geographic selectivity can be a problem for local advertisers such as retailers, since a station bases its rates on the total market area it reaches. For example, stations in Pittsburgh, Pennsylvania, reach viewers in western and central Pennsylvania, eastern Ohio, northern West Virginia, and even parts of Maryland. The small company whose market is limited to the immediate Pittsburgh area may find TV an inefficient media buy, since the stations cover a larger geographic area than the merchant's trade area. Geographic selectivity can be particularly problematic in large media markets.

Audience selectivity is improving as advertisers target certain groups of consumers through the type of program or day and/or time when they choose to advertise. However, TV still does not offer as much audience selectivity as radio, magazines, direct mail, or online ads for reaching precise segments of the market.

Fleeting Message   Most TV commercials last only 30 seconds or less and leave nothing tangible for the viewer to examine or consider. Commercials have become shorter and shorter as the demand for a limited amount of broadcast time has intensified and advertisers try to get more impressions from their media budgets. Thirty-second commercials became the norm in the mid-1970s, and in 1986, the three major networks began accepting 15-second spots across their full schedules (except during children's viewing time). However, 15-second spots have become more prevalent over the past 5 years and now account for nearly 60 percent of the commercial activity on network TV, while 30-second spots account for 30 percent. Fifteen-second spots are even more popular on cable networks, where they represent 64 percent of the commercials versus 29 percent for 30-second spots. The 30-second format remains the dominant commercial length for local nonnetwork advertising, accounting for 58 percent of spot TV ads versus 32 percent for 15-second spots.[10]

An important factor in the decline in commercial length has been the increase in media costs over the past decade, particularly for prime-time programs. With the average cost of a prime-time spot now exceeding $100,000, and the most popular shows commanding nearly $300,000 or more, advertisers see shorter commercials as the only way to keep their media costs in line. A 15-second spot typically sells for half the price of a 30-second spot. By using 15- or even 10-second commercials, advertisers can run additional spots to reinforce the message or reach a larger audience. Many advertisers also believe shorter commercials can deliver a message just as effectively as can longer spots for much less money.

Clutter   The problems of fleeting messages and shorter commercials are compounded by the fact that the advertiser's message is only one of many spots and other nonprogramming material seen during a commercial break, so it may have trouble being noticed. As noted in Chapter 6, one of advertisers' greatest concerns with TV advertising is the potential decline in effectiveness because of such *clutter*.

While the use of shorter commercials by advertisers has contributed to the problem, clutter also increases when the networks and individual stations run promotional announcements for their shows, make more time available for commercials, and redistribute time to popular programs. The next time you watch TV, count the number of commercials, promotions for the news or upcoming programs, or public service announcements that appear during a station break and you will appreciate why clutter is a major concern.

With all of these messages competing for our attention, it is easy to understand why the viewer comes away confused or even annoyed and unable to remember or properly identify the product or service advertised. Advertisers and agencies have been pressuring the networks to cut back on the commercials and other sources of clutter. However, the networks argue that they must maintain the number of commercials they show or increase advertising rates. Clutter has become even more of a problem on cable television as many networks have been packing in more ads to offset declines in viewership and a stagnant market for advertising sales.[11] In 2018, several of the major media companies, including NBC Universal and Fox, announced plans to reduce the number of commercials aired during prime-time shows over the next several years. However, these reductions have failed to materialize and many experts question whether the economics of decreasing ad loads is feasible. Advertisers have to be willing to pay more for commercial time in order to make up for the revenue the networks would lose from showing fewer commercials and most are unwilling to do so as they are more sensitive to prices increases than to clutter.[12]

Limited Viewer Attention   When advertisers buy time on a TV program, they are not purchasing guaranteed exposure but rather the opportunity to communicate a message to large numbers of consumers. But there is increasing evidence that the size of the viewing audience shrinks during a commercial break. People leave the room to go to the bathroom or to get something to eat or drink, or they are distracted in some other way during commercials.

A recent study by Matthew McGranaghan, Jura Liaukonyte, and Kenneth C. Wilbur used an innovative technology that installed microphones and cameras on a household's primary television set to passively monitor who is in the room and whether they are actually watching the TV during commercial breaks.[13] The study analyzed 4 million advertising exposures and found that nearly a third of TV commercials play to empty rooms, and that viewers are four times more likely to leave the room than change the channel. They also found that commercial viewing behaviors vary depending on channel, time of day, program genre, age, and gender. For example, older viewers are more likely to avoid ads by changing channels; younger viewers are more likely to avoid ads by leaving the room or diverting their visual attention—likely due to multitasking with a second screen. Additionally, ads for products such as beer and video games are best at retaining viewers, while among the worst at keeping eyes on the screen are prescription drug ads, particularly those for serious conditions. The study also found that ads that reduce viewing decrease the size of the audience paying attention to subsequent ads during the commercial break.

Getting consumers to pay attention to commercials has become an even greater challenge in recent years; 64 percent of television homes have DVRs and nearly 80 percent of households with income over $75,000 have them.[14] Most households have either cable or satellite service and receive more than 100 channels, which means there are more viewing options available. These factors have contributed to the problems of zipping and zapping. **Zipping** occurs when viewers fast-forward through commercials as they play back a previously recorded program. With the increased penetration of DVRs, more people are watching recorded shows and fast-forwarding through the commercials. The problem is being compounded by the fact that many of the networks schedule their most popular shows against one another on the same nights and in the same time slots. Thus, the most popular shows also end up being the most recorded. Moreover, the audience for these shows is composed of upscale viewers in the 18–49 age group that are highly coveted by many advertisers.

Zapping refers to changing channels to avoid commercials. Nearly all televisions come with remote controls, which enable viewers to switch channels easily. Studies have shown that as much as a third of program audiences may be lost to zapping when commercials appear.[15] Research by Nielsen has also found that most commercial zapping occurs at the beginning and, to a lesser extent, the end of a program. Zapping at these points is likely to occur because commercial breaks are so long and predictable. Research also shows that young adults zap more than do older adults and that men are more likely to zap than are women.[16]

Studies conducted on zapping behavior among television viewers have found that people stop viewing TV during a commercial break because they have a reason to stop watching television altogether or they want to find out what is being shown on other channels. The number of people zapping in and out was not related to the type of product being advertised or specific characteristics of the commercials.[17] Research has also shown that zappers recalled fewer of the brands advertised than did nonzappers and that most of the brands that were recalled by zappers were placed near the end of the commercial break, which is when viewers would be likely to return to a program.[18]

As more consumers become turned off by advertising and the number of channels available to them increases, the level of zapping is likely to increase. Thus, the challenge facing the networks, as well as advertisers, is how to discourage viewers from changing channels during commercial breaks and be more receptive to the advertising. Some advertisers believe that producing different executions of a campaign theme is one way to maintain viewers' attention. Others think the ultimate way to zap-proof commercials is to produce creative advertising messages that will attract and hold viewers' attention. However, this is easier said than done; many consumers just do not want to watch commercials.

One way television networks have been addressing the attention problem during sporting events is by reducing the number of commercial breaks and using a split-screen or "double box" format that continues to show the live action on one side of the screen while a commercial is shown on the other side, usually in a larger box. The use of the double box format has become common on telecasts of golf and tennis tournaments and has also been used during other sports programs such as soccer and college and NFL football games.[19] The GOLF Channel and parent NBC Sports have been using the split-screen "Playing Through" advertising format since 2016. Their research shows that the commercials draw higher viewership and consumers pay closer attention to the commercial using the format, which is favorable for both viewers and sponsors.[20] Exhibit 11-4, shows an example of the double box format being used during a telecast of a golf tournament on the Golf Channel.

Advances in technology are likely to continue to lead to changes in television viewing habits, which will impact the number of consumers who watch TV commercials. DVRs are expected to continue to present a problem for advertisers, particularly if devices such as the Dish Network's Hopper, which allows viewers to automatically skip ads on TV programs they record, become more prevalent. The Dish Hopper 3 Auto-Hop feature makes it possible to instantly skip all commercials in a recorded show (Exhibit 11-5). However, the feature is available only for prime-time recordings of shows on the major networks at varying times starting the day after airing. This restriction was the result of settlements between Dish and the major networks, which sued the company over the ad-skipping feature.[21] Also of concern to the television industry is how TV viewing patterns are being impacted by another time-shifting technology—video on demand (VOD)—that is offered by cable operators as well as satellite services. VOD services allow users to select and watch programs interactively, and pause, fast-forward, or rewind the program just as they might do with a DVR player.

For a number of years, TV shows available through VOD did not contain any ads. The networks made only a limited number of shows available because they were reluctant to allow viewers access to shows without commercials since they were concerned they would become accustomed to that type of viewing experience. However, the networks have begun to make their programs available with commercials, and the cable operators and other distributors have, in some cases, agreed to disable a viewer's ability to fast-forward through them. Some of the networks have also begun to include VOD viewership in the advertising packages they make available to advertisers, along with viewership on their websites and other devices such as tablets and smartphones.[22]

Viewers' interest in watching TV shows in alternative ways and on their own time schedule will increase as more homes acquire DVRs and VOD services. As discussed in the chapter opener, more people, particularly millennials, are watching TV shows online through video-streaming subscription services. The challenge

EXHIBIT 11-4

The "double box" format is sometimes used to show commercials during sporting events rather than having a commercial break.

NBCUniversal Media, LLC

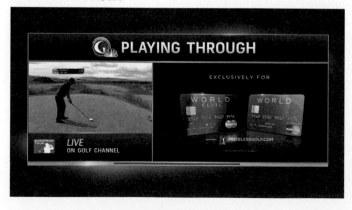

facing the TV industry is how to compete against these alternative viewing methods and protect their traditional advertising business model. They also must consider that the way many people watch television is changing as viewers are using their laptops, tablets, and smartphones to multitask when watching TV.

Distrust and Negative Evaluation   To many critics of advertising, TV commercials personify everything that is wrong with the industry. Critics often single out TV commercials because of their pervasiveness and the intrusive nature of the medium. Consumers are seen as defenseless against the barrage of TV ads, since they cannot control the transmission of the message and what appears on their screens. Viewers dislike TV advertising when they believe it is offensive, uninformative, or shown too frequently, or when they do not like its content.[23] Also, concern has been raised about the effects of TV advertising on specific groups, such as children and older adults.[24]

However, more recent studies have shown that trust in television advertising has increased. A survey of 1,200 U.S. consumers by Marketing Sherpa found that print ads were the most trusted form of advertising for making purchase decisions at 82 percent, followed by television at 80 percent.[25] The levels of trust in print and television advertising were significantly higher than for various forms of online advertising such as search (61 percent), social media (43 percent), and online banner ads (39 percent). The most recent Global Trust in Advertising study conducted by audience measurement company Nielsen found that 78 percent of consumers either somewhat or completely trust television advertising.[26] The high level of trust in TV advertising reflects consumer feelings that ads that appear on television are from legitimate businesses and that they are more trustworthy than newer forms of advertising such as online ads and those from influencers.

BUYING TELEVISION TIME

A number of options are available to advertisers that choose to use TV as part of their media mix. They can purchase time in a variety of program formats that appeal to various types and sizes of audiences. They can purchase time on a national, regional, or local basis. Or they can sponsor an entire program, participate in the sponsorship, or use spot announcements during or between programs.

The purchase of TV advertising time is a highly specialized phase of the advertising business, particularly for large companies spending huge sums of money. Large advertisers that do a lot of TV advertising generally use agency media specialists or specialized media buying services to arrange the media schedule and purchase TV time. Decisions have to be made regarding national or network versus local or spot purchases, selection of specific stations, sponsorship versus participation, different classes of time, and appropriate programs. Local advertisers may not have to deal with the first decision, but they do face all the others.

Network versus Spot

A basic decision for all advertisers is allocating their TV media budgets to network versus local or spot announcements. Most national advertisers use network schedules to provide national coverage and supplement this with regional or local spot purchases to reach markets where additional coverage is desired.

Network Advertising   A common way advertisers disseminate their messages is by purchasing airtime from a **television network**. A network assembles a series of affiliated local TV stations, or **affiliates**, to which it supplies programming and services. These affiliates, most of which are independently owned, contractually agree to preempt time during specified hours for programming provided by the networks and to carry the national advertising within the program. The networks share the advertising revenue they receive during these time periods with the affiliates. The affiliates are also free to sell commercial time in nonnetwork periods and during station breaks in the preempted periods to both national and local advertisers.

The three traditional major networks are NBC, ABC, and CBS. The Fox Broadcasting Co. broadcasts its programs over a group of affiliated independent stations and has become the fourth major network. A number of Fox's prime-time programs, such as *The Masked Singer* and *The Simpsons*, are popular, particularly among the 18–49 age group that is often targeted by advertisers. Fox has also become a major player in sports programming with its contracts to broadcast sporting events such as NFL football and Major League Baseball.[27] In 2022 Fox, along with CBS and NBC, signed a major deal with the Big Ten conference for the rights to televise college football as well as men's and women's basketball games through the 2029–30 seasons.[28]

The other television network in the United States is CW, which was formed in 2006 when two 11-year-old networks, WB and UPN, decided to merge.[29] The CW Network was co-owned by Warner Bros. Discovery and Paramount Global CBS Studios as a joint venture until 2022 when the majority ownership was sold to Nextstar, which owns nearly 200 local television stations and is the nation's largest local broadcasting company as well as the cable news network NewsNation. Nextstar has 75 percent ownership of The CW with Paramount and Warner Bros. Discovery retaining 12.5 percent each.[30] The CW is unique among the national broadcast networks as its strategy focuses on a more narrowly targeted demographic market of 18- to 34-year-olds and fewer hours of original programming than the four major networks. The network has a number of programs that are popular among its younger target market including *Kung Foo*, *Walker*, *DC's Stargirl*, and *The Flash* (Exhibit 11–6).

EXHIBIT 11–6

The CW Network has a number of popular shows such as *The Flash*.

CW Television Network/Photofest

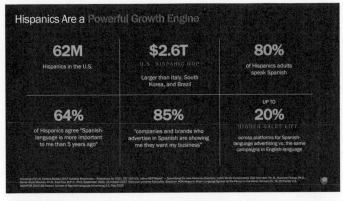

EXHIBIT 11–7

Univision is the leading
Spanish-language network.

Univision Communications Inc

In addition to The CW and the four major networks, there are also several Spanish-language networks in the United States. Spanish-language television networks such as Univision and Telemundo are becoming increasingly popular and provide advertisers a way to reach the fast-growing Hispanic market. Univision has become the nation's leading Hispanic media company and now challenges the four major broadcast TV networks with respect to size of its viewing audience. Hispanics now account for more than 62 million, or 19 percent, of the U.S. population, and advertising spending on Hispanic television continues to grow. The Hispanic population is also younger and is having a greater influence on the direction of pop culture, which makes them an important market for advertisers. Exhibit 11–7 shows a page from the Univision media kit promoting the size and importance of the Hispanic market.

The networks have affiliates throughout the nation for almost complete national coverage. When an advertiser purchases airtime from one of these national networks, the commercial is transmitted across the nation through the affiliate station network. Network advertising truly represents a mass medium, as the advertiser can broadcast its message simultaneously throughout the country.

A major advantage of network advertising is the simplification of the purchase process. The advertiser has to deal with only one party or media representative to air a commercial nationwide. The networks also offer many of the most popular and widely watched programs, particularly during prime time. Advertisers interested in reaching large national audiences generally buy commercials on shows that air during the prime-time viewing hours of 8 to 11 P.M. (7 to 10 P.M. in the Central and Mountain time zones).

While network advertising is an effective way to reach large audiences, the cost of advertising on prime-time shows is much higher because of the number of viewers they reach. Many of the popular prime-time shows such as *NCIS*, *The Voice*, and *The Masked Singer* can charge more than $200,000 for a 30-second spot. TV shows that do well among viewers in the 18–49 age group can often charge a premium since this demographic segment is very important to many advertisers. The most expensive TV program for the past several television seasons has been NBC's *Sunday Night Football*, which airs during the fall and charged over $800,000 for a 30-second commercial during the 2022–23 TV season. The cost of a commercial on one of the top 10 prime-time network shows can range from $150,000 to $200,000, depending on the size of the viewing audience, particularly the highly coveted 18–49 demographic age group.[31]

Availability of time can also be a problem because more advertisers turn to network advertising to reach mass markets. Traditionally, most prime-time commercial spots, particularly on the popular shows, are sold during the **up-front market**, a buying period that occurs before the TV season begins. Advertisers hoping to use prime-time network advertising must plan their media schedules and often purchase TV time as much as a year in advance. Demands from large clients who are heavy TV advertisers require agencies and media specialist companies to participate in the up-front market. However, TV time is also purchased during the **scatter market** that runs through the TV season. Some key incentives for buying up front, such as cancellation options and lower prices, are becoming more available in the quarterly scatter market. Network TV can also be purchased on a regional basis, so an advertiser's message can be aired in certain sections of the country with one media purchase.

The major networks as well as their cable counterparts often reserve at least 10 percent or more of their inventory of advertising time rather than offering all of it for sale during the up-front market. This is done when sales during the up-front buying period are weak in hopes of being able to sell the advertising time at higher prices on the scatter market.[32] Networks can also get higher prices for commercial time on the scatter market for new shows that end up attracting large audiences over the course of the television season. Fluctuations in supply and demand for network time can also work to the benefit of advertisers because they can often take advantage of weak demand for ad time on certain programs and purchase it at lower rates on the scatter market.

Spot and Local Advertising   **Spot advertising** refers to commercials shown on local TV stations, with time negotiated and purchased directly from the individual stations. All nonnetwork advertising done by a national advertiser is known as **national spot advertising**; airtime sold to local firms such as retailers, restaurants, banks, and auto dealers is known as **local advertising**. Local advertisers want media whose coverage is limited to the geographic markets in which they do business. This may be difficult to accomplish with TV, but many local businesses are large enough to make efficient use of TV advertising.

Spot advertising offers the national advertiser flexibility in adjusting to local market conditions. The advertiser can concentrate commercials in areas where market potential is greatest or where additional support is needed. This appeals to advertisers with uneven distribution or limited advertising budgets, as well as those interested in test marketing or introducing a product in limited market areas. National advertisers often use spot television advertising through local retailers or dealers as part of their cooperative advertising programs and to provide local dealer support.

A major problem for national advertisers is that spot advertising can be more difficult to acquire, since the time must be purchased from a number of local stations. Moreover, there are more variations in the pricing policies and discount structure of individual stations than of the networks. However, this problem has been reduced somewhat by the use of **station reps**, individuals who act as sales representatives for a number of local stations in dealings with national advertisers.

Spot ads are subject to more commercial clutter, since local stations can sell time on network-originated shows only during station breaks between programs, except when network advertisers have not purchased all the available time. Viewership generally declines during station breaks, as people may leave the room, zap to another channel, attend to other tasks, or stop watching TV.

While spot advertising is mostly confined to station breaks between programs on network-originated shows, local stations sell time on their own programs, which consist of news, movies, syndicated shows, or locally originated programs. Most cities have independent stations that spot advertisers use. Local advertisers find the independent stations attractive because they generally have lower rates than the major network affiliates do.

The decision facing most national advertisers is how to combine network and spot advertising to make effective use of their TV advertising budget. Another factor that makes spot advertising attractive to national advertisers is the growth in syndication.

Syndication   Advertisers may also reach TV viewers by advertising on **syndicated programs**, shows that are sold or distributed on a station-by-station, market-by-market basis. A syndicator seeks to sell its program to one station in every market. There are several types of syndicated programming. *Off-network syndication* refers to reruns of network shows that are bought by individual stations. Shows that are popular in off-network syndication include *The Big Bang Theory*, *Modern Family*, *Young Sheldon*, and *Family Guy*. Off-network syndication shows are very important to local stations because they provide quality programming with an established audience. The syndication market is also very important to the studios that produce programs and sell them to the networks. Most prime-time network shows initially lose money for the studios, since the licensing fee paid by the networks does not cover production costs. Over 4 years (the time it takes to produce the number of episodes needed to break into syndication), half-hour situation comedies often run up deficits of millions, and losses on one-hour drama shows are even higher. However, the producers recoup their money when they sell the show to syndication.

First-run syndication refers to shows produced specifically for the syndication market. The first-run syndication market is made up of a variety of shows, including some that did not make it as network shows. Examples of popular first-run syndication shows include talk shows such as *The Kelly Clarkson Show* and *The Dr. Phil Show*, entertainment shows such as *TMZ*, *Inside Edition*, and *Entertainment Tonight*, and court shows such as *Judge Judy*.

Advertiser-supported or *barter syndication* is the practice of selling shows to stations in return for a portion of the commercial time in the show, rather than (or in addition to) cash. The commercial time from all stations carrying the show is packaged into national units and sold to national advertisers. The station sells the remaining time to local and spot advertisers. Off-network as well as first-run syndicated programs are offered through barter syndication. Usually, more than half of the advertising time is presold, and the remainder is available for sale by the local advertiser. Barter syndication allows national advertisers to participate in the syndication market with the convenience of a network-type media buy, while local stations get free programming and can sell the remainder of the time to local or spot advertisers. Top-rated barter syndicated programs include *Wheel of Fortune* and *Jeopardy*.

Syndication now accounts for more than a third of the national broadcast audience and has become a very big business, generating ad revenue comparable to any of the big-four networks. Syndicated shows have become more popular than network shows in certain dayparts, such as daytime, early prime time, and late fringe. For example, during the 2021–22 television season, *Jeopardy* was the most-watched non-sports programming on television, averaging 9.2 million viewers per night, while *Wheel of Fortune* and *Family Feud* tied for second, drawing 8.4 million viewers per night (Exhibit 11–8).[33]

Many national advertisers use syndicated shows to broaden their reach, save money, and target certain audiences. For example, off-network syndication shows such as *The Big Bang Theory*, *Family Guy*, and *Modern Family* are popular with advertisers because they reach the highly sought after, and often difficult to reach, young-adult audience (ages 18 to 34) and are lower on a cost-per-thousand basis than network shows. Advertising rates for daytime syndicated shows are based primarily on the ratings among women 25 to 54. Syndication continues to gain in popularity, and more advertisers are making syndicated shows part of their television media schedules.

Syndication has certain disadvantages. The audience for some syndicated shows is often older and more rural, and syndicators do not supply as much research information as the networks do. Syndication also creates more problems for media buyers, since a syndicated show may not be seen in a particular market or may be aired during an undesirable time period. Thus, media buyers have to look at each market and check airtimes and other factors to put together a syndication schedule.

Methods of Buying Time

In addition to deciding whether to use network versus spot advertising, advertisers must decide whether to sponsor an entire program, participate in a program, or use spot announcements between programs. Sponsorship of a program and participations are available on either a network or a local market basis, whereas spot announcements are available only from local stations.

Sponsorship Under a **sponsorship** arrangement, an advertiser assumes responsibility for the production and usually the content of the program as well as the advertising that appears within it. In the early days of TV, most programs were produced and sponsored by corporations and were identified by their name, for example, *Texaco Star Theater* and *The Colgate Comedy Hour*. Today most shows are produced by either the networks or independent production companies that sell them to a network. Sole sponsorship of programs is usually limited to specials and has been declining. However, some companies, including Ford, Hallmark, AT&T, General Electric, and IBM, do sponsor programs occasionally.

A company might choose to sponsor a program for several reasons. Sponsorship allows the firm to capitalize on the prestige of a high-quality program, enhancing the image of the company and its products. Companies also sponsor programs to gain more control over the shows carrying their commercials, including the number, placement, and content of commercials. Commercials can be of any length, as long as the total amount of commercial time does not exceed network or station regulations. Advertisers introducing new products or brands sometimes sponsor a program and run commercials that are several minutes long to launch them.

Very few companies today are involved with the production of television shows. However, some do opt to be the single advertiser during a program as a way of enhancing their relationships with consumers by noting that the show is "being brought to you with limited commercial interruption." As was discussed in the chapter opener, with the growing popularity of streaming services like Netflix, Amazon Prime, Apple TV+, and others, the television networks are looking for ways to deliver an ad-reduced consumption experience for TV viewers. TV viewers may be more tolerant of single-sponsored shows with only a few commercial interruptions. For example, as part of its new initiative to reduce the number of commercials in its prime-time programming, Fox aired an episode of *Family Guy* that ran uninterrupted, with just two 1-minute spots from Sony PlayStation airing at the beginning and end of the episode.[34]

While these factors make sponsorship attractive to some companies, the high costs of sole sponsorship limit this option to large firms. Most commercial time is purchased through other methods, such as participations.

Participations   Most advertisers either cannot afford the costs of sponsorship or want greater flexibility than sole sponsorship permits. More than 90 percent of network advertising time is sold as **participations**, whereby network advertisers pay for commercial time during one or more programs. An advertiser can participate in a certain program once or several times on a regular or irregular basis. Participations provide advertisers with more flexibility in market coverage, scheduling, and budgeting. The advertiser has no long-term commitment to a program, and expenditures can be adjusted to buy whatever number of participation spots fit within the budget. This is particularly important to small advertisers with a limited budget. The second advantage is that the TV budget can be spread over a number of programs, thereby providing for greater reach in the media schedule.

The disadvantage of participations is that the advertiser has little control over the placement of ads, and there may also be problems with availability. Preference is given to advertisers willing to commit to numerous spots, and the firm trying to buy single spots in more than one program may find that time is unavailable in certain shows, especially during prime time.

Spot Announcements   As discussed previously, spot announcements are bought from the local stations and generally appear during time periods adjacent to network programs (hence the term **adjacencies**), rather than within them. Spot announcements are most often used by purely local advertisers but are also bought by companies with no network schedule (because of spotty or limited distribution) and by large advertisers that use both network and spot advertising.

Selecting Time Periods and Programs

Another consideration in buying TV time is selecting the right period and program for the advertiser's commercial messages. The cost of TV advertising time varies depending on the time of day and the particular program, since audience size varies as a function of these two factors. TV time periods are divided into **dayparts**, which are specific segments of a broadcast day.

The time segments that make up the programming day vary from station to station. A typical classification of dayparts for a weekday is shown in Figure 11–2. The various daypart segments attract different audiences in both size and nature, so advertising

FIGURE 11–2

Common Television
Dayparts

Early morning	5:00 A.M.–9:00 A.M.	Monday through Friday
Daytime	9:00 A.M.–3:00 P.M.	Monday through Friday
Early fringe	3:00 P.M.–5:00 P.M.	Monday through Friday
Early news	5:00 P.M.–7:00 P.M.	Monday through Saturday
Prime access	7:00 P.M.–8:00 P.M.	Monday through Saturday
Prime	8:00 P.M.–11:00 P.M.	Monday through Saturday
	7:00 P.M.–11:00 P.M.	Sunday
Late news	11:00 P.M.–11:30 P.M.	Sunday through Saturday
Late fringe	11:30 P.M.–2:00 A.M.	Monday through Friday
Overnight	2:00 A.M.–5:00 A.M.	Monday through Friday

Note: Times shown are for Eastern and Pacific time zones. Times may vary by market and station.

rates vary accordingly. Prime time draws the largest audiences, with 8:30 to 9 P.M. being the most watched half-hour time period and Sunday the most popular night for television. Since firms that advertise during prime time must pay premium rates, this daypart is dominated by the large national advertisers.

The various dayparts are important to advertisers since they attract different demographic groups. For example, daytime TV generally attracts women; early morning attracts women and children. The late-fringe (late-night) daypart period has become popular among advertisers trying to reach young adults who tune in to *The Late Show with Stephen Colbert* on CBS, *Jimmy Kimmel Live!* on ABC, and NBC's *The Tonight Show with Jimmy Fallon.* Audience size and demographic composition also vary depending on the type of program.

Cable Television

The Growth of Cable   Perhaps the most significant development in the television industry has been the expansion of **cable television**. Cable, or CATV (community antenna television), which delivers TV signals through fiber or coaxial wire rather than the airways, was developed to provide reception to remote areas that couldn't receive broadcast signals. Cable then expanded to metropolitan areas and grew rapidly due to the improved reception and wider selection of stations it offered subscribers. Several telecommunication services companies (telcos) also provide television signals through fiber-optic systems, including Verizon's Fios and AT&T's U-verse. Alternative delivery systems (ADS) such as direct broadcast satellite (DBS) companies DirecTV and Dish Network provide access to TV signals in areas where wired cable is not available. Cable, fiber-optic, and alternative delivery systems are sometimes referred to as **Multichannel Video Programming Distributors (MVPD)**, which are services that distribute or provide multiple television channels as part of a package that customers subscribe to for television programming. However, most of the ADS homes cannot receive advertising run on local cable stations.

Cable TV and ADS subscribers pay a monthly fee for which they receive an average of nearly 200 channels, including the local network affiliates and independent stations, various cable networks, superstations, and local cable system channels. Cable networks have a dual revenue stream; they are supported by both subscriber fees and ad revenue. Cable operators also offer programming that is not supported by commercial sponsorship and is available only to households willing to pay a fee beyond the monthly subscription charge. These premium channels include HBO, Showtime, and The Movie Channel.

Cable TV broadens the program options available to the viewer as well as the advertiser by offering specialty channels, including all-news, pop music, country music, sports, weather, educational, and cultural channels as well as children's programming. Figure 11-3 shows the most popular cable networks along with the types of

FIGURE 11-3 Major Cable Networks

Network	Description	Network	Description
ABC Family	Family/general/original	GSN: Game Show Network (GSN)	Game shows
A&E Network	Biographies/dramas/movies/documentaries	Golf Channel	Golf
Adult Swim	Young adult entertainment/programs	Hallmark Channel	Original movies/miniseries
AMC	Movies/documentaries	HLN	News/information
American Heroes	Military-focused programming/drama	HGTV	Decorating/gardening
Animal Planet	Wildlife and nature documentaries/adventure/children's entertainment	History Channel	Historical documentaries/movies
BBC America	Drama/comedy/news/arts	History En Espanol	Historical programming/documentaries (Spanish language)
BET	Entertainment/information for African Americans	ION	Family programs
Big 10 Network	College Sports	Lifetime Networks	News/information/women's interests
Bloomberg Television	Business and financial news	Logo TV	Movies/documentaries/gay-themed programming
Bravo	Drama/movies/reality shows	MLB Network	Major League Baseball
Cartoon Network	Cartoons	MSNBC	News/information
CBS Sports Network	College sports/events	MTV	Music/reality shows/drama
Centric	Entertainment/information for African Americans	MTV 2	Music/videos/popular culture
CMT Country	Country music video/concert/specials	mun2 Television	Bilingual programming for Hispanics/Latino youth culture
CNBC	Financial and business news/interviews and discussions	NBCSN	Sports
CNN	News/information	NGC (National Geographic Channel)	Adventure/exploration/science/culture
CNN Espanol	News/information (Spanish language)	NFL Network	NFL football
Comcast Sports Net	Regional sports	Nickelodeon/Nick at Nite	Youth interest/cartoons/comedy/game shows
Comedy Central	Comedy programs/original	OWN (Oprah Winfrey Netwok)	Entertainment/movies/talk/specials
Cooking Channel	Food/cooking	Oxygen	Movies/news/comedy/women's interests
Discovery Channel	Family/health/technology/science	Pac-12 Network	Colleges sports/Pac-12 Conference
Disney XD	Children's programming/entertainment	SOAPnet	Soap operas/drama
DIY Network	Home improvement/projects/crafts	Syfy Channel	Science fiction
E! Entertainment Television	Entertainment/celebrities/pop culture	Spike TV	Original programming/sports/entertainment for men
ESPN	Sports/specials/events	Superstation WGN	Movies/dramas/sports/sitcoms/reality-based programs
ESPN 2	Sports	TBS	Entertainment/movies/sports
ESPN Sports Classics	Sports history/biographies	TeenNick	Live-action for teens
ESPN Deportes	Sports (Spanish language)	Telemundo	Entertainment/news/sports (Spanish language)
ESPNEWS	Sports news	Tennis Channel	Tennis/health and fitness/lifestyle
Food Network	Food/cooking/entertainment	TLC (Learning Channel)	Science/history/adventure/behavior
Fox Business Network	Business news	TNT	Movies/general entertainment/sports
Fox News Channel	News/information	tru TV	Real-life stories/drama
Fox Soccer Plus	Soccer/rugby/sports	Travel Channel	Travel information
Fox Sports1	Sports	TV Guide Channel	Television entertainment information
Freeform	Family/general/original	Uni Mas	Novelas, reality shows for Hispanics
Fuse	Music/concerts	USA Network	Entertainment/movies/sports/drama
FX	Entertainment/original programs	VH1	Music videos/movies/concerts/documentaries
FYI	Lifestyle programs	Weather Channel	Weather
GAC: Great American Country	Country music/concerts	WGN	Entertainment/sports/movies
Galavision	Programming/entertainment for Hispanics	WE tv	Women's entertainment/fashion/health

Connecting brands to

7.6+ million households

22+ million consumers

72+ million screens

in the largest TV market.

That's the power of the New York Interconnect (NYI), a joint venture between Altice USA, Charter & Comcast.

altice + Charter + COMCAST

optimum. Spectrum xfinity flow dish Roku SAMSUNG

EXHIBIT 11—9

The New York Interconnect reaches over 7.6 million household in 75 zones.

NY Interconnect, LLC

programming they carry. Many cable and ADS also carry **superstations**, independent local stations that send their signals nationally via satellite to cable operators to make their programs available to subscribers. Programming on superstations such as TBS and WGN generally consists of sports, movies, and reruns of network shows. The superstations carry national advertising and are a relatively inexpensive option for reaching cable households across the country.

Cable has had a considerable influence on the nature of television as an advertising medium. First, the expanded viewing options have led to considerable audience fragmentation. Much of the growth in cable audiences has come at the expense of the four major networks. Cable channels now have more of the prime-time viewing audience than the major networks do. Many cable stations have become very popular among consumers, leading advertisers to reevaluate their media plans and the prices they are willing to pay for network and spot commercials on network affiliate stations.

Advertising on Cable Like broadcast TV, cable time can be purchased on a national, regional, or local (spot) level. Many large marketers advertise on cable networks to reach large numbers of viewers across the country with a single media buy. Regional advertising on cable is available primarily through sports and news channels that cover a certain geographic area.

Many national advertisers are turning to spot advertising on local cable systems to reach specific geographic markets. Spot cable affords them more precision in reaching specific markets, and they can save money by using a number of small, targeted media purchases rather than making one network buy. The growth in spot cable advertising is also being facilitated by the use of **interconnects**, where a number of cable systems and networks in a geographic area are joined for advertising purposes. These interconnects increase the size of the audience an advertiser can reach with a spot cable buy. For example, the New York Interconnect reaches over 22 million consumers across 75 different zones around the New York metropolitan area, which is the largest advertising market in the country. Exhibit 11–9 shows how the New York Interconnect promotes the number of households, consumers, and screens it reaches in the New York market.

Advantages of Cable Cable TV experienced tremendous growth as an advertising medium because it has some important advantages. A primary one is selectivity. Cable subscribers tend to be younger, more affluent, and better educated than nonsubscribers and have greater purchasing power. Moreover, the specialized programming on the various cable networks reaches very specific target markets.

EXHIBIT 11—10

MTV promotes its ability to reach a younger audience with programming built around music and pop culture.

MTV Entertainment

Many advertisers have turned to cable because of the opportunities it offers for **narrowcasting**, or reaching very specialized markets. For example, there are cable channels that focus on music and popular culture (MTV and VH1); food and cooking (Food Network); and home improvement and decorating (HGTV). CNBC, Fox Business, and Bloomberg TV focus on business and financial news and reach highly educated and affluent audiences. MTV is still viewed as the world's premiere youth entertainment channel and reaches millennials and gen Z age cohorts with programming that focuses on music and pop culture. Exhibit 11–10 is a page from the MTV media kit that shows the profile of the network's viewers. The profile includes demographics of MTV viewers as well as the index numbers for three lifestyle groups that watch the network.

VIEWER PROFILE

TOP THREE TARGET LIFESTYLE GROUPS WATCHING THIS NETWORK BY INDEX*:

Cultural Connections	144 or 44% more likely to watch (than the general population)
Aspirational Fusion	198 or 98% more likely to watch
Thrifty Habits	150 or 50% more likely to watch

GENDER		HOME OWNERSHIP	
Male:	43%	Own Home:	50%
Female:	57%	Rent:	46%

HOUSEHOLD INCOME		AGE	
$100K+:	24%	18 – 34:	43%
$75K - $99,999:	16%	35 – 54:	40%
$50K - $74,999:	14%	55+:	17%
$30K - $49,999:	23%		

EDUCATION		PRESENCE OF CHILDREN	
Graduated College:	22%	1+ Child in HH:	47%
Some College:	32%		

		MARITAL STATUS	
		Single (Never Married):	42%
		Married:	43%

FEATURED PROGRAMS

- Jersey Shore Family Vacation
- Floribama Shore
- Ex on the Beach
- Teen Mom
- Catfish: The TV Show
- MTV Video Music Awards
- The Hills: New Beginnings
- Are You The One?
- Ridiculousness

effectv

Advertisers are also interested in cable because of its low cost and flexibility. Advertising rates on cable programs are much lower than for the shows on the major networks. Advertising time on network shows can cost two to three times as much on a cost-per-thousand basis in some time periods. Spot advertising is also considerably cheaper on most cable stations, while local cable is the most affordable television advertising vehicle available. This makes TV a much more viable media option for smaller advertisers with limited budgets and those interested in targeting their commercials to a well-defined target audience. Also, cable advertisers generally do not have to make the large up-front commitments the networks require, which may be as much as a year in advance.

The low costs of cable make it a very popular advertising medium among local advertisers. Car dealers, furniture stores, restaurants, and many other merchants are switching advertising spending from traditional media such as radio, newspapers, and even magazines to take advantage of the low rates of local cable channels. Local cable advertising is an important segment of the advertising market, and cable systems are increasing the percentage of revenue they earn from local advertising.

Limitations of Cable   While cable has become increasingly popular among national, regional, and local advertisers, it still has some drawbacks. One major problem is that cable is still somewhat overshadowed by the major networks, as households with basic cable service watch considerably more network and syndicated programming than they do cable shows. This stems from the fact that cable generally has less popular programming than broadcast TV does.

Another drawback of cable is audience fragmentation. Although cable's share of the TV viewing audience has increased significantly, the viewers are spread out among the large number of channels available to cable subscribers. The number of viewers who watch any one cable channel is generally quite low. Even popular cable networks such as ESPN, CNN, and MTV have prime-time ratings of only about 1 or 2 for their regular programming. The large number of cable stations has fragmented audiences and made buying procedures more difficult, since numerous stations must be contacted to reach the majority of the cable audience in a market. There are also problems with the quality and availability of local ratings for cable stations as well as with research on audience characteristics.

Cable also still lacks total penetration, especially in some major markets. Overall cable penetration from both wired and alternative delivery systems such as satellite is less than 80 percent in markets such as Houston, Milwaukee, and Boise. In some designated market areas, wired cable penetration is low because many households receive cable programming from alternative delivery systems that do not offer local advertising. For example, penetration of wired cable is under 60 percent in some major DMAs such as Los Angeles, Denver, and Dallas–Fort Worth. Thus, local advertisers in these markets would not be able to reach a significant number of households by advertising on local cable networks.

The Future of Cable and Subscription Television   The future of cable as an advertising medium will ultimately depend on the size and quality of the audiences cable networks can reach with their programs. This in turn will depend on cable's ability to offer programs that attract viewers and subscribers. Cable's image as a stepchild in program development and acquisition has changed. Cable networks such as VH1, E!, TBS, FX, CNN, ESPN, and others have been creating original films, documentaries, and other programs that draw significant ratings. Networks like A&E, the Discovery Channel, the National Geographic Channel, and the History Channel provide outstanding cultural and educational programming. Cable news networks such as the Fox News Network, MSNBC, and CNN are also popular among many viewers, particularly those in the key 25–54 age segment.

Advertising and media experts note that many people, particularly children and young adults, really do not differentiate between cable and traditional broadcast television.[35] Cable programs generally cannot deliver the broad reach and mass audiences of popular network shows. However, cable networks have been developing high-quality and critically acclaimed programs such as AMC's *The Walking Dead*, which is a drama series about a postapocalyptic world overrun by zombies. The show has been one of the most popular programs on cable and attracts viewing audiences similar in size to those of network programs, particularly among the 18–49 age group. Other popular shows on cable networks include the *90 Day Fiance* franchise on TLC, *Real Housewives* shown on Bravo, *Better Call Saul* on AMC, and *American Horror Story* on FX.

Cable TV continues to be a popular source of sports programming and is very important to advertisers interested in reaching the male market. For example, ESPN has become synonymous with sports and is very popular among advertisers who want to target men of all ages. ESPN has become more than just a 24-hour sports network; it has changed the way sports are covered and played a major role in making sports programming very popular and lucrative. In addition to reaching nearly 75 million homes in the United States, ESPN has grown to include ESPN2, ESPN News, ESPNU, ESPN Deportes, and 47 international channels. ESPN receives more than $10 per household in subscriber fees, which is far and away the highest of any television network. In 2018, ESPN added a new streaming service, ESPN+ (Exhibit 11-11), whose programming includes Major League Baseball, the National League Hockey, Major League Soccer, collegiate and international sports, and the full library of ESPN films, including the popular *30 for 30* series. ESPN+ has also developed original content featuring former and current athletes such as former NFL quarterbacks Peyton and Eli Manning and NBA star LeBron James. The streaming service had nearly 23 million subscribers in 2022 and is a way for the sports media giant to offer an additional service to sports fans while also gaining a foothold in the rapidly growing subscription-based streaming market.[36]

A number of collegiate sports networks as well as regional sports networks (RSNs) provide sports programming to local markets. The most important programming on these RSNs is live broadcasts of professional and college sports—events such as football, basketball, and baseball. Many of these regional networks are associated with major media companies such as Spectrum Sports and Comcast SportsNet. In 2019, Sinclair Broadcasting Group, which is one of the largest owners of television stations in the United States, acquired 21 Fox regional sports networks from the Walt Disney Co., which Disney acquired in its takeover of the majority of 21st Century Fox. The RSNs

EXHIBIT 11–11

EPSN+ is a new streaming service targeted to sports fans.

ESPN, Inc.

EXHIBIT 11–12

YouTube TV is an over-the-top
streaming service delivered
over the Internet.

Google LLC

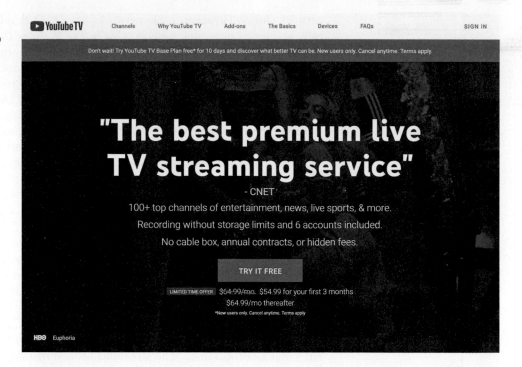

televise the live games of 42 Major League Baseball, National Basketball Association, and National Hockey League teams.[37]

Cable and ADS are important parts of the media strategy for nearly all advertisers using television. However, cable, like the major broadcast networks, faces competition from other viewing options such as streaming services. Over the past few years the MVPD and digital mediums have come together and yet another delivery system has emerged known as vMVPD, which stands for Virtual Multichannel Video Programming Distributor. This is also known as **OTT (over-the-top)** or streaming TV, which represents content that is delivered directly to viewers via a streaming service over the Internet, bypassing the traditional cable or satellite box. Examples of these streaming services include Sling TV, Hulu Live TV, fuboTV, and YouTube TV. The channel lineups for OTT streaming services are similar to cable packages as they include content from the major broadcast and cable networks as well as from other streaming providers. However, they often include fewer channels and lower subscription prices. Exhibit 11–13 shows how YouTube TV promotes the many channels available on its streaming service.

In 2022, 71 percent of the 122 million television households watched TV through a pay subscription service including those with OTT streaming services. However, a major problem facing the industry is the increase in **cord cutting**, which refers to households dropping traditional pay-TV services such as cable or satellite TV. The percentage of U.S. household with cable or an alternative delivery system has declined from 88 percent in 2013 to 66 percent in 2022. Cable and satellite TV providers are now losing nearly 2 million subscribers per year, and estimates are the number of households without traditional pay-TV service will reach 54 million by 2026, which represents about 45 percent of all U.S. homes.[38] Moreover, many of the pay-TV providers may have to offer subscribers "skinny bundles" that will include fewer channels so subscribers can save money on their monthly bills. ESPN, the cable network with the most subscribers, lost 11 million subscribers over the past 3 years and now has its lowest subscriber total in nearly a decade at 75 million.[39]

These are clearly challenging times for the television industry, and changes will be needed to retain viewers as well as advertisers, many of whom are shifting more of their media budgets to online and social media where they can reach younger consumers with highly targeted video ads on Google, Facebook, YouTube, TikTok, and Instagram. The broadcast and cable networks recognize that competing against streaming services requires quality programming, as well as finding ways to reduce the number of commercials in TV shows while maintaining revenue and profits. The networks must also move more quickly toward making **addressable TV advertising**, which allows different commercials to be shown to different households watching the same program, more available to marketers. An estimated 60 million households in the United States can be serviced via addressable ads on traditional cable and satellite TV, and the number will increase. However, it may take time for the broadcast and cable networks, as well as local stations, to gather the audience data needed to support the use of addressable ads on a large scale.[40]

Measuring the TV Audience

One of the most important considerations in TV advertising is the size and composition of the viewing audience. Audience measurement is critical to advertisers as well as to the networks and stations. Advertisers want to know the size and characteristics of the audience they are reaching when they purchase time on a particular program. And since the rates they pay are a function of audience size, advertisers want to be sure audience measurements are accurate.

Audience size and composition are also important to the networks and television stations, since they determine the amount they can charge for commercial time. Shows are frequently canceled because they fail to attract enough viewers to make their commercial time attractive to potential advertisers. Determining audience size is not an exact science and has been the subject of considerable controversy through the years. In this section, we examine how audiences are measured and how advertisers use this information in planning their media schedules.

Audience Measures The size and composition of television audiences are measured by ratings services. The sole source of network TV and local audience information is the Nielsen Company. Nielsen gathers viewership information from a sample of TV homes and then projects this information to the total viewing area. The techniques used to gather audience measurement information include electronic metering technology, diaries, and embedded software in devices. Nielsen provides various types of information that can be used to measure and evaluate a network and/or station's viewing audience. These measures are important to media planners because they weigh the value of buying commercial time on a program.

Television Households An important metric needed to measure the size of a viewing audience is an estimate of the number of households in a market that own a television or a computer that can be used to watch TV shows. Nielsen now defines a **television household** as a home with at least one operable TV or monitor with the ability to deliver video via traditional means of antenna, cable set-top-box, or satellite receiver and/or with a broadband connection. This updated definition accounts for households that do not have antenna, cable, or satellite access but can still watch video over the Internet. Since more than 98 percent of U.S. households own TVs and have access to TV shows, television households generally correspond to the number of households in a given market. According to Nielsen's National Television Household Universe Estimates there were nearly 122.4 million television households in the United States for the 2021–22 TV season.

Program Rating Probably the best known of all audience measurement figures is the **program rating**, the percentage of TV households in an area that are tuned to a specific program during a specific time period. The program rating is calculated by dividing the number of households tuned to a particular show by the total number of households in the area. For example, if 5 million households (HH) watched a popular show such as *The Voice*, the national rating would be 4.1, calculated as follows:

$$\text{Rating} = \frac{\text{HH tuned to show}}{\text{Total U.S. HH}} = \frac{5,000,000}{122,400,000} = 4.1$$

A **ratings point** represents 1 percent of all the television households in a particular area tuned to a specific program. On a national level, 1 ratings point represents 1,224,000. Thus, if a top-rated program like *The Voice* averages a rating of 4, it would reach 4,896,000 million households each week ($4 \times 1,224,000$).

The program rating is the key number to the television networks and stations, since the amount of money they can charge for commercial time is based on it. A small change in a program's ratings over the course of a viewing season can mean millions of dollars in advertising revenue to a broadcast or cable network. Advertisers also follow ratings closely, since they are the key measure for audience size and commercial rates.

Households Using Television The percentage of homes in a given area where TV is being watched during a specific time period is called **households using television (HUT)**. This figure, sometimes referred to as *sets in use*, is always expressed as a percentage. For example, if 72 million of the U.S. TV households have their sets turned on at 9 P.M. on a Thursday night, the HUT figure is 59 percent (72 million out of 122.4 million). Television usage varies widely depending on the time of day and season of the year.

Share of Audience Another important audience measurement figure is the **share of audience**, which is the percentage of households using TV in a specified time period that are tuned to a specific program. This figure considers variations in the number of sets in use and the total size of the potential audience, since it is based only on those households that have their sets turned on. Audience share is calculated by dividing the number of households (HH) tuned to a show by the number of households using television (HUT). Thus, if 72 million U.S. households had their sets turned on during the 8 P.M. time slot when *The Voice* is shown, the share of audience would be 6.9 calculated as follows:

$$\text{Share} = \frac{\text{HH tuned to show}}{\text{U.S. households using TV}} = \frac{5,000,000}{72,000,000} = 6.9$$

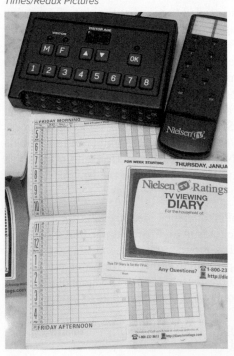

Audience share is always higher than the program rating unless all the households have their sets turned on (in which case they would be equal). Share figures are important since they reveal how well a program does with the available viewing audience. For example, late at night the size of the viewing audience drops substantially, so the best way to assess the popularity of a late-night program is to examine the share of the available audience it attracts relative to competing programs.

Ratings services also provide an audience statistic known as **total audience**, the total number of homes viewing any five-minute part of a telecast. This number can be broken down to provide audience composition figures that are based on the distribution of the audience into demographic categories.

National Audience Information Nielsen has a national TV ratings service that provides daily and weekly estimates of the size and composition of the national viewing audiences for programs aired on the broadcast and major cable networks. To measure the viewing audience, Nielsen uses a national sample of approximately 40,000 homes carefully selected to be representative of the population of U.S. households. The widely cited Nielsen ratings are based on the viewing patterns of this cross section of homes, which are measured using electronic metering technology. The **people meter** is an electronic measuring device that records not only what is being watched but also by whom in the measured households. It requires panel members to register their presence when they watch TV. The people meter records all their activities—whether they changed channels, watched through a streaming service, watched a recorded show, or even watched from their bedroom TV. The actual device is a small box with eight buttons—six for the family and two for visitors—that can be placed on the top of the TV (Exhibit 11-13). A remote-control unit permits electronic entries from anywhere in the room.

Each member of the sample household is assigned a button/number that indicates his or her presence as a viewer. The device is also equipped with a sonar sensor to remind viewers entering or leaving the room to log in or out on the meter.

The viewership information the people meter collects from the household is stored in the home system until it is retrieved by Nielsen's computers. Data collected include when the TV is turned on, which channel is viewed, when the channel is changed, and when the TV is off, in addition to who is viewing. The demographic characteristics of the viewers are also in the system, and viewership can be matched to these traits. Nielsen's operation center processes all this information each week for release to the TV and advertising industries. Nielsen uses a sample of metered households in 56 markets across the country to provide overnight viewing results.

Local Audience Information Information on local audiences is important to both local advertisers and firms making national spot buys. Nielsen's local market measurement service is called the Nielsen Station Index (NSI), which measures viewing audiences in 210 local markets known as **designated market areas (DMAs)**. DMAs are nonoverlapping areas used for planning, buying, and evaluating TV audiences and are generally a group of counties in which stations located in a metropolitan or central area achieve the largest audience share. NSI reports information on viewing by time periods and programs and includes audience size and estimates of viewing over a range of demographic categories for each DMA.

In addition to the national audience measurement, Nielsen also measures TV viewership in the 56 largest local markets using electronic or metered technology. This includes people meters as well as a **Portable People Meter (PPM)**, which is a wearable, page-size device that electronically tracks exposure to cable and satellite television; terrestrial, satellite, and online radio; as well as cinema advertising and many types of place-based digital media.[41] The device detects inaudible identification codes within embedded programs as they air or stream live. In 2017, Nielsen expanded the use of its PPM technology to 44 local markets and now gathers TV viewing data from more than 75,000 PPM panelists.[42] This information is augmented at least four times a year with demographic data that are collected from separate samples of households that fill out seven-day paper viewing diaries (or eight-day diaries in homes with DVRs). Smaller markets (DMAs ranked over 60) are currently measured using paper diaries only, although Nielsen plans to extend electronic measurement to some of these markets as well.

EXHIBIT 11–14

WJZ promotes its dominance of the sweeps rating period for local news.

WJZ-TV

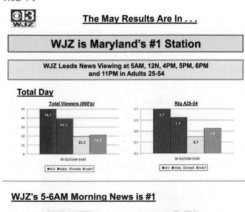

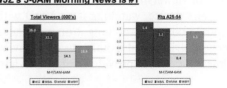

Nielsen measures viewing audiences in every local television market at least four times a year during rating periods known as **sweeps periods**. The term dates back to the 1950s, when Nielsen began mailing diaries to households and reporting the results, beginning with the East Coast markets before *sweeping* across the country. Sweeps rating periods are held in November, February, May, and July. In some of the larger markets, diaries provide viewer information for up to three additional sweeps months. The viewing information gathered during the sweeps periods is used for program scheduling decisions by local television stations and cable systems and is a basis for pricing and selling advertising time. Exhibit 11–14 shows how WJZ, the CBS affiliate in Baltimore, promotes its dominance of the sweeps ratings in various categories.

Many advertising executives and media buyers are skeptical of the local audience estimates gathered during the sweeps periods. They argue that special programming and promotion efforts are often used by the networks and their local affiliates to bolster their ratings during the sweeps and that the numbers gathered during these periods are not indicative of audience size for the remaining weeks of the year.[43]

Much of the concern over the measurement system used by Nielsen involves the use of the paper diaries to measure viewing in local markets. The system requires households in the sample to keep a tally of what is being watched and by whom. With so many channels now available, along with the increase in viewing through DVRs and on smartphones, tablets, and computers, it has become very challenging for the Nielsen panelists to accurately record all of their television viewing in the diaries. Many homes do not return completed diaries and many of those that are returned are often not filled out. Nielsen has acknowledged the problems with its measurement system for local markets and is working to correct them.[44]

Developments in Audience Measurement For years the television and advertising industries have been calling for changes in the way TV viewing audiences are measured at both the local and national levels. They have argued that new digital technologies are leading to major changes with regard to when, where, and how people watch television. Many of those working for the television networks as well as in advertising argue that the Nielsen measurement system is being overwhelmed by the explosion in the number of TVs, delivery systems, program options, and viewing platforms available. Advertisers and media planners have argued that these developments are having a major impact on audience size and composition and on the way advertisers use and should pay for TV as an advertising medium. A major issue in television audience measurement over the past decade has been the need to move beyond **linear TV**, where the viewer has to watch a scheduled TV program at the particular time it's offered and on the particular channel it's presented on.

One of the major concerns of advertisers for years has been the need to measure ratings for television commercials, not just for programs. In 2007 Nielsen began providing **commercial ratings** data, known as "C3," which includes measures of the average viewership of the commercials both live and up to 3 days after the ads are played back on a DVR.[45] The new ratings did not track individual ads or specific time slots, but rather offered an average viewership of all the national commercial minutes in a program. Thus advertisers began paying for advertising time on network shows based not just on linear TV usage, but based on measures of how many viewers watched commercials live and on DVR-recorded playback within 3 days of the airing of the show, rather than simply on the traditional program ratings.

While Nielsen's C3 ratings were an improvement over the old measurement system, many in the television and advertising industries were still dissatisfied with them, particularly as live viewing of television programs continued to decline and time-shifted viewing through DVRs and video on demand (VOD) became more prevalent. Many television network executives began pushing for "C7" ratings that include viewership of programs and commercials as many as 7 days after live airing of a TV show, arguing that viewership of many programs continued to increase over a 7-day period.[46] By 2014 Nielsen was providing C3 as well as C7 viewership numbers; however, the industry continued to argue that better measurement was still needed to account for viewership across all platforms to determine total viewership of a program as well as viewing patterns.

In 2016 Nielsen began rolling out its Total Audience Measurement system, which is a single-sourced platform that accounts for all viewing across linear TV, DVRs, VOD, and connected TV devices including streaming video devices and game consoles, enabled smart TVs, tablets, smartphones, and personal computers.[47] The measurement system accounts for viewers overlooked by current C3 and C7 metrics and also provides more insight into viewing patterns for television shows. The system is able to determine how much time people spend with devices overall and link program viewing to those specific devices. For example, in tests of its measurement system, Nielsen broke viewership of a television show into the six categories shown in Figure 11–4. As can be seen in this chart, 45 percent of viewers watched the show during its live airing while an additional 32 percent watched the show by playing it back on a DVR within 7 days after it aired. The remaining 23 percent of viewership came from people watching it digitally by streaming it on a PC or mobile device, watching it on VOD within 35 days, watching it on a DVR between 8 and 35 days, or watching it on a connected TV device. Nielsen is also developing a new metric called Total Use of Television (TUT), which adds connected TV usage to linear viewing to provide a complete view of TV usage.[48]

FIGURE 11-4

Viewership Categories for
Television Programs

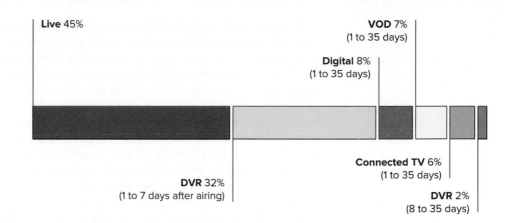

Live 45%

VOD 7%
(1 to 35 days)

Digital 8%
(1 to 35 days)

Connected TV 6%
(1 to 35 days)

DVR 32%
(1 to 7 days after airing)

DVR 2%
(8 to 35 days)

As part of its new Total Audience Measurement system, Nielsen increased the sample size of its national TV panel to 40,000 households, which represent a total of 100,000 viewers and include more than 100,000 TV sets and more than 50,000 connected devices.[49] While advertisers view Nielsen's new system as a significant improvement, there is still concern over how viewing audiences are measured. Expanded use of the people meter is seen as an improvement over the use of paper diaries, but critics note that these devices still require cooperation on an ongoing basis from people in the metered homes. Panelists in the Nielsen households, including children, must enter a preassigned number on the remote-control device every time they start or stop watching. Media researchers argue that children in particular often forget and adults tire of the task over the two years they are in the Nielsen sample. There has been a call for the use of more passive measurement systems that require less involvement by people in the metered homes and can produce more accurate measures of the program-viewing as well as commercial-viewing audiences.[50]

Nielsen is continually working to address the ongoing challenges of audience measurement, particularly as people watch TV shows on a variety of devices. In 2019, the company launched an enhanced cross-platform system that provides measurement of viewers watching programs on television, smartphones, tablets, or computers, as well as viewing across any combination of these platforms.[51] Nielsen's Total Ad Ratings report now includes measurement of mobile audiences as well as over-the-top audiences that watch television using a streaming device such as Roku, Google Chromecast, or Amazon Fire Stick. Nielsen also measures away-from-home viewing audiences, including places like health clubs, hotel rooms, bars, and transit locations. Nielsen provides these measurements for 44 DMAs to give local advertisers more insight into incremental viewing audiences in their markets. Nielsen also measures YouTube TV viewership as part of its national Digital TV ratings, as well as at the DMA level through its local TV audience measurement.[52]

Despite all of the changes Nielsen has made, the measurement company continues to come under attack, as was noted in Chapter 10. In 2021 the Media Rating Council, an industry organization that maintains research standards for the media industry, noted a consistent pattern of underreporting of viewing in Nielsen's February 2021 report. The MRC audit found that total usage of television that month for people between 18 and 49, which is the audience of most importance to advertisers, may have been underestimated by 2 to 6 percent. The problem resulted from a decision by Nielsen to stop sending field agents to homes in the Nielsen panel during the coronavirus pandemic. There was also concern that Nielsen's sample started to include homes whose residents may have moved elsewhere in the country during the pandemic, leaving the company tabulating results from homes where no TV watching was taking place.[53] Nielsen also came under criticism when it informed television networks and media buyers that it had been undercounting out-of-home viewers in its national ratings for more than a year from September 2020 to December 2021. The miscounting of viewers is a major concern to the television networks as even a 1 percent undercounting could represent millions of dollars of lost revenue.

Nielsen is also facing challenges as cord cutting continues and the traditional broadcast and cable networks lose viewers to streaming services. While Nielsen's ratings now include the measurement of over-the-top and mobile viewing audiences, some of the television networks are considering alternative methods and data providers to measure streaming audiences such as data from ad-server companies that insert the ads and subscriber data owned by streaming device companies such as Roku, Amazon, and Apple. Nielsen has acknowledged that its measurement system has problems and is taking steps to address them. The company is developing a new streamlined system to measure viewership of traditional TV and streaming that will be completed by 2024.[54] As part of this system, Nielsen has begun using its new Portable People Meter (PPM) wearable devices for its panelists along with a companion app that will help improve compliance and engagement. The new wearable PPM will serve as the foundation for Nielsen ONE, a cross-media solution that will deliver a single, unduplicated metric for total media consumption across TV, digital, and audio devices.[55] Despite the concerns with Nielsen, the company is deeply entrenched in the media ecosystem and it is unlikely that viable alternatives to its audience measurement system will emerge soon.

RADIO

Television has often been referred to as the ideal advertising medium, and to many people it personifies the glamour and excitement of the industry. Radio, on the other hand, is often viewed as old-school and is not the first medium that comes to mind when developing a media strategy. Dominated by network programming and national advertisers before the growth of TV, radio has evolved into a primarily local advertising medium. Network advertising generally accounts for less than 5 percent of radio's revenue. However, radio boasts the broadest mass reach among all media while simultaneously affording advertisers narrow targeting capabilities through numerous formats and networks. Radio has also become a medium characterized by highly specialized programming appealing to very narrow segments of the population.

The importance of radio to advertisers is best demonstrated by the numbers, as it is a pervasive medium. There are more than 11,300 commercial radio stations in the United States, including 4,700 AM and 6,600 FM stations. There are over 576 million radios in use, which is an average of 5.6 per household. Radio reaches 88 percent of all Americans over the age of 12 each week and has grown into a ubiquitous background to many activities, among them reading, driving, running, working, and socializing. The average American listens to radio for over 2 hours every weekday and 3 hours every weekend. Commercial radio dominates the time spent listening to some form of news or entertainment in a car, as nearly two-thirds of in-car listening time is on AM/FM radio. People are spending more time listening to the radio on computers and/or mobile devices; the online radio audience has doubled in the past 6 years and now exceeds more than 103 million monthly listeners. In 2021, 91 percent of Americans between the ages of 12 and 24, and 74 percent from the ages of 25 to 54, reported listening to radio online, with smartphones becoming the device of choice for doing so. Online listening to radio is expected to continue to grow, and this audience complements rather than substitutes for broadcast radio.[56] The pervasiveness of this medium has not gone unnoticed by advertisers; radio has continued to hold its own in attracting advertising revenue in a highly competitive media environment, spending on radio advertising declined significantly during the pandemic. Spending on radio declined 23 percent in 2020 from pre-COVID-19 levels, following pullbacks by advertisers in the auto, retail, travel, and entertainment industries, all of which were heavily impacted by the pandemic. However, in 2021 radio advertising rebounded to $13.7 billion and was expected to reach $15.8 billion in 2022.

Radio plays an integral role in the lifestyle of consumers and has the power to reach and influence their purchase behavior. It has survived and flourished as an advertising medium because it has a number of advantages that make it an effective way for marketers

EXHIBIT 11–15

The Radio Advertising Bureau promotes the value of radio to advertisers.

Radio Advertising Bureau

to communicate with consumers. The radio industry promotes these advantages to advertisers to encourage use of the medium. Exhibit 11–15 shows how the Radio Advertising Bureau promotes the broad reach of radio, which is America's No. 1 reach medium. The RAB also promotes the upscale audience that can be reached through radio.

Advantages of Radio

Radio has many advantages over other media, including cost and efficiency, receptivity, selectivity, flexibility, mental imagery, and integrated marketing opportunities.

Cost and Efficiency One of the main strengths of radio as an advertising medium is its low cost. Radio commercials are very inexpensive to produce. They require only a script of the commercial to be read by the radio announcer or a copy of a prerecorded message that can be broadcast by the station. The cost for radio time is also low. A minute on network radio may cost only $5,000, which translates into a cost per thousand of only $3 to $4. Local advertising on radio is lower on a cost-per-thousand basis, compared to local TV advertising. However, the CPM rate can vary greatly across different stations, markets, and listening audiences. For example, an average daytime CPM rate will be higher, particularly for stations reaching adults 18 to 49. CPM rates will be lower for programming with an audience over 50, as well as for evening and overnight radio programs. The low relative costs of radio make it one of the most efficient of all advertising media, and the low absolute cost means the budget needed for an effective radio campaign is often lower than that for other media.

The low cost of radio means advertisers can build more reach and frequency into their media schedule within a certain budget. They can use different stations to broaden the reach of their messages and multiple spots to ensure adequate frequency. Advertisers can use radio as a fast and relatively inexpensive way to get their names known. Radio commercials can be produced more quickly than TV spots, and the companies can run them more often. Many national advertisers also recognize the cost-efficiency of radio and use it as part of their media strategy.

Receptivity Radio often provides advertisers with a very receptive environment for their advertising messages. The Radio Advertising Bureau has conducted studies in conjunction with several research firms that show that consumers perceive radio advertising to be more personally relevant to them than ads on television or the Internet.[57] The studies have found that radio listeners have a unique relationship with radio as a medium because they often are more emotionally connected to the radio stations to which they listen. This emotional connection can make consumers more receptive to radio ads when the message is designed and placed properly. Figure 11–5 shows the main reasons consumers gave for listening to radio in a recent study that surveyed over 41,000 listeners of 220 radio stations in North America.[58] The survey found that while the primary reason cited was "easy to listen to in my car," many of the reasons for listening to radio are emotion-based as well as informational. Research has also shown that consumers perceive radio advertising as being more personally relevant to them. This may be due to the nature of radio ads usually being targeted to the demographic and psychographic characteristics of the listeners of particular stations, as discussed next.

Selectivity Another major advantage of radio is the high degree of audience selectivity available through the various program formats and geographic coverage of the numerous stations. Radio lets companies focus their advertising on specialized audiences such as certain demographic and lifestyle groups. Most areas have radio stations with formats such as adult contemporary, easy listening, classical music,

RADIO'S EQUATION
EASE + MUSIC + INFO + EMOTION

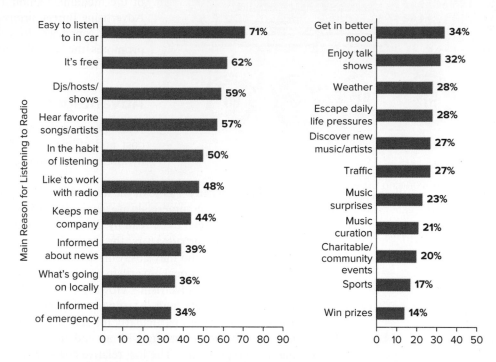

country, news/talk shows, jazz, and all news, to name a few. Figure 11–6 shows the percentage of the radio listening audience captured by radio formats for various age groups. As can be seen in these numbers, the Rock, CHR/Top 40, Rhythmic, and Alternative formats get a high percentage of their listeners from the 18–24 and 24–34 age groups, while News/Talk and Adult Standards formats get most of their listeners from adults over age 45. Elusive consumers like teenagers, college students, and working adults can be reached more easily through radio than through most other media.

Radio can reach consumers other media can't. Light television viewers spend considerably more time with radio than with TV and are generally an upscale market in terms of income and education level. Light readers of magazines and newspapers also spend more time listening to radio. Radio has become a popular way to reach specific non-English-speaking ethnic markets. Los Angeles, New York City, Dallas, and Miami have several radio stations that broadcast in Spanish and reach these areas' large Hispanic markets. As mass marketing gives way to market segmentation and regional marketing, radio will continue to grow in importance.

Flexibility   Radio is probably the most flexible of all the advertising media because it has a very short closing period, which means advertisers can change their message almost up to the time it goes on the air. Radio commercials can usually be produced and scheduled on very short notice. Radio advertisers can easily adjust their messages to local market conditions and marketing situations.

Mental Imagery   A potential advantage of radio that is often overlooked is that it encourages listeners to use their imagination when processing a commercial message. While the creative options of radio are limited, many advertisers take advantage of the absence of a visual element to let consumers create their own picture of what is happening in a radio message.

Radio may also reinforce television messages through a technique called **image transfer**, where the images of a TV commercial are implanted into a radio spot.[59] First the marketer establishes the video image of a TV commercial. Then it uses a similar, or even the same, audio portion (spoken words and/or jingle) as the basis for the radio

FIGURE 11-6 Radio Listening by Format and Age Groups

Format	Percentage of Age Groups					
	P 18–24	P 25–34	P 35–44	P 45–54	P 55–64	P 65+
AAA (Subset of Alternative)	6.0%	14.5%	17%	19.9%	24.2%	18.4%
Adult Contemporary	10.7	18.2	20	20.7	17	13.4
Adult Hits	8.2	15.4	19.9	27.4	18.6	10.6
Adult Standards	1.4	3.0	3.6	13.6	20.8	57.7
All News	2.1	5.6	11	16.9	24.9	39.5
All Sports	4.3	12.3	19.3	19	22.4	22.7
All Talk	1.6	5.2	10	16.3	24.5	42.3
Alternative	10.5	23.8	21.9	18.9	15.9	9.1
CHR/Top 40	19.2	27.6	23.3	15.9	8.8	5.3
Classic Hits	7.1	10.5	14	24.1	24.4	19.8
Classic Rock	6.8	12.3	13.8	26.1	28.9	12.1
Classical	3.3	7.1	11.2	10.7	19.1	49.0
Country	9.5	19.3	16.53	17.9	19	17.8
Ethnic	5.8	17.0	15.7	18.75	20.4	22.4
Gospel	5.5	11.4	12.7	22.2	20.1	28.0
Hispanic (All Genres)	11.7	24.0	23.5	17.6	12.2	11.0
Hot AC (Subset of Adult Contemporary)	13.3	20.9	23	19.2	13.7	9.9
Jazz	4.0	7.6	10.7	14.1	21.4	42.1
Mexican/Tejano/Ranchera (subset of Hispanic)	12.0	26.7	24.4	17.2	11.6	8.1
News/Talk	2.2	8.3	11.3	15.7	22.8	39.7
Oldies	7.7	7.9	8.7	18.1	21	36.6
Public/Non-Commercial	4.0	12.8	16	16.5	20.2	30.4
Religion/Christian	7.1	16.0	16.9	18.8	22.2	19.0
Rhythmic	22.5	28.7	23.1	14.5	7.6	3.6
Rock	8.0	22.5	21.5	24.9	16.1	7.2
Soft AC/Lite Rock	7.7	12.8	17	19.1	18.5	25.0
Spanish AC (subset of Hispanic)	9.5	28.9	22.8	21	10.66	7.2
Tropical (subset of Hispanic)	8.5	19.4	28.7	22.3	11.8	9.4
Urban	15.0	23.4	20.5	17.9	14.2	9.1
Urban AC (Subset of Urban)	8.3	14.7	17.5	24.1	22.5	12.9
Urban Contemporary (Subset of Urban)	18.7	28.3	23.2	16.2	8.8	4.9
Variety/Other	7.2	15.8	15.4	17.3	18.5	25.7

Source: MRI Simmons 2021 Fall Doublebase.

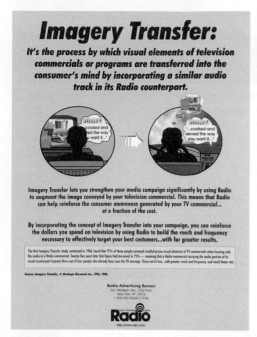

Imagery Transfer:

It's the process by which visual elements of television commercials or programs are transferred into the consumer's mind by incorporating a similar audio track in its Radio counterpart.

Imagery Transfer lets you strengthen your media campaign significantly by using Radio to augment the image conveyed by your television commercial. This means that Radio can help reinforce the consumer awareness generated by your TV commercial... at a fraction of the cost.

By incorporating the concept of Imagery Transfer into your campaign, you can reinforce the dollars you spend on television by using Radio to build the reach and frequency necessary to effectively target your best customers...with far greater results.

The first Imagery Transfer study, conducted in 1968, found that 72% of those people surveyed recalled prime visual elements of TV commercials when hearing only the audio in a Radio commercial. Twenty-five years later that figure had increased to 75% — meaning that a Radio commercial carrying the audio portion of its visual counterpart impacts three out of four people who already have seen the TV message. Three out of four...with greater reach and frequency and much lower cost.

Source: Imagery Transfer, © Strategic Research Inc, 1990, 1996.

Radio Advertising Bureau
261 Madison Ave., 23rd Floor
New York, NY 10016
1-800-252-RADIO (7234)

Radio
http://www.rab.com

EXHIBIT 11–16

The Radio Advertising Bureau promotes the concept of imagery transfer.

Radio Advertising Bureau

EXHIBIT 11–17

Radio stations are often involved in local community events.

Radio Advertising Bureau

LOCAL MATTERS
CONNECTION TO LISTENERS

* Local content and promotions that strengthen local community connections
* Audience engagement with sites that offer local music talent and playlist interactivity between listeners and station
* Community events driven by stations prove local radio's connection

counterpart. The idea is that when consumers hear the radio message, they will make the connection to the TV commercial, reinforcing its video images. Image transfer offers advertisers a way to make radio and TV ads work together synergistically. This promotional piece put out by the Radio Advertising Bureau shows how the image transfer process works (Exhibit 11–16).

Integrated Marketing Opportunities Radio provides marketers with a variety of integrated marketing opportunities. It can be used in combination with other media, including television, magazines, newspapers, the Internet, and social media, to provide advertisers with synergistic effects in generating awareness and communicating their message. The radio industry has sponsored research studies to determine how radio works in combination with other media. These studies have shown that the synergistic use of radio, television, newspapers, and the Internet has a positive impact on various measures such as brand awareness, brand consideration, emotional connections, purchase intentions, and website visitation.[60] Marketers can also use radio in conjunction with digital and social media applications such as Facebook and Twitter to allow listeners to publish audio content as well as receive song and station updates. Radio station websites as well as their Facebook, Instagram, and Twitter pages can be used to create listener databases and engage them by offering promotions and deals.

Radio can also be used in conjunction with a variety of other IMC tools such as sales promotion, event marketing, and cause-related marketing. Radio stations are an integral part of many communities, and the deejays and program hosts are often popular and influential figures. Advertisers often use radio stations and personalities to enhance their involvement with local markets and to gain influence with local retailers. Radio also works very effectively in conjunction with place-based/point-of-purchase promotions. Retailers often use on-site radio broadcasts combined with special sales or promotions to attract consumers to their stores and get them to make purchases. Live radio broadcasts are also used in conjunction with event marketing. Marketers often sponsor live broadcast promotions at beaches, sporting events, and festivals, setting up product booths for sampling and giveaways. Exhibit 11–17 shows how the Radio Advertising Bureau promotes the value of radio by showing how it can be used to strengthen local community connections.

Limitations of Radio

Several factors limit the effectiveness of radio as an advertising medium, among them creative limitations, fragmentation, difficult buying procedures, limited research data, limited listener attention, competition from digital media, and clutter. The media planner must consider them in determining the role the medium will play in the advertising program.

Creative Limitations A major drawback of radio as an advertising medium is the absence of a visual image. The radio advertiser cannot show the product, demonstrate it, or use any type of visual appeal or information. A radio commercial is, like a TV ad, a short-lived and fleeting message that is externally paced and does not allow the receiver to control the rate at which it is processed. Because of these creative limitations many companies tend to ignore radio, and agencies often assign junior people to the development of radio commercials.

EXHIBIT 11-18

HD radios in automobiles can display visual advertising messages that can improve awareness and brand recall.

Westwood One, LLC.

The creative possibilities of radio in terms of visual images are improving for commercials people hear when driving. The dashboard displays that come in new vehicles today are loaded with technology that includes navigation systems, maintenance and safety messages, and high-definition (HD) radio receivers that make it possible to pair radio commercials with visual images. More than half of the new vehicles come with HD radio receivers, and about 25 percent of the cars, trucks, and SUVs currently on the road have HD technology. HD radios provide station names, artist and song title information, and visual images of the artist or album. Of particular importance to marketers airing radio ads is the opportunity to provide visuals and messaging for consumers on the display screen by using HD radio image integration software (Exhibit 11-18). The ability to combine audio with visual imagery allows advertisers to make a deeper connection with consumers and may revolutionize the use of radio advertising targeted to consumers when driving. Studies have shown that the pairing of a radio commercial with a visual image increases brand awareness and recall, as well as intentions to visit a retail store.[61]

Fragmentation   Another problem with radio is the high level of audience fragmentation due to the large number of stations. The percentage of the market tuned to any particular station is usually very small. The top-rated radio station in many major metropolitan areas with a number of AM and FM stations may attract less than 10 percent of the total listening audience. Advertisers that want a broad reach in their radio advertising media schedule have to buy time on a number of stations to cover even a local market.

Difficult Buying Procedures   It should be readily apparent how difficult the media planning and purchasing process can become for the advertiser that wants to use radio on a nationwide spot basis. Acquiring information and evaluating and contracting for time with even a fraction of the 11,300 commercial stations that operate across the country can be very difficult and time-consuming. This problem has diminished somewhat in recent years as the number of radio networks and of syndicated programs offering a package of several hundred stations increases.

Limited Research Data   Audience research data on radio are often limited, particularly compared with TV, magazines, or newspapers. Most radio stations are small operations and lack the revenue to support detailed studies of their audiences. And most users of radio are local companies that cannot support research on radio listenership in their markets. Thus, media planners do not have as much audience information available to guide them in their purchase of radio time as they do with other media.

Limited Listener Attention   Another problem that plagues radio is that it is difficult to retain listener attention to commercials. Radio programming, particularly music, is often the background to some other activity and may not receive the listeners' full attention. Thus they may miss all or some of the commercials. One environment where radio has a more captive audience is in cars. But getting listeners to pay attention to commercials can still be difficult. Most people preprogram their car radio and change stations during commercial breaks. A study by Avery Abernethy found large differences between exposure to radio programs versus advertising for listeners in cars. They were exposed to only half of the advertising broadcast and changed stations frequently to avoid commercials.[62] Another factor that is detracting from radio listening in automotive vehicles is the high penetration of smartphones. Studies have found that commuters surveyed who own mobile phones reported listening to less radio than they previously did.[63] Many consumers spend time on their phones while driving and also can listen to music stored on their phones or through streaming services.

Competition from Digital Media   Radio is also facing threats from several digital-based technologies that are impacting the listening audience for commercial radio. A major source of competition for conventional broadcast radio is the growth of satellite radio, which bounces signals off satellites stationed over the East and West Coasts and back down to receivers that encode the signals digitally. The major satellite radio company, SiriusXM, was formed by the merger of the major two satellite radio companies (Sirius and XM Radio) in 2008 and now has nearly 30 million subscribers.[64] The primary market for satellite radio is vehicle owners who choose it as an option when purchasing a new car, or they purchase a receiver and pay a monthly subscription fee of around $13 for the digital quality radio service that includes 140+ channels of music, news, talk, sports, and children's programming. However, SiriusXM also targets other markets for its service, including homes, businesses, Internet/mobile devices, portable radios, boats, and planes.

The music stations on SiriusXM are commercial free, while talk channels have approximately 6 minutes of commercials every hour. Programming on SiriusXM features big-name entertainers and personalities such as shock jock Howard Stern, skateboarder Tony Hawk, Jenny McCarthy, Dr. Laura, and other personalities. The satellite network has also spent large amounts of money to acquire the broadcast rights for professional and college sports as well as NASCAR. SiriusXM has also been adding more locally tailored programming such as traffic and weather reports, which make them more competitive against terrestrial stations in local markets.

In addition to satellite, terrestrial radio is also being impacted by the popularity of music services that are streamed over the Internet, such as Pandora, Spotify, and Apple Music. However, the Radio Advertising Bureau has done studies that show that over 80 percent of drivers cite AM/FM radio as their primary in-car entertainment device (Exhibit 11–19). Digital and Social Media Perspective 11–1 discusses the growing popularity of podcasts, which are becoming a competitor for radio.

EXHIBIT 11–19

Radio is the most popular in-car entertainment device.

Radio Advertising Bureau

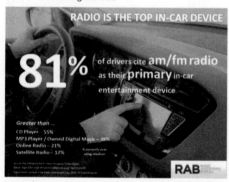

Clutter   Clutter is just as much a problem with radio as with other advertising media. Most radio stations carry an average of 10 minutes of commercials every hour. During the popular morning and evening rush hours, the amount of commercial time may exceed 12 minutes. Also contributing to the clutter problem is the practice of some stations offering "commercial-free" blocks of music to attract listeners. This practice results in more commercials being aired in a short time period and may also result in listeners switching to another station rather than listening through a long block of ads. Advertisers must create commercials that break through the clutter or use heavy repetition to make sure their messages reach consumers. In a study of radio listeners conducted by Edison Research, perceptions of increased ad clutter were cited by participants as a reason for spending less time listening to radio.[65]

Digital and Social Media Perspective 11–1 >>>

Podcasts Are Becoming Popular among Listeners and Advertisers

It was a century ago, in 1922, that America's airwaves changed forever when New York radio station WEAS broadcast the first radio commercial for the Hawthorne Court Apartments in the suburb of Jackson Heights. Eight years later the first radio was installed in an automobile, and while many drivers embraced the idea of having music and news in their cars, others were up in arms over the dangers they presented. It took several decades for radios to become standard equipment in cars, but once they did drivers loved being able to listen to music, news, or the broadcast of a sporting event whether driving across town or going on a long-distance trek. And advertisers loved it even more as they could deliver radio commercials to drivers and their passengers who were a captive audience, particularly during the morning and evening drive times when they often sat in traffic.

The availability of radios in vehicles helped make radio a major advertising medium, and it has remained so for the past 100 years despite competition from other media, as well as other forms of audio entertainment from devices such as cassette and CD players, satellite radio, iPods, smartphones, and streaming music services. However, radio is now facing yet another form of competition from the podcasting industry, which has exploded over the past decade. A podcast is a collection or series of digital audio files that are made available for downloading or listening via the Internet to a computer or mobile device. Each individual audio recording is known as a podcast episode and is typically hosted by an individual who shares a story, news, information, or entertainment. Podcasts began in 2004 when an MTV video jockey coded the iPodder program that let a user download Internet radio broadcasts to an Apple iPod. This is where the term and meaning podcast was born, taking its name from a blend of iPod and broadcasts.

Christian Horz/Shutterstock

The number of podcasts available to listeners has increased tremendously in the past few years. There were more than 2 million active podcasts available in 2022 (versus a quarter of that 3 years earlier), and there were over 48 million episodes. As with other forms of useful media and entertainment, marketers have recognized that podcasts are a very good medium for delivering an advertising message to promote their products, services, or businesses. Podcast advertising involves inserting an advertising message into the podcast content, either by having the host read a scripted message or using a pre-recorded message. As with other forms of digital advertising, podcast ads can appear at different times or positions. Pre-roll ads are inserted into the beginning of the podcast, usually before or after the introduction and typically are between 15 and 30 seconds. Mid-roll ads take place in the middle of a podcast episode, are often the longest, running between 30 and 90 seconds, and are also the least likely to be skipped since they fall directly in the middle of the content. Post-roll ads are played at the end of an episode, usually right before or after the closing lines of the podcast when the host thanks listeners and recaps the episode.

Podcast advertising is one of the fastest-growing channels in digital media. Revenues surpassed the $1 billion mark in 2021 for the first time. According to the IAB, podcast advertising grew 72 percent, twice as fast as the total Internet advertising market, and annual revenue is expected to reach $4 billion by 2024. The growth of podcast advertising is being fueled by a continually expanding user base that is consuming a growing library of engaging and diverse content. It is estimated that nearly 60 percent of U.S. consumers age 12 and older listen to podcasts. Podcast advertising is receiving increased ad spending by existing, as well as new, advertisers across a variety of industries.

In addition to the growth of podcast audiences, there are several more reasons for the growing popularity of podcasts among advertisers. Podcast listeners have a median age of 34, which is younger than that of broadcast radio (47) and network television (57). Moreover, the percentage of monthly podcast listeners among 12- to 34-year-olds has grown to just over 50 percent, which provides advertisers with another way to reach this coveted age group with their messages. Advertisers like podcasts as the audio content is amenable to conveying information and messages to listeners as they are generally a very captive audience. Studies by Edison Research show that podcast advertising generates four times better recall than online display advertising and is more effective in generating engagement because audiences pay such intense attention to and value the podcast content. Podcast hosts often are perceived as influencers in the sense they are making an implied endorsement of the brands being advertised, which can result in listeners taking action.

As podcasts grow in popularity, their use as an advertising medium will no doubt continue to grow as well. Large media companies are investing heavily in podcasts, as are major platform providers such as Spotify and Apple. However, as the industry grows and attracts more advertisers, there will be demand for better audience measurement and confirmation of impression delivery. The pricing structure for podcast advertising is currently using the basic cost-per-thousand (CPM) model, whereby the advertiser pays for every 1,000 plays of the episode. The typical CPM rate is around $18 for a 30-second ad and $25 for a 60-second spot. Some advertisers are using a cost-per-acquisition (CPA) model where the focus is on the number of conversions resulting from the podcast ad with the advertiser paying a predetermined fee. Podcast advertisers using the CPA model rely on promotion codes and click-throughs to URLs to measure performance.

Podcasting is becoming a big business and is yet another way for many marketers, including major advertisers such as Procter & Gamble, Amazon, Disney, and General Motors, to reach consumers with their ads. This advertising revenue is very important to the podcast creators, as for many of them it is turning a hobby into a lucrative profession. However, as is the case with other media, there is concern that clutter can become a problem if too many ads are inserted into podcasts. Listeners may fast-forward through them or decide not to listen to them at all. Hopefully, advertising won't kill the goose that has the potential to lay the golden egg when it comes to podcasts.

Sources: Ariel Shapiro, "Podcasting Will Be a $4 Billion Industry by 2024," *The Verge*, May 10, 2022, https://www.theverge.com/2022/5/10/23065056/podcasting-industry-iab-report-audacy-earnings-patreon-pulitzer; "U.S. Podcast Advertising Revenue Study," *Interactive Advertising Bureau*, https://www.iab.com/wp-content/uploads/2022/05/IAB-FY-2021-Podcast-Ad-Revenue-and-2022-2024-Growth-Projections_FINAL.pdf; Brad Adgate, "As Podcasts Continue to Grow in Popularity, Ad Dollars Follow," *Forbes*, February 11, 2021, https://www.forbes.com/sites/bradadgate/2021/02/11/podcasting-has-become-a-big-business/?sh=3db9fe22cfb4.

The radio industry is looking for other ways to make radio advertising more valuable to marketers. In 2010 Clear Channel, which is now known as iHeartMedia, Inc., began offering advertisers a new service known as contextual radio ads that can automatically insert radio commercials immediately after specific programming or certain kinds of content, including other ads.[66] A number of companies have been using the service to better target their radio advertising messages. For example, GEICO used the service to air commercials with its "Save 15 percent on insurance" after ads for cars, motorcycles, or RVs aired.

Buying Radio Time

The purchase of radio time is similar to that of television, as advertisers can make either network, spot, or local buys. Since these options were reviewed in the section on buying TV time, they are discussed here only briefly.

Network Radio Advertising time on radio can be purchased on a network basis using one of the national networks. There are currently seven major national radio networks such as CBS Radio, Cumulus, Westwood One, and Premiere. There are also more than 100 regional radio networks across the country. Using networks minimizes the amount of negotiation and administrative work needed to get national or regional coverage, and the costs are lower than those for individual stations. However, the number of affiliated stations on the network roster and the types of audiences they reach can vary considerably, so the use of network radio reduces advertisers' flexibility in selecting stations.

An important trend in radio is the increasing number of radio networks and syndicated programs that offer advertisers a package of several hundred stations. For example, *The Herd with Colin Cowherd* is a syndicated radio and television sports talk show hosted by sports personality Colin Cowherd that airs on Fox Sports radio and is syndicated nationally (Exhibit 11–20). The show is particularly popular among the 18–49 male audience. Another popular syndicated sports talk program is the *The Jim Rome Show* that airs on CBS Sports Radio and streams to over 2 million listeners on 200 stations across North America.

Politically focused talk radio shows have become a very popular format for nationally syndicated radio shows. Among the most popular are shows with a conservative political focus such as *The Sean Hannity Show* and *The Glenn Beck Program* that air on the Premiere Networks and *The Mark Levin Show* that airs on Westwood One. Syndication reduces audience fragmentation and purchasing problems and increases radio's appeal to national advertisers.

Spot Radio National advertisers can also use spot radio to purchase airtime on individual stations in various markets. The purchase of spot radio provides greater flexibility in selecting markets, individual stations, and airtime and adjusting the message for local market conditions. Spot radio accounts for about 20 percent of radio time sold.

EXHIBIT 11–20

The Herd With Colin Cowherd is a nationally syndicated sports talk show.

Local Radio By far the heaviest users of radio are local advertisers; nearly 80 percent of radio advertising time is purchased from individual stations by local companies. Auto dealers, retailers, restaurants, and financial institutions are among the heaviest users of local radio advertising. But a number of radio advertisers are switching to local cable TV because the rates are comparable and there is the added advantage of TV's visual impact.

Time Classifications

As with television, the broadcast day for radio is divided into various time periods or dayparts, as shown in Figure 11-7. The size of the radio listening audience varies widely across the dayparts, and advertising rates

FIGURE 11–7

Dayparts for Radio

Morning drive time	6:00–10:00 A.M.
Midday	10:00 A.M.–3:00 P.M.
Afternoon/evening drive time	3:00–7:00 P.M.
Nighttime	7:00 P.M.–12:00 A.M.
Overnight	12:00–6:00 A.M.

follow accordingly. The largest radio audiences (and thus the highest rates) occur during the early morning and late afternoon drive times. Radio rates also vary according to the number-of-spots or type-of-audience plan purchased, the supply and demand of time available in the local market, and the ratings of the individual station. Rate information is available directly from the stations and is summarized in Kantar Media's SRDS's Radio Advertising Source, which provides format detail, demographics, spot radio rates, and other data for local stations as well as radio networks. Some stations issue rate cards showing their ad rates across various dayparts. However, many stations do not adhere strictly to rate cards and the rates published in SRDS. Their rates are negotiable and depend on factors such as availability, time period, and number of spots purchased.

Audience Information

One problem with radio is the lack of audience information. Because there are so many radio stations and thus many small, fragmented audiences, the stations cannot support the expense of detailed audience measurement. Also, owing to the nature of radio as incidental or background entertainment, it is difficult to develop precise measures of who listens at various time periods and for how long. The major radio ratings service is Nielsen Audio, which provides audience information for local stations and network audiences. For many years radio audience information was provided by Arbitron. However, Nielsen acquired Arbitron in 2012 and the deal was approved by the Federal Trade Commission in 2013. The acquisition of Arbitron gives Nielsen nearly total control of the television and radio measurement industry.[67]

Nielsen Audio   Nielsen Audio covers about 265 local radio markets and provides two to four ratings reports per year using both diary and electronic measurements. In most markets, Nielsen has a sample of representative listeners who maintain a diary of their radio listening for 7 days. Audience estimates for the market are based on these diary records and reported by time period and selected demographics in the *Nielsen Topline Radio Rating,* to which clients subscribe. A market needs to meet certain basic criteria for Nielsen to measure it. These include population requirements, listening levels, and commuting patterns. Once a market meets those criteria, local radio stations must support the survey area with a subscription to Nielsen's service.[68] Figure 11–8 provides a sample page from the ratings report for people in the 18–49 age target audience across the various dayparts. The three basic estimates in the radio ratings report are

- Person estimates—the estimated number of people listening.
- Rating—the percentage of listeners in the survey area population.
- Share—the percentage of the total estimated listening audience.

These three estimates are further defined by using quarter-hour and cume figures. The **average quarter-hour (AQH) figure** expresses the average number of people estimated to have listened to a station for a minimum of 5 minutes during any quarter-hour in a time period. For example, station KCBQ has an average quarter-hour listenership of 2,500 during the weekday 6 to 10 A.M. daypart. This means that any weekday, for any 15-minute period during this time period, an average of 2,500 people between

FIGURE 11–8 Partial Sample Page from Nielsen Audio Radio Ratings Report

	Target Audience, Persons 18–49							
	Monday–Friday 6–10 A.M.				Monday–Friday 10 A.M.–3 P.M.			
	AQH (00)	CUME (00)	AQH Rtg	AQH Shr	AQH (00)	CUME (00)	AQH Rtg	AQH Shr
KCBQ								
METRO	25	263	.2	.8	40	365	.3	1.3
TSA	25	263			40	365		
KCBQ-FM								
METRO	101	684	.7	3.1	117	768	.9	3.7
TSA	101	684			117	768		
KCEO								
METRO	11	110	.1	.3	8	81	.1	.3
TSA	11	110			8	81		
KFMB								
METRO	171	790	1.3	5.3	106	678	.8	3.3
TSA	171	790			106	678		

EXHIBIT 11–21

Arbitron promoted its Portable People Meter.

Arbitron

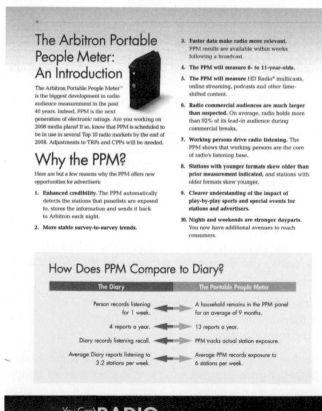

the ages of 18 and 49 are tuned to this station. This figure helps determine the audience and cost-of-a spot schedule within a particular time period.

Cume stands for "cumulative audience," the estimated total number of different people who listened to a station for at least 5 minutes in a quarter-hour period within a reported daypart. In Figure 11–8, the cumulative audience of people 18 to 49 for station KCBQ during the weekday morning daypart is 26,300. Cume estimates the reach potential of a radio station.

The **average quarter-hour rating (AQH RTG)** expresses the estimated number of listeners as a percentage of the survey area population. The **average quarter-hour share (AQH SHR)** is the percentage of the total listening audience tuned to each station. It shows the share of listeners each station captures out of the total listening audience in the survey area. The average quarter-hour rating of station KCBQ during the weekday 6 to 10 A.M. daypart is 0.2, while the average quarter-hour share is 0.8.

In 2008 Arbitron introduced the Portable People Meter (PPM), which is a wearable, pager-size device that electronically tracks what consumers listen to on the radio by detecting inaudible identification codes that are embedded in the programming. The PPM was developed in response to calls from the radio and advertising industries for Arbitron to provide more detailed measures of radio audiences.[69] Advertisers have welcomed the use of PPMs as they provide more detailed demographic information on radio listeners. Nielsen Audio now uses the PPM to measure radio audiences in the top 50 markets and is expected to continue to expand its use to other markets over the next several years.[70] Exhibit 11–21 shows an ad promoting the value of the Portable People Meter when it was developed by Arbitron.

RADAR   Another rating service now owned by Nielsen is RADAR (Radio's All Dimension Audience Research), which provides a national measurement of radio listening and audiences for network radio stations and syndicated radio shows. RADAR reports are based on a probability sample of nearly 400,000 respondents, aged 12 and older. Respondents record all radio listening for a 1-week period, including day of the week, time of day, and location. This information is merged with clearance records from the network affiliate stations to assure the accuracy of the ratings. RADAR reports are issued four times a year and include daypart averages and cumulative audience estimates for various demographic groups. Results are reported on a national basis as well as for all 210 television designated market areas (DMAs) used by Nielsen.

As with TV, media planners must use the audience measurement information to evaluate the value of various radio stations in reaching the advertiser's target audience and their relative cost. The media buyer responsible for the purchase of radio time works with information on target audience coverage, rates, time schedules, and availability to optimize the advertiser's radio media budget.

Summary

Television and radio are the most pervasive media in most consumers' daily lives and offer advertisers the opportunity to reach vast audiences. Both media are time- rather than space-oriented and organized similarly in that they use a system of affiliated stations belonging to a network, as well as individual stations, to broadcast their programs and commercial messages. Advertising on radio or TV can be done on national or regional network programs or purchased in spots from local stations.

TV has grown faster than any other advertising medium in history and has become the leading medium for national advertisers. No other medium offers its creative capabilities; the combination of sight, sound, and movement gives the advertiser a vast number of options for presenting a commercial message with high impact. Television also offers advertisers mass coverage at a low relative cost. Variations in programming and audience composition, along with the growth of cable, make it possible for TV to offer more audience selectivity to advertisers. While television is often viewed as the ultimate advertising medium, it has several limitations, including the high cost of producing and airing commercials, a lack of selectivity relative to other media, the fleeting nature of the message and shorter commercials, the problem of commercial clutter, limited viewer attention, and distrust of TV ads. The latter two problems have been compounded in recent years by the trend toward shorter commercials. Television viewing is being impacted by the Internet as more television programs are now available online, and consumers are "cord cutting" and subscribing to streaming services such as Netflix, Amazon Prime, Hulu, and Apple TV+, which they watch on smart TVs as well as on personal computers, tablets, and smartphones. Social media are also changing the way people watch television and how they interact with TV programs.

Information regarding the size and composition of national and local TV audiences is provided by the Nielsen Company.

The amount of money networks or stations can charge for commercial time on their programs is based on its audience measurement figures. This information is also important to media planners, as it is used to determine the combination of shows needed to attain specific levels of reach and frequency with the advertiser's target market.

As recording devices have proliferated and also more consumers watch television online using over-the-top streaming services, changes have occurred in the measurement of viewing audiences—such as the move to C3 and C7 ratings that include measures of viewing audiences both live and up to 3 and 7 days after a program airs live on television, and Nielsen's Total Audience Measurement system.

The role of radio as an entertainment and advertising medium changed with the growth of television. Radio has evolved into a primarily local advertising medium that offers highly specialized programming appealing to narrow segments of the market. Radio offers advertisers the opportunity to build high reach and frequency into their media schedules and to reach selective audiences at a very efficient cost. It also offers opportunities for integrated marketing programs such as place-based promotions and event sponsorships.

The major drawbacks of radio include its creative limitations owing to the absence of a visual image, the highly fragmented nature of the radio audience, difficult buying procedures, limited research data listener inattention, and clutter. Radio stations are also facing increased competition from online music services such as Pandora, Spotify, and Apple Music as well as podcasts.

As with TV, the rate structure for radio advertising time varies with the size of the audience delivered. The primary sources of audience information are Nielsen Audio for local radio and its RADAR studies for network audiences.

Key Terms

zipping 371
zapping 371
television network 374
affiliates 374
up-front market 375
scatter market 375
spot advertising 376
national spot advertising 376
local advertising 376
station reps 376
syndicated programs 376
sponsorship 377
participations 378
adjacencies 378
dayparts 378

cable television 379
Multichannel Video Programming
    Distributors (MVPD) 379
superstations 381
interconnects 381
narrowcasting 381
over-the-top (OTT) 384
cord cutting 384
addressable TV advertising 385
television household 385
program rating 385
ratings point 386
households using television
    (HUT) 386
share of audience 386

total audience 386
people meter 386
designated market areas
    (DMAs) 387
Portable People Meter (PPM) 387
sweeps periods 387
linear TV 388
commercial ratings 388
image transfer 392
average quarter-hour (AQH) figure 399
cume 400
average quarter-hour rating
    (AQH RTG) 400
average quarter-hour share
    (AQH SHR) 400

Discussion Questions

1. The chapter opener discusses the rapid adoption of streaming services by television viewers. Discuss how streaming is impacting the television industry and the business models of the major broadcast and cable networks. How can the networks respond to the challenges they are facing from streaming services? (LO 11-1, 11-2, 11-3)

2. Discuss the advantages and limitations of television as an advertising medium and how these factors affect its use by major national advertisers as well as smaller local companies. (LO 11-1, 11-2)

3. Discuss the reasons behind the popularity of live sports programming on television and why the networks are willing to pay such large sums of money for the rights to televise sporting events. How can the broadcast and cable networks respond to the challenges they are facing from streaming services owned by the major tech companies for the rights to sporting events? (LO 11-1, 11-2)

4. Discuss whether the major broadcast and cable networks should consider reducing the number of commercials that air during their programs. What are the pros and cons of doing so? (LO 11-1, 11-2)

5. What are the various options available to advertisers for purchasing advertising time on television? How does the use of these options differ for national versus local advertisers? (LO 11-2)

6. Choose one of the major cable networks listed in Figure 11–3 and analyze it as an advertising medium. Discuss the audience profile for viewers of programming on this cable network and the type of advertisers that might want to reach them. You might visit the website of the cable network for information on its viewing audience. (LO 11-2)

7. What is meant by over-the-top (OTT) viewing of television? Discuss how the growth in OTT is impacting the television industry and TV advertising. (LO 11-1, 11-2)

8. Discuss the methods used by Nielsen to measure the size of the viewing audience for national as well as local TV programs. Do you think the measurement techniques used provide valid estimates of the size of national and local viewing audiences? Do you think advertisers should have to pay for viewers who watch TV shows on a time-shifted basis on their DVRs or video on demand? (LO 11-3)

9. What are the advantages and disadvantages of advertising on radio? Discuss how radio advertising can be used by national versus local advertisers. (LO 11-4)

10. Discuss reasons for the growing popularity of podcasts and their impact on radio listenership. What types of companies are likely to advertise on podcasts? (LO 11-4, 11-5)

12 Evaluation of Media: Magazines and Newspapers

David Adamson/Alamy Stock Photo

Learning Objectives

LO 12-1 | Compare magazines and newspapers in terms of their value as advertising media.

LO 12-2 | Discuss magazine circulation and readership as well as audience information and research for magazines.

LO 12-3 | Describe how advertising space is purchased for magazines.

LO 12-4 | Discuss future trends and developments for magazines and how they will influence their use as advertising media.

LO 12-5 | Describe the newspaper audience and audience information and research for newspapers.

LO 12-6 | Discuss how advertising space is purchased for newspapers and rates are determined.

LO 12-7 | Discuss future trends and developments for newspapers and how they will influence their use as advertising media.

Can Newspapers Survive in the Digital World?

The past several years have been very challenging for the newspaper industry. Total advertising spending in newspapers declined by 45 percent from $20 billion in 2015 to $11 billion in 2022. Revenue from advertising has long been the primary source of income for newspapers in the United States, but has been in a steady decline since 2005 when newspapers generated a record high of $49 billion in ad revenue. The industry reached a major turning point in 2020 when newspapers generated more revenue from circulation than from advertising. Unfortunately for newspapers, it appears that it will be extremely difficult to pull out of the downward spiral that has seen many newspapers go out of business with many more likely to follow.

The decline in advertising income for newspapers reflects the dramatic declines in readership, as ad revenue is dependent on the number of eyeballs that newspapers can deliver to advertisers, and most papers have been struggling to attract and retain readers. The estimated total U.S. daily newspaper circulation (print and digital combined) in 2022 was 24.3 million for weekday and 25.8 million for Sunday. In contrast, a decade ago weekly circulation was at 43.4 million and for Sunday papers it was 44.8 million. The rise of the Internet and social media, along with the increasing use of mobile devices, such as tablets and smartphones, to access content has had a dramatic impact on the newspaper industry. A 2022 survey of frequency of newspaper readership in the United States revealed that nearly half of consumers never use newspapers as a source of news and only 10 percent of those between the ages of 18 and 64 read a newspaper daily, while 21 percent of adults aged 65 and above (who engage with newspapers the most) reported reading a newspaper every day.

This digital disruption has impacted not only the readership of newspapers, but also their value as an advertising medium. Traditionally newspapers bundled together an array of content offered in various sections such as national, international, and local news; business; sports; entertainment; local stories, editorials, and opinions; comics; and classified advertising for automobiles, real estate, rental, employment, and other products and services. Display advertising interspersed throughout the paper along with classified ads generated more than half of the revenue used to cover the costs of printing and distributing a physical paper. However, digital technology has led to the unbundling of the content provided by newspapers with the explosion of the news and information sources available on the Internet. Moreover, aggregation sites such as Apple News, Google News, Reddit, Flipboard and others consolidate news and information from a myriad of websites that are constantly updated, which means the news delivered by newspapers is "old news" when it is delivered a day later in a print edition. There are also aggregation sites for specific topics such as sports, business, entertainment, and most other areas of interest to readers.

Newspapers have also been impacted by the growth of "pure play" websites that focus on vertical markets such as real estate and employment that have taken away most of their revenue from classified advertising. For example, employment sites such as LinkedIn, Zip Recruiter, Indeed, CareerBuilder, and many others are now used for recruiting employees; sites such as AutoTrader Cars.com are used to buy and sell cars; people looking for a home go to Zillow, Redfin, and Realtor.com. Craigslist and Facebook Marketplace have classified sections for virtually every product and service category. Newspapers have experienced a dramatic decline in their revenue from classified advertising over the past two decades from nearly $17 billion in 2003 to just over $2 billion today. Revenue from display advertising has also been declining as many local retailers as well as national advertisers have been shifting their ad spending from newspapers to an array of digital alternatives.

The newspaper industry's response to the digital disruption they have been facing for the past decade or so has been to offer digital versions of their publications and sell display and video advertising in their digital editions as well as on their websites. Digital advertising revenue for newspapers has risen from 17 percent in 2011 to over 40 percent in 2022 and is expected to surpass print revenue by 2026. However, revenue from online advertising has not been able to compensate for the decline in monies received for print advertising as online ad rates are usually much lower than those for print

continued

ads. Digital advertising revenue for U.S. newspapers was just under $4 billion in 2022, just a third more than in 2014.

Newspapers trying to attract digital display and video advertising from marketers must also compete with other online media and websites as well as social media sites such as Facebook, LinkedIn, Instagram, TikTok, and Snapchat that offer advertisers very sophisticated ad-targeting techniques. The problem has become even greater recently with the growth in programmatic media buying whereby online ads are purchased in bulk through automated software programs that seek to maximize target audience coverage with little regard for the type of medium where the ad appears.

The challenges facing newspaper publishers have forced them to undergo significant cost-cutting measures while continuing to look for new sources of revenue. Many newspapers have tried to implement digital pay plans or "paywalls" that require readers to pay for a digital subscription or lose access. These digital pay plans may allow a certain number of free articles each month; however, users must pay for full access to the newspaper, which provides newspaper publishers with an additional source of revenue. Several major newspapers such as *The New York Times*, *The Wall Street Journal*, *The Los Angeles Times*, and *The Washington Post* have been successful in implementing paywalls as well as attracting digital subscribers. However, these paywalls are often easy to get around, and readers can generally find other ways to access articles or the news and information they are looking for on their social media feeds or through search engines.

Newspapers have little choice but to continue to respond to the digital disruption they have faced over the past decade and will continue to face in the future. Nearly every newspaper is increasingly relying on digital readership and utilizing interactive elements to appeal to both readers and advertisers. They are putting more emphasis on digital subscriptions and advertising to drive their revenue models. However, many experts question whether newspapers can survive in the new digital world.

Sources: Stephen Emrich, "Did COVID-19 End Newspapers? How Publishing Companies Are Compensating for Low Print Readership," *Entrepreneur*, June 6, 2022, https://www.entrepreneur.com/business-news/did-covid-19-end-newspapers-how-publishing-companies-are/426834; Mark Stenberg, "*The Wall Street Journal* Grew Digital Subscriptions 19% to 2.9 Million," *Adweek*, February 4, 2022, https://www.adweek.com/media/the-wall-street-journal-grew-digital-subscriptions/; Michael Barthel, "State of the News Media: Newspaper Fact Sheet," Pew Research Center, June 29, 2021, https://www.pewresearch.org/journalism/fact-sheet/newspapers/.

Magazines and newspapers have been advertising media for more than two centuries; for many years, they were the only major media available to advertisers. With the growth of the broadcast media, particularly television, reading habits declined. More consumers turned to TV viewing not only as their primary source of entertainment but also for news and information. But despite the competition from the broadcast media, newspapers and magazines remained important media vehicles to both consumers and advertisers.

Thousands of magazines are published in the United States and throughout the world. They appeal to nearly every specific consumer interest and lifestyle, as well as to thousands of businesses and occupations. By becoming a highly specialized medium that reaches specific target audiences, the magazine industry grew and became very important to advertisers. Although newspapers are facing major challenges from digital media, they still play an important role as a news and advertising medium. They are particularly important as a local advertising medium for hundreds of thousands of retail businesses and are often used by large national advertisers as well.

Magazines and newspapers are an important part of our lives. For many consumers, newspapers are an important source of product information. They would not think of going shopping without checking to see who is having a sale or clipping coupons from the weekly food section or Sunday inserts. Many people read a number of different magazines each week or month to become better informed or simply entertained. Individuals employed in various occupations rely on business magazines to keep them current about trends and developments in their markets and industries as well as in business in general.

While most of us are very involved with the print media, it is important to keep in mind that few newspapers or magazines could survive without the support of advertising revenue. Consumer magazines generate an average of around 50 percent of their revenues from advertising; business publications receive nearly 70 percent. Newspapers generate just under 50 percent of their total revenue from advertising. In many cities, the number of daily newspapers has declined because they could not attract enough advertising revenue to support their operations. The print media must be able to attract large numbers of readers or a very specialized audience to be of interest to advertisers.

Both magazines and newspapers are facing significant challenges from digital media, which is impacting the number of people who read the traditional print version of each medium and is also attracting an increasingly larger amount of marketers' advertising budgets each year. Many magazines and newspapers are struggling to get consumers to pay for their online editions and continue to look for ways to monetize them. Although they can sell banners, videos, and other forms of online advertising to marketers, the ad rates they can charge on the Web cannot match those in print and generate enough revenue to make up for the losses they are incurring from the decline in the sale of print ads. Thus, in the short term magazines and newspapers have to continue to search for ways to attract and retain readers and the advertising pages and revenue that accompany them. Despite the challenges they face, magazines and newspapers are still important media vehicles for many advertisers.[1]

THE ROLE AND VALUE OF MAGAZINES AND NEWSPAPERS

The role of magazines and newspapers in the advertiser's media plan differs from that of the broadcast media because they allow the presentation of detailed information that can be processed at the reader's own pace. The print media (including digital versions) are not intrusive like radio and TV, and they generally require some effort on the part of the reader for the advertising message to have an impact. For this reason, newspapers and magazines are often referred to as *high-involvement media*.[2] Magazine readership has remained strong despite the growth of new media options; nearly 90 percent of adults 18+ read print and digital editions of magazines, including 90 percent age 18 to 35.[3]

The majority of U.S. adults read a newspaper each week across a variety of technology platforms. Major newspapers still reach a broad target audience; specialized papers reach narrower or more specialized markets. Magazines are different from newspapers because the majority of them reach a selective audience and can be valuable in reaching specific types of consumers and market segments. Magazines and newspapers are the major forms of print media (although digital editions of most publications are now available), but the two are quite different, as are the types of advertising each attracts. This chapter focuses on these two major forms of print media (including their online versions) and examines the specific advantages and limitations of each, along with factors that are important in determining their role in the media plan, as well as the overall IMC program.

MAGAZINES

Over the past several decades, magazines have grown rapidly to serve the educational, informational, and entertainment needs of a wide range of readers in both the consumer and business markets. Magazines are the most specialized of all advertising media. While some magazines—such as *People* and *Reader's Digest*—are general mass-appeal publications, most are targeted to a very specific audience. There is a magazine designed to appeal to nearly every type of consumer in terms of demographics, lifestyle, activities, interests, or fascination. Numerous magazines are targeted toward specific businesses and industries as well as toward individuals engaged in various professions (Exhibit 12-1).

EXHIBIT 12–1

Magazines can be targeted to a specific industry or profession.

(left to right): ALM Media, LLC; Coyne & Blanchard, Inc.; Dentistry Today; EnsembleIQ

The wide variety makes magazines an appealing medium to a vast number of advertisers. Although TV accounts for the largest dollar amount of advertising expenditures among national advertisers, more companies advertise in magazines than in any other medium. Users of magazine ads range from large consumer-product companies such as Procter & Gamble and Johnson & Johnson, which spend over $200 million a year on magazine advertising, to a small company advertising scuba equipment in DIVER, which is an online magazine.

Classifications of Magazines

To gain some perspective on the various types of magazines available and the advertisers that use them, consider the way magazines are generally classified. The media research company SRDS, the primary reference source on periodicals for media planners, divides magazines into three broad categories based on the audience to which they are directed: consumer (which includes farm), business, and health care publications. Each category is then further classified according to the magazine's editorial content and audience appeal.

Consumer Magazines   Consumer magazines are bought by the general public for information and/or entertainment. The SRDS Consumer Media Advertising Source provides comprehensive planning data on U.S. print magazines and websites that reach consumer audiences. SRDS divides 2,800 domestic consumer magazines into 80 classifications, among them news, men's, sports, lifestyle, fitness, travel, and women's. Another way of classifying consumer magazines is by distribution: They can be sold through subscription or circulation, store distribution, or both. For example, whereas magazines such as *Time*, *People*, and *Sports Illustrated* are sold both through subscription and in stores, magazines such as *Woman's World* are sold primarily through stores. Magazines can also be classified by frequency; weekly, monthly, and bimonthly are the most common.

Consumer magazines represent the major portion of the magazine industry, accounting for nearly two-thirds of all advertising dollars spent in magazines. Consumer magazines are best suited to marketers interested in reaching general consumers of products and services as well as to companies trying to reach a specific target market. The most frequently advertised categories in consumer magazines are toiletries and cosmetics; drugs and remedies; food and food products; apparel and accessories; retail; and automotive.[4] Marketers of tobacco products spend most of their media budget in magazines, since they are prohibited from advertising in the broadcast media.

EXHIBIT 12–2

Ski magazine is an excellent medium for reaching skiers.

Outside Interactive, Inc

While large national advertisers tend to dominate consumer magazine advertising in terms of expenditures, the 2,800 consumer magazines are also important to smaller companies selling products that appeal to specialized markets. Special-interest magazines assemble consumers with similar lifestyles or interests and offer marketers an efficient way to reach these people with little wasted coverage or circulation. For example, companies marketing women's apparel, such as J.Crew, Anthropologie, H&M, and Forever 21, that target young adult females might find magazines such as *Elle*, *Allure*, *Cosmopolitan*, *Vogue*, or *Marie Claire* effective media vehicles for advertising to them.

Not only are these specialty magazines of value to firms interested in reaching a specific market segment, but their editorial content often creates a very favorable advertising environment for relevant products and services. For instance, avid skiers and snowboarders cannot wait for the first snowfall after reading the season's first issues of *Snowboarder* or *Ski* magazine and may be quite receptive to the ads they carry for skiing and snowboarding equipment and destination ski resorts. Exhibit 12–2 shows the annual gear guide issue of *Ski* magazine that provides readers with reviews of new skis, boots, and bindings.

EXHIBIT 12–3

Beef magazine provides cattle ranchers and others in the industry with market outlooks and other valuable information.

Informa Markets

Farm Publications The consumer SRDS category also consists of all the magazines directed to farmers and their families. About 300 publications are tailored to nearly every possible type of farming or agricultural interest. SRDS breaks farm publications into nine classifications, ranging from general-interest magazines aimed at all types of farmers (e.g., *Farm Journal, Successful Farming, Progressive Farmer*) to those in specialized agricultural areas such as poultry (*American Poultry Farmer*), hog farming (*National Hog Farmer*), or cattle raising (*Beef*—see Exhibit 12–3). A number of farm publications are directed at farmers in specific states or regions, such as *Nebraska Farmer*. Farm publications are not classified with business publications because historically farms were not perceived as businesses.

Business and Health Care Publications

Business publications are those magazines or trade journals published for specific businesses, industries, or occupations. SRDS breaks down nearly 4,700 print and 4,800 digital U.S. magazines and trade journals into nearly 200 market classifications. There are also approximately 2,700 publications in the health care category, of which 1,225 are digital. The major classifications include:

1. Magazines directed at specific professional groups, such as *National Law Review* for lawyers and *Architectural Forum* for architects.
2. Industrial magazines directed at businesspeople in various manufacturing and production industries—for example, *Automotive News, Chemical Week*, and *Industrial Engineer*.
3. Trade magazines targeted to wholesalers, dealers, distributors, and retailers, among them *Progressive Grocer, Drug Store News, Women's Wear Daily*, and *Restaurant Business*.
4. General business magazines aimed at executives in all areas of business, such as *Forbes, Fortune*, and *Bloomberg Businessweek*. (General business publications are also included in SRDS's consumer publications edition.)
5. Health care publications targeted to various areas including dental, medical and surgical, nursing, biotechnological sciences, hospital administration, veterinary medicine, and dentistry. Examples include *Modern Healthcare, Veterinary Practice News*, and *Dentistry Today*.

The numerous business publications reach specific types of professional people with particular interests and give them important information relevant to their industry, occupation, and/or careers. Business and health care publications are important to advertisers because they provide an efficient way of reaching the specific types of individuals who constitute their target market. Much marketing occurs at the trade and business-to-business level, where one company sells its products or services directly to another.

Advantages of Magazines

Magazines have a number of characteristics that make them attractive as an advertising medium. Strengths of magazines include their selectivity, excellent reproduction quality, creative flexibility, permanence, prestige, readers' high receptivity and involvement, and services they offer to advertisers.

Selectivity One of the main advantages of using magazines as an advertising medium is their **selectivity**, or ability to reach a specific target audience. Magazines are the most selective of all media except direct mail. Most magazines are published for

EXHIBIT 12–4

The number of new magazines launched each year continues to decline.

Magazine Consulting & Research, Inc.

special-interest groups. The thousands of magazines published in the United States reach all types of consumers and businesses and allow advertisers to target their advertising to segments of the population who buy their products. For example, *Shape* is a fitness magazine targeted toward active, professional women, *Rolling Stone* reaches those with an avid interest in music, and *Ebony* focuses on the upscale African American market. Many new magazines are introduced each year targeting new interests and trends. According to Dr. Samir Husni, who has been tracking magazine launches since 1985, the number of new magazines launched over the past several years has declined dramatically as only around 80 new titles were introduced in 2021 and 2022 versus double that number in previous years (Exhibit 12–4).[5] Publishers have also been launching special editions and *bookazines*, which contain the features of magazines such as glossy pages, photos, and easy-to-read layouts but are sold at higher price points. *U.S. News & World Report* has a number of bookazine products, including annual guidebooks based on its popular rankings such as "Best Colleges," "Best Graduate Schools," and "Best Hospitals." Many of these publications are sold at newsstands, in stores, or online. Many magazine publishers are launching bookazines and special editions to generate revenue as the number of subscribers to their publications declines. New consumer magazines are continually being introduced to meet the changing needs, interests, and passions of the public in areas such as sports/recreation, gaming, entertainment/celebrity, travel, fashion/apparel, and beauty/grooming.[6] New business publications are also frequently launched to respond to developments in business and industry.

In addition to providing selectivity based on interests, magazines can provide advertisers with high demographic and geographic selectivity. *Demographic selectivity*, or the ability to reach specific demographic groups, is available in two ways. First, as a result of editorial content, most magazines are aimed at fairly well-defined demographic segments. *Ladies' Home Journal*, *Elle*, and *Cosmopolitan* are read predominantly by women; *Esquire*, *Maxim*, *ESPN The Magazine*, and *Sports Illustrated* are read mostly by men. Older consumers can be reached through publications like *AARP The Magazine*. Celebrity-focused magazines such as *Us Weekly* and *People*, which are read primarily by women, have remained popular in recent years.

A second way magazines offer demographic selectivity is through special editions. Even magazines that appeal to broader audiences, such as *Reader's Digest*, *Time*, and *Good Housekeeping*, can provide a high degree of demographic selectivity through their special demographic editions. Some of the top consumer magazines publish different editions targeted at different demographic markets.

Geographic selectivity lets an advertiser focus ads in certain cities or regions. One way to achieve geographic selectivity is by using a magazine that is targeted toward a particular area. Magazines devoted to regional interests include *Yankee* (New England), *Southern Living* (South), *Sunset* (West), and *Texas Monthly* (guess where), among many others. One of the more successful media developments of recent years has been the growth of city magazines in most major American cities. *Los Angeles Magazine*, *Philadelphia*, and *Boston*, to name a few, provide residents of these areas with articles concerning lifestyle, events, and the like, in these cities and their surrounding metropolitan areas. City and regional magazines make it possible for advertisers to focus on specific local markets that may be of interest to them. They also have a readership profile that appeals to marketers of upscale brands: high income, college educated, loyal, and influential in their communities. Exhibit 12–5 shows a page from the media kit for *Portland* magazine that provides a reader profile which includes socioeconomic characteristics as well as their charitable behavior. Most of these publications belong to the City and Regional Magazine Association, which represents magazines in 78 different markets. An advertiser can run an ad in all of the magazines that belong to the association with one media buy.

Another way to achieve geographic selectivity in magazines is through purchasing ad space in specific geographic editions of national or regional magazines. A number of publications divide their circulation into groupings based on regions or major

Portland ≡

OVER **3 MILLION** PORTLANDERS
AND VISITORS RELY ON US TO MAKE
PLANS AND TAKE ACTION

Who is our reader?

MEDIAN AGE
39

They are well educated:

85%
GRADUATED COLLEGE

30%
HAVE A MASTERS OR DOCTORATE DEGREE

They are affluent:

$207k
AVERAGE HH INCOME

34%
NET WORTH > $1MM

They are social:

75%
HAVE A FACEBOOK ACCOUNT
(25% HAVE BROKEN UP WITH FB)

They are homeowners:

72%
OWN A HOME

They are generous:

83%
DONATE TO LOCAL OR NATIONAL CHARITIES

26%
DONATE OVER $2,500 ANNUALLY

EXHIBIT 12–5

Portland magazine promotes
the upscale socioeconomic
characteristics of its readers.

SagaCity Media

metropolitan areas and offer advertisers the option of concentrating their ads in these editions. A magazine may break the United States into geographic areas and offer regional editions for each and/or offer advertisers their choice of editions directed to specific states or metropolitan areas. Many magazines allow advertisers to combine regional or metropolitan editions to best match the geographic market of interest to them. Exhibit 12–6 shows the various regional marketing areas available to companies that advertise in *Better Homes & Gardens*. Information on the number of subscribers in each market area is important to advertisers and media planners.

SRDS lists more than 300 consumer magazines offering geographic and/ or demographic editions. Regional advertisers can purchase space in editions that reach only areas where they have distribution, yet still enjoy the prestige of advertising in a major national magazine. National advertisers can use the geographic editions to focus their advertising on areas with the greatest potential or those needing more promotional support. They can also use regional editions to test-market products or alternative promotional campaigns in various regions of the country.

Ads in regional editions can also list the names of retailers or distributors in various markets, thus encouraging greater local support from the trade. The trend toward regional marketing is increasing the importance of having regional media available to marketers. The availability of regional and demographic editions can also reduce the cost per thousand for reaching desired audiences.

Reproduction Quality   One of the most valued attributes of magazine advertising is the reproduction quality of the ads. Magazines are generally printed on high-quality paper stock and use printing processes that provide excellent reproduction in black and white or color. Since magazines are a visual medium where illustrations are often a dominant part of an ad, this is a very important property. The reproduction quality of most magazines is far superior to that offered by the other major print medium of newspapers, particularly when color is needed. The use of color has become a virtual necessity in most product categories, and more than two-thirds of all magazine ads now use color. The excellent reproduction quality of magazines provides the opportunity for innovative creative work by agencies. Many marketers are also integrating digital technology with print advertising.

Creative Flexibility   In addition to their excellent reproduction capabilities, magazines also offer advertisers a great deal of flexibility in terms of the type, size, and placement of the advertising material. Some magazines offer (often at extra charge) a variety of special options that can enhance the creative appeal of the ad and increase attention and readership. Examples include gatefolds, bleed pages, inserts, and creative space buys.

Gatefolds enable an advertiser to make a striking presentation by using a third page that folds out and gives the ad an extra-large spread. Gatefolds are often found at the inside cover of large consumer magazines or on some inside pages. Advertisers use gatefolds to make a very strong impression, especially on special occasions such as the introduction of a new product or brand. For example, automobile advertisers often use gatefolds to introduce new versions of their cars each model year. Not all magazines offer gatefolds, however, and they must be reserved well in advance and are sold at a premium.

Bleed pages are those where the advertisement extends all the way to the end of the page, with no margin of white space around the ad. Bleeds give the ad an impression of being larger and make a more dramatic impact. Many magazines charge an extra 10 percent to 20 percent for bleeds.

EXHIBIT 12–6

Better Homes & Gardens offers many regional marketing areas to advertisers.

Dotdash Meredith

Market	Value	Market	Value
Albany	28,400	Little Rock (state buy)	73,900
Atlanta	56,100	Los Angeles (includes Bakersfield)	256,600
Augusta, GA (state buy–includes Atlanta)	246,500	Louisville/Lexington (state buy)	120,400
Baltimore	41,200	Memphis	61,700
Birmingham/Montgomery (Birmingham only)	85,900	Miami	104,200
Boise (state buy)	34,900	Milwaukee/Madison/Green Bay (state buy)	141,000
Boston	103,600	Minneapolis/St.Paul (Minneapolis only)	34,800
Buffalo	34,600	Nashville	68,600
Charlotte (state buy–includes Raliegh)	279,500	New Orleans (state buy)	101,600
Chicago	138,400	New York (New York City only)	59,100
Cincinnati	67,700	Oklahoma City/Tulsa (state buy)	100,100
Cleveland	100,200	Omaha (state buy)	51,200
Columbia/Charleston, SC (state buy)	132,000	Orlando	63,400
Columbia/Springfield, MO (state buy–includes St. Louis)	121,900	Peoria (state buy–includes Chicago)	208,500
		Philadelphia	9,700
Columbus	57,500	Phoenix (includes Scottsdale)	35,400
Dallas/Ft.Worth (Dallas only)	146,800	Pittsburgh	101,100
Dayton/Toledo (state buy–includes Cincinnati, Cleveland, Columbus)	293,200	Portland, OR (state buy)	96,700
		Providence (state buy)	23,200
Denver (includes Boulder)	22,400	Raleigh	124,000
Des Moines (state buy)	71,800	Rochester/Syracuse (state buy–includes New York City, Albany, Buffalo)	265,000
Detroit	104,500		
Flint/Saginaw (state buy–includes Detroit)	239,800	Sacramento	89,800
Grand Rapids/Lansing (state buy–includes Detroit)	239,800	San Diego	68,800
Hartford/New Haven (state buy)	81,300	St. Louis	79,000
Houston	128,700	Salt Lake City	25,300
Indianapolis	13,800	San Antonio/Amarillo (San Antonio only)	99,400
Jackson, MS (state buy)	68,600	San Francisco/Oakland (includes Bay Area and Fresno)	152,896
Jacksonville/Tallahassee (state buy–includes Miami, Orlando, Tampa)	374,400	Santa Fe (state buy)	42,600
		Seattle/Tacoma/Spokane (Seattle only)	90,000
Kansas City (state buy–includes St. Louis)	121,900	Tampa	99,100
Knoxville (state buy–includes Memphis, Nashville)	226,000	Washington, D.C.	118,100
Las Vegas (state buy)	54,500	Wichita	32,500

Top markets may be purchased singularly, in combination with each other or in combination with state markets or segments of state markets.

BH&G For more information, please contact your *BH&G* Account Manager or Stephen Bohlinger, Senior Vice President/Publisher, at stephen.bohlinger@meredith.com.

In addition to gatefolds and bleed pages, creative options available through magazines include unusual page sizes and shapes. Some advertisers have grabbed readers' attention by developing three-dimensional pop-up ads that jump off the page. Various other *inserts* are used in many magazines. These include return cards, recipe booklets, coupons, records, and even product samples. Cosmetic companies use scratch-and-sniff inserts to introduce new fragrances, and some companies use them to promote deodorants, laundry detergents, or other products whose scent is important. Inserts are also used in conjunction with direct-response ads and as part of sales promotion strategies.

Scented ads, pop-ups, heavy card stock, stickers, and digital devices are among the types of inserts used by advertisers in magazines. Advertisers sometimes use special inserts to break through the clutter in magazines and to capture readers' attention. Marketers are becoming very strategic with regard to the type of inserts they are using in magazines and also continue to take advantage of technological advances in developing them. For example, the advertising agency for Audi of America developed a very creative insert that appeared in an issue of *Departures*, a magazine that focuses on travel,

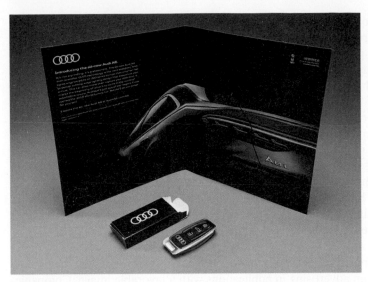

fashion arts, and culture and reaches a very upscale audience. The insert featured 49 LEDs firing in the same sequence as the lights on the Audi A8. Readers of the magazine received a faux luxury key fob with functioning lock and unlock buttons and, by clicking the key lock fob, could experience the lighting system that greets Audi A8 owners when they approach their cars (Exhibit 12–7). The insert was a unique way to capture the attention of *Departures* readers, many of whom are in the audience Audi is targeting, and to highlight the innovative and elegant lighting feature of the A8.[7]

Many magazine publishers are willing to work with advertisers who want to use creative inserts because they are eager to show that magazines can compete with new media as a way to showcase products. While the inserts pose challenges to production staff and printers, these costs along with any extra postage fees are generally passed on to the advertisers. The total cost of manufacturing inserts varies depending on the complexity, weight, assembly requirements, and other factors. Some of the very elaborate inserts can cost advertisers as much as several million dollars.[8]

Creative space buys are another option of magazines. Some magazines let advertisers purchase space units in certain combinations to increase the impact of their media budget. For example, WD-40, an all-purpose lubrication product, has used half- or quarter-page ads on consecutive pages of several magazines, mentioning a different use for the product on each page, as shown in Exhibit 12–8. This creative strategy gives the company greater impact for its media dollars and is helpful in promoting the product's variety of uses.

Permanence   Another distinctive advantage offered by magazines is their long life span. TV and radio are characterized by fleeting messages that have a very short life span; newspapers are generally discarded soon after being read. Magazines, however, are generally read over several days and are often kept for reference. They are retained in the home longer than any other medium and are generally referred to on several occasions. A study of magazine audiences found that readers spend an average of 51 minutes reading the print edition of a magazine and 48 minutes with a digital edition.[9] Studies have also found that the average magazine reader keeps 33 percent of their magazines for future reference.[10] One benefit of the longer life of magazines is that reading occurs at a less hurried pace and there is more opportunity to examine ads in considerable detail. This means ads can use longer and more detailed copy, which can be very important for high-involvement and complex products or services. The permanence of magazines also means readers can be exposed to ads on multiple occasions and can pass magazines along to other readers.

Prestige   Another positive feature of magazine advertising is the prestige the product or service may gain from advertising in publications with a favorable image. Companies whose products rely heavily on perceived quality, reputation, and/or image often buy space in prestigious publications with high-quality editorial content whose consumers have a high level of interest in the advertising pages. For example, *Esquire* and *GQ* cover men's fashions in a very favorable environment, and a clothing manufacturer may advertise its products in these magazines to enhance the prestige of its lines. *Architectural Digest* provides an impressive editorial environment that includes high-quality photography and artwork. The magazine's upscale readers are likely to have a favorable image of the publication that may transfer to the products advertised on its pages. *Good Housekeeping* has a unique consumer policy that states that if a product bearing its famous seal proves to be defective within 2 years of purchase, the magazine will replace the product or refund the purchase price. The research division of the company, now known as the Good Housekeeping Research Institute, has been evaluating products for more than a century. The seal may be used only by products whose ads have been reviewed and accepted for publication in *Good Housekeeping*. The seal can increase consumer confidence in a particular brand and reduce the amount of perceived risk associated with a purchase since it really is a money-back guarantee (Exhibit 12–9).[11]

While brands may enhance their prestige by advertising in magazines with a favorable image and high-quality editorial content, the type of ads that appear in a magazine may also influence readers' perceptions of a publication. The results of a study by Sara Rosengren and Micael Dahlén found that advertising content influences the perceptions of a magazine. Advertising for high-reputation brands or ads that were high in execution quality were beneficial to the evaluations of a magazine, while ads for brands with a poor reputation or that were low in execution quality were detrimental to the image of the publication.[12] These findings suggest that it is important for publishers to manage the advertising content of their magazines in both print and online editions. Some publishers have design guidelines stating that advertising should be treated as content and note that relevant, attractive advertising is an important part of the magazine experience as editorial content for readers.

While most media planners recognize that the environment created by a magazine is important, it can be difficult to identify it. Subjective estimates based on media planners' experience are often used to assess a magazine's prestige, as are objective measures such as reader opinion surveys.[13]

Consumer Receptivity and Engagement   With the exception of newspapers, consumers are more receptive to advertising in magazines than in any other medium. Magazines

EXHIBIT 12–9

The Good Housekeeping Seal gives consumers confidence in products advertised in the magazine. What are the benefits to including the Good Housekeeping Seal on advertisements?

Hearst Magazine Media, Inc.

are generally purchased because the information they contain interests the reader, and ads provide additional information that may be of value in making a purchase decision. Studies have shown that magazines are consumers' primary source of information for a variety of products and services, including automobiles, beauty and grooming, clothing and fashion, financial planning, and personal and business travel.[14] One of the reasons consumers are more receptive to advertising in magazines is trust. As was noted in Chapter 11, a survey by Marketing Sherpa found that print ads were the most trusted of all media, as 82 percent of respondents indicated they trust magazine and newspaper ads when making a purchase decision. Several other studies have also shown that consumers have a high level of trust in magazine ads.[15]

Media planners recognize that one of the major advantages of advertising in magazines is the ability of the medium to engage readers and hold their attention. Numerous studies have shown that consumers become involved with magazines when they read them and are also more likely to find ads acceptable, enjoyable, and even a valuable part of a publication. Intrusive media such as television, radio, and the Internet struggle with problems such as inattention and consumers trying to avoid advertising messages. And as advertisers try harder to get their commercials seen and heard in these media, the harder consumers search for ways to tune them out. However, magazine readers recognize that they control the rate and duration of their exposure to editorial content as well as advertisements and view ads as less disruptive to their media consumption experience.

Research has shown that engagement with an advertising medium is important because it is directly related to increased advertising recall and specific actions taken, such as searching for additional information about an advertiser's brand, visiting its website, saving an ad for future reference, purchasing a product or service, and recommending it to others. Exhibit 12-10 shows the various actions magazine readers take or plan as a result of exposure to specific magazine ads based on research by MRI-Simmons, which is one of the leading media and consumer research companies. This research shows that readers will take specific actions after seeing an ad regardless of its position in the publication.

Services A final advantage of magazines is the special services some publications offer advertisers. Some magazines have merchandising staffs that call on trade intermediaries like retailers to let them know a product is being advertised in their publication

EXHIBIT 12–10

Actions taken by consumers after exposure to magazine advertising.

The Association of Magazine Media

Regardless of placement within the book, **magazine readers notice ads and take action**

	noted	action taken
All ads	55%	68%
first quarter of book	57	68
second quarter of book	52	67
third quarter of book	52	68
fourth quarter of book	55	69

Note: Includes all ads, size/color and cover positions.
Source: **MRI-Simmons**, January-December 2020

Action taken includes:

• **have a more favorable opinion** about the advertiser

• **consider purchasing** the advertised product or service

• **gather more information** about the advertised product or service

• **recommend** the product or service

• **visit the advertiser's website**

• **purchase the product** or service

• **clip or save the ad**

• **visit a social media site/app**

• **watch a video** on a website, social media site, or app

and to encourage them to display or promote the item. Another service offered by magazines (usually the larger ones) is research studies that they conduct on consumers. These studies may deal with general consumer trends, changing purchase patterns, and media usage or may be relevant to a specific product or industry.

An important service offered by some magazines is **split runs**, where two or more versions of an ad are printed in alternate copies of a particular issue of a magazine. This service is used to conduct an A/B or split-run test, which allows the advertiser to determine which ad generates the most responses or inquiries, providing some evidence of their effectiveness. Technological developments have also made it possible for magazines to offer advertisers the opportunity to deliver personalized messages to tightly targeted audiences

Disadvantages of Magazines

Although the advantages offered by magazines are considerable, they have certain drawbacks too. These include the costs of advertising, their limited reach and frequency, the long lead time required in placing an ad, and the problem of clutter and heavy advertising competition.

Costs   The costs of advertising in magazines vary according to the size of the audience they reach and their selectivity. Advertising in large mass-circulation magazines like *People*, *Reader's Digest*, and *Better Homes and Gardens* can be very expensive. For example, a full-page, four-color ad in *People*'s national edition (circulation rate base of 3.4 million) cost $445,600 in 2022. Popular positions such as the back cover cost nearly $600,000. These are one-time rates and would be lower for advertisers running ads multiple times during a defined time period.

Like any medium, magazines must be considered not only from an absolute cost perspective but also in terms of relative costs. Most magazines emphasize their effectiveness in reaching specific target audiences at a low cost per thousand. Also, as discussed, an increasing number of magazines offer demographic and geographic editions, which helps lower their costs. Media planners generally focus on the relative costs of a publication in reaching their target audience. However, they may recommend a magazine with a high cost per thousand because of its ability to reach a small, specialized market segment. Of course, advertisers with limited budgets will be interested in the absolute costs of space in a magazine and the costs of producing quality ads for these publications.

Limited Reach and Frequency   Magazines are generally not as effective as other media in offering reach and frequency. While nearly 90 percent of adults in the United States read one or more consumer magazines each month, the percentage of adults reading any individual publication tends to be much smaller, so magazines have a thin penetration of households. For example, *Better Homes and Gardens* has the third-highest circulation of any magazine, at 7.6 million, but this represents only 6 percent of the 124.6 million households in the United States. The magazine does have 3.4 readers per copy, which increases its reach.

Even the most popular consumer magazines have a circulation of under 4 million, which means that they reach only about 2 to 4 percent of the households in the United States. While total readership of these magazines may be higher since there will be multiple readers of the publication, marketers seeking broad reach must run ads in a number of different magazines, which adds to the complexity of the media buying process. Marketers whose media plan calls for broad reach will often use magazines in conjunction with other media such as television as well the Internet and social media. Since most magazines are monthly or at best weekly publications, the opportunity for building frequency through the use of the same publication is limited. Using multiple ads in the same issue of a publication is an inefficient way to build frequency. Most advertisers try to achieve frequency by adding other magazines with similar audiences to the media schedule.

Long Lead Time Another drawback of magazines is the long lead time needed to place an ad in a print edition. Most major publications have a 30- to 60-day lead time, which means space must be purchased and the ad must be prepared well in advance of the actual publication date. No changes in the art or copy of the ad can be made after the closing date. This long lead time means magazine ads cannot be as timely as other media, such as radio or newspapers, in responding to current events or changing market conditions. However, as magazines face declines in ad pages and advertising revenue, many are shortening the lead times required to run ads in their publications. Advances in digital publishing and the use of computer-based production methods are also reducing the amount of lead time required to run an ad in a publication.

Clutter and Competition While the problem of advertising clutter is generally discussed in reference to the broadcast media, some magazines also have this drawback. The clutter problem for magazines is something of a paradox: The more successful a magazine becomes, the more advertising pages it attracts, and this leads to greater clutter. In fact, magazines generally gauge their success in terms of the number of advertising pages they sell.

Magazine publishers do attempt to control the clutter problem by maintaining a reasonable balance of editorial pages to advertising. For many years the number of advertising pages in consumer and business magazines was just under 50 percent, depending on the popularity of the publication. However by 2022 the ratio declined to 33 percent ad pages and 67 percent editorial and has continued to decline as marketers cut back advertising in print magazines and turn more to online versions as well as other digital media.[16] However, clutter is still a problem in some types of magazines that have remained popular among advertisers. Fashion magazines such as *Vogue*, *Elle*, *Harper's Bazaar*, and *Cosmopolitan* still have a high number of ad pages, although readers are generally receptive to the advertising in these publications. The high number of ads does make it difficult for an advertiser to gain readers' attention and draw them into the ad. Thus, many print ads use strong visual images, catchy headlines, or some of the creative techniques discussed earlier to grab the interest of magazine readers. Some advertisers create their own custom magazines to sidestep the advertising clutter problem as well as to have control over editorial content. A number of companies also publish their own magazines to build relationships with their customers. For example, Procter & Gamble began publishing *Home Made Simple* several years ago, and the custom publication branched into a television program on the OWN Network and shopper marketing programs. The online publication is now called P&G *Good Everyday*. Another company with a custom magazine is Red Bull, which publishes print and online versions of *The Red Bulletin* that focuses on the active lifestyle with stories from the worlds of sports, adventure, culture, and music that are delivered in the irreverent style that fits the brand Exhibit 12–11 shows an issue of *The Red Bulletin* that focuses on Formula 1 racing and other motorsports that are sponsored by Red Bull. A number of other companies have introduced their own magazines recently including online dating app Bumble that launched *Bumble Mag* in 2019, which offers stories and advice about dating, careers, friendship, and more to the apps of more than 50 million users. Airbnb launched *Airbnb Magazine* the same year, which is a

EXHIBIT 12–11

The Red Bulletin is an example of an in-house custom magazine with stories that fit with the active lifestyle of Red Bull drinkers.

Red Bull

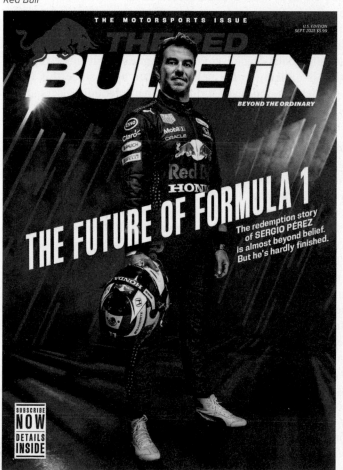

travel and lifestyle publication targeted to travelers who use the service as well as local hosts (Exhibit 12–12). However, publication of the magazine was suspended during the pandemic as travel declined.[17]

Clutter is not as serious an issue for the print media as for radio or TV, since consumers tend to be more receptive and tolerant of print advertising. They can also control their exposure to a magazine ad simply by turning the page.

Magazine Circulation and Readership

Two of the most important considerations in deciding whether to use a magazine in the advertising media plan are the size and characteristics of the audience it reaches. Media buyers evaluate magazines on the basis of their ability to deliver the advertiser's message to as many people as possible in the target audience. To do this, they must consider the circulation of the publication as well as its total readership and match these figures against the audience they are attempting to reach.

Circulation Circulation figures represent the number of individuals who receive a publication through either subscription or store purchase. The number of copies distributed to these original subscribers or purchasers is known as *primary circulation* and is the basis for the magazine's rate structure. Circulation fluctuates from issue to issue, particularly for magazines that rely heavily on retail or newsstand sales. Many publications base their rates on *guaranteed circulation* and give advertisers a rebate if the number of delivered magazines falls below the guarantee. To minimize rebating, most guaranteed circulation figures are conservative; that is, they are set safely below the average actual delivered circulation. Advertisers are not charged for any excess circulation.

Many publishers became unhappy with the guaranteed circulation concept, since it requires them to provide refunds if guarantees are not met but results in a bonus for advertisers when circulation exceeds the guarantee. Thus, many publications have gone to a circulation rate-based system. Rates are based on a set average circulation that is nearly always below the actual circulation delivered by a given issue but carries no guarantee. However, circulation is unlikely to fall below the rate base, since this would reflect negatively on the publication and make it difficult to attract advertisers at prevailing rates.

EXHIBIT 12–12

Airbnb has published its own travel and lifestyle magazine to connect with those who use its service.

Airbnb, Inc.

Circulation Verification Given that circulation figures are the basis for a magazine's advertising rates and one of the primary considerations in selecting a publication, the credibility of circulation figures is important. Most major publications are audited by one of the circulation verification services. Consumer magazines and farm publications are audited by the Alliance for Audited Media (AAM, formerly known as Audit Bureau of Circulations, or ABC), which is a membership organization consisting of North America's leading advertisers, advertising agencies, and content providers. AAM provides independently verified data and information critical to evaluating and purchasing media including consumer magazines and has also begun auditing digital replica editions of magazines that are available for tablets such as the iPad. A digital replica edition must include the print edition's full editorial content, including photography. In addition, any advertiser appearing in the print edition must have the opportunity to appear in the digital replica edition.

AAM collects and evaluates information regarding the subscriptions and sales of magazines and newspapers to verify their circulation figures. Only publications with 70 percent or more paid circulation are eligible for verification audits by AAM. In 2002 the former ABC approved new guidelines for counting magazine circulation and sales. The changes did away with the long-standing "50 percent rule," in which copies that sold for less than half the basic price of a magazine could not be counted as paid circulation. Under the new rules copies sold at any price may be counted, but the magazine must disclose sales and prices in its circulation statements.[18] More than 2,000 business publications are audited by BPA Worldwide, formerly known as Business Publications Audit (BPA) of Circulation. Many of these are published on a **controlled-circulation basis**, meaning copies are sent (usually free) to individuals the publisher believes can influence the company's purchases.

Circulation verification services provide media planners with reliable figures regarding the size and distribution of a magazine's circulation that help them evaluate its worth as a media vehicle. The AAM statement also provides other important information. It shows how a magazine is distributed by state and county size, as well as percentage of the circulation sold at less than full value and percentage arrears (how many subscriptions are being given away). Many advertisers believe that subscribers who pay for a magazine are more likely to read it than are those who get it at a discount or for free.

Media buyers are generally skeptical about publications whose circulation figures are not audited by one of the verification services, and some companies will not advertise in unaudited publications. Circulation data, along with the auditing source, are available from SRDS or from the publication itself. Exhibit 12-13 shows an example of a publisher's statement from the Alliance for Audited Media for both print and digital editions. As can be seen in this exhibit, the publisher's statement includes information

EXHIBIT 12–13

Example of an Alliance for Audited Media publisher's statement.

The Alliance for Audited Media

June 2022 - Paid, Verified, Analyzed Nonpaid with Digital

Alliance for Audited Media
TRANSACT WITH TRUST

Publisher's Statement
6 months ended June 30, 2022, Subject to Audit

Learn more about this media property at auditedmedia.com

Prototype Magazine

Annual Frequency: 10 times/year

Field Served: Consumers interested in healthy living.

Published by Magazine Inc.

EXECUTIVE SUMMARY: TOTAL AVERAGE CIRCULATION

Total Paid & Verified Subscriptions	Single Copy Sales	Total Paid & Verified Circulation	Analyzed Nonpaid Bulk	Total Circulation	Rate Base	Variance to Rate Base
760,435	48,550	808,985	1,550	810,535	802,000	8,535

TOTAL CIRCULATION BY ISSUE

	Paid Subscriptions			Verified Subscriptions				Single Copy Sales						Analyzed Nonpaid Bulk					
Issue	Print	Digital Issue	Total Paid Subscriptions	Print	Digital Issue	Total Verified Subscriptions	Total Paid & Verified Subscriptions	Print	Digital Issue	Total Single Copy Sales	Total Paid & Verified Circulation - Print	Total Paid & Verified Circulation - Digital Issue	Total Paid & Verified Circulation	Print	Digital Issue	Total Analyzed Nonpaid Bulk	Total Paid, Verified & Analyzed Nonpaid Bulk Circulation - Print	Total Paid, Verified & Analyzed Nonpaid Bulk Circulation - Digital Issue	Total Paid, Verified & Analyzed Nonpaid Bulk Circulation
Jan	632,381	70,000	702,381	61,300	1,025	62,325	764,706	49,825	2,000	51,825	743,506	73,025	816,531	1,550		1,550	745,056	73,025	818,081
Feb	631,848	70,000	701,848	58,300	1,000	59,300	761,148	44,750	2,000	46,750	734,898	73,000	807,898	1,550		1,550	736,448	73,000	809,448
Mar	629,100	70,000	699,100	58,255	1,000	59,255	758,355	46,375	2,000	48,375	733,730	73,000	806,730	1,550		1,550	735,280	73,000	808,280
Apr	626,899	70,000	696,899	59,000	1,000	60,000	756,899	46,375	2,000	48,375	732,274	73,000	805,274	1,550		1,550	733,824	73,000	806,824
May/Jun	630,818	70,000	700,818	59,250	1,000	60,250	761,068	45,425	2,000	47,425	735,493	73,000	808,493	1,550		1,550	737,043	73,000	810,043
Average	630,209	70,000	700,209	59,221	1,005	60,226	760,435	46,550	2,000	48,550	735,980	73,005	808,985	1,550		1,550	737,530	73,005	810,535

SUPPLEMENTAL ANALYSIS OF AVERAGE CIRCULATION

	Print	Digital Issue	Total	% of Circulation
Paid Subscriptions				
Individual Subscriptions	546,895	57,800	604,695	74.6
Membership	14,119		14,119	1.7
Multi-Title Digital Program		1,200	1,200	0.1
Partnership Deductible Subscriptions	48,210	1,000	49,210	6.1
Sponsored Subscriptions	20,985	10,000	30,985	3.8
Total Paid Subscriptions	630,209	70,000	700,209	86.4
Verified Subscriptions				
Public Place	50,500		50,500	6.2
Individual Use	8,721	1,005	9,726	1.2
Total Verified Subscriptions	59,221	1,005	60,226	7.4
Total Paid & Verified Subscrptions	689,430	71,005	760,435	93.8
Single Copy Sales				
Single Issue	43,420	2,000	45,420	5.6
Partnership Deductible Single Issue	1,000		1,000	0.1
Sponsored Single Issue	2,130		2,130	0.3
Total Single Copy Sales	46,550	2,000	48,550	6.0
Total Paid & Verified Circulation	735,980	73,005	808,985	99.8
Analyzed Nonpaid Bulk				
Nonpaid Bulk	1,550		1,550	0.2
Total Circulation	737,530	73,005	810,535	100.0

VARIANCE OF LAST THREE RELEASED AUDIT REPORTS

Audit Period Ended	Rate Base	Audit Report	Publisher's Statements	Difference	Percentage of Difference
12/31/2021	800,000	802,392	802,392		
12/31/2020	775,000	775,647	774,623	1,024	0.1
12/31/2019	700,000	705,825	706,250	-425	-0.0

Visit auditedmedia.com Media Intelligence Center for audit reports

PRICES

	Suggested Retail Prices	Average Price (1)
Single Copy	$3.95	
Subscription	$24.95	
Average Subscription Price Annualized (2)		$15.80
Average Subscription Price per Copy		$1.58

(1) Represents subscriptions sold for the 6 month period ended June 30, 2022
(2) Based on the following issues per year frequency: 10

on total circulation by issue including the number of print and digital subscriptions as well as single-copy sales. Publisher's statements also include circulation by issues, regions, and demographic editions; a trend analysis; and subscriptions and sales by state and county size.

Readership and Total Audience

Advertisers are often interested in the number of people a publication reaches as a result of secondary, or pass-along, readership. **Pass-along readership** can occur when the primary subscriber or purchaser gives a magazine to another person or when the publication is read in doctors' waiting rooms or beauty salons, on airplanes, and so forth.

Advertisers generally attach greater value to the primary in-home reader than to the pass-along reader or out-of-home reader, as the former generally spends more time with the publication, picks it up more often, and receives greater satisfaction from it. Thus, this reader is more likely to be attentive and responsive to ads. However, the value of pass-along readers should not be discounted. They can greatly expand a magazine's readership. *People* magazine commissioned a media research study to determine that its out-of-home audience spends as much time reading the publication as do its primary in-home readers.

You can calculate the **total audience/readership** of a magazine by multiplying the readers per copy (the total number of primary and pass-along readers) by the circulation of an average issue. For example, a magazine such as *People* may have a circulation base of 3.4 million but an audience of over 34 million readers since it has a high pass-along rate that yields nearly 10 readers per copy. However, rate structures are generally based on the more verifiable primary circulation figures, and many media planners devalue pass-along readers by as much as 50 percent. Total readership estimates are reported by major syndicated magazine research services (discussed next), but media buyers view these numbers with suspicion.

Audience Information and Research for Magazines

A very valuable source for information on magazines is SRDS, whose print and online service provides complete planning information on domestic and international consumer magazines as well as business and health care trade publications. The SRDS Consumer Media Advertising Source provides comprehensive planning data on U.S. print magazines and websites that reach consumer audiences, including standardized ad rates, circulation figures, dates, general requirements, contact information, and links to online media kits, websites, and audit statements that provide additional information on readership and positioning. The SRDS Business Media Advertising Source database provides this information for trade media, including print journals and websites that reach business-to-business audiences.

While circulation and total audience size are important in selecting a media vehicle, the media planner is also interested in the match between the magazine's readers and the advertiser's target audience. Information on readers is available from several sources, including the publication's own research and syndicated studies. Most magazines now have online media kits that provide basic information such as reader demographics, circulation, editorial calendars, rates, specifications, contact information, and other valuable data for advertisers. Exhibit 12-14 shows a page from the media kit for *Cosmopolitan* magazine that provides a profile of readers for its print edition. The index numbers show that Cosmo reaches gen Z and millennial women between the ages of 18 and 49. The magazine also

EXHIBIT 12-14

Cosmopolitan's online media kit contains useful information for advertisers such as this reader profile.

Hearst Magazine Media, Inc.

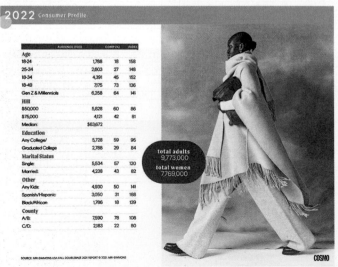

has a high index for African American as well as Hispanic women. Magazines generally provide media planners with even more detail than is available in online media kits. SRDS compiles these detailed media kits from most magazines and makes them available to advertisers and their agencies. Most magazines provide media planners with reports detailing readers' demographics, financial profile, lifestyle, and product usage characteristics. The larger the publication, the more detailed and comprehensive the information it usually can supply about its readers.

Syndicated research studies are also available. For consumer magazines, a primary source of information is MRI-Simmons, which was discussed in Chapter 10. These studies provide a broad range of information on the audiences of major national and regional magazines, including demographics, lifestyle characteristics, and product purchase and usage data. Most large ad agencies and media buying services also conduct ongoing research on the media habits of consumers. All this information helps determine the value of various magazines in reaching particular types of product users.

Audience information is generally more limited for business publications than for consumer magazines. The widely dispersed readership and nature of business publication readers make audience research more difficult. Media planners generally rely on information provided by the publication or by sources such as Business Publication Audits, which provide the titles of individuals who receive the publication and the type of industry in which they work. This information can be of value in understanding the audiences reached by various business magazines.

Purchasing Magazine Advertising Space

Cost Elements   Magazine rates are primarily a function of circulation. Other variables include the size of the ad, its position in the publication, the particular editions (geographic, demographic) chosen, any special mechanical or production requirements, and the number and frequency of insertions.

An important consideration for advertisers when buying space in a magazine is whether they want some type of preferred placement or just want to pay for a run-of-book ad that can appear anywhere in the magazine, at the discretion of the publisher. Most of the various preferred positions that magazines make available to advertisers are **first cover** (outside front), **second cover** (inside front), **third cover** (inside back), and **fourth cover** (outside back). These are considered to be very desirable positions in the magazine—particularly the fourth or back cover, for which there is often a waiting list. Because a cover ad position is a preferred position, it is almost always sold at a higher rate than any position inside the magazine. Very few publishers sell advertising space on the front cover of their magazines because the American Society of Magazine Editors guidelines discourage the practice. The front cover has always been considered editorial space and off limits to advertisers.[19]

Advertising space is generally sold on the basis of space units such as full page, half page, and quarter page, although some publications quote rates on the basis of column inches. The larger the ad, the greater the cost. However, many advertisers use full-page ads since they result in more attention and readership. Studies have found that full-page ads generated 30 percent more readership than did half-page ads.[20]

Ads can be produced or run using black and white, black and white plus one color, or four colors. The more color used in the ad, the greater the expense, because of the increased printing costs. On average, a four-color ad costs 30 percent more than a black-and-white ad. Advertisers generally prefer color ads because they have greater visual impact and are superior for attracting and holding attention.[21] Roper Starch Worldwide analyzed the effect of various factors on the readership of magazine ads. The "noted" scores (the percentage of readers who remember seeing the ad in a publication they read) are anywhere from 6 to 59 percent higher for a four-color full-page ad than for a black-and-white ad, depending on the product category. "Read-most" scores (the percentage who say they read more than half of the copy of an ad) are also higher

EXHIBIT 12–15

Advertisers can reach alumni of Ivy League schools through the Ivy League Magazine Network.

Ivy League Magazine Network

for four-color versus black-and-white ads, by about 25 percent on average.[22] Other studies have examined the impact of size and color and found that a four-color spread (two facing pages) outperforms a one-page color ad by 30 percent and a black-and-white spread by 35 percent in terms of ad recall.[23] Ads requiring special mechanical production such as bleed pages or inserts may also cost extra.

Rates for magazine ad space can also vary according to the number of times an ad runs and the amount of money spent during a specific period. The more often an advertiser contracts to run an ad, the lower are the space charges. Volume discounts are based on the total space purchased within a contract year, measured in dollars. Advertisers can also save money by purchasing advertising in magazine combinations, or networks.

Magazine networks offer the advertiser the opportunity to buy space in a group of publications as a package deal. The publisher usually has a variety of magazines that reach audiences with similar characteristics. Networks can also be publishers of a group of magazines with diversified audiences or independent networks that sell space in groups of magazines published by different companies. For example, the Ivy League Magazine Network is a consortium of alumni magazines of Ivy League schools and two non-Ivies—Stanford University and the University of Chicago. Advertisers can purchase ad space and reach the well-educated, affluent alumni of all nine schools with one media purchase through the network (Exhibit 12–15).

The Future for Magazines

The past few years have been very difficult for the magazine industry as advertising revenue has been declining for nearly a decade. In 2022 ad revenue for consumer magazines continued to decline and was forecast to be around $12.7 billion. However, print ad revenue represented less than half of the total as advertising in digital editions of magazines has now surpassed print. Advertising in business and trade magazines was forecast at $3.4 billion with nearly $1.9 billion in digital and $1.5 in print publications.[24] Most publications are experiencing reductions in revenue as advertisers shift more of their spending to digital media and other IMC tools and have been slow to increase their ad spending after reducing it during the pandemic and the latest economic downturn. Many publications have seen their number of advertising pages decline and have found it difficult to raise rates to offset the reduction in ad pages.[25] And while advertising revenue has been decreasing, publishers' other major revenue stream, circulation, has also been declining for most magazines. Many magazines have gone out of business in recent years, including some that were published for decades, such as *Transworld Snowboarding*, *The Weekly Standard*, and *Gourmet*. A number of well-known magazines have reduced the number of issues they publish each year including *The Atlantic*, *Men's Journal*, *Forbes*, and *Fortune*. One of the major changes impacting the magazine industry has been the shift from print to online editions made by many publications recently including *Entertainment Weekly*, *Shape*, *InStyle*, and *O, The Oprah Magazine*.[26] Digital and Social Media Perspective 12–1 discusses how a number of magazines have ceased publishing their print editions and are now available only online.

There are a number of challenges facing the magazine industry. The costs of paper and ink continue to rise, and the industry has had to weather several significant increases in postal rates, which have had a major impact on their cost.[27] Magazines are also facing strong competition for consumers' attention from television, streaming

Magazines Continue to Go Digital

The chapter opener discussed how the digital disruption has impacted the newspaper industry. The transition of readership from traditional print to online publications has resulted in declining circulation and lower advertising revenue for newspapers. Magazines, which are the other major category of traditional print media, are facing many of the same challenges as newspapers. Advertising revenue for print magazines, including both consumer and trade publications, declined from $17 billion in 2013 to $12.7 billion in 2022 and the decline is likely to continue. Like newspapers, magazines have been experiencing declines in readership, lower paid subscription numbers, and fewer single copy sales, as consumers increasingly switch to free or more affordable substitutes such as online publications.

Consumer magazines saw the number of advertising pages in their publications decline over the past several years as marketers cut back on advertising spending during the coronavirus pandemic. In 2022 the consumer magazine advertising market in the United States was estimated to be worth $8.5 billion with $5.1 billion coming from print ads and $3.4 from advertising in digital publications. However, by 2025 industry forecasts expect digital ad spending to surpass print, as both consumer and trade magazines shift their focus to digital editions of their publications.

For many years, digital editions of magazines were regarded as a side dish to the main course of a print edition, or an optional add-on to a subscription. Although the magazine industry recognized that it must embrace its digital future, most publishers were not ready to abandon their traditional print publications and went on the offensive to promote them. The Association of Magazine Media, the industry association that represents consumer magazines and works closely with them to promote their interest, ran several campaigns to promote the vitality of print magazines. The campaigns promoted the idea that print magazines remained an effective advertising medium in the age of the Internet because of the depth and lasting quality of print compared with the fleeting nature of much of the Web's content. The campaigns also reminded readers, as well as advertisers, that many of the popular digital brands are rooted in print publications that have tremendous cultural and commercial influence.

In 2011, Jan Wenner, the founder of the publishing company that owned popular magazines such as *Rolling Stone*, *Us Weekly*, and *Men's Journal*, argued there is still a place for traditional print magazines. Wenner predicted that it would take a decade or more before there was a decisive shift from print magazines to reading them on mobile devices and called the rush to digital editions of magazines the result of "sheer insanity, insecurity and fear." The decade or so has now passed since Wenner challenged magazine publishers' rush to digital, and it appears that the insecure and fearful are prevailing as more publications shutter their print editions in favor of digital editions only.

The exodus from print gained momentum in 2018 when the three major magazine publishers—Hearst, Conde Nast, and Meredith Corp.—ceased publishing the print versions of some of their magazines making them available only online. Among the magazines that Hearst has turned into digital-only publications are *Redbook* and *Seventeen*. In 2018, Conde Nast dropped its regular monthly print issue of *Glamour* as part of a "digital-first" strategy that now includes an online version along with special print editions published a few times a year. The magazine joined *Teen Vogue* as a digital-only publication since Conde Nast closed the print edition of the 80-year-old title, which had been publishing five times a year.

A year later The Walt Disney Co. ceased publishing regular monthly editions of *ESPN The Magazine*, which is part of the EPSN sports properties owned by the company, including the ESPN cable sports networks. In announcing the change to digital-only for the magazine, which published its first issue in 1998, ESPN stated that its research showed the vast majority of the magazine's readers already consumed its print journalism on digital platforms, and the shift will allow it to maximize its reach and impact. The company also noted that sports magazines are facing increased competition from other digital sports-focused platforms such as Bleacher Report, SB Nation, Deadspin, Ringer, and The Athletic. The shift to digital-only has continued over the past 3 years. In 2022 Dotdash Meredith announced that it would cut monthly print editions for six titles including *Eating Well*, *Entertainment Weekly*, *Health*, *InStyle*, *Parents*, and *People en Español*.

There are a number of reasons magazine publishers are moving to a digital-first or -only strategy. Closing print editions helps cut costs and copes with the loss of advertising revenue that most magazines are facing as marketers shift more of their media budgets from traditional to digital media. Another reason for the shift is that a number of magazines are facing competition from digital platforms that are continually updated and provide timely coverage of various topics, issues, and events as well as "breaking news."

A further reason publishers are going online is that digital editions of their magazines can help them better understand their readers and provide content that meets their needs and interests. They can detect clicks and time spent reading articles, which provides valuable insight into the topics, stories, and issues that attract the attention of readers and hold their interest. Many magazines are turning to sophisticated artificial intelligence–driven solutions to

(continued)

Victor J. Blue/Bloomberg/Getty Images

detailed information regarding readers and how best to engage them. Advertising in the digital editions of magazines provides marketers with the same advantages they have with other forms of digital media, including targeting and retargeting of advertising messages and detailed analytics that can be used to understand how well their ads are working.

The magazine industry continues to promote the value of print publications, noting that readers love the touch and feel of a printed magazine and that engagement is higher for print versus digital. They also point to studies that have shown a drop in engagement and time spent with magazines once a publication is no longer available in print. However, despite their efforts to promote the value of traditional print magazines, the shift to digital editions is very likely to continue. Many in the magazine publishing industry hoped that Jann Wenner was correct when he argued there was a still a place for print magazines. However, many publishers appear to be hedging their bets and embracing the digital future.

Sources: "*Entertainment Weekly, InStyle* Among Six Magazines Ending Print Issues," *Advertising Age*, February 9, 2022, https://adage.com/article/media/entertainment-weekly-instyle-among-six-iac-magazines-ending-print-issues/239887; "*ESPN The Magazine* to Abandon Print, Go Web-Only," *Advertising Age*, April, 20, 2019, https://adage.com/article/media/espn-magazine-abandon-print-go-web-only/2167836; Adam Rowe, "Magazines Lose Reader Engagement When They Go Digital-Only: Will Other Formats Suffer the Same Fate," *Forbes*, https://www.forbes.com/sites/adamrowe1/2019/11/19/magazines-lose-reader-engagement-when-they-go-digital-only-will-other-formats-suffer-the-same-fate/?sh=195eddc46c9c; Nat Ives, "Jann Wenner: Magazines' Rush to iPad Is 'Sheer Insanity and Insecurity and Fear,'" *Advertising Age*, May 29, 2011, adage.com/article/media/jann-wenner-magazines-tablet-migration-decades/227827.

conduct deep analyses of their audiences. This information is very valuable for enticing marketers to advertise in their digital publications because it can provide them with

---

services, the Internet and social media. Publishers are looking at a number of ways to improve their position—including stronger editorial platforms, better circulation management, cross-magazine and media deals, database marketing, technological advances, and digital delivery methods—to make advertising in magazines more appealing to marketers as well as to survive.

EXHIBIT 12–16

Men's Journal and *Men's Health* magazines have been very successful in attracting the male audience.

Source: (left to right) American Media, Inc.; Hearst Magazine Media, Inc.

Stronger Editorial Platforms   Magazines with strong editorial platforms that appeal to the interests, lifestyles, and changing demographics of consumers as well as business and market trends are in the best position to attract readers and advertisers. Lifestyle magazines targeted to women such as *Women's Health* and *Martha Stewart Living* have done well, as have magazines targeting specific interests, such as *Paws*, a magazine centered on pet care, and *Country Living*. Several publications with strong editorial platforms that appeal to younger male readers have also done very well, including *Men's Journal* and *Men's Health* (Exhibit 12–16).

Circulation Management   One of the major challenges facing magazine publishers is trying to increase or even maintain their circulation bases. Circulation is the second major source of revenue for most publications, and publishers must carefully manage the costs of attracting and maintaining additional readers or subscribers. The cost of acquiring subscribers has increased dramatically over the past decade. However, publishers have not been able to pass on these increased costs because the prices consumers pay for subscriptions as well as single copies of magazines have increased only slightly. Thus, publishers have to pay more to maintain their rate bases (the circulation level guaranteed to advertisers), but they make less money on each subscription sold.

Some publications have begun selling magazine subscriptions on Facebook by allowing users of the social media site to expand blurbs of magazine content that are common in news feeds into full articles that contain ads as well as options to subscribe.[28] Publishers have also been turning to daily-deal sites such as Groupon and Living Social as magazines such as *Esquire, Us Weekly, Reader's Digest, Allure, Men's Health,* and others have found them useful for attracting new subscribers. However, a major challenge publishers will face is getting subscribers to renew at higher rates once the discounted deals expire.[29]

Digital Magazines Many magazines are keeping pace with the digital revolution by making their publications available online.[30] The number of consumer and business magazine websites and digital versions has nearly doubled over the past 5 years. Digital versions of magazines offer the many advantages of the Internet to publishers as well as to advertisers. They provide advertisers with the opportunity for sponsorships as well as running video and banner ads and promotions on the online versions of the magazines. More and more people are becoming comfortable with reading magazines online rather than in traditional print form, which is leading many publications to expand beyond their basic print publications. A number of publishers are extending their magazine brands to include online, social networking, mobile, and user-generated content, which provides increasing readership as well as advertising reach opportunities.

Marketers are also recognizing that there are opportunities to integrate their advertising in online publications with the contextual environment and editorial content by using **native advertising.** As discussed in Chapter 9, a native online ad takes on the look and feel of the surrounding content, and its visual design and user experience are native or specific to the online site. A number of magazine and newspaper brands have been working with marketers to create native ads for their online publications, including *Forbes* and *The Atlantic. Forbes* has been at the forefront in the use of native advertising with an approach called BrandVoice that allows marketers to connect directly with its readers by enabling them to create content on the *Forbes* digital platforms. All content on the platforms is clearly labeled and transparent so readers know who is talking and the perspective from which they speak. Exhibit 12–17 shows how *Forbes* promotes its Forbes Connoisseur and Forbes Insights, which are both part of its Brand-Voice content marketing platform.

Another form of online delivery is digital editions of magazines developed specifically for tablets such as the iPad and devices using the Android operating system. There are several thousand apps for magazines available in the United States. The number of digital app editions of magazines will continue to grow as more consumers become comfortable with reading them on their tablets and advances in technology make the reading experience similar to that of a print publication. Digital editions of many magazines are now able to offer ads that can deliver the impact of full-page magazine ads, include video and TV commercials, and link directly to an advertiser's website. Although consumers who opt to read magazines on a mobile device enjoy the experience, magazine apps still account for a small share of total magazine readership. However, it is likely that readership of digital magazines will increase as magazine publishers

EXHIBIT 12–17

Forbes promotes two of the content marketing platforms it makes available to advertisers.

Forbes Media LLC

DISCOVER MORE CONTENT SOLUTIONS

FORBES CONNOISSEUR

Refining & Reimagining Your Brand's Storytelling

Take readers on an inspiring journey while showcasing your products or services to Forbes' influential global audiences. Ideal for luxury and travel brands, Connoisseur is an artful form of custom storytelling whose impactful design catches the attention of Forbes readers.

FORBES INSIGHTS

Share Insights That Move Your Business Forward

Demystify the future of business by partnering with Forbes to deliver data-driven perspectives on the issues that are most important to your brand—and your consumers. Tap into the power of Forbes Insights to ensure your brand has a say in the future of your industry.

What neuroscience says about why print magazine ads work

Paper readers remember more.

Paper-based reading	More focused attention, less distraction	Higher comprehension and recall	Stimulates emotions and desires
	Preferred by majority (even millennials)	Drives sensory involvement which contributes to reader impact	Slower reading speeds

EXHIBIT 12–18

Key findings from a study on the value of print advertising.

collaborate with technology companies to make digital versions of their publications more available. For example, in 2019 Apple launched its Apple News+ subscription service, which includes digital access to more than 300 popular magazines and leading newspapers. The digital versions of the magazines contain the same stories and photos as the print edition as well as the ads.[31]

The magazine industry recognizes that it must continue to respond to the changes in media consumption patterns and the challenges it faces as more marketers shift their advertising monies to digital. However, publishers still feel there are inherent advantages of traditional print magazines to advertisers and have gone on the offensive to promote them. For example, the Association for Magazine Media, which is now part of the News/Media Alliance, published a white paper titled "What Can Neuroscience Tell Us About Why Print Advertising Works?" that summarized the findings of numerous research papers, books, and reports regarding how consumers' brains process paper-based information.[32] The report concludes that print advertising is superior to online ads with regard to its ability to deliver a reading experience that supports comprehension of and connection with an advertiser's message. Exhibit 12–18 shows a summary of the key findings from the study regarding the value of print advertising.

Many magazines now offer more than their basic print publication to readers as they connect with them through various digital platforms including their websites, social media such as Twitter, Facebook, Instagram, and Pinterest, as well as YouTube channels. Exhibit 12–19 shows the digital ecosystem for *Women's Health* that extends well beyond its print edition, which is published 10 times a year, and includes its website and various social media extensions of the brand to post new content multiple times a day to attract and retain readers. Magazine publishers are hoping they can get advertisers to recognize that the digital editions of their magazines as well as the various extensions are rooted in print publications that are still valuable advertising platforms.

EXHIBIT 12–19

Women's Health uses a number of social media platforms to extend its connection to readers beyond the print edition of the magazine.

Hearst Magazine Media, Inc.

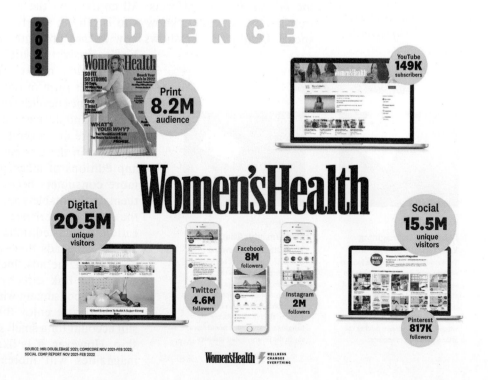

NEWSPAPERS

Newspapers, the second major form of print media after magazines, are increasingly being read online through digital formats. In 2022, an estimated $11.2 billion was spent on newspaper advertising, including print and digital, which was about 4 percent of the total advertising expenditures in the United States. Newspapers are an especially important advertising medium to local advertisers, particularly retailers. However, newspapers are also valuable to national advertisers. Many of the advertising dollars spent by local retailers are actually provided by national advertisers through cooperative advertising programs (discussed in Chapter 16). Newspapers vary in terms of their characteristics and their role as an advertising medium.

Types of Newspapers

The traditional role of newspapers has been to deliver prompt, detailed coverage of news as well as to supply other information and features that appeal to readers. The vast majority of newspapers are daily publications serving local communities. However, weekly, national, and special-audience newspapers have special characteristics that can be valuable to advertisers.

Daily Newspapers　Daily newspapers, which are published each weekday, are found in cities and larger towns across the country. Many areas have more than one daily paper. Readership of daily newspapers varies by age: 40 percent or more of older adults (55+) read a newspaper every day but only around 20 percent of younger adults (18 to 34) do so.[33] Newspapers provide detailed coverage of news, events, and issues concerning the local area as well as business, sports, and other relevant information and entertainment. Daily newspapers can further be classified as morning, evening, or Sunday publications. In 2022 there were 1,250 daily newspapers in the United States; of these, 30 percent were evening papers and 70 percent morning. There were also approximately 840 Sunday newspapers, most of which were published by daily newspapers.

Weekly Newspapers　Most weekly newspapers originate in small towns or suburbs where the volume of news and advertising cannot support a daily newspaper. These papers focus primarily on news, sports, and events relevant to the local area and usually ignore national and world news, sports, and financial and business news. There are approximately 5,100 weekly newspapers published in the United States, and they have an average circulation of close to 7,500. Weeklies appeal primarily to local advertisers because of their geographic focus and lower absolute cost. Most national advertisers avoid weekly newspapers because of their duplicate circulation with daily or Sunday papers in the large metropolitan areas and problems in contracting for and placing ads in these publications. However, the contracting and scheduling problems associated with these papers have been reduced by the emergence of syndicates that publish them in a number of areas and sell ad space in all of their local newspapers through one office.

National Newspapers　Newspapers in the United States with national circulation include *USA Today*, *The Wall Street Journal*, and *The New York Times*. All three are daily publications and have editorial content with a nationwide appeal. *The Wall Street Journal* has 650,000 subscribers to its print edition and another 3 million to its digital edition. The print and digital editions of the *WSJ* are an excellent way to reach businesspeople and its very affluent readership base. Another popular national newspaper is *USA Today*, which positions itself as "the nation's newspaper." *USA Today* is popular particularly among business and leisure travelers, with its coverage of national news as well as its money, sports, lifestyle, and entertainment sections. Like other national newspapers, the number of paid subscribers to the paper's print edition has declined

EXHIBIT 12–20

The New York Times has more than 10 million subscribers and attracts many national and regional advertisers.

The New York Times Company

significantly to 159,000 in 2022, but this has been offset by an increase in the number of digital-only subscribers. Gannett, the owner of *USA Today*, took a major step in 2021 by instituting a partial paywall for the digital edition of the paper.[34] The fastest growing national newspaper is *The New York Times*, which reached more than 10 million subscribers across its print and digital editions in 2022 and has a goal of reaching 15 million over the next 5 years.[35] *The New York Times* attracts a very upscale and engaged audience, which makes it popular among advertisers. The print edition of the newspaper is still widely read and promoted as its iconic product as shown in Exhibit 12–20. National newspapers appeal primarily to large national advertisers and to regional advertisers that use specific geographic editions of these publications. For example, *The Wall Street Journal* has three geographic editions covering 21 regions in which ads can be placed; *USA Today* offers advertisers the opportunity to run ads in its national edition or any of 25 regional markets.

Special-Audience Newspapers A variety of papers offer specialized editorial content and are published for particular groups, including labor unions, professional organizations, industries, and hobbyists. Many people working in advertising read *Advertising Age*, while those in the marketing area read *Marketing News*. Specialized newspapers are also published in areas with large foreign-language-speaking ethnic groups, among them Polish, Chinese, Hispanics, Vietnamese, and Filipinos. In the United States, there are newspapers printed in more than 40 languages.

Newspapers targeted at various religious groups compose another large class of special-interest papers. For example, more than 140 Catholic newspapers are published across the United States. Another type of special-audience newspaper is one most of you probably read regularly during the school year, the college newspaper. Nearly 1,300 colleges and universities publish newspapers and offer advertisers an excellent medium for reaching college students, who are a difficult target audience for marketers to reach. Many college newspapers are now being published online and either eliminating or reducing the number of print editions they publish each week. Some are facing major financial problems, and many have had to cease publication or become affiliated with their universities, which endangers independent coverage. Many are looking to alumni donations and have launched fundraising campaigns on social media to continue operating. Recently, many college papers have joined forces in the "Save Student Newsrooms" campaign started by the editors at *The Independent Florida Alligator* at the University of Florida (Exhibit 12–21). The goal of the campaign is to make people aware of the importance of student journalism and support college news organizations that are fighting for independence and financial stability.[36]

EXHIBIT 12–21

The "Save Student Newsrooms" campaign is addressing the challenges facing many college newspapers.

Save Student Newsrooms

Newspaper Supplements Although not a category of newspapers per se, many papers include magazine-type supplements, primarily in their Sunday editions. Sunday supplements have been part of most newspapers for many years and come in various forms. One type is the nationally syndicated Sunday magazine, such as *Parade*, which is distributed through nearly 500 newspapers and reaches over 40 million readers in markets across the country. These publications are similar to national magazines and carry both national and regional advertising. *Parade* is the only

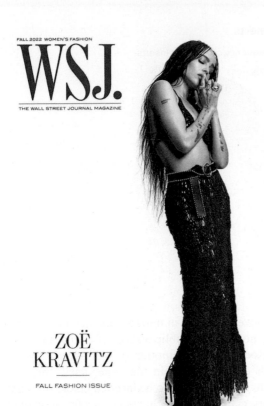

FALL 2022 WOMEN'S FASHION

WSJ.

THE WALL STREET JOURNAL MAGAZINE

ZOË
KRAVITZ

FALL FASHION ISSUE

EXHIBIT 12–22

WSJ Magazine is a very popular supplement to *The Wall Street Journal* and is a leading luxury magazine.

Dow Jones & Company, Inc

remaining nationally syndicated Sunday magazine since *USA Weekend* suspended publication in 2014. *Parade* has been distributed in newspapers nationwide for 80 years but published its last print edition in late 2022 and now appears in digital editions only.

Some large newspapers publish supplements distributed by the parent paper. These supplements contain stories of local, as well as national, interest, and both local and national advertisers buy ad space. *The New York Times Magazine* is the best-known newspaper supplement. *The Washington Post, San Francisco Examiner,* and *Los Angeles Times* have their own Sunday magazines. *The Wall Street Journal* also publishes *WSJ Magazine* eight times a year with its print publication and also has a digital edition. It covers contemporary culture, entertainment, fashion, art, travel, and other topics and is one of the leading luxury magazines. Exhibit 12–22 shows the cover of the annual fall fashion edition of the magazine, which is very popular among readers. In some areas, papers have begun carrying regional supplements as well as specialized weekday supplements that cover specific topics such as food, sports, or entertainment. Supplements are valuable to advertisers that want to use the newspaper yet get four-color reproduction quality in their ads.

Types of Newspaper Advertising

The ads appearing in print editions of newspapers can also be divided into different categories. The major types of newspaper advertising are display and classified. Other special types of ads and preprinted inserts also appear in newspapers.

Display Advertising   **Display advertising** is found throughout the newspaper and generally uses illustrations, headlines, white space, and other visual devices in addition to the copy text. The two types of display advertising in newspapers are local and national (general).

Local advertising refers to ads placed by local organizations, businesses, and individuals who want to communicate with consumers in the market area served by the newspaper. Supermarkets and department stores are among the leading local display advertisers, along with numerous other retailers and service operations such as banks and travel agents. Local advertising is sometimes referred to as retail advertising because retailers generally account for 85 percent of local display ads.

National or *general advertising* refers to newspaper display advertising done by marketers of branded products or services that are sold on a national or regional level. These ads are designed to create and maintain demand for a company's product or service and to complement the efforts of local retailers that stock and promote the advertiser's products. Major retail chains, automakers, and airlines are heavy users of newspaper advertising.

Classified Advertising   **Classified advertising** also provides newspapers with revenue. These ads are arranged under subheads according to the product, service, or offering being advertised. Employment, real estate, and automotive are the three major categories of classified advertising. While most classified ads are just text set in small type, some newspapers also accept classified display advertising. These ads are run in the classified section of the paper but use illustrations, larger type sizes, white space, borders, and even color to stand out. Many newspapers have moved classified ads online and do not publish them in their print editions or do so on a limited number of days.

EXHIBIT 12–23

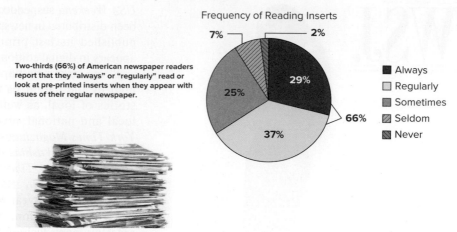

Pre-printed Inserts

Frequency of Reading Inserts

Two-thirds (66%) of American newspaper readers report that they "always" or "regularly" read or look at pre-printed inserts when they appear with issues of their regular newspaper.

7% 2%

29%

25%

37% 66%

■ Always
□ Regularly
■ Sometimes
▨ Seldom
■ Never

Special Ads and Inserts

Special advertisements in newspapers include a variety of government and financial reports and notices and public notices of changes in business and personal relationships. **Preprinted inserts** are another type of advertising distributed through newspapers. These ads do not appear in the paper itself; they are printed by the advertiser and then taken to the newspaper to be inserted before delivery. Many retailers use inserts such as circulars, catalogs, or brochures in specific circulation zones to reach shoppers in their particular trade areas. Inserts are used most often in Sunday editions of major newspapers since consumers spend more time with the Sunday paper and often look for inserts from retailers on weekends. Exhibit 12-23 shows how the News/Media Alliance promotes the value of preprinted inserts in newspapers.

Advantages of Newspapers

Newspapers have a number of characteristics that make them popular among both local and national advertisers. These include their extensive penetration of local markets, flexibility, geographic selectivity, reader involvement, and special services.

Market Penetration One of the advantages of newspapers is the market coverage or penetration they offer advertisers, particularly for older adult households. In most areas, daily readership of newspapers can be nearly 50 percent among households with higher incomes and education levels. The penetration of newspapers provides advertisers with an opportunity for reaching various segments of the population with their message. Also, since many newspapers are published and read daily, the advertiser can build a high level of frequency into the media schedule.

Flexibility Another advantage of newspapers is the flexibility they offer advertisers. First, they are flexible in terms of requirements for producing and running the ads. Newspaper ads can be written, laid out, and prepared in a matter of hours. For most dailies, the closing time by which the ad must be received is usually only 24 hours before publication (although closing dates for special ads, such as those using color, and Sunday supplements are longer). The short production time and closing dates make newspapers an excellent medium for responding to current events or presenting timely information to readers.

A second dimension of newspapers' flexibility stems from the creative options they make available to advertisers. Newspaper ads can be produced and run in various sizes, shapes, and formats; they can use color or special inserts to gain the interest of readers. Ads can be run in Sunday magazines or other supplements, and a variety of scheduling options are possible, depending on the advertiser's purpose.

EXHIBIT 12–24

The *Houston Chronicle* offers the opportunity to advertise in community newspapers.

Hearst Newspapers, LLC

Geographic Selectivity Newspapers generally offer advertisers more geographic or territorial selectivity than does any other medium except direct mail. Advertisers can vary their coverage by choosing a paper—or combination of papers—that reaches the areas with the greatest sales potential. National advertisers take advantage of the geographic selectivity of newspapers to concentrate their advertising in specific areas they can't reach with other media or to take advantage of strong sales potential in a particular area. For example, BMW, Mercedes, and Land Rover often run newspaper ads in major metropolitan markets such as major cities in California, Texas, and the New York/New Jersey area to capitalize on the high sales potential for luxury import cars in these markets. A number of companies use newspapers in their regional marketing strategies. Newspaper advertising lets them feature products on a market-by-market basis, respond and adapt campaigns to local market conditions, and tie into more retailer promotions, fostering more support from the trade.

Local advertisers such as retailers are interested in geographic selectivity or flexibility within a specific market or trade area. Their media goal is to concentrate their advertising on the areas where most of their customers are. Some major metropolitan newspapers offer advertisers various geographic areas or zones in which they can advertise. A number of media companies have also purchased community newspapers in their metropolitan areas and offer companies such as retailers the opportunity to run ads in these local markets. Exhibit 12-24 shows how the Houston Chronicle Media Group promotes community newspapers owned by the company.

Reader Involvement and Acceptance Another important feature of newspapers is consumers' level of acceptance and involvement with papers and the ads they contain. The typical daily newspaper reader spends time each day reading the weekday newspaper and even more time reading the Sunday paper. Recent studies have shown that around 54 percent of newspaper readers consume newspapers only in their printed form and are news enthusiasts. However, these print-only readers are older than those who read newspapers online and are less likely to have gone to college.[37] These consumers rely heavily on newspapers not only for news, information, and entertainment but also for assistance with consumption decisions.

One aspect of newspapers that is helpful to advertisers is readers' knowledge about particular sections of the paper. Most consumers know that ads for automotive products and sporting goods are generally found in the sports section, while ads for financial services are found in the business section. The weekly food section in many newspapers is popular for recipe and menu ideas as well as for the grocery store ads and coupons offered by many stores and companies.

The value of newspaper advertising as a source of information has been shown in several studies. One study found that consumers look forward to ads in newspapers more than in other media. In another study, 80 percent of consumers said newspaper ads were most helpful to them in doing their weekly shopping. Newspaper advertising has also been rated as one of the most trusted forms of advertising in numerous studies, along with magazines.

EXHIBIT 12–25

The *San Diego Union-Tribune*
promotes the services of
its advertising creative
department to advertisers.

The San Diego Union-Tribune

Services Offered   The special services newspapers offer can be valuable to advertisers. For example, many newspapers offer merchandising services and programs to manufacturers that make the trade aware of ads being run for the company's product and help convince local retailers they should stock, display, and promote the item.

Many newspapers are also excellent sources of local market information through their knowledge of market conditions and research like readership studies, consumer surveys, and various reports and market studies.

Newspapers can also assist small companies through free copywriting and art services. Small advertisers without an agency or advertising department often rely on the newspaper to help them write and produce their ads. Exhibit 12–25 shows how the *San Diego Union-Tribune* promotes the services of its advertising creative department to companies that advertise in the newspaper.

Limitations of Newspapers

While newspapers have many advantages, like all media they also have disadvantages that media planners must consider. The limitations of newspapers include their reproduction problems, short life span, lack of selectivity, and clutter.

Poor Reproduction   One of the greatest limitations of newspapers as an advertising medium is their poor reproduction quality. The coarse paper stock used for newspapers, the absence of color, and the lack of time papers have available to achieve high-quality reproduction limit the quality of most newspaper ads. Newspapers have improved their reproduction quality in recent years, and color reproduction has become more available. Also, advertisers desiring high-quality color in newspaper ads can turn to such alternatives as freestanding inserts or Sunday supplements. However, these are more costly and may not be desirable to many advertisers. As a general rule, if the visual appearance of the product is important, the advertiser will not rely on newspaper ads. Ads for food products and fashions generally use magazines to capitalize on their superior reproduction quality and color.

Short Life Span   Unlike magazines, which may be retained around the house for several weeks, a daily newspaper is generally kept less than a day. So an ad is unlikely to have any impact beyond the day of publication, and repeat exposure is very unlikely. Compounding this problem is the short amount of time many consumers spend with the newspaper and the possibility they may not even open certain sections of the paper. Media planners can offset these problems somewhat by using high frequency in the newspaper schedule and advertising in a section where consumers who are in the market for a particular product or service are likely to look.

Lack of Selectivity   While newspapers can offer advertisers geographic selectivity, they are not a selective medium in terms of demographics or lifestyle characteristics. Most newspapers reach broad and very diverse groups of consumers, which makes it difficult for marketers to focus on narrowly defined market segments. For example, manufacturers of fishing rods and reels will find newspapers very inefficient because of the wasted coverage that results from reaching all the newspaper readers who don't fish. Thus, they are more likely to use special-interest magazines such as *Field & Stream* and *Fishing World*.

Innovative Advertising

Bookend   Stairstep

14

EXHIBIT 12–26

The *Los Angeles Times* promotes the innovative advertising shapes it now offers.

Los Angeles Times

Clutter Newspapers, like most other advertising media, suffer from clutter because the advertiser's message must compete with other ads for consumers' attention and interest. Moreover, the creative options in newspapers are limited by the fact that most ads are black and white. Thus, it can be difficult for a newspaper advertiser to break through the clutter without using costly measures such as large space buys or color. However, clutter has become less of a problem as the number of ads appearing in print editions of newspapers declines.

Some newspapers offer advertisers the opportunity to use innovative shape-based ads that utilize unconventional sizes and formats such as stairsteps, bookends, U-shapes, island ads, spadea ads, and half-page spreads. Many newspapers are also now accepting ads on the front page of their publications as well as on the first page of various sections of the paper. The use of these innovative formats makes it possible for advertisers to more easily attract the attention of readers and increase recall of their advertising message. Exhibit 12–26 shows a page from the media kit for the *Los Angeles Times* promoting several of the innovative ad forms that the paper offers advertisers.

The Newspaper Audience

As with any medium, the media planner must understand the nature and size of the audience reached by a newspaper in considering its value in the media plan. Since newspapers as a class of media do an excellent job of penetrating their market, the typical daily newspaper gives advertisers the opportunity to reach most of the households in a market. But, while local advertisers aim to cover a particular market or trade area, national advertisers want to reach broad regions or even the entire country. They must purchase space in a number of papers to achieve the desired level of coverage.

The basic sources of information concerning the audience size of newspapers come from the circulation figures available through rate cards, publishers' statements, or SRDS's *Newspaper Advertising Source.* Circulation figures for many newspapers are verified by the Alliance for Audited Media (AAM), which was discussed earlier. Advertisers that use a number of papers in their media plan generally find SRDS the most convenient source.

Newspaper circulation figures are generally broken down into three categories: the city zone, the retail trading zone, and all other areas. The **city zone** is a market area composed of the city where the paper is published and contiguous areas similar in character to the city. The **retail trading zone** is the market outside the city zone whose residents regularly trade with merchants within the city zone. The "all other" category covers all circulation not included in the city or retail trade zone.

Sometimes circulation figures are provided only for the primary market, which is the city and retail trade zones combined, and the other areas. Local as well as national advertisers consider the circulation patterns across the various categories in evaluating and selecting newspapers.

National advertisers often buy newspaper space on the basis of the size of the market area they cover. For example, an advertiser might decide to purchase advertising in the top 10 markets, the top 50 markets, the top 100 markets, and so on. A national advertiser gets different levels of market coverage depending on the number of market areas purchased.

Audience Information Circulation figures provide the media planner with the basic data for assessing the value of newspapers and their ability to cover various market areas. However, the media planner also wants to match the characteristics of a

NEWSPAPERS

Newspaper Advertising Source

The **SRDS Newspaper Advertising Source** gives you comprehensive planning data on over 6,000 daily U.S. papers, newspaper groups, community papers, alternatives, shoppers, and classifieds.

Identify, Evaluate and Connect

Efficiently identify and evaluate national and local papers that meet your ad campaign needs

- Learn how to pinpoint national and local newspapers in over 210 Nielsen designated market areas (DMAs)
- Save time using enhanced search, filter and sort options, including market look-ups by zip code, county, city and state
- Access advertising rates, issue & closing dates
- Seamlessly analyze and verify circulation data with access to key industry audit reports from AAM and CVC
- Tap into county-defined maps and demographic profiles for all 210 DMAs
- Easily build consideration sets and export data to reports
- Quickly activate your plans by connecting with publishers

EXHIBIT 12–27

SRDS *Newspaper Advertising Source* provides advertisers with valuable Information on newspapers.

SRDS

newspaper's readers with those of the advertiser's target audience. Data on newspaper audience size and characteristics are available from studies conducted by the papers as well as from commercial research services. As with magazines, a valuable source for information on newspapers is SRDS, whose print and online service provides complete planning information on daily papers, newspaper groups, ethnic newspapers, college newspapers, comics, and newspaper-distributed magazines. The SRDS *Newspaper Advertising Source* data contains standardized ad rates, circulation figures, dates, general requirements, contact information, and other valuable information. As shown in Exhibit 12–27, this information can be used by media planners to identify and evaluate more than 6,000 newspapers across more than 200 designated market areas.

Companies such as MRI-Simmons provide syndicated research studies on lifestyles, media behavior, and product/brand preferences that include information on newspapers. These studies can be valuable for comparing newspapers with other media vehicles.

Many newspapers commission their own audience studies to provide current and potential advertisers with information on readership and characteristics of readers such as demographics, shopping habits, and lifestyles. These studies are often designed to promote the effectiveness of the newspaper in reaching various types of consumers. Since they are sponsored by the paper itself, many advertisers are skeptical of their results. Careful attention must be given to the research methods used and conclusions drawn by these studies.

Purchasing Newspaper Space

Advertisers are faced with a number of options and pricing structures when purchasing newspaper space. The cost of advertising space depends not only on the newspaper's circulation but also on factors such as premium charges for color or special sections as well as discounts available. The purchase process and the rates paid for newspaper space differ for general and local advertisers.

General versus Local Rates   Newspapers have different rate structures for general or national advertisers and local or retail advertisers. **General advertising rates** apply to display advertisers outside the newspaper's designated market area (DMA) and to any classification deemed by the publisher to be "general" in nature. This includes ads run by national advertisers such as automotive, tobacco, packaged-goods, and pharmaceutical companies. **Retail or local advertising rates** apply to advertisers that conduct business or sell goods or services within the DMA. The rates paid by general advertisers are, on average, higher than those paid by local advertisers. Newspaper publishers claim the rate differential is justified for several reasons. First, they argue it costs more to handle general advertising since ad agencies get a 15 percent commission and commissions must also be paid to the independent sales reps who solicit nonlocal advertising. Second, they note that general advertising is less dependable than local advertising; general advertisers usually don't use newspapers on a continual basis the way local advertisers do. Finally, newspaper publishers contend that demand for general advertising is inelastic—it will not increase if rates are lowered or decrease if rates are raised. This means there is no incentive to lower the national advertisers' rates.

National advertisers do not view these arguments as valid justification for the rate differential. They argue that the costs are not greater for handling national advertising than for local business and that many national advertisers use newspapers on a regular basis. Since they use an agency to prepare their ads, national advertisers are less likely to request special services. The large and costly staff maintained by many newspapers to assist in the design and preparation of advertising is used mostly by local advertisers. Many marketers sidestep the national advertiser label and the higher rates by channeling their newspaper ads through special category plans, cooperative advertising deals with retailers, and local dealers and distributors that pay local rates. However, the rate differential does keep many national advertisers from making newspapers a larger part of their media mix.

Rate Structures While the column inch and **standard advertising unit (SAU)** are used to determine basic newspaper advertising rates, the media planner must consider other options and factors. Many newspapers charge **flat rates**, which means they offer no discount for quantity or repeated space buys. Others have an **open-rate structure**, which means various discounts are available. These discounts are generally based on frequency or bulk purchases of space and depend on the number of column inches purchased in a year.

Newspaper space rates also vary with an advertiser's special requests, such as preferred position or color. The basic rates quoted by a newspaper are **run of paper (ROP)**, which means the paper can place the ad on any page or in any position it desires. While most newspapers try to place an ad in a requested position, the advertiser can ensure a specific section and/or position on a page by paying a higher **preferred position rate**. Color advertising is also available in many newspapers on an ROP basis or through preprinted inserts or Sunday supplements.

Advertisers can also buy newspaper space based on **combination rates**, where they get a discount for using several newspapers as a group. Typically, a combination rate occurs when a publisher owns both a morning and an evening newspaper or owns a number of community newspapers in a market and offers a reduced single rate for running the same ad in all of the newspapers, generally within a 24-hour period. Combination discounts are also available when the advertiser buys space in several newspapers owned by the publisher in a number of markets or in multiple newspapers affiliated in a syndicate or newspaper group.

The Future for Newspapers

Newspapers remain an important advertising medium; however, advertising revenue for traditional print papers has declined dramatically over the past several years. They generate most of their advertising revenue from local advertisers, particularly retailers who use display ads to advertise their products and services and inform consumers of sales and other types of promotions. Newspapers account for less than 5 percent of advertising expenditures for national advertisers, so they are very dependent on regional and local marketers for their advertising revenue.

Newspapers' major strength lies in their role as a medium that can be used effectively by local advertisers on a continual basis. However, there are a number of problems and issues newspapers must address to maintain their strong position as a dominant local advertising medium and to gain more national advertising: competition from digital and other advertising media, maintenance and management of circulation, and declining readership.

Competition from Other Media The newspaper industry's battle to increase its share of advertising revenue has been difficult. In addition to the problems of reproduction quality and rate differentials, newspapers face competition from other media for national and local advertisers' budgets.

The intermedia battle that newspapers find themselves involved in is no longer limited to other forms of traditional media. Many companies are using the Internet as a marketing tool and a place to invest advertising dollars that might otherwise go to newspapers. Local radio and TV stations (particularly cable stations), as well as the expanding number of Yellow Pages publishers, are aggressively pursuing local advertisers. Newspapers will have to fight harder to retain those advertisers.

Newspapers are also facing strong competition from various online sites for classified and employment advertising, which have long been major profit centers. Classified advertising revenue for U.S. newspapers has dropped steadily over the past decade, declining from $10 billion in 2008 to just $3 billion in 2018. Reductions in classified advertising have occurred across all three of the major categories, automotive, real estate, and recruitment ads. Newspapers must now compete against "pure play" online employment sites such as Indeed.com, Careerbuilder.com, Glassdoor .com, and Monster.com for job listings, as well as social media sites such LinkedIn. Websites such as eBay and Craigslist have become popular ways for selling a variety of merchandise that traditionally was sold through classified ads in local newspapers. Craigslist, which began as a type of counterculture message board for young people in the San Francisco area, has expanded to most major cities and become popular among people of all ages. The online site includes sections for selling merchandise, apartment rentals, services, personals, and job listings. Some newspapers are recognizing that it is very difficult to compete against online sites for classified ads and are responding by offering free classified ads for merchandise under certain price points as a way to grow readership.

Newspapers are doing a number of other things to respond to the challenges from other media. Many papers have expanded their marketing capabilities and are making efforts to develop and sustain relationships with their advertisers. Some have created sophisticated databases and direct-mail capabilities, which they offer as value-added services. Others are increasing their marketing research departments, preparing comprehensive market studies for major customers, and, in some cases, serving as media advisors and marketing partners.

Circulation   The newspaper industry has been struggling for years to reverse declining circulation.[38] Most of the major newspapers in the United States have been experiencing a decline in circulation and are seeking ways to respond to the problem, such as by emphasizing readership measures and developing online versions of their papers. Like magazines, many newspapers are taking a closer look at their circulation and analyzing whether the cost of getting additional circulation is justified by the advertising revenue it generates. Many papers are raising newsstand and home delivery rates, and circulation revenue is accounting for more of their total revenue.

Circulation revenue for some of the larger newspapers has held steady over the past few years, as many publishers are pursuing a "subscription-first model" by growing the number of print and/or digital subscribers rather than focusing on advertising revenue. They also have found that it is more cost-effective to focus on retaining subscribers than spending large sums of money to acquire new ones. The cancellation rate for newspaper subscribers has leveled off as many newspapers offer programs such as discounts for automatic renewal payment plans. However, gains in circulation revenue have not been nearly enough to make up for losses in advertising revenue—a pattern that holds true even at the large newspapers and major chains.

Attracting and Retaining Readers   The problems with newspapers as an advertising medium stem from the reduced popularity of the medium itself. Newspaper readership has been on a steady decline over the past decade.[39] The decline in newspaper readership can be attributed to several factors, including the fast-paced, time-poor lifestyle of the modern dual-income household and, of course, competition from the Internet and social media as many of those who used to read newspapers now get their news and information online.[40] Of particular concern to publishers is the decline in newspaper readership among important market segments such as women and young adults. Newspapers and advertisers are concerned because women are far more likely than men to make buying decisions. Many newspapers are introducing new women's sections and revising old ones to make them more appealing to modern women. This means including articles on such issues as health, parenting, and careers—for example, how women with children and jobs manage their time.

Newspapers are also concerned about where their future readers will come from, since many young people are now subscribing to TV streaming services and also spend more and more time surfing the Internet and on social media. A number of newspapers have been redesigned to be more interesting and easier and faster to read. Changes include the increased use of color and graphics as well as expanded coverage of sports and entertainment. Some papers have begun providing short summaries of articles in each section of the paper so readers can skim them and decide what they want to read. However, despite the best efforts of the industry, newspapers continue to lose readers and advertising revenue, which is resulting in many local papers going out of business. Ethical Perspective 12–1 discusses how this is impacting news coverage in local communities.

Ethical Perspective 12–1 > > >

The Decline in Newspapers Is Creating More "News Deserts"

Do You Live in a News Desert?

In the U.S., 225 counties do not have a local newspaper. Half of all counties - 1,528 - have only one newspaper, usually a weekly.

No newspapers
One newspaper

Hussman School of Journalism and Media

The newspaper industry has been in steady decline due to readership and advertising revenue shifting to digital media. This affects not only the companies that publish newspapers but also the local communities that depend on newspapers and their core offering of news and information. Newspapers closing leaves many areas with no local paper. Over the past two decades nearly 1,800 newspapers have shut down, most of them (1,700) weeklies. According to a 2022 report by Northwestern University's Medill School of Journalism and Integrated Marketing Communications, since 2005 newspapers in the United States have been closing at an average of two a week, and the United States now has around 6,300 newspapers compared to 8,891 in 2005.

As more newspapers close down, the number of "news deserts" grows and many parts of the country no longer have a local paper. The University of North Carolina's Hussman School of Journalism defines news deserts as communities in which the inhabitants have no local newspaper or are facing notably diminished access to the news and information that are necessary in a grassroots democracy. It is estimated that some 70 million Americans live in a county with either no local news organization or only one. Most of the areas without a source of local news tend to be poorer, older, and less educated than those covered well. As can be seen in the accompanying image, 200 counties in the United States do not have a local newspaper while half of the counties have only one newspaper, which is usually a weekly.

(continued)

Another manifestation of the problem is the emergence of "ghost newspapers," a term used by journalism professor Penelope Muse Abernathy to describe newspapers that still exist and publish, but do so as shadows of what they once were, with little original or in-depth reporting. The rise in ghost newspapers is caused by either the loss of jobs in the newsroom or the consolidation of newspaper ownership, which results in less attention to communities' local news. Media consultant Brad Adgate notes the number of mergers and acquisitions in the industry negatively impacting newspapers. Today, the 25 largest publishing companies control about one-third of all newspapers, up from 20 percent in 2004, and they control two-thirds of all daily newspapers. Hedge or private equity funds as owners of newspapers collectively control nearly half of daily newspapers in the United States. These large funds are known for cutting costs to make profit goals, which often means the laying off of journalists. About one-half of all newspapers have changed ownership in the past 15 years and most of those sold have been family run or operated by small private regional publishers. Newspapers have long been considered the primary source of local news for a community, and local interest has been a primary driver of their readership. Brad Adgate notes that the loss of independent ownership takes away the focus on community news and events that traditionally has kept local newspapers relevant.

After the initial waves of consolidation, there has been a recent trend of some smaller newspapers being sold back to local owners. Media experts such as Professor Abernathy note local ownership is always best for the community where the newspaper is located as local owners know the market and the residents. The importance and value of local newspapers to communities and their citizens and businesses has been recognized by the federal government, which is considering legislation to address the crisis facing local news outlets. The Local Journalism Sustainability Act introduced in 2021 would use tax credits to let news outlets hire more journalists and help subscribers and advertisers pay for their services. Under the proposed legislation, local newspaper subscribers could see up to $250 in tax credits to offset subscription costs while advertisers in local newspapers would get up to $500 in tax credits for purchasing ads in local newspapers. The measures could offer a temporary lifeline, while another bill, the Journalism Competition and Preservation Act, would address yet another problem facing newspapers by enabling news publishers to negotiate to get fair compensation for the content they create that is used by others, especially digital media. As news and advertising has moved from the printed page to the web page, tech giants such as Google and Facebook have reaped the benefits, scooping up ad revenue while squeezing the news outlets that create the content on which those online platforms rely. According to the News Media Alliance, an association that represents about 2,000 outlets, as much as 70 percent of digital ad revenue goes to Google and Facebook and their respective parent companies, Alphabet and Meta.

While politicians are paying more attention to the problem and the proposed legislation may help local newspapers, the collapse of newspapers' advertising-supported business model and the consolidation of the newspaper industry have not let up. Whether local newspapers can survive or more news deserts and ghost newspapers will emerge in the future remains a question.

Sources: David Bauder, "US Newspapers Continuing to Die at Rate of 2 Each Week," *AP News*, July 1, 2022, https://apnews.com/article/journalism-united-states-39ef84c1131267233768bbb4dcaa181b; Orion Donavon-Smith, "Can Congress Save Local News? Two Bills Backed by Northwest Lawmakers May Help," *The Spokesman-Review*, June 13, 2022, https://www.spokesman.com/stories/2022/jun/12/can-congress-save-local-news-two-bills-backed-by-n/; Brad Adgate, "Newspapers Have Been Struggling and Then Came the Pandemic," *Forbes*, August 20, 2021, https://www.forbes.com/sites/bradadgate/2021/08/20/newspapers-have-been-struggling-and-then-came-the-pandemic/?sh=1eba35512e64; Penelope Muse Abernathy, *News Deserts and Ghost Newspapers: Will Local News Survive?* (Chapel Hill, NC: University of North Carolina Press, 2020).

Online Delivery and Multiple Platforms

As we have seen, the digital transformation of media has hit the newspaper industry particularly hard and resulted in newspaper publishers broadening their portfolios well beyond the traditional print editions. Nearly every major newspaper now has a website, and most make their papers available online and through apps for mobile devices. Over the past decade, the digital newspaper audience has increased to just over 200 million unique users per month, with half of the newspaper digital audience composed of those using mobile devices (smartphones and tablets) to access newspaper content.[41] Publishers recognize that they must offer digital versions of their newspapers as this has become the preferred mode of reading for many people, particularly younger consumers. Studies have shown that people who read digital versions of newspapers are highly engaged and are an upscale audience—they spend more time online, are better educated, and have higher incomes than do online audiences in general. They are also more likely to make purchases online and to use the Internet to help them decide what to buy.[42]

The newspaper industry is focusing on increasing revenue generated by their digital editions from both advertising and subscription fees. Digital advertising accounted for nearly a third of newspaper ad revenue in 2018, up from 17 percent in 2011, and grew to nearly 40 percent in 2022. Over the next several years the United States is expected to become the first major media market in the world to see digital newspaper advertising revenue surpass that from print ads.[43] However, revenue from online advertising has not been able to compensate for the decline in money received for print advertising, as online ad rates are significantly lower than those for print ads. Marketers generally are not willing to pay as much for online newspaper ads as there are an enormous number of advertising options on the Internet and social media, driving down prices. Moreover, the click-through rates on most banner and video ads that appear in digital editions of newspaper are minuscule, meaning that newspapers have been trading traditional print advertising dollars for digital pennies.

Newspapers are trying to generate more revenue from circulation by charging readers for access to their digital content. The newspaper industry initially put content online for free to attract online readers. Display advertising on their websites and/or digital editions hopefully would generate revenue. To increase revenue from digital editions, a number of newspapers have implemented paywalls that require readers to pay for a digital subscription or be denied access. These digital pay plans may allow a certain number of free articles each month; however, readers must pay for full access to the newspaper and/or an unlimited number of articles. Digital editions of newspapers also help stabilize print circulation because access is often offered for free or at a reduced rate to print subscribers.

Newspapers are responding in other ways to the digital future. Many are working to attract advertising dollars from local as well as national advertisers. Networks are also forming to help local newspapers sell online ads on their websites to national advertisers. These networks provide national advertisers with access to digital editions of newspapers across the country and facilitate the purchase of online ads in the same way as with traditional print ads. While newspaper publishers are focusing more attention on the sale of digital advertising, they are also facing strong competition from the major Internet search players such as Google, Yahoo!, Bing, and Local.com because these companies have made it inexpensive and easy for local companies to run ads with them. Many newspapers are forming alliances with these Internet search competitors whereby they can use their technology to sell more sophisticated ad offerings, such as behaviorally targeted ads.[44]

Most newspaper publishers are transforming themselves into *media* companies with products that include print and online newspapers, apps for those who read newspapers on mobile devices, and websites that include multiple products and services. They are also working to generate revenue from a variety of other areas, including offering digital marketing services, providing analytics, helping businesses connect directly with consumers through e-commerce transactions, and expanding their integrated marketing capabilities to include event marketing and promotional services. Exhibit 12–28 shows how the *San Diego Union-Tribune* promotes the various digital and analytics solutions it offers to advertisers. By creating a variety of products and services and engaging consumers across multiple platforms, newspapers can capitalize on new revenue opportunities that will undoubtedly present themselves in the future.

EXHIBIT 12–28

The *San Diego Union-Tribune* offers a number of digital tools and analytics to advertisers.

The San Diego Union-Tribune

Summary

Magazines and newspapers, the two major forms of print media, play an important role in the media plans and strategy of many advertisers. Magazines are a very selective medium and are valuable for reaching specific types of customers and market segments. The three broad categories of magazines are consumer (which includes farm), business, and health care publications. Each of these categories can be further classified according to the publication's editorial content and audience appeal.

In addition to their selectivity, the advantages of magazines include their excellent reproduction quality, creative flexibility, long life, prestige, and readers' high receptivity to magazine advertising, as well as the services they offer to advertisers. Disadvantages of magazines include their high cost, limited reach and frequency, long lead time, and the advertising clutter in most publications.

Advertising space rates in magazines vary according to a number of factors, among them the size of the ad, position in the publication, particular editions purchased, use of color, and number and frequency of insertions. Rates for magazines are compared on the basis of cost per thousand, although other factors such as the editorial content of the publication and its ability to reach specific target audiences must also be considered.

Newspapers are a very important medium to local advertisers, especially retailers. They are also used by national advertisers, although the differential rate structure for national versus local advertisers is a source of controversy. Newspapers are a broad-based medium that reaches a large percentage of households in a particular area. Newspapers' other advantages include flexibility, geographic selectivity, reader involvement, and special services. Drawbacks of newspapers include their lack of high-quality ad reproduction, short life span, lack of audience selectivity, and clutter.

Both magazines and newspapers are facing major disruption from digital media. The popularity of social media along with the increasing use of mobile devices, such as tablets and smartphones, to access content has lowered circulation and readership of traditional magazines and newspapers, which has impacted their value as advertising media. Print editions have seen major declines in advertising revenue. Many magazines have ceased publishing print editions and offer digital versions only, while newspapers are focusing more on their digital publications. Magazines and newspapers are taking other steps to respond to the digital disruption such as broadening their platforms beyond print editions and working closely with advertisers to offer them more services and build stronger relationships with them.

Key Terms

selectivity 409

gatefolds 411

bleed pages 411

split runs 416

controlled-circulation
    basis 419

pass-along readership 420

total audience/readership 420

first cover 421

second cover 421

third cover 421

fourth cover 421

magazine networks 422

native advertising 425

display advertising 429

classified advertising 429

preprinted inserts 430

city zone 433

retail trading zone 433

general advertising rates 434

retail or local advertising rates 434

standard advertising unit (SAU) 435

flat rates 435

open-rate structure 435

run of paper (ROP) 435

preferred position rate 435

combination rates 435

Discussion Questions

1. Discuss the challenges facing the newspaper and magazine industries. How are these challenges affecting their role as advertising media? (LO 12-1, 12-4, 12-7)

2. Discuss the role of magazines as part of an advertiser's media strategy. What are the advantages and limitations of magazines? (LO 12-1, 12-2)

3. Find an example of a business or health care magazine and analyze the market that reads this publication. Discuss the types of companies that might advertise in this magazine. (LO 12-1, 12-2)

4. If you were purchasing magazine advertising space for marketers of fitness products such as workout clothing or athletic shoes, what type of magazines would you use? Would your media plan be limited to health and fitness magazines or would you run ads in other types of publications? Explain. (LO 12-3)

5. What are the different factors advertisers must consider in purchasing advertising space in magazines and newspapers? (LO 12-3, 12-6)

6. The Association for Magazine Media has promoted the value of advertising in traditional print magazines by citing research showing that print advertising is superior to online ads with regard to its ability to deliver a reading experience that supports comprehension of and connection with an advertiser's message. Discuss some of the reasons why print ads may be superior to online ads. (LO 12-4)

7. Discuss why so many magazines are ceasing publication of their print editions and publishing digital editions only. Do you think magazines can survive by publishing digital editions only? (LO 12-1, 12-4)

8. Why have national newspapers such as *The New York Times* and *The Wall Street Journal* been successful at increasing their subscribers despite the decline in newspaper readership? Discuss some of the reasons marketers advertise in these papers. (LO 12-1, 12-5)

9. Discuss how the factors involved in the decline in newspaper readership in the United States have impacted news coverage in many local markets. What are the implications of the closing of many local newspapers for advertising in addition to good journalism? (LO 12-5, 12-7)

10. What are the advantages online magazines and newspapers offer for advertisers? Find the online media kit of a magazine or newspaper and analyze how the publisher is promoting the digital edition to prospective advertisers. (LO 12-4, 12-7)

13 Support Media

Amazon.com, Inc.

Learning Objectives

LO13-1 | Describe the role of support media in an IMC program.

LO13-2 | Identify traditional and nontraditional support media in the development of an IMC program.

LO13-3 | Compare the advantages and disadvantages of support media.

LO13-4 | Describe how audiences for support media are measured.

LO13-5 | Describe how to measure the effectiveness of support media.

Now Streaming: Virtual Product Placements

We have all seen them—whether we noticed them or not—because they are in TV shows (both linear and streaming), movies, books, on the radio, in sports and music videos, in video games, and seemingly everywhere advertisers think they have a chance to expose you to their products and brands. Also referred to as imbedded marketing, the practice has been around since the 19th century when Jules Verne published his novel *Around the World in 80 Days* and was lobbied by shipping companies to include their names in his book. But what may have really led to product placement's current popularity started in the early 1980s when the alien in the movie *E.T.* was lured out of hiding by children giving him Reese's Pieces. It is now estimated that product placement is a $23 billion dollar industry with a very bright future.

As more and more consumers are "cutting the cord" and eschewing traditional programming in favor of streaming services (65 percent of paid video subscribers had three or more subscriptions in 2021), the opportunities for advertisers to get their products in front of consumers are on the decline. One of the popular reasons cited for switching to streaming is that consumers can often pay extra for ad-free programming and not have to watch commercials at all. The same is true online, as consumers become increasingly fed up with the number of ads they receive once they use search and/or through retargeting. One potential way of getting around this is through product placements, and while they may not be the same as a commercial, they also can get the product or brand in front of viewers without the intrusiveness of ads. For example, in the chapter opening photo, M&M's was able to get their product placed in this scene in a noticeable yet unobtrusive way. Advances in technology through artificial intelligence and machine learning are enhancing the efficacy of product placements.

For example, BENlabs, currently one of the leading product placement companies, which is owned by Microsoft founder Bill Gates, is teaming with data company 605, which captures information from set top boxes and smart TVs. The combination of the technologies of the two companies allows for sending targeted messages for different products to viewers watching the same scene of the same show. TripleLift offers a similar option instantly in which a viewer in Arizona could see a character in a scene drinking a can of Mt. Dew while one in Delaware will be drinking Dr Pepper. Unlike traditional placements, the amount of waste coverage is significantly reduced. Amazon and Peacock are taking product placements to a new level through virtual product placements (VPPs). In the past, product placements had to be inserted into the programming during production. Now, using VPP technology the placements can be digitally placed even *after* the filming has been completed. (The technology has already been used in sports broadcasts through virtual banners in NBA games or on pitchers' mounds in major league baseball.)

There are some who are not so enamored with the potential increase in product placements in shows that we watch. Their fear is if attention to ads continues to decline and revenues from advertisers decreases while use of product placements increases, viewers may become inundated with placements. As noted by Kelly Gilblom, "Still, more data-driven hypertargeting of product placement could stoke the same kind of consumer pushback that online digital ads have received." Others are concerned with placements' effectiveness. Carolina Portela, VP and director of strategic investment at Magna, asks, "What is the value of just having a branded soda on the table in the background? Are consumers even going to notice that? I'm not sure." Others ask if the viewer will become engaged given the brief exposure provided by a placement. Measurement issues continue to be an issue with some advertisers—an issue that BENlabs and others are aware of and addressing.

So, are product placements the potential savior for advertisers? While many think so—which accounts for the increases in placements and expenditures in this area—there are also many who say to move more slowly. And if Stacy Jones, CEO of Hollywood Branded, is correct that "The majority of product placement in film and television happens on a quid-pro-quo basis rather than in exchange for payment," it may be a different silver bullet that needs to be sought.

Sources: Sophie Haigney, "Anatomy of a Product Placement," *New York Times*, June 24, 2022, www.nytimes.com; Ryan Barwick, "Product Placement Is Going to Take Over Your Favorite Show," *Marketing Brew*, May 12, 2022, www.marketingbrew.com; Jeremy Goldman, "Amazon, NBCUniversal Take Product Placement to Another Level via Ad Formats Unveiled at NewFronts," *eMarketer*, May 6, 2022, www.emarketer.com; Kelly Gilblom, "Product Placement, Now Starring in the Streaming Era," *Bloomberg Businessweek*, August 16, 2021, www.bloombergbusinessweek.com.

We refer to the media discussed in this chapter as support media, but the fact is—as you will see—these media continue to grow in importance to the marketer, and the past decade or so has seen a significant increase in expenditures on them. As marketers look for more and more ways to get their messages to consumers, and consumers seemingly look for more and more ways to avoid them, many of these media have demonstrated their effectiveness. Over the past few years there has been significant growth in the use of support media—both traditional and new media forms. In many ways, the consumers' efforts to avoid commercial exposure may have had an opposite effect, as it seems ads now appear in many places not previously home to such messages.

Ads have appeared on manhole covers, inside restroom stalls, on bus shelters, in grocery stores, on hubcaps, on cell phones, and even on people's bodies. In this chapter, we review a number of support media, some that are new to the marketplace and others that have been around awhile. We discuss their relative advantages and disadvantages, how they are used, and audience measurement of each. We refer to them as **support media** because the media described in the previous chapters dominate the media strategies of large advertisers, particularly national advertisers. Support media are used to reach those people in the target market whom the primary media may not have effectively reached and to reinforce, or support, their messages. It is important to remember that some of these media are not used only for support, but for some companies they may be the primary or sole medium used.

You may be surprised at how many different ways there are to deliver the messages and how often you are exposed to them. You may also be surprised at how the number and types of media keep expanding and how effective they can be. Let's begin by examining the scope of the support media industry and some of the many alternatives available to marketers.

THE SCOPE OF THE SUPPORT MEDIA INDUSTRY

Support media are referred to by several titles, among them **alternative media**, **below-the-line media**, **nonmeasured media**, and **nontraditional media**. These terms describe a vast variety of channels used to deliver communications and to promote products and services. In this chapter we will discuss many of these media (though, as you might imagine, it would be impossible for us to discuss them all).

Many advertisers, as well as the top 100 advertising agencies, have increased their use of support media, and as new alternatives are developed, this use will continue to grow. Given the rapid emergence of a variety of new media, we will further divide support media into *traditional* and *nontraditional* support media categories. There are actually hybrids as well because some traditional media have adapted to the new media environment by updating their offerings. There is no particular necessity for this further distinction other than to demonstrate that many of the various forms of support media have been around for quite some time, while others have surfaced only recently. Let us examine some of these in more detail.

TRADITIONAL SUPPORT MEDIA

Out of home (OOH) advertising media encompass many advertising formats found out of the home (see Figure 13-1). As can be seen, the Out of Home Advertising Association of America (OAAA) categorizes these media as out of home—including billboards, street furniture, place-based media, and transit. As shown in Figure 13-2, billboards and transit constitute the majority of the outdoor billings. Given the similarity of these forms, we will discuss them together and then address other forms of media.

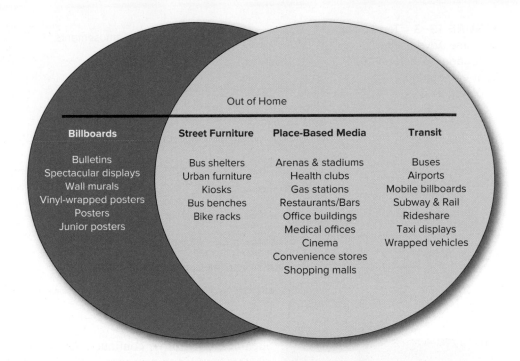

Out of Home

Billboards	Street Furniture	Place-Based Media	Transit
Bulletins	Bus shelters	Arenas & stadiums	Buses
Spectacular displays	Urban furniture	Health clubs	Airports
Wall murals	Kiosks	Gas stations	Mobile billboards
Vinyl-wrapped posters	Bus benches	Restaurants/Bars	Subway & Rail
Posters	Bike racks	Office buildings	Rideshare
Junior posters		Medical offices	Taxi displays
		Cinema	Wrapped vehicles
		Convenience stores	
		Shopping malls	

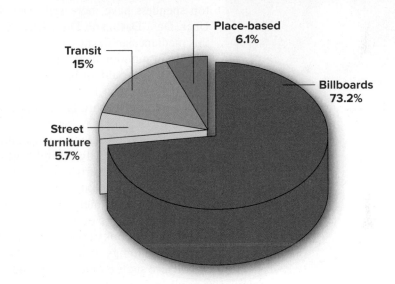

Place-based 6.1%

Transit 15%

Billboards 73.2%

Street furniture 5.7%

Out of Home Advertising (OOH)

OOH advertising has probably existed since the days of cave dwellers. The Egyptians and the Greeks used it as early as 5,000 years ago. OOH is certainly one of the more pervasive communication forms, particularly in urban and suburban areas.

While showing steady growth since 2000, OOH advertising has continued to grow in revenues to an estimated $8.6 billion for 2022.[1] Like all other media, the pandemic resulted in a decrease in expenditures in outdoor in 2020 following a decade in constant increases. However, in 2021 and 2022 revenues showed a strong rebound. The medium was once dominated by tobacco advertisers (25 percent of its $1.5 billion revenue came from cigarette advertising in 1991), so there were concerns in the industry when an agreement was reached with 46 states in November 1998 to ban all cigarette ads. Increased expenditures from local services and amusements, insurance, real estate, and telecom companies have more than made up for the losses. Companies like McDonald's, Apple, Geico, Amazon, AT&T, and Coca-Cola are some of the top spenders in this medium. As shown in Figure 13-3, OOH continues to be used by a broad client base, a

FIGURE 13–3 Top 10 Out of Home Advertising Categories (based on 2021 year-end outdoor expenditures)

1. Miscellaneous local services and amusements

2. Retail

3. Media and advertising

4. Restaurants

5. Government, politics, and organizations

6. Public transportation, hotels, and resorts

7. Financial services

8. Insurance and real estate

9. Schools, camps, and seminars

10. Automotive dealers and services

Reprinted with permission of Out of Home Advertising Association of America.

EXHIBIT 13–1

Billboards can be attention-getting.

Robert Landau/Alamy Stock Photo

EXHIBIT 13–2

This Oops campaign was designed to get attention.

Sam Mellish/Getty Images

demonstration of its continued acceptance in the industry. A number of factors have led to new entries into the top spenders in outdoor while past top spenders have increased expenditures as well. Advertisers including Uber, Door Dash, and Duck Duck Go have increased their expenditures in this medium significantly since 2020, while companies that have advertised heavily in outdoor in the past such as McDonald's and Apple have also increased their outdoor budgets.

A major reason for the continued success of outdoor is its ability to remain innovative through technology. As Exhibit 13–1 shows, billboards are no longer limited to standard sizes and two dimensions; 3-D forms and extensions are now used to attract attention. Digital OOH media have also contributed to the success. Digital messages on billboards, transit signs, and in stores have allowed more advertisers to participate since messages can be changed quickly and often. In addition, it allows OOH advertising to appear in places previously unavailable, and in a timely fashion (Exhibit 13–2). You probably have been exposed to either signboards or electronic billboards at sports stadiums, in supermarkets, in the campus bookstores and dining halls, in shopping malls, on freeways, or on the sides of buildings, from neon signs on skyscrapers in New York City to Mail Pouch Tobacco signs painted on the sides of barns in the Midwest. This is truly a pervasive medium.

Out of home advertising, particularly billboards, does have its critics. Ever since Lady Bird Johnson tried to rid the interstate highways of billboard advertising with the Highway Beautification Act of 1965 during her husband's presidency, there has been controversy regarding its use. As previously noted, legislation has passed in 46 states banning the advertising of cigarettes on billboards. In addition, a number of cities and states in the United States and internationally have banned or restricted the use of billboards. In some cities, existing billboards can remain, but once they are gone, they can no longer be replaced.

Digital Out of Home (DOOH) One of the fastest-growing out of home industries is that of **digital out of home (DOOH) media**. DOOH media take two forms: (1) video advertising networks, which include digital video screens that appear in offices, stores,

EXHIBIT 13–3

A variety of companies use blimps as an advertising medium.

SOPA Images Limited/Alamy Stock Photo

theaters, transit networks, and entertainment venues such as health clubs, sporting arenas, bars, and restaurants; and (2) digital billboards, or screens that transmit in LED (light-emitting diode) or LCD (liquid crystal display) technologies. Digital billboards include large boards found at sports and entertainment venues, retail locations (like malls), in transit locations (like terminals), and at roadsides or large traffic locations. Place-based advertising, which is not a purely DOOH medium, often uses digital technology to send its messages. These typically include smaller signs that appear in restrooms, on stairs, on personal vehicles, and on specialty items. The global DOOH signage segment is expected to reach $21.6 billion by 2027 due to its ability to be creative, attract attention, and engage the consumer.[2]

Place-Based Out of Home Media

Several other forms of OOH advertising are also available, including aerial advertising, interior and exterior place-based, and more. OAAA classifies these as place-based media. Let's examine a few of these.

Aerial Advertising   Airplanes pulling banners, skywriting (in letters as high as 1,200 feet), and blimps all constitute another form of outdoor advertising available to the marketer: **aerial advertising**. Generally these media are not expensive in absolute terms and can be useful for reaching specific target markets. For example, Coppertone has often used skywriting over beach areas to promote its tanning lotions, beer companies (among others) commonly employ aerial advertising at sporting events, and local advertisers promote special events, sales, and the like. Exhibit 13–3 shows one of the many products, services, and/or events that have used this medium and one that you are probably familiar with.

In-Store Media   Advertisers use **in-store media** such as in-store ads, aisle displays, store leaflets, shopping cart signage, and in-store TV to reach shoppers at the place where they buy, as discussed in IMC Perspective 13-1. A study by MEC Sensor and BMRB International revealed that one-third of shoppers say in-store ads influence them to make a purchase decision, 44 percent say they notice such ads, and 75 percent of those who noticed the ads said they are likely to purchase the advertised brand.[3]

Much of the attraction of point-of-purchase media is based on figures from the Point of Purchase Advertising International (POPAI) that states that approximately two-thirds of consumers' purchase decisions are made in the store; some impulse categories demonstrate an 82 percent rate.[4] Many advertisers are spending more of their dollars where decisions are made now that they can reach consumers at the point of purchase, providing additional product information while reducing their overall marketing efforts.

Miscellaneous Out of Home Media

As shown in Figure 13-4, there are numerous OOH media available, adding to the pervasiveness of this medium. The next time you are out, take a few moments to observe how many different forms of outdoor advertising you are exposed to.

Transit Advertising

Another form of OOH advertising is **transit advertising**. Transit is targeted at the millions of people who are exposed to commercial transportation facilities, including buses, taxis, commuter trains, trolleys, airplanes, and subways.

IMC Perspective 13–1 >>>

Now We Are Even Watched in Retail Stores: Is Privacy Dead?

Hardly a day goes by that you don't hear or read something about our rights to privacy. Your bank and/or credit card company sends you its privacy policy. Facebook and other sites are in the news for not protecting your personal information. You already know that the retail stores you visit online will lead to subsequent pop-up ads. Everywhere you go—from retail stores to banks to gas stations—you are on camera. While it may bother some of us, most people have become oblivious to being watched. One has to wonder just how far it will all go. In 2021 it was estimated that there were more than 85 million surveillance cameras deployed in the United States. Could it get worse? The answer is yes, and not just for security purposes.

Now, if you want privacy, it may not even be safe to shop at the grocery cooler. The next time you are standing in front of your cooler door looking over the contents, a camera could be watching you—and it's not because the grocer is making sure you don't steal something. Companies like Mood Media and Cooler Screens are now making a pitch to retailers to install cameras to watch shoppers while they stand in front of the cooler doors looking inside. Not only do the cameras watch you, they also use the information acquired to try to guess your age and gender—even your mood—and then send you a real-time target ad on an in-store video screen. You probably don't even know you are being watched, because the camera has only a penny-sized lens.

The Kroger Company (which owns Ralphs and Food 4 Less stores) and Walgreens (which owns more than 8,000 drugstores) have tested the technology, which uses the camera information to create ads that are displayed on a screen or, in the case of Walgreens, on the cooler doors along with a list of the contents inside. After discerning your gender and age range and tracking your eye movement and emotional response when looking at a product, an ad appears. For example, if someone the technology reads as a man is standing in front of a cooler containing drinks, a Coke Zero ad may appear because the product is more frequently purchased by men. A woman might receive a Diet Coke ad. A 20-year-old might receive a Red Bull ad, while a slightly older man might receive a Gatorade one. Later in the day, as dinner time approaches, if you pick up some beer, you might be sent a message offering you a special price on a DiGiorno pizza if you buy a six-pack of Coors Lite. You might also receive others reminding you that the diet drinks are zero calories or that the product you were just considering is now on sale. Cooler Screens has already booked advertising deals with Coca-Cola, Pepsi, Nestlé, Molson Coors, and Anheuser Busch, among other top consumer packaged-goods companies. This is not all that is being tracked while you are shopping. Ronny Max identifies 19 ways that retailers are now tracking your store movements including quantifying behaviors by motion (where customers go and how long they stay there); eye tracking and eye tilting, facial demographics, and so on; body movements; and emotional sentiments. Besides being mounted on coolers or other areas in the store, tracking

Cooler Screens Inc.

beacons can be mounted on shopping carts and baskets without the shopper knowing they are there. Companies like Mood Media, GeoCTRL, and Cooler Screens offer their own tracking tools to retailers.

While the tech companies and the packaged-goods sellers argue that the cameras and screens lead to a better shopping experience, not everyone is so sure. As noted earlier, the camera lenses are very small and not obvious to the customer. Supposedly, the data collected is anonymous. Pam Dixon, executive director of the World Privacy Forum, and Ryan Calo, a professor at the University of Washington School of Law, both contend that even if this is so, the use of the technology can lead to discriminatory practices in different ways. As noted by Dixon, "We shouldn't be gathering the emotional state of anyone." Consumers themselves seem to have mixed reactions. Most appear not to notice them, and at least one customer has said he wasn't concerned because there are "cameras everywhere." Others have expressed dislike about the fact they are being used if and when they do find out. Apparently not all stores notify customers they are being watched, which Katharine Schwab, writing in *Fast Company*, refers to as a "problematic lack of transparency that leads to serious privacy considerations." Some retail operations executives, including John Furner, CEO of Walmart Inc.'s Sam's Clubs, and Jon Reilly, VP of commerce for consulting agency Publicis Sapient, have also voiced privacy concerns.

Reilly expects that it won't be long before the cameras are widely used. Indeed, Cineplex Digital Media has screens that can be placed in malls or at bus stops and, eventually, at drive-through restaurants. I guess we'd better get used to it, as they will all know how we are feeling.

Sources: David Friend, "Why Smart Cities Will Accelerate Video's Move to the Cloud," *Security Info Watch*, November 26, 2021, www.securityinfowatch.com; Ronnie Max, "19 Technologies of People Tracking," Behavior Analytics Retail, October 6, 2022, www.behavioranalyticsretail.com; Joseph Pirani, "Smile, Say 'Cheese!' and Then Purchase It," *Los Angeles Times,* April 25, 2019, pp. C1, 3; Katharine Schwab, "It's Not Just Google or Facebook: The Freezer Aisle Is Ad Targeting You Now," *Fast Company*, February 6, 2019, www.fastcompany.com.

Number of Out of Home Displays (2022)			
Billboards	**Street Furniture**	**Transit**	**Place-Based**
Bulletins	**Bus Shelters**	**Airport**	**Arenas/Stadiums**
173,985	64,838	27,970	1,338
Digital Billboards	**Urban Street Furniture**	**Digital Airport**	**Cinema**
11,500	57,866	3,150	34,800
Posters	Bus benches	**Buses**	**Digital Place-Based**
145,000	Bike kiosks	1,354,842	750,000
Junior Posters	Newstands	**Rail/Subway**	**Interior Exterior Printed**
19,000	Outdoor kiosks	356,773	550,406
Wall Murals	Urban panels	**Digital Rail/Subway/ Transit**	Gas stations
2,310	**Digital Street Furniture**		Convenience stores
	10,815	16,466	Restaurants/bars
	Bus shelters	**Mobile Billboards**	Medical point of care
	Newsstands	4,515	Office buildings/elevators
	Outdoor kiosks	**Taxis**	Grocery stores
	Urban panels	21,000	**Shopping Malls**
		Digital Taxis/Rideshare	24,255
		71,400	**Digital Shopping Malls**
		Vehicle Wraps	12,507
		441,0000	

FIGURE 13-4

Out of Home Displays

Transit advertising has been around for a long time, but recent years have seen a renewed interest in this medium. While one might think that the increased usage of the Internet might have hurt transit advertising and out of home advertising in general, a number of other factors have contributed to its attractiveness. Studies have shown that (1) people are spending more time outdoors; (2) awareness and recall of transit ads is high; and (3) many consumers consider transit ads environmentally friendly. Add to this the fact that younger people often consider transit as more economically practical and you can see why this medium has remained popular.[5] McDonald's, Sprint, Frito-Lay, the United Way, numerous state lotteries, and others like transit's lower costs, frequency of exposures, flexibility, and point-of-sale presence. The California Beef Council found that 42 percent of rail commuters in Northern California saw its beef ads inside terminals in just one month and as a result developed more positive attitudes toward beef.[6]

Types of Transit Advertising There are actually four forms of transit advertising: (1) mobile billboards, (2) inside cards, (3) outside posters, and (4) station, platform, or terminal posters.

Mobile Billboards Another OOH medium is **mobile billboards**. Some companies paint their cars with ads; others paint trucks and vans. Still others put ads on small billboards, mount them on trailers, and drive around and/or park in the geographic areas being targeted (Exhibit 13-4). Costs depend on the area and the mobile board company's fees, though even small and large organizations have found the medium affordable. A number of studies have shown that mobile billboards can lead to a high number of impressions; a study conducted by the organization Product Acceptance & Research indicates that mobile ads lead to high levels of recall and readership and were likely to have an impact on sales.[7]

EXHIBIT 13-4

Mobile billboards can take interesting and unusual forms, from donkeys in Mexico to the sides of trucks.

Source: (left) (a) Michael Belch; (right) (b) Global Warming Images/Shutterstock.

A number of companies including Walmart, Home Depot, and State Farm are frequent users of mobile ads.

Inside Cards If you have ever ridden a commuter bus, you have probably noticed the **inside cards** placed above the seats and luggage area advertising restaurants, TV or radio stations, or myriad other products and services. As noted earlier, companies now advertise on digital screens in transit vehicles, which deliver news, video ads, restaurant information, and so forth. The ability to change the message and the visibility provide the advertiser with a more attention-getting medium.

Transit cards can be controversial. For example, in the New York subway system, many of the ads for chewing gum, soup, and Smokey the Bear have given way to public service announcements about AIDS, unwanted pregnancies, rape, and infant mortality. While subway riders may agree that such issues are important, many of them complain that the ads are depressing and intrusive.

Outside Posters Advertisers use various forms of outdoor transit posters to promote products and services. These **outside posters** may appear on the sides, backs, and/or roofs of buses, taxis, trains, and subway and trolley cars. In fact, some of the ads have become so popular that Uber and Lyft drivers have found them to be an excellent source of additional revenue. Some cities, like Los Angeles, have found them so common and distracting, they once considered legislation to ban them.[8]

The increasing sophistication of this medium is demonstrated by a technology, developed by Vert, Inc. (a division of Clear Channel), that transforms ads on top of taxicabs into real-time animated electronic billboards. A web server that communicates with a global positioning satellite (GPS) is built into the taxi-top screen. The GPS determines the taxi's location and sends it to the local server, which then delivers the relevant ads for a particular area. A taxi traveling through a Hispanic community can have a message in Spanish, stock quotes could appear in the financial district, and so on. The message can also be changed by time of day—for example, to advertise coffee in the mornings and dinner specials later in the day. The ads appear in color in a format similar to banner ads, at 10 times the brightness of a TV screen (see Exhibit 13-5).

Station, Platform, and Terminal Posters Floor displays, island showcases, electronic signs, and other forms of advertising that appear in train or subway stations, airline terminals, and the like are all forms of transit advertising. As Exhibit 13-6 shows, **terminal posters** can be very attractive and attention-getting. Bus shelters often

provide the advertiser with expanded coverage where other outdoor boards may be restricted. Digital signs on subway platforms have become a common sight.

Advantages and Disadvantages of OOH advertising OOH advertising offers a number of advantages:

1. *Wide coverage of local markets.* With proper placement, a broad base of exposure is possible in local markets, with both day and night presence. Think about the millions of people exposed to billboards in Times Square!
2. *Frequency.* Because purchase cycles are typically for 30-day periods, consumers are usually exposed a number of times, resulting in high levels of frequency.
3. *Geographic flexibility.* OOH can be placed along highways, near stores, or on mobile billboards, almost anywhere that laws permit. For local advertisers, outdoor can reach people in specific geographic and/or demographic areas. Local, regional, or even national markets may be covered.
4. *Creativity.* As shown earlier, OOH ads can be very creative. Large print, colors, and other elements like digital signs attract attention.

EXHIBIT 13–6

Terminal posters can be used to attract attention.

I Wei Huang/Shutterstock

5. *Ability to create awareness.* Because of its impact (and the need for a simple message), OOH can lead to a high level of awareness. Seventy-eight percent of U.S. travelers say they have seen a transit ad.[9]

6. *Efficiency.* OOH usually has a very competitive CPM when compared to other media. The average CPM of OOH is often one-half of radio and far less than that of TV, magazines, and newspapers. Transit is one of the least expensive media in both relative and absolute costs.

7. *Effectiveness.* OOH advertising can be effective, as demonstrated by the California Beef example. In a study reported by BBDO advertising, 35 percent of consumers surveyed said they had called a phone number they saw on an OOH ad.[10] A study reported by Mukesh Bhargava and Naveen Donthu showed that OOH advertising can have a significant effect on sales, particularly when combined with a promotion.[11]

8. *Production capabilities.* Modern technologies have reduced production times for OOH advertising to allow for rapid turnaround time, and digital messages can be changed in minutes.

9. *Timeliness.* Many outdoor ads appear in or near shopping areas or on or in the vehicles taking customers there, thus resulting in timely exposures.

At the same time, however, there are limitations to outdoor, many of them related to its advantages:

1. *Waste coverage.* While it is possible to reach very specific audiences, in many cases the purchase of OOH results in a high degree of waste coverage. It is not likely that everyone driving past a billboard is part of the target market.

2. *Limited message capabilities.* Because of the speed with which most people pass by OOH ads, exposure time is often short, so messages are limited to a few words and/or an illustration. Lengthy appeals are not likely to be effective. Some transit forms are not conducive to creative messages.

3. *Wearout.* Because of the high frequency of exposures, OOH may lead to a quick wearout. People are likely to get tired of seeing the same ad every day.

4. *Cost.* Because of the decreasing signage available and the higher cost associated with inflatables, in some markets outdoor advertising can be expensive in both an absolute and a relative sense.

5. *Measurement problems.* One of the more difficult problems of OOH advertising lies in the accuracy of measuring reach, frequency, and other effects. (As you will see in the measurement discussion, this problem is currently being addressed, though it has not been resolved.)

6. *Image problems.* OOH advertising has suffered some image problems as well as some disregard among consumers.

In sum, OOH advertising has both advantages and disadvantages for marketers. Some of these problems can be avoided with other forms of out of home advertising.

Advantages and Disadvantages of Transit Advertising
In addition to sharing some of the advantages and disadvantages of other outdoor media, transit has a few more that are specific to this medium. Advantages of using transit advertising include the following:

1. *Exposure.* Long length of exposure to an ad is one major advantage of indoor transit forms. The average ride on mass transit is 45 minutes, allowing for plenty of exposure time. As with airline terminals, the audience is essentially a captive one, with nowhere else to go and nothing much to do. As a result, riders are likely to read the ads—more than once. A second form of exposure transit advertising provides is the absolute number of people exposed. About 34 million people ride mass transit every day, and over 9.9 billion rides are taken each year, providing a substantial number of potential viewers.[12]

2. *Frequency.* Because our daily routines are standard, those who ride buses, subways, and the like are exposed to the ads repeatedly. If you rode the same subway to

work and back every day, in one month you would have the opportunity to see the ad 20 to 40 times. The locations of station and shelter signs also afford high frequency of exposure.
3. *Cost.* The CPM for transit advertising is low on a relative cost basis.

Some disadvantages are also associated with transit:

1. *Reach.* While an advantage of transit advertising is the ability to provide exposure to a large number of people, this audience may have certain lifestyles and/or behavioral characteristics that are not true of the target market as a whole. For example, in rural or suburban areas, mass transit is limited or nonexistent, so the medium is not very effective for reaching these people.
2. *Mood of the audience.* Sitting or standing on a crowded subway may not be conducive to reading advertising, let alone experiencing the mood the advertiser would like to create. Controversial ad messages may contribute to this less-than-positive feeling. Likewise, hurrying through an airport may create anxieties that limit the effectiveness of the ads placed there. Except for New York City, ridership is down in all major U.S. cities. Concerns with safety and other factors have led to less ridership.[13]

Measurement in Out of Home Media

In 2019 the OAAA announced a new audience measurement system that had been in development for the previous 5 years. For years, the Traffic Audit Bureau (TAB) was the organization responsible for measuring audience for the out of home media industry. Using the TAB methodology as a basis, a new system called Geopath developed a number of changes to the TAB system, including changes to sources of data, research methodology, and others. The new system provides some of the information provided by TAB as well as additional information to be more current with the changing U.S. environment and business practices. The new Geopath system is considered to be an improvement over the traditional measure of opportunity to see, with a "likely to see" metric that can also provide demographic and ethnographic data. The new data included a combination of eye tracking, circulation, and travel survey data all combined into one rating by a coalition of research companies.[14]

A number of other sources of audience measurement and information are available:

- Competitive Media Reports provides information on expenditures on outdoor media by major advertisers.
- MRI-Simmons conducts research for the OAAA providing demographic data, exposures, and the like.
- Point of Purchase Advertising International is a trade organization of point-of-purchase advertisers collecting statistical and other market information on POP advertising.
- The Out of Home Advertising Association of America (OAAA) is the primary trade association of the industry. It assists members with research, creative ideas, and more effective use of the medium and has a website at www.oaaa.org. OAAA commissions outside research as well as its own—for example, the Nielsen Outdoor Advertising Studies.
- The American Public Transportation Association (APTA) provides ridership statistics, studies, and other transit usage information.

PROMOTIONAL PRODUCTS MARKETING

According to the Promotional Products Association International (PPAI), **promotional products marketing** is "the advertising or promotional medium or method that uses promotional products, such as ad specialties, premiums, business gifts, awards, prizes,

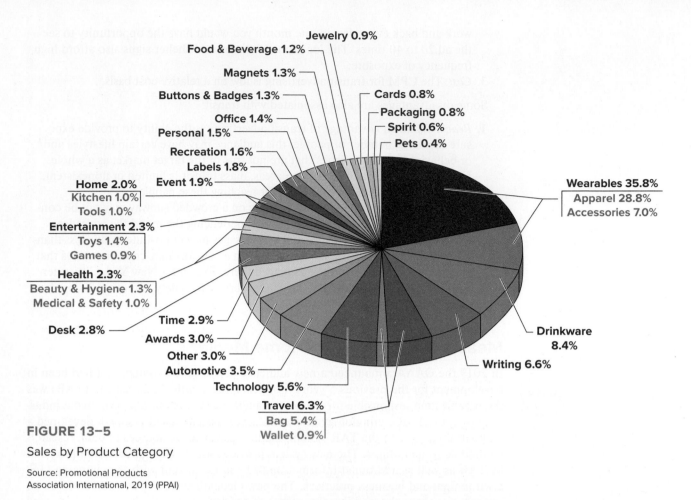

FIGURE 13–5

Sales by Product Category

Source: Promotional Products
Association International, 2019 (PPAI)

or commemoratives." Promotional products marketing is the more up-to-date name for what used to be called specialty advertising. **Specialty advertising** has now been provided with a new definition:

> A medium of advertising, sales promotion, and motivational communication employing imprinted, useful, or decorative products called advertising specialties, a subset of promotional products.
>
> Unlike premiums, with which they are sometimes confused (called advertising specialties), these articles are always distributed free—recipients don't have to earn the specialty by making a purchase or contribution.[15]

As you can see from these descriptions, specialty advertising is often considered both an advertising and a sales promotion medium. In our discussion, we treat it as a supportive advertising medium in the IMC program.

There are thousands of *advertising specialty* items, including ballpoint pens, coffee mugs, key rings, calendars, T-shirts, and matchbooks. Unconventional specialties such as plant holders, wall plaques, and gloves with the advertiser's name printed on them are also used to promote a company or its product; so are glassware, trophies, awards, and vinyl products. In fact, advertisers spend over $23.3 billion per year on specialty advertising items (Figure 13-5).[16]

If you stop reading for a moment and look around your desk (or bed or beach blanket), you'll probably find some specialty advertising item nearby. It may be the pen you are using, a thumb drive, or even a book cover with the campus bookstore name on it. Specialty items are used for many promotional purposes: to thank a customer for patronage, keep the name of the company in front of consumers, introduce new products, or reinforce the name of an existing company, product, or service. Advertising specialties are often used to support other forms of product promotions.

Advantages and Disadvantages of Promotional Products Marketing

Like any other advertising medium, promotional products marketing offers the marketer both advantages and disadvantages. Advantages include the following:

1. *Selectivity.* Because specialty advertising items are generally distributed directly to target customers, the medium offers a high degree of selectivity. The communication is distributed to the desired recipient, reducing waste coverage.
2. *Flexibility.* As the variety of specialty items in Figure 13–5 demonstrates, this medium offers a high degree of flexibility. A message as simple as a logo or as long as is necessary can be distributed through a number of means. Both small and large companies can employ this medium for a variety of objectives limited only by their own creativity.
3. *Frequency.* Most forms of specialty advertising are designed for retention. Key chains, calendars, and pens remain with the potential customer for a long time, providing repeat exposures to the advertising message at no additional cost.
4. *Cost.* Some specialty items are rather expensive (for example, leather goods), but most are affordable to almost any size organization. While they are costly on a CPM basis when compared with other media, the high number of repeat exposures drives down the relative cost per exposure of this advertising medium.
5. *Goodwill.* Promotional products are perhaps the only medium that generates goodwill in the receiver. Because people like to receive gifts and many of the products are functional (key chains, calendars, etc.), consumers are grateful to receive them. The products also lead to a favorable impression of the advertiser.
6. *High recall.* Specialties lead to high recall of both the advertisers' name and message.
7. *Supplementing other media.* A major advantage of promotional products marketing is its ability to supplement other media. Because of its low cost and repeat exposures, the simplest message can reinforce the appeal or information provided through other forms.

Promotional products have also been used to support trade shows, motivate dealers, recognize employees, and promote consumer and sales force contests.

Disadvantages of promotional products marketing include the following:

1. *Image.* While most forms of specialty advertising are received as friendly reminders of the store or company name, the firm must be careful choosing the specialty item. The company image may be cheapened by a chintzy or poorly designed advertising form.
2. *Saturation.* With so many organizations now using this advertising medium, the marketplace may become saturated. While you can always use another ballpoint pen or scratch pad, the value to the receiver declines if replacement is too easy, and the likelihood that you will retain the item or even notice the message is reduced. The more unusual the specialty, the more value it is likely to have to the receiver.
3. *Lead time.* The lead time required to put together a promotional products message is significantly longer than that for most other media.
4. *Reach.* Use of other media—such as television—leads to greater reach.

Even with its disadvantages, promotional products marketing can be an effective medium.

Measurement in Promotional Products Marketing

Owing to the nature of the industry, specialty advertising has no established ongoing audience measurement system. Research has been conducted in an attempt to determine the impact of this medium, leading to the following results:

- 70 percent report having received a promotional product in the last 12 months.
- 88 percent recalled the advertiser's name.
- 83 percent say they like receiving promotional products.

- 38 percent say it is a constant reminder of the advertiser.
- 53 percent of those using the promotion used it once a week.
- 71 percent generally keep it.[17]

In a study conducted at Georgia Southern University, it was shown that promotional products had a positive impact on brand image, leading to a more positive perception of the business and a higher likelihood of recommending the business.[18] In addition, another study showed that by adding promotional products to an integrated media mix, brand impressions and purchase intent could be increased.[19]

The Promotional Products Association International (www.ppai.org) and the Advertising Specialty Institute are two of the leading trade organizations of the field. The PPAI helps marketers develop and use specialty advertising forms. It also provides promotional and public relations support for specialty advertising and disseminates statistical and educational information.

OTHER TRADITIONAL SUPPORT MEDIA

There are numerous other traditional ways to promote products. Some are reviewed here.

Advertising in Movie Theaters

Another method of delivering a message that is increasing quickly (to the dismay of many) is the use of movie theaters to promote products and/or services. And while many moviegoers may still not like the fact that they are asked to watch ads after paying admission to the theater, recent research indicated that 62 percent of moviegoers claimed to enjoy the ads.[20] Commercials shown before the film and previews, with both local and national sponsorships, are now regularly shown in movie theaters. In addition, ads in theater lobbies, at kiosks, and on popcorn tubs and drink cups are used. Automotive, food, and package-goods companies and regional and local companies are just some of the product categories that find this medium attractive. Movie theater ad sales were expected to reach $444 million in 2022.[21]

Consumer reaction to ads in movie theaters is apparently mixed. A number of earlier studies showed that most people thought these ads were annoying or very annoying, although now people may be becoming more used to them or, as noted, actually are enjoying them. The Cinema Advertising Council (CAC) reported that 63 percent of moviegoers say they do not mind ads before the movie starts.[22] Another CAC study indicated that 72 percent of moviegoers who recalled an ad in cinema had not seen the ad on TV. Of those who had seen both TV and cinema ads, 32 percent preferred the cinema ad.[23] On the other hand, many consumers complain that having paid for a ticket, they shouldn't have to sit through ads and/or commercials.

Nevertheless, a number of products and brands have used this advertising medium, including IKEA, KFC, Google, BMW, Old Navy, and Taco Bell, among others Exhibit 13-7 is an example of an in-theater ad that Frito-Lay runs for two of its brands, Cheetos and Doritos. Numerous brands have developed commercials specifically for the purpose of being shown before movies. In addition, a research study commissioned by one in-theater advertising broker showed that the ads were three times more likely to be remembered than TV ads.[24]

Advantages of Movie Theater Advertising   Movies provide a number of advantages to advertisers, including the following:

1. *Exposure.* While a number of factors have led to declines in movie attendance from the over 1.3 billion tickets sold in 2018, including rising ticket costs, TV movie streaming, inflation, and the COVID-19 pandemic, the movie industry appeared to be gaining back viewers again in 2022. From a low of only 221 million attendees in 2020, 2021 showed an increase of 122 percent, and forecasts were optimistic that the growth would continue. Even at the lower figures, potential exposures are high.[25]

EXHIBIT 13-7

This Flamin' Hot Doritos and Cheetos ad features sloths and other animals having a party.

Zoonar GmbH/Alamy Stock Photo, Frito-Lay North America, Inc.

2. *Emotional attachment.* One report found that 41.5 percent of moviegoers say they become emotionally attached to cinema ads and brands—more than to the ads on the broadcasts of the *Super Bowl, Summer Olympics, World Series,* or the *Oscars.*[26] One neuromarketing research study showed movie-ad viewers to be much more engaged than those watching TV spots.[27]

3. *Cost.* The cost of advertising in a theater varies from one setting to the next. However, it is low in terms of both absolute and relative costs per exposure.

4. *Attention.* Movie watchers pay attention to the ads shown in theaters. Research indicates that cinema ads reach many consumers who say they are usually ad avoiders. These consumers are 157 percent more likely to see an ad in a movie than in any other medium.[28]

5. *Clutter.* Lack of clutter is another advantage offered by advertising in movie theaters. Most theaters limit the number of ads.

6. *Proximity.* Since many theaters are located in or adjacent to shopping malls, potential customers are "right next door." (Of moviegoers, 74 percent combine the activity with dining out.)[29]

7. *Segmentation.* A key advantage of movie advertising is the ability to target specific demographic segments. The profile of the moviegoer is above-average in education and affluence. The movie titles and ratings enable advertisements to reach specific groups.

8. *Quality.* The high-quality production including sight and sound allow more creative and attention-getting ads.

9. *Integration.* Those who download movies online are actually more likely to attend a movie than is the typical adult.[30]

Disadvantages of Movie Theater Advertising   Some of the disadvantages associated with movie theaters as advertising media follow:

1. *Irritation.* Perhaps the major disadvantage is that many people do not wish to see advertising in these media. A number of studies suggest these ads may create a high degree of annoyance. If true, this dissatisfaction may carry over to the product itself, to the movies, or to the theaters.

2. *Cost.* While the cost of advertising in local theaters has been cited as an advantage because of the low rates charged, ads exposed nationally are often as much as 20 percent higher than an equal exposure on television. CPMs also tend to be higher than in other media.

NONTRADITIONAL SUPPORT MEDIA

Branded Entertainment

As noted in the lead-in to this chapter, one of the major changes (along with the growth of social and mobile media) that has occurred in the area of integrated marketing communications over the past few years is the enormous growth associated with **branded entertainment**. Branded entertainment is a form of advertising that blends marketing and entertainment through television, film, music talent, and technology. Essentially, the goal is to use entertainment media to gain consumers' attention and exposure to products and/or brands. It is extremely difficult to place a dollar amount on branded entertainment, but there is no doubt that its use continues to increase yearly.

Let's take a look at the ways companies use branded entertainment. Simon Hudson, Endowed Chair in Tourism and Hospitality at the University of South Carolina, suggests that there is a subtle difference between product placements and branded entertainment that many overlook, and the two should be considered at opposite ends of a continuum.[31] On one end of the continuum are product placements, which Hudson describes as only a visual or verbal passive placement of the brand, with no integration into the program, movie, and so on. At the other end is branded entertainment, in which the brand is woven into the story line at a much higher level of integration. At the same time, the effectiveness of the strategy chosen (placement vs. branded entertainment) will be impacted by the media used, the brand characteristics, consumer attitudes toward brand placements, and other factors, including regulations.

Product Placements   While **product placements** account for only a small portion of major advertisers' budgets, the use of this medium has increased tremendously in recent years and is likely to continue to do so. Just a little over a decade ago, the majority of product placements were free or not offered in exchange for products or services. Estimates are that in 2012 paid product placement spending reached $4.75 billion—by 2019, it was $11.44 billion.[32] In 2020, it had reached $23 billion, most of which is in the United States.[33] It should be noted, however, that it is difficult to assess the accuracy of these figures, as many product placements are free or provided in exchange for trade. At one time, product placement agencies contended that as much as 70 percent to 95 percent of their placements were for trade;[34] an in-depth study of the product placement industry by Russell and Belch supported this contention and, as noted in the lead-in to this chapter, this appears to still be the case.[35] Industry analysts expect this trend to continue as placements move from traditional media to alternative media, providing additional communication outlets, and as people continue to attempt to avoid ads and marketers continue to look for more ways to get their products in front of you without actually advertising. Placements have caught on in Europe; the UK has now approved product placements on television, although they impose more restrictions than in the United States.[36]

Interestingly, product placement in movies and on TV is not a new phenomenon; placements are known to have existed as early as the 1930s and were commonly employed via soap operas in the 1950s. However, it was not until the turn of the century that the number of placements skyrocketed. Today, product placements are used to gain exposure by numerous companies large and small and are a very important part of the IMC strategy for companies like Apple, Nike, BMW, GM, and KFC, among others as noted in Figure 13-6. Much of the logic behind product placement is that since the placement is embedded in the script or program setting, it cannot be avoided, thereby increasing exposure. Given the lack of intrusiveness of the placement, consumers may not have the same negative reactions to it as they may have to a commercial. Further, research has demonstrated that association with a program or movie—or particularly with a celebrity—may enhance the image of the product and, in some instances, lead to increased engagement and sales.[37]

FIGURE 13–6

A Sampling of Product Placements	
Program	**Brand/Product**
Curb Your Enthusiasm	Clover cottage cheese; Perrier water; Pacific chicken broth
Euphoria	Cheerios
Riverdale; *How I Met Your Father*; *Love in the Time of Corona*; *Below Deck*; *Heels*; others	Core Hydration
Ozark; *Succession*; *The Sex Lives of College Girls*; *Sex and the City*; others	Dell computers
Grace and Frankie; *Dead to Me*; *Never Have I Ever*; *Book Club*; *Sweet Magnolias*; others	Zillow
And Just Like That	Peloton
House of Cards	Blackberry
Grace and Frankie; *Inventing Anna*; *Curb Your Enthusiasm*; *Fuller House*; others	Cheerios

Source: Sophie Haigney, "Anatomy of a Product Placement," *New York Times*, June 24, 2022, www.nytimes.com

Given the intense growth in the number of product placements, some marketers are concerned that placements may become too common. It is rare to watch a movie or TV show without being exposed to one or more placements. Given the obvious attempt to gain exposure in many of these, placements may become more obvious; consumers may perceive them more like ads and, as a result, they may have less impact on the viewer. Some industry watchdogs have called for more regulation of placements, contending that they blur the lines between advertising and programming and therefore may be deceptive.

At this time, however, product placements continue to increase in number. Films have included as many as 60 or more placements in less than a 2-hour movie. In addition, placements are appearing in media and situations never before imagined, including music videos, video games, and books. Subway, Coca-Cola, and even President Obama (when running for president) have used product placements in video games, while Oreos, Hershey Kisses, and Netflix have received plugs in books. Some of these were paid placements; others were not.

Product Integration A more involved form of product placements actually leads to the placement being integrated throughout the program content and/or script. In **product integration** the product is woven throughout the program or becomes the program itself. Like product placements, product integrations are on the increase as the networks continue to search for new program content, and the proliferation of cable media channels affords marketers with numerous integration opportunities. For example, on an episode of *Modern Family*, much of the show was devoted to the family's bumbling of the father's request for an Apple iPad for his birthday and their frantic efforts to find one. When the family actually obtained one, the program ended with the father sitting on the couch with the iPad in his lap, enjoying the product.[38]

In another instance, in the movie *Avengers: Age of Ultron*, 20 minutes of the action takes place in downtown Seoul, Korea, thanks to a contribution from the city of $3.6 million for production costs.[39] Under Armour collaborated with 20th Century Fox on production of the movie *The Martian* and created a microsite around star Matt Damon's training regimen. A full broadcast of *The Tonight Show Starring Jimmy Fallon* was done on Samsung Galaxy S10 cell phones. The phone was used to film

Jimmy Fallon and his guests at various New York locations in "an attempt to break through the noise and get people to engage in a way that best communicates the benefits of your products," said Patricio Paucar, Samsung's VP of marketing. Apparently, the collaboration was a part of a larger advertising deal between Samsung and NBC Universal.[40] Exhibit 13-8 shows how Lexus was integrated into the movie *Black Panther*.

Advertainment The creation of video and/or music content by an advertiser in an attempt to entertain viewers while advertising their products is known as **advertainment**. While companies make use of branded entertainment to link their brand with those forms of entertainment they want customers to identify them with, advertainment is "the blend of advertising and entertainment. The aim of advertainment is to make ads so entertaining that viewers genuinely want to keep watching them."[41] For example, Beyoncé's viral "I Was Here" music video designed to promote World Humanitarian Day was created by Droga5—an agency specializing in the creation of advertainment. The same agency created *Follow Phoenix* to promote Spotify's feature that allows users to follow musicians on their service with the click of a button. The 18-minute documentary, which lived on YouTube's homepage for a day, followed the band *Phoenix* for 24 hours in segments in an attempt to get more subscribers to Spotify. Perhaps the most classic piece of advertainment was the Red Bull-sponsored Stratos space jump (Exhibit 13-9). The live stream of skydiver Felix Baumgartner jumping from 127,900 feet and landing on his feet while breaking the record for the world's highest free fall was viewed live by 7.1 million viewers. That was way back in 2012!

Another form of advertainment is that of **advergames**. A number of companies including Chipotle and Burger King have developed online games designed to promote their products through electronic games. These games are designed to advertise products, brands, or organizations across social media, company websites, and mobile apps. For example, the Chipotle game called *Food With Integrity* guided players through 4 worlds and 20 levels. Those who made it through were rewarded with a "buy one, get one free" offer at Chipotle restaurants. The game led to 6.5 million users on YouTube in 2 weeks and a sales spike. On the flip side, the game (as well as those from other companies) has come under attack from some watchdog groups such as the Berkeley Studies Media Group and Bath University's Institute for Policy Research, among others, for being deceptive because those who played the games were not aware it was an advertisement.[42] Numerous other companies have created advergames with the purpose of getting potential consumers involved with their brand.

As noted by Helena Alcoverro, "Don't confuse advergaming with the ads that are inserted inside a video game. The ads that you see when playing a game are actually banners or display advertising. In advergaming, the presence of the brand is not secondary, but constitutes the core of the game." Alcoverro notes that the games are usually free, distributed online, and compatible with different types of devices.[43] In addition to Chipotle, other companies such as Chex, KFC, and LEGO have employed this form of marketing, as has Axe which has increased expenditures in an attempt to reach its gen Z target market.

Content Sponsorship   Rather than developing their own content, some advertisers agree to sponsor specific programs, receiving product placements, integration, and promotions in return. HGTV offers sponsorships to companies built around remodeling, gardening, home decorating, and more. Heineken has collaborated with the FIFA, and Rolex with the ATP World Tennis Tour. North Face had a significant content sponsorship in the Masters of Snowboarding webcast, and The Food Network and Travel Channel offer a variety of sponsorship opportunities. Turner Broadcasting offers content sponsorship opportunities on the Cartoon Network and Boomerang as well as some of its other channels. Content sponsorships are also common on the Internet; Calvin Klein and *Vanity Fair* and One a Day and *Eating Well* are just two examples of collaborations.

Ad-Supported Video on Demand (AVOD)   VODs are specialized content programs offered online and by some cable TV networks that are developed by advertisers and provided to the cable operators for free. For example, General Motors produced a short feature on the history of the Corvette to be shown on CNN through Time Warner and Comcast's VOD channels. MTV launched a series called *How to Show* in which musicians, athletes, and celebrities offer the "tricks of their trades" (the U.S. Air Force was the first advertiser). A number of TV shows have been made available as well; the San Diego Zoo provides a video tour to San Diego cable subscribers. Roku and Dish's Sling TV have some of the most robust VOD offerings, while Walmart is now offering original programming, as is Amazon. While ad-supported VOD has been around for a number of years, a number of factors resulting from changes in the way people watch TV have led *Ad Age* to consider AVOD as the hottest trend in streaming, expected to experience triple-digit growth from 2022 to 2027.[44] Disney has announced that they will launch ad-supported video on demand joining Roku, PlutoTV, Discovery+, Peacock, and Hulu.[45] A study conducted by *IPSOS* showed that running VOD ads in conjunction with regular TV advertising (versus just TV ads alone) could result in higher ad recall, purchase intent, and likelihood of talking about the brand with family and friends, as well as searching for the brand online and visiting the brand's website, than did TV ads alone.[46]

Others   While other forms of branded entertainment continue to develop through wireless, mobile, and "branded locations," space does not allow us to discuss each in detail. Suffice it to say that the use of branded entertainment continues to increase and will continue to do so as more and more technological innovations provide opportunities.

Advantages of Branded Entertainment   A number of advantages of branded entertainment have been suggested:

1. *Exposure*. In regard to product placements, a large number of people see movies each year. The average film is estimated to have a life span of 3.5 years (with 75 million exposures), and most moviegoers are very attentive audience members. When this is combined with the home video market and network and cable TV (including HBO, Showtime, and the Movie Channel), the potential exposure for a product placed in a movie and on television is enormous. And this form of exposure is not subject to zapping, at least not in the theater. High exposure numbers are also offered for TV placements, based on the ratings and the possibility to direct the ad to a defined target market.

2. *Frequency*. Depending on how the product is used in the movie (or program), there may be ample opportunity for repeated exposures (many, for those who like to watch a program or movie more than once). For example, if you are a regular watcher of the programs containing placements and/or integrations, you will be exposed to the products placed therein a number of times. Syndication will result in additional exposures.

3. *Support for other media*. Branded entertainment supports other promotional tools. A trend is to have the client that is placing the product cross-promote the product and movie tie-in in multiple media venues. As noted, the tie-ins reinforce and are reinforced by ads and commercials. It is now very common for advertisers to tie in to movies.

4. *Source association*. In Chapter 6 we discussed the advantages of source identification. When consumers see their favorite TV celebrities or movie stars using certain brands, the association may lead to a favorable product image or even to sales. In one study of 524 8- to 14-year-olds, 75 percent stated that they notice when brands are placed on their favorite shows, and 72 percent said that seeing a favorite character using a brand makes them want to purchase that brand.[47] Another study among adults showed that one-third of viewers said they try a product after seeing it on a TV show or movie.[48]

5. *Cost*. While the cost of branded entertainment may range from free to hundreds of thousands of dollars, the latter is an extreme. The CPM for this form of advertising can be very low, owing to the high volume of exposures it generates. For many products, like the Apple iPad in the *Modern Family* episode, the placements may be free because they save the TV or movie producers the expense of having to pay for the cost of the products.

6. *Recall*. A number of firms have measured the impact of product placements on next-day recall. Results ranged, but most show recall is higher than for TV commercials.

7. *Bypassing regulations*. In the United States as well as many foreign countries, some products are not permitted to advertise on television or to specific market segments. Product placements and integrations have allowed the cigarette and liquor industries to have their products exposed, circumventing these restrictions. For example, in the popular cable TV show *Jersey Shore*, in one scene a sack of Marlboro cigarettes washed up onto the beach, raising the specter of a placement. Philip Morris disclaimed any involvement.[49] The Marin Institute, an alcohol industry watchdog group, filed suit against Budweiser for its tie-ins to the movie *The Wedding Crasher*, arguing that the movie encouraged underage drinking. Spirits manufacturers Diageo, Bacardi USA, and Brown-Forman have also been named in lawsuits for similar reasons.[50] Other companies have been accused of advertising junk foods to kids through placements, and—as noted—through video games.[51]

8. *Acceptance*. Studies have shown that viewers are accepting of product placements and in general evaluate them positively, though some products (alcohol, guns, cigarettes) are perceived as less acceptable. Other studies report similar results, with one showing that as many as 80 percent of consumers say they have a positive attitude toward placements.[52] In a study conducted with tweens, 43 percent said they found placements to be funny, 39 percent found them to be

informative, and 35 percent found them entertaining and interesting.[53] A study by *eMarketer* reported similar results.[54] In a meta-analysis of 364 studies on various aspects of product placements appearing in *The International Journal of Research in Marketing* in 2021, the authors concluded that placements have (1) a strong effect on memory, (2) a small to modest effect on salience, attitudes, and conation, and (3) prominent effects on memory but not persuasion.[55]

9. *Targeting.* Content sponsorships and VOD may effectively reach potential customers with a strong interest in the subject matter (for example, fashion, football, biking).

Disadvantages of Branded Entertainment   Some disadvantages are also associated with branded entertainment:

1. *High absolute cost.* While the CPM may be very low for various forms of branded entertainment, the absolute costs may be very high, pricing some advertisers out of the market. The increased demand for branded entertainment, coupled with the rising emphasis by the studios on cross-promotions, drives costs up considerably. A study conducted by the National Association of Advertisers indicated that 79 percent of advertisers believe that the costs of branded entertainment deals are too high.[56] Some companies have ceased using this form of promotion, citing the rising costs.

2. *Time of exposure.* The way some products are exposed to the audience has an impact, but there is no guarantee viewers will notice the product. Some product placements are more conspicuous than others. When the product is not featured prominently, the advertiser runs the risk of not being seen (although, of course, the same risk is present in all forms of media advertising).

3. *Limited appeal.* The appeal that can be made in some of these media forms is limited. There is no potential for discussing product benefits or providing detailed information. Rather, appeals are limited to source association, use, and enjoyment. The endorsement of the product is indirect, and the flexibility for product demonstration is subject to its use in the medium.

4. *Lack of control.* In many movies, the advertiser has no say over when and how often the product will be shown. Many companies have found that their placements in movies did not work as well as expected. Fabergé developed an entire Christmas campaign around its Brut cologne and its movie placement, only to find the movie was delayed until February. Others have had their placements cut from the script.

5. *Public reaction.* Many TV viewers and moviegoers are incensed at the idea of placing ads in programs or movies. These viewers want to maintain the barrier between program content and commercials. If the placement is too intrusive, they may develop negative attitudes toward the brand. The increased use of placements and integrations has led many consumers to be annoyed by what they consider to be crass commercialization. The FTC has explored options for limiting placements without consumer notification, though they have not sought increased regulation to date. Still others are upset about programs such as *Undercover Boss* in which a CEO goes undercover in their own company to see how their employees work. Critics contend that these shows are nothing more than public relations disguised as programming.

6. *Competition.* The appeal of branded entertainment has led to increased competition to get one's product placed or integrated, increasing demand and costs. As noted, the number of product placements seems to be expanding exponentially.

7. *Negative placements.* Some products may appear in movie scenes that are disliked by the audience or create a less-than-favorable mood or reflect poorly on the brand. For example, in the movie *Missing*, a very good, loyal father takes comfort in a bottle of Coke; elsewhere in the movie, a Pepsi machine appears in a stadium where torturing and murders take place—not a good placement for Pepsi. Emerson—the manufacturer of the garbage

disposal brand In-Sink-Erator—sued NBC for showing a cheerleader getting her hand mangled in the program *Heroes*. NBC never received permission from Emerson to show the brand.

8. *Clutter*. The rapid growth of branded entertainment tie-ins has led to an overwhelming number of placements and integrations, as noted previously. Like other forms of advertising, too many placements and integrations will eventually lead to clutter and loss of effectiveness.

Measurement in Branded Entertainment   With the rapid growth in branded entertainment have come a number of research studies and companies attempting to monitor and measure the impact of this media form. At this time, there is no one accepted standard used by advertisers or industry members.[57] However, a number of high-profile companies now offer services in this area, including those listed below.

- *Nielsen Media Research*. The TV ratings company currently tracks product placements on network television. The company has plans to track cable programs in the near future.
- *Brandchannel Product Placement Watch*. While not specifically a measurement company, Brandchannel provides up-to-date information as to what is currently going on in the branded entertainment industry, including the annual Brandcameo Product Placement Awards.
- *Comscore*. The branded entertainment measurement service Comscore and product integration valuation company iTVX have combined efforts to measure Results-Oriented-Integration. The method values the quality of each hundredth of a second of an integration, and then translates them into a Product Placement/Commercial Cost Ratio to value the integration by comparing it to the value of a commercial.
- *BENlabs*. This company matches deterministic data from its viewership panel of over 22 million households with household-level data from third-party providers to measure sales across retail channels, in-store foot traffic, or visits to a website that stem directly from product placements.[58]

Guerrilla Marketing

In addition to branded entertainment, another nontraditional way that advertisers are now attempting to reach consumers is referred to by a variety of names, including guerrilla marketing, stealth, street, buzz, ambush, or viral marketing. Whatever it is called, there seems to be no end in sight to where advertisers will attempt to reach you. While previously targeted primarily to college students and others of the same age group, these efforts have now been expanded to reach additional audiences as well. Guerrilla marketers have benefited by technology in that they can be even more creative, as well as the fact that cell phones now have cameras, and through social media viewers can send pictures to others instantly.

A variety of well-known companies have used guerrilla tactics. Dominos employed "reverse graffiti" by stenciling removal graffiti clues in their "American Legends" campaign. The clues were part of a treasure hunt in which the brand invited people to find the ads, take a selfie, and upload them to the Internet for the chance to win a slice of pizza. With the help of a PR push, this campaign "produced 25 million online impressions in the first 3 months." To promote their movie *Red Sparrow*, 20th Century Fox used guerilla tactics to promote the film's upcoming release where 20 models were hired to dress up as Jennifer Lawrence's character and walk around the city handing out mysterious business cards. Each card had a kiss mark on one side and text on the other side, which read: "Red Sparrow Movie Premiere. All the showtimes in the nearest movie theatre." The models walked around handing out the cards to passers-by to promote the movie.[59]

Some marketers wonder if the guerrilla tactics are being taken too far. To promote the movie *Dead Man Down*, a viral agency tagged a scene with two men fighting on the floor of an elevator to the shock and chagrin of unsuspecting onlookers. In another, the floor seemingly falls out of an elevator while riders are in it (of course, there was a glass bottom). To promote Carlsberg beer, an unsuspecting man is aroused from his sleep by a friend who says he is desperate for money and asks him to bring $400 to a seedy bar. When the friend delivers, everyone raises a glass to salute friendship while it is all being caught on tape.

The stunts often go viral, but they are often very expensive to produce, risky, and sometimes even dangerous. Robert Thompson, a professor of popular culture at Syracuse University, thinks that the pranks may have gone "over the top."[60] Many others agree.

Miscellaneous Other Media

The variety of options for placing ads appears endless. Obviously, we have reported on only a few of these. Chapter 15 will discuss a few more, specifically online vehicles. Before leaving this chapter, however, we would like to mention a few of the faster-growing and more widely used options.

- *Branded phone calls.* First Orion, a communications agency, works with companies to replace the numbers displayed on phone calls by branded ad impressions. Each time the receiver gets a call, instead of the caller's phone number appearing on the phone screen, the name of the company calling does. A short targeted message can also be attached. The agency claims that the messages can improve answering rates by as much as 200 percent.
- *Satellite billboards.* A Canadian company has contracted with SpaceX to put a billboard into low-Earth orbit. Geometric Energy Corp. (GEC) announced that in 2022 it planned to blast a satellite into space aboard a SpaceX rocket that will allow advertising to be beamed from Earth and displayed on a pixelated screen on the side of the spacecraft.[61]
- *Parking lot ads.* An out of home medium showing increased growth is that of parking lot signage. From signs on cart docks to painting the walls of indoor parking garages, more companies are finding this medium attractive—particularly for point-of-purchase items. The ads reach a variety of demographics, depending on where they are placed. PepsiCo is just one of a number of companies employing this medium.
- *Gas station pump ads.* Screens appearing on gas pumps now reach you while you are pumping gas. What else do you have to do?

- *Place-based media.* The idea of bringing the advertising medium to the consumers wherever they may be underlies the strategy behind place-based media. TV monitors and magazine racks have appeared in classrooms, doctors' offices, and health clubs, among a variety of other locations. Many advertisers, particularly pharmaceutical companies, have found place-based media an effective way to reach their markets. Nielsen, MRI-Simmons, and others all provide audience reports. A study conducted by Millward Brown regarding customers' reactions to video ads at checkout counters in grocery stores indicated that over 70 percent of customers said they would watch the screen while in the checkout lines, 78 percent said the screens caught their attention, and 85 percent said the screens were entertaining and pleasant to watch.[62]
- *Others.* Just a few other examples of the use of support media: Coca-Cola installed 1,000 feet of light boxes in the Atlanta subway to show motion picture ads for Dasani; Muzak, a provider of background music, teamed with Tyme ATMs to broadcast ads at bank ATM sites; ads now appear on luggage conveyors at some airports, on MetroCards, on hubcaps, in elevators, on bowling balls, bike wheels, in people's homes, and on fruit. People are even allowing ads to be placed on their bodies, including their heads, necks, and thighs. A store in Kentucky offers a 20 percent discount to shoppers with the store's name tattooed in a visible location on the body, while the New Zealand Tourism Bureau uses heads (Exhibit 13–10). There are many other examples, as is demonstrated in Exhibit 13–11 (at least he earned something from the fight!).

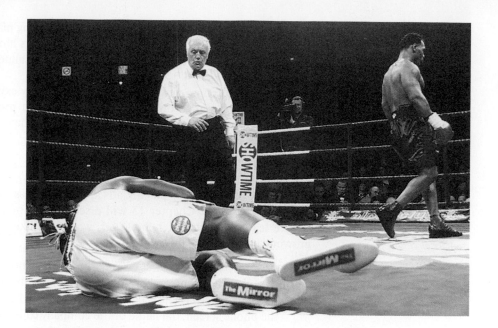

Advantages and Disadvantages of Miscellaneous Alternative Media

Advantages of alternative media include the following:

- *Awareness and attention.* Perhaps the major advantage of these tactics is their ability to attract attention. Given their novelty and the nontraditional locations in which they appear, they are likely to create awareness and gain attention.
- *Cost-efficiencies.* Because of the nontraditional nature of alternative media, many advertisers are using media not previously used for advertising or that, in general, do not require high expenditures. As such, the absolute and relative costs are not yet that high.
- *Targeting.* Depending on the tactic used, the campaign can be very targeted. It can be exposed only to a specific event, location, age, or interest group.

Disadvantages of alternative media include the following:

- *Irritation.* Unless the advertiser is careful, advertising placed in the wrong medium may have a negative impact, resulting in irritation, negative attitudes toward the advertiser, or even opportunities for the competitor. When Microsoft logos were painted on sidewalks, the city and consumers were not impressed and Microsoft was fined. One of its competitors gained significant public relations benefits when the company announced it would be happy to remove the paintings. (Reverse graffiti like that mentioned earlier is easy to wash off.) The City of New York was not very happy with Snapple when the company's giant Popsicle started to melt and created a flood in Union Square.
- *Wearout.* For now, many of these campaigns are novel and unique and are attracting consumer interest. As the number of efforts increases, however, there is the potential to lose the uniqueness associated with them.

Summary

This chapter introduced you to the vast number of support media available to marketers. These media, also referred to as nontraditional or alternative media, are just a few of the many ways advertisers attempt to reach their target markets. We have barely scratched the surface here. Support media include out of home advertising (outdoor, in-store, and transit), promotional products, and movie theater advertising, among many others.

The fastest-growing area is that of branded entertainment, including product placements, product integrations, and others.

Support media offer a variety of advantages. Cost, ability to reach the target market, and flexibility are just a few of those cited in this chapter. In addition, many of the media discussed here have effectively demonstrated the power of their specific medium to get results.

But each of these support media has disadvantages. Perhaps the major weakness with most is the lack of audience measurement and verification. Unlike many of the media discussed earlier in this text, most nontraditional media do not provide audience measurement figures. So the advertiser is forced to make decisions without hard data or based on information provided by the media.

As the number and variety of support media continue to grow, it is likely the major weaknesses will be overcome. When that occurs, these media may no longer be considered nontraditional or alternative.

Key Terms

support media 444
alternative media 444
below-the-line media 444
nonmeasured media 444
nontraditional media 444
out of home (OOH) advertising 444
digital out of home media 446

aerial advertising 447
in-store media 447
transit advertising 447
mobile billboard 449
inside cards 450
outside posters 450
terminal posters 450

promotional products marketing 453
specialty advertising 454
branded entertainment 458
product placements 458
product integration 459
advertainment 460
advergames 460

Discussion Questions

1. Product placements have continued to increase in use despite the fact that there are some who contend that they are ineffective. Cite reasons as to why these placements may or may not be effective. Provide examples to support your position. (LO 13-2)

2. As companies increase their efforts to track consumers' movements while shopping in a store, many consumers are concerned about these actions being an invasion of privacy. Explain why these consumers may feel this way. Should these tracking behaviors be curtailed? (LO 13-3)

3. Studies have shown that transit advertising—despite its sometimes being unattractive—continues to be an effective medium. Explain why this form of advertising is effective. (LO 13-5)

4. What are promotional products? Cite examples of how they are used by marketers. Explain whether or not they are effective. (LO 13-2)

5. The chapter identifies a number of "miscellaneous support media." Describe a number of other such media that you have seen. Who sponsored these ads? Explain whether you think they were effective. (LO 13-2)

6. Due to the variety of support media types, it is very difficult to provide a measure of effectiveness of these media as a whole. Discuss some of the methods used to attempt to measure the effectiveness of various types of support media. Are these measures useful to marketers? (LO 13-5)

7. This chapter discussed a number of new ways that marketers are trying to reach consumers. While some consider these media to be innovative, others are concerned that they may be an intrusion on consumers' privacy. What do you think? Should these methods be considered unethical? (LO 13-1)

8. The proliferation of places where ads now appear seems endless. From manhole covers to people's bodies, it seems like there is nowhere you can go without seeing an ad. Discuss some of the unusual places you have seen ads recently. Do you think this trend is likely to continue? Explain why or why not. (LO 13-3)

9. Advances in technology have allowed for the innovations that were discussed in this chapter. From billboards that track you on the highway to your digital home assistant, which may be tracking your conversations, it seems that our privacy is being infringed upon more and more. While some consumers do not care, others are outraged at what they consider to be an intrusion. Explain why this may be the case and give arguments on both sides. (LO 13-4)

10. When commercials first appeared in movie theaters, many moviegoers were outraged. Now one expects to see numerous commercials before the movie starts, with seemingly little pushback. Do you think commercials before the movie should be allowed? Why or why not? (LO 13-1)

14 Direct Marketing

Vantage_DS/Shutterstock

Learning Objectives

LO14-1 | Define direct marketing.

LO14-2 | Discuss the role of direct marketing in an IMC program.

LO14-3 | Identify strategies and tactics in the use of direct marketing.

LO14-4 | Compare the advantages and disadvantages of direct marketing.

Will Connected TV (CTV) Mean the End for DRTV?

In direct-response advertising, the new kid on the block is connected television (CTV). And like many newcomers entering a market, proponents of CTV believe it is the new Holy Grail. As noted by Natasia Langfelder, "CTV is television content streamed over apps and smart TVs, mobile devices, or over-the-top (OTT) devices such as gaming consoles, Amazon Firestick, Apple TV, Roku and other streaming devices." Also included in this list would be Hulu, YouTube Peach, and many others. Natasia also believes that direct-response TV as we have known it for decades is dead—killed by CTV.

Citing Nielsen figures that indicated the pandemic drove consumers indoors resulting in enormous gains in television viewing audiences and opportunities for direct-response marketers, she says even before that, CTV was starting to make inroads into the market. By the spring of 2021, the Leichtman Research Group had estimated that 80 percent of homes' televisions had at least one connected TV device, and as many as 64 percent had three or more. A report by Statista (among others) indicated that this number is likely to continue to grow, particularly among millennial audiences. Advertisers apparently share this optimism, as ad spend on CTV increased 57 percent in 2021 and was expected to grow an additional 39 percent in 2022.

In comparing CTV to traditional direct-response TV (DRTV), advocates believe there are a number of advantages to CTV besides the growing audience and the fact that it reaches the highly sought millennial audience. Proponents claim that CTV (1) can be better targeted and retargeted, (2) allows for types of data not available to linear or DRTV advertisers, (3) allows for more sophisticated testing of ads through A/B testing, and (4) avoids privacy issues due to noreliance on third-party cookies, among other factors. Natasia Langfelder provides three examples of successful use of CTV including the Defenders of Wildlife Organization, Fintech company Self, and Meineke, the national automotive repair franchiser.

But, as they say, look before you leap! Not everyone is so enthralled with CTV ads. An Ad Age–The Harris Poll study of television viewers revealed some "underwhelming" results regarding the "holy grailness" of shoppable ads. Nearly 80 percent of respondents said they don't want to watch ads during their programming, preferring to engage in multitasking activities like surfing other channels or checking their cell phones (certainly millennial activities!). Eighty percent prefer to see their ads before the program rather than during it, while 65 percent say they would turn off a show with too many ads in it while only 36 percent said they would buy from an in-show ad—a much lower percentage than touted by networks!

Perhaps most disturbing to the networks is the fact that the audience they very much want to reach, (e.g., millennials) may be the least likely to buy through shoppable ads as they are already some of the most likely to drop linear TV and subscribe to streaming programming, and are generally apathetic to advertising—particularly when frequency of exposure is high.

So, interestingly, while content providers are now pushing subscription services with tiered payment plans in which viewers can pay less to subscribe when ads are included or pay a premium for ad-free programming, on the other hand they are claiming the advantages of CTV. Among users of TV streaming platforms such as Sling and Hulu Live, 69 percent upgraded to the ad-free option. Of Xfinity Stream and Dish Anywhere the number is 65 percent, and among those who subscribe to Peacock and Discovery+ it is 61 percent.

So can these services have it both ways? Or is the Holy Grail really not a Holy Grail after all? If you are a direct-response marketer you need to know!

Sources: Interactive Advertising Bureau, "Digital Video Ad Spend Increased 49% in 2021 and Expected to Reach Nearly $50 Billion in 2022, According to IAB's 2021 Video Ad Spend and 2022 Outlook Report," May 2, 2022, www.IAB.org; Julia Stoll, "Number of Connected TV Users in the U.S. 2020–2025 by Generation," *Statista*, May 3, 2022, www.statista.com; Natasia Langfelder, "Direct Response TV Is Dead, Long Live Connected TV," Data Axle, April 14, 2021, www.dataaxle.com; Frankie Karrer, "Connected TV Statistics: Advertising, Viewership & Growth Trends," MNTN, October 17, 2022, www.mntn.com.

There were times when we thought of direct marketing as junk mail, direct-response ads on TV, telemarketing, infomercials, and other forms of marketing communication that we didn't hold in the highest esteem—and maybe we still think that. And the fact is that if we did (or do) think of direct marketers as unsophisticated, we would be dead wrong. Over the years, direct marketers have been some of the most effective and innovative practitioners of marketing strategies. The industry has always been adept at adapting to changes in the marketplace; from catalogs to direct-response TV ads, to infomercials to online, direct marketers have always been successful. Direct marketing has become a very important component of the IMC program, often working with other media as opposed to a stand-alone marketing tool. It is important to realize that there are numerous direct-marketing *tools* that can be used to reach one's target market. This chapter will focus our discussion on these direct media, their advantages and disadvantages, and their role in the IMC process.

DIRECT MARKETING

As we have discussed, many companies rely on a variety of promotional-mix elements to move their products and services through intermediaries, but an increasing number are going directly to the consumer. These companies believe that whereas promotional-mix tools such as advertising, sales promotion, support media, and personal selling are effective in creating brand image, conveying information, and/or creating awareness, going direct can generate an immediate behavioral response. Direct marketing is a valuable tool in the integrated communications program, though it usually seeks somewhat different objectives.

In this chapter, we discuss direct marketing and its role as a communications tool. Over the years companies have approached the market differently. There were companies who only sold to consumers directly, those who only sold through brick-and-mortar stores, and those who had physical environments and also sold through catalogs. The same is true today as you will see. Our focus here is more on direct marketing as a medium in the IMC program. For many companies and organizations, direct marketing is a key element in their IMC program, and for some marketers it has become the medium of choice for reaching consumers. We begin by defining direct marketing and then examine direct-marketing media and their use in the overall communications strategy. The section concludes with a basis for evaluating the direct-marketing program and a discussion of the advantages and disadvantages of this marketing tool.

Defining Direct Marketing

As noted in Chapter 1, **direct marketing** is a system of marketing by which organizations communicate directly with target customers to generate a response or transaction. By going directly to the consumer, the source avoids the extra costs and time involved in going through a middleman such as a retailer.

First we must distinguish between direct marketing and direct-marketing media. While direct marketing is now more commonly referred to as **direct to consumer (DTC)**, many business-to-business marketers also market this way. So as to be all inclusive, we will continue to use the term direct marketing. Direct to consumer marketing is an aspect of total marketing—that is, it involves marketing research, segmentation, evaluation, and the like, just as our planning model in Chapter 1 did. DTC marketing uses a set of **direct-response media**, including direct mail, telemarketing, interactive TV, print, the Internet, and other media. These media are the tools by which direct marketers implement the communication process.

The purchases of products and services through direct-response advertising currently exceed $155 billion in the United States.[1] Firms that use this marketing method range from major retailers such as the Gap, Restoration Hardware, and IKEA to airline companies to financial services and local companies as well as those who only sell direct such as dollarshaveclub.com and allbirds.com.

The Growth of Direct Marketing

Direct marketing has been around since the invention of the printing press in the 15th century. Ben Franklin was a very successful direct marketer in the early 1700s, and Warren Sears and Montgomery Ward were using this medium in the 1880s.

The major impetus behind the growth of direct marketing may have been the development and expansion of the U.S. Postal Service, which made catalogs available to both urban and rural dwellers. Catalogs revolutionized America's buying habits; consumers could now shop without ever leaving their homes.

But catalogs alone do not account for the rapid growth of direct marketing. A number of factors in American society have led to the increased attractiveness of this medium for both buyer and seller:

- *Consumer credit cards.* Estimates of the number of credit cards used by consumers in the United States vary widely, ranging from 365 million to 106 billion. Credit cards make it feasible for consumers to purchase both low- and high-ticket items through direct-response channels and assure sellers that they will be paid.[2] Americans hold about 3.84 cards each on average, with gen X, millennials, and gen Z charging the most.[3] Of course, not all of this is through direct marketing, but a high percentage of direct purchases do use this method of payment, and companies such as American Express, Discover, MasterCard, and Visa are among the heaviest direct advertisers, as well as the most commonly held. More and more companies are now requiring the use of a credit card (as opposed to checks or cash) for purchases, for example, airlines.
- *The changing structure of American society and the market.* One of the major factors contributing to the success of direct marketing is that so many Americans are now "money-rich and time-poor." The rapid increase in dual-income families has meant more income. An estimated 56 percent of women are now in the U.S. workforce, constituting 46.6 percent of all workers.[4] At the same time, the increased popularity of physical fitness, do-it-yourself crafts and repairs, and home entertainment has reduced the time available for shopping and has increased the attractiveness of direct purchases, as has the ease and time savings of online buying.
- *Technological advances.* The rapid technological advancement of electronic media and the Internet has made it easier for consumers to shop and for marketers to be successful in reaching the desired target markets. The ease and speed of shopping on the Internet, for example on Amazon.com, and having the purchase delivered to one's door is an attractive option that became even more so during the COVID-19 pandemic.
- *Miscellaneous factors.* A number of other factors have contributed to the increased effectiveness of direct marketing, including changing values and lifestyles, more sophisticated marketing techniques, more options, and the industry's improved image. These factors will also ensure the success of direct marketing in the future. The variety of companies employing direct marketing demonstrates its potential. Direct marketers are especially effective at adapting, as shown in IMC Perspective 14–1.

While some organizations rely on direct marketing solely to generate a behavioral response, for many others direct marketing is an integral part of the IMC program. They use direct marketing to achieve goals other than sales and integrate it with other program elements. We first examine the role of direct marketing in the IMC program and then consider its more *traditional* role.

IMC Perspective 14–1 >>>

The World of Direct Marketing

When you think of direct marketing, you might think of anything from Sears and Montgomery Ward catalogs to direct mail, infomercials, and other marketing tactics that have been used over the years to get your business. You may also think of competitors to retail. But you might not necessarily think of it as the powerful marketing tool that it is (isn't that why they call it junk mail?). One of the factors that has led to the success of marketing directly to the consumer is its ability to respond to marketing conditions and change as shown in the chapter opener. Well, direct marketing is changing again. This time it is the established companies and retailers that have now assumed the marketing strategies of an industry that for years they considered the competition. There was a time when some retailers would not carry items that were being sold direct. Those days have gone. Changing consumer behaviors and the adoption of new technologies have led to forecasts of triple direct marketing growth through 2025. For example, it seems that consumers *must* now have what they want in 2 days or less. Waiting is no longer an option. COVID-19 accelerated the growth of a storeless economy from a brick-and-mortar one by 200 to 300 percent according to a report by the IAB.

Legacy companies like P&G, Nike, Under Armour, and PetSmart are now entering the direct-to-consumer market. Walmart has expanded the number of in-store pickup kiosks to 1,700 stores so consumers can order online and pick up at the store. JCPenney has tested new in-store, interactive services including fitness and yoga classes, cooking demonstrations, kids clubhouses, relaxation lounges, and cafés.

Retailers and brands are reimagining in-store experiences to be multi-purpose (stores as lifestyle hangouts). They are leveraging technology for customer service experiences (e.g., cashierless stores and virtual try-ons) and utilizing shipping innovation to speed up delivery times points. Tesla Motors eschewed the long-established dealership model from the start, immediately going DTC. These brands, among many others, are growing their DTC businesses and counting on them for their future success. But why? And why now?

A number of reasons for the shift can be cited, but what it really comes down to is that market conditions have changed, and for many of these companies, the need to better understand the consumer has become even more critical. By dealing with their customers direct and establishing digital relationships, these companies feel they can develop a more personal relationship than was possible when it was the retailer making the contact. For example:

- *Consumers are demanding a better experience.* As consumers increasingly demand a more seamless purchase decision process, companies work harder and harder to keep them satisfied and (they hope) loyal. At the same time, if the manufacturer sells through a retailer, for example, it has no control over the selling interaction, how the product is sold, and whether or not the customer leaves happy and satisfied. The big brand companies realize that they may gain many more insights into what

factors influence the decision process and how, as well as gaining control over the interactions.
- *Relationship building.* While manufacturers feel the need to develop better relationships with their consumers, they also have to maintain positive relationships with their retailers. As noted, in the past, dealing direct could lead to the retailer refusing to carry a brand. Now that retailers are feeling the pinch of increased competition from some retailers, Amazon, and others, they are much more amenable to increased marketing support from manufacturers. By getting more involved with consumers directly, the Nikes and Under Armours of the world can provide more insights to the retailer, helping them sell more successfully as well. (Manufacturers have known this for years, but these relationships often have not worked out as planned.)
- *Data.* We exist in a world where, right now, big data is king. Many big companies are practically obsessed with gathering as much information about their customers and potential customers as they can. Direct to consumer (DTC) allows manufacturers to access data on buyers directly, more efficiently, and maybe more effectively than when there is a retailer involved. Effectively designed data collection can provide the manufacturer with a better understanding of the *why* behind the consumer's decision so that it can be used to develop strategies that increase engagement and loyalty.

The large legacy brands are attempting to enter the direct to consumer market in a variety of ways, including acquisitions (PetSmart buying e-commerce company Chewys, P&G acquiring Billie), mimicking successful strategies of competitors (AB InBev investing in e-commerce delivery, home brewers supplies, etc.), and strategic investments (PepsiCo partnering with food incubator The Hatchery and L'Oreal marketing a direct to consumer hair color brand). Retailer Lord & Taylor was sold to Le Tote. Having identified the need to engage in this market, they are now striving to find the best way to do so.

In their in-depth analysis of the DTC market, CB Insights provides examples of companies that have achieved success as start-ups challenging the larger companies by going direct—including Harry's Dollar Shave Club, Casper (mattresses), The Honest Company (baby products), Allbirds (sneakers), MeUndies with a subscription service to sell underwear, and a number of others. In short, each of these companies successfully provided what consumers wanted and the legacy companies either couldn't or wouldn't provide.

Isn't that what direct marketers always do?

Sources: "Brand Disruption 2022," IAB, November 28, 2021, www.iab.com; Natasia Langfelder, "5 Lessons from Thriving D2C Brands," Data Axle, August 30, 2022, www.dataaxle.com; "Big Brands Step into Direct-to-Consumer Space," WARC, February 18, 2019, www.warc.com; Claire Hopwood, "Why Direct-to-Consumer Is Becoming an Important Retail Channel," Alida, April 10, 2019, www.alida.com; "We Analyzed 12 of the Biggest Direct-to-Consumer Success Stories to Find Out the Secrets to Their Growth—Here's What We Learned," CB Insights, February 6, 2019, www.cbinsights.com.

EXHIBIT 14–1

This Vuori ad reflects who their target market is.

Vuori

The Role of Direct Marketing in the IMC Program

Long the stepchild of the promotional mix, direct marketing has now become an important component in the integrated marketing programs of many organizations. In fact, direct-marketing activities support and are supported by other elements of the promotional mix.

Combining Direct Marketing with Advertising

Obviously, direct marketing is in itself a form of advertising. Whether through mail, print, digital, or TV, the direct-response offer is an ad. It usually contains a toll-free number, always has a link, and sometimes has a form that requests mailing information. Sometimes the ad supports the direct-selling effort directly. For example, IKEA, Nordstrom, and Bloomingdale's among many others run image ads and commercials to support their store and catalog sales. Vuori Performance Apparel also markets through stores and online, supporting its efforts through advertising (Exhibit 14–1), which portrays the image of the Vuori user. In the past, some advertisers were reluctant to sell directly to customers, worrying that to do so might result in lost sales to retail stores. A study conducted by Forrester Research, Inc. showed just the opposite. More than half of manufacturers who sell on their e-commerce sites reported that the sites actually benefited stores, while only 9 percent said that it had a negative effect. In addition, 72 percent of responding companies said that selling online actually improved customer satisfaction.[5] Overall, the advertising was shown to support both direct and in-store sales positively.

Combining Direct Marketing with Public Relations   As you will see later in this text, public relations activities often employ direct-response techniques. Private companies may use telemarketing activities to solicit funds for charities or co-sponsor causes that use these and other direct-response techniques to raise funds. Likewise, corporations and organizations engaging in public relations activities may include toll-free numbers or website URLs in their ads or promotional materials. The ANA (Association of National Advertisers, formerly the Direct Marketing Educational Foundation) has worked with numerous organizations, small and large companies, and with students and faculty in support of environmental issues and assisting them in the use of direct media in their PR efforts.

Combining Direct Marketing with Personal Selling   Telemarketing and direct selling are two methods of personal selling used to generate sales. Nonprofit organizations like charities often use telemarketing (along with direct mail) to solicit funds. As you will see, for-profit companies—particularly those in the business-to-business market—have also used telemarketing to screen and qualify prospects (which reduces selling costs) and to generate leads. Direct-mail pieces are often used to invite prospective customers to visit auto showrooms to test-drive new cars; the salesperson then assumes responsibility for the selling effort. Automobile manufacturers and their dealers have both made effective use of this approach. Due to consumers' negative reactions to telemarketing, as well as a number of fraudulent activities perpetrated by unethical persons, telemarketing has seen a decline in use. The Federal Trade Commission's (FTC) passage of the Do Not Call Registry and actions that have been taken by consumers to screen calls have led to declines in this industry.

Combining Direct Marketing with Sales Promotions   How many times have you received a direct-mail piece notifying you of a sales promotion or event or inviting you to participate in a contest or sweepstakes? Ski shops regularly mail announcements of special end-of-season sales. Airlines send out mailers or e-mails announcing promotional airfares. Nordstrom and other retail outlets sometimes call

EXHIBIT 14-2

Costco sends promotional offers through the mail.

Costco Wholesale Corporation

EXHIBIT 14-3

BMW and Pinehurst Golf Resort partner on a direct-mail program.

Pinehurst, LLC

their existing customers to notify them of special sales promotions. Each of these is an example of a company using direct-marketing tools to inform customers of sales promotions. Costco regularly sends out flyers like the one shown in Exhibit 14-2 through direct mail that contain sales promotions being offered through both their warehouse and online sources. In turn, the sales promotion event may support the direct-marketing effort. A study conducted by Vertis indicated that marketers could increase the effectiveness of their direct-mail campaigns by offering exclusive deals and/or coupons. Seventy-two percent of adults surveyed said they had responded to a direct-mail offering of a buy-one-get-one-free offer, and 63 percent said they had responded to an offer of a percentage discount on merchandise. E-mails containing special offers, vouchers, or discounts have also been shown to be effective.[6] Databases are often built from the names and addresses acquired from a promotion, and direct mailers and/or telemarketing calls follow.

Combining Direct Marketing with Support Media Adding a promotional product to a direct mailer has proven to increase response rates. One company included a promotional product in half of its 10,000 mailers and not in the other half. The former generated 65 percent more orders. 3M used a promotional product as an incentive for people responding to a direct-mail offer. The incentive generated a 23 percent response rate versus only 9 percent for the regular mailer. Promotional products like refrigerator magnets, bookmarkers, and other items that can be easily inserted into the mailer are commonly used. A number of charitable organizations, such as Boys Town and St. Jude Children's Research Hospital, commonly send out notepads, mailing labels, pens, calendars, and notepads with requests for donations—particularly around the end of year holidays!

To successfully implement direct-marketing programs, companies must make a number of decisions. As in other marketing programs, they must determine (1) what the program's objectives will be, (2) which markets to target (through the use of a list or marketing database), (3) what direct-marketing strategies will be employed, and (4) how to evaluate the effectiveness of the program.

Direct-Marketing Objectives

Though more marketers now understand the contribution that direct marketing offers to the IMC program, the direct marketer usually seeks a direct response. The objectives of the program are typically defined in terms of behaviors—for example, test-drives, votes, contributions, and/or sales, and so on. A typical objective is defined through a sought response, perhaps a 2 to 3 percent response rate.

Not all direct marketing seeks a behavioral response, however. Many organizations use direct marketing to build an image, maintain customer satisfaction, and inform and/or educate customers in an attempt to lead to future actions. When President Obama kicked off his presidential reelection campaign, he did so with direct-response TV ads. The ads asked viewers to call an 888 phone number or visit JoinObama.com and enter their e-mail addresses and zip codes to get more involved in his reelection efforts. The success of the president's reelection campaign was attributed to these types of grassroots efforts. Exhibit 14-3 provides an example of how BMW and Pinehurst Golf Resort partnered to offer consumers special use of a BMW and a special package price for their vacation getaway. The two companies believe that they share a common target market profile and similar business philosophies of offering only the highest-quality product.

Direct-Marketing Strategies and Media

As with all other communications programs discussed in this text, marketers must decide the message to be conveyed, the size of the budget, and so on. Perhaps the major difference between direct-marketing programs and other promotional-mix programs regards the use of media.

Direct marketing employs a number of media, including direct mail, telemarketing, direct-response broadcasting, the Internet, and print. Each medium may be used to perform specific functions, although they all generally follow a one- or two-step approach.

In the **one-step approach**, the medium is used directly to obtain an order. You've probably seen TV commercials for products like wrench sets, workout equipment, or weight loss products in which the viewer is urged to phone a toll-free number to place an order immediately. Their goal is to generate an immediate sale when the ad is shown.

The **two-step approach** may involve the use of more than one medium. The first effort is designed to screen, or qualify, potential buyers. The second effort generates the response (that is, the order). For example, many companies use telemarketing to screen on the basis of interest and then follow up to interested parties with more information designed to achieve an order or use personal selling to close the sale. Some companies have evolved from a one-step to a two-step approach. For example, the magazine sales company Publishers Clearing House at one time employed a one-step approach by seeking subscriptions through direct mail. The company now has television commercials that tell potential consumers to watch for the mailers, or to go online to register to win (and buy magazine subscriptions!).

Direct Mail   Direct mail is often called "junk mail"—the unsolicited mail you receive. More advertising dollars continue to be spent in direct mail than in almost any other advertising medium—an estimated $43.3 billion in 2022. One study showed that 77 percent of respondents said they sorted through their mail immediately upon receiving it, while 48 percent indicated that they saved the mail for future reference—both percentages indicating the potential effectiveness of the medium.[7] Direct mail is not restricted to small companies seeking our business. Respected large companies and organizations in the retail, financial services, and fund-raising sectors (among others) commonly employ this medium.

Many advertisers shied away from direct mail in the past, fearful of the image it might create or harboring the belief that direct mail was useful only for low-cost products. But this is no longer the case. For example, Porsche Cars North America, Inc. uses direct mail to target high-income, upscale consumers who are most likely to purchase its expensive sports cars. Jaguar and Maserati have also employed this strategy. In one example, Porsche developed a direct-mail piece that was sent to a precisely defined target market: physicians in specialties with the highest income levels. This list was screened to match the demographics of Porsche buyers and narrowed further to specific geographic areas. The direct-mail piece was an X-ray of a Porsche 911 Carrera 4 written in the language of the medical audience. This creative campaign generated one of the highest response rates of any mailing Porsche has done in recent years. The piece shown in Exhibit 14–4 is one sent by Cadillac to market its new CT4 automobile.

Keys to the success of direct mail are the **mailing lists**, which constitute the database from which names are generated, the ability to segment markets, and, of course, the offer. It is now possible to buy mailing lists, e-mail lists, and sales leads. Lists for business-to-business purposes are also available. Lists have become more current and more selective, eliminating waste coverage. The data for these lists are derived from a variety of sources such as customer purchase history and third-party lists.

The importance of the list has led to a business of its own. It has been estimated that there are over 39 billion names on lists, and many companies have found it profitable to sell the names of purchasers of their products and/or services to list firms. (One of these companies claims to have over 245 million names on its e-mail list alone!) Companies like InfoUSA, Data Axle USA, and Experian (Exhibit 14–5) provide such lists on a national level, and in most metropolitan areas there are firms providing the same service locally.

While direct mail continues to be a favorite medium of many advertisers, and projections are that the market will grow, this medium has been seriously threatened by the Internet. The lower cost of e-mail and the convenience of the Internet have raised concerns among traditional direct-mail marketers. Interestingly, the Internet is both a threat and an opportunity, as Internet companies have increased their expenditures in direct mail to drive potential customers to their sites. Nevertheless, the traditional direct-mail business has experienced lower response rates from many consumers who see the offer first through direct mail and then go online to order. Many companies have shifted from print to online catalogs, saving money and remaining more current. However, the more traditional direct-mail piece is far from dead. As reported by Sarah Nassauer, the paper circular remains popular because retailers believe that consumers who do not read banner ads online or e-mails still read the mail delivered to their homes. Thus, stopping the mailing of print versions may lead to loss of sales. Some companies like Boxed.com have actually been increasing their print budgets, and for Stuller.com, direct mail constitutes its largest offline marketing expense. E-mail has also been shown to be an effective strategy for a variety of companies and organizations.

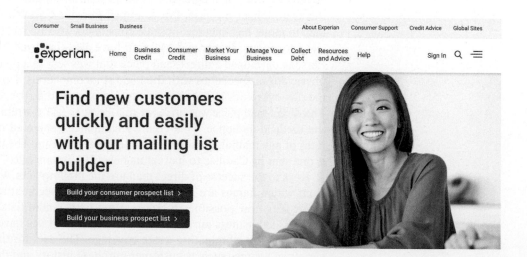

Catalogs Major participants in the direct-marketing business include retailers and other catalog companies. The number of catalogs mailed and the number of traditional catalog shoppers has decreased each year since 2007, with an estimated 18.5 billion sent out in 2006, down to about 10 billion to 12 billion in 2022.[8] Today's catalogs are much more targeted and specialized to meet consumers' needs.[9] Even though some companies now only publish a catalog online, the number of companies offering catalogs has been on the increase every year since 2015. Response rates have also continued to remain attractive.[10] Although some predicted that catalogs would cease to exist with more use of the Internet, traditional catalogs are still an effective way to reach consumers. The emotional appeal of the catalog exceeds that of online catalogs and ultimately is one of the best ways to drive consumers online.

Many companies use catalogs in conjunction with their more traditional sales and promotional strategies. For example, companies like Pottery Barn, Bloomingdale's, Nordstrom, and Patagonia sell directly through catalogs but also use them to inform consumers of product offerings available in the stores. Some companies rely solely on catalog sales. Others that started out exclusively as catalog companies have branched into retail outlets, among them Road Runner Sports, Eddie Bauer, Banana Republic, and Illuminations (Exhibit 14–6). The products being offered through this medium have reached new heights as well. The 2021 Neiman Marcus Christmas catalog featured:

—The Mughal Heart Diamond (30.86 carats)	$6,100,000.00
—Barrett-Jackson Hummer EV Edition 1	$285,000.00
—A Roaring Twenties Party	$395,000.00
—Ski with Lindsey Vonn at Jackson Hole, Wyoming	$235,000.00
—Vista Alegre Dinnerware and trip to Portugal	$80,000.00

EXHIBIT 14–6

Road Runner Sports started off as a direct-mail company and now has substantial retail store businesses.

Road Runner Sports, Inc.

Of course, these products were designed to attract publicity more than anything else—unless you have a lot of money!

In addition to the traditional hard copies, catalogs are now available on the Internet for consumers as well as business-to-business customers. In some instances in the consumer market, the catalog merchandise is available in retail stores as well. In others, the catalog and retail divisions are treated as separate entities. At the Gap, the catalog is used to supplement the inventory in stock, and phone orders for different sizes and so on can be made from the store and shipped for free.

E-mail Direct mail on the Internet (**e-mail**) is essentially an electronic version of regular mail. Like regular mail it is highly targeted, relies heavily on lists, and attempts to reach consumers with specific needs through targeted messages. The use of e-mail marketing by business-to-business and business-to-consumer marketers continues to grow; both the low cost and the higher effectiveness than traditional direct mail appeal to marketers. A study conducted by the Harvard Business School showed that e-mail campaigns were as much as 95 times more effective than traditional direct-marketing campaigns when return on investment (ROI) was used as the effectiveness measure.[11] Given the increase in the use of e-mail marketing over the years, this number is now likely to be lower.

Sometimes users may also receive less-targeted and unwanted e-mails. The electronic equivalent of junk mail, these messages are referred to as **spam**. Because of the high volumes of spam and the fact that many consumers consider it a nuisance, the U.S. government has passed laws regulating its use. In addition, antispam software has become effective in blocking most of the unwanted messages. Nevertheless, all indications are that the end of this form of advertising is not in sight.

Broadcast Media   The success of direct marketing in the broadcast industry has been truly remarkable; as far back as 1996 over 77 percent of the U.S. population reported that they had viewed a direct-response appeal on TV.[12] Direct-response TV advertising was predicted to be about $66 billion in 2021.[13]

While radio was used quite extensively in the 1950s, its use and effectiveness have dwindled substantially in recent years. Thus, the majority of direct-marketing broadcast advertising now occurs on TV, which receives the bulk of our attention here. It should be pointed out, however, that the two-step approach is still very common on the radio, particularly with local companies.

Direct marketing in the broadcast industry involves both direct-response advertising and support advertising. In **direct-response advertising**, the product or service is offered and a sales response is solicited, through either the one- or two-step approach previously discussed. Examples include ads for apparel, exercise equipment, collectables, and so on. Toll-free phone numbers are included so that the receiver can immediately call to order. **Support advertising** is designed to do exactly that—support other forms of advertising. Ads for Publishers Clearing House or *Reader's Digest* or other companies telling you to look in your mailbox for a sweepstakes entry are examples of support advertising.

Direct-response TV encompasses a number of media, including direct-response TV spots like those just mentioned, infomercials, connected TV, and home shopping shows (teleshopping).

TV Spots   Referred to in the direct-marketing industry as *short-form programs*, these spots include direct-response commercials commonly seen on television for products such as drugs and toiletries, audio and video supplies, household products, and more. Perfect Cushion and Pet Pain Away are examples of some of the more popular of these ads.

EXHIBIT 14–7

Bentley has successfully used an infomercial to attract buyers.

Bentley Motors

Arnage T

BENTLEY

The Ultimate Driver's Bentley

Infomercials   The lower cost of commercials on cable and satellite channels has led advertisers to another popular form of advertising. An **infomercial** is a long commercial that is designed to fit into a 30-minute or 1-hour time slot. Many infomercials are produced by the advertisers and are designed to be viewed as regular TV shows. Today's infomercials use both one- and two-step approaches. Programs such as *Liquid Luster*, *Amazing Discoveries*, and *Stainerator* (the so-called miracle-product shows) were the most common form of infomercial in the 1980s. While this form of show is still popular, the infomercial industry has been adopted by many large, mainstream marketers, including Coca-Cola, Braun, Disney, Nissan, Bentley, Apple, and Microsoft (see Exhibit 14–7).

The demographics of the infomercial shopper reflect a married female, mean age of 45, Caucasian, working full time with a household income of $55,000+ per year.[14] This advertising medium is indeed effective with a broad demographic base, not significantly different from the infomercial nonshopper in age, education, income, or gender. Retail stores are benefiting from infomercials as well, as brand awareness leads to increased in-store purchases. "As seen on TV" has benefited retailers as products seen on infomercials find their way onto TV. For example, a $500,000 print campaign combined with an infomercial for the George Foreman grill led to more sales at retail stores than through direct TV.[15]

The popularity of the infomercial has led companies to expand into the more frequently watched daytime TV market and the creation of infomercial networks. There is now an "As Seen on TV" website, store, and catalog.

However, some people are not sold on the idea of ads disguised as programs. For example, infomercials disguised as "ultrahip" TV shows have been targeted at teenagers, raising fears that kids under the age of 13 will be susceptible to their lure. Infomercials have become more popular on YouTube as well. Consumer complaints are on the rise, and the FTC has already levied fines for deceptive endorsements against infomercial sponsors and has taken legal action against those engaging in deceptive practices. Four consumer groups (the Consumer Federation of America, Center for the Study of Commercialism, Center for Media Education, and Telecommunications Research and Action Center) have asked the FCC to require all infomercials to display a symbol that indicates a "paid ad" or "sponsored by" so that viewers won't confuse them with regular programming.

Connected TV   As noted in the lead-in to this chapter, connected TV (CTV) advertising combines the ease of online advertising and reach of TV. Ads can be sent to audiences while they are streaming video content on their TVs before or during traditional commercial breaks. Because the viewer is connected, they can purchase the product being advertised when they see it. Spending in the United States in 2021 was estimated to be $14.19 billion, however due to its attractiveness to advertisers it is expected to grow to $38 billion by 2026.[16]

Home Shopping   Ever since home shopping channels came on air in the 1980s, their popularity has continued to increase. The Home Shopping Network, QVC, and Shop HQ are still among the leaders in sales, while Buy.com and Amazon.com also do well as do a number of traditional retailers like Hammacher Schlemmer. As you might imagine, home shopping channels thrived during the pandemic as shopping at home increased. Jewelry, kitchenware, fitness products, insurance, household products, and a variety of items are promoted (and sold) this way. The major shopping channel in the United States (QVC) broadcasts on TV 24 hours a day and online. In 2018, QVC purchased its major competitor—HSN—for $2.1 billion. While Internet e-commerce sales have hurt the TV home shopping channels, the channels have succeeded through adaptation: upgrading their product lines to include designer brand names and luxury goods at a lower price point and becoming more innovative to attract a broader audience. QVC has also purchased Zulily—a leading e-commerce site that targets millennial moms. Zulily, according to *The Wall Street Journal*, is "the web's version of QVC."[17] The success of home shopping networks has led to a proliferation of shopping channels, including the Gem Shopping Network, America's Auction Network, and the Liquidation Channel, to name just a few. As the demographics of shopping channel buyers continue to move younger and more upscale, the products offered on these channels continue to change as well. It is now possible to to shop on QVC on one's Apple Watch.

Print Media   Magazines and newspapers are difficult media to use for direct marketing. Because these ads have to compete with the clutter of other ads and because the space is relatively expensive, response rates and profits may be lower than in other media. Print direct-response ads can still be found in specific interest areas like financial newspapers or sports and hobby magazines, but they are being used less often.

Telemarketing   If you have a telephone, you probably do not have to be told about **telemarketing**, or sales by telephone. Both for-profit and charitable organizations have employed this medium effectively in one- and two-step approaches. Combined telemarketing sales (business-to-consumer and business-to-business) have continued to decrease since 2004. While business-to-business companies continue to employ this strategy with some success, in recent years the telemarketing industry has suffered from a decline due to a number of factors. Problems associated with telemarketing include its potential for fraud and deception and its potential for annoyance. These developments have led to the development of a Do Not Call list (DoNotCall.gov) for both landline and cell phones and the resulting decline in sales in the consumer market.

DIRECT SELLING

An additional element of the direct-marketing program is **direct selling**, the direct, personal presentation, demonstration, and sales of products and services to consumers in their homes. Amway, Avon, Cutco, Mary Kay, and Tupperware are some of the best-known direct-selling companies in the United States and have now extended these programs overseas (Exhibit 14–8). Tupperware (1949) and Amway (1959) have been employing direct selling for over 60 years. While some thought the pandemic might be a death knell for direct sellers, Tupperware not only survived but significantly increased its sales by 72 percent, the most in the last two decades, through "digital Tupperware parties."[18] Approximately 7.3 million people engage in direct selling throughout the United States, and 93 percent of them are independent contractors (not employees of the firm they represent). Direct selling generates over $42 billion in sales, selling to over 44 million customers.

The three forms of direct selling are:

1. *Repetitive person-to-person selling.* The salesperson visits the buyer's home, job site, or other location to sell frequently purchased products or services (e.g., Amway). Mary Kay has awarded more than 100,000 Cadillacs to successful salespersons—the company's symbol of sales success.
2. *Nonrepetitive person-to-person selling.* The salesperson visits the buyer's home, job site, or other location to sell infrequently purchased products or services (e.g., Cutco).
3. *Party plans.* The salesperson offers products or services to groups of people through home or office parties and demonstrations (e.g., Tupperware and PartyLite Gifts).

Whereas a number of products and services are sold through direct selling, home and family durables, weight loss and wellness products, and personal services are the most popular. The "typical" direct-selling representative is female (over 75 percent) and

FIGURE 14–1

Sales Strategy (methods used to generate sales)

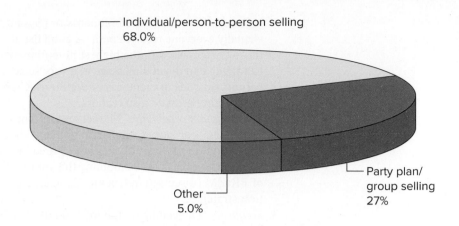

- Individual/person-to-person selling 68.0%
- Party plan/group selling 27%
- Other 5.0%

76 percent are between the ages of 25–54. For most of the representatives, direct selling is not a full-time job but an opportunity to earn additional income and a way to get the product at a discount for themselves. Over half of those in this industry spend fewer than 10 hours a week selling, and the vast majority spend less than 30 hours a week selling. Figure 14–1 reflects the means by which they sell.

EVALUATING THE EFFECTIVENESS OF DIRECT MARKETING

Because they generate a direct response, measuring the effectiveness of direct-marketing programs is not difficult. Using **cost per order (CPO)**, advertisers can evaluate the relative effectiveness of an ad in only a few minutes based on the number of calls generated. By running the same ad on different stations, a direct marketer can determine the relative effectiveness of the medium itself. For example, if the advertiser targets a $5 return per order and a broadcast commercial (production and print) costs $2,500, the ad is considered effective if it generates more than 500 orders. Similar measures have been developed for print and direct-mail ads.

Another commonly employed measure of effectiveness is **Customer Lifetime Value (CLTV)**. CLTV is a simple formula that is used to assist marketers in determining the dollar value associated with a long-term relationship with a customer, thus evaluating his or her worth. The value is used to determine whether or not a customer should be acquired, as well as to optimize service levels to existing customers. Companies use CLTV to assist them in assessing future revenues and profit streams from the customer, so that they can focus more on the satisfaction and retention of their more profitable customers. Thus, the company can focus more attention on profitable customers while spending less marketing effort on those with a low CLTV score.

Many companies use an **RFM analysis** (recency, frequency, monetary), a marketing technique used to determine quantitatively which customers are the most profitable by examining how recently a customer has purchased (recency), how often the customer purchases (frequency), and how much the customer spends (monetary).

For direct-marketing programs that do not have an objective of generating a behavioral response, traditional measures of effectiveness can be applied. (We discuss these measures in Chapter 18.)

Advantages and Disadvantages of Direct Marketing

Many of the advantages of direct marketing have already been presented. A review of these and some additions follow:

1. *Selective reach.* Direct marketing lets the advertiser reach a large number of people and reduces or eliminates waste coverage. Intensive coverage may be obtained through broadcast advertising or through the mail. While not everyone drives on

highways where there are billboards or pays attention to TV commercials, virtually everyone receives mail. A good list allows for minimal waste, as only those consumers with the highest potential are targeted. For example, a political candidate can direct a message at a very select group of people (those living in a certain zip code or members of the Sierra Club, say); a book club can target recent purchasers or avid readers.

2. *Segmentation capabilities*. Marketers can rent or purchase lists of recent product purchasers, car buyers, bank-card holders, and so on. These lists may allow segmentation on the basis of geographic area, occupation, demographics, and job title, to mention a few. Combining this information with the geocoding capabilities of PRIZM (discussed in Chapter 2), marketers can develop effective segmentation strategies.

3. *Frequency*. Depending on the medium used, it may be possible to build frequency levels. The program vehicles used for direct-response TV advertising are usually the most inexpensive available, so the marketer can afford to purchase repeat times. Frequency may not be so easily accomplished through the mail, since consumers may be annoyed to receive the same mail repeatedly.

4. *Testing*. Direct marketing allows for a strong ability to test the effectiveness of the overall program as well as specific elements.

5. *Timing*. While many media require long-range planning and have long closing dates, direct-response advertising can be much more timely. Direct mail and e-mail, for example, can be put together very quickly and distributed to the target population. TV programs typically used for direct-response advertising are older, less viewed programs that are likely to appear on the station's list of available spots. Another common strategy is to purchase available time at the last possible moment to get the best price.

6. *Personalization*. No other advertising medium can personalize the message as well as direct media can. Parents with children at different age levels can be approached, with their child's name included in the appeal. Car owners are mailed letters congratulating them on their new purchase and offering accessories. Computer purchasers are sent software solicitations. College students receive very personalized information that recognizes their specific needs and offers solutions, as well as college loan offers.

7. *Costs*. While the CPM for direct mail may be very high on an absolute and a relative basis, its ability to specifically target the audience and eliminate waste coverage reduces the actual CPM. Costs may be higher than in other media, but direct methods may be more profitable. The ads purchased on TV are often among the lowest-priced available. E-mail is extremely inexpensive. A second factor contributing to the cost-effectiveness of direct-response advertising is the cost per customer purchasing. Because of the low cost of media, each sale generated can be very inexpensive.

8. *Measures of effectiveness*. No other medium can measure the effectiveness of its efforts as well as direct response can. Feedback is often immediate and almost always accurate.

9. *Trustworthiness*. As reported in *eMarketer*, U.S. consumers indicate that direct mail and catalogs were the type of advertising they were most comfortable receiving (phone calls and texts were the least).[19]

Disadvantages of direct marketing include the following:

1. *Image factors*. As we noted earlier, the mail segment of this industry is often referred to as junk mail. Many people believe unsolicited mail promotes junk products, and others dislike being solicited. Even some senders of direct mail say they throw out most of the junk mail they receive. This problem is particularly relevant given the increased volume of mail being sent through e-mail.

Likewise, direct-response ads on TV are often low-budget ads for lower-priced products, which contributes to the image that something less than the best products are marketed in this way. (Some of this image is being overcome by the home shopping channels, which promote some very expensive products.) Telemarketing is found to be irritating to many consumers, as is "spam" or Internet junk mail. Other factors have also created image problems for the direct-marketing industry.

2. *Accuracy.* One of the advantages cited for direct mail and telemarketing was targeting potential customers specifically. But the effectiveness of these methods depends on the accuracy of the lists used. People move, change occupations, and so on, and if the lists are not kept current, selectivity will decrease. Computerization has greatly improved the currency of lists and reduced the incidence of bad names; however, the ability to generate lists is becoming a problem. The cost of generating a lead can range from a few dollars to as much as hundreds depending on its quality. Some states now have restrictions on how and where data on customers can be gathered.

3. *Content support.* In our discussion of media strategy objectives in Chapter 10, we said the ability of magazines to create mood contributes to the overall effectiveness of the ads they carry. In direct-response advertising, mood creation is limited to the surrounding program and/or editorial content.

4. *Rising costs.* As postal rates increase, direct-mail profits are immediately and directly impacted. The same is true for print costs, which drives up the costs of mailers and catalogs. The low cost of e-mail has led many companies to switch to this medium.

5. *Do Not Call lists.* Do Not Call lists now exist for both landline and cell phones. A "Do Not Contact" list in which consumers can choose not to receive junk mail is now available.

Summary

This chapter introduced you to the rapidly growing field of direct marketing, which involves a variety of methods and media beyond direct mail and telemarketing. The versatility of direct marketing offers many different types of companies and organizations a powerful promotional and selling tool.

Direct marketing continues to outpace other advertising and promotional areas in growth; many of the *Fortune* 500 companies now use sophisticated direct-marketing strategies. Database marketing has become a critical component of many marketing programs.

Advantages of direct marketing include its selective reach, segmentation, frequency, flexibility, and timing. Personalized and custom messages, low costs, and the ability to measure program effectiveness are also advantages of direct-marketing programs.

At the same time, a number of disadvantages are associated with the use of direct marketing. Image problems, deception, and the intrusive nature of the medium make some marketers hesitant to use direct-marketing tools. However, self-policing of the industry and involvement by large, sophisticated companies have led to significant improvements. As a result, the use of direct marketing will continue to increase.

Key Terms

direct marketing 470
direct to consumer (DTC) 470
direct-response media 470
one-step approach 475
two-step approach 475
mailing lists 475

e-mail 477
spam 478
direct-response advertising 478
support advertising 478
infomercial 478
telemarketing 479

direct selling 480
cost per order (CPO) 481
Customer Lifetime Value (CLTV) 481
RFM analysis 481

Discussion Questions

1. During the pandemic, direct-marketing transactions increased dramatically. Explain why this happened. Since the pandemic has lessened and people are now able to leave their homes, some companies have seen transactions decrease substantially while others have been able to maintain the levels (or close) to those attained at the peak of the pandemic. Give examples of each of these types of companies and explain why they are different. (LO 14-2)

2. Explain some of the factors that have made direct marketing attractive to many consumers. Then explain some that may make it less attractive. What do you think most motivates consumers to be attracted to direct marketing? (LO 14-4)

3. A common place for infomercials on television are in nonpeak hours—that is late at night, early morning, and other times when viewing is down. Explain why this is so and why infomercials are more common here than in prime time. (LO 14-3)

4. Some believe that digital catalogs will eventually mean the end for print versions. Others disagree, providing evidence that print catalogs are here to stay. Explain the arguments presented by both sides. (LO 14-3)

5. Direct mail—often referred to as junk mail—is often disliked by consumers. At the same time, the use of this medium continues and shows no indication of going away in the near future. Cite some of the reasons direct mail continues to thrive and remain effective. (LO 14-4)

6. Discuss the different methods direct marketers use to measure the effectiveness of their programs. Are there other methods that might be considered? Explain. (LO 14-3)

7. Explain what is meant by Customer Lifetime Value. How do marketers apply this formula to determine the effectiveness of their direct-marketing programs? (LO 14-4)

8. What are some advantages and disadvantages to direct marketing? There are some pundits that believe that direct marketing is in the decline stage of its product life cycle, while others believe that it will continue to be a successful means for marketing products. Discuss both of these positions. (LO 14-2)

9. When many people think of direct marketing they think of junk mail, infomercials, telemarketers, and catalogs that they don't want to receive. Given that so many people hold this attitude toward direct marketing, why does it continue to be so effective? (LO 14-4).

10. What is an infomercial? What are some of the reasons that infomercials have been so successful? Which types of products and services do you think are likely to be candidates for successful infomercials? (LO 14-3)

The Internet: Digital and Social Media

Learning Objectives

(LO15-1) Describe the role of the Internet and digital and social media in an IMC program.

(LO15-2) Discuss the use of media platforms in the IMC process.

(LO15-3) Explain how to evaluate the effectiveness of communications through the Internet and digital and social media.

(LO15-4) Compare the advantages and disadvantages of the Internet and digital and social media.

(LO15-5) Discuss the social and ethical issues associated with the Internet and digital and social media.

Let's Get Phygital! The Metaverse and the New Web 3.0

In 2021, Facebook shocked the world by changing its parent company's name to Meta! Well, not everyone in the world was shocked. A number of tech experts weren't all that surprised. But why would a company as successful as Facebook do such a thing you ask? Well, a year later some were still wondering.

According to Mark Zuckerberg, Facebook's CEO, the rebranding to Meta more closely reflects the future of the Internet, or what many now refer to as the *metaverse*. As the Internet continues to evolve, Zuckerberg and others see many changes taking place in version 3.0, through an increased integration of digital and real-life experiences including virtual reality (VR), augmented reality (AR), 3-D modeling, and gaming (NFTs). Marketers refer to this new version as *phygital marketing*—that is, the merging of digital and real-life experiences.

While the term *phygital* is not new (it actually goes back to 2007 when Australian ad agency Momentum used the term to describe the growing focus on digital advertising), as technology has advanced it has allowed the Internet to serve consumers' desire for real-life experiences, according to Asa Hiken writing in *AdAge.com*. The growth of digital and the new metaverse attracts both advertisers and customers, but not everyone is ready to walk away from the real world. In fact, a Harris Poll recently indicated that a majority of consumers worry that the metaverse will eventually cause them to lose touch with reality! Jeremy Cohen, the head of Web3 at Publicis Media, notes, "You can't just leave [physical] behind and jump into the virtual world. So how do you bridge that gap? Connect physical and digital." A number of companies are already doing just that.

- Wendy's launched Wendyverse, a virtual restaurant on Meta's *Horizon Worlds* platform. Consumers with a Quest 2 headset are able to visit the Wendyverse, which includes a "Town Square Central," the first Wendy's restaurant in virtual reality, and Partnership Plaza, a March Madness–themed experience in the Buck Biscuit Dome. "The basketball-themed experience lets Quest 2 users storm the court, shoot half court shots, and cut the net following the winning shot," and features ads about the chain's Buck Biscuit promotion. Other restaurants including Chipotle, which hosted a virtual restaurant on Roblox, have also entered the metaverse.

- A number of fashion brands have also employed phygital marketing. Puma created an experience allowing visitors to attend their brand's Fashion Week show interacting as if they were there in person. Gucci teamed with vinyl toy brand Superplastic to release ceramic figurines and SuperGucci NFTs based on the game platform "SuperGucci," while Prada paired its monthly online event Timecapsule with NFT versions of the apparel.

- Other companies marketing products from eyeglasses (Warby Parker) to whiskey (Jack Daniels) have also used AR, VR, or gaming successfully. Mountain Dew created a virtual watch e-sports party in VR platform Decentraland. But a gaming platform that claimed a connection between McDonald's and Nike had the permission of neither of them—a potential copyright infringement.

So did Facebook make the right move and is the future Internet going to be dominated by phygital marketers? Is the metaverse certain to be the new version? Maybe, maybe not! Approximately a year after the name change, nearly one-third of the U.S. population had never heard of the metaverse. Among 13- to 34-year-olds about one-quarter said they were fans of the metaverse, while the remainder said they had either never heard of it or disliked it. Many people who have heard of it are confused as to what it actually is or will be, and many are just not sold on the concept.

How has the rebranding worked out for Facebook—now Meta? About a year and $15 billion later, there has been little to show for it. Meta's value dropped 57 percent, and it had only 200,000 monthly active users on its platform called *Horizon World*. Much of the problem lies in the slow adoption of Meta's VR headsets due to high costs for the quality. Inflation hasn't helped either. Nevertheless, Meta is convinced that the future lies in the metaverse.

Sources: Arielle Feger, "A Year Later, Meta's Ambitious Plan for the Metaverse Falls Short," *eMarketer*, October 21, 2022, www.eMarketer.com; Sara Lebow, "Nearly a Third of US Population Has Never Heard of the Metaverse," *eMarketer*, July 25, 2022, www.eMarketer .com; Asa Hiken, "This McDonald's-themed Metaverse Restaurant Serves Food NFTs—But Was Built without

continued

the Chain's Permission," *Ad Age*, August 29, 2022, www
.adage.com; Patrick Kulp, "Mountain Dew Ventures into the
Metaverse with Virtual Esports Watch Party," *Ad Week*,
July 13, 2022, www.adweek.com; Amanda Jerelyn, "How
to Leverage AR in Your Digital Marketing Strategy," *ClickZ*,
January 21, 2021, www.clickz.com; Asa Hiken, "Blending
Digital and Physical May Not Be a New Practice, but It's
Gaining New Relevance from Web3," *Ad Age*, October 17,
2022, www.adage.com; Asa Hiken, "Phygital Marketing
in the Metaverse—How Brands Are Merging Digital and
Real-life Experiences," *Ad Age*, October 17, 2022, www
.adage.com; Eric Ravenscraft, "What Is the Metaverse,
Exactly?" *Wired*, April 25, 2022, www.wired.com; Chris
Kelly, "Wendy's Opens Metaverse Restaurant in Meta's
Horizon Worlds," *Restaurant Dive*, March 21, 2022, www
.restaurantdive.com.

As you can see from the lead-in to this chapter as well as previous chapters, the Internet has changed how we use media in ways unlike any medium has in the past. The incredibly rapid growth has been spurred by a number of factors, including the changing media habits of younger generations and the ever-evolving capabilities of digital media themselves. Social media has contributed to this growth in a very large way because the vast majority of Internet users are also on social media. But, like everything else, things change and so does the role of digital marketing in the IMC program.

This chapter will examine the role of the Internet and digital media in the IMC program. We will examine the growth of the Internet, how companies use the various platforms therein, its role in an IMC program, and the advantages and disadvantages associated with this medium. We will also discuss some of the various new media options that have resulted from the development of the Internet and their roles in an IMC program. The chapter will conclude with a discussion of the measurement of these media.

THE GROWTH OF THE INTERNET

Why the Rapid Adoption of the Internet?

The unprecedented growth of the Internet—the digital revolution—has led to changes in the marketing environment that have forced marketers to rethink almost everything they do. As the World Wide Web evolves, so too do marketing communications programs. There are now over 5 billion Internet users worldwide, accounting for over 63 percent of the world's population,[1] and over 4.7 billion social media users. Usage in some areas of the world—like northern Europe, western Europe, and North America—has reached 95 percent of the population.[2] A number of reasons can be cited as to why this growth has been so rapid. One is consumers' increased desire for information that they are now able to obtain easily. The speed and convenience of acquiring this information, as well as the ability to control what and how much is received, has had great appeal. The ability to conduct e-commerce through one's personal computer, tablet, or smartphone is also very attractive; it now seems there is almost nothing that one can't find or buy on the Web. It is as though the Internet has no bounds; every day one can find something new there.

Like the consumers', marketers' adoption of this medium has also soared. As shown in Figure 15-1, ad spending in industries like retail, travel, entertainment, telecom, and many others are now adopting this medium. The ability to target customers effectively through the Internet is attractive to marketers. The increased attention to accountability on the part of businesses has led to a view of the Internet as a medium that would provide more direct feedback on the value of marketing expenditures, customer satisfaction, trends, and the competition. As is true of direct marketing, companies like the fact that, unlike traditional media, it is often easier to account for the ROI of their expenditures. In fact, in its earliest stages a number of marketing companies perceived the Internet as a direct-response medium. While a large component of the Web is still e-commerce, today's marketers now employ the medium for numerous other communications and marketing objectives (as shown in Figure 15-2).

FIGURE 15–1

Companies in a variety of industries have increased their digital advertising expenditures.

eMarketer, July 2022.

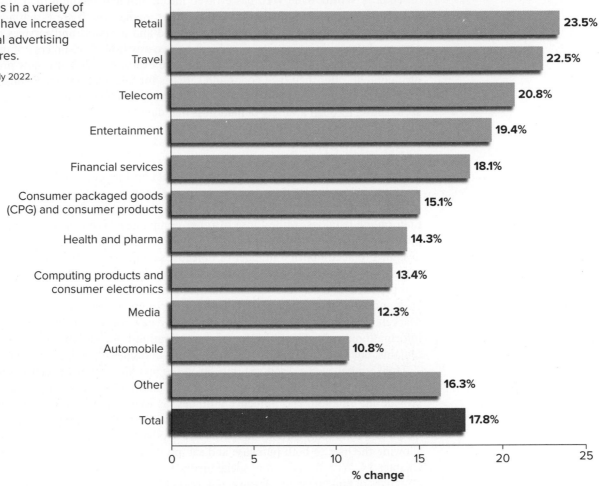

U.S. Digital Ad Spending Growth, by Industry, 2022

% change

FIGURE 15–2

Marketers' Use of the Internet

Today's World Wide Web has evolved into a different medium than anyone could have expected upon its inception. Unlike other media, which are essentially unidirectional and responsible for the content provided and products and services offered for sale, the Internet is interactive, allowing for a two-way flow. Consumers not only control when and which messages and content they are exposed to, but also now provide their own content, offer their own goods and services for sale, and provide feedback on what they use or purchase. As you will see, marketers are involving consumers in a way never seen before, through a variety of platforms that didn't exist just a few decades ago.

Web Objectives

When major corporations first began to conduct business on the Internet, they put up websites primarily for information purposes, and a one-way flow of information resulted. Companies like Kmart and Maytag had sites that were really not much more than online catalogs, while those of other companies were designed for information purposes only. The role of the website quickly changed, however, as sites are now designed to accomplish a number of objectives and have become much more creative promoting brand images, positioning, and offering promotions, product information, and products and services for sale. In addition, these sites allow for consumers' feedback and input that can be directly used by marketers to keep their customers engaged. Marketers are utilizing the Internet in entirely new ways, moving beyond the purely informational role. The objective of disseminating information and selling products remains, but many additional communications and sales objectives are being pursued.

Unlike other media discussed thus far in the text, the Internet is actually a hybrid of media. In part, it is a communications medium, allowing companies to create awareness, provide information, and influence attitudes, as well as pursue other communications objectives. Videos, display ads, and commercials—some of which may also appear in other media—are commonly used for this purpose. For others, it is also a direct-response medium, allowing the user to both purchase and sell products through e-commerce, as shown in Chapter 14. With the advent of social media, marketers have increasingly pursued other objectives of building brand image and developing a more direct and involved relationship with customers through engagement with the brand as well as selling through social media sites.

Figure 15-3 shows the many ways that marketers now use the Internet to reach out to consumers. As you can see, these efforts include outbound activities—those directed from the company to specific target markets—as well as inbound activities—such as

FIGURE 15-3

New Framework for Digital Marketing

Framework for Digital Marketing

1 Outbound
Ways firms reach out to target consumers

COMPANY

2 Inbound
Ways marketers ensure they can be found when consumers search for product or service

3 Social Media
Platforms where consumers create content to influence others

CONSUMERS

4 Mobile Technology
Activity done on smartphones, tablets, and other mobile devices

EXHIBIT 15–1

Start-up company SweetBling.com has benefited from the use of the Internet.

SweetBling

listening to gain feedback, interacting with customers, and so on. Note that this framework is circular in nature, reflecting the interactivity between companies and consumers. In addition to the firms making marketing efforts to be sure prospective consumers can find them when searching for a product or service, they also conduct activities to engage with consumers to better satisfy their needs. As is shown, social media are an important component of this mix as consumers interact with others in their spheres, influencing them in both positive and negative ways. As you will see, these social media networks have become a valuable marketing tool for marketers and have now become one of the most productive ways to sell products. The figure also shows some of the tools used to foster this communication process.

Let's now examine some of the objectives marketers may try to achieve in this process.

LO 15-1

Create Awareness Advertising on the Web can be useful in creating awareness of an organization as well as its specific product and service offerings. For small companies with limited budgets, the Web offers the opportunity to create awareness well beyond what might be achieved through traditional media. For example, a startup company like the one shown in Exhibit 15-1 can almost immediately gain worldwide exposure at a reasonable cost—something that was not possible before the Internet. Although a valuable tool for creating awareness—particularly for smaller companies that may have limited advertising budgets—the Internet is not likely to be the most effective of the IMC elements for achieving this objective for larger companies. Mass-media advertising may be more useful for this purpose, given its larger reach and lower cost per exposure (as the TV people will be glad to remind you!). Studies have continued to demonstrate the effectiveness of TV to create awareness and interest and drive visitors to websites. Nevertheless, even larger well-established companies have the creation of and increase in awareness as a primary objective.

Generate Interest A visit to RedBull.com will quickly demonstrate how a site can be used to generate interest. The site provides news, live streams, videos, and more from the "World of Red Bull" (Exhibit 15-2). The objectives of this site and many others like it are simple: Create interest that will bring visitors back to learn more about the products—and, of course, to sell stuff.

Disseminate Information One of the primary objectives for using the Web is to provide in-depth information about a company's products and services. Having a website

EXHIBIT 15–2

As shown in this image for the World of Red Bull, Elite Skydiving Series, Red Bull has used its website to generate interest and create a powerful brand image.

Red Bull/AP Images

has become a necessity, as more and more buyers expect that a company will have a site providing them with detailed information about its offerings, warranties, store locations, and so on. Think about the last time you tried to find information on a company and it didn't have a website. It is extremely rare for this to happen, and if it did, you would likely be hesitant to pursue a relationship with the company. In the government sector, contracts are often put out to bid on the Internet. Information regarding requirements, specifications, submission dates, and so forth is disseminated more quickly, to more potential candidates, and at a much lower cost via the Internet than it is through other media. Want information on filing federal income taxes? The first place you look would likely be www.irs.gov. Websites serve as a means of communicating

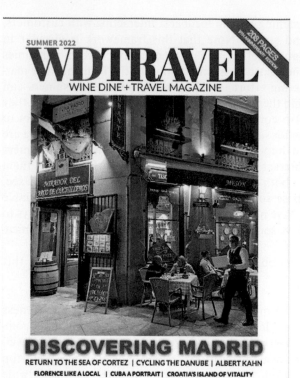

SUMMER 2022

WDTRAVEL
WINE DINE + TRAVEL MAGAZINE

DISCOVERING MADRID

RETURN TO THE SEA OF CORTEZ | CYCLING THE DANUBE | ALBERT KAHN
FLORENCE LIKE A LOCAL | CUBA A PORTRAIT | CROATIA'S ISLAND OF VITALITY

EXHIBIT 15–3

www.winedineandtravel.com creates a favorable brand image.

Wine Dine & Travel Magazine

information about a company's products and services, philanthropic efforts, contact information, and the company itself. Unfortunately, there has been a downside to this as well. Many companies now make it more difficult to obtain information in any way other than their website. Finding a phone number to contact them for more information, lodge a complaint, or other communications need seems to be getting more and more difficult.

Create an Image   Many websites are designed to reflect the image a company wants to portray. For example, check out the site www.winedineandtravel.com (Exhibit 15–3). The site is an excellent example of a website used for image building. *WD TRAVEL* is designed to appeal to upscale travelers looking for destinations and accommodations that reflect their lifestyles. Interestingly, one of the difficulties traditional marketers have experienced is that of creating a brand image on the Internet. While some of these companies have been successful, others have not fared as well and have come to realize that branding and image-creating strategies must be specifically adapted to this medium.

Create a Strong Brand   The Internet—as part of an integrated marketing communications program—can be a useful tool for branding. While originally many companies had difficulty using the Internet to establish their brand, this is no longer the case. Red Bull has used its site (shown earlier) as an integral part of its IMC campaign focusing on the "Red Bull Gives You Wings" image, positioning itself as a brand dedicated to excitement and daring through its motorsports, biking, surfing, and snowboarding news and videos as well as music and event sponsorships. Red Bull is one of the many companies that have "figured it out" in regard to successful branding.

Stimulate Trial   Many marketers have found the Internet to be an effective medium for stimulating trial of their products or services. Often websites offer electronic coupons in an attempt to stimulate trial of their products. Others offer samples, promotions, and sweepstakes designed to encourage trial. Music sites, like iTunes.com, allow for a "sampling" of songs before you purchase, while some business-to-business sites allow you to test their software online before purchasing.

Create Buzz   One of the many advantages of the Web is the ability to create buzz. The viral nature of social networking and other sites makes them attractive to marketers intending to spread the word and use word of mouth. In a very successful effort to go viral, Burger King's net neutrality video was designed to explain the issue of net neutrality. The video generated 1.5 million views on Twitter, 4.6 million views on YouTube, 15 million views on Facebook, and resulted in more than 206,000 conversations. *Stranger Things* star David Harbour encouraged his fans to give him 200,000 retweets so he could go on an expedition with Greenpeace. His tweet generated 376,000 retweets and more than 580,000 conversations. He went on the expedition.[3]

Gain Consideration   Many marketers believe that the Internet is an effective medium for achieving communications objectives such as consideration and/or evaluation. Blogs and discussion boards are considered particularly effective for providing information useful in evaluating products and brands. As seen earlier in this text, the use of influencers has become a very common strategy for marketers for this purpose and, as seen in the lead-in, is expected to continue into the foreseeable future.

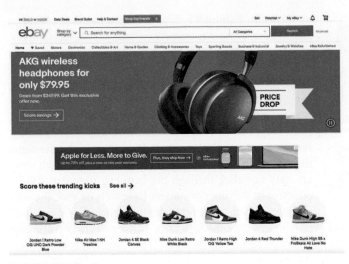

E-Commerce

The Internet also offers the opportunity to sell directly to customers in both the consumer market and the business-to-business market. This direct selling of goods and services has been labeled **e-commerce**. Sales through e-commerce reached over $959 billion in 2021, constituting 14.5 percent of all U.S. retail sales.[4] One of the more popular and successful sites is that of eBay, which positions itself as the world's online marketplace (Exhibit 15-4). Many of the sites already mentioned in this chapter have a sales component—as either a primary or secondary goal.

Many companies maintain their existing brick-and-mortar stores while also selling through the Internet. Walmart, Target, and The Home Depot are some of the leaders in e-commerce sales in the United States.

EXHIBIT 15-4

eBay is one of the most popular e-commerce sites.

eBay Inc.

Samsung, Apple, and others have added kiosks inside their stores where consumers can order online. Groceries and pharmacies are now allowing online orders and store pickup or home delivery.

We discussed e-commerce and strategies employed in this area in Chapter 14. Let's have a look at how the Internet can be used as part of an IMC program.

THE INTERNET AND INTEGRATED MARKETING COMMUNICATIONS

Up to this point, we have mentioned the need for using the Internet as part of an IMC program and the objectives sought. In this section, we discuss how the Web can be used with other program elements.

The most revolutionary change in the Internet came when it moved from what is referred to as Web 1.0 to Web 2.0. For the most part, Web 1.0 consisted mainly of static sites resulting in a one-way flow of communication. Web 2.0 led to dramatic changes in the World Wide Web, primarily as a result of decentralization of communications and interactivity, with information provided by users as contributors of content such as user-generated ads. As we write this edition of this text, Web 3.0 is expected to be introduced soon. The next iteration of the Web is, once again, expected to result in a major paradigm shift, with numerous changes expected including increases in decentralization, artificial intelligence, and machine learning and other changes. Everything we have discussed to this point still constitutes the way marketers use the Web; however, Web 2.0 has had a drastic impact on how the Internet is used in an IMC program.

Advertising on the Internet

Like broadcast or print, the Internet is an advertising medium. Companies and organizations working to promote their products and services must consider this medium as they would television, magazines, outdoor, and so on. Advertising on the Internet employs a variety of forms, display ads (including banners), sponsorships, pop-ups and pop-unders, interstitials, paid searches, behavioral targeting, and contextual ads.

Banners   The most common form of advertising on the Web is **banner ads**. It is difficult to get an accurate estimate of the number of times people see a banner or display ad as one's time spent online will make a difference. But one thing is for certain, online display ads are very common, as you no doubt are aware! Banner ads may be used for creating awareness or recognition, entering viewers into contests and sweepstakes, or direct-marketing objectives. Banner ads may take on a variety of forms,

EXHIBIT 15–5

An example of the variety of banner ad formats.

Oleg Romanko/Alamy Stock Photo

as shown in Exhibit 15–5, as well as a number of names such as *leader boards*, *rectangles*, *side panels*, *skyscrapers*, or *verticals.* They can also be static, animated, or in flash. Initially banner ads constituted the vast majority of advertising on the Internet, but studies indicating their questionable effectiveness have led some companies to reduce their usage. Reports on click-through rates vary, but most studies indicate a less than 1 percent response rate (and closer to 0.46 percent).[5] At the same time, a number of studies have shown that although viewers may not click through the banners, they can still be effective in driving consumers to search or visit the ad's website. A study reported in the *Journal of Consumer Research* showed evidence that even with low click-through rates, banner ads may still create a favorable attitude toward the ads through repeated exposures.[6] However, many consumers find banner ads annoying, leading many companies to avoid this advertising format.

Sponsorships   Another common form of advertising is **sponsorships**. There are two types of sponsorships. *Regular sponsorships* occur when a company pays to sponsor a section of a site—for example, a *House Beautiful* magazine or *Cosmopolitan* magazine sponsorship on Design.com or a corporate sponsorship of a page on Forbes.com. A more involved agreement is **content sponsorship**, in which the sponsor not only provides dollars in return for name association but also participates in providing the content itself. In some cases, the site is responsible for providing content and having it approved by the sponsor; in other instances, the sponsor may contribute all or part of the content. For example, Spotify sponsored content on Buzzfeed titled "15 Bands That Probably Wouldn't Exist Without Led Zeppelin," Taco Bell and Snapchat combined efforts on photo sharing, and Marks & Spencer and Daily Mail combined on an online article on the funky new flower trends for fall.

Pop-Ups/Pop-Unders   When you access the Internet, you no doubt have seen a window or a creature of some sort appear on your screen in an attempt to get your attention. These advertisements are known as **pop-ups**, and they often appear when you access certain sites. Pop-ups are usually larger than banner ads but smaller than a full screen. Instagram now accepts pop-up ads, to the dismay of many of its visitors.

Pop-unders are ads that appear underneath the web page and become visible only when the user leaves the site. As noted by Bartosz Bielecki, pop-under ads can be very effective: "The travel ecommerce giant Booking.com can serve as a good example of the thoughtful use of pop-under advertising. When you select and proceed with a hotel reservation, but ultimately don't make the booking, a new window may appear beneath your main browser screen with accommodation offers for the exact same dates and a similar pricing range you were interested in with your original search."[7]

While some companies believe that pop-ups and pop-unders are effective forms of advertising, others disagree. Consumer complaints have led some sites to no longer accept these advertising forms. A study conducted by TNS revealed that 93 percent of respondents found pop-up ads annoying or very annoying.[8] The frequency and effectiveness of pop-ups and pop-unders have been greatly reduced given the advent of pop-up screeners, which will block the ads before they appear on your screen.

Interstitials   **Interstitials** are full-page ads that appear on your screen while you are waiting for a site's content to download. Unlike banner ads, interstitials require the viewer to click off the ad to continue to the site they want to go to. Pinterest and Airbnb are just two of the many companies finding them to be effective. Because consumers have complained that mobile interstitials are irritating, in 2015 Google put into place a new policy to discourage their use by declaring the sites that use mobile interstitial apps as "mobile unfriendly."[9] The policy was updated and extended in 2022. Unfortunately

EXHIBIT 15–6

Results of a Google search for jeans.

Google LLC

for advertisers who may want to employ this medium, interstitials can also be blocked by pop-up blockers.

Searches Exhibit 15–6 shows the results of a **search** on Google. In general, the higher a site appears on a search page, the more visitors it will receive. (Studies suggest that 90 percent of searchers will not go past the first page of results.) **Organic search results** are those that appear because of their relevance to the search terms, not advertisements. In other words, consumers click on the site because their search request took them there. Organic search success is built by a combination of quality content and keyword optimization. Advertisers will also attempt to reach consumers through **nonorganic (paid) search results** such as **pay-per-click** advertising by placing their ads on web pages that display results from search engine queries.

While there are a number of search engines offering their services, Google is by far the dominant provider, accounting for 83 percent of all search ad revenues.[10] In an effort to more specifically target customers who may be interested in their offerings, advertisers employ **search engine optimization (SEO)**. SEO is the process of improving the volume of traffic driven to one's site by a search engine through unpaid (organic) results as opposed to paid inclusions. SEO considers how search engines work and edits its HTML and coding to increase its relevance to keywords and to remove barriers to the indexing activities of search engines. SEO content includes three types of media: (1) *owned media*—the content the company places on the website; (2) *earned media*—media the company does not create that directs readers back to its content through others including bloggers, publicity, and social media; and (3) *paid media*—media the company pays for in the form of ads. SEO has now become an integral part of the Internet marketing strategy of companies and organizations of all sizes.

Behavioral Targeting Another Internet advertising strategy that has seen rapid growth is **behavioral targeting**. Behavioral targeting is based on advertisers' targeting consumers by tracking their website surfing behaviors, such as which websites they have visited and/or searches they have made. By compiling clickstream data and Internet protocol (IP) information, segments of potential buyers can be identified and ads directed specifically to them. For example, by tracking an individual's visits to a number of automobile websites, an ad for cars or a dealership could be served to that individual in real time. As will be seen later in this chapter, behavioral targeting has been shown to be an effective, albeit controversial, strategy.

Advertisers have increased their use of **retargeting** (Figure 15-4). Once a user visits a website either on his or her desktop or mobile and leaves without purchasing the product, a specifically targeted ad will display on participating subsequent websites the user visits. Purchasing the space, however, is not a fixed transaction, but a bid process. Since each site has only so much space set aside for display ads, brands must bid against competitors for the space. The brand that puts in the highest bid is the one whose ads you will see. For example, let's say you were shopping for a pair of shoes at Nordstrom online but didn't purchase. The next time you visited a website, an ad for Nordstrom

FIGURE 15–4

Advertisers Attempt to
Reach Internet Users Who
Have Seen an Ad through
the Process of Retargeting

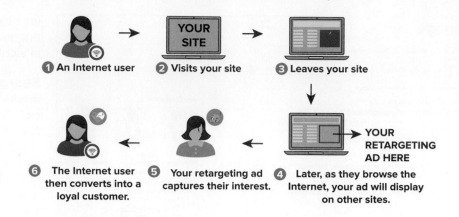

① An Internet user ② Visits your site ③ Leaves your site

⑥ The Internet user then converts into a loyal customer. ⑤ Your retargeting ad captures their interest. ④ Later, as they browse the Internet, your ad will display on other sites.

YOUR RETARGETING AD HERE

shoes would appear. Because advertisers find retargeting more successful than banner or display ads, their use is increasing. One blog estimates that such ads are 76 percent more likely to be clicked on than a regular display ad. The vast majority of over 1,000 market-ers surveyed are already retargeting on mobile—and 87 percent plan to increase this investment in the future.[11] Due to their rapid adoption, many advertisers are concerned that the ads may become as irritating as pop-up ads.

Contextual Ads   Advertisers who target their ads based on the content of the web page are using **contextual advertising**. Whereas behavioral advertising tracks surfing behaviors, contextual ad placements are determined by the content on the web page. For example, an advertiser may place an airline ad on a travel site, or a golf club ad on a golf site, or even in or near a story about golf on another site. As another example, Google's AdSense targets ads to match the content of a publisher's site. The ads come in a variety of formats including images and video ads and can be targeted to geo-graphic or local markets.

Recently, some marketers and policymakers have become concerned due to the increased popularity of native advertising. **Native advertising** is a form of paid media where the *ad* experience follows the natural form and function of the user experience in which it is placed.[12]

The goal of native ads is to be less intrusive while catching the attention of the reader who is likely interested in the content matter they reading. While these native ads have been shown to outperform the traditional banner ad, concern has been expressed that the ads sometimes appear as content, and not ads, leading the consumer to be misled. Marketers have expressed concern that when cookies are no longer allowed, there will be an increase in the use of native ads.

Rich Media   The increased penetration of broadband into households has increased the attention given to streaming video. **Rich media** is defined as "a broad range of inter-active digital media that exhibit dynamic motion, taking advantage of enhanced sensory features such as video, audio and animation."[13] Others state that rich media include all content that is created in Flash.[14] The successful adoption of music videos, sports clips, news, and more has led advertisers to create a variety of forms of streaming video adver-tising content. Types of rich media include the following.

Online Commercials The equivalent of traditional television commercials, **online commercials** are appearing more often on the Internet. Some of these commercials appear before the content that the user is seeking. These ads, called **pre-rolls**, are becoming more commonly employed by online advertisers, with some requiring that you watch the ad prior to receiving the content. (**Post-roll** ads run after the content is viewed.) Some companies have created their own web commercials to be shown only on the Internet, while others run the same spots they show on TV. For example, for years many fans were attracted to the Super Bowl football games to watch the commercials. The game became a forum for brands and agencies to demonstrate creativity in their ads, and the ads would not be released prior to the game, building expectations. This is rarely the case anymore, as advertisers often place their ads on Internet sites such as YouTube—much to the chagrin of viewers. Another trend has been to have consumers develop their own commercials to be shown online or on TV—or both. The Super Bowl has taken full advantage of this strategy along with Frito-Lay's Doritos. A number of companies have been successful in blending the two media, showing the commercial on TV and then directing interested viewers to the Web if they wish to see it again or to view longer versions. Online advertising spending continues to rise, and viewers have expressed displeasure with the frequency with which they see ads online.

Video on Demand As described in Chapter 13, **video on demand (VOD)** consists of video clips of various entertainment activities (which include ads or are sponsored) that are also available through the Internet and available to the viewer upon demand. Sporting events, FIFA World Cup highlights, and numerous other entertainment activities are just a few of the many options available.

Webisodes Short featured films created by the advertiser, such as those created by Jaguar and BMW, are examples of **webisodes**, in which companies create their own content to advertise their products. *The Walking Dead* is an example of a series that now has webisodes. IKEA, Target, Sara Lee, and Honda are just a few of the companies that have employed webisodes, but the range of these efforts also includes small jewelers, baking companies, cereal producers, and others. YouTube also carries a number of such webisodes.

Other Forms of Rich Media Advertising Advertising interactive banner ads, expandable ads, and rich media ads placed in video games, podcasts, and video ads within blogs are additional ways that rich media are currently employed. A number of advertisers are finding ads in gaming to be an effective strategy for marketing their brands, particularly to gen Z, millennials, and gen X.[15] As Fernando Machado, CMO of Activision Blizzard (the massive gaming leader responsible for *Call of Duty* and *World of Warcraft*), notes, "Gaming is a larger industry than the global film, global music, and North American sports industries combined." Given that ads and product placements are generally expected and accepted by players, Machado believes that the medium is often misunderstood.[16]

IMC Using Social and Other Media—Web 2.0

As noted earlier in the chapter, at the turn of the century the World Wide Web underwent significant changes. These changes led to the adoption of and the referral to the new Web as "Web 2.0." The birth of Web 2.0 has led to the development of many new media. As shown in Figure 15-5, these new media are designed for a number of purposes and contain a wide variety of materials for consumer use. While it is beyond the scope of this text to cover all of these new media, we will discuss many of them and their relevance to an IMC program. We will start our discussion with social networking sites, as the growth in this area has been literally astounding, and marketers have adopted these sites as an integral and critical part of their IMC programs.

Social media have been defined in numerous ways. Using the simplest definition from the *Merriam-Webster* dictionary, social media are defined as: "Forms of electronic communication (such as Web sites) through which people create online communities to share information, ideas, personal messages, etc."[17] As can be seen in Figure 15-6 there are numerous ways for consumers to access these sites (desktops, laptops, tablets, smartphones, and connected devices), as well as a variety of reasons for using them, including sharing information, networking, and so forth. The most popular of these are **social networking sites**, which are platforms for networks or social relations among people who share interests, activities, backgrounds, or real-life connections. While there are hundreds of social networks in existence, a small number of these dominate in terms of membership. Prior to discussing each of them and how marketers have used them, let's first examine the characteristics of the platforms.

FIGURE 15–5   Types of New Media

Types of New Media	Primary Purpose	Material	Examples
Forums and Chat Rooms	Discussion on topics, interest group sharing of information	Forums, discussion boards	Automobile forums
E-mail	Sending of electronic mail with file attachments	Web-based and non-Web-based e-mail platforms	Hotmail, Gmail, Yahoo! Mail
Social Networking Sites	Peer networking	Fan sites, alumni networks, personal news updates	Facebook, Twitter, LinkedIn
Content Aggregators	Hosting of content for information and entertainment	Informative content, podcasts, videos, channels	YouTube, Hulu
Virtual Reality	3-D experience, alternate space	Simulated environments, experiences	*Lowe's Holoroom How To*
Online Gaming	Alternate fantasy, entertainment, gaming	MMORPG (massively multiplayer online role-playing games), multiplayer online games	*World of Warcraft, StarCraft II*
Blogs	Opinions, information, viewpoints	Helpdesk, viewpoints, opinions	Hubspot.com
Portals	Aggregating news, communication tools	News studies, sponsored pages, ads	Asiaone.com, Yahoo!
Social News Sites	Peer-ranked news stories	News stories, popular blog content	Digg.com, Reddit.com
Augmented reality	An interactive experience of a real-world environment where the objects that reside in the real world are enhanced by computer-generated perceptual information	Multiple sensory modalities	*Pokemon Go, Harry Potter*

FIGURE 15–6

Social Media Landscape

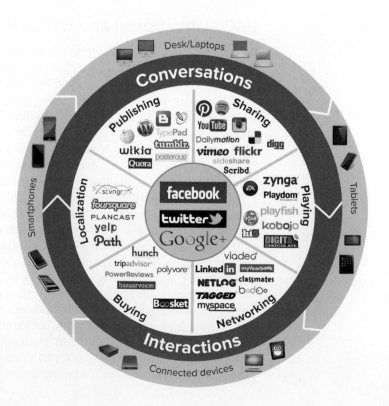

FIGURE 15–7

The Number of Global Social Media Users Continues to Grow.

www.oberlo.com/statistics/how-many-people-use-social-media

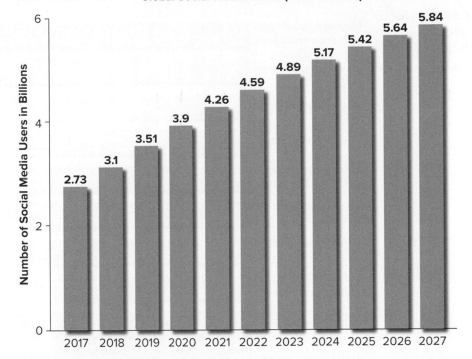

Global Social Media Users (2017 to 2027)

Who Uses Social Media and Why As you read earlier in this chapter, in 2021, about 63% of the world population used social media. This number is expected to reach nearly 6 billion by 2027, as shown in Figure 15-7.[18] Many of the top user sites are in China (where Facebook is not allowed). China is the most socially engaged social media market. As you will see when we discuss social networks, the demographics of the users of these sites vary, as do the reasons for using them. Let's start off by examining why users of these sites do so, and who they are.

Although a number of motivations for using social media have been identified (sharing ideas, activities, and events with others; community involvement, etc.), marketers are most interested in why individuals use these platforms from a consumer behavior perspective. In a series of studies, Muntinga examined the motivations for using social media in a brand-related context[19] (Consumers Online Brand-Related Activities–COBRAs). Specifically, the studies focused on why consumers (1) consume, (2) contribute to, and/or (3) create brand-related content. His results indicated that these COBRAs are driven by three primary motivations: to gain (1) information, (2) entertainment, and (3) remuneration. Gaining information included gathering prepurchase information, knowledge about brands, and new ideas. Entertainment involved enjoyment, relaxation, and passing time. Remuneration involved the potential to get something in return—for example, money, job-related benefits, or other rewards (social attraction, etc.). As social media have evolved, more recent research has added to this list, as shown in Figure 15–8. As will be seen throughout our further discussions, the ability for marketers to satisfy some of these motivations directly reflects their potential for success.

Although the networks are appealing to a range of demographics, they are particularly appealing to those between the ages of 18 and 29, and some are more appealing to women. As one might expect, the older age groups are less likely to engage in social media, particularly networks, though usage is on the increase in these segments as well.[20]

Prior to examining some of the most popular social media, let's examine how and why marketers use them in an IMC program. Again, the examples provided are but a sampling of the many ways marketers have used these media.

How Marketers Use Social Media In 2021, 91.9 percent of U.S. marketers in companies larger than 100 employees were expected to use social media for marketing purposes.[21] In a study of 3,000 marketers conducted by Social Media Examiner, an amazing 97 percent said they now include social media in their marketing plans,

FIGURE 15–8

Motivations for
Using Social
Media

Oberlo

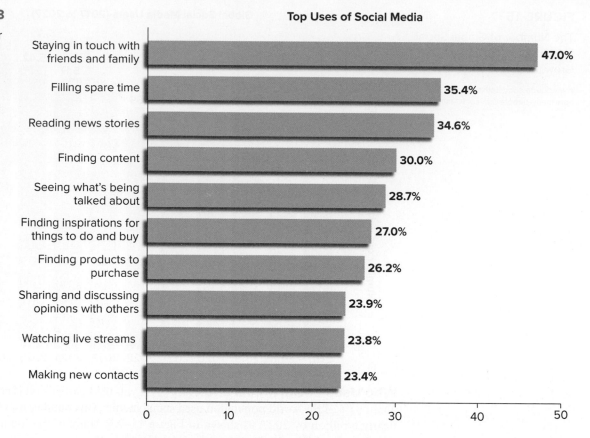

Top Uses of Social Media

Use	Percentage
Staying in touch with friends and family	47.0%
Filling spare time	35.4%
Reading news stories	34.6%
Finding content	30.0%
Seeing what's being talked about	28.7%
Finding inspirations for things to do and buy	27.0%
Finding products to purchase	26.2%
Sharing and discussing opinions with others	23.9%
Watching live streams	23.8%
Making new contacts	23.4%

with 92 percent stating that social media are important to their marketing success.[22] The primary reasons for marketers' using social media are to (1) drive traffic to one's site, (2) communicate with customers, and (3) gain brand exposure. The most important benefit these marketers believe they derive from the use of social media is increased brand awareness. Figure 15-9 shows that consumers use social media

FIGURE 15–9

How Consumers Use Social
Networks

Social Media Networks	Examples	Primary Use
Social	Facebook, Twitter, LinkedIn	Connect with others
Media Sharing	Instagram, Snapchat, YouTube	Share photos, videos, live videos, etc.
Discussion Forums	reddit, Quora, Digg	Share and discuss news, opinions, etc
Content Curation	Pinterest, Flipboard	Share and discuss news, trends, content
Consumer Review	Yelp, Trip Advisor, CNet	Review and share information about brands, products, services, etc.
Blogging and Publishing	Tumblr, Medium	Discover, comment, and publish
Social Shopping	Etsy, Fancy	Find and share trends, follow brands, purchase
Interest Based	Goodreads, Last.fm	Share interests, hobbies, etc.
Sharing Economy	Uber, Lyft, Airbnb	Advertise, find, share, sell, trade, services among peers

Source: Curtis Foreman, "10 Types of Social Media and How Each Can Benefit Your Business," Hoot Suite, June 20 2017, www.hootsuite.com.

networks for a variety of reasons. As a result, marketers find different media more effective for achieving specific objectives. For example, Twitter is considered the best channel for direct communication with consumers, while LinkedIn may be better for connecting with specific groups (like professionals). At the same time, LinkedIn may be the least effective for driving traffic. Each site contributes in more than one way.

Interestingly, while social media have grown in usage over the years and have certainly become an integral part of most Internet users' lives, they have also evolved in a more paradoxical fashion. A poll of more than 1,000 people conducted by *The Wall Street Journal* and *NBC News* indicated that while social media networks are considered divisive and a threat to privacy, people continue to use them—most use them every day. There also appears to be an increase in users feeling the need for government influence, with more and more people beginning to favor increased government legislation.[23]

Let's examine some of the more frequented social media, and how marketers use them in their IMC programs. We start our discussion with the most popular sites used by marketers. As can be seen in Figure 15-10, there is a lot of cross-usage among these sites.

The Most Popular Social Media

Facebook The largest of all social networks, Facebook has over 2.1 billion subscribers worldwide, covering six continents and 100 countries, who say they are active users of the site. Facebook was the most widely used social media platform in 2022. Site usage

FIGURE 15-10

Social Media Usage in the United States in 2021 | Pew Research Center

Use of online platforms, apps varies—sometimes widely—by demographic group										
% of U.S. adults in each demographic group who say they ever use ...										
	YouTube	Facebook	Instagram	Pinterest	LinkedIn	Snapchat	Twitter	WhatsApp	TikTok	Reddit	Nextdoor
Total	81	69	40	31	28	25	23	23	21	18	13
Men	82	61	36	16	31	22	25	26	17	23	10
Women	80	77	44	46	26	28	22	21	24	12	16
White	79	67	35	34	29	23	22	16	18	17	15
Black	84	74	49	35	27	26	29	23	30	17	10
Hispanic	85	72	52	18	19	31	23	46	31	14	8
Age 18–29	95	70	71	32	30	65	42	24	48	36	5
30–49	91	77	48	34	36	24	27	30	22	22	17
50–64	83	73	29	38	33	12	18	23	14	10	16
65+	49	50	13	18	11	2	7	10	4	3	8
<$30K	75	70	35	21	12	25	12	23	22	10	6
$30K–$49,999	83	76	45	33	21	27	29	20	29	17	11
$50K–$74,999	79	61	39	29	21	29	22	19	20	20	12
$75K+	90	70	47	40	50	28	34	29	20	26	20
HS or less	70	64	30	22	10	21	14	20	21	9	4
Some college	86	71	44	36	28	32	26	16	24	20	12
College+	89	73	49	37	51	23	33	33	19	26	24
Urban	84	70	45	30	30	28	27	28	24	18	17
Suburban	81	70	41	32	33	25	23	23	20	21	14
Rural	74	67	25	34	15	18	18	9	16	10	2

Note: White and Black adults include those who report being only one race and are not Hispanic. Hispanics are of any race. Not all numerical differences between groups shown are statistically significant (e.g., there are no statistically significant differences between the shares of White, Black, or Hispanic Americans who say the use Facebook). Respondents who did not give an answer are not shown.

Source: Survey of U.S. adults conducted Jan. 25–Feb. 8, 2021.

Pew Research Center

EXHIBIT 15-7

Banana Republic is one company that uses Facebook ads effectively.

Gap, Inc.

EXHIBIT 15-8

This Michael Kors ad allows potential buyers to see how they might look in various types of sunglasses.

Michael Kors

is just about equal across age groups, with approximately 75 percent saying they visit the site daily and more than 65 percent saying they visit more than once a day. While use of Facebook has, for the most part, stayed constant, growth in new users has been declining.[24] Interestingly, while teens tend to use Facebook less, they often find it hard to avoid, partly because those (like their parents) who tend to still use the platform make it necessary if they want to communicate with each other.[25] While the site has been somewhat controversial over the years as a result of frequently changing its privacy agreements, and other privacy-related issues, businesses have found Facebook to be a valuable communications medium. Even though Facebook has had a lot of negative publicity over the use of their users' data and other privacy matters and faced a boycott by over 400 brands,[26] and some in both the government and private sectors have called for the company to be broken up, ad revenues have actually increased. Based on advertising revenues, marketers consider Facebook to be the most important social platform for advertising.[27]

Just as individuals can exchange information by posting on the site, companies can also post information about the company and/or its products, photos, promotions, events, news, and so on. Facebook also allows advertising that can be targeted to subsets of Facebook users based on demographic and geographic data and interests and activities. In addition, because Facebook knows what pages its members like and visit, what their interests are, and even who is in their social network, targeting can become even more precise—and, as you might expect, create even more privacy concerns. Due to marketplace challenges, Facebook has evolved in an attempt to become an even more attractive medium for marketers by adding a number of new marketing tools such as sponsored stories, more targeted ads, and mobile video formats, including Facebook Live. The increased time being spent on mobile and engagement with video have led Facebook to continue to develop new programs and attract new advertisers.

Facebook has become a "must have" medium for many marketers who have used the site in a variety of ways. Throughout this text we have shown numerous examples of how companies use Facebook. Exhibit 15-7 is just one example of the many ways companies use Facebook ads.

Now the site offers advertisers the opportunity to employ both augmented and virtual reality. Mountain Dew, Vice, and Mondelēz have already placed such ads, along with Samsung and AT&T. The Michael Kors advertisement allows viewers to see what they would look like in various types of sunglasses right on their cellphones while avoiding having to make a trip to the store (Exhibit 15-8). As Facebook continues to move into the video arena, you can expect its ad revenues to continue to grow into the future. A major revision of the site in 2019 was favorably received.

TikTok Pamela Bump of Hubspot.com describes TikTok this way: "TikTok, created by a Chinese tech firm called ByteDance, is a social media app that allows you to record, edit, and share short, looping 15- or 60-second videos with musical overlays, sound effects, and visual effects."[28] The astounding growth of the app (1 billion downloads in its first year) immediately caught the attention of marketers and its growth continues to attract viewers and advertisers alike.[29] In addition to its incredible growth TikTok offers marketers a number of advantages including (1) a highly sought demographic audience (Figure 15–10); (2) the longer time spent on the app (particularly among gen Z users); (3) ads cost less than on other social media platforms; and (4) its attractiveness to influencer marketing, among others. As of December 2021, TikTok became the number 1 mobile app ranked by downloads, surpassing Instagram and Snapchat significantly. While YouTube still had more monthly users, forecasts predict that the platform will surpass YouTube in a few years if current growth continues.[30]

TikTok's success has led many companies and their agencies to move away from creating content for Instagram and YouTube, as a number of companies have achieved success on the new social media channel.[31] The NBA, for example, used TikTok to show a lighter side of the organization, posting videos of players working out to music, dancing on the court, and performing interesting antics. The San Diego Zoo posted videos with fun music featuring cute animals, while *The Washington Post* posted comedic skits about the late-breaking news. Numerous others including Chipotle, Gymshark, and Dunkin' have also successfully placed videos.

While the app continues to surprise marketers with its success, a number of businesses, government agencies, and users have raised less than positive issues. One is TikTok's ties to the Chinese state, which raises concerns with privacy issues including the protection of user data. Another concern is the lack of controls over content, particularly that involving sex and nudity—since young users constitute a high percentage of users and also spend a lot of time on the site. Some of the app's most expensive and high-profile ad formats have often failed, and direct-response marketing has so far been unsuccessful. Nevertheless, the app is likely to continue to be attractive to both users and advertisers.[32]

Twitter Twitter is an online social microblogging network that enables users to send and receive text-based messages (tweets) up to 280 characters. Twitter has about 436 million active users worldwide. Despite being made more popular by former President Trump—for whom it was a primary form of communication—and an increase of allowable characters to 280 from 140, Twitter experienced various negative publicity in 2022, but still gained users and ad revenues.[33]

As with Facebook, many marketers have found Twitter a useful tool for communicating with their existing and potential customers, and some marketers believe it may be the very best tool for establishing connections with them. A number of companies have found Twitter to be useful in promoting their brands, including Netflix, Greenhouse, and Close—a sales CRM for small businesses. The ASPCA used Twitter to send pictures of animals that had been mistreated, finding it more effective than words in generating responses. Converse made wise use of the Chinese social influencer and entertainer Zhang Yi Xing. Just by mentioning his name and showing him in a pair of Converse shoes, this tweet was successful in increasing engagement.

When Mercedes-Benz introduced its new A-Class automobile, a commercial was run on the popular TV show *X Factor* integrating the cast into a chase scene. Viewers were in control of the action in the scene and by tweeting #evade or #hide they determined the action in the 30-second spot. The "commercial you drive" was viewed by hundreds of thousands of viewers, and was considered a contributor to the product's launch success.

The City of St. Louis also found Twitter to be an effective medium for reaching its market. In this case, the medium was used in a nonprofit effort to find ways to improve the city, titled "Tweet Me in St. Louis." After establishing a community-based website (www.rallystl.org), the organization used Facebook and Twitter to crowdsource ideas on how to improve the city as well as crowdfunding to raise money to support the ideas generated. The public was asked to tweet ideas in regard to cultural arts, education,

EXHIBIT 15–9

Hostess ran this Twitter ad to celebrate the start of baseball season. With its mixed-sport message, it gained added attention.

Hostess Brands LLC

EXHIBIT 15–10

ECCO is considered one of the most successful users of Instagram.

ECCO

housing, or virtually anything else that they thought needed improvement. After the period for submitting ideas was closed, participants were asked to vote on the best ones—again by tweeting their vote. Those involved believed that the simplicity of the ability to tweet a response was a major factor contributing to the campaign's success. Virgin America, Sephora, and Starbucks, among others, have all used Twitter's enhanced promoted tweets program, which ensures that tweets from their brands will appear at the top of the timeline for those who follow the brand. Other companies have found that Twitter can be used to respond to customer complaints and/or inquiries, retweeting important information and monitoring the market to watch for opportunities or threats. Exhibit 15–9 shows a Twitter ad Hostess ran to celebrate the beginning of baseball season.

Like Facebook, Twitter has made substantial changes to the site in an effort to gain advertising revenues. Twitter now offers advertisers a "tailored audiences program" in which users who visit a website and also use Twitter can be found later for retargeting purposes.[34] Brands can also share their e-mail lists with Twitter and deliver ads to their customers. The idea is that companies can create tailored audiences using lists of Twitter IDs to build a more potentially interested database.[35] Database marketing companies Acxiom, Merkle, and Mailchimp, among others are assisting brands in this endeavor.

Instagram One of the rapidly growing platforms in users and popularity is Instagram, particularly among those in younger demographic segments. Since its acquisition by Facebook in 2012, Instagram has continued to be successful with this younger audience (particularly female millennials) and those advertisers targeting them, to the point where the site now accounts for about 50 percent of Meta's ad revenue.[36] While continuing to attract new companies, much of the growth has come from loyal advertisers who have continued—and increased—their advertising expenditures on the site. Instagram Stories has become a very attractive component to members and marketers and has accounted for much of Instagram's success. Instagram has proven to be an effective site for micro-influencers due to their closer personal networks and perceived authenticity and loyalty.[37] Marketers in numerous industries worldwide have found Instagram useful for a variety of communications activities. Instragram's visual content allows companies to post pictures and video news, events, new product introductions, and other company- or brand-related activities to increase exposure, showcase products in a creative way, establish visual brand identity, and more. As can be seen by the ad in Exhibit 15–10, the Instagram platform allows for an attractive option for marketing ones' products. Many marketers consider Instagram to be the most engaging of all social networks. Companies have initiated very successful contests in which they engage consumers by having them post pictures related to their brands. In its #SonyLove contest, Sony asked people to first follow the company on Instagram and then post pictures of anything that represented "love" to them. One entry was chosen every day to win a $50 Sony Store gift card or other Sony merchandise based on their entry. Virgin America surprised flyers with a gift and posted them in a picture on Instagram, or encouraged its followers to do the same. Given the ability to post pictures to garner engagement, the variety of uses of this site for marketers seem almost endless (Figure 15–11).

FIGURE 15–11

How Brands Use Instagram

Nike—The most followed brand on Instagram, Nike keeps it simple. For example, one photo shows a woman jogging through a beautiful row of cherry blossom trees with the caption "You don't have to stop and smell the flowers." Simple, but eye-catching and interesting. Nike also uses influencers such as soccer star Cristiano Ronaldo and other athletes.

Reebok—Taking a different approach from Nike, ReebockWomen inspires women to be better, stronger, and more determined. Visual content focuses on effort, action, and sweat with an emphasis on action images and sports while striking a balance between athletes and everyday women.

Chanel—Keeping it plain and simple like Nike, the product is always front and center. One series included Gisele Bündchen talking about her makeup secrets.

Staples—Attention-getting vivid colors exaggerated by a white background that appear hypnotic. Over 8 percent of Staples customers say they view the posts.

Saks Fifth Avenue—With a like2buy platform, the Saks posts are shoppable. The attractiveness and diversity of its photos including store windows, Gucci shoe displays, and Louis Vuitton shots lure consumers into the photos.

EXHIBIT 15–11

Macy's also runs ads on Snapchat.

Macy's, Inc.

Snapchat Originally developed as an app that had disappearing pictures, Snapchat has now evolved into a mix of private messaging and public content, including brand networks, publications, and live events such as sports and music. Snapchat is a popular messaging app that lets users exchange pictures and videos (called snaps) that are meant to disappear after they're viewed. It is primarily this feature that makes the app particularly interesting and appealing to a younger audience—with the prime advertising audience 18-24 and women 25-34.[38] Nevertheless, studies have shown that the personal-oriented messaging was still being accessed by users more than the publicly offered content that was being presented. In spite of users' preferences, Snapchat made changes to the app resulting in protests and a loss of users. As users declined, so too did advertising revenue, leading the company to lose value and the stock to plummet. Once an attractive medium to advertisers, many have departed and have yet to return. Amazon, Hollister, Macy's, Samsung, and Universal Pictures have all run Snapchat campaigns, and McDonald's, in particular, placed a lot of emphasis on marketing through snaps. Luxury brand Michael Kors used Snapchat's "Stories" feature at New York's Fashion Week showing content from runway pictures, backstage shots, and front-row pictures. Exhibit 15-11 shows an ad for Macy's that appeared on Snapchat, which reflects the fact that older, well-established stores have now adopted this new media platform.

By mid-2019, Snapchat was showing signs of resurgence after further design changes but was still facing stock declines in mid-2022 due to continued ad revenue declines.

Pinterest Pinterest is a pinboard-style photo-sharing website that allows users to create and manage theme-based image collections such as events, interests, and hobbies. Users can browse other pinboards for images, "re-pin" images to their own pinboards, or "like" photos. Pinterest is most attractive to females, with approximately 60 percent being younger women.[39] As with Instagram, Sony has found this site to be quite useful in its marketing efforts, as have numerous others such as Whole Foods, Southwest Airlines, and Banana Republic. The ad in Exhibit 15-12 for Toyota shows that, like the companies just mentioned, the platform appeals to a variety of advertisers. Nordstrom has used Pinterest to post pictures of new product offerings, to make its blog more appealing, and to sponsor a bridal contest in which brides-to-be could win prizes including cash, a bridal consultant, and a hotel stay at a J.W. Marriott Resort. Many other marketers targeting women have found Pinterest to be an effective medium. There were over 433 million Pinterest users in 2022.[40]

LinkedIn Another social networking site but with a different audience, LinkedIn now has over 810 million members who log in once a month or more.[41] While the site is primarily used by professionals to network, businesses have used banner ads on the site in an attempt to reach this professional audience to promote their products and services. LinkedIn offers marketers the opportunity to connect to customers with specific interests that may be related to their brand.

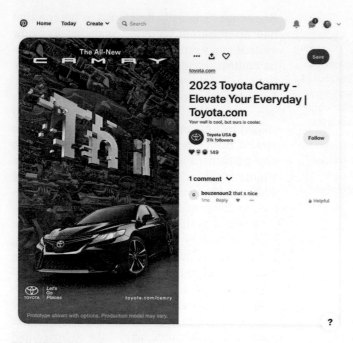

EXHIBIT 15–12

A number of companies like Toyota have found Pinterest to be useful in their IMC programs.

Toyota Motor Corporation

YouTube Another powerful social medium, YouTube is a content aggregator, hosting content for information and entertainment and, although it is a social network, is not a traditional one like Facebook or Snapchat. Users can upload and share their own videos, as well as those placed by others (including companies). Along with Facebook, YouTube dominates the social media domain. In fact, in a Pew Research study, 77 percent of U.S. users 18–25 say that they use YouTube (Facebook is at 65 percent). To put that into perspective, Instagram is third at 24 percent. Most millennials prefer YouTube to traditional television.[42]

What makes YouTube so effective for marketers is the ability to use the site as an advertising medium or as a search platform. Ads like the one for mountain biking (Exhibit 15–13) and the search option have led to the increased popularity of YouTube as an advertising medium. Marketers can post videos of their products or brands that can be informational (how to build an IKEA bookcase) or entertaining (as noted, companies posted TV commercials on the YouTube site prior to showing them on the Super Bowl). The site is particularly engaging to millennials, the segment much sought after by many marketers—so much so that YouTube has its own stars and vloggers and is now competing with advertising dollars that previously were targeted to broadcast television. However, there are some who are worried that the platform is abandoning what has led to its success in favor of more traditional content. Many companies have now established their own YouTube channels, which allows them to have a specifically branded URL and fully customized content. Among the top 10 advertisers on YouTube are Walmart, Target, Lowe's, Amazon, Walgreens, Squid Game, Samsung, and Apple.[43]

The potential for exposure on YouTube is one of the major attractions for marketers large and small. For example, as far back as 2015, Rachel Levin, a beauty vlogger sometimes referred to as "YouTubes's Cover Girl," had her antismoking commercial "It's A Trap" viewed 6.5 million times, while overall Levin's videos have been viewed over a billion times.[44] The Indian channel has over 227 million subscribers and has been viewed by over 227 trillion subscribers.[45] At the same time, a small brand, Orabrush, which had no sales online or offline, was able to successfully pull its product into large retail stores like Walmart as a result of its successful YouTube video. In less than 2 years the Orabush channel garnered over 45 million views, and consumers' demands for the tongue cleaner led to retail distribution. A study conducted by Defy Media showed that for teens, YouTube stars were much more influential on their purchase decisions than were either TV or movie stars, and they were fine with the fact that their stars were pushing products and trying to sell them things. In 2019, YouTube announced an editing tool that it claimed would help advertisers optimize their content for mobile audiences. The "Bumper Machine" would edit relevant content from longer ads down to 6 seconds (or help create a 6-second ad from scratch) to be more attractive to mobile video ad users, the main driver in the growing digital ad market, which is dominated by YouTube.

EXHIBIT 15–13

YouTube has become attractive to advertisers like Polygon Bikes.

YouTube, LLC

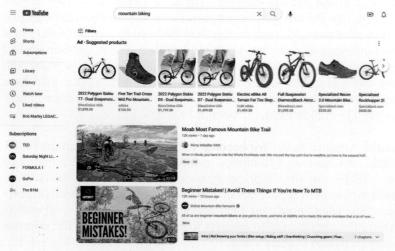

EXHIBIT 15–14

YouTube has its own celebrities like Rachel Levin shown here in her antismoking commerical "It's A Trap."

Rachel Levin, YouTube

EXHIBIT 15–15

Podcasts have become popular with a number of advertisers.

Ian Dagnall/Alamy Stock Photo

Other Social Sites As noted earlier, there are many more social media sites that are useful to marketers in their IMC programs. These sites have been used by marketers for marketing research, public relations, promotions, and a variety of other strategies. In addition, the three most popular sites previously discussed have broadened their offerings. See Digital and Social Media Perspective 15–1. A poll of 2,225 social media users conducted in 2022 showed an increase in purchases made through social media sites, particularly among gen Z and millennials. Approximately one-half of respondents from these age groups say they make purchases on social media (only 22 percent of baby boomers said they do).[46] As you can imagine, there are too many sites to discuss here.

Podcasting **Podcasting** is a medium that uses the Internet to distribute audio or video files for downloading onto desktops as well as iPods, iPads, tablets, and other portable devices, though smartphones are the most commonly used. As the market for these devices grows, the attractiveness of this medium does as well. An estimated 144 million Americans now listen to podcasts monthly, and over 420 million do worldwide. As this number has grown, so too have advertising revenues, with more than half of advertisers saying they will continue to increase spending in this medium.[47,48,49] Spotify and radio stations, including Clear Channel Communications and National Public Radio, and television programs, such as *60 Minutes*, now podcast entire programs or video clips. Traditional advertisers like Ford, Dunkin' Donuts, Wendy's, Allstate, and P&G are just a few of the many companies running ads or sponsorships in the medium, while others are finding it useful as well (Exhibit 15–15). Many travel-related companies have also found podcasts to be an attractive medium to advertise in, including Southwest Airlines, Marriott International, Cambria Hotels, and luxury travel company Truway Travel.[50] Durex, a condom manufacturer, purchased product placements in podcasts—in part to reach young listeners with risque marketing messages while skirting FCC decency rules. The typical podcast listener tends to be more upscale in income and education, and thus is an attractive target market for advertisers.[51]

Blogs A **blog** (or weblog) is a web-based publication consisting primarily of periodic articles, normally presented in reverse chronological order. As noted, blogs may reflect the writings of an individual, a community, a political organization, or a corporation, and they offer advertisers a new way to reach their target audiences. Alamo, Bacardi, Home Depot, and Coach are just a few companies who promote their products through blogs. For example, there are blogs about beer, current events, sports, raising children, and so on. In 2022, there were an estimated 600 million active blogs on the Internet.[52] Fashion, food, sewing, and travel are the most popular blog topics. Some marketers are excited about the potential of blogs to reach large or targeted audiences at a small cost. Besides banner ads, companies can buy pay-per-click ads and/or become an affiliate. As a result, these marketers attempt to keep the bloggers happy by feeding them exclusives, releasing product news to them before it hits the mainstream, and so on. Others are a bit more skeptical, noting that there are a number of problems with the use of blogs, including the potential for deception and limited reach. These critics cite the use of mommy bloggers and

Have the "Big Three" of the Internet Met Their Match?

When the new millennium began, digital technology was just starting to affect the world of marketing and advertising. The Internet was constrained by technological limitations such as bandwidth problems, and most consumers were accessing the Web via dial-up telephone services. The average consumer spent less than 30 minutes online each day versus nearly 7 hours today. However, technological advances such as wireless broadband (Wi-Fi) led to the growth of mobile devices such as tablets and smartphones, with the latter becoming an indispensable part of most people's daily lives. While a number of companies have been involved in the digital revolution, three in particular currently dominate the world of digital marketing and advertising: Google, Facebook, and Amazon accounting for 64 percent of all U.S. digital ad spending in 2021. It is interesting to examine the evolution of each company and how they have become so powerful.

Online search was in its infancy when Google was cofounded by Sergey Brin and Larry Page while they were graduate students at Stanford working on the problem of trying to improve the online search process. The system they developed delivered more relevant search results by favoring pages that were referenced and linked by other websites. Consumers fell in love with the simplicity of Google's search engine as well as the fast and accurate results it provided. Google attracted a loyal following among the growing number of Internet users and quickly became the dominant search engine and leading gateway to the vast amount of information available online. While Google helps Internet users search for information online, it also makes much of its revenue from selling advertisements associated with the keywords they use to do their searches. Google Ads is a platform where marketers pay to display brief advertising messages above the search results when people look for products and services. Online advertisers compete to have their ads displayed with the results of a particular keyword search in a higher position than competitors are given, and pay only when an ad is clicked (called cost-per-click), which in turn takes the Web surfer to a landing page on the advertiser's website.

In 2003, Google expanded beyond search-related advertising by launching contextual ads that appear on the websites of companies or online publishers with whom Google partners through its AdSense program. What are now known as display ads as well as videos can appear on more than 2 million websites and in over 650,000 mobile apps. In 2006, Google paid $1.6 billion for YouTube, which was launched just a year earlier by three former PayPal employees. YouTube quickly became the world's largest video-sharing website—people now watch over 1 billion hours of videos on YouTube each day. In late 2008, YouTube began accepting pre-roll ads that would appear before some of the videos, and in early 2009, it started accepting ads in seven other formats. Google has revolutionized the

This ad run by Google is designed to attract companies to advertise on the site.

HubSpot, Inc.

online advertising industry as well as the practice of marketing. The company has refined the concept of targeted advertising and taken it well beyond what traditional media can offer. Never before could marketers have their ads appear at the moment a potential customer was searching for a product. By the fourth quarter of 2021, YouTube advertising revenue had reached $8.6 billion.

Facebook was launched by Mark Zuckerberg in 2004 while he was a student at Harvard. Its membership was initially limited to Harvard students before quickly expanding to other colleges in the United States and Canada. By the end of 2006, the social networking site was available to everyone 13 years and older, and by 2010, Facebook had more than 500 million members. In September 2012, it reached a milestone of 1 billion monthly active users and in 2022, has 2.96 billion. In 2012, Facebook purchased Instagram, which reached 1 billion users by late 2018, nearly 90 percent of whom were outside the United States. In 2014, the company acquired WhatsApp, the world's most popular messaging platform, which now has over 1.5 billion users. Like Google, Facebook has had a tremendous impact on advertising and marketing because marketers can target Facebook and Instagram ads to users of the platforms by demographics such as age and gender, location, interests, behavior, and connections. Moreover, people spend a considerable amount of time on the two social media sites; the average daily Facebook user spends about 33 minutes on the app. Instagram users spend an average of 29 minutes per day on the platform, while those over the age of 35 spend 24 minutes a day.

The third major player in the digital advertising industry is now Amazon, which was founded in 1995 by Jeff Bezos as an e-commerce company that began by selling books online. Over the next several years, the company added more categories of merchandise, including toys, electronics, video games, software, and a variety of home goods. In 2005, the company launched Amazon Prime, which included free delivery for over a million eligible products, and free video streaming was added to the Prime offerings in 2011. By 2022, there were more than 200 million Prime members worldwide acquiring more than 25 billion items per year. Amazon has become the leading online retailer.

Amazon's dominance in e-commerce has made the company an important player in the advertising industry as companies selling their products on the site want to maintain a presence on it. As one marketing executive notes: "If you're selling on Amazon, you're advertising on Amazon." Amazon sells search ads similar to Google's cost-per-click search system as well as display and video ads. Its reach extends across the Web. Amazon generated $31 billion in ad revenue in 2021.

Evidence of how the three companies dominate the digital advertising market can be found in the numbers. Digital advertising revenue was expected to reach almost $240 billion in the United States in 2022. The dominance of Google, Facebook, and Amazon reflects how advertising is becoming less about developing creative ads run through high-profile media such as television and magazines and more about being able to use big data and analytics to target messages to individual consumers. All three companies have tremendous amounts of data on their members and consumers searching or shopping on their sites. For example, Facebook offers advertisers more than 1,300 categories that can be used for ad targeting. As one media agency executive notes, the advantage of being able to track online behavior is that "we know what you want even before you know you want it."

While clearly still the three major players in the ad revenue game, things are not going as smoothly as they were in the past. A number of factors have now resulted in some significant in-roads by competitors, for example, major gains by media platform TikTok. The incredible growth of the social media platform has now threatened the leaders, particularly Facebook and Instagram, but also others like YouTube, Snapchat, and Twitter. TikTok's greatest increase has come from gen Z who now spend more than 3 hours a day there—surpassing Facebook and Instagram. Where the crowd goes and spends its time attracts advertising revenues. Increased government regulation, privacy issues that have led some marketers to be less optimistic about digital advertising, and successful moves by Apple have also dented the armor of the top three. By late 2022, Facebook's newly named Meta had lost billions of dollars in ad revenue due to changes by Apple in its mobile operating system and concerns about their investments in the metaverse. Its stock price had fallen by 60 percent and layoffs were expected. While Google's revenues increased, they did so at the lowest rate in their history. Most of the other social networks were also showing declines. All of a sudden it's getting interesting!

Sources: Kevin Roose, "Top Social Media Apps Are Struggling after a Decade of Dominance," *New York Times*, October 26, 2022, www.nytimes.com; Claire Beveridge, "56 Important Social Media Advertising Statistics for 2022," Hootsuite, February 24, 2022, www.hootsuite.com; S. Dixon, "Number of Monthly Facebook Users Worldwide as of Third quarter 2022," *Statista*, October 22, 2022, www.statista.com; Brian Dean, "Amazon Prime User and Revenue Statistics," Back Linko, January 5, 2022, www.backlinko.com; Jordan Novet, "Amazon Has a $31 Billion a Year Advertising Business," *CNBC*, February 3, 2022, www.cnbc.com; Sara Lebon, "Google, Facebook and Amazon to Account for 64% of U.S. Digital Ad Spending This Year," *eMarketer*, November 3, 2022, www.emarketer.com; "People Spend Daily Average of 7 Hours Online Worldwide," TRT World, February 15, 2022, www.trtworld.com; Garett Sloane, "Advertisers Just Can't Quit Facebook," *Advertising Age*, February 4, 2019, p. 8; Ken Auletta, "How the Math Men Overthrew the Mad Men," *The New Yorker*, May 21, 2018, https://www.newyorker.com/news/annals-of-communications/how-the-math-men-overthrew-the-mad-men.

EXHIBIT 15–16

Virtual and augmented reality apps are used by marketers and consumers alike.

Monster Energy Company

teen bloggers who may support brands and promote them for compensation to unsuspecting audiences. Whether bloggers are full-time professionals or just hobbyists, many of them write about brands they love or hate (or love to hate!), and their influence on consumers is on the increase, as the consumers often use the information they obtain from blogs in their purchase decisions.

Other 2.0 Media Forms There are numerous other 2.0 media forms also available to marketers, including the use of virtual and augmented reality and QR codes.

Virtual/Augmented Reality While it may seem like something out of the future, **virtual and augmented reality** are very much here (Exhibit 15–16). As noted earlier in this chapter, the development of Web 3.0 has increased marketers' interest and emphasis on blending physical and digital environments. Aided by the pandemic having kept people at home, AR and

VR have seen rapid growth over the years. There were expected to be almost 90 million monthly AR users in the United States and approximately 59 million VR users in 2022.[53] There are now thousands of augmented reality apps currently being used by marketers and consumers alike, and the future promises much more. Macy's has used AR to help sell cosmetics. Rather than carry an enormous stock of lipsticks, potential buyers can see what they would look like with a thousand variety of colors. Ford used Snapchat to promote its Eco Sport mini SUV by taking the viewer into the AR version of the car to examine its interior and exterior. Lowe's and IKEA have both employed the technology to help those decorating their homes view the possibilities available to them, changing in and out the products to see how they look together. The use of AR is on a steady increase, with more and more companies exploring its capabilities.

Virtual reality (VR) has met with less success than AR at this point. While a number of companies like Nike, Wendy's, Samsung, McDonald's, and Coca-Cola have used VR for marketing purposes, Walmart has employed the technology for training, and other fields like sports and the medical field have recognized the advantages and capabilities of VR, the application of the concept has yet to gain traction.

QR Codes While **QR codes** (machine readable optical labels) initially may not have reached the potential expected, many marketers have used them effectively. A large percentage of print ads now carry the bar codes and their use on television is on the increase. More and more television ads are now displaying the codes, as are airlines, government agencies, and so on. An example of a successful application of this technology was a joint effort between Disney and Cargill (Honeysuckle White and Shady Brook Farms meats) that used mobile bar codes to entice consumers to buy through a *Wreck-It Ralph* Blu-ray combo pack promotion. Cargill placed QR bar codes on 7 million packages of turkey products that, when scanned, took consumers to a website where they could get a $5 mail-in rebate over their mobile device. The very popular app Shazam is another good example of the use of a form of QR code, in which radio listeners can immediately identify a song, artist, and album title through their cell phones. McDonald's, Burger King, and IKEA have made successful use of QR codes as have luxury brands like Lacoste, Louis Vuitton, adidas, Victoria's Secret, and Ralph Lauren among numerous others. It seems QR codes are finally living up to expectations.

Sales Promotion on the Internet

Companies have found the Internet to be a very effective medium for disseminating sales promotions. Numerous companies tie in sales promotions to their websites and/ or through other forms of digital and social media. Like many companies, Ghirardelli engages in the use of sales promotions with its website, as shown in Exhibit 15–17. Numerous companies now post online coupons. Other examples include the use of trivia games, contests, sweepstakes, instant win promotions, and so on.

EXHIBIT 15–17

Ghiradelli commonly runs ad promotions on its website.

Ghirardelli Chocolate Company

Personal Selling on the Internet

The Internet has been both a benefit and a detriment to many of those involved in personal selling—particularly those in the business-to-business market. For some, the Internet has been a threat that might take away job opportunities. Companies have found that they can remain effective, or even increase effectiveness, by building a strong online presence. The high-cost and poor-reach disadvantages of personal selling are allowing these companies to reduce new hires and even cut back on their existing sales forces.

On the positive side, websites have been used quite effectively to enhance and support the selling effort. As noted earlier, digital and social media have become primary sources of information for millions of customers in the consumer and business-to-business markets. Visitors to websites can gain volumes of information about a company's products and services. In return, the visitors become a valuable resource for leads that internal as well as external salespersons can follow up, and they become part of a prospect database. Not only can potential customers learn about the company's offerings, but the selling organization can serve and qualify prospects more cost-effectively.

The Web can also be used to stimulate trial. For many companies, personal salespersons can reach only a fraction of the potential customer base. Through trial demonstrations or samples offered online, customers can determine if the offering satisfies their needs and, if so, request a personal sales call. In such cases both parties benefit from time and cost savings.

Companies have used the Internet to improve their one-on-one relationships with customers. By providing more information in a more timely and efficient manner, a company enables customers to learn more about what it has to offer. This increases the opportunity for cross-selling and customer retention. Twitter has become a powerful tool for consumers to voice their opinions of companies or complaints, while also allowing the involved company to respond quickly.

In a well-designed IMC program, the Internet and personal selling are designed to be complementary tools, working together to increase sales. It appears that more and more companies are coming to this realization.

Public Relations on the Internet

The Internet is a useful medium for conducting public relations activities. Many sites devote a portion of their content to public relations activities, including the provision of information about the company, its philanthropic activities, annual reports, and more.

Companies, nonprofit organizations, and political parties have become quite adept at using the Internet for public relations purposes. An excellent example of the use of public relations on the Internet is provided by Chrysler (Exhibit 15–18). The site

EXHIBIT 15–18

Chrysler uses its website for public relations purposes as seen in this promotion for its Drive For the Kids School Fundraiser.

DoLightful, Inc.

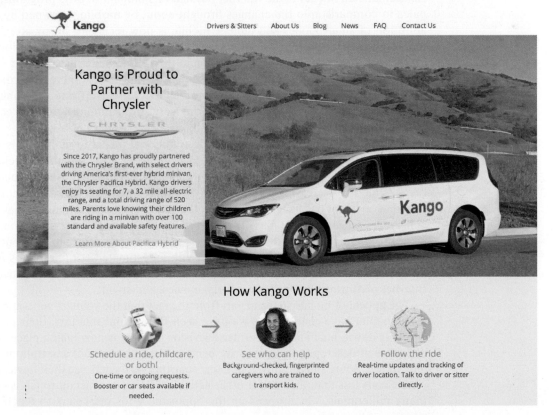

provides up-to-date news stories and other forms of content, photo images, and cross-references to other sites or media as well as press kits and a calendar of upcoming events. It also provides information about Chrysler automobiles and the corporation itself and allows for customer feedback and registration for updates. In addition, Chrysler's homepage contains many of the articles written about the corporation, including awards won and philanthropic efforts achieved, such as its concern for the environment and support for numerous causes.

Other examples of the effective use of public relations activities on the Internet are also available, as you will see in the chapter on public relations. The Web is a useful medium for conducting public relations activities, and its use for this function is on the increase.

At the same time, many philanthropic and nonprofit organizations have found the Internet to be a useful way to generate funds. As noted earlier, charitable organizations have also formed sites to handle public relations activities, provide information regarding the causes the charity supports, collect contributions, and so on. In an example of integrating the Internet with public relations and television, companies have found the Internet to be extremely useful for providing information in times of a crisis and for gathering feedback about their products and services and about themselves.

Direct Marketing on the Internet

Our discussion of direct marketing and the Internet approached the topic from two perspectives: the use of direct-marketing tools for communications objectives and e-commerce (as discussed in Chapter 14). As we stated previously, many direct-marketing tools like direct mail, infomercials, and the like have been adapted to the Internet. At the same time, e-commerce—selling directly to the consumer via the Internet—has become an industry all its own.

MOBILE

As dramatic an impact as the Internet has had on companies' IMC programs, it almost pales in comparison to the changes brought about by **mobile**. Spawned by the rapid adoption of smartphones and tablets, mobile is now receiving strong attention from marketers, and ad revenues continue to climb, primarily through applications (apps). Studies show that smartphone penetration in the United States has reached 77 percent of the population.[54] As adoption of these phones and tablets increases, content consumption will grow right along with it, and so too will advertising spending to reach these users. Marketers see mobile as offering very strong potential and will continue to move monies from traditional media to mobile.

As more dollars are being moved from traditional media to mobile, it is suggested that mobile devices have led to increases in search behavior and online purchasing and have dramatically changed the way we view television. One might think tablets may be responsible for decreasing TV watching, but this is not the case. The amount of TV watching may not be changing much, but the way that it is being watched has. Younger consumers are much more likely to report that they watch TV with their mobile device, posting, e-mailing, and texting friends as well as seeking information about program content and commercials while viewing. With an estimated 6 million apps now available, mobile users can watch just about anything including television programming, Internet platforms like YouTube, sports, movies, and so on.

The appeal of mobile stems in part from the fact that the younger generations' media usage habits have changed. As we have seen throughout this text, their use of print media is down, much of their former television viewing is now taking place on tablets, and sales of desktops and laptops are being replaced by sales of smartphones and tablets. In fact, some studies show that many smartphone owners use their devices to make phone calls less than they do for other activities. Being in constant touch is critical for many millennials, which opens up the opportunity for marketers to reach potential consumers at almost any time and any place—even at the point of purchase. (Next time you are in a public place, take a minute to look around at how many people are on their cell phones—although it might actually be easier to count the ones who are not!)

The Role of Mobile in the IMC Process

As you read in the previous sections of this chapter, mobile has already been integrated with other media. We have discussed mobile ads and provided examples of sales promotions and direct marketing and even product placements through the phones. We have also pointed out that marketing influencers can now reach consumers through their smartphones, and when users access social networks on their phones, marketers are provided with even more opportunities to reach them. The use of native ads on smartphones and tablets has been deemed to be quite effective and on the increase.

Let's look at some specific examples of successful mobile marketing tactics:

- The automobile industry has found that marketing through mobile is effective throughout the purchase funnel. At the top of the funnel, mobile, tablet, and video ads have all been shown to contribute to encouraging potential buyers to begin to look for a new car (exceeded only by direct mail). One study indicated that the automobile industry led all global industries in the number of video completions of mobile banner ads.[55]
- Advertising dollars being allocated to mobile search will continue to increase as marketers recognize that search on smartphone and tablet devices is on the increase. A study by FordDirect showed that 81 percent of auto shoppers used smartphones to research different autos. Twenty-five percent of these used smartphones exclusively, and once on the lot, 25 percent used their phones to access more sources of information.[56] Shoppers were also using their phones to arrange for financing options.
- In other examples, Burger King delivered mobile coupons to consumers within a geofence (virtual perimeter) (Exhibit 15–19); Hershey's offered to sponsor data costs for consumers who watched a video for its Scharffen Berger chocolate brand; JetBlue sent different messages to tablet and smartphone users, and offered a video game to the tablet users as they might have more time to watch; McDonald's used native ads touting the nature of their coffee. As you can see, mobile is integrating other promotional components into their campaigns while itself becoming more integrated into IMC programs.

Disadvantages of Mobile

Lest you be misled into believing that mobile is the be-all and end-all of media, the medium is not without its disadvantages:

- *Creative challenges*—While we have provided some excellent examples of the creative use of mobile, it is still a medium that challenges creative directors. The small screens limit what advertisers can do as compared to what they can do on the larger screens of TVs and even desktops. The JetBlue example provided earlier is one interesting approach to this challenge.
- *Time*—The very nature of being mobile means viewers may be on the move, thus providing less time to get attention and limiting message capabilities. Unlike the desktop and some traditional media, the viewer is not settled in to use the medium. Thus, it is more difficult to get, and hold, attention, and the message may have to be limited and short.
- *Sharing*—Maybe we should say *not sharing*. One study found that 99 percent of mobile users do not like to share what they see. One of the key objectives of digital advertisers is to get engagement, with viewers responding to the brand, providing feedback, and extending the reach to make the message viral. Desktop users are 35 percent more likely to click on a sharing button than are mobile users.[57]

EXHIBIT 15–19

Burger King has been very effective offering mobile coupons to consumers.

Burger King

- *Irritation and Privacy Issues*—As more and more monies go into advertising on mobile, there will be more and more ads sent to smartphones and other mobile devices. Over 50 percent of shopping apps run retargeting campaigns. The result is likely to be that consumers will become irritated with these ads—as with spam on computer desktops.[58] The result could be the development of negative attitudes toward the sender, increased use of ad blockers, and so on. It is now possible to get ad blockers for mobile devices, and marketers have already perceived this as a threat.

Despite its potential weaknesses, mobile will continue to be adopted and is expected to constitute a large share of the digital ad budget.

SOCIAL MEDIA MANAGEMENT PROGRAMS

As you read through all of the options for digital advertising, social media networks, and so on, you may feel overwhelmed by trying to figure out how to manage this whole process. Fortunately, there are a number of companies that provide **social media management** tools. Companies like Hootsuite, HubSpot, SocialPilot, and others provide management services for small, medium, and large companies. They offer media management, content development, publishing, monitoring the environment, and more. Typically, these companies will provide a dashboard to assist clients in the management of services to integrate with the major social networks.

INTERNET METRICS

Companies measuring the effectiveness of digital and social media employ a variety of methods, most of which are done electronically. A number of companies provide Internet measures as part of a package; that is, they provide audience measurement information (demographics, psychographics, etc.) as "up-front" information as well as some of the effectiveness measures described next. First, we will discuss some of the measures used to determine the effectiveness of a website. Then we will discuss some of the companies providing these measures.

Audience Measures and Measures of Effectiveness

When the Internet industry first developed its own measures of effectiveness, problems with these measures led to a slower rate of adoption by traditional media buyers. In an attempt to respond to criticism of the audience metrics employed, as well as to standardize some of the measures used to gauge effectiveness of the Internet, the Interactive Advertising Bureau (IAB)—the largest and most influential trade group—formed a task force in November 2004 consisting of major global corporations involved in advertising and research. The task force was created to examine and create standardized measures to measure advertising impact that could be used to assess the impact of ads and to eliminate confusion. The three key points of the new recommendations are detailed in a 20-page report available from www.iab.com. Industry experts believe that the adoption of these guidelines, along with objective auditing, would make the Internet a more attractive medium for many of those who advertise in traditional media. The guidelines have the support of major online publishers, as well as proprietary online ad-server technologies and major associations worldwide.[59]

Internet-Specific Measures
One of the perceived advantages of the Internet is a company's ability to measure commercial effectiveness, due in part to its ability to measure activity in real time. Google and Facebook both offer analytical tools that allow you to monitor your performance. **Facebook Analytics** "allows users to understand and optimize your complete customer journey across mobile, web, bots, offline,

EXHIBIT 15–20

An example of Google
Analytics output.

Alphabet Inc.

Google Analytics Website Overview

and more ..."; **Google Analytics** "is a web analytics service offered by Google that tracks and reports website traffic, currently as a platform inside the Google Marketing Platform brand" (Exhibit 15–20). Both of these programs offer a variety of valuable insights into how the product or brand is performing. In addition to these analytics, advertisers can determine effectiveness through a variety of measures. Figure 15–12 shows a comprehensive list suggested by Sonia Gregory, founder of freshsparks.com. These measures include audience measures specific to the Internet and interactive industry. (For a detailed explanation of each of these terms, visit www.iab.com.)

FIGURE 15–12

Digital Marketing Metrics Measures

1. Overall website traffic
2. Traffic by source
3. New visitors vs. returning visitors
4. Sessions
5. Average session duration
6. Page views
7. Most visited pages
8. Exit rate
9. Bounce rate
10. Conversion rate
11. Impressions
12. Social reach
13. Social engagement
14. E-mail open rate
15. E-mail click-through rate
16. Cost per click
17. Cost per conversion
18. Cost per acquisition
19. Overall ROI

Source: https://freshsparks.com/digital-marketing-success/.

Traditional Measures   In addition to the Internet-specific measures, companies employ a number of traditional marketing and communications measures, including the following:

- *Recall and retention.* A number of companies use traditional measures of recall and retention to test their Internet ads. These same measures have been used to pretest online commercials as well.
- *Surveys.* Survey research, conducted both online and through traditional methods, is employed to determine everything from site usage to attitudes toward a site.
- *Sales.* For the e-commerce marketers, a prime indicator of effectiveness is the volume of sales generated. Adding information regarding demographics, user behaviors, and so on can increase the effectiveness of this measure.
- *Tracking.* Some companies now offer more traditional tracking measures such as brand awareness, ad recall, message association, and purchase intent.
- *ROI.* A study conducted by comScore, MySpace, and dunnhumby measured the ROI of online sales generated by a $1 million campaign on MySpace.[60] As noted in previous chapters, ROI is difficult to measure and quantify.

The previously mentioned measures reveal that digital media have their own set of criteria for measuring effectiveness and are also borrowing from traditional measures; for example, brand recall has become a major area of focus. The American Association of Advertising Agencies and the Association of National Advertisers use a system called Advertising Digital Identification (Ad-Id). Ad-Id assigns advertising across all media a specific media code to facilitate cross-media buys. In 2008 Ad-Id became the official media coding standard. The goal of the coalition is to develop cross-media standards employing impression comparisons that include the Internet. Many of the companies that provide research information in traditional media (Nielsen, Ipsos-ASI) are now extending their reach into the Internet world. Others (Insights.com, Forrester) have developed measures specifically for online users. One of the commonly used Internet advertising effectiveness measurement companies is ComScore Media Metrix. The company offers a combination of effectiveness measures for marketers to use.[61] Academics are also beginning to publish articles related to measuring effectiveness of digital and social media. Studies on consumers' attitudes toward a site, response variations in e-mail surveys, and similarities between brick-and-mortar retailing and e-commerce are just a few of the many articles being published in academic journals to advance the measurement of Internet use.

In addition to the metrics provided here, there are numerous methods that have been suggested for measuring the effectiveness of social media. Note that the metrics shown in Figure 15–13 are not a complete list of effectiveness measures used, but they do provide an illustration of just some of the ways that marketers attempt to determine if they are accomplishing their goals when employing these media. Also keep in mind that many marketers are not enthralled with these measures, which has led to their reluctance to invest more monies in these new media, or to attempt to employ effectiveness measures at all.

Unfortunately, not all of the methods used to measure Internet activity and effectiveness are accurate. We discuss some of these problems next.

ADVANTAGES AND DISADVANTAGES OF THE INTERNET AND DIGITAL AND SOCIAL MEDIA

A number of advantages of the Internet and social media can be cited:

1. *Target marketing.* A major advantage of the Internet and digital and social media is the ability to target very specific groups of individuals with a minimum of waste coverage. For those in the business-to-business market, the Internet resembles a combination trade magazine and trade show, as only those most interested in the products and/or services a site has to offer will visit the site (others have little or no reason to do so). In the consumer market, through personalization, retargeting, and other techniques, sites are becoming more tailored to meet one's needs and wants.

2. *Message tailoring.* As a result of precise targeting, messages can be designed to appeal to the specific needs and wants of the target audience, much of which comes from behavior tracking. The interactive capabilities of social media make it possible to carry on one-to-one marketing with increased success in both the business and the consumer markets.

3. *Interactive capabilities.* Because these media are interactive, they provide strong potential for increasing customer involvement, engagement, satisfaction, and almost immediate feedback for buyers and sellers.

4. *Information access.* Perhaps the greatest advantage of the Internet is its availability as an information source. Internet users can find a plethora of information about almost any topic of their choosing merely by conducting a search. Once they have visited a particular site, users can garner a wealth of information regarding product specifications, costs, purchase information, and so on. Links will direct them to even more information if it is desired. Google and YouTube also offer a search function.

5. *Sales potential.* The sales numbers generated by Amazon and eBay alone (not to mention many, many more) demonstrate the incredible sales numbers being generated in both the business-to-business and the consumer segments.

FIGURE 15–13 Relevant Metrics for Social Media Applications Organized by Key Social Media Objectives

Social Media Application	Brand Awareness	Brand Engagement	Word of Mouth
Blogs	■ Number of unique visits ■ Number of return visits ■ Number of times bookmarked ■ Search ranking	■ Number of members ■ Number of RSS feed subscribers ■ Number of comments ■ Amount of user-generated content ■ Average length of time on site ■ Number of responses to polls, contests, surveys	■ Number of references to blog in other media (online/offline) ■ Number of reblogs ■ Number of times badge displayed on other sites ■ Number of "likes"
Microblogging (e.g., Twitter)	■ Number of tweets about the brand ■ Valence of tweets +/− ■ Number of followers	■ Number of followers ■ Number of @replies	■ Number of retweets
Cocreation (e.g., Nike By You)	■ Number of visits	■ Number of creation attempts	■ Number of references to project in other media (online/offline)
Social bookmarking (e.g., StumbleUpon)	■ Number of tags	■ Number of followers	■ Number of additional taggers
Forums and Discussion Boards (e.g., Google Groups)	■ Number of page views ■ Number of visits ■ Valence of posted content +/−	■ Number of relevant topics/threads ■ Number of individual replies ■ Number of sign-ups	■ Incoming links ■ Citations in other sites ■ Tagging in social bookmarking ■ Offline references to the forum or its members ■ In private communities: number of pieces of content (photos, discussions, videos); chatter pointing to the community outside of its gates ■ Number of "likes"
Product Reviews (e.g., Amazon)	■ Number of reviews posted ■ Valence of reviews ■ Number and valence of other users' responses to reviews (+/−) ■ Number of wish list adds ■ Number of times product included in users' lists (i.e., Listmanial on Amazon.com)	■ Length of reviews ■ Relevance of reviews ■ Valence of other users' ratings of reviews (i.e., how many found particular review helpful) ■ Number of wish list adds ■ Overall number of reviewer rating scores entered ■ Average reviewer rating score	■ Number of reviews posted ■ Valence of reviews ■ Number and valence of other users' responses to reviews (+/−) ■ Number of references to reviews in other sites ■ Number of visits to review site page ■ Number of times product included in users' lists (i.e., Listmanial on Amazon.com)
Social Networks (e.g., Facebook, LinkedIn)	■ Number of members/fans ■ Number of installs of applications ■ Number of impressions ■ Number of bookmarks ■ Number of reviews/ratings and valence +/−	■ Number of comments ■ Number of active users ■ Number of "likes" on friends' feeds ■ Number of user-generated items (photos, threads, replies) ■ Usage metrics of applications/widgets ■ Impressions-to-interactions ratio ■ Rate of activity (how often members personalize profiles, bios, links, etc.)	■ Frequency of appearances in timeline of friends ■ Number of posts on wall ■ Number of reposts/shares ■ Number of responses to friend referral invites
Video and Photosharing (e.g., Flickr, YouTube)	■ Number of views of video/photo ■ Valence of video/photo ratings +/−	■ Number of replies ■ Number of page views ■ Number of comments ■ Number of subscribers	■ Number of embeddings ■ Number of incoming links ■ Number of references in mock-ups or derived work ■ Number of times republished in other social media and offline ■ Number of "likes"

Source: *MIT Sloan Management Review*, Fall 2010.

Forecasts are for continued growth in the future. In addition, the number of persons who shop online and then purchase offline has continued to increase.

6. *Creativity.* Creatively designed sites can enhance a company's image, lead to repeat visits, and positively position the company or organization in the consumer's mind. Visit some of the sites mentioned earlier to see what we mean. Consumer-generated social media lead to even more creativity.

7. *Exposure.* For many smaller companies with limited budgets, the World Wide Web enables them to gain exposure to potential customers that in the past would have been impossible (recall the example of the tongue cleaner). For a fraction of the investment that would be required using traditional media, companies can gain national and even international exposure in a timely manner.

8. *Speed.* For those requesting information on a company, its products, and/or its service offerings, the Internet is the quickest means of acquiring and providing this information. Well-designed sites keep this information current, and search allows for additional sources.

9. *Complement to IMC.* The Internet and digital and social media complement and are complemented by other IMC media. As such, they serve as vital links in the integrative process. Marketers understand that these media support and are supported by traditional media.

10. *Timeliness.* The ability to communicate quickly and currently offer an advantage that no other media can match. Using social media and mobile, companies can keep consumers up to date with pretty much anything and everything—for example, think about product recalls.

While potentially effective, the Internet and digital and social media also have disadvantages, including the following:

1. *Measurement problems.* One of the greatest disadvantages of the Internet and new media is the lack of reliability of the research numbers generated. A quick review of forecasts and other statistics offered by research providers will demonstrate a great deal of variance—leading to a serious lack of validity and reliability. One company mentioned earlier, eMarketer, has attempted to reconcile such differences and explain the reasoning for the discrepancies (differences in methodologies employed), but the problem still exists. The actions taken by the IAB to standardize metrics will help in reducing some of this problem. But due to difficulties involved in both measuring and forecasting in this medium, it remains necessary to proceed with caution when using these numbers.

2. *Clutter.* As the number of ads proliferates, the likelihood of one's ad being noticed drops accordingly. The result is that some ads may not get noticed, and some consumers may become irritated by the clutter. Studies show that banner ads have lost effectiveness for this very reason, and that interstitials are irritating as well. Many ads others show consistently declining click-through rates.

3. *Potential for deception.* The Center for Media Education has referred to the Web as "a web of deceit" in regard to advertisers' attempts to target children with subtle advertising messages. The center, among others, has asked the government to regulate the Internet. In addition, data collection without consumers' knowledge and permission, hacking, and credit card theft are among the problems confronting Internet users. Bloggers, marketing influencers who endorse brands without revealing that they are being compensated to do so, and native ads can also be misleading. The problem with native ads may be particularly true on smartphones, where proper labeling of the ads as sponsored may be difficult to see.

4. *Privacy.* One of the many issues of concern for Internet users is privacy. Perhaps of most concern is the collection of personal data, subsequently provided to marketers, sometimes without the users' knowledge. While many younger users seem to be less worried about privacy, Facebook, among others, has had to deal with a number of issues regarding privacy, leading to legislation and bad public relations. The IAB has issued a policy on privacy to which it asks companies to adhere (see www.iab.com). See Digital and Social Media Perspective 15-2.

Changes in Privacy Regulations May Lead to Major Impacts for Consumers and Advertisers

You probably know about website cookies and are aware that they track your movements on a site that you visit to see where you go, and then follow you to other sites to see where else you go. Cookies are instrumental in companies' retargeting efforts and are promoted by marketers as a key tool used to improve the user experience, by collecting data that allows for more effective target marketing. But not everyone agrees with this description of a cookie, as many consumers and advocacy groups believe they are an invasion of privacy. They have lobbied for, and successfully achieved, a third-party cookie phaseout. While Safari and Firefox blocked third-party cookies in 2013, Google Chrome did not. Given that Chrome constitutes more than half of all searches, there were a lot of website visitors still being affected. But in 2020 Google announced that they too would phase out cookies (then later delayed the phaseout to 2022). The news sent panic among advertisers and led to significant changes given their heavy dependence on the identifiers.

In April 2021 Apple launched its App Tracking Transparency feature that gave iPhone users much more control over their privacy settings and their data. The impact was immediate and devastating to competitors. By the second half of the year Facebook, Snapchat, Twitter, and YouTube had lost $9.85 billion in revenue—that's 12.6 percent in the third and fourth quarters—as advertisers figured out how to transition to the new privacy measures. Most of the platforms had to figure out how to adapt, rebuild their infrastructures from scratch, and then test them before they could release them to the market. Meanwhile Apple's fourth quarter advertising revenues exceeded expectations by $700 million to a total of $18.3 billion.

Google announced in 2022 that they would not be building alternative identifiers, explaining, "We don't believe these solutions will meet rising consumer expectations for privacy," but instead would employ their own *privacy preserving APIs* to prevent individual tracking. (Google also did not stop all cookies and would continue to allow first-party tracking, which allows for tracking movements while on the advertisers' site.) In a survey conducted with ad agencies by Hubspot.com many advertisers were concerned that they would (1) not be able to track the right data; (2) need to increase spending by 5 to 25 percent to reach their previous year's goals; and (3) have to increase spending on e-mail marketing. Some relied on alternative tracking methods including a method called "fingerprinting." Tanvi Vyas, an engineer at Firefox, notes that this method is named so because, like your own unique fingerprints, your browser

Everything you need to know about cookies

JOE BOSSO | 25 NOV 2021

A guide to internet cookies and how you can control them

With the holidays right around the corner, many people are, like me, really looking forward to spending more time with family and friends. Another thing I'm looking forward to is the food we will be eating — specifically, the homemade cookies that are brought to these gatherings. A few can be a nice treat, but too many is always a bad thing for me.

The same can be said for the cookies that are dropped onto your computer or smartphone when you browse the internet. You will soon be flooded with different kinds of cookies, and there will be way more cookies than are good for you!

Some companies like Avast are providing individuals with information to assist them in making the transition away from cookies.

Avast Software s.r.o.

network and device data combined together can create a set of characteristics that are unique to you, and can track you as you move from one website to the next. This information can then be combined with personal information to collect more information on you that you know nothing about. Sometimes even the advertiser doesn't know. Attorney Elle Todd says that fingerprinting raises "serious data protection concerns," while others say it may actually be illegal.

So what about the consumers? How are they going to be impacted? It may be too early to tell, but some Internet researchers think that users will see an increase in contextual advertising, certainly a decrease in retargeting, a significant increase in requests for first-party data, and requests for users to grant permission to track their activities to other sites. Given that only 4 percent of iPhone users have agreed to allow tracking, you may not see much of this strategy.

Sources: Pamela Bump, "The Death of the Third-Party Cookie: What Marketers Need to Know about Google's 2022 Phase-Out," HubSpot, July 27, 2022, www.hubspot.com; Matt Burgess, "The Quiet Way Advertisers Are Tracking Your Browsing," *Wired*, February 26, 2022, www.wired.com; Alyse Stanley, "Apple's Privacy Policy Cost Snap, Facebook, Twitter, and YouTube an Estimated $9.85 Billion in Revenue," *Gizmodo*, October 31, 2021, www.gizmodo.com.

5. *Irritation.* Numerous studies have reported on the irritating aspects of some Web tactics. These studies have shown consumers' discontent with clutter, e-mail spam, and pop-ups and pop-unders. There is also a growing sense of irritation with retargeting ads and pre-rolls. As the use of retargeting increases, consumers are expressing more and more irritation with the frequency of ads. These irritating aspects can deter visitors from coming to or returning to the sites, or result in negative attitudes toward the advertiser.

Overall, the Internet and digital and social media offer marketers some very definite advantages over traditional media. At the same time, disadvantages and limitations render this medium as less than a one-stop solution. However, as part of an IMC program, these media are very valuable tools.

Summary

This chapter introduced you to the Internet and a variety of digital and social media. It explained some of the objectives for these media and how they can be used in an IMC program.

The discussion of the Internet focused on understanding the growth of the Internet, the objectives sought when using the Internet, and Internet communications strategies. In addition, we discussed the role of the Internet in an IMC program, explaining how all the IMC program elements can be used with the Internet.

The chapter discussed a number of online tools including paid search, behavioral targeting, contextual ads, rich media, and a number of Web 2.0 platforms including social media, social networks, user-generated content, blogs, and podcasting. We noted advantages of the Web 2.0 including targeting markets, using interactive capabilities, and building relationships.

In addition, we reviewed disadvantages—including high costs, unreliable measurements and statistics, and relatively low reach (compared to that of some traditional media), and the potential for deception.

The Internet has been the most rapidly adopted medium of our time (until mobile). The growth of mobile, due to smartphones, portable devices, and millions of apps, has led to very rapid growth in advertising expenditures in this area. Mobile holds great potential for business-to-business and consumer marketers.

Contrary to popular belief, digital media, the Internet, social media, and mobile are not stand-alone media for advertisers. Their role in an integrated marketing communications program strengthens the overall promotional program as well as the effectiveness of these media themselves.

Key Terms

e-commerce 493
banner ads 493
sponsorships 494
content sponsorship 494
pop-ups 494
pop-unders 494
interstitials 494
search 495
organic search results 495
nonorganic (paid) search results 495
pay-per-click 495

search engine optimization (SEO) 495
behavioral targeting 495
retargeting 495
contextual advertising 496
native advertising 496
rich media 496
online commercials 496
pre-rolls 496
post-rolls 496
video on demand (VOD) 497
webisodes 497

social media 497
social networking sites 497
podcasting 507
blog 507
virtual and augmented reality 509
QR codes 510
mobile 512
social media management 514
Facebook analytics 514
Google analytics 515

Discussion Questions

1. The lead-in to this chapter discusses the decision by Facebook to transform the company into one more focused on the "phygital" environment. Discuss what this means for Facebook. Do you think the move will be successful? Explain your answer. (LO 15-2)

2. One of the major success stories in recent years has been the growth of TikTok. Explain why the platform

has been so successful. Describe the audience for TikTok and why this group has become so enamored with the site. (LO 15-2)

3. Criticisms of social media are numerous leading some to refer to these social platforms as dangerous. Explain some of the reasons critics refer to social media as "out of control" and need to be under more government control. Take a position suggesting more or less control and support this position. (LO 15-5)

4. Recently there has been a significant shifting of media expenditures from traditional to digital media. Some believe this is not necessarily a smart move, but rather "jumping on the bandwagon." Discuss what you believe and explain your position. (LO 15-4)

5. Describe the evolution of the Internet from Web 1.0 to 2.0 to soon 3.0. What are the major differences between these versions? What are the implications of these changes for marketers? (LO 15-2)

6. In this chapter we discussed how Muntinga examined motivations for using social media using the acronym COBRAs. Explain what theses motivations are and discuss their meanings. Provide examples of each. (LO 15-1)

7. The appeal of Facebook is universal. However, in recent years growth in new members has leveled off. Give some of the reasons for this apparent maturing of the market. Where is new growth coming from? Where will future growth come from? (LO 15-2)

8. With all of its appeal, there are many who feel that social media are having negative consequences for society. Explain some of the reasons that people feel this way, citing examples. Take a position as to whether you believe their concerns have or do not have merit. (LO 15-4)

9. Explain some of the ways digital marketers attempt to measure the effectiveness of their programs. Discuss both digital and traditional measures and when each might be more appropriate to use. (LO 15-3)

10. Discuss some of the advantages and disadvantages of digital media. Give examples of each. (LO 15-4)

16 Sales Promotion

CHIPOTLE REWARDS The fastest way to free chipotle.   SIGN IN   JOIN NOW

CHIPOTLE REWARDS

THE FASTEST WAY TO FREE CHIPOTLE

Earn points just for rordering your faves and cash them out for a variety of rewards in the Rewards Exchange. Check out your Extras for ways to unlock extra points and collect exclusive badges. Not a member yet? Join now to start earning.

Program Terms

JOIN NOW

CONGRATULATIONS
YOU DID IT

CHIPOTLE
MEXICAN GRILL

Chipotle Mexican Grill, Inc

Learning Objectives

 | Describe the role of sales promotion in the IMC program.

 | Identify the objectives of sales promotion programs.

 | Explain how marketers use various types of consumer- and trade-oriented sales promotion tools.

 | Explain how to coordinate sales promotion with advertising.

 | Discuss potential problems in the use of sales promotion tools.

Fast-Food Restaurants Use Loyalty Programs to Engage Customers

Customer loyalty programs have been around for decades. They originated in the airline industry and then moved to other segments of the travel and hospitality industry including hotels, car rentals, and restaurants. In recent years they have also become popular among retailers, as well as other industries, as marketers look for ways to attract new customers and retain them. A customer loyalty program rewards customers who frequently engage with a brand. Most programs are designed to incentivize repeat purchases by providing members with discounts, free products, special offers, extra services, and other perks. Loyalty programs come in many forms—ranging from simple stamp or punch cards to sophisticated point-based tiers and reward systems—but all are geared toward bringing customers back to engage with a company or brand.

There is good reason for the increasing use of loyalty programs by marketers as studies show that 75 percent of consumers favor a brand if it has a loyalty program, 57 percent spend more on brands to which they are loyal, and 71 percent who are members of loyalty programs say membership is a meaningful part of their relationships with a company. Research has also shown that enhancing or expanding their loyalty program is a priority for marketers and many are developing strategies that will not only increase engagement and generate more sales, but also provide more touchpoints with their customers.

One area where loyalty programs have become extremely important is the quick-service and fast-food segments of the restaurant industry where several of the major players have recently introduced loyalty programs. Industry leader McDonald's launched its MyMcDonald's Rewards in 2021, and the long-awaited program quickly became one of the most popular programs just a few months after its debut, with more than 20 million members. McDonald's CEO Chris Kempczinski described the new loyalty program as "an instant fan favorite" that was leading to higher frequency and increased customer satisfaction, particularly among customers using its digital app. However, he also noted that the bigger long-term potential is with the data provided by customers in the program, which can be used to learn more about customers and their preferences. Kempczinski said that McDonald's knows who just 5 percent of its customers are and wants to increase this to 40 percent.

Another restaurant chain that has a popular loyalty program is Chipotle, which launched Chipotle Rewards in 2019 and now has more than 30 million members. Jason Scoggins, the senior director of loyalty & CRM at Chipotle, notes that the company uses promotions to engage loyalty program members and keeps them front and center as it plans its promotions calendar. Scoggins notes that Chipotle reserves the majority of its promotions for its members as a benefit for belonging to Chipotle Rewards. He says that while promotions are offered to the larger Chipotle bases, the company always makes sure there are added layers for members. These include Extras, which is a gamification layer of the program, or offering exclusive access to larger promotions such as Boorito at Halloween. Chipotle uses a mix of promotions that are linked with Chipotle Rewards and are data driven and target audiences based on their specific behaviors. For example, an Extras challenge is used to entice lunch customers to try a new daypart such as coming to Chipotle for dinner. The opening image shows how Chipotle promotes its rewards program on its website.

Some companies have developed loyalty programs that have subscription options where consumers can pay a fee for extra services and offerings. For example, Taco Bell introduced a new Taco subscription in early 2022 called the "Taco Lover's Pass," which was a limited-time offering that gave subscribers a daily taco for 30 days with a $10 subscription. The program helped foster customer loyalty, and after seeing the program's success, Taco Bell resurrected it for its Taco Bell Rewards loyalty program on National Taco Day in early October. Taco Bell's head of marketing and communications noted that the program has helped the company learn how digital consumers engage with its app and that the program paid for itself in just a few visits.

While fast-food restaurants are leveraging their loyalty programs to increase sales and customer engagement, they still must be careful when using them. For example, coffee and donut chain Dunkin' received backlash from its customers when it changed its rewards program from DD Perks to Dunkin' Rewards. Although Dunkin' viewed it as an

continued

improved loyalty program, some of its customers were quick to point out that the new system changed the point structure, making it more difficult to earn free drinks, which have become especially important during inflationary times. Dunkin' promoted the new program as better than the old one arguing that it has a more dynamic rewards structure whereby members can start earning rewards at a lower spending threshold and redeem points for a wider variety of food and beverages. It is likely that more companies will make changes to their loyalty programs, and some may reduce the value of the rewards or make them more difficult to earn, particularly as profit margins are squeezed. However, marketing experts note that customers are very savvy and transparency is key when making changes to loyalty programs.

Customer loyalty programs have become very important in the fast-food industry as companies look for one-to-one methods to lure customers in the door as well as collect more data on their preferences and behaviors. In an age when customers have access to a myriad of options, loyalty programs are becoming table stakes for fast-food restaurants, retailers, and many other companies as they compete for customers' share-of-wallet.

Sources: Adrienne Pasquarelli, "Brand Loyalty Programs Help Drive Engagement but Can Be Risky," *Advertising Age*, October 24, 2022, pp. 1, 5; Jonathan Maze, "McDonald's Gets Some Early Results from Its Loyalty Program," *Restaurant Business*, October 28, 2021, https://www.restaurant-businessonline.com/technology/mcdonalds-gets-some-early-results-its-loyalty-program; Jim Tierney, "How Chipotle Leverages Promotions to Keep Its Loyalty Program Members Front and Center," *Clarus Commerce*, https://www.claruscommerce.com/blog/how-chipotle-leverages-promotions-to-keep-its-loyalty-program-members-front-and-center-featuring-jason-scoggins/.

As discussed in the chapter opener about loyalty programs, marketers recognize that advertising and other IMC tools are not always enough to bring customers in the door or move products off store shelves and into the hands of consumers. They are using a variety of sales promotion methods targeted at both consumers and the wholesalers and retailers that distribute their products to stimulate demand. Most companies' IMC programs include consumer and trade promotions that are coordinated with their advertising, direct marketing, publicity/publications, and digital marketing as well as their personal-selling efforts.

This chapter focuses on the role of sales promotion in a firm's IMC program. We examine how marketers use both consumer- and trade-oriented promotions to influence the purchase behavior of consumers as well as wholesalers and retailers. We explore the objectives of sales promotion programs and the various types of sales promotion tools that can be used at both the consumer and trade level. We also consider how sales promotion can be integrated with other elements of the promotional mix and look at problems that can arise when marketers become overly dependent on consumer and trade promotions.

THE SCOPE AND ROLE OF SALES PROMOTION

Sales promotion has been defined as "a direct inducement that offers an extra value or incentive for the product to the sales force, distributors, or the ultimate consumer with the primary objective of creating an immediate sale."[1] Keep in mind several important aspects of sales promotion as you read this chapter.

First, sales promotion involves some type of inducement that provides an *extra incentive* to buy. This incentive is usually the key element in a promotional program; it may be a coupon or price reduction, the opportunity to enter a contest or sweepstakes, a money-back refund or rebate, or an extra amount of a product. The incentive may also be a free sample of the product, given in hopes of generating a future purchase or a premium such as the Mini Minion characters toy used by General Mills for Lucky Charms cereal (Exhibit 16–1). The Minion premium offer was part of a promotional tie-in to the movie *Despicable Me 2* that included packaging themed to the movie, eight collectible Minion premiums, and product integrations.[2] Most sales promotion offers attempt to add some value to the product or service. While advertising appeals to the mind and emotions to

EXHIBIT 16–1

A premium offer is used to provide extra incentive to purchase Lucky Charms.

Mark Dierker/McGraw Hill

give the consumer a reason to buy, sales promotion appeals more to the pocketbook and provides an incentive for purchasing a brand.

Sales promotion can also provide an inducement to marketing intermediaries such as wholesalers and retailers. A trade allowance or discount gives retailers a financial incentive to stock and promote a manufacturer's products. A trade contest directed toward wholesalers or retail personnel gives them extra incentive to perform certain tasks or meet sales goals.

A second point is that sales promotion is essentially an *acceleration tool*, designed to speed up the selling process and maximize sales volume.[3] By providing an extra incentive, sales promotion techniques can motivate consumers to purchase a larger quantity of a brand or shorten the purchase cycle of the trade or consumers by encouraging them to take more immediate action.

Companies also use limited-time offers such as price-off deals to retailers or a coupon with an expiration date to accelerate the purchase process.[4] Sales promotion attempts to maximize sales volume by motivating customers who have not responded to advertising. The ideal sales promotion program generates sales that would not be achieved by other means. However, as we will see later, many sales promotion offers end up being used by current users of a brand rather than attracting new users.

A final point regarding sales promotion activities is that they can be *targeted to different parties* in the marketing channel. As shown in Figure 16–1, sales promotion can be broken into two major categories: consumer-oriented and trade-oriented promotions. Activities involved in **consumer-oriented sales promotion** include sampling,

FIGURE 16–1

Types of Sales Promotion Activities

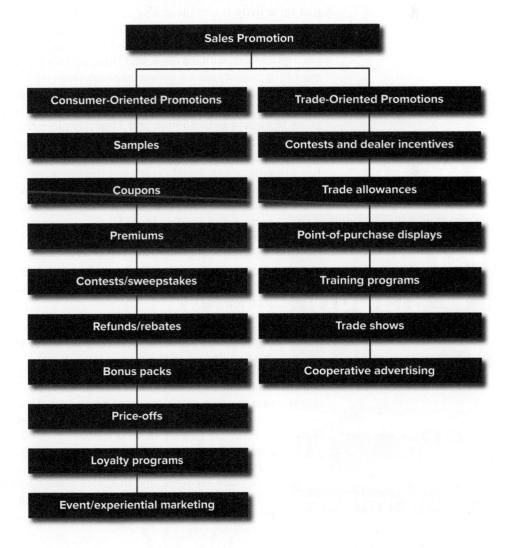

couponing, premiums, contests and sweepstakes, refunds and rebates, bonus packs, price-offs, loyalty programs, and event marketing. These promotions are directed at consumers, the end purchasers of goods and services, and are designed to induce them to purchase the marketer's brand.

As discussed in Chapter 2, consumer-oriented promotions are part of a promotional pull strategy; they work along with advertising to encourage consumers to purchase a particular brand and thus create demand for it. Consumer promotions are also used by retailers to encourage consumers to shop in their particular stores. Many grocery stores use their own coupons or sponsor contests and other promotions to increase store patronage.

Trade-oriented sales promotion includes dealer contests and incentives, trade allowances, point-of-purchase displays, sales training programs, trade shows, cooperative advertising, and other programs designed to motivate distributors and retailers to carry a product and make an extra effort to push it to their customers. Many marketing programs include both trade- and consumer-oriented promotions, since motivating both groups maximizes the effectiveness of the promotional program.

THE IMPORTANCE OF SALES PROMOTION

Sales promotion has been an integral part of the marketing process for a long time, and it continues to play an important role in the integrated marketing communications program of many companies. Marketers spent more than $200 billion on consumer and trade-related sales promotion in 2022.[5] Consumer packaged-goods (CPG) firms continue to be the core users of sales promotion programs and tools. However, sales promotion activity is also increasing in other categories, including health care, consumer electronics, fast-food, retailing, and service industries.

Estimates are that marketers spend more than half of their promotional budgets on sales promotion, with the remainder being allocated to media advertising.[6] Allocation of marketing budgets among consumer promotions, trade promotions, and media advertising varies by industry and company. For example, trade promotion accounts for about 43 percent of the budget for consumer packaged-goods companies, with 24 percent going to consumer promotion and 33 percent to media advertising.[7] Moreover, a portion of the monies that marketers allocate to media advertising is spent on ads that deliver promotional messages regarding contests, games, sweepstakes, and rebate offers. For example, when Wendy's entered the breakfast market in 2020, its strategy for attracting consumers and encouraging trial included the use of various promotions such as offers of two breakfast sandwiches for the price of one and free croissant sandwiches. Exhibit 16–2 shows a promotion that featured a $1 breakfast biscuit. Wendy's spent an estimated $25 million in media advertising to launch its breakfast menu and make consumers aware of the various promotions. Over the past 2 years Wendy's share of the breakfast market among fast-food chains has steadily increased, and morning sales now account for 10 percent of its total revenue.[8]

Reasons for the Increase and Importance of Sales Promotion

The increases in the percentage of the IMC budget allocated to sales promotion over the years concerned many marketers who still viewed media advertising as the primary tool for brand building and saw sales promotion programs as little more than gimmicks that contributed little to brand equity. However, most have recognized that consumers may love their brands but often want an extra incentive to buy them. Marketers also know they must partner effectively with trade accounts, and this often means providing them with an additional incentive to stock and promote their brands and participate in various promotional programs.

A major reason for the increase in spending on sales promotion is that the promotion industry has matured and become more specialized over the past several decades. Increased sophistication and a more strategic role and focus have elevated the discipline and its role in the IMC program of many companies. In the past, sales promotion specialists would be brought in after key strategic branding decisions were made. Promotional agencies were viewed primarily as tacticians whose role was to develop a promotional program such as a contest or sweepstakes or a coupon or sampling program that could create a short-term increase in sales. However, many companies are now making promotional specialists part of their strategic brand-building team. Many promotional agencies have expanded their capabilities and expertise and now offer clients a variety of integrated marketing services that extend beyond just sales promotion such as experiential, direct and digital marketing, analytics, PR, and social media.

There are a number of other factors that have led to the increase in the importance of sales promotion and the shift in marketing dollars from media advertising to consumer and trade promotions. Among them are the growing power of retailers, declining brand loyalty, increased promotional sensitivity, brand proliferation, short-term focus of many marketers, increased accountability, competition, and growth of digital and social media.

The Growing Power of Retailers One reason for the increase in sales promotion is the power shift in the marketplace from manufacturers to retailers. For many years, manufacturers of national brands had the power and influence; retailers were just passive distributors of their products. Consumer-product manufacturers created consumer demand for their brands by using heavy advertising and some consumer-oriented promotions, such as samples, coupons, and premiums, and exerted pressure on retailers to carry the products. Retailers did very little research and sales analysis; they relied on manufacturers for information regarding the sales performance of individual brands.

However, several developments have helped transfer power from the manufacturers to the retailers. With the advent of optical checkout scanners and sophisticated in-store computer systems, retailers gained access to data concerning how quickly products turn over, which sales promotions are working, and which products make money.[9] Companies such as IRI and NPD Group track sales of products in retail stores and provide the information to the retailers as well as marketers. For example, IRI tracks sales of consumer packaged-goods and combines this with information on consumers, including demographics, media habits, and other information. NPD Group's Retail Tracking Service sources point-of-sale (POS) data directly from more than 600,000 retail locations as well as e-commerce and mobile platforms (Exhibit 16–3). The service measures what consumers are buying, where they are buying it, and at what price.[10] Retailers use this information to analyze sales of manufacturers' products and then demand discounts and other promotional support from manufacturers of lagging brands. Companies that fail to comply with retailers' demands for more trade support often have their shelf space reduced or even have their product dropped.

Another factor that has increased the power of retailers is the consolidation of the retail industry, which has resulted in larger chains with greater buying power and clout. These large chains have become accustomed to trade promotions and can pressure manufacturers to provide deals, discounts, and allowances. Consolidation has also given large retailers more money for advancing already strong private-label initiatives, and sales promotion is the next step in the marketing evolution of private-label brands. Private-label brands in various packaged-goods categories such as foods, drugs, and health and beauty care products are giving national brands more competition for

EXHIBIT 16–3

NPD Group's Retail Tracking Service provides marketers with data to track their sale promotion effectiveness.

The NPD Group

retail shelf space and increasing their own marketing, including the use of traditional sales promotion tools. Sales of private brands have been increasing more rapidly than sales of national brands for many product categories. For example, the retail market share for private-label brands in the United States was nearly 17.7 percent in 2021. Private-label brands also accounted for nearly $200 billion (20 percent) of consumer packaged-goods sales.[11] Sales of private-label consumer packaged-goods brands increased during the initial year of the COVID-19 pandemic as sales of national brands disappeared from store shelves due to panic buying and consumers stockpiling them. Private-label sales have also increased as a result of the record inflation that has driven up prices and made financially strained consumers tighten their purse strings.[12]

Well-marketed private-label products are forcing national brand leaders, as well as second-tier brands, to develop more innovative promotional programs and to be more price-competitive. Many major consumer brands are struggling to compete with the growing number of popular private-label choices being offered by major retailers such as Aldi, Target, Trader Joe's, and Costco, which sells many items under the Kirkland Signature brand name. Amazon is also expanding the number of private-label brands that it sells under the AmazonBasics brand name.[13]

One of the most significant developments among retailers is the tremendous growth of Walmart, which has become the largest company in the world as well as the most powerful retailer[14] (Exhibit 16–4). Walmart operates nearly 10,500 stores in 26 countries, including nearly 4,725 in the United States, and had sales of $572 billion in fiscal 2022. It controls 20 percent of dry grocery, 29 percent of nonfood grocery, 30 percent of health and beauty aids, and 45 percent of general merchandise sales in the United States. Walmart accounts for a large share of the business done by every major U.S. consumer-products company and can use its power to influence the way marketers use sales promotions. Like many large retailers, Walmart often asks for account-specific promotions that are designed for and offered only through its stores. The company also has been known to mandate that marketers forgo promotional offers and use the monies to reduce prices.[15]

Declining Brand loyalty   Another major reason for the increase in sales promotion is that consumers have become less brand loyal and are purchasing more on the basis of price, value, and convenience. Some consumers are always willing to buy their preferred brand at full price without any type of promotional offer. However, many consumers are loyal coupon users and/or are conditioned to look for deals when they shop. They may switch back and forth among a set of brands they view as essentially equal. These brands are all perceived as being satisfactory and interchangeable, and consumers purchase whatever brand is on a special sale or for which they have a coupon.

Increased Promotional Sensitivity   Marketers are making greater use of sales promotion in their marketing programs because consumers respond favorably to the incentives it provides. An IRI Consumer Connect Survey in 2021 found that 85 percent of consumers make an effort to purchase consumer packaged-goods products such as groceries when they are on sale or on deal. The survey also found that consumers often make additional or unplanned purchases if in-store deals are good and that strong loyalty card discount programs are an important factor driving their shopping behavior.[16] An obvious reason for consumers' increased sensitivity to sales promotion offers is that they save them money. Another reason is that many purchase decisions are made at the point of purchase by consumers who are increasingly time-sensitive and facing too many choices. Some studies have found that up to 70 percent of purchase decisions are made in the store, where people are very likely to respond to promotional deals.[17]

EXHIBIT 16–4

Walmart is the world's largest and most powerful retailer.

Wolterk/iStock Editorial/Getty Images

Many marketers, as well as retailers, often condition consumers to wait for discounts through sales, special offers, and coupons, which make it very difficult to sell their merchandise at full price. Surveys have shown that consumers are more price-sensitive than they were years ago—and for good reason.[18] Marketers distribute nearly 170 billion coupons each year that can be used by price-conscious consumers to save money. They also use rebates, buy-one-get-one-free offers, special sales events, price-off deals, and other discounts to attract price-sensitive consumers. Consumers are not naive; they know that manufacturers or retailers will offer some type of promotion that encourages them to wait for the next deal rather than purchasing a product at full price.

Brand Proliferation   A major aspect of many firms' marketing strategies has been the development of new products. The market has become saturated with new brands, most of which lack any significant advantages. Research shows that about 75 percent of consumer packaged-goods and retail products fail in their first year—in large part because of ingrained consumer shopping habits.[19] Thus, companies increasingly depend on sales promotion to encourage consumers to try new brands. In Chapter 4, we saw how sales promotion techniques can be used as part of the shaping process to lead the consumer from initial trial to repeat purchase at full price. Marketers are relying more on samples, coupons, rebates, premiums, and other innovative promotional tools to achieve trial usage of their new brands and encourage repeat purchase (Exhibit 16–5).

Promotions are also important in getting retailers to allocate some of their precious shelf space to new brands. The competition for shelf space for new products in stores is enormous. Supermarkets carry an average of 30,000 products (compared with 13,067 in 1982). Retailers favor new brands with strong sales promotion support that will bring in more customers and boost their sales and profits. Many retailers require special discounts or allowances from manufacturers just to handle a new product. These slotting fees or allowances, which are discussed later in the chapter, can make it expensive for a manufacturer to introduce a new product.

Marketers are also shifting more of their promotional efforts to direct and digital marketing, which often includes some form of sales promotion incentive. Many marketers use information they get from premium offers, trackable coupons, rebates, and sweepstakes to build databases for future direct-marketing efforts. As marketers continue to shift from traditional media to digital marketing, promotional offers will probably be used even more to help build databases. The technology is already in place to enable marketers to communicate individually with target consumers and transform mass promotional tools into ways of doing one-to-one marketing.

EXHIBIT 16–5

Sales promotion tools such as this coupon for Purina Dog Chow are often used to encourage trial of a new brand or a repeat purchase.

Nestlé Purina Petcare

Short-Term Focus   Many businesspeople believe the increase in sales promotion is motivated by marketing plans and reward systems geared to short-term performance and the immediate generation of sales volume. Some think the packaged-goods brand management system has contributed to marketers' increased dependence on sales promotion. Brand managers use sales promotions routinely, not only to introduce new products or defend against the competition but also to meet quarterly or yearly sales and market share goals. The sales force, too, may have short-term quotas or goals to meet and may also receive requests from retailers and wholesalers for promotions. Thus, reps may pressure marketing or brand managers to use promotions to help them move the products into the retailers' stores.

Many managers view consumer and trade promotions as the most dependable way to generate short-term sales, particularly when they are price related. The reliance on sales promotion is particularly high in mature and slow-growth markets, where it is difficult to stimulate consumer demand through advertising. This has led to concern that managers have become too dependent on the quick sales fix that can result from a promotion and that the brand franchise may be eroded by too many deals.

Professors Leonard Lodish and Carl Mela have conducted research that suggests many companies are too focused on short-term results because the profusion of scanner data allows brand and marketing managers, as well as retailers, to see how sales often spike in response to promotional discounts.[20] They note how managers became enamored with these short-term increases in sales, which resulted in the allocation of the majority of their marketing budgets to consumer and trade promotions. Another problem they note is that many brand managers stay in their positions for only a short time, which motivates them to focus on the use of promotional tactics that can have more of an immediate impact. They often view investing in advertising or product development as benefiting the performance of subsequent managers rather than their own. When asked about why they take a short-term perspective, marketing and brand managers point out that they are judged on quarterly sales because investors focus on these numbers, and the link between promotion and sales is obvious.

Increased Accountability   In addition to pressuring their marketing or brand managers and sales force to produce short-term results, many companies are demanding to know what they are getting for their promotional expenditures. Results from sales promotion programs are generally easier to measure than those from advertising. Many companies are demanding measurable, accountable ways to relate promotional expenditures to sales and profitability.

Managers who are being held accountable to produce results often use price discounts or coupons, since they produce a quick and easily measured jump in sales. It takes longer for an ad campaign to show some impact, and the effects are more difficult to measure. Marketers are also feeling pressure from the trade as powerful retailers demand sales performance from their brands. Real-time data available from computerized checkout scanners make it possible for retailers to monitor promotions and track the results they generate on a daily basis.

Competition   Another factor that led to the increase in sales promotion is manufacturers' reliance on trade and consumer promotions to gain or maintain competitive advantage. The markets for many products are mature and stagnant, and it is increasingly difficult to boost sales through advertising. Exciting, breakthrough creative ideas are difficult to come by, and consumers' attention to mass-media advertising continues to decline. Rather than allocating large amounts of money to run dull ads, many marketers have turned to sales promotion.

Many companies are tailoring their trade promotions to key retail accounts and developing strategic alliances with retailers that include both trade and consumer promotional programs. A major development in recent years is **account-specific marketing** (also referred to as *comarketing*), whereby a manufacturer collaborates with an individual retailer to create a customized promotion that accomplishes mutual objectives. For example, Exhibit 16-6 shows an account-specific promotion the WD-40 Company ran in conjunction with the O'Reilly Auto Parts retail chain. The promotion included limited-edition, custom cans made to commemorate the 60th anniversary of WD-40's multiuse product, which has been made in the United States since 1953. The special cans were created as a salute to those who subscribe to the tradition of hard work and getting the job done.[21]

Retailers may use a promotional deal with one company as leverage to seek an equal or better deal with its competitors. Consumer and trade promotions are easily matched by competitors, and many marketers find themselves in a promotional trap where they must continue using promotions or be at a competitive disadvantage. (We discuss this problem in more detail later in the chapter.)

EXHIBIT 16–6

WD-40 developed an account-specific promotion for O'Reilly Auto Parts.

WD-40 Company

The Growth of Digital Marketing Another factor that has contributed to the increased use of sales promotion is the digital marketing revolution. Many marketers now use the various forms of online marketing to implement sales promotion programs as well as measure their effectiveness. Promotional offers have also become commonplace in various forms of online advertising including mobile marketing as a way of attracting the attention of consumers or encouraging them to take action. Various types of promotions such as coupons and discounts along with entry forms for contests and sweepstakes appear on marketers' websites as well as their social media pages on Facebook, Twitter, and Instagram.

Sales promotion offers are also used by marketers as a way to encourage consumers to "like" their brands on Facebook or follow them on Twitter. Figure 16–2 shows the results of a survey conducted by the research firm MarketingSherpa that examined why consumers follow brands on various social media platforms. The most popular reason cited by U.S. consumers who do connect with brands on social media was to get regular coupons/promotions (56 percent). Forty-eight percent of consumers said they connected to brands' social accounts because they were interested in buying the brand's products, and 44 percent said they connected because there was an incentive (e.g., sweepstakes, discount, or gift card).[22] Several other studies have found that the reasons consumers follow brands as well as retailers on social media is to learn about promotions or discounts.[23]

Concerns about the Increased Role of Sales Promotion

As discussed in the previous section, many factors have contributed to the increased use of sales promotion by consumer-product manufacturers. Marketing and advertising executives are concerned about how this shift in the allocation of the promotional budget

FIGURE 16–2

Reasons to Connect on
Social Media

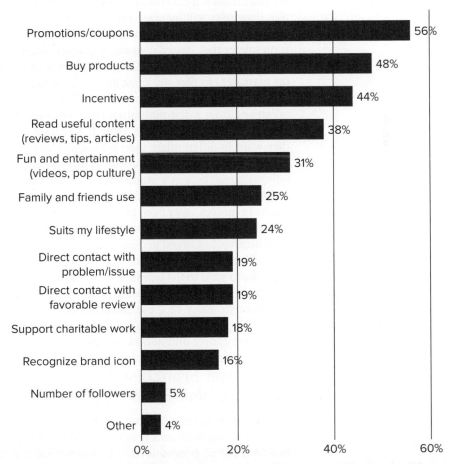

Source: From MarketingSherpa; www.marketingsherpa.com/article/chart/why-customers-follow-brandssocial-accounts.

last year

$70 original

49.99 sale

-$10 off with coupon

39.99

this year

$35 everyday

allen b. dress

fair and square.
no games. no gimmicks. learn more

do the math.

Last year price based on similar item, not clone.

store locator • customer service • privacy policy • unsubscribe here

EXHIBIT 16–7

Consumers reacted negatively when JCPenney tried to move to more everyday fair pricing and fewer promotions.

Jill Braaten/McGraw Hill

affects brand equity. Some critics argue that sales promotion increases come at the expense of brand equity and every dollar that goes into promotion rather than advertising devalues the brand.[24] They say trade promotions in particular contribute to the erosion of brand equity as they encourage consumers to purchase primarily on the basis of price.

Marketers often struggle with the problem of determining the extent to which they should use promotions to help generate sales for their brands or drive traffic to their retail stores versus relying on advertising as a way to build their brand image and avoid discounting and price competition. Given a choice, many companies would prefer to minimize their reliance on promotions and discounts and compete on the basis of product quality and/or brand image. However, many companies find it very difficult to avoid using promotions, particularly when consumers have become accustomed to them. For example, retailer JCPenney tried to reduce its reliance on promotions and move to a pricing and promotion model based on an everyday "fair" price (Exhibit 16–7). However, consumers reacted very negatively to the change, which resulted in a major decline in sales and the firing of the CEO who made the decision to reduce the number of promotions.[25]

Retailers are not the only companies being affected by the discounting trend; the vendors who supply them with merchandise are also being affected. Many marketers have turned to coupons, rebates, and other forms of discounts to appeal to promotion-sensitive consumers. These marketers and retailers have created a dilemma from which there is no easy escape. They know that discounts will increase sales in the short term, but the more marketers use these promotions, the more consumers become conditioned to purchase an item only when it is on sale or they have a coupon. Moreover, many consumers love to shop for deals and view it like playing a game; the money they save is how they keep score. The temptation for marketers to play the game and look for the quick fix and sales spike from a promotion will always be there as well. It is likely that many will continue to yield to the temptation and offer a discount rather than try to sell their brands at full price.

Proponents of advertising argue that marketers must maintain strong brand equity if they want to differentiate their brands and charge a premium price for them. They say advertising is still the most effective way to build the long-term franchise of a brand: It informs consumers of a brand's features and benefits, creates an image, and helps build and maintain brand loyalty. However, many marketers are not investing in their brands as they take monies away from media advertising to fund short-term promotions. Professors Lodish and Mela suggest that managers need to develop and arm themselves with long-term measures of brand performance and use them to make smarter marketing decisions that will not undermine brand equity.[26] However, it is likely that many marketers will continue to yield to the temptation rather than try to sell their brands at full price, particularly when competitors are using promotional tactics to attract their customers.

Although many of these concerns are justified, not all sales promotion activities detract from the value of a brand. It is important to distinguish between consumer franchise-building and nonfranchise-building promotions.

Consumer Franchise-Building versus Nonfranchise-Building Promotions

Sales promotion activities that communicate distinctive brand attributes and contribute to the development and reinforcement of brand identity are **consumer franchise-building (CFB) promotions**.[27] Consumer sales promotion efforts cannot make consumers loyal to a brand that is of little value or does not provide them with a specific

benefit. But they can make consumers aware of a brand and, by communicating its specific features and benefits, contribute to the development of a favorable brand image. Consumer franchise-building promotions are designed to build long-term brand preference and help the company achieve the ultimate goal of full-price purchases that do not depend on a promotional offer.

For years, franchise or image building was viewed as the exclusive realm of advertising, and sales promotion was used only to generate short-term sales increases. But now marketers are recognizing the image-building potential of sales promotion and paying attention to its CFB value. Surveys have found that nearly 90 percent of senior marketing executives believe consumer promotions can help build brand equity while nearly 60 percent think trade promotions can contribute.[28] Most sales promotion agencies recognize the importance of developing consumer and trade promotions that can help build brand equity. For example, Exhibit 16–8 shows a classic ad for Ryan Partnership that stresses how the agency develops trade promotions that help build brand equity.

Companies can use sales promotion techniques in a number of ways to contribute to franchise building. Rather than using a one-time offer, many companies are developing frequency programs that encourage repeat purchases and long-term patronage. Many credit cards have loyalty programs where consumers earn bonus points every time they use their card to charge a purchase. These points can then be redeemed for various items. Most airlines and many hotel chains offer frequent-flyer or guest programs to encourage repeat patronage. Many retail stores have also begun using frequency programs to build loyalty and encourage repeat purchases.

Nonfranchise-building (non-FB) promotions are designed to accelerate the purchase decision process and generate an immediate increase in sales. These activities do not communicate information about a brand's unique features or the benefits of using it, so they do not contribute to the building of brand identity and image. Price-off deals, bonus packs, and rebates or refunds are examples of non-FB sales promotion techniques. Trade promotions receive the most criticism for being nonfranchise building for good reason. First, many of the promotional discounts and allowances given to the trade are never passed on to consumers. And most trade promotions that are forwarded through the channels reach consumers in the form of lower prices or special deals and lead them to buy on the basis of price rather than brand equity.

Many specialists in the promotional area stress the need for marketers to use sales promotion tools to build a franchise and create long-term continuity in their promotional programs. Whereas non-FB promotions merely borrow customers from other brands, well-planned CFB activities can convert consumers to loyal customers. Short-term non-FB promotions have their place in a firm's promotional mix, particularly when competitive developments call for them. But their limitations must be recognized when a long-term marketing strategy for a brand is developed.

CONSUMER-ORIENTED SALES PROMOTION

Marketers have been using various types of sales promotion for more than a hundred years and have found a variety of ways to give consumers an extra incentive to purchase their products and services. In this section, we examine the various sales promotion tools and techniques marketers can use to influence consumers. We study the consumer-oriented promotions shown in Figure 16–1 and discuss their advantages and limitations. First, we consider some objectives marketers have for sales promotion programs targeted to the consumer market.

Objectives of Consumer-Oriented Sales Promotion

As the use of sales promotion techniques continues to increase, companies must consider what they hope to accomplish through their consumer promotions and how they interact with other promotional activities such as advertising, direct marketing, and personal selling. Not all sales promotion activities are designed to achieve the same objectives. As with any promotional-mix element, marketers must plan consumer promotions by conducting a situation analysis and determining sales promotion's specific role in the integrated marketing communications program. They must decide what the promotion is designed to accomplish and to whom it should be targeted. Setting clearly defined objectives and measurable goals for their sales promotion programs forces managers to think beyond the short-term sales fix (although this can be one goal).

While the basic goal of most consumer-oriented sales promotion programs is to induce purchase of a brand, the marketer may have a number of different objectives for both new and established brands—for example, obtaining trial and repurchase, increasing consumption of an established brand, defending current customers, targeting a specific market segment, or enhancing advertising and marketing efforts.

EXHIBIT 16–9

Gillette used a product sample and coupon to promote trial and continued product use.

Mark Dierker/McGraw Hill

Obtaining Trial and Repurchase One of the most important uses of sales promotion techniques is to encourage consumers to try a new product or service. While thousands of new products are introduced to the market every year, as noted earlier, the vast majority of them fail within the first year. Many of these failures are due to the fact that the new product or brand lacks the promotional support needed either to encourage initial trial by enough consumers or to induce enough of those trying the brand to repurchase it. Sales promotion tools have become an important part of new brand introduction strategies; the level of initial trial can be increased through techniques such as sampling, couponing, and refund offers. The success of a new brand depends not only on getting initial trial but also on inducing a reasonable percentage of people who try the brand to repurchase it and establish ongoing purchase patterns. Promotional incentives such as coupons or refund offers are often included with a sample to encourage repeat purchase after trial. For example, Exhibit 16–9 shows an account-specific promotion Gillette used for its Fusion ProGlide razor. Razors were mailed to members of the Rite Aid drug chain wellness +

EXHIBIT 16–10

Energizer used a sweepstakes to promote the use of its batteries in smoke and carbon monoxide detectors.

Energizer Brands, LLC

EXHIBIT 16–11

The "Where's The Mac?" promotion for Kraft Mac & Cheese was a clever way to engage consumers and encourage consumption of an established brand.

Kraft Foods

rewards program to encourage trial, while a $5 off coupon for cartridges was included to encourage consumers to continue to use the product.

Increasing Consumption of an Established Brand

Many marketing managers are responsible for established brands competing in mature markets, against established competitors, where consumer purchase patterns are often well set. Awareness of an established brand is generally high as a result of cumulative advertising effects, and many consumers have probably tried the brand. These factors can create a challenging situation for the brand manager. Sales promotion can generate some new interest in an established brand to help increase sales or defend market share against competitors.

Marketers attempt to increase sales for an established brand in several ways, and sales promotion can play an important role in each. One way to increase product consumption is by identifying new uses for the brand. Sales promotion tools like recipe books or calendars that show various ways of using the product often can accomplish this. An example of a brand that uses sales promotion to promote various uses of its product is Energizer batteries. Exhibit 16-10 shows how Energizer used a sweepstakes to encourage consumers to change the batteries in their smoke alarms and carbon monoxide detectors. Consumers could enter the sweepstakes by liking the Energizer Bunny on Facebook.

Another strategy for increasing sales of an established brand is to use promotions that attract nonusers of the product category or users of a competing brand. Attracting nonusers of the product category can be very difficult, as consumers may not see a need for the product. Sales promotions can appeal to nonusers by providing them with an extra incentive to try the product, but a more common strategy for increasing sales of an established brand is to attract consumers who use a competing brand. This can be done by giving them an incentive to switch, such as a coupon, premium offer, bonus pack, or price deal. Marketers can also get users of a competitor to try their brand through sampling or other types of promotional programs.

Sales promotion can also be used strategically to suggest new or additional uses for an established brand. For example, Johannes Leonardo, the agency for Kraft Heinz, developed a clever promotion for its Kraft Mac & Cheese brand called "Where's The Mac?" (Exhibit 16-11). The goal of the promotional campaign was to persuade fast-food giant McDonald's to add the cheesy noodle dish to its Big Mac to create a hybrid of the two popular foods. To gain public support for the proposal a website dedicated to the cause was created called WheresTheMac.com. Consumers were encouraged to use the site to prompt Twitter bots to send pre-drafted tweets addressed to McDonald's, to draft an original tweet from their personal account that automatically tagged McDonald's Twitter handle and add the hashtag #wheresthemac, or to fill out the McDonald's online customer feedback form and request that mac and cheese be added to the Big Mac. As an incentive for supporting the push to add mac and cheese to the Big Mac, Kraft Heinz offered coupons for a free box of its product to anyone tweeting in favor of the idea. McDonald's has not made changes to the iconic Big Mac in 55 years and was not involved in the promotion. However, it was viewed as

EXHIBIT 16–12

This promotion for Michelob ULTRA targeted social athletes.

Anheuser-Busch, Inc.

a clever way to attract attention and engagement with the brand and encourage more consumers to add mac and cheese to their burgers at home.[29]

Defending Current Customers   With more new brands entering the market every day and competitors attempting to take away their customers through aggressive advertising and sales promotion efforts, many companies are turning to sales promotion programs to hold present customers and defend their market share. A company can use sales promotion techniques in several ways to retain its current customer base. One way is to load them with the product, taking them out of the market for a certain time. Special price promotions, coupons, or bonus packs can encourage consumers to stock up on the brand. This not only keeps them using the company's brand but also reduces the likelihood they will switch brands in response to a competitor's promotion.

Targeting a Specific Market Segment   Most companies focus their marketing efforts on specific market segments and are always looking for ways to reach their target audiences. Many marketers are finding that sales promotion tools such as contests and sweepstakes, events, coupons, and samplings are very effective ways to reach specific geographic, demographic, psychographic, and ethnic markets. Sales promotion programs can also be targeted to specific user-status groups such as nonusers or light versus heavy users. For example, Anheuser-Busch created a clever promotion for its Michelob ULTRA to promote the brand to a new target audience they term the "social athlete." The promotion was called #WillRunforBeer and was targeted to beer drinkers who participate in 5K and 10K races on Thanksgiving Day. In recent years, Turkey Trots have become synonymous with the holiday, with over 1,300 races held in cities nationwide, and has become the largest race day of the year, bringing together more than 1 million runners to compete. To participate, consumers over the age of 21 in select markets across the country were invited to follow the brand on Twitter or Instagram and share a photo from their Turkey Trot using the #WillRunforBeer and tagging @MichelobULTRA (Exhibit 16–12). Participants were sent a Drizly promotion code that they could redeem for a free bottle or can of Michelob ULTRA.

Promotional programs also can be developed to coincide with peak sales periods for certain products and services. For example, candy companies such as Mars and Hershey often develop sales promotions that are run right before Halloween, while clothing and school supply companies targeting children and teens run promotions in late summer, when most of the back-to-school shopping occurs.

Enhancing Integrated Marketing Communications and Building Brand Equity   A final objective for consumer-oriented promotions is to enhance or support the integrated marketing communications effort for a brand or company. Building and/or maintaining brand equity was traditionally viewed as something that was done through media advertising, but it has also become an important goal for marketers as they develop their sales promotion programs. Companies are asking their advertising and promotion agencies to think strategically and develop promotional programs that can do more than simply generate short-term sales. They want promotions that require consumers to become more involved with their brands and offer a way of presenting the brand essence in an engaging way. Many marketers are recognizing that a well-designed and executed promotion can be a very effective way to engage consumers and to differentiate their brands. Sales promotion techniques such as contests or sweepstakes and premium offers are often used to draw attention to an advertising campaign, to increase involvement with the message and product or service, and to help build relationships with consumers. Digital & Social Media Perspective 16–1 discusses an award-winning promotion

Burger King Gets Consumers to Take a Whopper Detour

Just as Coke and Pepsi have been fighting the "cola wars" for decades, the battle between McDonald's and Burger King in the fast-food industry has been one of the greatest business rivalries in American history. Both started selling hamburgers in the mid-1950s, but McDonald's has since become the market leader in the United States, as well as around the world. Each chain has signature products: McDonald's has the Big Mac and Quarter Pounder, while Burger King counters with the flame-grilled Whopper. The Big Mac and Whopper are the two best-selling burgers of all time, with each selling hundreds of millions each year. McDonald's has always dominated the burger segment of the fast-food market, including in the United States, where the golden arches have a market share double that of Burger King.

One of the major advantages McDonald's has over Burger King—as well as other competitors such as Wendy's, Hardee's, Chick-fil-A, and Sonic—is the sheer number of restaurants. McDonald's has more than 14,000 restaurants in the United States, while Burger King has around 7,200. Because Burger King cannot compete on size, an important part of its strategy has been to challenge McDonald's products by introducing new menu items such as the Big King sandwich, as well as promoting its popular Whopper with advertising using the iconic "Have it your way" theme. However, Burger King periodically comes up with clever promotions to challenge McDonald's and get consumers to switch to a Whopper instead of having a Big Mac or Quarter Pounder. It is not easy to get fast-food loyalists to change their behavior because value menus, price promotions, and special deals are easy to match and usually do not result in a sustainable competitive advantage. However, Burger King used one of the most creative, as well as technologically challenging, promotions ever when it ran the "Whopper Detour" to entice consumers to drive to a McDonald's to order a Whopper—And yes, you read that right.

The big idea behind the Whopper Detour promotion was that consumers with the Burger King smartphone app and who were either inside or within 600 feet of a McDonald's could order a Whopper for one cent, as opposed to the regular price of $4 or more. The catch to the promotion was that the customer had to place the order on the app, which would then direct them to the nearest Burger King to redeem the offer. The promotion required a great deal of tech savvy to implement, as Burger King's advertising agency, FCB New York, had to work with a digital company to use geofencing to create a virtual geographic boundary around nearly every McDonald's restaurant in the country because the offer would unlock only within 600 feet of a McDonald's. The agency also had to make sure the app would work with geolocation, which uses a GPS chip in a smartphone to determine its exact location, and tag all of the McDonald's locations in the United States.

The strategy was to take advantage of the vast number of McDonald's locations (75 percent of the U.S. population lives within 3 miles of one) and, in a way, turn the competitor's stores into Burger Kings. An important part of the strategy behind the Whopper Detour promotion was the huge difference in the number of Burger King versus McDonald's restaurants, which means that ordinarily BK fans may have to drive further to get a Whopper. The promotion would activate on the BK app when people were close to a McDonald's and reward them with the discount for passing the McDonald's—and then heading to a Burger King to get it. Maybe they would get used to it.

For the detour campaign to work, Burger King and FCB had to make fast-food customers aware of the promotion as well as get those who did not have the BK mobile app on their smartphone to download it. Prior to launching the promotion, the agency team developed a short film where actors went to actual McDonald's restaurants in the New York area and told McDonald's crew members at the drive-thru that they were there to get a Whopper for a penny. Hidden cameras were used to film the interactions with the McDonald's drive-thru crews, whose faces were blurred and voices altered in the film for legal reasons. The film was shown online to promote the limited-time offer and was also used by the PR team to generate media attention. In addition to the online video, a print ad was created showing the arm of BK's king character changing a McDonald's sign to read "Billions Swerved" instead of "Billions Served."

The Whopper Detour ran for only 9 days but the numbers tell the story of just how successful it was. The Burger King app was downloaded to smartphones by 1.5 million people during the promotion, and more than a half-million people redeemed the one-cent Whopper offer, which was 40 times more than the previous record for a digital coupon promotion. Moreover, the impact of the promotion continued as downloads of the BK app were up by 4.5 million a few months later. The promotion also moved the sales needle for Burger King: Despite offering the Whopper for only one penny, total sales volume through the mobile app increased by 300 percent during the promotion. In addition, after the promotion, sales through the BK mobile app were two times higher than before the promotion. Burger King estimates consumers who redeemed the Whopper Detour promotion will spend around $15 million per year more on the BK app. The company's analysis of the promotion also showed that there was little cannibalization of the Whopper in BK restaurants because the people who came for the offer were actually new or lapsed customers, and they purchased more than just the Whopper-for-a-penny.

(continued)

Burger King

Cannes Lions Awards including the top awards for the Direct and Mobile categories as well as the Titanium Grand Prix. The latter award recognizes "out-of-the-box" ideas that are both bold and provocative but bring results and push the industry forward. The Detour promotion definitely pushed the promotion industry forward and got a lot of people to eat a Whopper in the process.

Sources: Ann-Christine Diaz, "Burger King's 'Whopper Detour' Campaign Wins the 2020 Grand Effie," *Advertising Age*, October 1, 2020, https://adage.com/article/advertising/burger-kings-whopper-detour-campaign-wins-2020-grand-effie/2285066; Fernando Machado, "The Inside Story of the Burger King Campaign That Changed the Brand's Entire Outlook on Marketing," *Adweek*, May 17, 2019, www.adweek.com/brand-marketing/the-inside-story-of-the-burger-kingcampaign-that-changed-the-brands-entire-outlook-onmarketing/; Jessica Wohl, "Burger King Offers a Whopper of a Deal with a McDonald's Catch," *Advertising Age*, December 4, 2018, adage.com/article/cmo-strategy/burger-kings-whopper-offer-a-mcdonald-s-related-catch/315822.

The Whopper Detour promotion won numerous awards, including the 2020 Grand Effie for the most effective marketing campaign, the 2019 Grand Clio Award, and three used by Burger King that was very effective in getting consumers to download the BK app to their smartphones and has helped increase sales from time-and-convenience-focused fast-food customers.

CONSUMER-ORIENTED SALES PROMOTION TECHNIQUES

Sampling

Marketers use a variety of consumer-oriented sales promotion tools to accomplish the objectives just discussed. We will discuss how these various sales promotion tools are used and factors marketers must consider in using them, beginning with sampling.

Sampling involves a variety of procedures whereby consumers are given some quantity of a product for no charge to induce trial. Sampling is generally considered the most effective way to generate trial, although it is also the most expensive. As a sales promotion technique, sampling is often used to introduce a new product or brand to the market. However, sampling is used for established products as well. Some companies do not use sampling for established products, reasoning that samples may not induce satisfied users of a competing brand to switch and may just go to the firm's current customers, who would buy the product anyway. This may not be true when significant changes (new and improved) are made in a brand.

Manufacturers of packaged-goods products such as food, health care items, cosmetics, and toiletries are heavy users of sampling since their products meet the three criteria for an effective sampling program:

1. The products are of relatively low unit value, so samples do not cost too much.
2. The products are divisible, which means they can be broken into small sample sizes that are adequate for demonstrating the brand's features and benefits to the user.
3. The purchase cycle is relatively short, so the consumer will consider an immediate purchase or will not forget about the brand before the next purchase occasion.

EXHIBIT 16–13

Jack in the Box's "Free Fryday" promotion was an effective way to encourage consumers to try its new French fries.

Jack In The Box Inc.

Benefits and Limitations of Sampling   Samples are an excellent way to induce trial as they provide consumers with a risk-free way to try new products. A major study by the Promotion Marketing Association (now the Brand Activation Division of the ANA) found that the vast majority of consumers receiving a sample either use it right away or save it to use sometime later.[30] Sampling generates much higher trial rates than do advertising or other sales promotion techniques.

Getting people to try a product leads to a second benefit of sampling: Consumers experience the brand directly, gaining a greater appreciation for its benefits. This can be particularly important when a product's features and benefits are difficult to describe through advertising. Many foods, beverages, and cosmetics have subtle features that are most appreciated when experienced directly. Thus, marketers in these industries often use samples as a way to introduce consumers to their new products. For example, Jack in the Box, one of the major fast-food restaurant chains in the Western region of the United States, used a "Free Fryday" promotion to give consumers the opportunity to sample its new French fries (Exhibit 16–13). Nearly 70 percent of the respondents in the PMA survey indicated they had purchased a product they did not normally use after trying a free sample. The study also found that samples are even more likely to lead to purchase when they are accompanied by a coupon.

While samples are an effective way to induce trial, the brand must have some unique or superior benefits for a sampling program to be worthwhile. Otherwise, the sampled consumers revert back to other brands and do not become repeat purchasers. The costs of a sampling program can be recovered only if it gets a number of consumers to become regular users of the brand at full retail price.

Another possible limitation to sampling is that the benefits of some products are difficult to gauge immediately, and the learning period required to appreciate the brand may require supplying the consumer with larger amounts of the brand than are affordable. An example would be an expensive skin cream that is promoted as preventing or reducing wrinkles but has to be used for an extended period before any effects are seen.

Sampling Methods   One basic decision the sales promotion or brand manager must make is how the sample will be distributed. The sampling method chosen is important not only in terms of costs but also because it influences the type of consumer who receives the sample. The best sampling method gets the product to the best prospects for trial and subsequent repurchase. Some basic distribution methods include door-to-door, direct-mail, in-store, and on-package approaches. *Door-to-door sampling*, in which the product is delivered directly to a residence, is used when it is important to control where the samples are delivered. For many years newspapers were used to achieve mass distribution of samples such as by using poly bags, with a promotional message printed on them along with the sample. However, less than half of U.S. households now subscribe to a print newspaper, which reduces their value as a sampling method for marketers who want mass distribution of their samples.

Sampling through the mail is common for small, lightweight, nonperishable products. A major advantage of this method is that the marketer has control over where and when the product will be distributed and can target the sample to specific market areas. Many marketers are using information from geodemographic target marketing programs such as Claritas' PRIZM Premier to better target their sample mailings. *In-store sampling* is sometimes used for food and beverage products since consumers get to taste the item and the demonstrator can give them more information about the product while it is being sampled. Although this sampling method can be very effective, it can also be expensive and requires a great deal of planning, as well as the cooperation of retailers. Many grocery and warehouse stores such as Whole Foods and Costco suspended in-store sampling of food items during the pandemic. Some stores have brought back samples, but on a more limited basis and by following more stringent safety protocols.[31]

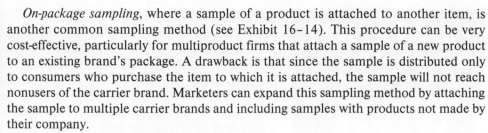

EXHIBIT 16–14

Armor All uses on-package samples for related products.

The Armor All/STP Products Company

EXHIBIT 16–15

Marketers of golf equipment often use demo days to give golfers the opportunity to sample their clubs.

Montana Pritchard/The PGA of America/Getty Images

On-package sampling, where a sample of a product is attached to another item, is another common sampling method (see Exhibit 16–14). This procedure can be very cost-effective, particularly for multiproduct firms that attach a sample of a new product to an existing brand's package. A drawback is that since the sample is distributed only to consumers who purchase the item to which it is attached, the sample will not reach nonusers of the carrier brand. Marketers can expand this sampling method by attaching the sample to multiple carrier brands and including samples with products not made by their company.

Event sampling has become one of the fastest-growing and most popular ways of distributing samples. Many marketers are using sampling programs that are part of integrated marketing programs that feature events, media tie-ins, and other activities that provide consumers with a total sense of a brand rather than just a few tastes of a food or beverage or a trial size of a packaged-goods product. Event sampling can take place in stores as well as at a variety of other venues such as concerts, sporting events, and other places. For example, marketers of sports equipment such as skis, snowboards, and golf clubs often hold "demo days" in cooperation with ski resorts, golf courses, driving ranges, and retail stores. Consumers can demo the equipment, and representatives from the companies usually work at these events to answer questions and promote their company's products (Exhibit 16–15).

Other Methods of Sampling The four sampling methods just discussed are the most common, but several other methods are also used. Several companies also use specialized sample distribution service companies. These firms help the company identify consumers who are nonusers of a product or users of a competing brand and develop appropriate procedures for distributing a sample to them. Many college students receive sample packs at the beginning of the semester that contain trial sizes of such products as mouthwash, toothpaste, headache remedies, and deodorant.

The Internet is yet another way companies are making it possible for consumers to sample their products, and it is adding a whole new level of targeting to the mix by giving consumers the opportunity to choose the samples they want. Several companies offer websites where consumers can register to receive free samples for products that interest them. Websites such as Sample A Day offer samples and other promotional offers. The service asks consumers qualifying questions on product usage that can be used by marketers to target their samples and other promotional offers more effectively.

Marketers also use various forms of social media as a way to distribute samples. For example, Splenda used Facebook to distribute samples of a pocket-size spray form of its sweetener. The company used engagement ads to direct consumers to the Splenda Mist page, where they could sign up for a "first look" at the new product and provide the company with information about themselves. Splenda also used its Facebook page to solicit valuable feedback from consumers who received the samples.[32]

Couponing

The oldest, most widely used, and most effective sales promotion tool is the cents-off coupon. Coupons have been around since 1895, when the C. W. Post Co. started using the penny-off coupon to sell its new Grape-Nuts cereal. In recent years, coupons have become increasingly popular with consumers, which may explain their explosive growth among manufacturers and retailers that use them as sales promotion incentives. Coupons are the most popular sales promotion technique as they are used by nearly all the packaged-goods firms.

Coupon distribution and use for consumer packaged goods (CPG) in the United States reached a record 332 billion in 2010, with 3.3 billion being redeemed.

However, as the economy recovered from the great recession, the number of coupons distributed declined to 258 billion in 2018, with 1.7 billion being redeemed. This decline has continued over the past several years as coupon distribution dropped to 171 billion in 2021 with redemption dropping to 865 million.[33] According to Vericast, a company that tracks coupon distribution and redemption patterns, over 60 percent of consumers in the United States use coupons and 13 percent say they always use them when they shop. The average face value of the 171 billion CPG coupons distributed in 2021 was $2.53. The average face value for nonfood CPG was $2.77 compared to $1.27 for food products.[34]

Advantages and Limitations of Coupons   Coupons have a number of advantages that make them popular sales promotion tools for both new and established products. First, coupons make it possible to offer a price reduction only to those consumers who are price-sensitive. Such consumers generally purchase *because* of coupons, while those who are not as concerned about price buy the brand at full value. Coupons also make it possible to reduce the retail price of a product without relying on retailers for cooperation, which can often be a problem. Coupons are generally regarded as second only to sampling as a promotional technique for generating trial. Since a coupon lowers the price of a product, it reduces the consumer's perceived risk associated with trial of a new brand. Coupons can encourage repurchase after initial trial. Many new products include a cents-off coupon inside the package to encourage repeat purchase.

Coupons can also be useful promotional devices for established products. They can encourage nonusers to try a brand, encourage repeat purchase among current users, and get users to try a new, improved version of a brand. Coupons may also help coax users of a product to trade up to more expensive brands. The product category where coupons are used most is disposable diapers, followed by cereal, detergent, and deodorant. Some of the product categories where coupons are used the least are carbonated beverages, candy, and gum.

But there are a number of problems with coupons. First, it can be difficult to estimate how many consumers will use a coupon and when. Response to a coupon is rarely immediate; it typically takes several months to redeem one. A study of coupon redemption patterns by Inman and McAlister found that many coupons are redeemed just before the expiration date rather than in the period following the initial coupon drop.[35] Many marketers are attempting to expedite redemption by shortening the time period before expiration. The average length of time from issue date to expiration date for CPG coupons in 2021 was 6 weeks, with the time being longer for consumer food products (10.8) than for nonfood products (5.1). However, coupons remain less effective than sampling for inducing initial product trial in a short period.

A problem associated with using coupons to attract new users to an established brand is that it is difficult to prevent the coupons from being used by consumers who already use the brand. Rather than attracting new users, coupons can end up reducing the company's profit margins among consumers who would probably purchase the product anyway. However, they can help retain users.

Other problems with coupons include low redemption rates and high costs. Couponing program expenses include the face value of the coupon redeemed plus costs for production, distribution, and handling of the coupons. Figure 16–3 shows the calculations used to determine the costs of a couponing program using an FSI (freestanding insert) in the Sunday newspaper and a coupon with a face value of $1. As can be seen from these figures, the cost of a couponing program can be very high. Marketers should track coupon costs very carefully to ensure their use is economically feasible.

Another problem with coupon promotions is misredemption, or the cashing of a coupon without purchase of the brand. Coupon misredemption or fraud occurs in a number of ways, including redemption of coupons by consumers for a product type or size not specified on the coupon; redemption by store managers and employees

FIGURE 16–3

Calculating Couponing Costs

Cost per Coupon Redeemed: An Illustration	
1. Distribution cost: 55,000,000 circulation × $6.25/M	$343,750
2. Redemptions at 1.5%	825,000
3. Redemption cost: 825,000 redemptions × $1.00 face value	$825,000
4. Retailer handling cost and processor fees: 825,000 redemptions × $0.10	$82,500
5. Creative costs	$1,500
6. Total program cost: Items 1 + 3 + 4 + 5	$1,252,750
Cost per coupon redeemed	$1.52
Cost divided by redemption	
7. Actual product sold on redemption (misredemption estimated at 20%): 825,000 × 80%	660,000
8. Cost per product moved: Program cost divided by amount of product sold	$1.90

without the accompanying sales of the product; printing of coupons by criminals who sell them to unethical merchants, who in turn redeem them; and online fraud, whereby phony coupons are produced and distributed online. Coupon fraud and misredemption cost manufacturers an estimated $500 million a year in the United States alone.

Many manufacturers hold firm in their policy to not pay retailers for questionable amounts or suspicious types of coupon submissions. However, some companies are less aggressive, and this affects their profit margins. Marketers must allow a certain percentage for misredemption when estimating the costs of a couponing program. Ways to identify and control coupon misredemption, such as improved coding, are being developed, but it still remains a problem. Many retailers are tightening their policies regarding Internet coupons. For example, Walmart will not accept Internet coupons unless they have a valid expiration date, remit address, and bar code.

Coupon Distribution Coupons can be disseminated to consumers by a number of means, including freestanding inserts in Sunday newspapers, direct mail, newspapers (either in individual ads or as a group of coupons in a cooperative format), magazines, on packages, and online. Distribution through newspaper **freestanding inserts (FSIs)** has historically been the most popular method for delivering coupons to consumers, accounting for nearly 80 percent of all coupons distributed. An FSI is a four-color multipage printed advertising booklet that contains consumer packaged-goods coupon offers delivered with newspapers (usually in Sunday editions). FSIs can also be delivered in direct-mail packages along with local retailer ads or can be cooperative booklets such as *RedPlum* or *SmartSource* as well as solo books done by companies. For example, Procter & Gamble uses its own *P&G brandSAVER* FSI booklet each month in newspapers throughout the country (Exhibit 16–16).

There are a number of reasons why FSIs are the most popular way of delivering coupons, including their high-quality four-color graphics, competitive distribution costs, national same-day

EXHIBIT 16–16

Procter & Gamble distributes its own FSI booklet.

Mark Dierker/McGraw Hill

circulation, market selectivity, and the fact that they can be competition-free due to category exclusivity (by the FSI company). Prices for a full-page FSI are currently about $6 to $7 per thousand, which makes FSI promotions very efficient and affordable. Because of their mass-market appeal among consumers and predictable distribution, coupons distributed in FSIs are also a strong selling point with the retail trade.

The increased distribution of coupons through FSIs has, however, led to a clutter problem. Consumers are being bombarded with too many coupons, and although each FSI publisher offers product exclusivity in its insert, this advantage may be negated when there are three inserts in a Sunday paper. Redemption rates of FSI coupons have declined from 4 percent to under 2 percent and even lower for some products. These problems are leading some marketers to look at other ways of delivering coupons that will result in less clutter and higher redemption rates, such as direct mail or by simply handing them out or dispensing them electronically in retail stores.

Couponing Trends Coupons continue to be the most effective sales promotion tool for influencing consumers' purchase decisions, as evidenced by the nearly 1 billion that are redeemed each year by U.S. consumers. The popularity of coupons reflects the fact that they are a way for the average household to save a considerable amount of money each year. Although coupon distribution and redemption has been declining, nearly 60 percent of consumers use coupons on a regular basis and some use them very heavily. In fact, the term *extreme couponing* has been coined to describe the activity of combining shopping skills with coupon use in an effort to save as much money as possible while shopping. The TLC network aired a reality show for many years titled *Extreme Couponing*, which focused on shoppers who save large amounts of money by using coupons (Exhibit 16–17). Casting recently began for a follow-up show titled *Extreme Couponing: The Next Generation*.

Coupons are often used by marketers as a way to compete against lower-priced competitors as well as private-label store brands.[36] While consumers are using more coupons, there are still a number of problems facing marketers in using them. The average U.S. household is still barraged with more than 1,000 coupons per year and consumers redeem less than 1 percent of the hundreds of billions of coupons distributed.

Concerns over the cost and effectiveness of coupons have led some marketers to cut back on their use and/or change the way they use them. For example, marketers have reduced the duration period, with expiration dates of 3 months or less becoming more common. Marketers are also moving to greater use of multiple-item purchase requirements for coupons, particularly for grocery products where nearly 40 percent of the coupons use this tactic. Despite the growing sentiment among major marketers that coupons are inefficient and costly, very few companies are likely to abandon them entirely. However, companies as well as the coupon industry are looking for ways to improve on their use. IMC Perspective 16–1 discusses why many marketers and retailers are cutting back on the use of coupons.

Many marketers and retailers are looking to the Internet as a medium for distributing coupons. A number of websites now offer coupons such as Coupon.com, RedPlum, and SmartSource. Consumers can also access coupons online through Valpak.com, which makes the same coupons and offers available to consumers that come in the Valpak direct-mail envelope.

Another way consumers access discounts and special offers online is through companies such as Groupon, Living Social, and others that connect local merchants, as well as national brands with consumers looking for deals. The best-known company in this promotional space is Groupon, which started in Chicago in 2008 and has expanded

EXHIBIT 16–17

Extreme Couponing was a popular reality TV show.

Mark Dierker/McGraw Hill

What's the Deal with Coupons?

Carolyn Franks/Shutterstock

Coupons as a promotional tool for marketers have influenced where consumers shop and what they buy for more than a century. The number of coupons distributed by consumer packaged-goods (CPG) marketers increased from 16 billion in 1968 to over 300 billion in 1994. However, over the next 7 years coupon distribution declined steadily and dropped to 239 billion in 2001. Over the next decade coupon use again increased steadily, particularly during the Great Recession of 2007 to 2009, which left millions of people out of work with much less financial assistance than they would receive during the later pandemic-induced recession. Vast numbers of coupons distributed by retailers were not even included in the distribution figures. Adding fuel to the coupon explosion, in some markets coupon wars broke out among grocery stores that would double the face value of coupons, making them even more attractive to consumers.

However, since peaking in 2010 at 332 billion, coupon distribution has been declining, falling to an estimated 160 billion in 2022. Not only is the number of coupons being sent to consumers falling, the redemption rate for all print and digital coupons has declined as well and is just 0.5 percent today. The decline in coupon distribution and use has marketing experts asking what is going on with the oldest and most widely used sales promotion tool. Surveys show that 60 percent of consumers still say coupons and discounts are more important than ever, particularly given the high inflation that has led to huge price increases for many products. Moreover, many marketers also still view coupons as an effective way to get consumers to try a new product or consider switching brands.

A major reason for the decline in coupon distribution, and subsequently, in redemption, has to do with the decline in newspaper circulation. At the beginning of the new millennium, nearly 60 million households received a Sunday newspaper each week and the free-standing inserts (FSIs) that contained scores of coupons for various CPGs. However, according to the Pew Research Center, that number had declined to about 25 million in 2021, which means that billions of coupons that were being distributed directly to consumers' homes are no longer available to them. FSIs have traditionally accounted for more than 80 percent of all coupons distributed to consumers and not only are there fewer of them being distributed, but those that do reach households contain fewer coupons. Direct mail and digital coupons have picked up some of the slack but not enough to offset the decline in FSI distribution.

While the decline in newspaper circulation and FSIs has been the primary reason for fewer coupons being distributed, there are several other factors contributing to the decline. Today, far fewer food coupons are being distributed. Traditionally, the mix of food versus nonfood coupons was about even, but that mix has been shifting toward nonfood items for the past several years. Data from the advertising and media research firm Kantar showed that only 12 percent of all FSI coupons available in 2022 were for food products, and those distributed digitally declined from 65 percent to just 54 percent in that year. Marketers relied less on food coupons during the pandemic because they didn't need to as many people avoided eating out and bought more food to prepare at home. With increasing demand and decreasing supply, due in part to supply chain disruptions, food marketers simply did not need to offer as many coupons.

Marketers would prefer not giving discounts to those who would buy the product even without a coupon. This has led to many companies pulling back on promotions and limiting the number of coupons that can be used in a given shopping trip. Grocery stores and mass merchandisers such as Target and Walmart have responded to pressure from e-commerce platforms such as Amazon by increasing their private-label brand offerings and asking major CPG markets to lower prices on name-brand items. Such trade discounts are having an impact on the profit margins and marketing budgets of many CPG companies, which is resulting in fewer coupons being offered.

If marketers are making coupons a smaller part of their marketing playbook, consumers are also using them less. One reason is that coupons' face value is not keeping pace with inflation, particularly for frequently purchased food products, which makes them less compelling to shoppers. Researchers who have been studying the decline in coupon use point to increasingly time-strapped consumers not wanting to deal with the hassle of using coupons just to save a few dollars on their purchases. Economists who

throughout the United States and around the world. The company has nearly 21 million active users, including 13 million in North America and 8 million internationally. Consumers can join the site for free and, once registered, receive notifications of discounted deals being offered in their area through e-mail notifications or by checking the Groupon website, Facebook, or Twitter pages. Groupon also utilizes mobile marketing; more than half of its transactions take place over smartphones and other mobile devices. Over 120 million people worldwide have downloaded the Groupon mobile app, which makes it possible for the company to use location-based marketing, whereby deals are sent to consumers based on their proximity to a specific merchant such as a restaurant or retail store. Exhibit 16–18 shows how Groupon's model works for both consumers and merchants.

Consumers seek out coupons and discounts from a number of different digital channels, including retailer and manufacturer websites, search engines, coupon-specific apps, e-mails from retailers, push notifications, and QR codes on digital signage or catalogs. Companies such as Scan, ShopSavvy, and RedLaser provide shopping apps that allow consumers to scan the UPC bar code with their phone to get a coupon for that product or a related one. Many consumers are downloading coupons linking mobile coupons and other promotional offers to their retailer loyalty cards. Some marketers work with companies that deliver coupons to mobile devices of consumers who sign up for its service. One such company, Cellfire, owned by Catalina Marketing, is the leading provider of load-to-card (L2C) digital coupons in the consumer packaged-goods market and works with marketers as well as more than 22,000 stores nationwide to offer mobile couponing services.

Mobile coupons are likely to become an even more important part of marketers' digital marketing programs because they recognize that mobile now represents nearly 65 percent of all digital media time for people online, with mobile apps dominating that usage. Another reason marketers are increasing their use of mobile coupons is that they are an effective way to measure the effectiveness of mobile advertising. *eMarketer* cites studies showing that almost two-thirds of U.S. marketers view mobile coupons as the most effective method for attributing in-store purchase to mobile ads.[37]

Premiums

Premiums are a sales promotion device used by many marketers. A **premium** is an offer of an item of merchandise or service either free or at a low price that is an extra incentive for purchasers. Many marketers are eliminating toys and gimmicks in favor of value-added premiums that reflect the quality of the product and are consistent with its image and positioning in the market. Marketers spend several billion dollars a year on value-added premium incentives targeted at the consumer market. The two basic types of offers are the free premium and the self-liquidating premium.

EXHIBIT 16–18

Groupon has become a very popular way for merchants to offer discounts and deals to consumers.

Groupon, Inc.

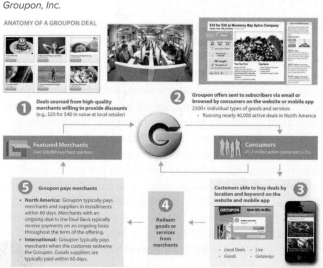

Free Premiums   Free premiums are usually small gifts or merchandise included in the product package or sent to consumers who mail in a request along with a proof of purchase. In/on-package free premiums include toys, balls, trading cards, or other items enclosed in cereal packages, as well as samples of one product included with another. Package-carried premiums have high impulse value and can provide an extra incentive to buy the product. However, several problems are associated with their use. First, there is the cost factor, which results from the premium itself as well as from extra packaging that may be needed. Finding desirable premiums at reasonable costs can be difficult, particularly for adult markets, and using a poor premium may do more harm than good.

Free mail-in premium offers require the consumer to send in more than one proof of purchase and thus can encourage repeat purchase and reward brand loyalty. But a major drawback of mail-in premiums is that they do not offer immediate reinforcement or reward to the purchaser, so they may not provide enough incentive to purchase the brand. Few consumers take advantage of mail-in premium offers as the average redemption rate for them is around 2 to 4 percent.

Free premiums have become very popular in the restaurant industry, particularly among fast-food chains such as McDonald's and Burger King, which use premium offers in their kids' meals to attract children. McDonald's has become the world's largest toymaker on a unit basis, commissioning about 750 million toys per year for its Happy Meals (Exhibit 16–19). Many of the premium offers used by the fast-food giants have cross-promotional tie-ins with popular movies and can be very effective at generating incremental sales. McDonald's negotiates movie tie-in deals with a number of studios, including DreamWorks Animation SKG and Pixar Animation Studios, as well as Disney. McDonald's uses movie tie-ins as the basis for many of its Happy Meal promotions.

A very popular type of incentive used by marketers is airline miles, which have literally become a promotional currency. U.S. airlines make more than an estimated $2 billion each year selling miles to other marketers. Consumers are now choosing credit-card services, phone services, hotels, and many other products and services on the basis of mileage premiums for major frequent-flyer programs such as American Airlines's AAdvantage program or United Airlines's Mileage Plus program. Exhibit 16–20 shows how American Airlines promotes the value of AAdvantage miles as a promotional incentive that companies can offer to help attract and retain customers.

Self-Liquidating Premiums   **Self-liquidating premiums** require the consumer to pay some or all of the cost of the premium plus handling and mailing costs. The marketer usually purchases items used as self-liquidating premiums in large quantities and offers them to consumers at lower-than-retail prices. The goal is not to make a profit on the premium item but rather just to cover costs and offer a value to the consumer.

In addition to cost savings, self-liquidating premiums offer several advantages to marketers. Offering values to consumers through the premium products can create interest in the brand and goodwill that enhances the brand's image. These premiums can also encourage trade support and gain in-store displays for the brand and the premium offer. Self-liquidating premiums are often tied directly to the advertising campaign, so they extend the advertising message and contribute to consumer franchise building for a brand. For example, Philip Morris offers Western wear, outdoor items, and other types of Marlboro gear through its Marlboro Country catalog, which reinforces the cigarette brand's positioning theme.

Self-liquidating premium offers have the same basic limitation as mail-in premiums: very low redemption rates that can leave the marketer with a large supply of items with a logo or some other brand identification that makes them hard to dispose of. Thus, it is important to test consumers' reaction to a premium incentive and determine whether they perceive the offer as a value. Another option is to use premiums with no brand identification, but that detracts from their consumer franchise-building value.

Contests and Sweepstakes

Contests and sweepstakes are still a very popular type of consumer-oriented promotion as marketers spend over $2 billion on them each year. These promotions seem to have an appeal and glamour that such tools as cents-off coupons lack. Contests and sweepstakes are exciting because, as one expert has noted, many consumers have a "pot of gold at the end of the rainbow mentality" and think they can win the big prizes being offered.[38] The lure of sweepstakes and promotions has also been influenced by the "instant-millionaire syndrome" that has derived from huge cash prizes given by many state lotteries in recent years. Marketers are attracted to contests and sweepstakes as a way of generating attention and interest among a large number of consumers.

There are differences between contests and sweepstakes. A **contest** is a promotion where consumers compete for prizes or money on the basis of skills or ability. The company determines winners by judging the entries or ascertaining which entry comes closest to some predetermined criterion (e.g., picking the winning teams and total number of points in the Super Bowl or NCAA basketball tournament). Contests usually provide a purchase incentive by requiring a proof of purchase to enter or an entry form that is available from a dealer or advertisement. Some contests require consumers to read an ad or package or visit a store display to gather information needed to enter. Marketers must be careful not to make their contests too difficult to enter, as doing so might discourage participation among key prospects in the target audience.

A **sweepstakes** is a promotion where winners are determined purely by chance; it cannot require a proof of purchase as a condition for entry. Entrants need only submit their names for the prize drawing. While there is often an official entry form, handwritten entries must also be permitted. One form of sweepstakes is a **game**, which also has a chance element or odds of winning. Scratch-off cards with instant winners are a popular promotional tool. Some games occur over a longer period and require more involvement by consumers. Promotions where consumers must collect game pieces are popular among retailers and fast-food chains as a way to build store traffic and repeat purchases.

Because they are easier to enter, sweepstakes attract more entries than contests. They are also easier and less expensive to administer, since every entry does not have to be checked or judged. Choosing the winning entry in a sweepstakes requires only the random selection of a winner from the pool of entries or generation of a number to match those held by sweepstakes entrants. Experts note that the costs of mounting a sweepstakes are also very predictable. Companies can buy insurance to indemnify them and protect against the expense of awarding a big prize. In general, sweepstakes present marketers with a fixed cost, which is a major advantage when budgeting for a promotion.

Contests and sweepstakes can involve consumers with a brand by making the promotion product relevant or by connecting the prizes to the lifestyle, needs, or interests of the target audience. Marketers often look for creative themes for contests and sweepstakes that will capture the attention and interest of consumers and generate entries, as well as excitement, over a company/brand and the product or service.

The nature of contests and sweepstakes, as well as the way they are deployed, is changing as many companies are delivering them online rather than through traditional entry forms that are submitted via the mail or dropped in an entry box. Marketers are using the Internet for their contests and sweepstakes because of its cost efficiency, immediate data collection capabilities, and ability to keep consumers engaged. Promotions are being designed to ensure an engaging consumer experience by making them more entering and interactive and also developing prizes that are not only larger but more customized and experiential-based.[39] A number of companies are also integrating user-generated content into their contests, which are often promoted on their Facebook pages. Contests that rely on *crowdsourcing*, whereby consumers enter ideas and they are voted on by others, are becoming increasingly popular. For example, Frito-Lay has run create-a-chip contests for Doritos as well as Lay's potato chips, while Samuel Adams has run contests asking consumers to create a crowdsourced beer, and Arizona Beverages USA has prodded the public to create new iced tea flavors.[40]

Problems with Contests and Sweepstakes   While the use of contests and sweepstakes continues to increase, there are some problems associated with these types of promotions. Many sweepstakes and/or contest promotions do little to contribute to consumer franchise building for a product or service and may even detract from it. The sweepstakes or contest often becomes the dominant focus rather than the brand, and little is accomplished other than giving away substantial amounts of money and/or prizes. Many promotional experts question the effectiveness of contests and sweepstakes. Some companies have cut back or even stopped using them because of concern over their effectiveness and fears that consumers might become dependent on them.

Another problem with contests and sweepstakes is the participation in them by hobbyists who submit entries but have no real interest in the product or service. Because most states make it illegal to require a purchase as a qualification for a sweepstakes entry, consumers can enter as many times as they wish. Entrants may enter a sweepstakes numerous times, depending on the nature of the prizes and the number of entries allowed. There are numerous websites on the Internet such as sweepsadvantage.com that inform consumers of all the contests and sweepstakes being held, the entry dates, estimated probabilities of winning, how to enter, and solutions to any puzzles or other information that might be needed. The presence of the professional entrants not only defeats the purpose of the promotion but also may discourage entries from consumers who feel that their chances of winning are limited. Exhibit 16–21 is a page from the website Giveaway Frenzy, which shows consumers various contests and sweepstakes being run by marketers and provides them with information on how to enter.

Numerous legal considerations affect the design and administration of contests and sweepstakes.[41] These promotions are regulated by several federal agencies, and each of the 50 states has its own rules. The regulation of contests and sweepstakes has helped clean up the abuses that plagued the industry for many years and has improved consumers' perceptions of these promotions. But companies must still be careful in designing a contest or sweepstakes and awarding prizes.[42] Most firms use consultants that specialize in the design and administration of contests and sweepstakes to avoid any legal problems, but they may still run into problems with them if they are not administered properly. Marketers are not the only ones who encounter problems with promotions; consumers who win contests and sweepstakes often learn that there may be unexpected tax consequences because the prizes are treated as income by the Internal Revenue Service. Many of the prizes offered in contests and sweepstakes go unclaimed because consumers do not want to pay taxes based on their face value.[43]

EXHIBIT 16–21

Giveaway Frenzy shows consumers various contests and sweepstakes being run by marketers.

Giveaway Frenzy

Refunds and Rebates

Refunds (also known as *rebates*) are offers by the manufacturer to return a portion of the product purchase price, usually after the consumer supplies some proof of purchase. Consumers are generally very responsive to rebate offers, particularly as the size of the savings increases. Rebates are used by makers of all types of products, ranging from packaged goods to major appliances, cars, and computer software.

EXHIBIT 16–22

Pennzoil uses a refund offer that is tied to a future purchase.

Pennzoil by Shell International B.V.

Marketers often use refund offers to induce trial of a new product or encourage users of another brand to switch. Refund offers can also encourage repeat purchase. Many offers require consumers to send in multiple proofs of purchase. The size of the refund offer may even increase as the number of purchases gets larger. Some packaged-goods companies are switching away from cash refund offers to coupons or cash/coupon combinations. Using coupons in the refund offer enhances the likelihood of repeat purchase of the brand. For example, Exhibit 16–22 shows a coupon refund offer used by Pennzoil that can be redeemed on the next oil change.

Evaluating Refunds and Rebates   Rebates can help create new users and encourage brand switching or repeat purchase behavior, or they can be a way to offer a temporary price reduction. This offer can influence purchase even if the consumer fails to realize the savings, so the marketer can reduce price for much less than if a direct price-off deal is used.

Some problems are associated with refunds and rebates. Many consumers are not motivated by a refund or rebate offer because of the delay and the effort required to obtain the savings. They do not want to be bothered saving cash register receipts and proofs of purchase, filling out forms, and mailing in the offer.[44] A study of consumer perceptions found a negative relationship between the use of rebates and the perceived difficulties associated with the redemption process.[45] The study also found that consumers perceive manufacturers as offering rebates to sell products that are not faring well. Nonusers of rebates were particularly likely to perceive the redemption process as too complicated and to suspect manufacturers' motives. This implies that companies using rebates must simplify the redemption process and use other promotional elements such as advertising to retain consumer confidence in the brand.

When small refunds are being offered, marketers may find other promotional incentives such as coupons or bonus packs more effective. They must be careful not to overuse rebate offers and confuse consumers about the real price and value of a product or service. Also, consumers can become dependent on rebates and delay their purchases or purchase only brands for which a rebate is available. Many retailers have become disenchanted with rebates and the burden and expense of administering them.[46]

However, despite the complaints consumers and retailers may have about them, marketers are unlikely to eliminate the use of rebates as they are a very effective promotion tool. A well-promoted, high-value rebate can increase sales significantly, and eliminating them can have a negative impact on sales, particularly in product categories where consumers have come to expect them. Marketers also recognize that they can accomplish a perceived price reduction among consumers who plan to redeem the rebates but never do so and factor the redemption rates into their pricing structure.[47]

Bonus Packs

Bonus packs offer the consumer an extra amount of a product at the regular price by providing larger containers or extra units. Exhibit 16–23 shows a bonus pack offer for Charmin toilet tissue. Bonus packs result in a lower cost per unit for the consumer and provide extra value as well as more product for the money. There are several advantages to bonus pack promotions. First, they give marketers a direct way to provide extra value without having to get involved with complicated coupons or refund offers. The additional value of a bonus pack is generally obvious to the consumer and can have a strong impact on the purchase decision at the time of purchase.

EXHIBIT 16–23

Charmin offers consumers 20 percent more toilet paper in this bonus pack.

Charmin by Procter & Gambl

EXHIBIT 16–24

Ban offers consumers a price-off deal in this promotion.

ban by KAO USA Inc.

Bonus packs can also be an effective defensive maneuver against a competitor's promotion or introduction of a new brand. By loading current users with large amounts of its product, a marketer can often remove these consumers from the market and make them less susceptible to a competitor's promotional efforts. Bonus packs may result in larger purchase orders and favorable display space in the store if relationships with retailers are good. They do, however, usually require additional shelf space without providing any extra profit margins for the retailer, so the marketer can encounter problems with bonus packs if trade relationships are not good. Another problem is that bonus packs may appeal primarily to current users who probably would have purchased the brand anyway or to promotion-sensitive consumers who may not become loyal to the brand.

Price-Off Deals

Another consumer-oriented promotion technique is the direct **price-off deal**, which reduces the price of the brand. Price-off reductions are typically offered right on the package through specially marked price packs, as shown in Exhibit 16–24. Typically, price-offs range from 10 to 25 percent off the regular price, with the reduction coming out of the manufacturer's profit margin, not the retailer's. Keeping the retailer's margin during a price-off promotion maintains its support and cooperation.

Marketers use price-off promotions for several reasons. First, since price-offs are controlled by the manufacturer, it can make sure the promotional discount reaches the consumer rather than being kept by the trade. Like bonus packs, price-off deals usually present a readily apparent value to shoppers, especially when they have a reference price point for the brand and thus recognize the value of the discount.[48] So price-offs can be a strong influence at the point of purchase when price comparisons are being made. Price-off promotions can also encourage consumers to purchase larger quantities, preempting competitors' promotions and leading to greater trade support.

Price-off promotions may not be favorably received by retailers, since they can create pricing and inventory problems. Most retailers will not accept packages with a specific price shown, so the familiar X amount off the regular price must be used. Also, like bonus packs, price-off deals appeal primarily to regular users instead of attracting nonusers. Finally, the Federal Trade Commission has regulations regarding the conditions that price-off labels must meet and the frequency and timing of their use.

A popular variation of a price-off promotion is the buy-one-get-one-free (BOGO) deal such as the offer for Purina Beneful dog food shown in Exhibit 16–25. These types of price promotions are an effective way to provide extra value for consumers and encourage them to make multiple purchases of a product.

EXHIBIT 16–25

Buy-one-get-one-free deals are often used to encourage multiple purchases of a brand.

Nestlé Purina Petcare

Loyalty Programs

One of the fastest-growing areas of sales promotion is the use of **loyalty programs** (also referred to as *continuity* or *frequency programs*). American Airlines was one of the first major companies to use loyalty programs when it introduced its AAdvantage frequent-flyer program in 1981. Since then frequency programs have become commonplace in a number of product and service categories, particularly travel and hospitality, as well as among retailers. Virtually every airline, car rental company, casino, and hotel chain has some type of frequency program. American Airlines has the largest airline loyalty program with over 115 million members in its AAdvantage program, while Marriott's Bonvoy program, which merged the Marriott Rewards, Ritz Carlton Rewards, and Starwood Preferred Guest programs, has over 140 million members. Consumers in the United States hold 3.8 billion memberships in loyalty programs.[49] The categories with the largest membership were retail with 1.6 billion, travel and hospitality with 1.1 billion, and financial services with 664 million.

Most of the fast-food and quick-serve restaurants have well-established loyalty programs with large numbers of members, including Starbucks (25 million),

EXHIBIT 16–26

Burger King offered free fries as an incentive to join its Royal Perks loyalty program.

Burger King

Domino's (20 million), Panera Bread (45 million), and Chipotle (30 million). The two largest fast-food restaurant chains, McDonald's and Burger King, launched loyalty programs in 2021. The MyMcDonald's loyalty program enrolled nearly 26 million members in its first year. Burger King began offering free fries with a purchase all year as an incentive for joining its Royal Perks loyalty program (Exhibit 16–26). Supermarkets were among the first retailers to develop card-based shopper loyalty programs and more than 7,000 of them now have loyalty programs that offer members discounts, a chance to accumulate points that can be redeemed for rewards, newsletters, and other special services. Loyalty programs are also used by a variety of other retailers, including department stores, home centers, bookstores, and even local bagel shops. Many specialty retailers such as consumer electronics stores also have launched loyalty programs. For example, Best Buy launched its Rewards Zone program in 2003, and the program, which is now called My Best Buy, has grown to include more than 10 million members.

There are a number of reasons why loyalty programs have become so popular. Marketers view these programs as a way of encouraging consumers to use their products or services on a continual basis and as a way of developing strong customer loyalty. Many companies are also realizing the importance of customer retention and understand that the key to retaining and growing market share is building relationships with loyal customers.[50] Frequency programs also provide marketers with the opportunity to develop databases containing valuable information on their customers that can be used to better understand their needs, interests, and characteristics as well as to identify and track a company's most valuable customers. These databases can also be used to target specific programs and offers to customers to increase the amount they purchase and/or to build stronger relationships with them. Many marketers find it more cost efficient and effective to communicate with their customers through their loyalty programs than through mass-media advertising.

As frequency programs become more common, marketers will be challenged to find ways to use them as a means of differentiating their product, service, business, or retail store. According to the most recent COLLOQUY Loyalty Census report, the average U.S. household belongs to 30 loyalty programs but is active in a little less than half of them.[51] Moreover, nearly 30 percent of loyalty program participants have left a program before redeeming a single reward. The primary reasons consumers drop out of loyalty programs are because of the length of time it takes to earn reward points (57 percent) and because the program did not provide rewards/offers they were interested in (53 percent). Participants also left loyalty programs because they send too many communications that they deemed to be irrelevant, which points to the importance of having a well-thought-out marketing communications strategy. The COLLOQUY report also found that loyalty program participants expect them to have smartphone apps to track rewards and redeem points. Marketers must find ways to make their loyalty programs more than just discount or frequent-buyer programs. This will require the careful management of databases to identify and track valuable customers and their purchase history and the strategic use of targeted loyalty promotions.

Some companies have already begun making changes in their loyalty programs to make them more appealing to members and encourage more purchases. Many companies are expanding their earn and redemption offerings outside of their own loyalty programs—specifically, through coalition loyalty programs. For example, airline loyalty programs such as Southwest Rapid Rewards allow members to exchange their points earned in hotel programs like Marriott Bonvoy and Hyatt Gold Passport for Southwest miles. Members of the Marriott Bonvoy program can redeem their points with 250 airlines and car rental companies around the world

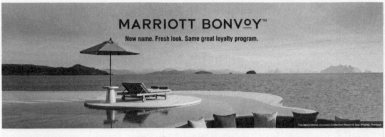

EXHIBIT 16–27

The Marriott Bonvoy loyalty program partners with other companies and programs.

Marriott International, Inc.

(Exhibit 16–27). By leveraging the loyalty of others, brands within coalition programs can benefit from increased engagement, heightened value, and growing loyalty to their own programs. Most of the loyalty programs for airlines and hotels have also entered into partnerships with credit card companies such as MasterCard, Visa, and American Express to create affinity cards that allow members to accumulate points or miles when they use the card. A number of companies have also made changes in the way rewards are earned in their loyalty programs. Several airlines such as American, Delta, United, and Southwest now base rewards on the amount of money spent for airline tickets rather than miles flown. Starbucks made changes to its My Starbucks Rewards program and customers now earn reward stars based on the amount of money they spend at the coffee retailer. Previously customers earned one star per transaction no matter how much money they spent.[52]

Event Marketing

Another type of consumer-oriented promotion that has become very popular in recent years is the use of event marketing. It is important to make a distinction between *event marketing* and *event sponsorships*, as the two terms are often used interchangeably yet they refer to different activities. **Event marketing** is a type of promotion where a company or brand is linked to an event or where a themed activity is developed for the purpose of creating experiences for consumers and promoting a product or service. Marketers often do event marketing by participating in and associating their product with some popular activity such as a sporting event, concert, fair, or festival. However, marketers also create their own events to use for promotional purposes. For example, PepsiCo has created an irreverent brand image for its popular Mountain Dew brand by associating it with action sports. Extreme sports are about a nonconforming lifestyle from clothes to music, and young people respond to brands that make an authentic connection and become part of the action sports community. In 2005, the brand raised its involvement with action sports to a new level when it became a founding partner of the Dew Tour, a five-event series that features competition in snowboarding, BMX, freestyle motocross, and skateboading. Exhibit 16–28 shows a page from the Dew Tour website promoting the tour as well as various Mountain Dew products. The Dew Tour has grown to become an innovative contest series and content platform that brings together the world's best skateboarders, snowboarders, skiers, artists, brands, and fans through the culture of action sports. A number of companies partner with the Dew Tour to promote their products

EXHIBIT 16–28

The Dew Tour provides Mountain Dew with event marketing opportunities.

PepsiCo, Inc.

and services. For example, many of the ski and snowboard manufacturers, as well as automotive brands, sponsor the snow events that are part of the Dew Tour. From an event marketing perspective, an important part of the Dew Tour is the promotional opportunities associated with the various events. These include custom art, interactive displays, athlete autograph sessions, lounges where fans can hang out and interact with their favorite extreme sport athletes, and the product sampling kitchen where they can try various Mountain Dew flavors, as well as other products.

An **event sponsorship** is an integrated marketing communications activity where a company develops actual sponsorship relations with a particular event and provides financial support in return for the right to display a brand name, logo, or advertising message and be identified as a supporter of the event. Event marketing often takes place as part of a company's sponsorship of activities such as concerts, the arts, social causes, and sporting events. Decisions and objectives for event sponsorships are often part of an organization's public relations activities and are discussed in Chapter 17.

Event marketing has become a very popular part of the integrated marketing communications programs of many companies as they view them as excellent promotional opportunities and a way to associate their brands with certain lifestyles, interests, and activities. Events can be an effective way to connect with consumers in an environment where they are comfortable with receiving a promotional message. Moreover, consumers often expect companies to be part of events and welcome their participation as they make the events more entertaining, interesting, and exciting. Marketers can use events to distribute samples as well as information about their products and services or to actually let consumers experience their brands. Events are also popular as they have become part of the growing emphasis marketers are placing on **experiential marketing**, which involves a live event or experience that provides consumers with the opportunity to see the product or service and experience it for themselves. The goal of experiential marketing is to connect brands with consumers in personally relevant and memorable ways.[53]

Summary of Consumer-Oriented Promotions and Marketer Objectives

The discussion of the various sales promotion techniques shows that marketers use these tools to accomplish a variety of objectives. Sales promotion techniques provide consumers with an *extra incentive* or *reward* for engaging in a certain form of behavior such as purchasing a brand. For some types of sales promotion tools, the incentive the consumer receives is immediate, while for others the reward is delayed. Marketers often evaluate sales promotion tools in terms of their ability to accomplish specific objectives and consider whether the impact of the promotion will be immediate or delayed. Figure 16–4 outlines which sales promotion tools can be used to accomplish various marketing objectives and identifies whether the extra incentive or reward is immediate or delayed.[54]

FIGURE 16–4

Consumer-Oriented Sales Promotion Tools for Various Marketing Objectives

Consumer Reward Incentive	Marketing Objective		
	Induce trial	Customer retention/loading	Support IMC program/ build brand equity
Immediate	• Sampling • Instant coupons • In-store coupons • In-store rebates	• Price-off deals • Bonus packs • In- and on-package free premiums • Loyalty programs	• Events • In- and on-package free premiums
Delayed	• Media- and mail-delivered coupons • Mail-in refunds and rebates • Free mail-in premiums • Scanner- and Internet-delivered coupons	• In- and on-package coupons • Mail-in refunds and rebates • Loyalty programs	• Self-liquidating premiums • Free mail-in premiums • Contests and sweepstakes • Loyalty programs

It should be noted that in Figure 16–4 some of the sales promotion techniques are listed more than once because they can be used to accomplish more than one objective. For example, loyalty programs can be used to retain customers by providing both immediate and delayed rewards. Shoppers who belong to loyalty programs sponsored by supermarkets and receive discounts every time they make a purchase are receiving immediate rewards that are designed to retain them as customers. Some loyalty promotions such as frequency programs used by airlines, car rental companies, and hotels offer delayed rewards by requiring that users accumulate points to reach a certain level or status before the points can be redeemed. Loyalty programs can also be used by marketers to help build brand equity. For example, when an airline or car rental company sends its frequent users upgrade certificates, the practice helps build relationships with these customers and thus contributes to brand equity.

While marketers use consumer-oriented sales promotions to provide current and/or potential customers with an extra incentive, they also use these promotions as part of their marketing program to leverage trade support. Retailers are more likely to stock a brand, purchase extra quantities, or provide additional support such as end-aisle displays when they know a manufacturer is running a promotion during a designated period. The development of promotional programs targeted toward the trade is a very important part of the marketing process and is discussed in the next section.

TRADE-ORIENTED SALES PROMOTION

Objectives of Trade-Oriented Sales Promotion

Like consumer-oriented promotions, sales promotion programs targeted to the trade should be based on well-defined objectives and measurable goals and a consideration of what the marketer wants to accomplish. Typical objectives for promotions targeted to marketing intermediaries such as wholesalers and retailers include obtaining distribution and support for new products, maintaining support for established brands, encouraging retailers to display established brands, and building retail inventories.

Obtain Distribution for New Products   Trade promotions are often used to encourage retailers to give shelf space to new products. Manufacturers recognize that only a limited amount of shelf space is available in supermarkets, drugstores, and other major retail outlets. Thus, they provide retailers with financial incentives to stock and promote new products. While trade discounts or other special price deals are used to encourage retailers and wholesalers to stock a new brand, marketers may use other types of promotions to get them to push the brand. Merchandising allowances can get retailers to display a new product in high-traffic areas of stores, while incentive programs or contests can encourage wholesale or retail store personnel to push a new brand.

Maintain Trade Support for Established Brands   Trade promotions are often designed to maintain distribution and trade support for established brands. Brands that are in the mature phase of their product life cycle are vulnerable to losing wholesale and/or retail distribution, particularly if they are not differentiated or face competition from new products. Trade deals induce wholesalers and retailers to continue to carry weaker products because the discounts increase their profit margins. Brands with a smaller market share often rely heavily on trade promotions, since they lack the funds required to differentiate themselves from competitors through media advertising. Even if a brand has a strong market position, trade promotions may be used as part of an overall marketing strategy. Many of the leading consumer packaged-goods companies such as Procter & Gamble, PepsiCo, Frito Lay, and Kraft Heinz rely heavily on trade promotions to maintain retail distribution and support for their brands, which in turn helps them maintain sales and market share.

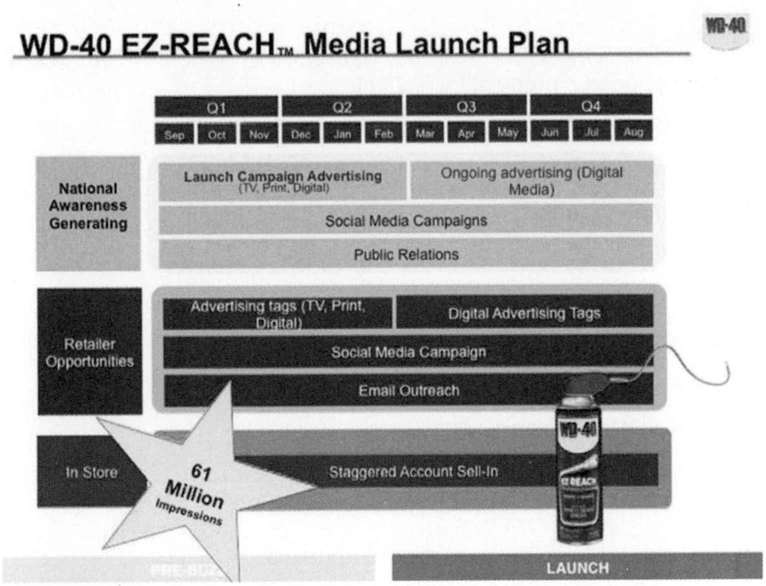

WD-40 EZ-REACH™ Media Launch Plan

EXHIBIT 16–29

WD-40's program calendar shows the retailers the marketing support planned to support its new EZ-REACH product.

WD-40 Company

Encourage Retailers to Display Established Brands Another objective of trade-oriented promotions is to encourage retailers to display and promote an established brand. Marketers recognize that many purchase decisions are made in the store, and promotional displays are an excellent way of generating sales. An important goal is to obtain retail store displays of a product away from its regular shelf location. A typical supermarket has approximately 50 display areas at the ends of aisles, near checkout counters, and elsewhere. Marketers want to have their products displayed in these areas to increase the probability shoppers will come into contact with them. Even a single display can increase a brand's sales significantly during a promotion.

Manufacturers often use multifaceted promotional programs to encourage retailers to promote their products at the retail level. For example, Exhibit 16–29 shows a program calendar the WD-40 Company provides to retailers showing the various marketing support programs the company would be using to support the launch of its new EZ-REACH product. The program included a variety of IMC tools including targeted advertising on television and in magazines; online videos and e-newsletters; social media banners and blogs; trade publication and blogger outreach; public relations; and various types of consumer and trade promotions.

Build Retail Inventories Manufacturers often use trade promotions to build the inventory levels of retailers or other channel members. There are several reasons manufacturers want to load retailers with their products. First, wholesalers and retailers are more likely to push a product when they have high inventory levels rather than storing it in their warehouses or back rooms. Building channel members' inventories also ensures they will not run out of stock and thus miss sales opportunities.

Some manufacturers of seasonal products offer large promotional discounts so that retailers will stock up on their products before the peak selling season begins. This enables the manufacturer to smooth out seasonal fluctuations in its production schedule and passes on some of the inventory carrying costs to retailers or wholesalers. When retailers stock up on a product before the peak selling season, they often run special promotions and offer discounts to consumers to reduce excess inventories.

Types of Trade-Oriented Promotions

Manufacturers use a variety of trade promotion tools as inducements for wholesalers and retailers. Next we examine some of the most often used types of trade promotions and some factors marketers must consider in using them. These promotions include contests and incentives, trade allowances, displays and point-of-purchase materials, sales training programs, trade shows, and cooperative advertising.

Contests and Incentives Manufacturers may develop contests or special incentive programs to stimulate greater selling effort and support from reseller management or sales personnel. Contests or incentive programs can be directed toward managers who work for a wholesaler or distributor as well as toward store or department managers at the retail level. Manufacturers often sponsor contests for resellers and use prizes such as trips or valuable merchandise as rewards for meeting sales quotas or other goals.

Contests or special incentives are often targeted at the sales personnel of the wholesalers, distributors/dealers, or retailers. These salespeople are an important link in the distribution chain because they are likely to be very familiar with the market, more

FIGURE 16–5

Three Forms of Promotion
Targeted to Reseller
Salespeople

- Product or Program Sales

  Awards are tied to the selling of a product; for example:

  Selling a specified number of cases

  Selling a specified number of units

  Selling a specified number of promotional programs

- New Account Placements

  Awards are tied to:

  The number of new accounts opened

  The number of new accounts ordering a minimum number of cases or units

  Promotional programs placed in new accounts

- Merchandising Efforts

  Awards are tied to:

  Establishing promotional programs (such as theme programs)

  Placing display racks, counter displays, and the like

frequently in touch with the customer (whether it be another reseller or the ultimate consumer), and more numerous than the manufacturer's own sales organization. Manufacturers often devise incentives or contests for these sales personnel. These programs may involve cash payments made directly to the retailer's or wholesaler's sales staff to encourage them to promote and sell a manufacturer's product. These payments are known as **push money (PM)** or *spiffs*. For example, an appliance manufacturer may pay a $25 spiff to retail sales personnel for selling a certain model or size. In sales contests, salespeople can win trips or valuable merchandise for meeting certain goals established by the manufacturer. As shown in Figure 16–5, these incentives may be tied to product sales, new account placements, or merchandising efforts.

While contests and incentive programs can generate reseller support, they can also be a source of conflict between retail sales personnel and management. Some retailers want to maintain control over the selling activities of their sales staffs. They don't want their salespeople devoting an undue amount of effort trying to win a contest or receive incentives offered by the manufacturer. Nor do they want their people becoming too aggressive in pushing products that serve their own interests instead of the product or model that is best for the customer.

Many retailers refuse to let their employees participate in manufacturer-sponsored contests or to accept incentive payments. Retailers that do allow them often have strict guidelines and require management approval of the program.

Trade Allowances   Probably the most common trade promotion is some form of **trade allowance**, a discount or deal offered to retailers or wholesalers to encourage them to stock, promote, or display the manufacturer's products. Types of allowances offered to retailers include buying allowances, promotional or display allowances, and slotting allowances.

Buying Allowances   A buying allowance is a deal or discount offered to resellers in the form of a price reduction on merchandise ordered during a fixed period. These discounts are often in the form of an **off-invoice allowance**, which means a certain per-case amount or percentage is deducted from the invoice. A buying allowance can also take the form of *free goods*; the reseller gets extra cases with the purchase of specific amounts (for example, 1 free case with every 10 cases purchased).

Buying allowances are used for several reasons. They are easy to implement and are well accepted, and sometimes expected, by the trade. They are also an effective way to encourage resellers to buy the manufacturer's product, since they will want to

BUMBLE BEE.

GOURMET BRISLING
WILD SARDINES

Pre-Packed Gourmet Brisling Wild Sardines Shippers Ready for Display!

★ Mixed Shippers Promote Trial and Impulse Sales. Perfect for secondary placements in perimeter areas to increase sales of related items

★ Generate higher category profit margin and larger basket rings

★ Customer friendly 48 count displays with eye catching graphics and clean designs

★ Available in two configurations

Extra Small Sardines: 48ct - 24/3.75oz Extra Virgin Olive Oil(EVOO) and 24/EVOO with Hot Jalapeño Peppers

Small Sardines: 48ct – 24/3.75oz Mediterranean-12/Water-12/Mango Habañero

EXHIBIT 16–30

Bumble Bee Seafoods uses a promotional allowance to encourage retailers to use in-store displays of its Wild Sardines products.

Bumble Bee Foods, LLC

take advantage of the discounts being offered during the allowance period. Manufacturers offer trade discounts expecting wholesalers and retailers to pass the price reduction through to consumers, resulting in greater sales. However, as discussed shortly, this is often not the case.

Promotional Allowances Manufacturers often give retailers allowances or discounts for performing certain promotional or merchandising activities in support of their brands. These merchandising allowances can be given for providing special displays away from the product's regular shelf position, running in-store promotional programs, or including the product in an ad. The manufacturer generally has guidelines or a contract specifying the activity to be performed to qualify for the promotional allowance. The allowance is usually a fixed amount per case or a percentage deduction from the list price for merchandise ordered during the promotional period.

Exhibit 16–30 shows a trade promotional piece used by Bumble Bee Seafoods to inform retailers of the merchandising opportunities available for its new Wild Sardines product and to encourage them to use in-store displays. An important goal of the company's trade marketing efforts is to get retailers to set up more displays of its products in various areas of their stores where related products are sold.

Slotting Allowances Some retailers demand a special allowance for agreeing to handle a new product. **Slotting allowances**, also called *stocking allowances*, *introductory allowances*, or *street money*, are fees retailers charge for providing a slot or position to accommodate the new product. Retailers justify these fees by pointing out the costs associated with taking on so many new products each year, such as redesigning store shelves, entering the product into their computers, finding warehouse space, and briefing store employees on the new product.[55] They also note they are assuming some risk, since so many new product introductions fail. Proponents of slotting fees argue that marketers often introduce new products with little consumer research and marketing support and do not consider the costs incurred by retailers when these products fail.[56]

Slotting fees can range from a few hundred dollars per store to $50,000 or more for an entire retail chain. Manufacturers that want to get their products on the shelves nationally can face several million dollars in slotting fees. Many marketers believe slotting allowances are a form of blackmail or bribery and say some 70 percent of these fees go directly to retailers' bottom lines.

Retailers can continue charging slotting fees because of their power and the limited availability of shelf space in supermarkets relative to the large numbers of products introduced each year. Some retailers have even been demanding **failure fees** if a new product does not hit a minimum sales level within a certain time. The fee is charged to cover the costs associated with stocking, maintaining inventories, and then pulling the product.[57] Large manufacturers with popular brands are less likely to pay slotting fees than smaller companies that lack leverage in negotiating with retailers.

In 1999, the Senate Committee on Small Business began taking action against the practice of using slotting fees in the grocery, drugstore, and computer software industries because of the fees' negative impact on small business.[58] The committee recommended that the Federal Trade Commission and Small Business Administration take steps to limit the use of slotting fees because they are anticompetitive. A study by Paul Bloom, Gregory Gundlach, and Joseph Cannon examined the views of manufacturers, wholesalers, and grocery retailers regarding the use of slotting fees. Their findings suggest that slotting fees shift the risk of new product introductions from retailers to manufacturers and help apportion the supply and demand of new products. They also found that slotting fees lead to higher retail prices, are applied in a discriminatory fashion, and place small marketers at a disadvantage.[59]

Despite the concerns over their use, many national and regional grocery store chains continue to charge slotting fees, arguing that there is a limit to the number of products they can carry on their shelves and these fees are warranted. However, some stores such as Costco, Whole Foods, and Walmart do not charge slotting fees. Walmart can use its size and buying power to negotiate low prices that it can pass on to its customers, while Costco and Whole Foods focus on selecting products that best fit their customers' needs.[60]

Displays and Point-of-Purchase Materials The next time you are in a store, take a moment to examine the various promotional materials used to display and sell products. Point-of-purchase (POP) displays are an important promotional tool because they can help a manufacturer obtain more effective in-store merchandising of products. Companies in the United States spend more than $20 billion a year on POP materials, including end-of-aisle displays, banners, posters, shelf cards, motion pieces, and stand-up racks, among others. Point-of-purchase displays are very important to marketers since many consumers make their purchase decisions in the store. In fact, some studies estimate that nearly two-thirds of a consumer's buying decisions are made in a retail store. Thus, it is very important for marketers to get the attention of consumers, as well as to communicate a sales or promotional message, through POP displays.

A measurement study from Point-of-Purchase Advertising International (an industry trade association) and the Advertising Research Foundation estimates that the cost-per-thousand-impressions figure for POPs is $6 to $8 for supermarket displays.[61] The CPM figure is based on findings that a grocery store display makes an average of 2,300 to 8,000 impressions per week, depending on store size and volume. Although this study has shown that POP displays are very effective at reaching consumers, difficulties in getting retail stores to comply with requests for displays often make it difficult for marketers to use them.[62] Moreover, many retailers are decreasing the amount of signage and displays they will accept as well as the messages they can communicate. Also, as account-specific promotions become more popular, some retailers are requiring customized POP materials. For example, 7-Eleven has taken over the responsibility for the production of all POP materials from vendors—who must still pay for them. The goal is to give 7-Eleven complete control over its in-store environment.

Despite these challenges, marketers recognize that point-of-purchase displays are an important part of their promotional programs. Many continue to develop innovative methods to display their products efficiently, make them stand out in the retail environment, and communicate a sales message to consumers. It should be noted that the importance of creative POP displays is not limited to grocery or convenience stores. Point-of-purchase displays are also important to companies that distribute their products through other types of retail outlets, such as home improvement, consumer electronic, and specialty retail stores. For example, Exhibit 16–31 shows an award-winning POP display created by Great Northern Instore for Logitech computer peripheral products including keyboards and mice. The display was used in consumer electronic and office supply stores such as Best Buy and Office Depot.

Many manufacturers help retailers use shelf space more efficiently through **planograms**, which are configurations of products that occupy a shelf section in a store. Some manufacturers are developing computer-based programs that allow retailers to input information from their scanner data and determine the best shelf layouts by experimenting with product movement, space utilization, profit yields, and other factors.[63]

Sales Training Programs Another form of manufacturer-sponsored promotional assistance is sales training programs for reseller personnel. Many products sold at the retail level require knowledgeable salespeople who can provide consumers with

EXHIBIT 16–31

This award-winning point-of-purchase display plays an important role in the merchandising of Logitech computer peripheral products.

Logitech

information about the features, benefits, and advantages of various brands and models. Cosmetics, appliances, computers, consumer electronics, and sporting equipment are examples of products for which consumers often rely on well-informed retail sales personnel for assistance.

Manufacturers provide sales training assistance to retail salespeople in a number of ways. They may conduct classes or training sessions that retail personnel can attend to increase their knowledge of a product or a product line. These training sessions present information and ideas on how to sell the manufacturer's product and may also include motivational components. Sales training classes for retail personnel are often sponsored by companies selling high-ticket items or complex products such as smartphones, cars, or ski equipment.

Another way manufacturers provide sales training assistance to retail employees is through their own sales force. Sales reps educate retail personnel about their product line and provide selling tips and other relevant information. The reps can provide ongoing sales training as they come into contact with retail sales staff members on a regular basis and can update them on changes in the product line, market developments, competitive information, and the like.

Manufacturers also give resellers detailed sales manuals, product brochures, reference manuals, and other material. Many companies provide DVDs or digital files for retail sales personnel that include product information, product-use demonstrations, and ideas on how to sell their product. These selling aids can often be used to provide information to customers as well.

Trade Shows   Another important promotional activity targeted to resellers is the **trade show**, a forum where manufacturers can display their products to current as well as prospective buyers. According to the Center for Exhibition Industry Research, prior to the COVID-19 pandemic, more than 100 million people attended the nearly 15,000 trade shows each year in the United States and Canada, and the number of exhibiting companies exceeded 1.3 million. In many industries, trade shows are a major opportunity to display one's product lines and interact with customers. They are often attended by important management personnel from large retail chains as well as by distributors and other reseller representatives. Trade show attendance was severely impacted by the pandemic but is slowly recovering. However, it is likely to take several years for the trade show industry to return to pre-pandemic levels for both exhibitors and attendees.

A number of promotional functions can be performed at trade shows, including demonstrating products, identifying new prospects, gathering customer and competitive information, and even writing orders for a product. Trade shows are particularly valuable for introducing new products because resellers are often looking for new

EXHIBIT 16–32

The International CES is a very popular industry trade show.

Seokyong Lee/Penta Press/ Shutterstock

merchandise to stock. Shows can also be a source of valuable leads to follow up on through sales calls or direct marketing. The social aspect of trade shows is also important. Many companies use them to entertain key customers and to develop and maintain relationships with the trade. An academic study demonstrated that trade shows generate product awareness and interest and can have a measurable economic return.[64] An example of a very high-profile trade show is the International Consumer Electronics Show (CES) that is held in Las Vegas each January. The show is owned and produced by the Consumer Electronics Association (CEA) and is often used as a platform for the announcement and release of new products such as computers, smartphones, HDTVs, and various other types of consumer electronic items. CES also receives extensive coverage from the media, which makes it a valuable promotional opportunity for markets launching new products. Exhibit 16–32 shows a picture from a recent CES.

Cooperative Advertising The final form of trade-oriented promotion we examine is **cooperative advertising**, where the cost of advertising is shared by more than one party. There are three types of cooperative advertising. Although the first two are not trade-oriented promotions, we should recognize their objectives and purpose.

Horizontal cooperative advertising is advertising sponsored in common by a group of retailers or other organizations providing products or services to the market. For example, automobile dealers who are located near one another in an auto park or along the same street often allocate some of their ad budgets to a cooperative advertising fund. Ads are run promoting the location of the dealerships and encouraging car buyers to take advantage of their close proximity when shopping for a new automobile. Many cities and resort areas use horizontal cooperative advertising by having hotels, theme parks, tourist attractions, and other businesses that benefit from tourism contribute monies to a fund to advertise and promote the area as a tourist destination and/or a place to hold meetings and conventions.

Ingredient-sponsored cooperative advertising is supported by raw materials manufacturers; its objective is to help establish end products that include the company's materials and/or ingredients. Companies that often use this type of advertising include DuPont, which promotes the use of its materials such as Teflon and Kevlar; 3M, which promotes Thinsulate; and NutraSweet, whose artificial sweetener is an ingredient in many food products and beverages.

Intel Inside® Program Associate Membership

The Intel brand represents "World-Class Technology and Manufacturing from Intel". When placed on devices or in marketing it's a reminder to end users that the devices they are purchasing contain Intel technology and offer performance, quality, reliability, and compatibility they expect from Intel.

The Intel Inside® Program Associate membership is designed for partnerships with Intel technology in personal computers, datacenters and IoT devices that define almost every aspect of our lives and transform industries.

The Intel Inside® Program Associate Membership is for customers that integrate Intel technology into their company branded devices.

Member Benefits

- Member access to Intel logos and trademarks for co-branding when they use Intel® technology in products they manufacture and sell, strengthening and promoting our respective brands

Perhaps the best-known, and most successful, example of this type of cooperative advertising is the "Intel Inside" program, sponsored by Intel Corporation, which the company has been using since 1991.[65] Under this program, personal computer manufacturers get back 5 percent of what they pay Intel for microprocessors in return for showing the "Intel Inside" logo in their advertising as well as on their PCs. The monies received from Intel must be applied to ads paid for jointly by the PC maker and Intel. Many of the print and online ads for PCs run in the United States and other countries carry the "Intel Inside" logo, and the program helped Intel grow its share of the microprocessor market from 56 percent in 1990 to nearly 80 percent over the next two decades.[66] Intel still has more than 60 percent market share for the worldwide computer microprocessor market, and ingredient branding through the "Intel Inside" program is still an important part of its promotional program. Exhibit 16–33 is a page from the Intel Inside website that shows how Intel promotes membership in the Intel Inside program, which now focuses on the use of Intel processors, Intel technology in personal computers, datacenters, and other Internet of Things (IoT) devices.

Another technology company that uses ingredient-sponsored advertising is Qualcomm, which has been running a brand-building campaign for its Snapdragon processor that powers many smartphones and other mobile devices. The company runs ads in the United States and several other countries to promote the features and benefits of the Snapdragon processor and how it contributes to the performance of mobile devices. In 2022 Qualcomm acquired the naming rights to the new football and events stadium built by San Diego State University as part of its efforts to build awareness of Snapdragon processors (Exhibit 16–34).

The most common form of cooperative advertising is the trade-oriented form, **vertical cooperative advertising**, in which a manufacturer pays for a portion of the advertising a retailer runs to promote the manufacturer's product and its availability in the retailer's place of business. Manufacturers generally share the cost of advertising run by the retailer on a percentage basis (usually 50–50) up to a certain limit.

The amount of cooperative advertising the manufacturer pays for is usually based on a percentage of dollar purchases. If a retailer purchases $100,000 of product from a manufacturer, it may receive 3 percent, or $3,000, in cooperative advertising money. Large retail chains often combine their co-op budgets across all of their stores, which gives them a larger sum to work with and more media options.

Cooperative advertising can take several forms. Retailers may advertise a manufacturer's product in, say, a newspaper ad featuring a number of different products, and the individual manufacturers reimburse the retailer for their portion of the ad. Or the ad may be prepared by the

EXHIBIT 16–35

This Bumble Bee Seafoods ad is provided to retailers for use as part of its vertical cooperative advertising program.

Bumble Bee Foods, LLC

manufacturer and placed in the local media by the retailer. Exhibit 16–35 shows a cooperative ad format for Bumble Bee Seafoods that retailers in various market areas can use by simply inserting into a newspaper circular or use as a display ad by adding their store name and location.

Once a cooperative ad is run, the retailer requests reimbursement from the manufacturer for its percentage of the media costs. Manufacturers usually have specific requirements the ad must meet to qualify for co-op reimbursement, such as size, use of trademarks, content, and format. Verification that the ad was run is also required, in the form of a digital copy of the ad and an invoice.

As with other types of trade promotions, manufacturers have been increasing their cooperative advertising expenditures. Some companies have been moving money out of national advertising into cooperative advertising because they believe they can have greater impact with ad campaigns in local markets. Historically, retailers have spent most cooperative advertising monies in traditional media such as newspaper, direct mail, and radio and until recently many marketers discouraged or did not allow the use of co-op funds in online channels. However, as audiences for newspapers and broadcast media decline, many companies have changed their policies and are allowing co-op funds to be spent in digital media.[67] Some retail chains now offer digital media buying platforms that are designed to help vendors better reach the retailer's customers, not just through the retailer website but through other online channels. Mass merchants such as Walmart and Target as well as supermarket chains such as Safeway/Albertsons, Food Lion, and ShopRite have set up digital media exchanges and are encouraging vendors to allocate some of their trade promotion dollars to them.[68]

COORDINATING SALES PROMOTION WITH ADVERTISING AND OTHER IMC TOOLS

Those involved in the promotional process must recognize that sales promotion techniques usually work best in conjunction with advertising and other integrated marketing tools and that the effectiveness of an IMC campaign can be enhanced by consumer-oriented sales promotion efforts. Rather than separate activities competing for a firm's promotional budget, advertising and sales promotion should be viewed as complementary tools. When properly planned and executed to work together, advertising and sales promotion can have a *synergistic effect* much greater than that of either promotional mix element alone.

Proper coordination of sales promotion with other IMC tools is essential for the firm to take advantage of the opportunities offered by each and get the most out of its promotional budget. Successful integration of advertising and sales promotion requires decisions concerning not only the allocation of the budget to each area but also the coordination of the ad and sales promotion themes, proper media support for, and timing of, the various promotional activities, and the target audience reached.

Budget Allocation

While many companies are spending more money on sales promotion than on media advertising, it is difficult to say just what percentage of a firm's overall promotional budget should be allocated to advertising versus consumer- and trade-oriented promotions. This allocation depends on a number of factors, including the specific promotional objectives of the campaign, the market and competitive situation, and the brand's stage in its life cycle.

Consider, for example, how allocation of the promotional budget may vary according to a brand's stage in the product life cycle. In the introductory stage, a large amount of the budget may be allocated to sales promotion techniques such as sampling and couponing to induce trial. In the growth stage, however, promotional dollars may be used primarily for advertising to stress brand differences and keep the brand name in consumers' minds.

When a brand moves to the maturity stage, advertising is primarily a reminder to keep consumers aware of the brand. Consumer-oriented sales promotions such as coupons, price-offs, premiums, and bonus packs may be needed periodically to maintain consumer loyalty, attract new users, and protect against competition. Trade-oriented promotions are needed to maintain shelf space and accommodate retailers' demands for better margins as well as encourage them to promote the brand. A study on the synergistic effects of advertising and promotion examined a brand in the mature phase of its life cycle and found that 80 percent of its sales at this stage were due to sales promotions. When a brand enters the decline stage of the product life cycle, most of the promotional support will probably be removed and expenditures on sales promotion are unlikely.

Coordination of Ad and Promotion Themes

To integrate the advertising and sales promotion programs successfully, the theme of consumer promotions should be tied in with the positioning platform for the company and/or their brand wherever possible. Sales promotion tools should attempt to communicate a brand's unique attributes or benefits and to reinforce the sales message or advertising campaign theme. In this way, the sales promotion effort contributes to the consumer franchise-building effort for the brand.

At the same time, media advertising and other IMC tools should be used to draw attention to a sales promotion program such as a contest, sweepstakes, or event or to a special promotion offer such as a price reduction or rebate program. An excellent example of the coordination of sales promotion with the advertising and positioning used for a brand is the "Countdown to Crunchtime" promotion used by Frito-Lay during the National Football League (NFL) Playoffs and Super Bowl, when snack food consumption such as chips and dips is at its highest as avid football fans host watch parties. Frito-Lay celebrated the pressure of Crunchtime in every NFL playoff game leading up to the Super Bowl to drive chip-buying urgency throughout the postseason. When the fourth quarter of each game began, an announcement on Frito-Lay's social channels alerted fans that the Countdown to Crunchtime was on and they had 60 minutes to enter for the chance to win $100,000 or other NFL prizes. Frito-Lay products acted as the entryway for the promotion to incentivize purchase and the time-pressured mechanic of the sweepstakes played off the idea of "Crunchtime."

A national advertising campaign was used as part of the integrated campaign with high-impact ads run on digital and social media as well as television. The ads featured former NFL stars and highlighted Frito-Lay chips and dips as an integral part of the experience when watching a playoff game. Situational and time-sensitive messaging was used to remind consumers "It's Crunchtime, don't forget the chips!" The promotion was also synchronized with retail stores as highly impactful point-of-purchase displays, such as the one shown in Exhibit 16–36, and thematic packaging were used to gain incremental shelf and end-of-aisle display space and leverage Frito-Lays NFL sponsorship. The promotion drove $104 million in retail sales for Frito-Lay chips during the playoffs, which was a 16 percent lift over the previous year and received a gold ANA REGGIE Award in 2022 for excellence in brand activation marketing.[69]

Media Support and Timing

Media support for a sales promotion program is critical and should be coordinated with the media program for the ad campaign. Media advertising is often needed to deliver such sales promotion materials as coupons, sweepstakes,

EXHIBIT 16–37

Unilever coordinates the advertising and sales promotion for the Dove Men + Care line.

Dove by Unilever

contest entry forms, premium offers, and even samples. It is also needed to inform consumers of a promotional offer as well as to create awareness, interest, and favorable attitudes toward the brand.

By using advertising in conjunction with a sales promotion program, marketers can make consumers aware of the brand and its benefits and increase their responsiveness to the promotion. Consumers are more likely to redeem a coupon or respond to a price-off deal for a brand they are familiar with than one they know nothing about. Moreover, product trial created through sales promotion techniques such as sampling or high-value couponing is more likely to result in long-term use of the brand when accompanied by advertising.[70]

Using a promotion without prior or concurrent advertising can limit its effectiveness and risk damaging the brand's image. If consumers perceive the brand as being promotion dependent or of lesser quality, they are not likely to develop favorable attitudes and long-term loyalty. Conversely, the effectiveness of an ad can be enhanced by a coupon, a premium offer, or an opportunity to enter a sweepstakes or contest.

An example of the effective coordination of advertising and sales promotion is the introductory campaign Unilever developed for its Dove Men + Care line. Unilever sent samples of the body and face wash product to more than half the households in the United States along with high-value coupons and also used trade promotions targeted to retailers as part of its introductory marketing blitz. The sales promotion efforts were accompanied by heavy advertising in print and on television, including a commercial in the Super Bowl, and follow-up spots featuring former New Orleans Saints quarterback Drew Brees. The launch campaign included the use of additional IMC tools, including public relations, mobile marketing, and digital and social media. Unilever continues to coordinate advertising and sales promotion for the Dove Men + Care line with ads such as the one shown in Exhibit 16–37, which featured a father's day promotion.

To coordinate their advertising and sales promotion programs more effectively, many companies are getting their sales promotion agencies more involved in the advertising and promotional planning process. Rather than hiring agencies to develop individual, nonfranchise-building types of promotions with short-term goals and tactics, many firms are having their sales promotion and advertising agencies work together to develop integrated promotional strategies and programs. Figure 16–6 shows how the role of promotional agencies is changing.

FIGURE 16–6

The Shifting Role of the Promotion Agency

Traditional	New and Improved
1. Primarily used to develop short-term tactics or concepts.	1. Used to develop long- and short-term promotional strategies as well as tactics.
2. Hired/compensated on a project-by-project basis.	2. Contracted on annual retainer, following formal agency reviews.
3. Many promotion agencies used a mix— each one hired for best task and/or specialty.	3. One or two exclusive promotion agencies for each division or brand group.
4. One or two contact people from agency.	4. Full team or core group on the account.
5. Promotion agency never equal to ad agency—doesn't work up front in annual planning process.	5. Promotion agency works on equal basis with ad agency—sits at planning table up front.
6. Not directly accountable for results.	6. Very much accountable—goes through a rigorous evaluation process.

SALES PROMOTION ABUSE

LO 16-5

The increasing use of sales promotion in marketing programs is more than a passing fad. It is a fundamental change in strategic decisions about how companies market their products and services. The value of this increased emphasis on sales promotion has been questioned by several writers, particularly with regard to the lack of adequate planning and management of sales promotion programs.[71]

Are marketers becoming too dependent on this element of the marketing program? As was discussed earlier, consumer and trade promotions can be a very effective tool for generating short-term increases in sales, and many brand managers would rather use a promotion to produce immediate sales than invest in advertising and build the brand's image over an extended time. As the director of sales promotion services at one large ad agency noted: "There's a great temptation for quick sales fixes through promotions. It's a lot easier to offer the consumer an immediate price savings than to differentiate your product from a competitor's."[72]

Overuse of sales promotion can be detrimental to a brand in several ways. A brand that is constantly promoted may lose perceived value. Consumers often end up purchasing a brand because it is on sale, they get a premium, or they have a coupon, rather than basing their decision on a favorable attitude they have developed. When the extra promotional incentive is not available, they switch to another brand. A study by Priya Raghubir and Kim Corfman examined whether price promotions affect pretrial evaluations of a brand.[73] They found that offering a price promotion is more likely to lower a brand's evaluation when the brand has not been promoted previously compared to when it has been frequently promoted; that price promotions are used as a source of information about a brand to a greater extent when the evaluator is not an expert but does have some product or industry knowledge; and that promotions are more likely to result in negative evaluations when they are uncommon in the industry. The findings from this study suggest that marketers must be careful in the use of price promotions as they may inhibit trial of a brand in certain situations.

Alan Sawyer and Peter Dickson have used the concept of *attribution theory* to examine how sales promotion may affect consumer attitude formation.[74] According to this theory, people acquire attitudes by observing their own behavior and considering why they acted in a certain manner. Consumers who consistently purchase a brand because of a coupon or price-off deal may attribute their behavior to the external promotional incentive rather than to a favorable attitude toward the brand. By contrast, when no external incentive is available, consumers are more likely to attribute their purchase behavior to favorable underlying feelings about the brand.

Another potential problem with consumer-oriented promotions is that a **sales promotion trap** or spiral can result when several competitors use promotions extensively.[75] Often a firm begins using sales promotions to differentiate its product or service from the competition. If the promotion is successful and leads to a differential advantage (or even appears to do so), competitors may quickly copy it. When all the competitors are using sales promotions, this not only lowers profit margins for each firm but also makes it difficult for any one firm to hop off the promotional bandwagon.[76] This dilemma is shown in Figure 16–7.

FIGURE 16–7

The Sales Promotion Trap

	Our Firm	
All Other Firms	**Cut back promotions**	**Maintain promotions**
Cut back promotions	Higher profits for all	Market share goes to our firm
Maintain promotions	Market share goes to all other firms	Market share stays constant; profits stay low

EXHIBIT 16-38

McDonald's created the $1 $2 $3 value menu to offer consumers more variety at different price points.

McDonald's Corporation

A number of industries have fallen into this promotional trap. In the cosmetics industry, gift-with-purchase and purchase-with-purchase promotional offers were developed as a tactic for getting buyers to sample new products. But they have become a common, and costly, way of doing business.[77] In many areas of the country, supermarkets fell into the trap of doubling coupons, which cut into their already small profit margins. Fast-food chains have also fallen into the trap with promotions featuring popular menu items for $0.99 or $1. Fast-food companies use their dollar menus to offer options to budget-conscious consumers and provide them with consistent everyday values. McDonald's introduced its value menu in 2003 and for many years it included popular items such as its double cheeseburger. However, competitors such as Burger King and Wendy's responded by putting popular items on their value meal menus in an effort to keep pace with the industry leader.[78] Other competitors also introduced dollar menu items such as Taco Bell, which introduced a "Cravings" value menu in 2013. McDonald's now has a $1 $2 $3 Dollar Menu that includes a wide variety of items at the three price points (Exhibit 16-38). In 2019, the company gave McDonald's restaurant operators more flexibility to tailor the value menu to meet the tastes and preferences of local customers.[79]

Marketers must consider both the short-term impact of a promotion and its long-term effect on the brand. The ease with which competitors can develop a retaliatory promotion and the likelihood of their doing so should also be considered. Marketers must be careful not to damage the brand franchise with sales promotions or to get the firm involved in a promotional war that erodes the brand's profit margins and threatens its long-term existence. Marketers are often tempted to resort to sales promotions to deal with declining sales and other problems when they should examine such other aspects of the marketing program as channel relations, price, packaging, product quality, or advertising.

After reading this chapter you can see that there are a number of factors that marketers must consider in developing and implementing effective sales promotion programs as they involve much more than just offering consumers an extra economic incentive to purchase a product. Priya Raghubir, Jeffrey Inman, and Hans Grande suggest that there are three aspects to consumer promotions, including economic, informative, and affective effects.[80] They note that in addition to economic effects, marketers must consider the information and signals a promotional offer conveys to the consumer as well as the affective influences. These include the consumer feelings and emotions aroused by exposure to a promotion or associated with purchasing the brand or company that is offering a deal. By considering all of these effects, managers can design and communicate consumer promotions more efficiently as well as more effectively.

Summary

For many years, advertising was the major promotional-mix element for most consumer-product companies. Over the past two decades, however, marketers have been allocating more of their promotional dollars to sales promotion. There has been a steady increase in the use of sales promotion techniques to influence consumers' purchase behavior. The growing power of retailers, erosion of brand loyalty, increase in consumers' sensitivity to promotions, increase in new product introductions, short-term focus of marketing and brand managers, competition, and growth of digital marketing are some of the reasons for this increase.

Sales promotions can be characterized as either franchise building or nonfranchise building. The former contribute to the long-term development and reinforcement of brand identity and image; the latter are designed to accelerate the purchase process and generate immediate increases in sales.

Sales promotion techniques can be classified as either trade- or consumer-oriented. A number of consumer-oriented sales promotion techniques were examined in this chapter, including sampling, couponing, premiums, contests and sweepstakes, rebates and refunds, bonus packs, price-off deals, loyalty programs, and event/experiential marketing. The characteristics of these promotional tools were examined, along with their advantages and limitations. Various trade-oriented promotions were also examined, including trade contests and incentives, trade allowances, displays and point-of-purchase materials, sales training programs, trade shows, and cooperative advertising.

Advertising and sales promotion should be viewed not as separate activities but rather as complementary tools. When planned and executed properly, advertising and sales promotion can produce a synergistic effect that is greater than the response generated from either promotional-mix element alone. To accomplish this, marketers must coordinate budgets, advertising and promotional themes, media scheduling and timing, and target audiences.

Sales promotion abuse can result when marketers become too dependent on the use of sales promotion techniques and sacrifice long-term brand position and image for short-term sales increases. Many industries experience sales promotion traps when a number of competitors use promotions extensively and it becomes difficult for any single firm to cut back on promotion without risking a loss in sales. Overuse of sales promotion tools can lower profit margins and threaten the image and even the viability of a brand.

Key Terms

sales promotion 524
consumer-oriented sales
   promotion 525
trade-oriented sales promotion 526
account-specific marketing 530
consumer franchise-building (CFB)
   promotions 532
nonfranchise-building (non-FB)
   promotions 533
sampling 538
freestanding insert (FSI) 542
premium 545

self-liquidating premium 546
contest 547
sweepstakes 547
game 547
refunds 548
bonus packs 549
price-off deal 550
loyalty programs 550
event marketing 552
event sponsorship 552
experiential marketing 553
push money (PM) 556

trade allowance 556
off-invoice allowance 556
slotting allowances 557
failure fees 557
planograms 558
trade show 559
cooperative advertising 560
horizontal cooperative advertising 560
ingredient-sponsored
   cooperative advertising 560
vertical cooperative advertising 561
sales promotion trap 565

Discussion Questions

1. Discuss the role of sales promotion as part of an integrated marketing communications program. How does the role of sales promotion differ from that of media advertising? (LO 16-1, 16-2)

2. Critics of sales promotion argue that retailers have become overly dependent on discounts and promotions. Discuss the reasons retailers have increased their reliance on discounts and promotions to drive store traffic and sales. How might they reduce their dependency on them? (LO 16-1, 16-5)

3. Discuss the difference between consumer-oriented promotions and trade-oriented promotions and the role each plays in marketers' IMC programs. What are the various objectives for each category of sales promotion? (LO 16-1, 16-2, 16-3)

4. Do you agree with those who argue that the use of sales promotion detracts from brand equity for many companies and/or brands? Evaluate the arguments on both sides of this issue. (LO 16-1, 16-5)

5. Digital & Social Media Perspective 16-1 discusses the "Whopper Detour" promotion used by Burger King to compete against McDonald's. Analyze the strategy behind this promotion and the reasons it was so successful. Do you think Burger King could use a similar type of promotion again to attract business from other competitors in the fast-food industry? Why or why not? (LO 16-1, 16-3)

6. Why has the number of coupons distributed to consumers declined so much over the past decade? Discuss why consumer packaged-goods companies are cutting back on the use of coupons as a sales promotion tool. (LO 16-3, 16-5)

7. Many companies are shifting more of their promotional dollars to experiential marketing events. Discuss the role of experiential marketing as part of an IMC program and the reasons it is becoming increasingly important. (LO 16-1, 16-2, 16-3)

8. A report by a rebate fulfillment service showed that the average redemption for a $50 rebate on a product that costs $200 is only 35 percent. Why do you think redemption rates for rebates are so low? How might a low redemption rate affect a marketer's decision to use rebates as a promotional tool? (LO 16-3)

9. The use of loyalty programs has been increasing in many industries including fast-food and quick-serve restaurants, retail, and travel/hospitality. Find an example of a loyalty program and analyze the way it is used as a promotional tool by the company. (LO 16-2, 16-3)

10. Discuss the various types of trade promotions used by marketers, giving attention to the objectives, as well as the pros and cons of each. (LO 16-3, 16-4)

11. What is a sales promotion trap? Find an example of an industry or market where a promotional battle is taking place. What are the options for marketers in deciding whether to participate in the promotional battle? (LO 16-5)

17 Public Relations, Publicity, and Corporate Advertising

Mario Fritz/Shutterstock

Learning Objectives

 LO17-1 Describe the roles of public relations, publicity, and corporate advertising in the promotional mix.

 LO17-2 Compare the advantages, disadvantages, and effectiveness of public relations and publicity.

 LO17-3 Discuss the advantages, disadvantages, and effectiveness of corporate advertising.

 LO17-4 Compare the different forms of corporate advertising.

What Do Kanye West and Cristiano Ronaldo Have in Common? A Lot of Lost Money!

It would be an understatement to say that companies are afraid of negative publicity. While some say that any publicity is good publicity, or negative publicity can be seen as an opportunity to promote the product or brand, Enron, Wells Fargo, Fox News, and others that have experienced negative publicity prove otherwise. Some affected by unfortunate events survive, while others are no longer around. Sometimes the wounds are self-inflicted, sometimes unavoidable, or sometimes caused by the actions of others. Even individuals, if they are famous or powerful enough, can create major crises. In the nature of things, the following are extreme examples, but they show what bad publicity is and can do.

If you are a European sports fan, or any fan of football (or soccer, as it is known in the United States), you are familiar with the global superstar captain of Portugal's team, Cristiano Ronaldo. In the 2020 European Championship he became the leading scorer in European history when he scored twice in Portugal's win over Hungary, but before the game Ronaldo damaged a company he has no relationship with at all! Prior to the game with Hungary during a press conference in Budapest, the Portuguese star moved away two bottles of Coca-Cola that were in front of him on a table and then held up a bottle of water, declaring in Portuguese, "Agua," appearing to encourage drinking the water instead of the Coca-Cola. Within an hour after his gesture, the company's share price dropped by $4 billion. Viewers claimed that the Portuguese captain was "visibly troubled" by the bottles but made no specific comments about the brand or product, though in the past he has spoken unfavorably about his son's drinking the soda. Cristiano is a renowned health fanatic and a strong advocate of a healthy diet. Coke's response for the most part was limited to the statement, "Everyone is entitled to their drink preferences, with different tastes and needs." Coca-Cola is an official sponsor of the European event, and its partnership with UEFA has been ongoing since 1988. A spokesperson for the European Championship stated, "Without the support of brands like Coca-Cola we could not organize a tournament with such success for players and fans, nor invest in the future of football at all levels."

If you are a music fan, or not, you may know Kanye West (or his preferred new name "Ye"), the hip-hop musician and producer turned fashion designer and founder of the brand Yeezy, who has been a controversial character over the years. In the fall of 2022 in a series of interviews conducted over a period of weeks, repeatedly expressing a "virulently antisemitic worldview," West created extremely negative publicity for himself and the brands that he is associated with, and damaged others as well. In one interview he spoke of a Jewish-controlled news media and suggested that Jewish doctors wrongly hospitalized him for treatment of bipolar disorder while publicizing his diagnosis. His comments led to the collapse of a number of businesses that handled the Yeezy brand, his brand's market value plummeted, and Ye's relationships with a number of high-profile brands were terminated. Fashion company Balenciaga, the Gap, Vogue, and adidas terminated their relationships with him, and his talent agency CAA dropped him. His deal with adidas had been ongoing since 2013, and with the Gap since 2020. Adidas estimated that Yeezy accounted for 4 to 8 percent of their sales, and the termination of the relationship would cost the company approximately a quarter of a billion dollars in 2022. Shoe stores in Los Angeles reported panic among consumers who said they were worried about being judged if they wore adidas. Ye's estimated $2 billion net worth was estimated to be about 75 percent based on his relationship with adidas. He is supposedly no longer a billionaire.

Sadly, and far more seriously, the damage was not limited to Ye and the companies he was associated with. The Holocaust Museum in Los Angeles said that they have received a "tremendous" amount of hate messages on social media. They invited Ye to visit them (he declined). Jewish individuals and organizations have received hate mail, flyers left at their homes, and antisemitic threats. West (or "Ye") has individually been blamed for a rise in antisemitism in the United States.

When Elon Musk purchased Twitter, promising a more open tolerance of tweets, over 1,200 antisemitic tweets occurred on the very first day after his takeover. As a result, a number of brands including Pfizer, Audi, General Motors, and General Mills halted all advertising on Twitter until they determined where the new owner would take the social media site and the impact it might have on their brands.

So, as you can see, negative publicity can cause serious damage at every level. It can also cost a lot of money!

Sources: Molly Schultz, "General Mills Pauses Its Ads on Twitter," *Los Angeles Times*, November 4, 2022, p. A9; Uday Sampath Kumar, "Adidas Ends Ye Deal over Hate Speech, Costing Rapper His Business Status," Reuters, October 26, 2022, www.reuters.com; Daniel Miller and Ronald D. White, "Collectors Dumping Kanye West Products," *Los Angeles Times*, October 26, 2022, p. A10; Adriana Garcia, "Cristiano Ronaldo Snub Wipes Billions off Coca-Cola's Market Value," *Guardian*, June 15, 2021, www.guardian.com.

LO 17-1

The power of negative publicity can be costly as you can see in the lead-in to this chapter. Likewise, positive publicity may be very rewarding. The results often directly impact the companies involved financially as well as in respect to trust, image, and other nonfinancial aspects. Brands and/or companies have ceased to exist as a result of negative publicity, and others can attribute their success to positive messages. As you will see in this chapter, publicity is often out of the control of the marketer, but increasingly the management of publicity as part of the overall public relations function is being adopted as a marketing strategy. While attempts to generate positive publicity are nothing new, as these efforts increase, they signify changes in the public relations functions of companies and organizations. Although the importance and role of public relations in the IMC program may be argued, one thing is clear: The role of public relations in the communications program has changed.

Public relations involves various management functions, which include the management of publicity and corporate image advertising. Public relations has now assumed a much more important role in IMC programs. This role is less philanthropic and much more marketing-oriented. In this chapter we will examine the role of public relations in the IMC program and how this role has changed over recent years. Like every other aspect of IMC, the public relations function has been changed significantly by digital and social media. Simply put, news travels faster and wider now for most companies and organizations. As a result, the role of public relations and the importance of managing publicity has taken on increased importance.

Publicity, public relations, and corporate advertising all have promotional program elements that may be of great benefit to marketers. They are integral parts of the overall promotional effort that must be managed and coordinated with the other elements of the promotional mix. However, these three tools do not always have the specific objectives of product and service promotion, nor do they always involve the same methods you have become accustomed to as you have read this text. Typically, these activities are designed more to change attitudes toward an organization or issue than to promote specific products or affect behaviors directly (though you will see that this role is changing in some organizations). This chapter explores the roles of public relations, publicity, and corporate advertising; the advantages and disadvantages of each; and the processes by which they are employed.

PUBLIC RELATIONS

What is public relations? How does it differ from other elements of marketing discussed thus far? Perhaps a good starting point is to define what the term *public relations* has traditionally meant and then to introduce its new role.

The Traditional Definition of PR

A variety of books define **public relations (PR)**, but perhaps the most comprehensive definition is that offered by *Public Relations News* (the weekly newsletter of the industry):

> The management function which evaluates public attitudes, identifies the policies and procedures of an organization with the public interest, and executes a program of action (and communication) to earn public understanding and acceptance.[1]

Public relations is indeed a management function. The term *management* should be used in its broadest sense; it is not limited to business management but extends to other types of organizations, including nonprofit institutions.

In this definition, public relations requires a series of stages, including:

1. The determination and evaluation of public attitudes.
2. The identification of policies and procedures of an organization with a public interest.
3. The development and execution of a communications program designed to bring about public understanding and acceptance.

This process does not occur all at once. An effective public relations program continues over months or even years.

Finally, this definition reveals that public relations involves much more than activities designed to sell a product or service. The PR program may involve some of the promotional program elements previously discussed but use them in a different way. For example, companies may send press releases to announce new products or changes in the organization, companies may organize special events to create goodwill in the community, and companies may use advertising to state the firm's position on a controversial issue; while these activities continue to be the responsibility of management, the means by which they take place have changed, as you will see.

The New Role of PR

An increasing number of marketing-oriented companies have established new responsibilities for public relations. In this new role PR takes on a much broader (and more marketing-oriented) perspective, designed to promote the organization as well as its products and/or services.

The way that companies and organizations use public relations might best be viewed as a continuum. On one end of the continuum is the use of PR from a traditional perspective. In this perspective, public relations is viewed as a nonmarketing function whose primary responsibility is to maintain mutually beneficial relationships between the organization and its publics. In this case, customers or potential customers are only part of numerous publics—employees, investors, neighbors, special-interest groups, and so on. Marketing and public relations are separate departments; if external agencies are used, they are often separate agencies. At the other end of the continuum, public relations is considered primarily a marketing communications function. All noncustomer relationships are perceived as necessary only in a marketing context.[2] In these organizations, public relations reports to marketing. At the same time, for many companies the PR function is moving more and more toward a new role, which is much closer to a marketing function than a traditional one.

In the new role of public relations, managers envision both strong marketing and strong PR departments. Rather than each department operating independently, the two work closely together, blending their talents to provide the best overall image of the firm and its product or service offerings. As noted by Jonah Bloom, there has always been a cultural gulf separating the two departments, but today's information age demands the two camps work together. Bloom comments, "You'll struggle to peddle your eco-friendly detergent if your company is being slammed for pouring chemicals into a river."[3] In a poll conducted among 200-plus PR professionals in the United States, 74 percent of the respondents said that the relationship between the PR department and marketing was strong to very strong, indicating that the silos that previously existed have pretty much been broken down. About 85 percent indicated that the two departments share information more willingly than before.[4]

Writing in *Advertising Age*, William N. Curry notes that organizations must use caution in establishing this relationship because PR and marketing are not the same thing, and when one department becomes dominant, the balance required to operate at maximum efficiency is lost.[5] He says losing sight of the objectives and functions of public relations in an attempt to achieve marketing goals may be detrimental in the long run. Others take an even stronger view that if public relations and marketing distinctions continue to blur, the independence of the PR function will be lost, and it will become much less effective.[6] In fact, as noted by Cutlip, Center, and Broom, marketing and public relations are complementary functions, "with each making unique but complementary contributions to building and maintaining the many relationships essential for organizational survival and growth. To ignore one is to risk failure in the other."[7] This position is consistent with our perception that public relations is an important part of the IMC process, contributing in its own way but also in a way consistent with marketing goals.

Integrating PR into the Promotional Mix

Given the broader responsibilities of public relations, the issue is how to integrate it into the promotional mix. Companies have a number of ways in which they organize the marketing and public relations functions. Others may outsource the public relations to outside agencies. In this text we regard public relations as an IMC program element. This means that its broad role must include traditional responsibilities, as well as new ones.

Whether public relations takes on a traditional role or a more marketing-oriented one, PR activities are still tied to specific communications objectives. Assessing public attitudes and creating a favorable corporate image are no less important than promoting products or services directly.

Marketing Public Relations Functions

Thomas L. Harris has referred to public relations activities designed to support marketing objectives as **marketing public relations (MPR)** functions.[8] Marketing objectives that may be aided by public relations activities include raising awareness, informing and educating, gaining understanding, building trust, giving consumers a reason to buy, and motivating consumer acceptance. MPR adds value to the integrated marketing program in a number of ways:

- *Building marketplace excitement before media advertising breaks.* The announcement of a new product, for example, is an opportunity for the marketer to obtain publicity and to dramatize the product, thereby increasing the effectiveness of ads. When Apple introduces any new product from its iPhones to Apple watches, a great deal of anticipation is created through public relations prior to the availability of the product. The result is that Apple receives a great deal of press coverage and word of mouth. It seems that upon release of any Apple product, consumers wait in lines—sometime for hours—to be the first to own the next innovation, with little or no advertising having been implemented.

- *Improving ROI.* By reducing overall marketing costs, while delivering meaningful marketing outcomes, MPR helps improve ROI.

- *Creating advertising news where there is no product news.* Ads themselves can be the focus of publicity. When an advertisement or commercial creates a great deal of "buzz," the exposure and interest that are generated result in much more value to the company than just the ad itself. A 2022 Super Bowl commercial for Salesforce.com featuring Matthew McConaughey that took a jab at the billionaire space race between Elon Musk and Jeff Bezos is a perfect example of this (Exhibit 17–1). There seems to be as much hype about the ads on the Super Bowl as there is for the game itself. TV commercials commonly find their ways to social sites on the Internet, where they are viewed time and time again and forwarded to others.

EXHIBIT 17–1

Salesforce.com used this advertisement to introduce a new service.

Salesforce, Inc.

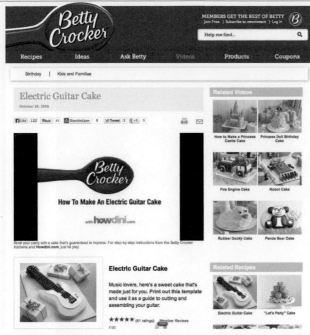

EXHIBIT 17-2

Betty Crocker's website is designed to create goodwill and build loyalty for its consumers by offering ideas, recipes, coupons, and even an "ask Betty" section where consumers can submit questions.

Betty Crocker by General Mills Marketing Inc. (GMMI)

- *Introducing a product with little or no advertising.* This strategy has been implemented successfully by a number of companies, including Tesla, Segway, Ty, Crayola, and, of course, Apple. Among others, Gillette uses PR as the lead medium in every new product launch. More and more companies seem to be taking this approach.

- *Providing a value-added customer service.* Butterball established a hotline where people can call in to receive personal advice on how to prepare their turkeys. The company handled 25,000 calls during the first holiday season. Many companies provide such services on their Internet sites. Chicken of the Sea provides recipes to visitors to its site (which, of course, suggest using Chicken of the Sea tuna).

- *Building brand-to-customer bonds.* The Pillsbury Bake-Off has led to strong brand loyalty among Pillsbury customers, who compete by submitting baked goods. The contest has taken place annually since 1949, and the winner now receives a $50,000 prize. The winning recipes are posted on the Pillsbury website. There is a significant part of the Pillsbury website that features the winning recipes, as well as a history of the contest and how it has evolved since its inception in 1949. Competitor Betty Crocker has used branded video to reach its MPR objectives and also has a helpful website (Exhibit 17-2).

- *Influencing the influentials.* That is, providing information to opinion leaders.

- *Defending products at risk and giving consumers a reason to buy.* By taking constructive actions to defend or promote a company's products, PR can actually give consumers a reason to buy the products. Energizer's national education campaign that urged consumers to change the batteries in their fire alarms when they reset their clocks in the fall resulted in a strong corporate citizen image and increased sales of batteries. Similarly, Arm & Hammer Baking Soda's website shows the multitude of uses for the product, as well as information on how to use it and when to replace it. There also is a section for an entry in a contest where consumers can win money by providing their unique use of the soda (Exhibit 17-3). Cessna's campaign to convince executives that there are legitimate reasons to buy corporate jets (Exhibit 17-4) is an excellent example of defending a product at risk. When sales were threatened, Cessna ran this attractive ad. Figure 17-1 shows a few more examples.

EXHIBIT 17-3

Arm & Hammer used this ad to show the multiple (and unique) uses for baking soda.

Church & Dwight Co., Inc.

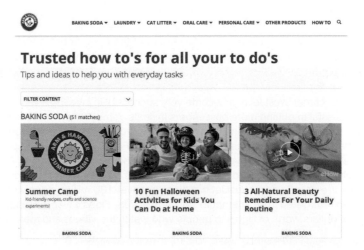

STATE-OF-THE-ART
CESSNA CITATION X

LUXURY BUSINESS JETS

FIGURE 17–1   Companies Use MPRs

Cessna

During the last big recession and auto industry sales slump, top executives of Detroit's Big Three car companies went to the nation's capital to ask for a bailout. When the execs traveled on a $50 million private plane rather than drive, the lawmakers and press bashed them for it. Unfortunately, the backlash had a profound negative effect on jet manufacturers, as numerous orders were canceled or deferred. Production was cut by as much as 56 percent, and as much as one-third of the industry's workers were laid off. One company, Cessna, decided to fight back and give corporate America a reason to buy.

In a hard-hitting print campaign starting in *The Wall Street Journal* called "Rise," Cessna challenged business leaders to not be timid, and recognize private planes are not about ego, but about having the right tools to be productive. Cessna said it was time for the other side of the story to be told. In addition to *The Wall Street Journal*, the ads were run in national business newspapers and magazines as well as aviation trade journals, together with an extensive PR campaign. Four years later Cessna was still receiving requests for reprints of the ads, and sales were on the increase.

Betty Crocker

Faced with the objective of getting more cake bakers to visit its website, Betty Crocker worked with digital video agency Touchstorm to create a series of informational videos targeted to mothers who bake their children's birthday cakes. Analyzing search terms, the two determined that when mothers want information or help in baking cakes, they don't search on brand names, but rather on specific solution terms like "birthday cake." Given this information, a series of high-quality HD videos approximately 5 minutes in length were created and posted on the Betty Crocker website. To convey the idea that the videos were instructional and not promotional, there was little reference to the Betty Crocker brand. The videos were very engaging, with an average of 75 percent of the content being watched. To date, the videos have driven over 70 million visitors to the website and, more important, are building brand loyalty due to their instructional nature.

WestJet

Canadian airlines carrier WestJet has become very successful in creating a variety of "PR stunts." The Calgary-based airline has also been successful in putting more passengers in seats. A much smaller airline than its main rival Air Canada, WestJet also has a much smaller marketing budget and knows it had to be creative. So to cut through the clutter, the airline began to pull the PR stunts and video them. The stunts have included an April Fool's ruse that asked passengers to put their hands up in the air during landing and take-off so as to improve aerodynamics that helped save fuel costs. Christmas videos showing the airline surprising people with gifts also proved to lead to popular videos, as have tie-ins to nonprofits. Poking fun at Air Canada is also positively received. Over the past 5 years, WestJet has amassed over 100 million video views and billions of impressions. Viewers of the videos are then retargeted in an attempt to sell them tickets. Does it work? WestJet says so as its tracking metrics show it has sold millions of dollars worth of flights to people who watch the videos and then immediately purchased tickets.

Source: "WestJet Taps Power of 'PR Stunts,'" WARC, June 10, 2019, www.warc.com.

FIGURE 17–2

Advantages and
Disadvantages of MPRs

Advantages
■ It is a cost-effective way to reach the market.
■ It is a highly targeted way to conduct public relations.
■ It benefits from the endorsement of independent and objective third parties who have no association with the product.
■ It achieves credibility.
■ It supports advertising programs by making messages more credible.
■ It breaks through the clutter.
■ It circumvents consumer resistance to sales efforts.
■ There can be improved media involvement among consumers.
■ It can create influence among opinion leaders and trendsetters.
■ It can improve ROI.

Disadvantages
■ There is a lack of control over the media.
■ It is difficult to tie in slogans and other advertising devices.
■ Media time and space are not guaranteed.
■ There are no standard effectiveness measures.

Sources: Thomas Harris, "Marketing PR—The Second Century," *Reputation Management*, January/February 1999, pp. 1–6, www.prcentral.com.

As shown in Figure 17–2, Harris notes that there are a number of advantages of using MPRs.[9]

One of the major threats of using an MPR structure, as expressed by Harris, is that public relations functions may become subservient to marketing efforts—a concern expressed by many opponents of MPR. However, if employed properly and used in conjunction with other traditional public relations practices as well as IMC elements, MPR can continue to be used effectively. Weiner also notes that the key to the successful use of MPRs is integration with IMC, though such a task may prove to be difficult to accomplish.

THE PROCESS OF PUBLIC RELATIONS

The actual process of conducting public relations and integrating it into the promotional mix involves a series of both traditional and marketing-oriented tasks.

Determining and Evaluating Public Attitudes

You have learned that public relations is concerned with people's attitudes toward the firm or specific issues beyond those directed at a product or service. The first question you may ask is why—why is the firm so concerned with the public's attitudes?

One reason is that these attitudes may affect sales of the firm's products. A number of companies have experienced sales declines as a result of consumer boycotts. BP, Amazon, Nike, Ben & Jerry's, Swatch, and Apple are just a few companies that have had to respond to organized pressures. PETA's 10-year campaign against Fortnum & Mason, a London-based company selling foie gras, finally led the company to stop selling the product. The campaign involved thousands of letters, advertising, and protests and was supported by celebrities Twiggy and Bill Oddie among others. PETA was also successful in getting Canada Goose to stop selling furs. Likewise, the media must be concerned with the attitudes of the public. *Fox News*, which is owned by News Corp., lost favor with many in the Republican base for its coverage of the 2016 Republican presidential primaries. Long known as a network favored by conservatives, the network saw a significant drop in perceptions of Fox as providing "fair and balanced coverage"; viewers were unhappy with the way *Fox News* treated candidate Donald Trump and ignored candidate Dr. Ben Carson. Thousands of #StopFundingHate group supporters were successful in getting "News UK"—a Fox news–style channel in the UK—to end its plans to start a new channel, by asking companies to agree not to advertise on the channel if launched.[10]

On the other hand, companies can gain favorable impressions and positive attitudes from consumers by doing the right thing. For example, Intuit sent consumers an apology letter and a free upgrade for changing its TurboTax software and not including a number of forms that were in previous versions, as well as not taking adequate measures to inform its customer base that it was doing so and why. The apology was used as an example of great customer service by bloggers and helped improve attitudes toward the TurboTax product.

Second, no one wants to be perceived as a bad citizen. Corporations exist in communities, and their employees generally both work and live there. Negative attitudes carry over to employee morale and may result in a less-than-optimal working environment internally and in the community.

Due to their concerns about public perceptions, many privately held corporations, publicly held companies, utilities, and media survey public attitudes. The reasons for conducting this research are many, but include the following:

1. *It provides input into the planning process.* Once the firm has determined public attitudes, they become the starting point in the development of programs designed to maintain favorable positions or change unfavorable ones.
2. *It serves as an early warning system.* Once a problem exists, it may require substantial time and money to correct. By conducting research, the firm may be able to identify potential problems and handle them effectively before they become serious issues.
3. *It secures support internally.* If research shows a problem or potential problem exists, it will be much easier for the public relations arm to gain the support it needs to address this problem.
4. *It increases the effectiveness of the communication.* The better it understands a problem, the better the firm can design communications to deal with it.

Establishing a PR Plan

For some companies, their PR programs involve little more than press releases, press kits for the media, and/or trade shows and new product announcements.

Further, these tools are often not designed into a formal public relations effort but rather are used only as needed. In other words, no structured program for conducting PR is evident. As we noted earlier, the public relations process is an ongoing one, requiring formalized policies and procedures for dealing with problems and opportunities. Just as you would not develop an advertising and/or a promotions program without a plan, you should not institute public relations efforts haphazardly. Moreover, the PR plan needs to be integrated into the overall marketing communications program. Figure 17–3 provides some questions marketers should ask to determine whether their PR plan is workable.

Cutlip and colleagues suggest a four-step process for developing a public relations plan: (1) define public relations problems, (2) plan and program, (3) take action and communicate, and (4) evaluate the program.[11] The questions in Figure 17–3 and the four-step planning process tie in with the promotional planning process stressed throughout this text.

Developing and Executing the PR Program

Because of the broad role that public relations may be asked to play, the PR program may need to extend beyond promotion. A broader definition of the target market, additional communications objectives, and different messages and delivery systems may be employed. Let us examine this process.

FIGURE 17–3

Ten Questions for Evaluating Public Relations Plans

1. Does the plan reflect a thorough understanding of the company's business situation?

2. Has the PR program made good use of research and background sources?

3. Does the plan include full analysis of recent editorial coverage?

4. Do the PR people fully understand the product's strengths and weaknesses?

5. Does the PR program describe several cogent, relevant conclusions from the research?

6. Are the program objectives specific and measurable?

7. Does the program clearly describe what the PR activity will be and how it will benefit the company?

8. Does the program describe how its results will be measured?

9. Do the research, objectives, activities, and evaluations tie together?

10. Has the PR department communicated with marketing throughout the development of the program?

EXHIBIT 17–5

An example of a newsletter used for internal communication by the Fowler College of Business Administration at San Diego State University.

San Diego State University

ADVANCE YOUR CAREER

Explore graduate programs at the Fowler College of Business. Applications open August 1st.

CLICK HERE FOR MORE INFO

Fowler College of Business Staff Spotlight

 FCB Staff Q&A
Jason Brown, Department Coordinator
Marketing, Management & Finance

Q: What are some of your responsibilities as Department Coordinator?

Some of my job responsibilities include the maintenance and reconciliation of departmental university accounts and Foundation funds, and the coordination of hiring new faculty for the university. While I am still learning many of the processes inherent to the position, I am excited that soon I will be able to bridge some of the gaps between the faculty and administrative areas to the overall benefit of the college.

Q: What or who inspires you?

My inspiration can change from moment to moment. Sometimes it may be my son, Aaron, or my granddaughter, Chloe, and other times it may be a song that I hear or melody that I play. Whichever it is, my hope is that I can capture the moment in some tangible form to reflect on later.

 FCB Staff Q&A
Zena Yang, Coordinator,
The Corky McMillin Center For Real Estate

Q: What are some of your responsibilities at The Corky McMillin Center for Real Estate?

My responsibilities include offering support for our students and our advisory board, marketing activities, engaging with the local real estate community, and event planning and implementation. I also manage the reservation schedules for the Page Pavilion and the college's conference rooms.

Q: Of all the places you've lived in the world, which one is your favorite and why?

I'd say my favorite is New Zealand. It is, without a doubt, the most jaw-droppingly beautiful country I have ever lived in. New Zealand is full of hidden gems from white sand beaches to secret coves and hiking trails. I do believe that Queenstown is one of the most beautiful places on earth.

San Diego State University, 5500 Campanile Drive, San Diego, CA 92182-8230

View Online © 2019 Copyright

Determining Relevant Target Audiences The targets of public relations efforts may vary, with different objectives for each. Some may be directly involved in selling the product; others may affect the firm in a different way (e.g., they may be aimed at stockholders or legislators). These audiences may be internal or external to the firm.

Internal audiences may include the employees, stockholders, and investors of the firm as well as members of the local community, suppliers, and current customers. As noted in Figure 17–1, Cessna's public relations programs were designed, in part, to reach buyers as well as to improve morale among employees. Why are community members and customers of the firm considered internal rather than external? According to John Marston, it's because these groups are already connected with the organization in some way, and the firm normally communicates with them in the ordinary routine of work.[12] **External audiences** are those people who are not closely connected with the organization (e.g., the public at large).

It may be necessary to communicate with these groups on an ongoing basis for a variety of reasons, ranging from ensuring goodwill to introducing new policies, procedures, or even products. A few examples may help.

Employees of the Firm Maintaining morale and showcasing the results of employees' efforts are often prime objectives of the public relations program. Organizational newsletters, notices on bulletin boards, awards ceremonies and events, direct mail, and annual reports are some of the methods used to communicate with these groups. Exhibit 17–5 shows one such internal communication used by the Fowler College of Business Administration at San Diego State University.

Personal methods of communicating may be as formal as an established grievance committee or as informal as an office Christmas party. Other social events, such as corporate bowling teams or picnics, are also used to create goodwill.

EXHIBIT 17–6

In addition to providing information regarding its finances, GE's annual report provides much more information regarding the companies activities.

General Electric

Stockholders and Investors You may think an annual report like the one in Exhibit 17-6 provides stockholders and investors only with financial information regarding the firm. While this is one purpose, annual reports are also a communications channel for informing this audience about why the firm is or is not doing well, outlining future plans, and providing other information that goes beyond numbers.

It has become very common for companies to use annual reports for public relations purposes—to generate additional investments, to bring more of their stocks "back home" (i.e., become more locally controlled and managed), and to produce funding to solve specific problems, as well as to promote goodwill.

Community Members People who live and work in the community where a firm is located or doing business are often the target of public relations efforts. Such efforts may involve ads informing the community of activities that the organization is engaged in, for example, reducing air pollution, cleaning up water supplies, or preserving wetlands. (The community can be defined very broadly.) As you can see in Exhibit 17-7, Tom's Shoes' Impact Report is an example of this form of public relations by demonstrating to people that the organization is a good citizen with their welfare in mind.

Suppliers and Customers An organization wishes to maintain *goodwill* with its suppliers as well as its consuming public. If consumers think a company is not socially conscious, they may take their loyalties elsewhere. Suppliers may be inclined to do the same.

Sometimes sponsoring a public relations effort results in direct evidence of success. Certainly Betty Crocker achieved its goal of getting consumers to the website and getting engaged with the brand. Indirect indications of the success of PR efforts may include more customer loyalty, less antagonism, or greater cooperation between the firm and its suppliers or consumers.

Public relations efforts are often targeted to more than one group and are a direct result of concerns initiated in the marketplace. As noted earlier, along with potential consumers, trade association members, human resource directors, buyers, and suppliers often constitute the target audience for PR efforts.

EXHIBIT 17–7

Tom's Shoes Impact Report demonstrates the company's focus on being a good citizen.

TOMS.com, LLC.

Relevant audiences may also include people not directly involved with the firm. The press, educators, civic and business groups, governments, and the financial community can be external audiences.

The Media Perhaps among the most critical external publics are the media, which determine what you will read in your newspapers or online, or see on TV and how this news will be presented. Because of the media's power, they should be informed of the firm's actions. Companies issue press releases and communicate through conferences, interviews, and special events. The media are generally receptive to such information as long as it is handled professionally; reporters are always interested in good stories. In turn, the media are also concerned about how the community perceives them. (Remember the *Fox News* example provided earlier.)

Educators A number of organizations provide educators with information regarding their activities. The Advertising Education Foundation (ANA); Direct Selling Education Foundation (DSEF); the Promotional Products Association International (PPAI); and the Outdoor Advertising Association of America (OAAA); among others, keep educators informed in an attempt to generate goodwill as well as exposure for their causes on both a local and national level. These groups and major corporations provide information regarding innovations, state-of-the-art research, and other items of interest. The ANA Educational Foundation works closely with colleges and universities, providing seminars, research information, and other forms of involvement including employment and internship opportunities for students (Exhibit 17–8).

Educators are a target audience because, like the media, they control the flow of information to certain parties—in this case, people like you. *The Bloomberg News* and *Fortune* magazines attempt to have professors use their magazines in their classes, as does *The Wall Street Journal*, *The New York Times*, and *Advertising Age*, among others. In addition to selling more magazines and newspapers, such usage also lends credibility to the medium, and (hopefully) the students will continue to use these media after they graduate and start a career.

EXHIBIT 17–8

The ANA strongly supports colleges and universities in a number of ways.

Association of National Advertisers

Become a Growth Champion

The ANA is the connective tissue marketers need to make better decisions and drive business growth. Representing more than 20,000 influential brands, we help our members become more effective marketers, build stronger brands, and drive industry and societal change through our CMO-endorsed Growth Agenda, which provides a 360-degree focus on all elements of the business enterprise.

We also empower marketing teams to become high performers through our unmatched proprietary intellectual capital, including insights, events, and professional development programs.

Read on for more on how we help marketers become growth champions.

What Marketing Leaders Are Saying

"The significance of the Growth Council is that for the first time, the ANA has brought together a group of very important people from all walks of industry around the world to work concertedly to ensure that our industry remains pertinent and relevant."

Tencent腾讯 — Sy Lau, CMO

"It is wonderful for us to bring our experiences together, to bring our learnings together, and to put a playbook together to collectively — as a trade, as a craft — lift ourselves up."

— Raja Rajamannar, Chief Marketing and Communications Officer and President, Healthcare Business

"There are so many actions we can take as individuals and as a group. There is power in the collective in terms of what we can do together to help shape the growth of the industry. This is an exciting place to be."

— Elizabeth Rutledge, CMO

Civic and Business Organizations The local Jaycees, Kiwanis, and other nonprofit civic organizations also serve as gatekeepers of information. Companies' financial contributions to these groups, speeches at organization functions, and sponsorships are all designed to create goodwill. Corporate executives' service on the boards of non-profit organizations also generates positive public relations.

Governments Public relations often attempts to influence government bodies directly at both local and national levels. Successful lobbying may mean immediate success for a product, while regulations detrimental to the firm may cost it millions. Imagine for a moment what FDA approval of a product can mean for sales, or what could happen to the beer and wine industries if TV advertising were banned. The pharmaceutical industry lobbied hard for permission to advertise prescription drugs directly to the consumer. Within the first 5 years of approval, an estimated 65 million consumers approached their doctors to inquire about the drugs as a result. The industry now spends an estimated $5.7 billion each year on TV advertising. When other media are included, advertising on TV, magazine, digital, newspaper, radio, and out-of-home advertising topped $5.5 billion in the first 6 months of 2022,[13] leading some organizations like the American Medical Association (AMA) to seek the ban to be continued.[14] While the AMA has not been successful in banning the TV ads, it lobbied hard enough to achieve legislation in 2019 that would require the ads to show prices of the drugs. In turn, environmentalists, trade unions, and other groups with specific agendas also attempt to influence government legislation in their behalf.

Financial Groups In addition to current shareholders, potential shareholders and investors may be relevant target markets for PR efforts. Financial advisors, lending institutions, and others must be kept abreast of new developments as well as of financial information, since they offer the potential for new sources of funding. Press releases and corporate reports play an important role in providing information to these publics.

Implementing the PR Program   Once the research has been conducted and the target audiences identified, the public relations program must be developed and delivered to the receivers. A number of PR tools are available for this purpose, including press releases, press conferences, exclusives, interviews, community involvement, the Internet, and social networks and blogs.

The Press Release One of the most important publics is the press. To be used by the press, information must be factual, true, and of interest to the medium as well as to its audience. The source of the **press release** can do certain things to improve the likelihood that the "news" will be disseminated, such as ensuring that it reaches the right target audience, making it interesting, and making it easy to pass along.

   The information in a press release won't be used unless it is of interest to the users of the medium it is sent to. For example, financial institutions may issue press releases to business trade media and to the editor of the business section of a general-interest newspaper. Organizations like the PR Newswire and PRLog provide services to help disseminate information.

Press Conferences We are all familiar with **press conferences** held by political figures. Press conferences are commonly used when organizations or companies experience negative publicity. Although used less often by organizations and corporations, this form of delivery can be very effective. The topic must be of major interest to a specific group before it is likely to gain coverage. Usually major accomplishments (such as the awarding of the next Super Bowl, FIFA, or Olympics location) and major breakthroughs (such as medical cures, emergencies, or catastrophes) warrant a national press conference. On a local level, community events, local developments, and the like may receive coverage. Companies often call press conferences when they

EXHIBIT 17–9

Dunkin' is a large supporter of community events.

Allen Creative/Steve Allen/Alamy Stock Photo

have significant news to announce, such as the introduction of a new product or advertising campaign. Sports teams use this tool to attract fan attention and interest when a new star is signed.

Exclusives Although most public relations efforts seek a variety of channels for distribution, an alternative strategy is to offer one particular medium exclusive rights to the story if that medium reaches a substantial number of people in the target audience. Offering an **exclusive** may enhance the likelihood of acceptance. If you happen to watch television over the next few weeks, watch for the various networks' and local stations' exclusives. Notice how the media actually use these exclusives to promote themselves.

Interviews When you watch TV or read magazines, pay close attention to the personal interviews. Usually someone will raise specific questions, and a spokesperson provided by the firm will answer them. For example, when NFL player Tyreek Hill of the Kansas City Chiefs was accused of domestic violence, a spokesperson for the Chiefs immediately announced Hill's suspension from the team and answered questions to reporters about his future with the team. Similar situations have become somewhat common with athletes in other sports as well. Depending on how significant the issue is, sometimes even top management will get involved. When consumers protested Chick-fil-A's support of antigay Christian organizations, the president, Dan Cahy, stood by his decision in an interview with *The Baptist Press* newspaper.

Community Involvement Many companies and individuals enhance their public image through involvement in the local community. This involvement may take many forms, including membership in local organizations like the Kiwanis, Jaycees, or other organizations and contributions to or participation in community events. Dunkin' has been involved in community events since its founding in 1950 (Exhibit 17–9).

The Internet As discussed in Chapter 15, the Internet has become a means by which companies and organizations can disseminate public relations information. Just as in the print media, companies have used the Web to establish media relations and government, investor, and community relationships; to deal with crises; and even to conduct cause marketing. Companies have used their websites to address issues, as well as to provide information about products and services, archive press releases, link to other articles and sites, and provide lists of activities and events. Many corporate websites have sections listing their press activities.

Social Networks and Blogs More and more companies and organizations are making use of social networks, blogs, and other web media for public relations purposes. It is now expected that companies will post information on their websites providing announcements and updates on product releases, recalls, or other issues. In addition, many of these companies are using digital media to disseminate this information. Many employed in PR consider themselves employed in a new form of PR they refer to as **digital public relations**. Digital PR, they say, is an intersection between traditional public relations activities as just discussed and new activities that incorporate digital marketing functions like SEO, social media, and influencer marketing. For example, a study by USC Annenberg School for Communication and Journalism indicated that "87% of PR executives believe the term 'public relations' won't accurately describe the work they will be doing in the near future." In the study of PR pros mentioned earlier, approximately 59 percent of the respondents indicated that they believed their colleagues had more business acumen than they had 5 years prior to the survey, and 73.5 percent believed that PR professionals delivered better results through social media than their marketing counterparts did.[16]

EXHIBIT 17–10

State Farm Insurance promotes its J.D. Power Award in this public relations ad that proclaims it ranked the "Highest Customer Satisfaction among Auto Insurance Providers."

State Farm Mutual Automobile Insurance Company

Advantages and Disadvantages of PR

Like the other program elements, public relations has both advantages and disadvantages.

Advantages include the following:

1. *Credibility.* Because public relations communications are not perceived in the same light as advertising—that is, the public does not realize the organization either directly or indirectly paid for them—they tend to have more credibility. The fact that the media are not being compensated for providing the information may lead receivers to consider the news more truthful and credible. For example, an article in newspapers or magazines discussing the virtues of aspirin may be perceived as much more credible than an ad for a particular brand of aspirin.

   Automotive awards presented in magazines such as *Motor Trend* have long been known to carry clout with potential car buyers. The influential J.D. Power Awards are now offered for a variety of reasons (quality, customer satisfaction, service, etc.) in a variety of industries (automobile, financial services, airports, etc.). It has become a common practice for car companies and others to promote their achievements (Exhibit 17–10). In one instance, the wife of a recently deceased spouse received a direct-mail piece from a funeral home touting its services and the fact that it was the recipient of a J.D. Power Award for funeral services. Let's hope they are better at providing funeral services than they are at maintaining their mailing lists!

   News about a product may in itself serve as the subject of an ad. Exhibit 17–11 demonstrates how General Mills used favorable publicity from a variety of sources to promote the importance of whole grain in a healthy diet and promote the use of whole grain in its cereals. Exhibit 17–11 shows the "white check" indicating that particular brand of General Mills cereal contains whole grain as the first and most prevalent ingredient. The symbol is carried on the front of each of 50 brands.

2. *Cost.* In both absolute and relative terms, the cost of public relations is very low, especially when the possible effects are considered. While a firm can employ public relations agencies and spend millions of dollars on PR, for smaller companies this form of communication may be the most affordable alternative available. As noted, many services exist to distribute this information at little or no cost. Many public relations programs require little more than the time and expenses associated with putting the program together and getting it distributed, yet they still accomplish their objectives.

3. *Avoidance of clutter.* Because they are typically perceived as news items, public relations messages are not subject to the clutter of ads. A story regarding a new product introduction or breakthrough is treated as a news item and is likely to receive attention.

4. *Lead generation.* Information about technological innovations, medical breakthroughs, and the like results almost immediately in a multitude of inquiries. These inquiries may give the firm some quality sales leads.

5. *Ability to reach specific groups.* Because some products appeal to only small market segments, it is not feasible to engage in advertising and/or promotions to reach them. If the firm does not have the financial capabilities to engage in promotional expenditures, the best way to communicate to these groups is through public relations. Social networks and blogs have become extremely valuable in this regard.

6. *Image building.* Effective public relations helps develop a positive image for the organization. A strong image is insurance against later misfortunes. The strength of the Toyota brand name made it possible for Toyota to get through a series of crises involving mechanical problems, while VW survived the extensive negative press received when it was shown to have manipulated emissions tests on its diesel vehicles.

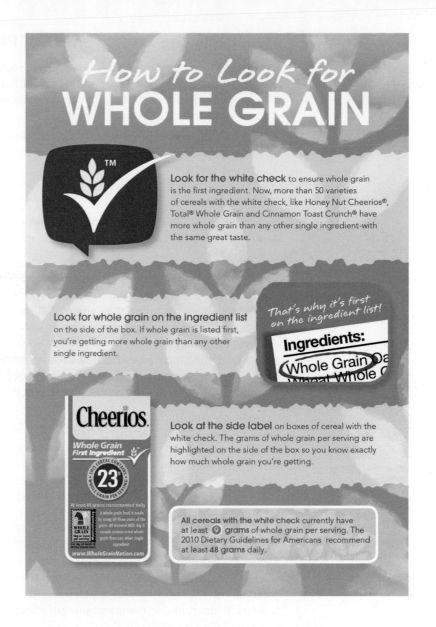

7. *Capitalizing on earned media.* One of the areas in which public relations practitioners believe they are very strong is achieving earned media through **storytelling**. Eddie Kim, founder and CEO of Memo, a PR measurement platform, believes that in regard to storytelling "there is no other medium that exists today where you can consistently get someone to spend the same amount of engaged time learning about your company's messaging, values, and products." Kim notes that while social posts are often "a flash in a pan," a well-placed article can remain in one's memory for years to come.[17]

Perhaps the major disadvantage of public relations is the potential for not completing the communications process. While public relations messages can break through the clutter of commercials, the receiver may not make the connection to the source. Many firms' PR efforts are never associated with their sponsors in the public mind.

Public relations may also misfire through mismanagement and a lack of coordination with the marketing department. When marketing and PR departments operate independently, there is a danger of inconsistent communications, redundancies in efforts, and so on.

The key to effective public relations is to establish a good program, worthy of public interest, and to manage it properly. To determine if this program is working, the firm must measure the effectiveness of the PR effort.

Measuring the Effectiveness of PR

As with the other promotional program elements, it is important to evaluate the effectiveness of the public relations efforts. In addition to determining the contribution of this program element to attaining communications objectives, the evaluation offers other advantages:

1. It tells management what has been achieved through public relations activities.
2. It provides management with a way to measure public relations achievements quantitatively.
3. It gives management a way to judge the quality of public relations achievements and activities.

According to the **Public Relations Society of America**, organizations that understand and subscribe to the benefits of public relations evaluation can effectively:

- Validate the results of their efforts.
- Link the results to business outcomes that further the realization of organizational goals.
- Credibly merchandise the impact of the results to those who fund PR programs.
- Set smarter objectives, develop better strategies, and employ more compelling and engaging tactics.
- Make midcourse adjustments and corrections.
- Regularly adapt their measurement approaches based on changing objectives, new competitors, and emerging best practices.[18]

In an extensive review of criteria used to measure effectiveness, Professor Jim Macnamara of the University of Technology, Sydney, identified 30 metrics that are broadly used for measuring PR and corporate communication today.[19] In a review of emerging models for measuring public relations effectiveness, Amit Jain concluded that traditional methods no longer work. Jain notes that as digital becomes more and more of the public relations process, new criteria need to be added to previous measures, and new models must be developed.[20] One company suggests that the digital PR organization use a framework based on the concept of a consumer funnel with three levels: (1) brand impact, (2) digital impact, and (3) bottom-line impact. As shown in Figure 17–4, these levels can be broken down into specific categories that can be specifically measured to determine the success of the PR efforts. Cision, along with many others in the PR industry, sees digital PR as the future of the industry.

Mark Weiner, in discussing measures of effectiveness specific to MPRs, also suggests using the following methods:[21]

- *Media content analysis.* Systematically and objectively identifying the characteristics of messages that appear in the media, analyzing the content to determine trends and perceptions relevant to the product or brand.
- *Survey research.* Quantitatively assessing consumers' attitudes toward the product or brand.
- *Marketing-mix modeling.* Drawing data from multiple sources and integrating them to provide insight into the process.

A model known as the PESO model, developed and championed by Gini Dietrich, a leading voice for the PR industry, has now been embraced by public relations practitioners.[22] The model has been shown to be successful in measuring the effectiveness of digital media in public relations. An excellent example of how the model works when combined with marketing is reflected by Dell at the company's Dell World conference. To communicate information about their first annual Global Technology Adoption Index (GTAI), the PR and marketing teams involved press, native ads, and owned and social media.

In the Dell example, here's how it went:

- Michael Dell announced the Global Technology Adoption Index (GTAI) during the Dell World press conference.

FIGURE 17–4

Communicators Funnel for Digital Public Relations

Cision Ltd. is a public relations and earned media software company and services provider assisting organizations in digital public relations. The Cision framework involves a communication funnel consisting of three levels:

Brand impact—examines how one's brand is perceived in the marketplace. Brand impact consists of three categories. These categories and their measures include:

1. Awareness—is the market aware of your brand? Is your brand being mentioned? (The number of mentions can serve as a proxy measure for awareness.)

2. Mindshare—finding trends in the mentions and share of voice (counting competitors' mentions compared to yours).

3. Reputation—determining if PR coverage is resonating with the target audience. (Social sharing is a good proxy for audience engagement, sentiment, and pull-through.)

Digital impact—the PR coverage driving traffic to the brand's website or other digital properties. In other words, what actions are the visitors taking?

1. Website traffic—tracking how many visits PR drives to the website. (Measure the percentage PR drives to the site versus overall site traffic. Use traffic measures to determine the effectiveness of the PR effort.)

2. SEO impact—examining referring domains to see how they impact the brands rankings. (Examine high-traffic and low-traffic websites and focus on high-authority sites while avoiding "toxic links.")

3. Social amplification—determining how viewers are extending the digital footprint across social media platforms. (Employ social media engagement metrics.)

Bottom line—taking behavioral measures such as sales, donations, and business transactions to determine whether they were influenced by the PR effort. (Use analytics provided by systems like Hubspot, Marketo, etc., to determine conversions, revenue, etc.)

Source: Cision.com, 2019

- The GTAI results were shared across Dell's social media platforms (e.g., LinkedIn, Twitter, Facebook), including tweets from the @Dell handle, and the social community was encouraged to use the hashtag #delltechindex.
- Dell's owned media site, Tech Page One, released a story called "Tech Hype Meets Tech Reality" that outlined some of the key findings from the GTAI.
- The PR team pitched the story to journalists and secured media coverage including online tech and business sites like the *Irish Times*, ZDnet, and eWeek.
- The *New York Times* GTAI native advertising campaign was released a day after the news media covered the announcement.
- Online video and content syndication ran on business and technology sites.
- Paid social posts promoted the campaign on LinkedIn and Twitter.
- Infographics were used to accompany all of the this content.

As the relationship between public relations and marketing continues to evolve and cooperation becomes more of the norm, the bases for measuring effectiveness of the PR effort will also evolve.

In summary, the role of public relations in the promotional mix is changing. As PR has become more marketing-oriented, and digital marketing has become increasingly important in PR, the criteria by which the programs are evaluated have also changed. At the same time, nonmarketing activities will continue to be part of the public relations department and part of the basis for evaluation.

PUBLICITY

Publicity refers to the generation of news about a person, product, or service that appears in broadcast, digital, or print media. To many marketers, publicity and public relations are synonymous. In fact, publicity is really a subset of the public relations effort.

But there are several major differences. First, publicity is typically a *short-term* strategy, while public relations is a concerted program extending over a period of time. Second, public relations is designed to provide positive information about the firm and is usually controlled by the firm or its agent. Publicity, on the other hand, is not always positive and is not always under the control of, or paid for by, the organization. Both positive and negative publicity often originate from sources other than the firm.

In most organizations, publicity is controlled and disseminated by the public relations department. In this section, we discuss the role publicity plays in the promotional program and some of the ways marketers use and react to these communications.

The Power of Publicity

One of the factors that most set off publicity from the other program elements is the sheer power this form of communication can generate. Unfortunately for marketers, this power is not always realized in the way they would like it to be. Publicity can make or break a product, a company, or even an individual. At one point, BP's stock dropped to less than one-half of what it was prior to the Gulf spill. The spill, which happened in 2010, cost BP more than $20 billion in funding the cleanup and lost economic value in the region. By 2013, the money in the fund was almost depleted, and by 2020, the environment had still not returned to normal. Fishermen in Mexico claim the supply of fish is still well below the amount prior to the spill, and the ecosystem would not recover before 2025 at best. Samsung's value declined by billions of dollars when it suffered negative publicity as a result of its exploding cell phone batteries. John Schnatter, founder of Papa John's, was ousted for making a racial slur on a call with investors. When the PR agency refused to defend him, he created his own website, SavePapaJohns.com, to get his message out to the public and Papa John's employees. The two have since parted ways. These are just a few of many examples of the impact that negative publicity can have. Other companies that have been affected over the years include Tylenol, McDonald's, Chipotle, and Johnson & Johnson, to name just a few.

Why is publicity so much more powerful than advertising or sales promotion—or even other forms of public relations? First, publicity is highly credible. Unlike advertising and sales promotions, publicity is not usually seen as being sponsored by the company (in negative instances, it never is). So consumers perceive this information as more objective and place more confidence in it. In fact, media often take great measures to ensure their objectivity and promote the fact that they are not influenced by advertisers or other outside sources.

Publicity may be perceived as endorsed by the medium in which it appears. For example, publicity regarding a breakthrough in the durability of golf balls will go far to promote them if it is reported by *Golf* magazine. *Car & Driver*'s award for car of the year reflects the magazine's perception of the quality of the auto selected.

Still another reason for publicity's power is its news value and the frequency of exposure it generates. When the publicity is positive, companies stand to benefit. When it is not, companies may suffer negative consequences such as lost sales, impacts on image, and even litigation.

The bottom line is that publicity is news, and people like to pass on information that has news value. Publicity thus results in a significant amount of free, credible, word-of-mouth information regarding the firm and its products.

The Control and Dissemination of Publicity

In some of the examples cited previously, the control of publicity was not always in the hands of the company. In some instances it is the firm's own blunder that allows information to leak out. Companies such as Papa John's, Samsung, BP, and others mentioned could do nothing to stop the media from releasing negative information about them. When publicity becomes news, it is reported by the media, sometimes despite efforts by the firm. In these instances, the organization needs to react to the potential threat created by the news. Unfortunately, simply ignoring the problem will not make it go away.

At Tree Top, 100% Pure Means 100% Safe.

Our business is children. And nobody goes to greater lengths to protect their health.

That's why Tree Top instituted strict safety procedures years ago to keep Alar out of our products.

Right from the start, we require growers to certify their fruit is not treated with Alar. Then we sample and test the fruit before it's processed. Over 8,000 of these tests have been conducted in the last year alone. Fact is, we've rejected tons of apples because they haven't measured up to Tree Top's high standards.

As a final safety check, the finished product is continuously sampled throughout the day, everyday.

As a result, we can assure you that all Tree Top juices and applesauce are 100% safe to consume.

There's been a lot said about Alar lately. But no matter what you've heard, they weren't talking about Tree Top.

We Always Give You 100%

EXHIBIT 17–12

Tree Top responds to the threat of negative publicity.

Tree Top, Inc

EXHIBIT 17–13

Publicity about *Fortnite* led to its very high popularity despite zero advertising expenditures.

Epic Games, Inc.

A good example of one company's efforts to respond to adverse publicity is shown in Exhibit 17–12. Tree Top's problems began when all the major news media reported that the chemical Alar, used by some growers to regulate the growth of apples, might cause cancer in children. (While this is an older example, we include it here because it is an excellent example of how to deal with a crisis resulting from negative publicity.) Despite published statements by reliable scientific and medical authorities (including the surgeon general) that Alar does not cause cancer, a few special-interest groups were able to generate an extraordinary amount of adverse publicity, causing concern among consumers and purchasing agents. A few school districts took apples off their menus, and even applesauce and juice were implicated. Tree Top ran the ad shown in Exhibit 17–12 to state its position and alleviate consumers' fears. It also sent a direct mailing to nutritionists and day care operators. The campaign was successful in assuring consumers of the product's safety and rebuilding their confidence.

Another example of effectively countering negative publicity is reflected in Budweiser's response to a class action lawsuit and negative publicity claiming that the brewer was watering down its beer, thereby reducing the alcoholic content and cheating consumers out of millions of dollars. Bud's response advertisement was particularly effective because it not only refuted the claim without giving it credence but at the same time turned the tables by indicating that not only does Bud maintain the brand's integrity, it also demonstrates the fact that they support causes by donating over 71 million cans of drinking water to those in need.

Publicity can also work for marketers. A number of video games have benefited from the publicity generated when they went viral on social media. *Pokemon Go* had so many visitors to its site, the site crashed. The app became the top grossing app within a day of its release. *Fortnite* became a sensation with no advertising dollars spent (Exhibit 17–13). Kids' toys frequently achieve significant sales due to high levels of positive publicity and word-of-mouth advertising. Sales of Cabernet Sauvignon increased an average of 45 percent in the month after a CBS *60 Minutes* report indicating that daily moderate consumption of red wine can reduce the risk of heart disease, and green tea sales skyrocketed when the word spread that consumption of the product was effective in preventing cancer. Products that contain antioxidants are now very popular due to their health benefits. There are many more examples of the positive impact publicity can have.

Marketers like to have as much control as possible over the time and place where information is released. One way to do this is with the **video news release (VNR)**, a publicity piece produced by publicists so that stations can air it as a news story. (Some agencies now offer social media news releases (SNRs), which are essentially news releases directed at a different target audience. As noted by one such agency, VNRs are targeted to broader target audiences, while SNRs are directed to one existing network.) The videos almost never mention that they are produced by the subject organization, and most news stations don't mention it either. Many government agencies and even countries have used VNRs, as have the American Dental Association, GM, Motorola, Sharp, the Mayo Clinic, and Nokia, among others. An example is Meghan Markle and Prince Harry's visit to Fraser Island, where King Fisher Bay Resort, which is part of the Accor group, was able to gain added media coverage because it provided content otherwise not available to mainstream media. The resort used a VNR to offer behind-the-scenes footage and interviews of the Royal couple's stay, which was used in news stories on local channels as well as on international news sites.[23] The use of VNRs without disclosing the source has led some consumer advocates to protest such actions. The Consumer Product Safety Commission has published guidelines for the appropriate use of VNRs at www.cpsp.gov.

In their efforts to manage publicity and public relations, marketers are continually learning more about these activities. Courses are offered, websites are devoted to the topic, and books are written on how to manage publicity. These books cover how to make a presentation, whom to contact, how to issue a press release, and what to know about each medium addressed, including TV, radio, newspapers, magazines, the Internet, and direct-response advertising. They discuss such alternative media as news conferences, seminars, events, and personal letters, as well as insights on how to deal with government and other legislative bodies. Because this information is too extensive to include as a single chapter in this text, we suggest you peruse one of the many books available on this subject for additional insights.

Advantages and Disadvantages of Publicity

Publicity offers the advantages of credibility, news value, significant word-of-mouth communications, and a perception of being endorsed by the media. Beyond the potential impact of negative publicity, other major problems arise from the use of publicity: lack of control, timing, and accuracy.

Lack of Control   In the viral world today, there is little control of what information is conveyed. Social networks, blogs, and so on have expanded the number of recipients of messages, while opening up the information stream to sources that are not confined by standards that may be imposed on traditional media. The result is that once public, the company or organization has lost control over the information. This can often become a costly experience.

Timing   Timing of the publicity is not always completely under the control of the marketer. Unless the press thinks the information has very high news value, the timing of the press release is entirely up to the media—if it gets released at all. Thus, the information may be released earlier than desired or too late to make an impact.

Accuracy   There are numerous ways to generate publicity. Quite often these means are not in the company's control. Unfortunately, the information sometimes gets lost in translation; that is, it is not always reported the way the provider wishes it to be. As a result, inaccurate information, omissions, or other errors may result. Sometimes when you see a publicity piece that was written from a press release, you wonder if the two are even about the same topic.

Measuring the Effectiveness of Publicity

The methods for measuring the effects of publicity are essentially the same as those discussed earlier under the broader topic of public relations. As noted at that point, traditional models of effectiveness are giving way to new measures as the digital world becomes a more important player in the communications programs of both large and small companies.

CORPORATE ADVERTISING

One of the more controversial forms of advertising is **corporate advertising**. Actually an extension of the public relations function, corporate advertising does not promote any one specific product or service. Rather, it is designed to promote the firm overall, by enhancing its image, assuming a position on a social issue or cause, or seeking direct involvement in something. Why is corporate advertising controversial? A number of reasons are offered:

1. *Consumers are not interested in this form of advertising.* Studies have shown that many consumers are not interested in corporate ads. At least part of this may be because consumers do not understand the reasons behind such ads. Of course, much of this confusion results from ads that are not very good from a communications standpoint.

2. *It's a costly form of self-indulgence.* Firms have been accused of engaging in corporate image advertising only to satisfy the egos of top management. This argument stems from the fact that corporate ads are not easy to write. The message to be communicated is not as precise and specific as one designed to position a product, so the top managers often dictate the content of the ad, and the copy reflects their ideas and images of the corporation.

3. *The firm must be in trouble.* Some critics believe the only time firms engage in corporate advertising is when they are in trouble—either in a financial sense or in the public eye—and are advertising to attempt to remedy the problem. There are a number of forms of corporate advertising, each with its own objectives. These critics argue that these objectives have become important only because the firm has not been managed properly.

4. *Corporate advertising is a waste of money.* Given that the ads do not directly appeal to anyone, are not understood, and do not promote anything specific, critics say the monies could be better spent in other areas. Again, much of this argument has its foundation in the fact that corporate image ads are often intangible. They typically do not ask directly for a purchase; they do not ask for investors. Rather, they present a position or try to create an image. Because they are not specific, many critics believe their purpose is lost on the audience and these ads are not a wise investment of the firm's resources.

Despite these criticisms and others, corporate advertising still enjoys wide usage. A variety of business-to-business and consumer-product companies continue to run corporate image ads, and numerous others have also increased expenditures in this area.

Since the term *corporate advertising* tends to be used as a catchall for any type of advertising run for the direct benefit of the corporation rather than its products or services, much advertising falls into this category. For purposes of this text (and to attempt to bring some perspective to the term), we use it to describe any type of advertising designed to promote the organization itself rather than its products or services.

Objectives of Corporate Advertising

Corporate advertising may be designed with two goals in mind: (1) creating a positive image for the firm and (2) communicating the organization's views on social, business, and environmental issues. More specific applications include:

- Boosting employee morale and smoothing labor relations.
- Helping newly deregulated industries ease consumer uncertainty and answer investor questions.
- Helping diversified companies establish an identity for the parent firm rather than relying solely on brand names.[24]

As these objectives indicate, corporate advertising is targeted at both internal and external audiences and involves the promotion of the organization as well as its ideas.

Types of Corporate Advertising

Marketers seek attainment of corporate advertising's objectives by implementing image, event sponsorships, advocacy, or cause-related advertising. Each form is designed to achieve specific goals.

EXHIBIT 17–14

Accenture uses corporate image advertising for positioning.

Accenture

FIGURE 17–5

2022 U.S. Olympic Sponsors and Partners

Airbnb

Alibaba Group

Allianz

Atos

Bridgestone

The Coca-Cola Company–Mengniu Dairy

Intel

Omega SA

Source: www.ispo.com, Nov. 9, 2022

Image Advertising   One form of corporate advertising is devoted to promoting the organization's overall image. **Image advertising** may accomplish a number of objectives, including creating goodwill both internally and externally, creating a position for the company, and generating resources, both human and financial. A number of methods are used:

1. *General image or positioning ads.* As shown in Exhibit 17–14, ads are often designed to create an image of the firm in mind. The exhibit shows how Accenture wants viewers to think about the company as large, but also as flexible enough to adapt to your needs.

2. *Sponsorships.* Firms often run corporate image advertising on TV programs or specials. For example, Ancestry.com and Consumer Cellular sponsor the program *Antiques Roadshow* on PBS. The sponsorship package includes on-air, online, and outdoor ads promoting the sponsorship and is designed to support Public Broadcasting. Other companies also sponsor programs on public TV and other educational programs designed to promote the corporation as a good citizen. By associating itself with high-quality or educational programming, companies like Fidelity Investments and Ford Motor Co. as well as local sponsors hope for a carryover effect that benefits their own images.

   Other examples of sponsorships include those run by P&G (Childrens' Safe Drinking Water Project), Accenture (UNICEF), and Nike (The Girl Effect). Exhibit 17–15 shows Whirlpool's sponsorship of the Habitat for Humanity and its efforts to fight poverty and increase affordable housing. Visa considers sponsorships an important part of its integrated marketing communications. It has sponsored the Olympics, the U.S. decathlon team, FIFA, NFL, NHL, the Toronto International Film Festival, and others. The sponsorships are designed to fulfill specific business objectives while providing support for the recipients. Figure 17–5 shows a few of the companies that decided an Olympic sponsorship would be good for them and were willing to pay hundreds of millions for a sponsorship.

3. *Recruiting.* The ad presented in Exhibit 17–16 is a good example of corporate image advertising designed to attract new employees. The ad–also for Whirlpool–portrays the company as a good place to work.

4. *Generating financial support.* Some corporate advertising is designed to generate investments in the corporation. By creating a more favorable image, the firm makes itself attractive to potential stock purchasers and investors. More investments mean more working capital, more monies for research and development, and so on. In this instance, corporate image advertising is almost attempting to make a sale; the product is the firm.

EXHIBIT 17–15

Whirlpool supports projects that help increase affordable housing.

Whirlpool

EXHIBIT 17–16

Corporate image advertising designed to attract employees.

Whirlpool

FIGURE 17–6

Corporate Reputations

Most Admired:
1. Apple
2. Amazon
3. Microsoft
4. Pfizer
5. Walt Disney

Best Corporate Citizens
1. Owens Corning
2. Pepsico, Inc
3. Apple, Inc
4. HP, Inc
5. Cisco Systems, Inc

Most Reputable
1. Trader Joe's
2. HEB Grocery
3. Patagonia
4. Hershey company
5. Wegmans

Source: Fortune 2022, CBL Media 2022, Harris Poll 2022

Although there is no concrete evidence that corporate image advertising leads directly to increased investment, many managers believe there is, and that there is a correlation between the price of stock and the amount of corporate advertising done. Firms that spend more on corporate advertising also tend to have higher-priced stocks (though a direct relationship is very difficult to substantiate).

This thing called *image* is not unidimensional. Many factors affect it. Figure 17–6 shows the results of three different rankings from three different sources. Note that none of the corporations appear on all three lists, which shows that companies can be respected and attain a strong corporate reputation in a number of ways. The most admired firms did not gain their positions merely by publicity and word of mouth (nor, we guess, did the least admired).

A positive corporate image cannot be created just from a few advertisements. Quality of products and services, innovation, sound financial practices, good corporate citizenship, and wise marketing are just a few of the factors that contribute to overall image. In addition, the type of product marketed and emotional appeal also contribute. The surveys cited above demonstrate that profits and stock performances have little to do with reputation and that once a reputation is acquired, it has lasting power. At the same time, IMC Perspective 17–1 demonstrates just how difficult it is to maintain a reputation.

Event Sponsorships   As we noted in the last section, corporate sponsorships of charities and causes have become a popular form of public relations. While some companies sponsor specific events or causes with primarily traditional public relations objectives in mind, a separate and more marketing-oriented use of sponsorships is also on the increase. Such **event sponsorships** take on a variety of forms, including sponsorship of the arts, concerts, entertainment, festivals, and so on. Sponsorship of sporting activities has been responsible for most of the spending in this area for a number of years. For example, the naming of sports stadiums and college football bowl games are now commonly used for corporate sponsorship. Like any other relationship, however, risks must be assumed by both sides in such agreements. For example, many companies that have had their names placed on stadiums—TWA Dome (St. Louis), PSINet (Baltimore), Fruit of the Loom (Miami)—have gone bankrupt, while others have had their images tarnished—Enron (Enron Field), MCI (MCI Center)—which is not good for the cities

My Reputation Was Tarnished! Now What Do I Do?

We all know that maintaining a good reputation is important. Movie stars, athletes, politicians, and regular everyday people try to avoid having their reputations tarnished. Sometimes these lost reputations can be repaired, but sometimes they just can't be retrieved. The same is true for organizations and corporations. Just one mistake can bring down a firm's image in a heartbeat. Sometimes the mistake may be of their own doing, but in other cases a slight error can create major damage. What is interesting and perhaps provides a lesson to be learned is how companies and/or organizations react when something goes wrong. Consider these examples:

Bud Light—As part of its "Up for Whatever" campaign, the beer company stamped some bottles with the tagline "the perfect beer for removing 'no' from your vocabulary for the night." Unfortunately, photos of the bottles were immediately picked up and posted on Reddit and the *Consumerist*. The next day it was circulated on social media with users claiming that it promoted a rape culture. The buzz got so great that it resulted in a tweet from U.S. Representative Nita Lowey (D-NY), criticizing the company saying that Bud Light should "promote responsible—not reckless—drinking." Brand perception scores took a major hit. After issuing an apology, Alexander Lambrecht, VP of Anheuser-Busch's Bud Light division, stated that the company would never condone disrespectful or irresponsible behavior and that the slogan would not be printed on any more bottles. He also noted that now in its second year, the campaign developed more than 140 messages that have been shown to lead to consumer engagement, but this one missed the mark, and it won't happen again.

Krispy Kreme—In a promotion of its "Krispy Kreme Klub," the company posted the acronym *KKK* on its Facebook page. Of course, Krispy Kreme immediately heard about it from social media followers, and issued an apology as well as the explanation for the mistake. Now the Krispy Kreme Club members can get rewards for eating KK donuts seven times a year including National Donut Day, their birthday, Veterans Day, and National Coffee Day. That's better!

Tom's of Maine—As a company that built its reputation for using only natural ingredients in its toothpastes, it wasn't exactly telling the truth. Once discovered, the misrepresentation led to a class action lawsuit and an eventual agreement to shell out $4.5 million and change its labeling practices. As noted by Mark Miller at www.brandchannel.com, the agreement didn't bring any smiles to the faces at Tom's or its parent company Colgate. Unfortunately for Tom's, after the lawsuit was settled a second lawsuit was brought in 2020 against Tom's and Colgate for using the word "natural" on their toothpaste and deodorant. As of this time the second suit is ongoing.

Chase Bank—Chase Bank's attempt to use a tweet to provide a little "Monday Motivation" encouraging people to become more fiscally responsible led to a backlash for "poor shaming." The since-deleted tweet was supposedly a hypothetical conversation between a bank customer and the bank, with the customer asking, "Why is my balance so low?"

Pacific Press Media Production Corp./Alamy Stock Photo

to which the bank responded, "Make coffee at home. . . eat the food that's already in the fridge. . . you don't need a cab, it's only three blocks." The response was quick and negative. Cale Weissman, a reporter for *Fast Company* noted that Chase charges customers overdraft fees as high as $34. Ben Walsh—a reporter at *Barrons*—tweeted that he "was sure" that CEO Jamie Dimon, who was making $31 million a year, "earned his riches making coffee at home and eating leftovers." Others argued that the bank and its CEO were "out of touch." After the tweet was deleted, a new one appeared stating, "Thanks for the feedback Twitter world."

Others—Urban Outfitters drew the ire of Kent State University for marketing a red-stained vintage sweatshirt with the college logo and what looked like blood stains. (In 1970 Ohio National Guardsmen shot and killed four Kent State students during Vietnam War protests.) Zara marketed a striped shirt with a six-pointed yellow badge that resembled uniforms worn at Holocaust concentration camps. Hermès, the maker of handbags that sell for $10,500 to $150,000, was asked by Jane Birkin (the actress and singer for whom the bags' line was named) to have her name taken off the bag line to protest the killing of crocodiles, ostriches, and lizards once it was brought to her attention by PETA.

How do these mistakes happen? Companies that are often cited for doing good things (Bud giving out cans of water; Tom's for supporting a number of environmental causes, etc.) can also be on the receiving end of negative publicity. Clearly someone in the organizations had to have noticed the slogan "Up for Whatever," or was aware of the meanings of the six-pointed badge, or knew about Kent State, and realized they would draw attention in this day and age—and not positive attention. Apologists claim that America is getting overly sensitive and that it was only a joke gone bad or a mistake, and mistakes happen. Unfortunately, sometimes mistakes can be very detrimental to a company's health. Interestingly, even when bad things happen to good companies, something positive can come out of it. In a study of 128 separate incidents in which a celebrity endorser generated negative publicity for a firm, it was shown that if the company takes the right steps, it could lead to a more positive value for the firm. Depending on how quickly the firm responds—it must be within 72 hours—the impact of the negative publicity can lead to about a 2 percent increase in stock value. After the 72-hour window, the impact gets more negative with each passing day. The study also concluded that even if the 72-hour "window of opportunity" is missed, the company must respond to avoid even more of a negative effect.

While the affected companies have survived, and are doing well, others have not been so fortunate. Their response was to change their names. Some of these are doing well again, some are not. Here are a few examples of name changes: Facebook to Meta (some say partly due to incriminating information leaked from internal documents, though the company denies this was a reason); British Petroleum to BP (after their massive oil spill); Blackwater to Xe to Academi (the name was changed twice, for negligent actions in Iraq); Phillip Morris to Altria (to end the association with cigarettes); and the Lance Armstrong Foundation to Live Strong Foundation (after the bicyclist's performance-enhancing drug use in winning the Tour de France bicycle race seven times in a row was discovered).

Sources: Cecily Mauran, "5 Companies with Horrible Reputations That Changed Their Names," *Mashable*, November 6, 2021, www.mashable.com; JND Legal Administration, "If You Purchased Tom's of Maine Deodorant or Toothpaste, on or after September 24, 2015 in California, New York, or Florida, a Class Action Lawsuit May Affect Your Rights," *PR Newswire*, October 19, 2021, www.prnewswire.com; Lindsey Rupp and Duane Stanford, "Bud Light Is Sorry for Slogan That Critics Say Endorsed Rape," *Bloomberg*, April 28, 2015, www.bloomberg.com; Elizabeth Bell, "Hermès, Bagged by PETA, Sees Jane Birkin Protest Her Namesake Bag," *Brand Channel*, July 29, 2015, www.brandchannel.com; Patricia Odell, "Krispy Kreme Gets Slammed for KKK Promo," *Chief Marketer*, February 9, 2015, www.chiefmarketer.com; Mark J. Miller, "Tom's of Maine Admits It's Not Totally Natural with $4.5M Settlement," *Brand Channel*, July 29, 2015, www.brandchannel.com. Michael Cappetta, "Chase Bank Deletes 'Monday Motivation' tweet after Drawing Social Media Outrage," *NBC News*, April 29, 2019, www.nbcnews.com; Jon Gingerich, "Negative Publicity Response Can Boost Brand Value," *O'Dwyer's*, March 27, 2019, www.odwyerpr.com.

or the companies themselves. A risk taken by a company in naming a stadium is the cost of hundreds of millions of dollars, which can cause stockholders and consumers concern over the value of such an investment. At the same time, naming a stadium can lead to increased name exposure—particularly for those companies that don't have strong brand recognition. For example, MetLife insurance, whose name is on the New York Jets and New York Giants stadium, believes it has been a very good investment, based on increased exposure alone. In addition, research has shown that 99 percent of fans can recall the name of the sponsors of their stadiums, and 35 percent say it causes them to have a more favorable impression of the brand.[25]

As can be seen in Figure 17-7, a number of traditional media are used to promote these sponsorships. You will also see that expenditures in all of these media except for newspapers and magazines is on the increase.

FIGURE 17–7 U.S. Offline Media Spending Review and Outlook

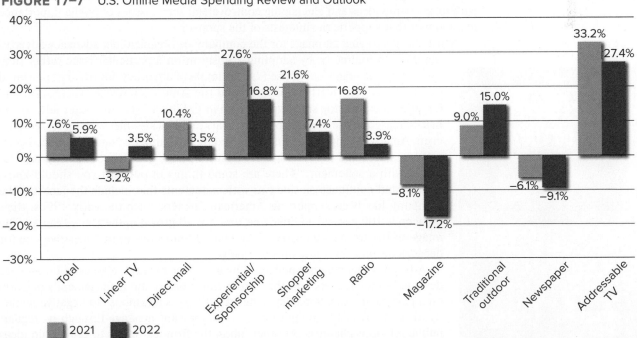

Source: Winterberry Group

The NASCAR Sprint Cup Series remains an attractive event to numerous companies, despite the increasing costs of sponsorship (Exhibit 17-17). Many companies are attracted to event sponsorships because effective IMC programs can be built around them, and promotional tie-ins can be made to local, regional, national, and even international markets. Companies are finding event sponsorships an excellent platform from which to build equity and gain affinity with target audiences as well as a good public relations tool. Interstate Batteries has been a sponsor of the NASCAR Series for over 30 years. The company obviously considers it one of the best ways to spend advertising dollars given the ability to reach the specific target market, as well as the number of impressions received for the investment.

Advocacy Advertising   A third major form of corporate advertising addresses social, business, or environmental issues. Such **advocacy advertising** is concerned with propagating ideas and elucidating controversial social issues of public importance in a manner that supports the interests of the sponsor.

While still portraying an image for the company or organization, advocacy advertising does so indirectly, by adopting a position on a particular issue rather than promoting the organization itself. An example of advocacy advertising sponsored by the American Heart Association and the American Stroke Association and targeting teens to stop smoking is shown in Exhibit 17-18. Advocacy advertising has increased in use over the past few years and has also met with increased criticism. An advertising campaign sponsored by the Santa Fe Natural Tobacco company was designed to create a more positive image of tobacco. The two-page ad began with a statement, "There are some things in our past you should know about," and continues on side two with statements that include the fact that the company has been supporting American farmers since the early 1990s, their tobacco is 100 percent additive-free, and it is all grown in the United States. The image of the tobacco industry in the United States has been a negative one for decades despite many attempts to change it.

Advocacy ads may be sponsored by a firm or by a trade association and are designed to tell readers how the firm operates or explain management's position on a particular issue. Sometimes the advertising is a response to negative publicity or to the firm's inability to place an important message through its regular public relations channels. At other times, the firm just wants to get certain ideas accepted or to have society understand its concerns.

EXHIBIT 17-19

Issue ads like these are increasingly appearing in the media.

(left): Campaign for Tobacco-Free Kids; (right): JUUL Labs, Inc.

Big Tobacco is back, thanks to JUUL — with a whole new way to get kids hooked on nicotine.

JUUL's flavored e-cigarettes deliver massive doses of nicotine

Don't let sweet-talking ads from JUUL fool you - each JUUL pod delivers the same amount of addictive nicotine as 20 cigarettes. It's no wonder Marlboro-maker Altria spent $12.8 billion buying into JUUL. Their mint, menthol, fruit, crème and mango flavors have fueled what the FDA warns is a "youth e-cigarette epidemic." It's time to act: Stop flavored e-cigarettes and give our kids, parents and teachers a fighting chance.

tobaccofreekids.org/JUUL
Paid for by Campaign for Tobacco-Free Kids

IT'S TIME TO RAISE THE LEGAL AGE TO PURCHASE TOBACCO PRODUCTS, INCLUDING VAPOR, FROM 18 TO 21.

BECAUSE WHEN YOUTH NEVER START SMOKING AND VAPING, THEY NEVER HAVE TO STOP.

About 80% of high school students turn 18 before graduating.

And in most states, they can then legally purchase tobacco and vapor products. Some illegally share with or sell those products to underage classmates.

This "social sourcing" accounts for nearly 80% of youth access to vapor products.*

Raising the legal age of purchase to 21+ reduces this social sourcing and can drive steep drops in underage usage.

JUUL Labs applauds the states that have gone to 21+ and supports making it the standard nationwide.

FOR ADULT SMOKERS ONLY

JUUL.com/T21

EXHIBIT 17-20

AT&T has used advocacy ads for years.

Jay Paul/Getty Images

Patrick Henry Addressing the First Continental Congress, Philadelphia, 1774

One Nation; One People

WHEN Patrick Henry declared that oppression had effaced the boundaries of the several colonies, he voiced the spirit of the First Continental Congress.

In the crisis, the colonies were willing to unite for their common safety, but at that time the people could not immediately act as a whole because it took so long for news to travel from colony to colony.

The early handicaps of distance and delay were greatly reduced and direct communication was established between communities with the coming of the railroads and the telegraph. They connected places. The telephone connects persons irrespective of place. The telephone system has provided the means of individual communication which brings into one national family, so to speak, the whole people.

Country wide in its scope, the Bell System carries the spoken word from person to person anywhere, annihilating both time and distance.

The people have become so absolutely unified by means of the facilities for transportation and communication that in any crisis they can decide as a united people and act simultaneously, wherever the location of the seat of government.

In the early days, the capital was moved from place to place because of sectional rivalry, but today Independence Hall is a symbol of union, revered alike in Philadelphia and the most distant American city.

AMERICAN TELEPHONE AND TELEGRAPH COMPANY
AND ASSOCIATED COMPANIES

One Policy   *One System*   *Universal Service*

Another form of advocacy advertising, **issue ads** are increasingly appearing in the media (Exhibit 17-19). While considered a form of advocacy advertising, issue ads may have no affiliation with a corporate or trade sponsor but may be sponsored by an organization to bring attention to what they consider to be an important issue. For example, after failed negotiations between the Humane Society of the United States and grocery store chain Trader Joe's, the animal welfare organization placed an issue ad with the headline "Why Won't Trader Joe's Give an Inch?" The response from Trader Joe's customers was enormous, leading the company to publicly announce that it would convert all of its brand eggs to cage free within 3 months. As evidence of the potentially harmful effects of vaping began to surface, issue ads were being run on both sides of the issue. The Campaign for Tobacco-Free Kids ran the ad shown on the left in Exhibit 17-19 in newspapers in a number of major markets in the United States. Interestingly, JUUL ran the ad shown on the right in Exhibit 17-19 at about the same time in *Time Magazine*. In 2007, the U.S. Supreme Court ruled that corporate and union sponsorships of issue ads (previously banned) must be permitted to run. Many believed this decision would lead to a significant increase in issue advertising.[26] Facebook and Twitter have both established guidelines regarding issue ads.

Advocacy advertising has been criticized by a number of sources. But as you can see in Exhibit 17-20, this form of communication has been around for a long time. AT&T engaged in issues-oriented advertising way back in 1908 and has continued to employ this form of communication into the 21st century. Critics contend that companies with large advertising budgets purchase too much ad space and time and that advocacy ads may be misleading, but the checks and balances of regular product advertising also operate in this area.

FIGURE 17–8

Reasons for Engaging in a
Cause-Marketing Program

- 91 percent of consumers are more likely to buy from a company that supports environmental or social issues.

- Consumers will publicly praise a company when their issues and those of the brand align.

- Consumers pay close attention to a brand's actions.

- Consumers say their impression of a brand is positively impacted by its association with a social cause.

- 1 percent of businesses offer more eco-friendly options than they did 3 years ago.

- U.S. consumers feel a deeper bond with firms that share their values, according to 79 percent of respondents.

- 25 percent of people stopped purchasing from a brand because it acted only in its own best interest.

- About 76 percent of millennials see business as a force for good in the world.

- Consumers said transparency in business practices is essential for brands to prove authenticity.

- Americans choose, switch, avoid, or boycott a brand based on its stand on societal issues.

Source: Cause Marketing Statistics Report for 2022, amraandelma.com, 2022; UBL 2022.

EXHIBIT 17–21

This ad was part of a campaign designed to stop domestic violence.

House of Ruth Maryland

Cause-Related Advertising   An increasingly popular method of image building is **cause-related marketing**, in which companies link with charities or nonprofit organizations as contributing sponsors. It is estimated that over $2 billion is spent on cause marketing in the United States each year.[27] The company benefits from favorable publicity, while the charity receives much-needed funds. Proponents of cause marketing say that association with a cause may differentiate one brand or store from another, increase consumer acceptance of price increases, generate favorable publicity, and even win over skeptical officials who may have an impact on the company. Indeed, association with a cause may impact consumers' purchase decisions—making them more likely to buy from the sponsor, while another showed that consumers are more likely to trust a brand that supports causes.[28] A number of studies have shown that companies can benefit by adopting a cause-marketing strategy (see Figure 17–8). Apple, Google, Microsoft, and Pepsi are just a few brands well known for their support of causes. Cause-marketing relationships can take a variety of forms. Making outright donations to a nonprofit cause, having companies volunteer for the cause, donating materials or supplies, running public service announcements, or even providing event refreshments are some of the ways companies get involved. Exhibit 17–21 shows an event titled "High Heels for Hope." The proceeds from this event went directly to the House of Ruth in Baltimore, Maryland—a cause supporting women and youth who have suffered from domestic violence. The campaign was targeted to those attempting to overcome the impact of domestic violence. Ethical Perspective 17–1 discusses another well-supported cause.

At the same time, not all cause marketing is a guarantee of success. Cause marketing requires more than just associating with a social issue, and it takes time and effort. Companies have gotten into trouble by misleading

Companies Show Their Good Side for Important Causes

Many small companies and corporations have been good citizens for years, but a lot of people didn't know it. In the past, advertising and promotion and public relations for the good of the corporation operated as separate managerial silos. While these companies and corporations often did many things that directly benefited the community—whether it be local or global—they usually did so without a lot of fanfare or "patting themselves on the back." Then someone must have turned on a light that said, "if you are doing these good things, why aren't you letting people know it?" Reluctantly, at first, the firms slowly started to let others know about their benevolence through corporate reports and maybe even a press release here and there. The first cracks started to appear in the silos. Then things started to change. Companies started to be less hesitant to let people know the good things they were doing—after all, the public always knew if they did something bad! Since there was no noticeable negative feedback, they expanded their PR efforts to be sure that people *did* know, and not long thereafter started to use PR more like a marketing tool. And why not? Many companies are doing very good things out there without recognition, and the positive publicity wouldn't hurt!

In 1993, the UN Conference on Environment and Development organized the first World Water Day. Based on the dire water conditions in many parts of the world today, 2.1 billion people live without safe water at home. Nearly 700 children die each day due to water shortages. Globally, 80 percent of the people who have unsafe water live in rural areas; diseases from dirty water kill more people every year than all forms of violence, including war; access to clean water can save around 16,000 lives a week; and more—CleanWater.org called on brands and media support to bring attention to the problem. And respond they did! CNBC International broadcast some of the lesser known facts about water. The beer brand Stella Artois, through Twitter, asked consumers to purchase a limited-edition chalice; the profits would help provide 5 years of clean water to a person in need. The children's TV show *Sesame Street* introduced Raya—a health superstar, whose birthday just happened to be on World Water Day. DAVIDsTEA created a whole new variety of tea, with each 50-gram purchase leading to a contribution of one month of clean water to a Kenyan child in need. Just a few of the other participants included Unilever, Georgio Armani Fragrances, Arrowhead Brand Mountain Spring Water, and the Surfrider Foundation who asked people to pledge to skip a shower for one day, which would save one million gallons of water that day. Numerous companies directly or indirectly involved with the use of water including Speakman (maker of high-end shower heads and plumbing products), water resource management company WaterStart, and Delta Faucets, among many more have joined in the cause. All of the participants put their own unique twist on their contribution to the effort (including *World of Warcraft!*).

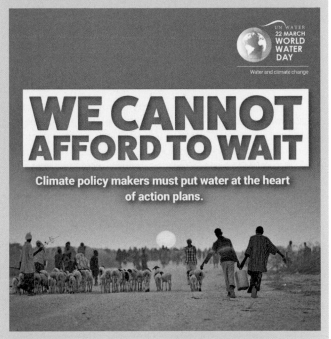

The United Nations

World Water Day is just one of thousands of causes being supported by numerous companies. Another is Earth Day. And just like World Water Day, companies have approached the cause in their own creative fashion. Earth Day—which is celebrated worldwide every April 22 since 1970—has now mobilized over 1 billion people in 196 countries and over 50,000 companies, along with a billion people who participated in the event in 2022. Earth Day offers a variety of causes to engage in—all designed to protect the earth. For example, Hershey has focused on sustainability challenges, tracing back through its supply chain that covers 94 percent of the mills that supply its palm and palm kernel oil globally to be sure they are compliant with environmentally friendly procedures. Hershey announced major progress in its push for 100 percent certified and sustainable cocoa worldwide by 2020. McDonald's has earned high praise for its deforestation plan, and Chipotle received kudos for its stance in dropping a major supplier that didn't meet the company's strict standards set as part of its sustainability commitment despite the fact that the move cost it a 5 percent drop in stock value. Of course, there are thousands more companies also supporting the cause in various ways—and more than 1.5 million other causes.

The world's top holding companies are also getting involved in Earth Day. Publicis Groupe has formed a business resource group called Écologique to support all

(continued)

Publicis Groupe agencies in the United States. For Earth Week, it offered

"a variety of programming and other opportunities for employees to celebrate their sustainability efforts and learn more about making an impact—everything from webinars on reaching net-zero emissions, to podcasts about greenwashing, to engaging our employees to share . . . corporate best practices and Earth Day resolutions. The team will also publish helpful content and articles throughout Earth Week and the remainder of the year."

Interpublic Group established programs to "work towards our climate goals by updating our travel and sustainability policies, launching a new tool to sort flight and travel accommodations by carbon emissions as well as cost, conducting an office audit to reduce our energy use, engaging with suppliers to monitor and support the reduction of supplier emissions." Other top-5 holding companies including the Omnicon Group, Havas, and Dentsu have also formulated and implemented programs to commit to the goals of Earth Day.

You have probably never heard of any of these companies' endeavors. So why are they doing it?

Well, clearly, a staggering number of people become exposed to their positive actions, creating a lot of goodwill while portraying the companies in a favorable light. Maybe some of that goodwill will directly benefit them through sales, financial investments, and so on. Being a good corporate brand certainly enhances their image as well—there are studies showing that many consumers prefer to purchase from "green" companies, all things being equal. Or, maybe they are just what they portend to be—good citizens that care about others!

As noted earlier, companies have only recently begun to recognize the power of public relations. In the past most PR activities were devoted to local activities, crisis management, or dealing with negative publicity. Once marketers realized the power and potential for integrating PR into the IMC mix, the nature and importance of this medium changed dramatically—not only for communicating positive information about the company's goodwill endeavors, but also for supporting their brands.

It is this last statement that has some PR people, and the general public as well, concerned that these small companies and large corporations are supporting causes in their own best interests. Or, maybe they just are altruistic and want to help others. If the world finds out about that, is that so bad?

Sources: "Water for All. World Water Day 2019," www.worldwaterday.org; Sheila Shayon, "World Water Day: Brands, Media Support Clean, Safe Water Efforts," *Brand Channel*, March 22, 2016, www.brandchannel.com; www.earthday.org; Dale Buss, "Earth Day 2015: Hershey Puts Sustainability Where Its Mouth Is," *Brand Channel*, April 22, 2015, www.brandchannel.com; Kendra Clark, "How the World's Top Holding Companies Are Celebrating Earth Day 2022," *The Drum*, April 18, 2022, www.thedrum.com; www.earthday.org, 2022; www.worldwaterday.org, 2022.

consumers about their relationships, and others have wasted money by supporting a cause that offered little synergism. One survey showed that more than 300 companies associated themselves with breast cancer concerns, but most became lost in sponsorship clutter. Another has shown that consumers are becoming more skeptical and are demanding more accountability from companies' cause-marketing efforts.[29] Others have simply picked the wrong cause—finding that their customers and potential customers either have little interest in or don't support the cause. In some cases, cause marketing is considered nothing more than shock advertising. Finally, the results of cause-marketing efforts can sometimes be hard to quantify.

Advantages and Disadvantages of Corporate Advertising

A number of reasons for the increased popularity of corporate advertising become evident when you examine the advantages of this form of communication:

1. *It is an excellent vehicle for positioning the firm.* Firms, like products, need to establish an image or position in the marketplace. Corporate image ads are one way to accomplish this objective. A well-positioned product is much more likely to achieve success than is one with a vague or no image. The same holds true of the firm. Stop and think for a moment about the image that comes to mind when you hear the name Apple, Johnson & Johnson, or Procter & Gamble.

    Now what comes to mind when you hear Unisys, USX, or Navistar? How many consumer brands can you name that fall under ConAgra's corporate umbrella (Hunts, Chef Boyardee, Pam, Slim-Jims, and many others)? While we are not saying these latter companies are not successful—because they certainly are—we are suggesting their corporate identities (or positions) are not as well entrenched as the identities of those first cited. Companies with strong positive corporate images have an advantage over competitors that may be enhanced when they promote the company overall.

2. *It takes advantage of the benefits derived from public relations.* As the PR efforts of firms have increased, the attention paid to these events by the media has lessened (not because they are of any less value, but because there are more events to cover). The net result is that when a company engages in a public relations effort, there is no guarantee it will receive press coverage and publicity. Corporate image advertising gets the message out, and though consumers may not perceive it as positively as information from an objective source, the fact remains that it can communicate what has been done.

3. *It reaches a select target market.* Corporate image advertising should not be targeted to the general public. It is often targeted to investors and managers of other firms rather than to the general public. It doesn't matter if the general public does not appreciate this form of communication, as long as the target market does. In this respect, this form of advertising may be accomplishing its objectives.

Some of the disadvantages of corporate advertising were alluded to earlier in the chapter. To these criticisms, we can add the following:

1. *Questionable effectiveness.* There is no strong evidence to support the belief that corporate advertising works. Many doubt the data cited earlier that demonstrated a correlation between stock prices and corporate image advertising as some studies show little support for this effect.

2. *Constitutionality and/or ethics.* Some critics contend that since larger firms have more money, they can control public opinion unfairly. This point was resolved in the courts in favor of the advertisers. Nevertheless, many consumers still see such advertising as unfair given the great disparities that sometimes exist in financial resources available to some but not others, and immediately take a negative view of the sponsor.

A number of valid points have been offered for and against corporate advertising. Two things are certain: (1) No one knows who is right, and (2) the use of this communications form continues to increase.

Measuring the Effectiveness of Corporate Advertising

As you can tell from our discussion of the controversy surrounding corporate advertising, there need to be methods for evaluating whether or not such advertising is effective:

- *Attitude surveys.* One way to determine the effectiveness of corporate advertising is to conduct attitude surveys to gain insights into both the public's and investors' reactions to ads. A study conducted by Janas Sinclair and Tracy Irani on advocacy advertising in the biotechnology industry employed a survey research methodology to demonstrate that public accountability was a good predictor of corporate trustworthiness, and this and the attitude toward the advertiser would predict consumers' attitude toward the ad, biotechnology, and purchase intentions.[30] Studies reported on earlier in this chapter show the many positive effects that companies that engage in corporate advertising might receive. The firm measured recall and attitude toward corporate advertisers and found that corporate advertising is more efficient in building recall for a company name than is product advertising alone. Frequent corporate advertisers rated better on virtually all attitude measures than those with low corporate ad budgets.

- *Studies relating corporate advertising and stock prices.* A number of studies have examined the effect of various elements of corporate advertising (position in the magazine, source effects, etc.) on stock prices. These studies have yielded conflicting conclusions, indicating that while the model for such measures seems logical, methodological problems may account for at least some of the discrepancies.

- *Focus group research.* Focus groups have been used to find out what investors want to see in ads and how they react after the ads are developed. As with product-oriented advertising, this method has limitations, although it does allow for some effective measurements.

While the effectiveness of corporate advertising has been measured by some of the methods used to measure product-specific advertising, reported research in this area has not kept pace with that of the consumer market. The most commonly offered reason for this lack of effort is that corporate ads are often the responsibility of those in the highest management positions in the firm, and these parties do not wish to be held accountable. It is interesting that those who should be most concerned with accountability are the most likely to shun this responsibility!

Summary

This chapter examined the role of the promotional elements of public relations, publicity, and corporate advertising. We noted that these areas are all significant to the marketing and communications effort and are usually considered different from the other promotional elements. Nevertheless, companies are increasing their use of these touch points in their IMC programs.

Public relations was shown to be useful in its traditional responsibilities as well as in a more marketing-oriented role. In many firms, PR is a separate department operating independently of marketing; in others, it is considered a support system. Many companies now effectively use PR as an IMC tool, with established MPR objectives. Many large firms have an external public relations agency, just as they have an outside ad agency. Digital PR agencies are developing to assist with digital communications.

In the case of publicity, another factor enters the equation: lack of control over the communication the public will receive. In public relations and corporate advertising, the organization remains the source and retains much more control. Publicity often takes more of a reactive than a proactive approach, yet it may be more instrumental (or detrimental) to the success of a product or organization than all other forms of promotion combined.

Although not all publicity can be managed, the marketer must nevertheless recognize its potential impact. Press releases and the management of information are just two of the factors under the company's control. Proper reaction and a strategy to deal with uncontrollable events are also critical responsibilities.

Corporate advertising was described as controversial, largely because the source of the message is often top management, so the rules for other advertising and promoting forms are often not applied. This element of communication definitely has its place in the promotional mix. But to be effective, it must be used with each of the other elements, with specific communications objectives in mind. The growing importance of cause, issue, and advocacy marketing was also discussed.

Finally, we noted that measures of evaluation and control are required for each of these program elements, just as they are for all others in the promotional mix. We presented some methods for taking such measurements and some evidence showing why it is important to use them. As long as the elements of public relations, publicity, and corporate advertising are considered integral components of the overall communications strategy, they must respect the same rules as the other promotional-mix elements to ensure success.

Key Terms

public relations (PR) 570
marketing public relations (MPR) 572
internal audiences 577
external audiences 577
press release 580
press conferences 580
exclusive 581

digital public relations 581
storytelling 583
Public Relations Society of America 584
publicity 585
video news release (VNR) 587
corporate advertising 588

image advertising 590
event sponsorships 591
advocacy advertising 594
issue advertising (issue ads) 595
cause-related marketing 596

Discussion Questions

1. Discuss the three levels of effectiveness described in the framework provided by Cision in Figure 17–4. Give an example of each of the three levels. (LO 17-2)
2. Discuss why publicity (positive or negative) can be so powerful. Cite examples of both positive and negative publicity's impact on brands, products, and so on. (LO 17-1)
3. Exhibit 17-19 shows an issue ad in opposition to JUUL, the vaping brand. It also shows JUUL's ad supporting a raise in the legal age necessary to purchase

vapor products. Both ads were run at approximately the same time. Give your opinion as to the motivations behind the JUUL ad. (LO 17-4)
4. Provide a number of examples of issue ads. Were these ads effective? Why or why not? (LO 17-4)
5. Companies that establish very positive reputations tend to maintain these reputations over time. What are some of the things that these companies do to maintain these positions? (LO 17-1)

6. Companies can't always predict or even avoid factors that lead to negative publicity. At the same time, many companies have made mistakes that have caused them problems. Cite a few examples of companies that may have caused their own negative publicity problems and discuss how they might have taken actions to avoid them. (LO 17-2)

7. As the silos constituting marketing and public relations continue to break down, there is some potential for both positive and negative ramifications. Discuss how the blending of PR and marketing activities could result in both positive and negative consequences. (LO 17-1)

8. There is an old saying that "any publicity is positive publicity," essentially meaning that anytime a company gets its name in the press, it is good for the company. Indicate whether you agree with this statement and explain why or why not. (LO 17-2)

9. Many marketers have expressed the belief that younger demographics (i.e., teens and preteens) are much more socially conscious than preceding generations, and therefore need to be shown that companies are environmentally and socially responsible. Do you agree with this belief? Explain how companies could use some of the various forms of corporate advertising discussed in this chapter to convey this to consumers. (LO 17-4)

10. Why are public relations and the tools used by PR potentially more effective than those employed by marketers even though the latter group may spend vastly more dollars to create a favorable image in the marketplace? (LO 17-2)

18 Measuring the Effectiveness of the Promotional Program

Words Marketers Use to Describe Effective TV Ads

sold think parents **fun** powerful woman
love showed **brand** beauty good
human created together
point **product** first message beef
feel effective identity later
crazy delicious **simple different**
story memorable campaign music
great positive **humor** kid real
funny **super-bowl** people new
know
years moment **remember**

Editorial Image, LLC

Learning Objectives

 Compare reasons for and against measuring the effectiveness of promotional programs.

 Describe the tools and processes available for assessing promotional program effectiveness.

 Discuss the limitations of current methods for measuring advertising effects.

 Compare different methods of measuring effectiveness of other promotional programs.

What Are the Best Commercials of All Time?

Recently a blog sponsored by marketing company Quality Logo Products posted a video called the "10 Best Commercials of All Time." Without really indicating the methodology used to make this determination, the commercials were well researched, and information was provided in support of the winners. Interestingly, the supporting evidence included a number of criteria including sales (Apple's "1984" ad), longevity (Tootsie Pop's "How Many Licks"; M&M's "They Do Exist"), awards won (Coca-Cola's "Mean Joe Greene"), and even cultural impact (Always' "Like a Girl"). The time period in which the ads ran was also quite interesting, as the Tootsie Pop ad first ran in 1968 and the most recent was Always, first aired in 2015. (In case you are wondering, there was one from the 60s; two from the 70s; one from the 80s; four from the 90s; and 11 since 2000.) As for the 60s, maybe you are surprised that they even had televisions way back then! (You can watch the commercials at www.https://www.qualitylogoproducts.com.) The blog also noted the "5 Worst Commercials," all of which aired since the year 2000. In explaining what makes for a good commercial, having a good storyline, emotional resonance, brevity, and having a catchphrase were cited as important criteria. Again, a significant number of resources were cited to lead to these conclusions including academic research, ad agencies personnel, business media, newspapers, and trade magazines.

Tim Edmundson, reporting for MNTN Research, conducted a survey asking what was the most effective ad ever seen. Sampling marketers (he doesn't say how many), he asked, "What was the most effective ad of all time that they had seen and why?" Once again, the M&M commercial, Mean Joe Greene, and 1984 were cited, as were Nike ads and Wendy's, which achieved runner-up status in the Quality Logo blog. The marketing professionals also cited catchphrases and emotional criteria as leading to effectiveness. The study identified a few other factors, for example, that (1) emotions have an "outsized impact on viewers"—especially humor; and (2) fast food, candy, and beer were the industries that had the most number of brands mentioned, while consumer electronics, soft drinks, and

athletic apparel were all dominated by single brands. Apple, Coca-Cola, Wendy's, and Nike were rated as the top advertisers. Celebrities factored into the determination of effectiveness, accounting for 14 percent of the reasons mentioned for why ads were so effective. Ten celebrities were mentioned the most often as a prominent factor in the respondents' responses, one being Mean Joe Greene.

The study's conclusion as to what makes an ad work? "A rough formula of hook + message = effective."

But the question remains, do memorable and popular ads really lead to effectiveness? There are no doubt numerous commercials, print ads, and even promotional products ("Where's the Beef?" t-shirts) that while memorable and likable may not have had an impact on the success of the product or brand. In a study of Super Bowl ads that ran in the 2021 and 2011 telecasts, Kantar examined some of the creative best practices involved in the advertising and whether these had an impact on the brand's ROI. Kantar noted that their previous studies showed that highly engaging ads did not automatically result in solid returns for a brand and there was no guarantee that they lead to the best results. In examining the effectiveness of the Super Bowl ads, the study focused on three measures: (1) *impact* (will it create a memory?), (2) *brand power* (will it contribute to brand equity?), and (3) *short-term sales lift* (will it drive sales in the short run?). While only 12 percent of the ads were scored as being "strong ads," each of these contributed positively to brand equity and ROI. What led to their strong showing?—creativity, making an emotional connection with the audience, and the ability to generate conversation and engagement. When the ads achieved these, the result was double-digit gains in ROI.

Of course, monetary value may not be the only criterion for determining effectiveness of ads. The Always campaign "Like a Girl" and the Old Spice "The Man Your Man Could Smell Like" campaign (also one of the top 10 in the Quality Logo research) have been cited by many as having a major positive impact if one considers cultural aspects. You may also be wondering if marketers only made good

continued

commercials in the old days, given the winners from decades ago. The answer is no, they still make great commercials (as well as bad ones). It may be that a focus on creativity and storytelling are giving way to using celebrities and getting attention as the major factors guiding ad creation. Maybe they should broaden the criteria?

Sources: "The 10 Greatest Commercials of All Time," Quality Logo Products Blog, https://www.qualitylogoproducts.com/blog/10-memorable-tv-commercials; Tim Edmundson, "What's the Most Effective TV Ad You've Seen and Why," MNTN Research, November 7, 2022, www.research.mountain.com; KANTAR, "The Power of Creative: How Ad Quality Improves ROI," *Ad Age*, March 2022, www.adage.com.

As the lead-in to this chapter shows, what makes an ad popular, memorable, or "the best" may have some consistent elements but also varies in the "eye of the beholder." Millions of dollars are spent on the production of ads, and as seen in earlier chapters, viewers are exposed to thousands per day. Yet most of these ads may be having little or no impact on viewers. Even if they are well liked and talked about, are they truly effective?

As noted throughout this text, the increased emphasis on accountability is forcing many companies to evaluate, or reevaluate, their IMC plans. Both clients and agencies are continually striving to determine whether their communications are working and how well they are working relative to other options. A number of studies indicate that marketing managers are not confident in the metrics they are currently using and are searching for new methods designed to assist in this endeavor. Companies and organizations continue to work together in an attempt to provide answers to these questions and to develop new ways to measure communications effectiveness.

Measuring the effectiveness of the promotional program is a critical element in the IMC planning process. Research allows the marketing manager to evaluate the performance of specific program elements and provides input into the next period's situation analysis. It is a necessary ingredient to a continuing planning process, yet it is often not carried out.

In this chapter, we discuss some reasons firms should measure the effectiveness of their IMC programs, as well as why many decide not to. We also examine how, when, and where such measurements can be conducted. Most of our attention is devoted to measuring the effects of advertising because much more time and effort have been expended developing evaluation measures in advertising than in the other promotional areas. We will, however, discuss measurement in other areas of the IMC program as well. You'll recall that we addressed the methods used to evaluate many of the other promotional elements in previous chapters.

It is important to understand that in this chapter we are concerned with research that is conducted in an evaluative role—that is, to measure the effectiveness of advertising and promotion and/or to assess various strategies before implementing them. This is not to be confused with research discussed earlier in the text to help develop the promotional program, although the two can (and should) be used together, as you will see. While evaluative research may occur at various times throughout the promotional process (including the development stage), it is conducted specifically to assess the effects of various strategies. We begin our discussion with the reasons effectiveness should be measured as well as some of the reasons firms do not do so.

ARGUMENTS FOR AND AGAINST MEASURING EFFECTIVENESS

Almost anytime one engages in a project or activity, whether for work or for fun, some measure of performance occurs. In sports, you may compare your golf score against par or your time on a ski course to other skiers' performances. In business, employees are generally given objectives to accomplish, and their job evaluations are based on their ability to achieve these objectives. Advertising and promotion should not be an exception. It is important to determine how well the communications program is working and to measure this performance against some standards.

Reasons to Measure Effectiveness

Assessing the effectiveness of ads both before they are implemented and after the final versions have been completed and fielded offers a number of advantages:

1. *Avoiding costly mistakes.* The top three advertisers in the United States were expected to spend over $21 billion in advertising and promotion in 2018. The top 10 spent a total of over $42 billion.[1] This is a lot of money to be throwing around without some understanding of how well it is being spent. If the program is not achieving its objectives, the marketing manager needs to know so he or she can stop spending (wasting) money on it.

   Just as important as the out-of-pocket costs is the opportunity loss due to poor communications. If the advertising and promotional program is not accomplishing its objectives, not only is the money spent lost but so too is the potential gain that could result from an effective program. Thus, measuring the effects of advertising does not just save money. It also helps the firm maximize its investment. Think about how many times you have seen an ad and had no idea what it was trying to communicate!

2. *Evaluating alternative strategies.* Typically a firm has a number of strategies under consideration. For example, there may be some question as to the degree to which each medium should be used or whether one message is more effective than another. Or the decision may be between two promotional program elements. A key issue for the manager is to be able to determine how effective each one was. As you have seen in previous chapters, numerous companies have also reallocated monies to nontraditional media, and studies have revealed that advertisers said they planned to spend more monies in digital and social media in the coming years. The question is, should research be spent on traditional, social, or digital advertising or other media and in what combination? Research may be designed to help the manager determine which strategy is most likely to be effective.

3. *Increasing the efficiency of advertising in general.* You may have heard the expression "can't see the forest for the trees." Sometimes advertisers get so close to the project they lose sight of what they are seeking, and because they know what they are trying to say, they expect their audience will also understand. They may use technical jargon that not everyone is familiar with. Or the creative department may get too creative or too sophisticated and lose the meaning that needs to be communicated. How many times have you seen an ad and asked yourself what it was trying to say, or how often have you seen an ad that you really like, but you can't remember the brand name? Conducting research helps companies develop more efficient and effective communications. An increasing number of clients are demanding accountability for their promotional programs and putting more pressure on the agencies to produce. As IMC Perspective 18–1 discussing the Ogilvy Award winners demonstrates, effective research can be used for both of these purposes.

4. *Determining if objectives are achieved.* In a well-designed IMC plan, specific communication objectives are established. If objectives are attained, new ones need to be established in the next planning period. An assessment of how program elements led to the attainment of the goals should take place, and/or reasons for less-than-desired achievements must be determined. Research should address whether the strategy delivers the stated objectives and how appropriate the measures used to make this assessment are.

Reasons Not to Measure Effectiveness

While it seems obvious that it makes sense to measure effectiveness, the fact remains that in too many instances this is not done. Whereas advertisers know that it is important to measure effectiveness, with as many as 90 percent considering it a priority, many do not do so, or if they do, they are not confident of the results.

The Winners of the Ogilvy Awards Rely on Research

The United States Census Bureau

One of the most prestigious awards an advertising agency and its client can receive is an Ogilvy Award. The award is named for longtime advertising executive David Ogilvy, who was always a strong advocate for the use of research in advertising. Sponsored by the Advertising Research Foundation (ARF), the awards are given for excellence in advertising research and/or the creative use of research in the advertising development process. While initially the awards were purely advertising related, awards are now given in a variety of communications areas. Here are a few of the winners in 2021.

The SeeHer Award Microsoft Teams—"Nothing Can Stop a Team"

Microsoft Teams was a new entrant to the communication market, competing head-to-head against Slack and Zoom for market share. When COVID-19 hit in 2020, it altered the marketing plan that had been formulated and raised the issue as to whether the program should continue to exist at all. To make this determination, Microsoft used extensive pretesting, message testing, weekly tracking, response-level modeling, and time-series modeling.

The research revealed a need for consumers to collaborate on work during the pandemic, as people were working from home and communication was a problem The research also indicated that a feeling of connection was crucial and missing in the lives of consumers. That was important to address in the creative strategy.

Creative was developed to demonstrate real-world solutions that were actually taking place, including doctors continuing to see patients, doctors screensharing to show X-rays, teachers using a whiteboard, and moms maintaining work continuity while still being moms. Given the many changes and challenges brought on by the pandemic,

Microsoft needed to know what impact Teams was currently having and how they could make it better. To do so Microsoft formed a research team called the Research + Insights Team that used the following tools to make the determination:

- Message testing
- Pretesting of the campaign
- Weekly brand/campaign measurement to understand recognition and impact
- Studies to understand impact of digital marketing
- Regular tracking of social conversations
- Structural equation modeling
- Marketing attribution modeling

Creative Strategy—Even though a campaign strategy had previously been developed, the impact of the pandemic rendered it useless. Based on the research, the objective of the new creative was to drive awareness of Teams targeting working people who were looking for a way to stay productive and connected during the pandemic. The research team identified businesses that were "on the front lines" responding to COVID-19. The businesses were filmed showing them using Teams to capture real stories of how they were effectively responding to the crisis.

A series of executions were created based on the information gleaned from the research. Each showed how different industries were using Teams to deal with issues resulting from the pandemic:

- "Nothing Can Stop a Team" featured the London Metropolitan Police Service, University of Bologna (Italy), L'Oreal, and St. Luke's University Health Service.
- "Mother's Day" highlighted the challenges of working at home while juggling family and work life.

- "More Ways to Be a Team" focused on announcing new features like "Together Mode" and "Large Gallery View" that delighted Teams users, helping people to feel better.
- "Teacher of the Year" focused on teachers and the amazing job they were doing to keep kids engaged and learning, with the help of Teams.
- "Where There's a Team, There's a Way" featured real customers and their stories, who had fully embraced Teams and this new way of working.

Campaign Results—The campaign not only achieved its objective, but surpassed expectations resulting in

- Unprecedented recognition of 76 percent
- Increased familiarity
- Closed the preference gap against Zoom
- Drove an increase of active usage by 13 percent

The "Nothing Can Stop a Team" campaign provides an excellent example of how research can be effective in developing a campaign, in this case effective enough to be the SeeHer Award winner, which is given for the best campaign that gives a realistic representation of women and girls.

Best Brand Transformation   Bank of Montreal—"Financial Fairness"

Banks are aware of women's lack of financial confidence but don't really understand its root cause. While many banks try to assist women customers in addressing financial literacy, they fail to ask why they lack confidence in the first place. Rather than just helping women "overcome" their lack of confidence, Bank of Montreal (BMO) wanted to uncover the real drivers behind it. Based on extensive research, focusing on the use of social listening, the bank uncovered a number of stereotypes about women's understanding of financial issues. The message line addressed the bias labels with a series of GIFs that "flipped the meaning of common stereotypes from harmful to empowering" to create labels with a positive meaning. For example, "Shopaholic" turned to "Stockaholic" and "Gold Digger" flipped to "Goal Digger." The campaign was extremely successful in brand favorability and engagement as well as internal engagement (employees who said they were proud to work at the bank).

Best Consumer Experience   Michelob—"Courtside"

Overall beer sales have been steadily declining since 2013, driven by a decrease in alcohol consumption and by new category exploration. Light beer was particularly challenged, declining 3–4 percent per year. In addition, the segment was being challenged by the growth of hard seltzers like White Claw and Truly.

After conducting extensive research on their target market, Michelob ULTRA virtually transported fans right back where they wanted to be at courtside. In partnership with the NBA and Microsoft, Michelob ULTRA Courtside reinvented the 124 games of the NBA season for the pandemic era by creating an immersive interactive experience and the tagline "It's Only Worth It If You Enjoy It."

The results showed a 32 percent increase in sales during basketball season—double that of its closest competitor. Michelob ULTRA also showed a growth of 69 share points while all other competitors' sales declined.

In addition to these categories, there were winners in a number of others including "Best New or Emerging Brand," "Brand Purpose," "Data Innovation," and "Social Responsibility," among others. And of course there was the overall grand prize winner—The U.S. Census "Shape Your Future—START HERE," which relied on insights from focus groups, community interviews, and predictive models, as well as other research methodologies to develop the top award-winning campaign.

The legacy of David Ogilvy lives on—demonstrated through strong research practices that guide campaigns.

Source: 2021 ARF David Ogilvy Awards.

Companies give a number of reasons for not measuring the effectiveness of advertising and promotions strategies:

1. *Cost.* Perhaps the most commonly cited reason for not testing (particularly among smaller firms) is the expense. In one of the surveys cited, it was noted that while some companies spend as much as 25 percent of their revenue on marketing and advertising, 70 percent of them spend less than 2 percent on measuring effectiveness.[2] Good research can be expensive in terms of both time and money. Many managers decide that time is critical, and they must implement the program while the opportunity is available. Many believe the monies spent on research could be better spent on improved production of the ad, additional media buys, and the like.

   While the first argument may have some merit, the second does not. Imagine what would happen if a poor campaign were developed or the incentive program did not motivate the target audience. Not only would you be spending money without the desired effects, but the effort could do more harm than good. Spending more money to buy media does not remedy a poor message or substitute for an improper promotional mix. For example, one of the nation's leading brewers watched its test-market sales for a new brand of beer fall short of expectations. The problem, it thought, was an insufficient media buy. The solution, it decided, was to buy all the TV time available that matched its target audience. After 2 months, sales had not improved and the product was abandoned in the test market. Analysis showed the problem was not in the media but rather in the message, which communicated no reason to buy. Research would have identified the problem, and millions of dollars and a brand might have been saved. The moral: Spending research monies to gain increased exposure to the wrong message is not a sound management decision.

2. *Research problems.* A second reason cited for not measuring effectiveness is that it is difficult to isolate the effects of promotional elements. Each variable in the marketing mix affects the success of a product or service. Because it is often difficult to measure the contribution of each marketing element directly, some managers become frustrated and decide not to test at all. They say, "If I can't determine the specific effects, why spend the money?" A study conducted by the Fournaise Marketing Group—a marketing performance and measurement business—reviewing over 500 marketing campaigns, briefs, and effectiveness reports concluded that the metrics being used were "shocking" in a very negative sense.[3] Simply put, the report concluded that marketers did not understand how to measure effectiveness.

   This argument that not being able to determine specific effects, so no measurement should take place, suffers from weak logic. While we agree that it is not always possible to determine the dollar amount of sales contributed by promotions, research can provide useful results and, as shown throughout this text, most have useful and specific metrics to evaluate their performance.

3. *Disagreement on what to test.* The objectives sought in the promotional program may differ by industry, by stage of the product life cycle, or even for different people within the firm. There are numerous ways to measure these and not always a consensus as to what measure should be used. The sales manager may want to see the impact of promotions on sales, top management may wish to know the impact on corporate image, and those involved in the creative process may wish to assess recall and/or recognition of the ad. The metrics used to measure effectiveness in traditional media are often quite different than those for digital media. Lack of agreement on what to test often results in no testing at all. A study conducted by the 4As and ANA revealed that many marketers were dissatisfied with their efforts to integrate traditional and digital media, and there is a need to develop appropriate metrics for doing so. At the same time there is much disagreement as to what to measure. As shown in Chapter 15, a variety of metrics are used in measuring the effectiveness of social media alone, and these measures continue to change. If you conduct a Google search on "measuring advertising effectiveness," you will see that the list of firms offering their services in this area is substantial. You will also see the key metrics they suggest measuring are not very consistent. One well-established organization provides a list of 21 KPIs to consider when trying to track activity by different objectives.[4]

   Again, there is little rationale for this position. With the proper design, many or even all of the above might be measured. Since every promotional element is designed to accomplish specific objectives while contributing to the overall program, research can be used to measure its effectiveness in doing so.

4. *The objections of creative.* It has been argued by many (and denied by others) that the creative department does not want its work to be tested and many agencies are reluctant to submit their work for testing. This is sometimes true. Ad agencies' creative departments argue that tests are not true measures of the creativity and effectiveness of ads; applying measures stifles their creativity; and the more creative the ad, the more likely it is to be successful. They want permission to be creative without the limiting guidelines marketing may impose. The

To advertisers interested in 'day after recall', we submit a case history:

"My friends... each of you is a single cell in the great body of the State. And today, that great body has purged itself of parasites."

We have triumphed over the unprincipled dissemination of facts. The thugs and wreckers have been cast out. And the poisonous weeds of disinformation have

been consigned to the dustbin of history... Let each and every cell rejoice! For today we celebrate the first glorious anniversary of the Information Purification Directives.

We have created, for the first time in all history, a garden of pure ideology, where each worker may bloom secure from the pests of contradictory and confusing truths.

Our Unification of Thought is more powerful a weapon than any fleet or army on earth. We are one people. With one will.

One resolve. One cause. Our enemies shall talk themselves to death. And we will bury them with their own confusion.

We shall prevail."

On January 24th, Apple Computer will introduce Macintosh. And you'll see why 1984 won't be like "1984"

Title and Voice Over: On January 24, Apple Computer will introduce Macintosh.

And you'll see why 1984 won't be like "1984"

On January 22, 1984, one commercial for Apple Computer ran on network television.

With all due respect to Burke, we didn't bother to test it.

Unlike a lot of advertising agencies, we prefer a different form of measurement:

When the product mentioned in the commercial, Apple's new Macintosh, was unveiled on January 24, over 200,000 people lined up to see it in person.

Within 6 hours, they bought $3,500,000 worth of Macintosh computers. And left cash deposits for $1,000,000 more.

ABC, CBS, NBC and CNN featured the commercial in network news segments.

Dan Rather covered it at night. Bryant Gumbel covered it at dawn.

The BBC ran it in England.

Associated Press put it on the wire.

27 TV stations in major U.S. markets ran it on local news programs.

Steven Spielberg called.

As did *The New York Times, The Wall Street Journal, The Washington Post,* the *Philadelphia Inquirer, USA Today,* the *Boston Globe,* the *Los Angeles Times,* the *San Francisco Chronicle* and, of course, the *San Jose Mercury News.*

Not to mention *Time, Newsweek, Fortune, Forbes, Business Week* and, of course, *Advertising Age.*

Apple is now producing one Macintosh every 27 seconds. And selling one every 20 seconds.

Not bad for one 60-second spot on the Super Bowl.

Chiat/Day
Los Angeles, San Francisco, New York

EXHIBIT 18–1

In this ad Chiat/Day expresses its opinion of recall tests by offering a case history of the 1984 Apple Commercial.

TBWA\CHIAT\DAY

Chiat/Day ad shown in Exhibit 18-1 reflects how many people in the advertising business feel about this subject. The 1984 commercial was designed by agency Chiat/Day to introduce the Apple MacIntosh. It was shown only one time in the United States—during the 1984 Super Bowl. Due to its creativity, the ad is considered by many to be the greatest commercial ever made and a large reason the Mac was so successful.

At the same time, the marketing manager is ultimately responsible for the success of the product or brand. Given the substantial sums being allocated to advertising and promotion, it is the manager's right, and responsibility, to know how well a specific program—or a specific ad—will perform in the market. As you have seen throughout this text, managers are placing much more emphasis on social and digital media at the expense of traditional strategies—not just media but creative strategies as well, much to the chagrin of creative directors. A very interesting study by comScore ARS measured the contribution that effective creative versus other marketing variables—ad quality, the media plan, effectiveness (Figure 18-1).[5]

5. *Time.* A final reason given for not testing is a lack of time. Managers believe they already have too much to do and just can't get around to testing, and they don't want to wait to get the message out because they might miss the window of opportunity. Planning might be the solution to the first problem. An article in *Advertising Age* indicates that time pressures are actually on the increase, particularly when it comes to digital. The speed to get content out in the digital age puts a spotlight on previous processes used to validate ad concepts before they are put into the market. As a result, many marketers are eschewing traditional copy testing methods and taking the risk that their ads will succeed on a hunch or gut feel. Although many managers are overworked and time poor, research is just too important to skip.

The second argument can also be overcome with proper planning. Responding to these needs, at least one research agency is in the process of developing new tools that will allow marketers to test different versions of creative ideas and get results back within hours. While timeliness is critical, getting the wrong message out is of little or no value and may even be harmful. There will be occasions where market opportunities require choosing between testing and immediate implementation. But even then some testing may help avoid mistakes or improve effectiveness.

FIGURE 18–1

Effective Creative Does Contribute to Campaign Effectiveness

Variables	Contribution to Sales Changes (Percent)*
Ad quality†	52%
Media plan‡	13
Other (price, promotion, distribution, etc.)	35

*Numbers represent the percent variance in market share shifts explained by the corresponding factors.

†Ad quality represents the quality of creative based on the ARS Persuasion Score, which measures changes in consumer preference through a simulated purchase.

‡Media plan includes variables such as GRPs, wearout, and continuity/flighting of airing.

Source: comScore ARS Global Validation Summary.

CONDUCTING RESEARCH TO MEASURE ADVERTISING EFFECTIVENESS

LO 18-2

What to Test

We now examine how to measure the effects of communications. This section considers what elements to evaluate, as well as where and how such evaluations should occur.

In Chapter 5 we discussed the components of the communication model (source, message, media, receiver) and the importance of each in the promotional program. Marketers need to determine how each is affecting the communication process. Other decisions made in the promotional planning process must also be evaluated.

Source Factors   An important question is whether the spokesperson being used is effective and how the target market will respond to him or her. Or a product spokesperson may be an excellent source initially but, owing to a variety of reasons, may lose impact over time. As shown in Chapter 17, negative publicity can easily change the value of a source. The fact that so many of the companies using Lance Armstrong as a spokesperson terminated their contracts with him was based on the expectation that the target audiences would no longer have positive perceptions of him. The list of celebrities who have fallen out of favor is a long one. Throughout this text we have discussed the role of the source as a celebrity, endorser, influencer, spokesperson, and so on. In the last chapter we discussed the impact on adidas that resulted from Kanye West's behaviors. It is obvious that the association between the source of the communication and the organization is critical.

Message Variables   Both the message and the means by which it is communicated are bases for evaluation. For example, in the beer example discussed earlier, the message never provided a reason for consumers to try the new product. In other instances, the message may not be strong enough to pull readers into the ad by attracting their attention or clear enough to help them evaluate the product. Sometimes the message is memorable but doesn't achieve the other goals set by management. For example, one study examined what effect sexually themed print ads would have on viewers. Among the numerous results were that men favor sex appeals more than women do and that recall of the brands was lower for sexual ads than for nonsexual ones. Whereas men responded that sexual ads have "high stopping power" for them, their lower brand recall seems to indicate that they are paying more attention to other aspects of the ad than the marketers would prefer.[6] In an extensive study of 1,400 TV ads involving 270 brands, Kantar examined the impact of creative messages on advertising effectiveness. The study concluded that when an ad's creativity was rated as "average" to "best," advertisers experienced an increase of 30 percent in ROI. One of the conclusions of the study was "Ads are more than what they say; great creative depends on how you say it."[7] A number of companies are now attempting to determine the specific reactions that viewers have to product and brand messages, including excitement, engagement, stress, and anxiety responses.

Media Strategies   Research may be designed in an attempt to determine which media class (for example, broadcast versus print), subclass (newspapers versus magazines), or specific vehicles (which newspapers or magazines) generate the most effective results. Likewise, how does one digital medium compare relative to others, or to traditional media? For example, an ad video for Tiffany & Co. featuring superstar Beyoncé was posted on Instagram where it drew 1.6 million views. One week later a different Tiffany video featuring social media personality Kate Bartlett was watched more than 5.2 million times on TikTok. In recent years TikTok has become one of the most effective social media sites for advertisers.[8] Perhaps most importantly, how does each medium contribute to the achievement of overall IMC objectives?

An important factor is the **vehicle option source effect**, "the differential impact that the advertising exposure will have on the same audience member if the exposure occurs in one media option rather than another." People perceive ads differently depending on their context.[9]

Another factor to consider in media decisions involves scheduling. The evaluation of flighting versus pulsing or continuous schedules is important, particularly given the increasing costs of media time. As discussed in Chapter 10, there is evidence to support the fact that continuity may lead to a more effective media schedule than does flighting. Likewise, there may be opportunities associated with increasing advertising weights in periods of downward sales cycles or recessions. A number of research studies have shown that overexposure to an ad can result in not only a lack of effectiveness, but negative reactions to that ad. The manager experimenting with these alternative schedules and/or budget outlays should attempt to measure their differential impact.

As more and more companies and organizations move toward an integrated media mix, it becomes increasingly important to attempt to determine the individual contributions of various media as well as their synergistic effect. As you will see later in this chapter, progress is being made in this regard, but making such a determination is not a simple task.

Budgeting Decisions   A number of studies have examined the effects of budget size on advertising effectiveness and the effects of various ad expenditures on sales. Many companies have also attempted to determine whether increasing their ad budget directly increases sales. This relationship is often hard to determine, perhaps because using sales as an indicator of effectiveness ignores the impact of other marketing-mix elements. More definitive conclusions may be possible if other dependent variables, such as the communications objectives stated earlier, are used.

When to Test

Virtually all test measures can be classified according to when they are conducted. **Pretests** are measures taken before the campaign is implemented; **posttests** occur after the ad or commercial has been in the field. A variety of pretests and posttests are available to the marketer, each with its own methodology designed to measure some aspect of the advertising program. Figure 18–2 classifies these testing methods.

Pretesting   Pretests may occur at a number of points, from as early on as idea generation to rough execution to testing the final version before implementing it.

FIGURE 18–2

Classification of Testing Methods

Pretests		
Laboratory Methods		
Consumer juries	Theater tests	Readability tests
Portfolio tests	Rough tests	Comprehension and reaction tests
	Focus groups	
Physiological measures	Concept tests	
Field Methods		
Dummy advertising vehicles	On-air tests	Online theater testing
Posttests		
Field Methods		
Recall tests	Single-source systems	Recognition tests
Association measures		Tracking studies
	Inquiry tests	

More than one type of pretest may be used. For example, concept testing (which is discussed later in this chapter) may take place at the earliest development of the ad or commercial, when little more than an idea, basic concept, or positioning statement is under consideration. In other instances, layouts of the ad campaign that include headlines, some body copy, and rough illustrations are used. For TV commercials, storyboards and animatics may be tested. In these tests specific shortcomings may be identified, and changes made to enhance certain executional elements. As noted by Cramphorn, the best reason to pretest is to identify winners, to enhance good ads, and to eliminate bad ones. He notes that it is important to know the probable effect the ad will have before committing to its use.[10]

The methodologies employed to conduct pretests vary. While many of the tests shown in Figure 18–2 have been conducted for years in personal settings, many are now conducted online. In focus groups, participants freely discuss the meanings they get from the ads, consider the relative advantages of alternatives, and even suggest improvements or additional themes. In addition to or instead of the focus groups, consumers are asked to evaluate the ad on a series of rating scales. (Different agencies use different measures.) In-home interviews, mall intercept, Internet surveys, or laboratory methods may be used to gather the data.

The advantage of pretesting at this stage is that feedback is relatively inexpensive. Any problems with the concept or the way it is to be delivered are identified before large amounts of money are spent in development. Sometimes more than one version of the ad is evaluated to determine which is most likely to be effective.

Because it costs so much less to find out that an ad may not work prior to making it public, rather than after doing so, it certainly makes sense to pretest.

The disadvantage is that mock-ups, storyboards, or animatics may not communicate nearly as effectively as the final product. The mood-enhancing and/or emotional aspects of the message are very difficult to communicate in this format. Another disadvantage is time delays. Many marketers believe being first in the market offers them a distinct advantage over competitors, so they forgo research to save time and ensure this position—even though this may be a risky strategy.

Posttesting   Posttesting is also common among both advertisers and ad agencies (with the exception of testing commercials for wearout). Posttesting is designed to (1) determine if the campaign is accomplishing the objectives sought and (2) serve as input into the next period's situation analysis.

Where to Test

In addition to when to test, decisions must be made as to *where*. These tests may take place in either laboratory or field settings.

Laboratory   In **laboratory tests**, people are brought to a particular location where they are shown ads and/or commercials. The testers either ask questions about them or measure participants' responses by other methods—for example, pupil dilation, eye tracking, biosciences, or neuroscience measures.

The major advantage of the lab setting is the *control* it affords the researcher. Changes in copy, illustrations, formats, colors, and the like can be manipulated inexpensively, and the differential impact of each assessed. This makes it much easier for the researcher to isolate the contribution of each factor.

The major disadvantage is the lack of *realism*. Perhaps the greatest effect of this lack of realism is a **testing bias**. When people are brought into a lab (even if it has been designed to look like a living room), they may scrutinize the ads much more closely than they would at home. The same is true of online tests, and respondents may know they are participating in a study. A second problem with this lack of realism is that it cannot duplicate the natural viewing situation, complete with the distractions or comforts of home. Looking at ads in a lab setting may not be the same as viewing at home on the couch, with the spouse, kids, dog, cat, and parakeet chirping in the background.

(A bit later you will see that some testing techniques have made progress in correcting this deficiency. No, they did not bring in the dogs and the parakeets.) Overall, however, the control offered by this method probably outweighs the disadvantages, which accounts for the frequent use of lab methods.

Field Tests **Field tests** are tests of the ad or commercial under natural viewing situations, complete with the realism of noise, distractions, and the comforts of home. Field tests take into account the effects of repetition, program content, and even the presence of competitive messages.

The major disadvantage of field tests is the lack of control. It may be impossible to isolate causes of viewers' evaluations. If atypical events occur during the test, they may bias the results. Competitors may attempt to sabotage the research. And field tests usually take more time and money to conduct, so the results are not available to be acted on quickly. Thus, realism is gained at the expense of other important factors. It is up to the researcher to determine which trade-offs to make.

How to Test

Our discussion of what should be tested, when, and where was general and designed to establish a basic understanding of the overall process as well as some key terms. In this section, we discuss more specifically some of the methods commonly used at each stage. First, however, it is important to establish some criteria by which to judge ads and commercials.

Conducting evaluative research is not easy. Twenty-one of the largest U.S. ad agencies have endorsed a set of principles aimed at "improving the research used in preparing and testing ads, providing a better creative product for clients, and controlling the cost of TV commercials."[11] This set of nine principles, called **Positioning Advertising Copy Testing (PACT)**, defines *copy testing* as research "that is undertaken when a decision is to be made about whether advertising should run in the marketplace. Whether this stage utilizes a single test or a combination of tests, its purpose is to aid in the judgment of specific advertising executions."[12] The nine principles of good copy testing are shown in Figure 18-3.

On the digital side, a blue ribbon task force has been assembled in an industrywide initiative dedicated to making digital media advertising friendlier to brands by evolving the way interactive advertising is measured. The project, titled "Making Measurement Make Sense," a joint effort of the 4As, the ANA, and the Interactive Advertising Bureau, has a goal of "making digital media measurements directly comparable to those of traditional media, while maintaining the ability to evaluate the unique value that

FIGURE 18–3

Positioning Advertising Copy Testing (PACT)

1. Provide measurements that are relevant to the objectives of the advertising.

2. Require agreement about how the results will be used in advance of each specific test.

3. Provide multiple measurements (because single measurements are not adequate to assess ad performance).

4. Be based on a model of human response to communications—the reception of a stimulus, the comprehension of the stimulus, and the response to the stimulus.

5. Allow for consideration of whether the advertising stimulus should be exposed more than once.

6. Require that the more finished a piece of copy is, the more soundly it can be evaluated and require, as a minimum, that alternative executions be tested in the same degree of finish.

7. Provide controls to avoid the biasing effects of the exposure context.

8. Take into account basic considerations of sample definition.

9. Demonstrate reliability and validity.

FIGURE 18–4

The Five Guiding Principles
of Digital Measurement

Principle #1	Move to a "viewable impressions" standard and count real exposures online.
Principle #2	Online advertising must migrate to a currency based on audience impressions, not gross impressions.
Principle #3	Because all ad units are not created equal, we must create a transparent classification system.
Principle #4	Determine interactivity "metrics that matter" for brand marketers, so that marketers can better evaluate the online's contribution to brand building.
Principle #5	Digital media measurement must become increasingly comparable and integrated with other media.

Source: Author created from www.measurementnow.net.

interactivity brings to brand campaigns."[13] The committee has established five guiding principles for this purpose (Figure 18-4).

As you can see, advertisers and their clients are concerned about developing *appropriate* testing methods. Adherence to these principles may not make for perfect testing, but it goes a long way toward improving the state of the art and alleviates at least one of the testing problems cited earlier.

THE TESTING PROCESS

Testing may occur at various points throughout the development of an ad or a campaign: (1) concept generation research; (2) rough, prefinished art, copy, and/or commercial testing; (3) finished art or commercial pretesting; and (4) market testing of ads or commercials (posttesting).

Concept Generation and Testing

Figure 18-5 describes the process involved in advertising **concept testing**, which is conducted very early in the campaign development process in order to explore the targeted consumer's response to a potential ad or campaign or have the consumer evaluate advertising alternatives. Positioning statements, copy, headlines, and/or illustrations may all be under scrutiny. The material to be evaluated may be just a headline or a rough sketch of the ad. The colors used, typeface, package designs, and even point-of-purchase materials may be evaluated.

FIGURE 18–5

Concept Testing

Objective
Explores consumers' responses to various ad concepts as expressed in words, pictures, or symbols.
Method
Alternative concepts are exposed to consumers who match the characteristics of the target audience. Reactions and evaluations of each are sought through a variety of methods, including focus groups, direct questioning, and survey completion. Sample sizes vary depending on the number of concepts to be presented and the consensus of responses.
Output
Qualitative and/or quantitative data evaluating and comparing alternative concepts.

■ The results are not quantifiable.

■ Sample sizes are too small to generalize to larger populations.

■ Group influences may bias participants' responses.

■ One or two members of the group may steer the conversation or dominate the discussion.

■ Consumers become instant "experts."

■ Members may not represent the target market. (Are focus group participants a certain type of person?)

■ Results may be taken to be more representative and/or definitive than they really are.

One of the more commonly used methods for concept testing is focus groups, which usually consist of 8 to 10 people in the target market for the product. Companies have tested everything from product concepts to advertising concepts using focus groups. For most companies, the focus group is the first step in the research process. The number of focus groups used varies depending on group consensus, strength of response, and/or the degree to which participants like or dislike the concepts. Some companies use 50 or more groups to develop a campaign, although fewer than 10 are usually needed to test a concept sufficiently.

While focus groups continue to be a favorite of marketers, they are often overused. The methodology is attractive in that results are easily obtained, directly observable, and immediate. A variety of issues can be examined, and consumers are free to go into depth in areas they consider important. Also, focus groups don't require quantitative analysis. Unfortunately, many managers are uncertain about research methods that require statistics; and focus groups, being qualitative in nature, don't demand much skill in interpretation. Weaknesses with focus groups are shown in Figure 18–6. Clearly, there are appropriate and inappropriate circumstances for employing this methodology.

Another way to gather consumers' opinions of concepts is mall intercepts, where consumers in shopping malls are approached and asked to evaluate rough ads and/or copy. Rather than participating in a group discussion, individuals assess the ads via questionnaires, rating scales, and/or rankings. New technologies allow for concept testing over the Internet, where advertisers can show concepts simultaneously to consumers throughout the United States, garnering feedback and analyzing the results almost instantaneously. In addition, online focus groups are being used more often to do concept testing (Exhibit 18–2). Internet methods are becoming increasingly popular given the cost savings and time efficiencies associated with these research methods, and some research firms now offer hybrid studies that involve a combination of online and traditional measures. Due in part to the pandemic, many research companies no longer conduct focus groups in person. Online groups, which some feel are not as effective as ones conducted in a research facility, are becoming more and more popular.

Rough Art, Copy, and Commercial Testing

Because of the high cost associated with the production of an ad or commercial (many network commercials cost hundreds of thousands of dollars to produce), advertisers are increasingly spending more monies testing a rendering of the final ad at early stages. Slides of the artwork posted on a screen or animatic and photomatic roughs may be used to test at this stage. (See Figure 18–7 for an explanation of terminology.) Because such tests can be conducted inexpensively, research at this stage is becoming ever more popular.

A rough commercial is an unfinished execution that may fall into three broad categories:

Animatic Rough	Photomatic Rough	Live-Action Rough
Succession of drawings/cartoons	Succession of photographs	Live motion
Rendered artwork	Real people/scenery	Stand-in/nonunion talent
Still frames	Still frames	Nonunion crew
Simulated movement:	Simulated movements:	Limited props/minimal opticals
Panning/zooming of frame/rapid sequence	Panning/zooming of frame/rapid sequence	Location settings

Finished Commercial Uses
Live motion/animation
Highly paid union talent
Full union crew
Exotic props/studio sets/special effects

FIGURE 18–7

Rough Testing Terminology

But cost is only one factor. The test is of little value if it does not provide relevant, accurate information. Rough tests must indicate how the finished commercial would perform. Studies have demonstrated that these testing methods are reliable and the results typically correlate well with the finished ad.

Most of the tests conducted at the rough stage involve lab settings, although some on-air field tests are also available. Popular tests include comprehension and reaction tests and consumer juries. Again, the Internet allows field settings to be employed at this stage.

1. *Comprehension and reaction tests.* One key concern for the advertiser is whether the ad or commercial conveys the meaning intended. The second concern is the reaction the ad generates. Obviously, the advertiser does not want an ad that evokes a negative reaction or offends someone. **Comprehension and reaction tests** are designed to assess these responses (which makes you wonder why some ads are ever brought to the marketplace).

   Tests of comprehension and reaction employ no one standard procedure. Personal interviews, group interviews, and focus groups have all been used for this purpose, as have online studies, and sample sizes vary according to the needs of the client; they typically range from 50 to 200 respondents.

2. *Consumer juries.* This method uses consumers representative of the target market to evaluate the probable success of an ad. **Consumer juries** may be asked to rate a selection of layouts or copy versions presented in pasteups on separate sheets. The objectives sought and methods employed in consumer juries are shown in Figure 18–8.

   While the jury method offers the advantages of control and cost effectiveness, serious flaws in the methodology limit its usefulness:

   • *The consumer may become a self-appointed expert.* One of the benefits sought from the jury method is the objectivity and involvement in the product or service that the targeted consumer can bring to the evaluation process. Sometimes, however, knowing they are being asked to critique ads, participants try to become more *expert* in their evaluations, paying more attention and being more critical than usual. The result may be a less than objective evaluation or an evaluation on elements other than those intended.

   • *The number of ads that can be evaluated is limited.* Whether *order of merit* or *paired comparison* methods are used, the ranking procedure becomes tedious as the number of alternatives increases. Consider the ranking of 10 ads. While the top 2 and the bottom 2 may very well reveal differences, those ranked in the middle may not yield much useful information.

FIGURE 18–8

Consumer Juries

Objective
Potential viewers (consumers) are asked to evaluate ads and give their reactions to and evaluation of them. When two or more ads are tested, viewers are usually asked to rate or rank order the ads according to their preferences.

Method
Respondents are asked to view ads and rate them according to either (1) the order of merit method or (2) the paired comparison method. In the former, the respondent is asked to view the ads and then rank them from one to *n* according to their perceived merit. In the latter, ads are compared only two at a time. Each ad is compared to every other ad in the group, and the winner is listed. The best ad is that which wins the most times. Consumer juries typically employ 50 to 100 participants.

Output
An overall reaction to each ad under construction as well as a rank ordering of the ads based on the viewers' perceptions.

In the paired comparison method, the number of evaluations required is calculated by the formula

$$\frac{n(n-1)}{2}$$

If six alternatives are considered, 15 evaluations must be made. As the number of ads increases, the task becomes even more unmanageable.

- *A halo effect is possible.* Sometimes participants rate an ad good on all characteristics because they like a few and overlook specific weaknesses. This tendency, called the **halo effect**, distorts the ratings and defeats the ability to control for specific components. (Of course, the reverse may also occur—rating an ad bad overall due to only a few bad attributes.)
- *Preferences for specific types of advertising may overshadow objectivity.* Ads that involve emotions or pictures may receive higher ratings or rankings than those employing copy, facts, and/or rational criteria. Even though the latter are often more effective in the marketplace, they may be judged less favorably by jurists who prefer emotional appeals.

Some of the problems noted here can be remedied by the use of ratings scales instead of rankings. But ratings are not always valid either. Thus, while consumer juries have been used for years, questions of bias have led researchers to doubt their validity. As a result, a variety of other methods (discussed later in this chapter) are more commonly employed.

A/B Testing   The process of **A/B testing** has been employed by marketers for years. The process involves the testing of two versions of an advertisement or homepage to see which will be the more effective prior to launch. In the vast majority (if not all) of these cases the ads or web pages are finished products. In making a case for using A/B testing earlier in the development process, Molly Soat makes the argument that waiting so long to test could be costing companies money, and at the same time be less effective. She notes that a number of advertising experts call for the testing of display art, or scripts, for example to gain insights into consumers' thinking rather than waiting to just have them choose between two finished ads. Besides saving a lot of money by not developing and producing a potentially ineffective ad, the results would likely lead to ads that use consumers' insights. The experts argue for using A/B testing earlier in the developmental process and measuring consumers' emotional and neurological responses rather than just have them choose between two finish products. Of course, the finished ads could be A/B tested as well.[14]

FIGURE 18–9

Conjointly.com

Objective
Pretesting print ads to determine the best print ads by (1) comparing respondents' attitudes toward the ad; (2) benchmarking ad against other good performing ads; and (3) garnering feedback regarding likes and dislikes about the ads.

Measures
A number of measures are taken for print ads, including:

1. Clarity and trustworthiness

2. How relevant and likeable the ad is

3. How easy it would be to spot the ad

4. Originality and authenticity

5. Whether respondents would follow the call to action (CTA) or discuss the ad further

6. Where they would expect to see the ad

Outputs
In addition to comparing the ads tested, additional measures of associations and likes and dislikes about the ads are provided.

Pretesting of Finished Ads

Pretesting finished ads is one of the more commonly employed studies among marketing researchers and their agencies. At this stage, a finished advertisement or commercial is used; since it has not been presented to the market, changes can still be made.

Many researchers believe testing the ad in final form provides better information. Several test procedures are available for print and broadcast ads, including both laboratory and field methodologies.

Print methods include portfolio tests, analyses of readability, and dummy advertising vehicles. Broadcast tests include theater tests and on-air tests. Both print and broadcast may use physiological measures.

Pretesting Finished Print Messages A number of methods for pretesting finished print ads are available. One is Conjointly.com, described in Figure 18-9. An example of the output from this is shown in Exhibit 18-3. Notice that the output compares a number of ads on a number of criteria. It also includes an analysis by different media. The most common of these methods are portfolio tests, readability tests, and hybrid measures.

Portfolio Tests Portfolio tests are a laboratory methodology designed to expose a group of respondents to a portfolio consisting of both control and test ads. Respondents are then asked what information they recall from the ads. The assumption is that the ads that yield the *highest recall* are the most effective.

While portfolio tests offer the opportunity to compare alternative ads directly, a number of weaknesses limit their applicability:

1. Factors other than advertising creativity and/or presentation may affect recall. Interest in the product or product category, the fact that respondents know they are participating in a test, or interviewer instructions (among others) may account for more differences than the ad itself.
2. Recall may not be the best test. Some researchers argue that for certain types of products (those of low involvement), ability to recognize the ad when shown may be a better measure than recall.

One way to determine the validity of the portfolio method is to correlate its results with readership scores once the ad is placed in the field. Whether such validity tests are

Print Ad Test
Comparison of ads tested

Feedbackers (N = 189)

KPIs	Print Ad 1	Print Ad 2	Print Ad 3	Print Ad 4	Average
Likeability	83%	84%	81%	79%	82%
Relevance	79%	69%	76%	73%	74%
Authenticity	80%	80%	73%	73%	77%
Originality	80%	80%	78%	73%	78%
Easy to spot	79%	71%	78%	74%	75%
Trustworthiness	85%	84%	78%	68%	79%
Clarity	84%	92%	85%	81%	86%
Intent to follow call to action	84%	71%	73%	71%	75%
Intent to discuss further	75%	66%	75%	73%	72%
Summary KPI performance	*81%*	*77%*	*78%*	*74%*	*77%*
Channel					
Website/blog	45%	47%	45%	48%	46%
Social media (e.g. Instagram, Facebo	61%	53%	70%	71%	64%
E-mail newsletter	18%	14%	19%	15%	17%
Google/Bing search results	42%	44%	34%	34%	39%
Mobile Games	20%	16%	35%	15%	22%
Print newspaper/magazine	42%	42%	35%	42%	40%
Outdoors	31%	31%	17%	18%	24%

Conjoint.ly   2

being conducted or not is not readily known, although the portfolio method remains popular in the industry. A variety of the portfolio test is the **mock magazine test** in which an ad is placed in an actual magazine and a similar methodology is employed.

Readability Tests The communications efficiency of the copy in a print ad can be tested without reader interviews. (Note: The tests are now also being used to test the readability of websites.) This test uses the **Flesch formula**, named after its developer, Rudolph Flesch, to assess readability of the copy by determining the average number of syllables per 100 words. Human interest appeal of the material, length of sentences, and familiarity with certain words are also considered and correlated with the educational background of target audiences. Test results are compared to previously established norms for various target audiences. The test suggests that copy is best comprehended when sentences are short, words are concrete and familiar, and personal references are drawn.

The Flesch Kincaid Reading Ease Score method eliminates many of the interviewee biases associated with other tests and avoids gross errors in understanding. The norms offer an attractive standard for comparison. Other readibility measures also exist, including the SMOG Readability Formula and the Fry Graph Readability Formula.

Disadvantages are also inherent, however. The copy may become too mechanical, and direct input from the receiver is not available. Without this input, contributing elements like creativity cannot be addressed. To be effective, this test should be used only in conjunction with other pretesting methods.

New Print Pretesting Measures In an effort to improve upon the traditional print pretest measures, a number of companies have introduced new methodologies or improved upon existing methods that employed dummy advertising vehicles. Many of these involve hybrid measures that either measure effectiveness in different ways or in different channels. For example, Ipsos-ASI Next*Connect has introduced an online copy testing tool (Figure 18-10) that can test ads on digital or traditional media. Consumers are recruited to complete an online survey where they are exposed to a variety of ad messages. The results are compared against a control group that was not exposed to the advertising. The methodology allows for testing ads in finished or rough formats, for individual executions or multiple campaign elements, and for determining ads' impact in traditional and new media (Exhibit 18-4).

FIGURE 18–10

Ipsos-ASI's Next*Connect

Objective
To assist advertisers in copy testing of rough or finished advertisements in traditional or digital form to determine the individual executions or multiple campaign elements across any platform.
Method
Consumers are recruited to complete an online survey where they are exposed to a variety of messages and results are compared against those from a control group not exposed to any ads.
Output
Standard scores, related recall, persuasion, and comprehensive diagnostics; potential ad-driven in-market sales.

EXHIBIT 18–4

Ipsos-ASI offers a comprehensive testing measure.

Ipsos

The PTG (PreTesting Group) methodology measures the time a respondent spends with a print ad or tablet or with a hidden camera in a store. The altered (dummy) magazines contain a number of ads targeted toward the interests of the consumers. Unknown to the consumers, as they go through the magazines, hidden cameras using eye-tracking technology record where their eyes go on the page, how long they stay on the page, and the stopping power of the ad. The studies can be conducted in person or online and can measure recall, main idea communication, and more.

Kantar offers its own trademarked methodology as well, called Link. According to the company, Link uses a comprehensive set of diagnostic questions to evoke viewer reactions to the ads. Nonverbal measures including eye tracking can also be used to determine consumers' enjoyment, comprehension, involvement, and other reactions to the ads. The three key metrics provided include awareness, persuasion, and short-term sales likelihood.

While other methods and measures are available, the most popular form of pretesting of print ads now involves a series of measures. The tests can typically be used for rough and/or finished ads and are most commonly conducted in a lab or online.

Pretesting Finished Broadcast Ads A variety of methods for pretesting broadcast ads are available. The tests can typically be used for rough and/or finished ads and are most commonly conducted in a lab or online. As noted, most of the companies that offer pretesting of print ads have expanded their services to include TV and other platforms. (The ASI method described in Figure 18–10 uses the same testing platform across media.) For example, MSW•ARS Research provides offerings that allow the advertiser to evaluate the impact of advertising messages and campaigns composed of any combination of touch points, including broadcast (television and radio), outdoor, and digital. The company provides research solutions in brand strategy, all stages of creative development from concept to fully finished ads, campaign evaluation across all channels, advertising and brand equity tracking, and additional consulting services.

Theater Tests In the past, one of the most popular laboratory methods for pretesting finished commercials was **theater testing**. In theater tests participants are invited to view pilots of proposed TV programs. In some instances, the show is actually being tested, but more commonly a standard program is used so audience responses can be compared with normative responses established by previous viewers. Sample sizes range from 250 to 600 participants, with 300 being most typical.

EXHIBIT 18–5

This ad for GfK promotes its research and testing as a smart business decision. Do you agree or disagree?

GfK

The methods of theater testing operations vary, though all measure brand preference changes. For example, many of the services now use programs with the commercials embedded for viewing in one's home or office rather than in a theater. Others establish viewing rooms in malls and/or hotel conference rooms. Some do not take all the measures listed here; others ask the consumers to turn dials or push buttons on a keypad to provide the continual responses.

Those opposed to theater tests cite a number of disadvantages. First, they say the environment is too artificial. The recruiting and lab testing conditions are likely to lead to testing effects, and consumers are exposed to commercials they might not even notice in a more natural environment. Second, the contrived measure of brand preference change seems too phony to believe. Critics contend that participants will see through it and make changes just because they think they are supposed to. Finally, the group effect of having others present and overtly exhibiting their reactions may influence viewers who did not have any reactions themselves.

Proponents argue that theater tests offer distinct advantages. In addition to control, the established norms (averages of commercials' performances) indicate how one's commercial will fare against others in the same product class that were already tested. Further, advocates say the brand preference measure is supported by actual sales results.

Despite the limitations of theater testing, most major consumer-product companies have used it to evaluate their commercials. This method may have shortcomings, but it allows them to identify strong or weak commercials and to compare them to other ads. Companies like Ipsos-ASI and Consumer Quest now offer in-home and online theater testing. While a number of research companies still offer theater testing services, the long-established traditional theater testing model is no longer the standard methodology used.

On-Air Tests Some of the firms conducting theater tests also insert the commercials into actual TV programs in certain test markets. Typically, the commercials are in finished form, although the testing of ads earlier in the developmental process is becoming more common. This is referred to as an **on-air test** and often includes single-source ad research (discussed later in this chapter). Decision Analyst, Ipsos-ASI, MSW•ARS, and Nielsen are well-known providers of on-air tests.

On-air testing techniques offer all the advantages of field methodologies, as well as all the disadvantages. The most commonly employed metric used in an on-air test is **recall**—that is, the number of persons able to recall the ad and/or its message. In an examination of real-world advertising tests reported in the *Journal of Advertising Research*, Hu and colleagues. conclude that recall and persuasion pretests, while often employed, do not fare well in respect to reliability and/or validity.[15] Nevertheless, most of the testing services have offered evidence of both validity and reliability for on-air pretesting of commercials. Both Ipsos-ASI and MSW•ARS claim their pretest and posttest results yield the same recall scores 9 out of 10 times—a strong indication of reliability and a good predictor of the effect the ad is likely to have when shown to the population as a whole (Exhibit 18–5).

In summary, on-air pretesting of finished or rough commercials offers some distinct advantages over lab methods and some indications of the ad's likely success. Whether the measures used are as strong an indication as the providers say remains in question.

Physiological Measures A less common but increasingly adopted method of pretesting finished commercials involves a laboratory setting in which physiological responses are measured. These measures indicate the receiver's *involuntary* response to the ad, theoretically eliminating biases associated with the voluntary measures reviewed to this point. (Involuntary responses are those over which the individual has no control, such

FIGURE 18-11

Eye Movement Research

Objective

Track viewers' eye movements to determine what viewers read or view in print ads and where their attention is focused in TV commercials, on websites, or on billboards.

Method

Fiber optics, digital data processing, and advanced electronics are used to follow eye movements of viewers and/or readers as they process an ad.

Output

Relationship among what readers see, recall, and comprehend. Scan movement paths in print ads, on billboards, in commercials, in print materials, and on websites. (Can also be used to evaluate package designs.)

as heartbeat and reflexes.) Physiological measures used to test both print and broadcast ads include pupil dilation, galvanic skin response, eye tracking, and brain waves:

1. *Pupil dilation.* Research in **pupillometrics** is designed to measure dilation and constriction of the pupils of the eyes in response to stimuli. Dilation is associated with action; constriction involves the body's conservation of energy.

    Advertisers have used pupillometrics to evaluate product and package design as well as to test ads. Pupil dilation suggests a stronger interest in (or preference for) an ad or implies arousal or attention-getting capabilities. Other attempts to determine the affective (liking or disliking) responses created by ads have met with less success.

    Because of high costs and some methodological problems, the use of pupillometrics has waned over the past decade. But it can be useful in evaluating certain aspects of advertising.

2. *Galvanic skin response (GSR).* Also known as **electrodermal response (EDR)**, GSR measures the skin's resistance or conductance to a small amount of current passed between two electrodes. Response to a stimulus activates sweat glands, which in turn increases the conductance of the electrical current. Thus, GSR/EDR activity might reflect a reaction to advertising. While there is evidence that GSR/EDR may be useful to determine the effectiveness of ads, difficulties associated with this testing method have resulted in its infrequent use at this time.

3. *Eye tracking.* A methodology that is more commonly employed is **eye tracking** (Figure 18-11), in which viewers are asked to view an ad while a sensor aims a beam of infrared light at the eye. The beam follows the movement of the eye and shows the exact spot on which the viewer is focusing, and for how long (Exhibit 18-6). The continuous reading of responses demonstrates which

EXHIBIT 18-6

SensoMotoric Instruments offers eye-tracking solutions as it becomes more commonly used in digital testing.

Tobii AB

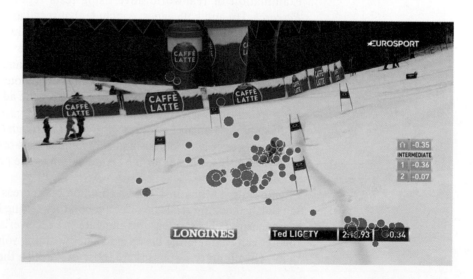

elements of the ad are attracting attention, how long the viewer is focusing on them, and the sequence in which they are being viewed.

Eye tracking can identify strengths and weaknesses in an ad. For example, attractive models or background action may distract the viewer's attention away from the brand or product being advertised. The advertiser can remedy this distraction before fielding the ad. In other instances, colors or illustrations may attract attention and create viewer interest in the ad.

Eye tracking has increasingly been used to measure the effectiveness of websites and online ads. Using eye tracking to examine how consumers view homepages, Steve Outing and Laura Roel were able to determine that (1) eyes first fixate on the upper left of the screen, (2) dominant headlines draw attention first, and (3) larger type promotes scanning, while small type encourages reading. The study drew other conclusions as well—too many to mention here.[16]

4. *Brain waves.* **Electroencephalographic (EEG) measures** can be taken from the skull to determine electrical frequencies in the brain. These electrical impulses are used in two areas of research, alpha waves and hemispheric lateralization:

- **Alpha activity** refers to the degree of brain activation. People are in an alpha state when they are inactive, resting, or sleeping. The theory is that a person in an alpha state is less likely to be processing information (recall correlates negatively with alpha levels) and that attention and processing require moving from this state. By measuring a subject's alpha level while viewing a commercial, researchers can assess the degree to which attention and processing are likely to occur.
- **Hemispheric lateralization** distinguishes between alpha activity in the left and right sides of the brain. It has been hypothesized that the right side of the brain processes visual stimuli and the left processes verbal stimuli. The right hemisphere is thought to respond more to emotional stimuli, while the left responds to logic. The right determines recognition, while the left is responsible for recall. If these hypotheses are correct, advertisers could design ads to increase learning and memory by creating stimuli to appeal to each hemisphere. However, some researchers believe the brain does not function laterally and an ad cannot be designed to appeal to one side or the other.
- Using technologies originally designed for the medical field such as positron emission tomography (PET), functional magnetic resonance imaging (fMRI), and electroencephalography (EEG), neuroscientists have teamed up with marketers to examine physiological reactions to ads and brands through brain scan imaging. By monitoring the brain activity directly, scientists are learning how consumers make up their minds by measuring chemical activity and/or changes in the magnetic fields of the brain as well as how they react to commercials.

EEG research has engaged the attention of academic researchers for some time, but recently the technology has gained in attractiveness to practioners as well. In addition to those examples cited earlier in the chapter and throughout this text, companies like the Nielsen Company—the world's largest audience measurement company—have invested in neuroscience measurement as *Fortune* 500 companies increasingly seek these services. Neuroscience measures have been used to determine viewers' responses to Super Bowl commercials, differences in responses to drinking Coke and Pepsi, political ads, and movie trailers, to name just a few of the many applications.

Market Testing of Ads

The fact that the ad and/or campaign has been implemented does not diminish the need for testing. The pretests were conducted on smaller samples and may in some instances have questionable merit, so the marketer must find out how the ad is doing in the field. In this section, we discuss methods for posttesting an ad. Many of the tests are similar to the pretests discussed in the previous section and are provided by the same companies.

Posttests of Print Ads   A variety of print posttests are available, including inquiry tests, recognition tests, and recall tests.

Inquiry Tests   Used in both consumer and business-to-business market testing, **inquiry tests** are designed to measure advertising effectiveness on the basis of inquiries generated from ads appearing in various print media, often referred to as "bingo cards." While still used, the response card is employed less often today as viewers can seek information merely by searching on the URL provided in the ad. Magazines used in B2B marketing are more likely to use inquiry cards. However, no one seems to know if the leads are followed up on. At least one study credits the cutback on the use of inquiry cards as responsible for declines in B2B magazine circulation.[17] The inquiry may take the form of the number of coupons returned, phone calls generated, or direct inquiries. Of course, on the Internet, there are a number of other measures used such as clicks, click-throughs, and so on. For local businesses distributing their ads through flyers or in direct mail pieces like the ones you receive in the weekly mail, the number of inquiries remains a useful measure of effectiveness. The ads shown in Exhibit 18–7 are good examples. Certainly measures such as the number of phone calls received, coupons redeemed, and so on, serve as a measure of the ad's effectiveness. If you called in response to an ad in a local medium recently, perhaps you were asked how you found out about the company or product or where you saw the ad. This is a very simple measure of the ad's or medium's effectiveness.

More complex methods of measuring effectiveness through inquiries may involve (1) running the ad in successive issues of the same medium; (2) running **split-run tests**, in which variations of the ad appear in different copies of the same newspaper or magazine; and/or (3) running the same ad in different media. Each of these methods yields information on different aspects of the strategy. The first measures the *cumulative* effects of the campaign; the second examines specific elements of the ad or variations on it. The final method measures the effectiveness of the medium rather than the ad itself.

While inquiry tests may yield useful information, weaknesses in this methodology limit its effectiveness. For example, inquiries may not be a true measure of the attention-getting or information-providing aspects of the ad. The reader may be attracted to an

EXHIBIT 18–7

For ads distributed through local direct mail pieces, catalogs, or flyers, the number of inquiries can be used as a measure of the ad's effectiveness.

cjmacer/iStock/Getty Images

FIGURE 18–12

MRI-Simmons Starch Ad Measure

Objective

Determining recognition of print ads and providing insight into the involvement readers have with specific ads. MRI-Simmons Starch Ad Measure now provides this service for ads appearing in magazines and/or digital.

Method

The test screens readers for qualifications and determines exposure and readership to specific issues of consumer magazines and measures each national ad (1/3 page or larger) in every issue of over 120 print titles. Participants are asked to go through the magazines, look at the ads, and provide specific responses.

Output

Starch Ad Readership Reports generate four recognition scores:

- Noting score—the percentage of readers who remember seeing the ad.
- Brand-associated score—the percentage of readers who recall seeing or reading any part of the ad identifying the product or brand.
- Read any score—the percentage of readers who read any of the ad's copy.
- Read-most score—the percentage of readers who report reading at least half of the copy portion of the ad. Ad norms provide a benchmark to provide a comparison to other ads in the issue.

These conventional scores have now been supplemented by additional measures, including brand disposition, purchase behavior or intention, actions taken, word-of-mouth opportunity, and publication and advertising engagement.

ad, read it, and even store the information but not be motivated to inquire at that particular time. Time constraints, lack of a need for the product or service at the time the ad is run, and other factors may limit the number of inquiries. But receiving a small number of inquiries doesn't mean the ad was not effective; attention, attitude change, awareness, and recall of copy points may all have been achieved. At the other extreme, a person with a particular need for the product may respond to any ad for it, regardless of specific qualities of the ad.

Major advantages of inquiry tests are that they are inexpensive to implement and they provide some feedback with respect to the general effectiveness of the ad or medium used. But they are usually not very effective for comparing different versions or specific creative aspects of an ad.

EXHIBIT 18–8

An ad scoring very high on the Starch rating scale.

GfK MRI

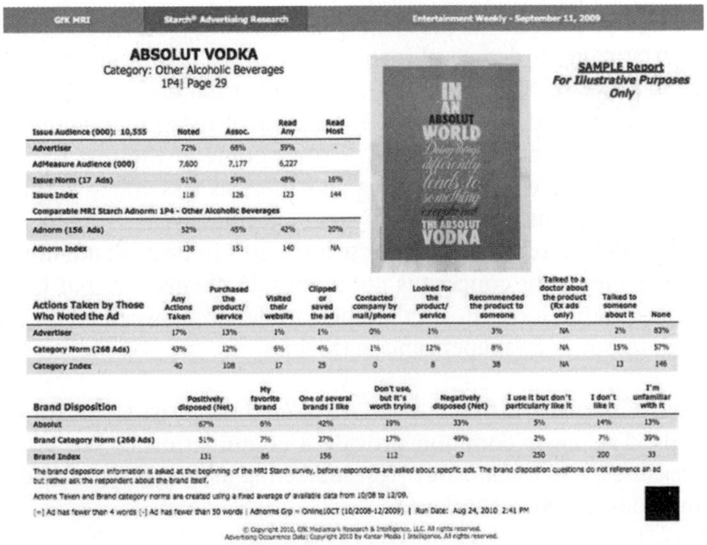

GfK MRI | Starch® Advertising Research | Entertainment Weekly - September 11, 2009

ABSOLUT VODKA
Category: Other Alcoholic Beverages
1P4| Page 29

SAMPLE Report
For Illustrative Purposes Only

Issue Audience (000): 10,555	Noted	Assoc.	Read Any	Read Most
Advertiser	72%	68%	59%	-
AdMeasure Audience (000)	7,600	7,177	6,227	
Issue Norm (17 Ads)	61%	54%	48%	16%
Issue Index	118	126	123	144
Comparable MRI Starch Adnorm: 1P4 - Other Alcoholic Beverages				
Adnorm (156 Ads)	52%	45%	42%	20%
Adnorm Index	138	151	140	NA

Actions Taken by Those Who Noted the Ad	Any Actions Taken	Purchased the product/ service	Visited their website	Clipped or saved the ad	Contacted company by mail/phone	Looked for the product/ service	Recommended the product to someone	Talked to a doctor about the product (Rx ads only)	Talked to someone about it	None
Advertiser	17%	13%	1%	1%	0%	1%	3%	NA	2%	83%
Category Norm (268 Ads)	43%	12%	6%	4%	1%	12%	8%	NA	15%	57%
Category Index	40	108	17	25	0	8	38	NA	13	146

Brand Disposition	Positively disposed (Net)	My favorite brand	One of several brands I like	Don't use, but it's worth trying	Negatively disposed (Net)	I use it but don't particularly like it	I don't like it	I'm unfamiliar with it
Absolut	67%	6%	42%	19%	33%	5%	14%	13%
Brand Category Norm (268 Ads)	51%	7%	27%	17%	49%	2%	7%	39%
Brand Index	131	86	156	112	67	250	200	33

The brand disposition information is asked at the beginning of the MRI Starch survey, before respondents are asked about specific ads. The brand disposition questions do not reference an ad but rather ask the respondent about the brand itself.

Actions Taken and Brand category norms are created using a fixed average of available data from 10/08 to 12/09.

[=] Ad has fewer than 4 words [-] Ad has fewer than 50 words | Adnorms Grp = Online10CT (10/2008-12/2009) | Run Date: Aug 24, 2010 2:41 PM

Recognition Tests Perhaps the most common posttest of print ads is the **recognition method**, most closely associated with Starch. The *Starch Ad Readership Report*, which has existed for over 85 years, lets the advertiser assess the impact of an ad in a single issue of a magazine, over time, and/or across different magazines. Starch measures hundreds of thousands of print ads representing more than 180 consumer magazines per year and provides a number of measures of an ad's effectiveness. In addition to the traditional *Starch Ad Readership Report*, Starch now offers syndicated and private studies, pretesting, out-of-home studies, and more. The measures used in the Starch test methodology are shown in Figure 18-12. An example of a Starch scored ad is shown in Exhibit 18-8.

Starch claims that (1) the pulling power of various aspects of the ad can be assessed through the control offered, (2) the effectiveness of competitors' ads can be compared through the norms provided, (3) alternative ad executions can be tested, and (4) readership scores are a useful indication of consumers' *involvement* in the ad or campaign. (The theory is that a reader must read and become involved in the ad before the ad can communicate. To the degree that this readership can be shown, it is a direct indication of effectiveness.) The MRI-Simmons Starch Ad Measure uses the traditional Starch measures and includes additional digital measures as well.

Of these claims, perhaps the most valid is the ability to judge specific aspects of the ad. Some researchers have criticized other aspects of the Starch recognition method (as well as other recognition measures) on the basis of problems of false claiming, interviewer sensitivities, and unreliable scores:

1. *False claiming.* Research shows that in recognition tests, respondents may claim to have seen an ad when they did not. False claims may be a result of having seen similar ads elsewhere, expecting that such an ad would appear in the medium, or wanting to please the questioner. Interest in the product category also increases reporting of ad readership. Whether this false claiming is deliberate or not, it leads to an overreporting of effectiveness. On the flip side, factors such as interview fatigue may lead to an underreporting bias—that is, respondents not reporting an ad they did see.

2. *Reliability of recognition scores.* Starch admits that the reliability and validity of its readership scores may increase with the number of insertions tested, which essentially means that to test just one ad on a single exposure may not produce valid or reliable results.

In sum, despite critics, the Starch readership studies continue to be used in the posttesting of print ads while the MRI-Simmons measure is also gaining acceptance in the market. The value provided by norms and the fact that multiple exposures can improve reliability and validity may underlie the decisions to employ this methodology. In addition, the long-standing reliability and trustworthiness of the test comes into play, as the Starch methodology has been used for almost 100 years, and has continued to evolve with the times.

Recall Tests   There are several tests to measure recall of print ads. Perhaps the best known of these is the Gallup & Robinson Magazine Impact Research Service (MIRS) described in Figure 18–13. (A number of other companies, including Kantar and Decision Analyst, offer similar services.) These **recall tests** are similar to those discussed in the section on pretesting broadcast ads in that they attempt to measure recall of specific ads.

In addition to having the same interviewer problems as recognition tests, recall tests have other disadvantages. The reader's degree of involvement with the product and/or the distinctiveness of the appeals and visuals may lead to higher-than-accurate recall scores, although in general the method may lead to lower levels of recall than actually exist (an error the advertiser would be happy with). Critics contend the test is not strong enough to reflect recall accurately, so many ads may score as less effective than they really are, and advertisers may abandon or modify them needlessly.

On the plus side, it is thought that recall tests can assess the ad's impact on memory. Proponents of recall tests say the major concern is not the results themselves but how they are interpreted. Previous studies have shown that the correlation between ad recall and recognition is very high in both newspapers and magazines.

Posttests of Broadcast Commercials   A variety of methods exist for posttesting broadcast commercials. The most common provide a combination of day-after recall tests, persuasion measures, and diagnostics. Test marketing and tracking studies, including single-source methods, are also employed.

FIGURE 18–13

G&R Magazine Impact
Research Service (MIRS)

Objective
Tracking recall of advertising (and client's ads) appearing in magazines to assess performance and effectiveness.

Method
Test magazines are placed in participants' homes and respondents are asked to read the magazine that day. Test ads are embedded with editorial content and other ads. A telephone interview is conducted the next day to assess recall of ads, idea communication, persuasion, brand rating, and ad liking. Both business-to-business and consumer magazine ads can be tested.

Output

Measures provided:

- Norms.
- Verbatim respondent playback.
- Performance summary.
- Diagnostics.

Day-After Recall Tests The most popular method of posttesting employed in the broadcasting industry for decades was the *Burke Day-After Recall test.* While a number of companies offered day-after recall (DAR) methodologies, the "Burke test" for all intents and purposes became the generic name attached to these tests. While popular, day-after recall tests also had problems, including limited samples, high costs, and security issues (ads shown in test markets could be seen by competitors). Because of their common usage, numerous studies have been conducted to determine the efficacy of DAR tests. Although these studies have been conducted quite some time ago, the conclusions seem to be relevant today and merit consideration here. In addition, the following disadvantages with recall tests were also suggested:

1. DAR tests may favor unemotional appeals because respondents are asked to verbalize the message. Thinking messages may be easier to recall than emotional communications, so recall scores for emotional ads may be lower.[18] A number of other studies have also indicated that emotional ads may be processed differently from thinking ones; some ad agencies, for example, Leo Burnett and BBDO Worldwide among others, have gone so far as to develop their own methods of determining emotional response to ads.[19]
2. Program content may influence recall. The programs in which the ad appears may lead to different recall scores for the same brand. The net result is a potential inaccuracy in the recall score and in the norms used to establish comparisons.
3. A pre-recruited sample may pay increased attention to the program and the ads contained therein because the respondents know they will be tested the next day. This testing effect would lead to a higher level of recall than really exists.
4. In addition, studies have shown that recall is a measure that the ad has been received, but not necessarily accepted, and not predictive of sales.[20,21]

The major advantage of day-after recall tests is that they are field tests. The natural setting is supposed to provide a more realistic response profile. These tests are also popular because they provide norms that give advertisers a standard for comparing how well their ads are performing. Companies including AXE, Coca-Cola, and numerous others continue to use day-after recall tests. In addition to recall, a number of different measures of the commercial's effectiveness are now offered, including persuasive measures and diagnostics. (The Burke test itself no longer exists under that name.)

Persuasive Measures As noted earlier in our discussion of pretesting broadcast commercials, a number of research firms now offer measures of a commercial's persuasive effectiveness. Some of the services offer additional persuasion measures, including purchase, intent, and frequency-of-purchase criteria.

Diagnostics In addition to measuring recall and persuasion, copy testing firms also provide diagnostic measures. These measures are designed to garner viewers' evaluations of the ads, as well as how clearly the creative idea is understood and how well the proposition is communicated. Rational and emotional reactions to the ads are also examined. A number of companies offer diagnostic measures, including G&R and Kantar among many others.

Comprehensive Measures While each of the measures just described provides specific input into the effectiveness of a commercial, many advertisers are interested in more than just one specific input. Thus, some companies provide comprehensive approaches in which each of the three measures just described can be obtained through one testing program.

Test Marketing Many companies conduct tests designed to measure their advertising effects in specific test markets before releasing them nationally. The markets chosen are representative of the target market. For example, a company may test its ads in Portland, Oregon; San Antonio, Texas; or Buffalo, New York, if the demographic and socioeconomic profiles of these cities match the product's target market. A variety of factors may be tested, including reactions to the ads (for example, alternative copy points), the effects of various budget sizes, or special offers. The ads run in finished form in the media where they might normally appear, and effectiveness is measured after the ads run.

The advantage of test marketing of ads is realism. Regular viewing environments are used and the testing effects are minimized. A high degree of control can be attained if the test is designed successfully. For example, an extensive test market study was designed and conducted by Seagram and Time, Inc. over a period of 3 years to measure the effects of advertising frequency on consumers' buying habits. This study demonstrated just how much could be learned from research conducted in a field setting but with some experimental controls. It also showed that proper research can provide strong insights into the impact of ad campaigns. (Many advertising researchers consider this study one of the most conclusive ever conducted in the attempt to demonstrate the effects of advertising on sales.)

The Seagram study also reveals some of the disadvantages associated with test market measures, not the least of which are cost and time. Few firms have the luxury to spend 3 years and hundreds of thousands of dollars on such a test. In addition, there is always the fear that competitors may discover and intervene in the research process.

A number of companies, including Procter & Gamble and Toyota, have test-marketed interactive commercials. Reckitt—the world's largest manufacturer of household cleaning products—and Whirlpool joined efforts to test iTV ads. Customers were offered three different enticements to interact with the campaign: (1) register to win a Whirlpool dishwasher, (2) register for free samples of Finish Dishwater Freshener, or (3) order money-off coupons for Finish Dishwater Tablets. After 8 months of testing, Reckitt reported that the target goal of 35,000 responses was exceeded.[22]

Test marketing can provide substantial insight into the effectiveness of advertising if care is taken to minimize the negative aspects of such tests.

Tracking Print/Broadcast Ads One of the more useful and adaptable forms of posttesting involves tracking the effects of the ad campaign by taking measurements at regular intervals. **Tracking studies** have been used to measure the effects of advertising on awareness, recall, interest, and attitudes toward the ad and/or brand as well as purchase intentions. (Ad tracking may be applied to print and digital ads.) Personal interviews, phone surveys, mall intercepts, and online surveys have been used. Tracking studies yield perhaps the most valuable information available to the marketing manager for assessing current programs and planning for the future.

The major advantage of tracking studies is that they can be tailored to each specific campaign and/or situation. A standard set of questions can track effects of the campaign over time or through the consumer purchase funnel. In a study by the research organization Yankelovich and the Television Bureau of Advertising (TVB), it was shown that the effectiveness of advertising depends on the product category and where the consumer is in the purchase funnel. The advertising medium impact varied as the consumer moved through the stages.[23] The effects of various media can also be determined, although with much less effectiveness. Tracking studies have also been used to measure the differential impact of different budget sizes, the effects of flighting, brand or corporate image, and recall of specific copy points. As you will see later in the chapter, however, it is often difficult to quantify some of the measures suggested. Finally, when designed properly, as shown in Figure 18-14, tracking studies offer a high degree of reliability and validity.

Some of the problems of recall and recognition measures are inherent in tracking studies, since many other factors may affect both brand and advertising recall. Despite these limitations, however, tracking studies are a very effective way to assess the effects of advertising campaigns.

In summary, you can see that each of the testing methods considered in this chapter has its strengths and its limitations. You may wonder: Can we actually test advertising effectiveness? What can be done to ensure a valid, reliable test? The next section of this chapter suggests some answers.

FIGURE 18-14

Factors That Make or Break Tracking Studies

1. Properly defined objectives.
2. Alignment with sales objectives.
3. Properly designed measures (e.g., adequate sample size, maximum control over interviewing process, adequate time between tracking periods).
4. Consistency through replication of the sampling plan.
5. Random samples.
6. Continuous interviewing (that is, not seasonal).
7. Evaluation of measures related to behavior (attitudes meet this criterion; recall of ads does not).
8. Critical evaluative questions asked early to eliminate bias.
9. Measurement of competitors' performance.
10. Skepticism about questions that ask where the advertising was seen or heard (TV always wins).
11. Building of news value into the study.
12. "Moving averages" used to spot long-term trends and avoid seasonality.
13. Data reported in terms of relationships rather than as isolated facts.
14. Integration of key marketplace events with tracking results (e.g., advertising expenditures of self and competitors, promotional activities associated with price changes in ad campaigns, introductions of new brands, government announcements, changes in economic conditions).

ESTABLISHING A PROGRAM FOR MEASURING ADVERTISING EFFECTS

There is no surefire way to test advertising effectiveness. However, in response to pressures to determine the contribution of ads—traditional and online—to the overall marketing effort, steps are being taken to improve this measurement task. Let's begin by reviewing the major problems with some existing methods and then examine possible improvements.

Problems with Current Research Methods

When current testing methods are compared to the criteria established by PACT (see Figure 18-3) and Making Measurement Make Sense (Figure 18-4), it is clear that some of the principles important to good testing can be accomplished readily, whereas others require substantially more effort. For example, PACT principle 6 (providing equivalent test ads) should require a minimum of effort. The researcher can easily control the state of completion of the test communications. Also fairly easy are principles 1 and 2 (providing measurements relative to the objectives sought and determining *a priori* how the results will be used). In regard to Figure 18-4 and digital measurement, some of the principles (for example, principle 2, the currency issue, and 5, comparable measures) may not be difficult to achieve.

We have seen throughout this text that each promotional medium, the message, and the budget all consider the marketing and communications objectives sought. The integrated marketing communications planning model establishes the roles of these elements. So by the time one gets to the measurement phase, the criteria by which these programs will be evaluated should simply fall into place.

Slightly more difficult are PACT principles 3, 5, and 8, although again these factors are largely in the control of the researcher. Principle 3 (providing multiple measurements) may require little more than budgeting to make sure more than one test is conducted. At the most, it may require considering two similar measures to ensure reliability. Likewise, principle 5 (exposing the test ad more than once) can be accomplished with a proper research design. Finally, principle 8 (sample definition) requires little more than sound research methodology; any test should use the target audience to assess an ad's effectiveness. You would not use a sample of nondrinkers to evaluate new liquor commercials. Likewise principles 3 and 4 on the digital side might take some time and give and take, but can be accomplished.

The most difficult factors to control—and the principles that may best differentiate between good and bad testing procedures—are PACT requirements 4, 7, and 9. Fortunately, however, addressing each of these contributes to the attainment of the others.

While it is important that marketers' attempts to measure effectiveness be guided by all of the principles stated, the research should be guided by a model of human response to communications that encompasses reception, comprehension, and behavioral response. It is the best starting point, in our opinion, because it is the principle least addressed by practicing researchers. If you recall, Chapter 5 proposed a number of models that could fulfill this requirement. Yet even though the models have existed for quite some time, few if any common research methods attempt to integrate them into their methodologies. Most current methods do little more than provide recall scores, despite the fact that many researchers have shown recall to be a poor measure of effectiveness. Models that do claim to measure such factors as attitude change or brand preference change are often fraught with problems that severely limit their reliability. Once again, a problem with digital metrics is that they often don't provide insights into the consumer response processes because the measures are behavioral and provide no insights into the emotional side. An effective measure must include some relationship to the communication process.

It might seem at first glance that PACT principle 7 (providing a nonbiasing exposure) would be easy to accomplish. But lab measures, while offering control, are artificial and vulnerable to testing effects. And field measures, although more realistic, often lose control. The Seagram and Time study may have the best of both worlds, but it is too large a task for most firms to undertake. Some of the improvements associated with the single-source systems help solve this problem. In addition, properly designed ad tracking studies provide truer measures of the impact of the communication. As technology develops and more attention is paid to this principle, we expect to see improvements in methodologies soon.

Last but not least is PACT principle 9, the concern for reliability and validity. This principle must carry over to online measures as well. Most of the measures discussed are lacking in at least one of these criteria, yet these are two of the most critical distinctions between good and bad research. If a study is properly designed, and by that we mean it addresses principles 1 through 8, it should be both reliable and valid. Studies designed to measure the impact of online advertising also need to adhere to the PACT principles as well as the Making Measurement Make Sense ones. As you have just read, many of the larger research firms mentioned here are now applying platforms to measure both traditional and digital ads.

Essentials of Effective Testing

Simply put, good tests of advertising effectiveness must address the nine principles established by PACT. One of the easiest ways to accomplish this is by following the decision sequence model in formulating promotional plans.

- *Establish communications objectives.* We have stated that except for a few instances (most specifically direct-response advertising), it is nearly impossible to show the direct impact of advertising on sales. So the marketing objectives established for the promotional program are not usually good measures of communication effectiveness. For example, it is very difficult (or too expensive) to demonstrate the effect of an ad on brand share or on sales. On the other hand, attainment of communications objectives can be measured and leads to the accomplishment of marketing objectives.
- *Use a consumer response model.* Early in this text we reviewed the hierarchy of effects models and cognitive response models, which provide an understanding of the effects of communications and lend themselves to achieving communications goals. Many companies including Honda, General Motors, Sprint, and others use hierarchy models to establish objectives and assess effectiveness in both the traditional and online environments.
- *Use both pretests and posttests.* From a cost standpoint—both actual cost outlays and opportunity costs—pretesting makes sense. It may mean the difference between success or failure of the campaign or the product. But it should work in conjunction with posttests, which avoid the limitations of pretests, use much larger samples, and take place in more natural settings. Posttesting may be required to determine the true effectiveness of the ad or campaign.
- *Use multiple measures.* Many attempts to measure the effectiveness of advertising focus on one major dependent variable—perhaps sales, recall, or recognition. At this time, many companies tend to be focusing on the attention-getting aspects of their ads, while ignoring other metrics. As noted earlier in this chapter, advertising may have a variety of effects on the consumer, some of which can be measured through traditional methods and others that require updated thinking (recall the discussion on physiological responses). For a true assessment of advertising effectiveness, a number of measures may be required. The Ogilvy Award winners mentioned earlier all employed multiple measures to track the effects on communications objectives.
- *Understand and implement proper research.* It is critical to understand research methodology. What constitutes a good design? Is it valid and reliable? Does it measure what we need it to? There is no shortcut to this criterion, and there is no way to avoid it if you truly want to measure the effects of advertising.

MEASURING THE EFFECTIVENESS OF OTHER PROGRAM ELEMENTS

Throughout this text, we have discussed how and when promotional program elements should be used, the advantages and disadvantages of each, and so on. In many chapters we have discussed measures of effectiveness used to evaluate these programs. In the final section of this chapter, we add a few measures that were not discussed earlier.

Measuring the Effectiveness of Sales Promotions

Sales promotions are not limited to retailers and resellers of products. Sports marketers have found them a very effective way to attract crowds and have been able to measure their relative effectiveness by the number of fans attending games. Major League Baseball teams have seen their attendance increase for those games in which promotions are offered.

A number of organizations measure the impact of sales promotions. The GfK National Shopper Lab (NSL) tracks the effectiveness of promotions leveraging data collected from more than 80 million consumers. NSL captures the data from shoppers' weekly transactions through Shopper ID, UPC, store, date, price, and coupon. NSL is a division of GfK—an international research company discussed at various points throughout this text. Promotion Decisions Inc. examines the impact of freestanding inserts (FSIs) in Figure 18–15.

Other measures of sales promotions are also available. For example, a number of research companies provide retailers visibility into the factors that influence the effectiveness of all of their promotions, allowing the retailer to make the right decision about the right products to promote using promotional vehicles and understanding the required inventory levels. Other companies have used awareness tracking studies and count the number of inquiries, coupon redemptions, and sweepstakes entries. They also track sales during promotional and nonpromotional periods while holding other factors constant. The Nielsen Company's ScanTrack methodology helps marketers answer the questions regarding how many promotions to do and how this promotion compares to competitors', and what overall sales lifts are associated with individual promotions using scanner data. An article by SAS concludes that retailers that make promotion decisions without considering measurable customer behavior are at a great disadvantage in the marketplace.[24]

FIGURE 18–15

Measuring the Effects of FSIs

A study by Promotion Decisions Inc. examined the actual purchase data of users and nonusers of 27 coupon promotions in its National Shopper Lab (75,000 households) over a period of 18 months. The findings are as follows:

- FSI coupons generated significant trial by new and lapsed users of a product (53 percent).

- Repeat purchase rates were 11.8 percent higher among coupon redeemers than nonredeemers.

- 64.2 percent of repeat volume among coupon redeemers was without a coupon.

- There was no significant difference in share of volume between buyers who used coupons and those who did not.

- Coupons returned between 71 and 79 percent of their cost within 12 weeks.

- Full-page ads provided higher redemption rates, incremental volume, redemption by new users, and a higher number of repeat buyers than half-page ads.

- Consumers who used coupons were brand loyal.

One interesting and useful technology designed to track the effectiveness of sales promotions at the point of sale is offered by Shopper Trak. Shopper Trak employs heat map technology in the store that views traffic; whether a person is coming or going; calculates the shopper's height (to differentiate between adults and children); and gauges traffic patterns and sales conversions, among other metrics. The system helps retailers evaluate the effectiveness of promotions or displays located throughout the store.[25]

Measuring the Effectiveness of Nontraditional Media

In Chapter 13, we noted that one of the disadvantages of employing nontraditional media (that is, nontraditional *traditional* media, in other words, less used but not digital) is that it is usually difficult to measure the effectiveness of the programs. But some progress has been made, as shown in these examples:

- *The effectiveness of print versus online flyers.* In an article published in the *Journal of Advertising Research*, Marco Ieva, Juan Carlos Gazquez-Abad, Ida D'ttoma, and Christina Ziliani examined the difference between online and traditional flyers' effects on memory and purchase behaviors. The measures were tracked in 37 supermarket chains over 9,902 consumers. The results indicated that there was no difference between the print and online flyers' impact on consumers.[26]
- *The effectiveness of parking lot–based media.* In Chapter 13, we discussed advertising on parking lot signage and other areas to attempt to reach selective demographic groups. Now the Traffic Audit Bureau (TAB) is tracking the effectiveness of this form of advertising to give advertisers more reliable criteria on which to base purchase decisions. The TAB data verify ad placements, while the media vendors have employed Experian Simmons Market Research and Nielsen Media Research to collect ad impressions and advertising recall information. These measures are combined with sales tracking data to evaluate the medium's effectiveness.
- *The effects of in-store radio and television.* Interactive Market Systems (IMS) introduced software that enables clients to measure the effectiveness of in-store radio. The company planned to introduce similar software designed to measure in-store television advertising effectiveness.[27]
- *The effectiveness of other media.* A number of companies provide effectiveness measures to determine the impact of package designs, POP displays, trade show exhibits, and the like. Nielsen Entertainment and Massivemedia now offer a service to measure video game advertising effectiveness as well as that of other outdoor media. While it is not possible to list them all here, suffice it to say that if one wants to measure the impact of various IMC elements, the resources are available.

Measuring the Effectiveness of Sponsorships

In earlier chapters we discussed the growth in sponsorships and the reasons why organizations have increased their investments in this area. Along with the increased expenditures have come a number of methods for measuring the impact of sponsorships. Essentially, measures of sponsorship effectiveness can be categorized as exposure-based methods or tracking measures:[28]

- *Exposure methods.* Exposure methods can be classified as those that monitor the quantity and nature of the media coverage obtained for the sponsored event and those that estimate direct and indirect audiences. While commonly employed by corporations, scholars have heavily criticized these measures. For example, Michel Pham argues that media coverage is not the objective of sponsorships and should not be considered as a measure of effectiveness. He argues that the measures provide no indication of perceptions, attitude change, or behavioral change.[29]

- *Tracking measures.* These measures are designed to evaluate the awareness, familiarity, and preferences engendered by sponsorship based on surveys. A number of empirical studies have measured recall of sponsors' ads, awareness of and attitudes toward the sponsors and their products, and image effect, including brand and corporate images.

A number of companies now measure the effectiveness of sports and other sponsorships. For example, companies assign a value referred to as media equivalency and assign a monetary value to the amount of exposure the sponsor receives during the event. They review broadcasts and add up the number of seconds a sponsor's product name or logo can be seen clearly (e.g., on signs or shirts). A total of 30 seconds is considered the equivalent of a 30-second commercial. An example of how marketers employ media equivalencies (though not specifically in a sponsorship role) occurred at the Coperni Fashion Show during Fashion Week in Paris in the fall of 2022 where a spray-paint dress was painted on Bella Hadid's mostly nude body. Besides inspiring a number of Halloween ideas, Launchmetrics—a firm that measures media impact value (MOV)—calculated that the monetary value generated from online posts, articles, news coverage, and so on was worth an estimated $26.3 million dollars within the first 48 hours, most of which came from social media where there were an estimated 2.8 million likes. Kim Kardashian's appearance at Balenciaga's show in July generated an estimated $935,000.[30,31] (Such measures are of questionable validity.)

As with all other IMC touch points, marketers would like to measure the ROI of event sponsorships. But—like these other means of communication—this is usually not possible, so the focus will be on other more communication-oriented objectives. Figure 18-16 shows a Sponsorship Performance Matrix used by one sponsor effectiveness measurement company. The vertical axis of this matrix measures the passion the target audience feels toward the sponsoring organization. The more emotionally attached to the property (sporting team, event, etc.), the higher the Passion Index. The horizontal axis measures sponsor appreciation—the Gratitude Index. Companies can achieve more appreciation by being more active, thus creating more goodwill. As can

FIGURE 18–16

Sponsorship Performance Matrix

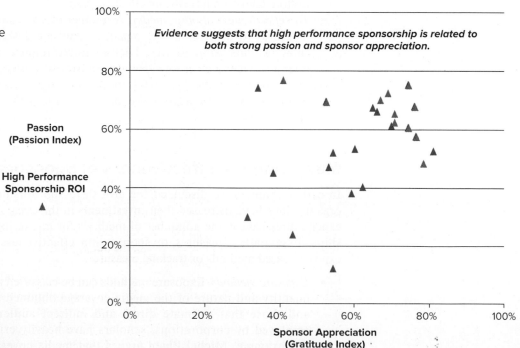

FIGURE 18–17

Eight Steps to Measuring
Event Sponsorship

1. Narrowly define objectives with specifics.

2. Establish solid strategies against which programming will be benchmarked and measure your programming and effectiveness against the benchmark.

3. Set measurable and realistic goals; make sure everything you do supports them.

4. Enhance, rather than just change, other marketing variables.

5. Don't pull Marketing Plan 101 off the shelf. Programming should be crafted to reflect the particulars of your company's constituencies and target audiences.

6. Define the scope of your involvement. Will it involve multiple areas within the company? Who internally and externally constitutes the team?

7. Think "long term." It takes time to build brand equity. Also, think of leveraging your sponsorship through programming for as long as possible, before and after the event.

8. Build evaluation and a related budget into your overall sponsoring program. Include items such as pre- and postevent attitude surveys, media analyses, and sales results.

be seen in Figure 18–16, the sponsor would want to be in the upper right-hand corner to achieve maximum effectiveness.

Performance research measures impact on brand awareness and image shifts. Tracking the number of website visits and buzz generated are also criteria that have been used.

While each of these measures has its advantages and disadvantages, most do not go far enough. As noted by John Nardone and Ed See, most marketers limit their sponsorship evaluations to brand awareness and impressions. The key question that needs to be asked, they say, is "how do you do sponsorships that build brand equity and maintain financial responsibility?"[32] We suggest using several measures in assessing the impact of sponsorships. In addition to those mentioned here, the eight-step process suggested in Figure 18–17 could be used to guide these evaluations.

Measuring the Effectiveness of Other IMC Program Elements

Many of the organizations mentioned in this chapter offer research services to measure the effectiveness of specific promotional program elements. As we noted at the outset of this chapter, the increased use of integrated marketing communications programs has led to more interest in determining the synergistic effects of all program elements. A review of the Ogilvy Award winners from 1993 to date demonstrates the increased integration of additional media (as opposed to specifically the best advertising campaign) and the value of measuring their contribution to the program's success. Also departing from the specific focus on advertising are the awards given by the London-based Institute of Practitioners, which has opened the competition to nontraditional media as well as public relations, sales promotions, and other entries.

As noted, a number of studies have been implemented to determine the combined effects of two or more media as well as their synergistic impact. The number of studies being designed to specifically measure synergistic effects continues to increase—most of which demonstrate a higher effectiveness when multiple media are employed.

Perhaps the major challenge facing the adoption of an IMC approach is determining the effectiveness and contribution of various elements of the IMC program. IMC Perspective 18-2 discusses how advertisers are using attribution models to make this determination. A number of academic studies have offered insights into this endeavor. For example, Dinner and colleagues examined the "presence, magnitude, and carryover of cross-channel effects for online advertising (display and search) and traditional media."[33] Their conclusion was that cross-channel effects do exist and are important.

Advertising Attribution: Is It the Holy Grail for Measuring Effectiveness?

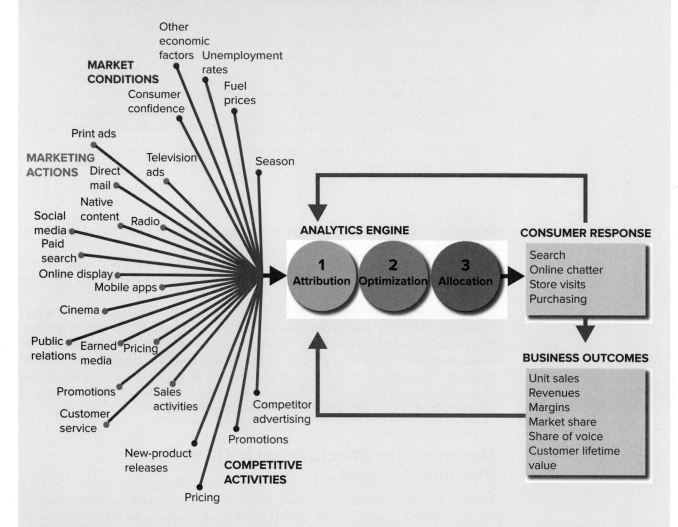

Throughout this text we have discussed how to measure various aspects of the IMC program including (but not limited to) advertising, sales promotions, digital marketing, public relations, and more. As you have seen, a number of measures may be used across these media, while each also has its own specific metrics for determining effectiveness. The logic is simple; managers want to know how each of these contributes to the specific objectives sought, in part, to determine how much of the budget should be allocated to that medium and whether its use should be continued or discontinued and to what degree. At the same time, we have discussed throughout the text the value of pursuing an integrated marketing communications approach as specific tools are often better than others for accomplishing specific objectives, and more importantly, they do not contribute to the program in isolation (often referred to as silos) but act synergistically with each other. In other words, "the whole is greater than the sum of its parts!" While most marketers agree with this integrated effect, many continue to measure the

effectiveness of their media strategies individually, primarily because it has been so difficult to measure the combined effects of all.

In reading this chapter you have seen a variety of measures offered by a number of companies designed to measure the effectiveness of specific program elements. While all of the measures discussed here still exist and are still relevant, the fact is the advertising world is changing and some may be used much less often than in the past. These tests were designed for a different time and a different media landscape. Take print media as an example. In this chapter we described the Starch Test methodology. The introduction of this test was in the 1920s—over 100 years ago! Advertising in newspapers and magazines has been replaced to a large extent by online ads. The heyday of the (Burke) day-after recall tests of television commercials was in the 1950s—but they are still in use, and still important, today. The increase in advertising budgets allocated to digital continues, but other ways to deliver the ad message, for example, outdoor, product placements, direct marketing, are still effective. But there was no method designed directly to measure the individual contribution in an IMC program.

In an article published in *the Harvard Business Review*, author Wes Nichols notes that marketers were aware of the need to measure the contribution of various media, using mixed-media modeling, surveys, focus groups, scanner data, and other research tools in this effort, but were still treating media contributions individually and not really getting at the combined contribution. Nichols contends that all of this changed in the 1990s with the growth of the Internet. He describes an excellent example of a scenario in which a person interested in purchasing a car does a search for sedans on a mobile device, and a paid pop-up ad appears. They then go to a *Car and Driver* website to read reviews, then watch a YouTube video where they see a Super Bowl ad from a few months back, see a billboard on the way to work, then later receive a direct mail piece offering a sales promotion. They then visit a showroom and talk to a salesperson. This hypothetical scenario provides an excellent example of potential media exposures and the necessity of measuring both the individual contribution of each exposure as well as the combined effects. Nichols

notes that as a result of Web 2.0 analytics, it is now possible to do exactly that through (1) *attribution* (the process of analyzing the contribution of each advertising element); (2) *optimization* (using predictive analytics to run planning scenarios); and (3) *allocation* (distributing resources across marketing activities to optimize scenarios).

Since the Nichols *HBR* article, numerous other articles on what has now become labeled "advertising attribution" have surfaced in the literature from academics as well as companies describing various models. In addition, a multitude of companies now offer their services, just like the providers that have traditionally been available, all of them now competing to offer companies the ability to measure how integrated marketing communications is working.

So are we finally moving out of the silos? It looks promising, but only time will tell.

Sources: Wes Nichols, "Advertising Analytics 2.0," *Harvard Business Review,* March 2013, pp. 60–68; Areg Vardanyan, "6 Types of Attribution Models That Marketers Should Know," *Hire Digital,* June 17, 2022, www.hiredigital.com; Katie Holmes, "What Is Advertising Attribution? A Guide to Attribution Models, Common Pitfalls and Tools," *Ruler,* October 23, 2020, www.ruleranalytics.com.

Practitioners obviously agree, as can be seen in Figure 18-18. Both agencies and brand managers consider cross-channel factors, determining the specific ROI of media, and cross-channel attribution as some of the most important factors in being able to measure effectiveness.

FIGURE 18-18

Factors in Effective Ad Measurement

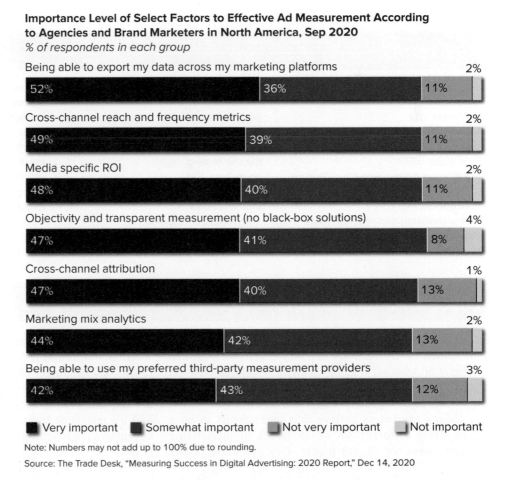

Importance Level of Select Factors to Effective Ad Measurement According to Agencies and Brand Marketers in North America, Sep 2020
% of respondents in each group

Being able to export my data across my marketing platforms — 2%
52% | 36% | 11%

Cross-channel reach and frequency metrics — 2%
49% | 39% | 11%

Media specific ROI — 2%
48% | 40% | 11%

Objectivity and transparent measurement (no black-box solutions) — 4%
47% | 41% | 8%

Cross-channel attribution — 1%
47% | 40% | 13%

Marketing mix analytics — 2%
44% | 42% | 13%

Being able to use my preferred third-party measurement providers — 3%
42% | 43% | 12%

■ Very important ■ Somewhat important ■ Not very important □ Not important

Note: Numbers may not add up to 100% due to rounding.

Source: The Trade Desk, "Measuring Success in Digital Advertising: 2020 Report," Dec 14, 2020

Despite these efforts, it appears we still have a long way to go to determine the overall effectiveness of an IMC program. All the advertising effectiveness measures discussed here have their inherent strengths and weaknesses. They offer the advertiser some information that may be useful in evaluating the effectiveness of promotional efforts. While not all promotional efforts can be evaluated effectively, progress is being made.

Summary

This chapter introduced you to issues involved in measuring the effects of advertising and promotions. These issues include reasons for testing, reasons companies do not test, and the review and evaluation of various research methodologies. We arrived at a number of conclusions: (1) Advertising research to measure effectiveness is important to the promotional program, (2) not enough companies test their ads, and (3) problems exist with current research methodologies. In addition, we reviewed the criteria for sound research and suggested some ways to accomplish effective studies.

All marketing managers should want to know how well their promotional programs are working. This information is critical to planning for the next period, since program adjustments and/or maintenance are based on evaluation of current strategies. Problems often result when the measures taken to determine such effects are inaccurate or improperly used.

This chapter demonstrated that testing must meet a number of criteria (defined by PACT and Making Measurement Make Sense) to be successful. These evaluations should occur both before and after the campaigns are implemented.

A variety of research methods were discussed, many provided by syndicated research firms such as Ipsos-ASI, MSW•ARS, Kantar, and the Nielsen Co. All of these companies have expanded their service offerings to assist in the evaluation of online and other advertising platforms. Many companies have developed their own testing systems. There has been an increase in testing through the Internet.

It is important to recognize that different measures of effectiveness may lead to different results. Depending on the criteria used, one measure may show that an ad or promotion is effective while another states that it is not. This is why clearly defined objectives and the use of multiple measures are critical to determining the true effects of an IMC program.

Key Terms

vehicle option source effect 610
pretests 611
posttests 611
laboratory tests 612
testing bias 612
field tests 613
Positioning Advertising Copy Testing
   (PACT) 613
concept testing 614
comprehension and reaction tests 616
consumer juries 616

halo effect 617
A/B testing 617
portfolio tests 618
mock magazine test 619
Flesch formula 619
theater testing 620
on-air test 621
recall 621
pupillometrics 622
electrodermal response
   (EDR) 622

eye tracking 622
electroencephalographic (EEG)
   measures 623
alpha activity 623
hemispheric lateralization 623
inquiry tests 624
split-run tests 624
recognition method 625
recall tests 626
tracking studies 629
advertising attribution 636

Discussion Questions

1. The chapter noted that many practitioners today focus their determination of an ad's effectiveness almost entirely on whether it achieves attention. Based on what you have learned throughout this text, explain why this is not likely to be a good strategy. (LO 18-3)
2. Many marketers believe that there needs to be a completely different set of measures of advertising effectiveness for digital media. Discuss some of the measures of effectiveness used in the digital domain and whether traditional measures such as those described in this chapter might also be used in the digital world. (LO 18-4)
3. Explain what is meant by "advertising attribution" and it's relevance to measuring ad effectiveness. What advantages are potentially accrued by using this method? (LO 18-2)

4. Explain why it is important to pretest ads. Why do many advertisers not do so? (LO 18-1)

5. Explain what factors should be tested when measuring advertising effectiveness. Also describe some of the dependent measures that should be considered in this process. Do you think advertisers test each of these measures and employ various dependent measures? (LO 18-4)

6. Describe the measures used to determine the effectiveness of sponsorships. Why is it important to attempt to measure sponsorship effectiveness? (LO 18-2)

7. In the decision sequence model presented in Chapter 1, the final stage is measuring effectiveness of the IMC program to provide feedback. This feedback is critical to the future planning process. Yet research shows that many companies do not conduct effectiveness research. Explain why they do not and why it is important that they do. (LO 18-1)

8. Creatives have long argued that measuring the effectiveness of their ads would stifle the creative process and lead to less creativity and more objective-seeking ads. The outstanding creative ads of the past would no longer be part of the future, they say. Some recent articles have contended that the ads of today are not creative and tend to copy each other. Take a side on this position, and cite examples to support it. (LO 18-1)

9. A/B testing has been used by marketers for decades to evaluate two different versions of finished ads and/or web pages. Some experts now believe that A/B testing would be more effective if employed earlier in the campaign development process. Explain what they mean by this, and argue for or against this position. (LO 18-1)

10. This chapter discussed the Ogilvy Awards. Describe what these awards are and how they have changed over time. Give examples of companies that have won these awards (you can find past winners online) and why they have won them. (LO 18-1)

19 International Advertising and Promotion

COME AND SAY G'day

Tourism Australia

Learning Objectives

LO19-1 | Describe the role and importance of international marketing and promotion.

LO19-2 | Discuss how economic, cultural, legal, and other factors in the international environment affect advertising and promotional decisions.

LO19-3 | Compare global versus localized advertising and promotion.

LO19-4 | Discuss the decision areas of international advertising.

LO19-5 | Describe the role of other elements of the promotional mix in the international IMC program.

Australia Invites Tourists to "Come and Say G'day"

Tourism is a major component of Australia's economy, which relies heavily on visitors from other countries to come and spend time in the land down under. To promote tourism the Australian government created Tourism Australia (TA), which is a government agency responsible for attracting international visitors to the country, both for leisure and business events. TA was created in 2004 for the purpose of growing demand and fostering a competitive and sustainable tourism industry. The vision of the agency is to make Australia the most desirable and memorable destination in the world by showcasing the diversity of places to visit and the experiences available across the country.

Australia has become a popular tourist destination, and prior to the COVID-19 pandemic it welcomed 9.5 million international visitors in 2019 who spent an estimated $45 billion. However, the country was closed to visitors for nearly 2 years during the pandemic, and finally reopened its borders in early 2022 to people from anywhere in the world as long as they were vaccinated. As Australia, and most other countries, reopened, the tourism and hospitality industry was still limping back into shape, challenged by widespread staff shortages, a lack of airline flights that was pushing up airfares, rising inflation, and a general reluctance of people still risk-averse from the pandemic to invest the time and money to travel to long-haul destinations such as Australia.

Facing these challenges, Tourism Australia recognized that it needed to let the world know that its doors were open again and to lure visitors to Australia, particularly big-spending travelers who stay longer, spend more money, and would value the country's unique offerings. However, the agency knew that the post-COVID-19 travel market was more competitive than ever with many destinations all fighting for the same slightly smaller pool of high-yielding travelers. Thus, it was important to create an advertising campaign that would stand out in a sea of sameness, advertising in the tourism industry often being laden with clichés and similar claims of great scenery, attractions, beaches, food, and nightlife.

To help rebuild its tourism industry, in late 2022 Tourism Australia launched its first global advertising campaign in 6 years. The campaign is called "Come and Say G'day" and features a 9-minute live action film that introduces Ruby, a CGI animated kangaroo who is the brand ambassador for the campaign. Ruby's voice is done by Australian actor Rose Bryne who is Tourism Australia's Global Ambassador and also makes an appearance in the film. During the film, Ruby is shown languishing in a souvenir shop, dreaming of travel until she finds herself on an adventure around Australia's most famous destinations—including the Sydney Opera House, Uluru-Kata Tjuta National Park, and the Great Barrier Reef—accompanied by her new sidekick Louie, a magical unicorn. To make it unmistakably Australian in flavor, the campaign includes a remake of the iconic song "Down Under" by Men at Work and the return of the "Come and Say G'day" slogan made famous by actor Paul Hogan during the 1980s in the *Crocodile Dundee* film series.

Tourism Australia and its agency, M&C Saatchi, viewed the short film as a way to provide mass reach and awareness to cut through the highly competitive and cluttered landscape of destination marketing. The goal of the film was to get the world, and the media, to take notice and talk about, write about, and share the campaign and put Australia in the consideration set of international travelers globally. The integrated campaign also includes television commercials (in 15-, 30-, and 60-second versions), print, and high-impact, out-of-home advertising placements, as well as social, digital, and content marketing initiatives. Tourism Australia has partnered with international airlines, state tourism organizations, and key distribution partners and travel agents around the world.

The focus on big-spending tourists is not a new strategy for Tourism Australia, which has run several campaigns targeting this market in various countries including the United States, China, Europe, and Southeast Asia. For example, to attract tourists from the United States, the agency created the popular Dundee campaign a few years ago, which launched with a commercial during the Super Bowl. The spot featured actor Paul Hogan in what appeared to be an official film trailer for a new *Crocodile Dundee* movie but then transformed into a commercial promoting Australia and its attractions.

continued

Tourism Australia is hoping the "Come and Say G'day" campaign will stand out on the global stage. It is seen as a critical part of the agency's efforts to rebuild its visitor economy and tourism industry. The global campaign developed around the famous Aussie greeting will hopefully serve as an invitation to come and experience all that Australia has to offer that will be accepted by tourists from around the world.

Sources: Danielle Long, "Can Ruby the Roo Drive Big-spending Travelers Downunder? Tourism Australia Thinks It Can," *The Drum*, October 26, 2022, https://www.thedrum.com/news/2022/10/26/can-ruby-the-roo-drive-big-spending-travellers-downunder-tourism-australia-thinks-it; Michele Hermann, "Tourism Australia Introduces 'Come and Say G'day' Global Campaign," *Forbes*, October 22, 2022, https://www.forbes.com/sites/micheleherrmann/2022/10/22/tourism-australia-introduces-new-come-and-say-gday-global-tourism-campaign/?sh=51f8707d74ef; "Come and Say G'day," Tourism Australia, https://www.tourism.australia.com/en/resources/campaign-resources/come-and-say-gday.html.

The primary focus of this book so far has been on integrated marketing communications programs for products and services sold in the U.S. market. Many American companies have traditionally devoted most of their marketing efforts to the domestic market, since they often lack the resources, skills, or incentives to go abroad. This is changing rapidly, however, as U.S. corporations recognize the opportunities that foreign markets offer for new sources of sales and profits as well as the need to market their products internationally. Many companies are striving to develop global brands that can be advertised and promoted the world over.

In this chapter, we look at international advertising and promotion and the various issues marketers must consider in communicating with consumers around the globe. We examine the environment of international marketing and how companies often must adapt their promotional programs to conditions in each country. We review the debate over whether a company should use a global marketing and advertising approach or tailor it specifically for various countries.

We also examine how firms organize for international advertising, select agencies, and consider various decision areas such as creative strategy and media selection. While the focus of this chapter is on international advertising, we also consider other promotional-mix elements in international marketing, including sales promotion, publicity/public relations, and digital and social media. Let's begin by discussing some of the reasons international marketing has become so important to companies.

THE IMPORTANCE OF INTERNATIONAL MARKETS

One of the major developments in the business world over the past several decades has been the globalization of markets. The emergence of a largely borderless world has created a new reality for all types of companies. Today, world trade is driven by global competition among global companies for global consumers.[1] With the development of faster communication, transportation, and financial transactions, time and distance are no longer barriers to global marketing. Products and services developed in one country quickly make their way to other countries, where they are finding enthusiastic acceptance. Consumers around the world wear Nike shoes and apparel and Levi's jeans; eat at McDonald's; shave with Gillette razors; use Dell and Lenovo computers as well as Apple, Samsung, and Huawei smartphones; drink Coca-Cola and Pepsi Cola soft drinks and Starbucks coffee; and drive cars made by global automakers such as Ford, Hyundai, Honda, General Motors, Toyota, BMW, and Volkswagen.[2]

Companies are focusing on international markets for a number of reasons. Many companies in the United States and Western Europe recognize that their domestic markets offer them limited opportunities for expansion because of slow population growth, saturated markets, intense competition, and/or an unfavorable marketing environment. For example, soft-drink consumption in the United States has been declining over the past decade as consumers turn to healthier beverages such as juices, teas, and fortified waters. The industry has also been under pressure from public health groups and regulatory agencies in both the United States and the European Union because of concerns over the consumption of sugared soft drinks and childhood obesity.[3] Thus companies like PepsiCo and Coca-Cola are looking to international markets in Asia, Africa, and Latin America for growth opportunities.[4]

Many companies must focus on foreign markets to survive. As discussed in the chapter opener, Australia's tourism industry is a major part of its economy and relies heavily on visitors from other countries. Most European nations are relatively small and without foreign markets would not have the economies of scale to compete against larger U.S. and Japanese companies. For example, Swiss-based Nestlé and London-based Unilever are two of the world's largest consumer-product companies because they have learned how to market their brands to consumers in countries around the world. Nestlé is a world-renowned manufacturer of consumer packaged goods and markets several thousand products and brands in nearly 200 countries. Its product portfolio includes well-known global brands such as KitKat, Nescafé, Perrier, Lean Cuisine, Häagen-Dazs, Nespresso, and Milo. Nestlé uses global advertising campaigns for many of its well-known products but also adapts its advertising to local markets to appeal to tastes and preferences of consumers in various countries. Exhibit 19–1 shows an ad for the company's Nespresso coffee machines and capsules featuring well-known actor George Clooney, who has been its global brand ambassador since 2006. Clooney has recently appeared in print, television, and digital ads as part of Nespresso's "Made With Care" campaign highlighting the threat that climate change is positing to global coffee production.[5]

EXHIBIT 19–1

Switzerland-based Nestlé markets its products and brands such as Nespresso to consumers around the world.

Nestlé Nespresso S.A.

Companies are also pursuing international markets because of the opportunities they offer for growth and profits. The dramatic economic, social, and political changes around the world in recent years have opened markets in China and Eastern Europe. China's joining of the World Trade Organization in 2001 has provided foreign competitors with access to 1.42 billion potential Chinese consumers, and Western marketers are eager to sell them a variety of products and services.[6] The growing markets of the Far East, Latin America, Africa, and other parts of the world present tremendous opportunities to marketers of consumer products and services as well as business-to-business marketers.

Many companies in the United States, as well as in other countries, are pursuing international markets out of economic necessity as they recognize that globalization is revolutionizing the world far more radically and rapidly than did industrial development and technological changes of previous eras. In his influential book *The World Is Flat: A Brief History of the Twenty-First Century*, Thomas L. Friedman discusses how the economic flattening of the earth is being stimulated by technology that is breaking down barriers that historically inhibited and restricted international trade. He notes that companies in the United States can prosper only if they are able to compete in the global marketplace that encompasses the 95 percent of the world's population that lives beyond our borders.[7]

Most major multinational companies have made the world their market and generate much of their sales and profits from abroad. However, international markets are important to small and midsize companies as well as the large multinational corporations. Many of these firms can compete more effectively in foreign markets, where they may face less competition or appeal

Nos momentos difíceis, é com
ele que você pode contar...

Feliz dia do amigo.

WWW.WD-40.COM.BR

EXHIBIT 19-2

The WD-40 Co. gets much of its sales growth from foreign markets such as Latin America.

WD-40 Company

to specific market segments or where products have not yet reached the maturity stage of their life cycle. For example, the WD-40 Co. has saturated the U.S. market with its lubricant product and now gets much of its sales growth from markets in Europe, Asia, Latin America, China, and Australia (Exhibit 19–2).

Another reason it is increasingly important for U.S. companies to adopt an international marketing orientation is that imports are taking a larger and larger share of the domestic market for many products. The United States has been running a continuing **balance-of-trade deficit**; the monetary value of our imports exceeds that of our exports. American companies are realizing that we are shifting from being an isolated, self-sufficient, national economy to being part of an interdependent *global economy*. This means U.S. corporations must defend against foreign inroads into the domestic market as well as learn how to market their products and services to other countries.

While many U.S. companies are becoming more aggressive in their pursuit of international markets, they face stiff competition from large multinational corporations from other countries. Some of the world's most formidable marketers are European companies such as Unilever, Nestlé, Siemens, Philips, and Reckitt Benckiser as well as the various Japanese and South Korean automotive and consumer electronic manufacturers such as Honda, Toyota, Sony, Samsung, Hyundai, and LG.

THE ROLE OF INTERNATIONAL ADVERTISING AND PROMOTION

Advertising and promotion are important parts of the marketing program of firms competing in the global marketplace. An estimated $330 billion was spent on advertising in the United States in 2022, with much of this money being spent by multinational companies headquartered outside this country. Advertising expenditures outside the United States have increased by nearly 70 percent since 1990, reaching over $450 billion in 2022. Global marketers based in the United States, as well as European and Asian countries, increased their worldwide advertising, particularly on digital marketing.[8] Figure 19–1 shows the top 10 companies in terms of worldwide advertising and promotion spending.

In addition, estimates are that another $500 billion is spent on sales promotion efforts targeted at consumers, retailers, and wholesalers around the world. The United States is still the world's major advertising market, accounting for over 40 percent of the nearly $800 billion in worldwide ad expenditures. Nearly 90 percent of the money spent on advertising products and services around the world is concentrated in the United States and Canada along with the industrialized countries of Western Europe and the Pacific Rim, including Japan, South Korea, and Australia. However, advertising spending is increasing rapidly in markets outside North America, Europe, and Japan such as India, China, and Brazil.[9]

More and more companies recognize that an effective promotional program is important for companies competing in foreign markets. As one international marketing scholar notes:

> Promotion is the most visible as well as the most culture bound of the firm's marketing functions. Marketing includes the whole collection of activities the firm performs in relating to its market, but in other functions the firm relates to the market in a quieter, more passive way. With the promotional function, however, the firm is standing up and speaking out, wanting to be seen and heard.[10]

Many companies have run into difficulties developing and implementing advertising and promotion programs for international markets. Companies that promote their products or services abroad face an unfamiliar marketing environment and customers with different sets of values, customs, consumption patterns, and habits, as well as differing purchase motives and abilities. Languages vary from country to country and even within a country, such as in India, Canada, or Switzerland. Media options are

FIGURE 19–1
Top 10 Companies by
Worldwide Advertising
Spending

	Advertising and Promotion Spending (billions US Dollars)		
		Worldwide	
Rank	Advertiser	Headquarters	Ad Spending
1.	Amazon	United States	$16.9
2.	Alibaba Group Holding	China	14.2
3.	L'Oreal	France	12.5
4.	Procter & Gamble Co.	United States	11.1
5.	Samsung Electronics	South Korea	10.1
6.	LVMH Moët Hennessy Louis Vuitton	France	8.6
7.	Unilever	United Kingdom	8.1
8.	Nestlé	Switzerland	8.0
9.	Alphabet (Google)	United States	7.9
10.	Comcast Corp.	United States	7.7

Source: "World's Largest Advertisers 2022" *Advertising Age*, December 5, 2022, www.adage.com/WLA2022topline.

quite limited in many countries, owing to lack of availability or limited effectiveness. These factors demand different creative and media strategies as well as changes in other elements of the advertising and promotional program for foreign markets.

THE INTERNATIONAL ENVIRONMENT

Just as with domestic marketing, companies engaging in international marketing must carefully analyze the major environmental factors of each market in which they compete, including economic, demographic, cultural, and political/legal variables. Figure 19-2 shows some of the factors marketers must consider in each category when analyzing the environment of each country or market. These factors are important in evaluating the potential of each country as well as designing and implementing a marketing and promotional program.

The Economic Environment

A country's economic conditions indicate its present and future potential for consuming, since products and services can be sold only to countries where there is enough income to buy them. This is generally not a problem in developed countries such as the United States, Canada, Japan, and most of Western Europe, where consumers generally have higher incomes and standards of living. Thus, they can and want to purchase a variety of products and services. Developed countries have the **economic infrastructure** in terms of the communications, transportation, financial, and distribution networks needed to conduct business in these markets effectively. By contrast, many developing countries lack purchasing power and have limited communications networks available to firms that want to promote their products or services to these markets.

For most companies, industrialized nations represent the greatest marketing and advertising opportunities. But most of these countries have stable population bases, and their markets for many products and services are already saturated. Many marketers are turning their attention to parts of the world whose economies and consumer markets

FIGURE 19-2

Forces in the International
Marketing Environment

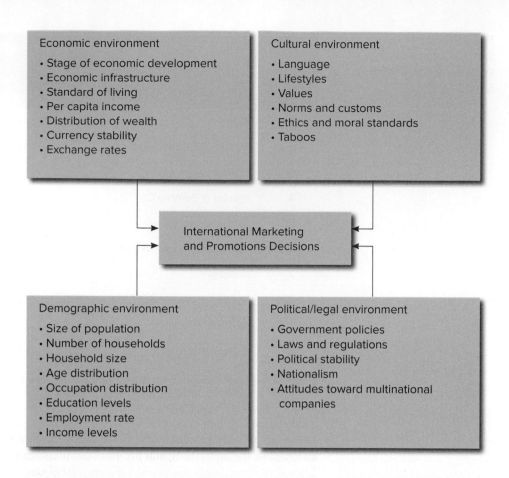

are growing. An important factor that many companies are using to assess various international markets is the growth of the consumer class, which is defined as a group of people who spend more than $11 per day as measured in purchasing power parity (PPP) terms. Asian countries are expected to exhibit the biggest growth of the consumer class among the world's 30 largest consumer markets.[11] Currently 55 percent of the global consumer class live in Asia, especially in the world's two largest consumer markets, India and China. However, other Asian countries such as Indonesia are also experiencing strong growth. By the end of the decade, nearly 76 million Indonesians will join the consumer class, making the country the fourth-largest consumer market in the world behind China, India, and the United States.

China and India in particular are two countries that are transforming the global economy. The two countries together account for a third of the world's population and both had economic (GDP) growth rates of 6 to 7 percent prior to the recent COVID-19 pandemic, much higher than other countries around the world. China's GDP growth slowed considerably from 2020 to 2022 as the Chinese government imposed a zero-COVID-19 policy that locked down most businesses and restricted consumers from traveling, shopping, and going to bars and restaurants. China's GDP growth was estimated at just 3 percent in 2022 but is expected to recover as COVID-19 restrictions are lifted.[12] India's economy has remained strong and has grown from the eleventh largest in the world to fifth, overtaking the United Kingdom. Both China and India have the fundamentals to sustain high growth rates, including large numbers of younger consumers, high savings rates, and a growing middle class of consumers who have the ability as well as the desire to purchase many products and services.[13]

Marketers of products such as mobile phones, TVs, personal computers, cars, as well as luxury items such as jewelry and designer clothing are focusing more attention on consumers in India and China.[14] The growing middle class in these countries is also creating growth opportunities for marketers of consumer packaged-goods products, who are focusing a great deal of attention and spending more on advertising to reach these consumers. For example, China has become Nike's second-largest market,

EXHIBIT 19–3

Nike targets women in China, encouraging them to break boundaries. China is Nike's second-largest market.

Nike, Inc.

and the company is spending large amounts of money there on media advertising, promotions, events, and sponsorship of sports teams and athletes. In 2019, Nike launched a campaign in China encouraging women to break boundaries and challenge stereotypes that features several prominent female athletes, including two-time tennis Grand Slam champion Li Na, Chinese women's national basketball captain Shao Ling, and high jumper Cecila Yeung (Exhibit 19–3). Nike also became the exclusive official apparel and footwear sponsor of esports *League of Legends* Pro League in China and provides clothes and shoes for the 16 competitive video gaming teams in the league, as well as developing training programs customized for esports athletes.[15] Video games are very popular in China as are esports, and *League of Legends* is a very popular multiplayer online video game. China has become the second-largest advertising market in the world, trailing only the United States, with Japan coming in third with expenditures estimated at $90 billion each year.

Many multinational companies are also turning their attention to other emerging markets such as Vietnam, the Philippines, and Bangladesh, which are some of the fastest-growing economies because they have become manufacturing hubs with the migration of manufacturing away from China. Sub-Saharan African nations such as Nigeria and Kenya are also experiencing economic growth but are still underdeveloped, particularly in rural areas.[16]

Many multinational companies have also been focusing their attention on the 4 billion consumers who live in the remote, rural communities of developing countries where consumer markets are slowly emerging. Packaged-goods companies such as Procter & Gamble and Unilever sell soap, toothpaste, shampoo, and laundry detergents to consumers in remote villages. Often they adapt their products for these markets by making them available in single-use sachets that cost the equivalent of pennies rather than dollars and can be easily distributed and sold through the small kiosks found in rural villages. Many developing countries are becoming more stable and open to trade and direct foreign investment, while education levels are also improving. Although investment in these markets still requires a long-term perspective, many companies are recognizing that the billions of people in developing countries are eager to become consumers and represent a major growth opportunity.

The Demographic Environment

Major demographic differences exist among countries as well as within them. Marketers must consider income levels and distribution, age and occupation distributions of the population, household size, education, and employment rates. In some countries, literacy rates are also a factor; people who cannot read will not respond well to print ads. Demographic data can provide insight into the living standards and lifestyles in a particular country to help companies plan ad campaigns.

Demographic information can reveal the market potential of various foreign markets. India's population reached 1.43 billion in 2023, surpassing China's 1.42 billion and making it the world's most populous country. Latin America remains one of the world's largest potential markets, although the meager income of most consumers in the region is still a problem. Brazil, the largest consumer market in South America, now has a population of 216 million, although recent political and economic problems are impacting the country and consumer spending.[17] Many European countries as well as the United States, Canada, Japan, and China are experiencing low or even negative population growth and an aging consumer base, which is leading many companies to look to other parts of the world for growth. For example, the average age in India in 2022 was 29, as compared to 38 in China and the United States, and 49 in Japan.

More than 50 percent of the Latin American market is younger than age 30; children are the fastest-growing demographic group in the region. These numbers have caught the attention of international advertisers such as Mattel, PepsiCo, Coca-Cola, Burger King, McDonald's, and others. Indonesia also has a very young population, with more people under the age of 16 than the United States, and they are very receptive to Western ways and products.

The Cultural Environment

Another important aspect of the international marketing environment is the culture of each country. Cultural variables that marketers must consider include language, customs, tastes, attitudes, lifestyles, values, and ethical/moral standards. Nearly every country exhibits cultural traits that influence not just the needs and wants of consumers but how they go about satisfying them.

Marketers must be sensitive not only in determining what products and services they can sell foreign cultures but also in communicating with them. Advertising is often the most effective way to communicate with potential buyers and create markets in other countries. But it can also be one of the most difficult aspects of the international marketing program because of problems in developing messages that will be understood in various countries.

International advertisers often have problems with language. The advertiser must know not only the native tongue of the country but also its nuances, idioms, and subtleties. International marketers must be aware of the connotations of words and symbols used in their messages and understand how advertising copy and slogans are translated. Marketers often encounter problems in translating their advertising messages and brand names into various languages. The ad for TaylorMade Burner Irons golf clubs shown in Exhibit 19–4 is one example. In the United States and other English-speaking countries, the tagline the advertising used is "The Set Is Dead." However, in Asian countries such as Japan and Korea, the word *dead* in the tagline did not translate well so it was changed to "The Set Is History," which made the meaning of the phrase easier to understand.

When the Colgate-Palmolive Co. launched its Colgate MaxFresh toothpaste brand in China, the company found that the brand name did not translate well, which led to it being changed to Icy Fresh. Colgate also had to change the description of the dissolvable mini breath strips that were part of the formulation of the product to cooling crystals since the concept of breath strips had no relevance to Chinese consumers.

Problems arising from language diversity and differences in signs and symbols that are used in marketing communications can usually be best solved with the help of local expertise. Marketers should consult local employees or use an ad agency knowledgeable in the local language that can help verify that the advertiser is saying what it wants to say. Many companies turn to agencies that specialize in translating advertising slogans and copy into foreign languages.[18]

Tastes, traditions, and customs are also an important part of cultural considerations. The customs of a society affect what products and services it will buy and how they must be marketed. In France, cosmetics are used heavily by men as well as women, and advertising to the male market is common. There are also cultural differences in the grooming and hygiene habits of consumers in various countries. For example, many consumers in the United States shower or bathe and use products such as mouthwash, body sprays, and deodorant daily. However consumers in many other Western countries have different ideas regarding the frequency of use of personal hygiene products, so consumption of these items is much lower than in the United States.

EXHIBIT 19–4

The tagline used in this TaylorMade ad had to be changed for Asian countries because of translation problems.

TaylorMade Golf Company, Inc.

Another aspect of culture that is very important for international marketers to understand is values. **Cultural values** are beliefs and goals shared by members of a society regarding ideal end states of life and modes of conduct. Society shapes consumers' basic values, which affect their behavior and determine how they respond to various situations. For example, cultural values in the United States place a major emphasis on individual activity and initiative, while many Asian societies stress cooperation and conformity to the group. Values and beliefs of a society can also affect its members' attitudes and receptivity toward foreign products and services.[19] Values such as *ethnocentrism*, which refers to the tendency for individuals to view their own group or society as the center of the universe, or nationalism often affect the way consumers in various countries respond to foreign brands or even advertising messages.[20] For many years, consumers in many European countries were reluctant to buy American brands, and there was even a backlash against American imagery. In fact, many U.S. companies doing business in Europe were careful not to flaunt their American roots.

In recent years, U.S. brands have become popular in many European countries as well as in other parts of the world. Marketers attribute the rising popularity of many U.S.-made products to the worldwide distribution of American music, films, and TV shows; the growth of the Internet; and the increase in travel to the United States. These factors have made consumers in foreign countries more familiar with American culture, values, and lifestyle. American brands have become increasingly popular among younger Europeans who follow American pop culture, want to work for American companies, and have even adopted holidays such as Halloween and rituals such as high school proms. A survey conducted in 2022 of gen Z and millennials in the United Kingdom, France, Germany, Italy, and Spain found that young Europeans' "top brands" lists are full of, and even topped by, popular brands from the United States, indicating their affinity for American brands. Nike and Apple top the list of young Europeans' favorite brands while other favorites include Ford, Levi's, Coca-Cola, Tesla, Amazon, and Starbucks.[21]

Attitudes toward American brands are shifting in some countries such as China, where consumers are putting less of a premium on foreign brands. The idea of **guochao**, which refers to the increase in favoritism toward Chinese brands, design, and culture, is being embraced by many consumers in China, increasing support for products made in the country. This is resulting in greater preference for Chinese brands in many product categories such as smartphones, consumer electronics, beauty, and automotive.[22]

Japan is one of the more difficult markets for many marketers to understand because of its unique values and customs.[23] For example, the Japanese have a very strong commitment to the group; social interdependence and collectivism are as important to them as individualism is to most Americans. Ads stressing individuality and nonconformity have traditionally not done well in Japan, but Westernized values have become more prevalent in Japanese advertising. However, the Japanese dislike ads that confront or disparage the competition and tend to prefer soft rather than hard sells.[24] A study found that Japanese and American magazine ads tend to portray teenage girls in different ways and that the differences correspond to each country's central concepts of self and society. In many American ads teens are associated with images of independence, rebelliousness, determination, and even defiance that are consistent with the American value of individuality. In contrast, Japanese ads tend to portray a happy, playful, childlike, girlish image that is consistent with the Japanese culture's sense of self, which is more dependent on others.[25] A study of the impact of the "Lost Decade," which refers to the period of economic stagnation and uncertainty that occurred during the 1990s and into the new millennium, on Japanese advertising resulted in a shift toward the use of more direct and persuasive selling approaches, but being too blatantly direct could still be problematic.[26]

As advertisers turn their attention to China, more consideration is also being given to understanding the cultural system and values of the world's most populous country. Chinese values are centered on Confucianism, which stresses loyalty and interpersonal relationships. Chinese culture also emphasizes passive acceptance of fate by seeking harmony with nature; inner experiences of meaning and feeling; stability and harmony; close family ties; and tradition.[27]

Nike ran into a problem over a commercial that aired in China showing NBA basketball star LeBron James winning a battle with a Chinese dragon and a kung fu master. The commercial was banned by government regulators who stated that it created indignant feelings among Chinese television viewers because it showed an American sports icon defeating the dragon, a symbol of Chinese culture, and the martial arts master, a symbol of national pride. A statement posted on the website of China's State Administration for Radio, Film, and Television stated that the ad violated the regulation that "all advertisements must uphold national dignity and interest, and respect the motherland's culture." Nike's China marketing director said that it was not the company's intention to show disrespect to the Chinese culture, explaining that the ad was meant to inspire youth to overcome internal fear and obstacles in order to improve themselves. Toyota Motor Co. of Japan also had to retract an ad and issue an apology for an ad that ran in magazines and newspapers in China depicting stone lions, a traditional sign of Chinese power, saluting and bowing to a Prado Land Cruiser sport-utility vehicle.[28] A study examined perceptions of offensive advertising among Chinese consumers living in Hong Kong and Shanghai. The study found that the central issue related to whether an ad was perceived as offensive by the type of execution and creative tactics used or by the offensiveness of the product or service being advertised. The researchers noted that despite the sophistication and modernization of these two major cities, consumers there remain conservative and, to some extent collectivist, as susceptibility to interpersonal influence affects this evaluation of offensive advertising. They recommended that marketers remain cautious when developing advertising for China and should not take too many risks with offensive advertising.[29]

Religion is another aspect of culture that affects norms, values, and behaviors and can have a strong influence on advertising in certain countries and regions. For example, in many Arab countries, religion has a major influence on cultural values and must be taken into consideration in developing advertising messages. Marketers must be aware of various taboos resulting from conservative applications of the Islamic religion. Alcohol and pork cannot be advertised in some countries. Human nudity is forbidden, as are pictures of anything sacred, such as images of a cross or photographs of Mecca. There are also strict guidelines regarding the use of women in advertising and the various roles to which they can be assigned. Women often do not appear in advertising and when they do only their eyes may be shown.

Marketers sometimes find creative ways to get around these restrictions. For example, when Saudi Arabia announced that it was lifting its ban on allowing women to drive in 2017, marketers began running advertising targeting the new female audience. In a clever ad posted on social media, Ford found a way to celebrate Saudi women's new sense of freedom in a way that was still respectful of the culture. Instead of showing the woman's face, the image focuses only on the eyes, with the blacked out background creating the illusion of a woman wearing a nijab, which is a veil for the face that leaves the area around the eyes clear (Exhibit 19-5). In conservative Islamic countries, many religious authorities are opposed to advertising on the grounds that it promotes Western icons and culture and the associated non-Islamic consumerism. Restrictions on advertising still exist in some countries such as Iran, which has particularly averse feelings toward Western-style advertising. However, Western-style ads have become more prevalent in many Middle Eastern countries such as Qatar, the United Arab Emirates, and Lebanon. Turkey is an interesting country from an advertising perspective as it is a member of the European Union but its Islamic roots are still prevalent, which results in a mix of both liberal European and moderate Islamic cultural values. Turkey has liberal policies regarding the use of female models in advertising but

EXHIBIT 19-5

Ford used this ad on social media to target women in Saudi Arabia that is respectful of the local culture.

Ford Motor Company

Welcome to the driver's seat.

#SaudiWomenMove

#SaudiWomenCanDrive

does not allow anything that goes against their cultural, moral, and religious values. Images, video, and other visual content that is seen as promoting sensuality, as well as homosexuality, are banned.[30]

Both Coca-Cola and PepsiCo have taken their cola wars to the Middle East and have been engaged in a battle to win the soft-drink allegiance of Arabs, especially the youth, in countries such as Lebanon, Saudi Arabia, Egypt, and Qatar. To reach the youth market, the two companies have used a variety of integrated marketing tools including media advertising, sponsorship of sports teams as well as sporting and musical events, and talent shows as well as branded entertainment. Global Perspective 19–1 discusses how the country of Qatar hosted the 2022 FIFA World Cup and the role IMC played in helping the Arab country secure the bid to host this popular sports event.

Global Perspective 19–1 >>>

Qatar Delivers "Amazing" as Host of the FIFA World Cup

The Fédération Internationale de Football Association (FIFA) World Cup is the largest single-event sporting competition in the world. The tournament is held every 4 years and is FIFA's flagship event, involving the national soccer (or football, as it is referred to in most countries) teams from 32 qualifying nations. The FIFA World Cup is also the world's most widely viewed sporting event. More than 3 billion people worldwide tune in to the month-long tournament on television, and over 3 million spectators usually attend the 64 matches played.

One of the goals of FIFA in awarding hosting rights is to promote football (soccer) around the globe, as well as in the host nation and region. The 2010 FIFA World Cup was played in South Africa, the 2014 tournament was held in Brazil, Russia hosted the event in 2018, and in 2026 the tournament will be jointly hosted by 16 cities in three North American countries: Canada, Mexico, and the United States. In 2022, the small Persian Gulf country of Qatar became the first Middle Eastern and Arab nation to host the prestigious event.

Qatar is the smallest nation, both by population and by area, ever to have hosted the FIFA World Cup; the country is approximately the size of the state of Connecticut and has a population of just under 3 million. Qatar recognized that its size could be perceived as a shortcoming in competing against Australia, Japan, South Korea, and the United States, the four other nations that bid for the right to host the 2022 tournament. Rather than shying away from the issue, Qatar turned its size into a positive by positioning itself as an environmentally and socially friendly host nation for the FIFA World Cup. As an example, the bid detailed how all of the stadiums, as well as nearly 90,000 hotel rooms and other amenities, would be within a 60-kilometer (37.3-mile) radius and easily accessible by public transportation from Doha, Qatar's capital. It also noted how the new, state-of-the-art stadiums would rely on solar power as part of a commitment to host the first ever carbon neutral FIFA World Cup, and use innovative cooling systems to provide maximum comfort for players and fans. The bid also outlined how most of the stadiums would be constructed using modular components, so they could be disassembled after the tournament and donated to developing countries, contributing to the tournament's legacy and leaving Qatar with stadiums suitable for its size.

Qatar's effort to win the right to host the 2022 FIFA World Cup entailed hard work and innovation, as well as an integrated marketing campaign designed to deliver the message of how this small country planned to transform various perceived challenges into unique assets. The process began with a positioning platform built around the tagline "Expect Amazing." The tagline was designed to communicate its intentions and dare people to believe in Qatar and its bid to host the FIFA World Cup. The "Expect Amazing" campaign was officially launched 1 year before FIFA made its decision to award hosting rights, with a TV commercial called "Puzzles." The goal of the spot was to gain global support for the bid by showcasing Qatar as a beautiful and vibrant country that welcomed people of all nations and was capable of hosting the World Cup. In addition, Qatar launched an official bid website that included a blog that allowed football fans to learn what was happening behind the scenes and kept them informed of the latest news so they would feel like partners in the bidding process. Social media, including Facebook, Twitter, and a YouTube channel, were also used to engage fans and supporters and provide another digital platform for what became known as the Qatar 2022 marketing effort.

The next phase of the campaign included a social responsibility initiative called "Generation Amazing." Football tournaments were held for underprivileged children from various countries in the Middle East and Asia, including Nepal, Pakistan, Lebanon, Syria, and Qatar. A select group of participants, chosen based on their football and leadership skills, were taken to South Africa to attend the 2010 FIFA World Cup. A documentary was created to capture the experiences of the children and posted on the Qatar 2022 Bid's YouTube channel to help generate publicity for the cause. Another video, called "Stadiums," was created and posted on YouTube, showcasing several of the stadiums that had been designed to host the football matches. Throughout the campaign, Qatar repeatedly grabbed the spotlight

(continued)

by introducing various legendary soccer players and coaches as ambassadors for its bid.

While Qatar utilized an effective IMC campaign to draw attention to its desire to host the FIFA World Cup, there were a number of other key strategic components to its bid. Qatar repeatedly emphasized the diversity of its population and the country's geographic location as a crossroads between the East and West. The Supreme Committee working on the bid also noted how hosting the FIFA World Cup would be a catalyst for driving growth and economic development by making Qatar a tourism and business destination on par with regional rivals Dubai and Abu Dhabi. They also argued that hosting the World Cup would leave a lasting legacy for Qatar, the Middle East, and beyond.

After being awarded the right to host the 2022 World Cup in 2010, Qatar spent more than a decade building seven new stadiums, 100 new hotels, a new airport, new highways, and a new driverless metro system to prepare for the players, media, and fans. However, in addition to these projects, Qatar had to deal with the fact that it was a very controversial choice to host the World Cup. Many questioned how a small nation of 3 million people and with no soccer pedigree managed to win the secret vote to host the event. Human-rights groups criticized Qatar's treatment of

foreign workers building the stadiums and accommodations, noting many were injured and died while working on the projects due to unsafe labor conditions. Qatar's stance on social issues also was a concern, as homosexuality is illegal in the country, women have limited rights, and alcohol is either banned or very scarce.

Concerns were also raised over holding the tournament during the traditional summertime slot given the intense heat in Qatar, so FIFA moved the 2022 World Cup to November and December. However, this created problems with television networks such as Fox and Telemundo, which paid large sums of money to televise the games and preferred to have them in the summer, so they would not overlap with football season in the United States. The November–December time period also fell in the middle of the European club season, drawing criticism from league officials and a number of teams, as play had to be suspended for more than a month and players had limited time to practice with their national teams.

Qatar addressed some of the controversies it faced by improving labor laws, raising the minimum wage, and creating an insurance fund for families of injured and deceased workers. The country also abolished kafala, a system that binds workers through contract to a sponsor who has full control over wages, accommodation, and immigration status. Qatar assured LGBTQ+ fans they would not face discrimination while attending the World Cup, and alcohol laws were loosened.

During the bidding process, Qatar told the world to "Expect Amazing." The tagline shifted to "Delivering Amazing" as the smallest nation ever to host the FIFA World Cup prepared for the big event. In 2022, Qatar's World Cup was held without any major problems and was won by Argentina. Given the various controversies surrounding Qatar's hosting of the World Cup, opinions will differ as to whether the country was able to truly deliver an amazing event. However, perhaps what is most amazing is that the tiny country persevered and indeed was able to host a successful World Cup.

Sources: Ishaan Tharoor, "The Political Debate Swirling Around the World Cup in Qatar," *The Washington Post*, November 14, 2022, https://www.washingtonpost.com/world/2022/11/14/qatar-world-cup-controversy-boycott-human-rights/; Joshua Robinson, "FIFA to Move 2022 Qatar World Cup to Winter," *The Wall Street Journal*, March 19, 2015, www.wsj.com/articles/fifa-to-move-2022-qatar-world-cup-to-winter-1426786731; Vivienne Walt, "Qatar Takes Over the World," *Fortune*, September 2, 2013, pp. 90–95.

The Political/Legal Environment

The political and legal environment in a country is one of the most important factors influencing the advertising and promotional programs of international marketers. Regulations differ owing to economic and national sovereignty considerations, nationalistic and cultural factors, and the goal of protecting consumers not only from false or misleading advertising but, in some cases, from advertising in general. It is difficult to generalize about advertising regulation at the international level, since some countries are increasing government control of advertising while others are decreasing it. Government regulations and restrictions can affect various aspects of a company's advertising and IMC program, including:

- The types of products that may be advertised.
- The content or creative approach that may be used.
- The media that all advertisers (or different classes of advertisers) are permitted to employ.
- The use of social and digital media.
- The amount of advertising a single advertiser may use in total or in a specific medium.
- The use of foreign languages in ads.
- The use of advertising material prepared outside the country.
- The use of local versus international advertising agencies.
- The specific taxes that may be levied against advertising.

A number of countries ban or restrict the advertising of various products. For example, countries vary in their regulation of alcoholic beverages such as beer, wine, and hard liquor. The United States and United Kingdom have voluntary self-regulation of advertising for alcoholic beverages while Australia and other countries have partial restrictions on the times they can be advertised and the media that can be used as well as the content of the advertising. A number of countries such as Norway, Iceland, and the UAE do not permit the advertising of any alcoholic beverages on television.[31] Cigarette advertising is banned in some or all media in numerous countries besides the United States including Argentina, Canada, France, Italy, Norway, Sweden, and Switzerland. The Australian government limits tobacco advertising to point of purchase. The ban also excludes tobacco companies from sponsoring sporting events.

In 2012 Australia's high court upheld the country's Plain Packaging Act, making it the first country to ban brand logos on all tobacco packages. The law requires tobacco and cigarettes to be sold in plain green packages that feature graphic pictures of the negative health effects of smoking such as blindness; mouth, throat, and lung cancer; and the dangers of secondhand smoke (Exhibit 19–6). The law has been challenged by tobacco companies through the World Trade Organization; they have concerns that it could set a marketing precedent that is adopted by other countries.[32] In Malaysia, a government ban on cigarette-related advertising and sponsorship was initiated in an effort to curb the rising number of smokers in the country.[33] In China, tobacco and liquor advertising are banned except in hotels for foreigners. In Europe there has been a long-standing ban on advertising for prescription-drug products, which is designed to keep government-subsidized health care costs under control. The European Union (EU) has argued that advertising increases the marketing budgets of drug companies and results in higher prices. The ban prevents prescription-drug companies from mentioning their products even on their websites or in brochures, although some relaxation of these restrictions is being considered by the European Commission for drugs used to treat AIDS, diabetes, and respiratory ailments.[34]

The advertising of tobacco and liquor is banned in India, although many companies have tried to get around the ban by using what are known as "surrogate advertisements." Instead of promoting tobacco and liquor products, these TV commercials and print ads market unrelated products that the company also happens to manufacture—such as CDs, playing cards, and bottled water—that carry the same brand name and allow them to build brand awareness. The Indian government has been clamping down on surrogate TV ads in response to complaints by health activists, which is leading marketers to look to other ways to promote their brands such as the branding of sports teams, concerts, and other entertainment events. They are also lobbying the Indian government for more flexibility in enforcing the crackdown such as allowing liquor ads on late-night television programs. Liquor marketers including beer and distilled spirits companies are also using social media to promote their brands as there are no clear rules covering the use of the medium in India.[35]

EXHIBIT 19–6

Australia bans brand logos on tobacco packages and requires graphic images of negative health effects.

Ella Pickover/AP Images

Many countries restrict the media that advertisers can use as well as the extent to which ads can appear in the media. In the EU, legislation limits the commercial time to 12 minutes per hour, and some countries require less frequent but longer advertising breaks that can be as long as 6 minutes. In 1999, the European Commission denied an appeal against Greece's national ban on toy advertising on daytime television. Thus, advertisers can advertise toys on TV only during the evening hours.[36] Some of the most stringent advertising regulations in the world are found in Scandinavian countries. Commercial TV advertising did not begin in Sweden until 1992, and both Sweden and Denmark limit the amount of time available for commercials. Both Sweden and Norway prohibit domestic advertising that targets children as their governments believe that young people are not able to differentiate between advertising and programming and are not capable of understanding the selling intent of commercials.[37] The move by Sweden to ban advertising aimed at children came following deregulation, which saw the country go from having just two state-funded TV channels to numerous commercial channels that show ads to generate revenue. Sweden moved quickly to protect children (and parents) from seeing TV commercials and even lobbied for the ban to be implemented across the EU, albeit unsuccessfully. While the restrictions remain in place in Sweden and other Scandinavian countries, households in these countries receive satellite TV channels containing commercials from the United Kingdom and other countries, which weakens the impact of the ban.[38] Saudi Arabia opened its national TV system to commercial advertising in 1986, but advertising is not permitted on the state-run radio system. Advertising in magazines and newspapers in the country is subject to government and religious restrictions.[39]

Many governments have rules and regulations that affect the advertising message. For example, comparative advertising is legal and widely used in the United States and Canada but is illegal in some countries, such as Korea and Belgium. In Europe, the European Commission has developed a directive to standardize the basic form and content of comparative advertising and develop a uniform policy. In 2012 the EU updated its Directive on Misleading and Comparative Advertising that specifies the conditions under which comparative advertising is permitted and requires marketers to make sure their advertisements are not misleading: compare "like with like"—goods and services meeting the same needs or intended for the same purpose; objectively compare important features of the products or services concerned; do not discredit other companies' trademarks; and do not create confusion among traders.[40] Comparative advertising is used on a limited basis in many EU countries, such as Germany.

Many Asian and South American countries have also begun to accept comparative ads. Brazil's self-regulatory advertising codes were so strict for many years that few advertisers were able to create a comparative message that could be approved. However, comparative advertising has become more common in the country although the comparison must be objective and supported by verifiable data and evidence.[41] Many countries restrict the types of claims advertisers can make, the words they can use, and the way products can be represented in ads. In Greece, specific claims for a product, such as "20 percent fewer calories," are not permitted in an advertising message.[42] Copyright and other legal restrictions make it difficult to maintain the same name from market to market. For example, Diet Coke is known as Coca-Cola Light in Germany, France, and many other countries because of legal restrictions prohibiting the word *diet* (Exhibit 19–7).

China has also begun cracking down on advertising claims as consumer groups slowly become a more powerful force in the country. For years, government regulation of advertising was less stringent than in developed markets and many companies were very aggressive with their advertising claims. However, government officials have begun enforcing a 1995 law that stipulates that statistical claims and quotations "should be true and accurate with sources clearly indicated." The Chinese government launched a crackdown on false and illegal ads with a focus on cosmetic, beauty, health, and pharmaceutical products.[43]

An area that is receiving a great deal of attention in Europe, as well as in the United States, is the marketing and advertising of food products that are considered to contribute to childhood obesity. The European Health Commission has called on advertisers of a variety of food products to set their own regulations to curb the advertising of so-called junk food to the 450 million consumers in the European Union. The commission has also recommended that these companies do not advertise directly to children and has even threatened to ban advertising icons such as Ronald McDonald and Tony the Tiger.[44] Another integrated marketing communications tool that is facing increasing regulatory challenges in many countries is online advertising as many countries are developing restrictions to protect the use of personal information. In 2018, the European Union enacted new General Data Protection Regulations (GDPR) that require organizations to meet stringent data protection requirements for personal data of EU citizens. The new rules also affect companies that are based outside of Europe but market their products and services in the EU.[45] These new regulations are discussed in Chapter 20.

GLOBAL VERSUS LOCALIZED ADVERTISING

The discussion of differences in the marketing environments of various countries suggests that each market is different and requires a distinct marketing and advertising program. However, through the years a great deal of attention has focused on the concept of **global marketing**, where a company uses a common marketing plan for all countries in which it operates, thus selling the product in essentially the same way everywhere in the world. **Global advertising** falls under the umbrella of global marketing as a way to implement this strategy by using the same basic advertising approach in all markets.

The debate over standardization versus localization of marketing and advertising programs began decades ago.[46] But the idea of global marketing was popularized by Professor Theodore Levitt, who says the worldwide marketplace has become homogenized and consumers' basic needs, wants, and expectations transcend geographic, national, and cultural boundaries.[47] More recently, support for the idea of global marketing has come from advocates of global consumer culture theory (GCCT) who argue that the globalization of markets has led to the existence of a global consumer culture in which many consumers share consumption values regardless of the countries in which they reside.[48] An outgrowth of this theory is the concept of global consumer culture positioning, which suggests that the shared consumption-related beliefs, symbols, and behaviors of many consumers across markets create an opportunity to use positioning strategies that transcend cultures. While this does not suggest complete homogenization or globalization of markets to the degree advocated by Levitt, it does suggest an opportunity for marketers to use global branding and positioning and to advertise their products and services in similar ways across markets.[49]

Not everyone agrees with the practicality of global marketing, particularly with respect to advertising. Many argue that products and advertising messages must be designed or at least adapted to meet the differing needs of consumers in different countries.[50] We will consider the arguments for and against global marketing and advertising, as well as situations where it is most appropriate.

Advantages of Global Marketing and Advertising

A global marketing strategy and advertising program offers certain advantages to a company, including the following:

- Economies of scale in production and distribution.
- Lower marketing and advertising costs as a result of reductions in planning and control.
- Lower advertising production costs.
- Abilities to exploit good ideas on a worldwide basis and introduce products quickly into various world markets.
- A consistent international brand and/or company image.
- Simplification of coordination and control of marketing and promotional programs.

EXHIBIT 19–8

Doritos uses global advertising to create a consistent image for the brand in various countries.

Doritos by Frito-Lay North America, Inc.

Advocates of global marketing and advertising contend that standardized products are possible in all countries if marketers emphasize quality, reliability, and low prices. They say people everywhere want to buy the same products and live the same way. Product standardization results in lower design and production costs as well as greater marketing efficiency, which translates into lower prices for consumers. Product standardization and global marketing also enable companies to roll out products faster into world markets, which is becoming increasingly important as product life cycles become shorter and competition increases.

A number of companies including IBM, De Beers, Red Bull, Nike, McDonald's, Coca-Cola, and American Express have successfully used the global advertising approach. Gillette has used the "Best a Man Can Get" as its global advertising theme for over a decade and has launched a number of new razor products including the Sensor, Mach3, and Fusion using a global approach.[51] Gillette uses the same advertising theme in each country and maintains websites and social media pages with similar content and layout, with only language differences.

Frito-Lay began using global advertising in 2013 for several of its snack food brands, including Doritos, which is the world's best-selling tortilla/corn-chip. Prior to launching its first global campaign, Doritos had a different look and feel across the 37 countries where the brand is sold; 25 packaging variations existed and different advertising approaches were used in various markets. Packaging for Doritos was standardized across all markets and the global campaign themed "For the Bold" was developed that included digital and television advertising, promotions on Facebook and Twitter, and sponsorship of concerts. The creative approach used in the campaign included humorous TV and print executions focusing on bold choices made to enjoy Doritos as shown in Exhibit 19–8. Frito-Lay's vice president of marketing explained the move to a global campaign: "With the rise of social media and technology, our world is smaller and more connected than ever before. We have found that our consumers across the world share very similar passions and interests, but until now may not have had a consistent way of speaking about the Doritos brand. The campaign is our way of connecting these fans worldwide, as we now provide a consistent storyline, and look and feel from the Doritos brand."[52]

Problems with Global Advertising

Opponents of the standardized global approach argue that very few products lend themselves to global advertising.[53] Differences in culture, market, and economic development; consumer needs and usage patterns; media availability; and legal restrictions make it extremely difficult to develop an effective universal approach to marketing and advertising. Advertising may be particularly difficult to standardize because of cultural differences in circumstances, language, traditions, values, beliefs, lifestyle, music, and so on. Moreover, some experts argue that cultures around the world are becoming more diverse, not less so. Thus, advertising's job of informing and persuading consumers and moving them toward using a particular brand can be done only within a given culture.

Consumer usage patterns and perceptions of a product may vary from one country to another, so advertisers must adjust their marketing and advertising approaches to different problems they may face in different markets. For example, while eating pizza is viewed as a casual affair in the United States and many other countries, in Japan it is perceived as an upscale meal that is consumed more on special occasions. Since entering the Japanese market in 1985, Domino's Pizza has been focusing on creating more usage occasions such as Valentine's Day and Mother's Day by delivering its pizza in heart-shaped, pink boxes. The company has also used clever promotions such as one where the chain offered 2.5 million yen (about $30,000) for 1 hour's work at a Domino's store. For another popular offbeat promotion, Domino's announced that it was working with

EXHIBIT 19–9

Domino's Pizza used its humorous Moon Branch Project promotion in Japan.

Domino's IP Holder LLC

space agency JAXA (the Japanese equivalent of NASA), Honda, and other high-profile companies to build the first-ever pizza store on the moon.[54] The CEO of Domino's Japan participated in the promotion by appearing in a full spacesuit, customized with a Domino's patch, and displaying a big picture of the Moon Branch Project (Exhibit 19–9).

Many experts believe that marketing a standardized product the same way all over the world can turn off consumers, alienate employees, and blind a company to diversities in customer needs. Multinational companies can also encounter problems when they use global advertising as local managers in countries or regions often resent the home office standardizing the advertising function and mandating the type of advertising to be used in their markets. Sir Martin Sorrell, the former chair of the United Kingdom–based WPP Group, argues that there are limits to global advertising and that the one-size-fits-all pendulum has gone too far. He urges his executives to focus on consumer needs in the countries they serve and advocates the use of country managers to build contacts and adapt campaigns to local markets.[55]

When Is Globalization Appropriate?

While globalization of advertising is viewed by many in the advertising industry as a difficult task, some progress has been made in learning what products and services are best suited to worldwide appeals:[56]

1. Brands or messages that can be adapted for a visual appeal, avoiding the problems of trying to translate words into dozens of languages.
2. Brands that are promoted with image campaigns that play to universal needs, values, and emotions.
3. High-tech products and new products coming to the world for the first time, not steeped in the cultural heritage of a country.
4. Products with nationalistic flavor if the country has a reputation in the field.
5. Products that appeal to a market segment with universally similar tastes, interests, needs, and values.

Many companies and brands in the first category rely on visual appeals that are easily adapted for use in global advertising campaigns. These companies are often marketing products in the second category, such as jewelry, cosmetics, liquor, and cigarettes, that appeal to universal needs, values, and emotions and lend themselves to global campaigns. Marketers recognize that emotions such as joy, sentiment, excitement, and pleasure are universal as are needs/values such as self-esteem, status, and achievement. Thus, it is common for global advertising campaigns to use emotional and image appeals. Global Perspective 19-2 discusses the "Real Magic" global advertising campaign developed recently by the Coca-Cola Company.

Global Perspective 19–2 >>>

Coca-Cola Wants to Create "Real Magic" Around the World

Coca-Cola is one of the most recognizable and valuable brands in the world, consistently ranking at or near the top of various brand value surveys. The flagship soft drink Coca-Cola, or Coke as it often referred to, is the world's number-one soft drink brand and is sold in more than 200 countries around the globe. The iconic brand has been around for more than 130 years and has never strayed from its timeless and basic ideals. While a number of different advertising campaigns have come and gone throughout the years, Coca-Cola has remained consistent in appealing to one

(continued)

The Coca-Cola Company

basic emotion: pleasure. Many of the popular advertising campaigns used to sell Coca-Cola have been built around simple slogans using words such as *smile*, *enjoy*, *feeling*, and *happiness* that translate easily to consumers everywhere.

From 2009 until 2016, Coca-Cola's global advertising used the slogan "Open Happiness," which was designed to appeal to consumers' desire for comfort and optimism and to be an invitation to consumers around the world to refresh themselves with a Coke and enjoy life. The "Open Happiness" campaign won numerous awards during its tenure as the global advertising theme for Coca-Cola. However, in 2016, the company announced a major shift in its marketing strategy whereby all Coke trademark brands were united in one global creative campaign called "Taste the Feeling." The new campaign put the product at the center of every ad as Coca-Cola sought to win over more drinkers in the struggling soda category. Coca-Cola's global vice president for creative noted that the new campaign was about living in the intimacy and simplicity of the moment and was similar to the classic tagline "Have a Coke and a smile." The "Taste the Feeling" campaign was designed to bring to mind the idea that drinking a Coca-Cola product is a simple pleasure that makes everyday moments more special and celebrates the experience of doing so.

Another major aspect of the new strategy was a "one-brand" approach designed to unite the various brands under the Coke trademark—Coca-Cola, Coca-Cola Light/Diet Coke, Coke Zero Sugar, and Coca-Cola Life—and under one personality, sharing the equity of the brand across all the products. The approach also underscored the company's commitment to providing consumers with more choices and healthier alternatives, including smaller package sizes. For example, Diet Coke and Coke Zero Sugar are positioned as customized choices for drinkers who want a sugar-free soft drink, while Coca-Cola Life is sweetened with cane sugar and stevia leaf extract.

The "Taste the Feeling" campaign ran for 5 years and helped Coca-Cola address some of the challenges the company faces in the global market, such as declining soda consumption in many markets amid growing health concerns and a shift to healthier lifestyles. However, in 2021 the company decided it was time to refresh the brand platform for its Coke trademark products, as well as alter its logo design and launch a new global campaign to support the changes. The new brand platform is called "Real Magic" and emphasizes the unexpected moments of togetherness between people in a connected yet diverse world. The Coca-Cola Company views "Real Magic" as a philosophy versus a tagline, describing it as follows: "The 'Real Magic' brand philosophy is rooted in the insight that magic lives in unexpected moments of connection that elevate the everyday into the extraordinary—a timeless learning that feels more relevant than ever in today's hyperconnected yet divided world. Real magic happens when people get together and when what we share in common is greater than what sets us apart."

The "Real Magic" platform includes a new design identity for the Coke trademark brands, anchored by a fresh expression of the Coca-Cola logo. The logo has been altered into a "hug" with the Coca-Cola letters resembling how they would appear wrapped around a bottle. The logo was inspired by iconic Coca-Cola packages wrapped with the signature logo.

To launch the new "Real Magic" platform, a global IMC campaign was created using the theme "One Coke Away From Each Other" with the tagline serving as a metaphor that celebrates our common humanity. The campaign targets gen Z consumers with a heavy emphasis on gaming, music, and sports. It was launched with a 2-minute, video game–focused spot featuring two battling armies in a video game who drop their weapons and come together while a real-life player raises a Coke, signaling the new platform's goal of bridging consumption occasions with consumer passion points. The spot featured three well-known gamers: DJ Alan Walker, Team Liquid's Aerial Powers, and AverageJonas. The integrated campaign also used social, digital, and out-of-home advertising, as well as a code hunt game where fans could win prizes including video gameplay sessions with celebrity gamers.

Coca-Cola's chief marketing officer notes that the goal of "Real Magic" is to put Coca-Cola trademark brands at the center of cultural conversations for which the brand is trying to increase consumption. This includes an ecosystem of experiences anchored in consumption occasions such as entertainment, meals, and refreshment breaks. He notes that Coke has always been part of culture: "For over a century we've been an icon of inclusion, diversity, of unity—an uplifting symbol of optimism or happiness. And that is what makes Coca-Cola more than just another drink. That is what actually makes Coca-Cola magical and yet undeniably very real." It will be interesting to see if the new global brand platform can work some real magic for Coca-Cola.

Sources: Kenneth Hein, "Breaking Down Coca-Cola's Marketing Spell Book as Real Magic Turns One," *The Drum*, October 13, 2022, https://www .thedrum.com/news/2022/10/13/breaking-down-coca-cola-s-marketing-spell-book-real-magic-turns-one; E. J. Schultz, "What to Expect as Coca-Cola's Massive Agency Review Comes to an End," *Advertising Age*, September 23, 2021, https://adage.com/article/marketing-news-strategy/behind-coca-colas-new-agency-and-marketing-approach/2367646; E. J. Schultz, "Coke Replaces 'Open Happiness' with 'Taste the Feeling' in Major Strategic Shift," *Advertising Age*, January 19, 2016, http://adage.com/article/cmo-strategy/coke-debuts-taste-feeling-campaign-strategic-shift/302184/.

EXHIBIT 19–10

High-tech companies such as Samsung often use global advertising campaigns to promote their products.

Samsung

High-tech products such as smartphones, personal computers, HDTV sets, video games, and fitness trackers are products in the third category. Many of the marketers of high-tech products use global campaigns to promote their brands. Samsung recently developed a global campaign called "#YouMake" to promote a marketing platform that allows consumers to customize various devices. As part of the global campaign, Samsung launched the #YouMake page on its website to introduce a lineup of products that can be personalized to fit users' style, space, and daily routine including smartphones, televisions, refrigerators, and wearables (Exhibit 19–10).

Products in the fourth category are those that come from countries with national reputations for quality and/or a distinctive image that can be used as the basis for global advertising. These products capitalize on the **country-of-origin effect**, which refers to consumers' general perceptions of quality for products made in a given country.[57] Examples include Swiss watches, French wine, and German beer or automobiles. Many U.S. companies such as Apple, Google, and Nike are also taking advantage of the cachet American brands have acquired among consumers around the world in recent years.[58]

A number of studies have shown a pronounced effect of country of origin on the quality perceptions of products, with the reputation of specific countries impacting consumers' evaluative judgments of brands.[59] Thus, companies and brands that originate in countries associated with quality may want to take advantage of this in their advertising. However, some marketing experts argue that in today's world of globalization, consumers are only vaguely aware of the country of origin for many of the brands they buy.[60] Thus, marketers need to understand whether product origin is relevant to the consumers in their target market.

In the final category for which globalization is appropriate are products and services that can be sold to common market segments around the world, such as those identified by Salah Hassan and Lea Katsansis.[61] One such segment is the world's elite—people who, by reason of their economically privileged position, can pursue a lifestyle that includes fine jewelry, expensive clothing, quality automobiles, and the like. Marketers of high-quality, luxury brands such as Tiffany, Prada, Cartier, Gucci, Chanel, and Louis Vuitton can use global advertising to appeal to the elite market segment around the world. Well-known international brands competing in the luxury goods marketplace often present a singular image of prestige and style to the entire world.

An example of a marketer of luxury products that uses global advertising is Swiss watchmaker TAG Heuer, which targets upscale consumers, many of whom are world travelers. Thus, the company feels that it is important to have a consistent advertising message and image in each country and uses global advertising to do so. The only element of its advertising that changes from country to country is the celebrity ambassador who appears in the ad. For nearly a decade, TAG Heuer has used its "#Don't Crack Under Pressure" global campaign, which includes a number of brand ambassadors from various countries in the ads such as Portuguese soccer star Cristiano Ronaldo, British model/actress Cara Delevingne in Europe, and musical artist Cai Xukun in China. In the United States the ambassadors have included NFL football star Tom Brady, skater and surfer Sky Brown, and actor Chris Hemsworth. Exhibit 19–11 shows TAG Heuer ads featuring Cara Delevingne and Patrick Dempsey who in addition to being a popular actor, is also a competitive racing driver and has his own racing team.

Another segment of global consumers who have similar needs and interests and seek similar features and benefits from products and services is teenagers. There are more

EXHIBIT 19–11

TAG Heuer uses a global campaign featuring different celebrity ambassadors for various countries.

left: LVMH Swiss Manufactures SA; right: TAG Heuer

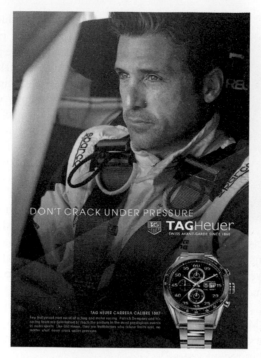

than 500 million teens in Asia and Latin America, whose lifestyles are converging with those of the 80 million teens in Europe and North America to create a vast, free-spending global market.[62] Teens now have intense exposure to the Internet, social media, television, movies, music, travel, and global advertising from companies such as Levi Strauss, Apple, Samsung, Nike, Coca-Cola, Pepsi, and many others.

Global Products, Local Messages

While the pros and cons of global marketing and advertising continue to be debated, many companies are taking an in-between approach by standardizing their products and basic marketing strategy but localizing their advertising messages. They recognize that it is difficult to create relevant and timely global advertising themes, positioning, and stories that appeal to consumers around the world and can be creatively executed across all touch points. The in-between approach recognizes similar desires, goals, needs, and uses for products and services but tailors advertising to the local cultures and conditions in each market. Some call this approach "think globally, act locally," others describe it as "global vision with a local touch," while more recently it has been referred to as *glocal* advertising strategy—locally adapting a universally embraced core idea that will resonate in any market anywhere in the world. Advocates of this approach argue that designers of global advertising strategy carry a creative concept most of the way to execution while regional marketers tailor the work to make it locally relevant and aligned to the different category and brand situations in different markets.[63]

PepsiCo-owned Frito-Lay is among the companies that use this approach. As noted earlier, the snack food giant began using global advertising for brands such as Doritos a decade ago. However, the company also has taken globally inspired ideas and adapted them to regional markets. For example, Frito-Lay signed on as a North American Regional Supporter of the 2022 FIFA World Cup held in Qatar as a way of getting its snack brands in front of a diverse global audience.[64] As part of the collaboration, Frito-Lay developed three new limited-edition Lay's products featuring World Cup–inspired flavors and also created a special promotion called the Pass the Ball Challenge. Soccer fans across North America could purchase any Frito-Lay product with specially marked FIFA World Cup packaging and scan a QR-code to

EXHIBIT 19-12

Frito-Lay used a regional sponsorship of the FIFA World Cup as a way to enhance the viewing experience of soccer fans in North America.

Frito-Lay North America, Inc.

join the challenge or visit a dedicated website (Fritolayscore.com) to join (Exhibit 19-12). Once there, fans could register on the platform where their faces would be feature on a giant digital soccer ball. They could also click on different images on the digital soccer ball to see which team others were rooting for during the World Cup. Every day during the month-long FIFA World Cup, there was a new game on the platform, ranging from soccer trivia to an AR challenge and more, granting users multiple opportunities to win unique prizes. Frito-Lay also partnered with adidas, giving fans the chance to win soccer-inspired merchandise and prizes, including a trip to the World Cup final in Qatar. Frito-Lay viewed the sponsorship as an excellent opportunity, as snacking is intrinsically tied to the home-viewing experience of sporting events such as the World Cup. It connected its brands with soccer, which is the fastest-growing sport in the United States, which will cohost the FIFA World Cup in 2026.

Although some marketers use global ads with little or no modification, most companies adapt their messages to respond to differences in language, market conditions, and other factors. Many global marketers use a strategy called **pattern advertising**: Their ads follow a basic approach, but themes, copy, and sometimes even visual elements are adapted to differences in local markets. For example, the TAG Heuer ads shown in Exhibit 19-11 are an example of pattern advertising. Creative elements of TAG Heuer ads such as the layout, logo, pictures of the product, slogan, and tagline remain clear, consistent, and visually recognizable all over the world.[65]

Another way global marketers adapt their campaigns to local markets is by producing a variety of ads with a similar theme and format and allowing managers in various countries or regions to select those messages they believe will work best in their markets. Some companies are also giving local managers more autonomy in adapting global campaign themes to local markets. They recognize that global advertising can rarely reflect the idiosyncratic characteristics of every market, but the alternative—locally designed advertising—often sacrifices a consistent global message and does not take advantage of economies of scale.

Most managers believe it is important to adapt components of their advertising messages—such as the language, models, scenic backgrounds, message content, and symbols—to reflect the culture and frame of reference of consumers in various countries. For example, global branding expert Nigel Hollis notes that research conducted by Kantar Millward Brown found that, all things being equal, brands that are identified with local culture will perform better than others.[66] He notes several reasons why it is important for brands to have a strong degree of identity to local culture and advises that the key to global brand success is to connect with consumers at the local level while capitalizing on the advantages offered by operating on a global scale.[67] Many companies are making these tactical adjustments to their advertising messages while still pursuing global strategies that will help them project a consistent global image and turn their products and services into global brands.

DECISION AREAS IN INTERNATIONAL ADVERTISING

LO 19-4

Companies developing advertising and promotional programs for international markets must make certain organizational and functional decisions similar to those for domestic markets. These decisions include organization style, agency selection, creative strategy and execution, and media strategy and selection.

Organizing for International Advertising

One of the first decisions a company must make when it decides to market its products to other countries is how to organize the international advertising and promotion function. This decision is likely to depend on how the company is organized overall for international marketing and business. Three basic options are centralization at the home office or headquarters, decentralization of decision making to local foreign markets, or a combination of the two.

Centralization Many companies prefer to *centralize* the international advertising and promotion function so that all decisions about agency selection, creative strategy and campaign development, media strategy, and budgeting are made at the firm's home office. Complete centralization is likely when market and media conditions are similar from one country to another, when the company has only one or a few international agencies handling all of its advertising, when the company can use standardized advertising, or when it desires a consistent image worldwide. Centralization may also be best when a company's international business is small and it operates through foreign distributors or licensees who do not become involved in the marketing and promotional process.

Many companies prefer the centralized organizational structure to protect their foreign investments and keep control of the marketing effort and corporate and/or brand image. Centralization can save money, since it reduces the need for staff and administration at the local subsidiary level. As the trend toward globalized marketing and advertising strategies continues, more companies are likely to move more toward centralization of the advertising function to maintain a unified world brand image rather than presenting a different image in each market. Some foreign managers may actually prefer centralized decision making, as it removes them from the burden of advertising and promotional decisions and saves them from defending local decisions to the home office. However, many marketing and advertising managers in foreign markets oppose centralized control. They say the structure is too rigid and makes it difficult to adapt the advertising and promotional program to local needs and market conditions.

Decentralization Under a *decentralized* organizational structure, marketing and advertising managers in each market have the authority to make their own advertising and promotional decisions. Local managers can select ad agencies, develop budgets, conduct research, approve creative themes and executions, and select advertising media. Companies using a decentralized approach put a great deal of faith in the judgment and decision-making ability of personnel in local markets. This approach is often used when companies believe local managers know the marketing situation in their countries the best. They may also be more effective and motivated when given responsibility for the advertising and promotional program in their markets. Decentralization also works well in small or unique markets where headquarters' involvement is not worthwhile or advertising must be tailored to the local market.

International fragrance marketer Chanel Inc. uses a decentralized strategy. Chanel found that many of its fragrance concepts do not work well globally and decided to localize advertising. For example, the U.S. office has the option of using ads created by the House of Chanel in Paris or developing its own campaigns for the U.S. market. Chanel executives in the United States think that the French concept of prestige is not the same as Americans' and the artsy ads created in France do not work well in this country. Advertising for various Chanel products such as fragrances, jewelry, and accessories has featured a number of high-profile fashion models and celebrities including Keira Knightley, Rihanna, Janelle Monáe, and Gisele Bündchen (Exhibit 19–13).

Combination While there is an increasing trend toward centralizing the international advertising function, many companies combine the two approaches. The home office, or headquarters, has the most control over advertising policy, guidelines, and operations in all markets. The international advertising or marketing communication manager works closely with local or regional marketing managers and personnel from the international

EXHIBIT 19–13

Advertising for Chanel in the United States often features high-profile celebrities and top fashion models.

Chanel

agency (or agencies) and sets advertising and promotional objectives, has budgetary authority, approves all creative themes and executions, and approves media selection decisions, especially when they are made on a regional basis or overlap with other markets.

Advertising managers in regional or local offices submit advertising plans and budgets for their markets, which are reviewed by the international advertising manager. Local managers play a major role in working with the agency to adapt appeals to their particular markets and select media.

The combination approach allows for consistency in a company's international advertising yet permits local input and adaptation of the promotion program. Most consumer-product companies find that local adaptation of advertising is necessary for foreign markets or regions, but they want to maintain control of the overall worldwide image they project. For example, Levi Strauss in 2010 hired its first global chief marketing officer to oversee the company's marketing operations in over 60 countries and try to make the Levi's brand more competitive against premium denim lines such as True Religion, 7 For All Mankind, AG Jeans, and Joe's Jeans.[68] However, the company still provides a great deal of autonomy to regional marketing directors. The Coca-Cola Company recently moved to a combination approach after going through a major agency review that resulted in the WPP Group being awarded the majority of the company's creative, data, and media across 200 brands in more than 200 countries.[69] However, Coca-Cola also has a roster of preferred agencies not owned by WPP that work in various other specialty areas including experiential, digital, shopper marketing, and design. The company is also using a network model whereby creative briefs are led globally with input from individual countries or regions who adjust the work where appropriate to ensure it is appropriate on a country-by-country basis. The network model approach was used in developing the "Real Magic" platform discussed in Global Perspective 19-2, as a global network of creative talent was used to craft the visual identity and bring the concept to life.[70]

Agency Selection

One of the most important decisions for a firm engaged in international marketing is the choice of an advertising agency. The company has three basic alternatives in selecting an agency to handle its international advertising. First, it can choose a major agency with both domestic and overseas offices. Many large agencies have offices all over the world and have become truly international operations. For example, a number of agencies have moved their offices from Hong Kong to Shanghai to be closer to the world's largest consumer market on the mainland of China.[71]

Many American companies prefer to use a U.S.-based agency with foreign offices; this gives them greater control and convenience and also facilitates coordination of overseas advertising. Companies often use the same agency to handle international and domestic advertising. As discussed in Chapter 3, the flurry of mergers and acquisitions in the ad agency business in recent years, both in the United States and in other countries, has created large global agencies that can meet the international needs of global marketers. A number of multinational companies have consolidated their advertising with one large agency. The consolidation trend began in 1994 when IBM dismissed 40 agencies around the world and awarded its entire account to Ogilvy & Mather Worldwide.[72] Since then a number of multinational companies such as Johnson & Johnson, Lenovo, and Samsung have consolidated their creative with one agency and/or holding company.

In addition to consolidating their creative work with one agency, many companies are also consolidating their global media planning and buying with a single agency to get greater efficiency and economies of scale. For example, Mars—whose businesses include snack foods, pet care, and confectionery products and brands such as M&M's, Snickers, Skittles, Pedigree, and Orbit gum—consolidated all of its global media business with WPP's GroupM media network. The move was made to allow the company to respond more quickly to the ever-changing media landscape and to move to a data-driven integrated media strategy.[73] In 2022 Nike consolidated its estimated $1 billion in worldwide media spending with two agencies. Independent media agency PMG is now its integrated media agency in North America and also handles digital media globally for the Nike and Jordan brands. Initiative, which is part of the Interpublic Group of Cos., handles integrated media globally including in Europe, the Middle East and Africa, Asia Pacific, and the Latin America regions.[74]

There are a number of reasons why global marketers consolidate their advertising with one agency. Many companies recognize they must develop a consistent global image for the company and/or its brands and speak with one coordinated marketing voice around the world. For example, IBM officials felt the company had been projecting too many images when its advertising was divided among so many agencies. The consolidation enabled IBM to present a single brand identity throughout the world while taking advantage of one of the world's best-known brand names.

Companies are also consolidating their global advertising in an effort to increase cost-efficiencies and gain greater leverage over their agencies. When a major client puts all of its advertising with one agency, that company often becomes the agency's most important account. And, as one IBM executive notes, "You become a magnet for talent and attention."[75] Consolidation can also lead to cost-efficiencies not only for creative but for media planning and buying as well.

Ogilvy has served as IBM's global creative agency for nearly 30 years. The effectiveness of the longstanding partnership was recognized in 2019 when IBM and Ogilvy were the recipients of the 5 for 50 Effie Award that honored five brands who most effectively adapted, stayed relevant, and sustained business success over time. In 2022 IBM was inducted into the Advertising Hall of Fame, just the 11th company to ever receive this distinct recognition and the first B2B brand to do so. Ogilvy recently launched the "Let's Create" integrated global campaign for IBM, which is the company's most significant brand initiative in more than a decade and reflects its vision, strategy, and purpose. The campaign invites IBM's clients and partners to co-create with the company using its hybrid cloud and artificial intelligence (AI) technology as well as consulting expertise (Exhibit 19–14).

Advertising executives also noted that a major reason for all of the account consolidation is that agencies now have the ability to communicate and manage globally. The Internet, e-mail, and videoconferencing capabilities through platforms such as Skype, Zoom, Microsoft Teams, and FaceTime make it much easier to manage accounts around the globe. Of course, placing an entire global advertising account with one agency can be risky. If the agency fails to deliver an effective campaign, the client has no backup agency to make a fast rebound and the search for a new agency can be very time-consuming. Clients who consolidate also face the problem of selling the idea to regional offices, which often previously enjoyed their own local agency relationships. However, it appears that more and more companies are willing to take these risks and rely on one agency to handle their advertising around the world.

A second alternative for the international marketer is to choose an agency that rather than having its own foreign offices or branches is affiliated with agencies in other countries or belongs to a network of foreign agencies.

EXHIBIT 19–14

Ogilvy has been the global creative agency for IBM for nearly 30 years and developed the Let's Create integrated campaign.

IBM

A domestic agency may acquire an interest in several foreign agencies or become part of an organization of international agencies. The agency can then sell itself as an international agency offering multinational coverage and contacts. Many of the large agency holding companies such as the WPP Group, Publicis Groupe, Omnicom, and Interpublic Group own agencies throughout the world that can handle their clients' advertising in various countries.

The advantage of this arrangement is that the client can use a domestic-based agency yet still have access to foreign agencies with detailed knowledge of market conditions, media, and so on in each local market. There may be problems with this approach, however. The local agency may have trouble coordinating and controlling independent agencies, and the quality of work may vary among network members. Companies considering this option must ask the local agency about its ability to control the activities of its affiliates and the quality of their work in specific areas such as creative and media.

The third alternative for the international marketer is to select a local agency for each national market in which it sells its products or services. Since local agencies often have the best understanding of the marketing and advertising environment in their country or region, they may be able to develop the most effective advertising.

Some companies like local agencies because they may provide the best talent in each market. In many countries, smaller agencies may, because of their independence, be more willing to take risks and develop the most effective, creative ads. Choosing local agencies also increases the involvement and morale of foreign subsidiary managers by giving them responsibility for managing the promotion function in their markets. Some companies have the subsidiary choose a local agency, since it is often in the best position to evaluate the agency and will work closely with it.

Criteria for Agency Selection   The selection of an agency to handle a company's international advertising depends on how the firm is organized for international marketing and the type of assistance it needs to meet its goals and objectives in foreign markets. Figure 19-3 lists some criteria a company might use in selecting an agency. In a study conducted among marketing directors of European companies, creative capability was ranked the most important factor in selecting an advertising agency network, followed by understanding the market, understanding marketing goals, and ability to produce integrated communications. Size of the agency and agency reputation were cited as important criteria by less than 2 percent of the respondents.[76] Another study found that most clients choose an agency based on its creative reputation and the

FIGURE 19-3

Criteria for Selecting an Agency to Handle International Advertising

- Ability of agency to cover relevant markets.

- Quality of agency work.

- Market research, public relations, and other services offered by agency.

- Digital marketing capabilities

- Relative roles of company advertising department and agency.

- Level of communication and control desired by company.

- Ability of agency to coordinate international campaign.

- Size of company's international business.

- Company's desire for local versus international image.

- Company organizational structure for international business and marketing (centralized versus decentralized).

- Company's level of involvement with international operations.

creative presentation it had made. However, a large number of clients felt their agencies lacked international expertise and account coordination ability.[77]

Some companies choose a combination of the three alternatives just discussed because their involvement in each market differs, as do the advertising environment and situation in each country. Several experts in international marketing and advertising advocate the use of international agencies by international companies, particularly those firms moving toward global marketing and striving for a consistent corporate or brand image around the world. The trend toward mergers and acquisitions and the formation of mega-agencies with global marketing and advertising capabilities suggests the international agency approach will become the preferred arrangement among large companies.

Creative Decisions

Another decision facing the international advertiser is determining the appropriate advertising messages for each market. Creative strategy development for international advertising is basically similar in process and procedure to that for domestic advertising. Advertising and communications objectives should be based on the marketing strategy and market conditions in foreign markets. Major selling ideas must be developed and specific appeals and execution styles chosen.

An important factor in the development of creative strategy is the issue of global versus localized advertising. If the standardized approach is taken, the creative team must develop advertising that will transcend cultural differences and communicate effectively in every country. For example, Airbnb launched a global advertising campaign several years ago titled "Live There" that was designed to appeal to consumers around the world and encourage them to use its online site to find lodging in a home or apartment rather than having a cookie cutter experience staying in a hotel. The campaign was based on research conducted by the company showing that 86 percent of Airbnb users pick the platform because they want to live more like a local than a tourist when visiting a destination. The campaign included television and digital ads as well as a series of print ads featuring Pinterest-style images of travelers who look at home in various locales such as a Tokyo artist's loft, a California poolside, or a cozy apartment in Paris (Exhibit 19–15). The various ads in the global campaign focused on the idea that people shouldn't simply go to a new place; they should live there, even if for only one night.[78]

Airbnb launched another global campaign in 2021 to appeal to people interested in traveling as they emerged from the lockdown created by the COVID-19 pandemic. The "Made Possible By Hosts" campaign focused on educating the world about hosted travel and what makes Airbnb unique.[79] The campaign also focused on the experiences Airbnb hosts make possible for guests staying at their properties. As discussed in Chapter 9, the campaign relied on user-generated content by creating a series of short films using pictures and videos shot by photographers on real trips while staying in the homes of Airbnb hosts around the world. The videos appearing in the ads were chosen to tap into a sense of nostalgia and encourage viewers to think of their own meaningful trips.

When companies follow a **localized advertising strategy**, the creative team must determine what type of selling idea, ad appeal, and execution style will work in each market. A product may have to be positioned differently in each market depending on consumers' usage patterns and habits. Emotional appeals such as humor may

EXHIBIT 19–15

Airbnb's "Live There" global campaign appeals to consumers' desire to live like a local when they visit a destination.

Airbnb, Inc

work well in one country but not in another because of differences in cultural backgrounds and perceptions of what is or is not funny. While humorous appeals are popular in the United States and Britain, they are not used often in Germany, where consumers do not respond favorably to them. German advertising typically uses rational appeals that are text-heavy and contain arguments for a product's superiority.[80] France, Italy, and Brazil are more receptive to sexual appeals and nudity in advertising than are most other countries. However, the French government stepped up its efforts to convince advertisers and their ad agencies to tone down the use of sexual imagery and violence in their advertising.[81] France's Truth in Advertising Commission, which is the main self-regulatory body, has standards regarding the presentation of human beings in advertising.

Countries such as Japan, Brazil, and Thailand appreciate creativity: Humorous and irreverent ads are often needed to catch the attention of consumers. In Thailand, which has become the creative nerve center of Asian advertising, the unusual blend of culture, religion, politics, and language influences the advertising. Thailand's *sabi-sabai* ("take it easy") attitude reflects the country's culture as well as its heritage as a peaceful kingdom. Thailand has a very high literacy rate but few people read as a leisure activity, which results in most ads being visual in nature rather than based upon language.[82] Many marketers have found that ads that are more humorous, irreverent, or adventurous break through the clutter and attract the attention of Thai consumers. Another area where creative strategies often differ by country is in the use of celebrities in advertisements. Over half of the TV commercials in countries such as Japan and South Korea feature a celebrity. There are several reasons celebrities are used so often in these countries. Most of the TV commercials are 10- or 15-second spots, and celebrities can help attract attention to the ad. Also, consumers in Japan often look to others for advice, especially from people they know and trust, and celebrities are often seen as trustworthy. The use of celebrities is lowest in European countries such as Belgium, Norway, and Sweden.

Another country where there is a major emphasis on creativity is India, where consumers are not as cynical toward advertising as they are in many other countries such as the United States.[83] Multinational marketers are recognizing that they must create ads specifically for the Indian market rather than trying to adapt campaigns being used globally or in their domestic markets.

In China, marketers must deal with a very decentralized market with distinct differences in culture, language, food preferences, and lifestyles among the various regions and 2,000 cities. In general, the Chinese place a high emphasis on group and family values. Advertisers must be careful when using humor and sexual appeal, particularly for national campaigns, since language and values vary greatly from province to province. Human interest stories are used as the basis for ads in southern China but less so in cities such as Beijing and Shanghai, where residents prefer more information-based ads.[84]

Media Selection

One of the most challenging areas for international marketers is media strategy and selection. Companies often find major differences in the media available outside their home markets, and media conditions may vary considerably from one country to another. Today advertising bombards consumers in countries around the world through a variety of media including print, radio, television, out-of-home, and digital media. However, marketers still face a number of problems in attempting to communicate advertising and promotional messages to consumers in various countries. For example, the amount of time people spend watching television varies from one country to the next. In the United States, the average person spends nearly 5 hours a day watching television. Most major European markets spend less time watching TV than the United States; however, it is higher in countries such as Saudi Arabia as well as Croatia and Romania. Brazil is one of the highest as the average Brazilian spends over 6 hours watching TV each day. Advertisers in Brazil spend the highest percentage of their media budget on television ads compared to other countries.[85] A comparative study of global media consumption showed that consumers in the United States and Western Europe watch a lot of TV, while Asia and other developing economies are disproportionately heavy in mobile and tablet use. But time spent online is increasing in the United States as well as other countries.[86]

In some countries, TV advertising is impacted by limits on the amount of commercial time available. For example, advertising time in countries that belong to the European Union have been limited to 12 minutes per hour. In 2016, the European Union changed the rules, limiting television advertising to a total of 3 hours per day while keeping a limit of 12 minutes of advertising per hour. The new rules also allow product placement in television shows, with the exception of children's and informational shows, and on condition that viewers are informed of the appearance of the placement either before or after the program. The new rules allow each country across the EU to set tighter advertising rules on television broadcasters if they choose to do so.[87]

The number of TV sets is increasing tremendously in India, but there is still controversy over TV advertising. Commercials are restricted to only 10 percent of programming time and must appear at the beginning or end of a program. Australia lifted a ban on cable TV advertising in 1997. However, some cable channels won't accept any advertising, and Australian consumers will not tolerate as much advertising on cable channels as on free TV networks.[88]

The characteristics of media differ from country to country in terms of coverage, cost, quality of reproduction, restrictions, and the like. In some countries, media rates are negotiable or may fluctuate owing to unstable currencies, economic conditions, or government regulations. For example, in China, TV stations charge a local rate for Chinese advertisers, a foreign rate, and a joint venture rate. Although the more than a billion TV viewers make China the world's largest television market, the medium is strictly controlled by the Communist Party. State-owned China Central Television (CCTV) controls the national networks. Politics frequently intrude into program selection and scheduling: A show might be delayed for several months to coincide with a key political event, or programs from foreign countries may be pulled off the air.[89] CCTV has developed its own version of an up-front market, as an auction is held each November to sell advertising time on prime-time programming for the coming year. The annual auction is generally considered a barometer for China's media market as local and regional channels will often hold off setting their advertising rates to see the level of demand for advertising time. While CCTV is China's only national broadcaster, it accounts for just 12 percent of the total television advertising revenue in China, with the remainder going to local TV channels, provincial satellite channels, and provincial TV stations.[90]

Another problem international advertisers face is obtaining reliable media information such as circulation figures, audience profiles, and costs. Many countries that had only state-owned TV channels are now experiencing a rapid growth in commercial channels, which is providing more market segmentation opportunities. However, reliable audience measurement data are not available, and media buyers often rely on their instincts when purchasing TV time. A number of research companies are developing audience measurement systems for countries in Eastern Europe, Russia, and China. In China, AGB Nielsen Media Research monitors TV-viewing audiences in 11 of China's biggest cities including Beijing, Shanghai, and Guangzhou as well as in the rural parts of several provinces, using nearly 10,000 households with people meters.[91] Audience measurement information is also available from CSM Media Research, a company that is a joint venture between CTR Market Research (the leading market research company in China) and Kantar.

The goal of international advertisers is to select media vehicles that reach their target audience most effectively and efficiently. Media selection is often localized even for a centrally planned, globalized campaign. Local agencies or media buyers generally have more knowledge of local media and better opportunities to negotiate rates, and subsidiary operations can maintain control and adapt to media conditions and options in

EXHIBIT 19–16

Jelly is a popular fashion magazine in Japan.

Mark Dierker/McGraw Hill

their market. Media planners have two options: using national or local media or using international media.

Local Media   Many advertisers choose the local media of a country to reach its consumers. While the print media are struggling in the United States, they are still popular in many countries where magazines are circulated nationwide and national or regional newspapers carry advertising directed to a national audience. While newspaper advertising has declined dramatically in the United States and other countries, it still accounts for 27 percent of the advertising spending in India. The country has 144,000 registered newspapers and periodicals. Advertisers in India often rely on newspapers to reach consumers, as well as television. Most countries also have magazines that appeal to special interests or activities, allowing for targeting in media selection. For example, Japan has numerous fashion magazines such as *Jelly*, which focuses on runway fashions, as well as street fashion and culture (Exhibit 19–16).

In addition to print and television, local media available to advertisers include radio, direct mail, billboards, cinema, and transit advertising. These media give international advertisers great flexibility and the opportunity to reach specific market segments and local markets within a country. Most international advertisers rely heavily on national and local media in their media plans for foreign markets.

International Media   The other way for the international advertiser to reach audiences in various countries is through international media that have multimarket coverage. The primary focus of international media has traditionally been magazines and newspapers. A number of U.S.-based consumer-oriented publications have international editions, including *Time*, *Reader's Digest*, and *National Geographic* as well as the newspaper *USA Today*. Hearst Magazines International is the largest U.S. publisher of magazines worldwide and oversees the publication of more than 200 print editions and more than 150 websites in 34 languages and more than 80 countries including *Esquire*, *Car and Driver*, *Men's Health*, *Good Housekeeping*, *Cosmo Girl*, and *Elle*. Hearst also publishes *Cosmopolitan*, which with 64 international editions is the largest-selling young women's magazine and has more editions than any other magazine in the world (Exhibit 19–17).[92] Other U.S.-based publications with foreign editions include *Bloomberg Businessweek*, *Fortune*, and *The Wall Street Journal*.

International publications offer advertisers a way to reach large audiences on a regional or worldwide basis. Readers of these publications are usually upscale, high-income individuals who are desirable target markets for many products and services. There are, however, several problems with these international media that can limit their attractiveness to many advertisers. Their reach in any one foreign country may be low, particularly for specific segments of a market. Also, while they deliver desirable audiences to companies selling business or upscale consumer products and services, they do not cover the mass consumer markets or specialized market segments very well. Other U.S.-based publications in foreign markets do offer advertisers ways to reach specific market segments.

The use of print media is declining in many countries as more marketers move more of their media spending to digital. However, television remains popular. Consumer product and service companies in particular view TV advertising as the best way to reach mass markets and effectively communicate their advertising messages. Satellite technology has helped spread the growth of TV in other countries through **direct broadcast by satellite (DBS)** to homes and communities equipped with small, low-cost receiving dishes. A number of satellite networks operate in Europe, Asia, and Latin America and beam entertainment programming across a number of countries.

EXHIBIT 19–17

International editions of *Cosmopolitan* magazine are distributed in more than 100 countries in 35 languages.

Hearst Magazines

EXHIBIT 19–18

STAR India reaches more than 600 million people every month.

Star India

For example, Exhibit 19–18 shows an ad for StarPlus, one of the channels owned by STAR India, which has become the leading television company in India, with 40 channels in eight languages that reach more than 600 million people every month across India and other countries around the world.

THE ROLES OF OTHER PROMOTIONAL-MIX ELEMENTS IN INTERNATIONAL MARKETING

This chapter has focused on advertising, since it is usually the primary element in the promotional mix of the international marketer. However, as in domestic marketing, promotional programs for foreign markets generally include other elements such as sales promotion, public relations, and digital and social media. The roles of these other promotional-mix elements vary depending on the firm's marketing and promotional strategy in foreign markets.

Sales promotion and public relations can support and enhance advertising efforts; the latter may also be used to create or maintain favorable images for companies in foreign markets. For some firms, personal selling may be the most important promotional element and advertising may play a support role. This final section considers the roles of some of these other promotional-mix elements in the international marketing program.

Sales Promotion

Sales promotion activity in international markets is growing due in part to the transfer of promotion concepts and techniques from country to country and in part to the proliferation of media. The growth also stems from the liberalization of trade, the rise of

EXHIBIT 19-19

WD-40 uses product samples in various countries to encourage trial.

WD-40 Company

global brands, the spread of cable and satellite TV, the growth of digital and social media as a result of greater Internet access, and the deregulation and/or privatization of media. Sales promotion and direct-response agencies have become more common, particularly in Europe and more recently in South American, Asian, and Middle Eastern countries. In many less developed countries, spending on sales promotion often exceeds media spending on TV, radio, and print ads.

As we saw in Chapter 16, sales promotion is a very important IMC tool for marketers in the United States, particularly for consumer packaged-goods marketers selling their products through retail channels. Both consumer and trade promotion schedules are planned in advance, and marketers work closely with channel members to get shelf space for their brands. They also use various promotional offers such as price discounts, buy-one-get-one-free offers, and other tactics to target promotion-sensitive consumers. Companies increasingly rely on consumer- and trade-oriented sales promotion to help sell their products in foreign markets as well. Many of the promotional tools that are effective in the United States, such as free samples, premiums, event sponsorships, contests, coupons, and trade promotions, are also used in foreign markets. For example, Häagen-Dazs estimates it gave out more than 5 million free tastings of its ice cream as part of its successful strategy for entering the European market. Since taste is the major benefit of this premium product, sampling was an appropriate sales promotion tool for entering foreign markets. The WD-40 Co. uses samples in the United States as well as foreign markets to educate consumers about the versatility of the product and encourage trial. The samples shown in Exhibit 19-19, which use the front headline "One Can. One Thousand Uses," was translated into 20 different languages. This makes it possible for the distributors in different countries to use a sampling tool in their local languages. Nestlé introduced its Nescafé brand to China by conducting the world's largest coffee-sampling program. Nescafé samples were passed out across 150 cities in China using 18 teams throughout the country. The sampling program helped increase sales by over 150 percent in the predominantly tea-drinking country.[93]

Unlike advertising, which can be done on a global basis, sales promotions must be adapted to local markets. Kamran Kashani and John Quelch noted several important differences among countries that marketers must consider in developing a sales promotion program.[94] They include the stage of economic development, market maturity, consumer perceptions of promotional tools, trade structure, and legal restrictions and regulations:

- *Economic development.* In highly developed countries such as the United States, Canada, Japan, and Western European nations, marketers can choose from a wide range of promotional tools. But in developing countries they must be careful not to use promotional tools such as in- or on-package premiums that would increase the price of the product beyond the reach of most consumers. Free samples and demonstrations are widely used as effective promotional tools in developing countries. But coupons, which are so popular with consumers in the United States, are rarely used because of problems with distribution and resistance from retailers. In the United States and Britain, most coupons are distributed through newspapers (including FSIs) or magazines. Low literacy rates in some countries make print media an ineffective coupon distribution method, so coupons are delivered door to door, handed out in stores, or placed in or on packages. Despite the decline over the past several years, the use of coupons by both marketers as well as consumers is much greater in the United States than other countries. Coupons are also very popular in China as nearly two-thirds of consumers use them. There are coupon kiosks in subways, malls, and supermarkets, and hundreds of thousands are printed and distributed every day for packaged goods products, restaurants, car rentals, and many other goods and services. The Chinese market is highly saturated with brand names and coupons, as well as other promotional offers, which can be important to consumers in making purchase decisions.

- *Market maturity.* Marketers must also consider the stage of market development for their product or service in various countries when they design sales promotions. To introduce a product to a country, consumer-oriented promotional tools such as sampling, high-value coupons, and cross-promotions with established products and brands are often effective. The competitive dynamics of a foreign market are also often a function of its stage of development. More competition is likely in well-developed mature markets, which will influence the types of sales promotion tools used. For example, there may be competitive pressure to use trade allowances to maintain distribution or consumer promotions that will maintain customer loyalty, such as bonus packs, price-off deals, or loyalty programs.

- *Consumer perceptions.* An important consideration in the design of sales promotion programs is how they are perceived by consumers as well as the trade. Consumer perceptions of various sales promotion tools vary from market to market. For example, Japanese women are less likely to take advantage of contests, coupons, or other promotions than are women in the United States. Premium offers in particular must be adapted to the tastes of consumers in various markets. A study by Huff and Alden examined consumers' opinions toward the use of coupons and sweepstakes in three Asian countries: Taiwan, Malaysia, and Thailand. The study found differences among the three countries, with consumers in Taiwan having more negative attitudes and lower levels of use of both sweepstakes and coupons than consumers in Malaysia and Thailand.[95]

- *Trade structure.* In areas with highly concentrated retailing systems, such as northern Europe, the trade situation is becoming much like the United States and Canada as pressure grows for more price-oriented trade and in-store promotions. In southern Europe, the retail industry is highly fragmented and there is less trade pressure for promotions. The willingness and ability of channel members to accommodate sales promotion programs must also be considered. Retailers in many countries do not want to take time to process coupons, post promotional displays, or deal with premiums or packaging that require special handling or storage. In countries like Japan or India, where retailing structures are highly fragmented, stores are too small for point-of-purchase displays or in-store sampling. In most Asian countries simple price-cut promotions that are supported by direct-mail leaflets and newspaper advertising are the primary promotional vehicles.[96]

- *Regulations.* An important factor affecting the use of sales promotions in foreign countries is the presence of legal restrictions and regulations. Laws affecting sales promotions are generally more restrictive in other countries than in the United States. Some countries ban contests, games, or lotteries, while others restrict the size or amount of a sample, premium, or prize. For example, fair-trade regulations in Japan limit the maximum value of premiums to 10 percent of the retail price; in France the limit is 5 percent. Canada prohibits games of pure chance unless a skill element is used to determine the winner. In Japan the amount of a prize offer is limited to a certain percentage of the product tied to the promotion.[97] In some countries, a free premium must be related to the nature of the product purchased. Many countries have strict rules when it comes to premium offers for children, and some ban them altogether.

Variations in rules and regulations mean marketers must often develop separate consumer sales promotion programs for each country. Many companies have found it difficult to do any promotions throughout Europe because sales promotion rules differ so much from one country to another. While the European Commission has considered various proposals to standardize regulations for sales promotions in countries that are members of the European Union, it has not been successful in doing so. Thus, many companies use local agencies or international sales promotion companies to develop sales promotion programs in Europe as well as other foreign markets.

Public Relations

Many companies involved in international marketing are recognizing the importance of using public relations to support and enhance their marketing and advertising efforts.[98] Public relations activities are needed to deal with local governments, media, trade associations, and the general public, any of which may feel threatened by the presence of a foreign multinational. The job of PR agencies in foreign markets is not only to help the company sell its products or services but also to present the firm as a good corporate citizen concerned about the future of the country.

Companies generally need a favorable image to be successful in foreign markets. Those perceived negatively may face pressure from the media, local governments, or other relevant publics or even boycotts by consumers. Often, public relations is needed to deal with specific problems a company faces in international markets. For example, McDonald's and a number of other companies have had to deal with PR problems arising from concerns over the nutritional value of their food. The latest controversy erupted in response to a report showing childhood obesity in France had doubled to 16 percent in 10 years. Concerns over the problem of childhood obesity have spread to other European countries, and other food companies such as Kraft and Kellogg are also being criticized. As noted earlier, the European Union called on the food industry to regulate so-called junk-food advertising aimed at consumers across the continent.[99]

The National Basketball Association (NBA) had to deal with a major public relations crisis in China when an executive with the Houston Rockets set off a geopolitical firestorm by sharing an image on Twitter expressing support for pro-democracy protests in Hong Kong.[100] The NBA has spent years building a fan base in China, where more than 300 million people play basketball and hundreds of millions more watch NBA games every season. NBA officials have cultivated lucrative deals with powerful investors and built large followings on social media platforms. However, there was an understanding that NBA officials would stay clear of political controversy, nor was it contemplated that they would risk alienating China's communist party leaders. The social media post angered the Chinese government, which pulled NBA games off the air. Chinese companies pulled sponsorships from the league. In response to the controversy, the Rockets executive was rebuked by the team's owner, and he issued a statement saying he did not intend to cause offense. The NBA later released a statement on Chinese social media that it was regrettable that the post had offended many of the league's friends and fans in China and expressed its respect for the country's history and culture (Exhibit 19-20). In the United States, the NBA's statement resulted in criticism at home, as it was viewed as an apology to the Chinese government and not supportive of free speech on social and political issues. NBA games did not appear on television in China for 3 years. In 2022, China Central Television (CCT), the state-run TV network, began broadcasting NBA games again, signaling that the rift between the league and the government was coming to an end.[101]

Google has also had to deal with negative publicity in foreign markets involving issues such as stifling competition and preventing competitors from being able to compete and innovate fairly. In 2019, the European Union ordered Google to pay $1.69 billion for stifling completion in the online advertising sector. The European Commission ruled that Google had placed exclusivity contracts on website publishers, prohibiting them from including search results from Google's rivals. A year earlier, Google was fined $5 billion for abusing the dominance of its Android operating system that is used in mobile devices such as smartphones and tablets. Google allowed smartphone manufacturers to use the Android OS for free but was accused of favoring its own services by forcing the smartphone makers to bundle products such as Google Search, Maps, and the Chrome browser along with its app store Play.[102]

EXHIBIT 19–20

The NBA has had to deal with a major public relations crisis in China. This apology statement appeared on social media sites in China.

The National Basketball Association

NBA STATEMENT

NEW YORK, October 7, 2019 – NBA Chief Communications Officer Mike Bass released the following statement:

"We recognize that the views expressed by Houston Rockets General Manager Daryl Morey have deeply offended many of our friends and fans in China, which is regrettable. While Daryl has made it clear that his tweet does not represent the Rockets or the NBA, the values of the league support individuals' educating themselves and sharing their views on matters important to them. We have great respect for the history and culture of China and hope that sports and the NBA can be used as a unifying force to bridge cultural divides and bring people together."

###

Digital and Social Media

Worldwide Growth of the Internet   The Internet has clearly come of age as a global marketing medium and is now an important IMC tool as well for companies around the world, both large and small. Marketers are using digital and social media to promote their companies, build their brands, and engage in e-commerce transactions in their own countries as well as across borders. As of 2022, there were nearly 5.5 billion Internet users around the world, with the largest number of users residing in Asia, followed by Europe and North America. China is now the country with the largest number of people online, with just over 1 billion users, followed by India with 834 million, the United States with 293 million, and Japan with 119 million. There are also 750 million Internet users in Europe.[103]

As noted, China now has the world's largest Internet population. There are key differences in the demographic and usage behavior of China's "digital elite" as they are younger, better educated, and more likely to be employed full time versus Internet users in other countries. They also spend more time online and are more involved with web activities such as participating in blogs and chats, posting product ratings and reviews, and using social media. They are also more likely to access the Internet from mobile devices. The look, feel, and features of many Chinese websites are similar to those in the United States and Europe, and China has search and e-commerce sites that function like Google, Amazon, and eBay. Baidu dominates online search in China today since Google closed its China site in March 2010 because of censorship by the Chinese government and cyberattacks from within the country. While Google Play and the Apple App Store dominate the mobile app market in the West, China's market makes it more challenging for them to compete. There is tight government control and censorship of apps, and the adoption of mobile technology and platforms from local Chinese companies is widespread. To conform to Chinese licensing laws, Apple has a different version of the Apple App Store available in China for iPhone users. Thus, app and game publishers and developers must launch their apps on both versions of the Apple App Store to reach the entirety of the world market. In late 2022 Google discontinued Google Translate, which was one of its last remaining services in China.[104] Alibaba is China's largest online commerce company and its three main sites—Taobao, Tmall, and Alibaba.com—have over 500 million active users, and host millions of merchants and businesses. Alibaba handles more business than any other e-commerce company and is the most popular destination for online shopping in China, which is the world's fastest-growing e-commerce market. Digital and Social Media Perspective 19–1 discusses how digital marketing has become dominant in China.

Digital and Social Media Perspective 19–1 > > >

China Leads the Way in Digital Marketing

Global expansion is an important goal of multinational companies as their domestic markets stagnate and they try to take advantage of the growth opportunities in international markets. And the market nearly every company has at the top of its list is China, whose 1.42 billion consumers and massive modernization drive over the past four decades have made the country the fastest-growing consumer market in the world. Advertising, once banned as a capitalist scourge, is now encouraged by the Chinese government, which views it as a catalyst that can accelerate China's economic development. There is also a new spirit of consumption, as reform in China has brought about dramatic increases in the purchasing power and size of the middle class. Over the next decade, China may add more consumption than any other country, and is expected to generate more than one-quarter of all global consumption growth. The average disposable income of Chinese consumers continues to rise, and demand is increasing for many products, including consumer electronics, automobiles, and luxury goods such as clothing, watches, jewelry, and fashion accessories.

BJI/Blue Jean Images/Getty Images

While China offers tremendous opportunities, many companies struggle to take advantage of them because they find China's market very different from the United States and other countries, requiring a different marketing mindset, as well as a different set of competencies. Marketers who hope to compete in China must understand that the country has moved away from traditional media and has become a digital and, more specifically, "mobile first" market. In 2022, 82 percent of total media advertising spending in China went to digital, with more than 80 percent of digital ad spending dedicated to mobile. The management consulting company McKinsey notes that vibrant digital ecosystems have developed in China that are steadily increasing their share of the country's economy. Chinese technology companies have created innovative business models, especially in all types of e-commerce, digital payments, food delivery, health care, and mobility services. China is the world's largest e-commerce market. More than 70 percent of China's consumers are true omnichannel shoppers combining both online and offline purchases.

Chinese consumers are enthusiast adopters and users of digital media and innovations with younger age cohorts including millennials and members of gen Z leading the way. Nearly 30 percent of gen Zers spend more than 6 hours a day on their mobile phones, with much of this time spent consuming digital content. This is nearly twice the amount of time as consumers in the United States and most European countries. Super apps are now well established and have become mainstream in China and further advanced than in most other countries.

The mobile advertising market is dominated by three powerful companies, Baidu, Alibaba, and Tencent, which are often referred to as BAT. Baidu is the leading Internet search company in China and is equivalent to Google in the United States. The company has 75 percent of the search market in China and has a variety of other products, including e-commerce and social media sites as well as a payment service. Tencent owns the world's largest gaming platform, a wide array of news agencies, as well as the dominant social media (Wexin and WeChat) and financial services platforms. More than half of all time spent online by Chinese consumers is within the Tencent ecosystem of companies. Alibaba has surpassed Amazon to become the world's leading e-commerce site, with more than 500 million active shoppers. The company's e-commerce platforms include not only business-to-consumer sales, but also business-to-business and consumer-to-consumer sales as well. Marketers trying to grow market share in China must learn to understand the BATs and develop close relationships with them.

Marketing Professor Kimberly Whitler at the University of Virginia's Darden School of Business notes that companies from the United States and Europe must learn to adapt their marketing strategies to compete successfully in China. One of the changes they must make is to adopt a mobile-first mindset because almost all media activity in China is consolidated on mobile devices. While U.S. companies are used to advertising and interacting with consumers on Facebook, Instagram, YouTube, Snapchat, and other social channels, these are not where Chinese audiences gather. They interact with brands on WeChat, Weibo, Douyin (the name for TikTok in China), and other platforms that have their own kind of Internet language, memes, and influencers.

Whitler recommends that companies competing in China must go all-in on social media, which is used extensively by consumers to research and share information about brands, and viral marketing, which includes learning how to use key opinion leaders (KOLs). The intensity associated with using KOLs in China is very unique relative to other countries and often involves livecasting and streaming. KOLs encompass a variety of areas, including sports, gaming, and dramas. China's "fan economy" is better developed and a much more important marketing vehicle than are tools such as Facebook and Instagram in the United States.

The size of the Chinese market and emerging middle class makes entering China a no-brainer for most multinational companies. The newly emerging middle class in China is very brand conscious, and demand for popular Western products from the United States and Europe is increasing. However, the realities of competing in China have changed because rather than evolving, the digital revolution in China has leapfrogged other countries, and as we have described, a different marketing approach and set of competencies are needed to compete there. Moreover, it will not be long before marketers must deal with these challenges in other countries, as the world moves to a digital and mobile-first mindset. As Kimberly Whitler notes, "Whether Western firms' leaders embrace or ignore the emerging mindset may very well determine their success in China—and eventually, their ability to compete around the world."

Sources: Daniel Zipser, Shenzhen Jeongmin Seong, and Jonathan Woetzel, "Five Consumer Trends Shaping the Next Decade in China," McKinsey & Company, November 2021, https://www.mckinsey.com/cn/our-insights/our-insights/five-consumer-trends-shaping-the-next-decade-of-growth-in-china; Irene Yang, "What Marketers Everywhere Are Getting Wrong about the Chinese Market," The Drum, August 27, 2021, https://www.thedrum.com/opinion/2021/08/27/what-marketers-everywhere-are-getting-wrong-about-the-chinese-market; Kimberly A. Whitler, "What Western Marketers Can Learn from China," Harvard Business Review, May–June 2019, pp. 75–82.

EXHIBIT 19–21

TaylorMade Golf develops a website specifically for countries such as Japan.

TaylorMade Golf Company

Use of Digital and Social Media in International Marketing

Digital media are becoming an integral part of the IMC program of marketers at a global, regional, and local level as Internet penetration increases in countries around the world and marketers become more adept at using social media, mobile marketing, and other forms of digital communication. Most multinational marketers now have websites for specific countries and/or regions that allow them to tailor the information they provide to the needs, interests, lifestyles, and subtleties of consumers in these markets. For example, Exhibit 19–21 shows a page from the website used by the Taylor-Made Golf Company in Japan. Marketers are also using mass-media advertising to drive consumers to their websites, where they provide them with detailed information about their products and services, encourage them to participate in promotions, or encourage them to make purchases.

International marketers are also allocating a large amount of their advertising budgets in various countries to digital media, with online advertising becoming the primary driver of global advertising spending growth. As is the case in the United States, much of this growth in digital advertising is being driven by ads on social media, online display and video, and paid search. The great majority of digital advertising is targeted at mobile devices, thanks to their widespread adoption and their ever-tighter integration into the daily lives of consumers around the world.

The use of social media is becoming very prevalent in countries around the world, and marketers are making social networking sites an integral part of their IMC programs. An estimated 4.7 billion people use social media, which represents more than half of the world's population. Nearly half of the active social media users worldwide live in Asian countries with China and India ranking first and second in number of users. Facebook has become the first truly global social media platform and now has 2.9 billion users around the world. Facebook's parent company Meta also owns Instagram, which had 1.4 billion users in 2022 and 500 million daily active users, 80 percent of whom live outside the United States. Facebook is the leading social networking site in the United States with 200 million users and is also popular in most other countries including Indonesia where it has 140 million users and Brazil with 130 million. Facebook is banned in China along with a number of other social media platforms including Instagram, Twitter, Snapchat, and YouTube. Its penetration is also low in many Asian and African countries, where local social networking sites are more popular.

A market of great importance to Facebook is India, which is now Facebook's largest market, with 340 million users and the potential for even more growth given the number of Internet users in the country and the population. Growing Internet penetration and a large youth population has helped Facebook expand its user base in India. Nearly 90 percent of those on Facebook in India are accessing the platform on their mobile phones at least once per month, and nearly half are using their mobile phones every day to connect with friends on Facebook. Facebook is now available in 12 languages in India, and more than 80 percent of the top revenue-generating apps in India are integrated with the platform.[105]

Twitter has also become a global social media platform as in 2022 the micro-blogging site had 368 million monthly active users. However, Twitter's growth has stagnated, which is creating concern over its viability as a marketing platform.[106] The way people around the world are using Twitter is also changing. Research shows that usage is becoming much more commercial, with consumers posting comments about brands, using branded apps, and asking friends about products. It is likely that global marketers will continue to use Twitter, particularly for publicity and public relations, while looking for other ways to leverage it as an IMC tool such as through the use of Promoted

Tweets as well as hashtag campaigns. However, it remains to be seen how the acquisition of Twitter by Elon Musk will impact the platform in various countries.[107]

As the digital revolution continues, marketers will be making greater use of digital and social media in their global as well as regional and local IMC programs. The use of social networking sites will become more prevalent, and marketers are also expected to increase their use of mobile marketing techniques since more consumers are now using their smartphones and other mobile devices to access and surf the Internet. As consumers become more reliant on the Internet and various forms of digital media for information, entertainment, and socializing, marketers must develop ways to reach them through these contact points.

Summary

Many companies are recognizing the opportunities as well as the necessity of marketing their products and services internationally because of saturated markets and intense competition from both domestic and foreign competitors. Advertising and promotion are important parts of the international marketing programs of these companies. Global marketers based in the United States, as well as European and Asian countries, have increased their advertising spending, particularly in digital media.

International marketers must carefully analyze the major environmental forces in each market where they compete, including economic, demographic, cultural, and political/legal factors. These factors are important not only in assessing the potential of each country as a market but also in designing and implementing advertising and promotional programs.

Much attention has focused on global marketing, where a standard marketing program is used in all markets. Part of global marketing is global advertising, where the same basic advertising approach is used in all markets. Opponents of the global (standardized) approach argue that differences in culture, market and economic conditions, and consumer needs and wants make a universal approach to marketing and advertising impractical. Many companies use an in-between approach, standardizing their basic marketing strategy but localizing advertising messages to fit each market.

There are a number of important decision areas in the development of advertising and promotional programs for international markets. These include organization, agency selection, creative strategy and execution, and media strategy and selection. An important decision facing international advertisers is determining the appropriate advertising messages for each market. Creative strategy development for international advertising is basically similar in process and procedure to that for domestic advertising.

Sales promotion, personal selling, public relations, and digital marketing are also part of the promotional mix of international marketers. Sales promotion programs usually must be adapted to local markets. Factors to consider include stage of market development, market maturity, consumer perceptions of promotional tools, trade structure, and legal restrictions and regulations. PR programs are also important to help international marketers develop and maintain favorable relationships with governments, media, and consumers in foreign countries. The use of digital and social media such as the Internet, social networking sites, and mobile marketing is becoming an important part of international marketers' IMC programs. Internet penetration is increasing rapidly in most countries, and as more consumers go online, marketers are developing websites for various countries and also using other forms of digital and social media to reach them.

Key Terms

balance-of-trade deficit 644
economic infrastructure 645
cultural values 649
guochao 649

global marketing 655
global advertising 655
country-of-origin effect 659

pattern advertising 661
localized advertising strategy 666
direct broadcast by satellite (DBS) 669

Discussion Questions

1. The chapter opener discusses how Tourism Australia uses global advertising. Discuss the importance of international markets to the Australian tourism industry and the role of advertising and other IMC tools in attracting tourists to Australia. (LO 19-1, 19-2, 19-5)

2. Find examples of companies that were official sponsors of the 2022 FIFA World Cup that was held in Qatar. Do you think the controversy surrounding Qatar's hosting of the Word Cup had a negative impact on these companies? Why or why not? (LO 19-1, 19-2)

3. What are some of the political/legal factors that marketers must consider in developing advertising and promotional programs in a foreign market? Choose one of these political/legal factors and discuss how it has created a problem or challenge for a company in developing an advertising or promotional program in a specific country. (LO 19-2)

4. What is meant by a country-of-origin effect? Choose a product category for which there is a country-of-origin effect and discuss how a company or brand might use it in developing an advertising message. (LO 19-3)

5. Global Perspective 19–2 discusses the "Real Magic" global marketing campaign for the Coca-Cola Company. Evaluate the creative strategy being used for this campaign as well as the "one-brand" approach that unites various Coca-Cola soft drink brands under one image, rather than positioning each brand differently. (LO 19-1, 19-2)

6. Discuss the advantages and disadvantages of using a global advertising campaign for a company or brand. For what types of products or services is a global advertising approach appropriate? (LO 19-3)

7. Many marketing and advertising experts argue there are limits to global advertising and the one-size-fits-all approach. Do you agree with their position? What are some of the reasons advertising needs to be more localized for specific regions or countries? (LO 19-2, 19-3)

8. What are the three options available to marketers when organizing for international advertising and promotion? Discuss factors that will influence which option a marketer might use. (LO 19-4)

9. Discuss some of the differences in media that exist across various countries and how they might impact the media strategy used by marketers. (LO 19-4)

10. Digital and Social Media Perspective 19–1 discusses the growth and prevalence of digital and mobile marketing in China. Discuss the challenges and opportunities this presents to companies from the United States and Europe that are marketing their products and services in China. (LO 19-1, 19-2, 19-5)

20 Regulation of Advertising and Promotion

Kim Kardashian/Instagram

Learning Objectives

 LO20-1 Explain the role and function of various regulatory agencies.

 LO20-2 Evaluate the effectiveness of self-regulation of advertising.

 LO20-3 Describe how advertising is regulated by federal and state regulatory bodies.

 LO20-4 Discuss the regulation of sales promotion and direct marketing.

 LO20-5 Discuss the regulation of marketing on the Internet including privacy and security, online endorsements, and native advertising.

High-Profile Celebrities Run into Trouble for Endorsing Failed Cryptocurrencies

In June 2021, at the height of the cryptocurrency craze, Kim Kardashian posted a message on Instagram promoting Ethereum Max (EMAX), a brand-new token. The headline of the reality star and social media influencer's post stated: "Are you guys into crypto????" The message then noted that she was not giving financial advice but was eager to share with her 330 million followers "what her friends had just told her about the Ethereum Max token—that they were reducing supply to give back to the entire E-max community." The post also included instructions for potential investors to access the EMAX website where they could purchase the tokens.

It turns out that some of those friends who had given Kardashian the information she was eager to share included EMAX, which had paid her $250,000 to promote its token. The U.S. Securities and Exchange Commission (SEC), the government agency charged with regulating the securities and investments market and protecting the investing public, decided that the queen of influencers did a little too much influencing when it came to EMAX. Even though Kardashian had labeled her Instagram post as an "ad," it wasn't enough to satisfy the government regulators. After a year-long investigation, the SEC ruled that Kardashian had failed to disclose how much she was paid for the post promoting EMAX tokens and fined her $1.26 million to settle the charges. She also agreed not to promote any cryptocurrency assets for 3 years. As part of the settlement, Kardashian did not admit to or deny the SEC allegations. However, the settlement helped her avoid a much more public and intrusive process that might have involved a deposition and document collection.

What got Kim Kardashian in trouble with the SEC is that she included only the hashtag "#Ad" at the bottom of the post and did not include a more detailed disclosure mentioning how much she was paid. While celebrities and influencers have long used disclosures like "#Ad" on Instagram, Facebook, and other social media sites to tell their followers that a post is sponsored or paid for, the disclosure requirements for promoting cryptocurrencies and tokens, which are considered securities by the SEC, are stricter. The director of the SEC's enforcement division noted that federal securities laws are clear that any celebrity or other individual who promotes a crypto asset security must disclose the nature, source, and amount of compensation they received in exchange for the promotion. Investors are entitled to know whether the publicity for a security is unbiased, and Kardashian failed to disclose the information.

Kardashian's $1.26 million settlement is only a tiny fraction of her net worth, which is estimated at nearly $2 billion, and it is unlikely she will miss the money. However, the settlement has symbolic value for the SEC as it shows the commission isn't afraid to go after some of the biggest celebrities in the world, as well as social media influencers, who can spread the word quickly about crypto and other investments. For example, the chair of the United Kingdom Financial Conduct Authority called Kardashian's post the "financial promotion with the single biggest audience reach in history." Many celebrities have made money promoting what have ended up being shady crypto schemes that quickly collapsed, leaving investors, many of whom are their fans and followers, with empty pockets. Ethereum Max is a good example; the company had a market capitalization of $250 million at the time Kardashian endorsed it but was virtually worthless a little more than a year later.

Kim Kardashian is not the only high-profile celebrity whose promotion of EMAX raised concern among investors. A class-action lawsuit was filed in California on behalf of around 100 plaintiffs who lost more than $5 million investing in EMAX and named Kardashian, former NBA star Paul Pierce, boxing legend Floyd Mayweather, Jr., and former NFL star Antonio Brown as defendants. The lawsuit claimed the celebrities worked to pump up the price of EMAX tokens and then sold them, leaving investors with huge losses. A number of Hollywood and sports celebrities including Tom Brady, Larry David, Shaquille O'Neal, and Stephen Curry were also named as defendants in a class-action lawsuit against cryptocurrency exchange FTX, which went bankrupt in late 2022. The lawsuit alleged that the sports stars and television celebrities, who appeared in ads endorsing FTX, brought instant credibility to the exchange and that their celebrity status made them culpable for promoting the company's failed business model.

A new generation of investors is emerging for whom social media sites such as Instagram, YouTube,

continued

Reddit, TikTok, and YouTube have become some of the most popular sources for financial information and investment advice. However, SEC chairman Gary Gensler has noted that the Ethereum Max case is a reminder that when celebrities or influencers endorse investment opportunities, including crypto asset securities, it doesn't mean that those investment products are right for all investors. Making investment decisions based on the advice of a celebrity may not be a good idea. Hopefully Kim Kardashian's 330 million followers, as well as those of other celebrities and influencers, will heed this advice.

Sources: Ken Sweet, "Tom Brady, Larry David, Other Celebrities Named in FTX Suit," *San Diego Union Tribune*, November 17, 2022, pp. C1, 3; Mike Calia and Jacqueline Corba, "Kim Kardashian Pays Over $1 Million to Settle SEC Charges Linked to a Crypto Promo on Her Instagram," *CNBC*, October 3, 2022, https://www.cnbc.com/2022/10/03/kim-kardashian-settles-sec-charges-instagram-crypto-promotion.html; Ryan Browne, "Kim Kardashian and Floyd Mayweather Sued by Investors over Alleged Crypto Scam," *CNBC*, January 12, 2022, https://www.cnbc.com/2022/01/12/kim-kardashian-and-floyd-mayweather-sued-over-alleged-crypto-scam.html.

Suppose you are the advertising manager for a consumer-products company and have just reviewed a new commercial your agency created. You are very excited about the ad. It presents new claims about your brand's superiority that should help differentiate it from the competition. However, before you approve the commercial you need answers. Are the claims verifiable? Did researchers use proper procedures to collect and analyze the data and present the findings? Do research results support the claims? Were the right people used in the study? Could any conditions have biased the results?

Before approving the commercial, you have it reviewed by your company's legal department and by your ad agency's attorneys. If both reviews are acceptable, you send the ad to the major networks, which have their censors examine it. They may ask for more information or send the ad back for modification. (No commercial can run without approval from a network's Standards and Practices Department.)

Even after approval and airing, your commercial is still subject to scrutiny from such state and federal regulatory agencies as the state attorney general's office and the Federal Trade Commission. Individual consumers or competitors who find the ad misleading or have other concerns may file a complaint with the National Advertising Division of the BBB National Programs, Inc. Finally, disparaged competitors may sue if they believe your ad distorts the facts and misleads consumers. If you lose the litigation, your company may have to retract the claims and pay the competitor damages, sometimes running into millions of dollars.

After considering all these regulatory issues, you must ask yourself if the new ad can meet all these challenges and is worth the risk. Maybe you ought to continue with the old approach that made no specific claims and simply said your brand was great.

OVERVIEW OF REGULATION

Regulatory concerns can play a major role in the advertising and promotion decision-making process. Advertisers operate in a complex environment of local, state, and federal rules and regulations. Additionally, a number of advertising and business-sponsored associations, consumer groups and organizations, and the media attempt to promote honest, truthful, and tasteful advertising through their own self-regulatory programs and guidelines. The legal and regulatory aspects of advertising are very complex. Many parties are concerned about the nature and content of advertising and its potential to offend, exploit, mislead, and/or deceive consumers.

Advertising has also become increasingly important in product liability litigation involving products that are associated with consumer injuries. In many of these cases the courts have been willing to consider the impact of advertising on behavior of consumers that leads to injury-causing situations. Thus advertisers must avoid certain practices and proactively engage in others to ensure that their ads are comprehended correctly and do not misrepresent their products or services.[1] The costs can be very high and consequences quite severe when companies become involved in legal proceedings regarding their advertising claims.

Numerous guidelines, rules, regulations, and laws constrain and restrict advertising. These regulations primarily influence individual advertisers, but they can also affect advertising for an entire industry. For example, cigarette advertising was banned from the broadcast media in 1970, and many groups continue to push for a total ban on the advertising of tobacco products, including e-cigarettes and other delivery forms.[2] As discussed later in the chapter, legislation is being considered that would either ban or impose major restrictions on direct-to-consumer advertising of drugs.[3] Advertising is controlled by internal self-regulation and by external state and federal regulatory agencies such as the Federal Trade Commission (FTC), the Federal Communications Commission (FCC), the Food and Drug Administration (FDA), and the U.S. Postal Service. State attorneys general also have become more active in advertising regulation. While only government agencies (federal, state, and local) have the force of law, most advertisers also abide by the guidelines and decisions of internal regulatory bodies. In fact, self-regulation from groups such as the media and BBB National Programs, Inc. probably has more influence on advertisers' day-to-day operations and decision making than do government rules and regulations.

Decision makers on both the client and agency side must be knowledgeable about these regulatory groups, including the intent of their efforts, how they operate, and how they influence and affect advertising and other promotional-mix elements. In this chapter, we examine the major sources of advertising regulation, including efforts by the industry at voluntary self-regulation and external regulation by government agencies. We also examine regulations involving sales promotion, direct marketing, and marketing on the Internet.

SELF-REGULATION

For many years, the advertising industry has practiced and promoted voluntary **self-regulation**. Most advertisers, their agencies, and the media recognize the importance of maintaining consumer trust and confidence. Advertisers also see self-regulation as a way to limit government interference, which, they believe, results in more stringent and troublesome regulations. Self-regulation and control of advertising emanate from all segments of the advertising industry, including individual advertisers and their agencies, business and advertising associations, and the media.

Self-Regulation by Advertisers and Agencies

Self-regulation begins with the interaction of client and agency when creative ideas are generated and submitted for consideration. Most companies have specific guidelines, standards, and policies to which their ads must adhere. Recognizing that their ads reflect on the company, advertisers carefully scrutinize all messages to ensure they are consistent with the image the firm wishes to project. Companies also review their ads to be sure any claims made are reasonable and verifiable and do not mislead or deceive consumers. Ads are usually examined by corporate attorneys to avoid potential legal problems and their accompanying time, expense, negative publicity, and embarrassment.

Internal control and regulation also come from advertising agencies. Most have standards regarding the type of advertising they either want or are willing to produce, and they try to avoid ads that might be offensive or misleading. Most agencies will ask their clients to provide verification or support for claims they might want to make in their advertising and will make sure that adequate documentation or substantiation is available. However, agencies will also take formal steps to protect themselves from legal and ethical perils through agency–client contracts. For example, many liability issues are handled in these contracts. Agencies generally use information provided by clients for advertising claims, and in standard contracts the agency is protected from suits involving the accuracy of those claims. Contracts will also absolve the agency of

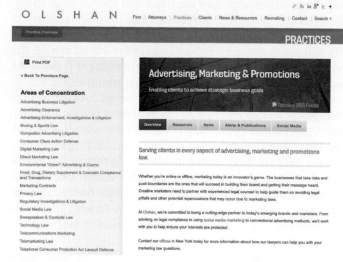

EXHIBIT 20–1

The Olshan firm specializes in advertising and integrated marketing communications law.

Olshan Frome Wolosky LLP

responsibility if something goes wrong with the advertised product and consumers suffer damages or injury or other product liability claims arise.[4] However, agencies have been held legally responsible for fraudulent or deceptive claims and in some cases have been fined when their clients were found guilty of engaging in deceptive advertising.[5] Many agencies have a creative review board or panel composed of experienced personnel who examine ads for content and execution as well as for their potential to be perceived as offensive, misleading, and/or deceptive. Most agencies also employ or retain lawyers who review the ads for potential legal problems. Exhibit 20-1 shows the homepage for the Advertising, Marketing & Promotions division of Olshan, a law firm in New York City whose specialities include advertising and integrated marketing communications law.

Self-Regulation by Trade Associations

Like advertisers and their agencies, many industries have also developed self-regulatory programs. This is particularly true in industries whose advertising is prone to controversy, such as liquor and alcoholic beverages, drugs, and various products marketed to children. Many trade and industry associations develop their own advertising guidelines or codes that member companies are expected to abide by including the Toy Industry Association, the Motion Picture Association of America, and the Pharmaceutical Research and Manufacturers of America (PHRMA). The Wine Institute, the Beer Institute, and the Distilled Spirits Council of the United States all have guidelines that member companies are supposed to follow in advertising alcoholic beverages.[6]

The advertising of hard liquor on television has been a very controversial issue as many consumer and public health groups argue that liquor is more dangerous than beer or wine because of its higher alcohol content. Critics also argue that airing liquor ads on TV glamorizes drinking and encourages children and teenagers to drink and were successful in keeping advertising for spirits off the major networks until recently. While no specific law prohibits the advertising of hard liquor on radio or television, it was effectively banned for over five decades as a result of a code provision by the National Association of Broadcasters and by agreement of liquor manufacturers and their self-governing body, the Distilled Spirits Council of the United States (DISCUS). However, in November 1996, DISCUS amended its code of good practice and overturned its self-imposed ban on broadcast advertising.[7]

After the DISCUS ban was lifted, the four major broadcast TV networks as well as major cable networks such as ESPN and MTV continued to refuse liquor ads, prompting consumer and public interest groups to applaud their actions.[8] However, the major networks cannot control the practices of affiliate stations they do not own, and many of them began accepting liquor ads, as did local cable channels and independent broadcast stations. While the national broadcast networks continued their self-imposed ban for many years, the amount of liquor advertising on television continued to increase as more cable and local broadcast stations began accepting the commercials. Over the past several years the major networks have been accepting commercials for liquor, although most of the ads do not air before 10 P.M., unlike on cable, where many networks allow them anytime.[9]

The airing of hard liquor ads on a network TV show represents a major victory for the distilled spirits industry, which has argued there should be a level playing field for alcohol advertising and that liquor should be viewed the same way as beer and wine. They also note that the Federal Trade Commission (FTC) has said there is no basis for treating liquor ads differently than advertising for other types of alcohol. For example, in 2017 the National Football League (NFL) changed its advertising policy and began

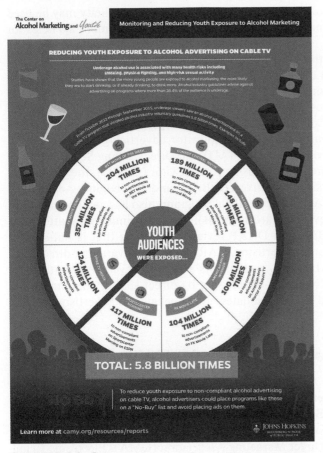

EXHIBIT 20–2

In this advertisement for The Center on Alcohol Marketing and Youth, it is apparent that they are opposed to the advertising of hard liquor on television.

Center on Alcohol Marketing and Youth

EXHIBIT 20–3

Advertising is often used by attorneys to promote their services.

The Law Office of J. Wyndal Gordon, P.A. Baltimore, Maryland

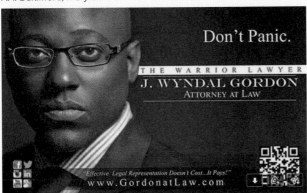

allowing the television networks to accept commercials for distilled spirits. The policy change limits hard liquor advertising to no more than four 30-second spots per game as well as two spots in any quarter or during halftime. The commercials also have to include a prominent social responsibility message and cannot use a football-related theme or target underage drinkers.[10] Thus, it appears that TV advertising for distilled spirits is here to stay, and it's likely that you will see a lot more liquor ads on network TV shows as well as on cable. However, as might be expected, public advocacy groups such as the Center for Science in the Public Interest and the Center on Alcohol Marketing and Youth remain opposed to the networks' softening of their stance, arguing that youth exposure to liquor ads on TV has already increased significantly (Exhibit 20–2).

Many professions also maintain advertising guidelines through local, state, and national organizations. For years professional associations like the American Medical Association (AMA) and the American Bar Association (ABA) restricted advertising by their members on the basis that such promotional activities lowered members' professional status and led to unethical and fraudulent claims. However, such restrictive codes have been attacked by both government regulatory agencies and consumer groups. They argue that the public has a right to be informed about a professional's services, qualifications, and background and that advertising will improve professional services as consumers become better informed and are better able to shop around.[11]

In 1977, the Supreme Court held that state bar associations' restrictions on advertising are unconstitutional and that attorneys have First Amendment freedom of speech rights to advertise.[12] Many professional associations subsequently removed their restrictions, and advertising by lawyers and other professionals is now common. Exhibit 20–3 shows an ad used by an attorney to promote his services and the value of effective legal representation.[13] Although industry associations are concerned with the impact and consequences of members' advertising, they have no legal way to enforce their guidelines. They can only rely on peer pressure from members or other nonbinding sanctions to get advertisers to comply. In 1982, the Supreme Court upheld an FTC order permitting advertising by dentists and physicians, and various forms of advertising are now used by both groups.[14]

Self-Regulation by Businesses

A number of self-regulatory mechanisms have been established by the business community in an effort to control advertising practices.[15] The largest and best known is the **Better Business Bureau (BBB)**, which promotes fair advertising and selling practices across all industries. The BBB was established in 1916 to handle consumer complaints about local business practices and particularly advertising. Local BBBs are located in most large cities throughout the United States and supported entirely by dues of the more than 100,000 member firms.

Local BBBs receive and investigate complaints from consumers and other companies regarding the advertising and selling tactics of businesses in their area. Each local office has its own operating procedures for handling complaints; generally, the office contacts the violator and, if the complaint proves true, requests that the practice be stopped or changed. If the violator does not respond, negative publicity may be used against the firm or the case may be referred to appropriate government agencies for further action.

While BBBs provide effective control over advertising practices at the local level, **BBB National Programs**, an independent nonprofit organization, is the third-party administrator of the advertising industry's system of self-regulation at the national level. Policies and procedures for industry self-regulation were established by the Advertising Self-Regulatory Council (ASRC), which merged into BBB National Programs, Inc. This system of industry self-regulation for advertising is implemented through the National Advertising Division (NAD), the Direct Selling Self-Regulatory Council (DSSRC), the Children's Advertising Review Unit (CARU), the Children's Food and Beverage Advertising Initiative (CFBAI), and the Digital Advertising Accountability Program (DAAP). BBB National Programs also has an appellate unit, the National Advertising Review Board (NARB). Staffed primarily by attorneys, NAD, DSSRC, CARU, CFBAI, and DAAP review advertising that is national in scope. NAD reviews all national advertising, CARU reviews advertising directed to children under age 13, CFBAI reviews participants' food and beverage advertising in child-directed media, DSSRC reviews advertising by direct selling companies and their salesforce members, and DAAP regulates online behavioral advertising (OBA) across the Internet.

BBB National Programs and the NAD/NARB

In 1971 four associations—the American Advertising Federation (AAF), the American Association of Advertising Agencies (the 4As), the Association of National Advertisers (ANA), and the Council of Better Business Bureaus—joined forces to establish the National Advertising Review Council (NARC). In 2009 the CEOs of three other major marketing organizations—the Direct Marketing Association (DMA), Electronic Retailing Association (ERA), and the Interactive Advertising Bureau (IAB)—joined the NARC Board of Directors, and in 2012 the organization changed its name to the Advertising Self-Regulatory Council (ASRC). As noted previously, the ASRC was merged into BBB National Programs in 2019.

BBB National Programs' mission is to sustain high standards of truth and accuracy in national advertising. The NAD has examined advertising for truth and accuracy since 1971 and has published more than 5,000 decisions, focusing on areas that include product performance claims, superiority claims against competitive products, and all kinds of scientific and technical claims. BBB National Programs has a process that it follows for self-regulation and follows a specific set of policies and procedures that can be found on its website (Exhibit 20-4).

Federal law requires that advertisers possess substantiation for their advertising claims before the claims are published. After initiating or receiving a complaint, the NAD requests the advertiser's substantiation, reviews the information, and reaches a determination. In cases where the substantiating evidence does not support the claim, the NAD recommends that the advertiser modify or discontinue the claim. When an advertiser or a challenger disagrees with the NAD's findings, its decision can be appealed to the NARB for additional review.

As can be seen in Figure 20-1, the vast majority of the complaints to the NAD come from marketers challenging claims made by their competitors, often in the context of a comparative advertising message.[16] For example, the online dating service eHarmony filed a complaint with the NAD over advertising used by competitor Chemistry.com, which claimed that it could use "the latest science of attraction to predict which single men and women [one] will have a relationship and dating chemistry with."[17] Chemistry.com's matchmaking system

EXHIBIT 20–4

BBB National Programs partners with advertising and marketing organizations to create an effective self-regulatory system.

Better Business Bureau

Revised effective September 19, 2022

THE ADVERTISING INDUSTRY'S PROCESS OF VOLUNTARY SELF-REGULATION

Policies and Procedures by:
BBB National Programs

Procedures for:

The National Advertising Division
(NAD)

The National Advertising Review Board
(NARB)

FIGURE 20-1   Sources of NAD Cases and Decisions, 2021

Sources	Number	Percentage	Decisions	Number	Percentage
Competitor challenges	80	75%	Modified/discontinued	40	37%
NAD monitoring	16	15	Substantiated/modified/discontinued	27	25
Council for Responsible Nutrition	11	10	Administratively closed	10	9
Consumer challenges	0	0	Compliance	23	22
Total	107	100%	Substantiated	3	3
			Referred to government	3	3
			Compliance/referred to government	1	1
			Total	107	100%

was developed by an anthropologist who studies mate selection and uses responses to an extensive survey to determine people who might be attracted to one another. The NAD concluded that the dating service could not substantiate many of the advertising claims and ruled that the company should discontinue them. Chemistry's parent company, Match.com, issued a statement saying that it disagreed with some of the NAD's findings, but agreed to discontinue the claims at issue.[18] Anheuser-Busch filed a claim with the NAD over advertising used by Molson Coors claiming that Miller Lite has more taste than Bud Light and Michelob ULTRA as part of its "Know Your Beer" campaign. The campaign included digital influencer videos featuring beer drinkers who were recruited to take part in on-camera taste tests. The NAD found that Molson Coors provided a reasonable basis for the more taste claim but also recommended that it discontinue using certain digital vignettes or modify them to remove statements suggesting that the consumers in the video participated in a taste test. Molson Coors agreed to comply with the NAD's decision and changed the videos but continued to use the "more taste" claim in its advertising.[19]

The NAD's advertising monitoring program is also the source of many of the cases it reviews (Figure 20-1). It also reviews complaints from consumers and consumer groups, trade associations, local BBBs, and competitors. For example, the NAD challenged an ad for CoverGirl mascara featuring singer Taylor Swift, arguing that it was misleading because her eyelashes had been enhanced after the fact to look fuller. The fine print under the photo of Swift read that her lashes had been "enhanced in post-production." However, the NAD considered the express claims made in the ad that indicated that the mascara would give eyelashes "2x more volume" and that the product was "20 percent lighter" than the most expensive mascara. The NAD attorneys argued that the photograph stood as a product demonstration and at issue was what one's lashes would look like when using the product. Procter & Gamble, the parent company of the CoverGirl brand at the time, fully cooperated with the NAD and voluntarily discontinued making the challenged claims as well as the photograph.[20]

Advertisers that disagree with NAD's findings have an automatic right to appeal NAD's decision to the **National Advertising Review Board (NARB)**. The NARB is made up of 83 professionals from three different categories: national advertisers (39 members), advertising agencies (30 members), and public members (14), which includes academics and other members of the public sector. Although the self-regulatory system has no power to order an advertiser to modify or stop running an ad and no sanctions it can impose, advertisers who participate in NAD/CARU/DSSRC or NARB proceedings generally comply. When companies refuse to participate in a self-regulatory proceeding or do not comply with the terms of a decision, their disputed advertising may be referred to the most appropriate federal agency for further review. In 2021, of the 107 cases handled by the NAD, 40 were modified or discontinued; 27 were substantiated, modified, or discontinued; 23 complied with the NAD; 10 were administratively closed; 3 were referred to government; 3 were substantiated; and 1 complied with the NAD and was referred to government (Figure 20-1).[21]

BBB National Programs' Children's Advertising Review Unit's (CARU) activities include the review and evaluation of child-directed advertising in all media as well as online privacy issues that affect children. CARU monitoring is under revised guidelines that went into effect at the beginning of 2022 that use widely recognized industry standards to assure that advertising directed to children is not deceptive, unfair, or inappropriate for its intended audience. CARU monitors child-directed media to ensure compliance with these guidelines, seeking voluntary cooperation of companies and, where necessary, referral for enforcement action to an appropriate federal regulatory body, usually the Federal Trade Commission (FTC), or to state Attorneys General. The steady growth in online platforms and new immersive, interactive forms of child-directed media is reflected in the revised guidelines, which now more specifically address digital and social media, video content, influencer advertising, apps, in-game advertising and purchasing, and other interactive children's spaces.[22]

BBB National Programs is also involved in the self-regulation of direct selling through the Direct Selling Self-Regulatory Council (DSSRC), which was established in 2019 in partnership with the Direct Selling Association (DSA). The mission of DSSRC is to enhance consumer and regulatory confidence in advertising and marketing in the direct selling marketplace through independent, third-party review of claims disseminated by or on behalf of direct selling companies. DSSRC offers the direct selling industry a system for expeditious review of earnings claims (including lifestyle representations) and product claims (including services) communicated by direct selling companies and their salesforce members. The goal of DSSRC is to discourage the use of false and unsubstantiated claims and to enhance the truthfulness, accuracy, and adequate substantiation of all advertising and marketing claims made in the direct selling industry.

Another area in which BBB National Programs is involved is the Digital Advertising Accountability Program (DAAP), which is a data privacy program that enforces self-regulatory standards for online and mobile advertising. Its mission is to build trust in the digital marketplace by ensuring that markets provide consumers with transparency and choice regarding the collection and use of their data for interest-based ads. The DAAP was developed at the request of the Digital Advertising Alliance (DAA), an alliance of the major advertising trade associations, as the third-party administrator for its suite of Self-Regulatory Principles for Online Behavioral Advertising (OBA). OBA uses information collected across multiple unaffiliated websites and mobile apps to predict a user's preferences and displays ads most likely to attract their interests. The principles correspond with tenets supported by the Federal Trade Commission, and also address public education and industry accountability issues raised by the FTC. The OBA Self-Regulatory Principles, which are shown in Figure 20-2, are designed to address consumer concerns about the use of personal information for interest-based advertising and focus on transparency and consumer-control issues. The OBA Principles are also the basis of additional guidance that applies self-regulatory principles developed by the DAA to mobile advertising as well as the practice of using multi-site data and cross-app data for interest-based advertising purposes. The Accountability Program also monitors the marketplace for compliance with the Political Advertising Principles, a set of best practices surrounding political advertising.

BBB National Programs, working through the NAD/NARB/CARU and DSSRC is a valuable and effective self-regulatory body. Cases brought to it are handled at a fraction of the cost (and with much less publicity) than those brought to court and are expedited more quickly than those reviewed by a government agency such as the FTC. The system also works because judgments are made by the advertiser's peers, and most companies feel compelled to comply. Firms may prefer self-regulation rather than government intervention in part because they can challenge competitors' unsubstantiated claims and achieve a more rapid resolution.[23]

FIGURE 20–2

Self-Regulatory Principles
for Online Behavioral
Advertising

Self-Regulatory Principles for Online
Behavioral Advertising, July 2009.
Developed by American Association of
Advertising Agencies, Association of
National Advertisers, Council of Better
Business Bureaus, Data and Marketing
Association, Network Advertising
Initiative, and Interactive Advertising
Bureau. Reprinted with permission
from Digital Advertising Alliance.

The Education Principle calls for organizations to participate in efforts to educate individuals and businesses about online behavioral advertising and the Principles.

The Transparency Principle calls for clearer and easily accessible disclosures to consumers about data collection and use practices associated with online behavioral advertising. It will result in new, enhanced notice on the page where data is collected through links embedded in or around advertisements, or on the web page itself.

The Consumer Control Principle provides consumers with an expanded ability to choose whether data is collected and used for online behavioral advertising purposes. This choice will be available through a link from the notice provided on the web page where data is collected.

The Consumer Control Principle also requires "service providers," a term that includes Internet access service providers and providers of desktop applications software such as web browser "tool bars" to obtain the consent of users before engaging in online behavioral advertising, and take steps to de-identify the data used for such purposes.

The Data Security Principle calls for organizations to provide appropriate security for, and limited retention of, data collected and used for online behavioral advertising purposes.

The Material Changes Principle calls for obtaining consumer consent before a Material Change is made to an entity's Online Behavioral Advertising data collection and use policies unless that change will result in less collection or use of data.

The Sensitive Data Principle recognizes that data collected from children and used for online behavioral advertising merits heightened protection, and requires parental consent for behavioral advertising to consumers known to be under 13 on child-directed websites. This Principle also provides heightened protections to certain health and financial data when attributable to a specific individual.

The Accountability Principle calls for development of programs to further advance these Principles, including programs to monitor and report instances of uncorrected non-compliance with these Principles to appropriate government agencies. The CBBB and DMA have been asked and agreed to work cooperatively to establish accountability mechanisms under the Principles.

Advertising Associations   Various groups in the advertising industry also favor self-regulation. The two major national organizations, the 4As and the American Advertising Federation, actively monitor and police industrywide advertising practices. The 4As, which is the major trade association of the ad agency business in the United States, has established standards of practice and its own creative code (Figure 20–3). The AAF

FIGURE 20–3

Standards of Practice of the
4A's: Creative Code

CREATIVE CODE

We, the members of the American Association of Advertising Agencies, in addition to supporting and obeying the laws and legal regulations pertaining to advertising, undertake to extend and broaden the application of high ethical standards. Specifically, we will not knowingly create advertising that contains:

a) False or misleading statements or exaggerations, visual or verbal

b) Testimonials that do not reflect the real opinion of the individual(s) involved

c) Price claims that are misleading

d) Claims insufficiently supported or that distort the true meaning or practicable application of statements made by professional or scientific authority

e) Statements, suggestions, or pictures offensive to public decency or minority segments of the population

"Creative Code" from Standards of Practice of the American Association of Advertising Agencies. © 2016. Reprinted with permission from 4A's.

UNHATE

UNITED COLORS
OF BENETTON.

Supports
the Unhate Foundation
unhatefoundation.org

EXHIBIT 20–5

A number of magazines
refused to run this
Benetton ad.

Benetton Group

consists of advertisers, agencies, media, and numerous advertising clubs. The association has standards for truthful and responsible advertising, is involved in advertising legislation, and actively influences agencies to abide by its code and principles.

Self-Regulation by Media

The media are another important self-regulatory mechanism in the advertising industry. Most media maintain some form of advertising review process and, except for political ads, may reject any they regard as objectionable. Some media exclude advertising for an entire product class; others ban individual ads they think offensive or objectionable. For example, *Reader's Digest* does not accept advertising for tobacco or liquor products. A number of magazines in the United States and other countries refused to run some of Benetton's shock ads on the grounds that their readers would find them offensive or disturbing (Exhibit 20-5).[24]

Newspapers and magazines have their own advertising requirements and restrictions, which often vary depending on the size and nature of the publication. Large, established publications, such as major newspapers or magazines, often have strict standards regarding the type of advertising they accept. Some magazines, such as *Parents* and *Good Housekeeping*, regularly test the products they advertise and offer a "seal of approval" and refunds if the products are later found to be defective. Such policies are designed to enhance the credibility of the publication and increase the reader's confidence in the products it advertises.

Advertising on television and radio has been regulated for years through codes developed by the industry trade association, the National Association of Broadcasters (NAB). Both the radio code (established in 1937) and the television code (1952) provided standards for broadcast advertising for many years. Both codes prohibited the advertising of certain products, such as hard liquor. They also affected the manner in which products could be advertised. However, in 1982 the NAB suspended all of its code provisions after the courts found that portions (dealing with time standards and required length of commercials in the TV code) were in restraint of trade. While the NAB codes are no longer in force, many individual broadcasters, such as the major TV networks, have incorporated major portions of the code provisions into their own standards.[25]

The four major television networks have the most stringent review process of any media. All four networks maintain standards and practices divisions, which carefully review all commercials submitted to the network or individual affiliate stations. Advertisers must submit for review all commercials intended for airing on the network or an affiliate.

A commercial may be submitted for review in the form of a script, storyboard, animatic, or finished commercial (when the advertiser believes there is little chance of objection). A very frustrating, and often expensive, scenario for both an agency and its client occurs when a commercial is approved at the storyboard stage but then is rejected after it is produced. Commercials are rejected for a variety of reasons, including violence, morbid humor, sex, politics, and religion. Network reviewers also consider whether the proposed commercial meets acceptable standards and is appropriate for certain audiences. For example, different standards are used for ads designated for prime-time versus late-night spots or for children's versus adults' programs (see Figure 20-4). Although most of these guidelines for children's advertising remain in effect, several networks have loosened their rules on celebrity endorsements.[26]

Each of the major TV networks has its own set of guidelines for children's advertising, although the basics are very similar. A few rules, such as the requirement of a static "island" shot at the end, are written in stone; others, however, can sometimes be negotiated. Many of the rules below apply specifically to toys. The networks also have special guidelines for kids' food commercials and for kids' commercials that offer premiums.

Must not overglamorize product

No exhortative language, such as "Ask Mom to buy . . ."

No realistic war settings

Generally no celebrity endorsements

Can't use "only" or "just" in regard to price

Show only two toys per child or maximum of six per commercial

Five-second "island" showing product against plain background at end of spot

Animation restricted to one-third of a commercial

Generally no comparative or superiority claims

No costumes or props not available with the toy

No child or toy can appear in animated segments

Three-second establishing shot of toy in relation to child

No shots under one second in length

Must show distance a toy can travel before stopping on its own

The four major networks receive nearly 50,000 commercials a year for review; nearly two-thirds are accepted, and only 3 percent are rejected. Most problems with the remaining 30 percent are resolved through negotiation, and the ads are revised and resubmitted.[27] Most commercials run after changes are made. For example, censors initially rejected a humorous "Got Milk?" spot that showed children watching an elderly neighbor push a wheelbarrow. Suddenly, the man's arms rip off, presumably because he doesn't drink milk. The spot was eventually approved after it was modified so that the man appears unhurt after losing his limbs and there was no expression of pain (Exhibit 20-6).[28]

The various social media platforms also have standards that restrict the advertising of certain products and services as well as the content.[29] Most of the restricted and

EXHIBIT 20-6

This humorous "Got Milk?" commercial had to be modified slightly to satisfy network censors.

The California Milk Advisory Board

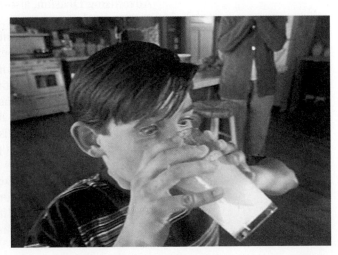

EXHIBIT 20-7

All ads running on Facebook and Instagram must meet Meta's advertising standards and policies.

PixieMe/Shutterstock

prohibited content includes the promotion of illegal products, use of trademarks belonging to others, and proscription of deceptive practices. For example, Meta, which is the parent company of Facebook and Instagram, has a set of Advertising Standards that provide policy detail and guidance on the types of ad content allowed on the social media platforms and the types of content prohibited. Each ad submitted by an advertiser is reviewed against these standards as well as Meta's advertising policy principles, which include protecting people from unsafe and discriminatory practices, protecting them from fraud or scam, promoting positive user experiences, and promoting transparency (Exhibit 20-7). In 2016 Facebook imposed a global ban on private gun sales on its social media platform as well as on Instagram, which it also owns. The policy does not apply to licensed retailers, which can market firearms on Facebook and Instagram while completing the transaction offline. The policy is designed to stop "peer-to-peer" sales of firearms by prohibiting people from using Facebook and Instagram to offer and coordinate private sales of firearms on the sites.[30]

Appraising Self-Regulation

The three major participants in the advertising process—advertisers, agencies, and the media—work individually and collectively to encourage truthful, ethical, and responsible advertising. The advertising industry views self-regulation as an effective mechanism for controlling advertising abuses and avoiding the use of offensive, misleading, or deceptive practices, and it prefers this form of regulation to government intervention. Self-regulation of advertising has been effective and in many instances probably led to the development of more stringent standards and practices than those imposed by or beyond the scope of legislation. Moreover, over 90 percent of advertisers comply with NAD decisions since failure to do so can result in government action, which can be very expensive to companies and result in more punitive measures.[31]

A senior vice president and general counsel at Kraft Foods, while praising the NAD, summarized the feelings of many advertisers toward self-regulation. In his testimonial he stated: "NAD is superior to its competition, which is regulation by the government or regulation by the courts. Accurate, prompt, and inexpensive decisions year in and year out have earned NAD its well-deserved credibility with the industry and with regulators." Laura Brett, vice president of BBB National Programs' National Advertising Division, also comments on the value of self-regulation: "With more than five decades of experience, the self-regulatory system built by the advertising industry is the gold standard of independent self-regulation: a strong example of how self-regulation can be used to build consumer trust." She notes that the self-regulatory system protects consumers from misleading advertising by acting quickly and decisively against misleading advertising claims; it leads the way in providing guidance as advertising evolves onto new platforms and new issues arise, providing advertisers with guidance that helps avoid missteps; it provides a fast, efficient, and expert forum that levels the playing field for all advertisers by holding them to high standards of truthfulness and claim substantiation; and it provides a roadmap for the development of strong, new self-regulation programs.[32]

Exhibit 20-8 summarizes how BBB National Programs helps create a more trustworthy marketplace for consumers and businesses.

There are, however, limitations to self-regulation, and the process has been criticized in a number of areas. For example, the NAD may take 3 or 4 months, and

Five Decades of Impact

While BBB National Programs was established as an independent non-profit entity in 2019, our program teams have worked with industry leaders and government regulatory agencies since 1971 to establish the standards that guide best practices in advertising, privacy, consumer warranty issues, children's and teen's marketing, and dispute resolution.

Our Programs:

- Monitor and enforce truth in national advertising

- Demonstrate respect for a consumer's privacy preferences through data privacy watchdog programs

- Manage corporate international data transfer compliance through monitoring, independent recourse mechanisms, and dispute resolution services

- Ensure consumer disputes are heard and addressed through the largest vehicle warranty dispute resolution program in the United States

- Strengthen the direct selling industry with accountability and dispute resolution mechanisms established with a leading industry association

- Protect young children from inappropriate child-directed advertising and improper online data collection practices and (coming soon) work to foster teen privacy protection practices

- Deliver arbitration services for customers of a leading telecommunications provider

- Address children's nutrition and advertising challenges through self-regulatory pledge programs with leading food, confectionary, beverage, and quick-service restaurants

Learn more about our programs →

National Programs

© BBB National Programs, 2022. All Rights Reserved.

EXHIBIT 20–8

BBB National Programs is an effective alternative to government intervention and/or litigation.

Better Business Bureau

sometimes even longer, to resolve a complaint, during which time a company often stops using the commercial anyway. Budgeting and staffing constraints may limit the number of cases the NAD/NARB system investigates and the speed with which it resolves them. Financial support remains an important challenge for the NAD/NARB as its programs are supported by about 200 major corporations through partnership with the BBB National Programs, Inc. Support for self-regulatory programs is much smaller in the United States than in many other countries despite the fact that the advertising market in the United States is much larger.[33] And some critics believe that self-regulation is self-serving to the advertisers and advertising industry because it lacks the power or authority to be a viable alternative to federal or state regulation. However, while state and federal agencies do not always pursue the cases referred by the NAD, the threat of referral serves as an important deterrent.[34]

An American Bar Association (ABA) working group consisting of attorneys who practice before the NAD released a report in 2015 that reviewed and suggested improvements to the advertising industry's self-regulatory system.[35] The ABA report concluded that the current system of advertising self-regulation administered by the NAD works well but did find areas for improvement. Among the recommendations were that the NAD issue its decisions in a timelier manner, as well as permitting advertisers to reach settlement agreements without the issuance of a press release and instead release only case abstracts or summaries taken from the NAD decision. However, press releases would continue to be used in cases where an advertiser has refused to participate or accept the NAD's recommendations and the case has been referred to federal regulatory agencies or law enforcement. One of the most important recommendations from the report was the need for additional funding for the NAD since implementation of the recommendations would require more staff.[36]

Many do not believe advertising can or should be controlled solely by self-regulation. They argue that regulation by government agencies is necessary to ensure that consumers get accurate information and are not misled or deceived. Moreover, since advertisers do not have to comply with the decisions and recommendations of self-regulatory groups, it is sometimes necessary to turn to the federal and/or state government.

FEDERAL REGULATION OF ADVERTISING

Advertising is controlled and regulated through federal, state, and local laws and regulations enforced by various government agencies. The federal government is the most important source of external regulation since many advertising practices come under the jurisdiction of the **Federal Trade Commission (FTC)**. In addition, depending on the advertiser's industry and product or service, other federal agencies such as the Federal Communications Commission, the Food and Drug Administration, the U.S.

Postal Service, and the Bureau of Alcohol, Tobacco, Firearms and Explosives may have regulations that affect advertising. We will begin our discussion of federal regulation of advertising by considering the basic rights of marketers to advertise their products and services under the First Amendment.

Advertising and the First Amendment

Freedom of speech or expression, as defined by the First Amendment to the U.S. Constitution, is the most basic federal law governing advertising in the United States. For many years, freedom of speech protection did not include advertising and other forms of speech that promote a commercial transaction. However, the courts have extended First Amendment protection to **commercial speech**, which is speech that promotes a commercial transaction. There have been a number of landmark cases where the federal courts have issued rulings supporting the coverage of commercial speech by the First Amendment.

In a 1976 case, *Virginia State Board of Pharmacy v. Virginia Citizens Consumer Council*, the U.S. Supreme Court ruled that states cannot prohibit pharmacists from advertising the prices of prescription drugs, because such advertising contains information that helps the consumer choose between products and because the free flow of information is indispensable.[37] As noted earlier, in 1977 the Supreme Court ruled that state bar associations' restrictions on advertising are unconstitutional and attorneys have a First Amendment right to advertise their services and prices.[38] In another landmark case in 1980, *Central Hudson Gas & Electric Corp. v. New York Public Service Commission*, the Supreme Court ruled that commercial speech was entitled to First Amendment protection in some cases. However, the Court ruled that the U.S. Constitution affords less protection to commercial speech than to other constitutionally guaranteed forms of expression. In this case the Court established a four-part test, known as the **Central Hudson Test**, for determining restrictions on commercial speech.[39] In another important case, the Supreme Court's 1996 decision in *44 Liquormart, Inc. v. Rhode Island* struck down two state statutes designed to support the state's interest in temperance. The first prohibited the advertising of alcoholic beverage prices in Rhode Island except on signs within a store, while the second prohibited the publication or broadcast of alcohol price ads. The Court ruled that the Rhode Island statutes were unlawful because they restricted the constitutional guarantee of freedom of speech, and the decision signaled strong protection for advertisers under the First Amendment.[40]

In the cases regarding advertising, the U.S. Supreme Court has ruled that freedom of expression must be balanced against competing interests. For example, the courts have upheld bans on the advertising of products that are considered harmful, such as tobacco. The Court has also ruled that only truthful commercial speech is protected, not advertising or other forms of promotion that are false, misleading, or deceptive.

In an important case involving Nike, the California Supreme Court issued a ruling that is likely to impact the way companies engage in public debate regarding issues that affect them. Nike was sued for false advertising under California consumer protection laws for allegedly making misleading statements regarding labor practices and working conditions in its foreign factories. Nike argued that statements the company made to defend itself against the charges should be considered political speech, which is protected by the First Amendment, rather than commercial speech, which is subject to advertising regulations. However, the California high court ruled that statements made by the company to defend itself against the allegations were commercial in nature and thus subject to the state's consumer protection regulations. Nike appealed the case to the U.S. Supreme Court, which sent it back to California for trial to determine if the company's statements were deceptive and misleading. However, Nike settled the case rather than risking a long and costly court battle. While the ruling in this case applies only to California, it is important as the courts ruled that speech in the form of press releases or public statements by company representatives can be considered commercial and subject to consumer protection laws.[41]

The job of regulating advertising at the federal level and determining whether advertising is truthful or deceptive is a major focus of the Federal Trade Commission. We now turn our attention to federal regulation of advertising and the FTC.

Background on Federal Regulation of Advertising

Federal regulation of advertising originated in 1914 with the passage of the **Federal Trade Commission Act**, which created the FTC, the agency that is today the most active in, and has primary responsibility for, controlling and regulating advertising. The FTC Act was originally intended to help enforce antitrust laws, such as the Sherman and Clayton Acts, by helping restrain unfair methods of competition. The main focus of the first five-member commission was to protect competitors from one another; the issue of false or misleading advertising was not even mentioned. In 1922, the Supreme Court upheld an FTC interpretation that false advertising was an unfair method of competition, but in the 1931 case *FTC v. Raladam Co.*, the Court ruled the commission could not prohibit false advertising unless there was evidence of injury to a competitor.[42] This ruling limited the power of the FTC to protect consumers from false or deceptive advertising and led to a consumer movement that resulted in an important amendment to the FTC Act.

In 1938, Congress passed the **Wheeler-Lea Amendment**. It amended section 5 of the FTC Act to read: "Unfair methods of competition in commerce and unfair or deceptive acts or practices in commerce are hereby declared to be unlawful." The amendment empowered the FTC to act if there was evidence of injury to the public; proof of injury to a competitor was not necessary. The Wheeler-Lea Amendment also gave the FTC the power to issue cease-and-desist orders and levy fines on violators. It extended the FTC's jurisdiction over false advertising of foods, drugs, cosmetics, and therapeutic devices. And it gave the FTC access to the injunctive power of the federal courts, initially only for food and drug products but expanded in 1972 to include all products in the event of a threat to the public's health and safety.

In addition to the FTC, numerous other federal agencies are responsible for, or involved in, advertising regulation. The authority of these agencies is limited, however, to a particular product area or service, and they often rely on the FTC to assist in handling false or deceptive advertising cases.

EXHIBIT 20–9

The Division of Advertising Practices protects consumers from deceptive and unsubstantiated advertising claims.

Federal Trade Commission

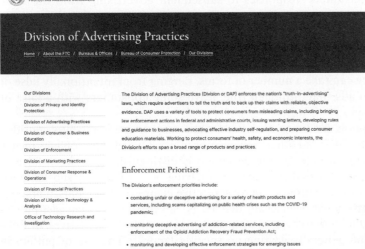

The Federal Trade Commission

The FTC is responsible for protecting both consumers and businesses from anti-competitive behavior and unfair and deceptive practices. The major divisions of the FTC include the bureaus of competition, economics, and consumer protection. The Bureau of Competition seeks to prevent business practices that restrain competition and is responsible for enforcing antitrust laws. The Bureau of Economics helps the FTC evaluate the impact of its actions and provides economic analysis and support to antitrust and consumer protection investigations and rule making. It also analyzes the impact of government regulation on competition and consumers. The Bureau of Consumer Protection's mandate is to protect consumers against unfair, deceptive, or fraudulent practices. This bureau also investigates and litigates cases involving acts or practices alleged to be deceptive or unfair to consumers. The Division of Advertising Practices protects consumers from deceptive and unsubstantiated advertising and enforces the provisions of the FTC Act that forbid misrepresentation, unfairness, and deception in general advertising at the national and regional level (Exhibit 20-9). The Division of Marketing Practices engages in activities that are related to various marketing and warranty practices such as fraudulent telemarketing schemes, 900-number programs, and disclosures relating to franchise and business opportunities.

Since the 1970s, the FTC has made enforcement of laws regarding false and misleading advertising a top priority. Several new programs were instituted, budgets were increased, and the commission became a very powerful regulatory agency. However, many of these programs, as well as the expanded powers of the FTC to develop regulations on the basis of "unfairness," became controversial. At the root of this controversy is the fundamental issue of what constitutes unfair advertising.

The Concept of Unfairness

Under section 5 of the FTC Act, the Federal Trade Commission has a mandate to act against unfair or deceptive advertising practices. However, this statute does not define the terms *unfair* and *deceptive*, and the FTC has been criticized for not doing so itself. While the FTC has taken steps to clarify the meaning of *deception*, people have been concerned for years about the vagueness of the term *unfair*.

The FTC responded to these criticisms in 1980 by sending Congress a statement containing an interpretation of unfairness. According to FTC policy, the basis for determining **unfairness** is that a trade practice (1) causes substantial physical or economic injury to consumers, (2) could not reasonably be avoided by consumers, and (3) must not be outweighed by countervailing benefits to consumers or competition. The agency also stated that a violation of public policy (such as other government statutes) could, by itself, constitute an unfair practice or could be used to prove substantial consumer injury. Practices considered unfair are claims made without prior substantiation, claims that might exploit such vulnerable groups as children and older adults, and instances where consumers cannot make a valid choice because the advertiser omits important information about the product or competing products mentioned in the ad.[43]

The FTC does have specific regulatory authority in cases involving deceptive, misleading, or untruthful advertising. The vast majority of advertising cases that the FTC handles concern deception and advertising fraud, which usually involve knowledge of a false claim.

Deceptive Advertising

In most economies, advertising provides consumers with information they can use to make consumption decisions. However, if this information is untrue or misleads the consumer, advertising is not fulfilling its basic function. Moreover, a study by Peter Darke and Robin Ritchie found that deceptive advertising engenders mistrust, which negatively affects consumers' responses to subsequent advertising from the same source as well as second-party sources. They note that deceptive advertising can seriously undermine the effectiveness and credibility of advertising and marketing in general by making consumers defensive toward future advertising and should be of concern to all marketers.[44] But what constitutes an untruthful or deceptive ad? Deceptive advertising can take a number of forms, ranging from intentionally false or misleading claims to ads that, although true, leave some consumers with a false or misleading impression.

The issue of deception, including its definition and measurement, receives considerable attention from the FTC and other regulatory agencies. One of the problems regulatory agencies deal with in determining deception is distinguishing between false or misleading messages and those that, rather than relying on verifiable or substantiated objective information about a product, make subjective claims or statements, a practice known as puffery. **Puffery** has been legally defined as "advertising or other sales presentations which praise the item to be sold with subjective opinions, superlatives, or exaggerations, vaguely and generally, stating no specific facts."[45] The use of puffery in advertising is common. For example, Bayer aspirin calls itself the "wonder drug that works wonders," Nestlé claims "Nestlé makes the very best chocolate," Snapple advertises that its beverages are "made from the best stuff on Earth," and Gillette uses the tagline "The Best a Man Can Get." Superlatives such as *greatest*, *best*, and *finest* are puffs that are often used.

Puffery has generally been viewed as a form of poetic license or allowable exaggeration. The FTC takes the position that because consumers expect exaggeration or inflated claims in advertising, they recognize puffery and don't believe it. But some studies show that consumers may believe puffery and perceive such claims as true.[46] One study found that consumers could not distinguish between a verifiable fact-based claim and puffery and were just as likely to believe both types of claims.[47] It has also been argued that puffery has a detrimental effect on consumers' purchase decisions by burdening them with untrue beliefs and refers to it as "soft-core deception" that should be illegal.[48]

Advertisers' battle to retain the right to use puffery was supported in the latest revision of the Uniform Commercial Code in 1996. The revision switches the burden of proof to consumers from advertisers in cases pertaining to whether certain claims were meant to be taken as promises. The revision states that the buyer must prove that an affirmation of fact (as opposed to puffery) was made, that the buyer was aware of the advertisement, and that the affirmation of fact became part of the agreement with the seller.[49]

One of the most intense battles regarding the use of puffery was fought by Papa John's and Pizza Hut and went all the way to the U.S. Supreme Court.[50] The central issue in the case was Papa John's use of the tagline "Better Ingredients. Better Pizza." Pizza Hut filed a lawsuit against Papa John's claiming that the latter's ads were false and misleading because it had failed to prove its sauce and dough were superior. Following a long, drawn-out legal battle that lasted nearly 5 years and cost the two companies millions of dollars, the U.S. Supreme Court issued a decision in support of the use of puffery as the basis for a comparative advertising claim. The advertising industry was relieved that the Supreme Court ruled in favor of Papa John's because a ruling against the puffery defense could have opened the door for other challenges and a redrawing of the blurry line between so-called puffery and outright false advertising.[51]

As an interesting by-product of the case, Domino's Pizza decided to take advantage of the appellate court ruling that Papa John's slogan was considered puffery and ran TV commercials showing the company's head chef, Brian Solano, standing outside a federal court of appeals building in New Orleans talking about Papa John's and its slogan. In the spot Solano says: "For years Papa John's has been telling us they have better ingredients and better pizza. But when challenged in this court, they stated their slogan is puffery." He then turns to a lawyer standing next to him and asks him: "What's puffery?" Reading from a law book, the lawyer says: "Puffery. An exaggerated statement based on opinion. Not fact" (Exhibit 20–10). Solano then says, "Here's what's not puffery" and goes on to explain how Domino's beat Papa John's in a national taste test. The spot ends with Solano stating, "Our pizza tastes better and that's not puffery, that's proven.[52]

EXHIBIT 20–10

Domino's poked fun at Papa John's puffery defense in a clever TV commercial.

Domino's IP Holder LLC

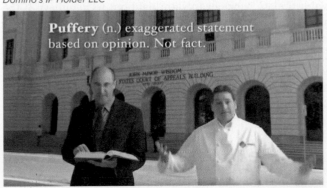

Since unfair and deceptive acts or practices have never been precisely defined, the FTC is continually developing and refining a working definition in its attempts to regulate advertising. The traditional standard used to determine deception was whether a claim had the "tendency or capacity to deceive." However, this standard was criticized for being vague and all-encompassing.

In 1983, the FTC put forth a new working definition of **deception**: "The commission will find deception if there is a misrepresentation, omission, or practice that is likely to mislead the consumer acting reasonably in the circumstances to the consumer's detriment."[53] There are three essential elements to this definition of deception.[54] The

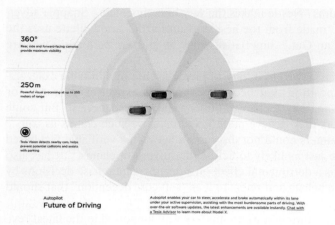

360°
Rear, side and forward-facing cameras provide maximum visibility

250 m
Powerful visual processing at up to 250 meters of range

Tesla Vision detects nearby cars, helps prevent potential collisions and assists with parking

Autopilot
Future of Driving

Autopilot enables your car to steer, accelerate and brake automatically within its lane under your active supervision, assisting with the most burdensome parts of driving. With over-the-air software updates, the latest enhancements are available instantly. Chat with a Tesla Advisor to learn more about Model X.

EXHIBIT 20–11

Tesla was accused of making deceptive advertising claims regarding its advanced driver-assistance system.

Tesla, Inc.

first element is that the representation, omission, or practice must be *likely to mislead* the consumer. The FTC defines *misrepresentation* as an express or implied statement contrary to fact, whereas a *misleading omission* occurs when qualifying information necessary to prevent a practice, claim, representation, or reasonable belief from being misleading is not disclosed.

The second element is that the act or practice must be considered from the perspective of *the reasonable consumer.* In determining reasonableness, the FTC considers the group to which the advertising is targeted and whether their interpretation of or reaction to the message is reasonable in light of the circumstances. The standard is flexible and allows the FTC to consider factors such as the age, education level, intellectual capacity, and frame of mind of the particular group to which the message or practice is targeted. For example, advertisements targeted to a particular group, such as children or older adults, are evaluated with respect to their effect on a reasonable member of that group.

The third key element to the FTC's definition of deception is *materiality.* According to the FTC a "material" misrepresentation or practice is one that is likely to affect a consumer's choice or conduct with regard to a product or service. What this means is that the information, claim, or practice in question is important to consumers and, if acted upon, would be likely to influence their purchase decisions. In some cases the information or claims made in an ad may be false or misleading but would not be regarded as material since reasonable consumers would not make a purchase decision on the basis of this information.

An example of a case where a potentially deceptive advertising claim was viewed as being material involved electric car manufacturer Tesla.[55] In 2022, the California Department of Motor Vehicles accused Tesla of falsely advertising its vehicles as operating autonomously (Exhibit 20–11). Teslas come equipped with an advanced driver-assistance system (ADAS) known as Autopilot that helps with tasks such as steering within a lane on a highway. Customers could also pay $12,000 for an enhanced set of features called "Full Self-Driving" that would make the vehicle fully self-driving in almost all circumstances with no action required by the person in the driver's seat. The California DMV complaint argued that Tesla vehicles equipped with these ADAS features could not operate as autonomous vehicles at the time the ads were run and still cannot do so. An additional class-action lawsuit was also filed around the same time on behalf of Tesla customers in California who paid for an upgraded autopilot system.[56] The complaint claimed that Tesla repeatedly made deceptive and misleading statements to consumers deceiving them about the abilities of its upgraded ADAS in order to get them to pay more for it. A **class action** is a legal proceeding in which one or more plaintiffs bring a lawsuit on behalf of a larger group, known as the class. This group, or class, is asserted to be affected by the defendant's actions, and the class action is often the only way for the individual consumers to pursue their claims, as it lower the costs of the legal pursuit. If the plaintiff class wins, awards are paid out to members of the class, though not necessarily in equal amounts. Many false or deceptive advertising or product labeling lawsuits are filed as class actions.

Determining what constitutes deception is still a gray area. Two of the factors the FTC considers in evaluating an ad for deception are (1) whether there are significant omissions of important information and (2) whether advertisers can substantiate the claims made for the product or service. The FTC has developed several programs to address these issues.

Affirmative Disclosure An ad can be literally true yet leave the consumer with a false or misleading impression if the claim is true only under certain conditions or circumstances or if there are limitations to what the product can or cannot do. Thus, under its **affirmative disclosure** requirement, the FTC may require advertisers to include certain types of information in their ads so that consumers will be aware of all the consequences, conditions, and limitations associated with the use of a product or service. The goal of affirmative disclosure is to give consumers sufficient information to make an informed decision. An ad may be required to define the testing situation, conditions, or criteria used in making a claim. For example, fuel mileage claims in car ads are based on Environmental Protection Agency (EPA) ratings since they offer a uniform standard for making comparisons. Cigarette ads must contain a warning about the health risks associated with smoking.

An example of a recent ruling involving affirmative disclosure is the FTC's case against PayPal Inc. over allegations that its Venmo peer-to-peer payment service misled consumers about their ability to transfer funds to external bank accounts and control the privacy of their transactions. In its complaint, the FTC alleged that when Venmo notified users that money had been credited to their balances and was available for transfer to an external account, it failed to disclose that those funds could be frozen or removed based on the results of Venmo's review of the underlying transaction. The FTC also ruled that Venmo misled consumers about the extent to which they could control the privacy of their transactions and misrepresented the extent to which consumers' financial accounts were protected by "bank grade security systems." As part of the settlement, Venmo was prohibited from misrepresenting any material restrictions on the use of its service, the extent of control provided by any privacy settings, and the extent to which Venmo implements or adheres to a particular level of security. The FTC ruled that Venmo also must make certain disclosures to consumers about its transaction and privacy practices and is required to obtain biennial third-party assessments of its compliance with these rules for 10 years.[57]

Another area where the Federal Trade Commission is seeking more specificity from advertisers is in regard to country-of-origin claims. The FTC has been working with marketers and trade associations to develop a better definition of what the "Made in USA" label means. The 50-year-old definition used until 1998 required full manufacturing in the United States, using U.S. labor and parts, with only raw materials from overseas.[58] Many companies argue that in an increasingly global economy, it very difficult to have 100 percent U.S. content and remain price-competitive. Moreover, for some products there is no domestic supply chain for making certain components and building manufacturing capabilities for them would be cost prohibitive. However, the FTC argues that advertising or labeling a product as "Made in USA" can provide a company with a competitive advantage, as for many products consumers do respond to the claim, as they trust the quality of domestic-made products and/or feel patriotic when they buy American. Recent research by the Alliance for American Manufacturing, as well as the FTC, found that when given a choice, most consumers prefer domestically made products to those that are imported and 60 percent are willing to pay up to 10 percent more for an American-made product.

In 1998, the FTC issued new guidelines for American-made products. The guidelines spell out what it means by "all or virtually all" in mandating how much U.S. content a product must have to wear a "Made in USA" label or be advertised as such. According to the FTC guidelines, all significant parts and processing that go into the product must be of U.S. origin and the product should have no or very little foreign content. Companies do not have to receive the approval of the FTC before making a "Made in USA" claim. However, the commission does have the authority to take action against false and unsubstantiated "Made in USA" claims just as it does with other advertising claims.[59] The FTC has become increasingly more aggressive in policing brands that claim to make products domestically. The agency forced the Detroit-based watch and bicycle brand Shinola to drop its slogan "Where American is Made" after it found that the company relied heavily on overseas parts to manufacture its products. The FTC also prosecuted Williams-Sonoma—the parent company of Pottery Barn, West Elm, and other brands—for making misleading claims that its home goods and furniture were "made in the USA," ultimately requiring the company to pay $1 million in penalties. In 2021 the FTC established new penalties for companies that

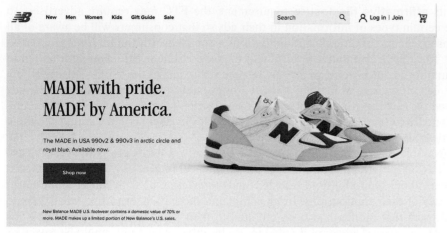

EXHIBIT 20–12

New Balance promotes its MADE product line which contains domestic content value of 70 percent or more.

New Balance

falsely market their products as American-made, seeking fines of up to $43,280 every time they falsely label a product.[60]

As a result of the FTC ruling, marketers must be careful in using "Made in the USA" or "American Made" claims in their advertising or on their product labels. For example, athletic shoe manufacturer New Balance has historically promoted its commitment to domestic manufacturing and that it is the only major athletic shoe company that assembles many of its shoes in the United States. However, the company is now careful to note that it is its MADE footwear collection that contains 70 percent domestic content and labor, which accounts for a limited portion of New Balance's U.S. sales (Exhibit 20–12).

Advertising Substantiation A major area of concern to regulatory agencies is whether advertisers can support or substantiate their claims. For many years, there were no formal requirements concerning substantiation of advertising claims. Many companies made claims without any documentation or support such as laboratory tests or clinical studies. In 1971, the FTC's **advertising substantiation** program required advertisers to have supporting documentation for their claims and to prove the claims are truthful.[61] Broadened in 1972, this program now requires advertisers to substantiate their claims before an ad appears. Substantiation is required for all express or implied claims involving safety, performance, efficacy, quality, or comparative price.

The FTC's substantiation program has had a major effect on the advertising industry because it shifted the burden of proof from the commission to the advertiser. Before the substantiation program, the FTC had to prove that an advertiser's claims were unfair or deceptive. However, ad substantiation seeks to provide a basis for believing advertising claims so consumers can make rational and informed decisions and companies are deterred from making claims they cannot adequately support. The FTC takes the perspective that it is illegal and unfair to consumers for a firm to make a claim for a product without having a "reasonable basis" for the claim. In their decision to require advertising substantiation, the commissioners made the following statement:

> Given the imbalance of knowledge and resources between a business enterprise and each of its customers, economically it is more rational and imposes far less cost on society, to require a manufacturer to confirm his affirmative product claims rather than impose a burden on each individual consumer to test, investigate, or experiment for himself. The manufacturer has the ability, the know-how, the equipment, the time and resources to undertake such information, by testing or otherwise, . . . the consumer usually does not.[62]

Many advertisers oppose the FTC's advertising substantiation program. They argue it is too expensive to document all their claims and most consumers either won't understand or aren't interested in the technical data. Some advertisers threaten to avoid the substantiation issue by using puffery claims, which do not require substantiation. Generally, advertisers making claims covered by the substantiation program must have available prior substantiation of all claims. However, in 1984, the FTC issued a policy statement that suggested after-the-fact substantiation might be acceptable in some cases and it would solicit documentation of claims only from advertisers that are under investigation for deceptive practices.

In a number of cases, the FTC has ordered advertisers to cease making inadequately substantiated claims. In the 1990s, the FTC took on the weight loss industry when it filed a complaint charging that none of five large, well-known diet program marketers had sufficient evidence to back up claims that their customers achieved their weight loss goals or maintained the loss. Three of the companies agreed to publicize the fact

10 Day Belly Buster Challenge

HERBALIFE. Independent Distributor

Are you serious about dropping a few pounds, losing inches and melting body fat fast?

Our healthy **BELLY BUSTER PROGRAM** is affordable, convenient & EASY to use

- It gives you 114 vital nutrients in out **Formula 1** pure food
- Breaks down, absorbs & eliminates fat in your body
- Eliminates food cravings
- Helps you lose weight and inches like crazy!
- And the best part is – it is completely natural.

HOW IT WORKS... It's so simple!

1. Replace any two meals a day with our **Formula 1** shake.
2. Take **Formula 2** multivitamin complex. A high quality product in a herbal base.
3. Take **Fibrebond** fat blocker to absorb and eliminate fats and toxins.
4. Take **Florafibre** to help with digesting, cleansing and elimination.
5. Eat a normal main meal, whatever you normally eat! The program will help you cut back (make sure you take the tablets before your meal).
6. Drink plenty of water between meals (you will naturally feel thirsty and feel like drinking water)

So... are you ready for it?

HERBALIFE. Nutrition for a better life.

EXHIBIT 20–13

Marketers are required to have scientific data to substantiate the weight loss claims such as those made in this Herbalife ad.

Herbalife Nutrition Ltd.

EXHIBIT 20–14

Skechers could not substantiate advertising claims made for its Shape-up toning shoes.

Kevan Brooks/AdMedia/Newscom

that most weight loss is temporary and to disclose how long their customers kept off the weight they lost. The agreement required the companies to substantiate their weight loss claims with scientific data and to document claims that their customers keep off the weight by monitoring a group of them for 2 years[63] (Exhibit 20–13).

The FTC has continued to take actions against companies that cannot adequately substantiate their advertising claims. For example, athletic shoe companies Reebok and Skechers agreed to pay large amounts of money to settle charges that they deceived consumers by making unsubstantiated claims regarding their toning shoes. Reebok ran ads for what became known as the "derriere-enhancing" shoes, making claims for its EasyTone shoes such as "Get a better butt" and "EasyTone shoes help you tone your butt and legs with every step." In 2011, following an investigation, the FTC alleged that the testing done by Reebok did not substantiate certain claims and charged the company with deceptive advertising. Reebok agreed to a $25 million settlement to resolve the charges but issued a statement saying that it was standing behind its shoes and agreed to the settlement only to avoid a protracted legal battle.[64] A few months after settling with Reebok, the FTC also settled with Skechers after charging the company with failure to substantiate its advertising for toning shoes. Skechers ran ads featuring celebrities such as Kim Kardashian and NFL Hall of Fame quarterback Joe Montana that included claims such as "Shape up while you walk" and "Get in shape without setting foot in a gym" (Exhibit 20–14). The ads also told women that wearing the toning shoes would help tone their buttocks, legs, and abdominal muscles; burn calories; fight cellulite; improve posture and circulation; and reduce joint stress. Following an investigation, the FTC charged Skechers with deceiving consumers with the claims made for its Shape-up shoes and other toning products, arguing that the results related to specific muscle activation results could not be substantiated. Skechers agreed to pay $40 million to settle the charges, which was one of the largest amounts ever agreed to with the FTC. The settlement also prohibited Skechers from making any claims about strengthening, weight loss, or any other health- or fitness-related benefits from its toning shoes.[65]

In another major case involving inadequate advertising substantiation the FTC took action against Volkswagen Group of America in 2016 charging that the company's "clean diesel" advertising campaign was deceptive. The U.S. Environmental Protection Agency discovered that special software installed in Volkswagen diesel-powered vehicles was designed to defeat emissions testing, making the cars seem far cleaner and safer for the environment than they actually were as the cars were emitting up to 40 times more toxic fumes than permitted. In its complaint the FTC alleged that during a 7-year period Volkswagen deceived consumers by selling or leasing more than 550,000 diesel cars based on false claims that the cars were low-emission, environmentally friendly, met emissions standards, and would maintain a high resale value. The FTC sought a court order requiring Volkswagen to compensate consumers who bought or leased any of the affected vehicles between late 2008 and late 2015, as well as an injunction to prevent Volkswagen from engaging in this type of conduct again. Volkswagen agreed to pay more than $4 billion to settle the deceptive advertising charges associated with the "Clean Diesel" advertising. This settlement was in addition to the estimated $25 billion in fines, penalties, and restitution the company has had to pay the U.S. government and consumers in connection with the case. Volkswagen ended up offering full compensation packages to the nearly 600,000 Volkswagen owners in the United States affected by their deception.[66]

The FTC's Handling of Deceptive Advertising Cases

Consent and Cease-and-Desist Orders   Allegations of unfair or deceptive advertising come to the FTC's attention from a variety of sources, including competitors, consumers, other government agencies, or the commission's own monitoring and investigations. Once the FTC decides a complaint is justified and warrants further action, it notifies the offender, who then has 30 days to respond. The advertiser can agree to negotiate a settlement with the FTC by signing a **consent order**, which is an agreement to stop the practice or advertising in question. This agreement is for settlement purposes only and does not constitute an admission of guilt by the advertiser. For example, the lawsuit filed by the SEC against Kim Kardashian discussed in the chapter opener was settled by a consent order. Most FTC inquiries are settled by consent orders because they save the advertiser the cost and possible adverse publicity that might result if the case went further.

If the advertiser chooses not to sign the consent decree and contests the complaint, a hearing can be requested before an administrative law judge employed by the FTC but not under its influence. The judge's decision may be appealed to the full five-member commission by either side. The commission either affirms or modifies the order or dismisses the case. If the complaint has been upheld by the administrative law judge and the commission, the advertiser can appeal the case to the federal courts.

The appeal process may take some time, during which the FTC may want to stop the advertiser from engaging in the deceptive practice. The Wheeler-Lea Amendment empowers the FTC to issue a **cease-and-desist order**, which requires that the advertiser stop the specified advertising claim within 30 days and prohibits the advertiser from engaging in the objectionable practice until after the hearing is held. Violation of a cease-and-desist order is punishable by a fine of up to $10,000 a day. Figure 20–5 summarizes the FTC complaint procedure.

Corrective Advertising   By using consent and cease-and-desist orders, the FTC can usually stop a particular advertising practice it believes is unfair or deceptive. However, even if an advertiser ceases using a deceptive ad, consumers may still remember some or all of the claim. To address the problem of residual effects, in the 1970s, the FTC developed a program known as **corrective advertising**. An advertiser found guilty of deceptive advertising can be required to run additional advertising designed to remedy the deception or misinformation contained in previous ads.

The impetus for corrective advertising was a case involving Campbell Soup, which when making a photo for an ad placed marbles in the bottom of a bowl of vegetable soup to force the solid ingredients to the surface, creating a false impression that the soup contained more vegetables than it really did. (Campbell Soup argued that if the marbles were not used, all the ingredients would settle to the bottom, leaving an impression of fewer ingredients than actually existed!) While Campbell Soup agreed to stop the practice, a group of law students calling themselves SOUP (Students Opposed to Unfair Practices) argued to the FTC that this would not remedy false impressions created by prior advertising and contended Campbell Soup should be required to run advertising to rectify the problem.[67]

Although the FTC did not order corrective advertising in the Campbell case, it has done so in many cases since then. Ocean Spray cranberry juice was found guilty of deceptive advertising because it claimed to have more "food energy" than orange or tomato juice but failed to note it was referring to the technical definition of food energy, which is calories. The STP Corporation was required to run corrective advertising for claims regarding the ability of its oil additive to reduce oil consumption. Many of the corrective ads run in the STP case appeared in business publications to serve notice to other advertisers that the FTC was enforcing the corrective advertising program. In each case, the companies were ordered to spend 25 percent of their annual media budgets to run corrective ads.

Corrective advertising is probably the most controversial of all the FTC programs.[68] Advertisers argue that corrective advertising infringes on First Amendment rights of

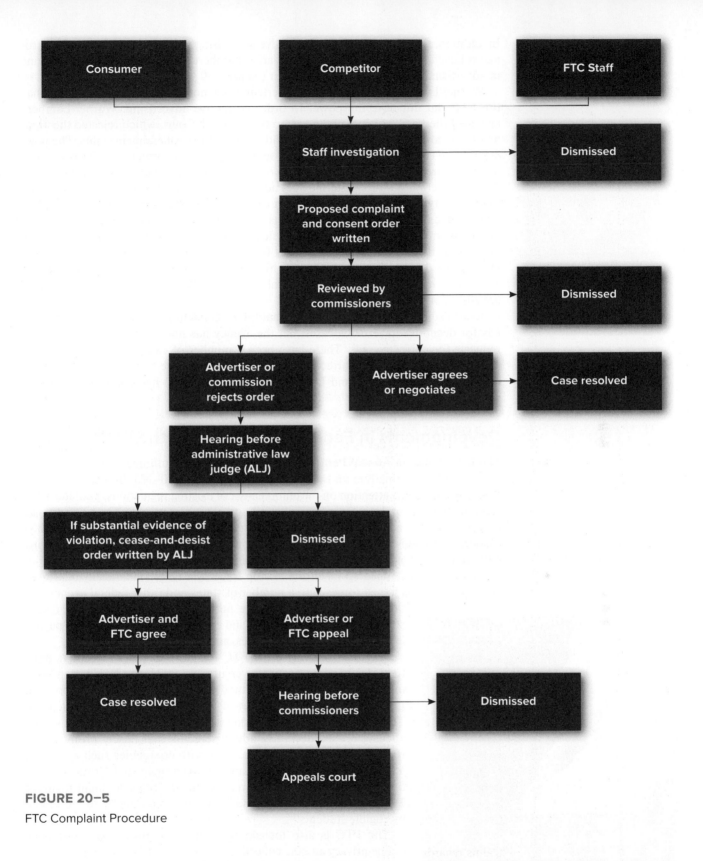

FIGURE 20–5

FTC Complaint Procedure

freedom of speech. In one of the most publicized corrective advertising cases ever, involving Listerine mouthwash, Warner-Lambert tested the FTC's legal power to order corrective messages.[69] For more than 50 years Warner-Lambert had advertised that gargling with Listerine helped prevent colds and sore throats or lessened their severity because it killed the germs that caused these illnesses. In 1975, the FTC ruled these claims could not be substantiated and ordered Warner-Lambert to stop making them.

In addition, the FTC argued that corrective advertising was needed to rectify the erroneous beliefs that had been created by Warner-Lambert as a result of the large amount of advertising it had run for Listerine over the prior 50 years.

Warner-Lambert argued that the advertising was not misleading and, further, that the FTC did not have the power to order corrective advertising. Warner-Lambert appealed the FTC decision all the way to the Supreme Court, which rejected the argument that corrective advertising violates advertisers' First Amendment rights. The powers of the FTC in the areas of both claim substantiation and corrective advertising were upheld. Warner-Lambert was required to run $10 million worth of corrective ads over a 16-month period stating, "Listerine does not help prevent colds or sore throats or lessen their severity." Since the Supreme Court ruling in the Listerine case, there have been several other situations where the FTC has ordered corrective advertising on the basis of the "Warner-Lambert test," which considers whether consumers are left with a latent impression that would continue to affect buying decisions and whether corrective ads are needed to remedy the situation. While the FTC's authority to order corrective advertising has been challenged in several cases, its right to do so has been upheld by appellate courts.[70]

Advertisers have expressed concern that the FTC might increase its use of the remedy for deceptive advertising cases, but the agency has not substantially changed its requests for corrective ads. There have been a number of cases where the FTC has required marketers to run corrective ads as a remedy for false and misleading advertising campaigns. The Food and Drug Administration (FDA) has also used corrective advertising in several cases.[71]

Developments in Federal Regulation by the FTC

The FTC issues an Annual Performance Report and Plan outlining its major achievements as well as initiatives for the upcoming year (Exhibit 20–15). In recent years the FTC has focused its attention on the enforcement of existing regulations, particularly in areas such as telemarketing, digital marketing, and consumer privacy. The FTC also has focused on false advertising sent via e-mail and stepped up its enforcement against senders of deceptive or misleading claims. The commission has been active in bringing enforcement actions against deceptive as well as unsubstantiated health claims.

The FTC has stepped up its efforts to stop fraud that targets financially distressed consumers. It has joined forces with a number of states and other federal agencies to take action against mortgage modification and foreclosure rescue scams; phony debt reduction and credit repair operations; and payday lenders, get-rich-quick schemes, and bogus government grants.

Another area where the FTC has been active is deceptive practices involving for-profit universities. In 2021, the FTC began sending nearly $50 million in refunds to students attending the for-profit University of Phoenix as part of a record $191 million settlement. The refunds stemmed from a lawsuit the FTC filed against the school alleging it used deceptive advertisements that falsely promoted its relationships and job opportunities with companies such as AT&T, Yahoo!, Microsoft, Twitter, and the American Red Cross. In addition to the $50 million in direct payments, the settlement included $141 million to cancel unpaid balances owed directly to the school by eligible students.[72]

The FTC is also focusing attention on protecting consumers' online privacy and the collection of sensitive information, particularly by social media platforms such as Facebook, Instagram, TikTok, Twitter, and Snapchat, as well as major technology companies such as Apple, Google, and Amazon.[73] The commission has expressed concern that developments in digital technology enable companies to collect vast amounts of data about individuals at a hyper-granular level and combine this data across various domains to develop very detailed

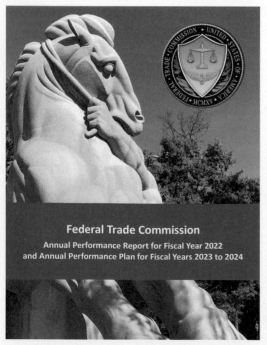

Federal Trade Commission
Annual Performance Report for Fiscal Year 2022
and Annual Performance Plan for Fiscal Years 2023 to 2024

user profiles that can be used to target individuals. These data practices pose several potential risks to consumers including allowing companies to target scams and deceptive ads to consumers who are most vulnerable to being lured by them as well as targeting ads in certain sectors based on race, gender, and age, resulting in potentially unlawful discrimination.[74]

The FTC will continue to be the primary regulator of advertising and marketing practices in the United States, although the direction of the commission is likely to be influenced by the political party controlling Congress as well as that of the presidential administration. While the FTC is the major regulator of advertising for products and services sold in interstate commerce, there are several other federal agencies and departments that regulate advertising and promotion that warrant discussion.

Additional Federal Regulatory Agencies

The Federal Communications Commission The Federal Communications Commission (FCC) was founded in 1934 to regulate broadcast communication and now regulates interstate and international communications by radio, television, wire, satellite, and cable in all 50 states, as well as U.S. territories. An independent U.S. government agency overseen by Congress, the commission is the primary authority for communications law, regulation, and technological innovation. The FCC has the authority to license broadcast stations as well as to remove a license or deny renewal to stations not operating in the public's interest. The commission's authority over the airways gives it the power to control advertising content and to restrict what products and services can be advertised on radio and TV. The FCC can eliminate obscene and profane programs and/or messages and those it finds in poor taste. While the FCC can purge ads that are deceptive or misleading, it generally works closely with the FTC in the regulation of advertising.

Many of the FCC's rules and regulations for TV and radio stations have been eliminated or modified. The FCC no longer limits the amount of television time that can be devoted to commercials. (But in 1991, the Children's Television Act went into effect. The act limits advertising during children's programming to 10.5 minutes an hour on weekends and 12 minutes an hour on weekdays.)

The FCC actively enforces laws governing the airing of obscene, indecent, and profane material. For example, in 2004 the commission fined "shock jock" Howard Stern $495,000 for broadcasting indecent content and also levied fines against Clear Channel Communications (now iHeart-Communications Inc.), the nation's largest owner of radio stations, which carried his syndicated show. Concern over Stern's constant battling with the FCC led to a decision by Clear Channel to drop his daily radio show.[75] Stern subsequently signed a contract with SiriusXM Satellite radio, the subscription-based radio service, where his show is not subject to FCC regulations. The FCC also stepped up its enforcement of obscenity in the wake of the controversy following the baring of Janet Jackson's breast during the halftime show of the 2004 Super Bowl (Exhibit 20-16).[76] These incidents resulted in federal legislation dramatically increasing the amount both radio and television networks and stations can be fined for broadcast obscenity violations.

The FCC has also become involved in issues affecting the area of publicity and public relations. In 2005, the commission issued a missive insisting that broadcasters screen video news releases to ensure that they clearly disclose "the nature, source and sponsorship" of the material. The crackdown was designed to address a marketing practice whereby prepackaged promotional videos sent to TV stations by companies, organizations, and government agencies are represented as news stories.[77]

The FCC is also currently considering the regulation of the use of product placements in television shows. Unlike some countries, the United States does not prohibit product placements in the broadcast or motion picture industries.

EXHIBIT 20–16

Janet Jackson's "wardrobe malfunction" during the 2004 Super Bowl halftime show led to greater enforcement of obscenity laws by the FCC.

Frank Micelotta/Staff/Getty Images

However, the use of undisclosed commercial messages in broadcasting has been regulated by section 317 of the Communications Act of 1934, which requires broadcasters to disclose "any money, service or valuable consideration" that is paid to, or promised to, or charged by the broadcaster in exchange for product placements. However, broadcasters do not have to disclose product placements when they are offered without charge or for a nominal fee. The FCC has basically interpreted the purpose of section 317 to be that the viewers in the TV audience must be clearly informed that what they are viewing has been paid for and that the entity paying for the broadcast must be clearly identifiable.

Critics are concerned not just by the prevalence of products appearing in shows but also by the various forms of integration whereby brands are actually written into TV plots. Some are calling on the FCC to require the TV networks to disclose product placements by using some form of onscreen notification system. Proposals range from requiring programs to run text along the bottom of the screen when a product appears in a scene, to using a flashing red light to alert viewers that a marketer is promoting a product in a TV show.[78]

The Food and Drug Administration Now under the jurisdiction of the Department of Health and Human Services, the FDA has authority over the labeling, packaging, branding, ingredient listing, and advertising of packaged foods and drug products, as well as cosmetics. The FDA is authorized to require caution and warning labels on potentially hazardous products and also has limited authority over nutritional claims made in food advertising. This agency has the authority to set rules for promoting these products and the power to seize food and drugs on charges of false and misleading advertising.

Like the FTC, the Food and Drug Administration has become a very aggressive regulatory agency in recent years. The FDA has cracked down on a number of commonly used descriptive terms it believes are often abused in the labeling and advertising of food products—for example, *natural*, *light*, *no cholesterol*, *fat free*, and *organic*. The FDA has also become tougher on nutritional claims implied by brand names that might send a misleading message to consumers. For example, Great Foods of America was not permitted to continue using the HeartBeat trademark under which it sold most of its foods. The FDA argued the trademark went too far in implying the foods have special advantages for the heart and overall health.

Many changes in food labeling are a result of the Nutritional Labeling and Education Act, which Congress passed in 1990. Under this law the FDA established legal definitions for a wide range of terms (such as *low fat*, *light*, and *reduced calories*) and required straightforward labels for all foods beginning in 1994 (Exhibit 20–17). The law has changed over the years with regular updates and changes to labeling requirements. A substantial update occurred in 2020 that included requiring more prominent print for serving size, larger print for displaying calories and calories per serving, a listing of added versus natural sugar, updated daily value for nutrients, and updates to nutrients required on the label including Vitamin D, calcium, iron, and potassium. The FTC issued a policy statement on food advertising that automatically makes claims acceptable for advertising if they conform to the FDA regulations. Claims inadmissible for labeling are not admissible in advertising.

The FDA has become increasingly active in policing health-related claims for food products. General Mills received a warning letter from the FDA for violations stemming from claims the company has been making that eating Cheerios cereal can reduce cholesterol by 4 to 6 percent in 6 weeks. The FDA charged that the claims made for the product based on clinical studies would make it a drug, not a food, because it is intended for use in the prevention, mitigation, and treatment of disease. General Mills worked with the FDA to resolve the

EXHIBIT 20–17

The Nutritional Labeling and Education Act requires that labels be easy for consumers to understand.

U.S. Food and Drug Administration

Nutrition Facts

8 servings per container

Serving size   **2/3 cup (55g)**

Amount per serving

Calories   230

	% Daily Value*
Total Fat 8g	**10%**
Saturated Fat 1g	**5%**
Trans Fat 0g	
Cholesterol 0mg	**0%**
Sodium 160mg	**7%**
Total Carbohydrate 37g	**13%**
Dietary Fiber 4g	**14%**
Total Sugars 12g	
Includes 10g Added Sugars	**20%**
Protein 3g	
Vitamin D 2mcg	10%
Calcium 260mg	20%
Iron 8mg	45%
Potassium 240mg	6%

* The % Daily Value (DV) tells you how much a nutrient in a serving of food contributes to a daily diet. 2,000 calories a day is used for general nutrition advice.

issue as the cholesterol-reduction claims are an important part of the brand's positioning and used as the basis for much of its advertising.[79] However, the company did remove the specific cholesterol reduction claim and replaced it with a more general statement that the toasted oats "can help reduce cholesterol" and "along with a diet low in saturated fat and cholesterol may reduce the risk of heart disease."[80] Over the past several years there has been a significant increase in the number of false advertising cases involving food and beverage products as both the FTC and FDA have been making the regulation of labeling, standards of identity, and advertising a priority. Ethical Perspective 20-1 discusses some of the high-profile cases involving false advertising of food and beverage products.

Ethical Perspective 20–1 > > >

False Advertising Lawsuits for Food and Beverage Products Surging

Food and beverage companies spend millions of dollars on advertising every year to promote their brands and differentiate them from competitors. Many of the ads rely on puffery or claims based on superlatives and subjective terms such as delicious, best, healthy, or nutritious. While consumers often expect some overhyping of products, some food and beverage marketers stray too far, making claims that cannot be substantiated or are false and misleading. Several governmental agencies, including the Federal Trade Commission (FTC) and Food and Drug Administration (FDA), as well as self-regulatory and consumer advocacy groups, monitor the advertising of food and beverage products in an effort to prevent marketers from making false or misleading claims. Advertising and labeling claims are also scrutinized by individual attorneys around the country who often file class-action lawsuits against companies on behalf of a larger group or "class" of consumers who have purportedly suffered common injury or damages.

Despite efforts of the FTC and FDA to regulate the advertising of food and beverage products, there has been a tremendous increase in the number of lawsuits brought against marketers over the past decade. Class-action litigation against food and beverage companies hit a record high in 2020 with 220 lawsuits filed compared to only 45 in 2010. Consumer advocates argue that a major reason for the increase in lawsuits is that federal regulators have made little progress in providing definitions and clarifying what terms such as *healthy*, *all natural*, or *artificially flavored* really mean. They also argue that for a number of years the FTC and FDA have been lax in addressing the problem of exaggerated food and beverage marketing claims. Many are calling for an overhaul of not only advertising, but front-of-package food labeling through a standardized system of symbols to convey whether a product is truly healthy. A bill was introduced in Congress in late 2021 that would address the problem and also direct federal regulators to specifically define terms like *healthy* and *natural*. However, opposition from food and beverage lobbyists has made its passage in a narrowly divided Congress very difficult.

While lawsuits regarding health-related claims are prevalent, food companies are also being challenged for touting their environmental actions and sustainability of their products in their advertising and labeling. Several lawsuits have alleged that companies "greenwash" their products for consumers by claiming them to be environmentally friendly in describing their farming processes and other practices. For example, a lawsuit and complaint filed with the FTC challenged a claim by Tyson Foods that its chickens are "all natural," arguing that its chickens are mass-produced in crowded sheds contaminated with antibiotic-resistant pathogens and that after slaughter, they are bathed in chemical disinfectants. Tyson has argued that it complies with all labeling regulations and was transparent about environmental and animal welfare efforts.

Another area that has been the focus of a large number of false advertising cases involves vanilla flavoring. A number of lawsuits have alleged that products labeled and advertised as "vanilla" contain flavoring ingredients that do not come from vanilla beans or vanilla extract. A number of companies have successfully defended claims against their vanilla products, including Wegmans vanilla ice cream and Blue Diamond's vanilla almond milk. Mars Wrigley Confectionary had a case dismissed alleging that the company misrepresented its Dove brand ice cream by claiming it "tastes like vanilla" when in reality the vanilla flavoring did not come exclusively from natural sources. The court dismissed the case on the grounds that at no point did Mars represent that the flavor came exclusively from natural sources, but rather that the product "tastes like" vanilla, which the court noted it does.

Artificial flavoring has been an issue for a number of other food and beverage products. For example, a case was filed against Frito-Lay North America alleging that the snack food maker advertised its Tostitos chips as having a "hint of lime" although the lime taste comes from artificial ingredients rather than actual limes. Several beverage products have also been charged with false advertising claims related to the flavoring of their beverages. A case filed against the grocery store chain Kroger alleged that the packaging for its sparkling water products sold with flavors such as "Black Cherry," "White Grape," and "Kiwi Strawberry" was misleading because

(continued)

the waters are purportedly artificially flavored rather than with extracts of the fruits. Kroger filed a motion to dismiss the case.

Consumer advocates argue that much of the litigation could be avoided through more stringent federal oversight of food marketing claims by the FTC and FDA. They note that without official FDA guidance, industry confusion and consumer class action lawsuits are likely to continue. In the interim, many view legal activism as the most effective way to hold food and beverage companies accountable for questionable advertising and labeling claims. However, critics also note that many of the class action suits brought against food and beverage companies are dubious and in some cases border on extortion as the plaintiffs are looking for settlements that include monetary compensation, much of which goes to the attorneys rather than the class of consumers.

In an effort to appeal to consumers and gain a competitive advantage, food and beverage companies are likely to continue to make claims for their products that are difficult to substantiate or are dubious or even outright false and misleading. Some of these claims may result in litigation, in some cases, for reasons that are debatable. For example, Ben & Jerry's stopped describing the cows that provide the milk for their ice cream as "happy" after being sued by a consumer advocacy group.

Another case that raised eyebrows was filed against Kraft Heinz in late 2022, accusing the company of misleading advertising, based on the time it takes to prepare a single-serving cup of its Velveeta microwavable macaroni and cheese. While Kraft Heinz markets the product as being ready in 3½ minutes, the plaintiff argues that this is only the amount of time each cup needs to be microwaved and the actual preparation process, from stirring in water to letting the cheese sauce thicken, takes longer. The class-action lawsuit claims that as a result of the false and misleading representation, the product is sold at a premium price

Sara Stathas/Alamy Stock Photo

versus similar products represented in a non-misleading way, and higher than it would be sold for absent the misleading representations and omissions.

Kraft Heinz called the lawsuit frivolous and stated that it will strongly defend against the allegations. Some news media, such as NPR, have questioned the legitimacy of the case, noting the plaintiffs' legal team includes an attorney who in recent years has filed hundreds of class-action suits alleging misleading claims in food advertising and labeling. We will leave it up to you to decide whether the complaint is legitimate or the case should be dismissed as "cheesy."

Sources: Rachel Treisman, "A Woman Sues Kraft, Claiming Velveeta Macaroni Preparation Time Is Misleading," *NPR*, November 28, 2022, https://www.npr.org/2022/11/28/1139415169/velveeta-mac-and-cheese-lawsuit-prep-time; Andrew Jacobs, "Lawsuits over 'Misleading' Food Labels Surge as Groups Cite Lax U.S. Oversight," *The New York Times*, September 7, 2021, https://www.nytimes.com/2021/09/07/science/food-labels-lawsuits.html; Pooja S. Nair and Cate Veeneman, "False Advertising Lawsuits Are Ramping Up in Food and Beverage," *Food Dive*, August 23, 2021, https://www.fooddive.com/news/false-advertising-lawsuits-are-ramping-up-in-food-and-beverage/604615/.

Another regulatory area where the FDA has been heavily involved is the advertising and promotion of tobacco products. In 1996, President Clinton signed an executive order declaring that nicotine is an addictive drug and giving the FDA broad jurisdiction to regulate cigarettes and smokeless tobacco. Many of the regulations resulting from this order were designed to keep teenagers from smoking.[81] However, the tobacco industry immediately appealed the order. While continuing to fight its legal battle with the federal government over the FDA regulations, the tobacco makers did agree to settle lawsuits brought by 46 states against the industry in 1998 by signing the Master Settlement Agreement. This settlement was considered a better deal for the tobacco industry, as many of the onerous cigarette marketing restrictions contained in the original FDA proposal settlement were missing. The agreement allows large outdoor signs at retailers, whereas the original proposal banned all outdoor ads. The original deal banned all use of humans and cartoons in ads, while the current settlement bans only cartoons and even permits their use on cigarette packs. And while the original proposal eliminated sports sponsorships, the agreement allowed each company to continue one national sponsorship.[82]

In 2000, the U.S. Supreme Court ruled that the Food and Drug Administration did not have the authority to regulate tobacco as a drug and that Congress would have to specifically enact legislation to allow the FDA to regulate tobacco. As a result, all FDA tobacco regulations were dropped. However, in June 2009 Congress

EXHIBIT 20–18

truth has been a very effective youth smoking prevention campaign developed by The Truth Initiative.

Truth Initiative

passed a tobacco-control bill giving the FDA sweeping new powers over the packaging, manufacturing, and marketing of tobacco products, and it was signed into law by President Obama shortly thereafter. The Family Smoking Prevention and Tobacco Control Act calls for restrictions on marketing and sales to youths, including a ban on all outdoor tobacco advertising within 1,000 feet of schools and playgrounds; a ban on all remaining tobacco-brand sponsorships of sports and entertainment events; a ban on free giveaways of nontobacco products with the purchase of a tobacco product; a limit on advertising in publications with significant teen readership as well as limiting outdoor and point-of-sale advertising, except in adult-only facilities, to black-and-white ads only; and a restriction on ads on vending machines and self-service displays to adult-only facilities.[83]

A number of consumer advocacy groups as well as health departments in many states run ads warning consumers about the dangers of smoking and tobacco-related diseases. For example, the American Legacy Foundation (ALF) was established as part of the 1998 tobacco settlement and funded primarily by payments designated by the settlement. The organization has four main goals: reducing youth tobacco use, decreasing exposure to second-hand smoke, increasing successful quit rates, and reducing disparities in access to prevention and cessation services and in exposure to second-hand smoke. The ALF developed a number of impactful advertising campaigns warning consumers of the risks of smoking and encouraging them to stop. One of the most successful programs developed by the ALF has been truth, which was launched in 2000 and is the largest national youth smoking prevention campaign. The truth campaign exposes the tactics of the tobacco industry, the truth about addiction, the health effects and consequences of smoking, and is designed to allow teens to make informed choices about tobacco use by giving them the facts about the industry and its products. The American Legacy Foundation delivered creative and effective public education messages to youth and young adults through its truth campaign for 15 years. However, in 2015 the ALF changed its name to the Truth Initiative and unveiled a new website for the organization: truthinitiative.org. Its mission has been broadened to "Inspiring lives free from smoking, vaping & nicotine" as vaping has become an important focus for the organization (Exhibit 20–18).

In 2016 the Food and Drug Administration was given the authority to regulate electronic cigarettes (e-cigarettes) as well as other tobacco products.[84] The new regulations cover products including hookah, cigar and pipe tobacco, vape pens, and refillable vaporizers. The rules prohibit sales to minors, ban free samples, require package warning labels, and call for makers of products released after 2007 to seek FDA per-

EXHIBIT 20–19

The use of e-cigarettes among young people is a major problem being addressed by the FDA.

JUUL Labs, Inc.

mission to remain on store shelves. While the tobacco industry has claimed that e-cigarettes help people trying to quit smoking, health experts argue that it is important for lawmakers to control their use as users of the product can still become hooked on nicotine and e-cigarette use has been rising steadily, especially among youth (Exhibit 20–19). According to the 2022 Annual National Youth Tobacco Survey, e-cigarette use or "vaping" among high school and middle school students has increased from just 1.5 percent in 2011 to 10 percent in 2022 with over 2.5 million teens and pre-teens using the products.[85] The survey found that 14.1 percent (2.14 million) of high school students and 3.3 percent (380,000) of middle school students reported current e-cigarette use and that 28 percent of current youth e-cigarette users vape every day while more than 40 percent report using e-cigarettes at least 20 days or more a month. Flavors in e-cigarettes are particularly problematic as they are very appealing to youth and are frequently cited as one of the top three reasons this population uses the product. The 2022 survey found that nearly 85 percent of current youth users used flavored e-cigarettes with fruit flavors being the most popular, followed by candy, desserts, or other sweets.

Another area where the Food and Drug Administration has become more involved is the advertising of prescription drugs. Tremendous growth in direct-to-consumer (DTC) drug advertising has occurred since the FDA issued new guidelines making it easier for pharmaceutical companies to advertise prescription drugs to consumers. In 2007, Congress passed legislation giving the FDA more power to regulate DTC drug advertising. The bill gives the FDA the power to require drug companies to submit TV ads for review before they run, but it can only recommend changes, not require them. The bill also granted the FDA the power to impose fines on a drug company if its ads are found to be false and misleading. The fines can amount to $250,000 a day for the first violation in any 3-year period and up to $5,000 for any subsequent violation.[86]

The advertising of prescription drugs directly to consumers has always been a very controversial issue; the United States and New Zealand are the only two countries in the world where the practice is permitted. The pharmaceutical companies contend that DTC advertising helps inform and educate consumers about diseases and treatment options, encourages people to seek medical advice, and helps remove stigmas associated with medical conditions. They also note that the advertising helps generate sales revenue needed to fund costly research and development of new drugs. However, groups such as the American Medical Association (AMA) are strongly opposed to the practice, arguing that DTC drug advertising misinforms patients; promotes the use of drugs before long-term safety profiles can be known; medicalizes and stigmatizes normal conditions and bodily functions, such as aging and low testosterone; and has led to society's overuse of prescription drugs. They also argue that drug advertising leads patients to ask their doctors to prescribe specific drugs when other treatments or lifestyle changes might be better for them.

The AMA, along with many other consumer and medical groups, has been calling for a total ban on DTC drug advertising. While the battle over drug advertising is likely to continue, many argue that DTC drug advertising in traditional media such as television and print is likely to fade away in the coming years as consumers go online to get information about drug products. It has been noted that more than 60 percent of consumers already get their first piece of health information by going online, e-mailing their friends, or checking social media.[87] Thus, banning DTC drug advertising will not really matter because the activity is happening in areas that companies cannot control and the government really cannot regulate.

Another drug-related area that falls under the jurisdiction of the Food and Drug Administration is cannabis or marijuana, which has been approved for medicinal use in 39 states, while recreational use by adults has been approved in 21 states. However, under federal law, cannabis is still considered a Schedule I dangerous drug that is highly addictive and has no acceptable medicinal value, and it is treated like other controlled substances, such as cocaine and heroin. Federal cannabis laws are very strict, and punishment for violating them is often very steep.

Individual states have varying regulations regarding the marketing and advertising of cannabis. For example, in California, it is common in many cities to see billboards for marijuana dispensaries as well as delivery services (Exhibit 20–20). However, many other states such as Maryland prohibit most cannabis ads, including billboards. And even in states where billboard advertising is

EXHIBIT 20–20

Regulations regarding the marketing and advertising of cannabis vary by state.

MME, LLC

permitted, there are often restrictions regarding the images that can be used or based on what percentage of people in the market likely to see the billboard are adults. Many municipalities have rules that restrict billboards from areas where young people congregate such as schools, libraries, and recreational centers. Digital platforms, including Facebook, Instagram, TikTok, YouTube, and Google, do not allow drug or drug-related promotions on their sites and are unlikely to change their policies until marijuana is legalized at the federal level.

In 2022 the Biden administration called for an administrative review to consider the reclassification of marijuana so it would no longer be considered a Schedule I drug.[88] However, it is difficult to predict if the FDA will change its position regarding the classification of marijuana, as there still are concerns regarding the long-term effects of cannabis use, potential abuse, use by minors, and impaired driving. The FDA has stated that it is committed to protecting public health while also taking steps to improve the efficiency of regulatory pathways for the lawful marketing of appropriate cannabis and cannabis-derived products. Any softening of the FDA's regulatory position could open the doors for widespread advertising and promotion of marijuana.

The U.S. Postal Service Many marketers use the U.S. mail to deliver advertising and promotional messages. The U.S. Postal Service has control over advertising involving the use of the mail and ads that involve lotteries, obscenity, or fraud. The regulation against fraudulent use of the mail has been used to control deceptive advertising by numerous direct-response advertisers. These firms advertise on TV or radio or in magazines and newspapers and use the U.S. mail to receive orders and payment. Many have been prosecuted by the Post Office Department for use of the mail in conjunction with fraudulent or deceptive offers.

Bureau of Alcohol, Tobacco, Firearms and Explosives The Bureau of Alcohol, Tobacco, Firearms and Explosives (ATF) is an agency within the Treasury Department that enforces laws, develops regulations, and is responsible for tax collection for the liquor industry. ATF regulates and controls the advertising of alcoholic beverages through the enforcement of the Federal Alcohol Administration Act, which is designed to prevent misleading labeling or advertising that may result in consumer deception and also includes provisions to regulate the marketing promotional practices concerning the sale of alcoholic beverages. The agency determines what information can be provided in ads as well as what constitutes false and misleading advertising. It is also responsible for including warning labels on alcohol advertising and banning the use of active athletes in beer commercials. ATF can impose strong sanctions for violators. As discussed earlier in the chapter, the advertising of alcoholic beverages has become a very controversial issue, with many consumer and public interest groups calling for a total ban on the advertising of beer, wine, and liquor.

The Lanham Act

While most advertisers rely on self-regulatory mechanisms and the FTC to deal with deceptive or misleading advertising by their competitors, many companies are filing lawsuits against competitors they believe are making false claims. One piece of federal legislation that has become increasingly important in this regard is the Lanham Act. This act was originally written in 1947 as the Lanham Trade-Mark Act to protect words, names, symbols, or other devices adopted to identify and distinguish a manufacturer's products. The **Lanham Act** was amended to encompass false advertising by prohibiting "any false description or representation including words or other symbols tending falsely to describe or represent the same." While the FTC Act did not give individual advertisers the opportunity to sue a competitor for deceptive advertising, civil suits are permitted under the Lanham Act.

Suing competitors for false claims was made even easier with passage of the Trade-Mark Law Revision Act of 1988. According to this law, anyone is vulnerable to civil action who "misrepresents the nature, characteristics, qualities, or geographical origin of his or her or another person's goods, services, or commercial activities." This wording closed a loophole in the Lanham Act, which prohibited only false claims about one's own goods or services. While many disputes over comparative claims are never contested or are resolved through the NAD, more companies are turning to lawsuits for several reasons: the broad information discovery powers available under federal civil procedure rules, the speed with which a competitor can stop the offending ad through a preliminary injunction, and the possibility of collecting damages.[89] However, companies do not always win their lawsuits. Under the Lanham Act you are required to prove five elements to win a false advertising lawsuit containing a comparative claim.[90] You must prove that:

- False statements have been made about the advertiser's product or your product.
- The ads actually deceived or had the tendency to deceive a substantial segment of the audience.
- The deception was "material" or meaningful and is likely to influence purchasing decisions.
- The falsely advertised products or services are sold in interstate commerce.
- You have been or likely will be injured as a result of the false statements, by either loss of sales or loss of goodwill.

Marketers using comparative advertising have to carefully consider whether their ads make claims that may misrepresent their company or brand relative to a competitor or make disparaging claims about a competitor that might result in a lawsuit. For example, the comparative advertising battle between Molson Coors and Anheuser-Busch over the use of corn syrup in Miller Lite and Coors Light beer, which was discussed in Chapter 6, resulted in a lawsuit under the Lanham Act. Molson Coors accused Anheuser-Busch InBev of false advertising for promoting Bud Light as having 100 percent less corn syrup than Coors/Light or Miller Lite.[91] Under the Lanham Act, companies can file lawsuits for harmful comparative advertising that often result in very large settlements if the defendant is found guilty of making a deceptive or unsubstantiated claim that is harmful to a competitor. A study by Michael J. Barone and his colleagues provides a framework for developing measures to assess the misleading effects that may arise from various types of comparative advertising.[92]

STATE REGULATION

In addition to the various federal rules and regulations, advertisers must also concern themselves with numerous state and local controls. An important early development in state regulation of advertising was the adoption in 44 states of the *Printers Ink* model statutes as a basis for advertising regulation. These statutes were drawn up in 1911 by *Printers Ink*, for many years the major trade publication of the advertising industry. Many states have since modified the original statutes and adopted laws similar to those of the Federal Trade Commission Act for dealing with false and misleading advertising.

In addition to recognizing decisions by the federal courts regarding false or deceptive practices, many states have special controls and regulations governing the advertising of specific industries or practices. As the federal government became less involved in the regulation of national advertising during the 1980s, many state attorneys general (AGs) began to enforce state laws regarding false or deceptive advertising.

The **National Association of Attorneys General (NAAG)** moved against a number of national advertisers as a result of inactivity by the FTC during the Reagan administration. In 1987, the NAAG developed enforcement guidelines on airfare advertising that were adopted by more than 40 states. The NAAG has also been involved in other regulatory areas, including car-rental price advertising as well as advertising dealing with nutrition and health claims in food ads. The NAAG's foray into regulating national advertising raises the issue of whether the states working together can create and implement uniform national advertising standards that will, in effect, supersede federal authority. However,

EXHIBIT 20–21

Fantasy sports betting sites must disclose information to players regarding the odds of winning.

Draft Kings

an American Bar Association panel concluded that the Federal Trade Commission is the proper regulator of national advertising and recommended the state AGs focus on practices that harm consumers within a single state.[93] This report also called for cooperation between the FTC and the state attorneys general.

In recent years state attorneys general have been working with the FTC and other federal government agencies on false advertising cases. For example, 27 state attorneys general worked with the FDA in the deceptive advertising case for Bayer's Yaz birth-control pill that resulted in corrective advertising. A group of state attorneys general also worked with the FTC in a case against the makers of Airborne, a multivitamin and herbal supplement whose labels and ads falsely claimed that the product cures and prevents colds. Airborne had been making the false claims for nearly a decade and agreed to refund the money to consumers who had bought the product, as part of a $23.3 million class action settlement.[94]

In another high-profile case, the State Attorney General in New York filed a lawsuit against daily fantasy sports betting sites DraftKings and FanDuel, the two biggest companies in the industry. The lawsuit claimed that the two companies consistently misled consumers with false advertising by making it appear that novice players had a realistic chance of winning big payouts when, in reality, most lost money over time. The attorney general alleged that casual and novice players were at a disadvantage when competing against frequent professional players, who often use sophisticated analytics and statistical information. Both DraftKings and FanDuel agreed to pay $6 million to settle the claims and also were required to maintain a web page that provides information about the rate of success of those who play in its fantasy contests, including the percentage of winnings captured by the top 1, 5, and 10 percent of players.[95] Deceptive advertising lawsuits were filed in several other states, and both companies have taken steps to provide more information to fantasy players regarding their odds of winning and to educate them regarding how their contests operate (Exhibit 20–21).

The Federal Trade Commission and seven states settled a case in late 2022 involving Google and iHeartMedia concerning misleading radio advertising about a Google smartphone. The case evolved from complaints that Google paid to have iHeartMedia radio personalities talk about their personal experiences using the Pixel 4 phone. The complaint alleged that a script was given to the radio DJs that included first-person language about using the Pixel 4's camera to take photos at night, as well as using the phone's voice activation system. However, at the time the phone was not available and many of the radio DJs had not used it. The FTC and the states noted that asking DJs to share personal experiences about a product they had not used was misleading and a violation of state consumer protection laws. As part of the settlement Google agreed to pay $9 million and iHeartMedia paid $400,000.[96]

Advertisers are concerned about the trend toward increased regulation of advertising at the state and local levels because it could mean that national advertising campaigns would have to be modified for every state or municipality. Yet the FTC takes the position that businesses that advertise and sell nationwide need a national advertising policy. While the FTC recognizes the need for greater cooperation with the states, the agency believes regulation of national advertising should be its responsibility.[97] However, the advertising industry is still keeping a watchful eye on changes in advertising rules, regulations, and policies at the state and local levels.

REGULATION OF OTHER PROMOTIONAL AREAS

So far we've focused on the regulation of advertising. However, other elements of the promotional mix also come under the surveillance of federal, state, and local laws and various self-regulatory bodies. This section examines some of the rules, regulations, and guidelines that affect sales promotion, direct marketing, and marketing on the Internet.

Sales Promotion

Both consumer- and trade-oriented promotions are subject to various regulations. The Federal Trade Commission regulates many areas of sales promotion through the Marketing Practices Division of the Bureau of Consumer Protection. Many promotional practices are also policed by state attorneys general and local regulatory agencies. Various aspects of trade promotion, such as allowances, are regulated by the Robinson-Patman Act, which gives the FTC broad powers to control discriminatory pricing practices.

Contest and Sweepstakes   As noted in Chapter 16, numerous legal considerations affect the design and administration of contests and sweepstakes, and these promotions are regulated by a number of federal and state agencies. There are two important considerations in developing contests (including games) and sweepstakes. First, marketers must be careful to ensure their contest or sweepstakes is not classified as a *lottery*, which is considered a form of gambling and violates the Federal Trade Commission Act and many state and local laws. A promotion is considered a lottery if a prize is offered, if winning a prize depends on chance and not skill, and if the participant is required to give up something of value in order to participate. The latter requirement is referred to as *consideration* and is the basis on which most contests, games, and sweepstakes avoid being considered lotteries. Generally, as long as consumers are not required to make a purchase to enter a contest or sweepstakes, consideration is not considered to be present and the promotion is not considered a lottery.

The second important requirement in the use of contests and sweepstakes is that the marketer provide full disclosure of the promotion. Regulations of the FTC, as well as many state and local governments, require marketers using contests, games, and sweepstakes to make certain all of the details are given clearly and to follow prescribed rules to ensure the fairness of the game.[98] Disclosure requirements include the exact number of prizes to be awarded and the odds of winning, the duration and termination dates of the promotion, and the availability of lists of winners of various prizes. The FTC also has specific rules governing the way games and contests are conducted, such as requirements that game pieces be randomly distributed, that a game not be terminated before the distribution of all game pieces, and that additional pieces not be added during the course of a game.

A number of states have responded to concerns over fraud on the part of some contest and sweepstakes operators and have either passed or tightened prize notification laws, requiring fuller disclosure of rules, odds, and the retail value of prizes. Some of the most ambitious legal actions are taking place in individual states, where prosecutors are taking sweepstakes and contest companies to court for misleading and deceptive practices.[99]

Many marketers are now using the Internet and social media sites such as Facebook, Instagram, TikTok, YouTube, and Twitter to run their contests and sweepstakes. This is creating additional issues that marketers must consider such as whether automated or repetitive electronic submissions will be accepted, how the contest website will detect violations, and restrictions on length, size, or format of content submitted. If the contest or sweepstakes is being marketed using e-mail, marketers must comply with online data privacy laws as well as the CAN-SPAM Act, which is discussed later in the chapter. If the online entry form collects personal information from persons under the age of 13 (including e-mail addresses), marketers must comply with the Children's Online Privacy Protection Act.[100]

Marketers that post audiovisual entries on YouTube or feature a contest on Facebook, Instagram, or Twitter must comply with each site's guidelines for on-site promotions. For contests that involve user-generated content, such as photos, videos, or short stories, the rules must contain specific language granting the company the necessary rights and licenses to use the content (Exhibit 20–22). Marketers that want to use the content for marketing purposes should obtain a liability and publicity release

iM SCION SELFIE CONTEST

INSTAGRAM CONTEST RULES:
- TAKE A SELFIE WITH THE SCION iM AND POST ON INSTAGRAM
- FOLLOW @SCIONRACING ON INSTAGRAM
- INCLUDE #SCIONiM HASHTAG IN YOUR POST
- FOR YOUR CHANCE TO WIN AN APEX SCION RACING RC CAR
- OFFICIAL RULES CAN BE FOUND AT SCIONRACING.COM

EXHIBIT 20-22

Contests involving user-generated content must provide specific rules regarding the use of photos, videos, or short stories.

Scion by Toyota Motor Sales USA, Inc

from every individual who appears in the photos or videos that are displayed on their website.[101] The Internet and social media provide marketers with a greater opportunity to promote their contests and sweepstakes to specific target audiences and make the administration of these promotions more efficient and cost effective. However, they also bring a host of additional legal factors that must be considered by companies.

Some social media sites are also imposing their own restrictions on how marketers can conduct contests and sweepstakes using their platforms. For example, Facebook changed its policy to prohibit marketers from "like-gating" a page to gain access to content or enter a contest. Facebook said the change was made to make sure people are liking pages because they truly want to connect with a business or brand, not because they were enticed by artificial incentives such as promotional offers.[102]

Premiums Another sales promotion area subject to various regulations is the use of premiums. A common problem associated with premiums is misrepresentation of their value. Marketers that make a premium offer should list its value as the price at which the merchandise is usually sold on its own. Marketers must also be careful in making premium offers to special audiences such as children. While premium offers for children are legal, their use is controversial; many critics argue that they encourage children to request a product for the premium rather than for its value. The Children's Advertising Review Unit has voluntary guidelines concerning the use of premium offers. These guidelines note that children have difficulty distinguishing a product from a premium. If product advertising contains a premium message, care should be taken that the child's attention is focused primarily on the product. The premium message should be clearly secondary. Conditions of a premium offer should be stated simply and clearly. "Mandatory" statements and disclosures should be stated in terms that can be understood by the child audience.[103]

Trade Allowances Marketers using various types of trade allowances must be careful not to violate any stipulations of the Robinson-Patman Act, which prohibits price discrimination. Certain sections of the act prohibit a manufacturer from granting wholesalers and retailers various types of promotional allowances and/or payments unless they are made available to all customers on proportionally equal terms.[104] Another form of trade promotion regulated by the Robinson-Patman Act is vertical cooperative advertising. The FTC monitors cooperative advertising programs to ensure that co-op funds are made available to retailers on a proportionally equal basis and that the payments are not used as a disguised form of price discrimination.

Direct Marketing

As we saw in Chapter 14, direct marketing is growing rapidly. Many consumers now purchase products directly from companies in response to TV and print advertising or direct selling. The Federal Trade Commission enforces laws related to direct marketing, including mail-order offers, the use of 900 telephone numbers, and direct-response TV advertising. The U.S. Postal Service enforces laws dealing with the use of the mail to deliver advertising and promotional messages or receive payments and orders for items advertised in print or broadcast media.

A number of laws govern the use of mail-order selling. The FTC and the Postal Service police direct-response advertising closely to ensure the ads are not deceptive or misleading and do not misrepresent the product or service being offered. Laws also forbid mailing unordered merchandise to consumers, and rules govern the use of "negative option" plans whereby a company proposes to send merchandise to consumers and

EXHIBIT 20–23

The National Do Not Call Registry protects consumers from calls by telemarketers.

Federal Trade Commission

expects payment unless the consumer sends a notice of rejection or cancellation.[105] FTC rules also encourage direct marketers to ship ordered merchandise promptly. Companies that cannot ship merchandise within the time period stated in the solicitation (or 30 days if no time is stated) must give buyers the option to cancel the order and receive a full refund.[106]

Another area of direct marketing facing increased regulation is telemarketing. With the passage of the Telephone Consumer Protection Act of 1991, marketers who use telephones to contact consumers must follow a complex set of rules developed by the Federal Communications Commission. These rules require telemarketers to maintain an in-house list of residential telephone subscribers who do not want to be called. Consumers who continue to receive unwanted calls can take the telemarketer to state court for damages of up to $500. The rules also ban telemarketing calls to homes before 8:00 A.M. and after 9:00 P.M.; automatic dialer calls; and recorded messages to emergency phones, health care facilities, and numbers for which the call recipient may be charged. They also ban unsolicited junk fax ads and require that fax transmissions clearly indicate the sender's name and fax number.[107]

In 2003, Congress approved a Federal Trade Commission proposal for the formation of a National Do Not Call Registry allowing consumers to opt out of most commercial telemarketing.[108] Consumers can place their home phone numbers, as well as personal cell phone numbers, on the National Do Not Call Registry (Exhibit 20–23). Commercial telemarketers must pay a fee to access the registry and generally are prohibited from calling the listed numbers. Telemarketers have 3 months to comply once a number goes on the list, and a consumer's registration lasts 5 years. Charities, political groups, debt collectors, and surveys are not affected by the regulation, and telemarketers can call consumers with whom they have an established relationship. Marketers face penalties of $11,000 per incident for calling someone on the list. The Federal Trade Commission, the Federal Communications Commission, and individual states are enforcing the National Do Not Call Registry, which contains nearly 250 million phone numbers.[109]

The National Do Not Call Registry affects the direct-marketing industry because it greatly reduces the number of households that telemarketers can call. As might be expected, the direct-marketing industry is strongly opposed to the registry, arguing that it violates their First Amendment rights and, further, that such a program is not needed. The Data & Marketing Association (DMA), which is the primary trade group for the direct-marketing industry, has argued that consumers already have a number of do-not-call options. They can ask to be excluded from an individual company's telemarketing list; at the same time they can sign up with state lists or pay $5 to sign up on the voluntary national list maintained by the Data & Marketing Association. The DMA argues that the national registry imposes more bureaucracy on the direct-marketing industry and that the same goal can be achieved by the industry itself with better education and enforcement.

The Data & Marketers Association and the American Teleservices Association (now known as the Professional Association for Customer Engagement or PACE), which represent callers, challenged the legality of the registry on the grounds that it took away their rights to First Amendment–protected speech and that it was excessive and poorly drafted, with competitive marketers forced to abide by different rules. However, in 2004 the U.S. Court of Appeals upheld the registry's validity, ruling that it is a valid commercial speech regulation. The appellate court said that because the registry doesn't affect political or charitable calls and because there is a danger of abusive telemarketing and invasion of consumer privacy from telemarketers, the government has a right to regulate its use.[110]

Direct marketers have been adjusting their telemarketing strategies to deal with the restrictions imposed by the Do Not Call Registry. They are focusing more attention on generating leads through promotional efforts such as sweepstakes and direct-mail programs, prompting consumers to opt in and agree to receive calls from direct marketers.[111] Some industry experts as well as academics argue that the Do Not Call Registry may actually improve telemarketing practice and the general efficiency of the business because direct marketers must focus more attention on consumers who are receptive to receiving their telemarketing calls.[112] However, there is also concern that some companies are finding loopholes in the rules governing the Do Not Call Registry. For example, one technique that has emerged is the use of a marketing tool called a "lead card," which invites a recipient to mail a reply card for free information. However, the cards often fail to warn consumers that by sending a reply, they are giving up their right to avoid telephone solicitations from the sender—even if their phone numbers are listed on the Do Not Call list.[113]

Another tactic being used by some companies to avoid the Do Not Call Registry is to use sweepstakes entry forms as a way to harvest consumers' telephone numbers for telemarketing purposes. When done correctly, this may be a legitimate direct-marketing tool; however, the FTC has cracked down on some companies that have violated Do Not Call regulations by calling phone numbers obtained via sweepstakes entry forms. Companies that want to collect telemarketing leads through a sweepstakes entry form must clearly and conspicuously disclose that their entry-form information will be used for telemarketing purposes and include a statement to be signed by consumers expressing agreement under the Do Not Call provision.[114]

The direct-marketing industry is also scrutinized by various self-regulatory groups, such as the Data & Marketing Association and the Direct Selling Association, that have specific guidelines and standards member firms are expected to adhere to and abide by. But some critics argue that these self-regulatory groups are not doing enough to keep consumers from receiving unwanted marketing messages, such as calls from telemarketers and direct-mail offers and solicitations. Thus, it is likely that they will continue to call for more government intervention and regulations.

Direct mail is also an area that has been under attack as many consumers are tired of seeing their mailboxes bulging with catalogs as well as other forms of direct mail and want to take action. Some states have considered legislation that would create state-run do-not-mail registries that would allow consumers to keep unsolicited direct mail out of their mailboxes. However, none of the proposed do-not-mail bills have made it beyond the hearing stage, and it may take years before any type of legislation is enacted. A number of advocacy groups are not waiting for the government to address the problem, though, and are taking steps to help consumers reduce the amount of unwanted direct mail they are receiving. Several of these initiatives have been started by groups that are interested in reducing the environmental impact created by the direct-mail industry.

One initiative having a significant impact in terms of reducing the amount of direct mail is Catalog Choice, which was launched in 2007 with the mission of reducing the number of repeat and unsolicited catalog mailings, and promoting the adoption of sustainable industry best practices.[115] The company offers an online service that allows people to compile a list of catalogs, coupons, credit card offers, and other types of direct mail they do not want to receive. The company then contacts the retailers with a request to take the person's name off their mailing list or makes a downloadable file available that merchants can then feed into their direct-mail database. Several thousand merchants and marketers have agreed to abide by the site's opt-out requests, including major companies such as Lands' End, Office Depot, and REI. Catalog Choice now operates as a nonprofit organization managed by the Story of Stuff Project.

EXHIBIT 20–24

DMAchoice is an online tool that can be used by consumers to manage direct mail and other types of direct marketing messages they receive.

The Association of National Advertisers

LO 20-5

The direct marketing industry has also taken steps to allow consumers to address the problem. The Data & Marketing Association has developed an online tool called DMAchoice that is offered through the Association of National Advertisers (ANA), which acquired the DMA in 2018, and allows consumers to manage the direct mail they receive from marketers (Exhibit 20–24). The tool allows consumers to pay a $2 fee and unsubscribe from entire categories of direct mail, such as catalogs and advertisements, or unsubscribe from specific catalogs. The service does not unsubscribe consumers from catalogs for companies they have already been a customer of, only those for which they may be a prospect.[116]

Marketing on the Internet

The rapid growth of the Internet as a marketing tool has created a new area of concern for regulators. The same consumer protection laws that apply to commercial activities in other media apply to online as well. The Federal Trade Commission Act, which prohibits "unfair or deceptive acts or practices," encompasses Internet advertising, marketing, and sales. Claims made in Internet ads or on websites must be substantiated, especially when they concern health, safety, or performance, and disclosures are required to prevent ads from being misleading and to ensure that consumers receive material information about the terms of a transaction. There are a number of regulatory areas companies must now adhere to when marketing on the Internet. These include privacy issues, data security, online marketing to children, endorsements made through social media or blogs, native advertising, and the use of spam or unsolicited e-mails for commercial purposes.

Privacy and Security Consumer privacy and security have become major issues among government regulators as a result of high-profile data breaches and concerns over the collection and use of consumer data for marketing purposes. Marketers must ensure that their online marketing programs are in compliance with consumer privacy and data security guidelines; failure to do so can lead to government enforcement actions, expensive litigation, and negative publicity that can be very damaging to their reputations and have long-term effects.

The major privacy issue regarding the Internet that has emerged involves undisclosed profiling whereby online marketers can profile a user on the basis of name, address, demographics, and online/offline purchasing data. Marketers argue that profiling offers them an opportunity to target specific niches and reach consumers with custom-tailored messages. However, the FTC has stated that Internet sites that claim they don't collect information but permit advertisers to surreptitiously profile viewer sites are violating consumer protection laws and are open to a charge of deception.[117] In 1999, DoubleClick, the company that is the leader in selling and managing online advertising as well as tracking web users and is now owned by Google, set off a controversy by connecting consumers' names, addresses, and other personal information with information it collects about where consumers go online. The controversy resulted in the company being investigated by the Federal Trade Commission and lawsuits being filed in some states.[118]

In response to the profiling controversy, companies that collect Internet usage data and information joined together under the banner of the Network Advertising Initiative (NAI) to develop a self-regulatory code.[119] The NAI has developed a set of privacy principles in conjunction with the Federal Trade Commission that provides consumers with explanations of Internet advertising practices and how they affect consumers. The NAI has also launched a website that provides consumers with

Home ❯ Opt Out ❯ AMA Opt Out

Want to Opt Out? ⊖

Opt Out of Audience Matched Advertising

EXHIBIT 20–25

The Network Advertising Initiative website provides consumers with information about online advertising practices.

Network Advertising Initiative

information about online advertising practices and gives them the choice to opt out of targeted advertising delivered by NAI member companies (Exhibit 20–25).

Consumer privacy and security have become major issues with the FTC in recent years.[120] The agency has requested that marketers voluntarily step up the disclosures they make about data they collect and seek permission from consumers before tracking their Internet surfing behavior.[121] Many marketers now adhere to the Digital Alliance Ad Choices program, which is a self-regulatory initiative that was implemented by BBB National Programs as part of its Digital Advertising Accountability Program discussed earlier in the chapter. However, critics have argued that the program only blocks behavioral ad targeting rather than actually stopping behavioral data collection. There continues to be calls for the FTC to oversee the development of a Do Not Track program that would prohibit websites or mobile app operators from compiling or disclosing personal data to third parties for targeted marketing purposes. The FTC began work as far back as 2010 on a Do Not Track initiative that would let consumers opt out of having any of their online data shared with third parties.[122] Although many digital advertising companies agreed to the idea in principle, it has been difficult to reach agreement over the definition, scope, and application of the program, and little progress has been made in finalizing a standard.[123]

Concerns over privacy and security have also increased with the explosion in the popularity of social media sites such as Facebook, Twitter, and others. For example, the FTC settled a complaint against Twitter charging it deceived consumers and put their privacy at risk by failing to safeguard their personal information, marking the agency's first such case against a social networking service. The FTC ordered Twitter to establish a security program subject to government monitoring for the next 10 years. Twitter agreed to the terms in exchange for the FTC not pursuing a civil lawsuit against the company.[124]

Privacy and data security are likely to remain at the top of the enforcement lists for the FTC as well as state attorneys general and other regulatory groups. The FTC won an important case against Wyndham Hotels & Resorts when an appeals court affirmed its authority to require companies to securely store customer data and punish them for failing to do so. The FTC charged that the company's security practices unfairly exposed the payment card information of hundreds of thousands of consumers to hackers in three separate data breaches. Wyndham challenged the scope of the FTC's authority to regulate data security arguing that the agency had no clear standards for what constitutes reasonable cyber security. However, the appellate court ruled in favor of the FTC, which was seen as a victory for consumer privacy, especially as companies collect increasing amounts of data and information about their customers. Many legal experts view this as a pivotal case that could lead to more scrutiny of companies' data security in the future.[125]

In 2022 the FTC announced that it was exploring rules to crack down on harmful commercial surveillance—the business of collecting, analyzing, and profiting from information about people—as well as lax data security. The agency notes that in the last two decades, it has used its existing authority under the FTC Act to bring hundreds of enforcement actions against companies for privacy and data security violations. These include cases involving the sharing of health-related data with third parties, the collection and sharing of sensitive television viewing data for targeted advertising, and the failure to implement reasonable security measures to protect sensitive personal data such as Social Security numbers. However, the FTC's ability to deter unlawful conduct is limited because the agency generally lacks authority to seek financial penalties for initial violations of the FTC Act. By contrast, rules that establish clear privacy and data security requirements across the board and provide the Commission the authority to seek financial penalties for first-time violations could incentivize all companies to invest more consistently in compliant practices. Digital and Social Media Perspective 20–1 discusses how the European Union is addressing privacy and data protection with the passage of the General Data Protection Regulation (GDPR) and how efforts are under way in California and other states to address the problem with similar regulations.

Digital and Social Media Perspective 20–1 >>>

Privacy Regulations Are Changing Digital Marketing

As discussed throughout the text, advertising through digital media has surpassed the use of traditional media such as television, radio, and print. One of the primary reasons marketers have shifted their advertising spending to search engines such as Google and Bing as well as display advertising on websites and social media platforms—such as Instagram, TikTok, and Facebook—is the tremendous amount of information they have about their users. For example, Google knows your location every time you turn on your phone; your online search history across all your devices; websites you have visited; the apps you use, including how often you use them, where you use them, and who you use them to interact with; and all your YouTube history. Google also creates profiles for advertisers based on consumers' location, age, gender, occupation, interests, purchase history, and other factors. Meta's two main social media sites, Facebook and Instagram, have similar profiles as well as articles and videos and other information consumers share with one another plus information from outside data providers and advertisers.

While many people trusted Google and Facebook, as well as other digital platforms, with their data for years, there have been significant developments over the past several years that have led to an awakening over the issue of privacy and the rights of companies to use the data they gather. The privacy issue took center stage in 2018 when a whistleblower came forward to reveal that the research firm Cambridge Analytica had improperly harvested the personal Facebook data of millions of Americans without their knowledge to create personality profiles and help target political ads that helped Donald Trump win the 2016 presidential election. When the news broke, Facebook founder and CEO Mark Zuckerberg apologized for his company's mistakes, and Facebook immediately banned Cambridge Analytica and its parent company SCL from the platform. However, these actions did little to stem the outrage of lawmakers, privacy advocates, and the media, as well as the public, as the Cambridge Analytica scandal became the poster child for how data can be misused as well as a catalyst for debates over the privacy rights of consumers.

Apple recognized that privacy was becoming a major issue and made significant changes to the privacy settings of its mobile operating system in 2021, allowing iPhone users to choose whether advertisers could track them. Apple has made privacy a key part of its marketing for the iPhone and other products, giving customers the ability to opt out of tracking and making tracking more difficult in its Safari web browser. Since Apple introduced the feature, the majority of iPhone users have opted to block tracking as only a quarter of iPhone users around the world have consented to being tracked by marketers. Apple's new policy has created major problems for social media platforms such as Facebook, Instagram, and Snapchat that rely on tracking as a major selling point to advertisers seeking to target their ads and measure their effectiveness by using post-ad data conversion metrics. Apple's new privacy features are costing Meta as well as Snap, the parent company of Snapchat, billions of dollars in lost advertising revenue each year.

While Facebook's data breaches and Apple's new privacy policies were bringing privacy and protection of people's data to the attention of federal and state regulatory bodies in the United States, efforts had already been well under way in Europe to address the problem. In 2012, the European Commission began developing plans for data protection reform across the European Union (EU) in order to make Europe fit for the digital age. One of the key components of the reform is the introduction of the General Data Protection Regulation (GDPR), which took effect in May 2018 across the 28-nation bloc of EU countries. The new regulations apply to any organization operating within the European Union, as well as any organization outside of the EU that offers goods and/or services to customers in the EU. This essentially means that nearly every major company in the world needs a GDPR compliance strategy because regulators in the EU can fine companies as much as 4 percent of annual sales for the most serious violations. Some of the key privacy and data protection requirements of the GDPR include requiring the consent of data subjects when collecting and processing data from them, making collected data anonymous to protect privacy, providing data breach notification, safely handling the transfer of data across borders, and requiring certain companies to appoint a data-protecting officer to oversee GDPR compliance.

Efforts are already under way in the United States to develop regulations similar to the sweeping privacy rules enacted in the European Union. California passed a new law, the California Consumer Privacy Act (CCPA), that went into effect in 2020, and gives the state's residents the most sweeping online privacy rights in the nation and also includes some of the most stringent rules for companies. Marketers began taking notice of California's new data privacy laws in 2022 after Sephora, one of the world's largest cosmetic retailers, settled a lawsuit claiming that the company sold customer information without proper notice in violation of the law. Sephora was charged with failing to tell customers it was selling their personal information, not allowing them to opt out of the sale, and not fixing the problem within 30 days as required by the law after it was notified of the violation. Sephora agreed to pay $1.2 million in penalties and immediately correct the problem.

The CCPA gives California the strongest data privacy law in the United States, providing consumers with the right to know what information companies collect about them online, to get that data deleted, and to opt out of the sale of their personal information. Several other states have passed similar laws regulating privacy that will go into effect in 2023, including Virginia, Colorado, Connecticut, Vermont, and Utah. However, the California Consumer Privacy Act is more comprehensive and is likely to be used as a guideline for other states as well as a possible model for national legislation. Several industry trade groups, including the Interactive Advertising Bureau (IAB) and Association of National Advertisers (ANA), are urging Congress to create a federal regulatory framework around privacy that will protect consumers and avoid the problem of conflicting and damaging state laws, which would create major challenges for companies.

Companies are taking steps to address the new privacy regulations because they really have no choice but to do so. It is likely that security breaches will continue, even as more strict regulations are enacted. However, technology companies must recognize failure to protect consumers' privacy may result in the greatest breach of all—the loss of consumer trust.

Sources: Kim S. Nash, "Sephora Agrees to $1.2 Million Settlement of Data Privacy Charges," *The Wall Street Journal*, August 24, 2022, https://www.wsj.com/articles/sephora-agrees-to-1-2-million-settlement-of-data-privacy-charges-11661372755; Kat Conger and Brian X. Chen, "A Change by Apple Is Tormenting Internet Companies, Especially Meta," *The New York Times*, February 3, 2022, https://www.nytimes.com/2022/02/03/technology/apple-privacy-changes-meta.html; Ronan Shields, "As CCPA's Deadline Looms, Tech and Media Brace for Another GDPR," *Adweek*, May 28, 2019, https://www.adweek.com/digital/as-ccpas-deadline-looms-tech-and-media-brace-for-another-gdpr/; Issie Lapowsky, "How Cambridge Analytica Sparked the Great Privacy Awakening," *Wired*, March 17, 2019, https://www.wired.com/story/cambridge-analytica-facebook-privacy-awakening/.

Online Marketing to Children　While various proposals are aimed at protecting the privacy rights of adults, one of the biggest concerns is over restricting marketers whose activities or websites are targeted at children. These concerns over online marketing to children led to the passage of the **Children's Online Privacy Protection Act (COPPA) of 1998**, which the FTC began enforcing in 2000.[126] This act places tight restrictions on collecting information from children via the Internet and requires that websites directed at children and young teens have a privacy policy posted on their home page and areas of the site where information is collected. The law also requires websites aimed at children under age 13 to obtain parental permission to collect most types of personal information and to monitor chat rooms and bulletin boards to make sure children do not disclose personal information there. When the law was enacted in 2000, it was left to the FTC to determine how to obtain the required permission, and the FTC temporarily allowed websites to let parents simply return an e-mail to approve certain information. Since then no other solution to the permission issue has surfaced, and the FTC has made the solution permanent.[127] However, the issue continues to be an area of concern since many marketers close their websites to children under the age of 13, but children under this age will often lie about their ages to gain access to the sites. The prevalence of social media is adding to the problem; many young people want access to fan clubs, blogs, and other websites that allow online interaction.

As of July 1, 2013, the FTC began enforcing updates to COPPA that are designed to bring the law in line with changes that have occurred in the market, including the explosive growth of mobile device usage among kids and the data collection that goes along with it. The changes include the categorization of geolocation information, photos, and videos as personal information, requiring parental consent before such data are collected on children under age 13. The changes also extended COPPA to cover persistent device identifiers such as IP addresses and mobile device IDs that allow companies to track a user across various personal devices but do not cover mobile app stores.

In 2019 Google and its subsidiary YouTube agreed to pay a record $170 million fine and make changes to protect children's privacy as regulators said the video sharing site had knowingly and illegally collected personal information from children—including identification codes used to track web browsing over time—without their parents' consent.[128] Google was accused of using the information to profit by targeting the children with ads. The penalty and charges were part of a settlement with the FTC and the New York attorney general which accused YouTube of violating the COPPA law. The $170 million Google agreed to pay to settle the charges was the largest penalty ever obtained by the FTC in a children's privacy case.

Another company fined for a COPPA violation was Epic Games Inc., developer of *Fortnite* which is one of the world's most popular video games. In late 2022, the company agreed to pay $520 million to resolve FTC allegations that it violated the COPPA by collecting personal information from *Fortnite* players under the age of 13 without notifying their parents or obtaining verifiable parental consent. The FTC accused Epic Games of illegally enabling real-time voice and text chat communications for children and teens playing the game and using the tactics to drive unintended purchases. The FTC also alleged that Epic Games intentionally obscured cancellation and refund features to make them more difficult to find and locked the accounts of customers who disputed unauthorized charges with their credit card companies. Epic did not admit or deny the FTC allegations as part of the settlement.[129]

Online Endorsements   The FTC has taken action to address the issue of endorsements made through social media sites and blogs and ensure that the same rules apply in this context as they do in traditional advertising and infomercials. As noted in the chapter opener, in 2009 the agency passed a new set of guidelines for online endorsements that require online endorsers and bloggers to disclose any "material connection" to an advertiser.[130] Under the guidelines, bloggers, influencers, and other paid endorsers who post on social media sites such as Facebook, Instagram, TikTok, Snapchat, or Twitter or post product reviews on sites such as Amazon can be held liable if they do not identify themselves as having a material connection to a company or brand. This means that any time an endorser receives money or something of value, such as free products or services, it must be clearly and conspicuously disclosed when they are discussing or promoting the brand on social media.

The FTC rules also apply to third-party networks that are paid by marketers and then turn around and pay influencers or others to promote their brands online. For example, the FTC settled a case against Machinima Inc., an online entertainment network, charging that it engaged in deceptive advertising by paying "influencers" to post YouTube videos endorsing Microsoft's Xbox One video system and several games as part of a marketing campaign being managed by Microsoft's ad agency. The influencers failed to adequately disclose their connection to Machinima and that they were being paid for their seemingly objective opinions. Microsoft and its ad agency reacted swiftly once they were aware that Microsoft's products were being endorsed by paid influencers by requiring Machinima to comply with FTC rules.[131] The FTC also settled a case with Warner Bros. Home Entertainment (WB) over its failure to adequately disclose that it had paid influencers on YouTube to promote the launch of a video game.

Another important part of the FTC guidelines involves requirements for disclosures (Exhibit 20–26). The FTC issued updates to its endorsement guidelines in 2013 and 2015 clarifying how much disclosure is required and whether it applies to short-form platforms such as Twitter. In the updated guidelines, the FTC discusses requirements related to factors such as proximity, prominence, and multimedia. With regard to proximity, even in a space-constrained ad or promotion, the disclosure must be physically close to the statement or endorsement. The FTC also requires that the disclosure must be in understandable language, which means that using a hashtag such as #spon may not be acceptable. The FTC recommends using #Ad, "Ad:," or "Sponsored" in tweets or on social media pages. Prominence requirements mean that the disclosures must be prominent or viewable on any device and not buried within a web

EXHIBIT 20-26

Endorsers must follow the FTC
guidelines when promoting a
brand on social media.

Federal Trade Commission

FEDERAL TRADE COMMISSION
PROTECTING AMERICA'S CONSUMERS

Enforcement ∨ | Policy ∨ | Advice and Guidance ∨ | News and Events ∨ | About the FTC ∨ | Q

Home / Business Guidance / Business Guidance Resources

Vea esta página en español

Disclosures 101 for Social Media Influencers

Tags: Advertising and Marketing | Endorsements, Influencers, and Reviews

📄 1001a-influencer-guide-508_1.pdf (257.15 KB)

The FTC works to stop deceptive ads, and its Endorsement Guides 🔖 go into detail about how advertisers and endorsers can stay on the right side of the law.

If you endorse a product through social media, your endorsement message should make it obvious when you have a relationship ("material connection") with the brand. A "material connection" to the brand includes a personal, family, or employment relationship or a financial relationship – such as the brand paying you or giving you free or discounted products or services.

Telling your followers about these kinds of relationships is important because it helps keep your recommendations honest and truthful, and it allows people to weigh the value of your endorsements.

As an influencer, it's **your responsibility** to make these disclosures, to be familiar with the Endorsement Guides, and to comply with laws against deceptive ads. Don't rely on others to do it for you.

---

page or a page on a mobile platform. The multimedia guidelines require disclosure for audio or video claims and endorsements in the same clear and conspicuous ways as expected for written media. They also require that the form of the disclosure should match the content, which means that if a video or sound file is used, the disclosure should be done in the native format rather than included in a post or annotation on a social media site.

The new FTC guidelines and updates require that marketers, as well as their advertising agencies and third-party networks, clearly understand how they can use endorsers and to make sure that they are in compliance with the rules and regulations. It is very important that they know what constitutes an endorsement because these do not always require explicit wording by the endorser stating that they approve of a product or service. Simply posting a video or photo on social media may convey that the poster likes and approves of the product and be viewed as an endorsement. Marketers must also consider whether they may be creating material connections by paying money to a celebrity or influencer to promote a brand, providing free products or discounts to influencers, offering entries into a contest or sweepstakes in exchange for posting pictures or statements about a brand, paying employees to post things about a brand on social media, or offering an incentive program to marketing affiliates.

As companies shift more of their marketing efforts online and make greater use of bloggers and other types of endorsers, it will be important for them to train their employees and monitor the way endorsers are being used. The FTC provides a very helpful and simple mnemonic for marketers it calls M.M.M.: *mandate* a disclosure policy that complies with the law, *make sure* people who work for you or with you know what the rules are, and *monitor* what they are doing on your behalf.

Native Ads   Another aspect of online marketing where the FTC has become involved is native advertising, which refers to online ads that are similar in format and topic to content on the publisher's website. As was discussed in Chapter 15, in late 2015 the FTC published its long-awaited guidelines for native advertising, which has become a very common practice as marketers shift more of their ad spending to digital media. A major goal of the FTC guidelines is to ensure that there is no misleading representations or omissions about an online advertisement's true nature or source. According to the policy statement: "In evaluating whether an ad's format is misleading, the Commission will scrutinize the entire ad, examining such factors as its overall appearance, the similarity of its written, spoken, or visual style to non-advertising content offered on a publisher's site, and the degree to which it is distinguishable from such other content."[132]

While the FTC has made it clear that it does not consider native ads inherently deceptive, the agency is very prescriptive about where and how disclosures should be made and what language is required. The guidelines state that when labels such as "advertisement" are necessary, they need to be prominent on first contact with consumers, and disclosures should appear near a native ad. They also emphasize the need to disclose that native content is an ad before the consumer clicks on it and note that labels such as "sponsored content" or "presented by" may not may be sufficient to avoid misleading consumers regarding the intention of the content. Many of these requirements are at odds with industry practices, which will mean that marketers and online publishers must reexamine their policies and procedures. It also means that the FTC is likely to take enforcement actions against marketers whose use of native advertising violates the new guidelines.[133]

Spamming   Another Internet-related marketing area receiving regulatory attention is **spamming**, which is the sending of unsolicited multiple commercial electronic messages. Spamming has become a major problem; studies show that the typical Internet user spends the equivalent of 10 working days a year dealing with incoming spam.[134] Spam also costs businesses billions of dollars every year in terms of lost worker productivity and network maintenance. Moreover, many of these messages are fraudulent or deceptive in one or more respects. A number of states have enacted antispamming legislation, and a comprehensive federal antispam bill, the Controlling the Assault of Non-Solicited Pornography and Marketing Act of 2003 (CAN-SPAM Act), went into effect in 2004. The act's general requirements for commercial e-mails include the following requirements:

- A prohibition against false or misleading transmission information.
- Conspicuous notice of the right to opt out and a functioning Internet-based mechanism that a recipient may use to request to not receive future commercial e-mail messages from the sender.
- Clear and conspicuous identification that the message is an advertisement.
- A valid physical postal address for the sender.

Violations of the CAN-SPAM law include both civil and criminal penalties, including a fine of $250 (calculated on a per e-mail basis) up to a maximum of $2 million. While the CAN-SPAM Act carries severe penalties for violators, thus far it has done little to stop unsolicited e-mail messages. Spammers have been able to stay one step ahead of law enforcement officials by operating offshore and by constantly moving the Internet hosting source.[135]

As marketers expend more of their IMC efforts online, they are facing many challenges as regulation of digital, social, and mobile advertising is becoming increasingly restrictive. They must understand and follow legal requirements in areas such as privacy and data security as well as guidelines regarding the use of endorsers and the types of online advertising formats they can use. Many companies work closely with law firms specializing in these areas to ensure that their digital marketing programs comply with rules and regulations governing online marketing. Marketers are recognizing that it is very important to embed privacy and data security considerations into their digital marketing campaigns and programs.[136] They must also understand rules and regulations regarding endorser disclosures as well as monitor what is being said and posted about their companies and brands online.

Summary

Regulation and control of advertising stem from internal regulation or self-regulation as well as from external control by federal, state, and local regulatory agencies. For many years the advertising industry has promoted the use of voluntary self-regulation to regulate advertising and limit government interference with and control over advertising. Self-regulation of advertising emanates from all segments of the advertising industry, including advertisers and their agencies, business and advertising associations, and the media.

BBB National Programs, Inc., the primary self-regulatory mechanism for national advertising, has been very effective in achieving its goal of voluntary regulation of advertising and other forms of marketing communication. Various media also have their own advertising guidelines. The major television networks maintain the most stringent review process and restrictions.

Advertising is viewed as commercial speech, which is speech promoting a commercial transaction, and is protected under the First Amendment. The federal government is the most important source of external regulation, with the Federal Trade Commission serving as the major watchdog of advertising in the United States. The FTC protects both consumers and businesses from unfair and deceptive practices and anticompetitive behavior. The FTC is very active in the regulation of advertising and other marketing practices and has authority in cases involving deceptive, misleading, or untruthful advertising. The agency has a number of tools and programs that are used to regulate advertising including affirmative disclosure, advertising substantiation, cease-and-desist orders, and corrective advertising. A number of other federal agencies regulate advertising and promotion including the Federal Communications Commission, the Food and Drug Administration, the U.S. Postal Service, and the Bureau of Alcohol, Tobacco, Firearms and Explosives. The FDA regulates the advertising and promotion of cigarettes and other tobacco-related products, as well as direct-to-consumer drug advertising.

While most advertisers rely on self-regulatory mechanisms and the FTC to deal with deceptive or misleading advertising by their competitors, many are filing lawsuits against competitors under the Lanham Act for making false or misleading claims through comparative advertising. Many states, as well as the National Association of Attorneys General, are also active in exercising their jurisdiction over false and misleading advertising.

A number of laws also govern the use of other promotional-mix elements, such as sales promotion and direct marketing. The Federal Trade Commission regulates many areas of IMC, including sales promotion as well as direct marketing. Various consumer-oriented sales promotion tools such as contests, games, sweepstakes, and premiums are subject to regulation. Trade promotion practices, such as the use of promotional allowances and vertical cooperative advertising, are regulated by the Federal Trade Commission under the Robinson-Patman Act. The FTC also enforces laws in a variety of areas that relate to direct marketing and mail-order selling as well as the Internet, while the FCC has rules governing telemarketing companies.

The rapid growth of the Internet as a marketing tool has created a new area of concern for regulators. The same consumer protection laws that apply to commercial activities in other media apply online as well. Major areas of concern with regard to advertising and marketing on the Internet are privacy and security, online marketing to children, and spamming or the sending of unsolicited commercial e-mail messages. Concerns over online marketing to children have led to the passage of the Children's Online Privacy Protection Act, which the FTC began enforcing in early 2000 and updated in 2013. The federal government passed the CAN-SPAM Act, which went into effect on January 1, 2004, and was updated in 2013. This legislation sets stringent requirements for commercial e-mail messages.

The Federal Trade Commission has become increasingly concerned over privacy issues related to the popularity of social media and is requiring various sites to protect the privacy of users. The FTC also has issued new guidelines covering online endorsements that require endorsers and bloggers to disclose any material connection to an advertiser. In 2015 the FTC published guidelines for native advertising, which has become a very common practice as marketers shift more of their ad spending to digital media. A major goal of the FTC guidelines is to ensure that there are no misleading representations or omissions about an online advertisement's true nature or source.

Key Terms

self-regulation 683
Better Business Bureau (BBB) 685
BBB National Programs 686
National Advertising Review Board (NARB) 687
Federal Trade Commission (FTC) 693
commercial speech 694
Central Hudson Test 694
Federal Trade Commission Act 695

Wheeler-Lea Amendment 695
unfairness 696
puffery 696
deception 697
class action 698
affirmative disclosure 699
advertising substantiation 700
consent order 702
cease-and-desist order 702

corrective advertising 702
Lanham Act 711
National Association of Attorneys General (NAAG) 712
Children's Online Privacy Protection Act (COPPA) of 1998 721
spamming 724

Discussion Questions

1. The chapter opener discusses how Kim Kardashian was fined $2.6 million by the Securities and Exchange Commission (SEC) for promoting a cryptocurrency on Instagram. Discuss why she was fined by the SEC and why she agreed to settle the case and pay the fine rather than challenging it. (LO 20-1, 20-5)

2. Discuss the need for regulation of advertising and other IMC tools. Do you advocate more or less regulation of advertising and other forms of promotion by governmental agencies such as the Federal Trade Commission and the Food and Drug Administration? (LO 20-1, 20-3, 20-4)

3. Discuss the role BBB National Programs, Inc., plays in the self-regulation of advertising and other forms of marketing communication. Evaluate the arguments for and against voluntary self-regulation as an effective way of protecting consumers from misleading or deceptive advertising and other marketing practices. (LO 20-2)

4. Do you agree with the DISCUS argument that advertising for hard liquor should be treated the same as advertising for beer and wine? Should advertising for spirits be confined to late night programs on the networks or should the ads be permitted to run earlier in the evening as well as during major sporting events such as National Football League (NFL) games? (LO 20-2)

5. The chapter discusses how Volkswagen was fined for making advertising claims that its diesel cars were low emission, environmentally friendly, and met government emission standards. The Federal Trade Commission argued the claims were false and misleading and could not be substantiated. Evaluate the claims made by Volkswagen from a deceptive advertising perspective. Why do you think the company agreed to pay large sums of money to settle the FTC allegations rather than appealing them? (LO 20-1, 20-2)

6. Find several examples of advertising claims or slogans based on puffery rather than substantiated claims. Discuss whether these advertising claims can be defended on the basis of puffery. (LO 20-3)

7. Ethical Perspective 20–1 discusses the significant increase in the number of false advertising cases involving food and beverage products in recent years. What are some of the reasons for this increase? Do you think the large number of class-action lawsuits being filed against food and beverage companies is justified? (LO 20-2)

8. Discuss the regulations governing the advertising and promotion of cannabis or marijuana in the United State and the challenges they present for marketers of cannabis products. Do you think the government should loosen the restrictions on how cannabis can be advertised? Defend your position. (LO 20-3, 20-4)

9. What are some of the regulatory issues marketers must take into consideration in using sales promotion and direct marketing as part of their IMC programs? (LO 20-4)

10. Digital and Social Media Perspective 20–1 discusses the GDPR program being used in the European Union and how it may be the basis for privacy regulations in the United States. Discuss the major issues facing digital marketing and social media platforms such as Google, Facebook, TikTok, and Instagram with regard to privacy. How will impending regulations affect the use of digital marketing by marketers? (LO 20-1, 20-5)

11. Evaluate the guidelines now used by the FTC requiring bloggers and social media influencers to disclose any material connection to a company whose product or service they are endorsing. How might this affect companies that use influencers as part of their digital marketing programs? (LO 20-1, 20-5)

Balenciaga

Learning Objectives

LO21-1 | Discuss various ethical perspectives on advertising and promotion.

LO21-2 | Discuss various social perspectives on advertising and promotion.

LO21-3 | Evaluate the social criticisms of advertising.

LO21-4 | Discuss the effect of advertising on consumer choice, competition, and prices.

Why Do Companies Continue to Run Offensive Ads?

Will they ever learn? Companies (and/or their agencies) have been accused of running offensive ads for decades. The pushback that they receive for doing so can be severe, yet it seems they just don't get the lesson. Interestingly, many of these companies are well respected, successful, and have been advertising for years. In a November 2022 blog post by Quality Logo Promotional Products, the authors listed a number of examples of offensive advertising that included ads run by Dove, Nike, Reebok, Peloton, and even PETA. While most, if not all, were not intended to be offensive, but humorous or attention-getting instead, nevertheless the consequences ranged from apologies from the sponsors to calls for boycotts from consumers.

At about the same time this blog was posted, yet another company apparently failed to learn the lesson. Balenciaga—the luxury brand owned by the French conglomerate Kering, which also owns Gucci and Saint Laurent—committed its own faux pas. (Or was it a faux pas at all?—more on this later.) In its 2022 holiday campaign, young girls were pictured on the website's gift shop holding teddy bears that were wearing what appeared to be bondage-style harnesses, chains, and other BDSM-style gear. The ads did not go over well with the public, leading to backlash on Twitter, extensive press coverage, and outright outrage from industry persons. Kim Kardashian, who previously walked in a Balenciaga runway show and wore the brand to a Met Gala, let it be known that she was "re-evaluating her relationship with the brand" after receiving a barrage of messages from fans urging her to denounce the brand. Balenciaga immediately apologized and announced that it had removed the ads from all of its platforms. They also took down all of the pictures from social media.

In many of the cases cited in the Quality Logo blog, one might argue that while offensive, it may not have been intentional. In the Balenciaga case, many are not so sure. In a different campaign featuring actor Nicole Kidman and Bella Hadid, in a scene meant to replicate a corporate office, a messy desk full of papers clearly included a page from the 2008 Supreme Court ruling that confirmed "as illegal and not protected by freedom of speech the promotion of child pornography." Once again, there was a public uproar, and once again, Balenciaga apologized and said that they were accountable for the "oversight." But this time, the company claimed that they had no responsibility or knowledge of the inclusion of the document and filed a $25 million lawsuit against the production company, arguing that the defendants' "inexplicable acts and omissions were malevolent or at the very least extraordinarily reckless." In other words, Balenciaga was placing the blame on someone else! The production company fired back, stating that they had no input over the shoot, that Balenciaga representatives were present when it was being made, and that absolutely no malevolent actions were involved.

Many observers think that Balenciaga's actions were not a mistake at all, but a planned strategy. They cite previous examples where the company was responsible for controversial ads including the remaking of IKEA's 99 cent shopping bag as a luxury item, placing heels on Crocs and sending models who looked like refugees down a runway carrying trash bags made of expensive leather, among others. The critics argue that the company creates the ads for shock value and thrives on the publicity that is generated by their outlandishness. But the brand has always contended that consumers must grapple with the meaning of "taste." After all, other companies have been doing this for years, and many of those campaigns were highly successful. Ads by Calvin Klein and Benetton are just two such examples, and Nike experienced a 10 percent sales increase while the Colin Kaepernick campaign was running.

So maybe it was a designed strategy after all? Did Balenciaga intentionally create the controversy in an attempt to bolster their image—or was it a mistake? The jury is still out. The controversial Always campaign by Procter & Gamble led to a number of positive results including successfully subverting gender stereotypes and increasing positive attitudes toward the brand and sales. Gillette's "Best a Man Can Be" campaign while controversial led to more positive feedback than negative and extensive exposure. There are examples where companies apparently were surprised at the feedback, as their goal may not have been to create shock.

continued

Nevertheless, if the strategy is intentional, it is a risky one. Not all publicity is good publicity, and sometimes the costs outweigh the benefits!

Sources: Alyssa Mertes et al., "15 Offensive Advertisements: Ads That Were Banned or Made People Angry," Quality Logo Products, November 28, 2022, www.qualitylogoproducts .com; Erin Keller, "Balenciaga Pulls Controversial Bear Ads amid Child Abuse Fears," *New York Post*, November 22, 2022, www.newyorkpost.com; Elizabeth Paton, Vanessa Friedman, and Jessica Testa, "When High Fashion and QAnon Collide," *New York Times*, November 28, 2022, www .nytimes.com; Jamie Wilde, "Balenciaga Ads Condemned by Customers, Kim Kardashian," *Morning Brew*, November 28, 2022, www.morningbrew.com; Jacqui Parr, "Shock Effect: The 5 Most Controversial Marketing Campaigns across Social Media," *Marketing Week*, July 27, 2022, www.marketing-week.co.uk.

> If I were to name the deadliest subversive force within capitalism, the single greatest source of its waning morality—I would without hesitation name advertising. How else should one identify a force that debases language, drains thought, and undoes dignity?[1]

As described in the chapter lead-in, many ads may be considered offensive or shocking and lead to controversy among viewers. Two schools of thought are prevalent as to why such ads are shown. The first is that they are designed to be intentionally shocking or offensive, which will hopefully result in significant publicity and exposure and create an image for the brand. The other is that they may be unintentional but lead to controversy that may result in discourse that can be either positive or negative for the brand and/or society as a whole. The same holds true of ads that may feature interracial and/or LGBTQ (lesbian, gay, bisexual, transgender, and queer) models. When advertisers choose to use these forms of advertising they must be aware of the impact they may have on viewers and society as a whole—as well as on themselves.

The primary focus of this text has been on the role of advertising and promotion as marketing activities used to convey information to, and influence the behavior of, consumers. We have been concerned with examining the advertising and promotion function in the context of a business and marketing environment and from a perspective that assumes these activities are appropriate. However, as you can see in the lead-in, not everyone shares this perspective. Advertising and promotion are the most visible of all business activities and are prone to scrutiny by those who are concerned about the methods that marketers use to sell their products and services.

Proponents of advertising argue that it is the lifeblood of business—it provides consumers with information about products and services and encourages them to improve their standard of living. They say advertising produces jobs and helps new firms enter the marketplace. Companies employ people who make the products and provide the services that advertising sells. Free-market economic systems are based on competition, which revolves around information, and nothing delivers information better and at less cost than advertising.

Not everyone, however, is sold on the value of advertising. Critics argue that most advertising is more propaganda than information; it creates needs and faults consumers never knew they had. Ads suggest that children need cell phones, that our bodies should be leaner, our faces younger, and our houses cleaner. They point to the sultry, scantily clad bodies used in ads to sell everything from perfume to beer to power tools and argue that advertising promotes materialism, insecurity, and greed.

One of the reasons advertising and other forms of integrated marketing communications are becoming increasingly criticized is that they are so prevalent. Not only are there more ads than ever, but there are more places where these ads appear. Advertising professor David Helm notes: "Between the stickered bananas and the ads over the urinals and the ones on the floor of the supermarkets, we're exposed to 3,000 commercial messages a day. That's one every 15 seconds, assuming we sleep for 8 hours, and I'd guess right now there's someone figuring out how to get us while our eyes are closed."[2] (You should recall from earlier chapters that the number of exposures is much higher now.)

As marketers intensify their efforts to get the attention of consumers, resentment against their integrated marketing communications efforts is likely to increase. Concern is growing that there may be a consumer backlash as integrated marketing efforts move

EXHIBIT 21–1

Commercial Alert, a project of Public Citizen, is concerned with the excessive amount of marketing messages consumers receive.

Public Citizen

to new heights and marketers become increasingly aggressive. The growing practice of placing ads and logos everywhere seems a desperate last attempt to make branding work according to the old rules. As telemarketing, advertising in the digital and social media, in movie theaters, in classrooms, and seemingly everywhere else continues at a frenzied pace, the value of the messages potentially decreases. The system seems headed for a large implosion. Groups such as Public Citizen.org's Commercial Alert are concerned about intrusion of advertising, social media, and other types of marketing messages into all aspects of consumers' lives. In addition to the pervasiveness of commercial messages, the organization is also concerned with other ad-related issues, as can be seen in Exhibit 21–1. Consumer advocacy groups also argue that many companies are obliterating the line between marketing communications and entertainment by creating and delivering ads and other messages that appear to be part of popular culture but have a persuasive intent.[3] (You may recall our earlier discussion on native ads.)

Advertising is a very powerful force, and this text would not be complete without a look at the criticisms regarding its social and economic effects as well as some defenses against these charges. We consider the various criticisms of advertising and promotion from an ethical and social perspective and then appraise the economic effects of advertising.

ADVERTISING AND PROMOTION ETHICS

EXHIBIT 21–2

Menthol cigarettes have been heavily advertiser to Black Americans in the past.

R. J. Reynolds Tobacco Company

In the previous chapter, we examined the regulatory environment in which advertising and promotion operate. While many laws and regulations determine what advertisers can and cannot do, not every issue is covered by a rule. Marketers must often make decisions regarding appropriate and responsible actions on the basis of ethical considerations rather than on what is legal or within industry guidelines. **Ethics** are moral principles and values that govern the actions and decisions of an individual or group.[4]

A particular action may be within the law and still not be ethical. A good example of this involves target marketing. No laws restrict tobacco companies from targeting advertising and promotion for new brands to African Americans. However, given the high levels of lung cancer and smoking-related illnesses among the Black population, many people would consider this an unethical business practice. The ad shown in Exhibit 21–2 is just one of many that have specifically targeted African Americans to sell menthol cigarettes to. For more than a decade menthol brands have been heavily marketed to this population as research indicated that 85 percent of African Americans who smoke opt for menthols. Additional research indicated that 44.5 percent who smoke menthols would try to quit if the flavor additive was banned. While advertising to the youth market has been banned since 1964, the same has not held true for menthol-flavored cigarettes (other flavors including cherry, vanilla, and clove have been banned since 2009). In April 2022 the Food and Drug Administration announced that they were considering banning menthols as well.[5,6] Ads targeting children even if not illegal are often questionable ethically.

Throughout this text we have presented a number of ethical perspectives to show how various aspects of advertising and promotion often involve ethical considerations. Ethical issues must be considered in integrated marketing communications decisions. And advertising and promotion are areas where a lapse in ethical standards or judgment can result in actions that are highly visible and often very damaging to a company.

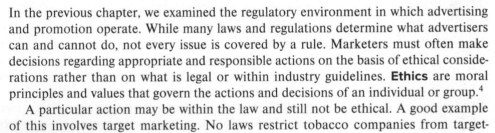

EXHIBIT 21-3

Many companies and organizations now run ads encouraging customers to drink responsibly.

Heineken N.V.

EXHIBIT 21-4

This image demonstrates just how big a problem drinking can be.

National Institute on Alcohol Abuse and Alcoholism

The role of advertising in society is controversial and has sometimes resulted in attempts to restrict or ban advertising and other forms of promotion to certain groups or for certain products. College students are one such group. The level of alcohol consumption and binge drinking by college students has become a serious problem. Alcohol-related problems have proliferated on college campuses in recent years and have resulted in many negative consequences including sexual abuse, assault, and even death, leading some companies to run ads like that shown in Exhibit 21-3.[7] Several studies have shown that there has been a significant increase in binge drinking among college students and have advocated a ban on alcohol-related advertising and promotion to this segment (Exhibit 21-4).[8] Many colleges and universities have imposed restrictions on the marketing of alcoholic beverages to their students. These restrictions include banning sponsorships or support of athletic, musical, cultural, or social events by alcoholic-beverage companies and limiting college newspaper advertising to price and product information ads.

A great deal of attention is being focused on the issue of whether alcoholic-beverage companies target not only college students but underage drinkers as well. The actions of beer, wine, and liquor marketers are being closely scrutinized in the wake of the distilled-spirits industry's decisions to reverse its long-standing ban on television and radio advertising. Alcohol advertising is regulated by the Tobacco Tax and Trade Bureau (TTB). In regard to the regulations of these ads, the TTB has made this statement: "The First Amendment allows for a lot of freedom of speech in general and therefore limits how much the federal government can regulate advertising, even in regard to alcohol. In general, advertisements of alcoholic products must be truthful and without deception. They must provide enough information about the identity of the product for the consumer's benefit and for them to be able to make an educated decision about what the product is or what it contains."[9] The U.S. surgeon general has issued a report stating that alcohol is the most widely used substance of abuse among America's youth and urged marketers of alcoholic beverages to cut back on outdoor advertising and end any remaining college newspaper advertising as well as event sponsorships.[10] The report also called on the media, alcohol marketers, and colleges and universities to work to address the problem

EXHIBIT 21-5

After receiving criticism, Anheuser-Busch issued an apology for the tagline on this label. To read the full statement, visit http://newsroom.anheuser-busch.com/statement-on-bud-light-bottle/.

Bud Light, Anheuser Busch+

EXHIBIT 21-6

Coors has advertised itself as the "Official No Bra Beer."

Coors Brewing Company

EXHIBIT 21-7

NOW posts ads depicting women in a positive light on its site.

Girl Scouts of the United States of America

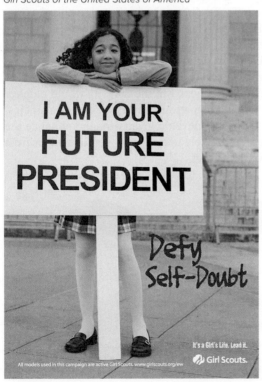

by not glamorizing underage alcohol use in movies and TV shows and minimizing youth exposure to alcohol advertising through the media as well as on the Internet.

Companies marketing alcoholic beverages such as beer and liquor recognize the need to reduce alcohol abuse and drunken driving, particularly among young people, as do government agencies. Many of these companies have developed programs and ads designed to address this problem. The same is true in Canada, where the Alberta Gaming, Liquor, and Cannabis Commission (AGLC) (Alberta, Canada) has been running an advertising campaign that uses ads to encourage drinkers to consume responsibly. The campaign also includes an age-verification splash page, a Facebook page, and images on Pinterest, Instagram, and Twitter. The AGLC has also developed programs designed to help maintain the ethical use of gaming activities and the proper use of cannabis. The Beer Institute and Distilled Spirits Council of the United States marketing codes also ban college newspaper ads, prohibit rite-of-passage ad appeals, and limit some outdoor ads. Both groups also require that ads be placed in media where 70 percent of the audience is 21 or older. Liquor ads have become much more frequently shown on cable TV in the United States.

Criticism often focuses on the actions of specific advertisers. Groups like the National Organization for Women and Women Against Pornography have been critical of advertisers for promoting sexual permissiveness and objectifying women in their ads. These groups have now been joined by the general public. You may recall from Chapter 17 the incident where Bud Light's "Up for Whatever" campaign was criticized for the tagline "The perfect beer for removing 'no' from your vocabulary for the night," which some people took as an endorsement of date rape. The company soon apologized and stopped printing the slogan on its labels. Nevertheless, the negative publicity that resulted was certainly not in Bud's best interest[11] (Exhibit 21-5). On the positive side, some beer companies are now thinking more about how their ads will be perceived by women. A recent Coors Light campaign titled "Made to Chill" targeted both men and women to let them know that in a world where they are "always on" it's important that they take a moment to turn off. One of the campaign's first ads titled "Official Beer of Being Done Wearing a Bra" (Exhibit 21-6) won praise from the media, which called the ad "refreshing and remarkable." Heineken introduced a campaign that suggested that women are more attracted to men who drink less. The campaign featured women singing the Bonnie Tyler song "I Need a Hero" as they walk away from ostensibly inebriated men. NOW posts ads it considers offensive to women, as well as ones they consider positive—like the young girl aspiring to be president—on its website (Exhibit 21-7).

As you read this chapter, remember that the various perspectives presented reflect judgments of people with different backgrounds, values, and interests. You may see nothing wrong with the ads for cigarettes or beer or sexually suggestive ads. Others, however, may oppose these actions on moral and ethical grounds. While we attempt to present the arguments on both sides of these controversial issues, you will have to draw your own conclusions as to what is right or wrong.

SOCIAL AND ETHICAL CRITICISMS OF ADVERTISING

Much of the controversy over advertising stems from the ways many companies use it as a selling tool and from its impact on society's tastes, values, and lifestyles. Specific techniques used by advertisers are criticized as deceptive or untruthful, offensive or in bad taste, and exploitative of certain groups, such as women or children. We discuss each of these criticisms, along with advertisers' responses. We then turn our attention to criticisms concerning the influence of advertising on values and lifestyles, as well as charges that it perpetuates stereotyping and that advertisers exert control over the media.

Advertising as Untruthful or Deceptive

One of the major complaints against advertising is that many ads are misleading or untruthful and deceive consumers. A number of studies have shown a general mistrust of advertising among consumers. These studies have shown that consumers don't find most commercials to be honest and do not trust them. Figure 21-1 shows that Americans' trust in media reporting continues to remain as it has since 2016. According to a Gallup survey conducted in 2022, only 34 percent said that they believe that mass media report the news "fully, accurately and fairly." Only 7 percent said they had a "great deal of trust," while 38 percent said they had "no trust at all" in reporting on television, newspapers, and radio (the Internet was not included in this study). Most marketers consider malware to be the most deceptive form of communication.[12]

Attempts by industry and government to regulate and control deceptive advertising were discussed in Chapter 20. We noted that advertisers should have a reasonable basis for making a claim about product performance and may be required to provide evidence to support their claims. However, deception can occur more subtly as a result of how consumers perceive the ad and its impact on their beliefs.[13] The difficulty of determining just what constitutes deception, along with the fact that advertisers have the right to use puffery and make subjective claims about their products, tends to complicate the issue. But a concern of many critics is the extent to which advertisers are *deliberately* untruthful or misleading.

Sometimes advertisers have made false or misleading claims or failed to award prizes promoted in a contest or sweepstakes. However, these cases usually involved smaller companies and only a tiny portion of the hundreds of billions of dollars spent on advertising and promotion each year. Most advertisers do not design their messages with the intention to mislead or deceive consumers or run sweepstakes with no intention of awarding prizes. Not only are such practices unethical, but the culprits would damage their reputation and risk prosecution by regulatory groups or government agencies. National advertisers invest large sums of money to develop loyalty to, and enhance the image of, their brands. These companies are not likely to risk hard-won consumer trust and confidence by intentionally deceiving consumers.

FIGURE 21-1 Global Trust in Advertising

Source: https://news.gallup.com/poll/403166/americans-trust-media-remains-near-record-low.aspx

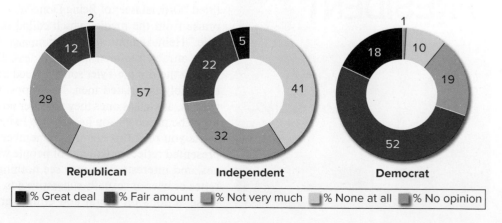

| ■ % Great deal | ■ % Fair amount | □ % Not very much | □ % None at all | □ % No opinion |

The problem of untruthful or fraudulent advertising and promotion exists more at the local level and in specific areas such as Internet fraud, telemarketing, and other forms of direct marketing. Yet there have been many cases where large companies were accused of misleading consumers with their ads or promotions. For example, automobile companies Kia and Hyundai were the targets of U.S. government and class action suits when the Environmental Protection Agency found both manufacturers guilty of posting inflated fuel-economy estimates on their vehicles.[14] Hyundai and Kia agreed to pay a $100 million fine, give up $200 million in emission credits, spend $50 million setting up independent tests to certify mileage claims to settle with the U.S. government, and settle the class actions. In another case, Ford was required to lower mileage ratings for a second time in a year on its hybrids and compensated more than 200,000 owners of models such as the C-Max and Fusion hybrid.[15] Mitsubishi admitted that it had manipulated fuel-economy tests, and Volkswagen was caught manipulating emissions tests. Some companies test the limits of industry and government rules and regulations to make claims in an attempt to give their brands an advantage in highly competitive markets. This seems to be the case in the auto industry. Of course, the auto industry is not the only one that has been accused or found guilty of deceptive advertising. In 2022 the FTC asked a federal court to rule against TurboTax's "Free" advertising campaign, and has done the same regarding Airborne (dietary supplements) and L'Oreal (cosmetics).[16]

Many critics of advertising would probably agree that most advertisers are not out to deceive consumers deliberately, but they are still concerned that consumers may not be receiving enough information to make an informed choice. They say advertisers usually present only information that is favorable to their position and do not always tell consumers the whole truth about a product or service.

Some critics believe advertising should be primarily informative in nature and should not be permitted to use puffery or embellished messages. Others argue that advertisers have the right to present the most favorable case for their products and services and should not be restricted to just objective, verifiable information. They note that consumers can protect themselves from being persuaded against their will and that the various industry and government regulations suffice to keep advertisers from misleading consumers. Figure 21–2 shows the advertising ethics and principles of the American Advertising Federation, which many advertisers use as a guideline in preparing and evaluating their ads.

Advertising as Offensive or in Bad Taste

Another common criticism of advertising, as discussed in the chapter's lead-in, is that ads are offensive, tasteless, irritating, boring, obnoxious, and so on. A number of studies have found that consumers feel that most advertising insults their intelligence and that many ads are in poor taste.

Sources of Distaste   Consumers can be offended or irritated by advertising in a number of ways. Some object when certain products or services such as contraceptives or personal hygiene products are advertised at all. Most media did not accept ads for condoms until the AIDS crisis forced them to reconsider their restrictions. The major TV networks gave their affiliates permission to accept condom advertising in 1987, but the first condom ad did not appear on network TV until 1991.

In 1994, the U.S. Department of Health's Centers for Disease Control and Prevention (CDC) began a new HIV prevention campaign that included radio and TV commercials urging sexually active people to use latex condoms. The commercials prompted strong protests from conservative and religious groups, which argued that the government should stress abstinence in preventing the spread of AIDS among young people. NBC and ABC agreed to broadcast all the commercials, while CBS said it would air certain spots.

Advertising for condoms has now been appearing on TV for over 20 years, but were only in late-night time slots or on cable networks. However, in 2005 the broadcast networks agreed to accept commercials for condoms during prime time by agreeing to run heath-oriented ads for the Trojan brand.[17] The tone of the Trojan advertising was

Principle 1	Advertising, public relations, marketing communications, news, and editorial all share a common objective of truth and high ethical standards in serving the public.
Principle 2	Advertising, public relations, and all marketing communications professionals have an obligation to exercise the highest personal ethics in the creation and dissemination of commercial information to consumers.
Principle 3	Advertisers should clearly distinguish advertising, public relations and corporate communications from news and editorial content and entertainment, both online and offline.
Principle 4	Advertisers should clearly disclose all material conditions, such as payment or receipt of a free product, affecting endorsements in social and traditional channels, as well as the identity of endorsers, all in the interest of full disclosure and transparency.
Principle 5	Advertisers should treat consumers fairly based on the nature of the audience to whom the ads are directed and the nature of the product or service advertised.
Principle 6	Advertisers should never compromise consumers' personal privacy in marketing communications, and their choices as to whether to participate in providing their information should be transparent and easily made.
Principle 7	Advertisers should follow federal, state and local advertising laws, and cooperate with industry self-regulatory programs for the resolution of advertising practices.
Principle 8	Advertisers and their agencies, and online and offline media, should discuss privately potential ethical concerns, and members of the team creating ads should be given permission to express internally their ethical concerns.

EXHIBIT 21–8

Many of the broadcast
networks now accept ads for
condoms during prime time
that promote health-related
uses.

Church & Dwight Co., Inc.

informational and provided facts and figures designed to raise viewers' consciousness and awareness about the potential consequences of unprotected sex among those who are sexually active (Exhibit 21–8). While condom ads remain scarce in traditional media, many such as this one appear frequently on YouTube or in print, like this tongue-in-cheek one (Exhibit 21–9).

There has been found to be a strong product class effect with respect to the types of ads consumers perceived as distasteful or irritating. The most irritating commercials tend to be for feminine hygiene products; ads for women's undergarments and hemorrhoid products were close behind. Ads for personal products have become more common on television and in print, and the public is more accepting of them. However, advertisers must still be careful of how these products are presented and the language and terminology used. There are still many rules, regulations, and taboos advertisers must deal with to have their TV commercials approved by the networks.

Another way advertising can offend consumers is by the type of appeal or the manner of presentation. For example, many people object to appeals that exploit consumer anxieties. Fear appeal ads, especially for products such as deodorants, mouthwash, and dandruff shampoos, are often criticized for attempting to create

EXHIBIT 21–9

Condom ads are still scarce in traditional media, but many appear on YouTube.

Durex

anxiety and using fear of social rejection to sell these products. Some ads for home computers were also criticized for attempting to make parents think that if their young children couldn't use a computer, they would fail in school.

Sexual Appeals The advertising appeals that have received the most criticism for being in poor taste are those using sexual appeals such as suggestiveness and/or nudity. In a longitudinal study of TV viewers in Australia, Michael Ewing found that the issue resulting in the most complaints to the country's advertising Standards Bureau involved sex, sexuality, and/or nudity—almost three times more than any other issue.[18] Similar attitudes have been demonstrated in other countries as well. These techniques are often used to gain consumers' attention and may not even be appropriate to the product being advertised. Even if the sexual appeal relates to the product, people may be offended by it.

A common criticism of sexual appeals is that they can demean women (or men) by depicting them as sex objects. Ads for cosmetics and lingerie are among the most criticized for their portrayal of women as sex objects and for being implicitly suggestive, though many other products also make use of this appeal, including a number of clothing companies and shoe and liquor brands. One of the reasons for using sexy ads is the attention they get as well as the free exposure that often results from the ads through publicity and/or word of mouth. For example, sexy ad campaigns using actor Megan Fox, singer Beyoncé, and soccer player David Beckham have each gathered over 12 million views in ads that have appeared for Armani, H&M, and H&M, respectively.[19]

A company that has used sexy ads in a direct attempt to garner publicity (and has done so quite successfully!) is Calvin Klein. Since the first controversial Brooke Shields ad in 1981, the company has released very sexy ads that push the limits of compliance and have been debated in a variety of media, from both pro and against perspectives—all the while gaining even more exposure for the ads (Exhibit 21-10).

No doubt viewers will continue to hold different perspectives of the use of sex in advertising. Advertisers, however, are not likely to discontinue the practice. As noted by one company spokesperson responding to the criticisms, "Style is a matter of interpretation and like with all art we appreciate all points of view."[20]

Attitudes toward the use of sex in advertising is a polarizing issue because opinions regarding its use vary depending on the individual's values and religious orientation, as well as by age, education, and gender. One study found major differences between men and women in their attitudes toward sex in advertising.[21] While almost half of men said they liked sexual ads, only 8 percent of women felt the same way. Women were also much more likely than men to say that sexual ads promote a deterioration of moral and social values and that they are demeaning of the models used in them (IMC Perspective 21-1).

Shock Advertising With the increasing clutter in the advertising environment, advertisers continue to use sexual appeals and other techniques that offend some people but catch the attention of consumers and may even generate publicity for their companies. In recent years, there has been an increase in what is often referred to as **shock advertising**, in which marketers use nudity, sexual suggestiveness, or other startling images to get consumers' attention. As discussed earlier in the chapter, shock advertising is nothing new; companies such as American Apparel and Calvin Klein have been using this tactic in their ads for quite a while. However, a number of other marketers have been criticized for using shock techniques in their ads as well as in other promotional materials. Mexican beer brand Tecate shocked people passing by its billboards in Los Angeles and San Francisco when the advertisement displayed a tree with the word *baño* (Spanish for "bathroom") overlaying the image. The tongue-in-cheek message was meant to imply that it is easier for guys to go to the bathroom. While Tecate said the ad was not intended for the U.S. market, and took it down, one still wonders what it was meant to

EXHIBIT 21–10

Calvin Klein started pushing the limits with this ad in 1981.

The Advertising Archives/Alamy Stock Photo

Was the Beginning of #MeToo the End of Sexy Advertising?

There was a time not that long ago when sexy ads were in vogue. Watch commercials featuring Kate Upton and Paris Hilton for Carl's Jr. and almost any commercial from AXE or GoDaddy from a decade or more ago, and you will see what we mean. But now, Carl's Jr. says it would "stop using boobs to sell burgers," beer commercials are targeting friendship and community more than sex, and AXE has rebranded—less sex in ads. What happened? Can it be attributed to a sense of enlightenment? Are these companies' target markets losing interest in sex? Or is it something else?

Many, like journalist Sheena Butler-Young, believe that much of the decline that we see in the use of sexy ads can be attributed to the #MeToo movement—a movement against sexual assault and sexual harassment that gained traction internationally around 2017. She cites the example of a recent Jimmy Choo's commercial that featured supermodel Cara Delevingne in a "barely there" minidress strutting down a street on a busy night in Manhattan to numerous catcalls and male gazes following her movements along the way. The commercial drew a great deal of scrutiny, and social media called out the spot as being "regressive" and "tone deaf" (and more!). After numerous complaints, the brand pulled the ad. While the company refused to comment on the incident, Butler-Young attributed the pulling of the ad to changing times in the wake of #MeToo.

Dafna Lemish, a professor of journalism and media studies at Rutgers University, notes that the overuse of sexy ads can be attributed to the feminist era of the 1960s, when positive movements in regard to sexual liberation, embracing the female form, and freedom of choice were won. Unfortunately, marketers commoditized the movement, and the trend in ads became the overuse of sexuality. The problem becomes amplified in advertising because "brands have mere seconds to make an impact, so they often rely on a shock factor," says Lemish. Unfortunately, the ads often distort men's perceptions of how to behave, thinking that women are available for sex at any time, she says.

Tamara Mellon, the cofounder of Jimmy Choo, makes the point that ads can be sexy without being sexist. Women can be sexy and empowered. She notes that in her current job (not at Jimmy Choo), the brand is extremely conscientious about how women are portrayed. She says they are never put in poses to make them look submissive, they are in strong athletic poses, and they are never under the age of 18. The very successful company Kate Spade has frequently run ads that featured women in high-fashion, yet modern garments.

An article in *Ad Age* by Jeanine Poggi also suggests the #MeToo movement may be affecting ads but from a slightly different perspective. Poggi agrees that GoDaddy and Carl's Jr. have cut back on their objectification of women in recent years, but she still sees a gap between the roles of women and men who are depicted in ads. Citing research conducted by Professor Raymond Taylor that analyzed Super Bowl ads over the past decade, Poggi notes that 76 percent of the ads featured men as the principle character, and twice as many male celebrities appeared than did females—only a slight improvement over the Super Bowl 5 years earlier. While 14 of the ads analyzed included no women, only one included no men. While one might attribute these results to the assumption that the Super Bowl is watched primarily by men and the ads are designed to appeal to men, the fact is that women constitute 49 percent of the audience, and prior research from years past indicate women are more likely than men to watch Super Bowl ads.

Professor Taylor explains that there is an opportunity to make "sensible, pro-women" statements that show empowerment that does not come "at the expense of men." He suggests that the #MeToo movement often "involves bad actions from men toward women, but how do you frame it positively toward women without coming across badly toward men?" He suggests that men must become part of the solution.

Others are less likely to attribute the decline in use of sexy ads all to the #MeToo movement, however. A study conducted by John Wirtz at the University of Illinois examined 78 studies conducted from 1969 to 2017 analyzing thousands of participants' reactions to sexy ads. Men were shown to like the ads more than women did, and sexy ads were remembered for a longer period of time. However, there was no impact on sales. So the old adage that "sex sells" is not necessarily true, according to Wirtz.

Maybe it is not all about #MeToo. Maybe it's the fact that sex doesn't sell. Or maybe, it's fear of reprisal in the form of bad publicity on social media. At this point, none of these factors can be held strictly responsible. Maybe they are all responsible. Nevertheless, #MeToo is a significant force to deal with and surely is contributing.

So the question is, does sexy advertising work? Have advertisers cut back on its use in response to the #MeToo movement, or have they determined that it is no longer an effective practice? Mike Rampton contends that while gen Z consumers may be less impacted by sexy ads because of their skepticism to advertising in general, it would be a mistake to conclude that sexy ads no longer work because they definitely do! An interview with four advertising industry experts in Australia, conducted by Seja Al Zaida, revealed some different perspectives. While overall the women all agreed that consumers' values have changed and that trying to sell a product with blatant sex is no longer an acceptable strategy, they were more hesitant to attribute this to the #MeToo movement itself. Rather, there was some consensus that sexy ads can and do work but must be appropriate to the brand or product being sold. They felt that sexy ads in themselves are not inherently wrong, but the strategy must be done in good taste and consistent with the product being sold not just blatant "sex sells" thinking.

Sources: Jeanine Poggi, "Where Are the Women? Super Bowl Ads Face Scrutiny amid #MeToo Movement," *Ad Age*, January 12, 2018, www.adage .com; Sheena Butler-Young, "The End of an Era: How the #MeToo Movement Is Raining on Advertising's 'Sex Sells' Parade," *Footwear News*, February 12, 2018, www.footwearnews.com; Sarah Rense, "The Sexiest Ads of All TIme Are Bullsh*t," *Esquire*, June 27, 2017, www.esquire.com.

EXHIBIT 21-11

Air Asia's billboard gained attention and criticism.

Air Asia

accomplish. The billboard for Air Asia shown in Exhibit 21-11 no doubt was designed to gain attention to the fact that the airline offered cheap airfares to Phuket, Thailand, albeit in a shocking manner. Clothing retailer Abercrombie & Fitch has been criticized numerous times for the content and images used in its quarterly catalogs, which have included sex tips from porn star Jenna Jameson, a spoof interview with a shopping mall Santa portrayed as a pedophile, and nude photos. A few years ago the retailer promoted its Christmas catalog with an advertisement across the plastic covering stating, "Two-hundred and eighty pages of sex and Xmas fun" (Exhibit 21-12). Officials in four states threatened or pursued legal action against the company, which responded by implementing a policy of carding would-be buyers of the catalog to ensure they were at least 18 years old.[22]

Many advertising experts argue that what underlies the increase in the use of shock advertising is the pressure on marketers and their agencies to do whatever it takes to get their ads noticed—we have seen this in earlier chapters. However, critics argue that the more advertisers use the tactic, the more shocking the ads have to be to get attention. How far advertisers can go with these appeals will probably depend on the public's reaction. When consumers think the advertisers have gone too far, they are likely to pressure the advertisers to change their ads and the media to stop accepting them.

Interestingly, one of the most well-known employers of shock advertising is fashion brand Benetton. As far back as 1965, Benetton's marketing strategy was to challenge social norms using very shocking ads to champion social issues. From ads featuring the Pope kissing Ahmed el-Tayeb, the imam of Egypt's al-Azhar Mosque, to a picture of an HIV-positive patient as he lay dying in a hospital bed, the controversy led to increased brand awareness for the brand, discussions, the opening of more stores, and increased sales. However, over time awareness remained high, but the controversy and accompanying discussions did not—nor did sales. By 2016 the company changed its creative from "shockvertising" to "never shocking."[23]

Not all shock ads are designed to gain one's attention to commercial products. Exhibit 21-13 is an excellent example of how cause marketers are now employing this tactic.

EXHIBIT 21-12

Abercrombie & Fitch's catalogs were criticized over the use of sex and nudity.

Splash News/Newscom

EXHIBIT 21-13

Not all shock ads are for commercial products. Here, Greenpeace asks people to rethink their use of plastic straws.

Greenpeace

IT'S TIME TO RAISE THE LEGAL AGE TO PURCHASE TOBACCO PRODUCTS, INCLUDING VAPOR, FROM 18 TO 21.

BECAUSE WHEN YOUTH NEVER START SMOKING AND VAPING, THEY NEVER HAVE TO STOP.

About 80% of high school students turn 18 before graduating.

And in most states, they can then legally purchase tobacco and vapor products. Some illegally share with or sell those products to underage classmates.

This "social sourcing" accounts for nearly 80% of youth access to vapor products.*

Raising the legal age of purchase to 21+ reduces this social sourcing and can drive steep drops in underage usage.

JUUL Labs applauds the states that have gone to 21+ and supports making it the standard nationwide.

FOR ADULT SMOKERS ONLY

JUUL.com/T21

© 2019 and TM JUUL Labs, Inc. All rights reserved.
Paid for by JUUL Labs, Inc.

*Suanne Tanski et al., "Youth Access to Tobacco Products in the United States: Findings from Wave 1 (2013-2014) of the Population Assessment of Tobacco and Health (PATH) Study," 2018, https://www.ncbi.nlm.nih.gov/pubmed/30407588.

EXHIBIT 21–14

Juul switched its emphasis to appeal more to adults as the FDA took notice of Juul's ads that seemed to target young people.

JUUL Labs, Inc

Advertising and Children

Another controversial topic advertisers must deal with is the issue of advertising to children. TV and the Internet are two vehicles through which advertisers can reach children easily. Estimates are that children between the ages of 8 and 12 in the United States spend approximately 5 hours and 33 minutes a day online on average, with those 13–18 spending 8 hours 39 minutes.[24] These numbers continue to increase. A study conducted by Fairplay for Kids.org, formerly the Campaign for a Commercial-Free Childhood, estimated that children ages 2 to 11 see more than 40,000 commercials a year on TV alone, not to mention the ones they may see on the Internet, cell phones, video games, and so on.[25] Companies spend approximately $12 billion a year advertising to children, with most of this advertising falling into four categories: toys, food, clothing, and accessories.[26] Children are targeted because the ads influence their purchases as well as influencing other family members' purchases. In addition, if the child continues to use the product into adulthood, his or her lifetime value as a customer increases significantly.

More recently, there has been strong public criticism of companies marketing vapes to children and teens (Exhibit 21–14). The e-cigarettes come in a variety of flavors, and the companies who market them are being purchased by the large cigarette companies. A review of the Silicon Valley startup Juul—purchased by Altria, one of the world's largest tobacco companies—by researchers from Stanford Research into the Impact of Tobacco Advertising studied thousands of Juul's Instagram posts, e-mails, and ads from 2015 to 2018 and came to the conclusion that they "were patently youth-oriented" and appeared to borrow directly from the tobacco industry playbook. The company's campaign also featured ads on Facebook and Twitter, as well as sampling events in major U.S. cities with social influencers distributing free Juuls at movie and music events. A later campaign employed social media as well as billboards. Katy Perry was shown with Juul's device at the Golden Globes. None of the promotions featured adults.

Juul argued that the product and its ads were targeted to adults who were having trouble quitting smoking. When the FDA and media took notice of the rising concern, the company switched its emphasis to the slogan "Make the switch," featuring testimonials from grown-ups.[27]

Concern has also been expressed about marketers' use of other promotional vehicles and techniques such as radio ads, point-of-purchase displays, premiums in packages, product placements, and commercial characters as the basis for TV shows. A number of advocacy groups petitioned the FTC to investigate a YouTube app that offers kids the opportunity to watch hundreds of channels of entertainment and educational programs. But, according to the watchdog groups, there were numerous branded content programs from McDonald's, Mattel, and Hasbro mixed in. In assisting the groups to draft the FTC complaint, University of Arizona professor Dale Kunkel said, "this is the most hyper-commercialized media for kids I have ever seen." A spokesperson for YouTube claimed that the company consulted with numerous child advocacy and privacy groups in the development of the app, and were always open to feedback on ways to improve the app.[28]

Critics argue that children, particularly young ones, are especially vulnerable to advertising because they lack the experience and knowledge to understand and critically evaluate the purpose of persuasive advertising appeals. Research has shown that preschool children cannot differentiate between commercials and programs, do not perceive the selling intent of commercials, and cannot distinguish between reality and fantasy.[29] The study also concluded that children must understand how advertising works in order to use their cognitive defenses against it effectively. Because of children's limited ability to interpret the selling intent of a message or identify a commercial, critics charge that advertising to them is inherently unfair and deceptive and should be banned or severely restricted.

At the other extreme are those who argue that advertising is a part of life and children must learn to deal with it in the **consumer socialization process** of acquiring the skills needed to function in the marketplace. They say existing restrictions are adequate for controlling children's advertising and that marketplace knowledge plays an important role in adolescents' skepticism toward advertising. They contend that greater knowledge of the marketplace appears to give teens a basis by which to evaluate ads and enables them to recognize the persuasion techniques used by advertisers.[30]

Children are also protected from the potential influences of commercials by network censors and industry self-regulatory groups such as the Council of Better Business Bureaus's Children's Advertising Review Unit (CARU). CARU has strict self-regulatory guidelines regarding the type of appeals, product presentation and claims, and disclosures and disclaimers, and the use of premiums, safety, and techniques such as special effects and animation. Commercial Alert's Parents' Bill of Rights is shown in Figure 21-3.

As we saw in Chapter 20, the major networks also have strict guidelines for ads targeted to children. For example, in network TV ads, only 10 seconds can be devoted to animation and special effects; the final 5 seconds are reserved for displaying all the toys shown in the ad and disclosing whether they are sold separately and whether accessories such as batteries are included.[31]

Concerns over advertising and other forms of promotion directed at children diminished somewhat during the late 1990s and the early part of the new century. However, the issue has once again begun receiving a considerable amount of attention as various groups are calling for restrictions on advertising targeted to children. The American Psychological Association (APA), the nation's largest organization of psychologists, issued a report criticizing the increasing commercialization of childhood and calling for new curbs on marketing aimed at children.[32] The APA report faulted marketers for taking advantage of an ever-fragmenting media landscape of cable channels and the Internet to target children. The report noted that marketing activities focused on America's youth have reached unprecedented levels and called for restrictions on advertising in TV programming that appeals primarily to children under the age of eight and a total ban on advertising in programs aimed at very young children in this group. The report also found that the Internet is a particularly effective, and thus potentially harmful, means of sending advertising messages to children as websites often blur or even ignore the boundaries between commercial and noncommercial content. Marketing and advertising trade groups have been critical of the report and continue to defend their right to advertise on the basis that parents of younger children, rather than the children themselves, make purchase decisions.[33]

In addition to concerns over the increasing amount of advertising targeted to children, there are a number of other issues that consumer groups and regulatory agencies have raised with respect to young people. These include an increase in the number of ads encouraging children to visit websites, and general concerns over the content of children's programming, particularly with regard to violence. The marketing of violent entertainment to minors and the advertising practices and rating systems of the film, music, and electronic game industries are also being monitored very carefully. The issue of what young consumers are watching, listening to, communicating, and playing and

PARENTS' BILL OF RIGHTS
Commercial Alert's

WHEREAS, the nurturing of character and strong values in children is one of the most important functions of any society;

WHEREAS, the primary responsibility for the upbringing of children resides in their parents;

WHEREAS, an aggressive commercial culture has invaded the relationship between parents and children, and has impeded the ability of parents to guide the upbringing of their own children;

WHEREAS, corporate marketers have sought increasingly to bypass parents, and speak directly to children in order to tempt them with the most sophisticated tools that advertising executives, market researchers and psychologists can devise;

WHEREAS, these marketers tend to glorify materialism, addiction, hedonism, violence and anti-social behavior, all of which are abhorrent to most parents;

WHEREAS, parents find themselves locked in constant battle with this pervasive influence, and are hard pressed to keep the commercial culture and its degraded values out of their children's lives;

WHEREAS, the aim of this corporate marketing is to turn children into agents of corporations in the home, so that they will nag their parents for the things they see advertised, thus sowing strife, stress and misery in the family;

WHEREAS, the products advertised generally are ones parents themselves would not choose for their children: violent and sexually suggestive entertainment, video games, alcohol, tobacco, gambling and junk food;

WHEREAS, this aggressive commercial influence has contributed to an epidemic of marketing-related diseases in children, such as obesity, type 2 diabetes, alcoholism, anorexia and bulimia, while millions will eventually die from the marketing of tobacco;

WHEREAS, corporations have latched onto the schools and compulsory school laws as a way to bypass parents and market their products and values to a captive audience of impressionable and trusting children;

WHEREAS, these corporations ultimately are creatures of state law, and it is intolerable that they should use the rights and powers so granted for the purpose of undermining the authority of parents in these ways;

THEREFORE, BE IT RESOLVED, that the U.S. Congress and the fifty state legislatures should right the balance between parents and corporations and restore to parents some measure of control over the commercial influences on their children, by enacting this Parents' Bill of Rights, including,

----

Leave Children Alone Act. This act bans television advertising aimed at children under 12 years of age. (federal)

Child Privacy Act. This act restores to parents the ability to safeguard the privacy of their own children. It gives parents the right to control any commercial use of personal information concerning their children, and the right to know precisely how such information is used. (federal, state)

Advertising to Children Accountability Act. This act helps parents affix individual responsibility for attempts to subject their children to commercial influence. It requires corporations to disclose who created each of their advertisements, and who did the market research for each ad directed at children under 12 years of age. (federal)

Commercial-Free Schools Act. Corporations have turned the public schools into advertising free-fire zones. This act prohibits corporations from using the schools and compulsory school laws to bypass parents and pitch their products to impressionable schoolchildren. (federal, state)

Fairness Doctrine for Parents. This act provides parents with the opportunity to talk back to the media and the advertisers. It makes the Fairness Doctrine apply to all advertising to children under 12 years of age, providing parents and community with response time on broadcast TV and radio for advertising to children. (federal)

Product Placement Disclosure Act. This law gives parents more information with which to monitor the influences that prey upon their children through the media. Specifically, it requires corporations to disclose, on packaging and at the outset, any and all product placements on television and videos, and in movies, video games and books. This prevents advertisers from sneaking ads into media that parents assume to be ad-free. (federal)

Child Harm Disclosure Act. Parents have a right to know of any significant health effects of products they might purchase for their children. This act creates a legal duty for corporations to publicly disclose all information suggesting that their product(s) could substantially harm the health of children. (federal)

Children's Food Labeling Act. Parents have a right to information about the food that corporations push upon their children. This act requires fast food restaurant chains to label contents of food, and provide basic nutritional information about it. (federal, state)

Children's Advertising Subsidy Revocation Act. It is intolerable that the federal government actually rewards corporations with a big tax write-off for the money they spend on psychologists, market researchers, ad agencies, media and the like in their campaigns to instill their values in our children. This act eliminates all federal subsidies, deductions and preferences for advertising aimed at children under 12 years of age. (federal)

Please make copies of the Parents' Bill of Rights, and give or mail them to your members of Congress, state legislators and candidates. Ask them to turn the provisions into law. Distribute this at day care centers, schools, churches, synagogues, coffee shops, grocery stores and other places where parents gather. Call 503.235.8012 to volunteer or to find out how you can help enact the Parents' Bill of Rights into law.

Commercial Alert • www.commercialalert.org • 4110 SE Hawthorne Blvd. #123, Portland, OR 97214-5246 • 503.235.8012

that's love™

BE YOURSELF, TOGETHER.

Build a Target® Wedding Gift Registry as unique as the two of you.

explore our catalog

EXHIBIT 21–15

Many companies now produce ads that are LGBTQ friendly like this Target ad.

Target Brands, Inc.

LO 21-2

how much violence that entertainment contains has become an area of great concern following numerous, well-publicized shootings at schools.

How marketers are using the Internet and social media to communicate with and sell to children is a growing concern. Studies have claimed that advertisers avoid many of the regulations designed to protect children by advertising on the Internet and mobile instead of traditional media. Noting that the Internet is less regulated, there are increasing claims that advertising regulators are failing to protect children who are the targets of aggressive marketing through ads as well as in Internet video games. They argue that children and youth can be reached through games, ads, brand pages, and social networking sites, and as a result, marketers have increased their efforts to reach these groups and that these efforts may be even more fruitful than TV given kids' strong attraction to online activities.

Advertising to children will remain a controversial topic. Some groups feel that the government is responsible for protecting children from the potentially harmful effects of advertising and other forms of promotion, while others argue that parents are ultimately responsible for doing so.

It is important to many companies to communicate directly with children. However, only by being sensitive to the naiveté of children as consumers will they be able to do so freely and avoid potential conflict with those who believe children should be protected from advertising and other forms of promotion.

Social and Cultural Consequences

Concern is often expressed over the impact of advertising on society, particularly on values and lifestyles. While a number of factors influence the cultural values, lifestyles, and behavior of a society, the overwhelming amount of advertising and its prevalence in the mass media lead many critics to argue that advertising plays a major role in influencing and transmitting social values. In his book *Advertising and Social Change*, Ronald Berman says:

> The institutions of family, religion, and education have grown noticeably weaker over each of the past three generations. The world itself seems to have grown more complex. In the absence of traditional authority, advertising has become a kind of social guide. It depicts us in all the myriad situations possible to a life of free choice. It provides ideas about style, morality, behavior.[34]

Mike Hughes, president and creative director of the Martin Agency, notes that advertising has a major impact on society: "Ads help establish what is cool in society; their messages contribute to the public dialogue. Gap ads show white, black, and Hispanic kids dancing together. Hilfiger ads showed it's cool for people to get along. IKEA showed a gay couple." He argues that advertising agencies have a social and ethical responsibility to consider the impact of the advertising messages they create for their clients.[35] Gap, JCPenney, McDonald's, Levis, Target, and Amazon Kindle among many others have all produced ads that are lesbian, gay, bisexual, and transgender friendly, like the one shown in Exhibit 21-15.[36]

While there is general agreement that advertising is an important social influence agent, opinions as to the value of its contribution are often negative. Advertising is criticized for encouraging materialism, manipulating consumers to buy things they do not really need, perpetuating stereotypes, and controlling the media.

Advertising Encourages Materialism Many critics claim advertising has an adverse effect on consumer values by encouraging **materialism**, a preoccupation with material things rather than intellectual or spiritual concerns. They argue that a major contributor to materialism is advertising that

- Seeks to create needs rather than merely showing how a product or service fulfills them.
- Surrounds consumers with images of the good life and suggests the acquisition of material possessions leads to contentment and happiness and adds to the joy of living.
- Suggests material possessions are symbols of status, success, and accomplishment and/or will lead to greater social acceptance, popularity, sex appeal, and so on.

Advertising for products such as expensive automobiles, like the one shown in this Maserati ad (Exhibit 21–16), and luxury goods like clothing, jewelry, and alcoholic beverages is often criticized for promoting materialistic values.

This criticism of advertising assumes that materialism is undesirable and is sought at the expense of other goals. But many believe materialism is an acceptable part of the **Protestant ethic**, which stresses hard work and individual effort and initiative and views the accumulation of material possessions as evidence of success. Others argue that the acquisition of material possessions has positive economic impact by encouraging consumers to keep consuming after their basic needs are met. Many Americans believe economic growth is essential and materialism is both a necessity and an inevitable part of this progress.

It has also been argued that an emphasis on material possessions does not rule out interest in intellectual, spiritual, or cultural values. Defenders of advertising say consumers can be more interested in higher-order goals when basic needs have been met and point out that consumers may purchase material things in the pursuit of nonmaterial goals. For example, a person may buy an expensive stereo system to enjoy music rather than simply to impress someone or acquire a material possession.

Even if we assume materialism is undesirable, there is still the question of whether advertising is responsible for creating and encouraging it. While many critics argue that advertising is a major contributing force to materialistic values, others say advertising merely reflects the values of society rather than shaping them. They argue that consumers' values are defined by the society in which they live and are the results of extensive, long-term socialization or acculturation.

The argument that advertising is responsible for creating a materialistic and hedonistic society is addressed by Stephen Fox in his book *The Mirror Makers: A History of American Advertising and Its Creators.* Fox concludes advertising has become a prime scapegoat for our times and merely reflects society. Regarding the effect of advertising on cultural values, he says:

> To blame advertising now for those most basic tendencies in American history is to miss the point. It is too obvious, too easy, a matter of killing the messenger instead of dealing with the bad news. The people who have created modern advertising are not hidden persuaders pushing our buttons in the service of some malevolent purpose. They are just producing an especially visible manifestation, good and bad, of the American way of life.[37]

The ad shown in Exhibit 21–17 was developed by the American Association of Advertising Agencies (4A's) and suggests that advertising is a reflection of society's tastes and values, not vice versa. The ad was part of a campaign that addressed criticisms of advertising.

EXHIBIT 21–16

Critics argue that advertising contributes to materialistic values.

Maserati S.p.A.

Some people say that advertising determines America's tastes.

Which is another way of saying that advertising determines your tastes.

Which is, in turn, another way of saying that you don't have a mind of your own.

Well, time and time again the advertising industry has found that you do have a mind of your own. If a product doesn't interest you, you simply don't buy it.

And if the product's advertising doesn't interest you, you don't buy that either.

Think of it as a sort of natural selection.

Good products and good advertising survive. Bad products and bad advertising perish. All according to the decisions you make in the marketplace.

So we've concluded that advertising is a mirror of society's tastes. Not vice versa.

Our conclusion is based on a great deal of thought. And many years of reflection.

ADVERTISING.
ANOTHER WORD FOR FREEDOM OF CHOICE.
American Association of Advertising Agencies

EXHIBIT 21–17

The advertising industry argues that advertising reflects society.

American Association of Advertising Agencies

EXHIBIT 21–18

The 4As responds to the claim that advertising makes consumers buy things they do not need.

American Association of Advertising Agencies

DESPITE WHAT SOME PEOPLE THINK, ADVERTISING CAN'T MAKE YOU BUY SOMETHING YOU DON'T NEED.

Some people would have you believe that you are putty in the hands of every advertiser in the country.

They think that when advertising is put under your nose, your mind turns to oatmeal.

It's mass hypnosis. Subliminal seduction. Brain washing. Mind control. It's advertising.

And you are a pushover for it.

It explains why your kitchen cupboard is full of food you never eat. Why your garage is full of cars you never drive.

Why your house is full of books you don't read, TV's you don't watch, beds you don't use, and clothes you don't wear.

You don't have a choice. You are forced to buy.

That's why this message is a cleverly disguised advertisement to get you to buy land in the tropics.

Got you again, didn't we? Send in your money.

ADVERTISING
ANOTHER WORD FOR FREEDOM OF CHOICE.
American Association of Advertising Agencies

Individuals from a variety of backgrounds are concerned over the values they see driving our society. They believe that materialism, greed, and selfishness increasingly dominate American life and that advertising is a major reason for these undesirable values. The extent to which advertising is responsible for materialism and the desirability of such values are deep philosophical issues that will continue to be part of the debate over the societal value and consequences of advertising.

Advertising Makes People Buy Things They Don't Need A common criticism of advertising is that it manipulates consumers into buying things they do not need. Many critics say advertising should just provide information useful in making purchase decisions and should not attempt to persuade. They view information advertising (which reports price, performance, and other objective criteria) as desirable, but persuasive advertising (which plays on consumers' emotions, anxieties, and psychological needs and desires such as status, self-esteem, and attractiveness) as unacceptable. Persuasive advertising is criticized for fostering discontent among consumers and encouraging them to purchase products and services to solve deeper problems.

Defenders of advertising offer a number of rebuttals to these criticisms. First, they point out that a substantial amount of advertising is essentially informational in nature. Also, it is difficult to separate desirable informational advertising from undesirable persuasive advertising. Shelby Hunt, in examining the *information-persuasion dichotomy*, points out that even advertising that most observers would categorize as very informative is often very persuasive. He says, "If advertising critics really believe that persuasive advertising should not be permitted, they are actually proposing that no advertising be allowed, since the purpose of all advertising is to persuade."[38]

Defenders of advertising also take issue with the argument that it should be limited to dealing with basic functional needs. In our society, most lower-level needs recognized in Maslow's hierarchy, such as the need for food, clothing, and shelter, are satisfied for most people. It is natural to move from basic needs to higher-order ones such as self-esteem and status or self-actualization. Consumers are free to choose the degree to which they attempt to satisfy their desires, and wise advertisers associate their products and services with the satisfaction of higher-order needs.

Proponents of advertising offer two other defenses against the charge that advertising makes people buy things they do not really need. First, this criticism attributes too much power to advertising and assumes consumers have no ability to defend themselves against it. Second, it ignores the fact that consumers have the freedom to make their own choices when confronted with persuasive advertising. While they readily admit the persuasive intent of their business, advertisers are quick to note it is extremely difficult to make consumers purchase a product they do not want or for which they do not see a personal benefit. If advertising were as powerful as the critics claim, we would not see products with multimillion-dollar advertising budgets failing in the marketplace. The reality is that consumers do have a choice, and they are not being forced to buy. Consumers ignore ads for products and services they do not really need or that fail to interest them (see Exhibit 21–18).

Advertising and Stereotyping Advertising is often accused of creating and perpetuating stereotypes through its portrayal of women, ethnic minorities, and other groups.

EXHIBIT 21–19

Many advertisers now portray women in powerful roles.

JPMorgan Chase & Co.

EXHIBIT 21–20

Many marketers are creating ads specifically for the culturally diverse market, such as this Stuart Weitzman ad featuring Kim Kardashian.

Stuart Weitzman

Women As you have read, the portrayal of women in advertising is an issue that has received a great deal of attention through the years. In addition to the sexual portrayals discussed, advertising has received much criticism for stereotyping women and failing to recognize the changing role of women in our society. Critics have argued that advertising often depicts women as preoccupied with beauty, household duties, and motherhood or shows them as decorative objects or sexually provocative figures. Portrayals of adult women in American television and print advertising have emphasized passivity, deference, lack of intelligence and credibility, and punishment for high levels of effort. In contrast, men have been portrayed as constructive, powerful, autonomous, and achieving.

While sexism and stereotyping certainly exist, advertising's portrayal of women is improving in many areas. Many advertisers have begun to recognize the importance of portraying women realistically. The increase in the number of working women has resulted not only in women having more influence in family decision making but also in more single-female households, which means more independent purchasers.

They note that as women have crossed the boundary from the domestic sphere to the professional arena, expectations and representations of women have changed as well. For example, a number of magazines, such as *Ms.*, now incorporate and appeal to the sociocultural shifts in women's lives. Many advertisers are now depicting women in a diversity of roles that reflect their changing place in society. In many ads, the stereotypic character traits attributed to women have shifted from weak and dependent to strong and autonomous. The Chase ad shown in Exhibit 21–19 is an example of how advertisers are changing the way they portray women in their ads. In addition to showing a professional woman, the copy attests to her success. The Stuart Weitzman ad featuring Kim Kardashian shown in Exhibit 21-20 is another example of a portrayal of a successful woman in a variety of fields including modeling, media, and business. One reason for these changes is the emergence of females in key agency roles. Women advertising executives are likely to be more sensitive to the portrayal of their own gender and to strengthen the role of women beyond stereotypical housewives or a position of subservience to men.

African Americans and Hispanics African Americans and Hispanics have also been the target of stereotyping in advertising. For many years, advertisers virtually ignored all non-white ethnic groups as identifiable subcultures and viable markets. Ads were rarely targeted to these ethnic groups, and the use of Black and Hispanic people as spokespeople, communicators, models, or actors in ads was very limited.

Ads are increasingly likely to be racially integrated. As seen in Digital and Social Media Perspective 21-1, advertisers have begun breaking the taboo against suggesting interracial attraction. A number of companies now run interracial ads—but not without risk. Advertisers are also finding that advertising developed specifically for the culturally diverse markets, is an effective way of reaching this ethnic market. A recent article in *Ad Age* took a historical perspective to cite five groundbreaking advertising campaigns that moved the needle on Black representation in ads. Campaigns by McDonald's, Pepsi, Nike, P&G, and Lexus were pointed out as examples of how things can change for the better.[39]

As We See More Interracial Ads, How Do Consumers React?

Singer Bob Dylan wrote "The times they are a changing" almost 50 years ago. A relatively unassuming commercial called "Just Checking" featuring an interracial family with a little girl expressing concern for her father's health was aired in 2013 by Cheerios. Yes, Cheerios, the cereal, not some edgy brand trying to get attention. (The iconic Cheerios brand has been around since 1945!) And there are still many out there who apparently haven't gotten Dylan's message. The response to the commercial, which was viewed over 2 million times on YouTube, received such racist and vitriolic feedback that General Mills had to disable the comments section of the posting. As noted by media and pop culture columnist Barbara Lippert, "A progressive-looking commercial collides with the ugliness of the Internet." At the same time, it should be reported that while comments referring to Nazis, "troglodytes," and even "racial genocide" were way too frequent, there were also many positive reactions to the commercial commending the brand for being progressive, timely, and considerate. Within a few days, Cheerio's Facebook page was flooded with positive comments praising the ad, with more than a million "likes," and YouTube ratings reflected over 21,000 "thumbs up" compared to less than 1,500 "thumbs down."

Three years later Old Navy received a similar reaction to its ad. The ad was simply supposed to promote a sale—30 percent off an entire Old Navy purchase. But some took the ad, which featured an interracial family, to promote a larger message on race. Social media users took to Twitter, calling the ad "absolutely disgusting," supportive of "the genocide of the white race," and threatened to boycott the store. Old Navy was not backing down and gave this response: "We are a brand with a proud history of championing diversity and inclusion. At Old Navy, everyone is welcome." Even then Senator John McCain's son—a Navy helicopter pilot whose wife is African American—responded to the racial accusations of "miscegenation," "anti-white propaganda," and "white genocide" being levied against Old Navy, calling them "ignorant racists." Later, Swift McCain tweeted a photo of herself and her husband with the caption: "I was just in @OldNavy this weekend! Bought something for me and my husband. #LoveWins." As with the Cheerios ad, the number of positive responses far outnumbered the negative ones—with many posting pictures of their interracial families online.

So what do you do if you are Old Navy or General Mills? Well—according to most marketing experts—the right thing. Other than disabling the comments section on the YouTube video, Cheerios stood by the spot, keeping it on the air, as well as on YouTube. As noted by Camille Gibson, vice president of marketing for Cheerios, in an e-mail comment, "There are many kinds of families, and Cheerios celebrates them all." Gibson explained that the comments section on the YouTube video was disabled because Cheerios is a family brand and not all of the comments were family-friendly. Old Navy stuck by its position stating that it was proud of the ad, calling it a message of diversity and inclusion.

Praise from the marketing community was overwhelmingly positive. (While some skeptics wondered if "Just Checking" was an attempt to get attention, they were few and far between.) Allen Adamson, managing director of Landor Associates, told *CBS News* that he applauded General Mills for standing by the ad, noting that "the traditional approach depicting the old 'Leave It to Beaver' family, while offending no one, is not very realistic." Meagan Hatcher-Mays, a celebrity fashion columnist, in a post on Jezebel commented, "This commercial is a huge step for interracial families like mine who want to be seen in public together and maybe eat some heart-healthy snacks." Numerous others took the same position, commending and cheering on Cheerios marketers for their actions. Old Navy received similar acclaim.

But in marketing, we also have to look at the bottom line. How did the commercials impact the brands? Besides the millions of exposures the brands received on social media, the publicity surrounding the ads and the brands was enormous. In many cases those posting said the ads made them want to buy them even more than before. But cultural strategist Denitria Lewis seemed to imply that the ads can cut both ways. Lewis notes that for some, "It's frightening to see a couple that is the antithesis of what you think a wholesome family would be. I don't know if the general public is prepared to have their brands tell them how to live." Lewis also stated that there are many people who believe we live in a post-racism society, but "If you pay only a modest bit of the attention to the news, you know we don't." And for those who still don't like the idea of being interracial, those who portray themselves as supporting this position are likely to lose their support.

The question is, given that these ads ran so long ago, what is the current status of perceptions of these ads now? Looking at the issue nearly a decade later, one wonders if anything has changed. As you might imagine, there have been a number of studies exploring this issue in both the academic and business communities. Larry Chiagouris, a marketing professor at Pace University in New York, considers it to be a smart move. He says that it is smart for brands to let customers know that they are listening and responsive to their needs. Chiagouris makes the point that the ads are not just targeted to interracial couples, but also to those whose values may be aligned with acceptance of interracial relationships. Subodh Bhat, a professor at San Francisco State, agrees, noting that consumers are no longer just interested in which product is better but now want more information about the company's values. They also want to feel good about the company's values.

(continued)

Oh, happy day! Our #ThankYouEvent is finally here. Take 30% off your entire purchase: oldnvy.me/1LUMNBd

Old Navy

An extensive study of consumers' views on diversity in advertising conducted by the research company Kantar led to a number of conclusions: (1) Not embracing diversity in advertising will negatively impact business growth, (2) positive representation of unrepresented individuals accelerates sales lift and long-term brand equity, (3) powerful stories that evoke an emotional response can be effective if the theme is relatable and authentic even if just one race is shown, and (4) the future is moving to a more diverse world, and marketers have the power to create a greater sense of community through diverse and inclusive advertising.

But not everyone agrees. A recent State Farm Insurance ad showing engagement between interracial couples recently received numerous comments on Twitter. As one person wrote, "This is disgusting and nobody wants to see this." Similar responses were common. An academic study conducted by Mai and associates concluded among other things that "consumers hold negative purchase intention for products featured in advertisements with actors of two different races, supporting previous literature." (They noted that negative responses could be lessened through authenticity.) Bhat notes that "ads depicting Black and white couples elicited more negative emotions and attitudes toward a brand than comparable ads showing same-race couples."

Others wonder why so many interracial ads focus on white and Black people and not other minority groups. Morgan State professor Jason Johnson notes that 70 percent of interracial ads over the past 4 years have shown a Black man with a white woman, the reality being that type of relationship is more common in the United States Johnson also believes that showing a white man with a Black woman is more comfortable to white people than a Black man with a white woman. Others note that other races in such ads are still underrepresented.

So while our cultural values continue to evolve, and ads become more diverse, there are many who believe that we still have a long way to go. As noted by Professor Johnson, while interracial ads may reflect an increasingly diverse America becoming more of a melting pot, they are not an accurate mirror of society. Charles Malik Whitfield, the father in the Cheerios ad, says, "Let's not pretend racism doesn't exist. Let's not pretend that we've come so far." We wonder what Bob Dylan would think.

Sources: Anna Wilgan and Deepak Varma, "Consumers' Views on Diversity in Advertising," Kantar, March 2021, www.kantar.com; Deborah Block, "Americans See More Interracial Relationships in Advertising," VOA News, March 7, 2021, www.voa.com; Enping (Shirley) Mai, Diana L. Haytko, and Brian J. Taillon, "How Advertisements Mixing Black and White Actors Affect Consumer Intent," Journal of Advertising Research, June 2022, pp. 1–18; Hallie Golden, "Inside the Biracial Advertising Boom," Daily Beast, February 5, 2018, www.thedailybeast.com; Joanne Kaufman, "A Sign of 'Modern Society': More Multiracial Families in Commercials," The New York Times, June 3, 2018, www.nytimes.com; Eun Kyung Kim, "Old Navy Ad with Interracial Family Prompts Social Media Outrage—and Support," USA Today, May 3, 2016, www.usatoday.com; Marie Solis, "Old Navy's Ad Showing an Interracial Family Drew Stomach-Churning Racist Backlash," MIC, September 30, 2016, www.mic.com; Christopher Heine, "Cheerios' Interracial Ad Spiked Its Online Branding by 77%," Adweek, June 7, 2013, www.adweek.com; Bruce Horovitz, "Hate Talk Won't Derail Mixed-Race Cheerios Ad," USA Today, June 3, 2013, www.usatoday.com; Morgan Whitaker, "Interracial Family in Cheerios Ad Sparks Online Backlash," Morgan Winn, June 3, 2013, www.morganwinn.com; Sheila Shayon, "General Mills Cheered for Defying Racial Backlash over Cheerios Ad," Brand Channel, June 6, 2013, www.brandchannel.com; Stacy Lambe, "An Internet High-Five to Cheerios for Showcasing Diverse Families," Queerty June 2, 2013, www.queerty.com.

There is little question that advertising has been guilty of stereotyping women and ethnic groups in the past and, in some cases, still does so. But as the role of women changes, advertisers are changing their portrayals to remain accurate and appeal to their target audience. Advertisers are also trying to increase the incidence of minority groups in ads while avoiding stereotypes and negative role portrayals. They are being careful to avoid ethnic stereotyping and striving to develop advertising that has specific appeals to various ethnic groups. Increases in the size and purchasing power of ethnic minorities are leading companies to give more attention to multicultural marketing.

EXHIBIT 21–21

Bud Light shows support for the LGBTQ community through its packaging.

Anheuser-Busch Inc.

Other Groups While the focus here has been on women and ethnic minorities, some other groups feel they are victims of stereotyping by advertisers. Many groups in our society are battling against stereotyping and discrimination, and companies must consider whether their ads might offend them. Creative personnel in agencies sometimes feel restricted as their ideas are squelched out of concern that they might offend someone or be misinterpreted. However, advertisers must be sensitive to the portrayal of specific types of people in their ads, for both ethical and commercial reasons.

One area where significant changes have taken place recently is in advertising targeted to LGBTQ consumers. In 1995 IKEA broke new ground with a TV commercial featuring a gay couple shopping for furniture. Target and Subaru have also aired gay-friendly ads, as have Kohl's, Tylenol, and Campbell's Soup, among many others. For years, beer companies targeted this market by placing ads in local gay media to support or sponsor AIDS awareness, Gay Pride festivals, and the Gay Games. A number of beer companies, including Anheuser-Busch and Molson Coors, now run gay-specific, brand-specific ads in national gay publications. Bud Lite featured the commemorative bottle in Exhibit 21–21.

More advertisers are turning to gay themes in their mainstream commercials, though often subtly. (Interestingly, sometimes ads are perceived as targeting gays when that was not the intention, resulting in very positive feedback from this segment nevertheless.) The Miller Brewing Co. took a bold step by airing one of the first gay-themed commercials on network television. One ad was for Miller Lite beer and showed a gay couple holding hands in a straight bar to the dismay of two women who are interested in them. Levi Strauss created a spot with alternative endings, one of which was designed to appeal to the gay market. The spot featured a young, attractive male in his second-floor apartment slipping on his Levi's. The motion of yanking up his jeans inexplicably causes the street below his apartment to get pulled up as well, crashing through his floor and bringing with it an attractive female in a telephone booth who he walks away with. In a version of the ad that aired on Logo, MTV's gay cable network seen in more than 27 million homes, an attractive man is in the phone booth and the two men run off together in the same manner as their heterosexual counterparts.[40]

Like the interracial discussion earlier in this chapter, not everyone approves of LGBTQ ads, however. An emotional 90-second McDonald's video for McCafé that was posted on the company's Facebook page in Taiwan depicted a young man coming out to his father. It was viewed more than 3.6 million times, with the original post gaining more than 92,000 likes and 11,800 shares. However, an anti-gay religious group called for a boycott of the video, saying it was inappropriate since many children eat at McDonald's (Exhibit 21–22). LGBTQ ads are now relatively common on TV.

EXHIBIT 21–22

McDonald's was threatened with a boycott by a religious group in Taiwan when it posted this video on its Facebook page.

McDonald's

Advertising and the Media The fact that advertising plays such an important role in financing the media has led to concern that advertisers may influence or even control the media. It is well documented that *economic censorship* occurs, whereby the media avoid certain topics or even present biased news coverage, in acquiescence to advertiser demands. In fact, as far back as 1992, Professors Lawrence Soley and Robert Craig said, "The assertion that advertisers attempt to influence what the public sees, hears, and reads in the mass media is perhaps the most damning of all criticisms of advertising, but this criticism isn't acknowledged in most advertising textbooks."[41] We will address this important issue in this book by considering arguments on both sides.

Arguments Supporting Advertiser Control
Advertising is the primary source of revenue for nearly

all the news and entertainment media in the United States. Some critics charge that the media's dependence on advertisers' support makes them susceptible to various forms of influence, including exerting control over editorial content; biasing editorial opinions to favor the position of an advertiser; limiting coverage of a controversial story that might reflect negatively on a company; and influencing the news and program content of television.

Newspapers and magazines receive the majority of their revenue from advertising; commercial TV and radio derive virtually all their income from advertisers. Advertising in digital media is increasing at a rapid rate and, as we have seen, now exceed all other media expenditures. Small, financially insecure newspapers, magazines, or broadcast stations are the most susceptible to pressure from advertisers, particularly companies that account for a large amount of the media outlet's advertising revenue. In some local markets, automobile and furniture advertisers may constitute as much as 80 percent of the TV stations' ad revenues. As you might imagine, the stations may tread lightly when reporting news that does not portray these industries positively. A local newspaper may be reluctant to print an unfavorable story about a car dealer or supermarket chain on whose advertising it depends. For example, a number of years ago more than 40 car dealers canceled their ads in the *San Jose Mercury News* when the paper printed an article titled "A Car Buyer's Guide to Sanity." The dealers objected to the tone of the article, which they felt implied consumers should consider car dealers unethical adversaries in the negotiation process. A study by Soontae An and Lori Bergen surveyed advertising directors at 219 daily newspapers in the United States and found frequent conflicts between the business side and editorial side of the newspaper operations. Advertising directors at small newspapers or chain-owned newspapers were more likely to endorse scenarios where editorial integrity was compromised to please, or refrain from offending, their advertisers.[42]

Individual TV stations and even the major networks also can be influenced by advertisers. Programming decisions are made largely on the basis of what shows will attract the most viewers and thus be most desirable to advertisers. Critics say this often results in lower-quality television as educational, cultural, and informative programming is usually sacrificed for shows that get high ratings and appeal to the mass markets. It is well recognized that advertisers often avoid TV shows that deal with controversial issues. Most advertisers also have contract stipulations allowing them to cancel a media buy if, after prescreening a show, they are uncomfortable with its content or feel sponsorship of it may reflect poorly on their company.

Advertisers have also been accused of pressuring the networks to change their programming. Many advertisers have withdrawn commercials from programs that contain too much sex or violence, often in response to threatened boycotts of their products by consumers if they advertise on these shows. For example, groups such as the American Family Association have been fighting sex and violence in TV programs by calling for boycotts. As you read in Chapter 17, ads have been pulled from Fox News. Advertisers pulled their ads from the *Roseanne* show after Roseanne Barr made racist comments, leading to the show's cancellation.

Arguments against Advertiser Control The commercial media's dependence on advertising means advertisers can exert influence on their character, content, and coverage of certain issues. However, media executives offer several reasons why advertisers do not exert undue influence over the media.

First, they point out it is in the best interest of the media not to be influenced too much by advertisers. To retain public confidence, they must report the news fairly and accurately without showing bias or attempting to avoid controversial issues. Media executives point to the vast array of topics they cover and the investigative reporting they often do as evidence of their objectivity. They want to build a large audience for their publications or stations so that they can charge more for advertising space and time.

Media executives also note that an advertiser needs the media more than the media need any individual advertiser, particularly when the medium has a large audience or does a good job of reaching a specific market segment. Many publications and stations have a broad base of advertising support and can afford to lose an advertiser that attempts to exert too much influence. This is particularly true for the larger, more established, financially secure media. For example, a consumer-product company would find it difficult to reach its target audience without network TV and could not afford to boycott a network if it disagreed with a station's editorial policy or program content. Even the local advertiser in a small community may be dependent on the local newspaper, since it may be the most cost-effective media option available.

Most media publishers insist they do not allow advertiser pressure to influence their editorial content. They argue that they have long regarded the formal separation of their news and business departments as essential to their independence and credibility. Many magazines and newspapers have traditionally discouraged employees on the publishing side—including advertising, circulation, and other business departments—from interacting with those on the editorial side, who write and edit the articles. This is done by separating editorial and advertising offices, barring the sales force from reading articles before they are printed, and prohibiting editorial employees from participating in advertising sales calls.

Most print media are very concerned over ensuring that decisions on the writing, editing, and publishing of stories are made on journalistic merit rather than on whether they will attract or repel advertisers. However, the new economics of the publishing industry is making it difficult to maintain the separation: Competition from TV, direct media, and the Internet is increasing, and newspaper and magazine readership and revenues continue to decline. There have been several well-publicized situations in the past where major magazines and newspapers were found to have given favorable editorial consideration to an advertiser. However, the media usually hold their ground when challenged by companies that threaten to pull their advertising, or even do so, when they find editorial coverage objectionable. For example, in April 2005 General Motors canceled all of its advertising in the *Los Angeles Times* after a series of articles in the newspaper were unflattering to the automaker. GM, which was spending an estimated $21 million in the *Times* each year, claimed that "factual errors and misrepresentations" in various articles led it to withdraw its advertising in the paper. The paper had run several articles that were critical of certain GM vehicles, and also suggested that some senior GM executives should be dismissed because of the company's sales and profit woes. GM's advertising boycott of the *Los Angeles Times* lasted 4 months and was finally ended after executives from the two sides met to resolve their differences.[43] At the same time, negative reports regarding the false mileage claims of Kia and Hyundai and other autos resulted in no backlash against the media.

The media in the United States are basically supported by advertising; this means we can enjoy them for free or for a fraction of what they would cost without advertising. The alternative to an advertiser-supported media system is support by users through higher subscription costs for print media and increased rates for cable and satellite TV access. Note that the decrease in newspaper subscriptions has led some papers to reduce their publication schedules and begin charging or increasing rates for online subscriptions. The ad in Exhibit 21-23, part of a campaign by the International Advertising Association, explains how advertising lowers the cost of print media for consumers. Another alternative is government-supported media like those in many other countries, but this runs counter to most people's desire for freedom of the press. Although not perfect, our system of advertising-supported media seems to provide the best option for receiving information and entertainment.

Summarizing Social Effects

We have examined a number of issues and have attempted to analyze the arguments for and against them. Many people have reservations about the impact of advertising and promotion on society. The numerous rules, regulations, policies, and guidelines marketers comply with do not cover every advertising and promotional situation. Moreover, what one individual views as distasteful or unethical may be acceptable to another.

EXHIBIT 21-23

This ad points out how advertising lowers the cost of newspapers for consumers.

International Advertising Association

WITHOUT ADVERTISING, YOUR NEWSPAPER WOULD COST YOU A BUNDLE.

Did you know that every ad in your newspaper helps pay for the rest of the essential pages? The fact is, your paper would cost you about $5.00 a day without advertisements. A price that would make news indeed.

Advertising. That's the way it works.

The global partnership of advertisers, agencies and media

EXHIBIT 21–24

In this commercial "Phases," a teen is shown stealing money from his mother's purse. The Partnership at Drugfree.org helps families address teen drug abuse.

Partnership for Drug-Free Kids

EXHIBIT 21–25

This Recycle Across America ad is one example of a pro bono space donated by media.

Recycle Across America

Negative opinions regarding advertising and other forms of promotion have been around almost as long as the field itself, and it is unlikely they will ever disappear. However, the industry must address the various concerns about the effects of advertising and other forms of promotion on society. Advertising is a very powerful institution, but it will remain so only as long as consumers have faith in the ads they see and hear every day. Many of the problems discussed here can be avoided if individual decision makers make ethics an important element of the IMC planning process.

The primary focus of this discussion of social effects has been on the way advertising is used (or abused) in the marketing of products and services. It is important to note that advertising and other IMC tools are also used to promote worthy causes and to deal with problems facing society (drunk driving, drug abuse, and the obesity crisis, among others). For example, the Partnership to End Addiction at Drugfree.org (formerly the Partnership for a Drug Free America) has created a website and uses social media, as well as print and TV ads, to drive awareness and action around teen substance abuse (Exhibit 21-24). The Partnership is funded primarily by donations from individuals, corporations, foundations, and the public sector. The organization has also partnered with the U.S. Office of National Drug Control Policy (ONDCP), and the joint campaign "Above the Influence." Above the Influence (ATI) won an Effie Award given for sustainability for its long-term effectiveness. Youth who are aware of anti-drug advertising are consistently more likely to have stronger anti-drug beliefs compared to those unaware of campaign advertising. However, concern with the misuse and abuse of prescription drugs is increasing and The Partnership created The Medicine Abuse Project, using ads to address this problem. (NOTE: Perhaps the first organization formed to fight the war on drugs was the Partnership for a Drug Free America. This organization changed its name in 2010 to Partnership at Drug Free.org, in an effort to include advertising on the Internet as part of its focus. A number of organizations like these mentioned here are now part of the coalition to fight drug use and addiction under the umbrella organization drugfree.org) As an example, when the organizations discovered that Urban Outfitters, the national retail store popular with teens, was selling products made to look like prescription pill bottles that made light of prescription drug misuse and abuse, they launched an advocacy effort and petition to ask the company to remove these products from their stores and website. The successful effort led Urban Outfitters to halt sales of the products. Campaigns for nonprofit organizations and worthy causes are often developed pro bono by advertising agencies, and free advertising time and space are donated by the media. Exhibit 21-25 shows an ad from a successful public service campaign for recycling. Notice how the ad includes a call to action asking the viewer to get involved. During the coronavirus pandemic, NBC Universal, Viacom CBS, and iHeartMedia used their channels to support consistent health messaging targeted to high-risk populations on how to protect themselves from the virus. The media companies worked with a number of government agencies and the AdCouncil by creating PSAs and donating free airtime to assist in fighting the pandemic.[44]

ECONOMIC EFFECTS OF ADVERTISING

LO 21-4

Advertising plays an important role in a free-market system like ours by making consumers aware of products and services and providing them with information for decision making. Advertising's economic role goes beyond this basic function, however. It is a powerful force that can affect the functioning of our entire economic system (Exhibit 21-26).

HOW TO BE A POWER HITTER IN ANY ECONOMY.

EXHIBIT 21–26

This ad from *Adweek* promotes the economic value of advertising by comparing the companies that continue to advertise as the all-stars of branding.

Adweek

EXHIBIT 21–27

Virgin Atlantic Airways chair Richard Branson acknowledges the importance of advertising.

Virgin Atlantic Airways

Advertising can encourage consumption and foster economic growth. It not only informs customers of available goods and services but also facilitates entry into markets for a firm or a new product or brand; leads to economies of scale in production, marketing, and distribution, which in turn lead to lower prices; and hastens the acceptance of new products and the rejection of inferior products.

Critics of advertising view it as a detrimental force that not only fails to perform its basic function of information provision adequately but also adds to the cost of products and services and discourages competition and market entry, leading to industrial concentration and higher prices for consumers.

In their analysis of advertising, economists generally take a macroeconomic perspective: They consider the economic impact of advertising on an entire industry or on the economy as a whole rather than its effect on an individual company or brand. Our examination of the economic impact of advertising focuses on these broader macro-level issues. We consider its effects on consumer choice, competition, and product costs and prices.

Effects on Consumer Choice

Some critics say advertising hampers consumer choice, as large advertisers use their power to limit our options to a few well-advertised brands. Economists argue that advertising is used to achieve (1) **differentiation**, whereby the products or services of large advertisers are perceived as unique or better than competitors', and (2) brand loyalty, which enables large national advertisers to gain control of the market, usually at the expense of smaller brands.

Larger companies often end up charging higher prices and achieve a more dominant position in the market than smaller firms that cannot compete against them and their large advertising budgets. When this occurs, advertising not only restricts the choice alternatives to a few well-known, heavily advertised brands but also becomes a substitute for competition based on price or product improvements.

Heavily advertised brands dominate the market in certain product categories, such as soft drinks, beer, and cereals. But advertising generally does not create brand monopolies and reduce the opportunities for new products to be introduced to consumers. In most product categories, a number of different brands are on the store shelves and thousands of new products are introduced every year. In 2022, there was over $83 billion worth of bottled water sold in the United States.[45] While there are about a dozen market leaders, the largest market share is held by hundreds of smaller companies.[46] The opportunity to advertise gives companies the incentive to develop new brands and improve their existing ones. When a successful new product such as a smartphone or tablet is introduced, competitors quickly follow and use advertising to inform consumers about their brand and attempt to convince them it is superior to the original. Companies like Virgin Atlantic Airways recognize that advertising has been an important part of their success (Exhibit 21–27).

Effects on Competition

One of the most common criticisms economists have about advertising concerns its effects on competition. They argue that power in the hands of large firms with huge advertising budgets creates a **barrier to entry**, which makes it difficult for other firms to enter the market. This results in less competition and higher prices. Economists note that smaller firms already in the market find it difficult to compete against the large advertising budgets of the industry leaders and are often driven out of business. Take the U.S. wireless market as an example. While there are a number of wireless providers, the market is dominated by seven major providers. Verizon and AT&T hold the major share of the market, with an estimated 300 million subscribers between them. These companies are also two of the largest advertisers, spending over $4 billion a year combined. As you might imagine, to try to break into this market would be extremely difficult, if not impossible.

Large advertisers clearly enjoy certain competitive advantages. First, there are **economies of scale** in advertising, particularly with respect to factors such as media costs. Firms such as Procter & Gamble and PepsiCo, which spend several billion dollars a year on advertising and promotion, are able to make large media buys at a reduced rate and allocate them to their various products.

Large advertisers usually sell more of their product or service, which means they may have lower production costs and can allocate more monies to advertising, so they can afford the costly but more efficient media like network television. Their large advertising outlays also give them more opportunity to differentiate their products and develop brand loyalty. To the extent that these factors occur, smaller competitors are at a disadvantage and new competitors are deterred from entering the market.

While advertising may have an anticompetitive effect on a market, there is no clear evidence that advertising alone reduces competition, creates barriers to entry, and thus increases market concentration. High levels of advertising are not always found in industries where firms have a large market share. These findings run contrary to many economists' belief that industries controlled by a few firms have high advertising expenditures, resulting in stable brand shares for market leaders.

Defenders of advertising say it is unrealistic to attribute a firm's market dominance and barriers to entry solely to advertising. There are a number of other factors, such as price, product quality, distribution effectiveness, production efficiencies, competitive strategies, and even government legislation. For many years, products such as Coors beer and Hershey's chocolate bars were dominant brands even though these companies spent little on advertising. Hershey did not advertise at all until 1970. For 66 years, the company relied on the quality of its products, its favorable reputation and image among consumers, and its extensive channels of distribution to market its brands. Industry leaders often tend to dominate markets because they have superior product quality and the best management and competitive strategies, not simply the biggest advertising budgets. SPANX is another good example. The billion-dollar company was started without a single cent being spent on advertising—primarily because founder Sara Blakely didn't have any money to buy it. Starting the company with only $5,000, Blakely relied on word of mouth and endorsements from celebrities like Oprah, Brooke Shields, Julia Roberts, and Gwyneth Paltrow, and other marketing factors like packaging and product benefits. Exhibit 21–28 shows that SPANX is now advertising though they do not spend much even today. This ad features an attractive woman and is designed to appeal to younger women.

While market entry against large, established competitors is difficult, companies with a quality product at a reasonable price often find a way to break in. Moreover, they usually find that advertising actually facilitates their market entry by making it possible to communicate the benefits and features of their new product or brand to consumers.

EXHIBIT 21–28

SPANX has been successful even with very little advertising.

Spanx, LLC

Effects on Product Costs and Prices

A major area of debate among economists, advertisers, consumer advocates, and policymakers concerns the effects of advertising on product costs and prices. Critics argue that advertising increases the prices consumers pay for products and services. First, they say the large sums of money spent on advertising a brand constitute an expense that must be covered and the consumer ends up paying for it through higher prices. As discussed in the previous chapter, concern has been expressed that the tremendous increase in direct-to-consumer drug advertising by pharmaceutical companies is driving up the cost of prescription drugs. Critics argue that the millions of dollars spent on advertising and other forms of promotion are an expense that must be covered by charging higher prices.

A second way advertising can result in higher prices is by increasing product differentiation and adding to the perceived value of the product in consumers' minds. The fundamental premise is that advertising increases the perceived differences between physically homogeneous products and enables advertised brands to command a premium price without an increase in quality.

Critics of advertising generally point to the differences in prices between national brands and private-label brands that are physically similar, such as aspirin or tea bags, as evidence of the added value created by advertising. They see consumers' willingness to pay more for heavily advertised national brands rather than purchasing the lower-priced, nonadvertised brand as wasteful and irrational. The prescription drug industry is again a very good example of this, as critics argue that the increase in advertising is encouraging consumers to request brand-name drugs and steering them away from lower-priced generics. However, consumers do not always buy for rational, functional reasons. The emotional, psychological, and social benefits derived from purchasing a national brand are important to many people.

Proponents of advertising offer several other counterarguments to the claim that advertising increases prices (one of the arguments of the anti-pharmaceutical groups). They acknowledge that advertising costs are at least partly paid for by consumers. But advertising may help lower the overall cost of a product more than enough to offset them. For example, advertising may help firms achieve economies of scale in production and distribution by providing information to and stimulating demand among mass markets. These economies of scale help cut the cost of producing and marketing the product, which can lead to lower prices—if the advertiser chooses to pass the cost savings on to the consumer. The ad in Exhibit 21–29, from a campaign sponsored by the American Association of Advertising Agencies, emphasizes this point.

Advertising can also lower prices by making a market more competitive, which usually leads to greater price competition. It has been shown that for some products, advertising has helped to keep the costs down. Finally, advertising is a means to market entry rather than a deterrent and helps stimulate product innovation, which makes markets more competitive and helps keep prices down.

Overall, it is difficult to reach any firm conclusions regarding the relationship between advertising and prices. After an extensive review of this area, Farris and Albion concluded, "The evidence connecting manufacturer advertising to prices is neither complete nor definitive . . . consequently, we cannot say whether advertising is a tool of market efficiency or market power without further research."[47]

We admit it. Advertising has a tremendous impact on prices. But you may be surprised by what *kind* of impact.
In addition to being informative, educational and sometimes entertaining, advertising can actually lower prices.
It works like this: Advertising spurs competition which holds down prices. And since advertising also creates a mass market for products, it can bring down the cost of producing each product, a savings that can be passed on to consumers.
Moreover, competition created by advertising provides an incentive for manufacturers to produce new and better products.
Which means advertising can not only reduce prices, **ANOTHER WORD FOR FREEDOM OF CHOICE.** but it can also help you avoid lemons. American Association of Advertising Agencies

ADVERTISING

EXHIBIT 21–29

This ad refutes the argument that reducing advertising expenditures will lead to lower prices.

The American Association of Advertising Agencies

Summarizing Economic Effects

Economists' perspectives can be divided into two principal schools of thought that make different assumptions regarding the influence of advertising on the economy.[48] Figure 21–4 summarizes the main points of the "advertising equals market power" and "advertising equals information" perspectives.

Advertising = Market Power	Advertising	Advertising = Information
Advertising affects consumer preferences and tastes, changes product attributes, and differentiates the product from competitive offerings.	Advertising	Advertising informs consumers about product attributes but does not change the way they value those attributes.
Consumers become brand-loyal and less price-sensitive and perceive fewer substitutes for advertised brands.	Consumer buying behavior	Consumers become more price-sensitive and buy best "value." Only the relationship between price and quality affects elasticity for a given product.
Potential entrants must overcome established brand loyalty and spend relatively more on advertising.	Barriers to entry	Advertising makes entry possible for new brands because it can communicate product attributes to consumers.
Firms are insulated from market competition and potential rivals; concentration increases, leaving firms with more discretionary power.	Industry structure and market power	Consumers can compare competitive offerings easily and competitive rivalry increases. Efficient firms remain, and as the inefficient leave, new entrants appear; the effect on concentration is ambiguous.
Firms can charge higher prices and are not as likely to compare on quality or price dimensions. Innovation may be reduced.	Market conduct	More informed consumers pressure firms to lower prices and improve quality; new entrants facilitate innovation.
High prices and excessive profits accrue to advertisers and give them even more incentive to advertise their products. Output is restricted compared with conditions of perfect competition.	Market performance	Industry prices decrease. The effect on profits due to increased competition and increased efficiency is ambiguous.

Advertising Equals Market Power   The belief that advertising equals market power reflects traditional economic thinking and views advertising as a way to change consumers' tastes, lower their sensitivity to price, and build brand loyalty among buyers of advertised brands. This results in higher profits and market power for large advertisers, reduces competition in the market, and leads to higher prices and fewer choices for consumers. Proponents of this viewpoint generally have negative attitudes regarding the economic impact of advertising.

Advertising Equals Information   The belief that advertising equals information takes a more positive view of advertising's economic effects. This model sees advertising as providing consumers with useful information, increasing their price sensitivity (which moves them toward lower-priced products), and increasing competition in the market. Advertising is viewed as a way to communicate with consumers and tell them about a product and its major features and attributes. More informed and knowledgeable consumers pressure companies to provide high-quality products at lower prices. Efficient firms remain in the market, whereas inefficient firms leave as new entrants appear. Proponents of this model believe the economic effects of advertising are favorable and think it contributes to more efficient and competitive markets.

There are many people who use the Internet as an information source for comparing prices and getting others' reviews of the products, often then going to a brick-and-mortar store to make the purchase.

It is unlikely the debate over the economic effects and value of advertising will be resolved soon. Many economists will continue to take a negative view of advertising and its effects on the functioning of the economy, while advertisers will continue to

WHEN ADVERTISING DOES ITS JOB, MILLIONS OF PEOPLE KEEP THEIRS.

Good advertising doesn't just inform. It sells. It helps move product and keep businesses in business. Every time an ad arouses a consumer's interest enough to result in a purchase, it keeps a company going strong. And it helps secure the jobs of the people who work there.

Advertising. That's the way it works.

INTERNATIONAL
ADVERTISING
ASSOCIATION

The global partnership of advertisers, agencies and media

EXHIBIT 21–30

This ad is part of a global campaign by the International Advertising Association to educate consumers about the economic value of advertising.

International Advertising Association

EXHIBIT 21–31

The AAF promotes the value of advertising in building strong brands.

American Advertising Federation

view it as an efficient way for companies to communicate with their customers and an essential component of our economic system. The International Advertising Association has been running a campaign for several years to convince consumers around the world of the economic value of advertising. Ads like the one shown in Exhibit 21–30 are used in countries where consumers may be less familiar with the concept of advertising. The goal of the campaign is to get consumers in these countries to recognize the role advertising plays in contributing to their economic well-being.

The advertising industry in the United States continually promotes the value of advertising. Major advertising associations, such as the 4As and the American Advertising Federation (AAF), along with trade associations for various media, often run campaigns reminding the general public of advertising's contributions to the economy as well as to consumers' social well-being. However, sometimes the industry must also remind advertisers themselves of the value of advertising. Recently the AAF, which is the advertising industry's primary trade organization, decided to take action to change the way advertising is viewed by companies. It decided that the best way to get marketers to recognize the value of advertising was to practice what it preaches, and thus an integrated marketing communications campaign was developed to redefine advertising in the eyes of corporate executives.

The campaign was targeted at corporate executives who were responsible for establishing and maintaining budget levels for advertising. The theme of the campaign, "Advertising. The way great brands get to be great brands" cautions corporate executives not to neglect their brand development. The great brands campaign promoted the economic power of advertising by featuring companies synonymous with quality advertising and for whom advertising has played a critical role in building brand equity. Exhibit 21–31 shows one of the ads from the campaign featuring Intel, the market leader for computer chips and microprocessors. Other brands' ads were also run.

FIGURE 21–5

This Message Describes the
Positive Economic Effects of
Advertising

To me it means that if we believe to any degree whatsoever in the economic system under which we live, in a high standard of living and in high employment, advertising is the most efficient known way of moving goods in practically every product class.

My proof is that millions of businessmen have chosen advertising over and over again in the operations of their business. Some of their decisions may have been wrong, but they must have thought they were right or they wouldn't go back to be stung twice by the same kind of bee.

It's a pretty safe bet that in the next 10 years many Americans will be using products and devices that no one in this room has even heard of. Judging purely by past performance, American advertising can be relied on to make them known and accepted overnight at the lowest possible prices.

Advertising, of course, makes possible our unparalleled variety of magazines, newspapers, business publications, and radio and television stations.

It must be said that without advertising we would have a far different nation, and one that would be much the poorer—not merely in material commodities, but in the life of the spirit.

Leo Burnett

Source: Excerpts from a speech given by Leo Burnett on the American Association of Advertising Agencies's 50th anniversary, April 20, 1967.

Figure 21-5, excerpts from a speech given by famous ad executive Leo Burnett, summarizes the perspective of most advertising people on the economic effects of advertising. Advertising and marketing experts agree that advertising and promotion play an important role in helping to expand consumer demand for new products and services and in helping marketers differentiate their existing brands.

Summary

Advertising is a powerful institution and has been the target of considerable criticism regarding its social and economic impact. The criticism of advertising concerns the specific techniques and methods used as well as its effect on societal values, tastes, lifestyles, and behavior. Critics argue that advertising is deceptive and untruthful; that it can be offensive, irritating, or in poor taste; and that it exploits certain groups, such as children. Many people believe advertising should be informative only and advertisers should not use subjective claims, puffery, embellishment, or persuasive techniques.

Advertising often offends consumers by the type of appeal or manner of presentation used; sexually suggestive ads and nudity receive the most criticism. Advertisers say their ads are consistent with contemporary values and lifestyles and are appropriate for the target audiences they are attempting to reach. Advertising to children is an area of particular concern, since critics argue that children lack the experience, knowledge, and ability to process and evaluate persuasive advertising messages rationally. Although an FTC proposal to severely restrict advertising to children was defeated, it remains an issue.

The pervasiveness of advertising and its prevalence in virtually all media have led critics to argue that it plays a major role in influencing and transmitting social values. Advertising has been charged with encouraging materialism; manipulating consumers to buy things they do not really want or need; perpetuating stereotypes through its portrayal of certain groups such as women, minorities, and older adults; and controlling the media.

Advertising has also been scrutinized with regard to its economic effects. The basic economic role of advertising is to give consumers information that helps them make consumption decisions. Some people view advertising as a detrimental force that has a negative effect on competition, product costs, and consumer prices. Economists' perspectives regarding the effects of advertising follow two basic schools of thought: the advertising equals market power model and the advertising equals information model. Arguments consistent with each perspective were considered in analyzing the economic effects of advertising.

Key Terms

Discussion Questions

1. There is some disagreement regarding Balenciaga's controversial ads discussed in the lead-in to this chapter. Do you think Balenciaga ran the ads intentionally or just made an unintended mistake? Explain why you took the position you did. (LO 21-1)

2. Many people believe that the U.S. government's control over advertising is increasing and that this control is contrary to the right to free speech. Explain why those taking this perspective believe this is the case and cite examples to support their position. Offer your thoughts on whether there has been an increase in government control. (LO 21-2).

3. As diversity in advertising appears to be on the increase, there are those who support this movement and those who believe that it is not in the best interest of companies. Focusing your attention specifically on the business aspects of increasing diversity in ads, take a position on whether you believe this is a good strategy to undertake. Support your position. (LO 21-4).

4. Are women portrayed differently in advertising now than they were 10 years ago? Explain why you feel this way, providing examples to support your position. (LO 21-3)

5. The Partnership to End Addiction at Drug Free.org is the new name for the organization originally titled The Partnership for a Drug Free America. The coalition of companies and ad agencies have worked together for decades to fight the war on drugs by creating ads and offering their services for the cause. Do you believe they are having an impact? Explain your position. (LO 21-4)

6. The war on cigarette smoking by teens has now been replaced by the war on vaping—particularly flavored vaping products. There are those who say that it is the responsibility of the government to protect teens, while others feel that teens must make their own decisions. Take a position on this issue and argue in support of that position. (LO 21-3)

7. There is little doubt that the use of sexy advertising like that employed by Calvin Klein and Carl's Jr. has declined over the past few years. Is this a result of #MeToo, or just advertisers changing attitudes toward the effectiveness of this form of advertising? Support your position. (LO 21-2)

8. Does advertising make college students drink or drink more, or not? Explain both sides of this issue and provide your decision. (LO 21-1)

9. Many people believe that there should be severe restrictions placed on advertising to children under the age of 13. Others believe that children must learn to discriminate truth from lies and that it is part of the learning process. Discuss both sides of this issue. (LO 21-3)

10. Various studies have indicated that younger consumers are less likely to watch TV, listen to the radio, or read magazines and newspapers. If this is true, one might expect a reduction in sales of heavily advertised products. Is this happening? If so, provide examples. If not, explain why this is not happening, again providing examples. (LO 21-4)

22 Personal Selling

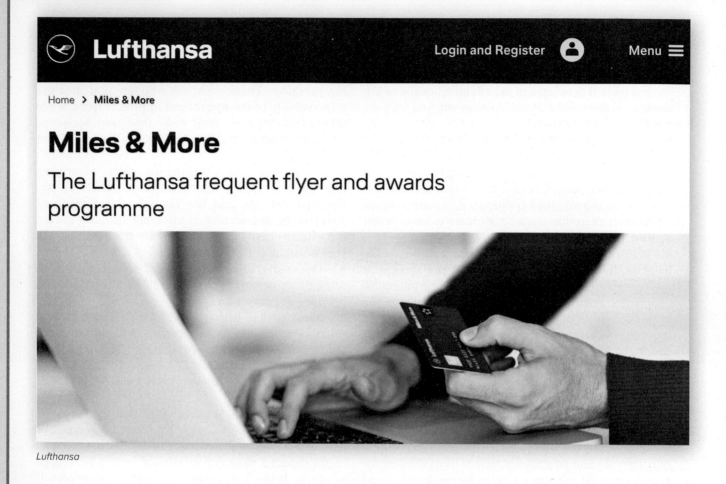

Lufthansa

Learning Objectives

LO 22-1 | Describe the role of personal selling in the IMC program.

LO 22-2 | Compare the advantages and disadvantages of personal selling as a promotional tool.

LO 22-3 | Explain how to combine personal selling with other elements in an IMC program.

LO 22-4 | Discuss how to measure the effectiveness of the personal-selling effort.

CHAPTER 22 IS AVAILABLE ONLINE THROUGH THE CONNECT PLATFORM.

Glossary of Advertising and Promotion Terms

A/B testing A process that involves the testing of two versions of an advertisement or homepage to see which will be the more effective prior to launch.

absolute cost The actual total cost of placing an ad in a particular media vehicle.

account executive The individual who serves as the liaison between the advertising agency and the client. The account executive is responsible for managing all of the services the agency provides to the client and representing the agency's point of view to the client.

account planner The individual who gathers information that is relevant to a client's product or service and can be used in the development of the creative strategy as well as other aspects of an IMC campaign.

account planning The process of conducting research and gathering all relevant information about a client's product, service, brand, and consumers in the target audience for use in the development of creative strategy as well as other aspects of an IMC campaign.

account-specific marketing Development of customized promotional programs for individual retail accounts by marketers.

ad execution–related thoughts A type of thought or cognitive response a message recipient has concerning factors related to the execution of the ad, such as creativity, visual effects, color, and style.

addressable TV advertising Advertising which allows different commercials to be shown to different households watching the same program.

adjacencies Commercial spots purchased from local television stations that generally appear during the time periods adjacent to network programs.

advergame Online game designed to promote a product and/or brand.

advertainment Media combining the use of advertising and entertainment (e.g., in-game advertising, advergaming).

advertising Any paid form of nonpersonal communication about an organization, product, service, or idea by an identified sponsor.

advertising agency A firm that specializes in the creation, production, and placement of advertising messages and may provide other services that facilitate the marketing communications process.

advertising appeal The basis or approach used in an advertising message to attract the attention or interest of consumers and/or influence their feelings toward the product, service, or cause.

advertising attribution The set of rules that determines how an ad account applies credit for clicks, conversions, and sales.

advertising campaign A comprehensive advertising plan that consists of a series of messages in a variety of media that center on a single theme or idea.

advertising creativity The ability to generate fresh, unique, and appropriate ideas that can be used as solutions to communication problems.

advertising disengagement A lack of excitement, interest, attention, or involvement intended to be aroused by an advertisement or advertising campaign.

advertising manager The individual in an organization who is responsible for the planning, coordinating, budgeting, and implementing of the advertising program.

advertising substantiation A Federal Trade Commission regulatory program that requires advertisers to have documentation to support the claims made in their advertisements.

advocacy advertising Advertising that is concerned with the propagation of ideas and elucidation of social issues of public importance in a manner that supports the position and interest of the sponsor.

aerial advertising A form of outdoor advertising where messages appear in the sky in the form of banners pulled by airplanes, skywriting, and on blimps.

affect referral decision rule A type of decision rule where selections are made on the basis of an overall impression or affective summary evaluation of the various alternatives under consideration.

affiliates Local television stations that are associated with a major network. Affiliates agree to preempt time during specified hours for programming provided by the network and carry the advertising contained in the program.

affirmative disclosure A Federal Trade Commission program whereby advertisers may be required to include certain types of information in their advertisements so consumers will be aware of all the consequences, conditions, and limitations associated with the use of the product or service.

affordable method A method of determining the budget for advertising and promotion where all other budget areas are covered and remaining monies are available for allocation.

agency of record (AOR) The agency that has primary responsibility for most of the integrated marketing communications services a company or brand might require, such as brand and creative strategy, media planning, development and maintenance of websites, and digital marketing.

AIDA model A model that depicts the successive stages a buyer passes through in the personal-selling process, including attention, interest, desire, and action.

alpha activity A measure of the degree of brain activity that can be used to assess an individual's reactions to an advertisement.

alternative media A term commonly used in advertising to describe support media.

animatic A preliminary version of a commercial whereby video of the frames of a storyboard is produced along with an audio soundtrack.

arbitrary allocation A method for determining the budget for advertising and promotion based on arbitrary decisions of executives.

attitude toward the ad A message recipient's affective feelings of favorability or unfavorability toward an advertisement.

attractiveness A source characteristic that makes him or her appealing to a message recipient. Source attractiveness can be based on similarity, familiarity, or likability.

audio logos A sound, an effect, a short music clip, a musical riff, or a voiceover that usually carries the advertising theme and a simple message.

average frequency The number of times the average household reached by a media schedule is exposed to a media vehicle over a specified period.

average quarter-hour (AQH) figure The average number of persons listening to a particular station for at least 5 minutes during a 15-minute period. Used by Arbitron in measuring the size of radio audiences.

average quarter-hour rating (AQH RTG) The average quarter-hour figure estimate expresses the estimated number of listeners as a percentage of the survey area population. Used by Nielsen in measuring the size of radio audiences.

average quarter-hour share (AQH SHR) The percentage of the total listening audience tuned to each station.

balance-of-trade deficit A situation where the monetary value of a country's imports exceeds its exports.

banner ad An ad on a web page that may be "hot-linked" to the advertiser's site.

barrier to entry Conditions that make it difficult for a firm to enter the market in a particular industry, such as high advertising budgets.

BBB National Programs Inc. A division of the Better Business Bureau that is home to national programs on dispute resolution, advertising review, privacy, and industry self-regulation.

behavioral targeting A basis for target marketing based on consumers' website surfing behaviors.

behavioristic segmentation A method of segmenting a market by dividing customers into groups based on their usage, loyalties, or buying responses to a product or service.

below-the-line media A term used to refer to support media whose costs are not assigned directly to advertising and/or promotional budgets.

benchmark measures Measures of a target audience's status concerning response hierarchy variables such as awareness, knowledge, image, attitudes, preferences, intentions, or behavior. These measures are taken at the beginning of an advertising or promotional campaign to determine the degree to which a target audience must be changed or moved by a promotional campaign.

benefit segmentation A method of segmenting markets on the basis of the major benefits consumers seek in a product or service.

Better Business Bureau (BBB) An organization established and funded by businesses that operate primarily at the local level to monitor activities of companies and promote fair advertising and selling practices.

bidding A digital pricing option in which the buyer participates in an auction to purchase placement for the ad format.

billings The amount of client money agencies spend on media purchases and other equivalent activities. Billings are often used as a way of measuring the size of advertising agencies.

bleed page Magazine advertisement where the printed area extends to the edge of the page, eliminating any white margin or border around the ad.

blog Also known as a weblog, a blog is a Web-based publication consisting primarily of periodic articles written and provided in reverse chronological order. Blogs may reflect the writings of an individual, community political organization, or corporation.

body copy The main text portion of a print ad. Also often referred to as copy.

bonus pack Special packaging that provides consumers with extra quantity of merchandise at no extra charge over the regular price.

brand activism A company or brand taking a stand and engaging in efforts to promote social, political, economic or environmental reform to help drive change in order to improve society.

brand development index (BDI) An index that is calculated by taking the percentage of a brand's total sales that occur in a given market as compared to the percentage of the total population in the market.

brand equity The intangible asset of added value or goodwill that results from the favorable image, impressions of differentiation, and/or the strength of consumer attachment of a company name, brand name, or trademark.

brand identity The combination of the name, logo, symbols, design, packaging, image, and associations held by consumers toward a brand.

brand loyalty Preference by a consumer for a particular brand that results in continual purchase of it.

brand manager The person responsible for the planning, implementation, and control of the marketing program for an individual brand.

branded entertainment The combined use of an audio-visual program (such as TV, radio, podcast, or videocast) and a brand to market a product or service. The purpose of a branded entertainment program is to entertain while providing the opportunity for brands or products to be promoted.

buildup approach A method of determining the budget for advertising and promotion by determining the specific tasks that have to be performed and estimating the costs of performing them. See also *objective and task method.*

buzz marketing The use of various activities that generate conversations and word-of-mouth communication about a particular topic such as a company, brand, or marketing activity.

cable television A form of television where signals are carried to households by wire rather than through the airways.

campaign theme The central message or idea that is communicated in all advertising and other promotional activities.

carryover effect A delayed or lagged effect whereby the impact of advertising on sales can occur during a subsequent time period.

category development index (CDI) An index that is calculated by taking the percentage of a product category's total sales that occur in a given market area as compared to the percentage of the total population in the market.

category management system An organizational system whereby managers have responsibility for the marketing programs for a particular category or line of products.

cause-related marketing Image-related advertising in which companies link with charities or nonprofit organizations as contributing sponsors.

cease-and-desist order An action by the Federal Trade Commission that orders a company to stop engaging in a practice that is considered deceptive or misleading until a hearing is held.

Central Hudson Test A four-part test used by the courts for determining restrictions on commercial speech.

central route to persuasion One of two routes to persuasion recognized by the elaboration likelihood model. The central route to persuasion views a message recipient as very active and involved in the communications process and as having the ability and motivation to attend to and process a message.

centralized system An organizational system whereby advertising along with other marketing activities such as sales, marketing research, and planning are divided along functional lines and are run from one central marketing department.

channel The method or medium by which communication travels from a source or sender to a receiver.

Children's Online Privacy Protection Act (COPPA) of 1998 Federal legislation that places restrictions on information collected from children via the Internet and requires that websites directed at children have a privacy policy posted on their home page and areas of the site where information is collected.

city zone A category used for newspaper circulation figures that refers to a market area composed of the city where the paper is published and contiguous areas similar in character to the city.

class action A legal proceeding in which one or more plaintiffs bring a lawsuit on behalf of a larger group, known as the class.

classical conditioning A learning process whereby a conditioned stimulus that elicits a response is paired with a neutral stimulus that does not elicit any particular response. Through repeated exposure, the neutral stimulus comes to elicit the same response as the conditioned stimulus.

classified advertising Advertising that runs in newspapers and magazines that generally contains text only and is arranged under subheadings according to the product, service, or offering. Employment, real estate, and automotive ads are the major forms of classified advertising.

clients The organizations with the products, services, or causes to be marketed and for which advertising agencies and other marketing promotional firms provide services.

clipping service A service that clips competitors' advertising from local print media, allowing the company to monitor the types of advertising that are running or to estimate their advertising expenditures.

close Obtaining the commitment of the prospect in a personal-selling transaction.

clutter The nonprogram material that appears in a broadcast environment, including commercials, promotional messages for shows, public service announcements, and the like.

cognitive dissonance A state of psychological tension or postpurchase doubt that a consumer may experience after making a purchase decision. This tension often leads the consumer to try to reduce it by seeking supportive information.

cognitive responses Thoughts that occur to a message recipient while reading, viewing, and/or hearing a communication.

collateral services Agencies that provide companies with specialized services such as package design, advertising production, and marketing research.

combination rate A special space rate or discount offered for advertising in two or more periodicals. Combination rates are often offered by publishers who own both morning and evening editions of a newspaper in the same market.

commercial ratings Measures of the average viewership of a television commercial both live and up to three days after the ads are played back on a digital video recorder (DVR).

commercial speech Speech that promotes a commercial transaction.

commission system A method of compensating advertising agencies whereby the agency receives a specified commission (traditionally 15 percent) from the media on any advertising time or space it purchases.

communication The passing of information, exchange of ideas, or process of establishing shared meaning between a sender and a receiver.

communication objectives Goals that an organization seeks to achieve through its promotional program in terms of communication effects such as creating awareness, knowledge, image, attitudes, preferences, or purchase intentions.

communications task Under the DAGMAR approach to setting advertising goals and objectives, something that can be performed by and attributed to advertising such as awareness, comprehension, conviction, and action.

comparative advertising The practice of either directly or indirectly naming one or more competitors in an advertising message and usually making a comparison on one or more specific attributes or characteristics.

competitive advantage Something unique or special that a firm does or possesses that provides an advantage over its competitors.

competitive parity method A method of setting the advertising and promotion budget based on matching the absolute level of percentage of sales expenditures of the competition.

compliance A type of influence process where a receiver accepts the position advocated by a source to obtain favorable outcomes or to avoid punishment.

comprehension and reaction tests Advertising testing to ensure receivers comprehend the message and to gauge their reaction to the same.

computer simulation models Quantitative-based models that are used to determine the relative contribution of advertising expenditures on sales response.

concave-downward function model An advertising/sales response function that views the incremental effects of advertising on sales as decreasing.

concentrated marketing A type of marketing strategy whereby a firm chooses to focus its marketing efforts on one particular market segment.

concept testing A method of pretesting alternative ideas for an advertisement or campaign by having consumers provide their responses and/or reactions to the creative concept.

conditioned response In classical conditioning, a response that occurs as a result of exposure to a conditioned stimulus.

conditioned stimulus In classical conditioning, a stimulus that becomes associated with an unconditioned stimulus and capable of evoking the same response or reaction as the unconditioned stimulus.

consent order A settlement between a company and the Federal Trade Commission whereby an advertiser agrees to stop the advertising or practice in question. A consent order is for settlement purposes only and does not constitute an admission of guilt.

consumer behavior The process and activities that people engage in when searching for, selecting, purchasing, using, evaluating, and disposing of products and services to satisfy their needs and desires.

consumer franchise-building (CFB) promotions Sales promotion activities that communicate distinctive brand attributes and contribute to the development and reinforcement of brand identity.

consumer juries A method of pretesting advertisements by using a panel of consumers who are representative of the target audience and provide ratings, rankings, and/or evaluations of advertisements.

consumer socialization process The process by which an individual acquires the skills needed to function in the marketplace as a consumer.

consumer-oriented sales promotion Sales promotion techniques that are targeted to the ultimate consumer such as coupons, samples, contests, rebates, sweepstakes, and premium offers.

content sponsorship The sponsor not only provides dollars in return for name association on the Internet but also participates in the provision of content itself.

contest A promotion whereby consumers compete for prizes or money on the basis of skills or ability, and winners are determined by judging the entries or ascertaining which entry comes closest to some predetermined criteria.

contextual advertising Internet advertising placed on the basis of the content of the web page.

continuity A media scheduling strategy where a continuous pattern of advertising is used over the time span of the advertising campaign.

contribution margin The difference between the total revenue generated by a product or brand and its total variable costs.

controlled-circulation basis Distribution of a publication free to individuals a publisher believes are of importance and responsible for making purchase decisions or are prescreened for qualification on some other basis.

cooperative advertising Advertising program in which a manufacturer pays a certain percentage of the expenses a retailer or distributor incurs for advertising the manufacturer's product in a local market area.

copywriter Individual who helps conceive the ideas for ads and commercials and writes the words or copy for them.

cord cutting Households dropping traditional pay-TV services such as cable or satellite TV.

corporate advertising Advertising designed to promote overall awareness of a company or enhance its image among a target audience.

corrective advertising An action by the Federal Trade Commission whereby an advertiser can be required to run advertising messages designed to remedy the deception or misleading impression created by its previous advertising.

cost per order (CPO) A measure used in direct marketing to determine the number of orders generated relative to the cost of running the advertisement.

cost per ratings point (CPRP) A computation used by media buyers to compare the cost-efficiency of broadcast programs that divides the cost of commercial time on a program by the audience rating.

cost per thousand (CPM) A computation used in evaluating the relative cost of various media vehicles that represents the cost of exposing 1,000 members of a target audience to an advertising message.

cost-plus system A method of compensating advertising agencies whereby the agency receives a fee based on the cost of the work it performs plus an agreed-on amount for profit.

counterargument A type of thought or cognitive response a receiver has that is counter or opposed to the position advocated in a message.

country-of-origin effect The impact on consumers' perceptions of products and/or brands that results from where the products are manufactured.

coverage A measure of the potential audience that might receive an advertising message through a media vehicle.

creative boutique An advertising agency that specializes in and provides only services related to the creative aspects of advertising.

creative brief A document that specifies the basic elements of the creative strategy such as the basic problem or issue the advertising must address, the advertising and communications objectives, target audience, major selling idea or key benefits to communicate, campaign theme or appeal, and supportive information or requirements.

creative execution style The manner or way in which a particular advertising appeal is transformed into a message.

creative strategy A determination of what an advertising message will say or communicate to a target audience.

creative tactics A determination of how an advertising message will be implemented to execute the creative strategy.

credibility The extent to which a source is perceived as having knowledge, skill, or experience relevant to a communication topic and can be trusted to give an unbiased opinion or present objective information on the issue.

cross sell A term used in personal selling that refers to the sale of additional products and/or services to the same customer.

cultural values Refers to beliefs and goals shared by members of a society regarding ideal end states of life and modes of conduct.

culture The complexity of learned meanings, values, norms, and customs shared by members of a society.

cume A term used for cumulative audience, which is the estimated total number of different people who listened to a radio station for a minimum of 5 minutes during a particular daypart.

Customer Lifetime Value (CLTV) An estimate of the total lifetime profit that can be generated from a specific customer.

customer relationship management (CRM) Programs that involve the systematic tracking of consumers' preferences and behaviors and modifying the product or service offers as much as possible to meet individual needs and wants.

DAGMAR An acronym that stands for defining advertising goals for measured advertising results. An approach to setting advertising goals and objectives developed by Russell Colley.

daily inch rate A cost figure used in periodicals based on an advertisement placed one inch deep and one column wide (whatever the column width).

dayparts The time segments into which a day is divided by radio and television networks and stations for selling advertising time.

decentralized system An organizational system whereby planning and decision-making responsibility for marketing, advertising, and promotion lies with a product/brand manager or management team rather than a centralized department.

deception According to the Federal Trade Commission, a misrepresentation, omission, or practice that is likely to mislead the consumer acting reasonably in the circumstances to the consumer's detriment.

decoding The process by which a message recipient transforms and interprets a message.

demographic segmentation A method of segmenting a market based on the demographic characteristics of consumers.

departmental system The organization of an advertising agency into departments based on functions such as account services, creative, media, marketing services, and administration.

designated market areas (DMAs) The geographic areas used by the Nielsen Station Index in measuring audience size. DMAs are non-overlapping areas consisting of groups of counties from which stations attract their viewers.

differentiated marketing A type of marketing strategy whereby a firm offers products or services to a number of market segments and develops separate marketing strategies for each.

differentiation A situation where a particular company or brand is perceived as unique or better than its competitors.

digital out of home (DOOH) media Traditional out of home media (billboards, transit ads, etc.), now presented in a digital format.

digital pricing models The options for pricing an ad in digital media entailing different bases for pricing, and different means for determining relative cost comparisons.

digital public relations The use of digital and social technologies to manage an organization's public relations functions.

digital agency Agencies that specialize in the development and strategic use of various digital and interactive marketing tools such as websites for the Internet, banner ads, search engine optimization, mobile marketing, and social media campaigns.

direct broadcast by satellite (DBS) A television signal delivery system whereby programming is beamed from satellites to special receiving dishes mounted in the home or yard.

direct channel A marketing channel where a producer and ultimate consumer interact directly with one another.

direct headline A headline that is very straightforward and informative in terms of the message it is presenting and the target audience it is directed toward. Direct headlines often include a specific benefit, promise, or reason for a consumer to be interested in a product or service.

direct marketing A system of marketing by which an organization communicates directly with customers to generate a response and/or a transaction.

direct selling The direct personal presentation, demonstration, and sale of products and services to consumers usually in their homes or at their jobs.

direct to consumer (DTC) A system of marketing by which organizations communicate directly with target customers to generate a response or transaction.

direct-marketing agency A company that provides a variety of direct-marketing services to its clients, including database management, direct mail, research, media service, creative, and production.

direct-response advertising A form of advertising for a product or service that elicits a sales response directly from the advertiser.

direct-response media Media used to seek a direct response from the consumer, including direct mail, telemarketing, interactive TV, print, the Internet, and other media.

display advertising Advertising in newspapers and magazines that uses illustrations, photos, headlines, and other visual elements in addition to copy text.

divergence The extent to which an advertisement contains certain creative elements that are novel, different, or unusual.

duplicated reach Individuals exposed to the same commercial on two or more media vehicles.

dyadic communication A process of direct communication between two persons or groups such as a salesperson and a customer.

e-commerce Direct selling of goods and services through the Internet.

e-mail Messages sent electronically over the Internet.

earned media Exposure for a company or brand that it did not have to pay for and is generated by entities outside the firms such as media coverage or through others sharing information via social media.

economic infrastructure A country's communications, transportation, financial, and distribution networks.

economies of scale A decline in costs with accumulated sales or production. In advertising, economies of scale often occur in media purchases as the relative costs of advertising time and/or space may decline as the size of the media budget increases.

effective reach A measure of the percentage of a media vehicle's audience reached at each effective frequency increment.

80–20 rule The principle that 80 percent of sales volume for a product or service is generated by 20 percent of the customers.

elaboration likelihood model (ELM) A model that identifies two processes by which communications can lead to persuasion—central and peripheral routes.

electrodermal response (EDR) A measure of the resistance the skin offers to a small amount of current passed between two electrodes. Used as a measure of consumers' reaction level to an advertisement.

electroencephalographic (EEG) measures Measures of the electrical impulses in the brain that are sometimes used as a measure of reactions to advertising.

emotional appeals Advertising messages that appeal to consumers' feelings and emotions.

encoding The process of putting thoughts, ideas, or information into a symbolic form.

ethics Moral principles and values that govern the actions and decisions of an individual or group.

ethnographic research A research technique that involves observing or studying consumers in their natural environment.

evaluative criteria The dimensions or attributes of a product or service that are used to compare different alternatives.

event marketing A type of promotion where a company or brand is linked to an event, or where a themed activity is developed for the purpose of creating experiences for consumers and promoting a product or service.

event sponsorship A type of promotion whereby a company develops sponsorship relations with a particular event such as a concert, sporting event, or other activity.

exchange Trade of something of value between two parties such as a product or service for money. The core phenomenon or domain for study in marketing.

exclusive A public relations tactic whereby one particular medium is offered exclusive rights to a story.

experiential marketing Involves a live event or experience that provides consumers with the opportunity to see the product or service and experience it for themselves.

external analysis The phase of the promotional planning process that focuses on factors such as the characteristics of an organization's customers, market segments, positioning strategies, competitors, and marketing environment.

external audiences In public relations, a term used in reference to individuals who are outside or not closely connected to the organization such as the general public.

external search The search process whereby consumers seek and acquire information from external sources such as advertising, other people, or public sources.

eye tracking A method for following the movement of a person's eyes as he or she views an ad or commercial. Eye tracking is used for determining which portions or sections of an ad attract a viewer's attention and/or interest.

Facebook analytics A free analytics tool provided by Facebook that allows users to measure the performance of their site. Measures include page views, reach, and more.

failure fee A trade promotion arrangement whereby a marketer agrees to pay a penalty fee if a product stocked by a retailer does not meet agreed-upon sales levels.

fear appeal An advertising message that creates anxiety in a receiver by showing negative consequences that can result from engaging in (or not engaging in) a particular behavior.

Federal Trade Commission (FTC) The federal agency that has the primary responsibility for protecting consumers and businesses from anticompetitive behavior and unfair and deceptive practices. The FTC regulates advertising and promotion at the federal level.

Federal Trade Commission Act Federal legislation passed in 1914 that created the Federal Trade Commission and gave it the responsibility to monitor deceptive or misleading advertising and unfair business practices.

fee–commission combination A type of compensation system whereby an advertising agency establishes a fixed monthly fee for its services to a client and media commissions received by the agency are credited against the fee.

feedback Part of the message recipient's response that is communicated back to the sender. Feedback can take a variety of forms and provides a sender with a way of monitoring how an intended message is decoded and received.

field of experience The experiences, perceptions, attitudes, and values that senders and receivers of a message bring to a communication situation.

field tests Tests of consumer reactions to an advertisement that are taken under natural viewing situations rather than in a laboratory.

financial audit An aspect of the advertising agency evaluation process that focuses on how the agency conducts financial affairs related to serving a client.

first cover The outside front cover of a magazine

fixed-fee method A method of agency compensation whereby the agency and client agree on the work to be done and the amount of money the agency will be paid for its services.

flat rate A standard newspaper advertising rate where no discounts are offered for large-quantity or repeated space buys.

Flesch formula A test used to assess the difficulty level of writing based on the number of syllables and sentences per 100 words.

flighting A media scheduling pattern in which periods of advertising are alternated with periods of no advertising.

focus groups A qualitative marketing research method whereby a group of 10 to 12 consumers from the target market is led through a discussion regarding a particular topic such as a product, service, or advertising campaign.

fourth cover The outside back cover position of a magazine where an ad can be placed

freestanding insert (FSI) A four-color multipage printed advertising booklet that contains consumer packaged-goods coupon offers delivered with newspapers (usually in Sunday editions). FSIs can also be delivered in direct-mail packages along with local retailer ads or can be cooperative booklets such as RedPlum or SmartSource as well as solo books done by companies.

frequency The number of times a target audience is exposed to a media vehicle(s) in a specified period.

full-service agency An advertising agency that offers clients a full range of marketing and communications services, including the planning, creating, producing, and placing of advertising messages and other forms of promotion.

functional consequences Outcomes of product or service usage that are tangible and can be directly experienced by a consumer.

game A promotion that is a form of sweepstakes because it has a chance element or odds of winning associated with it. Games usually involve game card devices that can be rubbed or opened to unveil a winning number or prize description.

gatefold An oversize magazine page or cover that is extended and folded over to fit into the publication. Gatefolds are used to extend the size of a magazine advertisement and are always sold at a premium.

general advertising rates Rates charged by newspapers to display advertisers outside the paper's designated market areas and to any classification deemed by the publisher to be general in nature.

general preplanning input Information gathering and/or market research studies on trends, developments, and happenings in the marketplace that can be used to assist in the initial stages of the creative process of advertising.

geographic segmentation A method of segmenting a market on the basis of different geographic units or areas.

global advertising The use of the same basic advertising message in all international markets.

global marketing A strategy of using a common marketing plan and program for all countries in which a company operates, thus selling the product or services the same way everywhere in the world.

Google analytics An analytical tool offered to Google users to assist advertisers in measuring your advertising ROI as well as tracking your Flash, video, and social networking applications.

gross ratings points (GRPs) A measure that represents the total delivery or weight of a media schedule during a specified time period. GRPs are calculated by multiplying the reach of the media schedule by the average frequency.

group system The organization of an advertising agency by dividing it into groups consisting of specialists from various departments such as creative, media, marketing services, and other areas. These groups work together to service particular accounts.

guochao The increase in favoritism toward Chinese brands, design, and culture.

halo effect The tendency for evaluations of one attribute or aspect of a stimulus to distort reactions to its other attributes or properties.

headline Words in the leading position of the advertisement; the words that will be read first or are positioned to draw the most attention.

hemispheric lateralization The notion that the human brain has two relatively distinct halves or hemispheres with each being responsible for a specific type of function. The right side is responsible for visual processing while the left side conducts verbal processing.

heuristics Simplified or basic decision rules that can be used by a consumer to make a purchase choice, such as buy the cheapest brand.

hierarchy of effects model A model of the process by which advertising works that assumes a consumer must pass through a sequence of steps from initial awareness to eventual action. The stages include awareness, interest, evaluation, trial, and adoption.

hierarchy of needs Abraham Maslow's theory that human needs are arranged in an order or hierarchy based on their importance. The need hierarchy includes physiological, safety, social/love and belonging, esteem, and self-actualization needs.

horizontal cooperative advertising A cooperative advertising arrangement where advertising is sponsored in common by a group of retailers or other organizations providing products or services to a market.

households using television (HUT) The percentage of homes in a given area that are watching television during a specific time period.

identification The process by which an attractive source influences a message recipient. Identification occurs when the receiver is motivated to seek some type of relationship with the source and adopt a similar position in terms of beliefs, attitudes, preferences, or behavior.

image advertising Advertising that creates an identity for a product or service by emphasizing psychological meaning or symbolic association with certain values, lifestyles, and the like.

image transfer A radio advertising technique whereby the images of a television commercial are implanted into a radio spot.

in-house agency An advertising agency set up, owned, and operated by an advertiser that is responsible for planning and executing the company's advertising program.

in-store media Advertising and promotional media that are used inside of a retail store such as point-of-purchase displays, ads on shopping carts, coupon dispensers, and display boards.

incentive-based system A form of compensation whereby an advertising agency's compensation level depends on how well it meets predetermined performance goals such as sales or market share.

index number A ratio used to describe the potential of a market. The index number is derived by dividing the percentage of users in a market segment by the percentage of population in the same segment and multiplying by 100.

indirect channel A marketing channel where intermediaries such as wholesalers and retailers are utilized to make a product available to the customer.

indirect headline Headline that is not straightforward with respect to identifying a product or service or providing information regarding the point of an advertising message.

influencer marketing Using social media to leverage the influence of individuals with a dedicated social media following.

infomercial Television commercial that is very long, ranging from several minutes to an hour. Infomercials are designed to provide consumers with detailed information about a product or service.

informational/rational appeals Advertising appeals that focus on the practical, functional, or utilitarian need for a product or service and emphasize features, benefits, or reasons for owning or using the brand.

ingredient-sponsored cooperative advertising Advertising supported by raw material manufacturers with the objective being to help establish end products that include materials and/or ingredients supplied by the company.

inherent drama An approach to advertising that focuses on the benefits or characteristics that lead a consumer to purchase a product or service and uses dramatic elements to emphasize them.

innovation adoption model A model that represents the stages a consumer passes through in the adoption process for an innovation such as a new product. The series of steps includes awareness, interest, evaluation, trial, and adoption.

inquiry tests Tests designed to measure advertising effectiveness on the basis of inquiries or responses generated from the ad such as requests for information, number of phone calls, or number of coupons redeemed.

inside cards A form of transit advertising where messages appear on cards or boards inside of vehicles such as buses, subways, or trolleys.

integrated marketing communications (IMC) A strategic business process used to develop, execute, and evaluate coordinated, measurable, persuasive brand communications programs over time with consumers, customers, prospects, employees, associates, and other targeted relevant external and internal audiences. The goal is to both generate short-term financial returns and build long-term brand and shareholder value.

integrated marketing communications management The process of planning, executing, evaluating, and controlling the use of various promotional-mix elements to effectively communicate with a target audience.

integrated marketing communications objectives Statements of what various aspects of the integrated marketing communications program will accomplish with respect to factors such as communication tasks, sales, market share, and the like.

integrated marketing communications plan A document that provides the framework for developing, implementing, and controlling an organization's integrated marketing communications program.

integration processes The way information such as product knowledge, meanings, and beliefs is combined to evaluate two or more alternatives.

interactive media A variety of media that allow the consumer to interact with the source of the message, actively receiving information and altering images, responding to questions, and so on.

interconnects Groups of cable systems in a geographic area joined together for advertising purposes.

internal analysis The phase of the promotional planning process that focuses on the product/service offering and the firm itself, including the capabilities of the firm and its ability to develop and implement a successful integrated marketing communications program.

internal audiences In public relations, a term used to refer to individuals or groups inside the organization or with a close connection to it.

internal search The process by which a consumer acquires information by accessing past experiences or knowledge stored in memory.

internalization The process by which a credible source influences a message recipient. Internalization occurs when the receiver is motivated to have an objectively correct position on an issue and the receiver will adopt the opinion or attitude of the credible communicator if he or she believes the information from this source represents an accurate position on the issue.

interstitial An advertisement that appears in a window on your computer screen while you are waiting for a web page to load.

issue advertising (issue ad) A form of advocacy advertising in which the advertiser wishes to bring attention to what it considers to be an important issue.

jingle Song about a brand or company that usually carries the advertising theme and a simple message.

laboratory tests Tests of consumer reactions to advertising under controlled conditions.

Lanham Act A federal law that permits a company to register a trademark for its exclusive use. The Lanham Act was amended to encompass false advertising and prohibits any false description or representation including words or other symbols tending falsely to describe or represent the same.

layout The physical arrangement of the various parts of an advertisement including the headline, subheads, illustrations, body copy, and any identifying marks.

lead A name given to a personal sales agent as a possible consumer.

linear TV Television service where the viewer has to watch a scheduled TV program at the particular time it's offered, and on the particular channel it's presented on.

local advertising Advertising done by companies within the limited geographic area where they do business.

localized advertising strategy Developing an advertising campaign specifically for a particular country or market rather than using a global approach.

low-involvement hierarchy A response hierarchy whereby a message recipient is viewed as passing from cognition to behavior to attitude change.

loyalty program Program designed to encourage repeat purchase or patronage of a specific brand of a product or service.

magazine network A group of magazines owned by one publisher or assembled by an independent network that offers advertisers the opportunity to buy space in a variety of publications through a package deal.

mailing list The database from which names are generated, and the ability to segment markets and, of course the offer.

major selling idea The basis for the central theme or message idea in an advertising campaign.

marginal analysis A principle of resource allocation that balances incremental revenues against incremental costs.

market opportunities Areas where a company believes there are favorable demand trends, needs, and/or wants that are not being satisfied, and where it can compete effectively.

market segmentation The process of dividing a market into distinct groups that have common needs and will respond similarly to a marketing action.

market segments Identifiable groups of customers sharing similar needs, wants, or other characteristics that make them likely to respond in a similar fashion to a marketing program.

marketing The activity, set of institutions, and processes for creating, communicating, delivering, and exchanging offerings that have value for customers, clients, partners, and society at large.

marketing channels The set of interdependent organizations involved in the process of making a product or service available to customers.

marketing mix The controllable elements of a marketing program including product, price, place (distribution), and promotion.

marketing objectives Goals to be accomplished by an organization's overall marketing program such as sales, market share, or profitability.

marketing plan A written document that describes the overall marketing strategy and programs developed for an organization, a particular product line, or a brand.

marketing public relations (MPR) Public relations activities designed to support marketing objectives and programs.

mass media Nonpersonal channels of communication that allow a message to be sent to many individuals at one time.

materialism A preoccupation with material things rather than intellectual or spiritual concerns.

media objectives The specific goals an advertiser has for the media portion of the advertising program.

media organizations One of the four major participants in the integrated marketing communications process whose function is to provide information or entertainment to subscribers, viewers, or readers while offering marketers an environment for reaching audiences with print and broadcast messages.

media planning The series of decisions involved in the delivery of an advertising message to prospective purchasers and/or users of a product or service.

media specialist companies Companies that specialize in the buying of advertising media time and space, particularly for television and digital advertising.

media strategies Plans of action for achieving stated media objectives such as which media will be used for reaching a target audience, how the media budget will be allocated, and how advertisements will be scheduled.

media vehicle The specific program, publication, or promotional piece used to carry an advertising message.

medium The general category of communication vehicles that are available for communicating with a target audience such as broadcast, print, direct mail, outdoor, and other support media.

message A communication containing information or meaning that a source wants to convey to a receiver.

mnemonics Basic cues such as symbols, rhymes, and associations that facilitate the learning and memory process.

mobile Type of services accessed through a portable communications device.

mobile billboard An out of home medium in which advertisements are able to be transported to different locations (signs painted on automobiles, trailers pulling billboards, and the like).

mobile marketing Promotional activity designed for delivery to cell phones, smartphones, tablets, and other handheld devices that includes apps, messaging, commerce, and customer relationship management.

mock magazine test Test in which an ad is placed in an actual magazine and a similar methodology is employed.

modular pricing A form of pricing costs based on the size of a set module such as full page, half page, quarter page or eighth page.

motivation research Qualitative research designed to probe the consumer's subconscious and discover deeply rooted motives for purchasing a product.

motive Something that compels or drives a consumer to take a particular action.

multiattribute attitude model A model of attitudes that views an individual's evaluation of an object as being a function of the beliefs that he or she has toward the object on various attributes and the importance of these attributes.

Multichannel Video Programming Distributors (MVPD) Services that distribute or provide multiple television channels as part of a package that customers subscribe to for television programming.

multiplexing An arrangement where multiple channels are transmitted by one cable network.

narrowcasting The reaching of a very specialized market through programming aimed at particular target audiences. Cable television networks offer excellent opportunities for narrowcasting.

National Advertising Review Board (NARB) A part of the National Advertising Division of the Council of Better Business Bureaus. The NARB is the advertising industry's primary self-regulatory body.

National Association of Attorneys General (NAAG) An organization consisting of state attorneys general that is involved in the regulation of advertising and other business practices.

national spot advertising All nonnetwork advertising done by a national advertiser in local markets.

native advertising Web advertising in which the advertiser attempts to gain attention by providing content in the context of the user's experience.

needledrop A term used in the advertising industry to refer to music that is prefabricated, multipurpose, and conventional and can be used in a commercial when a particular normative effect is desired.

negotiated commission A method of compensating advertising agencies whereby the client and agency negotiate the commission structure rather than relying on the traditional 15 percent media commission.

new media A term used to describe the proliferation of media resulting from the advent of Web 2.0.

noise Extraneous factors that create unplanned distortion or interference in the communications process.

nonfranchise-building (non-FB) promotions Sales promotion activities that are designed to accelerate the purchase decision process and generate an immediate increase in sales but do little or nothing to communicate information about a brand and contribute to its identity and image.

nonmeasured media A term commonly used in the advertising industry to describe support media.

nonorganic (paid) search results Internet search results that are impacted by advertisements paid for by marketers.

nontraditional media Newer media, including various forms of support media such as entertainment marketing, guerrilla marketing, product placements, and the like, as well as Internet and interactive media, such as blogs, podcasts, and more.

objective and task method A buildup approach to budget setting involving a three-step process: (1) determining objectives, (2) determining the strategies and tasks required to attain these objectives, and (3) estimating the costs associated with these strategies and tasks.

off-invoice allowance A promotional discount offered to retailers or wholesalers whereby a certain per-case amount or percentage is deducted from the invoice.

omnichannel retailing A strategy whereby companies sell their products through multiple distribution channels including retail stores, online, catalogs, and mobile apps.

on-air tests Testing the effectiveness of television commercials by inserting test ads into actual TV programs in certain test markets.

one-sided message Communications in which only positive attributes or benefits of a product or service are presented.

one-step approach A direct-marketing strategy in which the medium is used directly to obtain an order (for example, television direct-response ads).

online commercial The equivalent of a traditional television commercial that appears on the Internet.

open-rate structure A rate charged by newspapers in which discounts are available based on frequency or bulk purchases of space.

operant conditioning (instrumental conditioning) A learning theory that views the probability of a behavior as being dependent on the outcomes or consequences associated with it.

organic search results Search results that appear due to the relevance of the search terms, not advertisements.

out of home (OOH) advertising The variety of advertising forms including outdoor, transit, skywriting, and other media viewed outside the home.

outside posters Outdoor transit posters appearing on buses, taxis, trains, subways, and trolley cars.

over-the-top (OTT) Streaming TV representing content that is delivered directly to viewers via a streaming service over the Internet, bypassing the traditional cable or satellite box.

owned media Channels of marketing communication that a company controls, such as its websites, blogs, and mobile apps as well as social media channels.

paid media Channels of communication a marketer pays for including traditional advertising media such as television, radio, print, outdoor, and direct mail as well as various forms of digital advertising such as paid search and online display and video ads

participations The situation where several advertisers buy commercial time or spots on network television.

pass-along rate An estimate of the number of readers of a magazine in addition to the original subscriber or purchaser.

pass-along readership The audience that results when the primary subscriber or purchaser of a magazine gives the publication to another person to read, or when the magazine is read in places such as waiting rooms in doctors' offices.

pattern advertising Advertisements that follow a basic global approach although themes, copy, and sometimes even visual elements may be adjusted.

pay-per-click Advertisement payment method in which advertisers' costs are based on the number of times the ad is clicked on during a search.

payout plan A budgeting plan that determines the investment value of the advertising and promotion appropriation.

people meter An electronic device that automatically records a household's television viewing, including channels watched, number of minutes of viewing, and members of the household who are watching.

percentage charges The markups charged by advertising agencies for services provided to clients.

percentage-of-sales method A budget method in which the advertising and/or promotions budget is set based on a percentage of sales of the product.

perception The process by which an individual receives, selects, organizes, and interprets information to create a meaningful picture of the world.

peripheral route to persuasion In the elaboration likelihood model, one of two routes to persuasion in which the receiver is viewed as lacking the ability or motivation to process information and is not likely to be engaging in detailed cognitive processing.

personal selling Person-to-person communication in which the seller attempts to assist and/or persuade prospective buyers to purchase the company's product or service or to act on an idea.

persuasion matrix A communication planning model in which the stages of the response process (dependent variables) and the communication components (independent variables) are combined to demonstrate the likely effect that the independent variables will have on the dependent variables.

planogram A planning configuration of products that occupy a shelf section in a store that is used to provide more efficient shelf space utilization.

podcasting A medium using the Internet to distribute files for downloading into iPods and other MP3 players.

pop-under Ad that pops up as the user is leaving the website.

pop-up Advertisement window on the Internet usually larger than a banner ad and smaller than a full screen.

Portable People Meter (PPM) A wearable pager-sized device that electronically traces what consumers listen to on the radio by detecting inaudible identification codes that are embedded in the programming.

portfolio test A laboratory methodology designed to expose a group of respondents to a portfolio consisting of both control and test print ads.

positioning The art and science of fitting the product or service to one or more segments of the market in such a way as to set it meaningfully apart from competition.

Positioning Advertising Copy Testing (PACT) A set of principles endorsed by 21 of the largest U.S. ad agencies aimed at improving the research used in preparing and testing ads, providing a better creative product for clients, and controlling the cost of TV commercials.

post-roll Video display advertisement that plays on an Internet site after the video requested appears.

posttests Ad effectiveness measures that are taken after the ad has appeared in the marketplace.

pre-roll Video display advertisement that plays on an Internet site before the video requested appears.

preferred position rate A rate charged by newspapers that ensures the advertiser the ad will appear in the position required and/or in a specific section of the newspaper.

premium An offer of an item of merchandise or service either free or at a low price that is used as an extra incentive for purchasers.

preprinted insert Advertising distributed through newspapers that is not part of the newspaper itself, but is printed by the advertiser and then taken to the newspaper to be inserted.

press conference The calling together of the press to announce significant news and/or events.

press release Factual and interesting information released to the press.

pretests Advertising effectiveness measures that are taken before the implementation of the advertising campaign.

price-off deal A promotional strategy in which the consumer receives a reduction in the regular price of the brand.

primacy effect A theory that the first information presented in the message will be the most likely to be remembered.

problem detection A creative research approach in which consumers familiar with a product (or service) are asked to generate an exhaustive list of problems encountered in its use.

problem recognition The first stage in the consumer decision-making process in which the consumer perceives a need and becomes motivated to satisfy it.

product integration The act of integrating the product into television program content.

product placement A form of advertising and promotion in which products are placed in television shows and/or movies to gain exposure.

product symbolism The meaning that a product or brand has to consumers.

product- or service-specific preplanning input Specific studies provided to the creative department on the product or service, the target audience, or a combination of the two.

program rating The percentage of TV households in an area that are tuned to a program during a specific time period.

programmatic Computer-based advertising buying using a real-time bidding process.

programmatic buying A wide range of technologies that have begun automating the buying, placement, and optimization of advertising media time and space.

promotion The coordination of all seller-initiated efforts to set up channels of information and persuasion to sell goods and services or to promote an idea.

promotional mix The tools used to accomplish an organization's communications objective. The promotional mix includes advertising, direct marketing, digital/Internet marketing, sales promotion, publicity/public relations, and personal selling.

promotional products marketing The advertising or promotional medium or method that uses promotional products such as ad specialties, premiums, business gifts, awards, prizes, or commemoratives.

promotional pull strategy A strategy in which advertising and promotion efforts are targeted at the ultimate consumers to encourage them to purchase the manufacturer's brand.

promotional push strategy A strategy in which advertising and promotional efforts are targeted to the trade to attempt to get them to promote and sell the product to the ultimate consumer.

prospecting The process of seeking out prospective customers.

prospects Prospective customers.

Protestant ethic A perspective of life that stresses hard work and individual effort and initiative and views the accumulation of material possessions as evidence of success.

psychoanalytic theory An approach to the study of human motivations and behaviors pioneered by Sigmund Freud.

psychographic segmentation Dividing the product on the basis of personality and/or lifestyles.

psychosocial consequences Purchase decision consequences that are intangible, subjective, and personal.

public relations (PR) The management function that evaluates public attitudes, identifies the policies and procedures of an individual or organization with the public interest, and executes a program to earn public understanding and acceptance.

public relations firm An organization that develops and implements programs to manage a company's publicity, image, and affairs with consumers and other relevant publics.

Public Relations Society of America A nonprofit trade association for public relations professionals. It is the largest trade association in the United States serving the public relations industry.

publicity Communications regarding an organization, product, service, or idea that are not directly paid for or run under identified sponsorship.

puffery Advertising or other sales presentations that praise the item to be sold using subjective opinions, superlatives, or exaggerations, vaguely and generally, stating no specific facts.

pulsing A media scheduling method that combines flighting and continuous scheduling.

pupillometrics An advertising effectiveness methodology designed to measure dilation and constriction of the pupils of the eye in response to stimuli.

purchase intention The predisposition to buy a certain brand or product.

push money (PM) Cash payments made directly to the retailers' or wholesalers' sales force to encourage them to promote and sell a manufacturer's product.

QR code Short for quick response code; an optically machine-readable label attached to an item or advertisement that records information, which can be revealed to the viewer through an imaging device, which translates the code into content.

qualified prospects Those prospects that are able to make the buying decision.

qualitative audit An audit of the advertising agency's efforts in planning, developing, and implementing the client's communications programs.

qualitative media effect The positive or negative influence the medium may contribute to the message.

ratings point A measurement used to determine television viewing audiences in which one ratings point is the equivalent of 1 percent of all of the television households in a particular area tuned to a specific program.

reach The number of different audience members exposed at least once to a media vehicle (or vehicles) in a given period.

readers per copy A cost comparison figure used for magazines that estimates audience size based on pass-along readership.

recall An advertising effectiveness score indicating the number of persons who remember an ad.

recall tests Advertising effectiveness tests designed to measure advertising recall.

receiver The person or persons with whom the sender of a message shares thoughts or information.

recency The idea that advertising will have the most effect on someone who is in the market for the product and that planners should attempt to reach that consumer as close as possible to their purchase decision.

recency effect The theory that arguments presented at the end of the message are considered to be stronger and therefore are more likely to be remembered.

recency planning Media planning that attempts to reach the consumer in the period of time just before their purchase decision.

recognition method An advertising effectiveness measure of print ads that allows the advertiser to assess the impact of an ad in a single issue of a magazine over time and/or across alternative magazines.

reference group A group whose perspectives, values, or behavior is used by an individual as the basis for his or her judgments, opinions, and actions.

refund An offer by a manufacturer to return a portion of a product's purchase price, usually after the consumer supplies a proof of purchase.

refutational appeal A type of message in which both sides of the issue are presented in the communication, with arguments offered to refute the opposing viewpoint.

reinforcement The rewards or favorable consequences associated with a particular response.

relationship marketing An organization's effort to develop a long-term cost-effective link with individual customers for mutual benefit.

relative cost The relationship between the price paid for advertising time or space and the size of the audience delivered; it is used to compare the prices of various media vehicles.

relevance The degree to which the various elements of an advertisement are meaningful, useful, or valuable to the consumer.

reminder advertising Advertising designed to keep the name of the product or brand in the mind of the receiver.

repositioning The changing of a product or brand's positioning.

response The set of reactions the receiver has after seeing, hearing, or reading a message.

retail or local advertising rates Rates newspapers charge to advertisers that conduct business or sell goods and services within the paper's designated market area.

retail trading zone The market outside the city zone whose residents regularly trade with merchants within the city zone.

retargeting Resending an ad to a website visitor who previously visited the site seeking information but did not purchase, in an attempt to make a sale.

RFM analysis A marketing technique used to determine quantitatively which customers are the most profitable by examining how recently a customer has purchased (recency), how often he or she purchases (frequency), and how much the customer spends (monetary).

rich media A term for advanced technology used in Internet ads, such as a streaming video, which allows interaction and special effects.

ROI budgeting method (return on investment) A budgeting method in which advertising and promotions are considered investments, and thus measurements are made in an attempt to determine the returns achieved by these investments.

run of paper (ROP) A rate quoted by newspapers that allows the ad to appear on any page or in any position desired by the medium.

S-shaped response curve A sales response model that attempts to show sales responses to various levels of advertising and promotional expenditures.

sales promotion Marketing activities that provide extra value or incentives to the sales force, distributors, or the ultimate consumer and can stimulate immediate sales.

sales promotion agency An organization that specializes in the planning and implementation of promotional programs such as contests, sweepstakes, sampling, premiums, and incentive offers for its clients.

sales promotion trap A spiral that results when a number of competitors extensively use promotions. One firm uses sales promotions to differentiate its product or service and other competitors copy the strategy, resulting in no differential advantage and a loss of profit margins to all.

salient attributes Attributes considered important to consumers in the purchase decision process.

salient beliefs Beliefs concerning specific attributes or consequences that are activated and form the basis of an attitude.

sampling A variety of procedures whereby consumers are given some quantity of a product for no charge to induce trial.

scatter market A period for purchasing television advertising time that runs throughout the TV season.

schedules of reinforcement Schedules by which a behavioral response is rewarded.

script A written version of the commercial that provides a detailed description of its video and audio content.

search Looking for a term, company, and so forth on the Internet.

search engine optimization (SEO) The process of improving ranking in search engine results.

second cover The inside front cover position of a magazine where a print ad can be placed.

seeding The process of identifying and choosing the initial group of consumers who will be used to start the diffusion or spreading of a message.

selective attention A perceptual process in which consumers choose to attend to some stimuli and not others.

selective comprehension The perceptual process whereby consumers interpret information based on their own attitudes, beliefs, motives, and experiences.

selective exposure A process whereby consumers choose whether or not to make themselves available to media and message information.

selective perception The perceptual process involving the filtering or screening of exposure, attention, comprehension, and retention.

selective retention The perceptual process whereby consumers remember some information but not all.

selectivity The ability of a medium to reach a specific target audience.

self-liquidating premium Premium that requires the consumer to pay some or all of the cost of the premium plus handling and mailing costs.

self-regulation The practice by the advertising industry of regulating and controlling advertising to avoid interference by outside agencies such as the government.

sensation The immediate and direct response of the senses (taste, smell, sight, touch, and hearing) to a stimulus such as an advertisement, package, brand name, or point-of-purchase display.

shaping The reinforcement of successive acts that lead to a desired behavior pattern or response.

share of audience The percentage of households watching television in a special time period that are tuned to a specific program.

shock advertising Advertising in which marketers use nudity, sexual suggestiveness, or other startling images to get consumers' attention.

situational determinants Influences originating from the specific situation in which consumers are to use the product or brand.

sleeper effect A phenomenon in which the persuasiveness of a message increases over time.

slogan (tagline) A statement or phrase consisting of a few words that succinctly expresses the company image, identity, and/or positioning a company or brand wants to communicate.

slotting allowance Fees that must be paid to retailers to provide a "slot" or position to accommodate a new product on the store shelves.

social class Relatively homogeneous divisions of society into which people are grouped based on similar lifestyles, values, norms, interests, and behaviors.

social media Online means of communication and interactions among people that are used to create, share, and exchange content such as information, insights, experiences, perspectives, and even media themselves.

social media influencer Popular social media personalities who constantly create and disseminate useful and organic content within a knowledge domain, project authentic personae, curate intimate relations with a large following, and thus wield influence over followers' purchases and decision making.

social media management Services that include media management, content development, publishing, and monitoring this environment.

social networking sites Online platforms for networks or social relations among people who share interests, activities, backgrounds, or real-life connections.

source The sender—person, group, or organization—of the message.

source bolsters Favorable cognitive thoughts generated toward the source of a message.

source derogations Negative thoughts generated about the source of a communication.

source power The power of a source as a result of his or her ability to administer rewards and/or punishments to the receiver.

spam Unsolicited commercial e-mail.

spamming The sending of unsolicited multiple commercial electronic messages.

specialized marketing communication services Organizations that provide marketing communication services in their areas of expertise including direct marketing, public relations, and sales promotion firms.

specialty advertising An advertising, sales promotion, and motivational communications medium that employs useful articles of merchandise imprinted with an advertiser's name, message, or logo.

split runs Two or more versions of a print ad are printed in alternative copies of a particular issue of a magazine.

split-run test An advertising effectiveness measure in which different versions of an ad are run in alternate copies of the same newspaper and/or magazine.

sponsorship (television) When the advertiser assumes responsibility for the production and usually the content of a television program as well as the advertising that appears within it.

sponsorship (Internet) When an advertiser sponsors content on a website, it is considered a sponsorship.

spot advertising Commercials shown on local television stations, with the negotiation and purchase of time being made directly from the individual stations.

standard advertising unit (SAU) A standard developed in the newspaper industry to make newspaper purchasing rates more comparable to other media that sell space and time in standard units.

standard learning model Progression by the consumers through a learn-feel-do hierarchical response.

station reps Individuals who act as sales representatives for a number of local stations and represent them in dealings with national advertisers.

storyboard A series of drawings used to present the visual plan or layout of a proposed commercial.

storytelling Creating real, relevant, and emotionally resonant narratives for the target audience to communicate messages in a way that captures the audience's attention and motivates them to act.

strategic marketing plan The planning framework for specific marketing activities.

subcultures Smaller groups within a culture that possess similar beliefs, values, norms, and patterns of behavior that differentiate them from the larger cultural mainstream.

subhead Secondary headline in a print ad.

subliminal perception The ability of an individual to perceive a stimulus below the level of conscious awareness.

superagencies Large external agencies that offer integrated marketing communications on a worldwide basis.

superstations Independent local stations that send their signals via satellite to cable operators that, in turn, make them available to subscribers (e.g., WWOR, WPIX, WGN, WSBK, WTBS).

support advertising A form of direct marketing in which the ad is designed to support other forms of advertising appearing in other media.

support argument Consumers' thoughts that support or affirm the claims being made by a message.

support media Those media used to support or reinforce messages sent to target markets through other more "dominant" and/or more traditional media.

survey of buying power index An index that provides information regarding population, effective buying income, and total retail sales in an area.

sustainability Development that meets the needs of the current generation without compromising the ability of future generations to meet their needs.

sweeps periods The times of year in which television audience measures are taken (February, May, July, and November).

sweepstakes A promotion whereby consumers submit their names for consideration in the drawing or selection of prizes and winners are determined purely by chance. Sweepstakes cannot require a proof of purchase as a condition for entry.

syndicated programs Shows sold or distributed to local stations.

target CPM (TCPM) A relative cost comparison that calculates CPMs based on the target audience as opposed to the overall audience.

target marketing The process of identifying the specific needs of segments, selecting one or more of these segments as a target, and developing marketing programs directed to each.

target ratings points (TRPs) The number of persons in the primary target audience that the media buy will reach—and the number of times.

teaser advertising An ad designed to create curiosity and build excitement and interest in a product or brand without showing it.

telemarketing Selling products and services by using the telephone to contact prospective customers.

television household Defined by Nielsen as a home with at least one operable TV/monitor with the ability to deliver video via traditional means of antennae, cable set-top-box or satellite receiver and/or with a broadband connection.

television network The provider of news and programming to a series of affiliated local television stations.

terminal posters Floor displays, island showcases, electronic signs, and other forms of advertisements that appear in train or subway stations, airline terminals, and the like.

testing bias A bias that occurs in advertising effectiveness measures because respondents know they are being tested and thus alter their responses.

theater test An advertising effectiveness pretest in which consumers view ads in a theater setting and evaluate these ads on a variety of dimensions.

third cover The inside back cover position of a magazine where a print ad can be placed

top-down approaches Budgeting approaches in which the budgetary amount is established at the executive level and monies are passed down to the various departments.

total audience (television) The total number of homes viewing any five-minute part of a television program.

total audience/readership A combination of the total number of primary and pass-along readers multiplied by the circulation of an average issue of a magazine.

touch point Each and every opportunity a consumer has to see or hear about a company and/or its brands or have an encounter or experience with it.

tracking studies Advertising effectiveness measures designed to assess the effects of advertising on awareness, recall, interest, and attitudes toward the ad as well as purchase intentions.

trade advertising Advertising targeted to wholesalers and retailers.

trade allowance A discount or deal offered to retailers or wholesalers to encourage them to stock, promote, or display a manufacturer's product.

trade show A type of exhibition or forum where manufacturers can display their products to current as well as prospective buyers.

trade-oriented sales promotion A sales promotion designed to motivate distributors and retailers to carry a product and make an extra effort to promote or "push" it to their customers.

transformational ad An ad that associates the experience of using the advertised brand with a unique set of psychological characteristics that would not typically be associated with the brand experience to the same degree without exposure to the advertisement.

transit advertising Advertising targeted to target audiences exposed to commercial transportation facilities, including buses, taxis, trains, elevators, trolleys, airplanes, and subways.

two-sided message A message in which both good and bad points about a product or claim are presented.

two-step approach A direct-marketing strategy in which the first effort is designed to screen or qualify potential buyers, while the second effort has the responsibility of generating the response.

undifferentiated marketing A strategy in which market segment differences are ignored and one product or service is offered to the entire market.

unduplicated reach The number of persons reached once with a media exposure.

unfairness A concept used by the Federal Trade Commission to determine unfair or deceptive advertising practices. Unfairness occurs when a trade practice causes substantial physical or economic injury to consumers, could not be avoided by consumers, and must not be outweighed by countervailing benefits to consumers or competition.

unique selling proposition (USP) An advertising strategy that focuses on a product or service attribute that is distinctive to a particular brand and offers an important benefit to the customer.

up-front market A buying period that takes place prior to the upcoming television season when the networks sell a large part of their commercial time.

user-generated content (UGC) Advertising and/or other forms of content provided by consumers or other nonprofessional sources.

value The customer's perception of all the benefits of a product or service weighed against the costs of acquiring and consuming it.

vehicle option source effect The differential impact the advertising exposure will have on the same audience member if the exposure occurs in one media option rather than another.

vertical cooperative advertising A cooperative arrangement under which a manufacturer pays for a portion of the advertising a retailer runs to promote the manufacturer's product and its availability in the retailer's place of business.

video news release (VNR) News story produced by publicists so that television stations may air it as news.

video on demand (VOD) Video clips of various entertainment activities, which include ads or are sponsored, are also available through the Internet.

viral marketing The act of propagating marketing-relevant messages through the help and cooperation of individual consumers.

virtual and augmented reality View of the real-world environment supplemented by computer-generated sensory input.

voiceover A message or action on the screen in a commercial that is narrated or described by a narrator who is not visible.

want A felt need shaped by a person's knowledge, culture, and personality.

waste coverage A situation where the coverage of the media exceeds the target audience.

wearout The tendency for a television or radio commercial to lose its effectiveness when it is seen and/or heard repeatedly.

webisode Short featured film created by the advertiser.

Wheeler-Lea Amendment An act of Congress passed in 1938 that amended section 5 of the FTC Act to read that unfair methods of competition in commerce and unfair or deceptive acts or practices in commerce are declared unlawful.

word-of-mouth (WOM) communications Social channels of communication such as friends, neighbors, associates, coworkers, or family members.

zapping The use of a remote control device to change channels and switch away from commercials.

zero-based communications planning An approach to planning the integrated marketing communications program that involves determining what tasks need to be done and what marketing communication functions should be used to accomplish them and to what extent.

zipping Fast-forwarding through commercials during the playback of a program previously recorded on DVR.

Endnotes

Chapter 1

1. Emilia Kirk, "Looking Toward the Future of Advertising," *Forbes*, December 21, 2021, www.forbes.com/sites/forbesbusinessdevelopmentcouncil/2021/12/13/looking-toward-the-future-of-advertising/?sh=2f4240e53c87; Don Schultz, "The Future of Advertising or Whatever We're Going to Call It," *Journal of Advertising* 45, no. 3 (July 2016), pp. 276–85.

2. Robert J. Coen, *Insider's Report: Robert Coen Presentation on Advertising Expenditures*, (New York: Universal McCann, McCann Erickson Worldwide, December 2002).

3. "Traditional Media Resilient Through Economic Uncertainty—Social Media Stalls Under Headwinds," *MAGNA Global Ad Forecast*, December 4, 2022, www.magnaglobal.com/traditional-media-resilient-through-economic-uncertainty-social-media-stalls-under-headwinds/

4. Ibid.

5. Jessica Lis, "US Time Spent with Connected Devices 2022," *Insider Intelligence*, June 9, 2022, www.insiderintelligence.com/content/us-time-spent-with-connected-devices-2022.

6. Aleda Stam, "Magna Trims Industry Growth Expectations for 2022 2023 Amid Economic Worries," *Advertising Age*, December 4, 2022, www.adage.com/article/agency-news/magna-trims-industry-growth-expectations-2022-and-2023-amid-economic-worries/2456821.

7. Ethan Cramer Flood, "Worldwide Digital Ad Spending 2023," *Insider Intelligence*, January 9, 2023, www.insiderintelligence.com/content/worldwide-digital-ad-spending-2023.

8. "AMA Approves New Marketing Definition," *Marketing News*, March 1, 1985, p. 1

9. Richard P. Bagozzi, "Marketing as Exchange," *Journal of Marketing*, 39 (October 1975), pp. 32–39.

10. Lisa M. Keefe, "Marketing Defined," *Marketing News*, January 15, 2008, pp. 28–29.

11. Eric Almquist, John Senior and Nicholas Bloch, "The Elements of Value," *Harvard Business Review*, September 2016, pp. 47–53; Frederick E. Webster Jr., "Defining the New Marketing Concept," *Marketing Management* 3, no. 4 (1993), pp. 22–31.

12. Adrienne Ward Fawcett, "Integrated Marketing—Marketers Convinced: Its Time Has Arrived," *Advertising Age*, November 6, 1993, pp. S1–S2.

13. "Do Your Ads Need a SuperAgency?" *Fortune*, April 27, 1991, pp. 81–85; Faye Rice, "A Cure for What Ails Advertising?" *Fortune*, December 16, 1991, pp. 119–22.

14. Scott Hume, "Campus Adopts 'New' Advertising," *Advertising Age*, September 23, 1991, p. 17.

15. Don E. Schultz, "Integrated Marketing Communications: Maybe Definition Is in the Point of View," *Marketing News*, January 18, 1993, p. 17.

16. Jerry Kliatchko, "IMC 20 Years After: A Second Look at Definitions," *International Journal of Integrated Marketing Communications*, 2009 (Fall), pp. 7–12.

17. Nancy Olson, "Montblanc's What Moves You Makes You Campaign Introduces New 'Mark Makers'," *Forbes*, August 24, 2021, www.forbes.com/sites/nancyolson/2021/08/24/montblancs-what-moves-you-makes-you-campaign-introduces-new-mark-makers/

18. Joe P. Cornelissen and Andrew R. Lock, "Theoretical Concept or Management Fashion? Examining the Significance of IMC," *Journal of Advertising Research*, September/October 2000, pp. 7–15.

19. Philip J. Kitchen, Joanne Brignell, Tao Li, and Graham Spickett Jones, "The Emergence of IMC: A Theoretical Perspective," *Journal of Advertising Research*, March 2004, pp. 19–30.

20. Don E. Schultz, "IMC Receives More Appropriate Definition," *Marketing News*, September 15, 2004, pp. 8–9.

21. "Edwina Luck and Jennifer Moffatt," IMC: Has Anything Really Changed? A New Perspective on an Old Definition," *Journal of Marketing Communications*, Vol. 15, No. 5, December 2009, pp. 311–325.

22. Tom Duncan and Sandra E. Moriarty, "A Communication-Based Model for Managing Relationships," *Journal of Marketing* 62, no. 2 (April 1998), pp. 1–13.

23. Anthony J. Tortorici, "Maximizing Marketing Communications through Horizontal and Vertical Orchestration," *Public Relations Quarterly* 36, no. 1 (1991), pp. 20–22.

24. Emily Steel, "Advertising's Brave New World: Different Lineup of Players Emerges with Online's Rise," *The Wall Street Journal*, May 25, 2007, p. B1.

25. Hilde A. M. Voorveld, "Brand Communication in Social Media: A Research Agenda," *Journal of Advertising* 48, no. 1 (January–March 2019), pp. 14–26; W. Glynn Mangold and David J. Faulds, "Social Media: The New Hybrid Element of the Promotion Mix," *Business Horizons* 52, no. 4 (July/August 2009), pp. 52, 357–65.

26. Sreedhar Madhavaram and Robetrt E. Mcdonald, "Integrated Marketing Communication (IMC) and Brand Identity as Critical Components of Brand Equity," *Journal of Advertising*, Vol. 34, no. 4 (Winter 2005), pp. 69–80.

27. Jerry Kliatchko, "Revisiting the IMC Construct," *International Journal of Advertising*, 27 (1), (2008), pp. 133–160.

28. Lisa Du and Ellen Milligan, "Gen Zero," *Bloomberg Businessweek*, April 29, 2019, pp. 18–19; Adrianne Pasquarelli, "Marketers' Millennial Dilemma," *Advertising Age*, August 21, 2017, pp. 12–15.

29. Brian Dean, "Ad Blocker Usage and Demographic Statistics in 2022," *Backlinko*, March 9, 2021, www.backlinko.com/ad-blockers-users.

30. Stephen Shankland, "Ad Blocking Surges as Millions Seek Privacy, Security and Less Annoyance," *CNET*, May 3, 2021, www.cnet.com/news/privacy/ad-blocking-surges-as-millions-more-seek-privacy-security-and-less-annoyance.

31. Ibid.

32. Garett Sloane, "Spotify Tells Users with Ad Blockers to Get Lost," *Advertising Age*, February 2, 2019, www.adage.com/article/digital/spotify-tells-users-ad-blockers-lost/316593.

33. Expert Panel, "15 Key Marketing Trends Brands Need to Take Note of in 2022," *Forbes*, April 29, 2022, www.forbes.com/sites/forbesagencycouncil/2022/04/29/15-key-marketing-trends-brands-need-to-take-note-of-in-2022/; Bob Garfield, "The Chaos Scenario 2.0: The Post Advertising Age," *Advertising Age*, March 26, 2007, pp. 1, 12–14; Sergio Zyman, *The End of Marketing as We Know It* (New York: Harper Business, 1999).

34. Kevin Lane Keller, "The Brand Report Card," *Harvard Business Review* 78, no. 1 (January/February 2000), pp. 3–10.

35. Kevin Lane Keller, "Conceptualizing, Measuring, and Managing Customer-Based Brand Equity," *Journal of Marketing*, 57 (January 1993), pp. 1–22.

36. Doug Levy and Bob Garfield, "The Dawn of the Relationship Era," *Advertising Age*, January 2, 2013, pp. 1, 8–11.

37. Andrea Prothero, Susan Dobscha, Jim Freund, William E. Kilbourne, Michael G. Luchs, Lucie K. Ozanne, and John Thøgersen, "Sustainable Consumption: Opportunities for Consumer Research and Public Policy," *Journal of Public Policy & Marketing* 30, no. 1 (2011), pp. 31–38.

38. Rajeev Batra and Kevin Lane Keller, "Integrating Marketing Communications: New Findings, New Lessons, and New Ideas," *Journal of Marketing*, (November 2016), *80* (6), 122–145. https://doi.org/10.1509/jm.15.0419

39. Michael L. Ray, *Advertising and Communication Management* (Englewood Cliffs, NJ: Prentice Hall, 1982).

40. Ralph S. Alexander, ed., *Marketing Definitions* (Chicago: American Marketing Association, 1965), p. 9.

41. Parker Herren, "What TV Ads Cost in The 2022–23 Season," *Advertising Age*, October 26, 2022, www.adage.com/article/media/tv-commercial-prices-advertising-costs-2022-23-season/2437106.

42. Christine Moorman, Megan Ryan and Nadar Tavasolli, "Why Marketers Are Returning to Traditional Advertising," *Harvard Business Review*, April 29, 2022, www.hbr.org/2022/04/why-marketers-are-returning-to-traditional-advertising

43. Rance Crain, "Why Business-to-Business Advertising Is Increasingly Also Aimed at Consumers," *Advertising Age*, June 17, 2012, http://adage.com/article/rance-crain/b-b-advertising-increasingly-aimed-consumers/235413/.

44. Daniel Newman, "What You Need to Know About Omni-channel Marketing," *Entrepreneur*, September 21, 2015, www.entrepreneur.com/article/250833.

45. Barbara Conners, "Use CRM Data to Build Relevance—and Avoid Message Overload," *Advertising Age*, August 13, 2013, http://adage.com/article/datadriven-marketing/making-crm-data-work-avoiding-offer-overload/243441/.

46. *Internet World Stats: Usage and Population: Statistics 2022.* www.internetworldstats.com/stats.htm

47. Miley A Vogels, Risa Gelles-Watnick and Navid Massarat, "Teens, Social Media and Technology 2022," *Pew Research Center*, August 10, 2022, www.pewresearch.org/internet/2022/08/10/teens-social-media-and-technology-2022.

48. Todd Powers, Dorothy Advincula, Manila S. Austin, Stacy Graiko, and Jasper Snyder, "Digital and Social Media in the Purchase Decision Process: A Special Report from the Advertising Research Foundation," *Journal of Advertising Research* 52, no. 4 (December 2012), pp. 479–89.

49. "US Mobile Advertising Growth (2017–2026)" *Oberlo*, www.oberlo.com/statistics/mobile-advertising-growth.

50. Jennifer Valentino-Devries and Jeremy Singer-Vine, "They Know What You're Shopping For," *The Wall Street Journal*, December 7, 2012, pp. C1, C2.

51. Jennifer Valentino-Devries, Jeremy Singer-Vine, and Ashkan Soltani, "Websites Vary Prices, Deals Based on Users' Information," *The Wall Street Journal*, December 24, 2012, pp. A1, A10.

52. "2020 Marketing Spending Industry Study," *Cadent Consulting Group*, www.cadentcg.com/wp-content/uploads/2020-Marketing-Spending-Industry-Study.pdf.

53. Ryan Mac and Sheera Frenkel, "No More Apologies: Inside Facebook's Push to Defend Its Image," *The New York Times*, November 10, 2021, www.nytimes.com/2021/09/21/technology/zuckerberg-facebook-project-amplify.html

54. "About Public Relations," *Publication Relations Society of America*, www.prsa.org/aboutprsa/publicrelationsdefined/#.V5-nz4MrJaQ.

55. Jooyoung Kim, Hye Jin Yoon, and Sun Young Lee, "Integrating Advertising and Publicity," *Journal of Advertising* 39, no. 1 (Spring 2010), pp. 97–114; Paul Holmes, "Marketers See a Greater Role for Public Relations in the Marketing Mix," *Advertising Age*, January 24, 2005, pp. C4–C10; Jack Neff, "Ries' Thesis: Ads Don't Build Brands, PR Does," *Advertising Age*, July 15, 2002, pp. 14–15.

56. Tom Duncan, *Principles of Advertising & IMC*, 2nd ed. (New York: McGraw Hill/Irwin, 2005).

57. Ibid.

58. Daniel Newman, "The Role of Paid, Owned and Owned Media in Your Marketing Strategy," *Forbes*, December 3, 2014, www.forbes.com/sites/danielnewman/2014/12/03/the-role-of-paid-owned-and-earned-media-in-your-marketing-strategy/#112ddfd411d3.

59. Avery Hartmans, "Brands Like White Claw and Truly Changed the Way Americans Drink. But a Crowded Market and Changing Consumer Behavior May have Officially Ended the Hard Seltzer Craze," *Business Insider*, October 30, 2021, www.businessinsider.nl/brands-like-white-claw-and-truly-changed-the-way-americans-drink-but-a-crowded-market-and-changing-consumer-behavior-may-have-officially-ended-the-hard-seltzer-craze.

60. Anatoli Colicev, Ashwin Malshe, Koen Pauwels, and Peter O'Conor, "Improving Consumer and Shareholder Value through Social Media: The Different Roles of Owned and Earned Media," *Journal of Marketing* 82 (January 2018), pp. 37–56.

Chapter 2

1. "Chocolate Milk Market Size in 2022 by Fastest Growing Companies: Nestle SA, Arla Foods, Dean Foods with Top Countries Data" www.marketwatch.com, February 24, 2022.

2. "Global Luxury goods Market Report 2022: Watches & Jewelry Segment to

Reach $58.2 Billion by 2026," www
.ResearchandMarkets.com, March 21,
2022.

3. Charisse Jones, "Call It a Comeback but
   Hot Brands Fila, Dr. Martens, Polaroid
   Have Been Here for Years," *USA Today*,
   March 12, 2018, www.usatoday.com.
4. "National Beer Sales & Production
   Data," www.brewersassociation.org,
   May 20, 2022.
5. "AARP's Audience," 2022, www
   .advertise.AARP.org.
6. Jamie Beckland, "The End of
   Demographics: How Marketers Are
   Going Deeper with Personal Data,"
   Mashable, June 30, 2011, www
   .mashable.com.
7. Edward M. Tauber, "Research on Food
   Consumption Values Finds Four
   Market Segments: Good Taste Still
   Tops," *Marketing News*, May 15, 1981,
   p. 17; Rebecca C. Quarles, "Shopping
   Centers Use Fashion Lifestyle
   Research to Make Marketing
   Decisions," *Marketing News*, January
   22, 1982, p. 18; "Our Auto, Ourselves,"
   Consumer Reports, June 1985, p. 375.
8. Beckland, "The End of Demographics."
9. Andrew M. Carlo, "The Comfort
   Zone," *Home Channel News*, May 24,
   2004, pp. 3, 29; Davis A. Aaker and
   John G. Myers, *Advertising
   Management*, 3rd ed. (Englewood
   Cliffs, NJ: Prentice Hall, 1987), p. 125.
10. Jack Trout and Al Ries, "Positioning
    Cuts through Chaos in the
    Marketplace," *Advertising Age*, May 1,
    1972, pp. 51–53.
11. Jack Trout, "Branding Can't Exist
    without Positioning," *Advertising Age*,
    March 14, 2005, p. 28.
12. *Ayer's Dictionary of Advertising
    Terms* (Philadelphia: Ayer Press,
    1976).
13. David A. Aaker and J. Gary Shansby,
    "Positioning Your Product," *Business
    Horizons*, May/June 1982, pp. 56–62.
14. Aaker and Myers, *Advertising
    Management*.
15. J. Paul Peter and Jerry C. Olson,
    Consumer Behavior (Burr Ridge, IL:
    Irwin, 1987), p. 505.
16. Michael R. Solomon, "The Role of
    Products as Social Stimuli: A Symbolic
    Interactionism Perspective," *Journal of
    Consumer Research*, December 10,
    1983, pp. 319–329.
17. Don E. Schultz, Stanley I.
    Tannenbaum, and Robert F.
    Lauterborn, *Integrated Marketing
    Communications* (Lincolnwood, IL:
    NTC Publishing Group, 1993), p. 72.
18. Samantha Bomkamp, "Wrigley Wants
    Gum to Stick Out in Checkout Line,"
    San Diego Union Tribune, Jan 18, 2016,
    pp. C1, 3.
19. Peter and Olson, *Consumer Behavior*,
    p. 571.
20. Jack Neff, "Study: TV Spots Reduce
    Consumers' Sensitivity to Price
    Change," *Advertising Age*, October 10,
    2007.
21. Roger A. Kerin, Steven W. Hartley,
    Eric N. Berkowitz, and William
    Rudelius, *Marketing*, 8th ed. (Burr
    Ridge, IL: Irwin/McGraw Hill, 2006).
22. David W. Stewart, Gary L. Frazier,
    and Ingrid Martin, "Integrated
    Channel Management: Merging the
    Communication and Distribution
    Functions of the Firm," in *Integrated
    Communication: Synergy of Persuasive
    Voices*, Esther Thorson and Jeri
    Moore, eds. (Mahwah, NJ: Erlbaum,
    1996), pp. 185–215.
23. Varun Madan, Raghay Ranjan, and
    Vishal Garga, "The D2C Imperative
    in the Wake of the Pandemic,"
    www.Deloitte.com, September 1,
    2021, p. 3.

Chapter 3

1. Jade Yan, "Pernod Ricard USA Hires
   Four Multicultural Agencies,"
   Advertising Age, June 16, 2022, www
   .adage.com/article/marketing-news-
   strategy/pernod-ricard-usa-hires-
   four-multicultural-agencies/2420476.
2. Jack Neff, "P&G Redefines the Brand
   Manager," *Advertising Age*, October 13,
   1997, pp. 1, 18, 20.
3. Thomas J. Cosse and John E. Swan,
   "Strategic Marketing Planning by
   Product Managers—Room for
   Improvement?" *Journal of Marketing*
   47 (Summer 1983), pp. 92–102.
4. "Behind the Tumult at P&G," *Fortune*,
   March 7, 1994, pp. 74–82; "Category
   Management: New Tools Changing
   Life for Manufacturers, Retailers,"
   Marketing News, September 25, 1989,
   pp. 2, 19.
5. Timothy Dewhirst and Brad Davis,
   "Brand Strategy and Integrated
   Marketing Communications," *Journal
   of Advertising* 34, no. 4 (Winter 2005),
   pp. 81–92.
6. Cosse and Swan, "Strategic Marketing
   Planning by Product Managers."
7. Victor P. Buell, *Organizing for
   Marketing/Advertising Success*
   (New York: Association of National
   Adver-tisers, 1982).
8. Jean Halliday, "GM Puts Final Nail in
   Coffin of Brand-Management Effort,"
   Advertising Age, April 5, 2004, p. 8.
9. Jack Neff, "Why It's Time to Do Away
   with the Brand Manager," *Advertising
   Age*, October 12, 2009, http://adage
   .com/print?article_id=139593; Tom
   Hinkes, "Our Biggest Brands Can No
   Longer Be Managed by Nerds,"
   Advertising Age, March 17, 2010,
   www.adage.com/article/cmo-strategy/
   biggest-brands-longer-managed-
   nerds/142841/.
10. Jenna Schnuer, "How to Manage Your
    Brand's Social Life," *Advertising Age*,
    April 23, 2012, http://adage.com/
    article/digital/manage-brand-s-social-
    life/234309/; Douglas Holt, "Branding
    in the Age of Social Media," *Harvard
    Business Review*, (March 2016), www
    .hbr.org/2016/03/branding-in-the-age-of-
    social-media.
11. Rupal Parekh, "Thinking of Pulling a
    CareerBuilder? Pros and Cons of
    Bringing an Account In-House,"
    Advertising Age, May 18, 2009, http://
    adage.com/article/agency-news/pros-
    cons-house-careerbuilder/136701/.
12. Ibid.
13. Adrianne Pasquarelli, "New Report
    Cites Skyrocketing Growth of Internal
    Agencies," *Advertising Age*, October 15,
    2018, www.adage.com/article/cmo-
    strategy/report-cites-skyrocketing-
    growth-internal-agencies/315253;
    Bruce Horovitz, "Some Companies
    Say the Best Ad Agency Is No Ad
    Agency at All," *Los Angeles Times*,
    July 19, 1989, sec. IV, p. 5.
14. Ilyse Liffering, "Chobani CCO Lee
    Maschmeyer on Cutting Out Creative
    Agencies: 'We Can Make Our Dollars
    Work Harder,'" *Digiday*, February 13,
    2018, www.digiday.com/social/
    chobani-cco-lee-maschmeyer-cutting-
    creative-agencies-can-make-dollars-
    work-harder.
15. Olivia Morley, "Whirlpool Corp Shifts
    Entire Creative Investment and
    Launches Expansive in-House
    Agency," *Adweek*, May 22, 2023, www
    .adweek.com/agencies/whirlpool-corp-
    shifts-entire-creative-investment-and-
    launches-expansive-in-house-agency.
16. Joan Voight, "The Outsiders," *Adweek*,
    October 4, 2004, pp. 32–35.
17. Jeff Beer, "How Under Armour Uses a
    Scrappy Outsider Will to Get What It
    Wants," *FastCoCreate*, August 31, 2015,
    www.fastcocreate.com/3050420/behind-
    the-brand/how-under-armour-uses-a-
    scrappy-outsider-will-to-get-what-it-wants.

18. Olivia Morley, "State of In-House Agencies: Why They Aren't Expected to Shrink Anytime Soon," *Adweek*, December 21, 2021, www.adweek.com/agencies/state-of-in-house-agencies-why-they-arent-expected-to-shrink-anytime-soon.

19. "Ad Age Agency Report 2022," *Advertising Age*, April 25, 2022, www.adage.com/article/datacenter/agency-report-2022-whats-inside/2412576.

20. Sally Goll Beatty, "Global Needs Challenge Midsize Agencies," *The Wall Street Journal*, December 14, 1995, p. B9.

21. "Ad Age Agency Report 2022."

22. Bradley Johnson, "How Agency Revenue Growth Soared—And What It Means for the Industry," *Advertising Age*, April 25, 2022, www.adage.com/article/datacenter/agency-report-2022-how-agency-revenue-growth-soared/2411026.

23. Bob Lammons, "A Good Account Exec Makes a Big Difference," *Marketing News*, June 3, 1996, p. 12.

24. Maureen Morrison, "Wanted: Not Your Dad's Account Man," *Advertising Age*, May 2, 2016, pp. 36–37; Matthew Creamer, "The Demise of the Suit," *Advertising Age*, March 13, 2006, pp. 1, 41.

25. Phil Johnson, "A Vision for the Future of Account Management," *Advertising Age*, March 24, 2010, www.adage.com/article/small-agency-diary/account-management-entrepreneurs-suits/142947.

26. Jon Steel, *Truth, Lies & Advertising: The Art of Account Planning* (New York: Wiley, 1998).

27. Quote in Alice Z. Cuneo, "Account Planners at a Crossroads," *Advertising Age*, July 30, 2007, http://adage.com/article/news/account-planners-a-crossroads/119558/.

28. 4As Jay Chiat Awards, www.jaychiat.aaaa.org.

29. Jeff Beer, "Just Doing It," *Fast Company*, February 2019, pp. 73–78.

30. Emmy Liederman, "Why Do Agencies Stay Independent?," *Adweek*, August 11, 2022, www.adweek.com/agencies/why-do-agencies-stay-independent.

31. Mike Shields, "Programmatic for Dummies," *Adweek*, November 4, 2013, pp. 20–25.

32. Ashish Chordia, "Programmatic TV Future Coming into Focus Slowly, but Surely," *MediaPost*, May 6, 2018, www.mediapost.com/publications/article/318812/programmatic-tv-future-coming-into-focus-slowly-b.html.

33. Kendra Clark, "WPP Has a Coke and a Smile after Winning $4bn Pitch Prize," *The Drum*, November 8, 2021, www.thedrum.com/news/2021/11/08/wpp-has-coke-and-smile-after-winning-4bn-pitch-prize.

34. *Trends in Agency Compensation*, 17th Edition. (New York: Association of National Advertisers, 2017).

35. Alexandra Bruell, "It's Not Just Cyclical: Industry Change Is Driving Marketing Giants to Review Media Agencies," *Advertising Age*, May 12, 2015, www.adage.com/article/agency-news/industry-change-drives-massive-media-agency-reviews/298579.

36. *Trends in Agency Compensation*, 18th Edition (New York: Association of National Advertisers, 2022), www.ana.net/miccontent/show/id/rr-2022-11-ana-trends-in-agency-compensation.

37. Kate Maddox, "Fee-Based Model Dominant in Global Agency Compensation," *BtoB Magazine*, September 17, 2012, www.btobonline.com/article/20120917/AGENCIES/309179973/fee-based-model-dominant-in-global-agency-compensation.

38. Chris Kuenne, "Why Ad Agencies Need to Embrace Value-Based Compensation," *Advertising Age*, March 22, 2010, http://adage.com/article/agency-news/ad-agencies-embrace-based-compensation/142915/.

39. Michael J. Fanuele, "Let's Be Fans: How Clients Get the Best from Agencies," *Advertising Age*, May 29, 2019, www.adage.com/article/opinion/lets-be-fans-how-clients-get-best-agencies/2174331; Rupal Parekh, "ANA Survey: 52% of Marketers Will Ask Agencies to Lower Internal Costs," *Advertising Age*, April 2, 2012, www.adage.com/article/cmo-strategy/survey-majority-marketers-shops-lower-costs/233880/.

40. Jason Notte, "As Agencies and Brand Define the Value of Their Work, Compensation Models Merit Closer Scrutiny," *Adweek*, January 19, 2023, www.adweek.com/brand-marketing/agencies-brands-define-work-compensation-closer-scrutiny; Lindsay Stein, "How Much Are Your Ideas Worth?," *Advertising Age*, November 13, 2017, pp. 24–25

41. Alexandra Bruell, "In Unilateral Decision, ANA Hire Two Firms to Probe Agency Rebates," *Advertising Age*, October 26, 2015, pp. 2, 4.

42. David Beals, *Agency Compensation Methods: An ANA Guidebook*, Fourth Edition, January 21, 2022, www.ana.net/miccontent/show/id/aa-2022-01-agency-compentation-methods.

43. Jack Neff, "ANA Survey: Agency-Performance Reviews Are Now Business as Usual," *Advertising Age*, September 14, 2009, http://adage.com/article/agency-news/ana-surveyagency-performance-reviews-business-usual/138983/.

44. *Report on the Agency-Advertiser Value Survey*, American Association of Advertising Agencies and Association of National Advertisers, August 2007.

45. Tim Williams and Ronald Baker, "New Value-Based Comp Model Needed," *Advertising Age*, June 11, 2007, http://adage.com/article/cmo-strategy/based-comp-model-needed/117143/.

46. Lindsay Stein, "Love Me Tender: Why Agencies and Clients Stay—and Why They Stray," *Advertising Age*, February 12, 2016, www.adage.com/article/agency-news/longstanding-agency-client-relationships-highs-lows/302674.

47. Brian Bonilla, "12 Notable Agency Breakups of 2021," *Advertising Age*, December 21, 2021, www.adage.com/article/year-review/2021-review-12-notable-agency-breakups/2387906.

48. Lindsay Stein, "Deloitte's Heat Wins the Global Creative Account for John Hancock and Manulife," *Advertising Age*, July 3, 2017, www.adage.com/article/agency-news/deloitte-s-heat-wins-john-hancock-manulife-global-creative/309746.

49. Rupal Parekh, "Why the Client–Agency Bond Just Isn't What It Used to Be," *Advertising Age*, February 14, 2011, http://adage.com/article/agency-news/long-term-ad-agency-client-bonds-a-rarity/148787/.

50. Maureen Morrison, "Marketing Executives Reveal What They Want from Strong Client–Agency Relationship," *Advertising Age*, July 18, 2012, www.adage.com/article/cmo-strategy/marketers-ad-agency-relationships/236100/; "How to Be a Better Agency Client," *Advertising Age*, January 9, 2012, pp. 8, 9; Kathleen Sampley, "Love's Labors Lost: Behind the Breakups," *Adweek*, August 1, 2005, p. 8; Fred Beard, "Marketing Client Role Ambiguity as a Source of Dissatisfaction in Client–Ad Agency Relationships," *Journal of Advertising Research*, September/October 1996, pp. 9–20; Paul Michell, Harold Cataquet, and

Stephen Hague, "Establishing the Causes of Disaffection in Agency–Client Relations," *Journal of Advertising Research* 32, no. 2 (1992), pp. 41–48; Peter Doyle, Marcel Corstiens, and Paul Michell, "Signals of Vulnerability in Agency–Client Relations," *Journal of Marketing* 44 (Fall 1980), pp. 18–23.

51. E.J. Schultz, "Big Beer Churns Through Agencies," *Advertising Age*, August 24, 2015, p. 6.

52. Joan Voight and Wendy Melillo, "Study: Clients Want Multiple Partners," *Adweek*, May 14, 2007, pp. 20–21.

53. Alvin J. Silk, "Conflict Policy and Advertising Agency–Client Relations: The Problem of Competing Clients Sharing a Common Agency," *Working Knowledge, Harvard Business School Working Paper Number 12-104*, May 31, 2012, www.hbswk.hbs.edu/item/7021.html.

54. Mike Kapetanovic, "Surviving a Recession—How Agencies Can Continue to Grow and Become More Resilient," *Advertising Age*, August 1, 2022, www.adage.com/article/opinion/surviving-recession-how-agencies-can-continue-grow-and-become-more-resilient.

55. Jack Neff, "Why Spec Creative Should Go Away but Won't," *Advertising Age*, January 9, 2012, pp. 10, 11.

56. Jennifer Comiteau, "What Agencies Think of Search Consultants," *Adweek*, August 4, 2003, pp. 14–16.

57. Fred K. Beard, "Exploring the Use of Advertising Agency Review Consultants," *Journal of Advertising Research* 42, no. 1 (January/February) 2002, pp. 39–50.

58. E.J. Schultz, "The New Pitch Process: Shorter, Faster, Better," *Advertising Age*, April 2, 2018, pp. 22–23.

59. Ann-Christine Diaz, "Mischief Is Agency of the Year," *Advertising Age*, March 14, 2022, pp. 8–9; Jameson Fleming, "Here Are Adweek's 2022 Agency of the Year Winners," *Adweek*, December 11, 2022, https://www.adweek.com/agencies/here-are-adweeks-2022-agency-of-the-year-winners/

60. Jack Neff, "Ries' Thesis: Ads Don't Build Brands, PR Does," *Advertising Age*, July 15, 2002, pp. 14–15; Prema Nakra, "The Changing Role of Public Relations in Marketing Communications," *Public Relations Quarterly* 1 (1991), pp. 42–45.

61. Natalie Mortimer, "Dan Wieden Digital Revolution Will 'Transform Us or Render Us Inert'," *The Drum*, March 4, 2015, www.adweek.com/agencies/video-who-we-picked-for-our-agencies-of-the-year-and-why-we-picked-them.

62. Betsy Spathmann, "Sudden Impact," *Promo*, April 1999, pp. 42–48.

63. Quoted in Laura Q. Hughes and Kate MacArthur, "Soft Boiled," *Advertising Age*, May 28, 2001, pp. 3, 54.

64. Study cited in Michael Bush, "Memo to Marketers: It's Your Fault If Your Shops Flounder," *Advertising Age*, March 29, 2010, http://adage.com/article/cmo-strategy/marketers-fault-ad-agencies-flounder/143010/.

65. William N. Swain, "Perceptions of IMC after a Decade of Development: Who's at the Wheel and How Can We Measure Success?" *Journal of Advertising Research*, March 2004, pp. 46–67; Philip J. Kitchen and Don E. Schultz, "A Multi-Country Comparison of the Drive for IMC," *Journal of Advertising Research* 39, no. 1 (January 1999), pp. 21–38.

66. Mart Ots and Gergely Nyilasy, "Integrated Marketing Communications (IMC): Why Does It Fail?" *Journal of Advertising Research*, June 2015, pp. 132–145.

67. Lindsay Stein, "Agency of the Future: Survival of the Fittest," *Advertising Age*, April 2, 2018, www.adage.com/article/news/agency-future-survival-fittest/312949; David N. McArthur and Tom Griffin, "A Marketing Management View of Integrated Marketing Communications," *Journal of Advertising Research* 37, no. 5 (September/October) 1997, pp. 19–26; Adrienne Ward Fawcett, "Integrated Marketing—Marketers Convinced: Its Time Has Arrived," *Advertising Age*, November 6, 1993, pp. S1–S2.

68. Voight and Melillo, "Study: Clients Want Multiple Partners."

69. Quoted in Michael Bush, "Memo to Marketers: It's Your Fault If Your Shops Flounder," *Advertising Age*, March 2, 2010.

70. Tim Williams, "A Mind Map of the 2020 Agency," *Ignition Consulting Group*, May 27, 2015, www.ignitiongroup.com/propulsion-blog-post/mind-map-foundations-of-the-2020-agency.

Chapter 4

1. Dirk Zeims, "The Morphological Approach for Unconscious Consumer Motivation Research," *Journal of Advertising Research* 44, no. 2 (June 2004), pp. 210–215.

2. Jeffrey Ball, "But How Does It Make You Feel?" *The Wall Street Journal*, May 3, 1999, p. B1.

3. Ernest Dichter, *Getting Motivated* (New York: Pergamon Press, 1979).

4. Ball, "But How Does It Make You Feel?"

5. Gary Strauss, "TV Sex: Uncut, Unavoidable," *USA Today*, January 20, 2010, p. 1.

6. Business.com Editorial Staff, "Get a Whiff of This: Research Proves Marketing with a Scent Increases Sales," *Business.com*, February 22, 2017, www.business.com.

7. Joanne Lipman, "Leaders Turning Up Their Noses at 'Scent Strips' Ads in Magazines," *The Wall Street Journal*, December 6, 1989, p. 1.

8. Sheree Johnson, "New Research Sheds Light on Daily Ad Exposures," *Insights*, September 29, 2014, www.insights.com.

9. David Raab, "How Many Ads Do You See Each Day? Fewer Than It Seems (I Think)," *Customer Experience Matrix*, September 29, 2015, www.customerexperiencematrix.blogspot.com.

10. Sam Carr, "How Many Ads Do We See a Day in 2022?" www.lunio.ai, February 15, 2021.

11. Nadia, "How Many Ads Do We See a Day?" www.siteefy.com, May 13, 2022.

12. Gordon W. Allport, "Attitudes," in *Handbook of Social Psychology*, C. M. Murchison, ed. (Winchester, MA: Clark University Press, 1935), p. 810.

13. Robert B. Zajonc and Hazel Markus, "Affective and Cognitive Factors in Preferences," *Journal of Consumer Research* 9, no. 2 (June 1982), pp. 123–31.

14. Joel B. Cohen, Paul W. Minniard, and Peter R. Dickson, "Information Integration: An Information Processing Perspective," in *Advances in Consumer Research* (vol. 7), Jerry C. Olson, ed. (Ann Arbor, MI: Association for Consumer Research, 1980), pp. 161–70.

15. Matt Egan, "The 2-Year Wells Fargo Horror Story Just Won't End," *CNN Money*, September 7, 2018, www.money.cnn.com.

16. Geoffrey James, "The 7 Epic Brand Disasters of 2021," *Inc.*, December 27, 2021, www.inc.com.

17. Jason Aten, "Listen Carefully to What Mark Zuckerberg Is Saying About Facebook's Crisis—and More Closely to What He Isn't," *Inc.*, October 26, 2021, www.inc.com.

18. James F. Engel, "The Psychological Consequences of a Major Purchase Decision," in *Marketing in Transition*, William S. Decker, ed. (Chicago: American Marketing Association, 1963), pp. 462–75.

19. Leon G. Schiffman and Leslie Lazar Kannuk, *Consumer Behavior*, 4th ed. (Englewood Cliffs, NJ: Prentice Hall, 1991), p. 192.

20. Gerald J. Gorn, "The Effects of Music in Advertising on Choice: A Classical Conditioning Approach," *Journal of Marketing* 46 (Winter 1982), pp. 94–101.

21. James J. Kellaris, Anthony D. Cox, and Dena Cox, "The Effect of Background Music on Ad Processing: A Contingency Explanation," *Journal of Marketing* 57, no. 4 (Fall 1993), p. 114.

22. Brian C. Deslauries and Peter B. Everett, "The Effects of Intermittent and Continuous Token Reinforcement on Bus Ridership," *Journal of Applied Psychology* 62 (August 1977), pp. 369–75.

23. Rakesh Kochhar, "Are You in the American Middle Class?" *Pew Research Center*, September 6, 2018.

24. Lyman E. Ostlund, "Role Theory and Group Dynamics," in *Consumer Behavior: Theoretical Sources*, Scott Ward and Thomas S. Robertson, eds. (Englewood Cliffs, NJ: Prentice Hall, 1973), pp. 230–75.

Chapter 5

1. Wilbur Schram, *The Process and Effects of Mass Communications* (Urbana: University of Illinois Press, 1955).

2. Ibid.

3. Maureen Morrison, "Starbucks' New Logo Signals Intent to 'Think Beyond Coffee,'" *Advertising Age*, January 5, 2011, http://adage.com/article/news/starbucks-logo-signals-intent-coffee/148020/.

4. Andrew Hampp and Rupal Parekh, "Gap to Scrap New Logo, Return to Old Design Plans to Announce Change of Company Facebook Page," *Advertising Age*, October 11, 2010, http://adage.com/article/news/gap-scrap-logo-return-design/146417/.

5. India Roby, "Megan Thee Stallion Lands Another Fashion Campaign with Coach," *Nylon*, January 25, 2022, www.nylon.com/fashion/coach-spring-2022-campaign-megan-thee-stallion-jennifer-lopez#.

6. Joseph T. Plummer, "Word-of-Mouth—A New Advertising Discipline?," *Journal of Advertising Research* 47, no. 4 (December 2007), pp. 385–86; Dee T. Allsop, Bryce R. Bassett, and James A. Hoskins, "Word-of-Mouth Research: Principles and Applications," *Journal of Advertising Research* 47, no. 4 (December 2007), pp. 398–411; Robert E. Smith and Christine A. Vogt, "The Effects of Integrating Advertising and Negative Word-of-Mouth Communications on Message Processing and Response," *Journal of Consumer Psychology* 4, no. 2 (1995), pp. 133–51; Barry L. Bayus, "Word of Mouth: The Indirect Effect of Marketing Efforts," *Journal of Advertising Research* 25, no. 3 (June/July 1985), pp. 31–39.

7. Andrew M. Baker and Naveen Donthu, "Word-of-Mouth Processes in Marketing New Products: Recent Research and Future Opportunities," in *Handbook of Research on New Product Development*, Peter N. Golder and Debanjan Mitra (eds). 2018, (Northhampton, MA: Edgar Elgar Publishing).

8. Yuping Liu-Thompkins, "Seeding Viral Content," *Journal of Advertising Research* 52, no. 4 (December 2012), pp. 465–78; Kate Niederhoffer, Rob Mooth, David Wiesenfeld, and Jonathon Gordon, "The Origin and Impact of CPG New-Product Buzz: Emerging Trends and Implications," *Journal of Advertising Research*, December 2007, pp. 420–26

9. "GoPro Marketing: A Lesson on How Market Leaders Are Made," *KIMP*, January 11, 2023, www.kimp.io/gopro-marketing/

10. Yuping Liu-Thompkins, "Seeding Viral Content."

11. Peter Suciu, "Advertisers Shouldn't Overlook Social Media Before or After The Super Bowl, *Forbes*, February 11, 2022, www.forbes.com/sites/petersuciu/2022/02/11/advertisers-shouldnt-overlook-social-media-before-or-after-the-super-bowl/?sh=4f998f6d40ce.

12. H. C. Chiu, Y. C. Hsieh, Y. H. Kao, and M. Lee, "The Determinants of Email Receivers' Disseminating Behaviors on the Internet," *Journal of Advertising Research* 47, no. 4 (December 2007), pp. 524–34; T. Sun, S. Y. G. Wu, and M. Kuntaraporn, "Online Word-of-Mouth (or Mouse): An Exploration of Its Antecedents and Consequences," *Journal of Computer-Mediated Communication* 11, no. 4 (2006).

13. J. Y. C. Ho and M. Dempsey, "Viral Marketing Motivations to Forward Online Content," *Journal of Business Research* 63, no. 9/10 (2010), pp. 1000–06; Z. Katona, P. Zubcsek, and M. Sarvary, "Network Effect and Personal Influences: Diffusion of an Online Social Network," *Journal of Marketing Research* 48, no. 3 (2011), pp. 425–43; M. Trusov, A. V. Bodpati, and R. E. Bucklin, "Determining Influential Users in Internet Social Networks," *Journal of Marketing Research* 47, no. 4 (2010), pp. 643–58.

14. "Why Some Videos Go Viral," *Harvard Business Review*, September 2015, pp. 34–35.

15. Yuping Liu-Thompkins, "Seeding Viral Content."

16. Chen Lou, "Social Media Influencers and Followers: Theorization of a Trans-Parasocial Relation and Explication of Its Implications for Influencer Advertising," *Journal of Advertising* 51, no. 1 (2022), pp. 4–21 DOI: 10.1080/00913367.2021.1880345

17. Joachim Scholz, "How Consumers Consume Social Media Influence," *Journal of Advertising* 50, no. 5 (2021), pp. 510–27 DOI: 10.1080/00913367.2021.1980472

18. Werner Geyeser, "The State of Influencer Marketing 2022: Benchmark Report," *Influencer MarketingHub*, March 2, 2022, www.influencermarketinghub.com/ebooks/Influencer_Marketing_Benchmark_Report_2022.pdf.

19. *Aligning Marketers and Influencers: Shifting Perspectives on Influencer Marketing across the Funnel*, Impact.com/WARC, 2022, www.impact.com/press-releases/influencer-marketing-industry-research-report-warc/

20. Ed Keller and Brad Fay, "Word-of-Mouth Advocacy," *Journal of Advertising Research*, December 2012, pp. 459–64.

21. Ibid.

22. Ed Keller and Brad Fay, *The Face-to-Face Book: Why Real Relationships Rule in a Digital Marketplace* (New York: Free Press, 2012), pp. 103–06.

23. Taylor Evans and Mike Yagi, "New Study Reveals How Brand Conversations Influence Consumer Spending," *Advertising Age*, September 7, 2022, www.adage.com/article/twitter/

new-study-reveals-how-brand-conversations-influence-consumer-spending/242848.

24. Suzanne Vranica, "Getting Buzz Marketers to Fess Up," *The Wall Street Journal*, February 9, 2005, p. B9.

25. Ibid.

26. Keller and Fay, "Word-of-Mouth Advocacy."

27. Brad Fay and Rick Larkin, "Why Online Word-of-Mouth Measures Cannot Predict Brand Outcomes Offline: Volume, Sentiment, Sharing, and Influence Metrics Yield Scant Online–Offline WOM Correlations," *Journal of Advertising Research* 57, no, 2 (June 2017), pp. 132–143.

28. Quote by Gordon S. Bower in *Fortune*, October 14, 1985, p. 11.

29. Adrianne Pasquarelli, "The Other 'Ism'," *Advertising Age*, November 19, 2018, pp. 20–22; Ken Wheaton, "Think Twice Before You Kick All Those Middle Managers to the Curb," *Advertising Age*, March 21, 2016, p. 34.

30. Tiffany Hsu, "Older People Are Ignored and Distorted in Ageist Marketing, Report Finds," *The New York Times*, September 19, 2019, www.nytimes.com/2019/09/23/business/ageism-advertising-aarp.html.

31. Martin Eisend, "Older People in Advertising," *Journal of Advertising* 51, no. 3 (2022), pp. 308–22. DOI: 10.1080/00913367.2022.2027300

32. David Kirkpatrick, "EMarketer: 70% of US Adults 'Second Screen' while Watching TV," *MarketingDive*, November 8, 2017, www.marketingdive.com/news/emarketer-70-of-us-adults-second-screen-while-watching-tv/510341/.

33. "Most Digital Viewers Multitask While Watching Live TV," *eMarketer.com*, November 30, 2015, www.emarketer.com/Article/Most-Digital-Viewers-Multitask-While-Watching-Live-TV/1013281.

34. David Knox, "Survey: 91% of Viewers Multitask while Watching TV," *TV Tonight*, October 17, 2019, www.tvtonight.com.au/2019/10/survey-91-of-viewers-multitask-while-watching-tv.html.

35. Stephanie Prange, "Parrot Study: Major of Viewers Multitask While Watching TV," *MediaPlayNews*, August 19, 2018, www.mediaplaynews.com/parrot-study-majority-of-viewers-multitask-while-watching-tv/

36. Thomas V. Bonoma and Leonard C. Felder, "Nonverbal Communication in Marketing: Toward Communicational Analysis," *Journal of Marketing Research*, May 1977, pp. 169–80.

37. Jacob Jacoby and Wayne D. Hoyer, "Viewer Miscomprehension of Televised Communication: Selected Findings," *Journal of Marketing* 46, no. 4 (Fall 1982), pp. 12–26; Jacob Jacoby and Wayne D. Hoyer, "The Comprehension and Miscomprehension of Print Communications: An Investigation of Mass Media Magazines," *Advertising Education Foundation Study*, New York, 1987.

38. E. K. Strong, *The Psychology of Selling* (New York: McGraw Hill, 1925), p. 9.

39. Everett M. Rodgers, *Diffusion of Innovations* (New York: Free Press, 1962), pp. 79–86.

40. Robert J. Lavidge and Gary A. Steiner, "A Model for Predictive Measurements of Advertising Effectiveness," *Journal of Marketing* 24 (October 1961), pp. 59–62.

41. Thomas Barry, "The Development of the Hierarchy of Effects: An Historical Perspective," *Current Issues & Research in Advertising* 10, no. 2 (1987), pp. 251–95.

42. Herbert E. Krugman, "The Impact of Television Advertising: Learning without Involvement," *Public Opinion Quarterly* 29 (Fall 1965), pp. 349–56.

43. Scott A. Hawkins and Stephen J. Hoch, "Low-Involvement Learning: Memory without Evaluation," *Journal of Consumer Research* 19, no. 2 (September 1992), pp. 212–25.

44. Harry W. McMahan, "Do Your Ads Have VIP?" *Advertising Age*, July 14, 1980, pp. 50–51.

45. Robert E. Smith, "Integrating Information from Advertising and Trial: Processes and Effects on Consumer Response to Product Information," *Journal of Marketing Research* 30 (May 1993), pp. 204–19.

46. DeAnna S. Kempf and Russell N. Laczniak, "Advertising's Influence on Subsequent Product Trial Processing," *Journal of Advertising* 30, no. 3 (Fall 2001), pp. 27–38.

47. Judith L. Zaichkowsky, "Conceptualizing Involvement," *Journal of Advertising* 15, no. 2 (1986), pp. 4–14; Anthony G. Greenwald and Clark Leavitt, "Audience Involvement in Advertising: Four Levels," *Journal of Consumer Research* 11, no. 1 (June 1984), pp. 581–92; Richard Vaughn, "How Advertising Works: A Planning Model," *Journal of Advertising Research* 20, no. 5 (October 1980), pp. 27–33; Richard Vaughn, "How Advertising Works: A Planning Model Revisited," *Journal of Advertising Research* 26, no. 1 (February/March 1986), pp. 57–66.

48. Todd Powers, Dorothy Advincula, Manila S. Austin, Stacy Graiko, and Jasper Snyder, "Digital and Social Media in the Purchase Decision Process," *Journal of Advertising Research*, December 2012, pp. 479–89.

49. Roxane Divol, David Edelman, and Hugo Sarrazin, "Demystifying Social Media," *McKinsey Quarterly*, April 2012, www.mckinsey.com/insights/marketing_sales/demystifying_social_media.

50. Ibid.

51. David Court, Dave Elzinga, Susan Mulder, and Ole Jorgen Vetvik, "The Consumer Decision Journey," *McKinsey Quarterly*, June 2009, www.mckinsey.com/insights/marketing_sales/the_consumer_decision_journey.

52. Ibid.

53. Jerry C. Olson, Daniel R. Toy, and Phillip A. Dover, "Mediating Effects of Cognitive Responses to Advertising on Cognitive Structure," in *Advances in Consumer Research* (vol. 5), H. Keith Hunt, ed. (Ann Arbor, MI: Association for Consumer Research, 1978), pp. 72–78.

54. Anthony A. Greenwald, "Cognitive Learning, Cognitive Response to Persuasion and Attitude Change," in *Psychological Foundations of Attitudes*, A. G. Greenwald, T. C. Brock, and T. W. Ostrom, eds. (New York: Academic Press, 1968); Peter L. Wright, "The Cognitive Processes Mediating Acceptance of Advertising," *Journal of Marketing Research* 10 (February 1973), pp. 53–62; Brian Wansink, Michael L. Ray, and Rajeev Batra, "Increasing Cognitive Response Sensitivity," *Journal of Advertising* 23, no. 2 (June 1994), pp. 65–76.

55. Peter Wright, "Message Evoked Thoughts, Persuasion Research Using Thought Verbalizations," *Journal of Consumer Research* 7, no. 2 (September 1980), pp. 151–75.

56. Scott B. Mackenzie, Richard J. Lutz, and George E. Belch, "The Role of Attitude toward the Ad as a Mediator of Advertising Effectiveness: A Test of Competing Explanations," *Journal of Marketing Research* 23 (May 1986), pp. 130–43; Rajeev Batra and Michael L. Ray, "Affective Responses

Mediating Acceptance of Advertising," *Journal of Consumer Research* 13 (September 1986), pp. 234-49; Tim Ambler and Tom Burne, "The Impact of Affect on Memory of Advertising," *Journal of Advertising Research* 29, no. 3 (March/April 1999), pp. 25-34.

57. Edith G. Smits, Lex Van Meurs, and Peter C. Neijens, "Effects of Advertising Likeability: A 10-Year Perspective," *Journal of Advertising Research* 4, no. 1 (March 2006), pp. 73-83; Ronald Alsop, "TV Ads That Are Likeable Get Plus Rating for Persuasiveness," *The Wall Street Journal*, February 20, 1986, p. 23.

58. David J. Moore and William D. Harris, "Affect Intensity and the Consumer's Attitude toward High Impact Emotional Advertising Appeals," *Journal of Advertising* 25, no. 2 (Summer 1996), pp. 37-50; Andrew A. Mitchell and Jerry C. Olson, "Are Product Attribute Beliefs the Only Mediator of Advertising Effects on Brand Attitude?" *Journal of Marketing Research* 18 (August 1981), pp. 318-32.

59. David J. Moore, William D. Harris, and Hong C. Chen, "Affect Intensity: An Individual Difference Response to Advertising Appeals," *Journal of Consumer Research* 22 (September 1995), pp. 154-64; Julie Edell and Marian C. Burke, "The Power of Feelings in Understanding Advertising Effects," *Journal of Consumer Research* 14 (December 1987), pp. 421-33.

60. Richard E. Petty and John T. Cacioppo, "Central and Peripheral Routes to Persuasion: Application to Advertising," in *Advertising and Consumer Psychology*, Larry Percy and Arch Woodside, eds. (Lexington, MA: Lexington Books, 1983), pp. 3-23.

61. Ibid.

62. Richard E. Petty, John T. Cacioppo, and David Schumann, "Central and Peripheral Routes to Advertising Effectiveness: The Moderating Role of Involvement," *Journal of Consumer Research* 10 (September 1983), pp. 135-46.

63. Fred K. Beard, "Peer Evaluation and Readership of Influential Contributions to the Advertising Literature," *Journal of Advertising* 31, no. 4 (2002), pp. 65-75.

64. Philip J. Kitchen, Gayle Kerr, Don E. Schultz, Rod McColl, and Heather Pals, "The Elaboration Likelihood Model: Review, Critique and Research

Agenda," *European Journal of Marketing* 48, no. 11/12 (2014), pp. 2033-50; Catherine Cole, Richard Ettenson, Suzanne Reinke, and Tracy Schrader, "The Elaboration Likelihood Model (ELM): Replication, Extensions, and Some Conflicting Findings," *Advances in Consumer Research* 17 (1990), pp. 231-236.

65. Gayle Kerr, Don E. Schultz, Philip J. Kitchen, Frank J. Mulhern, and Park Beede, "Does Traditional Advertising Theory Apply to the Digital World?" *Journal of Advertising Research* 55, no. 1 (2015), pp. 1-11.

66. Demetrios Vakratsas and Tim Ambler, "How Advertising Works: What Do We Really Know?" *Journal of Marketing* 63 (January 1999), pp. 26-43.

67. Bruce F. Hall, "A New Model for Measuring Advertising Effects," *Journal of Advertising Research* 42, no. 2 (March/April 2002), pp. 23-31.

68. Thomas E. Barry, "In Defense of the Hierarchy of Effects: A Rejoinder to Weilbacher," *Journal of Advertising Research*, May/June 2002, pp. 44-47.

69. William M. Weilbacher, "Point of View: Does Advertising Cause a 'Hierarchy of Effects?,'" *Journal of Advertising Research* 41, no. 6 (November/December 2001), pp. 19-26.

Chapter 6

1. William J. McGuire, "An Information Processing Model of Advertising Effectiveness," in *Behavioral and Management Science in Marketing*, Harry J. Davis and Alvin J. Silk, eds. (New York: Ronald Press, 1978), pp. 156-80.

2. Selome Hailu and Jennifer Maas, "Yes, the CW's Average Viewer Is Actually 58—Here's How the Rest of Broadcast Stacks Up," *Variety*, August 17, 2022, www.variety.com/2022/tv/news/the-cw-age-average-viewer-broadcast-1235342962.

3. AFPRelaxnews, "Which TV Series Is the Gen Z and Millennial Favourite of 2021?," *Forbes India*, December 4, 2021, www.forbesindia.com/article/lifes/which-tv-series-is-the-gen-z-and-millennial-favourite-of-2021/71983/1.

4. Herbert C. Kelman, "Processes of Opinion Change," *Public Opinion Quarterly* 25 (Spring 1961), pp. 57-78.

5. William J. McGuire, "The Nature of Attitudes and Attitude Change," in

Handbook of Social Psychology (2nd ed.), G. Lindzey and E. Aronson, eds. (Cambridge, MA: Addison-Wesley, 1969), pp. 135-214; Daniel J. O'Keefe, "The Persuasive Effects of Delaying Identification of High- and Low-Credibility Communicators: A Meta-Analytic Review," *Central States Speech Journal* 38 (1987), pp. 63-72.

6. Roobina Ohanian, "The Impact of Celebrity Spokespersons' Image on Consumers' Intention to Purchase," *Journal of Advertising Research* 21 (February/March 1991), pp. 46-54.

7. Stephen W. Wang and Angeline Close Scheinbaum, "Enhancing Brand Credibility Via Celebrity Endorsement," *Journal of Advertising Research* 58, no. 1 (March 2018), pp. 16-32; Clinton Amos, Gary Holmes, and David Strutton, "Exploring the Relationship between Celebrity Endorser Effects and Advertising Effectiveness," *International Journal of Advertising* 27, no. 2 (2008), pp. 209-34.

8. "E-Score Celebrity Report 2022," E-Poll Market Research, www.blog.epollresearch.com/2022/10/12/e-score-celebrity-report-2022-2.

9. Ibid.

10. David P. Hamilton, "Celebrities Help 'Educate' Public on New Drugs," *The Wall Street Journal*, April 22, 2002, p. B1.

11. Ashley Rodriguez, "Best Practices: FTC Social Media Requirements," *Advertising Age*, April 21 2015, www.adage.com/article/cmo-strategy/practices-ftc-social-media-requirements/297950; Michael Learmonth, "FTC Cracks Down on Blogger Payola, Celebrity Tweets," *Advertising Age*, October 5, 2009, www.adage.com/article/digital/ftc-regulates-social-media-endorsements-blogger-payola/139457/.

12. Daniela Andreini, Marc Fetscherin, and Lia Zarantonello, "How a CEO's Personality, Performance, and Leadership Predict Advertising Credibility," *Journal of Advertising Research* 61, no. 1 (2021), pp. 110-124. DOI:10.2501/JAR-2020-003.

13. Frank Green, "Masters of the Pitch," *San Diego Union-Tribune*, January 30, 2000, pp. 1, 6.

14. Barbara Lippert, "A Winner out of the Gates," *Adweek*, September 22, 2008, p. 28.

15. Karlene Lukovitz, "Ads Starring CEOs: What Makes Winners, Losers?,"

Marketing Daily, March 13, 2012, www.mediapost.com/publications/article/170057.

16. Megan Mowery, "Our Timeline of the Papa John's Controversy Now Includes a Head-Scratching Website," *Advertising Age*, August 22, 2018, www.adage.com/article/digital/a-history-papa-john-s-controversy/314260.

17. Ben DiPietro, "Recent Controversies Spotlight Risks of Having CEO as Spokesman," *The Wall Street Journal*, July 24, 2018, www.wsj.com/riskandcompliance/2018/07/24/recent-controversies-spotlight-risks-of-having-ceo-as-spokesman; Rupal Parekh and Kunur Patel, "Ten Things to Think Hard about before Featuring the Chairman in Advertising," *Advertising Age*, September 14, 2009, www.adage.com/print?article_id=138984.

18. Nathalie Fleck-Dousteyssier, Géraldine Michel, and Valerie Zeiitoun," Brand Personification through the Use of Spokespeople: An Exploratory Study of Ordinary Employees, CEOs, and Celebrities Featured in Advertising," *Psychology and Marketing*, 31 (2014), pp. 84–92; Erick Reidenback and Robert Pitts, "Not All CEOs Are Created Equal as Advertising Spokespersons: Evaluating the Effective CEO Spokesperson," *Journal of Advertising* 20, no. 3 (1986), pp. 35–50.

19. Green, "Masters of the Pitch."

20. A. Eagly and S. Chaiken, "An Attribution Analysis of the Effect of Communicator Characteristics on Opinion Change," *Journal of Personality and Social Psychology* 32 (1975), pp. 136–44.

21. For a review of these studies, see Brian Sternthal, Lynn Philips, and Ruby Dholakia, "The Persuasive Effect of Source Credibility: A Situational Analysis," *Public Opinion Quarterly* 42 (Fall 1978), pp. 285–314.

22. Brian Sternthal, Ruby Dholakia, and Clark Leavitt, "The Persuasive Effects of Source Credibility: Tests of Cognitive Response," *Journal of Consumer Research* 4, no. 4 (March 1978), pp. 252–60; Robert R. Harmon and Kenneth A. Coney, "The Persuasive Effects of Source Credibility in Buy and Lease Situations," *Journal of Marketing Research* 19 (May 1982), pp. 255–60.

23. For a review, see Noel Capon and James Hulbert, "The Sleeper Effect: An Awakening," *Public Opinion Quarterly* 37 (1973), pp. 333–58.

24. Darlene B. Hannah and Brian Sternthal, "Detecting and Explaining the Sleeper Effect," *Journal of Consumer Research* 11, no. 2 (September 1984), pp. 632–42.

25. H. C. Triandis, *Attitudes and Attitude Change* (New York: Wiley, 1971).

26. J. Mills and J. Jellison, "Effect on Opinion Change Similarity between the Communicator and the Audience He Addresses," *Journal of Personality and Social Psychology* 9, no. 2 (1969), pp. 153–56.

27. Arch G. Woodside and J. William Davenport Jr., "The Effect of Salesman Similarity and Expertise on Consumer Purchasing Behavior," *Journal of Marketing Research* 11 (May 1974), pp. 198–202; Paul Busch and David T. Wilson, "An Experimental Analysis of a Salesman's Expert and Referent Bases of Social Power in the Buyer–Seller Dyad," *Journal of Marketing Research* 13 (February 1976), pp. 3–11.

28. Tim Nudd, "How Milan Vayntrub Became Advertising's New 'It' Girl," *Adweek*, January 13, 2015, www.adweek.com/news/advertising-branding/how-milana-vayntrub-became-advertisings-new-it-girl-162297.

29. Marshall McLuhan, "Top Ad Campaigns of the 21st Century," *Advertising Age*, January 12, 2015, pp. 14–22; Jeff Graham, "Whassup with All Those Award Wins?" *Advertising Age*, August 21, 2000, www.adage.com/article/cracks-in-the-foundation/defense-whassup/56775/.

30. Brett Knight, "The World's 10-Highest Paid Athletes, 2022," *Forbes*, www.forbes.com/sites/brettknight/2022/05/11/the-worlds-10-highest-paid-athletes-2022/?sh=69ec1aef1f6c.

31. Alexa Mancilla, "Endorsement Deals with Sofia Vergara—TV's Highest Paid Actress," *Hollywood Branded*, September 21, 2020, www.blog.hollywoodbranded.com/endorsement-deals-with-sofia-vergara-tvs-highest-paid-actress#.

32. Carsten Erfgen, Sebastian Zenker, and Henrik Sattler, "The Vampire Effect: When Do Celebrity Endorsers Harm Brand Recall?," *International Journal of Research in Marketing* 32 (January 2015), pp. 155–163; Utpal Dholakia, "Can a Celebrity Endorsement Hurt the Brand?," *Psychology Today*, November 3, 2015, www.psychologytoday.com/blog/the-science-behind-behavior/201511/can-celebrity-endorsement-hurt-the-brand.

33. Elena Gorgan, "Angelina Jolie Dumped by St. John for Overshadowing the Brand," *Softpedia*, January 9, 2010, www.news.softpedia.com/news/Angelina-Jolie-Dumped-by-St-John-for-Overshadowing-the-Brand-131636.shtml.

34. Jasmina Elicic and Cynthia M. Webster, "Eclipsing: When Celebrities Overshadow the Brand," *Psychology & Marketing* 31, no. 11 (November 2014), pp. 1040–50.

35. Valerie Folkes, "Recent Attribution Research in Consumer Behavior: A Review and New Directions," *Journal of Consumer Research* 14 (March 1988), pp. 548–65; John C. Mowen and Stephen W. Brown, "On Explaining and Predicting the Effectiveness of Celebrity Endorsers," in *Advances in Consumer Research* (vol. 8), K. B. Monroe, ed. (Ann Arbor, MI: Association for Consumer Research, 1981), pp. 437–41.

36. Stephen Rae, "How Celebrities Make Killings on Commercials," *Cosmopolitan*, January 1997, pp. 164–67.

37. "Impact of Celebrity Endorsement on Consumer Buying Behavior," *Guided Selling*, October 4, 2016, www.guided-selling.org/impact-of-celebrity-endorsement-on-consumer-buying-behavior.

38. Kenzie Bryant, "Why Everybody—Including the World's Biggest Brands—Wanted Selena Gomez in 2016," *Vanity Fair*, December 20, 2016, www.vanityfair.com/style/2016/12/selena-gomez-coach-coca-cola-verizon-endorsement-2016.

39. Margeaux Sippell, "Dwayne Johnson Tops Celebrity Endorsement Ranking among Actors," *Variety*, October 3, 2018, www.variety.com/2018/biz/news/older-celebrities-make-better-brand-endorsements-survey-finds-1202960720.

40. Brian D. Till and Terence A. Shimp, "Endorsers in Advertising: The Case of Negative Celebrity Information," *Journal of Advertising* 27, no. 1 (Spring 1998), pp. 67–82.

41. Shweta Ghandi, "From Nike to Rolex: Tiger Woods Career Endorsements Are Worth $1.7 Billion," *Regarding Luxury*, April 9, 2022, www.regardingluxury.com/from-nike-to-rolex-tiger-woods-career-endorsements-are-worth-1-7-billion; Merrit Kennedy,

"Tiger Woods Rises Again and Sponsors Are Celebrating His Resilience," *NPR*, April 15, 2019, www.npr.org/2019/04/15/713443562/tiger-woods-rises-again-and-sponsors-are-celebrating-his-resilience.

42. Shawn Medow, "Adidas Ends Tatis Jr.'s Contract after PED Suspension," *SportBusiness*, August 29, 2022, www.sportbusiness.com/news/adidas-ends-tatis-jr-s-contract-after-ped-suspension.

43. Rina Raphael, "YouTube Star Olivia Jade Dumped by Sephora over College Admissions Scandal," *Fast Company*, March 14, 2019, www.fastcompany.com/90320418/olivia-jade-lori-loughlin-daughter-dumped-by-sephora-after-college-scandal.

44. Stephanie Thompson, "Heroin Chic OK, Cocaine Use Not," *Advertising Age*, September 26, 2005, pp. 3, 80.

45. Cathy Yingling, "Beware the Lure of Celebrity Endorsers," *Advertising Age*, September 24, 2007, www.adage.com/article/cmo-strategy/beware-lure-celebrity-endorsers/120560/; James Tenser, "Endorser Qualities Count More Than Ever," *Advertising Age*, November 8, 2004, pp. S2, S4.

46. Anita Elberse and Jeroen Verleun, "The Economic Value of Celebrity Endorsements," *Journal of Advertising Research* 52, no. 2 (June 2012), pp. 149–65.

47. Matthew Schneier, "Coach Confirms Its Partenship with Selena Gomez," *The New York Times*, December 16, 2016, www.nytimes.com/2016/12/16/fashion/selena-gomez-coach-partnership-confirmed.html.

48. Amanda Ross, "Jennifer Aniston Is Now the Chief Creative Officer of a Leading Wellness Brand," BYRDIE, September 4, 2021, www.byrdie.com/jennifer-aniston-vital-proteins-collagen-partnership-5087995.

49. Natalie Zmuda, "Beverage Brand Swaps Equity for Met's Endorsements," *Advertising Age*, April 20, 2009, www.adage.com/article/news/beverage-brand-sonu-swaps-equity-mets-endorsements/136085.

50. Kevin Plank, "Under Armour's Founder on Learning to Leverage Celebrity Endorsements," *Harvard Busienss Review*, May 2012, pp. 45–48.

51. Kurt Badenhausen, "Kobe's $400 Million Leads Athlete Payouts after BodyArmor Sale," *Sportico*, November 1, 2021, www.sportico.com/business/commerce/2021/coca-cola-bodyarmor-purchase-1234645399.

52. Dave McCaughan, "The Fine Art of Matching a Celebrity with a Brand," *Advertising Age*, April 16, 2007, p. 34; Betsy Cummings, "Star Power," *Sales and Marketing Management*, April 2001, pp. 52–59; Michael A. Kamins, "An Investigation into the 'Match-Up' Hypothesis in Celebrity Advertising," *Journal of Advertising* 19, no. 1 (1990), pp. 4–13.

53. Grant McCracken, "Who Is the Celebrity Endorser? Cultural Foundations of the Endorsement Process," *Journal of Consumer Research* 16, no. 3 (December 1989), pp. 310–21.

54. Ibid., p. 315.

55. Molly Fitzpatrick, "The Business of Being Jennifer Aniston," *Elle*, July 12, 2018, www.elle.com/culture/celebrities/a21990794/the-business-of-being-jennifer-aniston/

56. B. Zafer Erdogan, Michael J. Baker, and Stephen Tagg, "Selecting Celebrity Endorsers: The Practitioner's Perspective," *Journal of Advertising Research* 41, no. 43 (May/June 2001), pp. 39–48.

57. "GfK MRI, E-Poll Partner to Deliver Unprecedented Alignment of Celebrities, Consumers, and Brands," *Business Wire*, September 5, 2018, www.marketwatch.com/press-release/gfk-mri-e-poll-partner-to-deliver-unprecedented-alignment-of-celebrities-consumers-and-brands-2018-09-05.

58. For an excellent review of these studies, see Marilyn Y. Jones, Andrea J. S. Stanaland, and Betsy D. Gelb, "Beefcake and Cheesecake: Insights for Advertisers," *Journal of Advertising* 27, no. 2 (Summer 1998), pp. 32–51; W. B. Joseph, "The Credibility of Physically Attractive Communicators," *Journal of Advertising* 11, no. 3 (1982), pp. 13–23.

59. Michael Solomon, Richard Ashmore, and Laura Longo, "The Beauty Match-Up Hypothesis: Congruence between Types of Beauty and Product Images in Advertising," *Journal of Advertising* 21, no. 4, pp. 23–34; M. J. Baker and Gilbert A. Churchill Jr., "The Impact of Physically Attractive Models on Advertising Evaluations," *Journal of Marketing Research* 14 (November 1977), pp. 538–55.

60. Robert W. Chestnut, C. C. La Chance, and A. Lubitz, "The Decorative Female Model: Sexual Stimuli and the Recognition of the Advertisements," *Journal of Advertising* 6 (Fall 1977),

pp. 11–14; Leonard N. Reid and Lawrence C. Soley, "Decorative Models and Readership of Magazine Ads," *Journal of Advertising Research* 23, no. 2 (April/May 1983), pp. 27–32.

61. Amanda B. Bower, "Highly Attractive Models in Advertising and the Women Who Loathe Them: The Implications of Negative Affect for Spokesperson Effectiveness," *Journal of Advertising* 30, no. 3 (Fall 2001), pp. 51–63; Amanda B. Bower and Stacy Landreth, "Is Beauty Best? Highly versus Normally Attractive Models in Advertising," *Journal of Advertising* 30, no. 1 (2001), pp. 1–12.

62. Rachelle Jantzon and Michael Basil, "Physical Attractiveness in Advertising: Can an Endorser Be Too Attractive," in N. Krey, P. Rossi (eds.), *Back to the Future: Using Marketing Basics to Provide Customer Value, Developments in Marketing Science: Proceedings of the Academy of Marketing Science*, DOI 10.1007/978-3-319-66023-3_194.

63. Jack Neff, "In Dove Ads, Normal Is the New Beautiful," *Advertising Age*, September 27, 2004, pp. 1, 80; Michelle Jeffers, "Behind Dove's 'Real Beauty,'" *Adweek*, September 12, 2005, pp. 34–35.

64. Herbert E. Krugman, "On Application of Learning Theory to TV Copy Testing," *Public Opinion Quarterly* 26 (1962), pp. 626–39.

65. C. I. Hovland and W. Mandell, "An Experimental Comparison of Conclusion Drawing by the Communicator and by the Audience," *Journal of Abnormal and Social Psychology* 47 (July 1952), pp. 581–88.

66. Alan G. Sawyer and Daniel J. Howard, "Effect of Omitting Conclusions in Advertisements to Involved and Uninvolved Audiences," *Journal of Marketing Research* 28 (November 1991), pp. 467–74.

67. Paul Chance, "Ads without Answers Make Brain Itch," *Psychology Today* 9 (1975), p. 78.

68. Connie Pechmann, "Predicting When Two-Sided Ads Will Be More Effective Than One-Sided Ads," *Journal of Marketing Research* 24 (November 1992), pp. 441–53; George E. Belch, "The Effects of Message Modality on One- and Two-Sided Advertising Messages," in *Advances in Consumer Research* (vol. 10), Richard P. Bagozzi and Alice M. Tybout, (eds.), (Ann

Arbor, MI: Association for Consumer Research, 1983), pp. 21–26.

69. Robert E. Settle and Linda L. Golden, "Attribution Theory and Advertiser Credibility," *Journal of Marketing Research* 11 (May 1974), pp. 181–85; Edmund J. Faison, "Effectiveness of One-Sided and Two-Sided Mass Communications in Advertising," *Public Opinion Quarterly* 25 (Fall 1961), pp. 468–69.

70. Martin Eisend, "Two-Sided Advertising: A Meta-Analysis," *International Journal of Research in Marketing* 23 (June 2006), pp. 187–98.

71. Paul Farhi, "Behind Domino's Mea Culpa Ad Campaign," *The Washington Post*, January 12, 2010, p. C7.

72. Brandon Shutt "How Digital Marketing Crowned Domino's the King of Pizza," *Online Marketing Institute*, May 22, 2018, www.medium .com/online-marketing-institute/how-digital-marketing-crowned-dominos-the-king-of-pizza-3d327d7350f8.

73. E.J. Schultz, "Why VW Is Bringing Up Its Emissions Scandal Again in the New Ad," *Advertising Age*, June 5, 2019, www.adage.com/article/cmo-strategy/why-vw-bringing-its-emissions-scandal-again-new-ad/217545.

74. Jeff Beer, "Why VW Decided to Reference Its Scandal in Its New Electric Car Ad Campaign," *Fast Company*, June 5, 2019, www .fastcompany.com/90359782/why-vw-decided-to-reference-its-scandal-in-its-new-electric-car-ad-campaign.

75. Alan G. Sawyer, "The Effects of Repetition of Refutational and Supportive Advertising Appeals," *Journal of Marketing Research* 10 (February 1973), pp. 23–37; George J. Szybillo and Richard Heslin, "Resistance to Persuasion: Inoculation Theory in a Marketing Context," *Journal of Marketing Research* 10 (November 1973), pp. 396–403.

76. Andrew A. Mitchell, "The Effect of Verbal and Visual Components of Advertisements on Brand Attitudes and Attitude toward the Advertisement," *Journal of Consumer Research* 13 (June 1986), pp. 12–24; Julie A. Edell and Richard Staelin, "The Information Processing of Pictures in Advertisements," *Journal of Consumer Research* 10, no. 1 (June 1983), pp. 45–60; Elizabeth C. Hirschmann, "The Effects of Verbal and Pictorial Advertising Stimuli on Aesthetic, Utilitarian and Familiarity Perceptions," *Journal of Advertising* 15, no. 2 (1986), pp. 27–34.

77. Jolita Kisielius and Brian Sternthal, "Detecting and Explaining Vividness Effects in Attitudinal Judgments," *Journal of Marketing Research* 21, no. 1 (1984), pp. 54–64.

78. H. Rao Unnava and Robert E. Burnkrant, "An Imagery-Processing View of the Role of Pictures in Print Advertisements," *Journal of Marketing Research* 28 (May 1991), pp. 226–31.

79. William L. Wilkie and Paul W. Farris, "Comparative Advertising: Problems and Potential," *Journal of Marketing* 39 (1975), pp. 7–15.

80. For a review of comparative advertising studies, see Fred K. Beard, "Practitioner View of Comparative Advertising," *Journal of Advertising Research* 53, no. 3 (September 2013), pp. 313–23; Cornelia Pechmann and David W. Stewart, "The Psychology of Comparative Advertising," in *Attention, Attitude and Affect in Response to Advertising*, E.M. Clark, T.C. Brock, and D.W. Stewart, eds. (Hillsdale, NJ: Erlbaum, 1994), pp. 79–96; Thomas S. Barry, "Comparative Advertising: What Have We Learned in Two Decades?" *Journal of Advertising Research* 33, no. 2 (1993), pp. 19–29.

81. Jennifer Maloney, "Coke to Pay $5.6 Billion for Full Control of BodyArmor," *The Wall Street Journal*, November 1, 2021, www.wsj.com/articles/coke-to-pay-5-6-billion-for-full-control-of-bodyarmor-11635713140.

82. Emily Bryson York, "Brand vs. Brand: Attack Ads on the Rise," *Advertising Age*, October 27, 2008, www.adage .com/article/news/brand-brand-attack-ads-rise/132028.

83. Gene Markin, "Anheuser-Busch Not Liable for False Advertising for Pointing Out to Consumers That Miller Lite and Coors Light Use Corn Syrup," *The National Law Review* 12, no. 250 (September 7, 2022).

84. Fred Beard, "The Effectiveness of Comparative versus Non-Comparative Advertising," *Journal of Advertising Research* 55, no. 3 (September 2015), pp. 296–306.

85. Patrick Meirick, "Cognitive Responses to Negative and Comparative Political Advertising," *Journal of Advertising* 31, no. 1 (Spring 2002), pp. 49–59.

86. Bruce E. Pinkleton, Nam-Hyun Um, and Erica Weintraub Austin, "An Exploration of the Effects of Negative Political Advertising on Political Decision Making," *Journal of Advertising* 31, no. 1 (Spring 2002), pp. 13–25.

87. Bruce E. Pinkleton, "The Effects of Negative Comparative Political Advertising on Candidate Evaluations and Advertising Evaluations: An Exploration," *Journal of Advertising* 26, no. 1 (1997), pp. 19–29.

88. Michael L. Ray and William L. Wilkie, "Fear: The Potential of an Appeal Neglected by Marketing," *Journal of Marketing* 34 (January 1970), pp. 54–62.

89. Brian Sternthal and C. Samuel Craig, "Fear Appeals Revisited and Revised," *Journal of Consumer Research* 1 (December 1974), pp. 22–34.

90. Punam Anand Keller and Lauren Goldberg Block, "Increasing the Persuasiveness of Fear Appeals: The Effect of Arousal and Elaboration," *Journal of Consumer Research* 22, no. 4 (March 1996), pp. 448–60.

91. John F. Tanner Jr., James B. Hunt, and David R. Eppright, "The Protection Motivation Model: A Normative Mode of Fear Appeals," *Journal of Marketing* 55 (July 1991), pp. 36–45.

92. Ibid.

93. Sternthal and Craig, "Fear Appeals Revisited and Revised."

94. Herbert Jack Rotfeld, "The Textbook Effect: Conventional Wisdom, Myth and Error in Marketing," *Journal of Marketing* 64 (April 2000), pp. 122–27.

95. Montana Meth Project, www .montanameth.org.

96. Andrea C. Morales, Eugenia C. Wu, and Gavan J. Fitzsimons, "How Disgust Enhances the Effectiveness of Fear Appeals," *Journal of Marketing Research*, June 2012, pp. 383–93.

97. Fred K. Beard, "One Hundred Years of Humor in American Advertising," *Journal of Macromarketing* 25, no. 2 (June 2005), pp. 54–65; C. Samuel Craig and Brian Sternthal, "Humor in Advertising," *Journal of Marketing* 37 (October 1973), pp. 12–18.

98. Martin Eisend, "A Meta-Analysis of Humor in Advertising," *Journal of the Academy of Marketing Science* 37, no. 2 (January 2009), pp. 191–203.

99. Bobby J. Calder and Brian Sternthal, "A Television Commercial Wearout: An Information Processing View," *Journal of Marketing Research* 17 (May 1980), pp. 173–87.

100. Dottie Enroco, "Humorous Touch Resonates with Consumers," *USA Today*, May 13, 1996, p. 3B.

101. Yong Zhang, "Response to Humorous Advertising: The Moderating Effect of Need for Cognition," *Journal of Advertising* 25, no. 1 (Spring 1996), pp. 15–32; Marc G. Weinberger and Charles S. Gulas, "The Impact of Humor in Advertising: A Review," *Journal of Advertising* 21 (December 1992), pp. 35–59.

102. Marc G. Weinberger and Leland Campbell, "The Use of Humor in Radio Advertising," *Journal of Advertising Research* 31 (December/ January 1990-91), pp. 44–52.

103. Yong Zhang and George M. Zinkhan, "Responses to Humorous Ads," *Journal of Advertising*, Winter 2006, pp. 113–27.

104. Harold C. Cash and W.J.E. Crissy, "Comparison of Advertising and Selling: The Salesman's Role in Marketing," *Psychology of Selling* 12 (1965), pp. 56–75.

105. Marshall McLuhan, *Understanding Media: The Extensions of Man* (New York: McGraw Hill, 1966).

106. Marvin E. Goldberg and Gerald J. Gorn, "Happy and Sad TV Programs: How They Affect Reactions to Commercials," *Journal of Consumer Research* 14, no. 3 (December 1987), pp. 387–403.

107. Andrew B. Aylesworth and Scott B. MacKenzie, "Context Is Key: The Effect of Program-Induced Mood on Thoughts about the Ad," *Journal of Advertising* 27, no. 2 (Summer 1998), pp. 17–32.

108. Michael T. Elliott and Paul Surgi Speck, "Consumer Perceptions of Advertising Clutter and Its Impact across Various Media," *Journal of Advertising Research* 38, no. 1 (January/February 1998), pp. 29–41; Peter H. Webb, "Consumer Initial Processing in a Difficult Media Environment," *Journal of Consumer Research* 6, no. 3 (December 1979), pp. 225–36.

109. Louisa Ha and Kim McCann, "An Integrated Model of Advertising Clutter in Offline and Online Media," *International Journal of Advertising* 27, no. 4 (2008), pp. 569–592, DOI: 10.2501/S0265048708080153

110. Peter H. Webb, "Consumer Initial Processing in a Difficult Media Environment"; Tom J. Brown and Michael L. Rothschild, "Reassessing the Impact of Television Advertising Clutter," *Journal of Consumer Research* 20, no. 1 (1993), pp. 138–146.

111. Advertising Research Foundation. "Disengagement," January 28, 2020, www.thearf.org/glossary/disengagement.

112. Sanjeev Tripathi, Varsha Jain, Jatin Pandey, Altaf Merchant, and Anupama Ambika, "When Consumers Tune Out Advertising Messages: Development and Validation of a Scale to Measure Advertising Disengagement," *Journal of Advertising Research* 62 (2021), pp. 1–17, DOI 10.2501/JAR-2021-020.

113. Sam Thielman, "You Endure More Commercials When Watching Cable Networks," *Adweek*, June 23, 2013, www.adweek.com/news/television/you-endure-more-commercials-when-watching-cable-networks-150575; "How Many Minutes of Commercials Are Shown in an Average TV Hour? The Number Has Been Steadily Climbing," *TV Week*, May 13, 2014, www.tvweek.com/tvbizwire/2014/05/how-many-minutes-of-commercial/.

114. Wayne Friedman, "TV Ad Load Spikes 6% in Q2, with A+E on Top, Disney at the Bottom," *MediaPost*, August 6, 2021, www.mediapost.com/publications/article/365761/tv-ad-load-spikes-6-in-q2-with-ae-on-top-disne.html?edition=123255.

115. Jason Lynch, "NBCUniversal Will Cut Prime-Time Ad Loads Another 10% by 2020," *Adweek*, January 8, 2019, www.adweek.com/tv-video/nbcuniversal-will-cut-prime-time-ad-loads-another-10-by-2020.

116. Katy Bachman, "Clutter Makes TV Ads Less Effective," *Adweek*, February 9, 2010, www.adweek.com/aw/content_display/news/media/e3i4f e3d67e44c8b3ad4c3fcbfe797fc862.

117. Louisa Ha and Kim McCann, "An Integrated Model of Advertising Clutter in Offline and Online Media."

118. Ibid, p. 576.

Chapter 7

1. "Do Marketers Rely on Instinct over ROI?" *eMarketer*, February 24, 2015, www.eMarketer.com.

2. "What Happened When Colgate-Palmolive Tasked AI with Finding ROI?" *WARC*, January 13, 2019, www.warc.com.

3. Roslyn McKenna, "10 Largest Auto Insurance Companies," *ValuePenguin*, August 17, 2022, www.valuepenguin.com.

4. Donald S. Tull, "The Carry-Over Effect of Advertising," *Journal of Marketing*, April 1965, pp. 46–53.

5. Darral G. Clarke, "Econometric Measurement of the Duration of Advertising Effect on Sales," *Journal of Marketing Research* 23 (November 1976), pp. 345–57.

6. Philip Kotler, *Marketing Decision Making: A Model Building Approach* (New York: Holt, Rinehart & Winston, 1971), Ch. 5.

7. Becky Ebencamp, "You Can Teach an Old Hot Dog Brand Some New Design Tricks," *Brandweek*, September 28, 2009, www.brandweek.com.

8. Stephanie Thompson, "Kellogg's Roars Back with Out of Box Ads," *Advertising Age*, May 3, 2004, pp. 4–5.

9. "Vans Shoemaker VF Quarterly Revenue Tops Estimates," *CNBC*, May 4, 2018, www.cnbc.com.

10. Russell H. Colley, *Defining Advertising Goals for Measured Advertising Results* (New York: Association of National Advertisers, 1961).

11. Don E. Schultz, Dennis Martin, and William Brown, *Strategic Advertising Campaigns*, 2nd ed. (Lincolnwood, IL: Crain Books, 1984).

12. Michael L. Ray, "Consumer Initial Processing: Definitions, Issues, Applications," in *Buyer/Consumer Information Processing*, G. David Hughes, ed. (Chapel Hill: University of North Carolina Press, 1974); David A. Aaker and John G. Myers, *Advertising Management*, 2nd ed. (Englewood Cliffs, NJ: Prentice Hall, 1982), pp. 122–23.

13. Aaker and Myers, *Advertising Management*.

14. Steven W. Hartley and Charles H. Patti, "Evaluating Business to Business Advertising: A Comparison of Objectives and Results," *Journal of Advertising Research*, 28 (April/May 1988), pp. 21–27.

15. Jerry Thomas, "Advertising Effectiveness, 2008," www.decisionanalyst.com.

16. Don E. Schultz, "Integration Helps You Plan Communications from Outside-In," *Marketing News*, March 15, 1993, p. 12.

17. Thomas R. Duncan, "To Fathom Integrated Marketing, Dive!" *Advertising Age*, October 11, 1993, p. 18.

18. G. Tellis and K. Tellis, "Research on Advertising in a Recession," *Journal of Advertising Research* 49, no. 3 (2009), pp. 304–27. Retrieved from

Communication & Mass Media Complete database.

19. Robert L. Steiner, "The Paradox of Increasing Returns to Advertising," *Journal of Advertising Research*, February/March 1987, pp. 45–53.

20. David A. Aaker and James M. Carman, "Are You Overadvertising?" *Journal of Advertising Research* 22, no. 4 (August/September 1982), pp. 57–70.

21. Julian A. Simon and Johan Arndt, "The Shape of the Advertising Response Function," *Journal of Advertising Research* 20, no. 4 (1980), pp. 11–28.

22. Melvin E. Salveson, "Management's Criteria for Advertising Effectiveness," in *Proceedings to the 5th Annual Conference, Advertising Research Foundation*, New York, 1959, p. 25.

23. Boonghee Yoo and Rujirutana Mandhachitara, "Estimating Advertising Effects on Sales in a Competitive Setting," *Journal of Advertising Research* 43, no. 3 (2003), pp. 310–20.

24. Dan Lippe, "Media Scorecard: How ROI Adds Up," *Advertising Age*, June 20, 2005, pp. S-6, S-42.

25. Landon Oakum, "Nielsen Report Finds Underspending in 50% of Media Plans Jeopardizing Maximum ROI", *Nielsen*, July 2022, www.nielsen.com.

26. Joe Mandese, "Half of Media Buys Driven by ROI, TV, Online Dominate," *MediaPost*, April 20, 2005, www.mediapost.com/publications/article/29392/half-of-media-buys-driven-by-roi-tv-online-domin.html.

27. Wayne Friedman, "ROI Measurement Still Falls Short," *TelevisionWeek*, January 31, 2005, p. 19.

28. Sarah Vizard, "Marketing's Importance Increasing During the Pandemic as Share of Company Spending Hits Record High," *Marketing Week*, June 22, 2020, www.marketingweek.com.

29. James O. Peckham, "Can We Relate Advertising Dollars to Market Share Objectives?" in *How Much to Spend for Advertising*, M. A. McNiven, ed. (New York: Association of National Advertisers, 1969), p. 30.

30. George S. Low and Jakki Mohr, "Setting Advertising and Promotion Budgets in Multi-Brand Companies," *Journal of Advertising Research* 39, no. 1 (January/February 1999), pp. 667–78.

31. John P. Jones, "Ad Spending: Maintaining Market Share," *Harvard Business Review* 68, no. 1 (January/February 1990), pp. 38–42; James C. Schroer, "Ad Spending: Growing Market Share," *Harvard Business Review* 68, no. 1 (January/February 1990), pp. 44–48.

32. Randall S. Brown, "Estimating Advantages to Large-Scale Advertising," *Review of Economics and Statistics* 60 (August 1978), pp. 428–37.

33. Kent M. Lancaster, "Are There Scale Economies in Advertising?" *Journal of Business* 59, no. 3 (1986), pp. 509–26.

34. Johan Arndt and Julian Simon, "Advertising and Economics of Scale: Critical Comments on the Evidence," *Journal of Industrial Economics* 32, no. 2 (December 1983), pp. 229–41; Aaker and Carman, "Are You Overadvertising?"

35. George S. Low and Jakki J. Mohr, "The Budget Allocation between Advertising and Sales Promotion: Understanding the Decision Process," *AMA Educators' Proceedings, Summer 1991* (Chicago: American Marketing Association 1991), pp. 448–57.

Chapter 8

1. Quoted in Werner Reinartz and Peter Saffert, "Creativity in Advertising: When It Works and When It Doesn't," *Harvard Business Review*, June 2013, pp. 4–8.

2. Keith Reinhard, "After 60 Years in Advertising, I Believe True Creativity Is More Powerful Than Ever," *Adweek*, May 22, 2016, http://www.adweek.com/news/advertising-branding/after-60-years-advertising-i-believe-true-creativity-more-powerful-ever-171542; Jeremy Mullman and Stephanie Thompson, "Burnett's Stumble Continues as Altoids Slips Away," *Advertising Age*, January 5, 2007, www.adage.com/article/agency-news/burnett-s-stumble-continues-altoids-slips/114094/.

3. Maureen Morrison, "DDB Cut from Bud Light Review, Move Ends 30 Year Relationship with Brand in U.S.," *Advertising Age*, October 11, 2011, p. 3.

4. Tripp Mickle, "Can Advertising Revive Light Beer?," *The Wall Street Journal*, October 12, 2015, pp. B1, 4.

5. Diane Christe, "Coors Light Breaks from Past Strategy in Millennial Focused Push," *MarketingDive*, July 31, 2019, www.marketingdive.com/news/coors-light-breaks-from-past-strategy-in-millennial-focused-push/559913.

6. Alex Parker, "Two Years on, Coors Light's 'Brilliant' 'Made to Chill' Campaign Keeps Paying Dividends. *Beer & Beyond*, November 23, 2021, www.molsoncoorsblog.com/coors-light-made-to-chill-momentum.

7. Avi Dan, "Agencies Are Questioning Just Who the Real Winners Are in the Business of Advertising Awards," *Forbes*, June 22, 2021, www.forbes.com/sites/avidan/2021/06/22/agencies-are-questioning-just-who-the-real-winners-are-in-the-business-of-advertising-awards/?sh=3567a112401e; Thom Forbes, "Is There Value in Advertising Awards," *Hispanic Ad.com*, October 7, 2017, www.hispanicad.com/agency/business/there-value-advertising-awards; Douglas West, Albert Caruana, and Kannika Leelapanyalert, "What Makes Win, Place, or Show: Judging Creativity in Advertising at Award Shows," *Journal of Advertising Research* 53, no. 3 (2013), pp. 324–38.

8. Patrick Collister, "Are Advertising Awards Important?," *Branding in Asia*, January 24, 2020, www.brandinginasia.com/are-advertising-awards-important.

9. Elizabeth C. Hirschman, "Role-Based Models of Advertising Creation and Production," *Journal of Advertising* 18, no. (1989), pp. 42–53.

10. Ibid., p. 51.

11. Edith G. Smits, Lex Van Meurs, and Peter C. Neijens, "Effects of Advertising Likeability: A 10-Year Perspective," *Journal of Advertising Research* 4, no. 1 (March 2006), pp. 73–83; Cyndee Miller, "Study Says 'Likability' Surfaces as Measure of TV Ad Success," *Marketing News*, January 7, 1991, pp. 6, 14; Ronald Alsop, "TV Ads That Are Likeable Get Plus Rating for Persuasiveness," *The Wall Street Journal*, February 20, 1986, p. 23.

12. Sheila L. Sasser and Scott Koslow, "Desperately Seeking Advertising Creativity: Engaging an Imaginative 3 P's Research Agenda," *Journal of Advertising* 37, no. 4 (2008), pp. 5–19.

13. Scott Koslow, "I Love Creative Advertising," *Journal of Advertising Research* 55, no. 1 (March 2015), pp. 5–8.

14. Brian D. Till and Daniel W. Baack, "Recall and Persuasion: Does Creativity Matter?" *Journal of Advertising* 34, no. 3 (2005), pp. 47–57.

15. Robert E. Smith, Scott B. MacKenzie, Xiaojing Yang, Laura Buchholz, William K. Darley, and Xiaojing Yang, "Modeling the Determinants and

Effects of Creativity in Advertising," *Marketing Science* 26, no. 6 (2007), pp. 819–33; Robert E. Smith and Xiaojing Yang, "Toward a General Theory of Creativity in Advertising: Examining the Role of Divergence," *Marketing Theory* 4, no. 1/2 (2004), pp. 29–55.

16. Deborah J. MacInnis and Bernard J. Jaworski, "Information Processing from Advertisement: Toward an Integrative Framework," *Journal of Marketing* 53, no. 4 (October 1989), pp. 1–23.

17. Robert E. Smith, Jiemiao Chen, and Xiaojing Yang, "The Impact of Advertising Creativity on the Hierarchy of Effects," *Journal of Advertising* 37, no. 4 (Winter 2008), pp. 47–61.

18. Smith et al., "Modeling the Determinants and Effects of Creativity in Advertising."

19. Swee Hoon Ang, Yih Hwai Lee, and Siew Meng Leong, "The Ad Creativity Cube: Conceptualization and Initial Validation," *Journal of the Academy of Marketing Science* 35, no. 23 (2007), pp. 220–32; Arthur J. Kover, Stephen M. Goldenberg, and William L. James, "Creativity vs. Effectiveness? An Integrative Classification for Advertising," *Journal of Advertising Research* 35 (November/December 1995), pp. 29–38.

20. Sara Rosengren, Martin Eisend, Scott Koslow, and Micael Kahlen, "A Meta-Analysis of When and How Advertising Creativity Works," *Journal of Marketing* 84, no. 6 (2020), pp. 39–56, doi.org/10.1177/0022242920929288

21. Reinartz and Saffert, "Creativity in Advertising: When It Works and When It Doesn't," *Harvard Business Review*, June 2013, pp. 4–8.

22. Smith et al., "Modeling the Determinants and Effects of Creativity in Advertising."

23. For an interesting discussion on the embellishment of advertising messages, see William M. Weilbacher, *Advertising*, 2nd ed. (New York: Macmillan, 1984), pp. 180–82.

24. David Ogilvy, *Confessions of an Advertising Man* (New York: Atheneum, 1963); Hanley Norins, *The Compleat Copywriter* (New York: McGraw Hill, 1966).

25. Hank Sneiden, *Advertising Pure and Simple* (New York: ANACOM, 1977).

26. Quoted in Valerie H. Free, "Absolut Original," *Marketing Insights*, Summer 1991, p. 65.

27. Scott Koslow, Sheila L. Sasser, and Edward A. Riordan, "Do Marketers Get the Advertising They Need or the Advertising They Deserve?" *Journal of Advertising* 35, no. 3 (Fall 2006), pp. 81–101.

28. I-Hsein Sherwood, "Ad Age 2019 Agency of the Year: Wieden & Kennedy," *Advertising Age*, April 15, 2019, www.adage.com/article/special-report-agency-list/ad-age-2019-agency-year-wieden-kennedy/2163301; Ann Christine Diaz, "Creativity's Agency of the Year," *Advertising Age*, January 28, 2013, p. 24; Cathy Taylor, "Risk Takers: Wieden & Kennedy," *Adweek's Marketing Week*, March 23, 1992, pp. 26–27.

29. Anthony Vagnoni, "Creative Differences," *Advertising Age*, November 17, 1997, pp. 1, 28, 30.

30. Jonathon Cranin, "Has Advertising Gone the Way of the Costra Nostra?" *Advertising Age*, June 6, 2005.

31. Vagnoni, "Creative Differences."

32. Cranin, "Has Advertising Gone the Way of the Costra Nostra?"

33. Arthur J. Kover, "Copywriters' Implicit Theories of Communication: An Exploration," *Journal of Consumer Research* 21, no. 4 (March 1995), pp. 596–611.

34. Kyle O'Brien, "How Global Media Agency of the Year MediaCom Stayed on Top for the Second Straight Year," *Adweek*, March 20, 2022, www.adweek.com/agencies/how-global-media-agency-of-the-year-mediacom-stayed-on-top-for-the-second-straight-year.

35. Sheila L. Sasser and Scott Koslow, "Desperately Seeking Advertising Creativity," *Journal of Advertising* 37, no. 4 (Winter 2008), pp. 5–19.

36. James Webb Young, *A Technique for Producing Ideas*, 3rd ed. (Chicago: Crain Books, 1975), p. 42.

37. Graham Wallas, *The Art of Thought* (New York: Harcourt Brace, 1926).

38. Jon Steel, *Truth, Lies & Advertising: The Art of Account Planning* (New York: Wiley, 1998).

39. John Parker, Lawrence Ang, and Scott Koslow, "The Creative Search for an Insight in Account Planning: An Absorptive Capacity Approach," *Journal of Advertising* 47, no. 3 (July/September 2018), pp. 237–54.

40. Sandra E. Moriarty, *Creative Advertising: Theory and Practice* (Englewood Cliffs, NJ: Prentice Hall, 1986).

41. E. E. Norris, "Seek Out the Consumer's Problem," *Advertising Age*, March 17, 1975, pp. 43–44.

42. Thomas L. Greenbaum, "Focus Groups Can Play a Part in Evaluating Ad Copy," *Marketing News*, September 13, 1993, pp. 24–25.

43. Emily Steel, "The New Focus Groups: Online Networks, Proprietary Panels Help Consumer Companies Shape Product Ads," *The Wall Street Journal*, January 14, 2008, p. B6.

44. Jennifer Comiteau, "Why the Traditional Focus Group Is Dying," *Adweek*, October 31, 2005, pp. 24–25, 32; Stephanie Thompson, "'Tipping Point' Guru Takes on Focus Groups," *Advertising Age*, January 24, 2005, pp. 4, 54; Malcolm Gladwell, *Blink: The Power of Thinking without Thinking* (New York: Little, Brown, 2004).

45. David Kiley, "Shoot the Focus Group," *BusinessWeek*, November 14, 2005, pp. 120–21.

46. Stephanie Thompson, "'Tipping Point' Guru Takes on Focus Groups."

47. Eric J. Arnould and Melanie Wallendorf, "Market-Oriented Ethnography: Interpretation Building and Marketing Strategy Formulation," *Journal of Marketing Research* 31 (November 1994), pp. 388–96.

48. ARF "David Ogilvy Awards 2021, as Real as It Tastes, Michelob ULTRA Organic Seltzer," www.thearf.org/arf-events/2021-arf-david-ogilvy-awards-winners.

49. Stephen Winzenburg, "Your Advertising Slogans Are Crummy. Can't You Do Better?" *Advertising Age*, January 14, 2008, p. 15; John Mathes, "Taglines That Stick; Here's How to Create an Effective Brand Summation Line. How Long Should It Be? Is It the Same as Your Brand Positioning? How Often Do You Need to Refresh It?" *ABA Bank Marketing*, December 1, 2008, pp. 22–25.

50. Chiranjeev Kohli, Lance Leuthesser, and Rajneesh Suri, "Got Slogan? Guidelines for Creating Effective Slogans," *Business Horizons* 50 (2007), pp. 415–22.

51. Ibid.

52. Denise Lee John, "The Death of the Tagline," *Adweek*, September 9, 2013, https://www.adweek.com/brand-marketing/death-tagline-152255/

53. *Better Creative Briefs*, ANA, November 2017, https://www.ana.net/magazines/show/id/ii-better-creative-briefs-2017.

54. Ibid.

55. John Sutherland, Lisa Duke, and Avery Abernethy, "A Model of

Marketing Information Flow," *Journal of Advertising* 22, no. 4 (Winter 2004), pp. 39–52.

56. Bill Duggan, "The ANA's Solution to Bad Creative Briefs (Of Which There Are Many)," *MediaPost*, November 30, 2017, www.mediapost.com/publications/article/310906/the-anas-solution-to-bad-creative-briefs-of-whic.html.

57. Jennifer Faull, "Clients Laud Improvements to Briefing Process, but Agencies Remain Skeptical," *The Drum*, April 19, 2017, www.thedrum.com/news/2017/04/19/clients-laud-improvements-briefing-process-agencies-are-sceptical.

58. A. Jerome Jeweler, *Creative Strategy in Advertising* (Belmont, CA: Wadsworth, 1981).

59. John O'Toole, *The Trouble with Advertising*, 2nd ed. (New York: Random House, 1985), p. 131.

60. David Ogilvy, *Ogilvy on Advertising* (New York: Crown, 1983), p. 16.

61. Ad Age Staff, "Top Ad Campaigns of the 21st Century," *Advertising Age*, January 12, 2015, pp. 14–22.

62. Arthur J. Kover, "Copywriters' Implicit Theories of Communication: An Exploration," *Journal of Consumer Research* 21, no. 4 (March 1995), pp. 596–611.

63. John R. Rossiter, "Defining the Necessary Components of Creative, Effective Ads," *Journal of Advertising Research* 37, no. 4 (Winter 2008), pp. 139–44.

64. Rosser Reeves, *Reality in Advertising* (New York: Knopf, 1961), pp. 47, 48.

65. Jeremy Mullman, "Hey, Those A-B Brands Look Like Miller Beers," *Advertising Age*, June 11, 2009, www.adage.com/article/news/beer-marketing-a-b-brands-miller-beers/137260/; Jeremy Mullman, "Miller Lightens Its Load: Will Go National with MGD 64 by Fall," *Advertising Age*, www.adage.com/article/news/miller-lightens-load-national-mgd-64-fall/127945.

66. M.T. Fletcher, "These Marketing Myths Are Killing Creativity," *Advertising Age*, November 9, 2021, www.adage.com/article/fletcher-marketing/these-marketing-myths-are-killing-creativity/2377836.

67. Ogilvy, *Confessions of an Advertising Man*.

68. Martin Mayer, *Madison Avenue, U.S.A.* (New York: Pocket Books, 1958).

69. Alexandra Jardine, "Pernod Ricard's Campaign That Calculates Time You Have Left with Loved Ones Wins Top Honors at AICP Next," *Advertising Age*, June 5, 2019, www.adage.com/article/creativity-news/pernod-ricards-campaign-calculates-time-you-have-left-loved-ones-wins-top-honors-aicp-next/2175571; "The Time We Have Left," D&D Awards 2020, www.dandad.org/awards/professional/2020/231683/the-time-we-have-left.

70. Al Ries and Jack Trout, *Positioning: The Battle for Your Mind* (New York: McGraw Hill, 1985); Jack Trout and Al Ries, "The Positioning Era Cometh," *Advertising Age*, April 24, 1972, pp. 35–38; May 1, 1972, pp. 51–54; May 8, 1972, pp. 114–16.

71. Jack Trout, "Brands Can't Exist without Positioning," *Advertising Age*, March 14, 2005, p. 28.

72. Jessica Wohl, "Subway Hits Refresh as It Tries to Rebound with Massive Overhaul, Media Push," *Advertising Age*, July 6, 2021, www.adage.com/article/marketing-news-strategy/subway-hits-refresh-it-tries-rebound-massive-overhaul-media-push/2348496.

73. Rajeev Batra, John G. Myers, and David A. Aaker, *Advertising Management*, 5th ed. (Upper Saddle River, NJ: Prentice Hall, 1996).

74. Jean Lin, "Liberating Creativity: The Old Agency Model Doesn't Work Anymore," *Advertising Age*, February 9, 2015, http://adage.com/article/agency-viewpoint/liberating-creativity-agency-model-work/296965/.

75. Rupal Parekh, "Lee Clow on Advertising, Then and Now," *Advertising Age*, June 11, 2013, ww.adage.com/article/agency-news/lee-clow-advertising/241987.

Chapter 9

1. Sandra E. Moriarty, *Creative Advertising: Theory and Practice*, 2nd ed. (Englewood Cliffs, NJ: Prentice Hall, 1991), p. 76.

2. William M. Weilbacher, *Advertising*, 2nd ed. (New York: Macmillan, 1984), p. 197.

3. William Wells, John Burnett, and Sandra Moriarty, *Advertising* (Englewood Cliffs, NJ: Prentice Hall, 1989), p. 330.

4. Hamish Pringle and Peter Field, "Why Emotional Messages Beat Rational Ones," *Advertising Age*, March 2, 2009, http://adage.com/article/cmo-strategy/emotional-messages-beat-rational/134920/; Stuart J. Agres, "Emotion in Advertising: An Agency Point of View," in *Emotion in Advertising: Theoretical and Practical Explanations*, Stuart J. Agres, Julie A. Edell, and Tony M. Dubitsky, eds. (Westport, CT: Quorom Books, 1991).

5. Edward Kamp and Deborah J. MacInnis, "Characteristics of Portrayed Emotions in Commercials: When Does What Is Shown in Ads Affect Viewers?" *Journal of Advertising Research* 22, no. 4 (November/December 1995), pp. 19–28.

6. For a review of research on the effect of mood states on consumer behavior, see Meryl Paula Gardner, "Mood States and Consumer Behavior: A Critical Review," *Journal of Consumer Research* 12, no. 3 (December 1985), pp. 281–300.

7. Cathy Madison, "Researchers Work Advertising into an Emotional State," *Adweek*, November 5, 1990, p. 30.

8. Hamish Pringle and Peter Field, *Brand Immortality: How Brands Can Live Long and Prosper* (London: Kogan Page Limited, 2009).

9. Pringle and Field, "Why Emotional Messages Beat Rational Ones."

10. Christopher P. Puto and William D. Wells, "Informational and Transformational Advertising: The Different Effects of Time," in *Advances in Consumer Research* (vol. 11), Thomas C. Kinnear, ed. (Ann Arbor, MI: Association for Consumer Research, 1984), p. 638.

11. Ibid.

12. Audrey Kemp, "VRBO's New Campaign Celebrates 'Only Your People'," *The Drum*, July 25, 2022, www.thedrum.com/news/2022/07/25/vrbos-new-campaign-celebrates-only-your-people.

13. Jason Notte, "VRBO Makes a Pregame Super Bowl Ad a Family Affair," *Adweek*, February 2, 2022, www.adweek.com/agencies/vrbo-super-bowl-pregame-ad.

14. David Ogilvy and Joel Raphaelson, "Research on Advertising Techniques That Work and Don't Work," *Harvard Business Review*, July/August 1982, p. 18.

15. Xiang Fang, Surendra Singh, and Rohini Ahluwalia, "An Examination of Different Explanations for the Mere Exposure Effect," *Journal of Consumer Research* 34 (June 2007), pp. 97–103.

16. Robert Zajonc, "Attitudinal Effects of Mere Exposure," *Journal of Personality and Social Psychology Monographs*, no. 2 (Pt. 2), pp. 1–27.

17. John Young, "Making Online Ads Suck Less in 8 Easy Steps," *Advertising Age*, April 10, 2010, www.adage.com/article/digitalnext/making-online-ads-suck-8-easy-steps/143368/.

18. Helge Thorbjornsen, Paul Ketelaar, Jonathan Van'T Riet, and Micael Dahlen, "How Do Teaser Advertisements Boost Word of Mouth about New Products?" *Journal of Advertising Research* 55, no. 1, (March 2015), pp. 73–80.

19. Quote by Irwin Warren, cited in Enrico, "Teaser Ads Grab Spotlight," *USA Today*, July 6, 1995, pp. 1B, 2B.

20. Colin Campbell, Leyland F. Pitt, Michael Parent, and Pierre R. Berthhon, "Understanding Consumer Conversations around Ads in a Web 2.0 World," *Journal of Advertising* 40, no. 1 (Spring 2011), pp. 87–102; E. J. Schultz, "Why 'Crash the Super Bowl' Hasn't Burned Out for Doritos," *Advertising Age*, January 24, 2013, www.adage.com/article/special-report-super-bowl/crash-super-bowl-burned-doritos/239373.

21. Pius Boachie, "User-Generated Content Brings Authenticity to Brands, " *Adweek*, April 13, 2018, www.adweek.com/digital/user-generated-content-brings-authenticity-to-brands.

22. Henley Worthen, "Airbnb's User Generated Campaign & The Post-Covid Traveler," *tubular*, February 28, 2022, www.tubularlabs.com/blog/airbnbs-user-generated-campaign-the-post-covid-traveler.

23. Martin Mayer, *Madison Avenue, U.S.A.* (New York: Pocket Books, 1958), p. 64.

24. Lynn Coleman, "Advertisers Put Fear into the Hearts of Their Prospects," *Marketing News*, August 15, 1988, p. 1.

25. Ibid.

26. Garett Sloane, "Amazon's Super Bowl Commercial Imagines If Alexa Were Psychic," *Advertising Age*, February 7, 2022, www.adage.com/article/special-report-super-bowl/amazons-super-bowl-commercial-imagines-if-alexa-were-psychic/2397611.

27. Stuart Elliott, "Look Who's Talking for Mr. Peanut Now," *The New York Times*, July 1, 2013, www.nytimes.com/2013/07/01/business/media/look-whos-talking-for-mr-peanut-now.html.

28. Jessica Wohl, "Chipotle Unveils Third Animated Film, Hopes Consumers Want It That Way," *Advertising Age*, July 6, 2016, www.adage.com/article/cmo-strategy/chipotle-takes-fast-food-love-animated-film/304824; Christine Diaz, "Chipotle and CAA Add a Film Grand Prix to Collection of Top Honors," *Advertising Age*, June 23, 2012, www.adage.com/article/special-report-cannes-2012/chipotle-caa-add-a-film-grand-prix-collection-top-honors/235603.

29. Jon Springer, "See Chipotle's Sequel to the 2011 Hit 'Back To the Start'," *Advertising Age*, November 16, 2021, www.adage.com/creativity/work/chipotles-sequel-2011-hit-back-start/2380546.

30. Leon William, "Benefits of Using Computer Animation in Advertising Industry," *Map Systems*, July 11, 2017, www.mapsystemsindia.com/blog/benefits-of-animation-in-advertising.html.

31. Theresa Howard, "Aflac Duck Gives Wings to Insurer's Name Recognition," *USA Today*, May 17, 2001, p. B9.

32. Barbara B. Stern, "Classical and Vignette Television Advertising: Structural Models, Formal Analysis, and Consumer Effects," *Journal of Consumer Research* 20, no. 4 (March 1994), pp. 601–15; John Deighton, Daniel Romer, and Josh McQueen, "Using Drama to Persuade," *Journal of Consumer Research* 15, no. 3 (December 1989), pp. 335–43.

33. Moriarty, *Creative Advertising*, p. 77.

34. Mario Pricken, *Creative Advertising* (New York: Thames & Hudson, 2009).

35. "The Truth About Opioids: Gold Distinction in Integrated Campaign," 11th Annual Shorty Awards, www.shortyawards.com/11th/know-more.

36. Charles Taylor, "What Makes Flo from Progressive Effective? Lessons for Using Humor in Advertising," *Forbes*, March 15, 2019, www.forbes.com/sites/charlesrtaylor/2019/03/15/what-makes-flo-from-progressive-effective-lessons-for-using-humor-in-advertising/#7492f1305216.

37. W. Keith Hafer and Gordon E. White, *Advertising Writing*, 3rd ed. (St. Paul, MN: West Publishing, 1989), p. 98.

38. Stacy Jones, "10 Celebrities Who Sell Brands with Their Voices," *Hollywood Branded*, May 30, 2022, www.blog.hollywoodbranded.com/5-celebrities-who-sell-brands-with-their-voices.

39. Siddarth Vodnala, "Voice-Over Actors Are Talking Up the Apps That Help Them Get Work," *The Los Angeles Times*, September 8, 2015, www.latimes.com/entertainment/envelope/cotown/la-et-ct-voiceover-tech-20150909-story.html.

40. David Allan, "A Content Analysis of Music Placement in Prime-Time Advertising," *Journal of Advertising Research*, September 2008, pp. 404–14.

41. Linda M. Scott, "Understanding Jingles and Needledrop: A Rhetorical Approach to Music in Advertising," *Journal of Consumer Research* 17, no. 2 (September 1990), pp. 223–36.

42. Kineta Hung, "Framing Meaning Perceptions with Music: The Case of Teaser Ads," *Journal of Advertising* 30, no. 3 (Fall 2001), pp. 39–49; Russell I. Haley, Jack Richardson, and Beth Baldwin, "The Effects of Nonverbal Communications in Television Advertising," *Journal of Advertising Research* 24, no. 4 (July/August 1984), pp. 11–18.

43. Steve Oakes, "Evaluating Empirical Research into Music in Advertising: A Congruity Perspective," *Journal of Advertising Research*, March 2007, pp. 38–50.

44. Gerald J. Gorn, "The Effects of Music in Advertising on Choice Behavior: A Classical Conditioning Approach," *Journal of Marketing* 46 (Winter 1982), pp. 94–100.

45. Donna DeMarco, "TV Ads Go Pop: Advertisers Marry Modern Music with Their Products," *The Washington Times*, May 12, 2002, p. A1.

46. Brie Barbee, "The Best Songs from Apple Commercials," *Digital Trends*, January 22, 2018, www.digitaltrends.com/music/best-apple-commercial-songs.

47. Christine Birkner, "Striking a Chord," *Marketing News*, October 2015, pp. 18–19.

48. Yadira Gonzalez, "The Top 10 Brand Audio Logos Ranked by Effectiveness," *Advertising Age*, March 24, 2022, www.adage.com/article/marketing-news-strategy/best-brand-audio-ads-and-jingles-2022-ranked/2407391.

49. Quote from Suzanne Vranica, "P&G Dusts Off a Familiar Tune," *The Wall Street Journal*, March 3, 2005, p. B2; Andrew Hampp, "A Reprise for Jingles on Madison Avenue, Brands, Agencies Rediscovering Power of Original Tunes in Ad Campaigns," *Advertising Age*, September 6, 2010, www.adage.com/article/madisonvine-news/a-reprise-jingles-madison–avenue/145744.

50. "Results of 4A's 2011 Television Production Costs Survey," American

Association of Advertising Agencies, Bulletin #7480, January 22, 2013.

51. "SAG-AFTRA and Joint Policy Committee Reach Tentative Agreement on Successor Contracts," *SAG-AFTRA*, April 2, 2019, www.sagaftra.org/sag-aftra-members-ratify-2019-commercials-contracts.

52. Dave Chaffey, "Average Display Advertising Cickthrough Rates," *Smart Insights*, April 10, 2019, www.smartinsights.com/internet-advertising/internet-advertising-analytics/display-advertising-clickthrough-rates.

53. David Griner, "Pepsi Shares the Story Behind Its Brilliant Burger-Wrapper Ads," *Adweek*, May 27, 2021, www.adweek.com/creativity/pepsi-shares-the-story-behind-its-brilliant-burger-wrapper-ads.

54. Eric Visser, "Why Online Advertising Is Killing Creativity," *The Drum*, July 19, 2017, www.thedrum.com/opinion/2017/07/19/why-online-advertising-killing-creativity; Kunar Pattel, "Online Ads Not Working for You? Blame the Creative," *Advertising Age*, October 20, 2009, www.adage.com/article/digital/digital-online-ads-working-blame-creative/139795.

55. Hernan Lopez, "Why Interactive Advertising Needs a Creative Revolution," *Advertising Age*, June 15, 2009, www.adage.com/article/digital/interactive-advertising-a-creative-revolution/137246.

56. Kendall Goodrich, Shu Z. Schiller, and Dennis Galletta, "Consumer Reactions to Intrusiveness of Online-Video Advertisements," *Journal of Advertising Research*, 55, no. 1, (March 2015), pp. 37–50.

57. Meg James, "Over 50 and out of Flavor," *Los Angeles Times*, May 10, 2005, pp. A1, A10.

58. Rupal Parekh, "Brand Awareness Was Only Half the Battle for Aflac," *Advertising Age*, June 22, 2009, www.adage.com/article/cmo-strategy/aflac-s-jeff-charney-insurance-brand-awareness/137392/; Suzanne Vranica, "Aflac Partly Muzzles Iconic Duck," *The Wall Street Journal*, December 2, 2004, p. B8.

59. Eric Oster, "KFC Responds to U.K. Chicken Scandal with a Timely 'FCK, We're Sorry'," *Adweek*, February 23, 2018, www.adweek.com/creativity/kfc-responds-to-u-k-chicken-shortage-scandal-with-a-timely-fck-were-sorry.

Chapter 10

1. Jamie Turner, "Top Social Media Platforms Every Marketer Should Know," *60 Second Marketer*, April 9, 2010, www.60secondmarketer.com.

2. Matthew Creamer, "Ad Groups Back Switch from 'Frequency' to 'Engagement,'" *Advertising Age*, July 21, 2005, http://adage.com/article/news/ad-groups-back-switch-frequency-engagement/46348/.

3. Mindi Chahal, "Is 'Brand Engagement' a Meaningless Metric?" *Marketing Week*, August 10, 2016.

4. "Marketers Shaky about Right Media Mix," eMarketer.com, July 1, 2015.

5. Chuck Ross, "Study Finds for Continuity vs. Flights," *Advertising Age*, April 19, 1999, p. 2.

6. Joseph W. Ostrow, "Setting Frequency Levels: An Art or a Science?" *Journal of Advertising Research* (August/September 1984), pp. 9–11.

7. David Crane, "Arnold vs Calbuzz, eMeg's Ad Buy: Memo to Media," *Calbuzz*, March 10, 2010, www.calbuzz.com.

8. Scott Walker, "Ratings and TV Advertising Sales," *Suite 101*, April 2, 2008, www.tvadvertising.suite101.com.

9. David Berger, "How Much to Spend," *Foote, Cone & Belding Internal Report*, in *Advertising*, Michael L. Rothschild (Lexington, MA: Heath, 1987), p. 468.

10. David W. Olson, "Real World Measures of Advertising Effectiveness for New Products," *Speech to the 26th Annual Conference of the Advertising Research Foundation*, New York, March 18, 1980.

11. Joseph W. Ostrow, "What Level Frequency?" *Advertising Age*, November 1981, pp. 13–18.

12. Susanne Schmidt and Martin Eisend, "Advertising Repetition: A Meta-Analysis on Effective Frequency in Advertising," *Journal of Advertising* no. 4 (March 25, 2015), pp. 415–28.

13. J. W. Smith, A. Clurman, and C. Wood, *Coming to Concurrence: Addressable Attitudes and the New Model for Marketing Productivity* (Chicago: Racom Communications, 2005).

14. Jim Surmanek, "One-Hit or Miss: Is a Frequency of One Frequently Wrong?" *Advertising Age*, November 27, 1995, p.46.

15. Erwin Ephron, "Back to the Future," *Ephron on Media*, April 14, 2010, www.ephrononmedia.com.

16. Sheree Johnson, "New Research Sheds Light on Daily Ad Exposures," *SJ Insights*, September 29, 2014, www.sjinsights.com.

17. Ostrow, "What Level Frequency?"

18. Schmidt and Eisend, "Advertising Repetition."

19. Erwin Ephron, "Recency Planning," *Ephron on Media*, March 18, 1998, www.ephrononmedia.com.

20. Erwin Ephron, "Sitting on the Shelf," *Ephron on Media*, October 1, 2009, www.ephrononmedia.com.

21. Susan Krashinsky, "Mood Mismatch between TV Shows and Ads May Hurt Advertisers: Study," *The Globe and Mail*, March 29, 2015, www.theglobeandmail.com.

Chapter 11

1. "Why Radio: Radio Facts," *Radio Advertising Bureau*, 2022, www.rab.com/whyradio/reportresults.cfm.

2. Diana T. Kurylko, "How Subaru Marketing Found the 'Love'," *Automotive News*, February 12, 2018, www.autonews.com/article/20180212/RETAIL03/180219982/how-subaru-marketing-found-the-love; Jake Holmes, "How 'Love' Helped Kick-Start Subaru Sales in the U.S.," *motor1.com*, April 17, 2017, www.motor1.com/news/142732/subaru-love-ad-campaign.

3. "Network Television Cost and CPM Trends," *Trends in Media*, Television Bureau of Advertising, www.tvb.org/rcentral.

4. Drew Fitzgerald and Benjamin Mullin, "Outlook for Traditional TV Goes from Bad to Worse," *The Wall Street Journal*, November 19, 2018, www.wsj.com/articles/outlook-for-traditional-tv-goes-from-bad-to-worse-1542632401.

5. Bennett Bennett, "ESPN and Dr Pepper Sweeten Deal, Add Six-Year Extension as Official Sponsor of College Football Playoff," *The Drum*, January 20, 2018, www.thedrum.com/news/2018/01/08/espn-and-dr-pepper-sweeten-deal-add-six-year-extension-official-sponsor-college.

6. Tyler Conway, "Report: 12-RTeam College Football Playoff Could Fetch $2.2B Annual Media Rights Deal," *Bleacher Report*, September 6, 2022, www.bleacherreport.com/articles/10047885-report-12-team-college-football-playoff-could-fetch-22b-annual-media-rights-deal.

7. Joe Flint, "CBS, Turner Strike $8.8 Billion Deal to Televise NCAA's March Madness Through 2032," *The Wall Street Journal*, April 12, 2016, pp. B1, 4.

8. "Results of 4A's 2011 Television Production Costs Survey," American Association of Advertising Agencies, Bulletin #7480, January 22, 2013.

9. Parker Morse, "How the U.S. Hispanic Market Is Changing This Year," *Forbes*, January 25, 2019, www.forbes.com/sites/forbesagencycouncil/2019/01/25/how-the-u-s-hispanic-market-is-changing-this-year/#3f12157464fc; Laurel Wentz, "Behind the Five Most Creative U.S. Hispanic Ideas," *Advertising Age*, May 1, 2013, www.adage.com/article/hispanic-marketing/creative-u-s-hispanic-ideas/241197.

10. "TV Activity by Commercial Length," *Television Advertising Bureau*, 2022, www.tvb.org/wp-content/uploads/portals/0/media/file/Commercial_Length.pdf.

11. Joe Mandese, "Cable, Broadcast Network Ad Clutter At or Near All-Time Highs," *MediaPost*, December 7, 2018, www.mediapost.com/publications/article/329018/cable-broadcast-network-ad-clutter-at-or-near-all.html.

12. Gerry Smith, "TV Networks Vowed to Cut Back on Commercials. Instead, They Stuffed in More," *Los Angeles Times*, August 3, 2019, www.latimes.com/business/story/2019-08-02/tv-networks-vowed-to-cut-back-on-commercials-instead-they-stuffed-in-more.

13. Matthew McGranaghan, Jura Liaukonyte, and Kenneth C. Wilbur, "How Viewer Tuning, Presence and Attention Respond to Ad Content and Predict Brand Search," *Marketing Science*, DOI: 10.1287/mksc.2021.1344.

14. "It's a Connected World, and That's a Boon for TV Viewers," *Nielsen*, June 13, 2018, www.nielsen.com/us/en/insights/article/2018/it-s-a-connected-world-and-that-s-a-boon-for-tv-viewers.

15. John J. Cronin, "In-Home Observations of Commercial Zapping Behavior," *Journal of Current Issues and Research in Advertising* 17, no. 2 (Fall 1995), pp. 69–75.

16. Suzanne Vranica, "TiVo Serves Up Portrait of the Ad-Zappers," *The Wall Street Journal*, November 8, 2007, p. B5; Carrie Heeter and Bradley S. Greenberg, "Profiling the Zappers," *Journal of Advertising Research* 25, no. 2 (April/May 1985), pp. 9–12; Fred S. Zufryden, James H. Pedrick, and Avu Sandaralingham, "Zapping and Its Impact on Brand Purchase Behavior," *Journal of Advertising*

Research 33, no. 1 (January/February 1993), pp. 58–66.

17. Lex van Meurs, "Zapp! A Study on Switching Behavior during Commercial Breaks," *Journal of Advertising Research*, (January/February 1998), pp. 43–53.

18. Alan Ching Biu Tse and Rub P. W. Lee, "Zapping Behavior during Commercial Breaks," *Journal of Advertising Research* 41, no. 3 (May/June 2001), pp. 25–29.

19. Michael McCarthy, "TV Viewers Thanking NBC/Golf Channel for 'Playing Through' Commercials," *Front Office Sports*, August 22, 2019, www.frontofficesports.com/golf-channel-playing-through.

20. Ibid.

21. Ted Johnson, "Fox, Dish Settle Lawsuit Over Ad-Skipping, Other Features," *Variety*, February 11, 2016, www.variety.com/2016/biz/news/fox-broadcasting-dish-network-autohop-1201703348/.

22. Dan Hurwitz, "Video on Demand's Future Requires an Ad Model Built around the Experience," *Marketing Land*, February 28, 2019, www.marketingland.com/video-on-demands-future-requires-an-ad-model-built-around-the-experience-257888.

23. Linda F. Alwitt and Paul R. Prabhaker, "Identifying Who Dislikes Television Advertising: Not by Demographics Alone," *Journal of Advertising Research* 34, no. 6 (November/December 1994), pp. 30–42.

24. Lucy L. Henke, "Young Children's Perceptions of Cigarette Brand Advertising Symbols: Awareness, Affect, and Target Market Identification," *Journal of Advertising* 24, no. 4 (Winter 1995), pp. 13–28.

25. "Advertising Chart: How Much Millennials, Gen X, and Other Age Groups Trust TV Ads When Making a Purchase," *Marketing Sherpa*, August 22, 2017, www.marketingsherpa.com/article/chart/do-millennials-gen-x-trust-tv-ads?_ga=2.89412443.1138828129.1561573138-1954659036.1561573138.

26. Mark Johnson, "New Global Nielsen Study Reveals Who Trusts What in Advertising," *Mediashotz*, November 1, 2022, www.mediashotz.co.uk/new-global-nielsen-study-reveals-who-trusts-what-in-advertising.

27. Brian Steinberg, "How Fox Went from Small Outcast to Broadcast Powerhouse," *Advertising Age*, April 18, 2011, pp. 2–3.

28. Adam Rittenberg, "Big Ten Completes 7-Year, $7 Billion Media Rights Agreement with Fox, CBS, NBC," *ESPN*, August 18, 2022, www.espn.com/college-football/story/_/id/34417911/big-ten-completes-7-year-7-billion-media-rights-agreement-fox-cbs-nbc.

29. Bill Mann, "What's with CW? Result of Merger between WB and UPN Targets 18-and-Ups," *The Press Democrat*, December 16, 2007, p. D8.

30. Alex Weprin and Lesley Goldberg, "Local TV Giant Nexstar Seals Deal to Buy 75 Percent Stake in The CW, Reshaping Broadcast Landscape," *The Hollywood Reporter*, August 15, 2022, www.hollywoodreporter.com/tv/tv-news/the-cw-sold-nexstar-1235141964.

31. Patrick Herren, "What TV Ads Cost in the 2022–23 Season," *Advertising Age*, October 26, 2022, www.adage.com/article/media/tv-commercial-prices-advertising-costs-2022-23-season/2437106.

32. Tim Peterson, "The Overhaul of TV Advertising's Upfront Model Is Underway," *Digiday*, January 23, 2023, www.digiday.com/future-of-tv/the-overhaul-of-tv-advertisings-upfront-model-is-underway.

33. John Consoli, "Top Syndie Shows Outdrawing Primetime," *TVNewsCheck*, October 4, 2022, www.tvnewscheck.com/programming/article/top-syndie-shows-outdrawing-primetime.

34. Stephen Battaglio, "TV Networks Shed Ad Time as Consumers Skip Commercials," *Los Angeles Times*, March 27, 2018, www.latimes.com/business/hollywood/la-fi-ct-commercials-clutter-20180327-story.html.

35. Jeanine Poggi, "Why Cable Has Become More Like Broadcast TV," *Advertising Age*, May 14, 2012, p. 16; Brian Steinberg, "Broadcast TV or Cable, It's All the Same to Consumers," *Advertising Age*, March 23, 2009, www.adage.com/print?article_id=135246.

36. Ed Dixon, "ESPN+ Reaches 22.8m Subs as Disney Post US$5.1bn Streaming Revenue for Q3," *SportsPro*, August 11, 2022, www.sportspromedia.com/news/disney-espn-plus-streaming-dtc-subscribers-q3-2022-earnings-revenue.

37. Kevin Draper and Edmund Lee, "Sinclair Buys Regional Sports Networks from Disney in $10.6 Billion

Deal," *The New York Times*, May 3, 2019, www.nytimes.com/2019/05/03/business/media/sinclair-disney-regional-sports-networks.html.

38. Eric Grunwedel, "Leichtman: Near 20% Drop in U.S. Pay-TV Subs in Past 15 Years, *MediaPlayNews*, October 24, 2022, www.mediaplaynews.com/leichtman-near-20-percent-drop-in-pay-tv-subs-in-past-15-years.

39. Clay Travis, "ESPN Lost 8 Million Subscribers in 2021, 10% of Its Overall Subscriber Base," *Outkick*, May 23, 2022, www.outkick.com/espn-lost-8-million-subscribers-in-2021-10-of-its-overall-subscriber-base.

40. Ross Benes, "Addressable TV Advertising Will Grow 33.1% This Year," *Insider Intelligence*, May 11, 2021, www.insiderintelligence.com/content/linear-addressable-tv-ad-spending-will-grow-33-percent-this-year.

41. Corey Dietz, "What Is the Portable People Meter and How Does It Work?," *Lifewire*, January 5, 2018, www.lifewire.com/what-is-the-portable-people-meter-2843405.

42. "Encoding for Nielsen PPM Measurement of Local TV Viewing," *Nielsen News Center*, December 8, 2016, www.sites.nielsen.com/newscenter/encoding-for-nielsens-local-out-of-home-measurement.

43. A. J. Frutkin, "Do Sweeps Still Matter?" *Mediaweek.com*, April 30, 2007.

44. Bennett Bennett, "The Future of Audience Measurement Is Getting Clearer, but Nielsen May not Carry the Torch," *The Drum*, May 3, 2018, www.lifewire.com/what-is-the-portable-people-meter-2843405.

45. Brian Steinberg and Andrew Hampp, "Commercial Ratings? Nets Talk TiVo Instead," *Advertising Age*, June 4, 2007, pp. 1, 60.

46. Antony Young, "Shifting to C7 - Ratings Would Be Good for TV and Advertisers," *Advertising Age*, May 12, 2014, p. 29.

47. Jason Lynch, "A First Look at Nielsen's Total Audience Measurement and How It Will Change the Industry," *Adweek*, October 20, 2015, www.adweek.com/news/television/first-look-nielsen-s-total-audience-measurement-and-how-it-will-change-industry-167661.

48. Jason Lynch, "With Its Total Audience Measurement Rollout Delayed, Nielsen Will Share More Connected TV Data," *Adweek*, March 23, 2016, www.adweek.com/news/television/its-total-audience-measurement-delayed-nielsen-will-share-more-connected-tv-data-170381.

49. Ibid.

50. Stephen Battaglio, "Facing Pressure from Clients, Nielsen Says It Is Changing How It Measures Television Ratings," *Los Angeles Times*, August 5, 1017, www.latimes.com/business/hollywood/la-fi-ct-nielsen-ratings-tca-20170805-story.html.

51. "Nielsen Launches Enhanced Cross-Platform Campaign Measurement Across TV and Digital Ads," *MarketWatch*, January 7, 2019, www.marketwatch.com/press-release/nielsen-launches-enhanced-cross-platform-campaign-measurement-across-tv-and-digital-ads-2019-01-07.

52. Alex Weprin, "Nielsen Adds YouTube to Total Ad Ratings," *MediaPost*, January 7, 2019, www.mediapost.com/publications/article/330163/nielsen-adds-youtube-to-total-ad-ratings.html.

53. Alexandra Bruell, "Nielsen's Grip Over TV Ratings Loosens Amid Streaming Boom," *The Wall Street Journal*, September 7, 2021, www.wsj.com/articles/nielsens-grip-over-tv-ratings-loosens-amid-streaming-boom-11631007002.

54. Ibid.

55. "Nielsen Readies Next-Gen Wearable Metering Technologies and Devices for National, Local and Audio Measurement," *Nielsen*, August 2021, www.nielsen.com/news-center/2021/nielsen-readies-next-gen-wearable-metering-technologies-and-devices-for-national-local-and-audio-measurement.

56. "Audio and Podcasting Fact Sheet," *State of the News Media 2021: Pew Research Center*, June 29, 2021, www.pewresearch.org/journalism/fact-sheet/audio-and-podcasting.

57. Radio Marketing Guide (Radio Advertising Bureau, 2010), www.rab.com

58. "Jacobs Media Unveils Tech Survey 11 at Worldwide Radio Summit 2015," *Allaccess.com*, April 23, 2015, www.allaccess.com/net-news/archive/story/140769/jacobs-media-unveils-techsurvey-11-at-worldwide-ra.

59. Verne Gay, "Image Transfer: Radio Ads Make Aural History," *Advertising Age*, January 24, 1985, p. 1.

60. *The Benefits of Synergy: Moving Money into Radio* (New York: Radio Ad Effectiveness Lab, Inc., December 2004), www.radioadlal.com.

61. Tim Higgins, "The Battle for the Last Unconquered Screen—The One in Your Car," *The Wall Street Journal*, April 6, 2019, pp. B1,3.

62. Avery Abernethy, "Differences between Advertising and Program Exposure for Car Radio Listening," *Journal of Advertising Research* 31, no. 2 (April/May 1991), pp. 33–42.

63. Martin Peers, "Radio Produces Both Gains and Skeptics," *The Wall Street Journal*, January 1, 1999, p. B6.

64. Andrew Hampp, "Liberty Media Rides in to Rescue Sirius XM," *Advertising Age*, February 17, 2009, www.adage.com/article/media/liberty-media-rides-rescue-sirius-xm/134661.

65. Heather Green, Tom Lowry, Catherine Young, and David Kiley, "The New Radio Revolution," *BusinessWeek*, March 14, 2005, pp. 32–35.

66. Andrew Hampp, "Contextual Radio Ads: Clear Channel's New Pitch to National Marketers," *Advertising Age*, January 15, 2010, http://adage.com/article/media/radio-clear-channel-rolls-contextual-radio–advertising/141533/.

67. David McLaughlin, "Nielsen's $1.26 Billion Arbitron Purchase Cleared by U.S.," *Bloomberg Businessweek*, September 20, 2013, www.bloomberg.com/news/2013-09-20/nielsen-s-1-26-billion-arbitron-purchase-cleared-by-u-s-.html.

68. "Nielsen Cancels Radio Ratings in Four More Small Markets," *Inside Radio.com*, September 13, 2018, www.insideradio.com/free/nielsen-cancels-radio-ratings-in-four-more-small-markets/article_95a5f6d0-b729-11e8-abc7-17430de684ed.html.

69. Jon Fine, "A Better Measure of Old Media," *BusinessWeek*, July 9, 2007, p. 20.

70. "Media Rating Council Grants Accreditation to Four Additional Arbitron Portable People Meter Markets," *PR Newswire*, February 5, 2013, www.prnewswire.com/news-releases/media-rating-council-grants-accreditation-to-four-additional-arbitron-portable-people-meter-markets-189901731.html.

Chapter 12

1. An excellent resource on the role of magazines and newspapers as advertising media vehicles is the News/Media Alliance website at: www.newsmediaalliance.org.

2. Herbert E. Krugman, "The Measurement of Advertising Involvement," *Public Opinion Quarterly* 30 (Winter 1966–67), pp. 583–96.

3. *Magazine Media Factbook 2021*, News/Media Alliance, www.newsmediaalliance.org/wp-content/uploads/2018/08/2021-MPA-Factbook_REVISED-NOV-2021.pdf.

4. Ibid.

5. *Mr. Magazine: Launch Monitor*, 2022, www.launchmonitor.wordpress.com.

6. Ibid.

7. Melynda Fuller, "Departures Teams with Audi for First Print User-Activated Ad," *MediaPost*, November 6, 2018, www.mediapost.com/publications/article/327630/departures-teams-with-audi-for-first-print-user-.html.

8. Brian Steinberg, "Gimmicky Magazine Inserts Aim to Grab Page Flippers," *The Wall Street Journal*, August 8, 2005, pp. B1, 2.

9. *Magazine Media Factbook 2021.*

10. Ibid.

11. Sarah Ellison, "Good Housekeeping Touts Its Test Lab to Seek New Readers' Seal of Approval," *The Wall Street Journal*, October 11, 2006, pp. B1, B4.

12. Sara Rosengren and Micael Dahlén, "Judging a Magazine by Its Advertising," *Journal of Advertising Research* 53, no. 1 (March 2013), pp. 61–70.

13. Steve Fajen, "Numbers Aren't Everything," *Media Decisions* 10 (June 1975), pp. 65–69.

14. "Marketing Chart: How Much Millennials, Gen X, and Other Age Groups Trust TV Ads When Making a Purchase," *Marketing Sherpa*, August 22, 2017, www.marketingsherpa.com/article/chart/do-millennials-gen-x-trust-tv-ads?_ga=2.89412443.1138828129.1561573138-1954659036.1561573138.

15. *Magazine Media Factbook, 2021.*

16. Ibid.

17. Kathryn Hopkins, "What Happened to the Brand Magazine?," *Yahoo!*, March 12, 2021, www.yahoo.com/video/happened-brand-magazine-130017551.html.

18. Jon Fine, "Audit Bureau to Change How It Counts Circulation," *Advertising Age*, July 17, 2001, http://adage.com/article/news/audit-bureau-change-counts-circulation/30030/.

19. "ASME Guidelines for Editors and Publishers Updated September 2013," *American Society of Magazine Editors*, www.magazine.org/asme/editorial-guidelines.

20. Study cited in Jim Surmanek, *Media Planning: A Practical Guide* (Lincolnwood, IL: Crain Books, 1985).

21. "How Advertising Readership Is Influenced by Ad Size," Report no. 110.1, *Cahners Advertising Research*, Newton, MA; "Larger Advertisements Get Higher Readership," *LAP Report no. 3102*, McGraw Hill Research, New York; "Effect of Size, Color and Position on Number of Responses to Recruitment Advertising," *LAP Report no. 3116*, McGraw Hill Research, New York.

22. "Almost Everything You Want to Know about Positioning in Magazines," study by Roper Starch Worldwide, Inc. 1999.

23. "Readership by Advertising Unit Type," *Magazine Dimensions*, 2001, Media Dynamics, Inc., www.magazine.org/resources/fact_sheets/adv.

24. "US Online and Traditional Media Advertising Outlook," *Marketing Charts*, July 27, 2022, www.marketingcharts.com/featured226320#:~:text=The%20latest%20estimates%20predict%20a,that%20of%20TV%20advertising%20spend.

25. Kathryn Hopkins, "Magazines Continue to Be Out of Favor with Advertisers," *Women's Wear Daily*, April 14, 2022, wwd.com/business-news/media/magazines-continue-to-be-out-of-favor-with-advertisers-1235159132.

26. "Entertainment Weekly, InStyle Among Six IAC Magazines Ending Print Issues," *Advertising Age*, February 9, 2022, www.adage.com/article/media/entertainment-weekly-instyle-among-six-iac-magazines-ending-print-issues/2398871; Sara Jerde, "All the Magazine Brands That Moved Away from Print This Year," *Adweek*, December 27, 2018, www.adweek.com/digital/all-the-magazine-brands-that-moved-away-from-print-this-year.

27. Beth Braverman, "How Magazine Publishers Are Cutting Print Costs to Improve Profits," *Folio*, August 2, 2021, www.archive.foliomag.com/magazine-publishers-cutting-print-costs-improve-profits.

28. Garett Sloane, "Facebook to Publishers: We Are Not There to Save You," *Advertising Age*, February 5, 2019, www.adage.com/article/digital/facebook-s-campbell-brown-publishers-talk/316541.

29. Rupal Parekh, "Daily-Deal Sites Offer Dose of Growth for Magazine Circulation," *Advertising Age*, February 27, 2012, p. 17; Nat Ives, "Many Magazines That Cut Subscription Prices Lose Subscribers Anyway," *Advertising Age*, February 5, 2010, www.adage.com/article/media/magazines-cheaper-subscriptions-win-subscribers/141945.

30. "Entertainment Weekly, InStyle Among Six IAC Magazines Ending Print Issues."

31. Garett Sloane, "How Publishers Are Eyeing Apple News Plus," *Advertising Age*, March 29, 2019, www.adage.com/article/digital/apple/317181.

32. Evan Tarantino, "What Your Digital Campaign Is Missing," *Adweek*, January 25, 2016, www.adweek.com/sponsored/3-reasons-why-print-advertising-makes-sense-169132.

33. "Newspapers Fact Sheet: The State of the News Media," *Pew Research Center*, June 29, 2021, www.pewresearch.org/journalism/fact-sheet/newspapers.

34. Marc Tracy, "USATODAY Will Introduce a Paywall, Joining News Rivals," *The New York Times*, July 7, 2021, www.nytimes.com/2021/07/07/business/usa-today-paywall.html.

35. Alexandra Bruell, "New York Times Tops 10 Million Subscriptions as Profit Soars," *The Wall Street Journal*, February 2, 2022, www.wsj.com/articles/new-york-times-tops-10-million-subscriptions-as-profit-soars-11643816086.

36. William Anderson, "Student-Run Newspapers Need Our Help—And They're Asking Together for It," *The Nation*, April 25, 2018, www.thenation.com/article/student-run-newspapers-need-our-help-and-theyre-coming-together-to-ask-for-it.

37. Michael Barthel, "Around Half of Newspaper Readers Rely Only on Print Edition," *Pew Research Center*, January 6, 2016, www.pewresearch.org/fact-tank/2016/01/06/around-half-of-newspaper-readers-rely-only-on-print-edition/.

38. Douglas McLennan and Jack Miles, "A Once Unimaginable Scenario: No More Newspapers," *The Washington Post*, March 21, 2018, https://www.washingtonpost.com/news/theworldpost/wp/2018/03/21/newspapers/?noredirect=on&utm_term=.a64fff11f63f;

39. "Newspapers Fact Sheet: The State of the News Media 2021."

40. Adam Grundy, "Internet Crushes Traditional Media: From Print to Digital," *United States Census Bureau*, June 7, 2022, www.census.gov/library/stories/2022/06/internet-crushes-traditional-media.html.

41. Katerina Eva Matsa and Kirsten Worden, "Local Newspapers Fact Sheet," *Pew Research Center*, May 26, 2022, www.pewresearch.org/journalism/fact-sheet/local-newspapers.

42. Julia Angwin, "Newspapers Set to Jointly Sell Ads on Web Sites," *The Wall Street Journal*, January 10, 2007, pp. A1, A8.

43. Sara Fischer, "U.S. Digital Newspaper Ad Revenue Expected to Surpass Print by 2026," *Axios*, June 21, 2022, www.axios.com/2022/06/21/digital-newspaper-ad-revenue-print.

44. Rebecca McPheters, "Magazines and Newspapers Need to Build Better Apps," *Advertising Age*, January 13, 2012, www.adage.com/article/media/viewpoint-magazines-newspapers-build-apps/232085/.

Chapter 13

1. Outdoor Advertising Association, 2022.
2. DOOH.com, 2022.
3. David Kaplan, "Agency Offers In-Store Insight: End-Aisles, Print Surpass TV," *Media Post*, June 23, 2005, www.mediapost.com.
4. Point of Purchase Advertising International, 2016.
5. "The Ultimate List of Transit Advertising Stats & 2022," www.contravision.com, September 28, 2022.
6. California Transit Association, 2017.
7. Product Acceptance & Research, 2007.
8. City News Service, "Los Angeles May Ban Digital Billboards on Uber, Lyft and Taxi Vehicles," *Daily News*, February 13, 2019, www.dailynews.com.
9. Ibid.
10. Outdoor Advertising Association of America, 2013.
11. Mukesh Bhargava and Naveen Donthu, "Sales Response to Outdoor Advertising," *Journal of Advertising Research* 39, no. 3 (July/August 1999).
12. "Public Transportation Facts Ridership Report," *American Public Transportation Association*, September 28, 2022, www.apta.com.
13. Aditi Shrikant, "Why U.S. Transportation Is So Bad—and Why Americans Don't Care," *Vox*, September 26, 2018, www.vox.com.
14. Ibid.

15. Promotional Products Association International, 2016.
16. Promotional Products Association International, 2019.
17. Promotional Products Association International, 2016.
18. Ibid.
19. Ibid.
20. Alissa Wilkinson, "Hollywood's Record Busting 2018 Explained," *Vox*, January 3, 2018, www.vox.com.
21. Michael Burgi, "Cinema Advertising Hopes to Get Close to Pre-Pandemic Ad Revenue Totals with New Tools, Services," *Digiday*, May 10, 2022, www.digiday.com.
22. Cinema Advertising Council, 2015.
23. Hank Kim, "Regal Pre-Movie Package Boosts Recall," *Advertising Age*, June 7, 2004, p. 21.
24. Joe Mandese, "And the Winner Is . . . Cinema Ads: Brain Research Shows They're More Emotionally Engaging Than TV Spots," *Media Post*, February 27, 2012, www.mediapost.com.
25. "Cinema Tickets–United States," *Statista*, May 2022, www.statista.com.
26. Hank Kim, "Regal Pre-Movie Package Boosts Recall."
27. Joe Mandese, "And the Winner Is . . . Cinema Ads."
28. _____ "Cinema Advertising Post-Pandemic: What Does the Future Hold for the Silver Screen?" *The Drum*, December 2021, www.thedrum.com.
29. Katy Bachman, "Taco Bell Goes Cinematic with Ad Campaign," *Media Week*, June 28, 2009, www.mediaweek.com.
30. "Online Viewers Are More Likely Than the Typical Adult to Go to the Movies," *Adweek*, February 20, 2012, p. 17.
31. Simon Hudson, "From Product Placement to Branded Entertainment," *Hotel Executive*, June 2010, http://hotelexecutive.com/business_review/4127/from-product-placement-to-branded-entertainment.
32. Sophie Haigney, "Anatomy of a Product Placement," *The New York Times*, June 24, 2022, www.nytimes.com.
33. Ryan Barwick, "Product Placement Is Going to Take Over Your Favorite Show," *Marketing Brew*, May 13, 2022, www.marketingbrew.com.
34. Mahmud Shahnaz, "Branded Content, Mobile to Grow," *Adweek*, August 8, 2007.
35. Michael Belch and Cristel A. Russell, "A Managerial Investigation into the Product Placement Industry," *Journal of Advertising Research*, March 2005, pp. 73–92.

36. Emma Hall, "UK Gives Product Placement Go-Ahead for February—with Conditions," *Advertising Age*, December 21, 2010, http://adage.com/article/global-news/product-placement-uk-start-date-official-rules/147786/.
37. Marc Graser, "Movie Placement Creates Demand for Nonexistent Show," *Advertising Age*, January 31, 2005, www.adage.com.
38. Brian Steinberg, "'Modern Family' Featured an iPad, but ABC Didn't Collect," *Advertising Age*, April 1, 2010, http://adage.com/article/media/modern-family-ipad-abc-collect/143105/.
39. Abe Sauer, "Product Placements (Including Seoul) Abound in *Avengers: Age of Ultron*," *Brand Channel*, May 5, 2015, www.brandchannel.com.
40. Angela Doland, "Jimmy Fallon's Entire Show Last Night Was a Samsung Ad: Tuesday Wake Up Call," *Advertising Age*, March 26, 2019, www.adage.com.
41. Julianna Rodriguez, "Branded Entertainment v. Advertainment: How to Display Your Logo at Events With Entertainment," *Scarlett Entertainment*, February 14, 2020, www.scarlettentertainment.com.
42. Lauren Maffeo, "The Legal Loophole of Advergames: How Ads Disguised as Video Games Are Impacting Today's Youth," *TNW*, June 29, 2014, www.thenextweb.com.
43. Helena Alcoverra, "What Is Advergaming? Uses and Examples", *CyberClick*, May 24, 2022, www.cyberclick.net.
44. "Ad Supported Video on Demand Is the TV Disruptor for 2022," *Kantar*, December 21, 2021, www.kantar.com.
45. Scott Halpert, "Advertising Based Video on Demand (AVOD) Services: The Complete Guide," *Penthera*, April 19, 2022, www.penthera.com.
46. "VOD Ads Can Complement TV," *WARC*, April 26, 2016, www.warc.com.
47. David G. Kennedy, "Coming of Age in Consumerdom," *Advertising Age*, April 1, 2004, www.adage.com.
48. David Kaplan, "Product Placement: Well-Placed among Consumers," *Media Post*, March 25, 2005, www.mediapost.com/publications/article/28530/.
49. Abe Sauer, "Marlboro Washes Up in *Jersey Shore*: Best Anti-Smoking Ad Ever?" *Brand Channel*, July 19, 2011, www.brandchannel.com.
50. Gail Schiller, "Tie-ins Often Sobering for Liquor Firms," *Hollywood Reporter*, August 1, 2005, pp. 1–3; MarinInstitute.org, 2006.

51. Katy Bachman, "Study: Industry's Found Sneaky Way to Keep Advertising Junk Food to Kids," *Adweek*, August 2, 2011, www.adweek.com.

52. John Consoli, "80% TV Viewers Approve Product Placement," *Inside Branded Entertainment*, March 28, 2005, www .insidebrandedentertainment.com.

53. Kennedy, "Coming of Age in Consumerdom."

54. Harris Interactive, "Attitudes of US Children and Teens toward Advertising Tactics, by Age," *eMarketer*, May 2006.

55. Barry J. Babin, Jean Luc-Herrmann, Mathieu Kacha, and Laurie A Babin, "The Effectiveness of Brand Placements: A Meta-Analytic Synthesis," *The International Journal of Research in Marketing*, December 2021, pp. 1017–1033.

56. Steve McClellan, "Branded Entertainment Finding Its Place (ment)," *Inside Branded Entertainment*, March 28, 2005, www .insidebrandedentertainment.com.

57. Belch and Russell, "A Managerial Investigation into the Product Placement Industry."

58. www.benlabs.com, 2023.

59. Cory Shroder, "3 Guerilla Marketing Methods to Try in 2022," *Latana*, June 27, 2022, www.latana.com.

60. "Branding Your Phone Calls," *First Orion*, 2022, www.firstorion.com.

61. Chandraveer Mathur, "Space X May Launch a Satelllite to Display Billboards in Space," *NewsBytes*, August 9, 2021, www.newsbytes.com.

62. Joe Liebkind, "Shoppers Take to In-Store Video Ads," *Venture Beat*, April 17, 2016, www.venturebeat.com.

Chapter 14

1. eMarketer.com, December 2021.

2. Stephen Dashiell and Megan Horner, "Credit Card Statistics In the United States 2023," *Finder*, February 2023, www.finder.com.

3. Ibid.

4. "U.S. Employed Women 1990–2022," *Statista*, February 3, 2023, www .statista.com.

5. Abby Callard, "When Manufacturers Sell Directly to Consumers Online, Retailers Benefit," *Internet Retailer*, June 10, 2014, www.internetretailer.com.

6. Erik Sass, "Survey Results Make a Case for Direct Mail," *MediaPost*, June 12, 2007.

7. "Direct Mail Marketing Statistics," *Modern Postcard*, 2022, www .modernpostcard.com.

8. Sarah Nassauer, "Why You Won't Stop Getting Junk Mail," *The Wall Street Journal*, January 11, 2018, www.wsj.com.

9. "Catalogs and the Mail Order Industry," *Postal Museum*, 2023, www.postalmuseum.si.edu.

10. Heather Brown, "Are Consumer Catalogs Making a Comeback?," *CBS*, November 7, 2018, www .minnesota.cbslocal.com.

11. Juliette Kopecky, "An Investigation into the ROI of Direct Mail versus E-mail Marketing," *HubSpot*, January 10, 2013, www.hubspot.com.

12. Elaine Underwood, "Is There a Future for the TV Mall?" *Brandweek*, March 25, 1996, pp. 24–26.

13. "TV Advertising Worldwide: Statistics and Facts," *Statista*, January 6, 2023, www.statista.com.

14. *Direct Marketing Association Statistal Fact Book* (New York: Direct Marketing Association, 2015).

15. Marianna Morello, "Print Media + DRTV = Retail Success," *Response*, September 2002, p. 6.

16. "Connected TV Advertising in the US: Statistics and Facts," *Statista*, January 6, 2023, www.statista.com.

17. Sheila Shayon, "QVC Acquires Zulily for $2.4 Billion to Attract a Younger Demographic," *Brand Channel*, August 18, 2015, www.brandchannel.com.

18. Direct Selling Association, 2022.

19. ____ "Direct Mail Data Shows How Important Catalogs Are for Promoting Sales," *Conquest Graphics*, May 13, 2022, www.conquestgraphics.com.

Chapter 15

1. Statista Research Department, "Number of Internet and Social Media Users Worldwide as of July 2022," *Statista*, September 20, 2022, www .statista.com.

2. Dave Chaffey, "Global Social Media Research Summary," *Smart Insights*, February 12, 2019, www.smartinsights .com.

3. Phillip Agnew, "15 Best Marketing Campaigns of 2018: Ranked by Data," *Brand Watch*, January 10, 2018, www .brandwatch.com.

4. U.S. Department of Commerce, "U.S. eCommerce Sales 2012–2022," *Oberlo*, October 21, 2022, www.oberlo.com.

5. Elisa Gabbert, "What's a Good Click Through Rate for . . .," *WordStream*, July 19, 2022, www.wordstream.com.

6. Xiang Fang, Surendra Singh, and Rohini Ahluwalia, "An Examination of Different Explanations for the Mere Exposure Effect," *Journal of Consumer Research*, June 2007.

7. Bartosz Bielecki, "Pop-Up and Pop-Under Ads Still Work: Here's How," *Zeropark*, July 18, 2018, www .zeropark.com.

8. "Consumers Unhappy with Web Site Simply Go Away," *Media Post*, August 23, 2005, www.mediapost .com/publications/article/33195/.

9. Barry Schwartz, "Google Warns It Will Crack Down on 'Intrusive Interstitials'," *Search Engine Land*, August 23, 2016, www.searchengineland.com.

10. Statista Research Dept, "Global Market Share of Search Engines 2010–2022," *Statista*, July 27, 2022, www.statista.com.

11. "State of the Industry 2016," *AdRoll*, January 2016, www.adroll.com.

12. "Native Advertising," *Sharethrough*, 2019, www.sharethrough.com.

13. Ian Schafer, "What Is Rich Media, Really?" *Clickz*, September 23, 2005, www.clickz.com/clickz/column/ 1692953/what-is-rich-media-really.

14. "Rich Media," *Techopedia*, 2019, www.techopedia.com.

15. Jeff Minsky, "Activision-Blizzard's Fernando Machado on Why Gaming Is (Candy) Crushing It as an Advertising Channel," *MediaVillage*, February 16, 2022, www.mediavillage.com.

16. Ibid.

17. "Dictionary and Thesaurus," Merriam-Webster, www.merriam-webster.com, August 10, 2016.

18. Pew Research Center, www .pewresearch.org, February 2019.

19. Daniel Muntinga, "Catching COBRAS," The Foundation for Scientific Research on Commercial Communication, Amsterdam, The Netherlands, 2013.

20. "Why Do People Use Social Media? (Oct 2022 Update)," *Oberlo*, October 2022, www.oberlo.com.

21. Statista Research Department, "Social Media Market Penetration in the U.S. 2013–2022," *Statista*, February 23, 2022, www.statista.com.

22. John D. McKinnon and Danny Dougherty, "Americans Hate Social Media But Can't Give It Up, WSJ/ NBC News Poll Finds," *The Wall Street Journal*, April 5, 2019, www.wsj.com.

23. Sara Lebow, "Facebook Hit 2 billion Users, But Growth is Slowing," *eMarketer*, February 2, 2022, www.emarketer.com.

24. Emily Dreyfuss, "Teens Don't Use Facebook, but They Can't Escape It Either," *Wired*, February 6, 2019, www.wired.com.

25. Gavin O'Malley, "Facebook Struggles to Contain Ad Boycott," *Digital Daily News*, July 20, 2020, www .digitaldailynews.com.

26. Shelly Walsh, "The Top Ten Social Media Sites & Platforms 2022," *Search Engine Journal*, May 30, 2022, www .searchenginejournal.com.

27. Pamela Bump, "What Is TikTok? And Why Marketers Need to Care," www .hubspot.com, July 28, 2022; Pamela Bump, "8 TikTok Marketing Examples to Inspire Your Brand in 2022," www .hubspot.com, April 18, 2022.

28. Daniel Konstantinovic, "TikTok Is Having Trouble Keeping Up with Its Own Growth," www.eMarketer.com, August 15, 2022.

29. Sara Lebow, "TikTok to Surpass YouTube in US–and Come After Other Apps in the Process," www .eMarketer.com, May 9, 2022.

30. Krystal Scanlon, "Prioritizing TikTok, Agencies Move Away from Creating Content for Instagram, YouTube," www.digiday.com, October 24, 2022.

31. Sara Lebow, "Marketers Increasingly Turn to TikTok for Influencer Marketing," www.eMarketer.com, January 19, 2022.

32. Mansoor Iqbal, "Twitter Revenue and Usage Statistics," www.businessofapps .com, September 6, 2022.

33. Garette Sloane, "Twitter's Tailored Audiences Program Gets More Targeted," www.adweek.com, January 14, 2014.

34. Amy Gesenhues, "Instagram Advertisers Stay Loyal, Keep Spending More," www.marketingland.com, February 7, 2018.

35. Mansoor Iqbal, "Instagram Revenue and Usage Statistics," www .businessofapps.com, January 11, 2023.

36. Pew Research Center, www .pewresearch.org, December 29, 2022.

37. Dan Milmo, "Shares in Snapchat Owner Slump Amid Slowdown in Ad Revenue," www.theguardian.com, July 22, 2022.

38. Ying Lin, "10 Pinterest Statistics Every Marketer Should Know in 2022," www.oberlo.com, August 5, 2022.

39. Ibid.

40. Althea Storm, "100 Most Important Social Media Demographics for 2022," www.hootsuite.com, June 6, 2022.

41. Julia Alexander, "The Golden Age of YouTube Is Over," www.theverge.com, April 5, 2019.

42. Todd Spangler, "Squid Game, Samsung, and Apple Top YouTube's 2022 Ad Global Leaderboard," www .variety.com, June 20, 2022.

43. Lauren Johnson, "How YouTube Beauty Star Rachel Levin Keeps 7 Million Subscribers Tuned In," www .adweek.com, May. 1, 2016; "Smosh YouTube Stats," www.socialblade.com, September 9, 2016.

44. Vlogger, "Top 100 YouTube Channels," www.socialblade.com, June 20, 2022.

45. Sara Lebow, "Half of Younger Consumers Buy Products on Social Media," www.eMarketer.com, October 26, 2022.

46. Jeremy Goldman, "Next Year for the First Time, Less Than Half of Digital Audio Listeners Won't Be Podcast Subscribers," www.eMarketer.com, October 4, 2022.

47. Ross Benes, "Podcasts Will Account for More Than One-Fourth of Digital Audio Ad Spending," www.eMarketer .com, August 2, 2022.

48. _____, "Podcast Listeners Worldwide, 2019–2024," www.eMarketer.com, July 2021.

49. Alyssa Meyers, "How Two Major Travel Brands Tell Their Stories Through Podcasting," www. morningbrew.com, July 8, 2022.

50. Alban Brooke, "Podcast Statistics and Data (September 2022)," www .buzzsprout.com, October 4, 2022.

51. Radoslav Chakarov, "How Many Blogs Are There? We Counted Them All," www.webtribunal.net, April 6, 2022.

52. _____ "US AR Users, 2020–2025," www.eMarketer.com, February 2022; Chris Kolmar, "25 Amazing Virtual Reality Statistics [2022]: The Future of AR + VR," www.zippia.com, October 9, 2022.

53. Teodora Dobrilova, "The Most Relevant Mobile Marketing Statistics in 2022," www.review42.com, May 29, 2022.

54. E. J. Schultz, "Mobile Becomes Engine for Auto Marketing," www .adage.com, February 23, 2016.

55. Ibid.

56. Yoram Wurmser, "Mobile Trends," www.emarketer.com, December 6, 2018.

57. _____ "Together, TV and Tablets Drive Brand Searches," www.emarketer.com, December 6, 2012.

58. "Measurement Guidelines and Measurement Certification," 2006, www.iab.net.

59. Jack Neff, "Study: ROI May Be Measurable in Facebook, MySpace After All," www.adage.com, April 13, 2009.

60. "Measurement Guidelines and Measurement Certification."

61. Gavin O'Malley, "Excessive Online Ads Curbed by Metric Standard," www.mediapost.com, August 16, 2012.

Chapter 16

1. Louis J. Haugh, "Defining and Redefining," *Advertising Age*, February 14, 1983, p. M44.

2. Wendy Goldman Getzier, "McDonald's, General Mills among *Despicable Me 2* Marketing Minions," *kidscreen*, May 21, 2013, http:// kidscreen.com/2013/05/21/ mcdonalds-general-mills-among-despicable-me-2-marketing-minions/.

3. Scott A. Nielsen, John Quelch, and Caroline Henderson, "Consumer Promotions and the Acceleration of Product Purchases," in *Research on Sales Promotion: Collected Papers*, Katherine E. Jocz, ed. (Cambridge, MA: Marketing Science Institute, 1984).

4. J. Jeffrey Inman and Leigh McAlister, "Do Coupon Expiration Dates Affect Consumer Behavior?" *Journal of Marketing Research* 31 (August 1994), pp. 423–28.

5. "The Myers Report/MediaVillage Marketing & Advertising Economic Data and Forecasts," MediaVillage, October 2022.

6. Minha Hwwang, Ryan Murphy, and Abdul Wahab Shaikh, "How Analytics Can Drive Growth in Consumer-Packaged-Goods Trade Promotions," McKinsey & Company, October 23, 2019, www.mckinsey.com/capabilities/ growth-marketing-and-sales/our-insights/how-analytics-can-drive-growth-in-consumer-packaged-goods-trade-promotions; Miguel Gomez and Vithala Rao, "Market Power and Trade Promotions in US Supermarkets," *British Food Journal* 111 (2009), pp. 866–877.

7. Jack Neff, "CPG Now Spends More on Digital Than Traditional Ads, But Shoppers Doubt They Work," *Advertising Age*, February 23, 2017, www.adage.com/article/cmo-strategy/ study-cpg-spends-digital-traditional-advertising-combined/308077.

8. Jonathan Maze, "As Its Breakfast Business Grows, Wendy's Takes Aim at Burger King," *Restaurant Business*, August 12, 2022, www.restaurantbusinessonline .com/financing/its-breakfast-business-grows-wendys-takes-aim-burger-king.

9. Ellen Byron and Suzanne Vranica, "Scanners Check Out Who's Browsing," *The Wall Street Journal*, September 27, 2006, p. B2.

10. "NPD Retail Tracking," www.npd.com/products/retail-tracking.

11. Errol Schweizer, "Why Private Label Brands Are Having Their Moment," *Forbes*, June 30, 2022, www.forbes.com/sites/errolschweizer/2022/06/30/why-store-brands-are-having-their-moment/?sh=66b374c038bf.

12. Rachel Wolff, "CPG Brands Lose Market Share to Private Labels as Consumers Focus on Price Tag," *Insider Intelligence*, June 1, 2022, www.insiderintelligence.com/content/cpg-brands-lose-market-share-private-labels-consumers-focus-on-price-tag.

13. Pamela N. Danziger, "How Amazon Plans to Dominate the Private Label Market," *Forbes*, May 6, 2018, www.forbes.com/sites/pamdanziger/2018/05/06/how-amazon-plans-to-dominate-the-private-label-market/#4e11fea772d9.

14. Sarah Nassauer, "Walmart's New Muscle," *The Wall Street Journal*, November 12–13, 2022, pp. B1-6.

15. Andy Serwer, "Bruised in Bentonville," *Fortune*, April 18, 2005, pp. 84–89.

16. Joan Driggs, "Consumer Connect: Pet Products Shopping Snapshot," IRI Worldwide, August 2021, www.iriworldwide.com/iri/media/library/Consumer-Connect-Q2-2021-Pet-Products.pdf.

17. Betsy Spethman, "Tuning in at the Shelf," *Promo 13th Annual Source Book*, 2006, pp. 22, 24.

18. "American Consumers Are Becoming More Price Sensitive," *The Economist*, October 13, 2022, www.economist.com/business/2022/10/13/american-consumers-are-becoming-more-price-sensitive-again.

19. Marc Emmer, "95 Percent of New Products Fail. Here Are 6 Steps to Make Sure Yours Don't," *Inc.*, July 6, 2028, www.inc.com/marc-emmer/95-percent-of-new-products-fail-here-are-6-steps-to-make-sure-yours-dont.html.

20. Leonard M. Lodish and Carl F. Mela, "If Brands Are Built Over Years, Why Are They Managed Over Quarters?" *Harvard Business Review*, 85, no. 7/8 (July/August 2007), pp. 104–12.

21. "Special 'Made in the U.S.A.' WD-40 Smart Straw Cans Celebrate Hard Work, Heritage," *WD-40 Product News and Information*, http://wd40.com/news/in-the-news/JUN0313/.

22. Liva LaMontagne, "MarketingSherpa Consumer Purchase Preference Survey: Why Customers Follow Brands' Social Accounts," *MarketingSherpa*, November 17, 2015, www.marketingsherpa.com/article/chart/why-customers-follow-brands-social-accounts.

23. Matt Southern, "The Top Reasons Consumers Follow and Engage with Brands on Social Media," *Search Engine Journal*, February 12, 2019, www.searchenginejournal.com/the-top-reasons-consumers-follow-and-engage-with-brands-on-social-media/293233/#close; "Why Do People Follow Brands on Social Media?" *Marketing Charts*, June 10, 2020, www.marketingcharts.com/digital/social-media-113405.

24. Lodish and Mela, "If Brands Are Built Over Years, Why Are They Managed Over Quarters?"

25. Jennifer Reingold, "How to Fail in Business While Really, Really Trying," *Fortune*, April 7, 2014, pp. 80–90.

26. Lodish and Mela, "If Brands Are Built Over Years, Why Are They Managed Over Quarters?"

27. R. M. Prentice, "How to Split Your Marketing Funds between Advertising and Promotion Dollars," *Advertising Age*, January 10, 1977, pp. 41–42, 44.

28. Betsy Spethman, "Money and Power," *Brandweek*, March 15, 1993, p. 21.

29. Ethan Jakob Craft, "Kraft Calls for McDonald's Crossover in New Brand Stunt, *Advertising Age*, October 12, 2022, www.adage.com/article/marketing-news-strategy/kraft-mac-cheese-wants-collab-mcdonalds-big-mac/2441721.

30. "Trial and Conversion VI: Consumers' Reactions to Samples and Demonstrations," Promotional Marketing Association, Inc., 2002.

31. Jaewon Kang and Annie Gasparro, "Cheapskates Rejoice: Free Samples Are Back," *The Wall Street Journal*, August 5, 2022, www.wsj.com/articles/free-samples-grocery-costco-whole-foods-11659709260.

32. Natalie Zmuda, "Facebook Turns Focus Group with Splenda Product-Sampling App," *Advertising Age*, July 13, 2009, http://adage.com/article?article_id=137851.

33. Megan O Gorden, "Why Coupons Still Matter," *Vericast*, June, 2022, www.vericast.com/insights/blog/why-coupons-still-matter.

34. Ibid.

35. Inman and McAlister, "Do Coupon Expiration Dates Affect Consumer Behavior?"

36. *Annual Topline View CPG Coupon Facts.* NCH Marketing Services, 2015.

37. "Most Effective Methods for Attributing In-Store Purchases to Mobile Ads According to US Marketers," *eMarketer*, October 16, 2016, www.emarketer.com/Chart/Most-Effective-Methods-Attributing-In-Store-Purchases-Mobile-Ads-According-US-Marketers-Oct-2015-of-respondents/180691.

38. Richard Sale, "Serving Up Sweeps," *Promo*, August 1999, pp. 70–78; "Sweepstakes Fever," *Forbes*, October 3, 1988, pp. 164–66.

39. Douglas Karr, "What Are the Most Popular Prizes for Your Promotion Giveaways?" *Marketing Tech Blog*, May 5, 2016, www.marketingtechblog.com/popular-prizes-promotion-giveaways.

40. David Kiefaber, "Lay's Crowdsourced Potato-Chip Finalists: Cheesy Garlic Bread, Chicken & Waffles, Sriracha," *Adweek*, February 11, 2013, www.adweek.com/adfreak/lays-crowdsourced-potato-chip-finalists-cheesy-garlic-bread-chicken-waffles-sriracha-147197; David Kiefaber, "Sam Adams Crowdsourcing Its Next Beer," *Adweek*, January 20, 2012, www.adweek.com/adfreak/sam-adams-crowdsourcing-its-next-beer-137619.

41. Bob Woods, "Picking a Winner," *Promo*, August 1998, pp. 57–62; Richard Sale, "Sweeping the Courts," *Promo*, May 1998, pp. 148–52, 422–45; Maxine S. Lans, "Legal Hurdles Big Part of Promotions Game," *Marketing News*, October 24, 1994, pp. 15–16.

42. Normandy Madden, "KFC Gets Burned by Digital Coupon Promotion," *Advertising Age*, April 14, 2010, www.adage.com/china/article/china-news/kfc-gets-burned-by-digital-coupon-promotion/143283; Kate McArthur, "McSwindle," *Advertising Age*, August 27, 2002, pp. 1, 22; Betsy Spethmann, "Harrah's Coupon Error to Cost $2.8 Billion," *promomagazine.com*, November 23, 2005; "User–Generated Content: The Good, the Bad and the Ugly," *Yahoo! Advertising Solutions*, December 19, 2011, www.advertising.yahoo.com/blogs/advertising/user-generated-content-good-bad-ugly-193505793.html.

43. Melanie Trottman and Ron Lieber, "Contest Winner Declines 'Free' Airline Tickets," *The Wall Street Journal*, July 6, 2005.

44. Kimberly Palmer, "Why Shoppers Love to Hate Rebates," January 18, 2008, www.usnews.com.

45. Peter Tat, William A. Cunningham III, and Emin Babakus, "Consumer Perceptions of Rebates," *Journal of Advertising Research* 28, no. 4 (August/September 1988), pp. 45–50.

46. "Rebates: Get What You Deserve," *Consumer Reports*, September 2009, p. 7; Brian Grow, "The Great Rebate Runaround," *BusinessWeek*, December 5, 2005, pp. 34–37.

47. Ashley Ketner, "Millennials More Motivated by Rebates Than Other Shoppers," *Intelligent Commerce*, April 2, 2019, www.inmar.com/blog/promotions/2019/04/02/millennials-more-motivated-by-rebates-than-other-shoppers; Brian Grow, "The Great Rebate Runaround."

48. Edward A. Blair and E. Lair Landon, "The Effects of Reference Prices in Retail Advertisements," *Journal of Marketing* 45, no. 2 (Spring 1981), pp. 61–69.

49. "2017 COLLOQUY Loyalty Census Report," *Loyalty One*, June 29, 2017, www.loyalty.com/home/insights/article-details/2017-colloquy-loyalty-census-report.

50. Suzette Parmley, "Loyalty Draws a Card," *San Diego Union-Tribune*, February 9, 2016, pp. C1, C4.

51. "2017 COLLOQUY Loyalty Census Report."

52. Kate Taylor, "Starbucks' Controversial New Rewards Program Launches Today—Here Are the Major Changes You Should Know About," *Business Insider*, April 12, 2016, www.businessinsider.com/starbucks-rewards-makes-major-change-2016-4.

53. Wided Batat, *Experiential Marketing: Consumer Behavior, Customer Experience and the 7Es*, first edition (Routledge, 2019). doi.org/10.4324/9781315232201.

54. Adapted from Terrence A. Shimp, *Advertising, Promotion, and Supplemental Aspects of Integrated Marketing Communication,* 6th ed. (Mason, OH: South-Western, 2003), p. 524.

55. William L. Wilkie, Debra M. Desrochers, and Gregory T. Gundlach, "Marketing Research and Public Policy: The Case of Slotting Fees," *Journal of Marketing & Public Policy* 21, no. 2 (Fall 2002), pp. 275–88; Frank Green, "Battling for Shelf Control," *San Diego Union-Tribune*, November 19, 1996, pp. C1, C6, C7.

56. Warren Thayer, "When Are Slotting Fees Warranted?" *RetailWire*, May 12, 2015, www.retailwire.com/discussion/when-are-slotting-fees-warranted/.

57. "Want Shelf Space at the Supermarket? Ante Up," *BusinessWeek*, August 7, 1989, pp. 60–61.

58. Ira Teinowitz, "Senators Berate Industry Abuse of Slotting Fees," *Advertising Age*, September 20, 1999, pp. 3, 66.

59. Paul N. Bloom, Gregory T. Gundlach, and Joseph P. Cannon, "Slotting Allowances and Fees: Schools of Thought and Views of Practicing Managers," *Journal of Marketing*, 64, (April 2000), pp. 92–108.

60. Brian Stoffel, "The Hidden Profit Machine for Grocery Stores," *The Motley Fool*, August 26, 2013, www.fool.com/investing/general/2013/08/26/the-hidden-profit-machine-for-grocery-stores.aspx.

61. "Crunching the Numbers," *Promo*, May 1, 2001, pp. 49–50.

62. Matthew Kinsman, "No Pain, No Gain," *Promo*, January 2002, pp. 26–28.

63. Tom Steinhagen, "Space Management Shapes Up with Planograms," *Marketing News*, November 12, 1990, p. 7.

64. Srinath Gopalakrishna, Gary L. Lilien, Jerome D. Williams, and Ian K. Sequeria, "Do Trade Shows Pay Off?" *Journal of Marketing* 59 (July 1995), pp. 75–83.

65. Beth Snyder Bulik, "Inside the 'Intel Inside' Campaign," *Advertising Age*, September 21, 2009, www.adage.com/article/news/advertising-inside-inside-intel-campaign/139128.

66. Stuart Elliott, "'Intel Inside' Ad Campaign Shifts Focus to the Web," *International Herald Tribune*, October 11, 2007, www.iht.com.

67. Rebecca Lieb, "Co-op Advertising: Digital's Lost Opportunity?" IAB, October 13, 2012, www.iab.com/insights/co-op-advertising-digitals-lost-opportunity-a-new-study-by-iab-local-search-association/.

68. Jack Neff, "As Retailer Digital Exchanges Proliferate, Will They Become the New Trade Promotion?" *Advertising Age*, October 26, 2015, p. 26.

69. Countdown to Crunchtime, 2022 Reggie Awards, Entertainment or Sports Marketing and/or Sponsorship, www.reggieawards.org/a/gallery/rounds/43/details/14059.

70. Edwin L. Artzt, "The Lifeblood of Brands," *Advertising Age*, November 4, 1991, p. 32.

71. Ana Andjelic, "Retailers: Stop Playing The Promotion Game," *Advertising Age*, November 16, 2016, www.adage.com/article/agency-viewpoint/retailers-stop-playing-promotion-game/306795; Lodish and Mela, "If Brands Are Built Over Years, Why Are They Managed Over Quarters?".

72. Quote by Thomas E. Hamilton, Director of Sales Promotion Service, William Esty Advertising, cited in Felix Kessler, "The Costly Couponing Craze," *Fortune*, June 9, 1986, p. 84.

73. Priya Raghubir and Kim Corfman, "When Do Price Promotions Affect Pretrial Brand Evaluations?" *Journal of Marketing Research* 36 (May 1999), pp. 211–22.

74. Alan G. Sawyer and Peter H. Dickson, "Psychological Perspectives on Consumer Response to Sales Promotion," in *Research on Sales Promotion: Collected Papers*, Katherine E. Jocz, ed. (Cambridge, MA: Marketing Science Institute, 1984).

75. William E. Myers, "Trying to Get Out of the Discounting Box," *Adweek*, November 11, 1985, p. 2.

76. Leigh McAlister, "Managing the Dynamics of Promotional Change," in *Looking at the Retail Kaleidoscope*, *Forum IX* (Stamford, CT: Donnelley Marketing, April 1988).

77. "Promotions Blemish Cosmetic Industry," *Advertising Age*, May 10, 1984, pp. 22–23, 26; Cliff Edwards, "Everyone Loves a Freebie—except Dell's Rivals," *BusinessWeek*, July 22, 2002, p. 41.

78. Lauren Shepherd, "Customers Getting More Burger for the Buck," *San Diego Union-Tribune*, February 13, 2008, pp. C1, C3.

79. Nancy Luna, "McDonald's Makes Two Key Changes to Value Menu," *Nation's Restaurant News*, December 20, 2018, www.nrn.com/quick-service/mcdonald-s-makes-two-key-changes-value-menu.

80. Priya Raghubir, J. Jeffrey Inman, and Hans Grande, "The Three Faces of Consumer Promotions," *California Management Review*, (Summer 2004), pp. 23–42.

Chapter 17

1. www.publicrelationsnewspr.com.

2. Scott M. Cutlip, Allen H. Center, and Glen M. Broom, *Effective Public Relations*, 11th ed. (Upper Saddle River, NJ: Prentice Hall, 2012).

3. Jonah Bloom, "The Cultural Gulf That Separates Marketing and PR," *Advertising Age*, March 11, 2007.

4. _____ "The Evolving PR and Marketing Partnership: Benefits of Self-Reflection," www.prweek.com, December 15, 2020.

5. William N. Curry, "PR Isn't Marketing," *Advertising Age*, December 18, 1991, p. 18.

6. Martha M. Lauzen, "Imperialism and Encroachment in Public Relations," *Public Relations Review* 17, no. 3 (Fall 1991), pp. 245–55.

7. Cutlip, Center, and Broom, *Effective Public Relations.*

8. Thomas L. Harris, "How MPR Adds Value to Integrated Marketing Communications," *Public Relations Quarterly*, Summer 1993, pp. 13–18.

9. Thomas L. Harris, "Marketing PR–The Second Century, Reputation Management," January/February 1999, www.prcentral.com.

10. _____, "History of Successful Boycotts", Ethical Consumer Research Association, Ltd, 2022.

11. Cutlip, Center, and Broom, *Effective Public Relations.*

12. John E. Marston, *Modern Public Relations* (New York: McGraw Hill, 1979).

13. Ben Adams, "Pharma Ad Spending up Just 1% This Year as the Slow Move Away from TV into Digital Continues," www.fiercepharma.com, August 22, 2022.

14. Beth Snyder Bulik, "In Another Record Year for Pharma TV Ads, Spending Soars to $3.7 Billion in 2018," January 2, 2019, www.fiercepharma.com.

15. "Measuring PR's Impact: The Framework for Digital PR," 2019, www.cision.com.

16. Ibid, "The Evolving PR and Marketing Partnership."

17. Eddie Kim, "Earned Media's Value: The True Story," www.prweek.com, July 21, 2022.

18. Stephen Sprayberry, "Measuring the Effectiveness of Your Public Relations Efforts," *PR Insights*, April 2, 2015, www.williammills.com.

19. Jim Macnamara, "PR Metrics: How to Measure Public Relations and Corporate Communications," www.researchgate.net, September 8, 2015.

20. Amit Jain, "Emerging Models of PR Measurement," July 16, 2014, www.prweek.com.

21. Mark Weiner, "Marketing PR Revolution," *Communication World*, January/February 2005, pp. 1–5.

22. Rebekah Iliff, "Why PR Is Embracing the PESO Model," December 4, 2014, www.themediabuy.com.

23. Leisa Goddard, "Why a Video News Release Needs to Be Part of Your PR Strategy," January 31, 2019, www.smartcompany.com.

24. Jaye S. Niefeld, "Corporate Advertising," *Industrial Marketing*, July 1980, pp. 64–74.

25. _____ "Naming Rights, Naming Wrongs," www.performanceresearch.com, October 2013.

26. Wayne Friedman, "Supreme Court OKs Corporate-Sponsored Issue Ads," *MediaPost*, June 27, 2007.

27. Sarah Fils, "The Rise of Cause Marketing," www.business2community.com, December 9, 2022.

28. Matt Petronzio, "90% of Americans More Likely to Trust Brands That Back Social Causes," January 11, 2015, www.mashable.com.

29. "Statistics Every Cause Marketer Should Know," 2016, www.causemarketingforum.com.

30. Janas Sinclair and Tracy Irani, "Advocacy Advertising for Biotechnology," *Journal of Advertising*, Fall 2005, pp. 59–74.

Chapter 18

1. Bradley Johnson, Kevin Brown, and Joy R. Lee, "Ad Age Leading National Advertisers 2022," www.adage.com, June 27, 2022.

2. Laurie Sullivan, "Marketing Budgets Rise, Determining Multichannel ROI, Metrics Remain a Challenge," February 5, 2013, www.mediapost.com.

3. Fournaise Marketing Group, "Marketers Use 'Shocking' Metrics," September 22, 2015, www.warc.com.

4. _____ "Building the Ultimate Dashboard with SAAS KPIs," www.adverity.com, 2022.

5. Peter Minnium, "It Is the Creative, Stupid: 3 Reasons Why Ad Creative Trumps Technology Every Time," February 4, 2015, www.marketingland.com.

6. _____ "The Power of Creative: How Ad Quality Improves ROI," www.adage.com, March 2022.

7. Kallly Huang, Isabella Simonetti, and Tiffany Shu, "TikTok Building Itself into Advertising Juggernaut," www.nytimes.com, November 15, 2022.

8. David A. Aaker and John G. Myers, *Advertising Management*, 3rd ed. (Englewood Cliffs, NJ: Prentice Hall, 1987), p. 474.

9. Spike Cramphorn, "What Advertising Testing Might Have Been, If We Had Only Known," *Journal of Advertising Research* 44, no. 2 (June 2004), pp. 170–80.

10. "21 Ad Agencies Endorse Copy Testing Principles," *Marketing News* 15 (February 19, 1982), p. 1.

11. Ibid.

12. http://measurementnow.net/principles-solution, 2016.

13. Molly Soat, "The Case for Earlier Insights," *Marketing News*, July 2015, pp. 16–17.

14. Ye Hu, Leonard Lodish, Abba Krieger, and Babak Hayati, "An Update of Real-World TV Advertising Tests," *Journal of Advertising Research*, June 2009, pp. 201–206.

15. Steve Outing and Laura Ruel, "The Best of Eyetrack III: What We Saw When We Looked through Their Eyes," 2004, www.poynterextra.org.

16. "The Response Card in Magazines: To Keep It or Not to Keep It?" May 28, 2019, www.a-i-m.com.

17. Hubert A. Zielske, "Does Day-After-Recall Penalize 'Feeling Ads'?" *Journal of Advertising Research* 22, no. 1 (1982), pp. 19–22.

18. Arthur J. Kover, "Why Copywriters Don't Like Advertising Research–and What Kind of Research Might They Accept," *Journal of Advertising Research* 36 (March/April 1996), pp. RC8–RC10; Gary Levin, "Emotion Guides BBDO's Ad Tests," *Advertising Age*, January 29, 1990, p. 12.

19. Terry Haller, "Day-After Recall to Persist Despite JWT Study; Other Criteria Looming," *Marketing News*, May 18, 1979, p. 4.

20. Joel Dubow, "Recall Revisited: Recall Redux," *Journal of Advertising Research* 34, no. 3 (May/June 1994), p. 92.

21. Ravi Chandiramani, "Reckitt Launches Debut iTV Campaign for Finish," *Marketing*, January 10, 2002, p.9

22. "Yankelovich Study Shows Advertising's Effects Vary, Depending on Category and Purchase Funnel Stage," April 16, 2009, www.tvb.org.

23. "Applying Customer Analytics to Promotion Decisions," 2012, www.sas.com.

24. ShopperTrak.com, 2016

25. "How Print and Online Flyers Impact Consumers," November 2, 2018, www.warc.com.

26. Steve McClellan, "New Software to Track In-Store Radio," *Adweek,* October 10, 2005, p. 10.

27. Michel Tuan Pham, "The Evaluation of Sponsorship Effectiveness: A Model and Some Methodological Considerations," *Gestion* 2000, pp. 47–65.

28. Ibid.

29. John Nardone and Ed See, "Measure Sponsorship to Drive Sales-Shift Gears: Move beyond Perceiving Them as Mere Brand Builders and Instead Assess ROI," *Advertising Age*, March 5, 2007.

30. Erin Keller, "Bella Hadid's Nude, Spray-Paint Dress Generated Millions by Going Viral," www.newyorkpost.com, October 3 , 2022.

31. Sarah Coffee, "Bella Hadid's Viral Coperni Look Was Inescapable This Halloween," www.vogue.com, October 31, 2022.

32. Isaac M. Dinner, Harald J. Van Heerde, and Scott A. Neslin, "Driving Online and Offline Sales: The Cross-Channel Effects of Traditional, Online Display, and Paid Search Advertising," *Journal of Marketing Research* 51 (October 2015), p. 527–45.

33. Marek Winearz, "The Market Contact Audit," 2010, www.integration-imc.com.

Chapter 19

1. Steven A. Altman and Caroline R. Bastian, "The State of Globalization in 2021," *Harvard Business Review*, April 12, 2022, www.hbr.org/2021/03/the-state-of-globalization-in-2021; Pankaj Ghemawat and Steven A. Altman, "The State of Globalization in 2019, and What It Means for Strategists," *Harvard Business Review*, February 6, 2019, www.hbr.org/2019/02/the-state-of-globalization-in-2019-and-what-it-means-for-strategist.

2. David Kiley and Burt Helm, "The Great Trust Offensive," *BusinessWeek*, September 28, 2009, pp. 38–42.

3. Emma Hall, "As Regulation Increases, WFA Must Decide What's Worth Protecting," *Advertising Age*, March 12, 2013, www.adage.com/article/cmo-interviews/pernod-ricard-cmo-riley-leads-wfa-amid-regulation-concerns/240222.

4. Geoff Colvin, "Indra Nooyi's Challenge," *Fortune*, June 11, 2012, pp. 149–56; Mutsa Chironga, Acha Leke, Susan Lund, and Arend van Wamelen, "Cracking the Next Growth Market: Africa," *Harvard Business Review*, May 2011, pp. 117–22.

5. Paolo Chua, "Nespresso Shares What's Behind Every Cup in Its Latest Campaign Starring George Clooney," *Esquire*, May 24, 2021, www.esquiremag.ph/culture/lifestyle/george-clooney-nespresso-campaign-a00297-20210524.

6. Hal Conick, "The West's Great Marketing Opportunity in China," *Marketing News*, June/July 2019, pp. 51–59.

7. Thomas L. Friedman, *The World Is Flat: A Brief History of the 21ˢᵗ Century*, (New York: Farrar, Straus and Giroux, 2005).

8. "Global Ad Market on Track for 8% Growth in 2022," Zenith Media, June 8, 2022, www.zenithmedia.com/global-ad-market-on-track-for-8-growth-in-2022.

9. "5 Global Advertising Trends Every Marketer Should Watch, July 10, 2018," *Marketing Insights MGD Advertising*, July 10, 2018, www.mdgadvertising.com/marketing-insights/5-global-advertising-trends-every-marketer-should-watch.

10. Vern Terpstra, *International Marketing*, 4th ed. (New York: Holt, Rinehart & Winston/Dryden Press, 1987), p. 427.

11. Katharina Buchholz, "Asia's Consumer Class Is Growing," *World Economic Forum*, October 22, 2021, www.weforum.org/agenda/2021/10/growth-consumers-asia-indonesia-bangladesh-pakistan-philippines.

12. Cynthia Li, "China's Growth Forecasts Raised into Next Year as Country Reopens," *Bloomberg*, January 18, 2023, www.bloomberg.com/news/articles/2023-01-19/china-s-growth-forecasts-raised-into-next-year-as-country-reopens.

13. Stuart Anderson, "Will China and India Become the World's Leading Economies?" *Forbes*, November 1, 2022, www.forbes.com/sites/stuartanderson/2022/11/01/will-china-and-india-become-the-worlds-top-economies-it-depends/?sh=205ce0697cfe.

14. Panos Mourdoukoutas, "India's Economy on Track to Beat China," *Forbes*, April 21, 2018, www.forbes.com/sites/panosmourdoukoutas/2018/04/21/indias-economy-on-track-to-beat china/#764a04045136.

15. Chris Morris, "Nike Signs Its First Esports Sponsorship Deal," *Fortune*, February 28, 2019, www.fortune.com/2019/02/28/nike-league-of-legends-esports-sponsorship.

16. "Have the BRICs Hit a Wall? The Next Emerging Markets," KNOWLEDGE@WHARTON, January 12, 2016, www.knowledge.wharton.upenn.edu/article/98411.

17. Bryan Harris, "Brazil Faces Economic Headwinds as Lula Prepares to Take Office," *Financial Times*, December 26, 2022, www.ft.com/content/c1b3d202-0d15-4ede-9e59-69dcf635e211.

18. Christel Grizaut, "Think Globally, Act Locally: Marketing to a Multinational Audience," *Advertising Age*, June 28, 2019, www.adage.com/article/industry-insights/think-globally-act-locally-marketing-multinational-audience/2180641.

19. Sophia Mueller, George Belch, and Heather Honea, "Testing a Model of Consumer Purchase Receptivity Toward Foreign Products," *Journal of Marketing Development and Competitiveness* 13, no. 4 (2019)

20. Subhash Sharma, Terrence Shimp, and Jeongshin Shin, "Consumer Ethnocentrism: A Test of Antecedents and Moderators," *Journal of the Academy of Marketing Science*, Winter 1995, pp. 26–37.

21. "Young Europeans Say These Are Their Favorite American Brands," *YPulse*, June 30, 2022, www.ypulse.com/article/2022/06/30/young-europeans-say-these-are-their-15-favorite-american-brands.

22. Daniel Zipser, Jeongmin Seong, and Jonathan Woetzel, "Five Consumer Trends Shaping the Next Decade of Growth in China," *McKinsey & Company*, November 2021, www.mckinsey.com/cn/our-insights/our-insights/five-consumer-trends-shaping-the-next-decade-of-growth-in-china.

23. For an excellent discussion of various elements of Japanese culture such as language and its implications for promotion, see John F. Sherry Jr. and Eduardo G. Camargo, "May Your Life Be Marvelous: English Language Labelling and the Semiotics of Japanese Promotion," *Journal of Consumer Research* 14, no. 2 (September 1987), pp. 174–88.

24. Barbara Mueller, "Reflections on Culture: An Analysis of Japanese and American Advertising Appeals," *Journal of Advertising Research*, June/July 1987, pp. 51–59; Barbara Mueller, "Standardization vs. Specialization:

An Examination of Westernization in Japanese Advertising," *Journal of Advertising Research* 31, no. 1 (January/February 1992), pp. 15–24; Johny K. Johansson, "The Sense of Nonsense: Japanese TV Advertising," *Journal of Advertising* 23, no. 1 (March 1994), pp. 17–26.

25. Michael L. Maynard and Charles R. Taylor, "Girlish Images across Cultures: Analyzing Japanese versus U.S. Seventeen Magazine Ads," *Journal of Advertising* 28, no. 1 (Spring 1999), pp. 39–49.

26. Shintaro Okazaki and Barbara Mueller, "The Impact of the Lost Decade on Advertising in Japan: A Grounded Theory Approach," *International Journal of Advertising* 30, no. 2 (December 2010), pp. 205–32.

27. Francis Hsu, *Americans and Chinese: Passage to Differences* (Honolulu: University Press of Hawaii, 1981).

28. Geoffrey A. Fowler, "China Bans Nike's LeBron Ad as Offensive to Nation's Dignity," *The Wall Street Journal*, December 7, 2004, p. B4.

29. Gerard Prendergast, Wah-Leung Cheung, and Douglas West, "How Far Is Too Far? The Antecedents of Offensive Advertising in Modern China," *Journal of Advertising Research* 48, no. 4 (December 2008), pp. 484–95.

30. "Image Censorship for the Middle East Market," *Color Experts International*, June 27, 2022, www.colorexpertsbd.com/blog/image-censorship-for-the-middle-east-market.

31. "Advertising Restrictions on National Advertising by Country," World Health Organization, www.apps.who.int/gho/data/view.main.54200.

32. Rich Thomaselli, "Will Australia's Cigarette Branding Ban Spread beyond Borders, Tobacco?" *Advertising Age*, August 19, 2012, http://adage.com/article/news/australia-s-cigarette-brand-ban-prompt-domino-effect/236761/.

33. "Malaysia Bans 'Sly' Tobacco Ads," *Marketing News*, September 1, 2002, p. 7.

34. Vanessa Fuhrmans, "In Europe, Prescription-Drug Ads Are Banned—and Health Costs Lower," *The Wall Street Journal*, March 15, 2002, pp. B1, B4.

35. Pritha Mitra Dasgupta, "In Absence of Any Clear Ad Rules, Liquor Companies Using Social Media to Promote Their Brands," *The Economic Times*, July 31, 2014, www.articles.economictimes.indiatimes.com/2014-07-31/news/52285216_1_social-media-liquor-companies-liquor-products; Niraj Sheth, "India Liquor, Tobacco Firms Shift Tack," *The Wall Street Journal*, May 6, 2008, p. B8.

36. Jeremy Slate, "EC Lets Stand Toy Ad Ban," *Advertising Age International*, August 1999, pp. 1, 11.

37. Sam Loewenberg, "Effort in EU to Ban TV Ads Aimed at Kids Gains Steam," *Los Angeles Times*, July 9, 2001, p. C3.

38. Judi Lembke, "Why Sweden Bans Advertising Targeted at Children," *Culture Trip*, February 5, 2018, www.theculturetrip.com/europe/sweden/articles/sweden-bans-advertising-targeted-children.

39. Safran S. Al-Makaty, G. Norman van Tubergen, S. Scott Whitlow, and Douglas S. Boyd, "Attitudes toward Advertising in Islam," *Journal of Advertising Research* 36, no. 3 (May/June 1996), pp. 16–26; Marian Katz, "No Women, No Alcohol: Learn Saudi Taboos before Placing Ads," *International Advertiser*, February 1986, pp. 11–12.

40. "Misleading Advertising," *European Commission*, www.ec.europa.eu/justice/consumer-marketing/unfair-trade/false-advertising; Naveen Donthu, "A Cross-Country Investigation of Recall of and Attitude toward Comparative Advertising," *Journal of Advertising* 27, no. 2 (Summer 1998), pp. 111–22.

41. Dannemann Siemsen Advogados, "Comparative Advertising and Ambush Marketing on the Rise in Brazil," *World Trademark Review*, December/January 2010, www.worldtrademarkreview.com.

42. J. Craig Andrews, Steven Lysonski, and Srinivas Durvasula, "Understanding Cross-Cultural Student Perceptions of Advertising in General: Implications for Advertising Educators and Practitioners," *Journal of Advertising* 20, no. 2 (June 1991), pp. 15–28.

43. Jonathan Cheng, "China Demands Concrete Proof of Ad Claims," *The Wall Street Journal*, July 8, 2005, pp. B1, B4.

44. Stephanie Thompson, "Europe Slams Icons as Food Fights Back," *Advertising Age*, January 31, 2005, pp. 1, 38.

45. Dipayan Ghosh, "How GDPR Will Transform Digital Marketing," *Harvard Business Review*, May 21, 2018, www.hbr.org/2018/05/how-gdpr-will-transform-digital-marketing.

46. Robert D. Buzzell, "Can You Standardize Multinational Marketing?" *Harvard Business Review*, November/December 1968, pp. 102–13; Ralph Z. Sorenson and Ulrich E. Wiechmann, "How Multinationals View Marketing," *Harvard Business Review*, May/June 1975, p. 38.

47. Theodore Levitt, "The Globalization of Markets," *Harvard Business Review*, May/June 1983, pp. 92–102; Theodore Levitt, *The Marketing Imagination* (New York: Free Press, 1986).

48. Melissa Akaka and Dana A. Alden, "Global Brand Positioning and Perceptions: International Advertising and Global Consumer Culture," *International Journal of Advertising* 29, no. 1 (2010), pp. 37–56.

49. Charles R. Taylor and Shintaro Okazaki, "Do Global Brands Use Similar Executional Styles across Cultures? A Comparison of U.S. and Japanese Television Advertising," *Journal of Advertising* 44, no. 3 (2015), pp. 276–88.

50. Maduh Agrawal, "Review of a 40-Year Debate in International Advertising," *International Marketing Review* 12, no. 1 (1995), pp. 26–48; William L. James and John S. Hill, "International Advertising Messages, to Adapt or Not to Adapt (That Is the Question)," *Journal of Advertising Research* 31 (June/July 1991), pp. 65–71; Keith Reinhard and W. E. Phillips, "Global Marketing: Experts Look at Both Sides," *Advertising Age*, April 15, 1988, p. 47.

51. Jack Neff, "Gillette Signs Three Sports Giants for Global Effort," *Advertising Age*, February 5, 2007, http://adage.com/article/news/gillette-signs-sports-giants-global-effort/114822/; Bernhard Warner, "IQ News: Gillette's Mach 3 Media Heft Hits Web: European Sites Next?" *Adweek Online*, August 24, 1998.

52. E. J. Schultz, "Doritos Launches First Global Campaign," *Advertising Age*, March 6, 2013, www.adage.com/article/news/doritos-launches-global-campaign/240173.

53. Kevin Goldman, "Professor Who Started Debate on Global Ads Still Backs Theory," *The Wall Street Journal*, October 13, 1992, p. B8.

54. Anita Chang Beattie, "In Japan, Pizza Is Recast as a Meal for Special Occasions," *Advertising Age*, April 2, 2012, p. 16.

55. Eric White and Jeffrey A. Trachtenberg, "One Size Doesn't Fit

All," *The Wall Street Journal*, October 1, 2003, pp. B1, B2.

56. Criteria cited by Edward Meyer, CEO, Grey Advertising, in Rebecca Fannin, "What Agencies Really Think of Global Theory," *Marketing & Media Decisions*, December 1984, p. 74.

57. Durairaj Maheswaran, "Country of Origin as a Stereotype: Effects on Product Evaluations," *Journal of Consumer Research*, September 1994, pp. 354–65.

58. Daniel Gross, "Yes We Can Still Market: Why U.S. Brands Remain World's Most Valuable," *The Daily Beast*, June 1, 2014, www.thedailybeast.com/articles/2014/06/01/yes-we-can-still-market-why-u-s-brands-remain-world-s-most-valuable.html.

59. Paul Chao, "The Moderating Effects of Country of Assembly, Country of Parts, and Country of Design on Hybrid Product Evaluations," *Journal of Advertising* 20, no. 4 (Winter 2001), pp. 67–82.

60. Beth Snyder Bulik, "Ditch the Flags, Kids Don't Care Where You Come From," *Advertising Age*, June 4, 2007, pp. 1, 59.

61. Salah S. Hassan and Lea P. Katsansis, "Identification of Global Consumer Segments: A Behavioral Framework," *Journal of International Consumer Marketing* 3, no. 2 (1991), pp. 11–28.

62. Arundhati Parmar, "Global Youth United," *Marketing News*, October 28, 2002, pp. 1, 49; "Ready to Shop until They Drop," *BusinessWeek*, June 22, 1998, pp. 104–10; "Teens Seen as the First Truly Global Consumers," *Marketing News*, March 27, 1995, p. 9; Shawn Tully, "Teens: The Most Global Market of All," *Fortune*, May 16, 1994, pp. 90–97.

63. Jerry Wind, Stan Sthanunathan, and Rob Malcolm, "Great Advertising Is Both Local and Global," *Harvard Business Review*, March 29, 2013, www.hbr.org/2013/03/great-advertising-is-both-local.

64. Jessica Dayo, "Frito-Lay Deepens World Cup Strategy with Age-Old Naming Debate," *Marketing Dive*, November 15, 2022, www.marketingdive.com/news/frito-lay-world-cup-marketing-Beckham-Manning/636564.

65. Jerry Wind, Stan Sthanunathan, and Rob Malcolm, "Great Advertising Is Both Local and Global,"

66. Nigel Hollis, *The Global Brand* (New York: Palgrave Macmillan, 2008).

67. Nigel Hollis, "Global Brands, Local Cultures," *Research World*, July/August 2009, pp. 20–24; Piet Levy, "10 Minutes with Nigel Hollis," *Marketing News*, August 30, 2009, pp. 18–19.

68. Natalie Zmuda, "Levi's Names Jaime Szulc Its First Global CMO," *Advertising Age*, August 26, 2009, www.adage.com/article/cmo-strategy/levi-s-names-jaime-szulc-global-cmo/138659.

69. E.J. Schultz, "WPP Wins Coca-Cola's Massive Agency Review," *Advertising Age*, November 8, 2021, www.adage.com/article/marketing-news-strategy/wpp-wins-coca-colas-massive-agency-review/2378756.

70. E. J. Schultz, "What to Expect as Coca-Cola's Massive Agency Review Comes to an End," *Advertising Age*, September 23, 2021, www.adage.com/article/marketing-news-strategy/behind-coca-colas-new-agency-and-marketing-approach/2367646.

71. Normandy Madden, "Shanghai Rises as Asia's Newest Marketing Capital," *Advertising Age*, October 14, 2002, pp. 1, 13.

72. Kevin Goldman, "Global Companies Hone Agency Rosters," *The Wall Street Journal*, July 25, 1995, p. B8.

73. Patrick Coffee, "Mars Consolidates $1.4 Billion Global Media Business with WPP's GroupM," *Adweek*, August 8, 2018, www.adweek.com/agencies/mars-consolidates-1-4-billion-global-media-business-with-wpps-groupm.

74. Brian Bonilla, "Nike Awards $1 Billion Media Account to PMG and Initiative," *Advertising Age*, July 26, 2022, www.adage.com/article/agency-news/nike-awards-media-account-pmg-and-initiative/2424381.

75. Goldman, "Global Companies Hone Agency Rosters."

76. "Advertising Is Indeed Going Global," *Market Europe*, October 1997, pp. 8–10.

77. Anne-Marie Crawford, "Clients and Agencies Split over Ad Superstars," *Ad Age Global* , no. 9 (May 2001), p. 16.

78. Katie Richards, "Put Away the Selfie Stick and Live Like a Local, Urges Airbnb's New Campaign," *Adweek*, April 19, 2016, www.adweek.com/news/advertising-branding/put-away-selfie-stick-and-live-local-urges–airbnbs-new-campaign-170920.

79. Dennis Schaal, "Airbnb Announces Major Global Advertising Campaign to Tout Hosting," *Skift*, February 18, 2021, www.skift.com/2021/02/18/airbnb-announces-major-global-advertising-campaign-to-tout-hosting.

80. Erin White, "German Ads Get More Daring, but Some Firms Aren't Pleased," *The Wall Street Journal*, November 22, 2002, p. B6.

81. Larry Speer, "French Government Attacks 'Sexist' Ads," *Ad Age Global*, May 2001, p. 7.

82. Normandy Madden, "Looking for the Next Brazil? Try Thailand," *Advertising Age*, April 11, 2005, p. 22.

83. Stephanie King, "Indian Ads Come into Their Own," *The Wall Street Journal*, December 12, 2007, p. B4.

84. Daniel Zipser, Jeongmin Seong, and Jonathan Woetzel, "Five Consumer Trends Shaping the Next Decade of Growth in China"; Normandy Madden, "Two Chinas," *Advertising Age*, August 16, 2004, pp. 1, 22.

85. A. Guttman, "Average Daily Time Spent Watching TV per Person in Brazil 2008–2019," Statista, January 23, 2023, www.statista.com/statistics/316111/brazil-time-spent-watching-tv.

86. "Global Media Outlook Report 2022," *YouGov*, www.business.yougov.com/sectors/media-content/global-media-outlook-report-2022.

87. Matthew Holehouse, "More Adverts in Prime Time under EU Rules Change, after Broadcasters Lose Viewers to Netflix," *The Telegraph*, May 26, 2016, www.telegraph.co.uk/news/2016/05/25/more-adverts-in-prime-time-shows-under-eu-rules-change-after-bro.

88. Rochell Burbury, "Australia Ends Ban on Cable TV Spots," *Advertising Age International*, March 1997, p. i22.

89. Leslie Chang, "Cracking China's Huge TV Market," *The Wall Street Journal*, August 1, 2000, pp. B1, B4.

90. "To Cope with New Rules, China TV Station Holds Ad Auction Do-Over," *Advertising Age*, December 9, 2011, www.adage.com/article/global-news/china-tv-station-holds-ad-auction-cope-rules/231492.

91. Jane Lanhee Lee, "TV Marketers Aim to Reap Rural China's Fertile Land," *The Wall Street Journal*, July 30, 2007, p. B2.

92. Hearst Magazines International, www.hearst.com/magazines/hearst-magazines-international.

93. Noreen O'Leary, "The Lay of the Land," *Adweek*, February 5, 2007, pp. 14–21.

94. Kamran Kashani and John A. Quelch, "Can Sales Promotion Go Global?"

Business Horizons, May/June 1990, pp. 37–43.

95. Lenard C. Huff and Dana L. Alden, "An Investigation of Consumer Response to Sales Promotion in Developing Markets: A Three Country Analysis," *Journal of Advertising Research* 26, no. 1 (May/June 1998), pp. 47–56.

96. "Global Consumers Go Sale Searching and Coupon Clipping," *Nielsen*, October 12, 2011, www.nielsen.com/us/en/newswire/2011/global-consumers-go-sale-searching-and-coupon-clipping.html.

97. Douglas J. Wood and Linda A. Goldstein, "A Lawyer's Guide to Going Global," *Promo Magazine*, Special Report, August 1998, p. S11.

98. "Foreign Ads Go Further with PR," *International Advertiser*, December 1986, p. 30.

99. Loewenberg, "Effort in EU to Ban TV Ads Aimed at Kids Gains Steam."

100. Laura He, "China Suspends Business Ties with NBA's Houston Rockets over Hong Kong Tweet," *CNN Business*, October 7, 2019, www.cnn.com/2019/10/07/business/houston-rockets-nba-china-daryl-morey/index.html.

101. Waiyee Yip, "Chinese State Broadcaster CCTV Aired Its First NBA Game Nearly 2 Years after the League Was Blacklisted," *Insider*, March 30, 2022, www.insider.com/china-state-broadcaster-airs-first-nba-game-nearly-two-years-2022-3.

102. Adam Satariano, "Google Fined $1.7 Billion by E.U. for Unfair Advertising Rules," *The New York Times*, March 20, 2019, www.nytimes.com/2019/03/20/business/google-fine-advertising.html.

103. World Internet, *Usage and Population Statistics, 2022*, www.internetworldstats.com/stats.htm.

104. Arjun Kharpal, "Google Shuts Down Translate Service in China," *CNBC*, October 3, 2022, www.cnbc.com/2022/10/03/google-shuts-down-translate-service-in-china-.html.

105. "India among Top 3 Countries for Active User Growth on Facebook, Says Meta," *India News*, February 2, 2023, www.ndtv.com/india-news/india-among-top-3-countries-for-active-users-growth-on-facebook-says-meta-3748341.

106. Itu Rathore, "Twitter Users Worldwide 2022–2024: 32.7 Million Users Are Expected to Leave in the Next Two Years," *DazeInfo Briefs*, December 14, 2022, www.dazeinfo.com/2022/12/14/twitter-users-worldwide-growth-2022-2024-over-30-million-users-are-expected-to-leave.

107. Mark Scott, "How Musk's Twitter Takeover Is Playing out Worldwide," *Politico*, December 29, 2022, www.politico.eu/article/elon-musk-twitter-takeover-is-playing-out-worldwide-activists-advertisers-nigeria-india.

Chapter 20

1. Fred W. Morgan and Jeffrey J. Stoltman, "Advertising and Product Liability Litigation," *Journal of Advertising* 26, no. 2 (Summer 1997), pp. 63–75.

2. Ira Teinowitz, "Curb Proposal Raises Tobacco Marketers' Ire," *Advertising Age*, March 18, 2002, p. 70; Myron Levin, "U.S. to Pursue Lawsuit to Curb Cigarette Marketing," *Los Angeles Times*, March 12, 2002, pp. C1, C15.

3. Reenita Das "Are Direct-to-Consumer Ads for Drugs Doing More Harm Than Good?" *Fortune*, May 14, 2019, www.forbes.com/sites/reenitadas/2019/05/14/direct-to-consumer-drug-ads-are-they-doing-more-harm-than-good; Christine Birkner, "With the Threat of an Ad Ban Looming, Pharma Is Fighting to Repair Its Reputation," *Adweek*, March 27, 2016, www.adweek.com/news/advertising-branding/threat-ad-ban-looming-pharma-fighting-repair-its-reputation-170409.

4. Alice Z. Cuneo, "Of Contracts and Claims; Agencies Face Liability Issues," *Advertising Age*, January 31, 2000, p. 25.

5. Alice Z. Cuneo, "Can an Agency Be Guilty of Malpractice?" *Advertising Age*, January 31, 2000, pp. 24–25; Steven W. Colford and Raymond Serafin, "Scali Pays for Volvo Ad: FTC," *Advertising Age*, August 26, 1991, p. 4.

6. Priscilla A. LaBarbera, "Analyzing and Advancing the State of the Art of Advertising Self-Regulation," *Journal of Advertising* 9, no. 4 (1980), pp. 27–38.

7. Ian P. Murphy, "Competitive Spirits: Liquor Industry Turns to TV Ads," *Marketing News*, December 2, 1996, pp. 1, 17.

8. Stuart Elliott, "Facing Outcry, NBC Ends Plan to Run Liquor Ads," *The New York Times*, March 21, 2002, p. C1.9.

9. E. J. Schultz, "Hard Time: Liquor Advertising Pours into TV," *Advertising Age*, May 14, 2012, pp. 1, 41; Mike Esterl, "Liquor Ads Win Airtime," *The Wall Street Journal*, August 2, 2012, p. B6.

10. Joe Flint and Suzanne Vranica, "NFL Adds Liquor to Menu of Advertisers," *The Wall Street Journal*, June 2, 2017, www.wsj.com/articles/nfl-adds-liquor-to-menu-of-advertisers-1496441710.

11. John F. Archer, "Advertising of Professional Fees: Does the Consumer Have a Right to Know?" *South Dakota Law Review* 21 (Spring 1976), p. 330.

12. *Bates v. State Bar of Arizona*, 97 S. Ct. 2691. 45, *U.S. Law Week* 4895 (1977).

13. Charles Laughlin, "Ads on Trial," *Link*, May 1994, pp. 18–22; "Lawyers Learn the Hard Sell—and Companies Shudder," *BusinessWeek*, June 10, 1985, p. 70.

14. Bruce H. Allen, Richard A. Wright, and Louis E. Raho, "Physicians and Advertising," *Journal of Health Care Marketing* 5 (Fall 1985), pp. 39–49.

15. LaBarbera, "Analyzing and Advancing the State of the Art of Advertising Self-Regulation."

16. "National Advertising Division Annual Report 2021—Summary of Case Work," p. 13. BBB National Programs.

17. Jessica E. Vascellaro, "Regulators Say Love Ain't 'Chemistry' after All," *The Wall Street Journal*, September 17, 2007, p. B5.

18. Ibid.

19. "Miller Lite Can Claim 'More Taste' Than Bud and Michelob Ultra, Says NAD; Recommends Changes to Its 'Know Your Beer' Campaign," *ASRC Reviews*, The Advertising Self-Regulatory Council, December 20, 2018, www.asrcreviews.org/miller-lite-can-claim-more-taste-than-bud-light-and-michelob-ultra-says-nad-recommends-changes-to-its-know-your-beer-campaign.

20. Tanzina Vega, "CoverGirl Withdraws 'Enhanced' Taylor Swift Ad," *The New York Times*, December 21, 2011, www.mediadecoder.blogs.nytimes.com/2011/12/21/covergirl-withdraws-enhanced-taylor-swift-ad/?_r=0.

21. "National Advertising Division Annual Report—2021 Summary of Case Work," p. 13. BBB National Programs.

22. "Children's Advertising Review Unit Issues Revised Guidelines for Responsible Advertising to Children," *BBB National Programs*, July 29, 2021,

www.bbbprograms.org/media-center/prd/CARU-revised-guidelines-for-advertising-to-children.

23. Dorothy Cohen, "The FTC's Advertising Substantiation Program," *Journal of Marketing* 44, no. 1 (Winter 1980), pp. 26–35.

24. Rupal Parekh, "Netanyahu, Abbas Smooch in Benetton Ad," *Advertising Age*, November 16, 2011, www.adage.com/article/agency-news/netanyahu-abbas-smooch-latest-benetton-ad-campaign/231037/; Eric J. Lyman, "The True Colors of Toscani," *Ad Age Global*, August 2001, www.ericjlyman.com/adageglobal.html.

25. Lynda M. Maddox and Eric J. Zanot, "The Suspension of the National Association of Broadcasters' Code and Its Effects on the Regulation of Advertising," *Journalism Quarterly* 61 (Summer 1984), pp. 125–30, 156.

26. Joe Mandese, "ABC Loosens Rules," *Advertising Age*, September 9, 1991, pp. 2, 8.

27. Avery M. Abernethy and Jan LeBlanc Wicks, "Self-Regulation and Television Advertising: A Replication and Extension," *Journal of Advertising Research* 41, no. 3 (May/June 2001), pp. 31–37; Eric Zanot, "Unseen but Effective Advertising Regulation: The Clearance Process," *Journal of Advertising* 14, no. 4 (1985), p. 48.

28. Joanne Voight and Wendy Melillo, "To See or Not to See?" *Adweek*, March 11, 2002, p. 30.

29. Taylor Clark, "The Complete List of Advertising Restrictions on Social Networks," *Ignite*, August 23, 2023, www.ignitesocialmedia.com/social-media-monitoring/the-complete-list-of-advertising-restrictions-on-social-networks.

30. Christopher Heine, "New Facebook Policy Bans Private Gun Sales from Its Platform and Instagram," *Adweek*, January 29, 2016, www.adweek.com/news/technology/facebook-no-longer-allowing-private-gun-sales-its-platform-169312.

31. Irina Slutsky, "Nine Things You Can't Do in Advertising If You Want to Stay on Right Side of the Law," *Advertising Age*, March 6, 2011, http://adage.com/article/news/advertising-regulation-nad-case-rulings-remember/149226/.

32. Quote by Laura Brett, Vice President of BBB National Programs' National Advertising Division, July 2022.

33. Stephen W. Colford, "Speed Up the NAD, Industry Unit Told," *Advertising Age*, May 1, 1989, p. 3.

34. Linda Goldstein, "The NAD Sets Precedent for Others in Media, Marketing," *Advertising Age*, March 6, 2011, www.adage.com/article/guest-columnists/nad-sets-precedent-media-marketing/149217.

35. "Self-Regulation of Advertising in the United States: An Assessment of the National Advertising Division," April 2015, www.olshanlaw.com/resources-publications-Self-Regulation–Advertising-US-NAD.html.

36. Ana Radelat, "Lawyers Recommend Slew of Changes to Advertising Self-Regulation," *Advertising Age*, April 15, 2015, www.adage.com/article/cmo-strategy/lawyers-recommend-slew-ad-regulation/298068.

37. *Virginia State Board of Pharmacy v. Virginia Citizens Consumer Council*, 425 U.S. 748, 96 S. Ct. 1817, 48 L. Ed. 2d 346 (1976).

38. *Bates v State Bar of Arizona*.

39. *Central Hudson Gas & Electric v. Public Service Commission*, 447 U.S. 557, 100 S. Ct. 2343, 65 L. Ed. 2d 341 (1980).

40. *Liquormart, Inc. v. Rhode Island*, 517 U.S. 484 (1996).

41. Erik L. Collins, Lynn Zoch, and Christopher S. McDonald, "When Professional Worlds Collide: Implications of *Kasky v. Nike* for Corporate Reputation Management," *Public Relations Review* 30, no. 4 (November 2004), pp. 411–18; Anne Gearan, "High Court Passes Up Decision on Nike Case," *San Diego Union-Tribune*, June 27, 2003, p. C1.

42. *FTC v. Raladam Co.*, 258 U.S. 643 (1931).

43. Federal Trade Commission Improvement Act of 1980, Pub. L. No. 96–252.

44. Peter R. Darke and Robin J. Ritchie, "The Defensive Consumer: Advertising Deception, Defensive Processing, and Distrust," *Journal of Marketing Research* 44 (February 2007), 114–27.

45. Ivan L. Preston, *The Great American Blow-Up: Puffery in Advertising and Selling* (Madison: University of Wisconsin Press, 1975), p. 3.

46. Isabella C. M. Cunningham and William H. Cunningham, "Standards for Advertising Regulation," *Journal of Marketing* 41 (October 1977), pp. 91–97; Herbert J. Rotfeld and Kim B. Rotzell, "Is Advertising Puffery Believed?" *Journal of Advertising* 9, no. 3 (1980), pp. 16–20.

47. Herbert J. Rotfeld and Kim B. Rotzell, "Puffery vs. Fact Claims—Really Different?" in *Current Issues and Research in Advertising*, James H. Leigh and Claude R. Martin Jr., eds. (Ann Arbor: University of Michigan, 1981), pp. 85–104.

48. Preston, *The Great American Blow-Up*.

49. Chuck Ross, "Marketers Fend Off Shift in Rules for Ad Puffery," *Advertising Age*, February 19, 1996, p. 41.

50. Louise Kramer, "Jury Finds Papa John's Ads Misled," *Advertising Age*, November 22, 1999, www.adage.com/article/news/jury-finds-papa-john-s-ads-misled/60251/.

51. Apryl Duncan, "Better Pizza? Bigger Lawsuit," *About Advertising*, www.advertising.about.com/od/foodrelatedadnews/a/papajohns.htm.

52. Emily Bryson York, "Domino's Claims Victory with Pizza Makeover Strategy," *Advertising Age*, May 20, 2010, www.advertising.about.com/od/foodrelatedadnews/a/papajohns.html.

53. Federal Trade Commission, "Policy Statement on Deception," 45 ATRR 689 (October 27, 1983), at p. 690.

54. For an excellent discussion and analysis of these three elements of deception, see Gary T. Ford and John E. Calfee, "Recent Developments in FTC Policy on Deception," *Journal of Marketing* 50, no. 3 (July 1986), pp. 86–87.

55. Orlando Mayorquin, "Elon Musk's Tesla Accused of Fraud, False Advertising of 'Autopilot' Technology in Lawsuit," *USA Today*, September 15, 2022, www.usatoday.com/story/money/2022/09/15/tesla-elon-musk-sued-autopilot/10386771002.

56. Rebecca Elliott, "California DMV Accused Tesla of False Advertising," *The Wall Street Journal*, August 5, 2022, www.wsj.com/articles/california-dmv-accuses-tesla-of-false-advertising-11659739771.

57. "FTC Gives Final Approval to Settlement with PayPal Related to Allegations Involving Its Venmo Peer-to-Peer Payment Service," *Federal Trade Commission Press Release*, May 24, 2018, www.ftc.gov/news-events/press-releases/2018/05/ftc-gives-final-approval-settlement-paypal-related-allegations.

58. Ira Teinowitz, "FTC Strives to Clarify 'Made in USA' Rules," *Advertising Age*, April 29, 1996, p. 12.

59. Kalpana Srinivasan, "FTC Spells Out Tough Standards for 'Made in USA,'"

Marketing News, January 18, 1999, p. 18.

60. "FTC Issues Rule to Deter Rampant Made in USA Fraud," Federal Trade Commission, July 1, 2021, www.ftc.gov/news-events/news/press-releases/2021/07/ftc-issues-rule-deter-rampant-made-usa-fraud.

61. Cohen, "The FTC's Advertising Substantiation Program."

62. *Trade Regulation Reporter*, Par. 20,056 at 22,033, 1970–1973 Transfer Binder, Federal Trade Commission, July 1972.

63. John E. Califee, "FTC's Hidden Weight-Loss Ad Agenda," *Advertising Age*, October 25, 1993, p. 29; Chester S. Galloway, Herbert Jack Rotfeld, and Jeff I. Richards, "Holding Media Responsible for Deceptive Weight-Loss Advertising," *West Virginia Law Review* 107, no. 2 (Winter 2005), pp. 353–84; Herbert Jack Rotfeld, "Desires versus the Reality of Self-Regulation," *The Journal of Consumer Affairs* 27, no. 2 (Winter 2003), pp. 424–27.

64. Natalie Zmuda, "Reebok Agrees to $25M Settlement Over Butt-Shaping Shoes," *Advertising Age*, September 28, 2011, www.adage.com/article/news/ftc-calls-butt-shaping-shoes-bogus-reebok-stands-claims/230082.

65. Natalie Zmuda, "Skechers Pays $40 Million to Settle Toning Claims FTC," *Advertising Age*, May 16, 2012, www.adage.com/article/news/skechers-pays-40-million-settle-toning-claims/234799.

66. Patrick Coffee, "Volkswagen Confirms $4.3 Billion False Advertising Settlement," *Adweek*, January 10, 2017, www.adweek.com/agencyspy/volkswagen-confirms-4-3-billion-false-advertising-emissions-settlement/123676.

67. For an excellent description of the Campbell Soup corrective advertising case, see Dick Mercer, "Tempest in a Soup Can," *Advertising Age*, October 17, 1994, pp. 25, 28–29.

68. William L. Wilkie, Dennis L. McNeill, and Michael B. Mazis, "Marketing's 'Scarlet Letter': The Theory and Practice of Corrective Advertising," *Journal of Marketing* 48 (Spring 1984), pp. 11–31.

69. *Warner-Lambert Co. v. Federal Trade Commission*, CCH P61, 563A-D.C., August 1977 and CCH P61, 646 CA-D.C., September 1977.

70. Ira Teinowitz, "Doan's Decision Sets Precedent for Corrective Ads,"

Advertising Age, September 4, 2000, www.adage.com/article/news/doan-s-decision-sets-precedent-corrective-ads/57074/.

71. Rich Thomaselli, "What Bayer Campaign Means for Pharma Ads," *Advertising Age*, February 16, 2009, www.adage.com/article/news/bayer–campaign-means-pharma-ads/134624/.

72. "FTC Sends Nearly $50 Million in Refunds to University of Phoenix Students," *Federal Trade Commission*, March 24, 2021, www.ftc.gov/news-events/news/press-releases/2021/03/ftc-sends-nearly-50-million-refunds-university-phoenix-students.

73. John D. McKinnon, "Federal Trade Commission Expected to Launch Effort to Expand Online Privacy Protection," *The Wall Street Journal*, August 10, 2022, www.wsj.com/articles/federal-trade-commission-expected-to-launch-effort-to-expand-online-privacy-protection-11660182122.

74. "FTC Explores Rules Cracking Down on Commercial Surveillance and Lax Data Security Practices," *Federal Trade Commission*, August 11, 2022, www.ftc.gov/news-events/news/press-releases/2022/08/ftc-explores-rules-cracking-down-commercial-surveillance-lax-data-security-practices.

75. Ira Teinowitz, "Howard Stern to Abandon FM Radio," *Advertising Age*, October 6, 2004, www.adage.com/article/media/howard-stern-abandon-fm-radio-move-sirius/41266/; Ira Teinowitz, "Clear Channel Drops Howard Stern," *Advertising Age*, February 26, 2004, www.adage.com/article/media/clear-channel-drops-howard-stern-fcc-indecency-fine/39530.

76. Ira Teinowitz, "FCC to Probe Super Bowl Halftime Breast Incident," *Advertising Age*, February 2, 2004, www.adage.com/article/media/fcc-probe-super-bowl-halftime-show-wardrobe-malfunction/39341.

77. Ira Teinowitz and Matthew Creamer, "Fake News Videos Unmasked in FCC Crackdown," *Advertising Age*, April 18, 2005, http://adage.com/article/news/fake-news-videos-unmasked-fcc-crackdown/102925/.

78. Daniel Hertzberg, "Blasting Away at Product Placement," *Bloomberg BusinessWeek*, October 26, 2010, p. 60.

79. Rich Thomaselli, "Cheerios First in FDA Firing Line. Who's Next?" *Advertising Age*, May 18, 2009, http://adage.com/print?article_id=136704.

80. E. J. Schultz, "Did FDA Cross the Line in Its 2009 Cheerios-Case Finding?" *Advertising Age*, March 6, 2011, www.adage.com/article/news/fda-cross-line-2009-cheerios-case-finding/149236/.

81. Sheryl Stolberg, "Clinton Imposes Wide Crackdown on Tobacco Firms," *Los Angeles Times*, August 24, 1996, pp. A1, A10.

82. Joy Johnson Wilson, "Summary of the Attorneys General Master Tobacco Settlement Agreement," National Conference of State Legislators, www.academic.udayton.edu/health/syllabi/tobacco/summary.

83. Rich Thomaselli, "FDA Set to Take Control of Tobacco Regulation," *Advertising Age*, June 11, 2009, http://adage.com/article/news/marketing-curbs-expected-fda-controls-tobacco/137253/.

84. "E-Cigarettes, Vapor Devices to Come under FDA Oversight," *Advertising Age*, May 5, 2016, www.adage.com/article/media/e-cigarettes-vapor-devices-fda-oversight/303899.

85. "Results from the Annual National Youth Tobacco Survey 2022," United States Food and Drug Administration, www.fda.gov/tobacco-products/youth-and-tobacco/results-annual-national-youth-tobacco-survey.

86. Jisu Huh and Rita Langteau, "Presumed Influence of Direct-to-Consumer (DTC) Prescription Drug Advertising on Patients: The Physician's Perspective," *Journal of Advertising* 36, no. 3 (Fall 2007), pp. 151–72; Sejung Marina Choi and Wei-Na Lee, "Understanding the Impact of Direct-to-Consumer (DTC) Pharmaceutical Advertising on Patient–Physician Interaction," *Journal of Advertising* 36, no. 3 (Fall 2007), pp. 137–49.

87. Ana Radelat, "Lawmaker Introduces Bill That Would Curb Drug Advertising," *Advertising Age*, February 22, 2016, www.adage.com/article/cmo-strategy/lawmaker-introduces-bill-curb-drug-advertising/302797.

88. Rachel Roubein, "Biden's Directive on Marijuana Faces a Catch-22," *The Washington Post*, October 10, 2022, www.washingtonpost.com/politics/2022/10/10/biden-directive-marijuana-faces-catch-22.

89. Bruce Buchanan and Doron Goldman, "Us vs. Them: The Minefield of Comparative Ads," *Harvard Business Review*, May/June 1989, pp. 38–50.

90. Maxine Lans Retsky, "Lanham Have It: Law and Comparative Ads," *Marketing News*, November 8, 1999, p. 16.

91. Jeunesse M. Rutledge, "Beer Wars Are Back: What Companies Can Learn from MillerCoors Suite against Anheuser-Busch in 'Corngate'," *Milwaukee Business Journal*, April 17, 2019, www.bizjournals.com/milwaukee/news/2019/04/17/beer-wars-are-back-what-companies-can-learn-from.html.

92. Michael J. Barone, Randall L. Rose, Paul W. Minniard, and Kenneth C. Manning, "Enhancing the Detection of Misleading Comparative Advertising," *Journal of Advertising Research* 39, no. 5 (September/October 1999), pp. 43–50.

93. Steven Colford, "ABA Panel Backs FTC over States," *Advertising Age*, April 10, 1994, p. 1.

94. "Airborne to Pay $23.3 Million for False Advertising," *Natural Standard Blog*, March 21, 2008, www.blog.naturalstandard.com/natural-standard-blog/2008/03/airborne.

95. George P. Slefo, "Fanduel, DraftKings to Pay $6 Million Each Amid False Advertising Claims," *Advertising Age*, October 26, 2016, www.adage.com/article/digital/fanduel-draftkings-agree-pay-6-million-amid-false-advertising-claims/306477.

96. "States Settle with Google and iHeartMedia," *Associated Press*, November 28, 2022, www.apnews.com/article/technology-business-california-federal-trade-commission-0df2707207b2bab0fcbb8dc0c65a9f5.

97. S. J. Diamond, "New Director Putting Vigor Back into FTC," *Los Angeles Times*, March 29, 1991, pp. D1, D4.

98. Federal Trade Commission, "Trade Regulation Rule: Games of Chance in the Food Retailing and Gasoline Industries," 16 CFR, Part 419 (1982).

99. Richard Sale, "Sweeping the Courts," *Promo*, May 1998, pp. 42–45, 148–52; Ira Teinowitz and Carol Krol, "Multiple States Scrutinize Sweepstakes Mailings," *Advertising Age*, February 9, 1998, p. 41; Mark Pawlosky, "States Rein in Sweepstakes, Game Operators," *The Wall Street Journal*, July 3, 1995, pp. B1, B3.

100. Steven Winters and Joann Kohl, "Keep Your Online Sweepstakes and Contests on the Right Side of the Law," *Advertising Age*, March 6, 2011, ww.adage.com/article/guest-columnists/online-sweepstakes-legal/149206.

101. Ibid.

102. Martin Beck, "Facebook Is Tearing Down the Like Gate: Are You Ready?" *Marketing Land*, November 4, 2014, www.marketingland.com/facebook-tearing-like-gate-ready-106611.

103. *Children Advertising Review Unit Self-Regulatory Guidelines for Children is Advertising*, Council of Better Business Bureaus, 2003, www.caru.org/guidelines/index.

104. Federal Trade Commission, "Guides for Advertising Allowances and Other Merchandising Payments and Services," 16 CFR, Part 240 (1983).

105. Federal Trade Commission, "Trade Regulation Rule: Use of Negative Option Plans by Sellers in Commerce," 16 CFR, Part 42 (1982).

106. For a more thorough discussion of legal aspects of sales promotion and mail-order practices, see Dean K. Fueroghne, *Law & Advertising* (Chicago: Copy Workshop, 1995).

107. Mary Lu Carnevale, "FTC Adopts Rules to Curb Telemarketing," *The Wall Street Journal*, September 18, 1992, pp. B1, B10.

108. Ira Teinowitz, "Congress Approves National 'Do Not Call'," *Advertising Age*, February 13, 2003, www.adage.com/article/news/congress-approves-national-call/36837.

109. Kathreine Skiba, "Do Not Call Registry Rises as Robocalls Drop," *AARP*, December 13, 2018, www.aarp.org/money/scams-fraud/info-2018/do-not-call-registry-growing.html.

110. Ira Teinowitz, "'Do Not Call' Law Upheld as Constitutional," *Advertising Age*, February 17, 2004, www.adage.com/article/news/call-law-upheld-constitutional/39453.

111. Ira Teinowitz, "'Do Not Call' Does Not Hurt Direct Marketers," *Advertising Age*, April 11, 2005, pp. 3, 95.

112. Herbert Jack Rotfeld, "Do-Not-Call as the US Government's Improvement to Telemarketing Efficiency," *Journal of Consumer Marketing* 21, no. 4 (2004), pp. 242–44.

113. Jennifer Levitz and Kelly Greene, "Marketers Use Trickery to Evade No-Call Lists," *The Wall Street Journal*, October 26, 2007, p. A1, A8.

114. Natasha Shabani, "Are You Using Sweepstakes to Skirt the Do-Not-Call List?" *Advertising Age*, April 12, 2010, www.adage.com/article/guest-columnists/sweepstakes-skirt-call-list/143190/.

115. Jenny Rough, "Saving Trees and Your Sanity by Managing Junk Mail," *The Examiner*, February 14, 2010, p. 31; Steven Swanson, "Up to Here in Catalogs? There Is a Solution Online," *Tribune Business News*, November 4, 2007.

116. Whitson Gordon, "How To Cut Down on Unwanted Junk Mail," *The New York Times*, March 8, 2018, www.nytimes.com/2018/03/08/smarter-living/how-to-cut-down-on-unwanted-junk-mail.html.

117. Ira Teinowitz and Jennifer Gilbert, "FTC Chairman: Stop Undisclosed Profiling on Net," *Advertising Age*, November 8, 1999, p. 2.

118. Andrea Petersen, "DoubleClick Reverses Course after Privacy Outcry," *The Wall Street Journal*, March 3, 2000, pp. B1, B6; Jennifer Gilbert and Ira Teinowitz, "Privacy Debate Continues to Rage," *Advertising Age*, February 7, 2000, pp. 44, 46.

119. "NAI Launches Privacy-Awareness Web Site," *Advertising Age*, May 28, 2001, www.adage.com/article/news/nai-launches-privacy-awareness-website/11226/; "Online Advertisers Launch Two Consumer Privacy Tools," *Network Advertising Initiative*, May 23, 2001, www.networkadvertising.org/aboutnai.

120. Cotton Delo, "FTC Privacy Report Urges Congress to Pass Data-Security Legislation," *Advertising Age*, March 26, 2012, www.adage.com/article/digital/ftc-urges-congress-pass-data-security-legislation/233719/; Larry Dobrow, "Privacy Issues Loom for Marketers," *Advertising Age*, March 13, 2006, www.adage.com/article/100-leading-media-companies/privacy-issues-loom-companies-marketing-kids-online/107066.

121. Ira Teinowitz, "Why Ignoring New Voluntary FTC Privacy Guidelines Could Be Perilous," *Advertising Age*, December 28, 2007, www.adage.com/article/digital/ignoring-voluntary-ftc-privacy-guidelines-perilous/122814/; Betsy Spethmann,"Private Eyes," *Promo*, January 2002, pp. 37–43; "Protecting Consumers' Privacy: 2002 and Beyond," Remarks of FTC chair Timothy J. Muris at the Privacy 2001 Conference, Cleveland, Ohio, October 4, 2001, www.ftc.gov/speeches/muris/privisp1002.

122. Kate Kaye, "Do-Not-Track Show Will Go on at W3C—for Now Group Names Two New Co-Chairs,"

Advertising Age, September 20, 2013, www.adage.com/article/privacy-and-regulation/track-show-w3c/244285/; Ira Teinowitz, "Consumer Groups Push Obama for 'Do Not Track' List," *Advertising Age*, December 16, 2008, www.adage.com/article/news/consumer-groups-push-obama-track-list/133329.

123. Dawn Chmielewski, "How 'Do Not Track' Ended Up Going Nowhere," *recode*, January 4, 2016, www.recode.net/2016/1/4/11588418/how-do-not-track-ended-up-going-nowhere; Fred B. Campbell, "The Slow Death of 'Do Not Track,'" *The New York Times*, December 26, 2014, www.nytimes.com/2014/12/27/opinion/the-slow-death-of-do-not-track.html.

124. Bryon Acohido, "FTC Tells Twitter to Protect the Private Data of Its Users," *USA Today*, June 25, 2010, p. 3B.

125. Stacey Higginbotham, "The FTC's Wyndham Victory Is Good for Privacy but Confusing for Business," *Fortune*, August 28, 2015, www.fortune.com/2015/08/28/ftc-wyndham-privacy-courts.

126. James Heckman, "COPPA to Bring No Surprises, Hefty Violation Fines in April," *Marketing News*, January 31, 2000, p. 6.

127. Ira Teinowitz, "FTC Proposal on Kids' Privacy Raises Ire of Watchdog Groups," *Advertising Age*, March 14, 2005, www.adage.com/article/digital/ftc-proposal-kids-privacy-raises-ire-watchdog-groups/102494.

128. Natasha Singer and Kate Conger, "Google Is Fined $170 Million for Violating Children's Privacy on YouTube," *The New York Times*, August 10, 2021, www.nytimes.com/2019/09/04/technology/google-youtube-fine-ftc.html.

129. Sarah E. Needleman, Aaron Tilley, and Brent Kendall, "Epic Games, Maker of 'Fortnite,' to Pay $520 Million to Resolve FTC Allegations," *The Wall Street Journal*, December 19, 2022, www.wsj.com/articles/epic-games-maker-of-fortnite-to-pay-520-million-to-resolve-ftc-allegations-11671456744.

130. Abbey Klassen and Michael Learmonth, "What You Need to Know about the New FTC Endorsement Rules and Why," *Advertising Age*, October 12, 2009, www.adage.com/article/digital/ftc-endorsement-rules/139595.

131. "Xbox One Promoter Settles FTC Charges That It Deceived Consumers with Endorsement Video Posted by Paid 'Influencers'," Federal Trade Commission Press Release, September 2, 2015 www.ftc.gov/news-events/news/press-releases/2015/09/xbox-one-promoter-settles-ftc-charges-it-deceived-consumers-endorsement-videos-posted-paid.

132. "FTC Issues Enforcement Policy Statement Addressing 'Native' Advertising and Deceptively Formatted Advertisements," *Federal Trade Commission*, December 22, 2015, www.ftc.gov/public-statements/2015/12/commission-enforcement-policy-statement-deceptively-formatted.

133. Jeremy Barr, "FTC Spells Out Its Guidelines for Native Ads," *Advertising Age*, December 22, 2015, www.adage.com/article/media/federal-trade-commission-releases-native-ad-guidelines/301921/.

134. Ira Teinowitz, "U.S. House Passes Anti-Spam Measure in Dawn Session," *Advertising Age*, November 23, 2003, www.adage.com/article/digital/u-s-house-passes-anti-spam-measure-dawn-session/38896/; Lisa Takeuchi Cullen, "Some More Spam, Please," *Time*, November 11, 2002, pp. 58–62.

135. Tom Zeller Jr., "Federal Law Hasn't Curbed Junk E-mail," *San Diego Union-Tribune*, February 1, 2005, pp. C1, C5.

136. David Normoyle, "Data Privacy for Marketers," *Digital Marketing Institute*, June 20, 2022, www.digitalmarketinginstitute.com/blog/data-privacy-for-marketers.

Chapter 21

1. Robert L. Heilbroner, "Demand for the Supply Side," *New York Review of Books* 38 (June 11, 1981), p. 40.

2. David Helm, "Advertising's Overdue Revolution," speech given to the Adweek Creative Conference, October 1, 1999.

3. Claire Atkinson, "FTC and FCC Nearing Product-Placement Decisions," *Advertising Age*, October 29, 2004, http://adage.com/article/news/ftc-fcc-nearing-product-placement-decisions/41433/; Daniel Eisenberg, "It's an Ad, Ad, Ad World," *Time*, September 2, 2002, pp. 38–41.

4. Eric N. Berkowitz, Roger A. Kerin, Steven W. Hartley, and William Rudelius, *Marketing*, 7th ed. (Burr Ridge, IL: Irwin/McGraw Hill, 2003), p. 21.

5. Andrew Limbong, "How the Tobacco Industry Targeted Black Americans with Menthol Smokes," www.npr.org, April 29, 2022.

6. Julia Craven, "How Menthol Cigarettes Became Black Americans' Preferred Smoke," www.slate.com, May 14, 2021.

7. "Binge Drinking and Alcoholism on College Campuses," July 5, 2019, www.alcohol.org.

8. Editorial Board, "Dartmouth College Tackles Campus Drinking with a Ban on Hard Alcohol," January 31, 2015, www.washingtonpost.com; Vivian B. Faden and Marcy L. Baskin, "Evaluation of College Alcohol Policies," 2014, www.collegedrinkingprevention.gov.

9. "Rules and Regulations about Marketing Alcohol," January 14, 2019, www.alcohol.org.

10. Ira Teinowitz, "Underage-Drinking Report Calls for Voluntary Alcohol Cutbacks," *Advertising Age*, March 6, 2007, http://adage.com/article/news/underage-drinking-report-calls-voluntary-alcohol-ad-cutbacks/115414/.

11. E. J. Schultz, "Bud Light Apologizes for Message on Its Bottle That Critics Linked to Rape Culture," April 28, 2015, www.adage.com.

12. Megan Brenan, "Americans Trust in Media Remains Near Record Low," www.gallup.com, October 18, 2022.

13. Gita Venkataramini Johar, "Consumer Involvement and Deception from Implied Advertising Claims," *Journal of Marketing Research* 32 (August 1995), pp. 267–79; J. Edward Russo, Barbara L. Metcalf, and Debra Stephens, "Identifying Misleading Advertising," *Journal of Consumer Research* 8 (September 1981), pp. 119–31.

14. Zach Bowman, "Hyundai, Kia Admit Exaggerated Mileage Claims, Will Compensate Owners," November 2, 2012, www.autoblog.com.

15. Danielle Ivory, "Ford Lowers Gas Mileage on 6 Models, All 2013–14s," www.nytimes.com, June 12, 2014.

16. Justin Elliott, "FTC Sues to Stop 'Deceptive' TurboTax 'Free' Campaign," www.propublica.com, March 29, 2022.

17. Jack Neff, "Trojan Ads Ready for Prime Time: NBC," *Advertising Age*, May 16, 2005, p. 3.

18. Michael T. Ewing, "The Good News about Television: Attitudes Aren't Getting Worse," *Journal of Advertising Research*, March 2013, p. 89.

19. Visible Measures, "The Most Successful Sexy Ads," www.adsoftheworld.com/blog/the_most_successful_sexy_ads.

20. James B. Arndorfer, "Skyy Hit the Limit with Racy Ad: Critics," *Advertising Age*, February 7, 2005, p. 6.

21. John G. Wirtz, Johnny V Sparks, and Thais M. Zimbres, "The Effect of Exposure Appeals in Advertisements on Memory, Attitude, and Purchase Intention: A Meta-Analytic Review," *Journal of Advertising Research* 37 (2018).

22. Leanne Potts, "Retailers, Ads Bare Flesh for Bottom Line," *Albuquerque Journal*, December 20, 2002, p. D1.

23. Natalie Mortimer, "How Benetton Moved from Shockvertising to Be Nevershocking," July 7, 2016, www.thedrum.com.

24. Melinda Wenner Moyer, "Kids as Young as 8 Are Using Social Media More Than Ever, Study Shows," www.nytimes.comm March 24, 2022.

25. _____, "Report of the APA Task Force on Advertising and Children," www.ap.org, 2022.

26. Mark J. Miller, "Camel Cigarettes Under Fire for Targeting Kids—Again," www.brandchannel.com, May 31, 2013.

27. Julia Belluz, "The Vape Company Juul Said It Doesn't Target Teens. Its Early Ads Tell a Different Story," January 25, 2019, www.vox.com.

28. Saba Hamedy, "Ad Overload?" *Los Angeles Times*, April 7, 2015, pp. C1, C3.

29. Merrie Brucks, Gary M. Armstrong, and Marvin E. Goldberg, "Children's Use of Cognitive Defenses against Television Advertising: A Cognitive Response Approach," *Journal of Consumer Research* 14, no. 4 (March 1988), pp. 471–82.

30. Tamara F. Mangleburg and Terry Bristol, "Socialization and Adolescents' Skepticism toward Advertising," *Journal of Advertising* 27, no. 3 (Fall 1998), pp. 11–21.

31. Ronald Alsop, "Watchdogs Zealously Censor Advertising Targeted to Kids," *The Wall Street Journal*, September 5, 1985, p. 35.

32. *Report of the APA Task Force on Advertising and Children*, February 20, 2004, www.apa.org.

33. Tiffany Meyers, "Marketing to Kids Comes under Fresh Attack," *Advertising Age*, February 21, 2005, pp. S2, S8.

34. Ronald Berman, *Advertising and Social Change* (Beverly Hills, CA: Sage, 1981), p. 13.

35. Joan Voight, "The Consumer Rebellion," www.adweek.com, January 10, 2000.

36. Glennisha Morgan, "Amazon Kindle Backs Gay Marriage with New Commercial," February 21, 2013, www.huffingtonpost.com.

37. Stephen Fox, *The Mirror Makers: A History of American Advertising and Its Creators* (New York: Morrow, 1984), p. 330.

38. Shelby D. Hunt, "Informational vs. Persuasive Advertising: An Appraisal," *Journal of Advertising*, Summer 1976, pp. 5–8.

39. "Historical Context," *Ad Age*, February 18, 2019, www.adage.com.

40. Andrew Hampp, "An Ad in Which Boy Gets Girl . . . or Boy," *Advertising Age*, August 6, 2007, http://adage.com.

41. Lawrence C. Soley and Robert L. Craig, "Advertising Pressure on Newspapers: A Survey," *Journal of Advertising*, December 1992, pp. 1–10.

42. Mark Simon, "Mercury News Ad Dispute Cooling Off: Advertisers Return while Reporters Stew," *San Francisco Business Chronicle*, July 15, 1994, p. B1.

43. Nat Ives, "GM Ends 'L.A.Times Boycott', Resumes Advertising," *Advertising Age*, August 2, 2005.

44. Laurie Sullivan, "NBC Universal, Viacom CBS, iHeart Media Run Coronavirus PSAs on Donated Media," www.mediadailynews.com, March 18, 2020.

45. _____ "Bottled Water Market Size, Proficient Market Insights," www.yahoofinance.com, October 6, 2022.

46. Clare O'Conner, "How Spanx Became a Billion-Dollar Business without Advertising," www.forbes.com, March 12, 2012.

47. Paul W. Farris and Mark S. Albion, "The Impact of Advertising on the Price of Consumer Products," *Journal of Marketing* 74, no. 3 (Summer 1980), pp. 17–35.

48. Ibid, p. 30.

Chapter 22

1. Ginger Conlon, "Cornering the Market," *Sales and Marketing Management*, March 1997, pp. 74–76.

2. Carl G. Stevens and David P. Keane, "How to Become a Better Sales Manager: Give Salespeople How to Not Rah Rah," *Marketing News*, May 30, 1980, p. 1.

3. Kevin Hoffberg and Kevin J. Corcoran, "Selling at the Speed of Change," *Customers 2000*, pp. S22-26.

4. Caroline Forsey, "The Ultimate Guide of Relationship Marketing," February 14, 2019, www.hubspot.com.

5. Sarita Harbour, "The Difference between Relationship Marketing & CRM," 2019, www.smallbusiness.chron.com.

6. Chuck Ingram, "Blogs by Chuck Ingram," www.tgribridge.com, November 21, 2016.

7. Bob Donath, "Move Over CRM, Marketing Automation Has Arrived," *Marketing News*, March 18, 2002, p. 6; Bob Sullivan, "Lower Cost per Sales with CRM, Mapping Software & Call Planning," www.inddist.com, August 12, 2013.

8. Russ Hill, "What Is the Cost of a BtoB Sales Call," www.ultimatelead.com, November 4, 2013.

9. Melinda Ligos, "Gimme, Gimme, Gimme," *Sales and Marketing Management*, March 2002, pp. 32–40.

10. Erin Strout, "Spy Games," *Sales & Marketing Management*, February 2002, pp. 30–33.

11. John E. Morrill, "Industrial Advertising Pays Off," *Harvard Business Review*, March/April 1970, p. 4.

12. "Salespeople Contact Fewer Than Ten Percent of Decision Makers in Last Two Months," McGraw Hill, 1987.

13. Ryan Scott, "10 Years after Hurricane Katrina, Companies Approach Disaster Relief Differently," www.causecast.com, August 25, 2015.

14. Steve Deist and Rick Johnson, "Developing an Effective Sales Force," *Industrial Distribution*, April 2005, p. 75.

15. "The Metrics of Bad Sales Interactions: A Sales Experience Benchmark Report," 2014, www.demandmetrics.com.

Name and Company Index

In this index "*f*" indicates figure and "n" indicates note.

A

AAdvantage program, 546, 550
Aaker, David A., 58, 58n, 61, 231n, 237, 237n, 253n, 610n
Aaker, Jennifer, 122
AARP, The Magazine, 55, 410
Abbott Laboratories Co., 307
Abboud, Shaq, 128
AbbVie, 19*f*, 366*f*
ABC, 11, 18, 364, 374, 379, 735
Abercrombie & Fitch, 739
Abernathy, Penelope Muse, 438
Abernethy, Avery M., 278n, 395, 395n, 691n
AB InBev, 472
Academi, 593
Academy Awards, 325
Accenture, 71–72, 190, 590
Accenture Interactive (AI), 71–72
Accenture Rose, 82
Accenture Song, 72, 82*f*
Accenture Song PwC Digital Services, 82
Ace Hardware, 57, 312
A-Class automobile, 503
Acohido, Bryon, 719n
Activision Blizzard, 497
Acxiom (IPG), 101, 504
Ad Age (AdAge.com), 71, 348, 461, 487, 738
Adage-Harris Poll, 469
Adams, Ben, 580n
Adamson, Allen, 747
AdBlock Plus, 13
Ad Council, 206, 306, 752
Adele, 194
Adgate, Brad, 438
Adidas, 22, 148, 190, 510, 569
AdSense, 508
Adult Swim, 380*f*
Advertisers Protection Society, 355
Advertising Age, 4, 13, 71, 100, 101, 143, 186, 201, 245, 270, 279, 294, 302, 304, 428, 487, 571, 579, 609
Advertising and Social Change (Berman), 743
Advertising Education Foundation (ANA), 579
Advertising Pure and Simple (Sneiden), 265
Advertising Research Foundation (ARF), 100, 168, 169, 212, 228, 271, 272, 330, 558, 606
Advertising Self-Regulatory Council (ASRC), 686
Advertising Specialty Institute, 456
Advincula, Dorothy, 23n, 168n
Advogados, Dannemann Siemsen, 654n
Adweek, 71, 100, 267, 270, 354, 753
Aegis Group, 245, 246*f*
A&E Network, 380*f*, 382
Aflac Incorporated, 271, 303, 304*f*, 321
Agassi, Andre, 188
AGB Nielsen Media Research, 668
Agency Compensation Methods (Beals), 94
Agnew, Phillip, 492n
Agrawal, Maduh, 655n
Agres, Stuart J., 293n
Ahluwalia, Rohini, 297n, 494n
Air Asia, 739
Airbnb, Inc., 129, 148, 276*f*, 298, 418, 494, 500*f*, 590*f*, 666
Air Max shoe, 128
AirTran, 46
Akaka, Melissa, 655n

Akech, Adut, 63
AKQA, 103
Alamo, 507
Alar, 587
Al-Azhar Mosque, 739
Alberta Gaming, Liquor, 733
Albion, Mark S., 755n
Alcorn, Chauncey, 44
Alcoverro, Helena, 461, 461n
Alden, Dana A., 655n, 672
Alden, Dana L., 672n
Aldi, 528
Alexa, 301
Alexander, Julia, 505n
Alexander, Ralph S., 18n
Alibaba Group Holding, 590*f*, 645*f*, 674, 675
Allan, David, 310n
Allbirds/allbirds.com, 471, 472
Allen, Bruce H., 685n
Alliance for Audited Media (AAM), 418, 419, 433
Allianz SE, 218, 590*f*
Allport, Gordon W., 126n
Allsop, Dee T., 150n
Allstate Corporation, 72, 127, 221, 262, 280, 303, 507
Allure magazine, 120, 408, 425
Ally Bank, 130
Al-Makaty, Safran S., 654n
ALM Media, LLC, 408
Almquist, Eric, 7n
Alphabet Inc., 19*f*, 46, 143, 203, 328*f*, 438, 459, 515, 645*f*
Alsop, Ronald, 172n, 261n, 741n
Altman, Steven A., 642n
Altria, 593
Alwitt, Linda F., 373n
Al Zaida, Seja, 738
Amazing Discoveries, 478
AmazonBasics, 528
Amazon.com, Inc., 4, 12, 19*f*, 56, 66, 111, 119*f*, 127*f*, 143, 148, 150, 208, 276*f*, 301, 327, 328*f*, 366*f*, 369, 390, 397, 471, 479, 505, 506, 508, 509, 516, 517*f*, 544, 575, 591*f*, 645*f*, 649, 674, 704
Amazon Firestick, 11, 389, 469
Amazon Fire TV, 363
Amazon Kindle, 743
Amazon Prime, 11, 12, 153, 363, 378, 509
Ambika, Anupama, 212n
Ambler, Tim, 172n, 175, 175n
AMC (cable network), 380*f*, 383
American Advertising Federation (AAF), 20, 269, 686, 689–690, 736*f*, 757
American Airlines, 76, 223, 546, 550
American Association of Advertising Agencies (4As), 9, 100, 120, 236, 269, 312, 330, 516, 686, 744, 745, 755
American Bar Association (ABA), 685, 693, 713
American Cancer Society, 62
American Council on Dental Therapeutics, 300
American Dental Association, 587
American Eurocopter Corp, 137
American Express Co., 19*f*, 291, 328*f*, 471, 552, 656
American Heart Association, 594
American Heroes, 380*f*
American Honda Motor Co., Inc., 26
American Horror Story, 383
American Legacy Foundation (ALF), 709
American Marketing Association (AMA), 6, 7, 100

American Medical Association (AMA), 580, 685, 710
American Poultry Farmer magazine, 409
American Psychological Association (APA), 741
American Public Transportation Association (APTA), 453
American Red Cross, 7, 704
American Society of Magazine Editors, 421
American Stroke Association, 594
American Teleservices Association, 716
America's Auction Network, 479
America's Milk Companies, 182
Ameritrade, 339
Amos, Clinton, 183n
Amtrak, 60
Amway, 22, 480
An, Soonate, 750
ANA Agency, 93
ANA Educational Foundation, 579
Anamoly, 98
ANA REGGIE Award, 563
Ancestry.com, 590
Anderson, 101
Anderson, Stuart, 646n
Anderson, William, 428n
Andjelic, Ana, 565n
Andreini, Daniela, 184n
Andrews, J. Craig, 654n
Android OS, 24, 673
Ang, Lawrence, 269n
Angie's List, 119
Angwin, Julia, 439n
Anheuser Busch+, 733
Anheuser-Busch InBev, 35, 97, 98, 204, 209, 260, 281, 448, 536, 712, 749
Animal Planet, 380*f*
Aniston, Jennifer, 183, 191, 192, 193, 194
Annual National Youth Tobacco Survey, 709
Anthropologie, 408
Antiques Roadshow, 590
Apatow, Judd, 310
Apple+, 11
Apple App Store, 674
Applebee's, 289–290
Apple Commercial, 609
Apple Computers, 46
Apple Inc., 12, 17, 34, 44, 46, 48, 58, 87, 115, 127*f*, 143, 146, 148, 190, 258, 259, 273, 285, 311, 312, 366*f*, 369, 390, 397, 426, 445, 458, 478, 493, 506, 509, 519, 572, 573, 575, 591*f*, 596, 598, 603, 642, 649, 659, 660, 704, 720
Apple MacIntosh, 609
Apple Music, 311
Apple News+, 426
Apple TV, 11, 363, 469
Apple TV+, 12, 192, 378
App Tracking Transparency, 519
Arbery, Ahmaud, 17
Arbitron, 400
Arby's, 312
Architectural Digest, 351, 414
Architectural Forum, 409
Arizona Beverages USA, 548
Arm & Hammer Baking Soda, 573
Armani, 737
Arm & Hammer, 59–60
Armor All, 540
Armstrong, Gary M., 741n
Armstrong, Lance, 190
Arndorfer, James B., 737n

Arndt, Johan, 238n, 253n
Arnold Worldwide, 306
Arnould, Eric J., 272n
Aronson, E., 183n
Arrowhead, 202
Arrowhead Brand Mountain Spring Water, 597
The Art of Thought (Wallas), 268
Artzt, Edwin L., 564n
Ashley Madison, 49
Ashmore, Richard, 195n
Asian Beauties, 49
AsianDating, 49
Asian Honeys, 49
Asian Melodies, 49
Asiaone.com, 498*f*
Asics, 104
ASPCA, 503
Aspen Skiing, 72
Association of Magazine Media, 423
Association of National Advertisers (ANA), 80, 89, 90, 91, 92, 94, 95, 100, 229, 277, 278, 325, 330, 473, 516, 579, 686, 718, 721
Association of Online Publishers, 355
Aten, Jason, 132n
Athletic, The, 423
Atkinson, Claire, 731n
Atlantic, The, 422, 425
Atos., 590*f*
ATP World Tennis Tour, 461
AT&T Inc., 19*f*, 48, 61, 125, 186, 190, 203, 236, 245, 259, 312, 366, 377, 379, 502, 595, 704, 754
Audi, 569
Audi of America, 413
Audit Bureau of Circulations (ABC), 418
Aunt Jemima, 43–44
Aussie, 78
Austin, Erica Weintraub, 204n
Austin, Manila S., 23n, 168n
Automotive News, 409
AutoTrader, 405
Aveeno Skin Care, 192
Avengers: Age of Ultron, 459
AverageJonas, 658
Avis, 48, 61
Avon, 22, 79, 480
AXE, 627, 738
Aylesworth, Andrew B., 211, 211n
Ayyoub, Joe, 227

B

Baack, Daniel W., 262n
Babakus, Emin, 549n
Babin, Barry J., 463n
Babin, Laurie A., 463n
Bacardi USA, 462, 507
Bachman, Katy, 212n, 457n, 462n
Badenhausen, Kurt, 192n
Bagozzi, Richard P., 7n, 200n
Baidu, 674, 675
Baker, Andrew M., 150, 150n
Baker, Michael J., 193n, 195n
Baker, Ronald, 95n
Baldwin, Beth, 310n
Balenciaga, 569, 729
Ball, Jeffrey, 117n, 118n
Ban, 550
Banana Bread, 190
Banana Republic, 79, 477, 502, 505
Bang VPX, 3
Bank of America, 125

Kisielius, Jolita, 202n
Kitchen, Philip J., 10n, 106n, 174n
KitchenAid, 80
KitKat, 643
Kiwanis, 580
Klassen, Abbey, 722n
Kliatchko, Jerry, 9n, 13, 13n
Kmart, 66, 490
Knight, Brett, 187n
Knight, Phil, 128, 148
Knightley, Keira, 662
Knox, David, 159n
Kohl, Joann, 714n, 715n
Kohli, Chiranjeev, 270, 275n
Kohl's, 59, 366, 749
Koki, 147
Kolmar, Chris, 507n
Konstantinovic, Daniel, 217, 503n
Kopecky, Juliette, 477n
Koslow, Scott, 262, 262n, 263n, 265, 265n, 267n, 269n
Kotler, Philip, 223n
Kover, Arthur J., 263n, 267, 267n, 281, 281n, 627n
Kraft Foods, 120, 302, 535, 692
Kraft-Heinz, Inc., 73, 163, 535, 554, 708
Kraft Mac & Cheese, 535
Kramer, Louise, 697n
Krashinsky, Susan, 351n
Krey, N., 196n
Krieger, Abba, 617n
Krispy Kreme, 592
Kroger Company, 448, 707
Krol, Carol, 714n
Krugman, Herbert E., 163, 163n, 198n, 348, 350, 407n
Kuenne, Chris, 93n
Kung Foo, 374
Kunkel, Dale, 740
Kuntaraporn, M., 151n
Kurylko, Diana T., 365n
Kyrgios, Nick, 188

L

LaBarbera, Priscilla A., 684n, 685n
La Chance, C. C., 196n
Lachinsky, Adam, 44
Lacoste, 510
Laczniak, Russell N., 165n
Ladies' Home Journal, 410
Lady Bird Johnson, 446
Lady Schick shaver, 53
Lambert, Miranda, 182
Lambrecht, Alexander, 592
Lame, Khaby, 194
Lammons, Bob, 83n
LaMontagne, Liva, 531n
Lancaster, Kent M., 253, 253n
Landon, E. Lair, 550n
Landreth, Stacy, 196n
Land Rover, 79, 431
Lands' End, 22
Langfelder, Natasia, 469
Langner, Tobias Dr., 122
Langteau, Rita, 710n
Lans, Maxine S., 548n
Larkin, Rick, 156n
Last.fm, 500f
Late Show with Stephen Colbert, The, 379
Lathan, Saundra, 44
Laughlin, Charles, 685n
Lauterborn, Robert F., 62n
Lauzen, Martha M., 571n
Lavidge, Robert J., 161, 161n
Law Office of J. Wyndal Gordon, 685
Lawrence, Jennifer, 464
Lay's, 548
La-Z-Boy, 62

LBrands, Inc., 63
Lean Cuisine, 643
Learmonth, Michael, 184n, 722n
Leavitt, Clark, 165n, 185n
Lebow, Sara, 501n, 503n, 506n
Lee, Ang, 87
Lee, Edmund, 384n
Lee, Jane Lanhee, 668n
Lee, Joy R., 605n
Lee, M., 151n
Lee, Rub P. W., 372n
Lee, Spike, 9, 87, 88
Lee, Sun Young, 26n
Lee, Wei-Na, 710n
Lee, Yih Hwai, 263n
Leelapanyalert, Kannika, 260n
Lego, 461
Leichtman Research Group, 469
Leigh, James H., 697n
Leke, Acha, 643n
Lembke, Judi, 654n
Lemish, Dafna, 738
Lenovo, 642, 663
Leo Burnett Co., 82, 283, 285
Leuthesser, Lance, 270, 275n
Levin, Gary, 627n
Levin, Myron, 683n
Levin, Rachel, 506, 507
Levis, 743
Levi Strauss & Co., 17, 283, 642, 649, 660, 663, 749
Levitt, Theodore, 655, 655n
Levitz, Jennifer, 717n
Levy, Doug, 15n
Lewis, Denitria, 747
Lexus, 55, 143, 144, 746
LG, 644
Li, Cynthia, 646n
Li, Tao, 10n
Li Na, 647
Liaukonyte, Jura, 371, 371n
Liberty Mutual Group, 280, 303, 304f
Lieb, Rebecca, 562n
Lieber, Ron, 548n
Liebkind, Joe, 465n
Liederman, Emmy, 88n
Lifetime Networks, 380f
Liffering, Ilyse, 80n
Ligos, Melinda, 774n
Lily, 186
Limbong, Andrew, 731n
Lin, Jean, 285n
Lin, Ying, 505n
Lincoln Financial, 130
Lindzey, G., 183n
LinkedIn, 11, 23, 37, 166, 405, 406, 436, 498f, 500f, 501, 501f, 505, 517f, 585
Lion of St. Mark Award, 285
Lipman, Joanne, 120n
Lippe, Dan, 245n
Lippert, Barbara, 184n, 747
Liquidation Channel, 479
Liquid Luster, 478
Lis, Jessica, 6n
Listerine, 704
Liu-Thompkins, Yuping, 150n, 151n, 152n
Liverpool, 128
Live Strong Foundation, 593
Living Social, 425, 543
L.L.Bean, 22
Local.com, 439
Lock, Andrew R., 10n
Lodish, Leonard M., 530, 530n, 532, 532n, 565n, 617n
Loewenberg, Sam, 654n, 673n
Logitech, 558, 559
Logo, 749
Logo TV, 380f
Longo, Laura, 195n
Lopez, Hernan, 316n

Lopez, Jennifer, 147, 194
L'Oréal International, 19f, 57, 136, 299, 472, 645f
Los Angeles Magazine, 410
Los Angeles Times, 406, 429, 433, 751
Lou, Chen, 152n
Loughlin, Lori, 190
Louisiana State University (LSU), 179
Louis Vuitton, 34, 111, 122, 187, 189, 505f, 510, 659
Low, George S., 249, 250n, 253, 253n
Lowe's, 498f, 506, 510
Lowey, Nita, 592
Lowry, Tom, 396n
Lubitz, A., 196n
Luc-Herrmann, Jean, 463n
Luchs, Michael G., 15n
Luck, Andrew, 192
Lucky Charms, 524–525
LuckyDate Asia, The, 49
Lukovitz, Karlene, 185n
LuLaRoe, 22
LuluLemon, 17, 72, 153, 276
Lulus, 190
Luna, Nancy, 566n
Lund, Susan, 643n
Lutz, Richard J., 172n
LVMH Moet Hennessy Louis Vuitton, 19f, 645f
LVMH Swiss Manufactures SA, 660
Lyft, 17, 500f
Lyman, Eric J., 690n
Lynch, Jason, 212n, 388n, 389n
Lynch, Marshawn, 284
Lysonski, Steven, 654n

M

Mac, Ryan, 26n
MacArthur, Kate, 106n
MacBooks, 369
Machado, Fernando, 497
Machinima Inc., 722
MacInnis, Deborah J., 262n, 293, 293n
MacKenzie, Scott B., 172n, 211, 211n, 262n
Macnamara, Jim, 583, 584n
Macy's, 366, 505, 510
Madan, Varun, 66n
Madden, Normandy, 548n, 663n, 667n
Maddox, Kate, 92n
Maddox, Lynda M., 690n
Madewell, 283
Madhavaram, Sreedhar, 13n
Madison, Cathy, 293n
Madison Avenue (Mayer), 299
Maffeo, Lauren, 461n
Magazine Consulting & Research, Inc., 410
Magazine Impact Research Service (MIRS), 626, 627f
Magazine Media, 269, 426
Maheswaran, Durairaj, 659n
Mahomes, Patrick, 280
Mailchimp, 504
Mail Pouch Tobacco, 446
Major League Baseball (MLB), 192, 367, 368, 369, 374, 383, 384, 632
Major League Soccer, 369, 383
Malcolm, Rob, 660n, 661n
Maloney, Jennifer, 203n
Malshe, Ashwin, 37n
Mancilla, Alexa, 187n
Mandell, W., 199n
Mandese, Joe, 245n, 371n, 456n, 690n
Mandhachitara, Rujirutana, 244, 244n
Mangleburg, Tamara F., 741n
Mangold, W. Glynn, 11n
Mann, Bill, 374n
Manning, Kenneth C., 712n
Manning, Peyton, 189
Manulife, 96

Marcus Thomas, LLC, 118
Marie Claire, 408
Marin Institute, 462
Marketing Evaluations, Inc., 193, 195–196
Marketing News, 270, 428
MarketingSherpa, 373, 415, 531
Marketing Technology Landscape, 104, 105
Markin, Gene, 204n
Markle, Meghan, 587
Mark Levin Show, The, 398
Mark Makers campaign, 9
Markus, Hazel, 127n
Marlboro, 96, 283, 462, 546
Marley, Bob, 311
Marly & Me, 192
Married With Children, 368
Marriott Bonvoy program, 551–552
Marriott International, Inc., 57, 507, 550, 552
Marriott Rewards, 550
Mars, Incorporated, 321, 664
Mars/BBDO, 96
Marston, John E., 577, 577n
Mars Wrigley Confectionary, 707
Martha Stewart Living, 424
Martian, The, 459
Martin, Claude R. Jr., 697n
Martin, Dennis, 229n
Martin, Ingrid, 66n
Martin Agency, 98, 280
Mary Kay, 22, 66, 480
Maserati S.p.A., 72, 475, 744
Masked Singer, The, 374, 375
Maslow, Abraham, 115–116
Maslow's hierarchy, 745
Massarat, Navid, 23n
Massivemedia, 633
MasterCard, 127, 149, 471, 552
Masters of Snowboarding, 461
Matchbox, 46
Match.com, 49, 50, 687
Mateschitz, Dietrich, 3
Mathur, Chandraveer, 465n
Matsa, Katerina Eva, 438n
Matsuyama, Hideki, 187
Mattel, 648, 740
Max, 11, 12, 363
Maxim, 410
Mayer, Martin, 283n, 299, 299n
Maynard, Michael L., 649n
Mayo Clinic, 587
Mayorquin, Orlando, 698n
Mays, Meagan Hatcher, 747
Maytag, 80, 283, 490
Mayweather, Floyd, 188
Mayweather, Floyd, Jr., 681
Maze, Jonathan, 526n
Mazis, Michael B., 702n
McAlister, Leigh, 525n, 541n, 565n
McArthur, David N., 106n
McArthur, Kate, 548n
McCafé, 749
McCaffrey, Christian, 203
McCain, John, 747
McCain, Swift, 747
McCann, Kim, 211, 211n, 212, 212n, 213, 213n
McCann Erickson, 118
McCarthy, Jenny, 396
McCarthy, Michael, 372n
McCaughan, Dave, 192n
McClellan, Steve, 463n, 633n
McColl, Rod, 174n
McConaughey, Matthew, 572
McCracken, Grant, 192, 192n, 193
McDonald, Christopher S., 694n
McDonald, Robert E., 13n
McDonald, Ronald, 655
McDonald's Corporation, 17, 47, 66, 88, 111, 147, 148, 205, 259, 276f, 283, 293, 308, 309, 312, 315, 355, 445, 446, 449, 487, 505, 510, 513, 523, 535, 537, 546, 551, 566, 586, 590, 597, 642, 648, 656, 673, 740, 743, 746, 749

Subject Index

Note: In this index f indicates figure.

Dramatization, 305–306
"Drive Something Bigger Than Yourself"
    campaign, 201
DRTV, 469
Duplicated reach, 344

E

Earned media, 29–30, 29f, 170, 495
    See also Media
"Eat Fresh Refresh" campaign, 284, 285
E-commerce, 493
Economic development, 671–672
Economic infrastructure, 645
Economies of scale, 252–253, 754
Editorial environment, 350f
Education principle, 689f
Educators, target audiences, 579
Effective advertising slogans, 276f
Effectiveness, 603–638
    of advertising
        budgeting decisions, 611
        copy testing, 613–614
        establishing a program for
            measuring, 630–631
        field tests, 613
        laboratory tests, 612–613
        media strategies, 610–611
        message variables, 610
        posttesting, 612
        pretesting/pretests, 611–612, 611f
        source factors, 610
    of commercial testing, 615–618
    of concept generation, 614–615
    of concept testing, 614–615, 614f
    of copy, 615–618
    of corporate advertising, 599–600
    of direct marketing, 481–483
    in foundational elements of advertising
        agencies, 107f
    of IMC program elements, 635–638
    of in-store radio and television, 633
    Internet metrics, 514
    market testing of ads, 623–629
    measuring of public relations,
        584–585
    of nontraditional media, 633
    of other media, 633
    out of home (OOH) advertising, 452
    of parking lot-based media, 633
    pretesting of finished ads,
        618–623
    of print versus online flyers, 633
    of publicity, 588
    reasons not to measure, 605–609
        costs, 607–608
        disagreement on what to test, 608
        objections of creative, 608–609
        research problems, 608
        time, 609
    reasons to measure
        avoiding costly mistakes, 605
        determining if objectives are
            achieved, 605
        evaluating alternative strategies, 605
        increasing the efficiency of
            advertising in general, 605
    rough art, 615–618
    of sales promotions, 632–633
    of sponsorships, 633–635
    See also Feedback
Effective reach, 347–349, 347f
Effective testing, essentials of, 631
Efficiency, out of home (OOH)
    advertising, 452
80-20 rule, 56
Elaboration, divergence in advertising, 262
Elaboration likelihood model (ELM),
    172–174, 173f

Electric vehicle (EV) market,
    143–144, 148
Electrodermal response (EDR), 622
Electroencephalographic (EEG)
    measures, 623
Electronic word-of-mouth (eWOM), 150
E-mail, 498f
    marketing, 6
    sampling through, 539
    strategies and media, 477–478
Emotional appeals, 292–297, 293f
Emotional attachment, advertising in
    movie theaters, 457
Emotional integration, 293
Emotional persuasion, 122
Emotions in consumer decision making,
    122–123
Employees of firm, as target
    audiences, 577
Encoding, 146–147
Endorsement, 300 See also Celebrities
Endorsers
    celebrity. See Celebrity endorser
    college athletes as, 179–180
Engagement and ad recall, 331f
Engineered WOM, 150
Environment
    analysis, 35f
    effect on channels, 210–211
    factors, 111–112
Environmental, social, and governance
    (ESG), 16
Environmental influences on consumer
    behaviors, 134–138
    culture, 135, 135f
    reference groups, 135f, 136–138
    situational determinants, 135f, 138
    social class, 135–136, 135f
    subcultures, 135, 135f
Esteem need, 115, 116f
Ethical perspective, 16–17
Ethics, 731
    advertising, 736f
Ethnocentrism, 649
Ethnographic research, 272
Evaluating agencies, 95–101
    gaining clients, 96–98, 99–101
        image and reputation, 100–101
        presentations, 99–100
        public relations, 100
        referrals, 99
        solicitations, 99
    losing clients, 96–98
        changes in client's corporate and/or
            marketing strategy, 96–97
        changes in policies, 98
        changes in size of client or
            agency, 96
        conflicting compensation
            philosophies, 97
        conflicts of interest, 96
        declining sales, 97
        disagreements over marketing and/or
            creative strategy, 98
        lack of integrated marketing
            capabilities, 98
        personality conflicts, 96
        personnel changes, 96
        poor communication, 96
        poor performance or service, 96
        unrealistic demands by the client, 96
Evaluation
    alternative in decision-making,
        123–124
    criteria in decision-making, 124
    media planning, 357
    objectives, 220
    refunds and rebates, 549
Event marketing, 552–553
Event sampling, 540

Event sponsorships, 552–553,
    591–594
    measuring, 635f
Ever evolving world of direct marketing,
    472 See also Direct marketing
Evoked set in decision-making, 123–124
Exchange, 6–7
Exclusives in public relations, 581
Execution in centralized system, 75
Execution style See Creative execution
Expenditures, buildup approach, 247
Experian National Consumer Study, 332
Experiential marketing, 553
Expertise
    credibility of sources, 183
    in foundational elements of advertising
        agencies, 107f
Exposure
    as advantages of the Internet and social
        media, 518
    advertising in movie theaters,
        456–457
    of branded entertainment, 462
    methods, 633–634
    in transit advertising, 452
External analysis, 34–35, 35f
External audiences, 577
External factors in media planning, 335
External influences on consumer
    behavior, 135f
External search, 119
Eye movement research, 622f
Eye tracking, 622–623

F

Failure fees, 557
False advertising lawsuits for food and
    beverage products, 707–708
False claiming, 626
Familiarity, source attractiveness, 185
Family decision making, 137, 138f
Family Smoking Prevention and Tobacco
    Control Act, 709
Farm publications, 409
Fast-food restaurants, use of loyalty
    programs to engage customers,
    523–524, 550–551
Favorable price appeal, 292
Fear appeals, 206
Fear levels and message acceptance,
    206, 607f
Fear operates, 206–208
Feature appeal, 291
Federal Alcohol Administration Act, 711
Federal regulation, 693–712
    agencies, 705–711
    background, 695
    See also Regulations
Federal Trade Commission Act, 695,
    718, 720
Fee arrangement, 92
Fee-based system, 92
Fee-commission combination, 92
Feedback, 159 See also Effectiveness
Field of experience, 156
Field tests, 613
Fifth-generation (5G), 20
Financial audit, 95
Financial groups, 580
First Amendment, 694–695
First cover (outside front), 421
First-run syndication, 376–377
Fixed-fee method, 92
Flat rates, 435
Fleeting message, as limitations of
    television, 370
Flesch formula, 619
Flesch Kincaid Reading Ease Score, 619

Flexibility, 264f
    advantages of newspapers, 430
    advantages of radio, 392
    availability of media, 352
    changes in media, 352
    divergence in advertising, 262
    market opportunities, 351–352
    market threats, 352
    media strategies, 351–352
    media vehicles, 352
    promotional products marketing, 455
Flighting, 342, 343f
Focus groups, 117f, 270–271
Follow-up, media planning, 357
Forums and chat rooms, 498f
Forums and discussion boards, 517f
4As, 95, 100
4As Awards for Account Planning, 86
Four Ps of marketing, 7
Fourth cover (outside back), 421
Frame of reference, 156
Freedom of speech See First Amendment
Free premiums, 546
Freestanding inserts (FSIs), 542–544
Frequency
    of branded entertainment, 462
    definition of, 327
    direct marketing, 482
    disadvantages of magazines, 416
    effects of, 346f
    factors, 350f
    media strategies, 342–351
    objectives, 344
    out of home (OOH) advertising, 451
    programs. See Loyalty programs
    representation of, 345f
    in transit advertising, 452–453
Fry Graph Readability Formula, 619
FSIs See Freestanding inserts
Full-service agency, 83, 84f
    research department of, 85
Functional consequences, 124

G

Gaining clients, 96–98, 99–101
Gaining consideration, web objectives,
    492
Galvanic skin response (GSR), 622
Game, 547
Gas station pump ads, 465
Gatefolds, 411
General advertising, 429
    rates, 434
General Data Protection Regulation
    (GDPR), 720–721
General image, 590
General preplanning input, 269
General versus local rates, purchasing
    newspaper space, 434–435
Generatiing interest, web objectives, 491
Generating financial support, 590
"Generation Amazing" initiative, 651
Generation X, 194
Generation Z, 181, 189, 193
Gen X, 497
Gen Z, 260, 497, 507, 675
Geographic coverage, media strategies,
    339
Geographic flexibility, out of home
    (OOH) advertising, 451
Geographic segmentation, 52f, 53
Geographic selectivity, 410
    advantages of newspapers, 431
Global advertising, 655
    problems with, 656–657
    See also Global marketing, advantages of
Global consumer culture theory
    (GCCT), 655

Research
    implement proper, 631
    for magazines, 420–421
Response/feedback, model in
    communication, 159
Response hierarchy, DAGMAR
    model, 231
Response process in communication,
    161–170, 175–176
    alternative response hierarchies,
        162–164
    hierarchy of effects model,
        161–162, 161f
    implications of models, 164–168
    social consumer decision,
        168–170, 169f
"Responses" campaign, 279
Retailers
    encouraged to display established
        brands, 555
    growing power of, 527–528
Retailing, omnichannel, 22
Retail inventories, 555
Retail/local advertising, 21f
    rate, 434
Retail stores, privacy in, 448
Retail trading zone, 433
Retargeting, 495
Retention as traditional measures, 515
Return on investment (ROI), 221, 245,
    319, 355, 477, 488
    celebrities, 191–192
    marketing public relations (MPR), 572
    as traditional measures, 515
Revenue, advertising, 12–13 See also
    Budgeting/budget
RFM analysis, 481
Rich media, 496–497
    advertising, 497
    online commercials, 496–497
    video on demand (VOD), 497
    webisodes, 497
Rising costs, direct marketing, 483
"Rising Stars" program, 317
Risks in creativity, 265–266
Risk to the advertiser, celebrities,
    190–191
Robinson-Patman Act, 714, 715
Roe v. Wade, 17
Rough art, effectiveness, 615–618
Run of paper (ROP), 435

S

Safety need, 115, 116f
Sales
    assumption as direct measure of
        advertising and promotion,
        237–238
    assumption that it is determined
        solely by advertising and
        promotion, 238
    potential, 516, 518
    as traditional measures, 515
    training programs, 558–559
Sales objectives, DAGMAR model, 231
Sales-oriented objectives, 221–224
    appropriateness of, 223–224
    factors influencing, 222f
    problems with, 222–223, 222f
Sales promotion, 5, 6, 8, 523–567,
    670–672
    abuse of, 565–566
    agencies, 101–102
    consumer franchise-building (CFB)
        promotions, 532–533
    consumer-oriented. See Consumer-
        oriented sales promotion
    contest and sweepstakes, 714–715

coordinating with advertising and IMC
    tools, 562–564
definition of, 524
direct marketing and, 8, 473–474
effectiveness of, 632–633
importance of, 526–534
    brand proliferation, 529
    competition, 530
    declining brand loyalty, 528
    growing power of retailers, 527–528
    growth of digital marketing, 531
    increased accountability, 530
    increased promotional sensitivity,
        528–529
    short-term focus, 529–530
increased role of, 531–532
on the Internet, 510
nonfranchise-building (non-FB)
    promotions, 533–534
premiums, 715
scope and role of, 524–526
spending on, 5
trade allowances, 715
trade-oriented. See Trade-oriented sales
    promotion
trap, 565, 565f
types of activities, 525f
See also Consumer-oriented sales
    promotion; Trade-oriented sales
    promotion
Sales response models, 238–239, 238f
Salient attributes, 58–59
Salient beliefs, 125
Sampling, 538–540
    benefits and limitations of, 539
    door-to-door, 539
    event, 540
    methods, 539–540
    on-package, 540
Sampling through mail, 539
Satellite billboards, 465
Satisfaction, postpurchase evaluation, 129
Saturation, promotional products
    marketing, 455
Save Student Newsrooms campaign, 428
Scatter market, 375
Schedules of reinforcement, 133
Scheduling, 350f
    media strategies, 339, 342
    methods, characteristics of, 343f
Scientific/technical evidence, 300
Seamless communication, 8
Search engine optimization (SEO), 495
    impact, 585
Searches, 495
Second cover (inside front), 421
Seeding strategy, 152
Segmentation
    advertising in movie theaters, 457
    capabilities, direct marketing, 482
Selecting target market, 57
Selective attention, 121
Selective comprehension, 121
Selective exposure, 121
Selective perception, 121, 121f
Selective reach, direct marketing, 481–482
Selective retention, 121
Selectivity
    advantages of magazines, 409–411
    advantages of radio, 391–392
    advantages of television, 367–368
    lacking, as limitations of television, 370
    promotional products marketing, 455
Self-actualization need, 115, 116f
Self-indulgence, costly form of, 589
Self-liquidating premiums, 546–547
Self-regulatory principles for online
    behavioral advertising, 689f
Self-satisfaction (reactor) strategy,
    166, 167

Sensation, 120
Sensitive data principle, 689f
Services, advantages of magazines,
    415–416
Services offered, advantages of
    newspapers, 432
Sexual advertising, 738
Sexual appeals, 737
Shaping, 133, 134f
Share of audience, 386
Share of voice (SOV), 252, 253f
"Share the Love" campaign, 297
Sharing, disadvantages of mobile, 513
Shifting role of promotion agency, 564f
Shock advertising, 737–739
Short-form programs, 478
Short life span, limitations of
    newspapers, 432
Short-term focus, sales promotion,
    529–530
Short-term strategy, 586
Sierra Club, 482
Similarity, source attractiveness, 185, 186
Situational determinants, consumer
    behaviors, 135f, 138
Situation analysis, promotional program,
    32f, 33–35 See also Media
    planning
Sleeper effect, 185
Slice-of-death advertising, 301
Slice of life advertising, 301–302
Slogan (tagline), 275
Slotting allowances, 557–558
SMOG Readability Formula, 619
Social amplification, 585
Social and cultural consequences of
    advertising, 743–751
Social bookmarking, 517f
Social class, consumer behaviors,
    135–136, 135f
Social consumer decision, 168–170, 169f
Social effects of advertising, 751–752
Social/love and belonging need, 115, 116f
Social media, 23, 497–510
    advantages of, 516–518
    classic model of, 166–167
    definition of, 497
    disadvantages of, 518–520
    global users, 499f
    influencers, 152, 194–195
    in international marketing, 676–677
    Internet and, 24
    landscape, 498f
    management programs, 514
    marketers use of, 499–501, 500f
    metrics for, 517f
    networks, consumer use of, 500f
    perspective, 12–13
    popular, 501–507
    reasons to connect on, 531f
    who and why use, 499
Social media news releases (SNRs), 587
Social networking sites, 497, 498f
Social networks, 517f
    public relations, 581
Social news sites, 498f
Solicitations in gaining clients, 99
Source/attention, persuasion matrix,
    180f, 181
Source bolsters, 171
Source derogations, 171
Source factors, 610
    association of branded
        entertainment, 462
    attractiveness, 185–193
    attributes and receiver processing
        modes, 182f
    credibility, 182–185
    definition of, 182
    direct, 182

indirect, 182
    model in communication, 146–147
Source-oriented thoughts, 171
Source power, spokespeople, 197–198
Sources of distaste, 735–737
Spam/spamming, 478
    marketing on the Internet, 724
Special ads and inserts, newspapers, 430
Special-audience newspapers, 427–428
Specialized marketing communication
    services, 74
Specialized services, 101–104
    digital agencies, 103–104
    direct-marketing agencies, 101
    public relations (PR) firms, 102–103
    sales promotion agencies, 101–102
Specialty advertising, 454
Specified time period, DAGMAR
    model, 230
Speed, as advantages of the Internet and
    social media, 518
Spending
    advertising, 6
    on digital advertising, 6, 12, 24
    on sales promotion, 5
    on social media platforms, 6
    See also Budgeting/budget
Spiffs, 556
Split-run, 416
    tests, 624
Sponsorships, 494, 590
    effectiveness of, 633–635
    event, 552–553
    performance matrix, 634f
    television buying time, 377–378
Spot advertising, 376
Spot announcements, television buying
    time, 378
Spot radio, buying radio time, 398
S-shaped response curve, 238–239,
    238f, 243
Standard advertising unit (SAU), 435
Standard learning model, 162
Standards manuals, 148
State regulation, 712–713 See also
    Regulations
Station posters, 450–451
Station reps, 376
Stereotyping, advertising and, 745–749
Stimulating trial, web objectives, 492
Stimulus-response orientation (S-R), 131
Stockholders and investors, target
    audiences, 578
Stocking allowances See Slotting
    allowances
Stock prices, corporate advertising and,
    599–600
Stopping power, 187
Store comes home, 111
Storyboard, 86, 274
Storytelling, 583
    marketing strategy in sports, 128–129
Straight-sell or factual message, 299
Strategic marketing plan, 45
Strategies and media, direct marketing,
    475–480
    broadcast media, 478
    catalogs, 477
    connected TV, 479
    direct mail, 475–476
    e-mail, 477–478
    home shopping, 479
    infomercials, 478–479
    print media, 479
    telemarketing, 479–480
    TV sports, 478
Strategy development, creativity, 275–285
    advertising campaigns, 275–276
    contemporary approaches to big idea,
        284–285

Wearout, 209, 350*f*
  of miscellaneous alternative media, 466
  of out of home (OOH) advertising, 452
Web 1.0, 493
Web 2.0, 23, 493, 497–510
Web 3.0, 487–488
Webisodes, 497
Weblog, 507–509
Web objectives, 490–492
  brand creation, 492
  buzz creation, 492
  creating awareness, 491
  disseminating information,
    491–492

  gaining consideration, 492
  generating interest, 491
  image creation, 492
  stimulating trial, 492
Website traffic, 585
Weekly newspapers, 427
Wheeler-Lea Amendment, 695
Where to promote, media planning,
  335–337
Whom to advertise, media
  planning, 332
Wide coverage of local markets, OOH
  advertising, 451
Women, 746

Word-of-mouth (WOM), 16, 143–144,
  150, 517*f*
  information, 182
  integrating with IMC, 153–156
World Water Day, 597
Worldwide advertising spending, 645*f*
Worldwide growth of the Internet, 674
World Wide Web, 49, 488, 490, 493

Y

"Yes To You" campaign, 305
Young's model of creative process, 268

Z

Zapping, 371
Zero-based communications
  planning, 233
Zero-sum competition, 244*f*
Zipping, 371
Zoo's objectives for various promotional
  elements, 235*f*